Collins
LATIN
DICTIONARY
& GRAMMAR

T0340407

Published by Collins
An imprint of HarperCollins Publishers
Westerhill Road
Bishopbriggs
Glasgow G64 2QT

HarperCollins Publishers
Macken House, 39/40 Mayor Street Upper
Dublin 1, D01 C9W8, Ireland

Second Edition 2016

10

ISBN   978-0-00-816767-7

collins.co.uk/languagesupport

Typeset by Sharon McTeir

Printed and bound in India by
Replika Press Pvt. Ltd.

A catalogue record for this book is available
from the British Library.

If you would like to comment on any aspect
of this book, please contact us at the given
address or online.
E-mail: dictionaries@harpercollins.co.uk
⬚ facebook.com/collinsdictionary
⬚ @collinsdict

Acknowledgements

We would like to thank those authors and
publishers who kindly gave permission for
copyright material to be used in the Collins
Corpus. We would also like to thank Times
Newspapers Ltd for providing valuable
data.

Dictionary based on the Collins Latin Gem
© 1957 by Professor D. A. Kidd, Canterbury
University

GRAMMAR TEXT AND DICTIONARY
SUPPLEMENTS BY
Mary Wade

FOR THE PUBLISHER
Susie Beattie
Gerry Breslin
Dave White
Sarah Woods

LATIN CONSULTANTS
Ian Brookes
Denis Bruce
Michael D. Igoe

CONTENTS

ABBREVIATIONS

adj	adjective	*MED*	medicine
abl	ablative	*MIL*	military
acc	accusative	*mod*	modern
adv	adverb	*n*	noun
AGR	agriculture	*NAUT*	nautical
ARCH	architecture	*neg*	negative
art	article	*nom*	nominative
ASTR	astronomy	*nt*	neuter
AUG	augury	*num*	numeral
COMM	business	*occ*	occasionally
CIRCS	circumstances	*p*	participle
compar	comparative	*pass*	passive
conj	conjunction	*perf*	perfect
cpd	compound	*perh*	perhaps
dat	dative	*pers*	person
defec	defective	*PHILOS*	philosophy
ECCL	ecclesiastical	*pl*	plural
esp	especially	*POL*	politics
excl	exclamatory	*ppa*	perfect participle active
f	feminine	*ppp*	perfect participle passive
fig	figurative	*prep*	preposition
fut	future	*pres*	present
gen	genitive	*pron*	pronoun
GEOG	geography	*prop*	properly
GRAM	grammar	*PROV*	proverb
impers	impersonal	*relat*	relative
imperf	imperfect	*RHET*	rhetoric
impv	imperative	*sg*	singular
indecl	indeclinable	*sim*	similarly
indic	indicative	*subj*	subjunctive
inf	informal	*superl*	superlative
infin	infinitive	*THEAT*	theatre
interj	interjection	*UNIV*	university
interrog	interrogative	*usu*	usually
LIT	literature	*vi*	intransitive verb
loc	locative	*voc*	vocative
m	masculine	*vt*	transitive verb
MATH	mathematics		

INTRODUCTION

Whether you are learning Latin for the first time or wish to "brush up" what you learned some time ago, this dictionary is designed to help you understand Latin and to express yourself in Latin, if you so wish.

HOW TO USE THE DICTIONARY

Entries are laid out as follows:

Headword

This is shown in **bold type**. On the Latin-English side all long vowels are shown by placing a ‾ above them. Latin nouns show the genitive singular form in bold. Latin verbs show the first person singular of the present indicative as the headword, followed by the infinitive, the first person singular of the perfect indicative and usually the past participle, all in bold type:

> **elegīa, -ae**
> **elementum, -ī**
> **ēlevō, -āre**
> **ēmātūrēscō, -ēscere, -uī**

Part of Speech

Next comes the part of speech (noun, verb, adjective etc), shown in *italics*. Part of speech abbreviations used in the dictionary are shown in the abbreviations list (p iv). Where a word has more than one part of speech, each new part of speech is preceded by a black lozenge (♦). If a Latin headword is a preposition, the case taken by the preposition comes immediately after the part of speech, in *italics* and in brackets.

> **era, -ae** *f*
> **ticklish** *adj*
> **thunder** *n* tonitrus *m* ♦ *vi* tonare, intonare.
> **ērgā** *prep (with acc)* towards; against.

Meanings

Where a word or a part of speech has only one meaning, the translation comes immediately after the part of speech. However, many words have more than one meaning. Where the context is likely to show which translation is correct, variations in meaning are simply separated by a semicolon. But usually there will also be an "indicator" in italics and in brackets. Some meanings relate to specific subject areas, for example religion, politics, military matters etc – these indicators are in small italic capitals.

ēnsiger, -ī *adj* with his sword.

toy *n* crepundia *ntpl* ♦ *vi* ludere.

toll collector *n* exactor *m*; portitor *m*.

eō, īre, īvī and **iī, itum** *vi* to go; (MIL) to march; (*time*) to pass; (*event*) to proceed, turn out.

Translations

Most words can be translated directly. On the English-Latin side, translations of nouns include the gender of the Latin noun in *italics*. However, sometimes a phrase is needed to show how a word is used, but in some cases a direct translation of a phrase would be meaningless - in these cases, an explanation in *italics* is given instead. In other cases, the user will need more information than simply the translation; in these cases, "indicators" are included in the translation(s), giving, for instance, the case required by a Latin verb or preposition or further details about a place or person.

> **thumb** *n* pollex *m*; **have under one's ~** in potestate sua habere.
>
> **elephantomacha, -ae** *m fighter mounted on an elephant.*
>
> **Erymanthus, -i** *m mountain range in Arcadia* (*where Hercules killed the boar*).
>
> **thwart** *vt* obstare (*dat*), officere (*dat*).

Pronunciation

Since Latin pronunciation is regular, once the basic rules have been learned (see pp *viii, ix*), the dictionary does not show phonetic transcriptions against each headword, but does show all long vowels.

Other Information

The dictionary also includes:

- basic grammar section
- information about life in Roman times:
  — how government and the army were organized — how numbers and dates were calculated and expressed — family relationships — geographical names — major Roman authors — key events in Roman history — (*important historical and mythological characters and events are listed within the body of the main text*).
- a section on Latin poetry and scansion
- a list of Latin expressions commonly used in English today

LATIN ALPHABET

The Latin alphabet is the one which has been almost universally adopted by the modern languages of Europe and America. In the Classical period it had 23 letters, namely the English alphabet without letters **j**, **v** and **w**.

Letter v

The symbol **v** was the capital form of the letter **u**, but in a later age the small **v** came into use to represent the consonantal **u**, and as it is commonly so employed in modern editions of Latin authors, it has been retained as a distinct letter in this dictionary for convenience.

Letter j

The symbol **j** came to be used as the consonantal **i**, and is found in older editions of the Classics, but as it has been almost entirely discarded in modern texts, it is not used in this dictionary, and words found spelt with a **j** must therefore be looked up under **i**.

Letters w, y, z

The letter **w** may be seen in the Latinized forms of some modern names, e.g. **Westmonasterium**, Westminster. The letters **y** and **z** occur only in words of Greek origin.

ORTHOGRAPHY

Many Latin words which begin with a prefix can be spelled in two ways. The prefix can retain its original spelling, or it can be assimilated, changing a letter depending on the letter which follows it. Compare the following:

ad before **g**, **l**, **r** and **p**:

adpropinquare	appropinquare
adgredi	aggredi
adloquor	alloquor
adrogans	arrogans

ad is also often assimilated before **f** and **n**:

adfectus	affectus
adnexus	annexus

and **ad** is often shortened to a before **sc**:

adscendere	ascendere

in changes to **il** before **l**, to **im** before **m** or **p** and to **ir** before **r**.

con becomes **cor** when followed by another **r** and **col** when followed by **l**.

We have provided cross-references in the text to draw your attention to the alternative forms of words. Thus, although **arrogantia** does not appear in the Latin-English section, the cross-reference at **arr-** will point you to the entry for **adrogantia**, where the translation is given.

PRONUNCIATION

The ancient pronunciation of Latin has been established with a fair degree of certainty from the evidence of ancient authorities and inscriptions and inferences from the modern Romance languages. It is not possible, of course, to recapture the precise nuances of Classical Latin speech, but what follows is now generally accepted and generally understood as a reasonably accurate guide to the sounds of Latin as spoken by educated Romans during the two centuries from Cicero to Quintilian.

ACCENT

The Latin accent in the Classical period was a weak stress, perhaps with an element of pitch in it. It falls, as in English, on the second last syllable of the word, if that syllable is long, and on the third last syllable if the second last is short. Disyllabic words take the accent on the first syllable, unless they have already lost a final syllable, e.g. **illīc**(**e**).

Inflected words are commonly learned with the accent wrongly placed on the last syllable, for convenience in memorizing the inflexions. But it is advisable to get the accent as well as the ending right.

The correct accent of other words can easily be found by noting carefully the quantity of the second last syllable and then accenting the word as in English, according to the rule given above. Thus **fuērunt** is accented on the second last syllable because the **e** is long, whereas **fuerant** is accented on the third last, because the **e** is short.

VOWELS

Vowels are pure and should not be diphthongized as in certain sounds of Southern English. They may be long or short. Throughout this Dictionary all vowels known or believed by the best authorities to be long are marked with a line above them; those unmarked are either known to be short or of uncertain quantity.

Short		Long	
agricol**a**	r**a**t	r**ā**mus	r**a**ther
h**e**d**e**ra	p**e**n	av**ē**	p**a**y
itaque	k**i**n	c**ī**vis	k**ee**n
fav**o**r	r**o**b	ampli**ō**	r**o**be
neb**u**la	f**u**ll	l**ū**na	f**oo**l

y is a Greek sound and is pronounced (both short and long) as **u** in French ie **rue**.

DIPHTHONGS

aestas	tr**y**	
audio	to**w**n	
h**ei**	p**ayee**	
m**eu**s	**ay-oo**	*with the accent on first sound*
mo**ec**ha	t**oy**	
t**ui**tus	L**oui**s	

CONSONANTS

balneae		**b**a**b**y	
a**bs**temius		a**ps**e	
su**bt**ractus		a**pt**	
castra		**c**ar	
chorda		sepul**ch**re	
inter**d**o		**d**og	
cōn**fl**ō		**f**ortune	
in**g**redior		**g**o	
habeō		**h**and	*(but faintly)*
iaceo		**y**es	*(consonantal i = j)*
Kalendae		oa**k**	
conge**l**ō		**l**et	
co**m**es		**m**an	*(final m was hardly sounded and may have simply nasalized the preceding vowel)*
pā**n**is		**n**o	
pa**ng**o		fi**ng**er	
stu**p**eō		a**p**t	
ra**ph**anus		**p**ill	
exse**qu**or		**qu**ite	
sup**r**emus		b**r**ae	*(Scottish)*
magnu**s**		**si**ster	*(never as in rose)*
lae**t**us		**st**op	
theātrum		**t**ake	
vapor	*(and consonantal u)*	**w**in	
de**x**tra		si**x**	*(ks, not gs)*
zona		**z**ero	

Double consonants lengthen the sound of the consonant.

QUICK REFERENCE
GRAMMAR

DECLENSIONS OF NOUNS

1st Declension

	mainly f		*m*	
SING				
Nom.	terra	crambē	Aenēās	Anchīsēs
Voc.	terra	crambē	Aenēā	Anchīsā,-ē
Acc.	terram	crambēn	Aenēam,-ān	Anchīsam, -ēn
Gen.	terrae	crambes	Aenēae	Anchīsae
Dat.	terrae	crambae	Aenēae	Anchīsae
Abl.	terra	cramba	Aenēā	Anchīsā

PLURAL		
Nom.	terrae	crambae
Voc.	terrae	crambae
Acc.	terrās	crambās
Gen.	terrārum	crambārum
Dat.	terrīs	crambīs
Abl.	terrīs	crambīs

2nd Declension

	mainly m				
SING					
Nom.	modus	Lūcius	Dēlos (f)	puer	liber
Voc.	mode	Lūcī	Dēle	puer	liber
Acc.	modum	Lūcium	Dēlon	puerum	librum
Gen.	modī	Lūcī	Dēlī	puerī	librī
Dat.	modō	Lūciō	Dēlō	puerō	librō
Abl.	modō	Lūciō	Dēlō	puerō	librō

PLURAL					
Nom.	modī			puerī	librī
Voc.	modī			puerī	librī
Acc.	modōs			puerōs	librōs
Gen.	modōrum			puerōrum	librōrum
Dat.	modīs			puerīs	librīs
Abl.	modīs			puerīs	librīs

nt

	SING
Nom.	dōnum
Voc.	dōnum
Acc.	dōnum
Gen.	dōnī
Dat.	dōnō
Abl.	dōnō

	PLURAL
Nom.	dōna
Voc.	dōna
Acc.	dōna
Gen.	dōnōrum
Dat.	dōnīs
Abl.	dōnīs

3rd Declension

Group I: *Vowel stems, with gen pl in* **-ium**

	m and f		*nt*	
SING				
Nom.	clādēs	nāvis	rēte	animal
Voc.	clādēs	nāvis	rēte	animal
Acc.	clādem	nāvem,-im	rēte	animal
Gen.	clādis	nāvis	rētis	animālīs
Dat.	clādī	nāvī	rētī	animālī
Abl.	clāde	nāve,-ī	rētī	animālī
PLURAL				
Nom.	clādēs	nāvēs	rētia	animālia
Voc.	clādēs	nāvēs	rētia	animālia
Acc.	clādēs, -īs	nāvēs, -īs	rētia	animālia
Gen.	clādium	nāvium	rētium	animālium
Dat.	clādibus	nāvibus	rētibus	animālibus
Abl.	clādibus	nāvibus	rētibus	animālibus

Group II: *Consonant stems, some with gen pl in* **-ium**, *some in* **-um** *and some in either.*
Monosyllabic nouns ending in two consonants (e.g. **urbs** *below) regularly have* **-ium**.

	m and f			*f*	*nt*
SING					
Nom.	urbs	amāns	laus	aetās	os
Voc.	urbs	amāns	laus	aetās	os
Acc.	urbem	amantem	laudem	aetātem	os
Gen.	urbis	amantis	laudis	aetātis	ossis
Dat.	urbī	amantī	laudī	aetātī	ossī
Abl.	urbe	amante	laude	aetāte	osse

PLURAL

Nom.	urbēs	amantēs	laudēs	aetātēs	ossa
Voc.	urbēs	amantēs	laudēs	aetātēs	ossa
Acc.	urbēs	amantēs	laudēs	aetātēs	ossa
Gen.	urbium	amantium, -um	laudum, -ium	aetātum, -ium	ossium
Dat.	urbibus	amantibus	laudibus	aetātibus	ossibus
Abl.	urbibus	amantibus	laudibus	aetātibus	ossibus

Group III: Consonant stems, with gen pl in **-um**

	m and f			nt	
SING					
Nom.	mōs	ratiō	pater	nōmen	opu
Voc.	mōs	ratiō	pater	nōmen	opus
Acc.	mōrem	ratiōnem	patrem	nōmen	opus
Gen.	mōris	ratiōnis	patris	nōminis	operis
Dat.	mōrī	ratiōnī	patrī	nōminī	operī
Abl.	mōre	ratiōne	patre	nōmine	opere

PLURAL

	m and f			nt	
Nom.	mōrēs	ratiōnēs	patrēs	nōmina	opera
Voc.	mōrēs	ratiōnēs	patrēs	nōmina	opera
Acc.	mōrēs	ratiōnēs	patrēs	nōmina	opera
Gen.	mōrum	ratiōnum	patrum	nōminum	operum
Dat.	mōribus	ratiōnibus	patribus	nōminibus	operibus
Abl.	mōribus	ratiōnibus	patribus	nōminibus	operibus

Group IV: Greek nouns

	m		f		nt
SING					
Nom.	āēr	hērōs	Periclēs	Naias	poēma
Voc.	āēr	hērōs	Periclē	Naias	poēma
Acc.	āera	hērōa	{ Periclem, Periclea	Naiada	poēma
Gen.	āeris	hērōis	Periclis, -i	Naiadis, -os	poēmatis
Dat.	āerī	hērōī	Periclī	Naiadī	poēmatī
Abl.	aere	hērōe	Pericle	Naiade	poēmate

PLURAL

	m		f		nt
Nom.	āeres	hērōes		Naiades	poēmata
Voc.	āeres	hērōes		Naiades	poēmata
Acc.	āeras	hērōas		Naiadas	poēmata
Gen.	āerum	hērōum		Naiadum	poēmatōrum
Dat.	āeribus	hērōibus		Naiadibus	poēmatīs
Abl.	āeribus	hērōibus		Naiadibus	poēmatīs

	4th Declension		**5th Declension**	
	mainly m	*nt*	*mainly f*	
SING				
Nom.	portus	genū	diēs	rēs
Voc.	portus	genū	diēs	rēs
Acc.	portum	genū	diem	rem
Gen.	portūs	genūs	diēī	reī
Dat.	portuī	genū	diēī	reī
Abl.	portū	genū	diē	rē
PLURAL				
Nom.	portūs	genua	diēs	rēs
Voc.	portūs	genua	diēs	rēs
Acc.	portūs	genua	diēs	rēs
Gen.	portuum	genuum	diērum	rērum
Dat.	portibus, -ubus	genibus, -ubus	diēbus	rēbus
Abl.	portibus, -ubus	genibus, -ubus	diēbus	rēbus

CONJUGATIONS OF VERBS

ACTIVE

PRESENT TENSE

	First **parāre** *prepare*	Second **habēre** *have*	Third **sūmere** *take*	Fourth **audīre** *hear*

Indicative

SING

1st pers	parō	habeō	sūmō	audiō
2nd pers	parās	habēs	sūmis	audīs
3rd pers	parat	habet	sūmit	audit

PLURAL

1st pers	parāmus	habēmus	sūmimus	audīmus
2nd pers	parātis	habētis	sūmitis	audītīs
3rd pers	parant	habent	sūmunt	audiunt

Subjunctive

SING

1st pers	parem	habeam	sūmam	audiam
2nd pers	parēs	habeās	sūmās	audiās
3rd pers	paret	habeat	sūmat	audiat

PLURAL

1st pers	parēmus	habeāmus	sūmāmus	audiāmus
2nd pers	parētis	habeātis	sūmātis	audiātis
3rd pers	parent	habeant	sūmant	audiant

IMPERFECT TENSE
Indicative

SING				
1st *pers*	parābam	habēbam	sūmēbam	audiēbam
2nd *pers*	parābās	habēbās	sūmēbās	audiēbās
3rd *pers*	parābat	habēbat	sūmēbat	audiēbat
PLURAL				
1st *pers*	parābāmus	habēbāmus	sūmēbāmus	audiēbāmus
2nd *pers*	parābātis	habēbātis	sūmēbātis	audiēbātis
3rd *pers*	parābant	habēbant	sūmēbant	audiēbant

Subjunctive

SING				
1st *pers*	parārem	habērem	sūmerem	audīrem
2nd *pers*	parārēs	habērēs	sūmerēs	audīrēs
3rd *pers*	parāret	habēret	sūmeret	audīret
PLURAL				
1st *pers*	parārēmus	habērēmus	sūmerēmus	audīrēmus
2nd *pers*	parārētis	habērētis	sūmerētis	audīrētis
3rd *pers*	parārent	habērent	sūmerent	audīrent

FUTURE TENSE
Indicative

SING				
1st *pers*	parābō	habēbō	sūmam	audiam
2nd *pers*	parābis	habēbis	sūmēs	audiēs
3rd *pers*	parābit	habēbit	sūmet	audiet
PLURAL				
1st *pers*	parābimus	habēbimus	sūmēmus	audiēmus
2nd *pers*	parābitis	habēbitis	sūmetis	audiētis
3rd *pers*	parābunt	habēbunt	sūment	audient

Subjunctive

SING

parātūrus, -a, -um	sim	*or*	essem
habitūrus, -a, -um	sis		essēs
sūmptūrus, -a, -um	sit		esset
audītūrus, -a, -um			

PLURAL

paratūrī, -ae, -a	simus	*or*	essēmus
habitūrī, -ae, -a	sitis		essētis
sūmptūrī, -ae, -a	sint		essent
audītūrī, -ae, -a			

PERFECT TENSE
Indicative

SING
1st pers	parāvī	habuī	sūmpsī	audīvī
2nd pers	parāvistī	habuistī	sūmpsistī	audīvistī
3rd pers	parāvit	habuit	sūmpsit	audīvit

PLURAL
1st pers	parāvimus	habuimus	sūmpsimus	audīvimus
2nd pers	parāvistis	habuistis	sūmpsistis	audīvistis
3rd pers	parāvērunt, -e	habuērunt, -e	sūmpsērunt, -e	audīvērunt, -e

Subjunctive

SING
1st pers	parāverim	habuerim	sūmpserim	audīverim
2nd pers	parāveris	habueris	sūmpseris	audīveris
3rd pers	parāverit	habuerit	sūmpserit	audīverit

PLURAL
1st pers	parāverimus	habuerimus	sūmpserimus	audīverimus
2nd pers	parāveritis	habueritis	sūmpseritis	audīveritis
3rd pers	parāverint	habuerint	sūmpserint	audīverint

PLUPERFECT TENSE
Indicative

SING
1st pers	parāveram	habueram	sūmpseram	audīveram
2nd pers	parāverās	habuerās	sūmpserās	audīverās
3rd pers	parāverat	habuerat	sūmpserat	audīverat

PLURAL
1st pers	parāverāmus	habuerāmus	sūmpserāmus	audīverāmus
2nd pers	parāverātis	habuerātis	sūmpserātis	audīverātis
3rd pers	parāverant	habuerant	sūmpserant	audīverant

Subjunctive

SING
1st pers	parāvissem	habuissem	sūmpsissem	audīvissem
2nd pers	parāvissēs	habuissēs	sūmpsissēs	audīvissēs
3rd pers	parāvisset	habuisset	sūmpsisset	audīvisset

PLURAL
1st pers	parāvissēmus	habuissēmus	sūmpsissēmus	audīvissēmus
2nd pers	parāvissētis	habuissētis	sūmpsissētis	audīvissētis
3rd pers	parāvissent	habuissent	sūmpsissent	audīvissent

FUTURE PERFECT TENSE
Indicative

SING				
1st *pers*	parāverō	habuerō	sūmpserō	audīverō
2nd *pers*	parāveris	habueris	sūmpseris	audīveris
3rd *pers*	parāverit	habuerit	sūmpserit	audīverit
PLURAL				
1st *pers*	parāverimus	habuerimus	sūmpserimus	audīverimus
2nd *pers*	parāveritis	habueritis	sūmpseritis	audīveritis
3rd *pers*	parāverint	habuerint	sūmpserint	audīverint

IMPERATIVE
Present

SING	parā	habē	sūme	audī
PLURAL	parāte	habēte	sūmite	audīte

Future

SING				
2nd *pers*	parātō	habētō	sūmitō	audītō
3rd *pers*	parātō	habētō	sūmitō	audītō
PLURAL				
2nd *pers*	parātōte	habētōte	sūmitōte	audītōte
3rd *pers*	parantō	habentō	sūmuntō	audiuntō

INFINITIVE
Present

parāre	habēre	sūmere	audīre

Perfect

parāvisse	habuisse	sūmpsisse	audīvisse

Future

parātūrus,	-a, -um, esse
habitūrus,	-a, -um, esse
sūmptūrus,	-a, -um, esse
audītūrus,	-a, -um, esse

PASSIVE

PRESENT TENSE

Indicative

SING				
1st pers	paror	habeor	sūmor	audior
2nd pers	parāris	habēris	sūmeris	audīris
3rd pers	parātur	habētur	sūmitur	audītur

PLURAL				
1st pers	parāmur	habēmur	sūmimur	audīmur
2nd pers	parāminī	habēminī	sūmiminī	audīminī
3rd pers	parantur	habentur	sūmuntur	audiuntur

Subjunctive

SING				
1st pers	parer	habear	sūmar	audiar
2nd pers	parēris	habeāris	sūmāris	audiāris
3rd pers	parētur	habeātur	sūmātur	audiātur

PLURAL				
1st pers	parēmur	habeāmur	sūmāmur	audiāmur
2nd pers	parēminī	habeāminī	sūmāminī	audiāminī
3rd pers	parentur	habeantur	sūmantur	audiantur

IMPERFECT TENSE

Indicative

SING				
1st pers	parābar	habēbar	sūmēbar	audiēbar
2nd pers	parābāris	habēbāris	sūmēbāris	audiēbāris
3rd pers	parābātur	habēbātur	sūmēbātur	audiēbātur

PLURAL				
1st pers	parābāmur	habēbāmur	sūmēbāmur	audiēbāmur
2nd pers	parābāmini	habēbāmini	sūmēbāminī	audiēbāminī
3rd pers	parābāntur	habēbantur	sūmēbantur	audiēbantur

Subjunctive

SING				
1st pers	parārer	habērer	sūmerer	audīrer
2nd pers	parārēris	habērēris	sūmerēris	audīrēris
3rd pers	parārētur	habērētur	sūmerētur	audīrētur

PLURAL				
1st pers	parārēmur	habērēmur	sūmerēmur	audīrēmur
2nd pers	parārēminī	habērēminī	sūmerēminī	audīrēminī
3rd pers	parārentur	habērentur	sūmerentur	audīrentur

FUTURE TENSE
Indicative

SING				
1st pers	parābor	habēbor	sūmar	audiar
2nd pers	parāberis	habēberis	sūmēris	audiēris
3rd pers	parābitur	habēbitur	sūmētur	audiētur

PLURAL				
1st pers	parābimur	habēbimur	sūmēmur	audiēmur
2nd pers	parābimini	habēbimini	sūmēminī	audiēminī
3rd pers	parābuntur	habēbuntur	sūmentur	audientur

PERFECT TENSE
Indicative

SING		PLURAL	
parātus, -a, -um	sum/es/est	parātī, -ae -a	sumus/estis/sunt
habitus, -a, -um	sum/es/est	habītī, -ae -a	sumus/estis/sunt
sūmptus, -a, -um	sum/es/est	sūmptī, -ae -a	sumus/estis/sunt
audītus, -a, -um	sum/es/est	audītī, -ae -a	sumus/estis/sunt

Subjunctive

SING		PLURAL	
parātus, -a, -um	sim/sīs/sit	parātī, -ae, -a	sumus/estis/sunt
habitus, -a, -um	sim/sīs/sit	habītī, -ae, -a	sumus/estis/sunt
sūmptus, -a, -um	sim/sīs/sit	sūmptī, -ae, -a	sumus/estis/sunt
audītus, -a, -um	sim/sīs/sit	audītī, -ae, -a	sumus/estis/sunt

PLUPERFECT TENSE
Indicative

SING		PLURAL	
parātus, -a, -um	eram/eras/erat	parātī, -ae, -a	eramus/eratis/erant
habitus, -a, -um	eram/eras/erat	habītī, -ae, -a	eramus/eratis/erant
sūmptus, -a, -um	eram/eras/erat	sūmptī, -ae, -a	eramus/eratis/erant
audītus, -a, -um	eram/eras/erat	audītī, -ae, -a	eramus/eratis/erant

Subjunctive

SING		PLURAL	
parātus, -a, -um	essem/essēs/esset	parātī, -ae, -a	essēmus/essētis/essent
habitus, -a, -um	essem/essēs/esset	habītī, -ae, -a	essēmus/essētis/essent
sūmptus, -a, -um	essem/essēs/esset	sūmptī, -ae, -a	essēmus/essētis/essent
audītus, -a, -um	essem/essēs/esset	audītī, -ae, -a	essēmus/essētis/essent

FUTURE PERFECT TENSE
Indicative

SING		PLURAL	
parātus, -a, -um	erō/eris/erit	parātī, -ae, -a	erimus/eritis/erunt
habitus, -a, -um	erō/eris/erit	habītī, -ae, -a	erimus/eritis/erunt
sūmptus, -a, -um	erō/eris/erit	sūmptī, -ae, -a	erimus/eritis/erunt
audītus, -a, -um	erō/eris/erit	audītī, -ae, -a	erimus/eritis/erunt

IMPERATIVE
Present

SING	parāre	habēre	sūmere	audīre
PLURAL	parāminī	habēminī	sūmiminī	audīminī

Future

SING				
2nd pers	parātor	habētor	sūmitor	audītor
3rd pers	parātor	habētor	sūmitor	audītor
PLURAL				
3rd pers	parantor	habentor	sūmuntor	audiuntor

INFINITIVE
Present

parārī	habērī	sūmī	audīrī

Perfect

parātus -a, -um, esse	habitus -a, -um, esse	sūmptus -a, -um, esse	audītus, -a, -um, esse

Future

parātum īrī	habitum īrī	sūmptum īrī	audītum īrī

VERBAL NOUNS AND ADJECTIVES

Present Participle Active

parāns	habēns	sūmēns	audiēns

Perfect Participle Passive

parātus	habitus	sūmptus	audītus

Future Participle Active

parātūrus	habitūrus	sūmptūrus	audītūrus

Gerund
(acc, gen, dat and abl)

parandum, -ī, -ō	habendum, -ī, -ō	sūmendum, -ī, -ō	audiendum, -ī, -ō

Gerundive

parandus	habendus	sūmendus	audiendus

Supines

1st	parātum	habitum	sūmptum	audītum
2nd	parātū	habitū	sūmptū	audītū

Note. *Some verbs of the 3rd conjugation have the present indicative ending in -io; e.g.* **capio,** *I capture.*

PRESENT TENSE

INDICATIVE		SUBJUNCTIVE	
Active	**Passive**	**Active**	**Passive**
capio	capior	capiam	capiar
capis	caperis	capias	capiāris
capit	capitur	capiat	capiātur
capimus	capimur	capiāmus	capiāmur
capitis	capiminī	capiātis	capiāminī
capiunt	capiuntur	capiant	capiantur

IMPERFECT TENSE

capiēbam *etc.*	capiēbar *etc.*	caperem *etc.*	caperer *etc.*

FUTURE TENSE

capiam	capiar
capiēs etc.	capiēris etc.

INFINITIVE MOOD

Present Active	capere
Present Passive	capī

PRESENT IMPERATIVE

Active		**Passive**	
cape	capite	capere	capiminī

	PARTICIPLE	GERUND	GERUNDIVE
Pres.	capiēns	capiendum	capiendus, -a, -um

In all other tenses and moods **capere** *is similar to* **sumere**.

IRREGULAR VERBS

	Esse *be*	**Posse** *be able*	**Velle** *wish*	**Ire** *go*
Present Indicative				
SING				
1st pers	sum	possum	volō	eō
2nd pers	es	potes	vīs	īs
3rd pers	est	potest	vult, volt	it
PLURAL				
1st pers	sumus	possumus	volumus	īmus
2nd pers	estis	potestis	vultis, voltis	ītis
3rd pers	sunt	possunt	volunt	eunt

Present Subjunctive

SING				
1st pers	sim	possim	velim	eam
2nd pers	sīs	possīs	velīs	eās
3rd pers	sit	possit	velit	eat
PLURAL				
1st pers	sīmus	possīmus	velīmus	eāmus
2nd pers	sītis	possītis	velītis	eātis
3rd pers	sint	possint	velint	eant

Imperfect Indicative

1st pers	eram	poteram	volēbam	ībam

Imperfect Subjunctive

1st pers	essem	possem	vellem	īrem

Future Indicative

1st pers	erō	poterō	volam	ībō

Future Subjunctive

1st pers	futūrus, -a, -um sim *or* essem	—	—	itūrus, -a, -um sim *or* essem

Perfect Indicative

1st pers	fuī	potuī	voluī	īvī, iī

Perfect Subjunctive

1ˢᵗ *pers*	fuerim	potuerim	voluerim	īverim, ierim

Pluperfect Indicative

1ˢᵗ *pers*	fueram	potueram	volueram	īveram, ieram

Pluperfect Subjunctive

1ˢᵗ *pers*	fuissem	potuissem	voluissem	īvissem, iissem

Future Perfect Indicative

1ˢᵗ *pers*	fuerō	potuerō	voluerō	īverō, ierō

Present Imperative

SING	es	—	—	ī
PLURAL	este	—	—	īte

Future Imperative

SING	estō	—	—	ītō
PLURAL	estōte	—	—	ītōte

Infinitives

PRES	esse	posse	velle	īre
PERF	fuisse	potuisse	voluisse	īvisse, iisse
FUT	futūrus, -a, -um, esse	—	—	itūrus, -a, -um, esse

Participles

PRES	—	—	—	iēns, euntis
FUT	futūrus	—	—	itūrus

Gerund and Supine

GERUND	—	—	—	eundum
SUPINE	—	—	—	itum

LATIN – ENGLISH

Aa

ā¹ *prep (with abl)* from; after, since; by, in respect of; **ab epistulīs, ā manū** secretary; **ab hāc parte** on this side; **ab integrō** afresh; **ā nōbīs** on our side; **ā tergō** in the rear; **cōpiōsus ā frūmentō** rich in corn; **usque ab** ever since

ā² *interj* ah!

ab *prep see* **ā¹**

abāctus *ppp of* **abigō**

abacus, -ī *m* tray; sideboard; gaming board; panel; counting table

abaliēnō, -āre, -āvī, -ātum *vt* to dispose of; to remove, estrange

Abantiadēs *m* Acrisius or Perseus

Abās, -antis *m a king of Argos*

abavus, -ī *m* great-great-grandfather

abbās, -ātis *m* abbot

abbātia *f* abbey

abbātissa *f* abbess

Abdēra, -ōrum or **-ae** *ntpl, fs a town in Thrace*

Abdērītānus *adj see* **Abdēra**

Abdērītēs *m* Democritus or Protagoras

abdicātiō, -ōnis *f* disowning, abdication

abdicō, -āre, -āvī, -ātum *vt* to disown; to resign; **sē abdicāre** abdicate

abdīcō, -īcere, -īxī, -ictum *vt* (AUG) to be unfavourable to

abditus *ppp of* **abdō**

abdō, -ere, -idī, -itum *vt* to hide; to remove

abdōmen, -inis *nt* paunch, belly; gluttony

abdūcō, -ūcere, -ūxi, -uctum *vt* to lead away, take away; to seduce

abductus *ppp of* **abdūcō**

abecedārium, -iī *nt* alphabet

abēgī *perf of* **abigō**

abeō, -īre, -iī, -itum *vi* to go away, depart; to pass away; to be changed; to retire *(from an office)*; **sīc abīre** turn out like this

abequitō, -āre, -āvī, -ātum *vi* to ride away

aberrātiō, -ōnis *f* relief *(from trouble)*

aberrō, -āre, -āvī, -ātum *vi* to stray; to deviate; to have respite

abfore *fut infin of* **absum**

abfuī *perf of* **absum**

abfutūrus *fut p of* **absum**

abhinc *adv* since, ago

abhorreō, -ēre, -uī *vi* to shrink from; to differ; to be inconsistent

abiciō, -icere, -iēcī, -iectum *vt* to throw away, throw down; to abandon, degrade

abiectus *ppp of* **abiciō** ✦ *adj* despondent; contemptible

abiēgnus *adj* of fir

abiēns, -euntis *pres p of* **abeō**

abiēs, -etis *f* fir; ship

abigō, -igere, -ēgī, -āctum *vt* to drive away

abitus, -ūs *m* departure; exit

abiūdicō, -āre, -āvī, -ātum *vt* to take away *(by judicial award)*

abiūnctus *ppp of* **abiungō**

abiungō, -ungere, -ūnxī, -ūnctum *vt* to unyoke; to detach

abiūrō, -āre, -āvī, -ātum *vt* to deny on oath

ablātus *ppp of* **auferō**

ablēgātiō, -ōnis *f* sending away

ablēgō, -āre, -āvī, -ātum *vt* to send out of the way

abligurriō, -īre, -īvī, -ītum *vt* to spend extravagantly

ablocō, -āre, -āvī, -ātum *vt* to let *(a house)*

ablūdō, -dere, -sī, -sum *vi* to be unlike

abluō, -uere, -uī, -ūtum *vt* to wash clean; to remove

abnegō, -āre, -āvī, -ātum *vt* to refuse

abnepōs, -ōtis *m* great-great-grandson

abneptis *f* great-great-granddaughter

abnoctō, -āre *vi* to stay out all night

abnōrmis *adj* unorthodox

abnuō, -uere, -uī, -ūtum *vt* to refuse; to deny

aboleō, -ēre, -ēvī, -itum *vt* to abolish

abolēscō, -ēscere, -ēvī *vi* to vanish

abolitiō, -ōnis *f* cancelling

abolla, -ae *f* greatcoat

abōminātus *adj* accursed

abōminor, -ārī, -ātus *vt* to deprecate; to detest

Aborīginēs, -um *mpl* original inhabitants

aborior, -īrī, -tus *vi* to miscarry

abortiō, -ōnis *f* miscarriage

abortīvus *adj* born prematurely

abortus, -ūs *m* miscarriage

abrādō, -dere, -sī, -sum *vt* to scrape off, shave

abrāsus *ppp of* **abrādō**

abreptus *ppp of* **abripiō**

abripiō, -ipere, -ipuī, -eptum *vt* to drag away, carry off

abrogātiō, -ōnis *f* repeal

abrogō, -āre, -āvī, -ātum *vt* to annul

abrotonum, -ī *nt* southernwood

abrumpō, -umpere, -ūpī, -uptum *vt* to break off

abruptus *ppp of* **abrumpō** ✦ *adj* steep; abrupt, disconnected

abs *etc see* **ā¹**

abscēdō, **-ēdere**, **-essi**, **-essum** *vi* to depart, withdraw; to cease

abscīdō, **-dere**, **-dī**, **-sum** *vt* to cut off

abscindō, **-ndere**, **-dī**, **-ssum** *vt* to tear off, cut off

abscissus *ppp of* **abscindō**

abscīsus *ppp of* **abscīdō** ♦ *adj* steep; abrupt

abscondō, **-ere**, **-ī** *and* **-idī**, **-itum** *vt* to conceal; to leave behind

absēns, **-entis** *pres p of* **absum** ♦ *adj* absent

absentia, **-ae** *f* absence

absiliō, **-īre**, **-iī** *and* **-uī** *vi* to spring away

absimilis *adj* unlike

absinthium, **-ī** *and* **-iī** *nt* wormwood

absis, **-īdis** *f* vault; (ECCL) chancel

absistō, **-istere**, **-titī** *vi* to come away; to desist

absolūte *adv* fully, unrestrictedly

absolūtiō, **-ōnis** *f* acquittal; perfection

absolūtus *ppp of* **absolvō** ♦ *adj* complete; (RHET) unqualified

absolvō, **-vere**, **-vī**, **-ūtum** *vt* to release, set free; (LAW) to acquit; to bring to completion, finish off; to pay off, discharge

absonus *adj* unmusical; incongruous; ~ **ab** not in keeping with

absorbeō, **-bēre**, **-buī**, **-ptum** *vt* to swallow up; to monopolize

absp- *etc see* **asp-**

absque *prep* (with abl) without, but for

abstēmius *adj* temperate

abstergeō, **-gēre**, **-sī**, **-sum** *vt* to wipe away; (fig) to banish

abstern̄eō, **-ēre**, **-ui**, **-itum** *vt* to scare away, deter

abstinēns, **-entis** *adj* continent

abstinenter *adv* with restraint

abstinentia, **-ae** *f* restraint, self-control; fasting

abstineō, **-inēre**, **-inuī**, **-entum** *vt* to withhold, keep off ♦ *vi* to abstain, refrain; **sē abstinēre** refrain

abstitī *perf of* **absistō**

abstō, **-āre** *vi* to stand aloof

abstractus *ppp of* **abstrahō**

abstrahō, **-here**, **-xī**, **-ctum** *vt* to drag away, remove; to divert

abstrūdō, **-dere**, **-sī**, **-sum** *vt* to conceal

abstrūsus *ppp of* **abstrūdō** ♦ *adj* deep, abstruse; reserved

abstulī *perf of* **auferō**

absum, **abesse**, **āfuī** *vi* to be away, absent, distant; to keep clear of; to be different; to be missing, fail to assist; **tantum abest ut** so far from; **haud multum āfuit quīn** I was (they were *etc*) within an ace of

absūmō, **-ere**, **-psī**, **-ptum** *vt* to consume; to ruin, kill; (time) to spend

absurdē *adv* out of tune; absurdly

absurdus *adj* unmusical; senseless, absurd

Absyrtus, **-ī** *m* brother of Medea

abundāns, **-antis** *adj* overflowing; abundant; rich; abounding in

abundanter *adv* copiously

abundantia, **-ae** *f* abundance, plenty; wealth

abundē *adv* abundantly, more than enough

abundō, **-āre**, **-āvī**, **-ātum** *vi* to overflow; to abound, be rich in

abūsiō, **-ōnis** *f* (RHET) catachresis

abusque *prep* (with abl) all the way from

abūtor, **-tī**, **-sus** *vi* (with abl) to use up; to misuse

Abydēnus *adj see* **Abȳdos**

Abȳdos, **Abȳdus**, **-ī** *m* a town on Dardanelles

ac *etc see* **atque**

Acadēmia, **-ae** *f* Plato's Academy at Athens; Plato's philosophy; Cicero's villa

Acadēmica *ntpl* book of Cicero on philosophy

Acadēmus, **-ī** *m* an Athenian hero

acalanthis, **-dis** *f* thistlefinch

acanthus, **-ī** *m* bear's-breech

Acarnānes, **-um** *mpl* the Acarnanians

Acarnānia, **-iae** *f* a district of N.W. Greece

Acarnānicus *adj see* **Acarnānia**

Acca Larentia, **Accae Larentiae** *f* Roman goddess

accēdō, **-ēdere**, **-essī**, **-essum** *vi* to come, go to, approach; to attack; to be added; to agree with; (duty) to take up; **ad rem pūblicam accēdere** to enter politics; **prope ~ ad** to resemble; **accēdit quod**, **hūc accēdit ut** moreover

accelerō, **-āre**, **-āvī**, **-ātum** *vt*, *vi* to hasten

accendō, **-endere**, **-endī**, **-ēnsum** *vt* to set on fire, light; to illuminate; (fig) to inflame, incite

accēnseō, **-ēre**, **-uī**, **-um** *vt* to assign

accēnsī *mpl* (MIL) supernumeraries

accēnsus¹ *ppp of* **accendō**, **accēnseō**

accēnsus², **-ī** *m* officer attending a magistrate

accentus, **-ūs** *m* accent

accēpī *perf of* **accipiō**

acceptiō, **-ōnis** *f* receiving

acceptum *nt* credit side (of ledger); **in ~ referre** place to one's credit

acceptus *ppp of* **accipiō** ♦ *adj* acceptable

accersō *etc see* **accessō**

accessiō, **-ōnis** *f* coming, visiting; attack; increase, addition

accessus, **-ūs** *m* approach, visit; flood tide; admittance, entrance

Acciānus *adj see* **Accius**

accidō, **-ere**, **-ī** *vi* to fall (at, on); (senses) to strike; (usu misfortune) to befall, happen

accīdō, **-dere**, **-dī**, **-sum** *vt* to fell, cut into; to eat up, impair

accingō, **-gere**, **-xī**, **-ctum** *vt* to gird on, arm; (fig) to make ready

acciō, **-īre**, **-īvī**, **-ītum** *vt* to summon; to procure

accipiō, **-ipere**, **-ēpī**, **-eptum** *vt* to take, receive, accept; (guest) to treat; (information) to hear; to interpret, take as; to suffer; to approve

accipiter, **-ris** *m* hawk

accīsus *ppp of* **accīdō**

accītus¹ *ppp of* **acciō**

accītus², **-ūs** *m* summons

Accius, **-ī** *m* Roman tragic poet

acclāmātiō, **-ōnis** *f* shout (of approval or disapproval)

acclāmō, **-āre**, **-āvī**, **-ātum** *vi* to cry out against; to hail

acclārō, **-āre**, **-āvī**, **-ātum** *vt* to make known

acclīnātus *adj* sloping

acclīnis *adj* leaning against; inclined

acclīnō, **-āre**, **-āvī**, **-ātum** vt to lean against; **sē acclīnāre** incline towards
acclīvis adj uphill
acclīvitās, **-ātis** f gradient
accola, **-ae** m neighbour
accolō, **-olere**, **-oluī**, **-ultum** vt to live near
accommodātē adv suitably
accommodātiō, **-ōnis** f fitting together; compliance
accommodātus adj suited
accommodō, **-āre**, **-āvī**, **-ātum** vt to fit, put on; to adjust, adapt, bring to; to apply; **sē accommodāre** devote oneself
accommodus adj suitable
accrēdō, **-ere**, **-idī**, **-itum** vi to believe
accrēscō, **-ēscere**, **-ēvī**, **-ētum** vi to increase, be added
accrētiō, **-ōnis** f increasing
accubitiō, **-ōnis** f reclining (at meals)
accubō, **-āre** vi to lie near; to recline (at meals)
accumbō, **-mbere**, **-buī**, **-bitum** vi to recline at table; **in sinū accumbere** sit next to
accumulātē adv copiously
accumulō, **-āre**, **-āvī**, **-ātum** vt to pile up, amass; to load
accūrātē adv painstakingly
accūrātiō, **-ōnis** f exactness
accūrātus adj studied
accūrō, **-āre**, **-āvī**, **-ātum** vt to attend to
accurrō, **-rrere**, **-currī** and **-rrī**, **-rsum** vi to hurry to
accursus, **-ūs** m hurrying
accūsābilis adj reprehensible
accūsātiō, **-ōnis** f accusation
accūsātor, **-ōris** m accuser, prosecutor
accūsātōriē adv like an accuser
accūsātōrius adj of the accuser
accūsō, **-āre**, **-āvī**, **-ātum** vt to accuse, prosecute; to reproach; **ambitūs accusāre** prosecute for bribery
acer, **-is** nt maple
ācer, **-ris** adj sharp; (sensation) keen, pungent; (emotion) violent; (mind) shrewd; (conduct) eager, brave; hasty, fierce; (circumstances) severe
acerbē adv see **acerbus**
acerbitās, **-ātis** f bitterness; (fig) harshness, severity; sorrow
acerbō, **-āre**, **-āvī**, **-ātum** vt to aggravate
acerbus adj bitter, sour; harsh; (fig) premature; (person) rough, morose, violent; (things) troublesome, sad
acernus adj of maple
acerra, **-ae** f incense box
acervātim adv in heaps
acervō, **-āre**, **-āvī**, **-ātum** vt to pile up
acervus, **-ī** m heap
acēscō, **-ere**, **acuī** vt to turn sour
Acestēs, **-ae** m a mythical Sicilian
acētum, **-ī** nt vinegar; (fig) wit
Achaemenēs, **-is** m first Persian king; type of Oriental wealth
Achaeus adj Greek
Achāia, **-ae** f a district in W. Greece; Greece; Roman province
Achāicus adj see **Achāia**

Achātēs, **-ae** m companion of Aeneas
Achelōius adj see **Achelōus**
Achelōus, **-ī** m river in N.W. Greece; river god
Acherōn, **-ontis** m river in Hades
Acherūsius adj see **Acherōn**
Achillēs, **-is** m Greek epic hero
Achillēus adj see **Achillēs**
Achīvus adj Greek
Acidālia, **-ae** f Venus
Acidālius adj see **Acidālia**
acidus adj sour, tart; (fig) disagreeable
aciēs, **-ēī** f sharp edge or point; (eye) sight, keen glance, pupil; (mind) power, apprehension; (MIL) line of troops, battle order, army, battle; (fig) debate; **prīma ~ van**; **novissima ~ rearguard**
acīnacēs, **-is** m scimitar
acinum, **-ī** nt berry, grape; fruit seed
acinus, **-ī** m berry, grape; fruit seed
acipēnser, **-eris** m sturgeon
acipēnsis, **-is** m sturgeon
aclys, **-dis** f javelin
aconītum, **-ī** nt monkshood; poison
acor, **-ōris** m sour taste
acquiēscō, **-ēscere**, **-ēvī**, **-ētum** vi to rest, die; to find pleasure (in); to acquiesce
acquīrō, **-rere**, **-sīvī**, **-sītum** vt to get in addition, acquire
Acragās, **-antis** m see **Agrigentum**
acrātophorum, **-ī** nt wine jar
acrēdula, **-ae** f a bird (unidentified)
ācriculus adj peevish
ācrimōnia, **-ae** f pungent taste; (speech, action) briskness, go
Acrisiōniadēs, **-ae** m Perseus
Acrisius, **-ī** m father of Danae
ācriter adv see **ācer**
ācroāma, **-tis** nt entertainment, entertainer
ācroāsis, **-is** f public lecture
Ācroceraunia, **-ōrum** ntpl a promontory in N.W. Greece
Ācrocorinthus, **-ī** f fortress of Corinth
acta, **-ae** f beach
ācta, **-ōrum** ntpl public records, proceedings; **~ diurna**, **~ pūblica** daily gazette
Actaeus adj Athenian
āctiō, **-ōnis** f action, doing; official duties, negotiations; (LAW) action, suit, indictment, pleading, case, trial; (RHET) delivery; (drama) plot; **~ grātiārum** expression of thanks; **āctiōnem intendere**, **āctiōnem īnstituere** bring an action
āctitō, **-āre**, **-āvī**, **-ātum** vt to plead, act often
Actium, **-ī** and **-iī** nt a town in N.W. Greece; Augustus's great victory
Actius, **Actiacus** adj see **Actium**
āctivus adj of action, practical
āctor, **-ōris** m driver, performer; (LAW) plaintiff, pleader; (COMM) agent; (RHET) orator; (drama) actor; **~ pūblicus** manager of public property; **~ summārum** cashier
āctuāria f pinnace
āctuāriolum, **-ī** m small barge
āctuārius adj fast (ship)
āctuōsē adv actively

āctuōsus *adj* very active

āctus[1] *ppp of* agō

āctus[2], **-ūs** *m* moving, driving; right of way for cattle or vehicles; performance; (*drama*) playing a part, recital, act of a play

āctūtum *adv* immediately

acuī *perf of* acēscō; acuō

acula, -ae *f* small stream

aculeātus *adj* prickly; (*words*) stinging; quibbling

aculeus, -ī *m* sting, prickle, barb; (*fig*) sting

acūmen, -inis *nt* point, sting; (*fig*) shrewdness, ingenuity; trickery

acuō, -uere, -uī, -ūtum *vt* to sharpen; to exercise; (*the mind*) to stimulate; to rouse (*to action*)

acus, -ūs *f* needle, pin; acū pingere embroider; rem acū tangere hit the nail on the head

acūtē *adv see* acūtus

acūtulus *adj* rather subtle

acūtus *adj* sharp, pointed; (*senses*) keen; (*sound*) high-pitched; severe; intelligent

ad *prep* (*with acc*) to, towards, against; near, at; until; (*num*) about; with regard to, according to; for the purpose of, for; compared with; besides; ad Castoris to the temple of Castor; ad dextram on the right; ad hōc besides; ad locum on the spot; ad manum at hand; ad rem to the point; ad summam in short; ad tempus in time; ad ūnum omnes all without exception; ad urbem esse wait outside the city gates; ad verbum literally; nīl ad nothing to do with; usque ad right up to

adāctiō, -ōnis *f* enforcing

adāctus[1] *ppp of* adigō

adāctus[2], **-ūs** *m* snapping (*of teeth*)

adaequē *adv* equally

adaequō, -āre, -āvī, -ātum *vt* to make equal, level; to equal, match ◆ *vi* to be equal

adamantēus, adamantinus *adj see* adamās

adamās, -antis *m* adamant, steel; diamond

adamō, -āre, -āvī, -ātum *vt* to fall in love with

adaperiō, -īre, -uī, -tum *vt* to throw open

adapertilis *adj* openable

adaquō, -āre, -āvī, -ātum *vt* (*plants, animals*) to water

adaquor *vi* to fetch water

adauctus, -ūs *m* growing

adaugeō, -gēre, -xī, -ctum *vt* to aggravate; (*sacrifice*) to consecrate

adaugēscō, -ere *vi* to grow bigger

adbibō, -ere, -ī *vt* to drink; (*fig*) to drink in

adbītō, -ere *vi* to come near

adc- *etc see* acc-

addecet, -ēre *vt* it becomes

addēnseō, -ēre *vt* to close (*ranks*)

addīcō, -īcere, -īxī, -ictum *vi* (AUG) to be favourable ◆ *vt* (LAW) to award; (*auction*) to knock down; (*fig*) to sacrifice, devote

addictiō, -ōnis *f* award (*at law*)

addictus *ppp of* addīcō ◆ *m* bondsman

addiscō, -scere, -dicī *vt* to learn more

additāmentum, -ī *nt* increase

additus *ppp of* addō

addō, -ere, -idī, -itum *vt* to add, put to, bring to; to impart; to increase; addere gradum quicken pace; adde quod besides

addoceō, -ēre, -uī, -tum *vt* to teach new

addubitō, -āre, -āvī, -ātum *vi* to be in doubt ◆ *vt* to question

addūcō, -ūcere, -ūxī, -uctum *vt* to take, bring to; to draw together, pull taut, wrinkle; (*fig*) to induce; (*pass*) to be led to believe

adductus *ppp of* addūcō ◆ *adj* contracted; (*fig*) severe

adedō, -edere, -ēdī, -ēsum *vt* to begin to eat; to eat up; to use up; to wear away

adēmī *perf of* adimō

ademptiō, -ōnis *f* taking away

ademptus *ppp of* adimō

adeō[1], **-īre, -iī, -itum** *vt, vi* to go to, approach; to address; to undertake, submit to, enter upon

adeō[2] *adv* so; (*after pron*) just; (*after conj, adv, adj: for emphasis*) indeed, very; (*adding an explanation*) for, in fact, thus; or rather; ~ nōn ... ut so far from; atque ~, sīve ~ or rather; usque ~ so far, so long, so much

adeps, -ipis *m/f* fat; corpulence

adeptiō, -ōnis *f* attainment

adeptus *ppa of* adipīscor

adequitō, -āre, -āvī, -ātum *vi* to ride up (to)

adesdum come here!

adesse *infin of* adsum

adēsus *ppp of* adedō

adfābilis *adj* easy to talk to

adfābilitās, -ātis *f* courtesy

adfabrē *adv* ingeniously

adfatim *adv* to one's satisfaction, enough, ad nauseam

adfātur, -rī, -tus *vt* (*defec*) to speak to

adfātus[1] *ppa of* adfātur

adfātus[2], **-ūs** *m* speaking to

adfectātiō, -ōnis *f* aspiring; (RHET) affectation

adfectātus *adj* (RHET) studied

adfectiō, -ōnis *f* frame of mind, mood; disposition; goodwill; (ASTR) relative position

adfectō, -āre, -āvī, -ātum *vt* to aspire to, aim at; to try to win over; to make pretence of; viam adfectāre ad try to get to

adfectus[1] *ppp of* adficiō ◆ *adj* affected with, experienced (*abl*); (*person*) disposed; (*things*) weakened; (*undertakings*) well-advanced

adfectus[2], **-ūs** *m* disposition, mood; fondness; (*pl*) loved ones

adferō, adferre, attulī, adlātum *and* allātum *vt* to bring, carry to; to bring to bear, use against; to bring news; (*explanation*) to bring forward; to contribute (*something useful*)

adficiō, -icere, -ēcī, -ectum *vt* to affect; to endow, afflict with (*abl*); exsiliō adficere banish; honōre adficere honour (*also used with other nouns to express the corresponding verbs*)

adfictus *ppp of* adfingō

adfīgō, -gere, -xi, -xum *vt* to fasten, attach; to impress (*on the mind*)

adfingō, -ngere, -nxī, -ctum *vt* to make, form (*as part of*); invent

adfīnis, -is *m/f* neighbour; relation (*by marriage*) ◆ *adj* neighbouring; associated with (*dat, gen*)

adfīnitās, -ātis f relationship (by marriage)
adfirmātē adv with assurance
adfirmātiō, -ōnis f declaration
adfirmō, -āre, -āvī, -ātum vt to declare; to confirm
adfīxus ppp of **adfīgō**
adflātus, -ūs m breath, exhalation; (fig) inspiration
adfleō, -ēre vi to weep (at)
adflīctātiō, -ōnis f suffering
adflīctō, -āre, -āvī, -ātum vt to harass, distress
adflīctor, -ōris m destroyer
adflīctus ppp of **adflīgō** ◆ adj distressed, ruined; dejected; depraved
adflīgō, -īgere, -īxī, -īctum vt to dash against, throw down; (fig) to impair, crush
adflō, -āre, -āvī, -ātum vt, vi to blow on, breathe upon
adfluēns, -entis adj rich (in)
adfluenter adv copiously
adfluentia, -ae f abundance
adfluō, -ere, -xī, -xum vi to flow; (fig) to flock in, abound in
adfore fut infin of **adsum**
adforem imperf subj of **adsum**
adfuī perf of **adsum**
adfulgeō, -gēre, -sī vi to shine on; to appear
adfundō, -undere, -ūdī, -ūsum vt to pour in; to rush (troops) to
adfūsus adj prostrate
adfutūrus fut p of **adsum**
adgemō, -ere vi to groan at
adglomerō, -āre vt to add on
adglūtinō, -āre vt to stick on
adgravēscō, -ere vi to become worse
adgravō, -āre, -āvī, -ātum vt to aggravate
adgredior, -dī, -ssus vt to approach, accost; to attack; (a task) to undertake, take up
adgregō, -āre, -āvī, -ātum vt to add, attach
adgressiō, -ōnis f introductory remarks
adgressus ppa of **adgredior**
adhaereō, -rēre, -sī, -sum vi to stick to; (fig) to cling to, keep close to
adhaerēscō, -ere vi to stick to or in; (speech) to falter
adhaesiō, -ōnis f clinging
adhaesus, -ūs m adhering
adhibeō, -ēre, -uī, -itum vt to bring, put, add; to summon, consult, treat; to use, apply (for some purpose)
adhinniō, -īre, -īvī, -ītum vi to neigh to; (fig) to go into raptures over
adhortātiō, -ōnis f exhortation
adhortātor, -ōris m encourager
adhortor, -ārī, -ātus vt to encourage, urge
adhūc adv so far; as yet, till now; still; ~ nōn not yet
adiaceō, -ēre, -uī vi to lie near, border on
adiciō, -icere, -iēcī, -iectum vt to throw to; to add; to turn towards (mind, eyes)
adiectiō, -ōnis f addition
adiectus¹ ppp of **adiciō**
adiectus², -ūs m bringing close

adigō, -igere, -ēgī, -āctum vt to drive (to); to compel; **iūs iūrandum adigere** put on oath; **in verba adigere** force to owe allegiance
adimō, -imere, -ēmī, -emptum vt to take away (from dat)
adipātum nt pastry
adipātus adj fatty; (fig) florid
adipīscor, -ipīscī, -eptus vt to overtake; to attain, acquire
aditus, -ūs m approach, access (to a person); entrance; (fig) avenue
adiūdicō, -āre, -āvī, -ātum vt to award (in arbitration); to ascribe
adiūmentum, -ī nt aid, means of support
adiūncta ntpl collateral circumstances
adiūnctiō, -ōnis f uniting; addition; (RHET) proviso; repetition
adiūnctus ppp of **adiungō** ◆ adj connected
adiungō, -ungere, -ūnxī, -ūnctum vt to yoke; to attach; (suspicion etc) to direct; (remark) to add
adiūrō, -āre, -āvī, -ātum vt, vi to swear, swear by
adiūtō, -āre, -āvī, -ātum vt to help
adiūtor, -ōris m helper; (MIL) adjutant; (POL) official; (THEAT) supporting cast
adiūtrīx, -rīcis f see **adiūtor**
adiūtus ppp of **adiuvō**
adiuvō, -uvāre, -ūvī, -ūtum vt to help; to encourage
adj- etc see **adi-**
adlābor, -bī, -psus vi to fall, move towards, come to
adlabōrō, -āre, -āvī, -ātum vi to work hard; to improve by taking trouble
adlacrimō, -āre, -āvī, -ātum vi to shed tears
adlāpsus¹ ppa of **adlābor**
adlāpsus², -ūs m stealthy approach
adlātrō, -āre, -āvī, -ātum vt to bark at; (fig) to revile
adlātus ppp of **adferō**
adlaudō, -āre, -āvī, -ātum vt to praise highly
adlectō, -āre, -āvī, -ātum vt to entice
adlectus ppp of **adliciō**
adlēctus ppp of **adlegō**
adlēgātī mpl deputies
adlēgātiō, -ōnis f mission
adlegō, -egere, -ēgī, -ēctum vt to elect
adlēgō, -āre, -āvī, -ātum vt to despatch, commission; to mention
adlevāmentum, -ī nt relief
adlevātiō, -ōnis f easing
adlevō, -āre, -āvī, -ātum vt to lift up; to comfort; to weaken
adliciō, -icere, -exī, -ectum vt to attract
adlīdō, -dere, -sī, -sum vt to dash (against); (fig) to hurt
adligō, -āre, -āvī, -ātum vt to tie up, bandage; (fig) to bind, lay under an obligation
adlinō, -inere, -ēvī, -itum vt to smear; (fig) to attach
adlīsus ppp of **adlīdō**
adlocūtiō, -ōnis f address, comforting words
adlocūtus ppa of **adloquor**
adloquium, -ī and **-iī** nt talk; encouragement
adloquor, -quī, -cūtus vt to speak to, address

adlūdiō, **-āre**, **-āvī**, **-ātum** *vi* to play (with)
adlŭdŏ, **-dere**, **-sī**, **-sum** *vi* to joke, play
adluŏ, **-ere**, **-ī** *vt* to wash
adluviēs, **-ēī** *f* pool left by flood water
adluviō, **-ōnis** *f* alluvial land
admātŭrŏ, **-āre**, **-āvī**, **-atum** *vt* to hurry on
admētior, **-tīrī**, **-nsus** *vt* to measure out
adminiculor, **-ārī**, **-ātus** *vt* to prop
adminiculum, **-ī** *nt* (AGR) stake; (*fig*) support
administer, **-rī** *m* assistant
administrātiō, **-ōnis** *f* services; management
administrātor, **-ōris** *m* manager
administrŏ, **-āre**, **-āvī**, **-ātum** *vt* to manage, govern
admīrābilis *adj* wonderful, surprising
admīrābilitās, **-ātis** *f* wonderfulness
admīrābiliter *adv* admirably; paradoxically
admīrātiō, **-ōnis** *f* wonder, surprise, admiration
admīror, **-ārī**, **-ātus** *vt* to wonder at, admire; to be surprised at
admīsceŏ, **-scēre**, **-scuī**, **-xtum** *vt* to mix in with, add to; (*fig*) to involve; **sē admīscēre** interfere
admissārius, **-ī** *and* **-iī** *m* stallion
admissum, **-ī** *nt* crime
admissus *ppp of* **admittŏ**
admittŏ, **-ittere**, **-īsī**, **-issum** *vt* to let in, admit; to set at a gallop; to allow; to commit (*a crime*); **equō admissō** charging
admixtiō, **-ōnis** *f* admixture
admixtus *ppp of* **admīsceŏ**
admoderātē *adv* suitably
admoderor, **-ārī**, **-ātus** *vt* to restrain
admodum *adv* very, quite; fully; yes; (*with neg*) at all
admoneŏ, **-ēre**, **-uī**, **-itum** *vt* to remind, suggest, advise, warn
admonitiō, **-ōnis** *f* reminder, suggestion, admonition
admonitor, **-ōris** *m* admonisher (*male*)
admonitrīx, **-rīcis** *f* admonisher (*female*)
admonitū at the suggestion, instance
admordeŏ, **-dēre**, **-sum** *vt* to bite into; (*fig*) to cheat
admorsus *ppp of* **admordeŏ**
admōtiō, **-ōnis** *f* applying
admōtus *ppp of* **admoveŏ**
admoveŏ, **-ovēre**, **-ōvī**, **-ōtum** *vt* to move, bring up, apply; to lend (*an ear*), direct (*the mind*)
admurmurātiō, **-ōnis** *f* murmuring
admurmurŏ, **-āre**, **-āvī**, **-ātum** *vi* to murmur (*of a crowd approving or disapproving*)
admutilŏ, **-āre**, **-āvī**, **-ātum** *vt* to clip close; (*fig*) to cheat
adnectŏ, **-ctere**, **-xuī**, **-xum** *vt* to connect, tie
adnexus, **-ūs** *m* connection
adnīsus *ppa of* **adnītor**
adnītor, **-tī**, **-sus** *and* **-xus** *vi* to lean on; to exert oneself
adnīxus *ppp of* **adnītor**
adnŏ, **-āre** *vt*, *vi* to swim to
adnotŏ, **-āre**, **-āvī**, **-ātum** *vt* to comment on
adnumerŏ, **-āre**, **-āvī**, **-ātum** *vt* to pay out; to reckon along with

adnuŏ, **-uere**, **-uī**, **-ūtum** *vi* to nod; to assent, promise; to indicate
adoleŏ, **-olēre**, **-oluī**, **-ultum** *vt* to burn; to pile with gifts
adolēscen- *etc see* **adulēscen-**
adolēscŏ, **-ēscere**, **-ēvī** *vi* to grow up, increase; to burn
Adōnis, **-is** *and* **-idis** *m* a beautiful youth loved by Venus
adopertus *adj* covered
adoptātiō, **-ōnis** *f* adopting
adoptiō, **-ōnis** *f* adoption
adoptīvus *adj* by adoption
adoptŏ, **-āre**, **-āvī**, **-ātum** *vt* to choose; to adopt
ador, **-ōris** *and* **-oris** *nt* spelt
adōrea *f* glory
adōreus *adj see* **ador**
adorior, **-īrī**, **-tus** *vt* to accost; to attack; to set about
adōrnŏ, **-āre**, **-āvī**, **-ātum** *vt* to get ready
adōrŏ, **-āre**, **-āvī**, **-ātum** *vt* to entreat; to worship, revere
adortus *ppa of* **adorior**
adp- *etc see* **app-**
adrādŏ, **-dere**, **-sī**, **-sum** *vt* to shave close
Adrastus, **-ī** *m* a king of Argos
adrāsus *ppp of* **adrādŏ**
adrēctus *ppp of* **adrigŏ** ✦ *adj* steep
adrēpŏ, **-ere**, **-sī**, **-tum** *vi* to creep, steal into
adreptus *ppp of* **adripiŏ**
Adria *etc see* **Hadria** *etc*
adrīdeŏ, **-dēre**, **-sī**, **-sum** *vt*, *vi* to laugh, smile at; to please
adrigŏ, **-igere**, **-ēxī**, **-ēctum** *vt* to raise; (*fig*) to rouse
adripiŏ, **-ipere**, **-ipuī**, **-eptum** *vt* to seize; to appropriate; to take hold of; to learn quickly; (LAW) to arrest; to satirize
adrōdŏ, **-dere**, **-sī**, **-sum** *vt* to gnaw, nibble at
adrogāns, **-antis** *adj* arrogant, insolent
adroganter *adv see* **adrogāns**
adrogantia, **-ae** *f* arrogance, presumption, haughtiness
adrogātiō, **-ōnis** *f* adoption
adrogŏ, **-āre**, **-āvī**, **-ātum** *vt* to ask; to associate; to claim, assume; (*fig*) to award
adsc- *etc see* **asc-**
adsecla *etc see* **adsecula**
adsectātiō, **-ōnis** *f* attendance
adsectātor, **-ōris** *m* follower
adsector, **-ārī**, **-ātus** *vt* to attend on, follow (*esp a candidate*)
adsecula, **-ae** *m* follower (*derogatory*)
adsēdī *perf of* **adsideŏ**; **adsīdŏ**
adsēnsiō, **-ōnis** *f* assent, applause; (PHILOS) acceptance of the evidence of the senses
adsēnsor, **-ōris** *m* one in agreement
adsēnsus¹ *ppa of* **adsentiō**
adsēnsus², **-ūs** *m* assent, approval; echo; (PHILOS) acceptance of the evidence of the senses
adsentātiō, **-ōnis** *f* flattery
adsentātiuncula *f* trivial compliments
adsentātor, **-ōris** *m* flatterer (*male*)
adsentātōriē *adv* ingratiatingly

adsentātrīx, -rīcis f flatterer (*female*)
adsentiō, -entīre, -ēnsī, -ēnsum, adsentior, -entīrī, -ēnsus vi to agree, approve
adsentor, -ārī, -ātus vi to agree, flatter
adsequor, -quī, -cūtus vt to overtake; to attain; to grasp (*by understanding*)
adserō[1], -ere, -uī, -tum vt (*LAW*) to declare free (*usu with* **manū**), liberate (*a slave*), lay claim to, appropriate; **adsere in servitūtem** claim as a slave
adserō[2], -erere, -ēvī, -itum vt to plant near
adsertiō, -ōnis f declaration of status
adsertor, -ōris m champion
adserviō, -īre vi to assist
adservō, -āre, -āvī, -ātum vt to watch carefully; to keep, preserve
adsessiō, -ōnis f sitting beside
adsessor, -ōris m counsellor
adsessus, -ūs m sitting beside
adsevēranter adv emphatically
adsevērātiō, -ōnis f assertion; earnestness
adsevērō, -āre, -āvī, -ātum vt to do in earnest; to assert strongly
adsideō, -idēre, -ēdī, -essum vi to sit by; to attend, assist; to besiege; to resemble
adsīdō, -īdere, -ēdī vi to sit down
adsiduē adv continually
adsiduitās, -ātis f constant attendance; continuance; frequent recurrence
adsiduō adv continually
adsiduus[1] adj constantly in attendance, busy; continual, incessant
adsiduus[2], -ī m taxpayer
adsignātiō, -ōnis f allotment (*of land*)
adsignō, -āre, -āvī, -ātum vt to allot (*esp land*); assign; to impute, attribute; to consign
adsiliō, -ilīre, -iluī, -ultum vi to leap at or on to
adsimilis adj like
adsimiliter adv similarly
adsimulātus adj similar; counterfeit
adsimulō, -āre, -āvī, -ātum vt, vi to compare; to pretend, imitate
adsistō, -istere, -titī vi to stand (by); to defend
adsitus ppp of **adserō[2]**
adsoleō, -ēre vi to be usual
adsonō, -āre vi to respond
adsp- etc see **asp-**
adsternō, -ere vt to prostrate
adstipulātor, -ōris m supporter
adstipulor, -ārī, -ātus vi to agree with
adstitī perf of **adsistō; adstō**
adstō, -āre, -itī vi to stand near, stand up; to assist
adstrepō, -ere vi to roar
adstrictē adv concisely
adstrictus ppp of **adstringō ♦** adj tight, narrow; concise; stingy
adstringō, -ngere, -nxī, -ctum vt to draw close, tighten; to bind, oblige; to abridge
adstruō, -ere, -xī, -ctum vt to build on; to add
adstupeō, -ēre vi to be astonished
adsuēfaciō, -acere, -ēcī, -actum vt to accustom, train
adsuēscō, -scere, -vī, -tum vi to accustom, train

adsuētūdō, -inis f habit
adsuētus ppp of **adsuēscō ♦** adj customary
adsultō, -āre, -āvī, -ātum vi to jump; to attack
adsultus, -ūs m attack
adsum, -esse, -fuī vi to be present; to support, assist (*esp at law*); to come; to appear before (*a tribunal*); **animo adesse** pay attention; **iam aderō** I'll be back soon
adsūmō, -ere, -psī, -ptum vt to take for oneself, receive; to take also
adsūmptiō, -ōnis f taking up; (*LOGIC*) minor premise
adsūmptīvus adj (*LAW*) which takes its defence from extraneous circumstances
adsūmptum, -ī nt epithet
adsūmptus ppp of **adsūmō**
adsuō, -ere vt to sew on
adsurgō, -gere, -rēxī, -rēctum vi to rise, stand up; to swell, increase
adt- etc see **att-**
adulātiō, -ōnis f (*dogs*) fawning; servility
adulātor, -ōris m sycophant
adulātōrius adj flattering
adulēscēns, -entis m/f young man or woman (*usu from 15 to 30 years*)
adulēscentia, -ae f youth (*age 15 to 30*)
adulēscentula, -ae f girl
adulēscentulus, -ī m quite a young man
adulō, -āre, -āvī, -ātum, adulor, -ārī, -ātus vt, vi to fawn upon, flatter, kowtow
adulter, -ī m, **adultera, -ae** f adulterer, adulteress ♦ adj adulterous
adulterīnus adj forged
adulterium, -ī and **-iī** nt adultery
adulterō, -āre, -āvī, -ātum vt, vi to commit adultery; to falsify
adultus ppp of **adolēscō ♦** adj adult, mature
adumbrātim adv in outline
adumbrātiō, -ōnis f sketch; semblance
adumbrātus adj false
adumbrō, -āre, -āvī, -ātum vt to sketch; to represent, copy
aduncitās, -ātis f curvature
aduncus adj hooked, curved
adurgeō, -ēre vt to pursue closely
adūrō, -rere, -ssī, -stum vt to burn; to freeze; (*fig*) to fire
adusque prep (*with acc*) right up to ♦ adv entirely
adūstus ppp of **adūrō ♦** adj brown
advectīcius adj imported
advectō, -āre vt to carry frequently
advectus[1] ppp of **advehō**
advectus[2], -ūs m bringing
advehō, -here, -xī, -ctum vt to carry, convey; (*pass*) to ride
advēlō, -āre vt to crown
advena, -ae m/f stranger ♦ adj foreign
adveniō, -enīre, -ēnī, -entum vi to arrive, come
adventīcius adj foreign, extraneous; unearned
adventō, -āre, -āvī, -ātum vi to come nearer and nearer, advance rapidly
adventor, -ōris m visitor
adventus, -ūs m arrival, approach
adversāria ntpl daybook

adversārius, **-i** *and* **-ii** *m* opponent ♦ *adj* opposing

adversātrīx, **-īcis** *f* antagonist

adversiō, **-ōnis** *f* turning (*the attention*)

adversor, **-ārī**, **-ātus** *vi* to oppose, resist

adversum, **-i** *nt* opposite; misfortune ♦ *prep* (+ *acc*) towards, against ♦ *adv* to meet

adversus *ppp of* **advertō** ♦ *adj* opposite, in front; hostile; **adversō flūmine** upstream; **adversae rēs** misfortune ♦ *prep* (+ *acc*) towards, against ♦ *adv* to meet

advertō, **-tere**, **-tī**, **-sum** *vt* to turn, direct towards; to call attention; **animum advertere** notice, perceive; (*with* **ad**) to attend to; (*with* **in**) to punish

advesperāscit, **-scere**, **-vit** *vi* it is getting dark

advigilō, **-āre** *vi* to keep watch

advocātiō, **-ōnis** *f* legal assistance, counsel

advocātus, **-ī** *m* supporter in a lawsuit; advocate, counsel

advocō, **-āre**, **-āvī**, **-ātum** *vt* to summon; (*LAW*) to call in the assistance of

advolō, **-āre**, **-āvī**, **-ātum** *vi* to fly to, swoop down upon

advolvō, **-vere**, **-vī**, **-ūtum** *vt* to roll to; to prostrate

advor- *etc see* **adver-**

adytum, **-ī** *nt* sanctuary

Aeacidēs, **-idae** *m* Achilles; Pyrrhus

Aeacus, **-ī** *m* father of Peleus, and judge of the dead

Aeaea, **-ae** *f* Circe's island

Aeaeus *adj* of Circe

aedēs, **-is** *f* temple; (*pl*) house

aedicula, **-ae** *f* shrine; small house, room

aedificātiō, **-ōnis** *f* building

aedificātiuncula, **-ae** *f* little house

aedificātor, **-ōris** *m* builder

aedificium, **-ī** *and* **-iī** *nt* building

aedificō, **-āre**, **-āvī**, **-ātum** *vt* to build, construct

aedīlicius *adj* aedile's ♦ *m* ex-aedile

aedīlis, **-is** *m* aedile

aedīlitās, **-ātis** *f* aedileship

aedis, **-is** *see* **aedēs**

aeditumus, **aedituus**, **-ī** *m* temple-keeper

Aeduī, **-ōrum** *mpl* a tribe of central Gaul

Aeëtēs, **-ae** *m* father of Medea

Aegaeus *adj* Aegean ♦ *nt* Aegean Sea

Aegātēs, **-um** *fpl* islands off Sicily

aeger, **-rī** *adj* ill, sick; sorrowful; weak

Aegīna, **-ae** *f* a Greek island

Aegīnēta, **-ae** *m* inhabitant of Aegina

aegis, **-dis** *f* shield of Jupiter or Athena, aegis

Aegisthus, **-ī** *m* paramour of Clytemnestra

aegocerōs, **-ōtis** *m* Capricorn

aegrē *adv* painfully; with displeasure; with difficulty; hardly; **~ ferre** be annoyed

aegrēscō, **-ere** *vi* to become ill; to be aggravated

aegrimōnia, **-ae** *f* distress of mind

aegritūdō, **-inis** *f* sickness; sorrow

aegror, **-ōris** *m* illness

aegrōtātiō, **-ōnis** *f* illness, disease

aegrōtō, **-āre**, **-āvī**, **-ātum** *vi* to be ill

aegrōtus *adj* ill, sick

Aegyptius *adj see* **Aegyptus**

Aegyptus, **-ī** *f* Egypt ♦ *m* brother of Danaus

aelinos, **-ī** *m* dirge

Aemiliānus *adj esp* Scipio, destroyer of Carthage

Aemilius, **-ī** Roman family name; **Via Aemilia** road in N. Italy

aemulātiō, **-ōnis** *f* rivalry (*good or bad*); jealousy

aemulātor, **-ōris** *m* zealous imitator

aemulor, **-ārī**, **-ātus** *vt* to rival, copy; to be jealous

aemulus, **-ī** *m* rival ♦ *adj* rivalling; jealous

Aeneadēs, **-ae** *m* Trojan; Roman

Aenēās, **-ae** *m* Trojan leader and hero of Virgil's epic

Aenēis, **-idis** *and* **-idos** *f* Aeneid

Aenēius *adj see* **Aenēās**

aēneus *adj* of bronze

aenigma, **-tis** *nt* riddle, mystery

aēnum, **-ī** *nt* bronze vessel

aēnus *adj* of bronze

Aeolēs, **-um** *mpl* the Aeolians

Aeolia *f* Lipari Island

Aeolidēs *m* a descendant of Aeolus

Aeolis¹, **-idis** *f* Aeolia (N.W. of Asia Minor)

Aeolis², **-idis** *f* daughter of Aeolus

Aeolius *adj see* **Aeolus**

Aeolus, **-ī** *m* king of the winds

aequābilis *adj* equal; consistent, even; impartial

aequābilitās, **-ātis** *f* uniformity; impartiality

aequābiliter *adv* uniformly

aequaevus *adj* of the same age

aequālis *adj* equal, like; of the same age, contemporary; uniform

aequālitās, **-ātis** *f* evenness; (*in politics, age*) equality, similarity

aequāliter *adv* evenly

aequanimitās, **-ātis** *f* goodwill; calmness of mind

aequātiō, **-ōnis** *f* equal distribution

aequē *adv* equally; (*with 'ac', 'atque', 'et', 'quam'*) just as; justly

Aequī, **-ōrum** *mpl* a people of central Italy

Aequicus, **Aequiculus** *adj see* **Aequī**

Aequimaelium, **-ī** *and* **-iī** *nt* an open space in Rome

aequinoctiālis *adj see* **aequinoctium**

aequinoctium, **-ī** *and* **-iī** *nt* equinox

aequiperābilis *adj* comparable

aequiperō, **-āre**, **-āvī**, **-ātum** *vt* to compare; to equal

aequitās, **-ātis** *f* uniformity; fair dealing, equity; calmness of mind

aequō, **-āre**, **-āvī**, **-ātum** *vt* to make equal, level; to compare; to equal; **solō aequāre** raze to the ground

aequor, **-is** *nt* a level surface, sea

aequoreus *adj* of the sea

aequum, **-i** *nt* plain; justice

aequus *adj* level, equal; favourable, friendly, fair, just; calm; **aequō animō** patiently; **aequō Marte** without deciding the issue; **aequum est** it is reasonable; **ex aequō** equally

āēr, **āeris** *m* air, weather; mist

aerāria *f* mine

aerārium *nt* treasury

aerārius *adj* of bronze; of money ♦ *m a citizen of the lowest class at Rome*; **tribūnī aerāriī** paymasters; *a wealthy middle class at Rome*

aerātus *adj* of bronze

aereus *adj* of copper or bronze

aerifer, -ī *adj* carrying cymbals

aeripēs, -edis *adj* bronze-footed

āerius *adj* of the air; lofty

aerūgō, -inis *f* rust; (*fig*) envy, avarice

aerumna, -ae *f* trouble, hardship

aerumnōsus *adj* wretched

aes, aeris *nt* copper, bronze; money; (*pl*) objects made of copper or bronze (*esp statues, instruments, vessels; soldiers' pay*); **aes aliēnum** debt; **aes circumforāneum** borrowed money; **aes grave** *Roman coin*, as

Aeschylus, -ī *m Greek tragic poet*

Aesculāpius, -ī *m god of medicine*

aesculētum, -ī *nt* oak forest

aesculeus *adj see* **aesculus**

aesculus, -ī *f* durmast oak

Aesōn, -onis *m father of Jason*

Aesonidēs, -ae *m* Jason

Aesōpius *adj see* **Aesōpus**

Aesōpus, -ī *m Greek writer of fables*

aestās, -ātis *f* summer

aestifer, -ī *adj* heat-bringing

aestimātiō, -ōnis *f* valuation, assessment; **lītis ~** assessment of damages

aestimātor, -ōris *m* valuer

aestimō, -āre, -āvī, -ātum *vt* to value, estimate the value of; **māgnī aestimāre** think highly of

aestīva, -ōrum *ntpl* summer camp, campaign

aestīvus *adj* summer

aestuārium, -ī *and* **-iī** *nt* tidal waters, estuary

aestuō, -āre, -āvī, -ātum *vi* to boil, burn; (*movement*) to heave, toss; (*fig*) to be excited; to waver

aestuōsus *adj* very hot; agitated

aestus, -ūs *m* heat; surge of the sea; tide; (*fig*) passion; hesitation

aetās, -ātis *f* age, life; time

aetātem *adv* for life

aetātula, -ae *f* tender age

aeternitās, -ātis *f* eternity

aeternō, -āre *vt* to immortalize

aeternus *adj* eternal, immortal; lasting; **in aeternum** for ever

aethēr, -eris *m* sky, heaven; air

aetherius *adj* ethereal, heavenly; of air

Aethiops, -is *adj* Ethiopian; (*fig*) stupid

aethra, -ae *f* sky

Aetna, -ae *f* Etna (*in Sicily*)

Aetnaeus, Aetnēnsis *adj see* **Aetna**

Aetōlia, -iae *f a district of W. Greece*

Aetōlus, Aetōlicus *adj see* **Aetōlia**

aevitās, -ātis *old form of* **aetās**

aevum, -ī *nt* age, lifetime; eternity; **in ~** for ever

Āfer, -rī *adj* African

āfore *fut infin of* **absum**

Āfrānius, -ī *m Latin comic poet*

Āfrica, -ae *f Roman province (now Tunisia)*

Āfricānae *fpl* panthers

Āfricānus *adj name of two Scipios*

Āfricus *adj* African ♦ *m* south-west (wind)

āfuī, āfutūrus *perf, fut p of* **absum**

Agamēmnōn, -onis *m leader of Greeks against Troy*

Agamēmnonius *adj see* **Agamēmnōn**

Aganippē, -ēs *f a spring on Helicon*

agāsō, -ōnis *m* ostler, footman

age, agedum come on!, well then

agellus, -ī *m* plot of land

Agēnōr, -oris *m father of Europa*

Agēnoreus *adj see* **Agēnōr**

Agēnoridēs, -ae *m* Cadmus; Perseus

agēns, -entis *adj* (RHET) effective

ager, -rī *m* land, field; countryside; territory

agg- *etc see* **adg-**

agger, -is *m* rampart; mound, embankment; *any built-up mass*

aggerō[1], -āre, -āvī, -ātum *vt* to pile up; to increase

aggerō[2], -rere, -ssi, -stum *vt* to carry, bring

aggestus, -ūs *m* accumulation

agilis *adj* mobile; nimble, busy

agilitās, -ātis *f* mobility

agitābilis *adj* light

agitātiō, -ōnis *f* movement, activity

agitātor, -ōris *m* driver, charioteer

agitō, -āre, -āvī, -ātum *vt* (*animals*) to drive; to move, chase, agitate; (*fig*) to excite (*to action*); to persecute, ridicule; to keep (*a ceremony*) ♦ *vi* to live; to deliberate

agmen, -inis *nt* forward movement, procession, train; army on the march; **~ claudere** bring up the rear; **novissimum ~** rearguard; **prīmum ~ van**

agna, -ae *f* ewe lamb; lamb (*flesh*)

agnāscor, -scī, -tus *vi* to be born after

agnātus, -ī *m* relation (*by blood on father's side*)

agnellus, -ī *m* little lamb

agnīnus *adj* of lamb

agnitiō, -ōnis *f* recognition, knowledge

agnitus *ppp of* **agnōscō**

agnōmen, -inis *nt* an extra surname (*eg Africanus*)

agnōscō, -ōscere, -ōvī, -itum *vt* to recognize; to acknowledge, allow; to understand

agnus, -ī *m* lamb

agō, agere, ēgī, āctum *vt* to drive, lead; to plunder; to push forward, put forth; (*fig*) to move, rouse, persecute; to do, act, perform; (*time*) to pass, spend; (*undertakings*) to manage, wage; (*public speaking*) to plead, discuss; to negotiate, treat; (THEAT) to play, act the part of; **agere cum populō** address the people; **age** come on!, well then; **age age** all right!; **āctum est dē** it is all up with; **aliud agere** not attend; **animam agere** expire; **annum quartum agere** be three years old; **causam agere** plead a cause; **hōc age** pay attention; **id agere ut** aim at; **lēge agere** go to law; **nīl agis** it's no use; **quid agis?** how are you?; **rēs agitur** interests are at stake; **sē agere** go, come

agrāriī *mpl* the land reform party

agrārius *adj* of public land; **lēx agrāria** land law

agrestis *adj* rustic; boorish, wild, barbarous ♦ *m* countryman

agricola, -ae *m* countryman, farmer

Agricola, **-ae** m a Roman governor of Britain; his biography by Tacitus
Agrigentīnus adj see **Agrigentum**
Agrigentum, **-ī** nt a town in Sicily
agripeta, **-ae** m landgrabber
Āgrippa, **-ae** m Roman surname (esp Augustus's minister)
Āgrippīna, **-ae** f mother of Nero; **Colōnia ~** or **Āgrippīnēnsis** Cologne
Agyīeus, **-eī** and **-eos** m Apollo
āh interj ah! (in sorrow or joy)
aha interj expressing reproof or laughter
ahēn- etc see **aēn-**
Āiāx, **-ācis** m Ajax (name of two Greek heroes at Troy)
āiō vt (defec) to say, speak; **ain tū?/ain vērō?** really?; **quid ais?** I say!
āla, **-ae** f wing; armpit; (MIL) wing of army
alabaster, **-rī** m perfume box
alacer, **-ris** adj brisk, cheerful
alacritās, **-ātis** f promptness, liveliness; joy, rapture
alapa, **-ae** f slap on the face; a slave's freedom
ālāriī mpl allied troops
ālārius adj (MIL) on the wing
ālātus adj winged
alauda, **-ae** f lark; name of a legion of Caesar's
alāzōn, **-onis** m braggart
Alba Longa, **Albae Longae** f a Latin town (precursor of Rome)
Albānus adj Alban; **Lacus ~**, **Mōns ~** lake and mountain near Alba Longa
albātus adj dressed in white
albeō, **-ēre** vi to be white; to dawn
albēscō, **-ere** vi to become white; to dawn
albicō, **-āre** vi to be white
albidus adj white
Albiōn, **-ōnis** f ancient name for Britain
albitūdō, **-inis** f whiteness
Albula, **-ae** f old name for the Tiber
albulus adj whitish
album, **-ī** nt white; records
Albunea, **-ae** f a spring at Tibur; a sulphur spring near Alban Lake
albus adj white, bright
Alcaeus, **-ī** m Greek lyric poet
alcēdō, **-inis** f kingfisher
alcēdōnia ntpl halcyon days
alcēs, **-is** f elk
Alcibiadēs, **-is** m brilliant Athenian politician
Alcīdēs, **-ae** m Hercules
Alcinous, **-ī** m king of Phaeacians in the Odyssey
ālea, **-ae** f gambling, dice; (fig) chance, hazard; **iacta ~ est** the die is cast; **in āleam dare** to risk
āleātor, **-ōris** m gambler
āleātōrius adj in gambling
ālēc etc see **allēc**
āleō, **-ōnis** m gambler
āles, **-itis** adj winged; swift ♦ m/f bird; omen
alēscō, **-ere** vi to grow up
Alexander, **-rī** m a Greek name; Paris (prince of Troy); Alexander (the Great) (king of Macedon)
Alexandrēa (later **-īa**), **-ēae** f Alexandria (in Egypt)
alga, **-ae** f seaweed

algeō, **-gēre**, **-sī** vi to feel cold; (fig) to be neglected
algēscō, **-ere** vi to catch cold
Algidus, **-ī** m mountain in Latium
algidus adj cold
algor, **-ōris** m cold
algū abl sg m with cold
aliā adv in another way
aliās adv at another time; at one time ... at another
alibī adv elsewhere; otherwise; in one place ... in another
alicubī adv somewhere
alicunde adv from somewhere
alid old form of **aliud**
aliēnātiō, **-ōnis** f transfer; estrangement
aliēnigena, **-ae** m foreigner
aliēnigenus adj foreign; heterogeneous
aliēnō, **-āre**, **-āvī**, **-ātum** vt to transfer (property by sale); to alienate, estrange; (mind) to derange
aliēnus adj of another, of others; alien, strange; (with abl or **ab**) unsuited to, different from; hostile ♦ m stranger
āliger, **-ī** adj winged
alimentārius adj about food
alimentum, **-ī** nt nourishment, food; obligation of children to parents; (fig) support
alimōnium, **-i** and **-iī** nt nourishment
aliō adv in another direction, elsewhere; one way ... another way
aliōquī, **aliōquīn** adv otherwise, else; besides
aliōrsum adv in another direction; differently
ālipēs, **-edis** adj wing-footed; fleet
alīptēs, **-ae** m sports trainer
aliquā adv some way or other
aliquam adv: **~ diū** for some time; **~ multī** a considerable number
aliquandō adv sometime, ever; sometimes; once, for once; now at last
aliquantisper adv for a time
aliquantō adv (with comp) somewhat
aliquantulum nt a very little ♦ adv somewhat
aliquantulus adj quite small
aliquantum adj a good deal ♦ adv somewhat
aliquantus adj considerable
aliquātenus adv to some extent
aliquī, **-quae**, **-quod** adj some, any; some other
aliquid adv at all
aliquis, **-quid** pron somebody, something; someone or something important
aliquō adv to some place, somewhere else
aliquot adj (indecl) some
aliquotiēns adv several times
aliter adv otherwise, differently; in one way ... in another
alitus ppp of **alō**
ālium, **-i** and **-iī** nt garlic
aliunde adv from somewhere else
alius, **alia**, **aliud** adj other, another; different; **~ ... ~** some ... others; **~ ex aliō** one after the other; **in alia omnia īre** oppose a measure; **nihil aliud quam** only
all- etc see **adl-**
allēc, **-is** nt fish pickle

allex, -icis m big toe

Allia, -ae f tributary of the Tiber (scene of a great Roman defeat)

Alliēnsis adj see **Allia**

Allobrogēs, -um mpl a people of S.E. Gaul

Allobrogicus adj see **Allobrogēs**

almus adj nourishing; kindly

alnus, -ī f alder

alō, -ere, -uī, -tum and **-itum** vt to nourish, rear; to increase, promote

Alpēs, -ium fpl Alps

Alphēus, -ī m river of Olympia in S.W. Greece

Alpīnus adj see **Alpēs**

alsī perf of **algeō**

alsius, alsus adj cold

altāria, -ium ntpl altars, altar; altar top

altē adv on high, from above; deeply; from afar

alter, -īus adj the one, the other (of two); second, the next; fellow man; different; ~ **ego**, ~ **īdem** a second self; **alterum tantum** twice as much; **ūnus et ~** one or two

altercātiō, -ōnis f dispute, debate

altercor, -ārī, -ātus vi to wrangle, dispute; to cross-examine

alternīs adv alternately

alternō, -āre, -āvī, -ātum vt to do by turns, alternate

alternus adj one after the other, alternate; elegiac (verses)

alteruter, -īusutrīus adj one or the other

altilis adj fat (esp fowls)

altisonus adj sounding on high

altitonāns, -antis adj thundering on high

altitūdō, -inis f height, depth; (fig) sublimity; (mind) secrecy

altivolāns, -antis adj soaring on high

altor, -ōris m foster father

altrīnsecus adv on the other side

altrīx, -īcis f nourisher, foster mother

altum, -ī nt heaven; sea (usu out of sight of land); **ex altō repetītus** far-fetched

altus adj high, deep; (fig) noble; profound

ālūcinor, -ārī, -ātus vi to talk wildly; (mind) to wander

aluī perf of **alō**

alumnus, -ī m, **alumna, -ae** f foster child; pupil

alūta, -ae f soft leather; shoe, purse, face patch

alveārium, -ī and **-iī** nt beehive

alveolus, -ī m basin

alveus, -eī m hollow; trough; (ship) hold; bath tub; riverbed

alvus, -ī f bowels; womb; stomach

amābilis adj lovely, lovable

amābilitās, -ātis f charm

amābiliter adv see **amābilis**

Amalthēa, -ae f nymph or she-goat; **cornū Amalthēae** horn of plenty

Amalthēum, -ī nt Atticus's library

āmandātiō f sending away

āmandō, -āre, -āvī, -ātum vt to send away

amāns, -antis adj fond ♦ m lover

amanter adv affectionately

āmanuēnsis, -is m secretary

amāracinum, -inī nt marjoram ointment

amāracum, -ī nt, **amāracus, -ī** m/f sweet marjoram

amārē adv see **amārus**

amāritiēs, -ēī f, **amāritūdō, -inis** f, **amāror, -ōris** m bitterness

amārus adj bitter; (fig) sad; ill-natured

amāsius, -ī and **-iī** m lover

Amathūs, -ūntis f town in Cyprus

Amathūsia f Venus

amātiō, -ōnis f lovemaking

amātor, -ōris m lover, paramour

amātorculus m poor lover

amātōriē adv amorously

amātōrius adj of love, erotic

amātrīx, -rīcis f mistress

Amāzōn, -onis f Amazon, warrior woman

Amāzonides fpl Amazons

Amāzonius adj see **Amāzōn**

ambāctus, -ī m vassal

ambāgēs, -is f windings; (speech) circumlocution, quibbling; enigma

ambedō, -edere, -ēdī, -ēsum vt to consume

ambēsus ppp of **ambedō**

ambigō, -ere vt, vi to wander about; to be in doubt; to argue; to wrangle

ambiguē adv doubtfully

ambiguitās, -ātis f ambiguity

ambiguus adj changeable, doubtful, unreliable; ambiguous

ambiō, -īre, -iī, -ītum vt to go round, encircle; (POL) to canvass for votes; (fig) to court (for a favour)

ambitiō, -ōnis f canvassing for votes; currying favour; ambition

ambitiōsē adv ostentatiously

ambitiōsus adj winding; ostentatious, ambitious

ambitus, -ūs m circuit, circumference; circumlocution; canvassing, bribery; **lēx de ambitū** a law against bribery

ambītus ppp of **ambiō**

ambō, ambae, ambō num both, two

Ambracia, -ae f district of N.W. Greece

Ambraciēnsis, Ambraciēnsus adj see **Ambracia**

ambrosia, -ae f food of the gods

ambrosius adj divine

ambūbāia, -ae f Syrian flute-girl

ambulācrum, -ī nt avenue

ambulātiō, -ōnis f walk, walking; walk (place)

ambulātiuncula f short walk

ambulō, -āre, -āvī, -ātum vi to walk, go; to travel

ambūrō, -rere, -ssī, -stum vt to burn up; to make frostbitten; (fig) to ruin

ambūstus ppp of **ambūrō**

amellus, -ī m Michaelmas daisy

āmēns, -entis adj mad, frantic; stupid

āmentia, -ae f madness; stupidity

āmentum, -ī nt strap (for throwing javelin)

ames, -itis m fowler's pole

amfr- etc see **anfr-**

amīca, -ae f friend; mistress

amiciō, -īre, -tus vt to clothe, cover

amīciter, -ē *adv see* **amīcus**
amīcitia, -ae *f* friendship; alliance
amictus¹ *ppp of* **amiciō**
amictus², -ūs *m* (manner of) dress; clothing
amiculum, -ī *nt* cloak
amīculus, -ī *m* dear friend
amīcus, -ī *m* friend ♦ *adj* friendly, fond
āmissiō, -ōnis *f* loss
āmissus *ppp of* **āmittō**
amita, -ae *f* aunt (*on father's side*)
āmittō, -ittere, -īsī, -issum *vt* to let go, lose
Ammōn, -is *m* Egyptian god identified with Jupiter
Ammōniacus *adj see* **Ammōn**
amnicola, -ae *m/f* sth growing by a river
amniculus *m* brook
amnicus *adj see* **amnis**
amnis, -is *m* river
amō, -āre, -āvī, -ātum *vt* to love, like; (*colloq*) to be obliged to; **ita mē dī ament** bless my soul!; **amābō** please!
amoenitās, -ātis *f* delightfulness (*esp of scenery*)
amoenus *adj* delightful
āmōlior, -īrī, -ītus *vt* to remove
amōmum, -ī *nt* cardamom
amor, -ōris *m* love; (*fig*) strong desire; *term of endearment*; Cupid; (*pl*) love affairs
āmōtiō, -ōnis *f* removal
āmōtus *ppp of* **āmoveō**
āmoveō, -ovēre, -ōvī, -ōtum *vt* to remove; to banish
amphibolia, -ae *f* ambiguity
Amphīōn, -onis *m* musician and builder of Thebes
Amphīonius *adj see* **Amphīōn**
amphitheātrum, -ī *nt* amphitheatre
Amphitrītē, -ēs *f* sea goddess; the sea
Amphitryō, -ōnis *m* husband of Alcmena
Amphitryōniadēs *m* Hercules
amphora, -ae *f* a two-handled jar; liquid measure; (NAUT) measure of tonnage
Amphrȳsius *adj* of Apollo
Amphrȳsus, -ī *m* river in Thessaly
ample *adv see* **amplus**
amplector, -ctī, -xus *vt* to embrace, encircle; (*mind*) to grasp; (*speech*) to deal with; (*fig*) to cherish
amplexor, -ārī, -ātus *vt* to embrace, love
amplexus¹ *ppa of* **amplector**
amplexus², -ūs *m* embrace, encircling
amplificātiō, -ōnis *f* enlargement; (RHET) a passage elaborated for effect
amplificē *adv* splendidly
amplificō, -āre, -āvī, -ātum *vt* to increase, enlarge; (RHET) to enlarge upon
ampliō, -āre, -āvī, -ātum *vt* to enlarge; (LAW) to adjourn
ampliter *adv see* **amplus**
amplitūdō, -inis *f* size; (*fig*) distinction; (RHET) fullness
amplius *adv* more (*esp amount or number*), further, longer; **~ ducentī** more than 200; **~ nōn petere** take no further legal action; **~ prōnūntiāre** adjourn a case
amplus *adj* large, spacious; great, abundant; powerful, splendid, eminent; (*superl*) distinguished

ampulla, -ae *f* a two-handled flask; (*fig*) high-flown language
ampullārius, -ārī *m* flask-maker
ampullor, -ārī *vi* to use high-flown language
amputātiō, -ōnis *f* pruning
amputatus *adj* (RHET) disconnected
amputō, -āre, -āvī, -ātum *vt* to cut off, prune; (*fig*) to lop off
Amūlius, -ī *m* king of Alba Longa, grand-uncle of Romulus
amurca, -ae *f* lees of olive oil
amussitātus *adj* nicely adjusted
Amȳclae, -ārum *fpl* town in S. Greece
Amȳclaeus *adj see* **Amȳclae**
amygdalum, -ī *nt* almond
amystis, -dis *f* emptying a cup at a draught
an *conj* or; perhaps; (*with single question*) surely not; **haud sciō an** I feel sure
Anacreōn, -ontis *m* Greek lyric poet
anadēma, -tis *nt* headband
anagnōstēs, -ae *m* reader
anapaestum, -ī *nt* poem in anapaests
anapaestus *adj*: **~ pēs** anapaest
anas, -tis *f* duck
anaticula *f* duckling
anatīnus *adj see* **anas**
anatocismus, -ī *m* compound interest
Anaxagorās, -ae *m* early Greek philosopher
Anaximander, -rī *m* early Greek philosopher
anceps, -ipitis *adj* two-headed; double; wavering, doubtful; dangerous ♦ *nt* danger
Anchīsēs, -ae *m* father of Aeneas
Anchīsēus *adj* Aeneas
Anchīsiadēs *m* Aeneas
ancīle, -is *nt* oval shield (*esp one said to have fallen from heaven in Numa's reign*)
ancilla, -ae *f* servant
ancillāris *adj* of a young servant
ancillula *f* young servant
ancīsus *adj* cut round
ancora, -ae *f* anchor
ancorāle, -is *nt* cable
ancorārius *adj see* **ancora**
Ancus Marcius, Anci Marcii *m* 4th king of Rome
Ancȳra, -ae *f* Ankara (*capital of Galatia*)
andabata, -ae *m* blindfold gladiator
Andrius *adj see* **Andros**
androgynē, -ēs *f* hermaphrodite
androgynus, -ī *m* hermaphrodite
Andromachē, -ēs *f* wife of Hector
Andromeda, -ae *f* wife of Perseus; a constellation
Andronicus, -ī *m* Livius (*earliest Latin poet*)
Andros, Andrus, -ī *f* Aegean island
ānellus, -ī *m* little ring
anēthum, -ī *nt* fennel
ānfrāctus, -ūs *m* bend, orbit; roundabout way; (*words*) digression, prolixity
angelus, -ī *m* angel
angina, -ae *f* quinsy
angiportum, -ī *nt* alley
angiportus, -ūs *m* alley
angō, -ere *vt* to throttle; (*fig*) to distress, torment
angor, -ōris *m* suffocation; (*fig*) anguish

anguicomus *adj* with snakes for hair
anguiculus, -ī *m* small snake
anguifer, -ī *adj* snake-carrying
anguigena, -ae *m* one born of serpents; Theban
anguilla, -ae *f* eel
anguimanus *adj* with a trunk
anguipēs, -edis *adj* serpent-footed
anguis, -is *m/f* snake, serpent; *(constellation)* Draco
Anguitenēns, -entis *m* Ophiuchus
angulātus *adj* angular
angulus, -ī *m* angle, corner; out-of-the-way place; **ad parēs angulōs** at right angles
angustē *adv* close, within narrow limits; concisely
angustiae, -ārum *fpl* defile, strait; *(time)* shortness; *(means)* want; *(circumstances)* difficulty; *(mind)* narrowness; *(words)* subtleties
angusticlāvius *adj* wearing a narrow purple stripe
angustō, -āre *vt* to make narrow
angustum, -ī *nt* narrowness; danger
angustus *adj* narrow, close; *(time)* short; *(means)* scanty; *(mind)* mean; *(argument)* subtle; *(circumstances)* difficult
anhēlitus, -ūs *m* panting; breath, exhalation
anhēlō, -āre, -āvī, -ātum *vi* to breathe hard, pant; to exhale
anhēlus *adj* panting
anicula, -ae *f* poor old woman
Aniēnsis, Aniēnus *adj* of the river Anio
Aniēnus *m* Anio
anīlis *adj* of an old woman
anīlitās, -tātis *f* old age
anīliter *adv* like an old woman
anima, -ae *f* wind, air; breath; life; soul, mind; ghost, spirit; **animam agere, animam efflāre** expire; **animam comprimere** hold one's breath
animadversiō, -ōnis *f* observation; censure, punishment
animadversor, -ōris *m* observer
animadvertō, -tere, -tī, -sum *vt* to pay attention to, notice; to realise; to censure, punish; **animadvertere in** punish
animal, -ālis *nt* animal; living creature
animālis *adj* of air; animate
animāns, -antis *m/f/nt* living creature; animal
animātiō, -ōnis *f* being
animātus *adj* disposed; *in a certain frame of mind*; courageous
animō, -āre, -āvī, -ātum *vt* to animate; *to give a certain temperament to*
animōsē *adv* boldly, eagerly
animōsus *adj* airy; lifelike; courageous, proud
animula, -ae *f* little soul
animulus, -ī *m* darling
animus, -ī *m* mind, soul; consciousness; reason, thought, opinion, imagination; heart, feelings, disposition; courage, spirit, pride, passion; will, purpose; *term of endearment*; **animī** in mind, in heart; **animī causā** for amusement; **animō fingere** imagine; **animō male est** I am fainting; **aequō animō esse** be patient, calm; **bonō animō esse** take

courage; be well-disposed; **ex animō** sincerely; **ex animō effluere** be forgotten; **in animō habēre** purpose; **meō animō** in my opinion
Aniō, -ēnis *m tributary of the Tiber*
annālēs, -ium *mpl* annals, chronicle
annālis *adj* of a year; **lēx ~** law prescribing ages for public offices
Anna Perenna, Annae Perennae *f Roman popular goddess*
anne *etc see* **an**
anniculus *adj* a year old
anniversārius *adj* annual
annōn or not
annōna, -ae *f* year's produce; grain; price of corn; the market
annōsus *adj* aged
annōtinus *adj* last year's
annus, -ī *m* year; **~ māgnus** astronomical great year; **~ solidus** a full year
annuus *adj* a year's; annual
anquīrō, -rere, -sīvī, -sītum *vt* to search for; to make inquiries; *(LAW)* to institute an inquiry **(dē)** or prosecution *(abl, gen)*
ānsa, -ae *f* handle; *(fig)* opportunity
ānsātus *adj* with a handle; *(comedy)* with arms akimbo
ānser, -is *m* goose
ānserīnus *adj see* **ānser**
ante *prep (with acc)* before *(in time, place, comparison)* ♦ *adv (place)* in front; *(time)* before
anteā *adv* before, formerly
antecapiō, -apere, -ēpī, -eptum *vt* to take beforehand, anticipate
antecēdō, -ēdere, -essī, -essum *vt* to precede; to surpass
antecellō, -ere *vi* to excel, be superior
anteceptus *ppp of* **antecapiō**
antecessiō, -ōnis *f* preceding; antecedent cause
antecessor, -ōris *m* forerunner
antecursor, -ōris *m* forerunner, pioneer
anteeō, -īre, -īī *vi* to precede, surpass
anteferō, -ferre, -tulī, -lātum *vt* to carry before; to prefer; to anticipate
antefīxus *adj* attached (in front) ♦ *ntpl* ornaments on roofs of buildings
antegredior, -dī, -ssus *vt* to precede
antehabeō, -ēre *vt* to prefer
antehāc *adv* formerly, previously
antelātus *ppp of* **anteferō**
antelūcānus *adj* before dawn
antemerīdiānus *adj* before noon
antemittō, -ittere, -īsī, -issum *vt* to send on in front
antenna, -ae *f* yardarm
antepīlānī, -ōrum *mpl (MIL)* the front ranks
antepōnō, -ōnere, -osuī, -ositum *vt* to set before; to prefer
antequam *conj* before
Anterōs, -ōtis *m avenger of slighted love*
antēs, -ium *mpl* rows
antesignānus, -ī *m (MIL)* leader; *(pl)* defenders of the standards

antestō, antistō, -āre, -ētī vi to excel, distinguish oneself

antestor, -ārī, -ātus vi to call a witness

anteveniō, -enīre, -ēnī, -entum vt, vi to anticipate; to surpass

antevertō, -tere, -tī, -sum vt to precede; to anticipate; to prefer

anticipātiō, -ōnis f foreknowledge

anticipō, -āre, -āvī, -ātum vt to take before, anticipate

antīcus adj in front

Antigonē, -ēs f daughter of Oedipus

Antigonus, -ī m name of Macedonian kings

Antiochēnsis adj see **Antiochīa**

Antiochīa, -īae f Antioch (capital of Syria)

Antiochus, -ī m name of kings of Syria

antīquārius, -ī and **-iī** m antiquary

antīquē adv in the old style

antīquitās, -ātis f antiquity, the ancients; integrity

antīquitus adv long ago, from ancient times

antīquō, -āre, -āvī, -ātum vt to vote against (a bill)

antīquus adj ancient, former, old; good old-fashioned, honest, illustrious; **antīquior** more important; **antīquissimus** most important

antistēs, -itis m/f high priest, chief priestess; (fig) master (in any art)

Antisthenēs, -is and **-ae** m founder of Cynic philosophy

antistita, -ae f chief priestess

antistō etc see **antestō**

antitheton, -ī nt (RHET) antithesis

Antōnīnus, -ī m name of Roman emperors (esp Pius and Marcus Aurelius)

Antōnius, -ī m Roman name (esp the famous orator, and Mark Antony)

antrum, -ī nt cave, hollow

ānulārius, -i m ringmaker

ānulātus adj with rings on

ānulus, -ī m ring; equestrian rank

ānus, -ī m rectum; ring

anus, -ūs f old woman ♦ adj old

ānxiē adv see **ānxius**

ānxietās, -ātis f anxiety, trouble (of the mind)

ānxifer, -ī adj disquieting

ānxitūdō, -inis f anxiety

ānxius adj (mind) troubled; disquieting

Āones, -um adj Boeotian

Āonia f part of Boeotia

Āonius adj of Boeotia, of Helicon

Aornos, -ī m/f lake Avernus

apage interj away with!, go away!

apēliōtēs, -ae m east wind

Apellēs, -is m Greek painter

aper, -rī m boar

aperiō, -īre, -uī, -tum vt to uncover, disclose, open; (country) to open up; (fig) to unfold, explain, reveal

apertē adv clearly, openly

apertum, -ī nt open space; **in apertō esse** be well known; be easy

apertus ppp of **aperiō** ♦ adj open, exposed; clear, manifest; (person) frank

aperuī perf of **aperiō**

apex, -icis m summit; crown, priest's cap; (fig) crown

aphractus, -ī f a long open boat

apiārius, -ī and **-iī** m beekeeper

Apīcius, -ī m Roman epicure

apicula, -ae f little bee

apis, -is f bee

apīscor, -īscī, -tus vt to catch, get, attain

apium, -ī and **-iī** nt celery

aplustre, -is nt decorated stern of a ship

apoclētī, -ōrum mpl committee of the Aetolian League

apodytērium, -ī and **-iī** nt dressing room

Apollināris, -ineus adj: **lūdī Apollinārēs** Roman games in July

Apollō, -inis m Greek god of music, archery, prophecy, flocks and herds, and often identified with the sun

apologus, -ī m narrative, fable

apophorēta, -ōrum ntpl presents for guests to take home

apoproēgmena, -ōrum ntpl (PHILOS) what is rejected

apostolicus adj see **apostolus**

apostolus, -ī m (ECCL) apostle

apothēca, -ae f storehouse, wine store

apparātē adv see **apparātus¹**

apparātiō, -ōnis f preparation

apparātus¹ adj ready, well-supplied, sumptuous

apparātus², -ūs m preparation; equipment; munitions; pomp, ostentation

appāreō, -ēre, -uī, -itum vi to come in sight, appear; to be seen, show oneself; to wait upon (an official); **appāret** it is obvious

appāritiō, -ōnis f service; domestic servants

appāritor, -ōris m attendant

apparō, -āre, -āvī, -ātum vt to prepare, provide

appellātiō, -ōnis f accosting, appeal; title; pronunciation

appellātor, -ōris m appellant

appellitātus adj usually called

appellō¹, -āre, -āvī, -ātum vt to speak to; to appeal to; (for money) to dun; (LAW) to sue; to call, name; to pronounce

appellō², -ellere, -ulī, -ulsum vt to drive, bring (to); (NAUT) to bring to land

appendicula, -ae f small addition

appendix, -icis f supplement

appendō, -endere, -endī, -ensum vt to weigh, pay

appetēns, -entis adj eager; greedy

appetenter adv see **appetēns**

appetentia, -ae f craving

appetītiō, -ōnis f grasping, craving

appetītus¹ ppp of **appetō**

appetītus², -ūs m craving; natural desire (as opposed to reason)

appetō, -ere, -īvī, -ītum vt to grasp, try to get at; to attack; to desire ♦ vi to approach

appingō, -ere vt to paint (in); (colloq) to write more

Appius, -ī m Roman first name; **Via Appia** main road from Rome to Capua and Brundisium

applaudō, -dere, -sī, -sum vt to strike, clap ♦ vi to applaud

applicātiō, **-ōnis** f applying (of the mind); **iūs applicātiōnis** the right of a patron to inherit a client's effects

applicātus, applicitus ppp of **applicō**

applicō, **-āre**, **-āvī** and **-uī**, **ātum** and **itum** vt to attach, place close (to); (NAUT) to steer, bring to land; **sē applicāre, animum applicāre** devote self, attention (to)

applōrō, **-āre** vt to deplore

appōnō, **-ōnere**, **-osuī**, **-ositum** vt to put (to, beside); (meal) to serve; to add, appoint; to reckon

apporrēctus adj stretched nearby

apportō, **-āre**, **-āvī**, **-ātum** vt to bring, carry (to)

apposcō, **-ere** vt to demand also

appositē adv suitably

appositus ppp of **appōnō** ✦ adj situated near; (fig) bordering on; suitable

apposuī perf of **appōnō**

appōtus adj drunk

apprecor, **-ārī**, **-ātus** vt to pray to

apprehendō, **-endere**, **-endī**, **-ēnsum** vt to take hold of; (MIL) to occupy; (argument) to bring forward

apprīmē adv especially

apprimō, **-imere**, **-essī**, **-essum** vt to press close

approbātiō, **-ōnis** f acquiescence; proof

approbātor, **-ōris** m approver

approbē adv very well

approbō, **-āre**, **-āvī**, **-ātum** vt to approve; to prove; to perform to someone's satisfaction

apprōmittō, **-ere** vt to promise also

approperō, **-āre**, **-āvī**, **-ātum** vt to hasten ✦ vi to hurry up

appropinquō, **-āre**, **-āvī**, **-ātum** vi to approach

appropinquātiō, **-ōnis** f approach

appugnō, **-āre** vt to attack

appulsus¹ ppp of **appellō²**

appulsus², **-ūs** m landing; approach

aprīcātiō, **-ōnis** f basking

aprīcor, **-ārī** vi to bask

aprīcus adj sunny; basking; **in aprīcum prōferre** bring to light

Aprīlis adj April, of April

aprūgnus adj of the wild boar

aps- etc see **abs-**

aptē adv closely; suitably, rightly

aptō, **-āre**, **-āvī**, **-ātum** vt to fit, put on; (fig) to adapt; to prepare, equip

aptus adj attached, joined together, fitted (with); suitable

apud prep (with acc) **1**. (with persons) beside, by, with, at the house of, among, in the time of; (speaking) in the presence of, to; (judgment) in the opinion of; (influence) with; (faith) in; (authors) in **2**. (with places) near, at, in; **est ~ mē** I have; **sum ~ mē** I am in my senses

Āpūlia, **-iae** f district of S.E. Italy

Āpūlus adj see **Āpūlia**

aput prep see **apud**

aqua, **-ae** f water; **~ mihī haeret** I am in a fix; **~ intercus** dropsy; **aquam adspergere** revive; **aquam praebēre** entertain; **aquam et terram petere** demand submission; **aquā et ignī interdīcere** outlaw

aquae fpl medicinal waters, spa

aquaeductus, **-ūs** m aqueduct; right of leading water

aquāliculus m belly

aquālis, **-is** m/f washbasin

aquārius adj of water ✦ m water carrier, water inspector; a constellation

aquāticus adj aquatic; humid

aquātilis adj aquatic

aquātiō, **-ōnis** f fetching water; watering place

aquātor, **-ōris** m water carrier

aquila, **-ae** f eagle; standard of a legion; (ARCH) gable; a constellation; **aquilae senectūs** a vigorous old age

Aquilēia, **-ae** f town in N. Italy

Aquilēiēnsis adj see **Aquilēia**

aquilifer, **-i** m chief standard-bearer

aquilīnus adj eagle's

aquilō, **-ōnis** m north wind; north

aquilōnius adj northerly

aquilus adj swarthy

Aquīnās, **-ātis** adj see **Aquīnum**

Aquīnum, **-i** nt town in Latium

Aquītānia, **-iae** f district of S.W. Gaul

Aquītānus adj see **Aquītānia**

aquor, **-ārī**, **-ātus** vi to fetch water

aquōsus adj humid, rainy

aquula, **-ae** f little stream

āra, **-ae** f altar; (fig) refuge; a constellation; **ārae et focī** hearth and home

arabarchēs, **-ae** m customs officer (in Egypt)

Arabia, **-iae** f Arabia

Arabicē adv with all the perfumes of Arabia

Arabicus, Arabicius, Arabus adj see **Arabia**

Arachnē, **-s** f Lydian woman changed into a spider

arānea, **-ae** f spider; cobweb

arāneola f, **-olus** m small spider

arāneōsus adj full of spiders' webs

arāneum, **-ī** nt spider's web

arāneus, **-i** m spider ✦ adj of spiders

Arar, **-is** m (river) Saône

Arātēus adj see **Arātus**

arātiō, **-ōnis** f ploughing, farming; arable land

arātiuncula f small plot

arātor, **-ōris** m ploughman, farmer; (pl) cultivators of public land

arātrum, **-ī** nt plough

Arātus, **-ī** m Greek astronomical poet

Araxēs, **-is** m river in Armenia

arbiter, **-rī** m witness; arbiter, judge, umpire; controller; **~ bibendī** president of a drinking party

arbitra, **-ae** f witness

arbitrāriō adv with some uncertainty

arbitrārius adj uncertain

arbitrātus, **-ūs** m decision; **meō arbitrātū** in my judgment

arbitrium, **-ī** and **-iī** nt decision (of an arbitrator), judgment; mastery, control

arbitror, **-ārī**, **-ātus** vt, vi to be a witness of; to testify; to think, suppose

arbor, arbōs, **-oris** f tree; ship, mast, oar; **~ īnfēlix** gallows

arboreus adj of trees, like a tree

arbustum, **-ī** *nt* plantation, orchard; (*pl*) trees
arbustus *adj* wooded
arbuteus *adj* of the strawberry tree
arbutum, **-ī** *nt* fruit of strawberry tree
arbutus, **-ī** *f* strawberry tree
arca, **-ae** *f* box; moneybox, purse; coffin; prison cell; **ex arcā absolvere** pay cash
Arcades, **-um** *mpl* Arcadians
Arcadia, **-iae** *f* district of E. Greece
Arcadicus, **-ius** *adj see* **Arcadia**
arcānō *adv* privately
arcānum, **-ī** *nt* secret, mystery
arcānus *adj* secret; able to keep secrets
arceō, **-ēre**, **-uī**, **-tum** *vt* to enclose; to keep off, prevent
accessītū *abl sg m* at the summons
accessītus *ppp of* **accessō** ♦ *adj* far-fetched
accessō, **-ere**, **-īvī**, **-ītum** *vt* to send for, fetch; (*LAW*) to summon, accuse; (*fig*) to derive
archetypus, **-ī** *m* original
Archilochus, **-ī** *m* Greek iambic and elegiac poet
archimagīrus, **-i** *m* chief cook
Archimēdēs, **-is** *m* famous mathematician of Syracuse
archipīrāta, **-ae** *m* pirate chief
architectōn, **-onis** *m* master builder; master in cunning
architector, **-ārī**, **-ātus** *vt* to construct; (*fig*) to devise
architectūra, **-ae** *f* architecture
architectus, **-ī** *m* architect; (*fig*) author
archōn, **-ontis** *m* Athenian magistrate
Archytās, **-ae** *m* Pythagorean philosopher of Tarentum
arcitenēns, **-entis** *adj* holding a bow ♦ *m* Apollo
Arctophylax, **-cis** *m* (*constellation*) Bootes
arctos, **-ī** *f* Great Bear, Little Bear; north, north wind; night
Arctūrus, **-ī** *m* brightest star in Boōtēs
arctus *etc see* **artus'** *etc*
arcuī *perf of* **arceō**
arcula, **-ae** *f* casket; (*RHET*) ornament
arcuō, **-āre**, **-āvī**, **-ātum** *vt* to curve
arcus, **-ūs** *m* bow; rainbow; arch, curve; (*MATH*) arc
ardea, **-ae** *f* heron
Ardea, **-ae** *f* town in Latium
ardeliō, **-ōnis** *m* busybody
ārdēns, **-entis** *adj* hot, glowing, fiery; (*fig*) eager, ardent
ārdenter *adv* passionately
ārdeō, **-dēre**, **-sī**, **-sum** *vi* to be on fire, burn, shine; (*fig*) to be fired, burn
ārdēscō, **-ere** *vi* to catch fire, gleam; (*fig*) to become inflamed, wax hotter
ārdor, **-ōris** *m* heat, brightness; (*fig*) ardour, passion
arduum, **-ī** *nt* steep slope; difficulty
arduus *adj* steep, high; difficult, troublesome
ārea, **-ae** *f* vacant site, open space, playground; threshing-floor; (*fig*) scope (*for effort*)
ārefaciō, **-acere**, **-ēcī**, **-actum** *vt* to dry
arēna *etc see* **harēna**
ārēns, **-entis** *adj* arid; thirsty

āreō, **-ēre** *vi* to be dry
āreola, **-ae** *f* small open space
Arēopagītēs *m* member of the court
Arēopagus, **-ī** *m* Mars' Hill in Athens; a criminal court
Arēs, **-is** *m* Greek god of war
ārēscō, **-ere** *vi* to dry, dry up
Arestoridēs, **-ae** *m* Argus
aretālogus, **-ī** *m* braggart
Arethūsa, **-ae** *f* spring near Syracuse
Arethūsis *adj* Syracusan
Argēī, **-ōrum** *mpl* sacred places in Rome; effigies thrown annually into the Tiber
argentāria, **-ae** *f* bank, banking; silver mine
argentārius *adj* of silver, of money ♦ *m* banker
argentātus *adj* silver-plated; backed with money
argenteus *adj* of silver, adorned with silver; silvery (*in colour*); of the silver age
argentum, **-ī** *nt* silver, silver plate; money
Argēus, **Argīvus**, **Argolicus** *adj* Argive; Greek
Argīlētānus *adj see* **Argīlētum**
Argīlētum, **-ī** *nt* part of Rome (noted for bookshops)
argilla, **-ae** *f* clay
Argō, **-ūs** *f* Jason's ship
Argolis, **-olidis** *f* district about Argos
Argonautae, **-ārum** *mpl* Argonauts
Argonauticus *adj see* **Argonautae**
Argos *nt*, **Argī**, **-ōrum** *mpl* town in S.E. Greece
Argōus *adj see* **Argō**
argūmentātiō, **-ōnis** *f* adducing proofs
argūmentor, **-ārī**, **-ātus** *vt*, *vi* to prove, adduce as proof; to conclude
argūmentum, **-ī** *nt* evidence, proof; (*LIT*) subject matter, theme, plot (*of a play*); (*art*) subject, motif
arguō, **-uere**, **-uī**, **-ūtum** *vt* to prove, make known; to accuse, blame, denounce
Argus, **-ī** *m* monster with many eyes
argūtē *adv* subtly
argūtiae, **-ārum** *fpl* nimbleness, liveliness; wit, subtlety, slyness
argūtor, **-ārī**, **-ātus** *vi* to chatter
argūtulus *adj* rather subtle
argūtus *adj* (*sight*) clear, distinct, graceful; (*sound*) clear, melodious, noisy; (*mind*) acute, witty, sly
argyraspis, **-dis** *adj* silver-shielded
Ariadna, **-ae** *f* daughter of Minos of Crete
Ariadnaeus *adj see* **Ariadna**
āridulus *adj* rather dry
āridum, **-ī** *nt* dry land
āridus *adj* dry, withered; meagre; (*style*) flat
ariēs, **-etis** *m* ram; 1st sign of Zodiac; battering ram; beam used as a breakwater
arietō, **-āre** *vt*, *vi* to butt, strike hard
Ariōn, **-onis** *m* early Greek poet and musician
Ariōnius *adj see* **Ariōn**
arista, **-ae** *f* ear of corn
Aristaeus, **-ī** *m* legendary founder of beekeeping
Aristarchus, **-ī** *m* Alexandrian scholar; a severe critic
Aristīdēs, **-is** *m* Athenian statesman noted for integrity
Aristippēus *adj see* **Aristippus**
Aristippus, **-ī** *m* Greek hedonist philosopher

aristolochia, -ae f birthwort
Aristophanēs, -is m *Greek comic poet*
Aristophanēus, Aristophanīus adj *see*
  Aristophanēs
Aristotelēs, -is m Aristotle *(founder of Peripatetic*
  school of philosophy)
Aristotelēus, Aristotelīus adj *see* **Aristotelēs**
arithmētica, -ōrum ntpl arithmetic
āritūdō, -inis f dryness
Ariūsius adj of Ariusia *(in Chios)*
arma, -ōrum ntpl armour, shield; arms,
  weapons *(of close combat only)*; warfare, troops;
  (fig) defence, protection; implements, ship's
  gear
armāmenta, -ōrum ntpl implements, ship's
  gear
armāmentārium, -ī and **-iī** nt arsenal
armāriolum, -ī nt small chest
armārium, -ī and **-iī** nt chest, safe
armātū abl m armour; **gravī ~** with heavy-
  armed troops
armatūra, -ae f armour, equipment; **levis**
  ~ light-armed troops
armatus adj armed
Armenia, -ae f Armenia
Armeniaca, -acae f apricot tree
Armeniacum, -acī nt apricot
Armenius adj *see* **Armenia**
armentālis adj of the herd
armentārius, -ī and **-iī** m cattle herd
armentum, -ī nt cattle *(for ploughing)*, herd *(cattle*
  etc)
armifer, -ī adj armed
armiger, -ī m armour-bearer ♦ adj armed;
  productive of warriors
armilla, -ae f bracelet
armillātus adj wearing a bracelet
armipotēns, -entis adj strong in battle
armisonus adj resounding with arms
armō, -āre, -āvī, -ātum vt to arm, equip; to
  rouse to arms *(against)*
armus, -ī m shoulder *(esp of animals)*
Arniēnsis adj *see* **Arnus**
Arnus, -ī m *(river)* Arno
arō, -āre, -āvī, -ātum vt to plough, cultivate; to
  live by farming; *(fig: sea, brow)* to furrow
Arpīnās, -ātis adj *see* **Arpīnum**
Arpīnum, -ī nt *town in Latium (birthplace of Cicero)*
arquātus adj jaundiced
arr- *etc see* **adr-**
arrabō, -ōnis m earnest money
ars, artis f skill *(in any craft)*; the art *(of any*
  profession); science, theory; handbook; work of
  art; moral quality, virtue; artifice, fraud
ārsī perf of **ārdeō**
ārsus ppp of **ārdeō**
artē adv closely, soundly, briefly
artēria¹, -ae f windpipe; artery
artēria², -ōrum ntpl trachea
arthrīticus adj gouty
articulātim adv joint by joint; *(speech)* distinctly
articulō, -āre, -āvī, -ātum vt to articulate
articulōsus adj minutely subdivided

articulus, -ī m joint, knuckle; limb; *(words)*
  clause; *(time)* point, turning point; **in ipsō**
  articulō temporis in the nick of time
artifex, -icis m artist, craftsman, master;
  (fig) maker, author ♦ adj ingenious, artistic,
  artificial
artificiōsē adv skilfully
artificiōsus adj ingenious, artistic, artificial
artificium, -ī and **-iī** nt skill, workmanship;
  art, craft; theory, rule of an art; ingenuity,
  cunning
artō, -āre vt to compress, curtail
artolaganus, -ī m *kind of cake*
artopta, -ae m baker; baking tin
artus¹ adj close, narrow, tight; *(sleep)* deep; *(fig)*
  strict, straitened
artus², -ūs m joint; *(pl)* limbs, body; *(fig)*
  strength
ārula, -ae f small altar
arundō *etc see* **harundō** *etc*
arvīna, -ae f grease
arvum, -ī nt field; land, country, plain
arvus adj ploughed
arx, arcis f fortress, castle; height, summit; *(fig)*
  bulwark, stronghold; **arcem facere ē cloācā**
  make a mountain out of a molehill
ās, assis m *(weight)* pound; *(coin)* bronze unit, of low
  value; *(inheritance)* the whole *(subdivided into 12*
  parts); **ad assem** to the last farthing; **hērēs ex**
  asse sole heir
Ascānius, -ī m son of Aeneas
ascendō, -endere, -endī, -ēnsum vt, vi to go up,
  climb, embark; *(fig)* to rise
ascēnsiō, -ōnis f ascent; *(fig)* sublimity
ascēnsus, -ūs m ascent, rising; way up
ascia, -ae f axe; mason's trowel
asciō, -īre vt to admit
ascīscō, -īscere, -īvī, -ītum vt to receive with
  approval; to admit *(to some kind of association)*; to
  appropriate, adopt *(esp customs)*; to arrogate to
  oneself
ascītus adj acquired, alien
Ascra, -ae f birthplace of Hesiod in Boeotia
Ascraeus adj of Ascra; of Hesiod; of Helicon
ascrībō, -bere, -psī, -ptum vt to add *(in writing)*;
  to attribute, ascribe; to apply *(an illustration)*; to
  enrol, include
ascrīptīcius adj enrolled
ascrīptiō, -ōnis f addition *(in writing)*
ascrīptīvus adj *(MIL)* supernumerary
ascrīptor, -ōris m supporter
ascrīptus ppp of **ascrībō**
asella, -ae f young ass
asellus, -ī m young ass
Āsia, -ae f Roman province; Asia Minor; Asia
asīlus, -ī m gad fly
asinus, -ī m ass; fool
Āsis, -dis f Asia
Āsius, Āsiānus, Āsiāticus adj *see* **Āsia**
Āsōpus, -ī m river in Boeotia
asōtus, -ī m libertine
asparagus, -ī m asparagus
aspargō *etc see* **aspergō¹**
aspectābilis adj visible

aspectō, -āre *vt* to look at, gaze at; to pay heed to; (*places*) to face

aspectus¹ *ppp of* **aspiciō**

aspectus², -ūs *m* look, sight; glance, sense of sight; aspect, appearance

aspellō, -ere *vt* to drive away

asper, -ī *adj* rough; (*taste*) bitter; (*sound*) harsh; (*weather*) severe; (*style*) rugged; (*person*) violent, exasperated, unkind, austere; (*animal*) savage; (*circumstances*) difficult

asperē *adv see* **asper**

aspergō¹, -gere, -sī, -sum *vt* to scatter, sprinkle; to bespatter, besprinkle; **aquam aspergere** revive

aspergō², -inis *f* sprinkling; spray

asperitās, -ātis *f* roughness, unevenness, harshness, severity; (*fig*) ruggedness, fierceness; trouble, difficulty

aspernātiō, -ōnis *f* disdain

aspernor, -ārī, -ātus *vt* to reject, disdain

asperō, -āre, -āvī, -ātum *vt* to roughen, sharpen; to exasperate

aspersiō, -ōnis *f* sprinkling

aspersus *ppp of* **aspergō¹**

aspiciō, -icere, -exī, -ectum *vt* to catch sight of, look at; (*places*) to face; (*fig*) to examine, consider

aspīrātiō, -ōnis *f* breathing (on); evaporation; pronouncing with an aspirate

aspīrō, -āre, -āvī, -ātum *vi* to breathe, blow; to favour; to aspire, attain (to) ♦ *vt* to blow, instil

aspis, -dis *f* asp

asportātiō, -ōnis *f* removal

asportō, -āre *vt* to carry off

asprēta, -ōrum *ntpl* rough country

ass- *etc see* **ads-**

Assaracus, -ī *m* Trojan ancestor of Aeneas

asser, -is *m* pole, stake

assula, -ae *f* splinter

assulātim *adv* in splinters

assum, -ī *nt* roast; (*pl*) sweating-bath

assus *adj* roasted

Assyria, -ae *f* country in W. Asia

Assyrius *adj* Assyrian; oriental

ast *conj* (*laws*) and then; (*vows*) then; (*strong contrast*) and yet

ast- *etc see* **adst-**

Astraea, -ae *f* goddess of Justice

Astraeus, -ī *m* father of winds; **Astraeī frātrēs** the winds

astrologia, -ae *f* astronomy

astrologus, -ī *m* astronomer; astrologer

astrum, -ī *nt* star, heavenly body, constellation; a great height; heaven, immortality, glory

astu *nt* (*indecl*) city (*esp Athens*)

astus, -ūs *m* cleverness, cunning

astūtē *adv* cleverly

astūtia, -ae *f* slyness, cunning

astūtus *adj* artful, sly

Astyanax, -ctis *m* son of Hector and Andromache

asȳlum, -ī *nt* sanctuary

asymbolus *adj* with no contribution

at *conj* (*adversative*) but, on the other hand; (*objecting*) but it may be said; (*limiting*) at least, but at least; (*continuing*) then, thereupon;

(*transitional*) now; (*with passionate appeals*) but oh!, look now!; **at enim** yes, but; **at tamen** nevertheless

Atābulus, -ī *m* sirocco

atat *interj* (*expressing fright, pain, surprise*) oh!

atavus, -ī *m* great-great-great-grandfather; ancestor

Atella, -ae *f* Oscan town in Campania

Ātellānicus, Ātellānius *adj see* **Atella**

Ātellānus *adj*: **fābula Atellāna** *kind of comic show popular in Rome*

āter, -rī *adj* black, dark; gloomy, dismal; malicious; **diēs ātrī** unlucky days

Athamantēus *adj see* **Athamās**

Athamantiadēs *m* Palaemon

Athamantis *f* Helle

Athamās, -antis *m* king of Thessaly (*who went mad*)

Athēnae, -ārum *fpl* Athens

Athēnaeus, Athēniēnsis *adj see* **Athēnae**

atheos, -ī *m* atheist

athlēta, -ae *m* wrestler, athlete

athlēticē *adv* athletically

Athos (*dat* **-ō**, *acc* **-ō, -on, -ōnem**) *m* mount Athos (*in Macedonia*)

Atlantiadēs *m* Mercury

Atlanticus *adj*: **mare Atlanticum** Atlantic Ocean

Atlantis *f* lost Atlantic island; a Pleiad

Atlās, -antis *m* giant supporting the sky; Atlas mountains

atomus, -ī *m* atom

atque (*before consonants* **ac**) *conj* (*connecting words*) and, and in fact; (*connecting clauses*) and moreover, and then, and so, and yet; (*in comparison*) as, than, to, from; **~ adeō** and that too; or rather; **~ nōn** and not rather; **~ sī** as if; **alius ~** different from; **contrā ~** opposite to; **īdem ~** same as; **plūs ~** more than

atquī *conj* (*adversative*) and yet, nevertheless, yes but; (*confirming*) by all means; (*minor premise*) now; **~ sī** if now

ātrāmentum, -ī *nt* ink; blacking

ātrātus *adj* in mourning

Atreus, -eī *m* son of Pelops (king of Argos)

Atrīdēs *m* Agamemnon; Menelaus

ātriēnsis, -is *m* steward, major-domo

ātriolum, -ī *nt* anteroom

ātrium, -ī *and* **-iī** *nt* hall, open central room in Roman house; forecourt of a temple; hall (*in other buildings*)

atrōcitās, -ātis *f* hideousness; (*mind*) brutality; (PHILOS) severity

atrōciter *adv* savagely

Atropos, -ī *f* one of the Fates

atrōx, -ōcis *adj* hideous, dreadful; fierce, brutal, unyielding

attāctus¹ *ppp of* **attingō**

attāctus², -ūs *m* contact

attagēn, -is *m* heathcock

Attalica *ntpl* garments of woven gold

Attalicus *adj* of Attalus; of Pergamum; ornamented with gold cloth

Attalus, -ī *m* king of Pergamum (*who bequeathed his kingdom to Rome*)

attamen *conj* nevertheless

attat *see* **atat**
attegia, -ae *f* hut
attemperātē *adv* opportunely
attempto *etc see* **attentō**
attendō, -dere, -dī, -tum *vt* to direct (*the attention*); attend to, notice
attentē *adv* carefully
attentiō, -ōnis *f* attentiveness
attentō, -āre, -āvī, -ātum *vt* to test, try; (*loyalty*) to tamper with; to attack
attentus¹ *ppp of* **attendō** ◆ *adj* attentive, intent; businesslike, careful (*esp about money*)
attentus² *ppp of* **attineō**
attenuātē *adv* simply
attenuātus *adj* weak; (*style*) brief; refined; plain
attenuō, -āre, -āvī, -ātum *vt* to weaken, reduce; to diminish; to humble
atterō, -erere, -rīvī, -rītum *vt* to rub; to wear away; (*fig*) to impair, exhaust
attestor, -ārī, -ātus *vt* to confirm
attexō, -ere, -uī, -tum *vt* to weave on; (*fig*) to add on
Atthis, -dis *f* Attica
Attiānus *adj see* **Attius**
Attica, -ae *f district of Greece about Athens*
Atticē *adv* in the Athenian manner
Atticissō *vi* to speak in the Athenian manner
Atticus *adj* Attic, Athenian; (RHET) of a plain and direct style
attigī *perf of* **attingō**
attigō *see* **attingō**
attineō, -ēre, -uī, -entum *vt* to hold fast, detain; to guard; to reach for ◆ *vi* to concern, pertain, be of importance, avail
attingō, -ingere, -igī, -āctum *vt* to touch; to strike, assault; to arrive at; to border on; to affect; to mention; to undertake; to concern, resemble
Attis, -dis *m Phrygian priest of Cybele*
Attius, -ī *m Latin tragic poet*
attollō, -ere *vt* to lift up, erect; (*fig*) to exalt, extol
attondeō, -ondēre, -ondī, -ōnsum *vt* to shear, prune, crop; (*fig*) to diminish; (*comedy*) to fleece
attonitus *adj* thunderstruck, terrified, astonished; inspired
attonō, -āre, -uī, -itum *vt* to stupefy
attōnsus *ppp of* **attondeō**
attorqueō, -ēre *vt* to hurl upwards
attractus *ppp of* **attrahō**
attrahō, -here, -xī, -ctum *vt* to drag by force, attract; (*fig*) to draw, incite
attrectō, -āre *vt* to touch, handle; to appropriate
attrepidō, -āre *vi* to hobble along
attribuō, -uere, -uī, -ūtum *vt* to assign, bestow; to add; to impute, attribute; to lay as a tax
attribūtiō, -ōnis *f* (*money*) assignment; (GRAM) predicate
attribūtum, -ī *nt* (GRAM) predicate
attribūtus *ppp of* **attribuō** ◆ *adj* subject
attrītus *ppp of* **atterō** ◆ *adj* worn; bruised; (*fig*) impudent
attulī *perf of* **adferō**
au *interj* (*expressing pain, surprise*) oh!

auceps, -upis *m* fowler; (*fig*) eavesdropper; a pedantic critic
auctārium, -ī *and* **-iī** *nt* extra
auctificus *adj* increasing
auctiō, -ōnis *f* increase; auction sale
auctiōnārius *adj* auction; **tabulae auctiōnāriae** catalogues
auctiōnor, -ārī, -ātus *vi* to hold an auction
auctitō, -āre *vt* to greatly increase
auctō, -āre *vt* to increase
auctor, -ōris *m/f* 1. (*originator: of families*) progenitor; (: *of buildings*) founder; (: *of deeds*) doer 2. (*composer: of writings*) author, historian; (: *of knowledge*) investigator, teacher; (: *of news*) informant 3. (*instigator: of action*) adviser; (: *of measures*) promoter; (: *of laws*) proposer, supporter; ratifier 4. (*person of influence: in public life*) leader; (: *of conduct*) model; (: *of guarantees*) witness, bail; (: *of property*) seller; (: *of women and minors*) guardian; (: *of others' welfare*) champion; **mē auctōre** at my suggestion
auctōrāmentum, -ī *nt* contract; wages
auctōrātus *adj* bound (*by a pledge*); hired out (*for wages*)
auctōritās, -ātis *f* 1. source; lead, responsibility 2. judgment; opinion; advice, support; bidding, guidance; (*of senate*) decree; (*of people*) will 3. power; (*person*) influence, authority, prestige; (*things*) importance, worth; (*conduct*) example; (*knowledge*) warrant, document, authority; (*property*) right of possession
auctumn- *etc see* **autumn-**
auctus¹ *ppp of* **augeō** ◆ *adj* enlarged, great
auctus², -ūs *m* growth, increase
aucupium, -i *and* **-iī** *nt* fowling; birds caught; (*fig*) hunting (after); quibbling
aucupō, -āre *vt* to watch for
aucupor, -ārī, -ātus *vi* to go fowling ◆ *vt* to chase; (*fig*) to try to catch
audācia, -ae *f* daring, courage; audacity, impudence; (*pl*) deeds of daring
audācter, audāciter *adv see* **audāx**
audāx, -ācis *adj* bold, daring; rash, audacious, proud
audēns, -entis *adj* bold, brave
audenter *adv see* **audēns**
audentia, -ae *f* boldness, courage
audeō, -dēre, -sus *vt, vi* to dare, venture; to be brave
audiēns, -entis *m* hearer ◆ *adj* obedient
audientia, -ae *f* hearing; **audientiam facere** gain a hearing
audiō, -īre, -īvī, -iī, -ītum *vt* to hear; to learn, be told; to be called; to listen, attend to, study under (*a teacher*); to examine (a case); to agree with; to obey, heed; **bene/male audīre** have a good/bad reputation
audītiō, -ōnis *f* listening; hearsay, news
audītor, -ōris *m* hearer; pupil
audītōrium, -i *and* **-iī** *nt* lecture room, law court; audience
audītus, -ūs *m* (sense of) hearing; a hearing; rumour
auferō, auferre, abstulī, ablātum *vt* to take away, carry away; to mislead, lead into a

digression; to take by force, steal; to win, obtain (as the result of effort); **aufer** away with!

Aufidus, -ō m river in Apulia

aufugiō, -ugere, -ūgī vi to run away ♦ vt to flee from

Augēās, -ae m king of Elis (whose stables Hercules cleaned)

augeō, -gēre, -xī, -ctum vt to increase; to enrich, bless (with); to praise, worship ♦ vi to increase

augēscō, -ere vi to begin to grow, increase

augmen, -inis nt growth

augur, -is m/f augur; prophet, interpreter

augurāle, -is nt part of camp where auspices were taken

augurālis adj augur's

augurātiō, -ōnis f soothsaying

augurātō adv after taking auspices

augurātus, -ūs m office of augur

augurium, -ī and **-iī** nt augury; an omen; prophecy, interpretation; presentiment

augurius adj of augurs

augurō, -āre vt, vi to take auguries; to consecrate by auguries; to forebode

auguror, -ārī, -ātus vt, vi to take auguries; to foretell by omens; to predict, conjecture

Augusta, -ae f title of the emperor's wife, mother, daughter or sister

Augustālis adj of Augustus; **lūdī Augustālēs** games in October; **praefectus** ~ governor of Egypt; **sodālēs Augustālēs** priests of deified Augustus

augustē adv see augustus

Augustus, -ī m title given to C Octavius, first Roman emperor, and so to his successors ♦ adj imperial; (month) August, of August

augustus adj venerable, august, majestic

aula¹, -ae f courtyard (of a Greek house); hall (of a Roman house); palace, royal court; courtiers; royal power

aula² etc see olla

aulaeum, -ī nt embroidered hangings, canopy, covering; (THEAT) curtain

aulicī, -ōrum mpl courtiers

aulicus adj of the court

Aulis, -idis and **-is** f port in Boeotia from which the Greeks sailed to Troy

auloedus, -ī m singer accompanied by flute

aura, -ae f breath of air, breeze, wind; air, upper world; vapour, odour, sound, gleam; (fig) winds (of public favour), breeze (of prosperity), air (of freedom), daylight (of publicity)

aurāria, -ae f gold mine

aurārius adj of gold

aurātus adj gilt, ornamented with gold; gold

Aurēlius, -ī m Roman name; **lēx Aurēlia** law on the composition of juries; **via Aurēlia** main road running NW from Rome

aureolus adj gold; beautiful, splendid

aureus adj gold, golden; gilded; (fig) beautiful, splendid ♦ m gold coin

aurichalcum, -ī nt a precious metal

auricomus adj golden-leaved

auricula, -ae f the external ear; ear

aurifer, -ī adj gold-producing

aurifex, -icis m goldsmith

aurīga, -ae m charioteer, driver; groom; helmsman; a constellation

aurigena, -ae adj gold-begotten

auriger, -ī adj gilded

aurigō, -āre vi to compete in the chariot race

auris, -is f ear; (RHET) judgment; (AGR) earthboard (of a plough); **ad aurem admonēre** whisper; **in utramvis aurem dormīre** sleep soundly

aurītulus, -ī m "Long-Ears"

aurītus adj long-eared; attentive

aurōra, -ae f dawn, morning; goddess of dawn; the East

aurum, -ī nt gold; gold plate, jewellery, bit, fleece etc; money; lustre; the Golden Age

auscultātiō, -ōnis f obedience

auscultātor, -ōris m listener

auscultō, -āre, -āvī, -ātum vt to listen to; to overhear ♦ vi (of servants) to wait at the door; to obey

ausim subj of audeō

Ausones, -um mpl indigenous people of central Italy

Ausonia f Italy

Ausonidae mpl Italians

Ausonius, -is adj Italian

auspex, -icis m augur, soothsayer; patron, commander; witness of a marriage contract

auspicātō adv after taking auspices; at a lucky moment

auspicātus adj consecrated; auspicious, lucky

auspicium, -ī and **-iī** nt augury, auspices; right of taking auspices; power, command; omen; ~ **facere** give a sign

auspicō, -āre vi to take the auspices

auspicor, -ārī, -ātus vi to take the auspices; to make a beginning ♦ vt to begin, enter upon

auster, -rī m south wind; south

austērē adv see austērus

austēritās, -ātis f severity

austērus adj severe, serious; gloomy, irksome

austrālis adj southern

austrīnus adj from the south

ausum, -ī nt enterprise

ausus ppa of audeō

aut conj or; either ... or; or else, or at least, or rather

autem conj (adversative) but, on the other hand; (in transitions, parentheses) moreover, now, and; (in dialogue) indeed

authepsa, -ae f stove

autographus adj written with his own hand

Autolycus, -ī m a robber

automaton, -ī nt automaton

automatus adj spontaneous

Automedōn, -ontis m a charioteer

autumnālis adj autumn, autumnal

autumnus, -ī m autumn ♦ adj autumnal

autumō, -āre vt to assert

auxī perf of augeō

auxilia, -iōrum ntpl auxiliary troops; military force

auxiliāris adj helping, auxiliary; of the auxiliaries ♦ mpl auxiliary troops

auxiliārius adj helping; auxiliary

auxiliātor, **-ōris** *m* helper
auxiliātus, **-ūs** *m* aid
auxilior, **-āri**, **-ātus** *vi* to aid, support
auxilium, **-ī** *and* **-iī** *nt* help, assistance
avārē, **avāriter** *adv see* **avārus**
avāritia, **-ae** *f* greed, selfishness
avāritiēs, **-ēī** *f* avarice
avārus *adj* greedy, covetous; eager
avē, **avēte**, **avētō** *impv* hail!, farewell!
āvehō, **-here**, **-xī**, **-ctum** *vt* to carry away; (*pass*) to ride away
āvellō, **-ellere**, **-ellī** *and* **-ulsī**, **(-olsī)**, **-ulsum**, **(-olsum)** *vt* to pull away, tear off; to take away (by force), remove
avēna, **-ae** *f* oats; (*music*) reed, shepherd's pipe
avēns, **-entis** *adj* eager
Aventīnum, **-ī** *nt* Aventine hill
Aventīnus, **-ī** *m* Aventine (hill) (*in Rome*) ◆ *adj* of Aventine
aveō, **-ēre** *vt* to desire, long for
Avernālis *adj* of lake Avernus
Avernus, **-ī** *m* lake near Cumae (*said to be an entrance to the lower world*); the lower world ◆ *adj* birdless; of Avernus; infernal
āverruncō, **-āre** *vt* to avert
āversābilis *adj* abominable
āversor[1], **-ārī**, **-ātus** *vi* to turn away ◆ *vt* to repulse, decline
āversor[2], **-ōris** *m* embezzler
āversūm, **-ī** *nt* back
āversus *ppp of* **āvertō** ◆ *adj* in the rear, behind, backwards; hostile, averse

āvertō, **-tere**, **-tī**, **-sum** *vt* to turn aside, avert; to divert; to embezzle; to estrange ◆ *vi* to withdraw
avia[1], **-ae** *f* grandmother
avia[2], **-ōrum** *ntpl* wilderness
aviārium, **-ī** *nt* aviary, haunt of birds
aviārius *adj* of birds
avidē *adv see* **avidus**
aviditās, **-ātis** *f* eagerness, longing; avarice
avidus *adj* eager, covetous; avaricious, greedy; hungry; vast
avītus *adj* of a grandfather; ancestral
āvius *adj* out of the way, lonely, untrodden; wandering, astray
āvocāmentum, **-ī** *nt* relaxation
āvocātiō, **-ōnis** *f* diversion
āvocō, **-āre** *vt* to call off; to divert, distract; to amuse
āvolō, **-āre** *vi* to fly away, hurry away; to depart, vanish
āvolsus, **avulsus** *ppp of* **āvellō**
avunculus, **-ī** *m* uncle (*on mother's side*); ~ **māgnus** great-uncle
avus, **-ī** *m* grandfather; ancestor
Axenus, **-ī** *m* Black Sea
axicia, **axitia**, **-ae** *f* scissors
āxilla, **-ae** *f* armpit
axis, **-is** *m* axle, chariot; axis, pole, sky, clime; plank
azȳmus *adj* unleavened

Bb

babae *interj* (*expressing wonder or joy*) oho!
Babylōn, -ōnis *f* ancient city on the Euphrates
Babylōnia *f* the country under Babylon
Babylōnicus, Babylōniēnsis *adj see* **Babylōnia**
Babylōnius *adj* Babylonian; Chaldaean, versed in astrology
bāca, -ae *f* berry; olive; fruit; pearl
bācātus *adj* of pearls
bacca *etc see* **bāca**
baccar, -is *nt* cyclamen
Baccha, -ae *f* Bacchante
Bacchānal, -ālis *nt* place consecrated to Bacchus; (*pl*) festival of Bacchus
bacchātiō, -ōnis *f* revel
Bacchēus, Bacchĭcus, Bacchius *adj see* **Bacchus**
Bacchiadae, -ārum *mpl* kings of Corinth (*founders of Syracuse*)
bacchor, -ārī, -ātus *vi* to celebrate the festival of Bacchus; to revel, rave; to rage
Bacchus, -ī *m* god of wine, vegetation, poetry, and religious ecstasy; vine, wine
bācifer, -ī *adj* olive-bearing
bacillum, -ī *nt* stick, lictor's staff
Bactra, -ōrum *ntpl* capital of Bactria in central Asia (*now Balkh*)
Bactriāna *f* Bactria
Bactriānus, Bactrius *adj* Bactrian
baculum, -ī *nt*, **baculus, -ī** *m* stick, staff
Baetica *f* Roman province (*now Andalusia*)
Baeticus *adj see* **Baetis**
Baetis, -is *m* river in Spain (*now* Guadalquivir)
Bagrada, -ae *m* river in Africa (*now* Medjerda)
Bāiae, -ārum *fpl* Roman spa on Bay of Naples
Bāiānus *adj see* **Bāiae**
bāiulō, -āre *vt* to carry (*something heavy*)
bāiulus, -ī *m* porter
bālaena, -ae *f* whale
balanus, -ī *f* balsam (*from an Arabian nut*); a shellfish
balatrō, -ōnis *m* jester
bālātus, -ūs *m* bleating
balbus *adj* stammering
balbūtiō, -īre *vt, vi* to stammer, speak indistinctly; (*fig*) to speak obscurely
Baleārēs, -ium *fpl* Balearic islands
Baleāris, Baleāricus *adj see* **Baleārēs**
balineum *etc see* **balneum** *etc*
ballista, -ae *f* (MIL) catapult for shooting stones and other missiles; (*fig*) weapon
ballistārium, -ī *and* **-iī** *nt* catapult

balneae, -ārum *fpl* bath, baths
balneāria, -ōrum *ntpl* bathroom
balneārius *adj* of the baths
balneātor, -ōris *m* bath superintendent
balneolum, -ī *nt* small bath
balneum, -ī *nt* bath
bālō, -āre *vi* to bleat
balsamum, -ī *nt* balsam, balsam tree
baltea, -ōrum *ntpl* belt (*esp swordbelt; woman's girdle; strapping*)
balteus, -ī *m* belt (*esp swordbelt; woman's girdle; strapping*)
Bandusia, -ae *f* spring near Horace's birthplace
baptisma, -tis *nt* baptism
baptizō, -āre *vt* (ECCL) to baptize
barathrum, -i *nt* abyss; the lower world; (*fig*) a greedy person
barba, -ae *f* beard
barbarē *adv* in a foreign language (*to a Greek*), in Latin; in an uncivilized way; roughly, cruelly
barbaria, -ae, barbariēs (*acc* **-em**) *f* a foreign country (*outside Greece or Italy*); (*words*) barbarism; (*manners*) rudeness, stupidity
barbaricus *adj* foreign, outlandish (*to a Greek*), Italian
barbarus *adj* foreign, barbarous; (*to a Greek*) Italian; rude, uncivilized; savage, barbarous ♦ *m* foreigner, barbarian
barbātulus *adj* with a little beard
barbātus *adj* bearded, adult; ancient (*Romans*); of philosophers
barbiger, -ī *adj* bearded
barbitos (*acc* **-on**) *m* lyre, lute
barbula, -ae *f* little beard
Barcās, -ae *m* ancestor of Hannibal
Barcīnus *adj see* **Barcās**
bardus¹ *adj* dull, stupid
bardus², -ī *m* Gallic minstrel
bārō, -ōnis *m* dunce
barrus, -ī *m* elephant
bascauda, -ae *f* basket (*for the table*)
bāsiātiō, -ōnis *f* kiss
basilica, -ae *f* public building used as exchange and law court
basilicē *adv* royally, in magnificent style
basilicum, -ī *nt* regal robe
basilicus *adj* royal, magnificent ♦ *m* highest throw at dice
bāsiō, -āre *vt* to kiss
basis, -is *f* pedestal, base
bāsium, -ī *and* **-iī** *nt* kiss

Bassareus, -eī m Bacchus
Batăvī, -ōrum mpl people of Batavia (now Holland)
batillum, -ī nt firepan
Battiadēs, -ae m Callimachus
bătuŏ, -ere, -ī vt to beat
baubor, -ārī vi (of dogs) to howl
Baucis, -idis f wife of Philemon
beătē adv see **beătus**
beătitās, -ātis f happiness
beătitūdŏ, -inis f happiness
beătulus, -ī m the blessed man
beătus adj happy; prosperous, well-off; rich,
   abundant
Bēdriacēnsis adj see **Bēdriăcum**
Bēdriăcum, -ī nt village in N. Italy
Belgae, -ārum mpl people of N. Gaul (now Belgium)
Bēlides, -um fpl Danaids
Bēlīdēs, -īdae m Danaus, Aegyptus, Lynceus
bellăria, -ōrum ntpl dessert, confectionery
bellător, -ōris m warrior, fighter ♦ adj warlike
bellătōrius adj aggressive
bellătrīx, -īcis f warrioress ♦ adj warlike
bellē adv well, nicely; ~ **habēre** be well (in health)
Bellerophŏn, -ontis m slayer of Chimaera, rider of
   Pegasus
Bellerophontēus adj see **Bellerophŏn**
bellicōsus adj warlike
bellicus adj of war, military; **bellicum canere**
   give the signal for marching or attack
belliger, -ī adj martial
belligerŏ, -āre, -āvī, -ātum vi to wage war
bellipotēns, -entis adj strong in war
bellŏ, -āre, -āvī, -ātum vi to fight, wage war
Bellŏna, -ae f goddess of war
bellor, -ārī vi to fight
bellulus adj pretty
bellum, -ī nt war, warfare; battle; ~ **gerere** wage
   war; **bellī** in war
bellus adj pretty, handsome; pleasant, nice
bēlua, -ae f beast, monster (esp large and fierce),
   any animal; (fig) brute; ~ **Gaetula** Indian
   elephant
bēluătus adj embroidered with animals
bēluōsus adj full of monsters
Bēlus, -ī m Baal; an oriental king
Bēnācus, -ī m lake in N. Italy (now Garda)
bene adv (compar **melius**, superl **optimē**) well;
   correctly; profitably; very ♦ interj bravo!, good!;
   ~ **dīcere** speak well; speak well of, praise;
   ~ **emere** buy cheap; ~ **est tibi** you are well off;
   ~ **facere** do well; do good to; ~ **facis** thank you;
   rem ~ **gerere** be successful; ~ **sē habēre** have
   a good time; ~ **habet** all is well, it's all right;
   ~ **merērī dē** do a service to; ~ **partum** honestly
   acquired; ~ **tē** your health!; ~ **vēndere** sell at a
   high price; ~ **vīvere** live a happy life
benedīcŏ, -īcere, -īxī, -ictum vt to speak well of,
   praise; (ECCL) to bless
benedictiŏ, -ōnis f (ECCL) blessing
beneficentia, -ae f kindness
beneficiăriī, -ōrum mpl privileged soldiers
beneficium, -ī and **-iī** nt benefit, favour; (POL, MIL)
   promotion; **beneficiō tuō** thanks to you
beneficus adj generous, obliging
Beneventānus adj see **Beneventum**

Beneventum, -ī nt town in S. Italy (now
   Benevento)
benevolē adv see **benevolus**
benevolēns, -entis adj kind-hearted
benevolentia, -ae f goodwill, friendliness
benevolus adj kindly, friendly; (of servants)
   devoted
benīgnē adv willingly, courteously; generously;
   (colloq) no thank you; ~ **facere** do a favour
benīgnitās, -ātis f kindness; liberality, bounty
benīgnus adj kind, friendly; favourable; liberal,
   lavish; fruitful, bounteous
beŏ, -āre, -āvī, -ātum vt to gladden, bless,
   enrich
Berecyntia f Cybele
Berecyntius adj of Berecyntus; of Cybele
Berecyntus, -ī m mountain in Phrygia sacred to
   Cybele
Berenīcē, -ēs f a queen of Egypt; **coma Berenīcēs**
   a constellation
bēryllus, -ī m beryl
bēs, bessis m two-thirds of the as; two-thirds
bēstia, -ae f beast; wild animal (for the arena)
bēstiārius adj of beasts ♦ m beast fighter (in the
   arena)
bēstiola, -ae f small animal
bēta¹, -ae f beet
bēta² nt indecl (Greek letter) beta
bibī perf of **bibŏ**
bibliopōla, -ae m bookseller
bibliothēca, -ae, bibliothēcē, -ēs f library
bibŏ, -ere, -ī vt to drink; to live on the banks
   of (a river); to drink in, absorb; (fig) to listen
   attentively, be imbued; **bibere aquas** be
   drowned; **Graecō mōre bibere** drink to someone's
   health
Bibulus, -ī m consul with Caesar in 59 BC
bibulus adj fond of drink, thirsty; (things) thirsty
biceps, -ipitis adj two-headed
biclīnium, -ī and **-iī** nt dining couch for two
bicolor, -ōris adj two-coloured
bicorniger, -ī adj two-horned
bicornis adj two-horned, two-pronged; (rivers)
   two-mouthed
bicorpor, -is adj two-bodied
bidēns, -entis adj with two teeth or prongs ♦ m
   hoe ♦ f sheep (or other sacrificial animal)
bidental, -ālis nt a place struck by lightning
biduum, -ī nt two days
biennium, -ī and **-iī** nt two years
bifāriam adv in two parts, twice
bifer, -ī adj flowering twice a year
bifidus adj split in two
biforis adj double-doored; double
bifōrmātus, bifōrmis adj with two forms
bifrōns, -ontis adj two-headed
bifurcus adj two-pronged, forked
bīgae, -ārum fpl chariot and pair
bīgātus adj stamped with a chariot and pair
biiugī, -ōrum mpl two horses yoked abreast;
   chariot with two horses
biiugis, biiugus adj yoked
bilībra, -ae f two pounds
bilībris adj holding two pounds

bilinguis *adj* double-tongued; bilingual; deceitful

bīlis, -is *f* bile, gall; (*fig*) anger, displeasure; ~ **ātra**, ~ **nigra** melancholy; madness

bilīx, -īcis *adj* double-stranded

bilūstris *adj* ten years

bimaris *adj* between two seas

bimarītus, -ī *m* bigamist

bimāter, -ris *adj* having two mothers

bimembris *adj* half man, half beast; (*pl*) Centaurs

bimēstris *adj* of two months, two months old

bimulus *adj* only two years old

bimus *adj* two years old, for two years

bīnī, bīnae, bīna *num* two each, two by two; a pair; (*with pl nouns having a meaning different from sg*) two

binoctium, -ī and -iī *nt* two nights

binōminis *adj* with two names

Biōn, -ōnis *m* satirical philosopher

Biōnēus *adj* satirical

bipalmis *adj* two spans long

bipartītō *adv* in two parts, in two directions

bipartītus *adj* divided in two

bipatēns, -entis *adj* double-opening

bipedālis *adj* two feet long, broad or thick

bipennifer, -ī *adj* wielding a battle-axe

bipennis *adj* two-edged ♦ *f* battle-axe

bipertītō *etc see* **bipartītō**

bipēs, -edis *adj* two-footed ♦ *m* biped

birēmis *adj* two-oared; with two banks of oars ♦ *f* two-oared skiff; galley with two banks of oars

bis *adv* twice, double; **bis ad eundem** make the same mistake twice; **bis diē, in diē** twice a day; **bis tantō, bis tantum** twice as much; **bis terque** frequently; **bis terve** seldom

bissextus, -ī *m* intercalary day after 24th Feb

Bistones, -um *mpl people of Thrace*

Bistonis *f* Thracian woman, Bacchante

Bistonius *adj* Thracian

bisulcilingua, -ae *adj* fork-tongued, deceitful

bisulcus *adj* cloven

Bīthȳnia, -iae *f province of Asia Minor*

Bīthȳnicus, Bīthȳnius *adj see* **Bīthȳnia**

bītō, -ere *vi* to go

bitūmen, -inis *nt* bitumen, *a kind of pitch*

bitūmineus *adj see* **bitūmen**

bivium *nt* two ways

bivius *adj* two-way

blaesus *adj* lisping, indistinct

blandē *adv see* **blandus**

blandidicus *adj* fair-spoken

blandiloquentia, -ae *f* attractive language

blandiloquus, blandiloquentulus *adj* fair-spoken

blandīmentum, -ī *nt* compliment, allurement

blandior, -īrī, -ītus *vi* to coax, caress; to flatter, pay compliments; (*things*) to please, entice

blanditia, -ae *f* caress, flattery; charm, allurement

blandītim *adv* caressingly

blandus *adj* smooth-tongued, flattering, fawning; charming, winsome

blaterō, -āre *vi* to babble

blatiō, -īre *vt* to babble

blatta, -ae *f* cockroach

blennus, -ī *m* idiot

bliteus *adj* silly

blitum, -ī *nt kind of spinach*

boārius *adj* of cattle; **forum boārium** cattle market in Rome

Bodotria, -ae *f* Firth of Forth

Boeōtarchēs *m chief magistrate of Boeotia*

Boeōtia, -iae *f district of central Greece*

Boeōtius, Boeōtus *adj see* **Boeōtia**

boiae, -ārum *fpl* collar

Boiī, -ōrum *mpl people of S.E. Gaul*

Boiohaemī, -ōrum *mpl* Bohemians

bōlētus, -ī *m* mushroom

bolus, -ī *m* (*dice*) throw; (*net*) cast; (*fig*) haul, piece of good luck; titbit

bombus, -ī *m* booming, humming, buzzing

bombȳcinus *adj* of silk

bombȳx, -ȳcis *m* silkworm; silk

Bona Dea, Bonae Deae *f goddess worshipped by women*

bonitās, -ātis *f* goodness; honesty, integrity; kindness, affability

Bonōnia, -ae *f town in N. Italy (now Bologna)*

Bonōniēnsis *adj see* **Bonōnia**

bonum, -ī *nt* a moral good; advantage, blessing; (*pl*) property; **cuī bonō?** who was the gainer?

bonus *adj* (*compar* **melior**, *superl* **optimus**) good; kind; brave; loyal; beneficial; lucky ♦ *mpl* upper class party, conservatives; **bona aetās** prime of life; **bonō animō** of good cheer; well-disposed; **bonae artēs** integrity; culture, liberal education; **bona dicta** witticisms; **bona fidēs** good faith; **bonī mōrēs** morality; **bonī nummī** genuine money; **bona pars** large part; conservative party; **bonae rēs** comforts, luxuries; prosperity; morality; **bonā veniā** with kind permission; **bona verba** words of good omen; well-chosen diction; **bona vōx** loud voice

boō, -āre *vi* to cry aloud

Boōtēs, -ae *m* constellation containing Arcturus*

Boreās, -ae *m* north wind; north

Boreus *adj see* **Boreās**

Borysthenēs, -is *m* (river) Dnieper

Borysthenidae *mpl dwellers near the Dnieper*

Borysthenius *adj see* **Borysthenidae**

bōs, bovis *m/f* ox, cow; kind of turbot; **bōs Lūca** elephant; **bovī clitellās impōnere** put a round peg in a square hole

Bosporānus, Bosporius *adj see* **Bosporus**

Bosporus, -ī *m strait from Black Sea to Sea of Marmora*

Bosporus Cimmerius *m strait from Sea of Azov to Black Sea*

Boudicca, -ae *f British queen (falsely called Boadicea)*

bovārius *etc see* **boārius**

Bovillae, -ārum *fpl ancient Latin town*

Bovillānus *adj see* **Bovillae**

bovillus *adj* of oxen

brācae, -ārum *fpl* trousers

brācātus *adj* trousered; barbarian (*esp of tribes beyond the Alps*)

bracchiālis *adj* of the arm

bracchiolum, -ī *nt* dainty arm
bracchium, -ī *and* **-iī** *nt* arm, forearm; (*shellfish*) claw; (*tree*) branch; (*sea*) arm; (*NAUT*) yardarm; (*MIL*) outwork, mole; **levī bracchiō, mollī bracchiō** casually
bractea *etc see* **brattea**
brassica, -ae *f* cabbage
brattea, -ae *f* gold leaf
bratteola, -ae *f* very fine gold leaf
Brennus, -ī *m Gallic chief who defeated the Romans*
brevī *adv* shortly, soon; briefly, in a few words
brevia, -ium *ntpl* shoals
breviārium, -ī *and* **-iī** *nt* summary, statistical survey, official report
breviculus *adj* shortish
breviloquēns, -entis *adj* brief
brevis *adj* short, small, shallow; brief, short-lived; concise
brevitās, -ātis *f* shortness, smallness; brevity, conciseness
breviter *adv* concisely
Brigantēs, -um *mpl British tribe in N. England*
Briganticus *adj see* **Brigantēs**
Brīsēis, -idos *f captive of Achilles*
Britannia, -iae *f* Britain; the British Isles
Britannicus *m son of emperor Claudius*
Britannus, Britannicus *adj see* **Britannia**
Bromius, -ī *and* **-iī** *m* Bacchus
brūma, -ae *f* winter solstice, midwinter; winter
brūmālis *adj* of the winter solstice; wintry; ~ **flexus** tropic of Capricorn
Brundisīnus *adj see* **Brundisium**
Brundisium, -ī *and* **-iī** *nt* port in S.E. Italy (now Brindisi)
Bruttiī, -ōrum *mpl people of the toe of Italy*
Bruttius *adj see* **Bruttiī**
Brūtus, -ī *m liberator of Rome from kings; murderer of Caesar*
brūtus *adj* heavy, unwieldy; stupid, irrational

bubīle, -is *nt* stall
būbo, -ōnis *m/f* owl
būbula, -ae *f* beef
bubulcitor, -ārī *vi* to drive oxen
bubulcus, -ī *m* ploughman
būbulus *adj* of cattle
būcaeda, -ae *m* flogged slave
bucca, -ae *f* cheek; mouth; ranter
buccō, -ōnis *m* babbler
buccula, -ae *f* visor
bucculentus *adj* fat-cheeked
būcerus *adj* horned
būcina, -ae *f* shepherd's horn; military trumpet; night watch
būcinātor, -ōris *m* trumpeter
būcolica, -ōrum *ntpl* pastoral poetry
būcula, -ae *f* young cow
būfō, -ōnis *m* toad
bulbus, -ī *m* bulb; onion
būlē, -es *f* Greek senate
būleuta *m* senator
būleutērium *nt* senate house
bulla, -ae *f* bubble; knob, stud; *gold charm worn round the neck by children of noblemen*
bullātus *adj* wearing the bulla; still a child
būmastus, -ī *f kind of vine*
būris, -is *m* plough-beam
Burrus *old form of* **Pyrrhus**
Busīris, -idis *m Egyptian king killed by Hercules*
bustirapus, -ī *m* graverobber
bustuārius *adj* at a funeral
bustum, -ī *nt* funeral place; tomb, grave
buxifer, -ī *adj* famed for its box trees
buxum, -ī *nt* boxwood; flute, top, comb, tablet
buxus, -ī *f* box tree; flute
Byzantium, -ī *and* **-iī** *nt* city on Bosporus (*later* Constantinople, *now* Istanbul)
Byzantius *adj see* **Byzantium**

Cc

caballīnus *adj* horse's

caballus, -ī *m* horse

cacātus *adj* impure

cachinnātiō, -ōnis *f* loud laughter

cachinnō¹, -āre *vi* to laugh, guffaw

cachinnō², -ōnis *m* scoffer

cachinnus, -ī *m* laugh, derisive laughter; (*waves*) splashing

cacō, -āre *vi* to evacuate the bowels

cacoëthes, -is *nt* (*fig*) itch

cacula, -ae *m* soldier's slave

cacūmen, -inis *nt* extremity, point, summit, treetop; (*fig*) height, limit

cacūminō, -āre *vt* to make pointed

Cācus, -ī *m* giant robber, son of Vulcan

cadāver, -is *nt* corpse, carcass

cadāverōsus *adj* ghastly

Cadmēa, -ēae *f* fortress of Thebes

Cadmēis, -ēidis *f* Agave; Ino; Semele

Cadmēus, Cadmēius *adj* of Cadmus; Theban

Cadmus, -ī *m* founder of Thebes

cadō, -ere, cecidī, cāsum *vi* to fall; to droop, die, be killed; (ASTR) to set; (*dice*) to be thrown; (*events*) to happen, turn out; (*money*) to be due; (*strength, speech, courage*) to diminish, cease, fail; (*wind, rage*) to subside; (*words*) to end; **cadere in** suit, agree with; come under; **cadere sub** be exposed to; **animīs cadere** be disheartened; **causā cadere** lose one's case

cādūceātor, -ōris *m* officer with flag of truce

cādūceus, -ī *m* herald's staff; Mercury's wand

cādūcifer, -ī *adj* with herald's staff

cadūcus *adj* falling, fallen; (*fig*) perishable, fleeting, vain; (LAW) without an heir ♦ *nt* property without an heir

Cadurcī, -ōrum *mpl* Gallic tribe

Cadurcum, -ī *nt* linen coverlet

cadus, -ī *m* jar, flask (*esp for wine*); urn

caecigenus *adj* born blind

Caeciliānus *adj see* **Caecilius**

Caecilius, -ī *m* Roman name (*esp early Latin comic poet*)

caecitās, -ātis *f* blindness

caecō, -āre, -āvī, -ātum *vt* to blind; to make obscure

Caecubum, -ī *nt* choice wine from the Ager Caecubus in S. Latium

caecus *adj* blind; invisible, secret; dark, obscure; (*fig*) aimless, unknown, uncertain; **appāret caecō** it's as clear as daylight; **domus caeca** a house with no windows; **caecā diē emere** buy on credit; **caecum corpus** the back

caedēs, -is *f* murder, massacre; gore; the slain

caedō, -ere, cecīdī, caesum *vt* to cut; to strike; to kill, cut to pieces; (*animals*) to sacrifice

caelāmen, -inis *nt* engraved work

caelātor, -ōris *m* engraver

caelātūra, -ae *f* engraving in bas-relief

caelebs, -ibis *adj* unmarried (*bachelor or widower*); (*trees*) with no vine trained on

caeles, -itis *adj* celestial ♦ *mpl* the gods

caelestis, -is *adj* of the sky, heavenly; divine; glorious ♦ *mpl* the gods ♦ *ntpl* the heavenly bodies

Caeliānus *adj see* **Caelius**

caelibātus, -ūs *m* celibacy

caelicola, -ae *m* god

caelifer, -ī *adj* supporting the sky

Caelius, -ī *m* Roman name; Roman hill

caelō, -āre, -āvī, -ātum *vt* to engrave (*in relief on metals*), carve (*on wood*); (*fig*) to compose

caelum¹, -ī *nt* engraver's chisel

caelum², -ī *nt* sky, heaven; air, climate, weather; (*fig*) height of success, glory; **~ ac terrās miscēre** create chaos; **ad ~ ferre** extol; **dē caelō dēlāpsus** a messiah; **dē caelō servāre** watch for omens; **dē caelō tangī** be struck by lightning; **digitō ~ attingere** be in the seventh heaven; **in caelumō esse** be overjoyed

caementum, -ī *nt* quarrystone, rubble

caenōsus *adj* muddy

caenum, -ī *nt* mud, filth

caepa, -ae *f*, **caepe, -is** *nt* onion

Caere (*gen* **-itis**, *abl* **-ēte**) *nt indecl*, *f* ancient Etruscan town

Caerēs, -itis *and* **-ētis** *adj*: **Caerite cērā dignī** like the disfranchised masses

caerimōnia, -ae *f* sanctity; veneration (*for gods*); religious usage, ritual

caeruleus, caerulus *adj* blue, dark blue, dark green, dusky ♦ *ntpl* the sea

Caesar, -is *m* Julius (*great Roman soldier, statesman, author*); Augustus; the emperor

Caesareus, Caesariānus, Caesarīnus *adj see* **Caesar**

caesariātus *adj* bushy-haired

caesariēs, -ēī *f* hair

caesīcius *adj* bluish

caesim *adv* with the edge of the sword; (RHET) in short clauses

caesius *adj* bluish grey, blue-eyed

caespes, -itis *m* sod, turf; mass of roots
caestus, -ūs *m* boxing glove
caesus *ppp of* **caedō**
caetra, -ae *f* targe
caetrātus *adj* armed with a targe
Caīcus, -ī *m river in Asia Minor*
Cāiēta, -ae, Cāiētē, -ēs *f town in Latium*
Cāius *etc see* **Gāius**[1]
Calaber, -rī *adj* Calabrian
Calabria *f S.E. peninsula of Italy*
Calamis, -idis *m Greek sculptor*
calamister, -rī *m,* **calamisterum, -rī** *nt* curling iron; (RHET) flourish
calamistrātus *adj* curled; foppish
calamitās, -ātis *f* disaster; (MIL) defeat; (AGR) damage, failure
calamitōsē *adv see* **calamitōsus**
calamitōsus *adj* disastrous, ruinous; blighted, unfortunate
calamus, -ī *m* reed; stalk; pen, pipe, arrow, fishing rod
calathiscus, -ī *m* small basket
calathus, -ī *m* wicker basket; bowl, cup
calātor, -ōris *m* servant
calcāneum, -ī *nt* heel
calcar, -āris *nt* spur
calceāmentum, -ī *nt* shoe
calceātus *ppp* shod
calceolārius, -ī *and* **-iī** *m* shoemaker
calceolus, -ī *m* small shoe
calceus, -ī *m* shoe
Calchās, -antis *m Greek prophet at Troy*
calcitrō, -āre *vi* to kick; (*fig*) to resist
calcō, -āre, -āvī, -ātum *vt* to tread, trample on; (*fig*) to spurn
calculus, -ī *m* pebble, stone; draughtsman, counting stone, reckoning, voting stone; **calculum redūcere** take back a move; **calculōs subdūcere** compute; **ad calculōs vocāre** subject to a reckoning
caldārius *adj* with warm water
caldus *etc see* **calidus**
Calēdonia, -ae *f the Scottish Highlands*
Calēdonius *adj see* **Calēdonia**
calefaciō, calfaciō, -facere, -fēcī, -factum *vt* to warm, heat; (*fig*) to provoke, excite
calefactō, -āre *vt* to warm
Calendae *see* **Kalendae**
Calēnus *adj* of Cales ♦ *nt* wine of Cales
caleō, -ēre *vi* to be warm, be hot, glow; (*mind*) to be inflamed; (*things*) to be pursued with enthusiasm; to be fresh
Calēs, -ium *fpl town in Campania*
calēscō, -ere, -uī *vi* to get hot; (*fig*) to become inflamed
calidē *adv* promptly
calidus *adj* warm, hot; (*fig*) fiery, eager; hasty; prompt ♦ *f* warm water ♦ *nt* warm drink
caliendrum, -ī *nt* headdress of hair
caliga, -ae *f* soldier's boot
caligātus *adj* heavily shod
cālīginōsus *adj* misty, obscure
cālīgō[1], -inis *f* mist, fog; dimness, darkness; (*mind*) obtuseness; (*circumstances*) trouble

cālīgō[2], -āre *vi* to be misty, be dim; to cause dizziness
Caligula, -ae *m emperor Gaius*
calix, -cis *m* wine cup; cooking pot
calleō, -ēre *vi* to be thick-skinned; (*fig*) to be unfeeling; to be wise, be skilful ♦ *vt* to know, understand
callidē *adv see* **callidus**
calliditās, -ātis *f* skill; cunning
callidus *adj* skilful, clever; crafty
Callimachus, -ī *m Greek poet of Alexandria*
Calliopē, -ēs, Calliopēa, -ēae *f Muse of epic poetry*
callis, -is *m* footpath, mountain track; pass; hill pastures
Callistō, -ūs *f daughter of Lycaon;* (*constellation*) Great Bear
callōsus *adj* hard-skinned; solid
callum, -ī *nt* hard or thick skin; firm flesh; (*fig*) callousness
cālō, -ōnis *m* soldier's servant; drudge
calō, -āre, -āvī, -ātum *vt* to convoke
calor, -ōris *m* warmth, heat; (*fig*) passion, love
Calpē, -ēs *f Rock of Gibraltar*
Calpurniānus *adj see* **Calpurnius**
Calpurnius, -ī *m Roman name*
caltha, -ae *f* marigold
calthula, -ae *f* yellow dress
caluī *perf of* **calēscō**
calumnia, -ae *f* chicanery, sharp practice; subterfuge; misrepresentation; (LAW) dishonest accusation, blackmail; being convicted of malicious prosecution; **calumniam iūrāre** swear that an action is brought in good faith
calumniātor, -ōris *m* legal trickster, slanderer
calumnior, -ārī, -ātus *vt* to misrepresent, slander; (LAW) to bring an action in bad faith; **sē calumniārī** deprecate oneself
calva, -ae *f* bald head
calvitium, -ī *and* **-iī** *nt* baldness
calvor, -ārī *vt* to deceive
calvus *adj* bald
calx[1], -cis *f* heel; foot; **calce petere, calce ferīre** kick; **adversus stimulum calcēs** kicking against the pricks
calx[2], -cis *f* pebble; lime, chalk; finishing line, end; **ad carceres ā calce revocārī** have to begin all over again
Calydōn, -ōnis *f town in Aetolia*
Calydōnis *adj* Calydonian
Calydōnius *f* Deianira; **~ amnis** Achelous; **~ hērōs** Meleager; **Calydōnia rēgna** *Daunia in S. Italy*
Calypsō, -ūs (*acc* **-ō**) *f nymph who detained Ulysses in Ogygia*
camēlīnus *adj* camel's
camella, -ae *f* wine cup
camēlus, -ī *m* camel
Camēna, -ae *f* Muse; poetry
camera, -ae *f* arched roof
Camerīnum, -ī *nt town in Umbria*
Camers, -tis, -tīnus *adj* of Camerinum
Camillus, -ī *m* Roman hero (*who saved Rome from the Gauls*)

camīnus, **-ī** m furnace, fire; forge; **oleum addere camīnō** add fuel to the flames

cammarus, **-ī** m lobster

Campānia, **-iae** f district of W. Italy

Campānicus, **Campānicius** adj Campanian, Capuan

campē, **-ēs** f evasion

campester, **-ris** adj of the plain; of the Campus Martius ♦ nt loincloth ♦ ntpl level ground

campus, **-ī** m plain; sports field; any level surface; (fig) theatre, arena (of action, debate); ~ **Martius** level ground by the Tiber (used for assemblies, sports, military drills)

Camulodūnum, **-ī** nt town of Trinobantes (now Colchester)

camur, **-ī** adj crooked

canālis, **-is** m pipe, conduit, canal

cancellī, **-ōrum** mpl grating, enclosure; barrier (in public places), bar of law court

cancer, **-rī** m crab; (constellation) Cancer; south, tropical heat; (MED) cancer

candefaciō, **-ere** vt to make dazzlingly white

candēla, **-ae** f taper, tallow candle; waxed cord; **candēlam appōnere valvīs** set the house on fire

candēlābrum, **-ī** nt candlestick, chandelier, lampstand

candēns, **-entis** adj dazzling white; white-hot

candeō, **-ēre** vi to shine, be white; to be white-hot

candēscō, **-ere** vi to become white; to grow white-hot

candidātōrius adj of a candidate

candidātus adj dressed in white ♦ m candidate for office

candidē adv in white; sincerely

candidulus adj pretty white

candidus adj white, bright; radiant, beautiful; clothed in white; (style) clear; (mind) candid, frank; (circumstances) happy; **candida sententia** acquittal

candor, **-ōris** m whiteness, brightness, beauty; (fig) brilliance, sincerity

cānēns, **-entis** adj white

cāneō, **-ēre**, **-uī** vi to be grey, be white

cānēscō, **-ere** vi to grow white; to grow old

canīcula, **-ae** f (dog) bitch; Dog Star, Sirius

canīnus adj dog's, canine; snarling, spiteful; **canīna littera** letter R

canis, **-is** m/f dog, bitch; (fig) shameless or angry person; hanger-on; (dice) lowest throw; (ASTR) Canis Major, Canis Minor; (myth) Cerberus

canistrum, **-ī** nt wicker basket

cānitiēs, **-ēī** f greyness; grey hair; old age

canna, **-ae** f reed; pipe; gondola

cannabis, **-is** f hemp

Cannae, **-ārum** fpl village in Apulia (scene of great Roman defeat by Hannibal)

Cannēnsis adj see **Cannae**

canō, **canere**, **cecinī** vt, vi to sing; to play; to sing about, recite, celebrate; to prophesy; (MIL) to sound; (birds) to sing, crow

canor, **-ōris** m song, tune, sound

canōrus adj musical, melodious; singsong ♦ nt melodiousness

Cantaber, **-rī** m Cantabrian

Cantabria, **-riae** f district of N Spain

Cantabricus adj see **Cantabria**

cantāmen, **-inis** nt charm

cantharis, **-idis** f beetle; Spanish fly

cantharus, **-ī** m tankard

canthērīnus adj of a horse

canthērius, **-ī** and **-iī** m gelding

canticum, **-ī** nt aria in Latin comedy; song

cantilēna, **-ae** f old song, gossip; **cantilēnam eandem canere** keep harping on the same theme

cantiō, **-ōnis** f song; charm

cantitō, **-āre**, **-āvī**, **-ātum** vt to sing or play often

Cantium, **-ī** and **-iī** nt Kent

cantiunculae, **-ārum** fpl fascinating strains

cantō, **-āre**, **-āvī**, **-ātum** vt, vi to sing; to play; to sing about, recite, celebrate; to proclaim, harp on; to use magic spells; to sound; to drawl

cantor, **-ōris** m, **cantorīx**, **-rīcis** f singer, musician, poet; actor

cantus, **-ūs** m singing, playing, music; prophecy; magic spell

cānus adj white, grey, hoary; old ♦ mpl grey hairs

Canusīnus adj see **Canusium**

Canusium, **-ī** nt town in Apulia (famous for wool)

capācitās, **-ātis** f spaciousness

capāx, **-ācis** adj capable of holding, spacious, roomy; capable, able, fit

capēdō, **-inis** f sacrificial dish

capēduncula f small dish

capella, **-ae** f she-goat; (ASTR) bright star in Auriga

Capēna, **-ae** f old Etruscan town

Capēnās, **Capēnus** adj: **Porta Capēna** Roman gate leading to the Via Appia

caper, **-rī** m goat; odour of the armpits

caperrō, **-āre** vi to wrinkle

capessō, **-ere**, **-īvī**, **-ītum** vt to seize, take hold of, try to reach, make for; to take in hand, engage in; **rem pūblicam capessere** go in for politics

capillātus adj long-haired; ancient

capillus, **-ī** m hair (of head or beard), a hair

capiō, **-ere**, **cēpī**, **captum** vt to take, seize; to catch, capture; (MIL) to occupy, take prisoner; (NAUT) to make, reach (a goal); (fig) to captivate, charm, cheat; (pass) to be maimed, lose the use of; to choose; (appearance) to assume; (habit) to cultivate; (duty) to undertake; (ideas) to conceive, form; (feeling) to experience; (harm) to suffer; to receive, get, inherit; to contain, hold; (fig) to bear; (mind) to grasp; **cōnsilium capere** come to a decision; **impetum capere** gather momentum; **initium capere** start; **oculō capī** lose an eye; **mente captus** insane; **cupīdō eum cēpit** he felt a desire

capis, **-dis** f sacrificial bowl with one handle

capistrātus adj haltered

capistrum, **-ī** nt halter, muzzle

capital, **-ālis** nt capital crime

capitālis adj mortal, deadly, dangerous; (LAW) capital; important, excellent

capitō, **-ōnis** m bighead

Capitōlīnus *adj* of the Capitol; of Jupiter
Capitōlium, **-ī** *nt* Roman hill with temple of Jupiter
capitulātim *adv* summarily
capitulum, **-ī** *nt* small head; person, creature
Cappadocia, **-ae** *f country of Asia Minor*
capra, **-ae** *f* she-goat; odour of armpits; (ASTR) Capella
caprea, **-ae** *f* roe
Capreae, **-ārum** *fpl* island of Capri
capreolus, **-ī** *m* roebuck; (*pl*) crossbeams
Capricornus, **-ī** *m* (*constellation*) Capricorn (*associated with midwinter*)
caprificus, **-ī** *f* wild fig tree
caprigenus *adj* of goats
caprimulgus, **-ī** *m* goatherd, rustic
caprīnus *adj* of goats
capripēs, **-edis** *adj* goat-footed
capsa, **-ae** *f* box (*esp for papyrus rolls*)
capsō *archaic fut of* **capiō**
capsula, **-ae** *f* small box; **dē capsulā tōtus** out of a bandbox
Capta, **-ae** *f* Minerva
captātiō, **-ōnis** *f* catching at
captātor, **-ōris** *m* one who courts; legacy hunter
captiō, **-ōnis** *f* fraud; disadvantage; (*argument*) fallacy, sophism
captiōsē *adv see* **captiōsus**
captiōsus *adj* deceptive; dangerous; captious
captiuncula, **-ae** *f* quibble
captīvitās, **-ātis** *f* captivity; capture
captīvus *adj* captive, captured; of captives ♦ *m/f* prisoner of war
captō, **-āre**, **-āvī**, **-ātum** *vt* to try to catch, chase; to try to win, court, watch for; to deceive, trap
captus¹ *ppp of* **capiō** ♦ *m* prisoner
captus², **-ūs** *m* grasp, notion
Capua, **-ae** *f chief town of Campania*
capulāris *adj* due for a coffin
capulus, **-ī** *m* coffin; handle, hilt
caput, **-itis** *nt* head; top, extremity; (*rivers*) source; (*more rarely*) mouth; person, individual; life; civil rights; (*person*) chief, leader; (*towns*) capital; (*money*) principal; (*writing*) substance, chapter; principle, main point, the great thing; **~ cēnae** main dish; **capitis accūsāre** charge with a capital offence; **capitis damnāre** condemn to death; **capitis dēminūtiō** loss of political rights; **capitis poena** capital punishment; **capita cōnferre** confer in secret; **in capita** per head; **suprā ~ esse** be imminent
Cǎr, **-is** *m* Carian
carbaseus *adj* linen, canvas
carbasus, **-ī** *f*, **carbasa**, **-ōrum** *ntpl* Spanish flax, fine linen; garment, sail, curtain
carbō, **-ōnis** *m* charcoal, embers
carbōnārius, **-ī** *and* **-iī** *m* charcoal burner
carbunculus, **-ī** *m* small coal; *precious stone*
carcer, **-is** *m* prison; jailbird; barrier, starting place (*for races*); **ad carcerēs ā calce revocārī** have to begin all over again
carcerārius *adj* of a prison
carchēsium, **-ī** *and* **-iī** *nt* drinking cup; (NAUT) masthead

cardiacus, **-ī** *m* dyspeptic
cardō, **-inis** *m* hinge; (ASTR) pole, axis, cardinal point; (*fig*) juncture, critical moment
carduus, **-ī** *m* thistle
cārē *adv see* **cārus**
cārectum, **-ī** *nt* sedge
cāreō, **-ēre**, **-uī** *vi* (*with abl*) to be free from, not have, be without; to abstain from, be absent from; to want, miss
cārex, **-icis** *f* sedge
Cāria, **-ae** *f district of S.W. Asia Minor*
Cāricus *adj* Carian ♦ *f* dried fig
cariēs (*acc* **-em**, *abl* **-ē**) *f* dry rot
carīna, **-ae** *f* keel; ship
Carīnae, **-ārum** *fpl district of Rome*
carīnārius, **-ī** *and* **-iī** *m* dyer of yellow
cariōsus *adj* crumbling; (*fig*) withered
cāris, **-idis** *f kind of crab*
cāritās, **-ātis** *f* dearness, high price; esteem, affection
carmen, **-inis** *nt* song, tune; poem, poetry, verse; prophecy; (*in law, religion*) formula; moral text
Carmentālis *adj see* **Carmentis**
Carmentis, **-is**, **Carmentia**, **-ae** *f prophetess, mother of Evander*
carnārium, **-ī** *and* **-iī** *nt* fleshhook; larder
Carneadēs, **-is** *m Greek philosopher (founder of the New Academy)*
Carneadēus *adj see* **Carneadēs**
carnifex, **-icis** *m* executioner, hangman; scoundrel; murderer
carnificīna, **-ae** *f* execution; torture; **carnificīnam facere** be an executioner
carnificō, **-āre** *vt* to behead, mutilate
carnuf- *etc see* **carnif-**
cārō, **-ere** *vt* to card
carō, **-nis** *f* flesh
Carpathius *adj see* **Carpathus**
Carpathus, **-ī** *f island between Crete and Rhodes*
carpatina, **-ae** *f* leather shoe
carpentum, **-ī** *nt* two-wheeled coach
carpō, **-ere**, **-sī**, **-tum** *vt* to pick, pluck, gather; to tear off; to browse, graze on; (*wool*) to card; (*fig*) to enjoy, snatch; to carp at, slander; to weaken, wear down; to divide up; (*journey*) to go, travel
carptim *adv* in parts; at different points; at different times
carptor, **-ōris** *m* carver
carptus *ppp of* **carpō**
carrus, **-ī** *m* wagon
Carthāginiēnsis *adj see* **Carthāgō**
Carthāgō, **-inis** *f* Carthage (*near Tunis*); **~ Nova** town in Spain (*now* Cartagena)
caruncula, **-ae** *f* piece of flesh
cārus *adj* dear, costly; dear, beloved
Carystēus *adj see* **Carystos**
Carystos, **-ī** *f town in Euboea (famous for marble)*
casa, **-ae** *f* cottage, hut
cascus *adj* old
cāseolus, **-ī** *m* small cheese
cāseus, **-ī** *m* cheese
casia, **-ae** *f* cinnamon; spurge laurel
Caspius *adj* Caspian

Cassandra, **-ae** f *Trojan princess and prophetess, doomed never to be believed*

cassēs, **-ium** mpl net, snare; spider's web

Cassiānus adj see **Cassius**

cassida, **-ae** f helmet

Cassiopēa, **-ae**, **Cassiopē**, **-ēs** f *mother of Andromeda; a constellation*

cassis, **-idis** f helmet

Cassius, **-ī** m *Roman family name*

cassō, **-āre** vi to shake

cassus adj empty; devoid of, without (abl); vain, useless; ~ **lūmine** dead; **in cassum** in vain

Castalia, **-ae** f *spring on Parnassus, sacred to Apollo and the Muses*

Castalides, **-dum** fpl Muses

Castalius, **-is** adj see **Castalia**

castanea, **-ae** f chestnut tree; chestnut

castē adv see **castus**

castellānus adj of a fortress ♦ mpl garrison

castellātim adv in different fortresses

castellum, **-ī** nt fortress, castle; (fig) defence, refuge

castēria, **-ae** f rowers' quarters

castīgābilis adj punishable

castīgātiō, **-ōnis** f correction, reproof

castīgātor, **-ōris** m reprover

castīgātus adj small, slender

castīgō, **-āre**, **-āvī**, **-ātum** vt to correct, punish; to reprove; to restrain

castimōnia, **-ae** f purity, morality; chastity, abstinence

castitās, **-ātis** f chastity

Castor, **-oris** m *twin brother of Pollux (patron of sailors)*; star in Gemini

castor, **-oris** m beaver

castoreum, **-ī** nt *odorous secretion of the beaver*

castra, **-ōrum** ntpl camp; day's march; army life; (fig) party, sect; ~ **movēre** strike camp; ~ **mūnīre** construct a camp; ~ **pōnere** pitch camp; **bīna** ~ two camps

castrēnsis adj of the camp, military

castrō, **-āre** vt to castrate; (fig) to weaken

castrum, **-ī** nt fort

castus adj clean, pure, chaste, innocent; holy, pious

cāsū adv by chance

casula, **-ae** f little cottage

cāsus, **-ūs** m fall, downfall; event, chance, accident; misfortune, death; opportunity; (time) end; (GRAM) case

Catadūpa, **-ōrum** ntpl *Nile cataract near Syene*

catagraphus adj painted

Catamītus, **-ī** m Ganymede

cataphractēs, **-ae** m coat of mail

cataphractus adj wearing mail

cataplus, **-ī** m ship arriving

catapulta, **-ae** f (MIL) catapult; (fig) missile

catapultārius adj thrown by catapult

cataracta, **-ae** f waterfall; sluice; drawbridge

catasta, **-ae** f stage, scaffold

catē adv see **catus**

catēia, **-ae** f javelin

catella, **-ae** f small chain

catellus, **-ī** m puppy

catēna, **-ae** f chain; fetter; (fig) bond, restraint; series

catēnātus adj chained, fettered

caterva, **-ae** f crowd, band; flock; (MIL) troop, body; (THEAT) company

catervātim adv in companies

cathedra, **-ae** f armchair, sedan chair; teacher's chair

catholicus adj (ECCL) orthodox, universal

Catilīna, **-ae** m Catiline (*conspirator suppressed by Cicero*)

Catilīnārius adj see **Catilīna**

catillō, **-āre** vt to lick a plate

catillus, **-ī** m small dish

catīnus, **-ī** m dish, pot

Catō, **-ōnis** m *famous censor and author, idealized as the pattern of an ancient Roman; famous Stoic and republican leader against Caesar*

Catoniānus adj see **Catō**

Catōnīnī mpl Cato's supporters

catōnium, **-ī** and **-iī** nt the lower world

Catulliānus adj see **Catullus**

Catullus, **-ī** m *Latin lyric poet*

catulus, **-ī** m puppy; cub, *young of other animals*

catus adj clever, wise; sly, cunning

Caucasius adj see **Caucasus**

Caucasus, **-ī** m Caucasus (mountains)

cauda, **-ae** f tail; **caudam iactāre** fawn; **caudam trahere** be made a fool of

caudeus adj wooden

caudex, **-icis** m trunk; block of wood; book, ledger; (fig) blockhead

caudicālis adj of woodcutting

Caudīnus adj see **Caudium**

Caudium, **-ī** nt *Samnite town*

caulae, **-ārum** fpl opening; sheepfold

caulis, **-is** m stalk; cabbage

Cauneus adj Caunian

Caunus, **-ī** f *town in Caria* ♦ fpl dried figs

caupō, **-ōnis** m shopkeeper, innkeeper

caupōna, **-ae** f shop, inn

caupōnius adj see **caupō**

caupōnor, **-ārī** vt to trade in

caupōnula, **-ae** f tavern

Caurus, **-ī** m north-west wind

causa, **-ae** f cause, reason; purpose, sake; excuse, pretext; opportunity; connection, case, position; (LAW) case, suit; (POL) cause, party; (RHET) subject matter; **causam agere**, **causam ōrāre** plead a case; **causam dēfendere** speak for the defence; **causam dīcere** defend oneself; **causā** for the sake of; **cum causā** with good reason; **quā dē causā** for this reason; **in causā esse** be responsible; **per causam** under the pretext

causārius adj (MIL) unfit for service

causia, **-ae** f Macedonian hat

causidicus, **-ī** m advocate

causificor, **-ārī** vi to make a pretext

causor, **-ārī**, **-ātus** vt, vi to pretend, make an excuse of

caussa etc see **causa**

causula, **-ae** f petty lawsuit; slight cause

cautē adv carefully, cautiously; with security

cautēla, **-ae** f caution

cautēs, -is f rock, crag

cautim adv warily

cautiō, -ōnis f caution, wariness; (LAW) security, bond, bail; **mihi ~ est** I must take care; **mea ~ est** I must see to it

cautor, -ōris m wary person; surety

cautus ppp of **caveō** ♦ adj wary, provident; safe, secure

cavaedium, -ī and **-iī** nt inner court (of a house)

cavea, -ae f cage, stall, coop, hive; (THEAT) auditorium; theatre; **prīma ~** upper class seats; **ultima ~** lower class seats

caveō, -ēre, cāvī, cautum vt to beware of, guard against ♦ vi (+ **ab** or abl) to be on one's guard against; (with dat) to look after; (with **nē**) to take care that ... not; (with **ut**) to take good care that; (with subj or inf) to take care not to, do not; (LAW) to stipulate, decree; (COMM) to get a guarantee, give a guarantee, stand security; **cavē** look out!

caverna, -ae f hollow, cave, vault; (NAUT) hold

cavilla, -ae f jeering

cavillātiō, -ōnis f jeering, banter; sophistry

cavillātor, -ōris m scoffer

cavillor, -ārī, -ātus vt to scoff at ♦ vi to jeer, scoff; to quibble

cavō, -āre, -āvī, -ātum vt to hollow, excavate

cavus adj hollow, concave, vaulted; (river) deep-channelled ♦ nt cavity, hole

Caystros, Caystrus, -ī m river in Lydia (famous for swans)

-ce demonstrative particle appended to pronouns and adverbs

Cēa, -ae f Aegean island (birthplace of Simonides)

cecidī perf of **cadō**

cecīdī perf of **caedō**

cecinī perf of **canō**

Cecropidēs, -idae m Theseus; Athenian

Cecropis, -idis f Aglauros; Procne; Philomela; Athenian, Attic

Cecropius adj Athenian ♦ f Athens

Cecrops, -is m ancient king of Athens

cedo (pl **cette**) impv give me, bring here; tell me; let me; look at!

cēdō, -ere, cessī, cessum vi to go, walk; to depart, withdraw, retreat; to pass away, die; (events) to turn out; to be changed (into); to accrue (to); to yield, be inferior (to) ♦ vt to give up, concede, allow; **cēdere bonīs, cēdere possessiōne** make over property (to); **cēdere forō** go bankrupt; **cēdere locō** leave one's post; **cēdere memoriā** be forgotten

cedrus, -ī f cedar, perfumed juniper; cedar oil

Celaenō, -ūs f a Harpy; a Pleiad

cēlāta ntpl secrets

celeber, -ris adj crowded, populous; honoured, famous; repeated

celebrātiō, -ōnis f throng; celebration

celebrātus adj full, much used; festive; famous

celebritās, -ātis f crowd; celebration; fame

celebrō, -āre, -āvī, -ātum vt to crowd, frequent; to repeat, practise; to celebrate, keep (a festival); to advertise, glorify

celer, -is adj quick, swift, fast; hasty

Celerēs, -um mpl royal bodyguard

celeripēs, -edis adj swift-footed

celeritās, -ātis f speed, quickness

celeriter adv see **celer**

celerō, -āre vt to quicken ♦ vi to make haste

cella, -ae f granary, stall, cell; garret, hut, small room; sanctuary (of a temple)

cellārius adj of the storeroom ♦ m steward

cellula, -ae f little room

cēlō, -āre, -āvī, -ātum vt to hide, conceal, keep secret; **id mē cēlat** he keeps me in the dark about it

celōx, -ōcis adj swift ♦ f fast ship, yacht

celsus adj high, lofty; (fig) great, eminent; haughty

Celtae, -ārum mpl Celts (esp of central Gaul) ♦ nt the Celtic nation

Celtibērī, -ōrum mpl people of central Spain

Celtibēria, -iae f Central Spain

Celtibēricus adj see **Celtibēria**

Celticus adj Celtic

cēna, -ae f dinner (the principal Roman meal); **inter cēnam** at table

cēnāculum, -ī nt dining-room; upper room, garret

cēnāticus adj of dinner

cēnātiō, -ōnis f dining-room

cēnātus ppa having dined, after dinner ♦ ppp spent in feasting

Cenchreae, -ārum fpl harbour of Corinth

cēnitō, -āre vi to be accustomed to dine

cēnō, -āre, -āvī, -ātum vi to dine ♦ vt to eat, dine on

cēnseō, -ēre, -uī, -um vt (census) to assess, rate, take a census, make a property return; (fig) to estimate, appreciate, celebrate; (senate or other body) to decree, resolve; (member) to express an opinion, move, vote; to advise; to judge, think, suppose, consider; **cēnsuī cēnsendō** for census purposes

cēnsiō, -ōnis f punishment; expression of opinion

cēnsor, -ōris m censor; (fig) severe judge, critic

cēnsōrius adj of the censors, to be dealt with by the censors; (fig) severe; **homō ~** an ex-censor

cēnsūra, -ae f censorship; criticism

cēnsus¹ ppp of **cēnseō**; **capite cēnsī** the poorest class of Roman citizens

cēnsus², -ūs m register of Roman citizens and their property, census; registered property; wealth; **cēnsum agere, cēnsum habēre** hold a census; **sine cēnsū** poor

centaurēum, -ī nt centaury

Centaurēus adj see **Centaurus**

Centaurus, -ī m Centaur, half man, half horse

centēnī, -um num a hundred each, a hundred

centēsimus adj hundredth ♦ f hundredth part; (interest) 1 per cent monthly (12 per cent per annum)

centiceps adj hundred-headed

centiēns, -ēs adv a hundred times

centimanus adj hundred-handed

centō, -ōnis m patchwork; **centōnēs sarcīre** tell tall stories

centum num a hundred

centumgeminus adj hundred-fold

centumplex adj hundred-fold

31

centumpondium, **-ī** *and* **-iī** *nt* a hundred pounds

centumvirālis *adj* of the centumviri

centumvirī, **-ōrum** *mpl* a bench of judges who heard special civil cases in Rome

centunculus, **-ī** *m* piece of patchwork, saddlecloth

centuria, **-ae** *f* (MIL) company; (POL) century (a division of the Roman people according to property)

centuriātim *adv* by companies, by centuries

centuriātus¹ *adj* divided by centuries; **comitia centuriāta** assembly which voted by centuries

centuriātus², **-ūs** *m* division into centuries; rank of centurion

centuriō¹, **-āre**, **-āvī**, **-ātum** *vt* (MIL) to assign to companies; (POL) to divide by centuries

centuriō², **-ōnis** *m* (MIL) captain, centurion

centussis, **-is** *m* a hundred asses

cēnula, **-ae** *f* little dinner

Cēōs (*acc* **-ō**) *see* **Cēa**

Cēphēis *f* Andromeda

Cēphēius *adj* of Cepheus

Cēpheus, **-eī** (*acc* **-ea**) *m* king of Ethiopia (father of Andromeda)

Cēphēus *adj* Ethiopian

Cēphīsis *adj* see **Cēphīsus**

Cēphīsius *m* Narcissus

Cēphīsus, **-ī** *m* river in central Greece

cēpī *perf of* **capiō**

cēra, **-ae** *f* wax; honey cells; writing tablet, notebook; seal; portrait of an ancestor; **prīma ~** first page

Ceramīcus, **-ī** *m* Athenian cemetery

cērārium, **-ī** *and* **-iī** *nt* seal-duty

cerastēs, **-ae** *m* a horned serpent

cerasus, **-ī** *f* cherry tree; cherry

cērātus *adj* waxed

Ceraunia, **-ōrum** *nt*, **Cerauniī** *m* mountains in Epirus

Cerbereus *adj* see **Cerberus**

Cerberus, **-ī** *m* three-headed watchdog of Hades

cercopithēcus, **-ī** *m* monkey

cercūrus, **-ī** *m* Cyprian type of ship

cerdō, **-ōnis** *m* tradesman

Cereālia, **-ium** *ntpl* festival of Ceres

Cereālis *adj* of Ceres; of corn, of meal

cerebrōsus *adj* hot-headed

cerebrum, **-ī** *nt* brain; understanding; quick temper

Cerēs, **-eris** *f* goddess of agriculture; (fig) grain, bread

cēreus *adj* waxen; wax-coloured; (fig) supple, easily led ♦ *m* taper

cēriāria, **-ae** *f* taper maker

cērina, **-ōrum** *ntpl* wax-coloured clothes

cērintha, **-ae** *f* honeywort

cernō, **-ere**, **-crēvī**, **crētum** *vt* to see, discern; to understand, perceive; to decide, determine; (LAW) to decide to take up (an inheritance)

cernuus *adj* face downwards

cērōma, **-atis** *nt* wrestlers' ointment

cērōmaticus *adj* smeared with wax ointment

cerrītus *adj* crazy

certāmen, **-inis** *nt* contest, match; battle, combat; (fig) struggle, rivalry

certātim *adv* emulously

certātiō, **-ōnis** *f* contest; debate; rivalry

certē *adv* assuredly, of course; at least

certō¹ *adv* certainly, really

certō², **-āre**, **-āvī**, **-ātum** *vi* to contend, compete; (MIL) to fight it out; (LAW) to dispute; (with inf) to try hard

certus *adj* determined, fixed, definite; reliable, unerring; sure, certain; **mihi certum est** I have made up my mind; **certum scīre**, **prō certō habēre** know for certain, be sure; **certiōrem facere** inform

cērula, **-ae** *f* piece of wax; **~ miniāta** red pencil

cērussa, **-ae** *f* white lead

cērussātus *adj* painted with white lead

cerva, **-ae** *f* hind, deer

cervīcal, **-ālis** *nt* pillow

cervīcula, **-ae** *f* slender neck

cervīnus *adj* deer's

cervīx, **-īcis** *f* neck; **in cervīcibus esse** be a burden (to), threaten

cervus, **-ī** *m* stag, deer; (MIL) palisade

cessātiō, **-ōnis** *f* delaying; inactivity, idleness

cessātor, **-ōris** *m* idler

cessī *perf of* **cēdō**

cessiō, **-ōnis** *f* giving up

cessō, **-āre**, **-āvī**, **-ātum** *vi* to be remiss, stop; to loiter, delay; to be idle, rest, do nothing; (land) to lie fallow; to err

cestrosphendonē, **-ēs** *f* (MIL) engine for shooting stones

cestus, **-ī** *m* girdle (esp of Venus)

cētārium, **-ī** *and* **-iī** *nt* fishpond

cētārius, **-ī** *and* **-iī** *m* fishmonger

cētera *adv* in other respects

cēterī, **-ōrum** *adj* the rest, the others; (sg) the rest of

cēterōquī, **cēterōquīn** *adv* otherwise

cēterum *adv* for the rest, otherwise; but for all that; besides

Cethēgus, **-ī** *m* a conspirator with Catiline

cētr- *etc see* **caetr-**

cette *etc see* **cedo**

cētus, **-ī** *m*, **cētē** *ntpl* sea monster, whale

ceu *adv* just as, as if

Cēus *adj* see **Cēa**

Cēyx, **-ȳcis** *m* husband of Alcyone, changed to a kingfisher

Chalcidēnsis, **Chalcidiscus** *adj* see **Chalcis**

Chalcis, **-dis** *f* chief town of Euboea

Chaldaeī, **-aeōrum** *mpl* Chaldeans; astrologers

Chaldāicus *adj* see **Chaldaeī**

chalybēius *adj* of steel

Chalybes, **-um** *mpl* a people of Pontus (famous as ironworkers)

chalybs, **-is** *m* steel

Chāones, **-um** *mpl* a people of Epirus

Chāonia, **-iae** *f* Epirus

Chāonius, **-is** *adj* see **Chāonia**

Chaos (*abl* **-ō**) *nt* empty space, the lower world, chaos

chara, **-ae** *f* an unidentified vegetable

charistia, **-ōrum** *ntpl* a Roman family festival

Charites, **-um** *fpl* the Graces

Charōn, -ontis m Charon (ferryman of Hades)
charta, -ae f sheet of papyrus, paper; writing
chartula, -ae f piece of paper
Charybdis, -is f monster personifying a whirlpool in the Straits of Messina; (fig) peril
Chattī, -ōrum mpl a people of central Germany
Chēlae, -ārum fpl (ASTR) the Claws (of Scorpio), Libra
chelydrus, -ī m watersnake
chelys (acc -yn) f tortoise; lyre
cheragra, -ae f gout in the hands
Cherronēsus, Chersonēsus, -ī f Gallipoli peninsula; Crimea
chīliarchus, -ī m officer in charge of 1000 men; chancellor of Persia
Chimaera, -ae f fire-breathing monster formed of lion, goat and serpent
Chimaeriferus adj birthplace of Chimaera
Chios, -ī f Aegean island (famous for wine)
chīrographum, -ī nt handwriting; document
Chīrōn, -ōnis m a learned Centaur (tutor of heroes)
chīronomos, -ī m/f, **chīronomōn, -untis** and **-ontis** m mime actor
chīrūrgia, -ae f surgery; (fig) violent measures
Chīus adj Chian ♦ nt Chian wine; Chian cloth
chlamydātus adj wearing a military cloak
chlamys, -dis f Greek military cloak
Choerilus, -ī m inferior Greek poet
chorāgium, -i and **-iī** nt producing of a chorus
chorāgus, -ī m one who finances a chorus
choraulēs, -ae m flute-player (accompanying a chorus)
chorda, -ae f string (of an instrument); rope
chorēa, -ae f dance
chorēus, -ī m trochee
chorus, -ī m choral dance; chorus, choir of singers or dancers; band, troop
Christiānismus, -ī m Christianity
Christiānus adj Christian
Christus, -ī m Christ
Chrȳsēis, -ēidis f daughter of Chrȳsēs
Chrȳsēs, -ae m priest of Apollo in the Iliad
Chrȳsippēus adj see **Chrȳsippus**
Chrȳsippus, -ī m Stoic philosopher
chrȳsolithos, -ī m/f topaz
chrȳsos, -ī m gold
cibārius adj food (in cpds) ♦ ntpl rations
cibātus, -ūs m food
cibōrium, -ī and **-iī** nt kind of drinking cup
cibus, -ī m food, fodder, nourishment
cicāda, -ae f cicada, cricket
cicātrīcōsus adj scarred
cicātrīx, -īcis f scar; (plants) mark of an incision
ciccus, -ī m pomegranate pip
cicer, -is nt chickpea
Cicerō, -ōnis m famous Roman orator and author
Cicerōniānus adj see **Cicerō**
cichorēum, -ī nt chicory
Cicōnēs, -um mpl people of Thrace
cicōnia, -ae f stork
cicur, -is adj tame
cicūta, -ae f hemlock; pipe

cieō, ciēre, cīvī, citum vt to move, stir, rouse; to call, invoke; (fig) to give rise to, produce; **calcem ciēre** make a move (in chess)
Cilicia, -ae f country in S. Asia Minor (famous for piracy)
Ciliciēnsis, Ciliciēnsus adj see **Cilicia**
Cilix, -cis, Cilissa adj Cilician ♦ nt goats' hair garment
Cimbrī, -ōrum mpl people of N. Germany
Cimbricus adj see **Cimbrī**
cīmex, -icis m bug
Cimmeriī, -ōrum mpl people of the Crimea; mythical race in caves near Cumae
Cimmerius adj see **Cimmeriī**
cinaedus adj lewd
cinaedus, -ī m sodomite; lewd dancer
Cincinnātus, -ī m ancient Roman dictator
cincinnātus adj with curled hair
cincinnus, -ī m curled hair; (fig) rhetorical ornament
Cincius, -ī m Roman tribune; Roman historian
cincticulus, -ī m small girdle
cinctus¹ ppp of **cingō**
cinctus², -ūs m girding; ~ **Gabīnus** a ceremonial style of wearing the toga
cinctūtus adj girded
cinefactus adj reduced to ashes
cinerārius, -ī and **-iī** m hair curler
cingō, -gere, -xī, -ctum vt to surround, enclose; to gird, crown; (MIL) to besiege, fortify; to cover, escort; **ferrum cingor** I put on my sword
cingula, -ae f girth (of animals)
cingulum, -ī nt belt
cingulus, -ī m zone
ciniflō, -ōnis m hair curler
cinis, -eris m ashes; (fig) ruin
Cinna, -ae m colleague of Marius; poet friend of Catullus
cinnamōmum, cinnamum, -ī nt cinnamon
cinxī perf of **cingō**
Cīnyphius adj of the Cinyps (river of N. Africa); African
Cinyrās, -ae m father of Adonis
Cinyrēius adj see **Cinyrās**
cippus, -ī m tombstone; (pl) palisade
circā adv around, round about ♦ prep (with acc) (place) round, in the vicinity of, in; (time, number) about; with regard to
Circaeus adj see **Circē**
circamoerium, -ī and **-iī** nt space on both sides of a wall
Circē, -ēs and **-ae** f goddess with magic powers living in Aeaea
circēnsēs, -ium mpl the games
circēnsis adj of the Circus
circinō, -āre vt to circle through
circinus, -ī m pair of compasses
circiter adv (time, number) about ♦ prep (with acc) about, near
circueō, circumeō, -ire, -īvī and **-iī, -itum** vt, vi to go round, surround; (MIL) to encircle; to visit, go round canvassing; to deceive
circuitiō, -ōnis f (MIL) rounds; (speech) evasiveness
circuitus¹ ppp of **circueō**

circuitus², **-ūs** *m* revolution; way round, circuit; (RHET) period, periphrasis

circulātor, **-ōris** *m* pedlar

circulor, **-ārī** *vi* to collect in crowds

circulus, **-ī** *m* circle; orbit; ring; social group

circum *adv* round about ♦ *prep (with acc)* round, about; near; ~ **īnsulās mittere** send to the islands round about

circumagō, **-agere**, **-ēgī**, **-āctum** *vt* to turn, move in a circle, wheel; (*pass*, *time*) to pass; (*mind*) to be swayed

circumarō, **-āre** *vt* to plough round

circumcaesūra, **-ae** *f* outline

circumcīdō, **-dere**, **-dī**, **-sum** *vt* to cut round, trim; to cut down, abridge

circumcircā *adv* all round

circumcīsus *ppp of* **circumcīdō** ♦ *adj* precipitous

circumclūdō, **-dere**, **-sī**, **-sum** *vt* to shut in, hem in

circumcolō, **-ere** *vt* to live round about

circumcursō, **-āre** *vi* to run about

circumdō, **-are**, **-edī**, **-atum** *vt* to put round; to surround, enclose

circumdūcō, **-ūcere**, **-ūxī**, **-uctum** *vt* to lead round, draw round; to cheat; (*speech*) to prolong, drawl

circumductus *ppp of* **circumdūcō**

circumeō *etc see* **circueō**

circumequitō, **-āre** *vt* to ride round

circumferō, **-ferre**, **-tulī**, **-lātum** *vt* to carry round, pass round; to spread, broadcast; to purify; (*pass*) to revolve

circumflectō, **-ctere**, **-xī**, **-xum** *vt* to wheel round

circumflō, **-āre** *vt* (*fig*) to buffet

circumfluō, **-ere**, **-xī**, **-xum** *vt*, *vi* to flow round; (*fig*) to overflow, abound

circumfluus *adj* flowing round; surrounded (*by water*)

circumforāneus *adj* itinerant; (*money*) borrowed

circumfundō, **-undere**, **-ūdī**, **-ūsum** *vt* to pour round, surround; (*fig*) to crowd round, overwhelm; (*pass*) to flow round

circumgemō, **-ere** *vt* to growl round

circumgestō, **-āre** *vt* to carry about

circumgredior, **-dī**, **-ssus** *vt*, *vi* to make an encircling move, surround

circumiaceō, **-ēre** *vi* to be adjacent

circumiciō, **-icere**, **-iēcī**, **-iectum** *vt* to throw round, put round; to surround

circumiecta *ntpl* neighbourhood

circumiectus¹ *adj* surrounding

circumiectus², **-ūs** *m* enclosure; embrace

circumit- *etc see* **circuit-**

circumitiō, **-ōnis** *f see* **circuitiō**

circumitus, **-ūs** *m see* **circuitus²**

circumlātus *ppp of* **circumferō**

circumligō, **-āre**, **-āvī**, **-ātum** *vt* to tie to, bind round

circumlinō, **-ere**, **-tum** *vt* to smear all over, bedaub

circumluō, **-ere** *vt* to wash

circumluviō, **-ōnis** *f* alluvial land

circummittō, **-ittere**, **-īsī**, **-issum** *vt* to send round

circummoeniō, **circummūniō**, **-īre**, **-īvī**, **-ītum** *vt* to fortify

circummūnītiō, **-ōnis** *f* investing

circumpadānus *adj* of the Po valley

circumpendeō, **-ēre** *vi* to hang round

circumplaudō, **-ere** *vt* to applaud on all sides

circumplector, **-ctī**, **-xus** *vt* to embrace, surround

circumplicō, **-āre**, **-āvī**, **-ātum** *vt* to wind round

circumpōnō, **-pōnere**, **-posuī**, **-positum** *vt* to put round

circumpōtātiō, **-ōnis** *f* passing drinks round

circumrētiō, **-īre**, **-īvī**, **-ītum** *vt* to ensnare

circumrōdō, **-rodere**, **-rosī** *vt* to nibble round about; (*fig*) to slander

circumsaepiō, **-īre**, **-sī**, **-tum** *vt* to fence round

circumscindō, **-ere** *vt* to strip

circumscrībō, **-bere**, **-psī**, **-ptum** *vt* to draw a line round; to mark the limits of; to restrict, circumscribe; to set aside; to defraud

circumscrīptē *adv* in periods

circumscrīptiō, **-ōnis** *f* circle, contour; fraud; (RHET) period

circumscrīptor, **-ōris** *m* defrauder

circumscrīptus *ppp of* **circumscrībō** ♦ *adj* restricted; (RHET) periodic

circumsecō, **-āre** *vt* to cut round

circumsedeō, **-edēre**, **-ēdī**, **-essum** *vt* to blockade, beset

circumsēpiō *etc see* **circumsaepiō**

circumsessiō, **-ōnis** *f* siege

circumsessus *ppp of* **circumsedeō**

circumsīdō, **-ere** *vt* to besiege

circumsiliō, **-īre** *vi* to hop about; (*fig*) to be rampant

circumsistō, **-sistere**, **-stetī** surround

circumsonō, **-āre** *vi* to resound on all sides ♦ *vt* to fill with sound

circumsonus *adj* noisy

circumspectātrīx, **-īcis** *f* spy

circumspectiō, **-ōnis** *f* caution

circumspectō, **-āre** *vt*, *vi* to look all round, search anxiously, be on the lookout

circumspectus¹ *ppp of* **circumspiciō** ♦ *adj* carefully considered, cautious

circumspectus², **-ūs** *m* consideration; view

circumspiciō, **-icere**, **-exī**, **-ectum** *vi* to look all round; to be careful ♦ *vt* to survey; (*fig*) to consider, search for

circumstantēs, **-antium** *mpl* bystanders

circumstetī *perf of* **circumsistō**; **circumstō**

circumstō, **-āre**, **-etī** *vt*, *vi* to stand round; to besiege; (*fig*) to encompass

circumstrepō, **-ere** *vt* to make a clamour round

circumsurgēns, **-entis** *pres p* rising on all sides

circumtentus *adj* covered tightly

circumterō, **-ere** *vt* to crowd round

circumtextus *adj* embroidered round the edge

circumtonō, **-āre**, **-uī** *vt* to thunder about

circumvādō, **-dere**, **-sī** *vt* to assail on all sides

circumvagus *adj* encircling

circumvallō, **-āre**, **-āvī**, **-ātum** *vt* to blockade, beset

circumvectiō, -ōnis f carrying about; (sun) revolution

circumvector, -ārī vi to travel round, cruise round; (fig) describe

circumvehor, -hī, -ctus vt, vi to ride round, sail round; (fig) to describe

circumvēlō, -āre vt to envelop

circumveniō, -enīre, -ēnī, -entum vt to surround, beset; to oppress; to cheat

circumvertō, circumvortō, -ere vt to turn round

circumvestiō, -īre vt to envelop

circumvinciō, -īre vt to lash about

circumvīsō, -ere vt to look at all round

circumvolitō, -āre, -āvī, -ātum vt, vi to fly round; to hover around

circumvolō, -āre vt to fly round

circumvolvō, -vere vt to roll round

circus, -ī m circle; the Circus Maximus (famous Roman racecourse), a racecourse

Cirrha, -ae f town near Delphi (sacred to Apollo)

Cirrhaeus adj see **Cirrha**

cirrus, -ī m curl of hair; fringe

cis prep (with acc) on this side of; (time) within

Cisalpīnus adj on the Italian side of the Alps, Cisalpine

cisium, -ī and **-iī** nt two-wheeled carriage

Cissēis, -dis f Hecuba

cista, -ae f box, casket; ballot box

cistella, -ae f small box

cistellātrīx, -īcis f keeper of the moneybox

cistellula, -ae f little box

cisterna, -ae f reservoir

cistophorus, -ī m an Asiatic coin

cistula, -ae f little box

citātus adj quick, impetuous

citerior (superl **-imus**) adj on this side, nearer

Cithaerōn, -ōnis m mountain range between Attica and Boeotia

cithara, -ae f lyre, lute

citharista, -ae m, **citharistria, -ae** f lyre player

citharizō, -āre vi to play the lyre

citharoedus, -ī m a singer who accompanies himself on the lyre

citimus adj nearest

cito (compar **-ius**, superl **-issimē**) adv quickly, soon; **nōn ~** not easily

citō, -āre, -āvī, -ātum vt to set in motion, rouse; to call (by name), appeal to, cite, mention

citrā adv on this side, this way, not so far ◆ prep (with acc) on this side of, short of; (time) before, since; apart from; **~ quam** before

citreus adj of citrus wood

citrō adv hither, this way; **ultrō citrōque** to and fro

citrus, -ī f citrus tree; citron tree

citus ppp of **cieō** ◆ adj quick

cīvicus adj civic, civil; **corōna cīvica** civic crown (for saving a citizen's life in war)

cīvīlis adj of citizens, civil; political, civilian; courteous, democratic; **iūs cīvīle** civil rights; Civil Law; code of legal procedure

cīvīlitās, -ātis f politics; politeness

cīvīliter adv like citizens; courteously

cīvis, -is m/f citizen, fellow citizen

cīvitās, -ātis f citizenship; community, state; city; **cīvitāte dōnāre** naturalize

clādēs, -is f damage, disaster, ruin; defeat; (fig) scourge; **dare clādem** make havoc

clam adv secretly; unknown ◆ prep (with acc) unknown to; **~ mē habēre** keep from me

clāmātor, -ōris m bawler

clāmitātiō, -ōnis f bawling

clāmitō, -āre, -āvī, -ātum vt, vi to bawl, screech, cry out

clāmō, -āre, -āvī, -ātum vt, vi to shout, cry out; to call upon, proclaim

clāmor, -ōris m shout, cry; acclamation

clāmōsus adj noisy

clanculum adv secretly ◆ prep (with acc) unknown to

clandestīnō adv see **clandestīnus**

clandestīnus adj secret

clangor, -ōris m clang, noise

clārē adv brightly, loudly, clearly, with distinction

clāreō, -ēre vi to be bright, be clear; to be evident; to be renowned

clārēscō, -ere, clāruī vi to brighten, sound clear; to become obvious; to become famous

clārigātiō, -ōnis f formal ultimatum to an enemy; fine for trespass

clārigō, -āre vi to deliver a formal ultimatum

clārisonus adj loud and clear

clāritās, -ātis f distinctness; (RHET) lucidity; celebrity

clāritūdō, -inis f brightness; (fig) distinction

Clarius adj of Claros ◆ m Apollo

clārō, -āre vt to illuminate; to explain; to make famous

Claros, -ī f town in Ionia (famous for worship of Apollo)

clārus adj (sight) bright; (sound) loud; (mind) clear; (person) distinguished; **~ intonāre** thunder from a clear sky; **vir clārissimus** a courtesy title for eminent men

classiārius adj naval ◆ mpl marines

classicula, -ae f flotilla

classicum, -ī nt battle-signal; trumpet

classicus adj of the first class; naval ◆ mpl marines

classis, -is f a political class; army; fleet

clāthrī, -ōrum mpl cage

clāthrātus adj barred

clātrī, -ōrum mpl see **clāthrī**

claudeō, -ēre vi to limp; (fig) to be defective

claudicātiō, -ōnis f limping

claudicō, -āre vi to be lame; to waver, be defective

Claudius[1], -ī m patrician family name (esp Appius Claudius Caecus, famous censor); Emperor Claudius

Claudius[2], Claudiānus, Claudiālis adj see **Claudius[1]**

claudō[1], -dere, -sī, -sum vt to shut, close; to cut off, block; to conclude; to imprison, confine, blockade; **agmen claudere** bring up the rear

claudō[2], -ere etc see **claudeō**

claudus adj lame; (verse) elegiac; (fig) wavering

clausī perf of **claudō[1]**

claustra, -ōrum ntpl bar, bolt, lock; barrier, barricade, dam

clausula, **-ae** f conclusion; (RHET) ending of a period

clausum, **-ī** nt enclosure

clausus ppp of **claudō**[1]

clāva, **-ae** f club, knotty branch; (MIL) foil

clāvārium, **-ī** and **-iī** nt money for buying shoe nails

clāvātor, **-ōris** m cudgel-bearer

clāvicula, **-ae** f vine tendril

clāviger, **-ī** m (Hercules) club bearer; (Janus) key-bearer

clāvis, **-is** f key

clāvus, **-ī** m nail; tiller, rudder; *purple stripe on the tunic (broad for senators, narrow for equites)*; **clāvum annī movēre** reckon the beginning of the year

Cleanthēs, **-is** m *Stoic philosopher*

clēmēns, **-entis** adj mild, gentle, merciful; (*weather, water*) mild, calm

clēmenter adv gently, indulgently; gradually

clēmentia, **-ae** f mildness, forbearance, mercy

Cleopatra, **-ae** f *queen of Egypt*

clepō, **-ere**, **-sī**, **-tum** vt to steal

clepsydra, **-ae** f waterclock (*used for timing speakers*); **clepsydram dare** give leave to speak; **clepsydram petere** ask leave to speak

clepta, **-ae** m thief

cliēns, **-entis** m client, dependant; follower; vassal-state

clienta, **-ae** f client

clientēla, **-ae** f clientship, protection; clients

clientulus, **-ī** m insignificant client

clīnāmen, **-inis** nt swerve

clīnātus adj inclined

Cliō, **-ūs** f *Muse of history*

clipeātus adj armed with a shield

clipeus, **-ī** m, **clipeum**, **-ī** nt round bronze shield; disc; *medallion on a metal base*

clitellae, **-ārum** fpl packsaddle (*attribute of an ass*)

clitellārius adj carrying packsaddles

Clitumnus, **-ī** m *river in Umbria*

clīvōsus adj hilly

clīvus, **-ī** m slope, hill; ~ **sacer** *part of the Via Sacra*

cloāca, **-ae** f sewer, drain

Cloācīna, **-ae** f *Venus*

Clōdius, **-ī** m *Roman plebeian name (esp the tribune, enemy of Cicero)*

Cloelia, **-ae** f *Roman girl hostage (who escaped by swimming the Tiber)*

Clōthō (*acc* **-ō**) f *one of the Fates*

clueō, **-ēre**, **-eor**, **-ērī** vi to be called, be famed

clūnis, **-is** m/f buttock

clūrīnus adj of apes

Clūsīnus adj see **Clūsium**

Clūsium, **-ī** nt *old Etruscan town (now Chiusi)*

Clūsius, **-ī** m *Janus*

Clytaemnēstra, **-ae** f *wife of Agamemnon (whom she murdered)*

Cnidius adj see **Cnidus**

Cnidus, **-ī** f *town in Caria (famous for worship of Venus)*

coacervātiō, **-ōnis** f accumulation

coacervō, **-āre** vt to heap, accumulate

coacēscō, **-ēscere**, **-uī** vi to become sour

coāctō, **-āre** vt to force

coāctor, **-ōris** m collector (*of money*)

coāctōrēs agminis rearguard

coāctum, **-ī** nt thick coverlet

coāctus[1] adj forced

coāctus[2] ppp of **cōgō**

coāctus[3], **-ūs** m compulsion

coaedificō, **-āre**, **-āvī**, **-ātum** vt to build on

coaequō, **-āre**, **-āvī**, **-ātum** vt to make equal, bring down to the same level

coagmentātiō, **-ōnis** f combination

coagmentō, **-āre**, **-āvī**, **-ātum** vt to glue, join together

coagmentum, **-ī** nt joining, joint

coagulum, **-ī** nt rennet

coalēscō, **-ēscere**, **-uī**, **-itum** vi to grow together; (*fig*) to agree together; to flourish

coangustō, **-āre** vt to restrict

coarct- etc see **coart-**

coarguō, **-ere**, **-ī** vt to convict, prove conclusively

coartātiō, **-ōnis** f crowding together

coartō, **-āre**, **-āvī**, **-ātum** vt to compress, abridge

coccineus, **coccinus** adj scarlet

coccum, **-ī** nt scarlet

cochlea, **coclea**, **-ae** f snail

cocleāre, **-is** nt spoon

cocles, **-itis** m man blind in one eye; *surname of Horatius who defended the bridge*

coctilis adj baked; of bricks

coctus ppp of **coquō** ♦ adj (*fig*) well considered

cocus etc see **coquus**

Cōcȳtius adj see **Cōcȳtos**

Cōcȳtos, **-us**, **-ī** m *river in the lower world*

cōda etc see **cauda**

cōdex etc see **caudex**

cōdicillī, **-ōrum** mpl letter, note, petition; codicil

Codrus, **-ī** m *last king of Athens*

coēgī perf of **cōgō**

coel- etc see **cael-**

coemō, **-emere**, **-ēmī**, **-emptum** vt to buy up

coemptiō, **-ōnis** f a form of Roman marriage; mock sale of an estate

coemptiōnālis adj used in a mock sale; worthless

coen- etc see **caen-** or **cēn-**

coeō, **-īre**, **-īvī** and **-iī**, **-itum** vi to meet, assemble; to encounter; to combine, mate; (*wounds*) to close; to agree, conspire ♦ vt: **coīre societātem** make a compact

coepiō, **-ere**, **-ī**, **-tum** vt, vi begin (*esp in perf tenses*); **rēs agī coeptae sunt** things began to be done; **coepisse** to begin

coeptō, **-āre**, **-āvī**, **-ātum** vt, vi to begin, attempt

coeptum, **-ī** nt beginning, undertaking

coeptus[1] ppp of **coepiō**

coeptus[2], **-ūs** m beginning

coepulōnus, **-ī** m fellow-banqueter

coerātor etc see **cūrātor**

coerceō, **-ēre**, **-uī**, **-itum** vt to enclose; to confine, repress; (*fig*) to control, check, correct

coercitiō, **-ōnis** f coercion, punishment

coetus, **coitus**, **-ūs** m meeting, joining together; assembly, crowd

cōgitātē adv deliberately

cōgitātiō, -ōnis f thought, reflection; idea, plan; faculty of thought, imagination

cōgitātus adj deliberate ♦ ntpl ideas

cōgitō, -āre, -āvī, -ātum vt, vi to think, ponder, imagine; to feel disposed; to plan, intend

cognātiō, -ōnis f relationship (by blood); kin, family; (fig) affinity, resemblance

cognātus, -ī m, **cognāta, -ae** f relation ♦ adj related; (fig) connected, similar

cognitiō, -ōnis f acquiring of knowledge, knowledge; idea, notion; (LAW) judicial inquiry; (comedy) recognition

cognitor, -ōris m (LAW) attorney; witness of a person's identity; (fig) defender

cognitus¹ adj acknowledged

cognitus² ppp of **cognōscō**

cognōmen, -inis nt surname; name

cognōmentum, -ī nt surname, name

cognōminis adj with the same name

cognōminō, -āre, -āvī, -ātum vt to give a surname to; **verba cognōmināta** synonyms

cognōscō, -ōscere, -ōvī, -itum vt to get to know, learn, understand; to know, recognize, identify; (LAW) to investigate; (MIL) to reconnoitre

cōgō, -ere, coēgī, coāctum vt to collect, gather together; (liquids) to thicken, curdle; to contract, confine; to compel, force; to infer; **agmen cōgere** bring up the rear; **senātum cōgere** call a meeting of the senate

cohaerentia, -ae f coherence

cohaereō, -rēre, -sī, -sum vi to stick together, cohere; to cling to; (fig) to be consistent, harmonize; to agree, be consistent with

cohaerēscō, -ere vi to stick together

cohaesus ppp of **cohaereō**

cohērēs, -ēdis m/f co-heir

cohibeō, -ēre, -uī, -itum vt to hold together, encircle; to hinder, stop; (fig) to restrain, repress

cohonestō, -āre vt to do honour to

cohorrēscō, -ēscere, -uī vi to shudder all over

cohors, -tis f courtyard; (MIL) cohort (about 600 men); retinue (esp of the praetor in a province); (fig) company

cohortātiō, -ōnis f encouragement

cohorticula, -ae f small cohort

cohortor, -ārī, -ātus vt to encourage, urge

coitiō, -ōnis f encounter; conspiracy

coitus etc see **coetus**

colaphus, -ī m blow with the fist, box

Colchis¹, -idis f Medea's country (at the E. end of the Black Sea)

Colchis², Colchius, Colchicus adj Colchian

cōleus etc see **culleus**

cōlis etc see **caulis**

collabāscō, -ere vi to waver also

collabefactō, -āre vt to shake violently

collabefīō, -fierī, -factus vi to be destroyed

collābor, -bī, -psus vi to fall in ruin, collapse

collacerātus adj torn to pieces

collacrimātiō, -ōnis f weeping

collactea, -ae f foster-sister

collāpsus ppa of **collābor**

collāre, -is nt neckband

Collātia, -iae f ancient town near Rome

Collātīnus adj of Collatia ♦ m husband of Lucretia

collātiō, -ōnis f bringing together, combination; (money) contribution; (RHET) comparison; (PHILOS) analogy

collātor, -ōris m contributor

collātus ppp of **cōnferō**

collaudātiō, -ōnis f praise

collaudō, -āre, -āvī, -ātum vt to praise highly

collaxō, -āre vt to make porous

collēcta, -ae f money contribution

collēctīcius adj hastily gathered

collēctiō, -ōnis f gathering up; (RHET) recapitulation

collēctus¹ ppp of **colligō²**

collēctus², -ūs m accumulation

collēga, -ae m colleague; associate

collēgī perf of **colligō²**

collēgium, -ī and **-iī** nt association in office; college, guild (of magistrates, etc)

collībertus, -ī m fellow freedman

collibet, collubet, -uit and **-itum est** vi it pleases

collīdō, -dere, -sī, -sum vt to beat together, strike, bruise; (fig) to bring into conflict

colligātiō, -ōnis f connection

colligō¹, -āre, -āvī, -ātum vt to fasten, tie up; (fig) to combine; to restrain, check

colligō², -igere, -ēgī, -ēctum vt to gather, collect; to compress, draw together; to check; (fig) to acquire; to think about; to infer, conclude; **animum colligere, mentem colligere** recover, rally; **sē colligere** crouch; recover one's courage; **vāsa colligere** (MIL) pack up

Collīna Porta gate in N.E. of Rome

collīneō, -āre vt, vi to aim straight

collinō, -inere, -ēvī, -itum vt to besmear; (fig) to deface

colliquefactus adj dissolved

collis, -is m hill, slope

collīsi perf of **collīdō**

collīsus ppp of **collīdō**

collitus ppp of **collinō**

collocātiō, -ōnis f arrangement; giving in marriage

collocō, -āre, -āvī, -ātum vt to place, station, arrange; to give in marriage; (money) to invest; (fig) to establish; to occupy, employ

collocuplētō, -āre, -āvī vt to enrich

collocūtiō, -ōnis f conversation

colloquium, -ī and **-iī** nt conversation, conference

colloquor, -quī, -cūtus vi to converse, hold a conference ♦ vt to talk to

collubet etc see **collibet**

collūceō, -ēre vi to shine brightly; (fig) to be resplendent

collūdō, -dere, -sī, -sum vi to play together or with; to practise collusion

collum, -ī nt neck; ~ **torquēre**, ~ **obtorquēre**, ~ **obstringere** arrest

colluō, -uere, -uī, -ūtum vt to rinse, moisten

collus etc see **collum**

collūsiō, -ōnis f secret understanding

collūsor, -ōris *m* playmate, fellow gambler

collūstrō, -āre, -āvī, -ātum *vt* to light up; to survey

colluviō, -ōnis, colluviēs (*acc* -em, *abl* -ē) *f* sweepings, filth; (*fig*) dregs, rabble

collybus, -ī *m* money exchange, rate of exchange

collȳra, -ae *f* vermicelli

collȳricus *adj see* **collȳra**

collȳrium, -ī *and* **-iī** *nt* eye lotion

colō, -ere, -uī, cultum *vt* (AGR) to cultivate, work; (*place*) to live in; (*human affairs*) to cherish, protect, adorn; (*qualities, pursuits*) to cultivate, practise; (*gods*) to worship; (*men*) to honour, court; **vītam colere** live

colocāsia, -ae *f*, **colocāsia, -ōrum** *ntpl* Egyptian bean, caladium

colōna, -ae *f* country-woman

colōnia, -ae *f* settlement, colony; settlers

colōnicus *adj* colonial

colōnus, -ī *m* crofter, farmer; settler, colonist

color, colōs, -ōris *m* colour; complexion; beauty, lustre; (*fig*) outward show; (RHET) style, tone; colourful excuse; **colōrem mūtāre** blush, go pale; **homō nullīus colōris** an unknown person

colōrātus *adj* healthily tanned

colōrō, -āre, -āvī, -ātum *vt* to colour, tan; (*fig*) to give a colour to

colossus, -ī *m* gigantic statue (*esp that of Apollo at Rhodes*)

colostra, colustra, -ae *f* beestings

coluber, -rī *m* snake

colubra, -ae *f* snake

colubrifer, -ī *adj* snaky

colubrīnus *adj* wily

coluī *perf of* **colō**

cōlum, -ī *nt* strainer

columba, -ae *f* dove, pigeon

columbar, -āris *nt* kind of collar

columbārium, -ī *and* **-iī** *nt* dovecote

columbīnus *adj* pigeon's ♦ *m* little pigeon

columbus, -ī *m* dove, cock-pigeon

columella, -ae *f* small pillar

columen, -inis *nt* height, summit; pillar; (*fig*) chief; prop

columna, -ae *f* column, pillar; *a pillory in the Forum Romanum*; waterspout

columnārium, -ī *and* **-iī** *nt* pillar tax

columnārius, -ī *m* criminal

columnātus *adj* pillared

colurnus *adj* made of hazel

colus, -ī *and* **-ūs** *m/f* distaff

cōlȳphia, -ōrum *ntpl* *food of athletes*

coma, -ae *f* hair (*of the head*); foliage

comāns, -antis *adj* hairy, plumed; leafy

cōmarchus, -ī *m* burgomaster

comātus *adj* long-haired; leafy; **Gallia comāta** Transalpine Gaul

combibō¹, -ere, -ī *vt* to drink to the full, absorb

combibō², -ōnis *m* fellow-drinker

combūrō, -rere, -ssī, -stum *vt* to burn up; (*fig*) to ruin

combūstus *ppp of* **combūrō**

comedō, -ēsse, -ēdī, -ēsum *and* **-ēstum** *vt* to eat up, devour; (*fig*) to waste, squander; **sē comedēsse** pine away

Cōmēnsis *adj see* **Cōmum**

comes, -itis *m/f* companion, partner; attendant, follower; one of a magistrate's or emperor's retinue; (*medieval title*) count

comēs, comēst *pres of* **comedō**

comēstus, comēsus *ppp of* **comedō**

comētēs, -ae *m* comet

cōmicē *adv* in the manner of comedy

cōmicus, -ī *m* comedy actor, comedy writer ♦ *adj* of comedy, comic

cōmis *adj* courteous, friendly

cōmissābundus *adj* carousing

cōmissātiō, -ōnis *f* Bacchanalian revel

cōmissātor, -ōris *m* reveller

cōmissor, -ārī, -ātus *vi* to carouse, make merry

cōmitās, -ātis *f* kindness, affability

comitātus, -ūs *m* escort, retinue; company

cōmiter *adv see* **cōmis**

comitia, -iōrum *ntpl* assembly for the election of magistrates and other business (*esp the comitia centuriāta*); elections

comitiālis *adj* of the elections; ~ **morbus** epilepsy

comitiātus, -ūs *m* assembly at the elections

comitium, -ī *and* **-iī** *nt* place of assembly

comitō, -āre, -āvī, -ātum *vt* to accompany

comitor, -ārī, -ātus *vt, vi* to attend, follow

commaculō, -āre, -āvī, -ātum *vt* to stain, defile

commanipulāris, -is *m* soldier in the same company

commeātus, -ūs *m* passage; leave, furlough; convoy (*of troops or goods*); (MIL) lines of communication, provisions, supplies

commeditor, -ārī *vt* to practise

commeminī, -isse *vt, vi* to remember perfectly

commemorābilis *adj* memorable

commemorātiō, -ōnis *f* recollection, recounting

commemorō, -āre, -āvī, -ātum *vt* to recall, remind; to mention, relate

commendābilis *adj* praiseworthy

commendātīcius *adj* of recommendation or introduction

commendātiō, -ōnis *f* recommendation; worth, excellence

commendātor, -ōris *m* commender (*male*)

commendātrīx, -rīcis *f* commender (*female*)

commendātus *adj* approved, valued

commendō, -āre, -āvī, -ātum *vt* to entrust, commit, commend (*to one's care or charge*), recommend, set off to advantage

commēnsus *ppa of* **commētior**

commentāriolum, -ī *nt* short treatise

commentārius, -ī *and* **-iī** *m*, **commentārium, -ī** *and* **-iī** *nt* notebook; commentary, memoir; (LAW) brief

commentātiō, -ōnis *f* studying, meditation

commentīcius *adj* fictitious, imaginary; false

commentor¹, -ārī, -ātus *vt, vi* to study, think over, prepare carefully; to invent, compose, write

commentor², -ōris *m* inventor

commentum, **-ī** *nt* invention, fiction; contrivance

commentus *ppa of* **commīniscor** ♦ *adj* feigned, fictitious

commeō, **-āre** *vi* to pass to and fro; to go or come often

commercium, **-ī** *and* **-iī** *nt* trade, commerce; right to trade; dealings, communication

commercor, **-ārī**, **-ātus** *vt* to buy up

commereō, **-ēre**, **-uī**, **-itum**, **commereor**, **-ērī**, **-itus** *vt* to deserve; to be guilty of

commētior, **-tīrī**, **-nsus** *vt* to measure

commētō, **-āre** *vi* to go often

commictus *ppa of* **commingō**

commigrō, **-āre**, **-āvī**, **-ātum** *vi* to remove, migrate

commīlitium, **-ī** *and* **-iī** *nt* service together

commīlitō, **-ōnis** *m* fellow soldier

comminātiō, **-ōnis** *f* threat

commingō, **-ingere**, **-īnxī**, **-ictum** *vt* to pollute

commīniscor, **-ī**, **commentus** *vt* to devise, contrive

comminor, **-ārī**, **-ātus** *vt* to threaten

comminuō, **-uere**, **-uī**, **-ūtum** *vt* to break up, smash; to diminish; to impair

comminus *adv* hand to hand; near at hand

commīsceō, **-scēre**, **-scuī**, **-xtum** *vt* to mix together, join together

commiserātiō, **-ōnis** *f* (RHET) *passage intended to arouse pity*

commiserēscō, **-ere** *vt* to pity

commiseror, **-ārī** *vt* to bewail ♦ *vi* (RHET) to try to excite pity

commissiō, **-ōnis** *f* start (*of a contest*)

commissum, **-ī** *nt* enterprise; offence, crime; secret

commissūra, **-ae** *f* joint, connection

commissus *ppa of* **committō**

committō, **-ittere**, **-īsī**, **-issum** *vt* to join, connect, bring together; to begin, undertake; (*battle*) to join, engage in; (*offence*) to commit, be guilty of; (*punishment*) to incur, forfeit; to entrust, trust; **sē urbī committere** venture into the city

commīxtus *ppa of* **commīsceō**

commodē *adv* properly, well; aptly, opportunely; pleasantly

commoditās, **-ātis** *f* convenience, ease, fitness; advantage; (*person*) kindliness; (RHET) apt expression

commodō, **-āre**, **-āvī**, **-ātum** *vt* to adjust, adapt; to give, lend, oblige with; (*with dat*) to oblige

commodulē, **-um** *adv* conveniently

commodum¹, **-ī** *nt* convenience; advantage, interest; pay, salary; loan; **commodō tuō** at your leisure; **commoda vītae** the good things of life

commodum² *adv* opportunely; just

commodus *adj* proper, fit, full; suitable, easy, opportune; (*person*) pleasant, obliging

commōlior, **-īrī** *vt* to set in motion

commonefaciō, **-facere**, **-fēcī**, **-factum** *vt* to remind, recall

commoneō, **-ēre**, **-uī**, **-itum** *vt* to remind, impress upon

commōnstrō, **-āre** *vt* to point out

commorātiō, **-ōnis** *f* delay, residence; (RHET) dwelling (*on a topic*)

commoror, **-ārī**, **-ātus** *vi* to sojourn, wait; (RHET) to dwell ♦ *vt* to detain

commōtiō, **-ōnis** *f* excitement

commōtiuncula *f* slight indisposition

commōtus *ppp of* **commoveō** ♦ *adj* excited, emotional

commoveō, **-ovēre**, **-ōvī**, **-ōtum** *vt* to set in motion, move, dislodge, agitate; (*mind*) to unsettle, shake, excite, move, affect; (*emotions*) to stir up, provoke

commūne, **-is** *nt* common property; state; **in ~** for a common end; equally; in general

commūnicātiō, **-ōnis** *f* imparting; (RHET) *making the audience appear to take part in the discussion*

commūnicō, **-āre**, **-āvī**, **-ātum** *vt* to share (*by giving or receiving*); to impart, communicate; **cōnsilia commūnicāre cum** make common cause with

commūniō¹, **-īre**, **-īvī** *and* **-iī**, **-ītum** *vt* to build (*a fortification*), fortify, strengthen

commūniō², **-ōnis** *f* sharing in common, communion

commūnis *adj* common, general, universal; (*person*) affable, democratic; **commūnia loca** public places; **commūnēs locī** general topics; **~ sēnsus** popular sentiment; **aliquid commūne habēre** have something in common

commūnitās, **-ātis** *f* fellowship; sense of fellowship; affability

commūniter *adv* in common, jointly

commūnītiō, **-ōnis** *f* preparing the way

commurmuror, **-ārī**, **-ātus** *vi* to mutter to oneself

commūtābilis *adj* changeable

commūtātiō, **-iōnis** *f* change

commūtātus, **-ūs** *m* change

commūtō, **-āre**, **-āvī**, **-ātum** *vt* to change, exchange, interchange

cōmō, **-ere**, **-psī**, **-ptum** *vt* to arrange, dress, adorn

cōmoedia, **-ae** *f* comedy

cōmoedicē *adv* as in comedy

cōmoedus, **-ī** *m* comic actor

cōmōsus *adj* shaggy

compāctiō, **-ōnis** *f* joining together

compāctus *ppp of* **compingō**

compāgēs, **-is**, **compāgō**, **-inis** *f* joint, structure, framework

compār, **-aris** *m/f* comrade, husband, wife ♦ *adj* equal

comparābilis *adj* comparable

comparātē *adv* by bringing in a comparison

comparātiō, **-ōnis** *f* comparison; (ASTR) relative positions; agreement; preparation, procuring

comparātīvus *adj* based on comparison

compāreō, **-ēre** *vi* to be visible; to be present, be realized

comparō, **-āre**, **-āvī**, **-ātum** *vt* to couple together, match; to compare, (POL) to agree (*about respective duties*); to prepare, provide; (*custom*) to establish; to procure, purchase, get

compāscō, -ere vt to put (cattle) to graze in common

compāscuus adj for common pasture

compecīscor, -īscī, -tus vi to come to an agreement

compectum, -tī nt agreement

compediō, -īre, -ītum vt to fetter

compēgī perf of **compingō**

compellātiō, -ōnis f reprimand

compellō¹, -āre, -āvī, -ātum vt to call, address; to reproach; (*LAW*) to arraign

compellō², -ellere, -ulī, -ulsum vt to drive, bring together, concentrate; to impel, compel

compendiārius adj short

compendium, -ī and **-iī** nt saving; abbreviating; short cut; **compendiī facere** save; abridge; **compendiī fierī** be brief

compēnsātiō, -ōnis f (*fig*) compromise

compēnsō, -āre, -āvī, -ātum vt to balance (against), make up for

compercō, -cere, -sī vt, vi to save; to refrain

comperendinātiō, -iōnis f adjournment for two days

comperendinātus, -ūs m adjournment for two days

comperendinō, -āre vt to adjourn for two days

comperiō, -īre, -ī, -tum, comperior vt to find out, learn; **compertus** detected; found guilty; **compertum habēre** know for certain

compēs, -edis f fetter, bond

compēscō, -ere, -uī vt to check, suppress

competītor, -ōris m, **competītrīx, -rīcis** f rival candidate

competō, -ere, -īvī and **-iī, -ītum** vi to coincide, agree; to be capable

compīlātiō, -ōnis f plundering; compilation

compīlō, -āre, -āvī, -ātum vt to pillage

compingō, -ingere, -ēgī, -āctum vt to put together, compose; to lock up, hide away

compitālia, -ium and **-iōrum** ntpl festival in honour of the Lares Compitales

compitālicius adj of the Compitalia

compitālis adj of crossroads

compitum, -ī nt crossroads

complaceō, -ēre, -uī and **-itus sum** vi to please (someone else) as well, please very much

complānō, -āre vt to level, raze to the ground

complector, -ctī, -xus vt to embrace, clasp; to enclose; (*speech, writing*) to deal with, comprise; (*mind*) to grasp, comprehend; to honour, be fond of

complēmentum, -ī nt complement

compleō, -ēre, -ēvī, -ētum vt to fill, fill up; (*MIL*) to man, make up the complement of; (*time, promise, duty*) to complete, fulfil, finish

complētus adj perfect

complexiō, -ōnis f combination; (*RHET*) period; (*LOGIC*) conclusion of an argument; dilemma

complexus, -ūs m embrace; (*fig*) affection, close combat; (*speech*) connection

complicō, -āre vt to fold up

complōrātiō, -iōnis f, **complōrātus, -ūs** m loud lamentation

complōrō, -āre, -āvī, -ātum vt to mourn for

complūrēs, -ium adj several, very many

complūriēns adv several times

complūsculī, -ōrum adj quite a few

compluvium, -ī and **-iī** nt roof opening in a Roman house

compōnō, -ōnere, -osuī, -ositum vt to put together, join; to compose, construct; to compare, contrast; to match, oppose; to put away, store up, stow; (*dead*) to lay out, inter; to allay, quieten, reconcile; to adjust, settle, arrange; to devise, prepare ♦ vi to make peace

comportō, -āre vt to collect, bring in

compos, -tis adj in control, in possession; sharing; **vōtī ~** having got one's wish

compositē adv properly, in a polished manner

compositiō, -ōnis f compounding, system; (*words*) arrangement; reconciliation; matching (*of fighters*)

compositor, -ōris m arranger

compositūra, -ae f connection

compositus ppp of **compōnō** ♦ adj orderly, regular; adapted, assumed, ready; calm, sedate; (*words*) compound; **compositō, ex compositō** as agreed

compōtātiō, -ōnis f drinking party

compotiō, -īre vt to put in possession (of)

compōtor, -ōris m, **compōtrīx, -rīcis** f fellow drinker

comprānsor, -ōris m fellow guest

comprecātiō, -ōnis f public supplication

comprecor, -ārī, -ātus vt, vi to pray to; to pray for

comprehendō, comprendō, -endere, -endī, -ēnsum vt to grasp, catch; to seize, arrest, catch in the act; (*words*) to comprise, recount; (*thought*) to grasp, comprehend; to hold in affection; **numerō comprehendere** count

comprehēnsibilis adj conceivable

comprehēnsiō, -ōnis f grasping, seizing; perception, idea; (*RHET*) period

comprehēnsus, comprēnsus ppp of **comprehendō**

comprendō etc see **comprehendō**

compressī perf of **comprimō**

compressiō, -ōnis f embrace; (*RHET*) compression

compressus¹ ppp of **comprimō**

compressus², -ūs m compression, embrace

comprimō, -imere, -essī, -essum vt to squeeze, compress; to check, restrain; to suppress, withhold; **animam comprimere** hold one's breath; **compressīs manibus** with hands folded, idle

comprobātiō, -ōnis f approval

comprobātor, -ōris m supporter

comprobō, -āre, -āvī, -ātum vt to prove, make good; to approve

comprōmissum, -ī nt mutual agreement to abide by an arbitrator's decision

comprōmittō, -ittere, -īsī, -issum vt to undertake to abide by an arbitrator's decision

cōmpsī perf of **cōmō**

cōmptus¹ ppp of **cōmō** ♦ adj elegant

cōmptus², -ūs m coiffure; union

compulī *perf of* **compellō²**
compulsus *ppp of* **compellō²**
compungō, -ungere, -ūnxī, -ūnctum *vt* to prick, sting, tattoo
computō, -āre, -āvī, -ātum *vt* to reckon, number
Cōmum, -ī *nt* (*also* **Novum Cōmum**) *town in N. Italy* (*now* Como)
cōnāmen, -inis *nt* effort; support
cōnāta, -ōrum *ntpl* undertaking, venture
cōnātus, -ūs *m* effort; endeavour; inclination, impulse
concaedēs, -ium *fpl* barricade of felled trees
concalefaciō, -facere, -fēcī, -factum *vt* to warm well
concaleō, -ēre *vi* to be hot
concalēscō, -ēscere, -uī *vi* to become hot, glow
concallēscō, -ēscere, -uī *vi* to become shrewd; to become unfeeling
concastīgō, -āre *vt* to punish severely
concavō, -āre *vt* to curve
concavus *adj* hollow; vaulted, bent
concēdō, -ēdere, -essī, -essum *vi* to withdraw, depart; to disappear, pass away, pass; to yield, submit, give precedence, comply ♦ *vt* to give up, cede; to grant, allow; to pardon, overlook
concelebrō, -āre, -āvī, -ātum *vt* to frequent, fill, enliven; (*study*) to pursue eagerly; to celebrate; to make known
concēnātiō, -ōnis *f* dining together
concentiō, -ōnis *f* chorus
concenturiō, -āre *vt* to marshal
concentus, -ūs *m* chorus, concert; (*fig*) concord, harmony
conceptiō, -ōnis *f* conception; drawing up legal formulae
conceptīvus *adj* (*holidays*) movable
conceptus¹ *ppp of* **concipiō**
conceptus², -ūs *m* conception
concerpō, -ere, -sī, -tum *vt* to tear up; (*fig*) to abuse
concertātiō, -ōnis *f* controversy
concertātor, -ōris *m* rival
concertātōrius *adj* controversial
concertō, -āre, -āvī, -ātum *vi* to fight; to dispute
concessiō, -ōnis *f* grant, permission; (*LAW*) pleading guilty and asking indulgence
concessō, -āre *vi* to stop, loiter
concessus¹ *ppp of* **concēdō**
concessus², -ūs *m* permission
concha, -ae *f* mussel, oyster, murex; mussel shell, oyster shell, pearl; purple dye; trumpet, perfume dish
conchis, -is *f* kind of bean
conchīta, -ae *m* catcher of shellfish
conchȳliātus *adj* purple
conchȳlium, -ī *and* **-iī** *nt* shellfish, oyster, murex; purple
concidō, -ere, -ī *vi* to fall, collapse; to subside, fail, perish
concīdō, -dere, -dī, -sum *vt* to cut up, cut to pieces, kill; (*fig*) to ruin, strike down; (*RHET*) to dismember, enfeeble

concieō, -iēre, -īvī, -itum, conciō, -īre, -ītum *vt* to rouse, assemble; to stir up, shake; (*fig*) to rouse, provoke
conciliābulum, -ī *nt* place for public gatherings
conciliātiō, -ōnis *f* union; winning over (*friends, hearers*); (*PHILOS*) inclination
conciliātor, -ōris *m* promoter
conciliātrīx, -īcis *m*, **conciliātrīcula, -ae** *f* promoter, matchmaker
conciliātus¹, -ūs *m* combination
conciliātus² *adj* beloved; favourable
conciliō, -āre, -āvī, -ātum *vt* to unite; to win over, reconcile; to procure, purchase, bring about, promote
concilium, -ī *and* **-iī** *nt* gathering, meeting; council; (*things*) union
concinnē *adv see* **concinnus**
concinnitās, -ātis, concinnitūdō, -ūdinis *f* (*RHET*) rhythmical style
concinnō, -āre, -āvī, -ātum *vt* to arrange; to bring about, produce; (*with adj*) to make
concinnus *adj* symmetrical, beautiful; (*style*) polished, rhythmical; (*person*) elegant, courteous; (*things*) suited, pleasing
concinō, -ere, -uī *vi* to sing, play, sound together; (*fig*) to agree, harmonize ♦ *vt* to sing about, celebrate, prophesy
concio- *etc see* **contio-**
conciō *etc see* **concieō**
concipiō, -ipere, -ēpī, -eptum *vt* to take to oneself, absorb; (*women*) to conceive; (*senses*) to perceive; (*mind*) to conceive, imagine, understand; (*feelings, acts*) to harbour, foster, commit; (*words*) to draw up, intimate formally
concīsiō, -ōnis *f* breaking up into short clauses
concīsus *ppp of* **concīdō** ♦ *adj* broken up, concise
concitātē *adv see* **concitātus**
concitātiō, -ōnis *f* acceleration; (*mind*) excitement, passion; riot
concitātor, -ōris *m* agitator
concitātus *ppp of* **concitō** ♦ *adj* fast; excited
concitō, -āre, -āvī, -ātum *vt* to move rapidly, bestir, hurl; to urge, rouse, impel; to stir up, occasion
concitor, -ōris *m* instigator
concitus, concītus *ppp of* **concieō; conciō**
conclāmātiō, -ōnis *f* great shout
conclāmitō, -āre *vi* to keep on shouting
conclāmō, -āre, -āvī, -ātum *vt, vi* to shout, cry out; to call to help; (*MIL*) to give the signal; (*dead*) to call by name in mourning; **vāsa conclāmāre** give the order to pack up; **conclāmātum est** it's all over
conclāve, -is *nt* room
conclūdō, -dere, -sī, -sum *vt* to shut up, enclose; to include, comprise; to end, conclude, round off (*esp with a rhythmical cadence*); (*PHILOS*) to infer, demonstrate
conclūsē *adv* with rhythmical cadences
conclūsiō, -ōnis *f* (*MIL*) blockade; end, conclusion; (*RHET*) period, peroration; (*LOGIC*) conclusion
conclūsiuncula, -ae *f* quibble
conclūsum, -ī *nt* logical conclusion
conclūsus *ppp of* **conclūdō**

concoctus *ppp of* **concoquō**

concolor, -ōris *adj* of the same colour

concomitātus *adj* escorted

concoquō, -quere, -xī, -ctum *vt* to boil down; to digest; (*fig*) to put up with, stomach; (*thought*) to consider well, concoct

concordia, -ae *f* friendship, concord, union; *goddess of Concord*

concorditer *adv* amicably

concordō, -āre *vi* to agree, be in harmony

concors, -dis *adj* concordant, united, harmonious

concrēbrēscō, -ēscere, -uī *vi* to gather strength

concrēdō, -ere, -idī, -itum *vt* to entrust

concremō, -āre, -āvī, -ātum *vt* to burn

concrepō, -āre, -uī, -itum *vi* to rattle, creak, clash, snap (fingers) ♦ *vt* to beat

concrēscō, -scere, -vī, -tum *vi* to harden, curdle, congeal, clot; to grow, take shape

concrētiō, -ōnis *f* condensing; matter

concrētum, -ī *nt* solid matter, hard frost

concrētus *ppp of* **concrēscō** ♦ *adj* hard, thick, stiff, congealed; compounded

concrīminor, -ārī, -ātus *vi* to bring a complaint

concruciō, -āre *vt* to torture

concubīna, -ae *f* (*female*) concubine

concubīnātus, -ūs *m* concubinage

concubīnus, -ī *m* (*male*) concubine

concubitus, -ūs *m* reclining together (*at table*); sexual union

concubius *adj*: **concubiā nocte** during the first sleep ♦ *nt* the time of the first sleep

conculcō, -āre *vt* to trample under foot, treat with contempt

concumbō, -mbere, -buī, -bitum *vi* to lie together, lie with

concupīscō, -īscere, -īvī, -ītum *vt* to covet, long for, aspire to

concūrō, -āre *vt* to take care of

concurrō, -rere, -rī, -sum *vi* to flock together, rush in; (*things*) to clash, meet; (MIL) to join battle, charge; (*events*) to happen at the same time, concur

concursātiō, -ōnis *f* running together, rushing about; (MIL) skirmishing; (*dreams*) coherent design

concursātor, -ōris *m* skirmisher

concursiō, -ōnis *f* meeting, concourse; (RHET) repetition for emphasis

concursō, -āre *vi* to collide; to rush about, travel about; (MIL) to skirmish ♦ *vt* to visit, go from place to place

concursus, -ūs *m* concourse, gathering, collision; uproar; (*fig*) combination; (MIL) assault, charge

concussī *perf of* **concutiō**

concussus¹ *ppp of* **concutiō**

concussus², -ūs *m* shaking

concutiō, -tere, -ssī, -ssum *vt* to strike, shake, shatter; (*weapons*) to hurl; (*power*) to disturb, impair; (*person*) to agitate, alarm; (*self*) to search, examine; to rouse

condalium, -ī *and* **-iī** *nt* slave's ring

condecet, -ēre *vt impers* it becomes

condecorō, -āre *vt* to enhance

condemnātor, -ōris *m* accuser

condemnō, -āre, -āvī, -ātum *vt* to condemn, sentence; to urge the conviction of; to blame, censure; **ambitūs condemnāre** convict of bribery; **capitis condemnāre** condemn to death; **vōtī condemnātus** obliged to fulfil a vow

condēnsō, -āre, -eō, -ēre *vt* to compress, move close together

condēnsus *adj* very dense, close, thick

condiciō, -ōnis *f* arrangement, condition, terms; marriage contract, match; situation, position, circumstances; manner, mode; **eā condiciōne ut** on condition that; **sub condiciōne** conditionally; **hīs condiciōnibus** on these terms; **vītae** ~ way of life

condīcō, -īcere, -īxī, -ictum *vt, vi* to talk over, agree upon, promise; **ad cēnam condīcere** have a dinner engagement

condidī *perf of* **condō**

condignē *adv see* **condignus**

condignus *adj* very worthy

condīmentum, -ī *nt* spice, seasoning

condiō, -īre, -īvī, -ītum *vt* to pickle, preserve, embalm; to season; (*fig*) to give zest to, temper

condiscipulus, -ī *m* school-fellow

condiscō, -scere, -dicī *vt* to learn thoroughly, learn by heart

conditiō *etc see* **condiciō**

condītiō, -ōnis *f* preserving, seasoning

conditor, -ōris *m* founder, author, composer

conditōrium, -ī *and* **-iī** *nt* coffin, urn, tomb

condītus¹ *ppp of* **condō**

condītus² *ppp of* **condiō**

condītus¹ *adj* savoury; (*fig*) polished

condō, -ere, -idī, -itum *vt* **1**. (*build, found: arts*) to make, compose, write; (: *institutions*) to establish **2**. (*put away for keeping, store up: fruit*) to preserve; (: *person*) to imprison; (: *dead*) to bury; (: *memory*) to lay up; (: *time*) to pass, bring to a close **3**. (*put out of sight, conceal: eyes*) to close; (: *sword*) to sheathe, plunge; (: *troops*) to place in ambush

condocefaciō, -ere *vt* to train

condoceō, -ēre, -uī, -tum *vt* to train

condolēscō, -ēscere, -uī *vi* to begin to ache, feel very sore

condōnātiō, -ōnis *f* giving away

condōnō, -āre, -āvī, -ātum *vt* to give, present, deliver up; (*debt*) to remit; (*offence*) to pardon, let off

condormīscō, -īscere, -īvī *vi* to fall fast asleep

condūcibilis *adj* expedient

condūcō, -ūcere, -ūxī, -uctum *vt* to bring together, assemble, connect; to hire, rent, borrow; (*public work*) to undertake, get the contract for; (*taxes*) to farm ♦ *vi* to be of use, profit

conductī, -ōrum *mpl* hirelings, mercenaries

conductīcius *adj* hired

conductiō, -ōnis *f* hiring, farming

conductor, -ōris *m* hirer, tenant; contractor

conductum, -ī *nt* anything hired or rented

conductus *ppp of* **condūcō**

conduplicō, -āre *vt* to double

condūrō, -āre *vt* to make very hard
condus, -ī *m* steward
cōnectō, -ctere, -xuī, -xum *vt* to tie, fasten, link, join; (LOGIC) to state a conclusion
cōnexum, -ī *nt* logical inference
cōnexus¹ *ppp of* **cōnectō** ♦ *adj* connected; (*time*) following
cōnexus², -ūs *m* combination
cōnfābulor, -ārī, -ātus *vi* to talk (to), discuss
cōnfarreātiō, -ōnis *f the most solemn of Roman marriage ceremonies*
cōnfarreō, -āre, -ātum *vt* to marry by cōnfarreātiō
cōnfātālis *adj* bound by the same destiny
cōnfēcī *perf of* **cōnficiō**
cōnfectiō, -ōnis *f* making, completion; (*food*) chewing
cōnfector, -ōris *m* maker, finisher; destroyer
cōnfectus *ppp of* **cōnficiō**
cōnferciō, -cīre, -sī, -tum *vt* to stuff, cram, pack closely
cōnferō, -ferre, -tulī, -lātum *vt* to gather together, collect; to contribute; to confer, talk over; (MIL) to oppose, engage in battle; to compare; (*words*) to condense; to direct, transfer; to transform (into), turn (to); to devote, bestow; to ascribe, assign, impute; (*time*) to postpone; **capita cōnferre** put heads together, confer; **gradum cōnferre cum** walk beside; **sē cōnferre** go, turn (to); **sermōnēs cōnferre** converse; **signa cōnferre** join battle
cōnfertim *adv* in close order
cōnfertus *ppp of* **cōnferciō** ♦ *adj* crowded, full; (MIL) in close order
cōnfervēscō, -vēscere, -buī *vi* to boil up, grow hot
cōnfessiō, -ōnis *f* acknowledgement, confession
cōnfessus *ppa of* **cōnfiteor** ♦ *adj* acknowledged, certain; **in cōnfessō esse/in cōnfessum venīre** be generally admitted
cōnfestim *adv* immediately
cōnficiō, -icere, -ēcī, -ectum *vt* to make, effect, complete, accomplish; to get together, procure; to wear out, exhaust, consume, destroy; (COMM) to settle; (*space*) to travel; (*time*) to pass, complete; (PHILOS) to be an active cause; (LOGIC) to deduce; (*pass*) it follows
cōnfictiō, -ōnis *f* fabrication
cōnfictus *ppp of* **cōnfingō**
cōnfīdēns, -entis *pres p of* **cōnfīdō** ♦ *adj* self-confident, bold, presumptuous
cōnfīdenter *adv* fearlessly, insolently
cōnfīdentia, -ae *f* confidence, self-confidence; impudence
cōnfīdentiloquus *adj* outspoken
cōnfīdō, -dere, -sus sum *vi* to trust, rely, be sure; **sibi cōnfīdere** be confident
cōnfīgō, -gere, -xī, -xum *vt* to fasten together; to pierce, shoot; (*fig*) to paralyse
cōnfingō, -ingere, -inxī, -ictum *vt* to make, invent, pretend
cōnfinis *adj* adjoining; (*fig*) akin

cōnfīnium, -ī *nt* common boundary; (*pl*) neighbours; (*fig*) close connection, borderland between
cōnfīō, -fierī *occ pass of* **cōnficiō**
cōnfirmātiō, -ōnis *f* establishing; (*person*) encouragement; (*fact*) verifying; (RHET) adducing of proofs
cōnfirmātor, -ōris *m* guarantor (*of money*)
cōnfirmātus *adj* resolute; proved, certain
cōnfirmō, -āre, -āvī, -ātum *vt* to strengthen, reinforce; (*decree*) to confirm, ratify; (*mind*) to encourage; (*fact*) to corroborate, prove, assert; **sē cōnfirmāre** recover; take courage
cōnfiscō, -āre *vt* to keep in a chest; to confiscate
cōnfisiō, -ōnis *f* assurance
cōnfīsus *ppa of* **cōnfīdō**
cōnfiteor, -itērī, -essus *vi* to confess, acknowledge; to reveal
cōnfīxus *ppp of* **cōnfīgō**
cōnflagrō, -āre, -āvī, -ātum *vi* to burn, be ablaze
cōnflīctiō, -ōnis *f* conflict
cōnflīctō, -āre, -āvī, -ātum *vt* to strike down, contend (with); (*pass*) to fight, be harassed, be afflicted
cōnflīctus, -ūs *m* striking together
cōnflīgō, -gere, -xī, -ctum *vt* to dash together; (*fig*) to contrast ♦ *vi* to fight, come into conflict
cōnflō, -āre, -āvī, -ātum *vt* to ignite; (*passion*) to inflame; to melt down; (*fig*) to produce, procure, occasion
cōnfluēns, -entis, cōnfluēntēs, -entium *m* confluence of two rivers
cōnfluō, -ere, -xī *vi* to flow together; (*fig*) to flock together, pour in
cōnfodiō, -odere, -ōdī, -ossum *vt* to dig; to stab
cōnfore *fut infin of* **cōnsum**
cōnfōrmātiō, -ōnis *f* shape, form; (*words*) arrangement; (*voice*) expression; (*mind*) idea; (RHET) figure
cōnfōrmō, -āre, -āvī, -ātum *vt* to shape, fashion
cōnfossus *ppp of* **cōnfodiō** ♦ *adj* full of holes
cōnfrāctus *ppp of* **cōnfringō**
cōnfragōsus *adj* broken, rough; (*fig*) hard
cōnfrēgī *perf of* **cōnfringō**
cōnfremō, -ere, -uī *vi* to murmur aloud
cōnfricō, -āre *vt* to rub well
cōnfringō, -ingere, -ēgī, -āctum *vt* to break in pieces, wreck; (*fig*) to ruin
cōnfugiō, -ugere, -ūgī *vi* to flee for help (to), take refuge (with); (*fig*) to have recourse (to)
cōnfugium, -ī and -iī *nt* refuge
cōnfundō, -undere, -ūdī, -ūsum *vt* to mix, mingle, join; to mix up, confuse, throw into disorder; (*mind*) to perplex, bewilder; to diffuse, spread over
cōnfūsē *adv* confusedly
cōnfūsiō, -ōnis *f* combination; confusion, disorder; **ōris ~** going red in the face
cōnfūsus *ppp of* **cōnfundō** ♦ *adj* confused, disorderly, troubled
cōnfūtō, -āre, -āvī, -ātum *vt* to keep from boiling over; to repress; to silence, confute

congelō, **-āre**, **-āvī**, **-ātum** vt to freeze, harden ◆ vi to freeze over, grow numb

congeminō, **-āre**, **-āvī**, **-ātum** vt to double

congemō, **-ere**, **-uī** vi to groan, sigh ◆ vt to lament

conger, **-rī** m sea eel

congeriēs, **-ēī** f heap, mass, accumulation

congerō¹, **-rere**, **-ssī**, **-stum** vt to collect, accumulate, build; (missiles) to shower; (speech) to comprise; (fig) to heap (upon), ascribe

congerō², **-ōnis** m thief

congerrō, **-ōnis** m companion in revelry

congestīcius adj piled up

congestus¹ ppp of **congerō¹**

congestus², **-ūs** m accumulating; heap, mass

congiālis adj holding a congius

congiārium, **-ī** and **-iī** nt gift of food to the people, gratuity to the army

congius, **-ī** and **-iī** m Roman liquid measure (about 6 pints)

conglaciō, **-āre** vi to freeze up

conglīscō, **-ere** vi to blaze up

conglobātiō, **-ōnis** f mustering

conglobō, **-āre**, **-āvī**, **-ātum** vt to make round; to mass together

conglomerō, **-āre** vt to roll up

conglūtinātiō, **-ōnis** f gluing, cementing; (fig) combination

conglūtinō, **-āre**, **-āvī**, **-ātum** vt to glue, cement; (fig) to join, weld together; to contrive

congraecō, **-āre** vt to squander on luxury

congrātulor, **-ārī**, **-ātus** vi to congratulate

congredior, **-dī**, **-ssus** vt, vi to meet, accost; to contend, fight

congregābilis adj gregarious

congregātiō, **-ōnis** f union, society

congregō, **-āre**, **-āvī**, **-ātum** vt to collect, assemble, unite

congressiō, **-ōnis** f meeting, conference

congressus¹ ppa of **congredior**

congressus², **-ūs** m meeting, association, union; encounter, fight

congruēns, **-entis** adj suitable, consistent, proper; harmonious

congruenter adv in conformity

congruō, **-ere**, **-ī** vi to coincide; to correspond, suit; to agree, sympathize

congruus adj agreeable

coniciō, **-icere**, **-iēcī**, **-iectum** vt to throw together; to throw, hurl; to put, fling, drive, direct; to infer, conjecture; (AUG) to interpret; **sē conicere** rush, fly; devote oneself

coniectiō, **-ōnis** f throwing; conjecture, interpretation

coniectō, **-āre** vt to infer, conjecture, guess

coniector, **-ōris** m (male) interpreter, diviner

coniectrīx, **-rīcis** f (female) interpreter, diviner

coniectūra, **-ae** f inference, conjecture, guess; interpretation

coniectūrālis adj (RHET) involving a question of fact

coniectus¹ ppp of **coniciō**

coniectus², **-ūs** m heap, mass, concourse; throwing, throw, range; (eyes, mind) turning, directing

cōnifer, **cōniger**, **-ī** adj cone-bearing

cōnītor, **-tī**, **-sus** and **-xus** vi to lean on; to strive, struggle on; to labour

coniugālis adj of marriage, conjugal

coniugātiō, **-ōnis** f etymological relationship

coniugātor, **-ōris** m uniter

coniugiālis adj marriage- (in cpds)

coniugium, **-ī** and **-iī** nt union, marriage; husband, wife

coniugō, **-āre** vt to form (a friendship); **coniugāta verba** words related etymologically

coniūnctē adv jointly; on familiar terms; (LOGIC) hypothetically

coniūnctim adv together, jointly

coniūnctiō, **-ōnis** f union, connection, association; (minds) sympathy, affinity; (GRAM) conjunction

coniūnctum, **-ī** nt (RHET) connection; (PHILOS) inherent property (of a body)

coniūnctus ppp of **coniungō** ◆ adj near; connected, agreeing, conforming; related, friendly, intimate

coniungō, **-ungere**, **-ūnxī**, **-ūnctum** vt to yoke, join together, connect; (war) to join forces in; to unite in love, marriage, friendship; to continue without a break

coniūnx, **-ugis** m/f consort, wife, husband, bride

coniūrātī, **-ōrum** mpl conspirators

coniūrātiō, **-ōnis** f conspiracy, plot; alliance

coniūrātus adj (MIL) after taking the oath

coniūrō, **-āre**, **-āvī**, **-ātum** vi to take an oath; to conspire, plot

coniux etc see **coniūnx**

cōnīveō, **-vēre**, **-vī** and **-xī** vi to shut the eyes, blink; (fig) to be asleep; to connive at

conj- etc see **coni-**

conl- etc see **coll-**

conm- etc see **comm-**

conn- etc see **cōn-**

Conōn, **-is** m Athenian commander; Greek astronomer

cōnōpēum, **cōnōpeum**, **-ēī** nt mosquito net

cōnor, **-ārī**, **-ātus** vt to try, attempt, venture

conp- etc see **comp-**

conquassātiō, **-ōnis** f severe shaking

conquassō, **-āre**, **-ātum** vt to shake, upset, shatter

conqueror, **-rī**, **-stus** vt, vi to complain bitterly of, bewail

conquestiō, **-ōnis** f complaining; (RHET) appeal to pity

conquestus¹ ppa of **conqueror**

conquestus², **-ūs** m outcry

conquiēscō, **-scere**, **-vī**, **-tum** vi to rest, take a respite; (fig) to be at peace, find recreation; (things) to stop, be quiet

conquīnīscō, **-ere** vi to cower, squat, stoop down

conquīrō, **-rere**, **-sīvī**, **-sītum** vt to search for, collect

conquīsītē adv carefully

conquīsītiō, **-ōnis** f search; (MIL) levy

conquīsītor, **-ōris** m recruiting officer; (theatre) claqueur

conquīsītus ppp of **conquīrō** ◆ adj select, costly

conr- *etc see* **corr-**

cōnsaepiō, -īre, -sī, -tum *vt* to enclose, fence round

cōnsaeptum, -tī *nt* enclosure

cōnsalūtātiō, -ōnis *f* mutual greeting

cōnsalūtō, -āre, -āvī, -ātum *vt* to greet, hail

cōnsānēscō, -ēscere, -uī *vi* to heal up

cōnsanguineus *adj* brother, sister, kindred ♦ *mpl* relations

cōnsanguinitās, -ātis *f* relationship

cōnscelerātus *adj* wicked

cōnscelerō, -āre, -āvī, -ātum *vt* to disgrace

cōnscendō, -endere, -endī, -ēnsum *vt*, *vi* to climb, mount, embark

cōnscēnsiō, -ōnis *f* embarkation

cōnscēnsus *ppp of* **cōnscendō**

cōnscientia, -ae *f* joint knowledge, being in the know; (*sense of*) consciousness; moral sense, conscience, guilty conscience

cōnscindō, -ndere, -dī, -ssum *vt* to tear to pieces; (*fig*) to abuse

cōnsciō, -īre *vt* to be conscious of guilt

cōnscīscō, -scere, -vī *and* **-iī, -ītum** *vt* to decide on publicly; to inflict on oneself; **mortem (sibi) cōnscīscere** commit suicide

cōnscīssus *ppp of* **cōnscindō**

cōnscītus *ppp of* **cōnscīscō**

cōnscius *adj* sharing knowledge, privy, in the know; aware, conscious (of); conscious of guilt ♦ *m/f* confederate, confidant

cōnscreor, -ārī *vi* to clear the throat

cōnscrībō, -bere, -psī, -ptum *vt* to enlist, enrol; to write, compose, draw up, prescribe

cōnscrīptiō, -ōnis *f* document, draft

cōnscrīptus *ppp of* **cōnscrībō; patrēs cōnscrīptī** *patrician and elected plebeian members*; senators

cōnsecō, -āre, -uī, -tum *vt* to cut up

cōnsecrātiō, -ōnis *f* consecration, deification

cōnsecrō, -āre, -āvī, -ātum *vt* to dedicate, consecrate, deify; (*fig*) to devote; to immortalise; **caput cōnsecrāre** doom to death

cōnsectārius *adj* logical, consequent ♦ *ntpl* inferences

cōnsectātiō, -ōnis *f* pursuit

cōnsectātrīx, -īcis *f* (*fig*) follower

cōnsectiō, -ōnis *f* cutting up

cōnsector, -ārī, -ātus *vt* to follow, go after, try to gain; to emulate, imitate; to pursue, chase

cōnsecūtiō, -ōnis *f* (*PHILOS*) consequences, effect; (*RHET*) sequence

cōnsēdī *perf of* **cōnsīdō**

cōnsenēscō, -ēscere, -uī *vi* to grow old, grow old together; (*fig*) to fade, pine, decay, become obsolete

cōnsēnsiō, -ōnis *f* agreement, accord; conspiracy, plot

cōnsēnsū *adv* unanimously

cōnsēnsus[1] *ppp of* **cōnsentiō**

cōnsēnsus[2], -ūs *m* agreement, concord; conspiracy; (*PHILOS*) common sensation; (*fig*) harmony

cōnsentāneus *adj* agreeing, in keeping with; **cōnsentāneum est** it is reasonable

cōnsentiō, -entīre, -ēnsī, -ēnsum *vi* to agree, determine together; to plot, conspire; (*PHILOS*) to have common sensations; (*fig*) to harmonize, suit, be consistent (with); **bellum cōnsentīre** vote for war

cōnsequēns, -entis *pres p of* **cōnsequor** ♦ *adj* coherent, reasonable; logical, consequent ♦ *nt* consequence

cōnsequor, -quī, -cūtus *vt* to follow, pursue; to overtake, reach; (*time*) to come after; (*example*) to follow, copy; (*effect*) to result, be the consequence of; (*aim*) to attain, get; (*mind*) to grasp, learn; (*events*) to happen to, come to; (*standard*) to equal, come up to; (*speech*) to do justice to

cōnserō[1], -erere, -ēvī, -itum *vt* to sow, plant; (*ground*) to sow with, plant with; (*fig*) to cover, fill

cōnserō[2], -ere, -uī, -tum *vt* to join, string together, twine; (*MIL*) to join battle; **manum/manūs ~** engage in close combat; **ex iūre manum ~** lay claim to (*in an action for possession*)

cōnsertē *adv* connectedly

cōnsertus *ppp of* **cōnserō[2]**

cōnserva, -ae *f* fellow slave

cōnservātiō, -ōnis *f* preserving

cōnservātor, -ōris *m* preserver

cōnservitium, -ī *and* **-iī** *nt* being fellow slaves

cōnservō, -āre, -āvī, -ātum *vt* to preserve, save, keep

cōnservus, -ī *m* fellow slave

cōnsessor, -ōris *m* companion at table, fellow spectator; (*LAW*) assessor

cōnsessus, -ūs *m* assembly; (*LAW*) court

cōnsēvī *perf of* **cōnserō[1]**

cōnsīderātē *adv* cautiously, deliberately

cōnsīderātiō, -ōnis *f* contemplation

cōnsīderātus *adj* (*person*) circumspect; (*things*) well-considered

cōnsīderō, -āre, -āvī, -ātum *vt* to look at, inspect; to consider, contemplate

cōnsīdō, -īdere, -ēdī, -essum *vi* to sit down, take seats; (*courts*) to be in session; (*MIL*) to take up a position; (*residence*) to settle; (*places*) to subside, sink; (*fig*) to sink, settle down, subside

cōnsignō, -āre, -āvī, -ātum *vt* to seal, sign; to attest, vouch for; to record, register

cōnsilēscō, -ere *vi* to calm down

cōnsiliārius, -ī *and* **-iī** *m* adviser, counsellor; spokesman ♦ *adj* counselling

cōnsiliātor, -ōris *m* counsellor

cōnsilior, -ārī, -ātus *vi* to consult; (*with dat*) to advise

cōnsilium, -ī *and* **-iī** *nt* deliberation, consultation; deliberating body, council; decision, purpose; plan, measure, stratagem; advice, counsel; judgement, insight, wisdom; **~ capere, ~ inīre** come to a decision, resolve; **cōnsiliī esse** be an open question; **cōnsiliō** intentionally; **eō cōnsiliō ut** with the intention of; **prīvātō cōnsiliō** for one's own purposes

cōnsimilis *adj* just like

cōnsipiō, -ere *vi* to be in one's senses

cōnsistō, -istere, -titī *vi* to stand, rest, take up a position; to consist (of), depend (on); to exist, be; (*fig*) to stand firm, endure; (*liquid*) to solidify, freeze; to stop, pause, halt, come to rest; (*fig*) to come to a standstill, come to an end

cōnsitiō, -ōnis *f* sowing, planting

cōnsitor, -ōris *m* sower, planter

cōnsitus *ppp of* **cōnserō**[1]

cōnsōbrīnus, -ī *m*, **cōnsōbrīna, -ae** *f* cousin

cōnsociātiō, -ōnis *f* society

cōnsociō, -āre, -āvī, -ātum *vt* to share, associate, unite

cōnsōlābilis *adj* consolable

cōnsōlātiō, -ōnis *f* comfort, encouragement, consolation

cōnsōlātor, -ōris *m* comforter

cōnsōlātōrius *adj* of consolation

cōnsōlor, -ārī, -ātus *vt* to console, comfort, reassure; (*things*) to relieve, mitigate

cōnsomniō, -āre *vt* to dream about

cōnsonō, -āre, -uī *vi* to resound; (*fig*) to accord

cōnsonus *adj* concordant; (*fig*) suitable

cōnsōpiō, -īre, -īvī, -ītum *vt* to put to sleep

cōnsors, -tis *adj* sharing in common; (*things*) shared in common ♦ *m/f* partner, colleague

cōnsortiō, -ōnis *f* partnership, fellowship

cōnsortium, -ī *and* **-iī** *nt* society, participation

cōnspectus[1] *ppp of* **cōnspiciō** ♦ *adj* visible; conspicuous

cōnspectus[2], **-ūs** *m* look, view, sight; appearing on the scene; (*fig*) mental picture, survey; **in cōnspectum venīre** come in sight, come near

cōnspergō, -gere, -sī, -sum *vt* to besprinkle; (*fig*) to spangle

cōnspiciendus *adj* noteworthy, distinguished

cōnspiciō, -icere, -exī, -ectum *vt* to observe, catch sight of; to look at (*esp with admiration*), contemplate; (*pass*) to attract attention, be conspicuous, be notorious; (*mind*) to see, perceive

cōnspicor, -ārī, -ātus *vt* to observe, see, catch sight of

cōnspicuus *adj* visible; conspicuous, distinguished

cōnspīrātiō, -ōnis *f* concord, unanimity; plotting, conspiracy

cōnspīrō, -āre, -āvī, -ātum *vi* to agree, unite; to plot, conspire; (*music*) to sound together

cōnspōnsor, -ōris *m* co-guarantor

cōnspuō, -ere *vt* to spit upon

cōnspurcō, -āre *vt* to pollute

cōnspūtō, -āre *vt* to spit upon (*with contempt*)

cōnstabiliō, -īre, -īvī, -itum *vt* to establish

cōnstāns, -antis *pres p of* **cōnstō** ♦ *adj* steady, stable, constant; consistent; faithful, steadfast

cōnstanter *adv* steadily, firmly, calmly; consistently

cōnstantia, -ae *f* steadiness, firmness; consistency, harmony; self-possession, constancy

cōnsternātiō, -ōnis *f* disorder, tumult; (*horses*) stampede; (*mind*) dismay, alarm

cōnsternō[1], **-ernere, -rāvī, -rātum** *vt* to spread, cover, thatch, pave; **cōnstrāta nāvis** decked ship

cōnsternō[2], **-āre, -āvī, -ātum** *vt* to startle, stampede; to alarm, throw into confusion

cōnstīpō, -āre *vt* to crowd together

cōnstitī *perf of* **cōnsistō**

cōnstituō, -uere, -uī, -ūtum *vt* to put, place, set down; (MIL) to station, post, halt; to establish, build, create; to settle, arrange, organize; to appoint, determine, fix; to resolve, decide; **bene cōnstitūtum corpus** a good constitution

cōnstitūtiō, -ōnis *f* state, condition; regulation; decree; definition, point at issue

cōnstitūtum, -ūtī *nt* agreement

cōnstō, -āre, -itī, -ātum *vi* to stand together; to agree, correspond, tally; to stand firm, remain constant; to exist, be; to consist (of), be composed (of); (*facts*) to be established, be well-known; (COMM) to cost; **sibi cōnstāre** be consistent; **inter omnēs cōnstat** it is common knowledge; **mihi cōnstat** I am determined; **ratiō cōnstat** the account is correct

cōnstrātum, -ī *nt* flooring, deck

cōnstrātus *ppp of* **cōnsternō**[1]

cōnstringō, -ingere, -inxī, -ictum *vt* to tie up, bind, fetter; (*fig*) to restrain, restrict; (*speech*) to compress, condense

cōnstructiō, -ōnis *f* building up; (*words*) arrangement, sequence

cōnstruō, -ere, -xī, -ctum *vt* to heap up; to build, construct

cōnstuprātor, -ōris *m* debaucher

cōnstuprō, -āre *vt* to debauch, rape

cōnsuādeō, -ēre *vi* to advise strongly

Cōnsuālia, -ium *ntpl* festival of Consus

cōnsuāsor, -ōris *m* earnest adviser

cōnsūdō, -āre *vi* to sweat profusely

cōnsuēfaciō, -facere, -fēcī, -factum *vt* to accustom

cōnsuēscō, -scere, -vī, -tum *vt* to accustom, inure ♦ *vi* to get accustomed; to cohabit (with); (*perf tenses*) to be accustomed, be in the habit of

cōnsuētūdō, -inis *f* custom, habit; familiarity, social intercourse; love affair; (*language*) usage, idiom; **cōnsuētūdine/ex cōnsuētūdine** as usual; **epistulārum** ~ correspondence

cōnsuētus *ppp of* **cōnsuēscō** ♦ *adj* customary, usual

cōnsuēvī *perf of* **cōnsuēscō**

cōnsul, -is *m* consul; ~ **dēsignātus** consul elect; ~ **ōrdinārius** regular consul; ~ **suffectus** *successor to a consul who has died during his term of office*; ~ **iterum/tertium** consul for the second/third time; **cōnsulem creāre, cōnsulem dīcere, cōnsulem facere** elect to the consulship; **L. Domitiō App. Claudiō cōnsulibus** in the year 54 B.C.

cōnsulāris *adj* consular, consul's; of consular rank ♦ *m* ex-consul

cōnsulāriter *adv* in a manner worthy of a consul

cōnsulātus, -ūs *m* consulship; **cōnsulātum petere** stand for the consulship

cōnsulō, -ere, -uī, -tum *vi* to deliberate, take thought; (*with dat*) to look after, consult the interests of; (*with dē or in*) to take measures against, pass sentence on ♦ *vt* to consult, ask advice of; to consider; to advise (*something*); to decide; **bonī/optimī cōnsulere** take in good part, be satisfied with

cōnsultātiō, **-ōnis** f deliberation; inquiry; case
cōnsultē adv deliberately
cōnsultō¹ adv deliberately
cōnsultō², **-āre**, **-āvī**, **-ātum** vt, vi to deliberate, reflect; to consult; (with dat) to consult the interests of
cōnsultor, **-ōris** m counsellor; **consulter** client
cōnsultrīx, **-īcis** f protectress
cōnsultum, **-ī** nt decree (esp of the Senate); consultation; response (from an oracle)
cōnsultus ppp of **cōnsulō** ♦ adj considered; experienced, skilled ♦ m lawyer; **iūris ~** lawyer
cōnsuluī perf of **cōnsulō**
(cōnsum), **-futūrum**, **-fore** vi to be all right
cōnsummātus adj perfect
cōnsummō, **-āre** vt to sum up; to complete, perfect
cōnsūmō, **-ere**, **-psī**, **-ptum** vt to consume, use up, eat up; to waste, squander; to exhaust, destroy, kill; to spend, devote
cōnsūmptiō, **-ōnis** f wasting
cōnsūmptor, **-ōris** m destroyer
cōnsūmptus ppp of **cōnsūmō**
cōnsuō, **-uere**, **-uī**, **-ūtum** vt to sew up; (fig) to contrive
cōnsurgō, **-gere**, **-rēxī**, **-rēctum** vi to rise, stand up; to be roused (to); to spring up, start
cōnsurrēctiō, **-ōnis** f standing up
Cōnsus, **-ī** m ancient Roman god (connected with harvest)
cōnsusurrō, **-āre** vi to whisper together
cōnsūtus ppp of **cōnsuō**
contābefaciō, **-ere** vt to wear out
contābēscō, **-ēscere**, **-uī** vi to waste away
contabulātiō, **-ōnis** f flooring, storey
contabulō, **-āre**, **-āvī**, **-ātum** vt to board over, build in storeys
contāctus¹ ppp of **contingō¹**
contāctus², **-ūs** m touch, contact; contagion, infection
contāgēs, **-is** f contact, touch
contāgiō, **-ōnis** f, **contāgium**, **-ī** and **-iī** nt contact; contagion, infection; (fig) contamination, bad example
contāminātus adj impure, vicious
contāminō, **-āre**, **-āvī**, **-ātum** vt to defile; (fig) to mar, spoil
contechnor, **-ārī**, **-ātus** vi to think out plots
contegō, **-egere**, **-ēxī**, **-ēctum** vt to cover up, cover over; to protect; to hide
contemerō, **-āre** vt to defile
contemnō, **-nere**, **-psī**, **-ptum** vt to think light of, have no fear of, despise, defy; to disparage
contemplātiō, **-ōnis** f contemplation, surveying
contemplātor, **-ōris** m observer
contemplātus, **-ūs** m contemplation
contemplō, **-āre**, **-āvī**, **-ātum**, **contemplor**, **-ārī**, **-ātus** vt to look at, observe, contemplate
contempsī perf of **contemnō**
contemptim adv contemptuously, slightingly
contemptiō, **-ōnis** f disregard, scorn, despising
contemptor, **-ōris** m (male) despiser, defier
contemptrīx, **-rīcis** f (female) despiser, defier

contemptus¹ ppp of **contemnō** ♦ adj contemptible
contemptus², **-ūs** m despising, scorn; being slighted; **contemptuī esse** be despised
contendō, **-dere**, **-dī**, **-tum** vt to stretch, draw, tighten; (instrument) to tune; (effort) to strain, exert; (argument) to assert, maintain; (comparison) to compare, contrast; (course) to direct ♦ vi to exert oneself, strive; to hurry; to journey, march; to contend, compete, fight; to entreat, solicit
contentē¹ adv (from **contendō**) earnestly, intensely
contentē² adv (from **contineō**) closely
contentiō, **-ōnis** f straining, effort; striving (after); struggle, competition, dispute; comparison, contrast, antithesis
contentus¹ ppp of **contendō** ♦ adj strained, tense; (fig) intent
contentus² ppp of **contineō** ♦ adj content, satisfied
conterminus adj bordering, neighbouring
conterō, **-erere**, **-rīvī**, **-rītum** vt to grind, crumble; to wear out, waste; (time) to spend, pass; (fig) to obliterate
conterreō, **-ēre**, **-uī**, **-itum** vt to terrify
contestātus adj proved
contestor, **-ārī**, **-ātus** vt to call to witness; **lītem ~** open a lawsuit by calling witnesses
contexō, **-ere**, **-uī**, **-tum** vt to weave, interweave; to devise, construct; (recital) to continue
contextē adv in a connected fashion
contextus¹ adj connected
contextus², **-ūs** m connection, coherence
conticēscō, **conticīscō**, **-ēscere**, **-uī** vi to become quiet, fall silent; (fig) to cease, abate
contigī perf of **contingō¹**
contignātiō, **-ōnis** f floor, storey
contignō, **-āre** vt to floor
contiguus adj adjoining, near; within reach
continēns, **-entis** pres p of **contineō** ♦ adj bordering, adjacent; unbroken, continuous; (time) successive, continual, uninterrupted; (person) temperate, continent ♦ nt mainland, continent; essential point (in an argument)
continenter adv (place) in a row; (time) continuously; (person) temperately
continentia, **-ae** f moderation, self-control
contineō, **-inēre**, **-inuī**, **-entum** vt to hold, keep together; to confine, enclose; to contain, include, comprise; (pass) to consist of, rest on; to control, check, repress
contingō¹, **-ingere**, **-igī**, **-āctum** vt to touch, take hold of, partake of; to be near, border on; to reach, come to; to contaminate; (mind) to touch, affect, concern ♦ vi to happen, succeed
contingō², **-ere** vt to moisten, smear
continuātiō, **-ōnis** f unbroken succession, series; (RHET) period
continuī perf of **contineō**
continuō¹ adv immediately, without delay; (argument) necessarily

continuō², **-āre**, **-āvī**, **-ātum** vt to join together, make continuous; to continue without a break; **verba continuāre** form a sentence

continuus adj joined (to); continuous, successive, uninterrupted; **continuā nocte** the following night; **triduum continuum** three days running

cōntiō, **-ōnis** f public meeting; speech, address; rostrum; **cōntiōnem habēre** hold a meeting; deliver an address; **prō cōntiōne** in public

cōntiōnābundus adj delivering a harangue, playing the demagogue

cōntiōnālis adj suitable for a public meeting, demagogic

cōntiōnārius adj fond of public meetings

cōntiōnātor, **-ōris** m demagogue

cōntiōnor, **-ārī**, **-ātus** vi to address a public meeting, harangue; to declare in public; to come to a meeting

cōntiuncula, **-ae** f short speech

contorqueō, **-quēre**, **-sī**, **-tum** vt to twist, turn; (weapons) to throw, brandish; (words) to deliver forcibly

contortē adv intricately

contortiō, **-ōnis** f intricacy

contortor, **-ōris** m perverter

contortulus adj somewhat complicated

contortuplicātus adj very complicated

contortus ppp of **contorqueō** ♦ adj vehement; intricate

contrā adv (place) opposite, face to face; (speech) in reply; (action) to fight, in opposition, against (someone); (result, with **esse**) adverse, unsuccessful; (comparison) the contrary, conversely, differently; (argument) on the contrary, on the other hand; **~ atque** contrary to what, otherwise than ♦ prep (with acc) facing, opposite to; against; contrary to, in violation of

contractiō, **-ōnis** f contracting; shortening; despondency

contractiuncula, **-ae** f slight despondency

contractus ppp of **contrahō** ♦ adj contracted, narrow; short; in seclusion

contrādīcō (usu two words), **-dīcere**, **-dīxī**, **-dictum** vi to oppose, object; (LAW) to be counsel for the other side

contrādictiō, **-ōnis** f objection

contrahō, **-here**, **-xī**, **-ctum** vt to draw together, assemble; to bring about, achieve; (COMM) to contract, make a bargain; to shorten, narrow; to limit, depress; (blame) to incur; (brow) to wrinkle; (sail) to shorten; (sky) to overcast

contrāriē adv differently

contrārius adj opposite, from opposite; contrary; hostile, harmful ♦ nt opposite, reverse; **ex contrāriō** on the contrary

contrectābiliter adv so as to be felt

contrectātiō, **-ōnis** f touching

contrectō, **-āre**, **-āvī**, **-ātum** vt to touch, handle; (fig) to consider

contremīscō, **-īscere**, **-uī** vi to tremble all over; (fig) to waver ♦ vt to be afraid of

contremō, **-ere** vi to quake

contribuō, **-uere**, **-uī**, **-ūtum** vt to bring together, join, incorporate

contristō, **-āre**, **-āvī**, **-ātum** vt to sadden, darken, cloud

contrītus ppp of **conterō** ♦ adj trite, well-worn

contrōversia, **-ae** f dispute, argument, debate, controversy

contrōversiōsus adj much disputed

contrōversus adj disputed, questionable

contrucīdō, **-āre**, **-āvī**, **-ātum** vt to massacre

contrūdō, **-dere**, **-sī**, **-sum** vt to crowd together

contruncō, **-āre** vt to hack to pieces

contrūsus ppp of **contrūdō**

contubernālis, **-is** m/f tent companion; junior officer serving with a general; (fig) companion, mate

contubernium, **-ī** and **-iī** nt service in the same tent, mess; service as junior officer with a general; common tent; slaves' home

contueor, **-ērī**, **-itus** vt to look at, consider, observe

contuitus, **-ūs** m observing, view

contulī perf of **cōnferō**

contumācia, **-ae** f obstinacy, defiance

contumāciter adv see **contumāx**

contumāx, **-ācis** adj stubborn, insolent, pig-headed

contumēlia, **-ae** f (verbal) insult, libel, invective; (physical) assault, ill-treatment

contumēliōsē adv insolently

contumēliōsus adj insulting, outrageous

contumulō, **-āre** vt to bury

contundō, **-undere**, **-udī**, **-ūsum** vt to pound, beat, bruise; (fig) to suppress, destroy

contuor etc see **contueor**

conturbātiō, **-ōnis** f confusion, mental disorder

conturbātus adj distracted, diseased

conturbō, **-āre**, **-āvī**, **-ātum** vt to throw into confusion; (mind) to derange, disquiet; (money) to embarrass

contus, **-ī** m pole

contūsus ppp of **contundō**

contūtus see **contuitus**

cōnūbiālis adj conjugal

cōnūbium, **-ī** and **-iī** nt marriage; **iūs cōnūbiī** right of intermarriage

cōnus, **-ī** m cone; (helmet) apex

convador, **-ārī**, **-ātus** vt (LAW) to bind over

convalēscō, **-ēscere**, **-uī** vi to recover, get better; (fig) to grow stronger, improve

convallis, **-is** f valley with hills on all sides

convāsō, **-āre** vt to pack up

convectō, **-āre** vt to bring home

convector, **-ōris** m fellow passenger

convehō, **-here**, **-xī**, **-ctum** vt to bring in, carry

convellō, **-ellere**, **-ellī**, **-ulsum** and **-olsum** vt to wrench, tear away; to break up; (fig) to destroy, overthrow; **signa convellere** decamp

convena, **-ae** adj meeting

convenae, **-ārum** mpl/fpl crowd of strangers, refugees

conveniēns, **-entis** pres p of **conveniō** ♦ adj harmonious, consistent; fit, appropriate

convenienter *adv* in conformity (with), consistently; aptly

convenientia, -ae *f* conformity, harmony

conveniō, -enīre, -ēnī, -entum *vi* to meet, assemble; (*events*) to combine, coincide; (*person*) to agree, harmonize; (*things*) to fit, suit; (*impers*) to be suitable, be proper ♦ *vt* to speak to, interview

conventīcium, -ī *and* **-iī** *nt* payment for attendance at assemblies

conventīcius *adj* visiting regularly

conventiculum, -ī *nt* gathering; meeting place

conventiō, -ōnis *f* agreement

conventum, -ī *nt* agreement

conventus¹ *ppp of* **conveniō**

conventus², -ūs *m* meeting; (*LAW*) local assizes; (*COMM*) corporation; agreement; **conventūs agere** hold the assizes

converrō, -rere, -rī, -sum *vt* to sweep up, brush together; (*comedy*) to give a good beating to

conversātiō, -ōnis *f* associating (with)

conversiō, -ōnis *f* revolution, cycle; change over; (*RHET*) well-rounded period; verbal repetition at end of clauses

conversō, -āre *vt* to turn round

conversus *ppp* **converrō; convertō**

convertō, -tere, -tī, -sum *vt* to turn round, turn back; (*MIL*) to wheel; to turn, direct; to change, transform; (*writings*) to translate ♦ *vi* to return, turn, change

convestiō, -īre, -īvī, -ītum *vt* to clothe, encompass

convexus *adj* vaulted, rounded; hollow; sloping ♦ *nt* vault, hollow

convīciātor, -ōris *m* slanderer

convīcior, -ārī, -ātus *vt* to revile

convīcium, -ī *and* **-iī** *nt* loud noise, outcry; invective, abuse; reproof, protest

convīctiō, -ōnis *f* companionship

convīctor, -ōris *m* familiar friend

convīctus *ppp of* **convincō**

convīctus, -ūs *m* community life, intercourse; entertainment

convincō, -incere, -īcī, -ictum *vt* to refute, convict, prove wrong; to prove, demonstrate

convīsō, -ere *vt* to search, examine; to pervade

convītium *see* **convīcium**

convīva, -ae *m/f* guest

convīvālis *adj* festive, convivial

convīvātor, -ōris *m* host

convīvium, -ī *and* **-iī** *nt* banquet, entertainment; guests

convīvor, -ārī, -ātus *vi* to feast together, carouse

convocātiō, -ōnis *f* assembling

convocō, -āre, -āvī, -ātum *vt* to call a meeting of, muster

convolnerō *see* **convulnerō**

convolō, -āre, -āvī, -ātum *vi* to flock together

convolsus *see* **convulsus**

convolvō, -vere, -vī, -ūtum *vt* to roll up, coil up; to intertwine

convomō, -ere *vt* to vomit over

convorrō *see* **converrō**

convortō *see* **convertō**

convulnerō, -āre *vt* to wound seriously

convulsus *ppp of* **convellō**

cooperiō, -īre, -uī, -tum *vt* to cover over, overwhelm

cooptātiō, -ōnis *f* electing, nominating (*of new members*)

cooptō, -āre, -āvī, -ātum *vt* to elect (*as a colleague*)

coorior, -īrī, -tus *vi* to rise, appear; to break out, begin

coortus, -ūs *m* originating

cōpa, -ae *f* barmaid

cophinus, -ī *m* basket

cōpia, -ae *f* abundance, plenty, number; resources, wealth, prosperity;·(*MIL, usu pl*) troops, force; (*words, thought*) richness, fulness, store; (*action*) opportunity, facility, means, access; **prō cōpiā** according to one's resources, as good as possible considering

cōpiolae, -ārum *fpl* small force

cōpiōsē *adv* abundantly, fully, at great length

cōpiōsus *adj* abounding, rich, plentiful; (*speech*) eloquent, fluent

cōpis *adj* rich

cōpula, -ae *f* rope, leash, grapnel; (*fig*) bond

cōpulātiō, -ōnis *f* coupling, union

cōpulātus *adj* connected, binding

cōpulō, -āre, -āvī, -ātum *vt* to couple, join; (*fig*) to unite, associate

coqua, -ae *f* cook

coquīnō, -āre *vi* to be a cook

coquīnus *adj* of cooking

coquō, -quere, -xī, -ctum *vt* to cook, boil, bake; to parch, burn; (*fruit*) to ripen; (*stomach*) to digest; (*thought*) to plan, concoct; (*care*) to disquiet, disturb

coquus, cocus, -ī *m* cook

cor, cordis *nt* heart; (*feeling*) heart, soul; (*thought*) mind, judgement; **cordī esse** please, be agreeable

cōram *adv* in one's presence; in person ♦ *prep* (*with abl*) in the presence of, before

corbis, -is *m/f* basket

corbīta, -ae *f* slow boat

corbula, -ae *f* little basket

corculum, -ī *nt* dear heart

Corcȳra, -ae *f* island off W. coast of Greece (*now Corfu*)

Corcȳraeus *adj see* **Corcȳra**

cordātē *adv see* **cordātus**

cordātus *adj* wise

cordolium, -ī *and* **-iī** *nt* sorrow

Corfiniēnsis *adj see* **Corfinium**

Corfinium, -ī *nt* town in central Italy

coriandrum, -ī *nt* coriander

Corinthiacus, Corinthiēnsis, Corinthius *adj*: **Corinthium aes** Corinthian brass (*an alloy of gold, silver and copper*)

Corinthus, -ī *f* Corinth

corium, -ī *and* **-iī** *nt*, **corius, -ī** *and* **-iī** *m* hide, skin; leather, strap

Cornēlia, -iae *f* mother of the Gracchi

Cornēliānus, Cornēlius *adj*: **lēgēs Cornēliae** Sulla's laws

Cornēlius, -ī *m famous Roman family name (esp Scipios, Gracchi, Sulla)*

corneolus *adj* horny

corneus[1] *adj* of horn

corneus[2] *adj* of the cornel tree, of cornel wood

cornicen, -cinis *m* horn-blower

cornīcula, -ae *f* little crow

corniculārius, -ī *and* **-iī** *m* adjutant

corniculum, -ī *nt* a horn-shaped decoration

corniger, -ī *adj* horned

cornipēs, -edis *adj* horn-footed

cornīx, -īcis *f* crow

cornū, -ūs, cornum, -ī *nt* horn; *anything horn-shaped*; *(army)* wing; *(bay)* arm; *(book)* roller-end; *(bow)* tip; *(helmet)* crest-socket; *(land)* tongue, spit; *(lyre)* arm; *(moon)* horn; *(place)* side; *(river)* branch; *(yardarm)* point; *anything made of horn*: bow, funnel, lantern; *(music)* horn; *(oil)* cruet; *anything like horn, beak, hoof, wart*; *(fig)* strength, courage; **~ cōpiae** *Amalthea's horn, symbol of plenty*

cornum[1], **-ī** *nt* cornelian cherry

cornum[2] *see* **cornū**

cornus, -ī *f* cornelian cherry tree; javelin

corōlla, -ae *f* small garland

corōllārium, -ī *and* **-iī** *nt* garland for actors; present, gratuity

corōna, -ae *f* garland, crown; *(ASTR)* Corona Borealis; *(people)* gathering, bystanders; *(MIL)* cordon of besiegers or defenders; **sub corōnā vēndere, sub corōnā vēnīre** sell, be sold as slaves

Corōnaeus, Corōnēus, Corōnēnsis *adj see* **Corōnēa**

corōnārium aurum *gold collected in the provinces for a victorious general*

Corōnēa, -ēae *f town in central Greece*

corōnō, -āre, -āvī, -ātum *vt* to put a garland on, crown; to encircle

corporeus *adj* corporeal; of flesh

corpulentus *adj* corpulent

corpus, -oris *nt* body; substance, flesh; corpse; trunk, torso; person, individual; *(fig)* structure, corporation, body politic

corpusculum, -ī *nt* particle; *term of endearment*

corrādō, -dere, -sī, -sum *vt* to scrape together, procure

corrēctiō, -ōnis *f* amending, improving

corrēctor, -ōris *m* reformer, critic

corrēctus *ppp of* **corrigō**

corrēpō, -ere, -sī *vi* to creep, slink, cower

correptē *adv* briefly

correptus *ppp of* **corripiō**

corrīdeō, -ēre *vi* to laugh aloud

corrigia, -ae *f* shoelace

corrigō, -igere, -ēxī, -ēctum *vt* to make straight; to put right, improve, correct

corripiō, -ipere, -ipuī, -eptum *vt* to seize, carry off, get along quickly; *(speech)* to reprove, reproach, accuse; *(passion)* to seize upon, attack; *(time, words)* to cut short; **sē gradum corripere, sē viam corripere** hasten, rush

corrōborō, -āre, -āvī, -ātum *vt* to make strong, invigorate

corrōdō, -dere, -sī, -sum *vt* to nibble away

corrogō, -āre *vt* to gather by requesting

corrūgō, -āre *vt* to wrinkle

corrumpō, -umpere, -ūpī, -uptum *vt* to break up, ruin, waste; to mar, adulterate, falsify; *(person)* to corrupt, seduce, bribe

corruō, -ere, -ī *vi* to fall, collapse ◆ *vt* to overthrow, heap up

corruptē *adv* perversely; in a lax manner

corruptēla, -ae *f* corruption, bribery; seducer

corruptiō, -ōnis *f* bribing, seducing; corrupt state

corruptor, -ōris *m*, **corruptrīx, -rīcis** *f* corrupter, seducer

corruptus *ppp of* **corrumpō** ◆ *adj* spoiled, corrupt, bad

Corsus *adj* Corsican

cortex, -icis *m/f* bark, rind; cork

cortīna, -ae *f* kettle, cauldron; tripod of Apollo; *(fig)* vault, circle

corulus, -ī *f* hazel

Cōrus *see* **Caurus**

coruscō, -āre *vt* to butt; to shake, brandish ◆ *vi* to flutter, flash, quiver

coruscus *adj* tremulous, oscillating; shimmering, glittering

corvus, -ī *m* raven; *(MIL)* grapnel

Corybantēs, -ium *mpl priests of Cybele*

Corybantius *adj see* **Corybantēs**

cōrycus, -ī *m* punchbag

corylētum, -ī *nt* hazel copse

corylus, -ī *f* hazel

corymbifer *m* Bacchus

corymbus, -ī *m* cluster *(esp of ivy berries)*

coryphaeus, -ī *m* leader

cōrytos, cōrytus, -ī *m* quiver

cōs, cōtis *f* hard rock, flint; grindstone

Cōs, Coī *f Aegean island (famous for wine and weaving)* ◆ *nt* Coan wine ◆ *ntpl* Coan clothes

cosmēta, -ae *m* master of the wardrobe

costa, -ae *f* rib; side, wall

costum, -ī *nt* an aromatic plant, perfume

cothurnātus *adj* buskined, tragic

cothurnus, -ī *m* buskin, hunting boot; tragedy, elevated style

cotīd- *see* **cottīd-**

cōtis *f see* **cōs**

cottabus, -ī *m* game of throwing drops of wine

cottana, -ōrum *ntpl* Syrian figs

cottīdiānō *adv* daily

cottīdiānus *adj* daily; everyday, ordinary

cottīdiē *adv* every day, daily

coturnīx, -īcis *f* quail

Cotyttia, -ōrum *ntpl festival of Thracian goddess Cotytto*

Cōus *adj* Coan

covinnārius, -ī *and* **-iī** *m* chariot fighter

covinnus, -ī *m* war chariot; coach

coxa, -ae, coxendīx, -īcis *f* hip

coxī *perf of* **coquō**

crābrō, -ōnis *m* hornet

crambē, -ēs *f* cabbage; **~ repetīta** stale repetitions

Crantor, -oris *m Greek Academic philosopher*

crāpula, -ae *f* intoxication, hangover

crāpulārius *adj* for intoxication

crās *adv* tomorrow

crassē *adv* grossly, dimly

Crassiānus *adj see* **Crassus**

crassitūdō, -inis *f* thickness, density

crassus *adj* thick, gross, dense; *(fig)* dull, stupid

Crassus, -ī *m* famous orator; wealthy politician, triumvir with Caesar and Pompey

crāstinum, -ī *nt* the morrow

crāstinus *adj* of tomorrow; **diē crāstinī** tomorrow

crātēr, -is *m*, **crātēra, -ae** *f* bowl (*esp for mixing wine and water*); crater; *a constellation*

crātis, -is *f* wickerwork, hurdle; (AGR) harrow; (MIL) faggots for lining trenches; (*shield*) ribs; *(fig)* frame, joints

creātiō, -ōnis *f* election

creātor, -ōris *m*, **creātrīx, -rīcis** *f* creator, father, mother

creātus *m* (*with abl*) son of

crēber, -rī *adj* dense, thick, crowded; numerous, frequent; *(fig)* prolific, abundant

crēbrēscō, -ēscere, -uī *vi* to increase, become frequent

crēbritās, -ātis *f* frequency

crēbrō *adv* repeatedly

crēdibilis *adj* credible

crēdibiliter *adv see* **crēdibilis**

crēditor, -ōris *m* creditor

crēditum, -itī *nt* loan

crēdō, -ere, -idī, -itum *vt, vi* to entrust, lend; to trust, have confidence in; to believe; to think, suppose; **crēderēs** one would have thought

crēdulitās, -ātis *f* credulity

crēdulus *adj* credulous, trusting

cremō, -āre, -āvī, -ātum *vt* to burn, cremate

Cremōna, -ae *f* town in N. Italy

Cremōnēnsis *adj see* **Cremōna**

cremor, -ōris *m* juice, broth

creō, -āre, -āvī, -ātum *vt* to create, produce, beget; to elect (*to an office*), cause, occasion

creper, -ī *adj* dark; doubtful

crepida, -ae *f* sandal; **nē sūtor suprā crepidam** let the cobbler stick to his last

crepidātus *adj* wearing sandals

crepīdō, -inis *f* pedestal, base; bank, pier, dam

crepidula, -ae *f* small sandal

crepitācillum, -ī *nt* rattle

crepitō, -āre *vi* to rattle, chatter, rustle, creak

crepitus, -ūs *m* rattling, chattering, rustling, creaking

crepō, -āre, -uī, -itum *vi* to rattle, creak, snap (*fingers*) ♦ *vt* to make rattle, clap; to chatter about

crepundia, -ōrum *ntpl* rattle, babies' toys

crepusculum, -ī *nt* twilight, dusk; darkness

Crēs, -ētis *m* Cretan

crēscō, -scere, -vī, -tum *vi* to arise, appear, be born; to grow up, thrive, increase, multiply; to prosper, be promoted, rise in the world

Crēsius *adj* Cretan

Crēssa, -ae *f* Cretan

Crēta, -ae *f* Crete

crēta, -ae *f* chalk; good mark

Crētaeus, Crēticus, Crētis, -idis *adj see* **Crēta**

crētātus *adj* chalked; dressed in white

Crētē *see* **Crēta**

crēteus *adj* of chalk, of clay

crētiō, -ōnis *f* declaration of accepting an inheritance

crētōsus *adj* chalky, clayey

crētula, -ae *f* white clay for sealing

crētus *ppp of* **cernō** ♦ *ppa of* **crēscō** ♦ *adj* descended, born

Creūsa, -ae *f* wife of Jason; wife of Aeneas

crēvī *perf of* **cernō**; **crēscō**

crībrum, -ī *nt* sieve

crīmen, -inis *nt* accusation, charge, reproach; guilt, crime; cause of offence; **esse in crīmine** stand accused

crīminātiō, -ōnis *f* complaint, slander

crīminātor, -ōris *m* accuser

crīminō, -āre *vt* to accuse

crīminor, -ārī, -ātus *dep* to accuse, impeach; (*things*) to complain of, charge with

crīminōsē *adv* accusingly, slanderously

crīminōsus *adj* reproachful, slanderous

crīnālis *adj* for the hair, hair- (*in cpds*) ♦ *nt* hairpin

crīnis, -is *m* hair; (*comet*) tail

crīnītus *adj* long-haired; crested; **stēlla crīnīta** comet

crīspāns, -antis *adj* wrinkled

crīspō, -āre *vt* to curl, swing, wave

crīspus *adj* curled; curly-headed; wrinkled; tremulous

crista, -ae *f* cockscomb, crest; plume

cristātus *adj* crested, plumed

criticus, -ī *m* critic

croceus *adj* of saffron, yellow

crocinus *adj* yellow ♦ *nt* saffron oil

crōciō, -īre *vi* to croak

crocodīlus, -ī *m* crocodile

crocōtārius *adj* of saffron clothes

crocōtula, -ae *f* saffron dress

crocus, -ī *m*, **crocum, -ī** *nt* saffron; yellow

Croesus, -ī *m* king of Lydia (*famed for wealth*)

crotalistria, -ae *f* castanet dancer

crotalum, -ī *nt* rattle, castanet

cruciābilitās, -ātis *f* torment

cruciāmentum, -ī *nt* torture

cruciātus, -ūs *m* torture; instrument of torture; *(fig)* ruin, misfortune

cruciō, -āre, -āvī, -ātum *vt* to torture; to torment

crūdēlis *adj* hard-hearted, cruel

crūdēlitās, -ātis *f* cruelty, severity

crūdēliter *adv see* **crūdēlis**

crūdēscō, -ēscere, -uī *vi* to grow violent, grow worse

crūditās, -ātis *f* indigestion

crūdus *adj* bleeding; (*food*) raw, undigested; (*person*) dyspeptic; (*leather*) rawhide; (*fruit*) unripe; (*age*) immature, fresh; (*voice*) hoarse; *(fig)* unfeeling, cruel, merciless

cruentō, -āre *vt* to stain with blood, wound

cruentus *adj* bloody, gory; bloodthirsty, cruel; blood-red

crumēna, -ae *f* purse; money

crumilla, -ae *f* purse

cruor, -ōris *m* blood; bloodshed

cruppellāriī, -ōrum *mpl* mail-clad fighters

crūrifragius, -ī *and* **-iī** *m* one whose legs have been broken

crūs, -ūris *nt* leg, shin

crūsta, -ae *f* hard surface, crust; stucco; embossed *or* inlaid work

crūstulum, -ī *nt* small pastry

crūstum, -ī *nt* pastry

crux, -ucis *f* gallows, cross; (*fig*) torment; **abī in malam crucem** go and be hanged!

crypta, -ae *f* underground passage, grotto

cryptoporticus, -ūs *f* covered walk

crystallinus *adj* of crystal ♦ *ntpl* crystal vases

crystallum, -ī *nt*, **crystallus, -ī** *m* crystal

cubiculāris, cubiculārius *adj* of the bedroom ♦ *m* valet de chambre

cubiculum, -ī *nt* bedroom

cubīle, -is *nt* bed, couch; (*animals*) lair, nest; (*fig*) den

cubital, -ālis *nt* cushion

cubitālis *adj* a cubit long

cubitō, -āre *vi* to lie (*in bed*)

cubitum, -ī *nt* elbow; cubit

cubitus, -ūs *m* lying in bed

cubō, -āre, -uī, -itum *vi* to lie in bed; to recline at table; (*places*) to lie on a slope

cucullus, -ī *m* hood, cowl

cucūlus, -ī *m* cuckoo

cucumis, -eris *m* cucumber

cucurbita, -ae *f* gourd; cupping glass

cucurrī *perf of* **currō**

cūdō, -ere *vt* to beat, thresh; (*metal*) to forge; (*money*) to coin

cūiās, -tis *pron* of what country?, of what town?

cuicuimodī (*gen of* **quisquis** *and* **modus**) of whatever kind, whatever like

cūius *pron* (*interrog*) whose?; (*rel*) whose

culcita, -ae *f* mattress, pillow; eyepatch

cūleus *see* **culleus**

culex, -icis *m/f* gnat

culīna, -ae *f* kitchen; food

culleus, cūleus, -ī *m* leather bag for holding liquids; *a fluid measure*

culmen, -inis *nt* stalk; top, roof, summit; (*fig*) height, acme

culmus, -ī *m* stalk, straw

culpa, -ae *f* blame, fault; mischief; **in culpā sum, mea ~ est** I am at fault *or* to blame

culpātus *adj* blameworthy

culpitō, -āre *vt* to find fault with

culpō, -āre, -āvī, -ātum *vt* to blame, reproach

cultē *adv* in a refined manner

cultellus, -ī *m* small knife

culter, -rī *m* knife, razor

cultiō, -ōnis *f* cultivation

cultor, -ōris *m* cultivator, planter, farmer; inhabitant; supporter, upholder; worshipper

cultrīx, -īcis *f* inhabitant; (*fig*) nurse, fosterer

cultūra, -ae *f* cultivation, agriculture; (*mind*) care, culture; (*person*) courting

cultus¹ *ppp of* **colō** ♦ *adj* cultivated; (*dress*) well-dressed; (*mind*) polished, cultured ♦ *ntpl* cultivated land

cultus², -ūs *m* cultivation, care; (*mind*) training, culture; (*dress*) style, attire; (*way of life*)

refinement, civilization; (*gods*) worship; (*men*) honouring

culullus, -ī *m* goblet

cūlus, -ī *m* buttocks

cum¹ *prep* (*with abl*) with; **cum decimō** tenfold; **cum eō quod, cum eō ut** with the proviso that; **cum prīmīs** especially; **cum māgnā calamitāte cīvitātis** to the great misfortune of the community; **cum perīculō suō** at one's own peril

cum² *conj* (*time*) when, whenever, while, as, after, since; (*cause*) since, as, seeing that; (*concession*) although; (*condition*) if; (*contrast*) while, whereas; **multī annī sunt cum in aere meō est** for many years now he has been in my debt; **aliquot sunt annī cum vōs dēlēgī** it is now some years since I chose you; **cum māximē** just when; just then, just now; **cum prīmum** as soon as; **cum ... tum** not only ... but also; both ... and

Cūmae, -ārum *fpl* town near Naples (*famous for its Sibyl*)

Cūmaeānum, -āni *nt* Cicero's Cumaean residence

Cūmaeus, -ānus *adj see* **Cūmae**

cumba, cymba, -ae *f* boat, skiff

cumera, -ae *f* grain chest

cumīnum, -ī *nt* cumin

cumque, quomque *adv* -ever, -soever; at any time

cumulātē *adv* fully, abundantly

cumulātus *adj* increased; complete

cumulō, -āre, -āvī, -ātum *vt* to heap up; to amass, increase; to fill up, overload; (*fig*) to fill, overwhelm, crown, complete

cumulus, -ī *m* heap, mass; crowning addition, summit

cūnābula, -ōrum *ntpl* cradle

cūnae, -ārum *fpl* cradle

cunctābundus *adj* hesitant, dilatory

cunctāns, -antis *adj* dilatory, reluctant; sluggish, tough

cunctanter *adv* slowly

cunctātiō, -ōnis *f* delaying, hesitation

cunctātor, -ōris *m* loiterer; one given to cautious tactics (*esp Q Fabius Maximus*)

cunctor, -ārī, -ātus *vi* to linger, delay, hesitate; to move slowly

cūnctus *adj* the whole of; (*pl*) all together, all

cuneātim *adv* in the form of a wedge

cuneātus *adj* wedge-shaped

cuneus, -ī *m* wedge; (MIL) wedge-shaped formation of troops; (*theatre*) block of seats

cunīculus, -ī *m* rabbit; underground passage; (MIL) mine

cunque *see* **cumque**

cūpa, -ae *f* vat, tun

cupidē *adv* eagerly, passionately

Cupīdineus *adj see* **Cupīdō**

cupiditās, -ātis *f* desire, eagerness, enthusiasm; passion, lust; avarice, greed; ambition; partisanship

cupīdō, -inis *f* desire, eagerness; passion, lust; greed

Cupīdō, -inis *m* Cupid (*son of Venus*)

cupidus *adj* desirous, eager; fond, loving; passionate, lustful; greedy, ambitious; partial

cupiēns, -ēntis *pres p of* **cupiō ♦** *adj* eager, desirous

cupienter *adv see* **cupiēns**

cupiō, -ere, -īvī *and* **-iī, -ītum** *vt* to wish, desire, long for; (*with dat*) to wish well

cupītor, -ōris *m* desirer

cupītus *ppp of* **cupiō**

cuppēdia¹, -ae *f* fondness for delicacies

cuppēdia², -ōrum *ntpl* delicacies

cuppēdinārius, -ī *m* confectioner

cuppēdō, -inis *f* longing, passion

cuppes, -dis *adj* fond of delicacies

cupressētum, -ī *nt* cypress grove

cupresseus *adj* of cypress wood

cupressifer, -ī *adj* cypress-bearing

cupressus, -ī *f* cypress

cūr *adv* why?; (*indirect*) why, the reason for

cūra, -ae *f* care, trouble, pains (bestowed); anxiety, concern, sorrow (felt); attention (to), charge (of), concern (for); (MED) treatment, cure; (*writing*) work; (LAW) trusteeship; (*poet*) love; (*person*) mistress, guardian; ~ **est** I am anxious; **cūrae esse** be attended to, looked after

cūrābilis *adj* troublesome

cūralium, -ī *and* **-iī** *nt* red coral

cūrātē *adv* carefully

cūrātiō, -ōnis *f* charge, management; office; treatment, healing

cūrātor, -ōris *m* manager, overseer; (LAW) guardian

cūrātūra, -ae *f* dieting

cūrātus *adj* cared for; earnest, anxious

curculiō, -ōnis *m* weevil

curculiunculus, -ī *m* little weevil

Curēnsis *adj see* **Curēs**

Curēs, -ium *mpl* ancient Sabine town

Cūrētēs, -um *mpl attendants of Jupiter in Crete*

Cūrētis, -idis *adj* Cretan

cūria, -ae *f* earliest division of the Roman people; meeting-place of a curia; senate house; senate

cūriālis, -is *m* member of a curia

cūriātim *adv* by curia

cūriātus *adj* of the curiae; **comitia cūriāta** earliest Roman assembly

cūriō¹, -ōnis *m* president of a curia; ~ **māximus** head of all the curiae

cūriō², -ōnis *adj* emaciated

cūriōsē *adv* carefully; inquisitively

cūriōsitās, -ātis *f* curiosity

cūriōsus *adj* careful, thoughtful, painstaking; inquiring, inquisitive, officious; careworn

curis, -ītis *f* spear

cūrō, -āre, -āvī, -ātum *vt* to take care of, attend to; to bother about; (*with gerundive*) to get something done; (*with inf*) to take the trouble; (*with* **ut**) to see to it that; (*public life*) to be in charge of, administer; (MED) to treat, cure; (*money*) to pay, settle up; **aliud cūrā** never mind; **corpus/cutem** ~ take it easy; **prōdigia** ~ avert portents

curriculum, -ī *nt* running, race; course, lap; (*fig*) career; **curriculō** at full speed

currō, -ere, cucurrī, cursum *vi* to run; to hasten, fly ♦ *vt* to run through, traverse; **currentem incitāre** spur a willing horse

currus, -ūs *m* car, chariot; triumph; team of horses; ploughwheels

cursim *adv* quickly, at the double

cursitō, -āre *vi* to run about, fly hither and thither

cursō, -āre *vi* to run about

cursor, -ōris *m* runner, racer; courier

cursūra, -ae *f* running

cursus, -ūs *m* running, speed; passage, journey; course, direction; (*things*) movement, flow; (*fig*) rapidity, flow, progress; ~ **honōrum** succession of magistracies; ~ **rērum** course of events; **cursum tenēre** keep on one's course; **cursū** at a run; **māgnō cursū** at full speed

curtō, -āre *vt* to shorten

curtus *adj* short, broken off; incomplete

cūrūlis *adj* official, curule; **aedīlis** ~ patrician aedile; **sella** ~ magistrates' chair; **equī** ~ *horses provided for the games by the state*

curvāmen, -inis *nt* bend

curvātūra, -ae *f* curve

curvō, -āre, -āvī, -ātum *vt* to curve, bend, arch; (*fig*) to move

curvus *adj* bent, curved, crooked; (*person*) aged; (*fig*) wrong

cuspis, -dis *f* point; spear, javelin, trident, sting

custōdēla, -ae *f* care, guard

custōdia, -ae *f* watch, guard, care; (*person*) sentry, guard; (*place*) sentry's post, guardhouse; custody, confinement, prison; **lībera** ~ confinement in one's own house

custōdiō, -īre, -īvī *and* **-iī, -ītum** *vt* to guard, defend; to hold in custody, keep watch on; to keep, preserve, observe

custōs, -ōdis *m/f* guard, bodyguard, protector, protectress; jailer, warder; (MIL) sentry, spy; container

cutīcula, -ae *f* skin

cutis, -is *f* skin; **cutem cūrāre** take it easy

cyathissō, -āre *vi* to serve wine

cyathus, -ī *m* wine ladle; (*measure*) one-twelfth of a pint

cybaea, -ae *f* kind of merchant ship

Cybēbē, Cybelē, -ēs *f* Phrygian mother-goddess, Magna Mater

Cybelēius *adj see* **Cybēbē**

Cyclades, -um *fpl group of Aegean islands*

cyclas, -adis *f* formal dress with a border

cyclicus *adj* of the traditional epic stories

Cyclōpius *adj see* **Cyclōps**

Cyclōps, -is *m* one-eyed giant (*esp Polyphemus*)

cycnēus *adj* of a swan, swan's

cycnus, -ī *m* swan

Cydōnius *adj* Cretan ♦ *ntpl* quinces

cygnus *see* **cycnus**

cylindrus, -ī *m* cylinder; roller

Cyllēnē, -ēs *and* **-ae** *f* mountain in Arcadia

Cyllēnēus, Cyllēnis, Cyllēnius *adj see* **Cyllēnē**

Cyllēnius, -ī *m* Mercury

cymba *see* **cumba**

cymbalum, -ī *nt* cymbal

cymbium, -ī *and* -iī *nt* cup
Cynicē *adv* like the Cynics
Cynicus, -ī *m* a Cynic philosopher (*esp Diogenes*) ♦ *adj* Cynic
cynocephalus, -ī *m* dog-headed ape
Cynosūra, -ae *f* (constellation of) Ursa Minor
Cynosūris, -idis *adj see* **Cynosūra**
Cynthia, -iae *f* Diana
Cynthius, -ī *m* Apollo
Cynthus, -ī *m* hill in Delos (*birthplace of Apollo and Diana*)
cyparissus, -ī *f* cypress
Cypris, -idis *f* Venus
Cyprius *adj* Cyprian; copper
Cyprus, -ī *f* (island of) Cyprus (*famed for its copper and the worship of Venus*)
Cyrēnaeī, **Cyrēnaicī** *mpl* followers of Aristippus

Cyrēnaeus, **Cyrēnaicus**, **Cyrēnēnsis** *adj see* **Cyrēnē**
Cyrēnē, -ēs *f*, **Cyrēnae**, -ārum *fpl* town and province of N. Africa
Cyrnēus *adj* Corsican
Cȳrus, -ī *m* Persian king
Cytaeis, -idis *f* Medea
Cythēra, -ae *f* island S. of Greece (*famed for its worship of Venus*)
Cytherēa, -ēae, **Cytherēia**, -ēiae, **Cytherēis**, -ēidis *f* Venus
Cytherēus, **Cythēriacus** *adj* Cytherean; of Venus
cytisus, -ī *m/f* cytisus (a kind of clover)
Cyzicēnus *adj see* **Cyzicum**
Cyzicum, -ī *nt*, **Cyzicus**, -ī, **Cyzicos**, -ī *f* town on Sea of Marmora

Dd

Dăcī, -ōrum *mpl* Dacians (*a people on the lower Danube*)
Dăcia, -iae *f* the country of the Dacians (*now Romania*)
Dăcicus, -icī *m* gold coin of Domitian's reign
dactylicus *adj* dactylic
dactylus, -ī *m* dactyl
Daedalēus *adj see* **Daedalus**
Daedalus, -ī *m* mythical Athenian craftsman and inventor
daedalus *adj* artistic, skilful in creating; skilfully made, variegated
Dalmatae, -ārum *mpl* Dalmatians (*a people on the East coast of the Adriatic*)
Dalmatia, -iae *f* Dalmatia
Dalmaticus *adj see* **Dalmatia**
dāma, -ae *f* deer; venison
Damascēnus *adj see* **Damascus**
Damascus, -ī *f* Damascus
damma *f see* **dāma**
damnātiō, -ōnis *f* condemnation
damnātōrius *adj* condemnatory
damnātus *adj* criminal; miserable
damnificus *adj* pernicious
damnō, -āre, -āvī, -ātum *vt* to condemn, sentence; to procure the conviction of; (*heirs*) to oblige; to censure; **capitis/capite damnāre** condemn to death; **māiestātis damnāre, dē māiestāte damnāre** condemn for treason; **vōtī damnāre** oblige to fulfil a vow
damnōsē *adv* ruinously
damnōsus *adj* harmful, ruinous; spendthrift; wronged
damnum, -ī *nt* loss, harm, damage; (*LAW*) fine, damages; **~ facere** suffer loss
Danaē, -ēs *f* mother of Perseus
Danaēius *adj see* **Danaē**
Danaī, -ōrum *and* **-um** *mpl* the Greeks
Danaides, -idum *fpl* daughters of Danaus
Danaus¹, -ī *m* king of Argos and father of 50 daughters
Danaus² *adj* Greek
danīsta, -ae *m* moneylender
danīsticus *adj* moneylending
danō *see* **dō**
Dānuvius, -ī *m* upper Danube
Daphnē, -ēs *f* nymph changed into a laurel tree
Daphnis, -idis (*acc* **-im** *and* **-in**) *m* mythical Sicilian shepherd
dapinō, -āre *vt* to serve (*food*)
daps, dapis *f* religious feast; meal, banquet
dapsilis *adj* sumptuous, abundant

Dardania, -iae *f* Troy
Dardanidēs, -idae *m* Trojan (*esp Aeneas*)
Dardanus¹, -ī *m* son of Jupiter and ancestor of Trojan kings
Dardanus², Dardanius, Dardanis, -idis *adj* Trojan
Darēus, -ī *m* Persian king
datārius *adj* to give away
datātim *adv* passing from one to the other
datiō, -ōnis *f* right to give away; (*laws*) making
datō, -āre *vt* to be in the habit of giving
dator, -ōris *m* giver; (*sport*) bowler
Daulias, -adis *adj see* **Daulis**
Daulis, -dis *f* town in central Greece (*noted for the story of Procne and Philomela*)
Daunias, -iadis *f* Apulia
Daunius *adj* Rutulian; Italian
Daunus, -ī *m* legendary king of Apulia (*ancestor of Turnus*)
dē *prep* (*with abl*) (*movement*) down from, from; (*origin*) from, of, out of; (*time*) immediately after, in; (*thought, talk, action*) about, concerning; (*reason*) for, because of; (*imitation*) after, in accordance with; **dē industriā** on purpose; **dē integrō** afresh; **dē nocte** during the night; **diem dē diē** from day to day
dea, -ae *f* goddess
dealbō, -āre *vt* to whitewash, plaster
deambulātiō, -ōnis *f* walk
deambulō, -āre, -āvī, -ātum *vi* to go for a walk
deamō, -āre, -āvī, -ātum *vt* to be in love with; to be much obliged to
dearmātus *adj* disarmed
deartuō, -āre, -āvī, -ātum *vt* to dismember, ruin
deasciō, -āre *vt* to smooth with an axe; (*fig*) to cheat
dēbacchor, -ārī, -ātus *vi* to rage furiously
dēbellātor, -ōris *m* conqueror
dēbellō, -āre, -āvī, -ātum *vi* to bring a war to an end ♦ *vt* to subdue; to fight out
dēbeō, -ēre, -uī, -itum *vt* to owe; (*with inf*) to be bound, ought, should, must; to have to thank for, be indebted for; (*pass*) to be destined
dēbilis *adj* frail, weak
dēbilitās, -ātis *f* weakness, infirmity
dēbilitātiō, -ōnis *f* weakening
dēbilitō, -āre, -āvī, -ātum *vt* to cripple, disable; (*fig*) to paralyse, unnerve
dēbitiō, -ōnis *f* owing
dēbitor, -ōris *m* debtor

dēbitum, **-ī** nt debt

dēblaterō, **-āre** vt to blab

dēcantō, **-āre**, **-āvī**, **-ātum** vt to keep on repeating ♦ vi to stop singing

dēcēdō, **-ēdere**, **-essī**, **-essum** vi to withdraw, depart; to retire from a province (after term of office); to abate, cease, die; (rights) to give up, forgo; (fig) to go wrong, swerve (from duty); **viā dēcēdere** get out of the way

decem num ten

December, **-ris** adj of December ♦ m December

decempeda, **-ae** f ten-foot rule

decempedātor, **-ōris** m surveyor

decemplex, **-icis** adj tenfold

decemprīmī, **-ōrum** mpl civic chiefs of Italian towns

decemscalmus adj ten-oared

decemvirālis adj of the decemviri

decemvirātus, **-ūs** m office of decemvir

decemvirī, **-ōrum** and **-um** mpl commission of ten men (for public or religious duties)

decennis adj ten years'

decēns, **-entis** adj seemly, proper; comely, handsome

decenter adv with propriety

decentia, **-ae** f comeliness

dēceptus ppp of **dēcipiō**

dēcernō, **-ernere**, **-rēvī**, **-rētum** vt to decide, determine; to decree; to fight it out, decide the issue

dēcerpō, **-ere**, **-sī**, **-tum** vt to pluck off, gather; (fig) to derive, enjoy

dēcertātiō, **-ōnis** f deciding the issue

dēcertō, **-āre**, **-āvī**, **-ātum** vi to fight it out, decide the issue

dēcessiō, **-ōnis** f departure; retirement (from a province); deduction, disappearance

dēcessor, **-ōris** m retiring magistrate

dēcessus, **-ūs** m retirement (from a province); death; (tide) ebbing

decet, **-ēre**, **-uīt** vt, vi it becomes, suits; it is right, proper

dēcidō, **-ere**, **-ī** vi to fall down, fall off; to die; (fig) to fail, come down

dēcīdō, **-dere**, **-dī**, **-sum** vt to cut off; to settle, put an end to

deciēns, **deciēs** adv ten times

decimus, **decumus** adj tenth; **cum decimō** tenfold; **decimum** for the tenth time

dēcipiō, **-ipere**, **-ēpī**, **-eptum** vt to ensnare; to deceive, beguile, disappoint

dēcīsiō, **-ōnis** f settlement

dēcīsus ppp of **dēcīdō**

Decius[1], **-ī** m Roman plebeian name (esp P Decius Mus, father and son, who devoted their lives in battle)

Decius[2], **Deciānus** adj see **Decius**[1]

dēclāmātiō, **-ōnis** f loud talking; rhetorical exercise on a given theme

dēclāmātor, **-ōris** m apprentice in public speaking

dēclāmātōrius adj rhetorical

dēclāmitō, **-āre** vi to practise rhetoric; to bluster ♦ vt to practise pleading

dēclāmō, **-āre**, **-āvī**, **-ātum** vi to practise public speaking, declaim; to bluster

dēclārātiō, **-ōnis** f expression, making known

dēclārō, **-āre**, **-āvī**, **-ātum** vt to make known; to proclaim, announce, reveal, express, demonstrate

dēclīnātiō, **-ōnis** f swerving; avoidance; (RHET) digression; (GRAM) inflection

dēclīnō, **-āre**, **-āvī**, **-ātum** vt to turn aside, deflect; (eyes) to close; to evade, shun ♦ vi to turn aside, swerve; to digress

declive nt slope, decline

dēclīvis adj sloping, steep, downhill

dēclīvitās, **-ātis** f sloping ground

dēcocta, **-ae** f a cold drink

dēcoctor, **-ōris** m bankrupt

dēcoctus ppp of **dēcoquō** ♦ adj (style) ripe, elaborated

dēcōlō, **-āre** vi to run out; (fig) to fail

dēcolor, **-ōris** adj discoloured, faded; **~ aetās** a degenerate age

dēcolōrātiō, **-ōnis** f discolouring

dēcolōrō, **-āre**, **-āvī**, **-ātum** vt to discolour, deface

dēcoquō, **-quere**, **-xī**, **-ctum** vt to boil down; to cook ♦ vi to go bankrupt

decor, **-ōris** m comeliness, ornament, beauty

decorē adv becomingly, beautifully

decorō, **-āre**, **-āvī**, **-ātum** vt to adorn, embellish; (fig) to distinguish, honour

decōrum, **-ī** nt propriety

decōrus adj becoming, proper; beautiful, noble; adorned

dēcrepitus adj decrepit

dēcrēscō, **-scere**, **-vī**, **-tum** vi to decrease, wane, wear away; to disappear

dēcrētum, **-ī** nt decree, resolution; (PHILOS) doctrine

dēcrētus ppp of **dēcernō**

dēcrēvī perf **dēcernō**; **dēcrēscō**

decuma, **-ae** f tithe; provincial land tax; largesse

decumāna, **-ae** f wife of a tithe-collector

decumānus adj paying tithes; (MIL) of the 10th cohort or legion ♦ m collector of tithes; **decumānī decumānōrum** mpl men of the 10th legion; **porta decumāna** main gate of a Roman camp

decumātēs, **-ium** adj, pl subject to tithes

dēcumbō, **-mbere**, **-buī** vi to lie down; to recline at table; to fall (in fight)

decumus see **decimus**

decuria, **-ae** f group of ten; panel of judges; social club

decuriātiō, **-ōnis** f, **decuriātus**, **-ūs** m dividing into decuriae

decuriō[1], **-āre**, **-āvī**, **-ātum** vt to divide into decuriae or groups

decuriō[2], **-ōnis** m head of a decuria; (MIL) cavalry officer; senator of a provincial town or colony

dēcurrō, **-rrere**, **-currī** and **-rrī**, **-rsum** vt, vi to run down, hurry, flow, sail down; to traverse; (MIL) to parade, charge; (time) to pass through; (fig) to have recourse to

dēcursiō, **-ōnis** f military manoeuvre

dēcursus[1] ppp of **dēcurrō**

dēcursus[2], **-ūs** m descent, downrush; (MIL) manoeuvre, attack; (time) career

dēcurtātus – dēfundō

dēcurtātus *adj* mutilated

decus, -oris *nt* ornament, glory, beauty; honour, virtue; (*pl*) heroic deeds

dēcussō, -āre *vt* to divide crosswise

dēcutiō, -tere, -ssī, -ssum *vt* to strike down, shake off

dēdecet, -ēre, -uit *vt* it is unbecoming to, is a disgrace to

dēdecorō, -āre *vt* to disgrace

dēdecōrus *adj* dishonourable

dēdecus, -oris *nt* disgrace, shame; vice, crime

dedī *perf of* **dō**

dēdicātiō, -ōnis *f* consecration

dēdicō, -āre, -āvī, -ātum *vt* to consecrate, dedicate; to declare (*property in a census return*)

dēdidī *perf of* **dēdō**

dēdignor, -ārī, -ātus *vt* to scorn, reject

dēdiscō, -scere, -dicī *vt* to unlearn, forget

dēditīcius, -ī *and* **-iī** *m* one who has capitulated

dēditiō, -ōnis *f* surrender, capitulation

dēditus *ppp of* **dēdō** ♦ *adj* addicted, devoted; **dēditā operā** intentionally

dēdō, -ere, -idī, -itum *vt* to give up, yield, surrender; to devote

dēdoceō, -ēre *vt* to teach not to

dēdoleō, -ēre, -uī *vi* to cease grieving

dēdūcō, -ūcere, -ūxī, -uctum *vt* to bring down, lead away, deflect; (MIL) to lead, withdraw; (*bride*) to bring home; (*colony*) to settle; (*hair*) to comb out; (*important person*) to escort; (LAW) to evict, bring to trial; (*money*) to subtract; (*sail*) to unfurl; (*ship*) to launch; (*thread*) to spin out; (*writing*) to compose; (*fig*) to bring, reduce, divert, derive

dēductiō, -ōnis *f* leading off; settling a colony; reduction; eviction; inference

dēductor, -ōris *m* escort

dēductus *ppp of* **dēdūcō** ♦ *adj* finely spun

deerrō, -āre, -āvī, -ātum *vi* to go astray

deesse *infin of* **dēsum**

dēfaecō, -āre, -āvī, -ātum *vt* to clean; (*fig*) to make clear, set at ease

dēfatīgātiō, -ōnis *f* tiring out; weariness

dēfatīgō, -āre, -āvī, -ātum *vt* to tire out, exhaust

dēfatīscor *etc see* **dēfetīscor**

dēfectiō, -ōnis *f* desertion; failure, faintness; (ASTR) eclipse

dēfector, -ōris *m* deserter, rebel

dēfectus¹ *ppp of* **dēficiō** ♦ *adj* weak, failing

dēfectus², -ūs *m* failure; eclipse

dēfendō, -dere, -dī, -sum *vt* to avert, repel; to defend, protect; (LAW) to speak in defence, urge, maintain; (THEAT) to play (*a part*); **crīmen dēfendere** answer an accusation

dēfēnsiō, -ōnis *f* defence, speech in defence

dēfēnsitō, -āre *vt* to defend often

dēfēnsō, -āre *vt* to defend

dēfēnsor, -ōris *m* averter; defender, protector, guard

dēferō, -ferre, -tulī, -lātum *vt* to bring down, bring, carry; to bear away; (*power, honour*) to offer, confer; (*information*) to report; (LAW) to inform against, indict; to recommend (*for*

public services); **ad cōnsilium dēferre** take into consideration

dēfervēscō, -vēscere, -vī *and* **-buī** *vi* to cool down, calm down

dēfessus *adj* tired, exhausted

dēfetīgō *etc see* **dēfatīgō**

dēfetīscor, -tīscī, -ssus *vi* to grow weary

dēficiō, -icere, -ēcī, -ectum *vt, vi* to desert, forsake, fail; to be lacking, run short, cease; (ASTR) to be eclipsed; **animō dēficere** lose heart

dēfīgō, -gere, -xī, -xum *vt* to fix firmly; to drive in, thrust; (*eyes, mind*) to concentrate; (*fig*) to stupefy, astound; (*magic*) to bewitch

dēfingō, -ere *vt* to make, portray

dēfīniō, -īre, -īvī, -ītum *vt* to mark the limit of, limit; to define, prescribe; to restrict; to terminate

dēfīnītē *adv* precisely

dēfīnītiō, -ōnis *f* limiting, prescribing, definition

dēfīnītīvus *adj* explanatory

dēfīnītus *adj* precise

dēfīō, -ierī *vi* to fail

dēflagrātiō, -ōnis *f* conflagration

dēflagrō, -āre, -āvī, -ātum *vi* to be burned down, perish; to cool down, abate ♦ *vt* to burn down

dēflectō, -ctere, -xī, -xum *vt* to bend down, turn aside; (*fig*) to pervert ♦ *vi* to turn aside, deviate

dēfleō, -ēre, -ēvī, -ētum *vt* to lament bitterly, bewail ♦ *vi* to weep bitterly

dēflexus *ppp of* **dēflectō**

dēflōrēscō, -ēscere, -uī *vi* to shed blooms; (*fig*) to fade

dēfluō, -ere, -xī, -xum *vi* to flow down, float down; to fall, drop, droop; (*fig*) to come from, be derived; to flow past; (*fig*) to pass away, fail

dēfodiō, -ōdere, -ōdī, -ossum *vt* to dig, dig out; to bury; (*fig*) to hide away

dēfore *fut infin of* **dēsum**

dēfōrmis *adj* misshapen, disfigured, ugly; shapeless; (*fig*) disgraceful, disgusting

dēfōrmitās, -ātis *f* deformity, hideousness; baseness

dēfōrmō, -āre, -āvī, -ātum *vt* to form, sketch; to deform, disfigure; to describe; to mar, disgrace

dēfossus *ppp of* **dēfodiō**

dēfraudō, -āre *vt* to cheat, defraud; **genium dēfraudāre** deny oneself

dēfrēnātus *adj* unbridled

dēfricō, -āre, -uī, -ātum *and* **-tum** *vt* to rub down; (*fig*) to satirize

dēfringō, -ingere, -ēgī, -āctum *vt* to break off, break down

dēfrūdō *etc see* **dēfraudō**

dēfrutum, -ī *nt* new wine boiled down

dēfugiō, -ugere, -ūgī *vt* to run away from, shirk ♦ *vi* to flee

dēfuī *perf of* **dēsum**

dēfūnctus *ppa of* **dēfungor** ♦ *adj* discharged; dead

dēfundō, -undere, -ūdī, -ūsum *vt* to pour out

dēfungor, -ungī, -ūnctus vi (with abl) to discharge, have done with; to die

dēfutūrus fut p of **dēsum**

dēgener, -is adj degenerate, unworthy, base

dēgenerātum, -ātī nt degenerate character

dēgenerō, -āre, -āvī, -ātum vi to degenerate, deteriorate ◆ vt to disgrace

dēgerō, -ere vt to carry off

dēgō, -ere, -ī vt (time) to pass, spend; (war) wage ◆ vi to live

dēgrandinat it is hailing heavily

dēgravō, -āre vt to weigh down, overpower

dēgredior, -dī, -ssus vi to march down, descend, dismount

dēgrunniō, -īre vi to grunt hard

dēgustō, -āre vt to taste, touch; (fig) to try, experience

dehinc adv from here; from now, henceforth; then, next

dehīscō, -ere vi to gape, yawn

dehonestāmentum, -ī nt disfigurement

dehonestō, -āre vt to disgrace

dehortor, -ārī, -ātus vt to dissuade, discourage

Dēianīra, -ae f wife of Hercules

dēiciō, -icere, -iēcī, -iectum vt to throw down, hurl, fell; to overthrow, kill; (eyes) to lower, avert; (LAW) to evict; (MIL) to dislodge; (ship) to drive off its course; (hopes, honours) to foil, disappoint

dēiectiō, -ōnis f eviction

dēiectus¹ ppp of **dēiciō** ◆ adj low-lying; disheartened

dēiectus², -ūs m felling; steep slope

dēierō, -āre, -āvī, -ātum vi to swear solemnly

dein etc see **deinde**

deinceps adv successively, in order

deinde, dein adv from there, next; then, thereafter; next in order

Dēiotarus, -ī m king of Galatia (defended by Cicero)

Dēiphobus, -ī m son of Priam (second husband of Helen)

dēiungō, -ere vt to sever

dēiuvō, -āre vt to fail to help

dej- etc see **dei-**

dēlābor, -bī, -psus vi to fall down, fly down, sink; (fig) to come down, fall into

dēlacerō, -āre vt to tear to pieces

dēlāmentor, -ārī vt to mourn bitterly for

dēlāpsus ppa of **dēlābor**

dēlassō, -āre vt to tire out

dēlātiō, -ōnis f accusing, informing

dēlātor, -ōris m informer, denouncer

dēlectābilis adj enjoyable

dēlectāmentum, -ī nt amusement

dēlectātiō, -ōnis f delight

dēlectō, -āre vt to charm, delight, amuse

dēlēctus¹ ppp of **dēligō**

dēlēctus², -ūs m choice; see also **dīlēctus²**

dēlēgātiō, -ōnis f assignment

dēlēgī perf of **dēligō**

dēlēgō, -āre, -āvī, -ātum vt to assign, transfer, make over; to ascribe

dēlēnificus adj charming

dēlēnīmentum, -ī nt solace, allurement

dēlēniō, -īre, -īvī, -ītum vt to soothe, solace; to seduce, win over

dēlēnītor, -ōris m cajoler

dēleō, -ēre, -ēvī, -ētum vt to destroy, annihilate; to efface, blot out

Dēlia, -ae f Diana

Dēliacus adj of Delos

dēlīberābundus adj deliberating

dēlīberātiō, -ōnis f deliberating, consideration

dēlīberātīvus adj deliberative

dēlīberātor, -ōris m consulter

dēlīberātus adj determined

dēlīberō, -āre, -āvī, -ātum vt, vi to consider, deliberate, consult; to resolve, determine; **dēlīberārī potest** it is in doubt

dēlībō, -āre, -āvī, -ātum vt to taste, sip; to pick, gather; to detract from, mar

dēlībrō, -āre vt to strip the bark off

dēlibuō, -uere, -uī, -ūtum vt to smear, steep

dēlicātē adv luxuriously

dēlicātus adj delightful; tender, soft; voluptuous, spoiled, effeminate; fastidious

dēliciae, -ārum fpl delight, pleasure; whimsicalities, sport; (person) sweetheart, darling

dēliciolae, -ārum fpl darling

dēlicium, -ī and **-iī** nt favourite

dēlicō, -āre vt to explain

dēlictum, -ī nt offence, wrong

dēlicuus adj lacking

dēligō, -āre, -āvī, -ātum vt to tie up, make fast

dēligō, -igere, -ēgī, -ēctum vt to select, gather; to set aside

dēlingō, -ere vt to have a lick of

dēlīni- etc see **dēlēni-**

dēlinquō, -inquere, -īquī, -ictum vi to fail, offend, do wrong

dēliquēscō, -quēscere, -cuī vi to melt away; (fig) to pine away

dēliquiō, -ōnis f lack

dēlīrāmentum, -ī nt nonsense

dēlīrātiō, -ōnis f dotage

dēlīrō, -āre vi to be crazy, drivel

dēlīrus adj crazy

dēlitēscō, -ēscere, -uī vi to hide away, lurk; (fig) to skulk, take shelter under

dēlītigō, -āre vi to scold

Dēlius, -iacus adj see **Dēlos**

Delmatae see **Dalmatae**

Dēlos, -ī f sacred Aegean island (birthplace of Apollo and Diana)

Delphī, -ōrum mpl town in central Greece (famous for its oracle of Apollo); the Delphians

Delphicus adj see **Delphī**

delphīnus, -ī, delphīn, -is m dolphin

Deltōton, -ī nt (constellation) Triangulum

dēlubrum, -ī nt sanctuary, temple

dēluctō, -āre, dēluctor, -ārī vi to wrestle

dēlūdificō, -āre vt to make fun of

dēlūdō, -dere, -sī, -sum vt to dupe, delude

dēlumbis adj feeble

dēlumbō, -āre vt to enervate

dēmadēscō, -ēscere, -uī vi to be drenched

dēmandō, -āre vt to entrust, commit

dēmarchus, **-ī** *m* demarch *(chief of a village in Attica)*

dēmēns, **-entis** *adj* mad, foolish

dēmēnsum, **-ī** *nt* ration

dēmēnsus *ppa of* **dēmētior**

dēmenter *adv see* **dēmēns**

dēmentia, **-ae** *f* madness, folly

dēmentiō, **-īre** *vi* to rave

dēmereō, **-ēre**, **-uī**, **-itum**, **dēmereor**, **-ērī** *vt* to earn, deserve; to do a service to

dēmergō, **-gere**, **-sī**, **-sum** *vt* to submerge, plunge, sink; *(fig)* to overwhelm

dēmessus *ppp of* **dēmetō**

dēmētior, **-tīrī**, **-nsus** *vt* to measure out

dēmetō, **-tere**, **-ssuī**, **-ssum** *vt* to reap, harvest; to cut off

dēmigrātiō, **-ōnis** *f* emigration

dēmigrō, **-āre** *vi* to move, emigrate

dēminuō, **-uere**, **-uī**, **-ūtum** *vt* to make smaller, lessen, detract from; **capite dēminuere** deprive of citizenship

dēminūtiō, **-ōnis** *f* decrease, lessening; *(LAW)* right to transfer property; **capitis ~** loss of political rights

dēmīror, **-ārī**, **-ātus** *vt* to marvel at, wonder

dēmissē *adv* modestly, meanly

dēmissīcius *adj* flowing

dēmissiō, **-ōnis** *f* letting down; *(fig)* dejection

dēmissus *ppp of* **dēmittō** ♦ *adj* low-lying; drooping; humble, unassuming; dejected; *(origin)* descended

dēmītigō, **-āre** *vt* to make milder

dēmittō, **-ittere**, **-īsī**, **-issum** *vt* to let down, lower, sink; to send down, plunge; *(beard)* to grow; *(ship)* to bring to land; *(troops)* to move down; *(fig)* to cast down, dishearten, reduce, impress; **sē dēmittere** stoop; descend; be disheartened

dēmiūrgus, **-ī** *m* chief magistrate in a Greek state

dēmō, **-ere**, **-psī**, **-ptum** *vt* to take away, subtract

Dēmocriticus, **Dēmocritius**, **Dēmocritēus** *adj see* **Dēmocritus**

Dēmocritus, **-ī** *m* Greek philosopher *(author of the atomic theory)*

dēmōlior, **-īrī** *vt* to pull down, destroy

dēmōlītiō, **-ōnis** *f* pulling down

dēmōnstrātiō, **-ōnis** *f* pointing out, explanation

dēmōnstrātīvus *adj* *(RHET)* for display

dēmōnstrātor, **-ōris** *m* indicator

dēmōnstrō, **-āre**, **-āvī**, **-ātum** *vt* to point out; to explain, represent, prove

dēmorior, **-ī**, **-tuus** *vi* to die, pass away ♦ *vt* to be in love with

dēmoror, **-ārī**, **-ātus** *vi* to wait ♦ *vt* to detain, delay

dēmortuus *ppa of* **dēmorior**

Dēmosthenēs, **-is** *m* greatest Athenian orator

dēmoveō, **-ovēre**, **-ōvī**, **-ōtum** *vt* to remove, turn aside, dislodge

dēmpsī *perf of* **dēmō**

dēmptus *ppp of* **dēmō**

dēmūgītus *adj* filled with lowing

dēmulceō, **-cēre**, **-sī** *vt* to stroke

dēmum *adv* *(time)* at last, not till; *(emphasis)* just, precisely; **ibi ~** just there; **modo ~** only now; **nunc ~** now at last; **post ~** not till after; **tum ~** only then

dēmurmurō, **-āre** *vt* to mumble through

dēmūtātiō, **-ōnis** *f* change

dēmūtō, **-āre** *vt* to change, make worse ♦ *vi* to change one's mind

dēnārius, **-ī** *and* **-iī** *m* Roman silver coin

dēnārrō, **-āre** *vt* to relate fully

dēnāsō, **-āre** *vt* to take the nose off

dēnatō, **-āre** *vi* to swim down

dēnegō, **-āre**, **-āvī**, **ātum** *vt* to deny, refuse, reject ♦ *vi* to say no

dēnī, **-ōrum** *adj* ten each, in tens; ten; tenth

dēnicālis *adj* for purifying after a death

dēnique *adv* at last, finally; *(enumerating)* lastly, next; *(summing up)* in short, briefly; *(emphasis)* just, precisely

dēnōminō, **-āre** *vt* to designate

dēnōrmō, **-āre** *vt* to make irregular

dēnotō, **-āre**, **-āvī**, **-ātum** *vt* to point out, specify; to observe

dēns, **dentis** *m* tooth; ivory; prong, fluke

dēnsē *adv* repeatedly

dēnsō, **-āre**, **-āvī**, **-ātum**, **dēnseō**, **-ēre** *vt* to thicken; *(ranks)* to close

dēnsus *adj* thick, dense, close; frequent; *(style)* concise

dentālia, **-ium** *ntpl* ploughbeam

dentātus *adj* toothed; *(paper)* polished

dentiō, **-īre** *vi* to cut one's teeth; *(teeth)* to grow

dēnūbō, **-bere**, **-psī**, **-ptum** *vi* to marry, marry beneath one

dēnūdō, **-āre**, **-āvī**, **-ātum** *vt* to bare, strip; *(fig)* to disclose

dēnūntiātiō, **-ōnis** *f* intimation, warning

dēnūntiō, **-āre**, **-āvī**, **-ātum** *vt* to intimate, give notice of, declare; to threaten, warn; *(LAW)* to summon as witness

dēnuō *adv* afresh, again, once more

deonerō, **-āre** *vt* to unload

deorsum, **deorsus** *adv* downwards

deōsculor, **-ārī** *vt* to kiss warmly

dēpacīscor *etc see* **dēpecīscor**

dēpāctus *adj* driven in firmly

dēpāscō, **-scere**, **-vī**, **-stum**, **dēpāscor**, **dēpāscī** *vt* to feed on, eat up; *(fig)* to devour, destroy, prune away

dēpecīscor, **-īsci**, **-tus** *vt* to bargain for, agree about

dēpectō, **-ctere**, **-xum** *vt* to comb; *(comedy)* to flog

dēpectus *ppa of* **dēpecīscor**

dēpecūlātor, **-ōris** *m* embezzler

dēpecūlor, **-ārī**, **-ātus** *vt* to plunder

dēpellō, **-ellere**, **-ulī**, **-ulsum** *vt* to expel, remove, cast down; *(MIL)* to dislodge; *(infants)* to wean; *(fig)* to deter, avert

dēpendeō, **-ēre** *vi* to hang down, hang from; to depend on; to be derived

dēpendō, **-endere**, **-endī**, **-ēnsum** *vt* to weigh, pay up

dēperdō, **-ere**, **-idī**, **-itum** *vt* to lose completely, destroy, ruin

dēpereō, **-īre**, **-iī** vi to perish, be completely destroyed; to be undone ♦ vt to be hopelessly in love with

dēpexus ppp of **dēpectō**

dēpingō, **-ingere**, **-inxī**, **-ictum** vt to paint; (fig) to portray, describe

dēplangō, **-gere**, **-xī** vt to bewail frantically

dēplexus adj grasping

dēplōrābundus adj weeping bitterly

dēplōrō, **-āre**, **-āvī**, **-ātum** vi to weep bitterly ♦ vt to bewail bitterly, mourn; to despair of

dēpluit, **-ere** vi to rain down

dēpōnō, **-ōnere**, **-osuī**, **-ositum** vt to lay down; to set aside, put away, get rid of; to wager; to deposit, entrust, commit to the care of; (fig) to give up

dēpopulātiō, **-ōnis** f ravaging

dēpopulātor, **-ōris** m marauder

dēpopulor, **-ārī**, **-ātus**, **dēpopulō**, **-āre** vt to ravage, devastate; (fig) to waste, destroy

dēportō, **-āre**, **-āvī**, **-ātum** vt to carry down, carry off; to bring home (from a province); (LAW) to banish for life; (fig) to win

dēposcō, **-scere**, **-poscī** vt to demand, require, claim

dēpositum, **-ī** nt trust, deposit

dēpositus ppp of **dēpōnō** ♦ adj dying, dead, despaired of

dēprāvāte adv perversely

dēprāvātiō, **-ōnis** f distorting

dēprāvō, **-āre**, **-āvī**, **-ātum** vt to distort; (fig) to pervert, corrupt

dēprecābundus adj imploring

dēprecātiō, **-ōnis** f averting by prayer; imprecation, invocation; plea for indulgence

dēprecātor, **-ōris** m intercessor

dēprecor, **-ārī**, **-ātus** vt to avert (by prayer); deprecate, intercede for

dēprehendō, **dēprendō**, **-endere**, **-endī**, **-ēnsum** vt to catch, intercept; to overtake, surprise; to catch in the act, detect; (fig) to perceive, discover

dēprehēnsiō, **-ōnis** f detection

dēprehēnsus, **dēprēnsus** ppp of **dēprehendō**

dēpressī perf of **dēprimō**

dēpressus ppp of **dēprimō** ♦ adj low

dēprimō, **-imere**, **-essī**, **-essum** vt to press down, weigh down; to dig deep; (ship) to sink; (fig) to suppress, keep down

dēproelior, **-ārī** vi to fight it out

dēprōmō, **-ere**, **psī**, **-ptum** vt to fetch, bring out, produce

dēproperō, **-āre** vi to hurry up ♦ vt to hurry and make

depsō, **-ere** vt to knead

dēpudet, **-ēre**, **-uit** v impers not to be ashamed

dēpūgis adj thin-buttocked

dēpugnō, **-āre**, **-āvī**, **-ātum** vi to fight it out, fight hard

dēpulī perf of **dēpellō**

dēpulsiō, **-ōnis** f averting; defence

dēpulsō, **-āre** vt to push out of the way

dēpulsor, **-ōris** m repeller

dēpulsus ppp of **dēpellō**

dēpūrgō, **-āre** vt to clean

dēputō, **-āre** vt to prune; to consider, reckon

dēpȳgis etc see **dēpūgis**

dēque adv down

dērēctā, **dērēctē**, **dērēctō** adv straight

dērēctus ppp of **dērigō** ♦ adj straight, upright, at right angles; straightforward

dērelictiō, **-ōnis** f disregarding

dērelinquō, **-inquere**, **-īquī**, **-ictum** vt to abandon, forsake

dērepente adv suddenly

dērēpō, **-ere** vi to creep down

dēreptus ppp of **dēripiō**

dērīdeō, **-dēre**, **-sī**, **-sum** vt to laugh at, deride

dērīdiculum, **-ī** nt mockery, absurdity; object of derision

dērīdiculus adj laughable

dērigēscō, **-ēscere**, **-uī** vi to stiffen, curdle

dērigō, **-igere**, **-ēxī**, **-ēctum** vt to turn, aim, direct; (fig) to regulate

dēripiō, **-ipere**, **-ipuī**, **-eptum** vt to tear off, pull down

dērīsor, **-ōris** m scoffer

dērīsus¹ ppp of **dērīdeō**

dērīsus², **-ūs** m scorn, derision

dērīvātiō, **-ōnis** f diverting

dērīvō, **-āre**, **-āvī**, **-ātum** vt to lead off, draw off

dērogō, **-āre** vt (LAW) to propose to amend; (fig) to detract from

dērōsus adj gnawed away

dēruncinō, **-āre** vt to plane off; (comedy) to cheat

dēruō, **-ere**, **-ī**, **-tum** vt to demolish

dēruptus adj steep ♦ ntpl precipice

dēsaeviō, **-īre** vi to rage furiously; to cease raging

dēscendō, **-endere**, **-endī**, **-ēnsum** vi to come down, go down, descend, dismount; (MIL) to march down; (things) to fall, sink, penetrate; (fig) to stoop (to), lower oneself

dēscēnsiō, **-ōnis** f going down

dēscēnsus, **-ūs** m way down

dēscīscō, **-īscere**, **-īvī** and **-iī**, **-ītum** vi to desert, revolt; to deviate, part company

dēscrībō, **-bere**, **-psī**, **-ptum** vt to copy out; to draw, sketch; to describe; see also **dīscrībō**

dēscrīptiō, **-ōnis** f copy; drawing, diagram; description

dēscrīptus ppp of **dēscrībō**; see also **dīscrīptus**

dēsecō, **-āre**, **-uī**, **-tum** vt to cut off

dēserō, **-ere**, **-uī**, **-tum** vt to desert, abandon, forsake; (bail) to forfeit

dēsertor, **-ōris** m deserter

dēsertus ppp of **dēserō** ♦ adj desert, uninhabited ♦ ntpl deserts

dēserviō, **-īre** vi to be a slave (to), serve

dēses, **-idis** adj idle, inactive

dēsiccō, **-āre** vt to dry, drain

dēsideō, **-idēre**, **-ēdī** vi to sit idle

dēsīderābilis adj desirable

dēsīderātiō, **-ōnis** f missing

dēsīderium, **-ī** and **-iī** nt longing, sense of loss; want; petition; **mē ~ tenet urbis** I miss Rome

dēsīderō, **-āre**, **-āvī**, **-ātum** vt to feel the want of, miss; to long for, desire; (casualties) to lose

dēsidia, **-ae** f idleness, apathy

dēsidiōsē adv idly

dēsidiōsus *adj* lazy, idle; relaxing

dēsīdō, -īdere, -ēdī *vi* to sink, settle down; *(fig)* to deteriorate

dēsignātiō, -ōnis *f* specifying; election *(of magistrates)*

dēsignātor *etc see* **dissignātor**

dēsignātus *adj* elect

dēsignō, -āre, -āvī, -ātum *vt* to trace out; to indicate, define; *(POL)* to elect; *(art)* to depict

dēsiī *perf of* **dēsinō**

dēsiliō, -ilīre, -iluī, -ultum *vi* to jump down, alight

dēsinō, -nere, -ī *vt* to leave off, abandon ♦ *vi* to stop, desist; to end *(in)*

dēsipiēns, -ientis *adj* silly

dēsipientia, -ae *f* folly

dēsipiō, -ere *vi* to be stupid, play the fool

dēsistō, -istere, -titī, -titum *vi* to stop, leave off, desist

dēsitus *ppp of* **dēsinō**

dēsōlō, -āre, -āvī, -ātum *vt* to leave desolate, abandon

dēspectō, -āre *vt* to look down on, command a view of; to despise

dēspectus¹ *ppp of* **dēspiciō** ♦ *adj* contemptible

dēspectus², -ūs *m* view, prospect

dēspēranter *adv* despairingly

dēspērātiō, -ōnis *f* despair

dēspērātus *adj* despaired of, hopeless; desperate, reckless

dēspērō, -āre, -āvī, -ātum *vt, vi* to despair, give up hope of

dēspexī *perf of* **dēspiciō**

dēspicātiō, -ōnis *f* contempt

despicātus *adj* despised, contemptible

dēspicātus, -ūs *m* contempt

dēspicientia, -ae *f* contempt

dēspiciō, -icere, -exī, -ectum *vt* to look down on; to despise ♦ *vi* to look down

dēspoliātor, -ōris *m* robber

dēspoliō, -āre *vt* to rob, plunder

dēspondeō, -ondēre, -ondī *and* **-opondī, -ōnsum** *vt* to pledge, promise; to betroth; to devote; to give up, despair of; **animum** **dēspondēre** despair

dēspūmō, -āre *vt* to skim off

dēspuō, -ere *vi* to spit on the ground ♦ *vt* to reject

dēsquāmō, -āre *vt* to scale, peel

dēstillō, -āre *vi* to drop down ♦ *vt* to distil

dēstimulō, -āre *vt* to run through

dēstinātiō, -ōnis *f* resolution, appointment

dēstinātus *adj* fixed, decided

dēstinō, -āre, -āvī, -ātum *vt* to make fast; to appoint, determine, resolve; *(archery)* to aim at; *(fig)* to intend to buy ♦ *nt ppp* mark; intention; **dēstinātum est mihi** I have decided

dēstitī *perf of* **dēsistō**

dēstituō, -uere, -uī, -ūtum *vt* to set apart, place; to forsake, leave in the lurch

dēstitūtiō, -ōnis *f* defaulting

dēstitūtus *ppp of* **dēstituō**

dēstrictus *ppp of* **dēstringō** ♦ *adj* severe

dēstringō, -ingere, -inxī, -ictum *vt* *(leaves)* to strip; *(body)* to rub down; *(sword)* to draw; to graze, skim; *(fig)* to censure

dēstruō, -ere, -xī, -ctum *vt* to demolish; to destroy

dēsubitō *adv* all of a sudden

dēsūdāscō, -ere *vi* to sweat all over

dēsūdō, -āre *vi* to exert oneself

dēsuēfactus *adj* unaccustomed

dēsuētūdō, -inis *f* disuse

dēsuētus *adj* unaccustomed, unused

dēsultor, -ōris *m* circus rider; *(fig)* fickle lover

dēsultūra, -ae *f* jumping down

dēsum, deesse, -fuī *vi* to be missing, fail, fail in one's duty

dēsūmō, -ere, -psī, -ptum *vt* to select

dēsuper *adv* from above

dēsurgō, -ere *vi* to rise

dētegō, -egere, -ēxī, -ēctum *vt* to uncover, disclose; *(fig)* to reveal, detect

dētendō, -endere, -ēnsum *vt* *(tent)* to strike

dētentus *ppp of* **dētineō**

dētergō, -gere, -sī, -sum *vt* to wipe away, clear away; to clean; to break off

dēterior, -ōris *adj* lower; inferior, worse

dēterius *adv* worse

dēterminātiō, -ōnis *f* boundary, end

dēterminō, -āre, -āvī, -ātum *vt* to bound, limit; to settle

dēterō, -erere, -rīvī, -rītum *vt* to rub, wear away; *(style)* to polish; *(fig)* to weaken

dēterreō, -ēre, -uī, -itum *vt* to frighten away; to deter, discourage, prevent

dētersus *ppp of* **dētergō**

dētestābilis *adj* abominable

dētestātiō, -ōnis *f* execration, curse; averting

dētestor, -ārī, -ātus *vt* to invoke, invoke against; to curse, execrate; to avert, deprecate

dētexō, -ere, -uī, -tum *vt* to weave, finish weaving; *(comedy)* to steal; *(fig)* to describe

dētineō, -inēre, -inuī, -entum *vt* to hold back, detain; to keep occupied

dētondeō, -ondēre, -ondī, -ōnsum *vt* to shear off, strip

dētonō, -āre, -uī *vi* to cease thundering

dētorqueō, -quēre, -sī, -tum *vt* to turn aside, direct; to distort, misrepresent

dētractātiō, -ōnis *f* declining

dētractiō, -ōnis *f* removal, departure

dētractō *etc see* **dētrectō**

dētractus *ppp of* **dētrahō**

dētrahō, -here, -xī, -ctum *vt* to draw off, take away, pull down; to withdraw, force to leave; to detract, disparage

dētrectātor, -ōris *m* disparager

dētrectō, -āre, -āvī, -ātum *vt* to decline, shirk; to detract from, disparage

dētrīmentōsus *adj* harmful

dētrīmentum, -ī *nt* loss, harm; *(MIL)* defeat; **~ capere** suffer harm

dētrītus *ppp of* **dēterō**

dētrūdō, -dere, -sī, -sum *vt* to push down, thrust away; to dislodge, evict; to postpone; *(fig)* to force

dētruncō, -āre, -āvī, -ātum *vt* to cut off, behead, mutilate

dētrūsus *ppp of* **dētrūdō**

dēturbō, -āre, -āvī, -ātum *vt* to dash down, pull down; *(fig)* to cast down, deprive

Deucaliōn, -ōnis *m* son of Prometheus (survivor of the Flood)

Deucaliōnēus *adj see* **Deucaliōn**

deūnx, -cis *m* eleven twelfths

deūrō, -rere, -ssī, -stum *vt* to burn up; to frost

deus, -ī *(voc* **deus**, *pl* **dī, deos, deum, dis)** *m* god; **dī meliōra** Heaven forbid!; **dī tē ament** bless you!

deūstus *ppp of* **deūrō**

deūtor, -ī *vi* to maltreat

dēvastō, -āre *vt* to lay waste

dēvehō, -here, -xī, -ctum *vt* to carry down, convey; *(pass)* to ride down, sail down

dēvellō, -ellere, -ellī *and* **-olsī, -ulsum** *vt* to pluck, pull out

dēvēlō, -āre *vt* to unveil

dēveneror, -ārī *vt* to worship; to avert by prayers

dēveniō, -enīre, -ēnī, -entum *vi* to come, reach, fall into

dēverberō, -āre, -āvī, -ātum *vt* to thrash soundly

dēversor¹, -ārī *vi* to lodge, stay *(as guest)*

dēversor², -ōris *m* guest

dēversōriolum, -ī *nt* small lodging

dēversōrium, -ī *and* **-iī** *nt* inn, lodging

dēversōrius *adj* for lodging

dēverticulum, -ī *nt* by-road, by-pass; digression; lodging place; *(fig)* refuge

dēvertō, -tere, -tī, -sum *vi* to turn aside, put up; to have recourse to; to digress

dēvertor, -tī, -versus *vi see* **dēvertō**

dēvexus *adj* sloping, going down, steep

dēvinciō, -cīre, -xī, -ctum *vt* to tie up; *(fig)* to bind, lay under an obligation

dēvincō, -incere, -īcī, -ictum *vt* to defeat completely, win the day

dēvītātiō, -ōnis *f* avoiding

dēvītō, -āre *vt* to avoid

dēvius *adj* out of the way, devious; *(person)* solitary, wandering off the beaten track; *(fig)* inconstant

dēvocō, -āre, -āvī, -ātum *vt* to call down, fetch; to entice away

dēvolō, -āre *vi* to fly down

dēvolvō, -vere, -vī, -ūtum *vt* to roll down, fall; *(wool)* to spin off

dēvorō, -āre, -āvī, -ātum *vt* to swallow, gulp down; to engulf, devour; *(money)* to squander; *(tears)* to repress; *(trouble)* to endure patiently

dēvors-, dēvort- *see* **dēvers-, dēvert-**

dēvortia, -ōrum *ntpl* byways

dēvōtiō, -ōnis *f* devoting; *(magic)* spell

dēvōtō, -āre *vt* to bewitch

dēvōtus *ppp of* **dēvoveō** ♦ *adj* faithful; accursed

dēvoveō, -ovēre, -ōvī, -ōtum *vt* to devote, vow, dedicate; to give up; to curse; to bewitch

dēvulsus *ppp of* **dēvellō**

dextella, -ae *f* little right hand

dexter, -erī *and* **-rī** *adj* right, right-hand; handy, skilful; favourable

dexteritās, -ātis *f* adroitness

dextrā *prep (with acc)* on the right of

dextra *f* right hand, right-hand side; hand; pledge of friendship

dextrē *(compar* **-erius)** *adv* adroitly

dextrōrsum, dextrōrsus, dextrōvorsum *adv* to the right

dī *pl of* **deus**

diabathrārius, -ī *and* **-iī** *m* slipper maker

diabolus, -ī *m* devil

diāconus, -ī *m* (ECCL) deacon

diadēma, -tis *nt* royal headband, diadem

diaeta, -ae *f* diet; living room

dialectica, -ae, dialecticē, -ēs *f* dialectic, logic ♦ *ntpl* logical questions

dialecticē *adv* dialectically

dialecticus *adj* dialectical ♦ *m* logician

Diālis *adj* of Jupiter ♦ *m* high priest of Jupiter

dialogus, -ī *m* dialogue, conversation

Diāna, -ae *f* virgin goddess of hunting (also identified with the moon and Hecate, and patroness of childbirth)

Diānius *adj* of Diana ♦ *nt* sanctuary of Diana

diāria, -ōrum *ntpl* daily allowance of food or pay

dibaphus, -ī *f* Roman state robe

dica, -ae *f* lawsuit

dicācitās, -ātis *f* raillery, repartee

dicāculus *adj* pert

dicātiō, -ōnis *f* declaration of citizenship

dicāx, -ācis *adj* witty, smart

dichorēus, -ī *m* double trochee

diciō, -ōnis *f* power, sway, authority

dicis causā for the sake of appearance

dicō, -āre, -āvī, -ātum *vt* to dedicate, consecrate; to deify; to devote, give over

dīcō, -cere, -xī, dictum *vt* to say, tell; to mention, mean, call, name; to pronounce; (RHET) to speak, deliver; (LAW) to plead; *(poetry)* to describe, celebrate; *(official)* to appoint; *(time, place)* to settle, fix ♦ *vi* to speak (in public); **causam dīcere** plead; **iūs dīcere** deliver judgment; **sententiam dīcere** vote; ~ namely; **dīxī** I have finished; **dictum factum** no sooner said than done

dicrotum, -ī *nt* bireme

Dictaeus *adj* Cretan

dictamnus, -ī *f* dittany (a kind of wild marjoram)

dictāta, -ōrum *ntpl* lessons, rules

dictātor, -ōris *m* dictator

dictātōrius *adj* dictator's

dictātūra, -ae *f* dictatorship

Dictē, -ēs *f* mountain in Crete (where Jupiter was brought up)

dictiō, -ōnis *f* speaking, declaring; style, expression, oratory; *(oracle)* response

dictitō, -āre *vt* to keep saying, assert; to plead often

dictō, -āre, -āvī, -ātum *vt* to say repeatedly; to dictate; to compose

dictum, -ī *nt* saying, word; proverb; bon mot, witticism; command

dictus *ppp of* **dīcō**

Dictynna, -ae *f* Britomartis; Diana

Dictynnaeus *adj see* **Dictynna**

didicī *perf of* **discō**

Dīdō, -ūs *and* **-ōnis** *(acc* **-ō)** *f* Queen of Carthage

dīdō, -ere, -idī, -itum *vt* to distribute, broadcast

dīdūcō, -ūcere, -ūxī, -uctum *vt* to separate, split, open up; (*MIL*) to disperse; (*fig*) to part, divide

diēcula, -ae *f* one little day

diērēctus *adj* crucified; **abī ~** go and be hanged

diēs, -ēī *m/f* day; set day (*usu fem*); a day's journey; (*fig*) time; **~ meus** my birthday; **diem dīcere** impeach; **diem obīre** die; **diem dē diē, diem ex diē** from day to day; **in diem** to a later day; for today; **in diēs** daily

Diēspiter, -ris *m* Jupiter

diffāmō, -āre, -āvī, -ātum *vt* to divulge; to malign

differentia, -ae *f* difference, diversity; species

differitās, -ātis *f* difference

differō, -erre, distulī, dīlātum *vt* to disperse; to divulge, publish; (*fig*) to distract, disquiet; (*time*) to put off, delay ♦ *vi* to differ, be distinguished

differtus *adj* stuffed, crammed

difficilis *adj* difficult; (*person*) awkward, surly

difficiliter *adv* with difficulty

difficultās, -ātis *f* difficulty, distress, hardship; surliness

difficulter *adv* with difficulty

diffīdēns, -entis *adj* nervous

diffīdenter *adv* without confidence

diffīdentia, -ae *f* mistrust, diffidence

diffīdō, -dere, -sus *vi* to distrust, despair

diffindō, -ndere, -dī, -ssum *vt* to split, open up; (*fig*) to break off

diffingō, -ere *vt* to remake

diffissus *ppp of* **diffindō**

diffisus *ppa of* **diffīdō**

diffiteor, -ērī *vt* to disown

diffluēns, -entis *adj* (*RHET*) loose

diffluō, -ere *vi* to flow away; to melt away; (*fig*) to wallow

diffringō, -ere *vt* to shatter

diffugiō, -ugere, -ūgī *vi* to disperse, disappear

diffugium, -ī *and* **-iī** *nt* dispersion

diffunditō, -āre *vt* to pour out, waste

diffundō, -undere, -ūdī, -ūsum *vt* to pour off; to spread, diffuse; to cheer, gladden

diffūsē *adv* expansively

diffūsilis *adj* diffusive

diffūsus *ppp of* **diffundō** ♦ *adj* spreading; (*writing*) loose

Dīgentia, -ae *f* tributary of the Anio (near Horace's villa)

dīgerō, -rere, -ssī, -stum *vt* to divide, distribute; to arrange, set out; to interpret

dīgestiō, -ōnis *f* (*RHET*) enumeration

dīgestus *ppp of* **dīgerō**

digitulus, -ī *m* little finger

digitus, -ī *m* finger; toe; inch; (*pl*) skill in counting; **digitum porrigere, digitum prōferre** take the slightest trouble; **digitum trānsversum nōn discēdere** not swerve a finger's breadth; **attingere caelum digitō** reach the height of happiness; **licērī digitō** bid at an auction; **mōnstrārī digitō** be a celebrity; **extrēmī digitī, summī digitī** the fingertips; **concrepāre digitīs** snap the fingers

dīgladior, -ārī *vi* to fight fiercely

dignātiō, -ōnis *f* honour, dignity

dignē *adv see* **dignus**

dignitās, -ātis *f* worth, worthiness; dignity, rank, position; political office

dignō, -āre *vt* to think worthy

dignor, -ārī *vt* to think worthy; to deign

dīgnōscō, -ere, -ōvī *vt* to distinguish

dignus *adj* worth, worthy; (*things*) fitting, proper

dīgredior, -dī, -ssus *vi* to separate, part; to deviate, digress

dīgressiō, -ōnis *f* parting; deviation, digression

dīgressus[1] *ppa of* **dīgredior**

dīgressus[2]**, -ūs** *m* parting

dīiūdicātiō, -ōnis *f* decision

dīiūdicō, -āre *vt* to decide; to discriminate

dīiun- *etc see* **disiun-**

dīlābor, -bī, -psus *vi* to dissolve, disintegrate; to flow away; (*troops*) to disperse; (*fig*) to decay, vanish

dīlacerō, -āre *vt* to tear to pieces

dīlāminō, -āre *vt* to split in two

dīlaniō, -āre, -āvī, -ātum *vt* to tear to shreds

dīlapidō, -āre *vt* to demolish

dīlāpsus *ppa of* **dīlābor**

dīlargior, -īrī *vt* to give away liberally

dīlātiō, -ōnis *f* putting off, adjournment

dīlātō, -āre, -āvī, -ātum *vt* to expand; (*pronunciation*) to broaden

dīlātor, -ōris *m* procrastinator

dīlātus *ppp of* **differō**

dīlaudō, -āre *vt* to praise extravagantly

dīlēctus[1] *ppp of* **dīligō** ♦ *adj* beloved

dīlēctus[2]**, -ūs** *m* selection, picking; (*MIL*) levy; **dīlēctum habēre** hold a levy, recruit

dīlēxī *perf of* **dīligō**

dīligēns, -entis *adj* painstaking, conscientious, attentive (to); thrifty

dīligenter *adv see* **dīligēns**

dīligentia, -ae *f* carefulness, attentiveness; thrift

dīligō, -igere, -ēxī, -ēctum *vt* to prize especially, esteem, love

dīlōrīcō, -āre *vt* to tear open

dīlūceō, -ēre *vi* to be evident

dīlūcēscit, -cēscere, -xit *vi* to dawn, begin to grow light

dīlūcidē *adv see* **dīlūcidus**

dīlūcidus *adj* clear, distinct

dīlūculum, -ī *nt* dawn

dīlūdium, -ī *and* **-iī** *nt* interval

dīluō, -uere, -uī, -ūtum *vt* to wash away, dissolve, dilute; to explain; (*fig*) to weaken, do away with

dīluviēs, -iēī *f*, **dīluvium, -ī** *and* **-iī** *nt* flood, deluge

dīluviō, -āre *vt* to inundate

dīmānō, -āre *vi* to spread abroad

dīmēnsiō, -ōnis *f* measuring

dīmēnsus *adj* measured

dīmētior, -tīrī, -nsus *vt* to measure out

dīmētō, -āre, dīmētor, -ārī vt to mark out

dīmicātiō, -ōnis f fighting, struggle

dīmicō, -āre, -āvī, -ātum vi to fight, struggle, contend

dīmidiātus adj half, halved

dīmidius adj half ♦ nt half

dīmissiō, -ōnis f sending away; discharging

dīmissus ppp of **dīmittō**

dīmittō, -ittere, -īsī, -issum vt to send away, send round; to let go, lay down; (meeting) to dismiss; (MIL) to disband, detach; (fig) to abandon, forsake

dimminuō, -ere vt to dash to pieces

dīmoveō, -ovēre, -ōvī, -ōtum vt to part, separate; to disperse; to entice away

Dindymēnē, -ēnēs f Cybele

Dindymus, -ī m mountain in Mysia (sacred to Cybele)

dīnōscō see **dīgnōscō**

dīnumerātiō, -ōnis f reckoning up

dīnumerō, -āre vt to count, reckon up; to pay out

diōbolāris adj costing two obols

dioecēsis, -is f district; (ECCL) diocese

dioecētēs, -ae m treasurer

Diogenēs, -is m famous Cynic philosopher; a Stoic philosopher

Diomēdēs, -is m Greek hero at the Trojan War

Diomēdēus adj see **Diomēdēs**

Diōnaeus adj see **Diōnē**

Diōnē, -ēs, Diōna, -ae f mother of Venus; Venus

Diōnȳsia, -iōrum ntpl Greek festival of Bacchus

Diōnȳsius, -ī m tyrant of Syracuse

Diōnȳsus, -ī m Bacchus

diōta, -ae f a two-handled wine jar

diplōma, -tis nt letter of recommendation

Dipylon, -ī nt Athenian gate

Dircaeus adj Boeotian

Dircē, -ēs f famous spring in Boeotia

dīrēctus ppp of **dīrigō** ♦ adj straight; straightforward, simple; see also **dērēctus**

dīrēmī perf of **dirimō**

diremptus' ppp of **dirimō**

diremptus², -ūs m separation

dīreptiō, -ōnis f plundering

dīreptor, -ōris m plunderer

dīreptus ppp of **dīripiō**

dīrēxī perf of **dīrigō**

dīribeō, -ēre vt to sort out (votes taken from ballot-boxes)

dīribitiō, -ōnis f sorting

dīribitor, -ōris m ballot-sorter

dīrigō, -igere, -ēxī, -ēctum vt to put in line, arrange; see also **dērigō**

dirimō, -imere, -ēmī, -emptum vt to part, divide; to interrupt, break off; to put an end to

dīripiō, -ipere, -ipuī, -eptum vt to tear in pieces; to plunder, ravage; to seize; (fig) to distract

dīritās, -ātis f mischief, cruelty

dīrumpō, disrumpō, -umpere, -ūpī, -uptum vt to burst, break in pieces; (fig) to break off; (pass) to burst (with passion)

dīruō, -ere, -ī, -tum vt to demolish; to scatter; **aere dīrutus** having one's pay stopped

dīruptus ppp of **dīrumpō**

dīrus adj ominous, fearful; (person) dread, terrible ♦ fpl bad luck; the Furies ♦ ntpl terrors

dīrutus ppp of **dīruō** ♦ adj bankrupt

Dīs, Dītis m Pluto

dīs, dītis adj rich

discēdō, -ēdere, -ēssī, -essum vi to go away, depart; to part, disperse; (MIL) to march away; (result of battle) to come off; (POL) to go over (to a different policy); to pass away, disappear; to leave out of consideration; **ab signīs discēdere** break the ranks; **victor discēdere** come off best

disceptātiō, -ōnis f discussion, debate

disceptātor, -ōris m, **disceptātrīx, -rīcis** f arbitrator

disceptō, -āre vt to debate, discuss; (LAW) to decide

discernō, -ernere, -rēvī, -rētum vt to divide, separate; to distinguish between

discerpō, -ere, -sī, -tum vt to tear apart, disperse; (fig) to revile

discessiō, -ōnis f separation, departure; (senate) division

discessus, -ūs m parting; departure; marching away

discidium, -ī and **-iī** nt disintegration; separation, divorce; discord

discīdō, -ere vt to cut in pieces

discinctus ppp of **discingō** ♦ adj ungirt; negligent; dissolute

discindō, -ndere, -dī, -ssum vt to tear up, cut open

discingō, -gere, -xī, -ctum vt to ungird

disciplīna, -ae f teaching, instruction; learning, science, school, system; training, discipline; habits

discipulus, -ī m, **discipula, -ae** f pupil, apprentice

discissus ppp of **discindō**

disclūdō, -dere, -sī, -sum vt to keep apart, separate out

discō, -ere, didicī vt to learn, be taught, be told

discolor, -ōris adj of a different colour; variegated; different

discondūcit it is not worthwhile

disconveniō, -īre vi to disagree, be inconsistent

discordābilis adj disagreeing

discordia, -ae f discord, disagreement

discordiōsus adj seditious

discordō, -āre vi to disagree, quarrel; to be unlike

discors, -dis adj discordant, at variance; inconsistent

discrepantia, -ae f disagreement

discrepātiō, -ōnis f dispute

discrepitō, -āre vi to be quite different

discrepō, -āre, -uī vi to be out of tune; to disagree, differ; to be disputed

discrētus ppp of **discernō**

dīscrībō, -bere, -psī, -ptum vt to distribute, apportion, classify

discrīmen, -inis *nt* interval, dividing line; distinction, difference; turning point, critical moment; crisis, danger

discrīminō, -āre *vt* to divide

dīscrīptē *adv* in good order

dīscrīptiō, -ōnis *f* apportioning, distributing

dīscrīptus *ppp of* **dīscrībō ♦** *adj* secluded; well-arranged

discruciō, -āre *vt* to torture; (*fig*) to torment, trouble

discumbō, -mbere, -buī, -bitum *vi* to recline at table; to go to bed

discupiō, -ere *vi* to long

discurrō, -rrere, -currī *and* **-rrī, -rsum** *vi* to run about, run different ways

discursus, -ūs *m* running hither and thither

discus, -ī *m* quoit

discussus *ppp of* **discutiō**

discutiō, -tere, -ssī, -ssum *vt* to dash to pieces, smash; to scatter; to dispel

disertē, disertim *adv* distinctly; eloquently

disertus *adj* fluent, eloquent; explicit

disiciō, -icere, -iēcī, -iectum *vt* to scatter, cast asunder; to break up, destroy; (*MIL*) to rout

disiectō, -āre *vt* to toss about

disiectus¹ *ppp of* **disiciō**

disiectus², -ūs *m* scattering

disiūnctiō, -ōnis *f* separation, differing; (*LOGIC*) statement of alternatives; (*RHET*) a sequence of short co-ordinate clauses

disiūnctius *adv* rather in the manner of a dilemma

disiūnctus *ppp of* **disiungō ♦** *adj* distinct, distant, removed; (*speech*) disjointed; (*LOGIC*) opposite

disiungō, -ungere, -ūnxī, -ūnctum *vt* to unyoke; to separate, remove

dispālēscō, -ere *vi* to be noised abroad

dispandō, -āndere, -andī, -ānsum *and* **-essum** *vt* to spread out

dispār, -aris *adj* unlike, unequal

disparilis *adj* dissimilar

disparō, -āre, -āvī, -ātum *vt* to segregate

dispart- *etc see* **dispert-**

dispectus *ppp of* **dispiciō**

dispellō, -ellere, -ulī, -ulsum *vt* to scatter, dispel

dispendium, -ī *and* **-iī** *nt* expense, loss

dispennō *etc see* **dispandō**

dispēnsātiō, -ōnis *f* management, stewardship

dispēnsātor, -ōris *m* steward, treasurer

dispēnsō, -āre, -āvī, -ātum *vi* to weigh out, pay out; to manage, distribute; (*fig*) to regulate

dispercutiō, -ere *vt* to dash out

disperdō, -ere, -idī, -itum *vt* to ruin, squander

dispereō, -īre, -iī *vi* to go to ruin, be undone

dispergō, -gere, -sī, -sum *vt* to disperse, spread over, space out

dispersē *adv* here and there

dispersus *ppp of* **dispergō**

dispertiō, -īre, -īvī, -ītum, dispertior, -īrī *vt* to apportion, distribute

dispertītiō, -ōnis *f* division

dispessus *ppp of* **dispandō**

dispiciō, -icere, -exī, -ectum *vt* to see clearly, see through; to distinguish, discern; (*fig*) to consider

displiceō, -ēre *vi* (*with dat*) to displease; **sibi displicēre** be in a bad humour

displōdō, -dere, -sī, -sum *vt* to burst with a crash

dispōnō, -ōnere, -osuī, -ositum *vt* to set out, arrange; (*MIL*) to station

dispositē *adv* methodically

dispositiō, -ōnis *f* arrangement

dispositūra, -ae *f* arrangement

dispositus¹ *ppp of* **dispōnō ♦** *adj* orderly

dispositus², -ūs *m* arranging

dispudet, -ēre, -uit *v impers* to be very ashamed

dispulsus *ppp of* **dispellō**

disputātiō, -ōnis *f* argument

disputātor, -ōris *m* debater

disputō, -āre, -āvī, -ātum *vt* to calculate; to examine, discuss

disquīrō, -ere *vt* to investigate

disquīsītiō, -ōnis *f* inquiry

disrumpō *etc see* **dīrumpō**

dissaepiō, -īre, -sī, -tum *vt* to fence off, separate off

dissaeptum, -ī *nt* partition

dissāvior, -ārī *vt* to kiss passionately

dissēdī *perf of* **dissideō**

dissēminō, -āre *vt* to sow, broadcast

dissēnsiō, -ōnis *f* disagreement, conflict

dissēnsus, -ūs *m* dissension

dissentāneus *adj* contrary

dissentiō, -entīre, -ēnsī, -ēnsum *vi* to disagree, differ; to be unlike, be inconsistent

dissēp- *etc see* **dissaep-**

disserēnō, -āre *vi* to clear up

disserō¹, -erere, -ēvī, -itum *vt* to sow, plant at intervals

disserō², -ere, -uī, -tum *vt* to set out in order, arrange; to examine, discuss

disserpō, -ere *vi* to spread imperceptibly

dissertō, -āre *vt* to discuss, dispute

dissideō, -idēre, -ēdī, -essum *vi* to be distant; to disagree, quarrel; to differ, be unlike, be uneven

dissignātiō, -ōnis *f* arrangement

dissignātor, -ōris *m* master of ceremonies; undertaker

dissignō, -āre *vt* to arrange, regulate; *see also* **dēsignō**

dissiliō, -īre, -uī *vi* to fly apart, break up

dissimilis *adj* unlike, different

dissimiliter *adv* differently

dissimilitūdō, -inis *f* unlikeness

dissimulanter *adv* secretly

dissimulantia, -ae *f* dissembling

dissimulātiō, -ōnis *f* disguising, dissembling; Socratic irony

dissimulātor, -ōris *m* dissembler

dissimulō, -āre, -āvī, -ātum *vt* to dissemble, conceal, pretend that ... not, ignore

dissipābilis *adj* diffusible

dissipātiō, -ōnis *f* scattering, dispersing

dissipō, dissupō, -āre, -āvī, -ātum vt to scatter, disperse; to spread, broadcast; to squander, destroy; (MIL) to put to flight
dissitus ppp of **disserō¹**
dissociābilis adj disuniting; incompatible
dissociātiō, -ōnis f separation
dissociō, -āre, -āvī, -ātum vt to disunite, estrange
dissolūbilis adj dissoluble
dissolūtē adv loosely, negligently
dissolūtiō, -ōnis f breaking up, destruction; looseness; (LAW) refutation; (person) weakness
dissolūtum, -ī nt asyndeton
dissolūtus ppp of **dissolvō ♦** adj loose; lax, careless; licentious
dissolvō, -vere, -vī, -ūtum vt to unloose, dissolve; to destroy, abolish; to refute; to pay up, discharge (debt); to free, release
dissonus adj discordant, jarring, disagreeing, different
dissors, -tis adj not shared
dissuādeō, -dēre, -sī, -sum vt to advise against, oppose
dissuāsiō, -ōnis f advising against
dissuāsor, -ōris m opposer
dissultō, -āre vi to fly asunder
dissuō, -ere vt to undo, open up
dissupō etc see **dissipō**
distaedet, -ēre v impers to weary, disgust
distantia, -ae f diversity
distendō, distenō, -dere, -dī, -tum vt to stretch out, swell
distentus ppp of **distendō ♦** adj full ♦ ppp of **distineō ♦** adj busy
disterminō, -āre vt to divide, limit
distichon, -ī nt couplet
distinctē adv distinctly, lucidly
distinctiō, -ōnis f differentiating, difference; (GRAM) punctuation; (RHET) distinction between words
distinctus¹ ppp of **distinguō ♦** adj separate, distinct; ornamented, set off; lucid
distinctus², -ūs m difference
distineō, -inēre, -inuī, -entum vt to keep apart, divide; to distract; to detain, occupy; to prevent
distinguō, -guere, -xī, -ctum vt to divide, distinguish, discriminate; to punctuate; to adorn, set off
distō, -āre vi to be apart, be distant; to be different
distorqueō, -quēre, -sī, -tum vt to twist, distort
distortiō, -ōnis f contortion
distortus ppp of **distorqueō ♦** adj deformed
distractiō, -ōnis f parting, variance
distractus ppp of **distrahō ♦** adj separate
distrahō, -here, -xī, -ctum vt to tear apart, separate, estrange; to sell piecemeal, retail; (mind) to distract, perplex; **aciem distrahere** break up a formation; **contrōversiās distrahere** end a dispute; **vōcēs distrahere** leave a hiatus
distribuō, -uere, -uī, -ūtum vt to distribute, divide

distribūtē adv methodically
distribūtiō, -ōnis f distribution, division
districtus ppp of **distringō ♦** adj busy, occupied; perplexed; severe
distringō, -ngere, -nxī, -ctum vt to draw apart; to engage, distract; (MIL) to create a diversion against
distruncō, -āre vt to cut in two
distulī perf of **differō**
disturbō, -āre, -āvī, -ātum vt to throw into confusion; to demolish; to frustrate, ruin
dītēscō, -ere vi to grow rich
dīthyrambicus adj dithyrambic
dīthyrambus, -ī m dithyramb
dītiae, -ārum fpl wealth
dītiō etc see **diciō**
dītō, -āre vt to enrich
diū (compar **diūtius**, superl **diūtissimē**) adv long, for a long time; long ago; by day
diurnum, -ī nt day-book; **ācta diurna** Roman daily gazette
diurnus adj daily, for a day; by day, day- (in cpds)
dīus adj divine, noble
diūtinē adv long
diūtinus adj long, lasting
diūtissimē, -ius etc see **diū**
diūturnitās, -ātis f long time, long duration
diūturnus adj long, lasting
dīva, -ae f goddess
dīvāricō, -āre vt to spread
dīvellō, -ellere, -ellī, -ulsum vt to tear apart, tear in pieces; (fig) to tear away, separate, estrange
dīvēndō, -ere, -itum vt to sell in lots
dīverberō, -āre vt to divide, cleave
dīverbium, -ī and **-iī** nt (comedy) passage in dialogue
dīversē adv in different directions, variously
dīversitās, -ātis f contradiction, disagreement, difference
dīversus, dīvorsus ppp of **dīvertō ♦** adj in different directions, apart; different; remote; opposite, conflicting; hostile ♦ mpl individuals
dīvertō, -tere, -tī, -sum vi to turn away; differ
dīves, -itis adj rich
dīvexō, -āre vt to pillage
dīvidia, -ae f worry, concern
dīvidō, -idere, -īsī, -īsum vt to divide, break open; to distribute, apportion; to separate, keep apart; to distinguish; (jewel) to set off; **sententiam dīvidere** take the vote separately on the parts of a motion
dīviduus adj divisible; divided
dīvīnātiō, -ōnis f foreseeing the future, divination; (LAW) inquiry to select the most suitable prosecutor
dīvīnē adv by divine influence; prophetically; admirably
dīvīnitās, -ātis f divinity; divination; divine quality
dīvīnitus adv from heaven, by divine influence; excellently
dīvīnō, -āre, -āvī, -ātum vt to foresee, prophesy

dīvīnus *adj* divine, of the gods; prophetic; superhuman, excellent ♦ *m* soothsayer ♦ *nt* sacrifice; oath; **rēs dīvīna** religious service, sacrifice; **dīvīna hūmānaque** all things in heaven and earth; **dīvīnī crēdere** believe on oath

dīvīsī *perf of* **dīvidō**

dīvīsiō, -ōnis *f* division; distribution

dīvīsor, -ōris *m* distributor; bribery agent

dīvīsus¹ *ppp of* **dīvidō** ♦ *adj* separate

dīvīsus², -ūs *m* division

dīvitiae, -ārum *fpl* wealth; (*fig*) richness

dīvor- *etc see* **dīver-**

dīvortium, -ī *and* **-iī** *nt* separation; divorce (*by consent*), road fork, watershed

dīvulgātus *adj* widespread

dīvulgō, -āre, -āvī, -ātum *vt* to publish, make public

dīvulsus *ppp of* **dīvellō**

dīvum, -ī *nt* sky; **sub dīvō** in the open air

dīvus *adj* divine; deified ♦ *m* god

dīxī *perf of* **dīcō**

dō, dare, dedī, datum *vt* to give; to permit, grant; to put, bring, cause, make; to give up, devote; to tell; to impute; **fābulam dare** produce a play; **in fugam dare** put to flight; **litterās dare** post a letter; **manūs dare** surrender; **nōmen dare** enlist; **operam dare** take pains, do one's best; **poenās dare** pay the penalty; **vēla dare** set sail; **verba dare** cheat

doceō, -ēre, -uī, -tum *vt* to teach; to inform, tell; **fābulam docēre** produce a play

dochmius, -ī *and* **-iī** *m* dochmiac foot

docilis *adj* easily trained, docile

docilitās, -ātis *f* aptness for being taught

doctē *adv* skilfully, cleverly

doctor, -ōris *m* teacher, instructor

doctrīna, -ae *f* instruction, education, learning; science

doctus *ppp of* **doceō** ♦ *adj* learned, skilled; cunning, clever

documentum, -ī *nt* lesson, example, proof

Dōdōna, -ae *f town in Epirus (famous for its oracle of Jupiter)*

Dōdōnaeus, Dōdōnaeis, -idis *adj see* **Dōdōna**

dōdrāns, -antis *m* three-fourths

dogma, -tis *nt* philosophical doctrine

dolābra, -ae *f* pickaxe

dolēns, -entis *pres p of* **doleō** ♦ *adj* painful

dolenter *adv* sorrowfully

doleō, -ēre, -uī, -itum *vt, vi* to be in pain, be sore; to grieve, lament, be sorry (for); to pain; **cuī dolet meminit** once bitten, twice shy

dōliāris *adj* tubby

dōliolum, -ī *nt* small cask

dōlium, -ī *and* **-iī** *nt* large wine jar

dolō¹, -āre, -āvī, -ātum *vt* to hew, shape with an axe

dolō², -ōnis *m* pike; sting; fore-topsail

Dolopes, -um *mpl people of Thessaly*

Dolopia, -iae *f the country of the people of Thessaly*

dolor, -ōris *m* pain, pang; sorrow, trouble; indignation, resentment; (*RHET*) pathos

dolōsē *adv see* **dolōsus**

dolōsus *adj* deceitful, crafty

dolus, -ī *m* deceit, guile, trick; **~ malus** wilful fraud

domābilis *adj* tameable

domesticus *adj* domestic, household; personal, private; of one's own country, internal ♦ *mpl* members of a household; **bellum domesticum** civil war

domī *adv* at home

domicilium, -ī *and* **-iī** *nt* dwelling

domina, -ae *f* mistress, lady of the house; wife, mistress; (*fig*) lady

domināns, -antis *pres p of* **dominor** ♦ *adj* (*words*) literal ♦ *m* tyrant

dominātiō, -ōnis *f* mastery, tyranny

dominātor, -ōris *m* lord

dominātrīx, -rīcis *f* queen

dominātus, -ūs *m* mastery, sovereignty

dominicus *adj* (*ECCL*) the Lord's

dominium, -ī *and* **-iī** *nt* absolute ownership; feast

dominor, -ārī, -ātus *vi* to rule, be master; (*fig*) to lord it

dominus, -ī *m* master, lord; owner; host; despot; (*ECCL*) the Lord

Domitiānus *adj, m Roman Emperor*

Domitius, -ī *m Roman plebeian name (esp with surname Ahenobarbus)*

domitō, -āre *vt* to break in

domitor, -ōris *m*, **domitrīx, -rīcis** *f* tamer; conqueror

domitus¹ *ppp of* **domō**

domitus², -ūs *m* taming

domō, -āre, -uī, -itum *vt* to tame, break in; to conquer

domus, -ūs *and* **-ī** *f* house (*esp in town*); home, native place; family; (*PHILOS*) sect; **domī** at home; in peace; **domī habēre** have of one's own, have plenty of; **domum** home(wards); **domō** from home

dōnābilis *adj* deserving a present

dōnārium, -ī *and* **-iī** *nt* offering; altar, temple

dōnātiō, -ōnis *f* presenting

dōnātīvum, -ī *nt* largesse, gratuity

dōnec, dōnicum, dōnique *conj* until; while, as long as

dōnō, -āre, -āvī, -ātum *vt* to present, bestow; to remit, condone (*for another's sake*); (*fig*) to sacrifice

dōnum, -ī *nt* gift; offering

dorcas, -dis *f* gazelle

Dōrēs, -um *mpl* Dorians (*mostly the Greeks of the Peloponnese*)

Dōricus *adj* Dorian; Greek

Dōris, -dis *f a sea nymph*; the sea

dormiō, -īre, -īvī, -ītum *vi* to sleep, be asleep

dormītātor, -ōris *m* dreamer

dormītō, -āre *vi* to be drowsy, nod

dorsum, -ī *nt* back; mountain ridge

dōs, dōtis *f* dowry; (*fig*) gift, talent

Dossēnus, -ī *m* hunchback, clown

dōtālis *adj* dowry (*in cpds*), dotal

dōtātus *adj* richly endowed

dōtō, -āre *vt* to endow

drachma, drachuma, -ae *f a Greek silver coin*

dracō, **-ōnis** m serpent, dragon; (ASTR) Draco
dracōnigena, **-ae** adj sprung from dragon's teeth
drāpeta, **-ae** m runaway slave
Drepanum, **-ī**, **Drepana**, **-ōrum** nt town in W. Sicily
dromas, **-dis** m dromedary
dromos, **-ī** m racecourse (at Sparta)
Druidēs, **-um**, **Druidae**, **-ārum** mpl Druids
Drūsiānus adj see **Drūsus**
Drūsus, **-ī** m Roman surname (esp famous commander in Germany under Augustus)
Dryades, **-um** fpl wood nymphs, Dryads
Dryopes, **-um** mpl a people of Epirus
dubiē adv doubtfully
dubitābilis adj doubtful
dubitanter adv doubtingly, hesitatingly
dubitātiō, **-ōnis** f wavering, uncertainty, doubting; hesitancy, irresolution; (RHET) misgiving
dubitō, **-āre**, **-āvī**, **-ātum** vt, vi to waver, be in doubt, wonder, doubt; to hesitate, stop to think
dubium nt doubt
dubius adj wavering, uncertain; doubtful, indecisive; precarious; irresolute ♦ nt doubt; **in dubium vocāre** call in question; **in dubium venīre** be called in question; **sine dubiō**, **haud dubiē** undoubtedly
ducēnī, **-ōrum** adj 200 each
ducentēsima, **-ae** f one-half per cent
ducentī, **-ōrum** num two hundred
ducentiēs, **-iēns** adv 2 times
dūcō, **-cere**, **-xī**, **ductum** vt to lead, guide, bring, take; to draw, draw out; to reckon, consider; (MIL) to lead, march, command; (breath) to inhale; (ceremony) to conduct; (changed aspect) to take on, receive; (dance) to perform; (drink) to quaff; (metal) to shape, beat out; (mind) to attract, induce, deceive; (oars) to pull; (origin) to derive, trace; (time) to prolong, put off, pass; (udders) to milk; (wool) to spin; (a work) to construct, compose, make; (COMM) to calculate; **īlia dūcere** become broken-winded; **in numerō hostium dūcere** regard as an enemy; **ōs dūcere** make faces; **parvī dūcere** think little of; **ratiōnem dūcere** have regard for; **uxōrem dūcere** marry
ductim adv in streams
ductitō, **-āre** vt to lead on, deceive; to marry
ductō, **-āre** vt to lead, draw; to take home; to cheat
ductor, **-ōris** m leader, commander; guide, pilot
ductus¹ ppp of **dūcō**
ductus², **-ūs** m drawing, drawing off; form; command, generalship
dūdum adv a little while ago, just now; for long; **haud ~** not long ago; **iam ~ adsum** I have been here a long time; **quam ~** how long
duellum etc see **bellum**
Duillius, **-ī** m consul who defeated the Carthaginians at sea
duim pres subj of **dō**

dulce, **dulciter** adv see **dulcis**
dulcēdō, **-inis** f sweetness; pleasantness, charm
dulcēscō, **-ere** vi to become sweet
dulciculus adj rather sweet
dulcifer, **-ī** adj sweet
dulcis adj sweet; pleasant, lovely; kind, dear
dulcitūdō, **-inis** f sweetness
dūlicē adv like a slave
Dūlichium, **-ī** nt island in the Ionian Sea near Ithaca
Dūlichius adj of Dulichium; of Ulysses
dum conj while, as long as; provided that, if only; until ♦ adv (enclitic) now, a moment; (with neg) yet
dūmētum, **-ī** nt thicket, thornbushes
dummodo conj provided that
dūmōsus adj thorny
dumtaxat adv at least; only, merely
dūmus, **-ī** m thornbush
duo, **duae**, **duo** num two
duodeciēns, **-ēs** adv twelve times
duodecim num twelve
duodecimus adj twelfth
duodēnī, **-ōrum** adj twelve each, in dozens
duodēquadrāgēsimus adj thirty-eighth
duodēquadrāgintā num thirty-eight
duodēquīnquāgēsimus adj forty-eighth
duodētrīciēns adv twenty-eight times
duodētrīgintā num twenty-eight
duodēvīcēnī adj eighteen each
duodēvīgintī num eighteen
duoetvīcēsimānī, **-ānōrum** mpl soldiers of the 22nd legion
duoetvīcēsimus adj twenty-second
duovirī, **duumvirī**, **-ōrum** mpl a board of two men; colonial magistrates; **~ nāvālēs** naval commissioners (for supply and repair); **~ sacrōrum** keepers of the Sibylline Books
duplex, **-icis** adj double, twofold; both; (person) false
duplicārius, **-ī** and **-iī** m soldier receiving double pay
dupliciter adv doubly, on two accounts
duplicō, **-āre**, **-āvī**, **-ātum** vt to double, increase; to bend
duplus adj double, twice as much ♦ nt double ♦ f double the price
dupondius, **-ī** and **-iī** m coin worth two asses
dūrābilis adj lasting
dūrāmen, **-inis** nt hardness
dūrateus adj wooden
dūrē, **dūriter** adv stiffly; hardily; harshly, roughly
dūrēscō, **-ēscere**, **-uī** vi to harden
dūritās, **-ātis** f harshness
dūritia, **-ae**, **dūritiēs**, **-ēī** f hardness; hardiness; severity; want of feeling
dūrō, **-āre**, **-āvī**, **-ātum** vt to harden, stiffen; to make hardy, inure; (mind) to dull ♦ vi to harden; to be patient, endure; to hold out, last; (mind) to be steeled

dūruī *perf of* **dūrēscō**
dūrus *adj* hard, harsh, rough; hardy,
tough; rude, uncultured; (*character*) severe,
unfeeling, impudent, miserly; (*circumstances*)
hard, cruel
duumvirī *etc see* **duovirī**
dux, **ducis** *m* leader, guide; chief, head; (MIL)
commander, general

dūxī *perf of* **dūcō**
Dymantis, **-antidis** *f* Hecuba
Dymās, **-antis** *m father of Hecuba*
dynamis, **-is** *f* plenty
dynastēs, **-ae** *m* ruler, prince
Dyrrhachīnus *adj see* **Dyrrhachium**
Dyrrhachium, **Dyrrachium**, **-ī** *nt Adriatic port*
(*now* Durrës)

Ee

ē *prep see* **ex**
eā *adv* there, that way
ea *f, pron* she, it ♦ *adj see* **is**
eadem *f, pron see* **īdem**
eādem *adv* the same way; at the same time
eaīdem, eapse *f of* **ipse**
eapse *f of* **ipse**
eātenus *adv* so far
ebenus *etc see* **hebenus**
ēbibō, -ere, -ī *vt* to drink up, drain; to squander; to absorb
ēblandior, -īrī *vt* to coax out, obtain by flattery; **ēblandītus** obtained by flattery
Eborācum, -ī *nt* York
ēbrietās, ātis *f* drunkenness
ēbriolus *adj* tipsy
ēbriōsitās, -ātis *f* addiction to drink
ēbriōsus *adj* drunkard; (*berry*) juicy
ēbrius *adj* drunk; full; (*fig*) intoxicated
ēbulliō, -īre *vi* to bubble up ♦ *vt* to brag about
ebulus, -ī *m*, **ebulum, -ī** *nt* danewort, dwarf elder
ebur, -is *nt* ivory; ivory work
Eburācum, -ī *nt* York
eburātus *adj* inlaid with ivory
eburneolus *adj* of ivory
eburneus, eburnus *adj* of ivory; ivory-white
ēcastor *interj* by Castor!
ecce *adv* look!, here is!, there is!; lo and behold!; **ecca, eccam, eccillam, eccistam** here she is!; **eccum, eccillum** here he is!; **eccōs, eccās** here they are!
eccerē *interj* there now!
eccheuma, -tis *nt* pouring out
ecclēsia, -ae *f* a Greek assembly; (*ECCL*) congregation, church
eccum *etc see* **ecce**
ecdicus, -ī *m* civic lawyer
ecf- *see* **eff-**
echidna, -ae *f* viper; **~ Lernaea** hydra
echīnus, -ī *m* sea-urchin; hedgehog; a rinsing bowl
Echīōn, -onis *m* Theban hero
Echīonidēs *m* Pentheus
Echīonius *adj* Theban
Ēchō, -us *f* wood nymph; echo
ecloga, -ae *f* selection; eclogue
ecquandō *adv* ever
ecquī, -ae, -od *adj interrog* any
ecquid, ecquidī *adv* whether
ecquis, -id *pron interrog* anyone, anything

ecquō *adv* anywhere
eculeus, -ī *m* foal; rack
edācitās, -ātis *f* gluttony
edāx, -ācis *adj* gluttonous; (*fig*) devouring, carking
ēdentō, -āre *vt* to knock the teeth out of
ēdentulus *adj* toothless; old
edepol *interj* by Pollux, indeed
ēdī *perf of* **edō**
ēdīcō, -īcere, -īxī, -ictum *vt* to declare; to decree, publish by an edict
ēdictiō, -ōnis *f* decree
ēdictō, -āre *vt* to proclaim
ēdictum, -ī *nt* proclamation, edict (*esp a praetor's*)
ēdidī *perf of* **edō**
ēdiscō, -ere, ēdidicī *vt* to learn well, learn by heart
ēdisserō, -ere, -uī, -tum *vt* to explain in detail
ēdissertō, -āre *vt* to explain fully
ēditīcius *adj* chosen by the plaintiff
ēditiō, -ōnis *f* publishing, edition; statement; (*LAW*) designation of a suit
ēditus *ppp of* **ēdō** ♦ *adj* high; descended ♦ *nt* height; order
edō, edere *and* **ēsse, ēdī, ēsum** *vt* to eat; (*fig*) to devour
ēdō, -ere, -idī, -itum *vt* to put forth, discharge; to emit; to give birth to, produce; (*speech*) to declare, relate, utter; (*action*) to cause, perform; (*book*) to publish; (*POL*) to promulgate; **lūdōs ēdere** put on a show; **tribūs ēdere** nominate tribes of jurors
ēdoceō, -ere, -uī, -ctum *vt* to instruct clearly, teach thoroughly
ēdomō, -āre, -uī, -itum *vt* to conquer, overcome
Ēdōnus *adj* Thracian
ēdormiō, -īre *vi* to have a good sleep ♦ *vt* to sleep off
ēdormīscō, -ere *vt* to sleep off
ēducātiō, -ōnis *f* bringing up, rearing
ēducātor, -ōris *m* foster father, tutor
ēducātrīx, -īcis *f* nurse
ēducō, -āre, -āvī, -ātum *vt* to bring up, rear, train; to produce
ēdūcō, -ūcere, -ūxī, -uctum *vt* to draw out, bring away; to raise up, erect; (*LAW*) to summon; (*MIL*) to lead out, march out; (*ship*) to put to sea; (*young*) to hatch, rear, train
edūlis *adj* edible
ēdūrō, -āre *vi* to last out
ēdūrus *adj* very hard

effarciō *etc see* **efferciō**

effātus *ppa* (*occ pass*) *of* **effor** ♦ *adj* solemnly pronounced, declared ♦ *nt* axiom; (*pl*) predictions

effectiō, -ōnis *f* performing; efficient cause

effector, -ōris *m*, **effectrīx, -rīcis** *f* producer, author

effectus¹ *ppp of* **efficiō**

effectus², -ūs *m* completion, performance; effect

effēmināte *adv see* **effēminātus**

effēminātus *adj* effeminate

effēminō, -āre, -āvī, -ātum *vt* to make a woman of; to enervate

efferātus *adj* savage

efferciō, -cīre, -sī, -tum *vt* to cram full

efferitās, -ātis *f* wildness

efferō¹, -āre, -āvī, -ātum *vt* to make wild; (*fig*) to exasperate

efferō², ecferō, -re, extulī, ēlātum *vt* to bring out, carry out; to lift up, raise; (*dead*) to carry to the grave; (*emotion*) to transport; (*honour*) to exalt; (*news*) to spread abroad; (*soil*) to produce; (*trouble*) to endure to the end; **sē efferre** rise; be conceited

effertus *ppp of* **efferciō** ♦ *adj* full, bulging

efferus *adj* savage

effervēscō, -vēscere, -buī *vi* to boil over; (*fig*) to rage

effervō, -ere *vi* to boil up

effētus *adj* exhausted

efficācitās, -ātis *f* power

efficāciter *adv* effectually

efficāx, -ācis *adj* capable, effective

efficiēns, -entis *pres p of* **efficiō** ♦ *adj* effective, efficient

efficienter *adv* efficiently

efficientia, -ae *f* power, efficacy

efficiō, -icere, -ēcī, -ectum *vt* to make, accomplish; to cause, bring about; (*numbers*) to amount to; (*soil*) to yield; (*theory*) to make out, try to prove

effictus *ppp of* **effingō**

effigiēs, -ēī, effigia, -ae *f* likeness, copy; ghost; portrait, statue; (*fig*) image, ideal

effingō, -ngere, -nxī, -ctum *vt* to form, fashion; to portray, represent; to wipe clean; to fondle

efflāgitātiō, -ōnis *f* urgent demand

efflāgitātus, -ūs *m* urgent request

efflāgitō, -āre *vt* to demand urgently

efflīctim *adv* desperately

efflīctō, -āre *vt* to strike dead

effligō, -gere, -xī, -ctum *vt* to exterminate

efflō, -āre, -āvī, -ātum *vt* to breathe out, blow out ♦ *vi* to billow out; **animam efflāre** expire

efflōrēscō, -ēscere, -uī *vi* to blossom forth

effluō, -ere, -xī *vi* to run out, issue, emanate; (*fig*) to pass away, vanish; (*rumour*) to get known; **ex animō effluere** become forgotten

effluvium, -ī *and* **-iī** *nt* outlet

effodiō, -odere, -ōdī, -ossum *vt* to dig up; (*eyes*) to gouge out; (*house*) to ransack

effor, -ārī, -ātus *vt* to speak, utter; (*AUG*) to ordain; (*LOGIC*) to state a proposition

effossus *ppp of* **effodiō**

effrēnātē *adv see* **effrēnātus**

effrēnātiō, -ōnis *f* impetuousness

effrēnātus *adj* unbridled, violent, unruly

effrēnus *adj* unbridled

effringō, -ingere, -ēgī, -āctum *vt* to break open, smash

effugiō, -ugere, -ūgī *vi* to run away, escape ♦ *vt* to flee from, escape; to escape the notice of

effugium, -ī *and* **-iī** *nt* flight, escape; means of escape

effulgeō, -gēre, -sī *vi* to shine out, blaze

effultus *adj* supported

effundō, -undere, -ūdī, -ūsum *vt* to pour forth, pour out; (*crops*) to produce in abundance; (*missiles*) to shoot; (*rider*) to throw; (*speech*) to give vent to; (*effort*) to waste; (*money*) to squander; (*reins*) to let go; **sē effundere, sē effundī** rush out; indulge (in)

effūsē *adv* far and wide; lavishly, extravagantly

effūsiō, -ōnis *f* pouring out, rushing out; profusion, extravagance; exuberance

effūsus *ppp of* **effundō** ♦ *adj* vast, extensive; loose, straggling; lavish, extravagant

effūtiō, -īre *vt* to blab, chatter

ēgelidus *adj* mild, cool

egēns, -entis *pres p of* **egeō** ♦ *adj* needy

egēnus *adj* destitute

egeō, -ēre, -uī *vi* to be in want; (*with abl or gen*) to need, want

Ēgeria, -ae *f* nymph who taught Numa

ēgerō, -rere, -ssī, -stum *vt* to carry out; to discharge, emit

egestās, -ātis *f* want, poverty

ēgestus *ppp of* **ēgerō**

ēgī *perf of* **agō**

ego *pron* I; **egomet** I (*emphatic*)

ēgredior, -dī, -ssus *vi* to go out, come out; to go up, climb; (*MIL*) to march out; (*NAUT*) to disembark, put to sea; (*fig*) to overstep, surpass ♦ *vt* to go beyond, quit; (*fig*) to overstep, surpass

ēgregiē *adv* uncommonly well, singularly

ēgregius *adj* outstanding, surpassing; distinguished, illustrious

ēgressus¹ *ppa of* **ēgredior**

ēgressus², -ūs *m* departure; way out; digression; (*NAUT*) landing; (*river*) mouth

eguī *perf of* **egeō**

ēgurgitō, -āre *vt* to lavish

ehem *interj* (*expressing surprise*) ha!, so!

ēheu *interj* (*expressing pain*) alas!

eho *interj* (*expressing rebuke*) look here!

ei *interj* (*expressing alarm*) oh!

eī *dat of* **is**

eia *interj* (*expressing delight, playful remonstrance, encouragement*) aha!, come now!, come on!

ēiaculor, -ārī *vt* to shoot out

ēiciō, -icere, -iēcī, -iectum *vt* to throw out, drive out, put out; (*joint*) to dislocate; (*mind*) to banish; (*NAUT*) to bring to land, run aground, wreck; (*rider*) to throw; (*speech*) to utter; (*THEAT*) to hiss off; **sē ēicere** rush out, break out

ēiectāmenta, -ōrum *ntpl* refuse

ēiectiō, -ōnis *f* banishment

ēiectō, -āre *vt* to throw up

ēiectus¹ *ppp of* **ēiciō** ♦ *adj* shipwrecked

ēiectus², **-ūs** *m* emitting
ēierō, ēiūrō, -āre *vt* to abjure, reject on oath, forswear; *(office)* to resign; **bonam cōpiam ēierāre** declare oneself bankrupt
ēiulātiō, -ōnis *f*, **ēiulātus, -ūs** *m* wailing
ēiulō, -āre *vi* to wail, lament
ēius *pron* his, her, its; **ēiusmodī** such
ej- *etc see* **ei-**
ēlābor, -bī, -psus *vi* to glide away, slip off; to escape, get off; to pass away
ēlabōrātus *adj* studied
ēlabōrō, -āre, -āvī, -ātum *vi* to exert oneself, take great pains ♦ *vt* to work out, elaborate
ēlāmentābilis *adj* very mournful
ēlanguēscō, -ēscere, -ī *vi* to grow faint; to relax
ēlāpsus *ppa of* **ēlābor**
ēlātē *adv* proudly
ēlātiō, -ōnis *f* ecstasy, exaltation
ēlātrō, -āre *vt* to bark out
ēlātus *ppp of* **efferō** ♦ *adj* high; exalted
ēlavō, -avāre, -āvī, -autum *and* **-ōtum** *vt* to wash clean; *(comedy)* to rob
Ēlea, -ae *f* town in S. Italy *(birthplace of Parmenides)*
Ēleātēs, Ēleāticus *adj see* **Ēlea**
ēlecebra, -ae *f* snare
ēlēctē *adv* choicely
ēlēctilis *adj* choice
ēlēctiō, -ōnis *f* choice, option
ēlēctō, -āre *vt* to coax out
ēlēctō, -āre *vt* to select
Ēlectra, -ae *f* a Pleiad *(daughter of Atlas; sister of Orestes)*
ēlectrum, -ī *nt* amber; *an alloy of gold and silver*
ēlēctus¹ *ppp of* **ēligō** ♦ *adj* select, choice
ēlēctus², -ūs *m* choice
ēlegāns, -antis *adj* tasteful, refined, elegant; fastidious; *(things)* fine, choice
ēleganter *adv* with good taste
ēlegantia, -ae *f* taste, finesse, elegance; fastidiousness
elegī, -ōrum *mpl* elegiac verses
ēlēgī *perf of* **ēligō**
elegīa, -ae *f* elegy
Eleleides, -eidum *fpl* Bacchantes
Eleleus, -eī *m* Bacchus
elementum, -ī *nt* element; *(pl)* first principles, rudiments; beginnings; letters *(of alphabet)*
elenchus, -ī *m* a pear-shaped pearl
elephantomacha, -ae *m* fighter mounted on an elephant
elephantus, -ī, elephās, -antis *m* elephant; ivory
Ēleus, Ēlēius, Ēlēias *adj* Elean; Olympian
Eleusīn, -is *f* Eleusis *(Attic town famous for its mysteries of Demeter)*
Eleusīus *adj see* **Eleusīn**
eleutheria, -ae *f* liberty
ēlevō, -āre *vt* to lift, raise; to alleviate; to make light of, lessen, disparage
ēliciō, -ere, -uī, -itum *vt* to lure out, draw out; *(god)* to call down; *(spirit)* to conjure up; *(fig)* to elicit, draw
ēlīdō, -dere, -sī, -sum *vt* to dash out, squeeze out; to drive out; to crush, destroy

ēligō, -igere, -ēgī, -ēctum *vt* to pick, pluck out; to choose
ēlīminō, -āre *vt* to carry outside
ēlīmō, -āre *vt* to file; *(fig)* to perfect
ēlinguis *adj* speechless; not eloquent
ēlinguō, -āre *vt* to tear the tongue out of
Ēlis, -idis *f* district and town in W. Peloponnese *(famous for Olympia)*
Elissa, -ae *f* Dido
ēlīsus *ppp of* **ēlīdō**
ēlixus *adj* boiled
elleborōsus *adj* quite mad
elleborus, -ī *m*, **elleborum, -ī** *nt* hellebore
ellum, ellam there he/she is!
ēlocō, -āre *vt* to lease, farm out
ēlocūtiō, -ōnis *f* delivery, style
ēlocūtus *ppa of* **ēloquor**
ēlogium, -ī *and* **-iī** *nt* short saying; inscription; *(will)* clause
ēloquēns, -entis *adj* eloquent
ēloquenter *adv see* **ēloquēns**
ēloquentia, -ae *f* eloquence
ēloquium, -ī *and* **-iī** *nt* eloquence
ēloquor, -quī, -cūtus *vt, vi* to speak out, speak eloquently
ēlūceō, -cēre, -xī *vi* to shine out, glitter
ēluctor, -ārī, -ātus *vi* to struggle, force a way out ♦ *vt* to struggle out of, surmount
ēlūcubrō, -āre, ēlūcubror, -ārī, -ātus *vt* to compose by lamplight
ēlūdificor, -ārī, -ātus *vt* to cheat, play up
ēlūdō, -dere, -sī, -sum *vt* to parry, ward off, foil; to win off at play; to outplay, outmanoeuvre; to cheat, make fun of ♦ *vi* to finish one's sport
ēlūgeō, -gēre, -xī *vt* to mourn for
ēlumbis *adj* feeble
ēluō, -uere, -uī, -ūtum *vt* to wash clean; *(money)* to squander; *(fig)* to wash away, get rid of
ēlūsus *ppp of* **ēlūdō**
ēlūtus *ppp of* **ēluō** ♦ *adj* insipid
ēluviēs *(acc* **-em,** *abl* **-ē)** discharge; overflowing
ēluviō, -ōnis *f* deluge
Ēlysium, -ī *nt* Elysium
Ēlysius *adj* Elysian
em *interj* there you are!
ēmancipātiō, -ōnis *f* giving a son his independence; conveyance *(of property)*
ēmancipō, -āre *vt* to declare independent; to transfer, give up, sell
ēmānō, -āre, -āvī, -ātum *vi* to flow out; to spring (from); *(news)* to leak out, become known
Ēmathia, -ae *f* district of Macedonia; Macedonia, Thessaly
Ēmathides, -idum *fpl* Muses
Ēmathius *adj* Macedonian, Pharsalian
ēmātūrēscō, -ēscere, -uī *vi* to soften
emāx, -ācis *adj* fond of buying
emblēma, -tis *nt* inlaid work, mosaic
embolium, -ī *and* **-iī** *nt* interlude
ēmendābilis *adj* corrigible
ēmendātē *adv see* **ēmendātus**
ēmendātiō, -ōnis *f* correction

ēmendātor, -ōris m, **ēmendātrīx, -rīcis** f corrector

ēmendātus adj faultless

ēmendō, -āre, -āvī, -ātum vt to correct, improve

ēmēnsus ppa of **ēmētior** ♦ adj traversed

ēmentior, -īrī, -ītus vi to tell lies ♦ vt to pretend, fabricate; **ēmentītus** pretended

ēmercor, -ārī vt to purchase

ēmereō, -ēre, -uī, -itum, ēmereor, ēmerērī vt to earn fully, deserve; to lay under an obligation; to complete one's term of service

ēmergō, -gere, -sī, -sum vt to raise out; (fig) to extricate ♦ vi to rise, come up, emerge; (fig) to get clear, extricate oneself; (impers) it becomes evident

ēmeritus ppa of **ēmereōr** ♦ adj superannuated, worn-out ♦ m veteran

ēmersus ppp of **ēmergō**

emetica, -ae f emetic

ēmētior, -tīrī, -nsus vt to measure out; to traverse, pass over; (time) to live through; (fig) to impart

ēmetō, -ere vt to harvest

ēmī perf of **emō**

ēmicō, -āre, -uī, -ātum vi to dart out, dash out, flash out; (fig) to shine

ēmigrō, -āre, -āvī, -ātum vi to remove, depart

ēminēns, -entis pres p of **ēmineō** ♦ adj high, projecting; (fig) distinguished, eminent

ēminentia, -ae f prominence; (painting) light

ēmineō, -ēre, -uī vi to stand out, project; to be prominent, be conspicuous, distinguish oneself

ēminor, -ārī vi to threaten

ēminus adv at or from a distance

ēmīror, -ārī vt to marvel at

ēmissārium, -ī and **-iī** nt outlet

ēmissārius, -ī and **-iī** m scout

ēmissīcius adj prying

ēmissiō, -ōnis f letting go, discharge

ēmissus¹ ppp of **ēmittō**

ēmissus², -ūs m emission

ēmittō, -ittere, -īsī, -issum vt to send out, let out; to let go, let slip; (missile) to discharge; (person) to release, free; (sound) to utter; (writing) to publish

emō, -ere, ēmī, emptum vt to buy, procure; to win over; **bene emere** buy cheap; **male emere** buy dear; **in diem emere** buy on credit

ēmoderor, -ārī vt to give expression to

ēmodulor, -ārī vt to sing through

ēmōlior, -īrī vt to accomplish

ēmolliō, -īre, -iī, -ītum vt to soften; to mollify; to enervate

ēmolumentum, -ī nt profit, advantage

ēmoneō, -ēre vt to strongly advise

ēmorior, -ī, -tuus vi to die; (fig) to pass away

ēmortuālis adj of death

ēmoveō, -ovēre, -ōvī, -ōtum vt to remove, drive away

Empedoclēs, -is m Sicilian philosopher

Empedoclēus adj see **Empedoclēs**

empīricus, -ī m empirical doctor

emporium, -ī and **-iī** nt market, market town

emptiō, -ōnis f buying; a purchase

emptitō, -āre vt to often buy

emptor, -ōris m purchaser

emptus ppp of **emō**

ēmulgeō, -ēre vt to drain

ēmunctus ppp of **ēmungō** ♦ adj discriminating

ēmungō, -gere, -xī, -ctum vt to blow the nose of; (comedy) to cheat

ēmūniō, -īre, -īvī, -ītum vt to strengthen, secure; to build up; to make roads through

ēn interj (drawing attention) look!, see!; (excited question) really, indeed; (command) come now!

ēnārrābilis adj describable

ēnārrō, -āre, -āvī, -ātum vt to describe in detail

ēnāscor, -scī, -tus vi to sprout, grow

ēnatō, -āre vi to swim ashore; (fig) to escape

ēnātus ppa of **ēnāscor**

ēnāvigō, -āre vi to sail clear, clear ♦ vt to sail over

Enceladus, -ī m giant under Etna

endromis, -dis f sports wrap

Endymiōn, -ōnis m a beautiful youth loved by the Moon, and doomed to eternal sleep

ēnecō, -āre, -uī and **-āvī, -tum** and **-ātum** vt to kill; to wear out; to torment

ēnervātus adj limp

ēnervis adj enfeebled

ēnervō, -āre, -āvī, -ātum vt to weaken, unman

ēnicō etc see **ēnecō**

enim conj (affirming) yes, truly, in fact; (explaining) for, for instance, of course; (anticipating) it will be objected; **quid ~?** well?; **sed ~** but actually

enimvērō conj certainly, yes indeed

Enīpeus, -eī m river in Thessaly

ēnīsus ppa of **ēnītor**

ēniteō, -ēre, -uī vi to shine, brighten up; (fig) to be brilliant, distinguish oneself

ēnitēscō, -ēscere, -uī vi to shine, be brilliant

ēnītor, -tī, -sus and **-xus** vi to struggle up, climb; to strive, make a great effort ♦ vt to give birth to; to climb

ēnīxē adv earnestly

ēnīxus ppa of **ēnītor** ♦ adj strenuous

Enniānus adj see **Ennius**

Ennius, -ī m greatest of the early Latin poets

Ennosigaeus, -ī m Earthshaker, Neptune

ēnō, -āre, -āvī vi to swim out, swim ashore; to fly away

ēnōdātē adv lucidly

ēnōdātiō, -ōnis f unravelling

ēnōdis adj free from knots; plain

ēnōdō, -āre, -āvī, -ātum vt to elucidate

ēnōrmis adj irregular; immense

ēnōtēscō, -ēscere, -uī vi to get known

ēnotō, -āre vt to make a note of

ēnsiculus, -ī m little sword

ēnsiger, -ī adj with his sword

ēnsis, -is m sword

enthȳmēma, -tis nt argument

ēnūbō, -bere, -psī vi to marry out of one's station; to marry and go away

ēnucleātē adv plainly

ēnucleātus adj (style) straightforward; (votes) honest

ēnucleō, -āre vt to elucidate

ēnumerātiō, -ōnis f enumeration; (RHET) recapitulation

ēnumerō, -āre vt to count up; to pay out; to relate

ēnūntiātiō, -ōnis f proposition

ēnūntiātum, -ī nt proposition

ēnūntiō, -āre vt to disclose, report; to express; to pronounce

ēnūptiō, -ōnis f marrying out of one's station

ēnūtriō, -īre vt to feed, bring up

eō¹, īre, īvī and iī, itum vi to go; (MIL) to march; (time) to pass; (event) to proceed, turn out; **in alia omnia īre** vote against a bill; **in sententiam īre** support a motion; **sīc eat** so may he fare!; **ī** (mocking) go on!

eō² adv (place) thither, there; (purpose) with a view to; (degree) so far, to such a pitch; (time) so long; (cause) on that account, for the reason; (with comp) the; **accēdit eō** besides; **rēs erat eō locī** such was the state of affairs; **eō magis** all the more

eōdem adv to the same place, purpose or person; **~ locī** in the same place

Ēōs f dawn

Ēōus adj at dawn, eastern ♦ m morning star; Oriental

Ēpamīnōndās, -ae m Theban general

epāstus adj eaten up

ephēbus, -ī m youth (18 to 20)

ephēmeris, -idis f diary

Ephesius adj see **Ephesus**

Ephesus, -ī f Ionian town in Asia Minor

ephippiātus adj riding a saddled horse

ephippium, -ī and -iī nt saddle

ephorus, -ī m a Spartan magistrate, ephor

Ephyra, -ae, Ephyrē, -ēs f Corinth

Ephyrēius adj see **Ephyra**

Epicharmus, -ī m Greek philosopher and comic poet

epichysis, -is f kind of jug

epicōpus adj rowing

Epicūrēus adj Epicurean

Epicūrus, -ī m famous Greek philosopher

epicus adj epic

Epidaurius adj see **Epidaurus**

Epidaurus, -ī f town in E. Peloponnese

epidīcticus adj (RHET) for display

epigramma, -tis nt inscription; epigram

epilogus, -ī m peroration

epimēnia, -ōrum ntpl a month's rations

Epimēthis, -dis f Pyrrha (daughter of Epimetheus)

epirēdium, -ī and -iī nt trace

Ēpīrōtēs, -ōtae m native of Epirus

Ēpīrōticus, Ēpīrēnsis adj see **Ēpīrus**

Ēpīrus, Ēpīros, -ī f district of N.W. Greece

episcopus, -ī m bishop

epistolium, -ī and -iī nt short note

epistula, -ae f letter; **ab epistulīs** secretary

epitaphium, -ī and -iī nt funeral oration

epithēca, -ae f addition

epitoma, -ae, epitomē, -ēs f abridgement

epitȳrum, -ī nt olive salad

epops, -is m hoopoe

epos (pl **-ē**) nt epic

ēpōtō, -āre, -āvī, -um vt to drink up, drain; to waste in drink; to absorb

epulae, -ārum fpl dishes; feast, banquet

epulāris adj at a banquet

epulō, -ōnis m guest at a feast; priest in charge of religious banquets

epulor, -ārī, -ātus vi to be at a feast ♦ vt to feast on

epulum, -ī nt banquet

equa, -ae f mare

eques, -itis m horseman, trooper; (pl) cavalry; knight, member of the equestrian order

equester, -ris adj equestrian, cavalry- (in cpds)

equidem adv (affirming) indeed, of course, for my part; (concessive) to be sure

equīnus adj horse's

equīria, -ōrum ntpl horseraces

equitātus, -ūs m cavalry

equitō, -āre vi to ride

equuleus etc see **eculeus**

equulus, -ī m colt

equus, -ī m horse; (ASTR) Pegasus; **~ bipēs** seahorse; **equō merēre** serve in the cavalry; **equīs virīsque** with might and main

era, -ae f mistress (of the house); (goddess) Lady

ērādīcō, -āre vt to root out, destroy

ērādō, -dere, -sī, -sum vt to erase, obliterate

Eratō f Muse of lyric poetry

Eratosthenēs, -is m famous Alexandrian geographer

Erebēus adj see **Erebus**

Erebus, -ī m god of darkness; the lower world

Erechtheus, -eī m legendary king of Athens

Erechthēus adj see **Erechtheus**

Erechthīdae mpl Athenians

Erechthis, -idis f Orithyia; Procris

ērēctus ppp of **ērigō** ♦ adj upright, lofty; noble, haughty; alert, tense; resolute

ērēpō, -ere, -sī vi to creep out, clamber up ♦ vt to crawl over, climb

ēreptiō, -ōnis f seizure, robbery

ēreptor, -ōris m robber

ēreptus ppp of **ēripiō**

ergā prep (with acc) towards; against

ergastulum, -ī nt prison (esp for slaves); (pl) convicts

ergō adv therefore, consequently; (questions, commands) then, so; (resuming) well then; (with gen) for the sake of, because of

Erichthonius, -ī m a king of Troy; a king of Athens ♦ adj Trojan; Athenian

ēricius, -ī and -iī m hedgehog; (MIL) beam with iron spikes

Ēridanus, -ī m mythical name of river Po

erifuga, -ae m runaway slave

ērigō, -igere, -ēxī, -ēctum vt to make upright, raise up, erect; to excite; to encourage

Ērigonē, -ēs f (constellation) Virgo

Ērigonēius adj see **Ērigonē**

erīlis adj the master's, the mistress's

Erīnys, -yos f Fury; (fig) curse, frenzy

Eriphȳla, -ae f mother of Alcmaeon (who killed her)

ēripiō, -ipere, -ipuī, -eptum vt to tear away, pull away, take by force; to rob; to rescue; **sē ēripere** escape

ērogātiō, -ōnis f paying out

ērogitō, -āre vt to enquire

ērogō, -āre, -āvī, -ātum vt to pay out, expend; to bequeath

errābundus adj wandering

errāticus adj roving, shifting

errātiō, -ōnis f wandering, roving

errātum, -ī nt mistake, error

errātus, -ūs m wandering

errō¹, -āre, -āvī, -ātum vi to wander, stray, lose one's way; to waver; to make a mistake, err ♦ vt to traverse; **stēllae errantēs** planets

errō², -ōnis m vagabond

error, -ōris m wandering; meander, maze; uncertainty; error, mistake, delusion; deception

ērubēscō, -ēscere, -uī vi to blush; to feel ashamed ♦ vt to blush for, be ashamed of; to respect

ērūca, -ae f colewort

ēructō, -āre vt to belch, vomit; to talk drunkenly about; to throw up

ērudiō, -īre, -iī, -ītum vt to educate, instruct

ērudītē adv learnedly

ērudītiō, -ōnis f education, instruction; learning, knowledge

ērudītulus adj somewhat skilled

ērudītus ppp of **ērudiō** ♦ adj learned, educated, accomplished

ērumpō, -umpere, -ūpī, -uptum vt to break open; to make break out ♦ vi to burst out, break through; to end (in)

ēruō, -ere, -ī, -tum vt to uproot, tear out; to demolish, destroy; to elicit, draw out; to rescue

ēruptiō, -ōnis f eruption; (MIL) sally

ēruptus ppp of **ērumpō**

erus, -ī m master (of the house); owner

ērutus ppp of **ēruō**

ervum, -ī nt vetch

Erycīnus adj of Eryx; of Venus; Sicilian ♦ f Venus

Erymanthius, -is adj see **Erymanthus**

Erymanthus, Erymanthī m mountain range in Arcadia (where Hercules killed the boar)

Eryx, -cis m town and mountain in the extreme W. of Sicily

esca, -ae f food, titbits; bait

escārius adj of food; of bait ♦ ntpl dishes

ēscendō, -endere, -endī, -ēnsum vi to climb up, go up ♦ vt to mount

ēscēnsiō, -ōnis f raid (from the coast), disembarkation

esculentus adj edible, tasty

Esquiliae, -iārum fpl Esquiline hill (in Rome)

Esquilīnus adj Esquiline ♦ f Esquiline gate

essedārius, -ī and -iī m chariot fighter

essedum, -ī nt war chariot

essitō, -āre vt to usually eat

ēst pres of **edō**

ēstrīx, -īcis f glutton

ēsuriālis adj of hunger

ēsuriō, -īre, -ītum vi to be hungry ♦ vt to hunger for

ēsurītiō, -ōnis f hunger

ēsus ppp of **edō**

et conj and; (repeated) both ... and; (adding emphasis) in fact, yes; (comparing) as, than ♦ adv also, too; even

etenim conj (adding an explanation) and as a matter of fact, in fact

etēsiae, -ārum fpl Etesian winds

etēsius adj see **etēsiae**

ēthologus, -ī m mimic

etiam adv also, besides; (emphatic) even, actually; (affirming) yes, certainly; (indignant) really!; (time) still, as yet; again; **~ atque ~** again and again; **~ cavēs** do be careful!; **nihil ~** nothing at all

etiamdum adv still, as yet

etiamnum, etiamnunc adv still, till now, till then; besides

etiamsī conj even if, although

etiamtum, etiamtunc adv till then, still

Etrūria, -ae f district of Italy north of Rome

Etruscus adj Etruscan

etsī conj even if, though; and yet

etymologia, -ae f etymology

eu interj well done!, bravo!

Euan m Bacchus

Euander, Euanderus, -rī m Evander (ancient king on the site of Rome)

Euandrius adj see **Euander**

euax interj hurrah!

Euboea, -oeae f Greek island

Euboicus adj Euboean

euge, eugepae interj bravo!, cheers!

Euhan m Bacchus

euhāns, -antis adj shouting the Bacchic cry

Euhias f Bacchante

Euhius, -ī m Bacchus

euhoe interj ecstatic cry of Bacchic revellers

Euius, -i m Bacchus

Eumenides, -um fpl Furies

eunūchus, -ī m eunuch

Euphrātēs, -is m (river) Euphrates

Eupolis, -dis m Athenian comic poet

Eurīpidēs, -is m Athenian tragic poet

Eurīpidēus adj see **Eurīpidēs**

Eurīpus, -ī m strait between Euboea and mainland; a channel, conduit

Eurōpa, -ae, Eurōpē, -ēs f mythical princess of Tyre (who was carried by a bull to Crete); (continent of) Europe

Eurōpaeus adj see **Eurōpa**

Eurōtās, -ae m river of Sparta

Euroüs adj eastern

Eurus, -ī m east wind; south-east wind

Eurydicē, -ēs f wife of Orpheus

Eurystheus, -eī m king of Mycenae (who imposed the labours on Hercules)

euschēmē adv gracefully

Euterpē, -ēs f Muse of music

Euxīnus m the Black (Sea)

ēvādō, -dere, -sī, -sum vi to come out; to climb up; to escape; to turn out, result, come true ♦ vt to pass, mount; to escape from

ēvagor, -ārī, -ātus vi (MIL) to manoeuvre; (fig) to spread ♦ vt to stray beyond

ēvalēscō, -ēscere, -uī vi to grow, increase; to be able; to come into vogue

Ēvander etc see **Euander**

ēvānēscō, -ēscere, -uī vi to vanish, die away, lose effect

ēvangelium, -ī and **-iī** nt (ECCL) Gospel

ēvānidus adj vanishing

ēvāsī perf of **ēvādō**

ēvastō, -āre vt to devastate

ēvehō, -here, -xī, -ctum vt to carry out; to raise up, exalt; to spread abroad; (pass) to ride, sail, move out

ēvellō, -ellere, -ellī, -ulsum vt to tear out, pull out; to eradicate

ēveniō, -enīre, -ēnī, -entum vi to come out; to turn out, result; to come to pass, happen, befall

ēventum, -ī nt result, issue; occurrence, event; fortune, experience

ēventus, -ūs m result, issue; success; fortune, fate

ēverberō, -āre vt to beat violently

ēverriculum, -ī nt dragnet

ēverrō, -rere, -rī, -sum vt to sweep out, clean out

ēversiō, -ōnis f overthrow, destruction

ēversor, -ōris m destroyer

ēversus ppp of **ēverrō**; **ēvertō**

ēvertō, -tere, -tī, -sum vt to turn out, eject; to turn up, overturn; to overthrow, ruin, destroy

ēvestīgātus adj tracked down

ēvictus ppp of **ēvincō**

ēvidēns, -entis adj visible, plain, evident

ēvidenter adv see **ēvidēns**

ēvidentia, -ae f distinctness

ēvigilō, -āre, -āvī, -ātum vi to be wide awake ♦ vt to compose carefully

ēvīlēscō, -ere vi to become worthless

ēvinciō, -cīre, -xī, -ctum vt to garland, crown

ēvincō, -incere, -īcī, -ictum vt to overcome, conquer; to prevail over; to prove

ēvirō, -āre vt to castrate

ēviscerō, -āre vt to disembowel, tear to pieces

ēvītābilis adj avoidable

ēvītō, -āre, -āvī, -ātum vt to avoid, clear

ēvocātī, -ōrum mpl veteran volunteers

ēvocātor, -ōris m enlister

ēvocō, -āre, -āvī, -ātum vt to call out, summon; to challenge; to call up; to call forth, evoke

ēvolō, -āre, -āvī, -ātum vi to fly out, fly away; to rush out; (fig) to rise, soar

ēvolūtiō, -ōnis f unrolling (a book)

ēvolvō, -vere, -vī, -ūtum vt to roll out, roll along; to unroll, unfold; (book) to open, read; (fig) to disclose, unravel, disentangle

ēvomō, -ere, -uī, -itum vt to vomit up, disgorge

ēvulgō, -āre, -āvī, -ātum vt to divulge, make public

ēvulsiō, -ōnis f pulling out

ēvulsus ppp of **ēvellō**

ex, ē prep (with abl) (place) out of, from, down from; (person) from; (time) after, immediately after, since; (change) from being; (source, material) of; (cause) by reason of, through; (conformity) in accordance with; **ex itinere** on the march; **ex parte** in part; **ex quō** since; **ex rē** for the good of; **ex ūsū** for the good of; **ē rē pūblicā** constitutionally; **ex sententiā** to one's liking; **aliud ex aliō** one thing after another; **ūnus ex** one of

exacerbō, -āre vt to exasperate

exāctiō, -ōnis f expulsion; supervision; tax; (debts) calling in

exāctor, -ōris m expeller; superintendent; tax collector

exāctus ppp of **exigō** ♦ adj precise, exact

exacuō, -uere, -uī, -ūtum vt to sharpen; (fig) to quicken, inflame

exadversum, exadversus adv, prep (with acc) right opposite

exaedificātiō, -ōnis f construction

exaedificō, -āre vt to build up; to finish the building of

exaequātiō, -ōnis f levelling

exaequō, -āre, -āvī, -ātum vt to level out; to compensate; to put on an equal footing; to equal

exaestuō, -āre vi to boil up

exaggerātiō, -ōnis f exaltation

exaggerō, -āre, -āvī, -ātum vt to pile up; (fig) to heighten, enhance

exagitātor, -ōris m critic

exagitō, -āre, -āvī, -ātum vt to disturb, harass; to scold, censure; to excite, incite

exagōga, -ae f export

exalbēscō, -ēscere, -uī vi to turn quite pale

exāmen, -inis nt swarm, crowd; tongue (of a balance); examining

examinō, -āre, -āvī, -ātum vt to weigh; to consider, test

examussim adv exactly, perfectly

exanclō, -āre vt to drain; to endure to the end

exanimālis adj dead; deadly

exanimātiō, -ōnis f panic

exanimis adj lifeless, breathless; terrified

exanimō, -āre, -āvī, -ātum vt to wind; to kill; to terrify, agitate; (pass) to be out of breath

exanimus see **exanimis**

exārdēscō, -dēscere, -sī, -sum vi to catch fire, blaze up; (fig) to be inflamed, break out

exārēscō, -ēscere, -uī vi to dry, dry up

exarmō, -āre vt to disarm

exarō, -āre, -āvi, -ātum vt to plough up; to cultivate, produce; (brow) to furrow; (writing) to pen

exārsī perf of **exārdēscō**

exasciātus adj hewn out

exasperō, -āre, -āvī, -ātum vt to roughen; (fig) to provoke

exauctōrō, -āre, -āvī, -ātum vt (MIL) to discharge, release; to cashier

exaudiō, -īre, -īvī, -ītum vt to hear clearly; to listen to; to obey

exaugeō, -ēre vt to increase

exaugurātiō, -ōnis f desecrating

exaugurō, -āre vt to desecrate

exauspicō, -āre vi to take an omen

exbibō etc see **ēbibō**

excaecō, -āre vt to blind; (river) to block up

excandēscentia, -ae f growing anger

excandēscō, -ēscere, -uī vi to burn, be inflamed

excantō, -āre vt to charm out, spirit away

excarnificō, -āre *vt* to tear to pieces
excavō, -āre *vt* to hollow out
excēdō, -ēdere, -essī, -essum *vi* to go out, go
away; to die, disappear; to advance, proceed
(to); to digress ♦ *vt* to leave; to overstep, exceed
excellēns, -entis *pres p of* **excellō** ♦ *adj*
outstanding, excellent
excellenter *adv see* **excellēns**
excellentia, -ae *f* superiority, excellence
excellō, -ere *vi* to be eminent, excel
excelsē *adv* loftily
excelsitās, -ātis *f* loftiness
excelsum, -ī *nt* height
excelsus *adj* high, elevated; eminent,
illustrious
exceptiō, -ōnis *f* exception, restriction; (*LAW*)
objection
exceptō, -āre *vt* to catch, take out
exceptus *ppp of* **excipiō**
excernō, -ernere, -rēvī, -rētum *vt* to sift out,
separate
excerpō, -ere, -sī, -tum *vt* to take out; to select,
copy out extracts; to leave out, omit
excessus, -ūs *m* departure, death
excetra, -ae *f* snake
excidiō, -ōnis *f* destruction
excidium, -ī *and* **-iī** *nt* overthrow, destruction
excidō, -ere, -ī *vi* to fall out, fall; (*speech*) to slip
out, escape; (*memory*) to get forgotten, escape;
(*person*) to fail, lose; (*things*) to disappear, be lost
excīdō, -dere, -dī, -sum *vt* to cut off, hew out,
fell; to raze; (*fig*) to banish
excieō *vt see* **exciō**
exciō, -īre, -īvī *and* **-iī, -itum** *and* **-ītum** *vt* to call
out, rouse, summon; to occasion, produce; to
excite
excipiō, -ipere, -ēpī, -eptum *vt* to take out,
remove; to exempt, make an exception
of, mention specifically; to take up, catch,
intercept, overhear; to receive, welcome,
entertain; to come next to, follow after,
succeed
excīsiō, -ōnis *f* destroying
excīsus *ppp of* **excīdō**
excitātus *adj* loud, strong
excitō, -āre, -āvī, -ātum *vt* to rouse, wake up,
summon; to raise, build; to call on (*to stand up*);
(*fig*) to encourage, revive, excite
excitus, excītus *ppp of* **exciō**
exclāmātiō, -ōnis *f* exclamation
exclāmō, -āre, -āvī, -ātum *vi* to cry out, shout
♦ *vt* to exclaim, call
exclūdō, -dere, -sī, -sum *vt* to shut out, exclude;
to shut off, keep off; (*egg*) to hatch out; (*eye*) to
knock out; (*fig*) to prevent, except
exclūsiō, -ōnis *f* shutting out
exclūsus *ppp of* **exclūdō**
excoctus *ppp of* **excoquō**
excōgitātiō, -ōnis *f* thinking out, devising
excōgitō, -āre, -āvī, -ātum *vt* to think out,
contrive
excolō, -olere, -oluī, -ultum *vt* to work
carefully; to perfect, refine
excoquō, -quere, -xī, -ctum *vt* to boil away; to
remove with heat, make with heat; to dry up

excors, -dis *adj* senseless, stupid
excrēmentum, -ī *nt* excretion
excreō *etc see* **exscreō**
excrēscō, -scere, -vī, -tum *vi* to grow, rise up
excrētus *ppp of* **excernō**
excruciō, -āre, -āvī, -ātum *vt* to torture,
torment
excubiae, -ārum *fpl* keeping guard, watch;
sentry
excubitor, -ōris *m* sentry
excubō, -āre, -uī, -itum *vi* to sleep out of doors;
to keep watch; (*fig*) to be on the alert
excūdō, -dere, -dī, -sum *vt* to strike out,
hammer out; (*egg*) to hatch; (*fig*) to make,
compose
exculcō, -āre *vt* to beat, tramp down
excultus *ppp of* **excolō**
excurrō, -rrere, -currī *and* **-rrī, -rsum** *vi* to run
out, hurry out; to make an excursion; (*MIL*) to
make a sortie; (*place*) to extend, project; (*fig*) to
expand
excursiō, -ōnis *f* raid, sortie; (*gesture*) stepping
forward; (*fig*) outset
excursor, -ōris *m* scout
excursus, -ūs *m* excursion, raid, charge
excūsābilis *adj* excusable
excūsātē *adv* excusably
excūsātiō, -ōnis *f* excuse, plea
excūsō, -āre, -āvī, -ātum *vt* to excuse; to
apologize for; to plead as an excuse
excussus *ppp of* **excutiō**
excūsus *ppp of* **excūdō**
excutiō, -tere, -ssī, -ssum *vt* to shake out,
shake off; to knock out, drive out, cast off; (*fig*)
to discard, banish; to examine, inspect
exdorsuō, -āre *vt* to fillet
exec- *etc see* **exsec-**
exedō, -ēsse, -ēdī, -ēsum *vt* to eat up; to wear
away, destroy; (*feelings*) to prey on
exedra, -ae *f* hall, lecture room
exedrium, -ī *and* **-iī** *nt* sitting room
exēmī *perf of* **eximō**
exemplar, -āris *nt* copy; likeness; model, ideal
exemplārēs *mpl* copies
exemplum, -ī *nt* copy; example, sample,
precedent, pattern; purport, nature; warning,
object lesson; ~ **dare** set an example; **exemplī
causā, exemplī gratiā** for instance
exemptus *ppp of* **eximō**
exenterō, -āre *vt* (*comedy*) to empty, clean out;
to torture
exeō, -īre, -iī, -itum *vi* to go out, leave; to come
out, issue; (*MIL*) to march out; (*time*) to expire;
to spring up, rise ♦ *vt* to pass beyond; to avoid;
exīre ex potestāte lose control
exeq- *etc see* **exseq-**
exerceō, -ēre, -uī, -itum *vt* to keep busy,
supervise; (*ground*) to work, cultivate; (*MIL*)
to drill, exercise; (*mind*) to engage, employ;
(*occupation*) to practise, follow, carry on; (*trouble*)
to worry, harass; **sē exercēre** practise, exercise
exercitātiō, -ōnis *f* practice, exercise,
experience
exercitātus *adj* practised, trained, versed;
troubled

exercitium, **-ī** *and* **-iī** *nt* exercising

exercitō, **-āre** *vt* to exercise

exercitor, **-ōris** *m* trainer

exercitus' *ppp of* **exerceō** ♦ *adj* disciplined; troubled; troublesome

exercitus², **-ūs** *m* army (*esp the infantry*); assembly; troop, flock; exercise

exerō *etc see* **exserō**

exēsor, **-ōris** *m* corroder

exēsus *ppp of* **exedō**

exhālātiō, **-ōnis** *f* vapour

exhālō, **-āre** *vt* to exhale, breathe out ♦ *vi* to steam; to expire

exhauriō, **-rīre**, **-sī**, **-stum** *vt* to drain off; to empty; to take away, remove; (*fig*) to exhaust, finish; (*trouble*) to undergo, endure to the end

exhērēdō, **-āre** *vt* to disinherit

exhērēs, **-ēdis** *adj* disinherited

exhibeō, **-ere**, **-uī**, **-itum** *vt* to hold out, produce (*in public*); to display, show; to cause, occasion

exhilarātus *adj* delighted

exhorrēscō, **-ēscere**, **-uī** *vi* to be terrified ♦ *vt* to be terrified at

exhortātiō, **-ōnis** *f* encouragement

exhortor, **-ārī**, **-ātus** *vt* to encourage

exigō, **-igere**, **-ēgī**, **-āctum** *vt* to drive out, thrust; (*payment*) to exact, enforce; to demand, claim; (*goods*) to dispose of; (*time*) to pass, complete; (*work*) to finish; (*news*) to ascertain; to test, examine, consider

exiguē *adv* briefly, slightly, hardly

exiguitās, **-ātis** *f* smallness, meagreness

exiguus *adj* small, short, meagre ♦ *nt* a little bit

exiliō *etc see* **exsiliō**

exīlis *adj* thin, small, meagre; poor; (*style*) flat, insipid

exīlitās, **-ātis** *f* thinness, meagreness

exīliter *adv* feebly

exilium *etc see* **exsilium**

exim *see* **exinde**

eximiē *adv* exceptionally

eximius *adj* exempt; select; distinguished, exceptional

eximō, **-imere**, **-ēmī**, **-emptum** *vt* to take out, remove; to release, free; to exempt; (*time*) to waste; (*fig*) to banish

exin *see* **exinde**

exināniō, **-īre**, **-iī**, **-ītum** *vt* to empty; to pillage

exinde *adv* (*place*) from there, next; (*time*) then, thereafter, next; (*measure*) accordingly

exīstimātiō, **-ōnis** *f* opinion, judgment; reputation, character; (*money*) credit

exīstimātor, **-ōris** *m* judge, critic

exīstimō, **-āre**, **-āvī**, **-ātum** *vt* to value, estimate, judge, think, consider

existō *etc see* **exsistō**

exīstumō *vt see* **exīstimō**

exitiābilis *adj* deadly, fatal

exitiālis *adj* deadly

exitiōsus *adj* pernicious, fatal

exitium, **-ī** *and* **-iī** *nt* destruction, ruin

exitus, **-ūs** *m* departure; way out, outlet; conclusion, end; death; outcome, result

exlēx, **-ēgis** *adj* above the law, lawless

exoculō, **-āre** *vt* to knock the eyes out of

exodium, **-ī** *and* **-iī** *nt* afterpiece

exolēscō, **-scere**, **-vī**, **-tum** *vi* to decay, become obsolete

exolētus *adj* full-grown

exonerō, **-āre**, **-āvī**, **-ātum** *vt* to unload, discharge; (*fig*) to relieve, exonerate

exoptātus *adj* welcome

exoptō, **-āre**, **-āvī**, **-ātum** *vt* to long for, desire

exōrābilis *adj* sympathetic

exōrātor, **-ōris** *m* successful pleader

exōrdior, **-dīrī**, **-sus** *vt* to lay the warp; to begin

exōrdium, **-ī** *and* **-iī** *nt* beginning; (RHET) introductory section

exorior, **-īrī**, **-tus** *vi* to spring up, come out, rise; to arise, appear, start

exōrnātiō, **-ōnis** *f* embellishment

exōrnātor, **-ōris** *m* embellisher

exōrnō, **-āre**, **-āvī**, **-ātum** *vt* to equip, fit out; to embellish, adorn

exōrō, **-āre**, **-āvī**, **-ātum** *vt* to prevail upon, persuade; to obtain, win by entreaty

exōrsus' *ppa of* **exōrdior** ♦ *adj* begun ♦ *ntpl* preamble

exōrsus², **-ūs** *m* beginning

exortus' *ppa of* **exorior**

exortus², **-ūs** *m* rising; east

exos, **-ossis** *adj* boneless

exōsculor, **-ārī**, **-ātus** *vt* to kiss fondly

exossō, **-āre** *vt* to bone

exōstra, **-ae** *f* stage mechanism; (*fig*) public

exōsus *adj* detesting

exōticus *adj* foreign

expallēscō, **-ēscere**, **-uī** *vi* to turn pale, be afraid

expalpō, **-āre** *vt* to coax out

expandō, **-ere**, **-nsī**, **-nsum** *and* **-ssum** *vt* to unfold

expatrō, **-āre** *vt* to squander

expavēscō, **-ere**, **expāvī** *vi* to be terrified ♦ *vt* to dread

expect- *etc see* **exspect-**

expediō, **-īre**, **-īvī** *and* **-iī**, **-ītum** *vt* to free, extricate, disentangle; to prepare, clear (*for action*); to put right, settle; to explain, relate; (*impers*) it is useful, expedient

expedītē *adv* readily, freely

expedītiō, **-ōnis** *f* (MIL) expedition, enterprise

expedītus *ppp of* **expediō** ♦ *adj* light-armed; ready, prompt; at hand ♦ *m* light-armed soldier; **in expedītō esse habēre** be, have in readiness

expellō, **-ellere**, **-ulī**, **-ulsum** *vt* to drive away, eject, expel; to remove, repudiate

expendō, **-endere**, **-endī**, **-ēnsum** *vt* to weigh out; to pay out; (*penalty*) to suffer; (*mind*) to ponder, consider, judge

expēnsum, **-ī** *nt* payment, expenditure

expergēfaciō, **-facere**, **-fēcī**, **-factum** *vt* to rouse, excite

expergīscor, **-gīscī**, **-rēctus** *vi* to wake up; to bestir oneself

expergō, **-ere**, **-ī**, **-itum** *vt* to awaken

experiēns, **-entis** *pres p of* **experior** ♦ *adj* enterprising

experientia, -ae *f* experiment; endeavour; experience, practice

experīmentum, -ī *nt* proof, test; experience

experior, -īrī, -tus *vt* to test, make trial of; to attempt, experience; (*LAW*) to go to law; (*perf tenses*) to know from experience

experrēctus *ppa of* **expergīscor**

expers, -tis *adj* having no part in, not sharing; free from, without

expertus *ppa* (*occ pass*) *of* **experior** ♦ *adj* proved, tried; experienced

expetessō, -ere *vt* to desire

expetō, -ere, -īvī *and* **-iī, -ītum** *vt* to aim at, tend towards; to desire, covet; to attack; to demand, require ♦ *vi* to befall, happen

expiātiō, -ōnis *f* atonement

expictus *ppp of* **expingō**

expīlātiō, -ōnis *f* pillaging

expīlātor, -ōris *m* plunderer

expīlō, -āre, -āvī, -ātum *vt* to rob, plunder

expingō, -ingere, -inxī, -ictum *vt* to portray

expiō, -āre, -āvī, -ātum *vt* to purify; to atone for, make amends for; to avert (*evil*)

expīrō *etc see* **exspīrō**

expiscor, -ārī, -ātus *vt* to try to find out, ferret out

explānātē *adv see* **explānātus**

explānātiō, -ōnis *f* explanation

explānātor, -ōris *m* interpreter

explānātus *adj* distinct

explānō, -āre, -āvī, -ātum *vt* to state clearly, explain; to pronounce clearly

explaudō *etc see* **explōdō**

explēmentum, -ī *nt* filling

expleō, -ēre, -ēvī, -ētum *vt* to fill up; to complete; (*desire*) to satisfy, appease; (*duty*) to perform, discharge; (*loss*) to make good; (*time*) to fulfil, complete

explētiō, -ōnis *f* satisfying

explētus *ppp of* **expleō** ♦ *adj* complete

explicātē *adv* plainly

explicātiō, -ōnis *f* uncoiling; expounding, analysing

explicātor, -ōris *m*, **explicātrīx, -rīcis** *f* expounder

explicātus¹ *adj* spread out; plain, clear

explicātus², **-ūs** *m* explanation

explicitus *adj* easy

explicō, -āre, -āvī *and* **-uī, -ātum** *and* **-itum** *vt* to unfold, undo, spread out; (*book*) to open; (*MIL*) to deploy, extend; (*difficulty*) to put in order, settle; (*speech*) to develop, explain; to set free

explōdō, -dere, -sī, -sum *vt* to hiss off, drive away; (*fig*) to reject

explōrātē *adv* with certainty

explōrātiō, -ōnis *f* spying

explōrātor, -ōris *m* spy, scout

explōrātus *adj* certain, sure

explōrō, -āre, -āvī, -ātum *vt* to investigate, reconnoitre; to ascertain; to put to the test

explōsī *perf of* **explōdō**

explōsiō, -ōnis *f* driving off (the stage)

explōsus *ppp of* **explōdō**

expoliō, -īre, -īvī, -ītum *vt* to smooth off, polish; (*fig*) to refine, embellish

expolītiō, -ōnis *f* smoothing off; polish, finish

expōnō, -ōnere, -osuī, -ositum *vt* to set out, put out; (*child*) to expose; (*NAUT*) to disembark; (*money*) to offer; (*fig*) to set forth, expose, display; (*speech*) to explain, expound

exporrigō, -igere, -ēxī, -ēctum *vt* to extend, smooth out

exportātiō, -ōnis *f* exporting

exportō, -āre, -āvī, -ātum *vt* to carry out, export

exposcō, -ere, expoposcī *vt* to implore, pray for; to demand

expositīcius *adj* foundling

expositiō, -ōnis *f* narration, explanation

expositus *ppp of* **expōnō** ♦ *adj* open, affable; vulgar

expostulātiō, -ōnis *f* complaint

expostulō, -āre, -āvī, -ātum *vt* to demand urgently; to complain of, expostulate

expōtus *ppp of* **ēpōtō**

expressus *ppp of* **exprimō** ♦ *adj* distinct, prominent

exprimō, -imere, -essī, -essum *vt* to squeeze out, force out; to press up; (*fig*) to extort, wrest; (*art*) to mould, model; (*words*) to imitate, portray, translate, pronounce

exprobrātiō, -ōnis *f* reproach

exprobrō, -āre, -āvī, -ātum *vt* to reproach, cast up

exprōmō, -ere, -psī, -ptum *vt* to bring out, fetch out; (*acts*) to exhibit, practise; (*feelings*) to give vent to; (*speech*) to disclose, state

expugnābilis *adj* capable of being taken by storm

expugnācior, -ōris *adj* more effective

expugnātiō, -ōnis *f* storming, assault

expugnātor, -ōris *m* stormer

expugnō, -āre, -āvī, -ātum *vt* to storm, reduce; to conquer; (*fig*) to overcome, extort

expulī *perf of* **expellō**

expulsiō, -ōnis *f* expulsion

expulsor, -ōris *m* expeller

expulsus *ppp of* **expellō**

expultrīx, -īcis *f* expeller

expungō, -ungere, -ūnxī, -ūnctum *vt* to prick out, cancel

expūrgātiō, -ōnis *f* excuse

expūrgō, -āre *vt* to purify; to justify

exputō, -āre *vt* to consider, comprehend

exquīrō, -rere, -sīvī, -sītum *vt* to search out, investigate; to inquire; to devise

exquīsītē *adv* with particular care

exquīsītus *ppp of* **exquīrō** ♦ *adj* well thought out, choice

exsaeviō, -īre *vi* to cease raging

exsanguis *adj* bloodless, pale; feeble

exsarciō, -cīre, -tum *vt* to repair

exsatiō, -āre *vt* to satiate, satisfy

exsaturābilis *adj* appeasable

exsaturō, -āre *vt* to satiate

exsce- *etc see* **esce-**

exscindō, -ndere, -dī, -ssum *vt* to extirpate

exscreō, -āre *vt* to cough up

exscrībō, -bere, -psī, -ptum *vt* to copy out; to note down

exsculpō, -ere, -sī, -tum *vt* to carve out; to erase; (*fig*) to extort

exsecō, -āre, -uī, -tum *vt* to cut out; to castrate

exsecrābilis *adj* cursing, deadly

exsecrātiō, -ōnis *f* curse; solemn oath

exsecrātus *adj* accursed

exsecror, -ārī, -ātus *vt* to curse; to take an oath

exsectiō, -ōnis *f* cutting out

exsecūtiō, -ōnis *f* management; discussion

exsecūtus *ppa of* **exsequor**

exsequiae, -ārum *fpl* funeral, funeral rites

exsequiālis *adj* funeral

exsequor, -quī, -cūtus *vt* to follow, pursue; to follow to the grave; (*duty*) to carry out, accomplish; (*speech*) to describe, relate; (*suffering*) to undergo; (*wrong*) to avenge, punish

exserciō *vt see* **exsarciō**

exserō, -ere, -uī, -tum *vt* to put out, stretch out; to reveal

exsertō, -āre *vt* to stretch out repeatedly

exsertus *ppp of* **exserō** ♦ *adj* protruding

exsībilō, -āre *vt* to hiss off

exsiccātus *adj* (*style*) uninteresting

exsiccō, -āre, -āvī, -ātum *vt* to dry up; to drain

exsicō *etc see* **exsecō**

exsignō, -āre *vt* to write down in detail

exsiliō, -īre, -uī, -sultum *vi* to jump up, spring out; to start

exsilium, -ī *and* **-iī** *nt* banishment, exile; retreat

exsistō, -istere, -titī, -titum *vi* to emerge, appear; to arise, spring (from); to be, exist

exsolvō, -vere, -vī, -ūtum *vt* to undo, loosen, open; to release, free; to get rid of, throw off; (*debt, promise*) to discharge, fulfil, pay up; (*words*) to explain

exsomnis *adj* sleepless, watchful

exsorbeō, -ēre, -uī *vt* to suck, drain; to devour, endure

exsors, -tis *adj* chosen, special; free from

exspargō *etc see* **exspergō**

exspatior, -ārī, -ātus *vi* to go off the course

exspectābilis *adj* to be expected

exspectātiō, -ōnis *f* waiting, expectation

exspectātus *adj* looked for, welcome

exspectō, -āre, -āvī, -ātum *vt* to wait for/till; to see; to expect; to hope for, dread; to require

exspergō, -gere, -sum *vt* to scatter; to diffuse

exspēs *adj* despairing

exspīrātiō, -ōnis *f* exhalation

exspīrō, -āre, -āvī, -ātum *vt* to breathe out, exhale; to emit ♦ *vi* to rush out; to expire, come to an end

exsplendēscō, -ere *vi* to shine

exspoliō, -āre *vt* to pillage

exspuō, -uere, -uī, -ūtum *vt* to spit out, eject; (*fig*) to banish

exsternō, -āre *vt* to terrify

exstillō, -āre *vi* to drip

exstimulātor, -ōris *m* instigator

exstimulō, -āre *vt* to goad on; to excite

exstinctiō, -ōnis *f* annihilation

exstinctor, -ōris *m* extinguisher; destroyer

exstinguō, -guere, -xī, -ctum *vt* to put out, extinguish; to kill, destroy, abolish

exstirpō, -āre *vt* to root out, eradicate

exstitī *perf of* **exsistō**

exstō, -āre *vi* to stand out, project; to be conspicuous, be visible; to be extant, exist, be

exstructiō, -ōnis *f* erection

exstruō, -ere, -xī, -ctum *vt* to heap up; to build up, construct

exsūdō, -āre *vi* to come out in sweat ♦ *vt* (*fig*) to toil through

exsūgō, -gere, -xī, -ctum *vt* to suck out

exsul, -is *m/f* exile

exsulō, -āre, -āvī, -ātum *vi* to be an exile

exsultātiō, -ōnis *f* great rejoicing

exsultim *adv* friskily

exsultō, -āre, -āvī, -ātum *vi* to jump up, prance; (*fig*) to exult, run riot, boast; (*speech*) to range at will

exsuperābilis *adj* superable

exsuperantia, -ae *f* superiority

exsuperō, -āre, -āvī, -ātum *vi* to mount up; to gain the upper hand, excel ♦ *vt* to go over; to surpass; to overpower

exsurdō, -āre *vt* to deafen; (*fig*) to dull

exsurgō, -gere, -rēxī, -rēctum *vi* to rise, stand up; to recover

exsuscitō, -āre *vt* to wake up; (*fire*) to fan; (*mind*) to excite

exta, -ōrum *ntpl* internal organs

extābēscō, -ēscere, -uī *vi* to waste away; to vanish

extāris *adj* sacrificial

extemplō *adv* immediately, on the spur of the moment; **quom ~** as soon as

extemporālis *adj* extempore

extempulō *see* **extemplō**

extendō, -dere, -dī, -tum *and* **extēnsum** *vt* to stretch out, spread, extend; to enlarge, increase; (*time*) to prolong; **sē extendere** exert oneself; **īre per extentum fūnem** walk the tightrope

extēnsus *ppp of* **extendō**

extentō, -āre *vt* to strain, exert

extentus *ppp of* **extendō** ♦ *adj* broad

extenuātiō, -ōnis *f* (*RHET*) diminution

extenuō, -āre, -āvī, -ātum *vt* to thin out, rarefy; to diminish, weaken

exter *adj* from outside; foreign

exterebrō, -āre *vt* to bore out; to extort

extergeō, -gēre, -sī, -sum *vt* to wipe off, clean; to plunder

exterior, -ōris *adj* outer, exterior

exterius *adv* on the outside

exterminō, -āre *vt* to drive out, banish; (*fig*) to put aside

externus *adj* outward, external; foreign, strange

exterō, -erere, -rīvī, -rītum *vt* to rub out, wear away

exterreō, -ēre, -uī, -itum *vt* to frighten

extersus *ppp of* **extergeō**

exterus *see* **exter**

extexō, -ere *vt* to unweave; (*fig*) to cheat

extimēscō, -ēscere, -uī *vi* to be very frightened ♦ *vt* to be very afraid of

extimus *adj* outermost, farthest

extin- *etc see* **exstin-**

extispex, -icis *m* diviner

extollō, -ere, -tulī *vt* to lift up, raise; (*fig*) to exalt, beautify; (*time*) to defer

extorqueō, -quēre, -sī, -tum *vt* to wrench out, wrest; to dislocate; (*fig*) to obtain by force, extort

extorris *adj* banished, in exile

extortor, -ōris *m* extorter

extortus *ppp of* **extorqueō**

extrā *adv* outside; ~ **quam** except that, unless ♦ *prep* (*with acc*) outside, beyond; free from; except

extrahō, -here, -xī, -ctum *vt* to draw out, pull out; to extricate, rescue; to remove; (*time*) to prolong, waste

extrāneus, -ī *m* stranger ♦ *adj* external, foreign

extraōrdinārius *adj* special, unusual

extrārius *adj* external; unrelated ♦ *m* stranger

extrēmitās, -ātis *f* extremity, end

extrēmum¹, -ī *nt* end; **ad ~** at last

extrēmum² *adv* for the last time

extrēmus *adj* outermost, extreme; last; utmost, greatest, meanest

extrīcō, -āre, -āvī, -ātum *vt* to disentangle, extricate; to clear up

extrīnsecus *adv* from outside, from abroad; on the outside

extrītus *ppp of* **exterō**

extrūdō, -dere, -sī, -sum *vt* to drive out; to keep out; (*sale*) to push

extulī *perf of* **efferō²**

extumeō, -ēre *vi* to swell up

extundō, -undere, -udī, -ūsum *vt* to beat out, hammer out; (*comedy*) to extort; (*fig*) to form, compose

exturbō, -āre, -āvī, -ātum *vt* to drive out, throw out, knock out; (*wife*) to put away; (*fig*) to banish, disturb

exūberō, -āre *vi* to abound

exul *etc see* **exsul**

exulcerō, -āre, -āvī, -ātum *vt* to aggravate

exululō, -āre *vi* to howl wildly ♦ *vt* to invoke with cries

exūnctus *ppp of* **exungō**

exundō, -āre *vi* to overflow; to be washed up

exungō, -ere *vt* to anoint liberally

exuō, -uere, -uī, -ūtum *vt* to draw out, put off; to lay aside; to strip

exūrō, -rere, -ssī, -stum *vt* to burn up; to dry up; to burn out; (*fig*) to inflame

exūstiō, -ōnis *f* conflagration

exūtus *ppp of* **exuō**

exuviae, -ārum *fpl* clothing, arms; hide; spoils

Ff

faba, -ae f bean
fabālis adj bean- (in cpds)
fabella, -ae f short story, fable; play
faber, -rī m craftsman (in metal, stone, wood), tradesman, smith; (MIL) artisan; ~ **ferrārius** blacksmith; ~ **tignārius** carpenter ◆ adj skilful
Fabius¹, -ī m Roman family name (esp Q F Maximus Cunctator, dictator against Hannibal)
Fabius², Fabiānus adj see **Fabius¹**
fabrē adv skilfully
fabrēfaciō, -facere, -fēcī, -factum vt to make, build, forge
fabrica, -ae f art, trade; work of art; workshop; (comedy) trick
fabricātiō, -ōnis f structure
fabricātor, -ōris m artificer
Fabricius¹, -ī m Roman family name (esp C F Luscinus, incorruptible commander against Pyrrhus)
Fabricius², Fabriciānus adj see **Fabricius¹**
fabricō, -āre, fabricor, -ārī, -ātus vt to make, build, forge
fabrīlis adj artificer's ◆ ntpl tools
fābula, -ae f story; common talk; play, drama; fable; **fābulae** nonsense!; **lupus in fābulā** talk of the devil!
fābulor, -ārī, -ātus vi to talk, converse ◆ vt to say, invent
fābulōsus adj legendary
facessō, -ere, -īvī, -ītum vt to perform, carry out; to cause (trouble) ◆ vi to go away, retire
facētē adv humorously; brilliantly
facētiae, -ārum fpl wit, clever talk, humour
facētus adj witty, humorous; fine, genteel, elegant
faciēs, -ēī f form, shape; face, looks; appearance, aspect, character
facile adv easily; unquestionably; readily; pleasantly
facilis adj easy; well-suited; ready, quick; (person) good-natured, approachable; (fortune) prosperous
facilitās, -ātis f ease, readiness; (speech) fluency; (person) good nature, affability
facinorōsus adj criminal
facinus, -oris nt deed, action; crime
faciō, -ere, fēcī, factum (impv **fac**, pass **fīō**) vt to make, create, compose, cause; to do, perform; (profession) to practise; (property) to put under; (value) to regard, think of; (words) to represent, pretend, suppose ◆ vi to do, act; (religion) to offer (sacrifice); (with **ad** or dat) to be of use; **cōpiam facere** afford an opportunity;

damnum facere suffer loss; **metum facere** excite fear; **proelium facere** join battle; **rem facere** make money; **verba facere** talk; **māgnī facere** think highly of; **quid tibi faciam?** how am I to answer you?; **quid tē faciam?** what am I to do with you?; **fac sciam** let me know; **fac potuisse** suppose one could have
factiō, -ōnis f making, doing; group, party, faction (esp in politics and chariot racing)
factiōsus adj factious, oligarchical
factitō, -āre, -āvī, -ātum vt to keep making or doing; to practise; to declare (to be)
factor, -ōris m (sport) batsman
factum, -ī nt deed, exploit
factus ppp of **faciō**
facula, -ae f little torch
facultās, -ātis f means, opportunity; ability; abundance, supply, resources
fācundē adv see **fācundus**
fācundia, -ae f eloquence
fācundus adj fluent, eloquent
faeceus adj impure
faecula, -ae f wine lees
faenebris adj of usury
faenerātiō, -ōnis f usury
faenerātō adv with interest
faenerātor, -ōris m moneylender
faenerō, -āre, faeneror, -ārī, -ātus vt to lend at interest; to ruin with usury; (fig) to trade in
faenīlia, -um ntpl hayloft
faenum, -ī nt hay; ~ **habet in cornū** he is dangerous
faenus, -oris nt interest; capital lent at interest; (fig) profit, advantage
faenusculum, -ī nt a little interest
Faesulae, -ārum fpl town in Etruria (now Fiesole)
Faesulānus adj see **Faesulae**
faex, faecis f sediment, lees; brine (of pickles); (fig) dregs
fāgineus, fāginus adj of beech
fāgus, -ī f beech
fala, -ae f siege tower (used in assaults); (Circus) pillar
falārica, -ae f a missile, firebrand
falcārius, -ī and **-iī** m sicklemaker
falcātus adj scythed; sickle-shaped
falcifer, -ī adj scythe-carrying
Falernus adj Falernian (of a district in N. Campania famous for its wine) ◆ nt Falernian wine
Faliscī, -ōrum mpl a people of S.E. Etruria (with chief town Falerii)

Faliscus *adj see* **Faliscī**
fallācia, -ae *f* trick, deception
fallāciter *adv see* **fallāx**
fallāx, -ācis *adj* deceitful, deceptive
fallō, -lere, fefellī, -sum *vt* to deceive, cheat, beguile; to disappoint, fail, betray; (*promise*) to break; to escape the notice of, be unknown to; (*pass*) to be mistaken; **mē fallit** I am mistaken; I do not know
falsē *adv* wrongly, by mistake; fraudulently
falsidicus *adj* lying
falsificus *adj* deceiving
falsiiūrius *adj* perjurious
falsiloquus *adj* lying
falsiparēns, -entis *adj* with a pretended father
falsō *adv see* **falsē**
falsus *ppp of* **fallō** ◆ *adj* false, mistaken; deceitful; forged, falsified; sham, fictitious ◆ *nt* falsehood, error
falx, falcis *f* sickle, scythe; pruning hook; (MIL) siege hook
fāma, -ae *f* talk, rumour, tradition; public opinion; reputation, fame; infamy
famēlicus *adj* hungry
famēs, -is *f* hunger; famine; (*fig*) greed; (RHET) poverty of expression
fāmigerātiō, -ōnis *f* rumour
fāmigerātor, -ōris *m* telltale
familia, -ae *f* domestics, slaves of a household; family property, estate; family, house; school, sect; **pater familiās** master of a household; **familiam dūcere** be head of a sect, company *etc*
familiāris *adj* domestic, household, family; intimate, friendly; (*entrails*) relating to the sacrificer ◆ *m* servant; friend
familiāritās, -ātis *f* intimacy, friendship
familiāriter *adv* on friendly terms
fāmōsus *adj* celebrated; infamous; slanderous
famula, -ae *f* maidservant, handmaid
famulāris *adj* of servants
famulātus, -ūs *m* slavery
famulor, -ārī *vi* to serve
famulus, -ī *m* servant, attendant ◆ *adj* serviceable
fānāticus *adj* inspired; frantic, frenzied
fandī *gerund of* **for**
fandum, -ī *nt* right
fānum, -ī *nt* sanctuary, temple
fār, farris *nt* spelt; corn; meal
farciō, -cīre, -sī, -tum *vt* to stuff, fill full
farīna, -ae *f* meal, flour
farrāgō, -inis *f* mash, hotch-potch; medley
farrātus *adj* of corn; filled with corn
farsī *perf of* **farciō**
fartem, -im *f acc* filling; mincemeat
fartor, -ōris *m* fattener, poulterer
fartus *ppp of* **farciō**
fās *nt* divine law; right; **fās est** it is lawful, possible
fascia, -ae *f* band, bandage; streak of cloud
fasciculus, -ī *m* bundle, packet
fascinō, -āre *vt* to bewitch (*esp with the evil eye*)
fascinum, -ī *nt*, **fascinus, -ī** *m* charm
fasciola, -ae *f* small bandage

fascis, -is *m* bundle, faggot; soldier's pack, burden; (*pl*) rods and axe (*carried before the highest magistrates*); high office (*esp the consulship*)
fassus *ppa of* **fateor**
fāstī, -ōrum *mpl register of days for legal and public business*; calendar; *registers of magistrates and other public records*
fastīdiō, -īre, -īī, -ītum *vt* to loathe, dislike, despise ◆ *vi* to feel squeamish, be disgusted; to be disdainful
fastīdiōsē *adv* squeamishly; disdainfully
fastīdiōsus *adj* squeamish, disgusted; fastidious, nice; disagreeable
fastīdium, -ī *and* **-iī** *nt* squeamishness, distaste; disgust, aversion; disdain, pride
fastīgātē *adv* in a sloping position
fastīgātus *adj* sloping up or down
fastīgium, -ī *and* **-iī** *nt* gable, pediment; slope; height, depth; top, summit; (*fig*) highest degree, acme, dignity; (*speech*) main headings
fāstus *adj* lawful for public business
fastus, -ūs *m* disdain, pride
Fāta *ntpl* the Fates
fātālis *adj* fateful, destined; fatal, deadly
fātāliter *adv* by fate
fateor, -tērī, -ssus *vt* to confess, acknowledge; to reveal, bear witness to
fāticanus, -inus *adj* prophetic
fātidicus *adj* prophetic ◆ *m* prophet
fātifer, -ī *adj* deadly
fatīgātiō, -ōnis *f* weariness
fatīgō, -āre, -āvī, -ātum *vt* to tire, exhaust; to worry, importune; to wear down, torment
fātiloqua, -ae *f* prophetess
fatīscō, -ere, fatīscor, -ī *vi* to crack, split; (*fig*) to become exhausted
fatuitās, -ātis *f* silliness
fātum, -ī *nt* divine word, oracle; fate, destiny; divine will; misfortune, doom, death; **fātō obīre** die a natural death
fātur, fātus *3rd pers and ppa of* **for**
fatuus *adj* silly; unwieldy ◆ *m* fool
faucēs, -ium *fpl* throat; pass, narrow channel, chasm; (*fig*) jaws
Faunus, -ī *m father of Latinus* (*god of forests and herdsmen, identified with Pan*); (*pl*) woodland spirits, Fauns
faustē *adv see* **faustus**
faustitās, -ātis *f* good fortune, fertility
faustus *adj* auspicious, lucky
fautor, -ōris *m* supporter, patron
fautrīx, -īcis *f* protectress
favea, -ae *f* pet slave
faveō, -ēre, fāvī, fautum *vi* (*with dat*) to favour, befriend, support; **favēre linguīs** keep silence
favilla, -ae *f* embers, ashes; (*fig*) spark
favitor *etc see* **fautor**
Favōnius, -ī *m* west wind, zephyr
favor, -ōris *m* favour, support; applause
favōrābilis *adj* in favour; pleasing
favus, -ī *m* honeycomb
fax, facis *f* torch, wedding torch, funeral torch; marriage, death; (ASTR) meteor; (*fig*) flame, fire, instigator; guide; **facem praeferre** act as guide

faxim, faxō *archaic subj and fut of* **faciō**

febrīcula, -ae *f* slight fever

febris, -is *f* fever

Februārius, -ī *m* February ♦ *adj* of February

februum, -ī *nt* purification; **Februa** *pl festival of purification in February*

fēcī *perf of* **faciō**

fēcunditās, -ātis *f* fertility; (*style*) exuberance

fēcundō, -āre *vt* to fertilize

fēcundus *adj* fertile, fruitful; fertilizing; (*fig*) abundant, rich, prolific

fefellī *perf of* **fallō**

fel, fellis *nt* gall bladder, bile; poison; (*fig*) animosity

fēlēs, -is *f* cat

fēlīcitās, -ātis *f* happiness, good luck

fēlīciter *adv* abundantly; favourably; happily

fēlīx, -īcis *adj* fruitful; auspicious, favourable; fortunate, successful

fēmella, -ae *f* girl

fēmina, -ae *f* female, woman

fēmineus *adj* woman's, of women; unmanly

femur, -oris *and* **-inis** *nt* thigh

fēn- *etc see* **faen-**

fenestra, -ae *f* window; (*fig*) loophole

fera, -ae *f* wild beast

ferācius *adv* more fruitfully

fērālis *adj* funereal; of the Feralia; deadly ♦ *ntpl festival of the dead in February*

ferāx, -ācis *adj* fruitful, productive

ferbuī *perf of* **ferveō**

ferculum, -ī *nt* litter, barrow; dish, course

ferē *adv* almost, nearly, about; quite, just; usually, generally, as a rule; (*with neg*) hardly; **nihil ~** hardly anything

ferentārius, -ī *m* a light-armed soldier

Feretrius, -ī *m* an epithet of Jupiter

feretrum, -ī *nt* bier

fēriae, -ārum *fpl* festival, holidays; (*fig*) peace, rest

fēriātus *adj* on holiday, idle

ferīnus *adj* of wild beasts ♦ *f* game

feriō, -īre *vt* to strike, hit; to kill, sacrifice; (*comedy*) to cheat; **foedus ferīre** conclude a treaty

feritās, -ātis *f* wildness, savagery

fermē *see* **ferē**

fermentum, -ī *nt* yeast; beer; (*fig*) passion, vexation

ferō, ferre, tulī, lātum *vt* to carry, bring, bear; to bring forth, produce; to move, stir, raise; to carry off, sweep away, plunder; (*pass*) to rush, hurry, fly, flow, drift; (*road*) to lead; (*trouble*) to endure, suffer, sustain; (*feelings*) to exhibit, show; (*speech*) to talk about, give out, celebrate; (*bookkeeping*) to enter; (*circumstances*) to allow, require; **sē ferre** rush, move; profess to be, boast; **condiciōnem ferre, lēgem ferre** propose terms, a law; **iūdicem ferre** sue; **sententiam ferre, suffrāgium ferre** vote; **signa ferre** march; attack; **aegrē ferre** be annoyed at; **laudibus ferre** extol; **in oculīs ferre** be very fond of; **prae sē ferre** show, declare; **fertur, ferunt** it is said, they say; **ut mea fert opīniō** in my opinion

ferōcia, -ae *f* courage; spirit; pride, presumption

ferōcitās, -ātis *f* high spirits, aggressiveness; presumption

ferōciter *adv* bravely; insolently

Fērōnia, -ae *f* old Italian goddess

ferōx, -ōcis *adj* warlike, spirited, daring; proud, insolent

ferrāmentum, -ī *nt* tool, implement

ferrārius *adj* of iron; **faber ~** blacksmith ♦ *f* iron-mine, iron-works

ferrātus *adj* ironclad, ironshod ♦ *mpl* men in armour

ferreus *adj* of iron, iron; (*fig*) hard, cruel; strong, unyielding

ferrūgineus *adj* rust-coloured, dark

ferrūgō, -inis *f* rust; dark colour; gloom

ferrum, -ī *nt* iron; sword; *any iron implement*; force of arms; **~ et ignis** devastation

fertilis *adj* fertile, productive; fertilizing

fertilitās, -ātis *f* fertility

ferula, -ae *f* fennel; staff, rod

ferus *adj* wild; uncivilized; cruel ♦ *m* beast

fervēfaciō, -ere, -fēcī, -factum *vt* to boil

fervēns, -entis *pres p of* **ferveō** ♦ *adj* hot; raging; (*fig*) impetuous, furious

ferventer *adv* hotly

ferveō, -vēre, -buī *vi* to boil, burn; (*fig*) to rage, bustle, be agitated

fervēscō, -ere *vi* to boil up, grow hot

fervidus *adj* hot, raging; (*fig*) fiery, violent

fervō, -vere, -vī *vi see* **ferveō**

fervor, -ōris *m* seething; heat; (*fig*) ardour, passion

Fescennīnus *adj* Fescennine (*a kind of ribald song, perhaps from Fescennium in Etruria*)

fessus *adj* tired, worn out

festīnanter *adv* hastily

festīnātiō, -ōnis *f* haste, hurry

festīnō, -āre *vi* to hurry, be quick ♦ *vt* to hasten, accelerate

festīnus *adj* hasty, quick

fēstīvē *adv* gaily; humorously

fēstīvitās, -ātis *f* gaiety, merriment; humour, fun

fēstīvus *adj* gay, jolly; delightful; (*speech*) humorous

festūca, -ae *f* rod (*with which slaves were manumitted*)

fēstus *adj* festal, on holiday ♦ *nt* holiday; feast

fētiālis, -is *m* priest who carried out the ritual in making war and peace

fētūra, -ae *f* breeding; brood

fētus¹ *adj* pregnant; newly delivered; (*fig*) productive, full of

fētus², -ūs *m* breeding, bearing, producing; brood, young; fruit, produce; (*fig*) production

fiber, -rī *m* beaver

fibra, -ae *f* fibre; section of lung or liver; entrails

fībula, -ae *f* clasp, brooch; clamp

ficedula, -ae *f* fig pecker

fictē *adv* falsely

fictilis *adj* clay, earthen ♦ *nt* jar; clay figure

fictor, -ōris *m* sculptor; maker, inventor

fictrīx, -īcis *f* maker

fictūra, -ae f shaping, invention
fictus ppp of **fingō** ♦ adj false, fictitious ♦ nt falsehood
ficulnus adj of the fig tree
ficus, -ī and **-ūs** f fig tree; fig
fidēle adv faithfully, surely, firmly
fidēlia, -ae f pot, pail; **dē eādem fidēliā duōs parietēs dealbāre** kill two birds with one stone
fidēlis adj faithful, loyal; trustworthy, sure
fidēlitās, -ātis f faithfulness, loyalty
fidēliter adv faithfully, surely, firmly
Fīdēnae, -ārum fpl ancient Latin town
Fīdēnās, -ātis adj see **Fīdēnae**
fidēns, -entis pres p of **fīdō** ♦ adj bold, resolute
fidenter adv see **fidēns**
fidentia, -ae f self-confidence
fidēs¹, -eī f trust, faith, belief; trustworthiness, honour, loyalty, truth; promise, assurance, word; guarantee, safe-conduct, protection; (COMM) credit; (LAW) good faith; ~ **mala** dishonesty; **rēs fidēsque** entire resources; **fidem facere** convince; **fidem servāre ergā** keep faith with; **dī vostram fidem** for Heaven's sake!; **ex fidē bonā** in good faith
fidēs², -is f (usu pl) stringed instrument, lyre, lute; (ASTR) Lyra
fidī perf of **findō**
fidicen, -inis m musician; lyric poet
fidicina, -ae f music girl
fidicula, -ae f small lute
Fidius, -ī m an epithet of Jupiter
fīdō, -dere, -sus vi (with dat or abl) to trust, rely on
fidūcia, -ae f confidence, assurance; self-confidence; (LAW) trust, security
fidūciārius adj to be held in trust
fīdus adj trusty, reliable; sure, safe
fīgō, -gere, -xī, -xum vt to fix, fasten, attach; to drive in, pierce; (speech) to taunt
figulāris adj a potter's
figulus, -ī m potter; builder
figūra, -ae f shape, form; nature, kind; phantom; (RHET) figure of speech
figūrō, -āre vt to form, shape
fīlātim adv thread by thread
fīlia, -ae f daughter
fīlicātus adj with fern patterns
fīliola, -ae f little daughter
fīliolus, -ī m little son
fīlius, -ī and **-iī** m son; **terrae ~** a nobody
filix, -cis f fern
fīlum, -ī nt thread; band of wool, fillet; string, shred, wick; contour, shape; (speech) texture, quality
fimbriae, -ārum fpl fringe, end
fimus, -ī m dung; dirt
findō, -ndere, -dī, -ssum vt to split, divide; to burst
fingō, -ere, finxī, fictum vt to form, shape, make; to mould, model; to dress, arrange; to train; (mind, speech) to imagine, suppose, represent, sketch; to invent, fabricate; **vultum fingere** compose the features

fīniō, -īre, -īvī, -ītum vt to bound, limit; to restrain; to prescribe, define, determine; to end, finish, complete ♦ vi to finish, die
fīnis, -is m/f boundary, border; (pl) territory; bound, limit; end; death; highest point, summit; aim, purpose; ~ **bonōrum** the chief good; **quem ad fīnem?** how long?; **fīne genūs** up to the knee
fīnītē adv within limits
fīnitimus adj neighbouring, adjoining; akin, like ♦ mpl neighbours
fīnītor, -ōris m surveyor
fīnitumus adj see **fīnitimus**
fīnītus ppp of **fīniō** ♦ adj (RHET) well-rounded
finxī perf of **fingō**
fīō, fierī, factus vi to become, arise; to be made, be done; to happen; **quī fit ut?** how is it that?; **ut fit** as usually happens; **quid mē fīet?** what will become of me?
firmāmen, -inis nt support
firmāmentum, -ī nt support, strengthening; (fig) mainstay
firmātor, -ōris m establisher
firmē adv powerfully, steadily
firmitās, -ātis f firmness, strength; steadfastness, stamina
firmiter adv see **firmē**
firmitūdō, -inis f strength, stability
firmō, -āre, -āvī, -ātum vt to strengthen, support, fortify; (mind) to encourage, steady; (fact) to confirm, prove, assert
firmus adj strong, stable, firm; (fig) powerful, constant, sure, true
fiscella, -ae f wicker basket
fiscina, -ae f wicker basket
fiscus, -ī m purse, moneybox; public exchequer; imperial treasury, the emperor's privy purse
fissilis adj easy to split
fissiō, -ōnis f dividing
fissum, -ī nt slit, fissure
fissus ppp of **findō**
fistūca, -ae f rammer
fistula, -ae f pipe, tube; panpipes; (MED) ulcer
fistulātor, -ōris m panpipe player
fīsus ppa of **fīdō**
fīxī perf of **fīgō**
fīxus ppp of **fīgō** ♦ adj fixed, fast, permanent
flābellifera, -ae f fanbearer
flābellum, -ī nt fan
flābilis adj airy
flābra, -ōrum ntpl blasts, gusts; wind
flacceō, -ēre vi to flag, lose heart
flaccēscō, -ere vi to flag, droop
flaccidus adj flabby, feeble
flaccus adj flap-eared
Flaccus, -ī m surname of Horace
flagellō, -āre vt to whip, lash
flagellum, -ī nt whip, lash; strap, thong; (vine) shoot; (polyp) arm; (feelings) sting
flāgitātiō, -ōnis f demand
flāgitātor, -ōris m demander, dun
flāgitiōsē adv infamously
flāgitiōsus adj disgraceful, profligate
flāgitium, -ī and **-iī** nt offence, disgrace, shame; scoundrel

flāgitō, -āre, -āvī, -ātum vt to demand, importune, dun; (LAW) to summon

flagrāns, -antis pres p of **flagrō ♦** adj hot, blazing; brilliant; passionate

flagranter adv passionately

flagrantia, -ae f blazing; (fig) shame

flagrō, -āre vi to blaze, burn, be on fire; (feelings) to be excited, be inflamed; (ill-will) to be the victim of

flagrum, -ī nt whip, lash

flāmen¹, -inis m priest (of a particular deity)

flāmen², -inis nt blast, gale, wind

flāminica, -ae f wife of a priest

Flāminīnus, -ī m Roman surname (esp the conqueror of Philip V of Macedon)

flāminium, -ī and **-iī** nt priesthood

Flāminius¹, -ī m Roman family name (esp the consul defeated by Hannibal)

Flāminius², Flāminiānus adj: **Via Flāminia** road from Rome N.E. to Ariminum

flamma, -ae f flame, fire; torch, star; fiery colour; (fig) passion; danger, disaster

flammeolum, -ī nt bridal veil

flammēscō, -ere vi to become fiery

flammeus adj fiery, blazing; flame-coloured ♦ nt bridal veil

flammifer, -ī adj fiery

flammō, -āre, -āvī, -ātum vi to blaze ♦ vt to set on fire, burn; (fig) to inflame, incense

flammula, -ae f little flame

flātus, -ūs m blowing, breath; breeze; (fig) arrogance

flāvēns, -entis adj yellow, golden

flāvēscō, -ere vi to turn yellow

Flāviānus adj see **Flāvius**

Flāvius, -ī m Roman family name (esp the emperors Vespasian, Titus and Domitian)

flāvus adj yellow, golden

flēbilis adj lamentable; tearful, mournful

flēbiliter adv see **flēbilis**

flectō, -ctere, -xī, -xum vt to bend, turn; to turn aside, wheel; (promontory) to round; (mind) to direct, persuade, dissuade ♦ vi to turn, march

fleō, -ēre, -ēvī, -ētum vi to weep, cry ♦ vt to lament, mourn for

flētus, -ūs m weeping, tears

flexanimus adj moving

flexī perf of **flectō**

flexibilis adj pliant, flexible; fickle

flexilis adj pliant

flexiloquus adj ambiguous

flexiō, -ōnis f bending, winding; (voice) modulation

flexipēs, -edis adj twining

flexuōsus adj tortuous

flexūra, -ae f bending

flexus¹ ppp of **flectō ♦** adj winding

flexus², -ūs m winding, bending; change

flīctus, -ūs m collision

flō, -āre, -āvī, -ātum vt, vi to blow; (money) to coin

floccus, -ī m bit of wool; triviality; **floccī nōn faciō** I don't care a straw for

Flōra, -ae f goddess of flowers

Flōrālis adj see **Flōra**

flōrēns, -entis pres p of **flōreō ♦** adj in bloom; bright; prosperous, flourishing

flōreō, -ēre, -uī vi to blossom, flower; (age) to be in one's prime; (wine) to froth; (fig) to flourish, prosper; (places) to be gay with

flōrēscō, -ere vi to begin to flower; to grow prosperous

flōreus adj of flowers, flowery

flōridulus adj pretty little

flōridus adj of flowers, flowery; fresh, pretty; (style) florid, ornate

flōrifer, -ī adj flowery

flōrilegus adj flower-sipping

flōrus adj beautiful

flōs, -ōris m flower, blossom; (wine) bouquet; (age) prime, heyday; (youth) downy beard, youthful innocence; (fig) crown, glory; (speech) ornament

flōsculus, -ī m little flower; (fig) pride, ornament

flūctifragus adj surging

flūctuātiō, -ōnis f wavering

flūctuō, -āre vi to toss, wave; (fig) to rage, swell, waver

flūctuōsus adj stormy

flūctus, -ūs m wave; flowing, flood; (fig) disturbance; **flūctūs in simpulō** a storm in a teacup

fluēns, -entis pres p of **fluō ♦** adj lax, loose, enervated; (speech) fluent

fluenta, -ōrum ntpl stream, flood

fluenter adv in a flowing manner

fluentisonus adj wave-echoing

fluidus adj flowing, fluid; lax, soft; relaxing

fluitō, -āre vi to flow, float about; to wave, flap, move unsteadily; (fig) to waver

flūmen, -inis nt stream, river; (fig) flood, flow, fluency; **adversō flūmine** upstream; **secundō flūmine** downstream

flūmineus adj river- (in cpds)

fluō, -ere, -xī, -xum vi to flow; to overflow, drip; (fig) to fall in, fall away, vanish; (speech) to run evenly; (circumstances) to proceed, tend

flūtō etc see **fluitō**

fluviālis adj river- (in cpds)

fluviātilis adj river- (in cpds)

flūvidus etc see **fluidus**

fluvius, -ī and **-iī** m river, stream

fluxī perf of **fluō**

fluxus adj flowing, loose, leaky; (person) lax, dissolute; (thing) frail, fleeting, unreliable

fōcāle, -is nt scarf

foculus, -ī m stove, fire

focus, -ī m hearth, fireplace; pyre, altar; (fig) home

fodicō, -āre vt to nudge, jog

fodiō, -ere, fōdī, fossum vt to dig; to prick, stab; (fig) to goad

foedē adv see **foedus¹**

foederātus adj confederated

foedifragus adj perfidious

foeditās, -ātis f foulness, hideousness

foedō, -āre, -āvī, -ātum vt to mar, disfigure; to disgrace, sully

foedus¹ *adj* foul, hideous, revolting; vile, disgraceful

foedus², **-eris** *nt* treaty, league; agreement, compact; law

foen- *etc see* **faen-**

foeteō, **-ēre** *vi* to stink

foetidus *adj* stinking

foetor, **-ōris** *m* stench

foetu- *etc see* **fētu-**

foliātum, **-ī** *nt* nard oil

folium, **-ī** *and* **-iī** *nt* leaf

folliculus, **-ī** *m* small bag; eggshell

follis, **-is** *m* bellows; punchball; purse

fōmentum, **-ī** *nt* poultice, bandage; (*fig*) alleviation

fōmes, **-itis** *m* tinder, kindling

fōns, **fontis** *m* spring, source; water; (*fig*) origin, fountainhead

fontānus *adj* spring- (*in cpds*)

fonticulus, **-ī** *m* little spring

for, **fārī**, **fātus** *vt*, *vi* to speak, utter

forābilis *adj* penetrable

forāmen, **-inis** *nt* hole, opening

forās *adv* out, outside

forceps, **-ipis** *m/f* tongs, forceps

forda, **-ae** *f* cow in calf

fore, **forem** *fut infin and imperf subj of* **sum**

forēnsis *adj* public, forensic; of the marketplace

foris, **-is** *f* (*usu pl*) door; (*fig*) opening, entrance

forīs *adv* out of doors, outside, abroad; from outside, from abroad; ~ **cēnāre** dine out

fōrma, **-ae** *f* form, shape, appearance; mould, stamp, last; (*person*) beauty; (*fig*) idea, nature, kind

fōrmāmentum, **-ī** *nt* shape

fōrmātūra, **-ae** *f* shaping

Formiae, **-ārum** *fpl town in S. Latium*

Formiānus *adj* of Formiae ♦ *nt* villa at Formiae

formīca, **-ae** *f* ant

formīcinus *adj* crawling

formīdābilis *adj* terrifying

formīdō¹, **-āre**, **-āvī**, **-ātum** *vt*, *vi* to fear, be terrified

formīdō², **-inis** *f* terror, awe, horror; scarecrow

formīdolōsē *adv see* **formīdolōsus**

formīdolōsus *adj* fearful, terrifying; afraid

fōrmō, **-āre**, **-āvī**, **-ātum** *vt* to shape, fashion, form

fōrmōsitās, **-ātis** *f* beauty

fōrmōsus *adj* beautiful, handsome

fōrmula, **-ae** *f* rule, regulation; (LAW) procedure, formula; (PHILOS) principle

fornācula, **-ae** *f* small oven

fornāx, **-ācis** *f* furnace, oven, kiln

fornicātus *adj* arched

fornix, **-icis** *m* arch, vault; brothel

forō, **-āre** *vt* to pierce

Foroiūliēnsis *adj see* **Forum Iūlī**

fors, **fortis** *f* chance, luck ♦ *adv* perchance; **forte** by chance, as it happened; perhaps; **nē forte** in case; **sī forte** if perhaps; in the hope that

forsan, **forsit**, **forsitan** *adv* perhaps

fortasse, **-is** *adv* perhaps, possibly; (*irony*) very likely

forticulus *adj* quite brave

fortis *adj* strong, sturdy; brave, manly, resolute

fortiter *adv* vigorously; bravely

fortitūdō, **-inis** *f* courage, resolution; strength

fortuītō *adv* by chance

fortuītus *adj* casual, accidental

fortūna, **-ae** *f* chance, luck, fortune; good luck, success; misfortune; circumstances, lot; (*pl*) possessions; **fortūnae fīlius** Fortune's favourite; **fortūnam habēre** be successful

fortūnātē *adv see* **fortūnātus**

fortūnātus *adj* happy, lucky; well off, rich, blessed

fortūnō, **-āre** *vt* to bless, prosper

forulī, **-ōrum** *mpl* bookcase

forum, **-ī** *nt* public place, market; market town; *Roman Forum between the Palatine and Capitol*; public affairs, law courts, business; ~ **boārium** cattle market; ~ **olitōrium** vegetable market; ~ **piscātōrium** fish market; ~ **agere** hold an assize; ~ **attingere** enter public life; **cēdere forō** go bankrupt; **utī forō** take advantage of a situation

Forum Iūlī *colony in S. Gaul* (*now* Fréjus)

forus, **-ī** *m* gangway; block of seats; (*bees*) cell frame

fossa, **-ae** *f* ditch, trench

fossiō, **-ōnis** *f* digging

fossor, **-ōris** *m* digger

fossus *ppp of* **fodiō**

fōtus *ppp of* **foveō**

fovea, **-ae** *f* pit, pitfall

foveō, **-ēre**, **fōvī**, **fōtum** *vt* to warm, keep warm; (MED) to foment; to fondle, keep; (*fig*) to cherish, love, foster, pamper, encourage; **castra fovēre** remain in camp

frāctus *ppp of* **frangō** ♦ *adj* weak, faint

frāga, **-ōrum** *ntpl* strawberries

fragilis *adj* brittle, fragile; frail, fleeting

fragilitās, **-ātis** *f* frailness

fragmen, **-inis** *nt* (*pl*) fragments, ruins, wreck

fragmentum, **-ī** *nt* fragment, remnant

fragor, **-ōris** *m* crash, din; disintegration

fragōsus *adj* crashing, roaring, breakable; rough

frāgrāns, **-antis** *adj* fragrant

framea, **-ae** *f* German spear

frangō, **-angere**, **-ēgī**, **-āctum** *vt* to break, shatter, wreck; to crush, grind; (*fig*) to break down, weaken, humble; (*emotion*) to touch, move; **cervīcem frangere** strangle

frāter, **-ris** *m* brother; cousin; (*fig*) friend, ally

frāterculus, **-ī** *m* brother

frāternē *adv* like a brother

frāternitās, **-ātis** *f* brotherhood

frāternus *adj* brotherly, a brother's, fraternal

frātricīda, **-ae** *m* fratricide

fraudātiō, **-ōnis** *f* deceit, fraud

fraudātor, **-ōris** *m* swindler

fraudō, **-āre**, **-āvī**, **-ātum** *vt* to cheat, defraud; to steal, cancel

fraudulentus *adj* deceitful, fraudulent

fraus, **-audis** *f* deceit, fraud; delusion, error; offence, wrong; injury, damage; **lēgī fraudem**

facere evade the law; **in fraudem incidere** be disappointed; **sine fraude** without harm

fraxineus, fraxinus *adj* of ash

fraxinus, -ī *f* ash tree; ashen spear

Fregellae, -ārum *fpl town in S. Latium*

Fregellānus *adj see* **Fregellae**

frēgī *perf of* **frangō**

fremebundus *adj* roaring

fremitus, -ūs *m* roaring, snorting, noise

fremō, -ere, -uī, -itum *vi* to roar, snort, grumble
  ◆ *vt* to shout for, complain

fremor, -ōris *m* murmuring

frendō, -ere *vi* to gnash the teeth

frēnō, -āre, -āvī, -ātum *vt* to bridle; (*fig*) to curb, restrain

frēnum, -ī *nt* (*pl* **-a, -ōrum** *nt*, **-ī, -ōrum** *m*) bridle, bit; (*fig*) curb, check; **frēnōs dare** give vent to;
  ~ mordēre take the bit between one's teeth

frequēns, -entis *adj* crowded, numerous, populous; regular, repeated, frequent;
  ~ senatus a crowded meeting of the senate

frequentātiō, -ōnis *f* accumulation

frequenter *adv* in large numbers; repeatedly, often

frequentia, -ae *f* full attendance, throng, crowd

frequentō, -āre, -āvī, -ātum *vt* to crowd, populate; to visit repeatedly, frequent; to repeat; (*festival*) to celebrate, keep

fretēnsis *adj* of the Straits of Messina

fretum, -ī *nt* strait; sea; (*fig*) violence;
  ~ Siciliēnse Straits of Messina

fretus, -ūs *m* strait

frētus *adj* relying, confident

fricō, -āre, -uī, -tum *vt* to rub, rub down

frictus *ppp of* **frigō**

frīgefactō, -āre *vt* to cool

frīgeō, -ēre *vi* to be cold; (*fig*) to be lifeless, flag; to be coldly received, fall flat

frīgerāns *adj* cooling

frīgēscō, -ere, frixī *vi* to grow cold; to become inactive

frīgida, -ae *f* cold water

frīgidē *adv* feebly

frīgidulus *adj* rather cold, faint

frīgidus *adj* cold, cool; chilling; (*fig*) dull, torpid; (*words*) flat, uninteresting

frīgō, -gere, -xī, -ctum *vt* to roast, fry

frīgus, -oris *nt* cold; cold weather, winter; death; (*fig*) dullness, inactivity; coldness, indifference

friguttiō, -īre *vi* to stammer

friō, -āre *vt* to crumble

fritillus, -ī *m* dice box

frīvolus *adj* empty, paltry

frixī *perf of* **frigō**

frondātor, -ōris *m* vinedresser, pruner

frondeō, -ēre *vi* to be in leaf

frondēscō, -ere *vi* to become leafy, shoot

frondeus *adj* leafy

frondifer, -ī *adj* leafy

frondōsus *adj* leafy

frōns¹, -ondis *f* leaf, foliage; garland of leaves

frōns², -ontis *f* forehead, brow; front, facade; (*fig*) look, appearance, exterior; **frontem**

contrahere frown; **ā fronte** in front; **in fronte** in breadth

frontālia, -um *ntpl* frontlet

frontō, -ōnis *m* a broad-browed man

frūctuārius *adj* productive; paid for out of produce

fructuōsus *adj* productive; profitable

frūctus¹ *ppa of* **fruor**

frūctus², -ūs *m* enjoyment; revenue, income; produce, fruit; (*fig*) consequence, reward; **frūctuī esse** be an asset (to); **frūctum percipere** reap the fruits (of)

frūgālis *adj* thrifty, worthy

frūgālitās, -ātis *f* thriftiness, restraint

frūgāliter *adv* temperately

frūgēs *etc see* **frūx**

frūgī *adj* (*indecl*) frugal, temperate, honest; useful

frūgifer, -ī *adj* fruitful, fertile

frūgiferēns, -entis *adj* fruitful

frūgilegus *adj* food-gathering

frūgiparus *adj* fruitful

frūmentārius *adj* of corn, corn- (*in cpds*) ◆ *m* corn dealer; **lēx frūmentāria** *law about the distribution of corn*; **rēs frūmentāria** commissariat

frūmentātiō, -ōnis *f* foraging

frūmentātor, -ōris *m* corn merchant, forager

frūmentor, -ārī, -ātus *vi* to go foraging

frūmentum, -ī *nt* corn, grain; (*pl*) crops

frūnīscor, -ī *vt* to enjoy

fruor, -uī, -ūctus *vt, vi* (*usu with abl*) to enjoy, enjoy the company of; (*LAW*) to have the use and enjoyment of

frūstillātim *adv* in little bits

frūstrā *adv* in vain, for nothing; groundlessly; in error; **~ esse** be deceived; **~ habēre** foil

frūstrāmen, -inis *nt* deception

frūstrātiō, -ōnis *f* deception, frustration

frūstrō, -āre, frūstror, -ārī, -ātus *vt* to deceive, trick

frūstulentus *adj* full of crumbs

frūstum, -ī *nt* bit, scrap

frutex, -icis *m* bush, shrub; (*comedy*) blockhead

fruticētum, -ī *nt* thicket

fruticor, -ārī *vi* to sprout

fruticōsus *adj* bushy

frūx, -ūgis *f*, **-ūgēs, -ūgum** *pl* fruits of the earth, produce; (*fig*) reward, success; virtue; **sē ad frūgem bonam recipere** reform

fuam *old pres subj of* **sum**

fūcātus *adj* counterfeit, artificial

fūcō, -āre, -āvī, -ātum *vt* to paint, dye (*esp red*)

fūcōsus *adj* spurious

fūcus¹, -ī *m* red dye, rouge; bee glue; (*fig*) deceit, pretence

fūcus², -ī *m* drone

fūdī *perf of* **fundō²**

fuga, -ae *f* flight, rout; banishment; speed, swift passing; refuge; (*fig*) avoidance, escape; **fugam facere, in fugam dare** put to flight

fugācius *adv* more timidly

fugāx, -ācis *adj* timorous, shy, fugitive; swift, transient; (*with gen*) avoiding

fūgī *perf of* **fugiō**

fugiēns, -entis *pres p of* **fugiō** ♦ *adj* fleeting, dying; averse (to)

fugiō, -ere, fūgī, -itum *vi* to flee, run away, escape; to go into exile; (*fig*) to vanish, pass swiftly ♦ *vt* to flee from, escape from; to shun, avoid; (*fig*) to escape, escape notice of; **fuge quaerere** do not ask; **mē fugit** I do not notice or know

fugitīvus, -ī *m* runaway slave, truant, deserter ♦ *adj* fugitive

fugitō, -āre *vt* to flee from, shun

fugō, -āre, -āvī, -ātum *vt* to put to flight; to banish; to rebuff

fulcīmen, -inis *nt* support

fulciō, -cīre, -sī, -tum *vt* to prop, support; to strengthen, secure; (*fig*) to sustain, bolster up

fulcrum, -ī *nt* bedpost; couch

fulgeō, -gēre, -sī *vi* to flash, lighten; to shine; (*fig*) to be illustrious

fulgidus *adj* flashing

fulgō *etc see* **fulgeō**

fulgor, -ōris *m* lightning; flash, brightness; (*fig*) splendour

fulgur, -is *nt* lightning; thunderbolt; splendour

fulgurālis *adj* of lightning (*as an omen*)

fulgurātor, -ōris *m* interpreter of lightning

fulgurītus *adj* struck by lightning

fulgurō, -āre *vi* to lighten

fulica, -ae *f* coot

fūlīgō, -inis *f* soot; black paint

fulix, -cis *f see* **fulica**

fullō, -ōnis *m* fuller

fullōnius *adj* fuller's

fulmen, -inis *nt* thunderbolt; (*fig*) disaster

fulmenta, -ae *f* heel (*of a shoe*)

fulmineus *adj* of lightning; (*fig*) deadly

fulminō, -āre *vi* to lighten; (*fig*) to threaten

fulsī *perf of* **fulciō; fulgeō**

fultūra, -ae *f* support

fultus *ppp of* **fulciō**

Fulvia, -iae *f wife of M. Antony*

Fulvius, -ī *m Roman family name*

fulvus *adj* yellow, tawny, dun

fūmeus *adj* smoking

fūmidus *adj* smoky, smoking

fūmifer, -ī *adj* smoking

fūmificō, -āre *vi* to burn incense

fūmificus *adj* steaming

fūmō, -āre *vi* to smoke, steam

fūmōsus *adj* smoky, smoked

fūmus, -ī *m* smoke, steam

fūnāle, -is *nt* cord; wax torch; chandelier

fūnambulus, -ī *m* tightrope walker

fūnctiō, -ōnis *f* performance

fūnctus *ppa of* **fungor**

fūnda, -ae *f* sling; dragnet

fundāmen, -inis *nt* foundation

fundāmentum, -ī *nt* foundation; **fundāmenta agere, fundāmenta iacere** lay the foundations

Fundānus *adj see* **Fundī**

fundātor, -ōris *m* founder

Fundī, -ōrum *mpl coast town in Latium*

funditō, -āre *vt* to sling

funditor, -ōris *m* slinger

funditus *adv* utterly, completely; at the bottom

fundō¹, -āre, -āvī, -ātum *vt* to found; to secure; (*fig*) to establish, make secure

fundō², -ere, fūdī, fūsum *vt* to pour, shed, spill; (*metal*) to cast; (*solids*) to hurl, scatter, shower; (*MIL*) to rout; (*crops*) to produce in abundance; (*speech*) to utter; (*fig*) to spread, extend

fundus, -ī *m* bottom; farm, estate; (*LAW*) authorizer

fūnebris *adj* funeral- (*in cpds*); murderous

fūnerātus *adj* killed

fūnereus *adj* funeral- (*in cpds*), fatal

fūnestō, -āre *vt* to pollute with murder, desecrate

fūnestus *adj* deadly, fatal; sorrowful, in mourning

fungīnus *adj* of a mushroom

fungor, -gi, fūnctus *vt, vi* (*usu with abl*) to perform, discharge, do; to be acted on

fungus, -ī *m* mushroom, fungus; (*candle*) clot on the wick

fūniculus, -ī *m* cord

fūnis, -is *m* rope, rigging; **fūnem dūcere** be the master

fūnus, -eris *nt* funeral; death; corpse; ruin, destruction

fūr, fūris *m* thief; slave

fūrācissimē *adv* most thievishly

fūrāx, -ācis *adj* thieving

furca, -ae *f* fork; fork-shaped pole; pillory

furcifer, -ī *m* gallows rogue

furcilla, -ae *f* little fork

furcillō, -āre *vt* to prop up

furcula, -ae *f* forked prop; **furculae Caudīnae** Pass of Caudium

furenter *adv* furiously

furfur, -is *m* bran; scurf

Furia, -ae *f* Fury, avenging spirit; madness, frenzy, rage

furiālis *adj* of the Furies; frantic, fearful; infuriating

furiāliter *adv* madly

furibundus *adj* mad, frenzied

furiō, -āre, -āvī, -ātum *vt* to madden

furiōsē *adv* in a frenzy

furiōsus *adj* mad, frantic

furnus, -ī *m* oven

furō, -ere *vi* to rave, rage, be mad, be crazy

furor, -ōris *m* madness, frenzy, passion

fūror, -ārī, -ātus *vt* to steal; to pillage; to impersonate

fūrtificus *adj* thievish

fūrtim *adv* by stealth, secretly

fūrtīvē *adv* secretly

fūrtīvus *adj* stolen; secret, furtive

fūrtō *adv* secretly

fūrtum, -ī *nt* theft, robbery; (*pl*) stolen goods; (*fig*) trick, intrigue

fūrunculus, -ī *m* pilferer

furvus *adj* black, dark

fuscina, -ae *f* trident

fuscō, -āre *vt* to blacken

fuscus *adj* dark, swarthy; (*voice*) husky, muffled

fūsē *adv* diffusely

fūsilis *adj* molten, softened
fūsiō, -ōnis *f* outpouring
fūstis, -is *m* stick, club, cudgel; (MIL) beating to death
fūstuārium, -ī *and* **-iī** *nt* beating to death
fūsus¹ *ppp of* **fundō²** ✦ *adj* broad, diffuse; copious

fūsus², **-ī** *m* spindle
futile *adv* in vain
futilis *adj* brittle; worthless
futilitās, -ātis *f* futility
futūrum, -ī *nt* future
futūrus *fut p of* **sum** ✦ *adj* future, coming

Gg

Gabiī, -iōrum *mpl* ancient town in Latium

Gabinius¹, -ī *m* Roman family name (*esp Aulus, tribune 67 B.C.*)

Gabinius², Gabiniānus *adj*: **lēx Gabinia** *law giving Pompey command against the pirates*

Gabīnus *adj see* **Gabiī**

Gādēs, -ium *fpl* town in Spain (*now* Cadiz)

Gāditānus *adj see* **Gādēs**

gaesum, -ī *nt* Gallic javelin

Gaetūlī, -ōrum *mpl* African people N. of Sahara

Gaetūlus, -icus *adj* Gaetulian; African

Gāius¹, -ī *m* Roman praenomen (*esp emperor Caligula*)

Gāius², Gāia *m/f* (*wedding ceremony*) bridegroom, bride

Galatae, -ārum *mpl* Galatians of Asia Minor

Galatia, -iae *f* Galatia

Galba, -ae *m* Roman surname (*esp emperor 68–9*)

galbaneus *adj* of galbanum (*a Syrian plant*)

galbinus *adj* greenish-yellow ♦ *ntpl* pale green clothes

galea, -ae *f* helmet

galeātus *adj* helmeted

galērītus *adj* rustic

galērum, -ī *nt*, **galērus, -ī** *m* leather hood, cap; wig

galla, -ae *f* oak apple

Gallī, -ōrum *mpl* Gauls (*people of what is now France and N. Italy*)

Gallia, -iae *f* Gaul

Gallicānus *adj* of Italian Gaul

Gallicus *adj* Gallic ♦ *f* a Gallic shoe

gallīna, -ae *f* hen; **gallīnae albae fīlius** fortune's favourite

gallīnāceus *adj* of poultry

gallīnārius, -ī *and* **-iī** *m* poultry farmer

Gallograecī, -ōrum *mpl* Galatians

Gallograecia, -iae *f* Galatia

Gallus, -ī *m* Gaul; Roman surname (*esp the lyric poet*); priest of Cybele

gallus, -ī *m* cock

ganēa, -ae *f* low eating house

ganeō, -ōnis *m* profligate

ganeum, -ī *nt* low eating house

Gangaridae, -ārum *mpl* a people on the Ganges

Gangēs, -is *m* (*river*) Ganges

Gangēticus *adj see* **Gangēs**

ganniō, -īre *vi* to yelp; (*fig*) to grumble

gannītus, -ūs *m* yelping

Ganymēdēs, -is *m* Ganymede (*cup bearer in Olympus*)

Garamantes, -um *mpl* N. African tribe

Garamantis, -idis *adj see* **Garamantes**

Gargānus, -ī *m* mountain in S. Italy

garriō, -īre *vi* to chatter

garrulitās, -ātis *f* chattering

garrulus *adj* talkative, babbling

garum, -ī *nt* fish sauce

Garumna, -ae *f* (*river*) Garonne

gaudeō, -ēre, gāvīsus *vt, vi* to rejoice, be pleased, delight (in); **in sē gaudēre, in sinū gaudēre** be secretly pleased

gaudium, -ī *and* **-iī** *nt* joy, delight, enjoyment

gaulus, -ī *m* bucket

gausape, -is *nt*, **gausapa, -ōrum** *pl* a woollen cloth, frieze

gāvīsus *ppa of* **gaudeō**

gāza, -ae *f* treasure, riches

gelidē *adv* feebly

gelidus *adj* cold, frosty; stiff, numb; chilling ♦ *f* cold water

gelō, -āre *vt* to freeze

Gelōnī, -ōrum *mpl* Scythian tribe (*in what is now Ukraine*)

gelū, -ūs *nt* frost, cold; chill

gemebundus *adj* groaning

gemellipara, -ae *f* mother of twins

gemellus *adj* twin, double; alike ♦ *m* twin

geminātiō, -ōnis *f* doubling

geminō, -āre, -āvī, -ātum *vt* to double, bring together; to repeat ♦ *vi* to be double

geminus *adj* twin, double, both; similar ♦ *mpl* twins (*esp Castor and Pollux*)

gemitus, -ūs *m* groan, sigh, moaning sound

gemma, -ae *f* bud, precious stone, jewel; jewelled cup, signet

gemmātus *adj* bejewelled

gemmeus *adj* jewelled; sparkling

gemmifer, -ī *adj* gem-producing

gemmō, -āre *vi* to bud, sprout; to sparkle

gemō, -ere, -uī, -itum *vi* to sigh, groan, moan ♦ *vt* to bewail

Gemōniae, -ārum *fpl* steps in Rome on which bodies of criminals were thrown

genae, -ārum *fpl* cheeks; eyes, eye sockets

geneālogus, -ī *m* genealogist

gener, -ī *m* son-in-law

generālis *adj* of the species; universal

generāliter *adv* generally

generāscō, -ere *vi* to be produced

generātim *adv* by species, in classes; in general

generātor, -ōris *m* producer

generō, -āre, -āvī, -ātum *vt* to breed, procreate

generōsus *adj* high-born, noble; well-stocked; generous, chivalrous; (*things*) noble, honourable

genesis, -is *f* birth; horoscope

genethliacon, -ī *nt* birthday poem

genetīvus *adj* native, inborn

genetrīx, -īcis *f* mother

geniālis *adj* nuptial; joyful, genial

geniāliter *adv* merrily

geniculātus *adj* jointed

genista, -ae *f* broom

genitābilis *adj* productive

genitālis *adj* fruitful, generative; of birth

genitāliter *adv* fruitfully

genitor, -ōris *m* father, creator

genitus *ppp of* **gignō**

genius, -ī *and* **-iī** *m* guardian spirit; enjoyment, inclination; talent; **geniō indulgēre** enjoy oneself

gēns, gentis *f* clan, family, stock, race; tribe, people, nation; descendant; (*pl*) foreign peoples; **minimē gentium** by no means; **ubi gentium** where in the world

genticus *adj* national

gentīlicius *adj* family

gentīlis *adj* family, hereditary; national ♦ *m* kinsman

gentīlitās, -ātis *f* clan relationship

genū, -ūs *nt* knee

genuālia, -um *ntpl* garters

genuī *perf of* **gignō**

genuīnus¹ *adj* natural

genuīnus² *adj* of the cheek ♦ *mpl* back teeth

genus, -eris *nt* birth, descent, noble birth, descendant; race; kind, class, species, respect, way; (LOGIC) genus, general term; **id ~** of that kind; **in omnī genere** in all respects

geōgraphia, -ae *f* geography

geōmetrēs, -ae *m* geometer

geōmetria, -ae *f* geometry

geōmetricus *adj* geometrical ♦ *ntpl* geometry

germānē *adv* sincerely

Germānī, -ōrum *mpl* Germans

Germānia, -iae *f* Germany

Germānicus *adj*, *m cognomen of Nero Claudius Drusus and his son*

germānitās, -ātis *f* brotherhood, sisterhood; relation of sister colonies

germānus *adj* of the same parents, full (brother, sister); genuine, true ♦ *m* full brother ♦ *f* full sister

germen, -inis *nt* bud, shoot; embryo; (*fig*) germ

gerō¹, -rere, -ssī, -stum *vt* to carry, wear; to bring; (*plants*) to bear, produce; (*feelings*) to entertain, show; (*activity*) to conduct, manage, administer, wage; (*time*) spend; **mōrem gerere** comply, humour; **persōnam gerere** play a part; **sē gerere** behave; **sē medium gerere** be neutral; **prae sē gerere** exhibit; **rēs gestae** exploits

gerō², -ōnis *nt* carrier

gerrae, -ārum *fpl* trifles, nonsense

gerrō, -ōnis *m* idler

gerulus, -ī *m* carrier

Gēryōn, -onis *m mythical three-bodied king killed by Hercules*

gessī *perf of* **gerō¹**

gestāmen, -inis *nt* arms, ornaments, burden; litter, carriage

gestiō¹, -ōnis *f* performance

gestiō², -īre *vi* to jump for joy, be excited; to be very eager

gestitō, -āre *vt* to always wear *or* carry

gestō, -āre *vt* to carry about, usually wear; to fondle; to blab; (*pass*) to go for a ride, drive, sail

gestor, -ōris *m* telltale

gestus¹ *ppp of* **gerō¹**

gestus², -ūs *m* posture, gesture; gesticulation

Getae, -ārum *mpl Thracian tribe on the lower Danube*

Geticus *adj* Getan, Thracian

gibbus, -ī *m* hump

Gigantes, -um *mpl* Giants, *sons of Earth*

Gigantēus *adj see* **Gigantes**

gignō, -ere, genuī, genitum *vt* to beget, bear, produce; to cause

gilvus *adj* pale yellow, dun

gingīva, -ae *f* gum

glaber, -rī *adj* smooth, bald ♦ *m* favourite slave

glaciālis *adj* icy

glaciēs, -ēī *f* ice

glaciō, -āre *vt* to freeze

gladiātor, -ōris *m* gladiator; (*pl*) gladiatorial show

gladiātōrius *adj* of gladiators ♦ *nt* gladiators' pay

gladiātūra, -ae *f* gladiator's profession

gladius, -ī *and* **-iī** *m* sword; (*fig*) murder, death; **gladium stringere** draw the sword; **suō sibi gladiō iugulāre** beat at his own game

glaeba, -ae *f* sod, clod of earth; soil; lump

glaebula, -ae *f* small lump; small holding

glaesum *etc see* **glēsum**

glandifer, -ī *adj* acorn-bearing

glandium, -ī *and* **-iī** *nt* glandule (*in meat*)

glāns, -andis *f* acorn, nut; bullet

glārea, -ae *f* gravel

glāreōsus *adj* gravelly

glaucōma, -ae *f* cataract; **glaucōmam ob oculōs obicere** throw dust in the eyes of

glaucus *adj* bluish grey

glēba *etc see* **glaeba**

glēsum, -ī *nt* amber

glīs, -īris *m* dormouse

glīscō, -ere *vi* to grow, swell, blaze up

globōsus *adj* spherical

globus, -ī *m* ball, sphere; (MIL) troop; mass, crowd, cluster

glōmerāmen, -inis *nt* ball

glomerō, -āre, -āvī, -ātum *vt* to form into a ball, gather, accumulate

glomus, -eris *nt* ball of thread, clue

glōria, -ae *f* glory, fame; ambition, pride, boasting; (*pl*) glorious deeds

glōriātiō, -ōnis *f* boasting

glōriola, -ae *f* a little glory

glōrior, -ārī, -ātus *vt, vi* to boast, pride oneself

glōriōsē *adv see* **glōriōsus**

glōriōsus *adj* famous, glorious; boastful

glūten, -inis *nt* glue
glūtinātor, -ōris *m* bookbinder
gluttiō, -īre *vt* to gulp down
gnāruris, gnārus *adj* knowing, expert; known
gnātus *see* **nātus**
gnāvus *see* **nāvus**
Gnōsis, -idis *f* Ariadne
Gnōsius, Gnōsiacus, Gnōsias *adj* of Cnossos, Cretan ♦ *f* Ariadne
Gnōsus, -ī *f* Cnossos (*ancient capital of Crete*)
gōbiō, -ōnis, gōbius, -ī *and* **-iī** *m* gudgeon
Gorgiās, -ae *m* Sicilian sophist and teacher of rhetoric
Gorgō, -ōnis *f* mythical monster capable of turning men to stone, Medusa
Gorgoneus *adj*: **equus** ~ Pegasus; **lacus** ~ Hippocrene
Gortȳna, -ae *f* Cretan town
Gortȳnius, Gortȳniacus *adj* Gortynian, Cretan
gōrȳtos, -ī *m* quiver
grabātus, -ī *m* camp bed, low couch
Gracchānus *adj see* **Gracchus**
Gracchus, -ī *m* Roman surname (*esp the famous tribunes Tiberius and Gaius*)
gracilis *adj* slender, slight, meagre, poor; (*style*) plain
gracilitās, -ātis *f* slimness, leanness; (*style*) simplicity
grāculus, -ī *m* jackdaw
gradātim *adv* step by step, gradually
gradātiō, -ōnis *f* (RHET) climax
gradior, -adī, -essus *vi* to step, walk
Grādīvus, -ī *m* Mars
gradus, -ūs *m* step, pace; stage, step towards; firm stand, position, standing; (*pl*) stair, steps; (*hair*) braid; (MATH) degree; (*fig*) degree, rank; **citātō gradū, plēnō gradū** at the double; **suspēnsō gradū** on tiptoe; **dē gradū deicī** be disconcerted
Graecē *adv* in Greek
Graecia, -iae *f* Greece; **Māgna** ~ S. Italy
graecissō, -āre *vi* to ape the Greeks
graecor, -ārī *vi* to live like Greeks
Graeculus *adj* (*contemptuous*) Greek
Graecus *adj* Greek
Grāiugena, -ae *m* Greek
Grāius *adj* Greek
grallātor, -ōris *m* stiltwalker
grāmen, -inis *nt* grass; herb
grāmineus *adj* grassy; of cane
grammaticus *adj* literary, grammatical ♦ *m* teacher of literature and language ♦ *f, ntpl* grammar, literature, philology
grānāria, -ōrum *ntpl* granary
grandaevus *adj* aged, very old
grandēscō, -ere *vi* to grow
grandiculus *adj* quite big
grandifer, -ī *adj* productive
grandiloquus, -ī *m* grand speaker; boaster
grandinat, -āre *vi* it hails
grandis *adj* large, great, tall; old; strong; (*style*) grand, sublime; ~ **nātū** old
granditās, -ātis *f* grandeur
grandō, -inis *f* hail
grānifer, -ī *adj* grain-carrying

grānum, -ī *nt* seed, grain
graphicē *adv* nicely
graphicus *adj* fine, masterly
graphium, -ī *and* **-iī** *nt* stilus, pen
grassātor, -ōris *m* vagabond; robber, footpad
grassor, -ārī, -ātus *vi* to walk about, prowl, loiter; (*action*) to proceed; (*fig*) to attack, rage against
grātē *adv* with pleasure; gratefully
grātēs *fpl* thanks
grātia, -ae *f* charm, grace; favour, influence, regard, friendship; kindness, service; gratitude, thanks; **grātiam facere** excuse; **grātiam referre** return a favour; **in grātiam redīre cum** be reconciled to; **grātiās agere** thank; **grātiās habēre** feel grateful; **grātiā** (*with gen*) for the sake of; **eā grātiā** on that account; **grātīs** for nothing
Grātiae, -ārum *fpl* the three Graces
grātificātiō, -ōnis *f* obligingness
grātificor, -ārī *vi* to do a favour, oblige ♦ *vt* to make a present of
gratiīs, grātīs *adv* for nothing
grātiōsus *adj* in favour, popular; obliging
grātor, -ārī, -ātus *vi* to rejoice, congratulate
grātuītō *adv* for nothing
grātuītus *adj* free, gratuitous
grātulābundus *adj* congratulating
grātulātiō, -ōnis *f* rejoicing; congratulation; public thanksgiving
grātulor, -ārī, -ātus *vt, vi* to congratulate; to give thanks
grātus *adj* pleasing, welcome, dear; grateful, thankful; (*acts*) deserving thanks; **grātum facere** do a favour
gravātē *adv* reluctantly, grudgingly
gravātim *adv* unwillingly
gravēdinōsus *adj* liable to colds
gravēdō, -inis *f* cold in the head
graveolēns, -entis *adj* strong-smelling
gravēscō, -ere *vi* to become heavy; to grow worse
graviditās, -ātis *f* pregnancy
gravidō, -āre *vt* to impregnate
gravidus *adj* pregnant; loaded, full
gravis *adj* heavy; loaded, pregnant; (*smell*) strong, offensive; (*sound*) deep, bass; (*body*) sick; (*food*) indigestible; (*fig*) oppressive, painful, severe; important, influential, dignified
gravitās, -ātis *f* weight, severity, sickness; importance, dignity, seriousness; **annōnae** ~ high price of corn
graviter *adv* heavily; strongly, deeply; severely, seriously, violently; gravely, with dignity; ~ **ferre** be vexed at
gravō, -āre *vt* to load, weigh down; to oppress, aggravate
gravor, -ārī *vt, vi* to feel annoyed, object to, disdain
gregālis *adj* of the herd, common ♦ *m* comrade
gregārius *adj* common; (MIL) private
gregātim *adv* in crowds
gremium, -ī *nt* bosom, lap
gressus[1] *ppa of* **gradior**

gressus², **-ūs** m step; course
grex, **-egis** m flock, herd; company, troop
grunniō, **-īre** vi to grunt
grunnītus, **-ūs** m grunting
grūs, **-uis** f crane
grȳps, **-ȳpis** m griffin
gubernāclum, **gubernāculum**, **-ī** nt rudder, tiller; helm, government
gubernātiō, **-ōnis** f steering, management
gubernātor, **-ōris** m steersman, pilot, governor
gubernātrīx, **-īcis** f directress
gubernō, **-āre**, **-āvī**, **-ātum** vt to steer, pilot; to manage, govern
gula, **-ae** f gullet, throat; gluttony, palate
gulōsus adj dainty
gurges, **-itis** m abyss, deep water, flood; (person) spendthrift
gurguliō, **-ōnis** f gullet, windpipe
gurgustium, **-ī** and **-iī** nt hovel, shack
gustātus, **-ūs** m sense of taste; flavour

gustō, **-āre**, **-āvī**, **-ātum** vt to taste; to have a snack; (fig) to enjoy, overhear; **prīmīs labrīs gustāre** have a superficial knowledge of
gustus, **-ūs** m tasting; preliminary dish
gutta, **-ae** f drop; spot, speck
guttātim adv drop by drop
guttur, **-is** nt throat, gluttony
gŭttus, **-ī** m flask
Gyās, **-ae** m giant with a hundred arms
Gȳgaeus adj see **Gȳgēs**
Gȳgēs, **-is** and **-ae** m king of Lydia (famed for his magic ring)
gymnasiarchus, **-ī** m master of a gymnasium
gymnasium, **-ī** and **-iī** nt sports ground, school
gymnasticus adj gymnastic
gymnicus adj gymnastic
gynaecēum, **-ēī**, **gynaecīum**, **-ī** nt women's quarters
gypsātus adj coated with plaster
gypsum, **-ī** nt plaster of Paris; a plaster figure
gȳrus, **-ī** m circle, coil, ring; course

Hh

ha *interj* (*expressing joy or laughter*) hurrah!, ha ha!

habēna, -ae *f* strap; (*pl*) reins; (*fig*) control; **habēnās dare, habēnās immittere** allow to run freely

habeō, -ēre, -uī, -itum *vt* to have, hold; to keep, contain, possess; (*fact*) to know; (*with inf*) to be in a position to; (*person*) to treat, regard, consider; (*action*) to make, hold, carry out ◆ *vi* to have possessions; **ōrātiōnem habēre** make a speech; **in animō habēre** intend; **prō certō habēre** be sure; **sē habēre** find oneself, be; **sibi habēre, sēcum habēre** keep to oneself; (*fight*); **habet** a hit!; **bene habet** it is well; **sīc habet** so it is; **sīc habētō** be sure of this

habilis *adj* manageable, handy; suitable, nimble, expert

habilitās, -ātis *f* aptitude

habitābilis *adj* habitable

habitātiō, -ōnis *f* dwelling, house

habitātor, -ōris *m* tenant, inhabitant

habitō, -āre, -āvī, -ātum *vt* to inhabit ◆ *vi* to live, dwell; to remain, be always (in)

habitūdō, -inis *f* condition

habitus¹ *ppp of* **habeō** ◆ *adj* stout; in a humour

habitus², -ūs *m* condition, appearance; dress; character, quality; disposition, feeling

hāc *adv* this way

hāctenus *adv* thus far, so far; till now

Hadria, -ae *f town in N. Italy*; Adriatic Sea

Hadriānus, -ānī *m* (*emperor*) Hadrian

Hadriāticus, Hadriacus *adj* of (*emperor*) Hadrian

haedilia, -ae *f* little kid

haedinus *adj* kid's

haedulus, -ī *m* little kid

haedus, -ī *m* kid; (*ASTR, usu pl*) the Kids (*a cluster in Auriga*)

Haemonia, -ae *f* Thessaly

Haemonius *adj* Thessalian

Haemus, -ī *m* mountain range in Thrace

haereō, -rēre, -sī, -sum *vi* to cling, stick, be attached; (*nearness*) to stay close, hang on; (*continuance*) to linger, remain (at); (*stoppage*) to stick fast, come to a standstill, be at a loss

haerēscō, -ere *vi* to adhere

haeresis, -is *f* sect

haesī *perf of* **haereō**

haesitantia, -ae *f* stammering

haesitātiō, -ōnis *f* stammering; indecision

haesitō, -āre *vi* to get stuck; to stammer; to hesitate, be uncertain

hahae, hahahae *see* **ha**

haliaeetos, -ī *m* osprey

hālitus, -ūs *m* breath, vapour

hallex, -icis *m* big toe

hāllūcinor *etc see* **ālūcinor**

hālō, -āre *vi* to be fragrant ◆ *vt* to exhale

hālūcinor *etc see* **ālūcinor**

hama, -ae *f* water bucket

Hamādryas, -adis *f* woodnymph

hāmātilis *adj* with hooks

hāmātus *adj* hooked

Hamilcar, -is *m father of Hannibal*

hāmus, -ī *m* hook; talons

Hannibal, -is *m famous Carthaginian general in 2nd Punic War*

hara, -ae *f* sty, pen

harēna, -ae *f* sand; desert, seashore; arena (*in the amphitheatre*)

harēnōsus *adj* sandy

hariola, -ae *f*, **hariolus, -ī** *m* soothsayer

hariolor, -ārī *vi* to prophesy; to talk nonsense

harmonia, -ae *f* concord, melody; (*fig*) harmony

harpagō¹, -āre *vt* to steal

harpagō², -ōnis *m* grappling hook; (*person*) robber

harpē, -ēs *f* scimitar

Harpȳiae, -ārum *fpl* Harpies (*mythical monsters, half woman, half bird*)

harundifer, -ī *adj* reed-crowned

harundineus *adj* reedy

harundinōsus *adj* abounding in reeds

harundō, -inis *f* reed, cane; fishing rod; shaft, arrow; (*fowling*) limed twig; (*music*) pipe, flute; (*toy*) hobbyhorse; (*weaving*) comb; (*writing*) pen

haruspex, -icis *m* diviner (*from entrails*); prophet

haruspica, -ae *f* soothsayer

haruspicīnus *adj* of divination by entrails ◆ *f* art of such divination

haruspicium, -ī and -iī *nt* divination

Hasdrubal, -is *m* brother of Hannibal

hasta, -ae *f* spear, pike; sign of an auction sale; **sub hastā vēndere** put up for auction

hastātus *adj* armed with a spear ◆ *mpl* first line of Roman army in battle; **prīmus ~** 1st company of hastati

hastīle, -is *nt* shaft, spear, javelin; vine prop

hau, haud *adv* not, not at all

hauddum *adv* not yet

haudquāquam *adv* not at all, not by any means**

haurio, -rīre, -sī, -stum vt to draw, draw off, derive; to drain, empty, exhaust; to take in, drink, swallow, devour

haustus¹ ppp of **haurio**

haustus², -ūs m drawing (water); drinking; drink, draught

haut see **hau**

hebdomas, -dis f week

Hēbē, -ēs f goddess of youth (cup bearer to the gods)

hebenus, -ī f ebony

hebeō, -ēre vi to be blunt, dull, sluggish

hebes, -tis adj blunt, dull, sluggish; obtuse, stupid

hebēscō, -ere vi to grow dim or dull

hebetō, -āre vt to blunt, dull, dim

Hebrus, -ī m Thracian river (now Maritza)

Hecatē, -ēs f goddess of magic (and often identified with Diana)

Hecatēius, Hecatēis adj see **Hecatē**

hecatombē, -ēs f hecatomb

Hector, -is m son of Priam (chief warrior of the Trojans against the Greeks)

Hectoreus adj of Hector; Trojan

Hecuba, -ae, Hecubē, -ēs f wife of Priam

hedera, -ae f ivy

hederiger, -ī adj wearing ivy

hederōsus adj covered with ivy

hēdychrum, -ī nt a cosmetic perfume

hei, heia see **eia**

Helena, -ae, Helenē, -ēs f Helen (wife of Menelaus, abducted by Paris)

Helenus, -ī m son of Priam (with prophetic powers)

Hēliades, -um fpl daughters of the Sun (changed to poplars or alders, and their tears to amber)

Helicē, -ēs f the Great Bear

Helicōn, -ōnis m mountain in Greece sacred to Apollo and the Muses

Helicōniades, -um fpl the Muses

Helicōnius adj see **Helicōn**

Hellas, -dis f Greece

Hellē, -ēs f mythical Greek princess (carried by the golden-fleeced ram, and drowned in the Hellespont)

Hellēspontius, Hellēspontiacus adj see **Hellēspontus**

Hellēspontus, -ī m Hellespont (now Dardanelles)

helluō, -ōnis m glutton

helluor, -ārī vi to be a glutton

helvella, -ae f a savoury herb

Helvētiī, -ōrum mpl people of E. Gaul (now Switzerland)

Helvētius, Helvēticus adj see **Helvētiī**

hem interj (expressing surprise) eh?, well well!

hēmerodromus, -ī m express courier

hēmicillus, -ī m mule

hēmicyclium, -ī and **-iī** nt semicircle with seats

hēmīna, -ae f half a pint

hendecasyllabī, -ōrum mpl hendecasyllabics, verses of eleven syllables per line

heptēris, -is f ship with seven banks of oars

hera etc see **era**

Hēra, -ae f Greek goddess identified with Juno

Hēraclītus, -ī m early Greek philosopher

Hēraea, -aeōrum ntpl festival of Hera

herba, -ae f blade, young plant; grass, herb, weed

herbēscō, -ere vi to grow into blades

herbeus adj grass-green

herbidus adj grassy

herbifer, -ī adj grassy

herbōsus adj grassy, made of turf; made of herbs

herbula, -ae f little herb

hercīscō, -ere vt to divide an inheritance

hercle interj by Hercules!

herctum, -ī nt inheritance

Hercule interj by Hercules!

Herculēs, -is and **-ī** m mythical Greek hero, later deified

Herculeus adj: **arbor** ~ poplar; **urbs** ~ Herculaneum

here see **herī**

hērēditārius adj inherited; about an inheritance

hērēditās, -ātis f inheritance; ~ **sine sacrīs** a gift without awkward obligations

hērēdium, -ī and **-iī** nt inherited estate

hērēs, -ēdis m/f heir, heiress; (fig) master, successor

herī adv yesterday

herīlis etc see **erīlis**

Hermēs, -ae m Greek god identified with Mercury; Hermes pillar

Hernicī, -ōrum mpl people of central Italy

Hernicus adj see **Hernicī**

Hērodotus, -ī m first Greek historian

hērōicus adj heroic, epic

hērōīna, -ae f demigoddess

hērōis, -dis f demigoddess

hērōs, -is m demigod, hero

hērōus adj heroic, epic

herus etc see **erus**

Hēsiodēus, -īus adj see **Hēsiodus**

Hēsiodus, -ī m Hesiod (Greek didactic poet)

Hesperia, -iae f Italy; Spain

Hesperides, -idum fpl keepers of a garden in the far West

Hesperius, -is adj western

Hesperus, -ī m evening star

hesternus adj of yesterday

heu interj (expressing dismay or pain) oh!, alas!

heus interj (calling attention) ho!, hallo!

hexameter, -rī m hexameter verse

hexēris, -is f ship with six banks of oars

hiātus, -ūs m opening, abyss; open mouth, gaping; (GRAM) hiatus

Hibērēs, -um mpl Spaniards

Hibēria, -iae f Spain

hiberna, -ōrum ntpl winter quarters

hībernācula, -ōrum ntpl winter tents

Hibernia, -ae f Ireland

hībernō, -āre vi to winter, remain in winter quarters

hībernus adj winter, wintry

Hibērus¹, Hibēricus adj Spanish

Hibērus², -ī m (river) Ebro

hibīscum, -ī nt marsh mallow

hibrida, hybrida, -ae m/f (dog) mongrel

hīc¹, haec, hōc *pron, adj* this; he, she, it; my, the latter, the present; **hīc homō** I; **hōc magis** the more; **hōc est** that is

hīc² *adv* here; herein; *(time)* at this point

hīce, haece, hōce *emphatic forms of* **hīc¹, haec, hōc**

hīcine, haecine, hōcine *emphatic forms of* **hīc¹, haec, hōc**

hiemālis *adj* winter, stormy

hiemō, -āre *vi* to pass the winter; to be wintry, stormy

hiems, (hiemps), -is *f* winter; stormy weather, cold

Hierōnymus, -ī *m* Jerome

Hierosolyma, -ōrum *ntpl* Jerusalem

Hierosolymārius *adj see* **Hierosolyma**

hietō, -āre *vi* to yawn

hilare *adv see* **hilaris**

hilaris *adj* cheerful, merry

hilaritās, -ātis *f* cheerfulness

hilaritūdō, -inis *f* merriment

hilarō, -āre *vt* to cheer, gladden

hilarulus *adj* a gay little thing

hilarus *etc see* **hilaris**

hīllae, -ārum *fpl* smoked sausage

Hīlōtae, -ārum *mpl* Helots *(of Sparta)*

hīlum, -ī *nt* something, a whit

hinc *adv* from here, hence; on this side; from this source, for this reason; *(time)* henceforth

hinniō, -īre *vi* to neigh

hinnītus, -ūs *m* neighing

hinnuleus, -ī *m* fawn

hiō, -āre *vi* to be open, gape, yawn; *(speech)* to be disconnected, leave a hiatus ♦ *vt* to sing

hippagōgī, -ōrum *fpl* cavalry transports

hippocentaurus, -ī *m* centaur

hippodromos, -ī *m* racecourse

Hippolytus, -ī *m son of Theseus (slandered by stepmother Phaedra)*

hippomanes, -is *nt* mare's fluid; membrane on foal's forehead

Hippōnactēus *adj* of Hipponax ♦ *m* iambic verse used by Hipponax

Hippōnax, -ctis *m Greek satirist*

hippotoxotae, -ārum *mpl* mounted archers

hīra, -ae *f* the empty gut

hircīnus *adj* of a goat

hircōsus *adj* goatish

hircus, -ī *m* he-goat; goatish smell

hirnea, -ae *f* jug

hirq- *etc see* **hirc-**

hirsūtus *adj* shaggy, bristly; uncouth

hirtus *adj* hairy, shaggy; rude

hirūdō, -inis *f* leech

hirundinīnus *adj* swallows'

hirundō, -inis *f* swallow

hīscō, -ere *vi* to gape; to open the mouth ♦ *vt* to utter

Hispānia, -iae *f* Spain

Hispāniēnsis, Hispānus *adj* Spanish

hispidus *adj* hairy, rough

Hister, -rī *m* lower Danube

historia, -ae *f* history, inquiry; story

historicus *adj* historical ♦ *m* historian

histricus *adj* of the stage

histriō, -ōnis *m* actor

histriōnālis *adj* of an actor

histriōnia, -ae *f* acting

hiulcē *adv* with hiatus

hiulcō, -āre *vt* to split open

hiulcus *adj* gaping, open; *(speech)* with hiatus

hodiē *adv* today; nowadays, now; up to the present

hodiernus *adj* today's

holitor, -ōris *m* market gardener

holitōrius *adj* for market gardeners

holus, -eris *nt* vegetables

holusculum, -ī *nt* small cabbage

Homēricus *adj see* **Homērus**

Homērus, -ī *m Greek epic poet*, Homer

homicīda, -ae *m* killer, murderer

homicīdium, -ī *and* **-iī** *nt* murder

homō, -inis *m/f* human being, man; *(pl)* people, the world; *(derogatory)* fellow, creature; **inter hominēs esse** be alive; see the world

homullus, -ī, homunciō, -ōnis, homunculus, -ī *m* little man, poor creature, mortal

honestās, -ātis *f* good character, honourable reputation; sense of honour, integrity; *(things)* beauty

honestē *adv* decently, virtuously

honestō, -āre *vt* to honour, dignify, embellish

honestus *adj* honoured, respectable; honourable, virtuous; *(appearance)* handsome ♦ *m* gentleman ♦ *nt* virtue, good; beauty

honor, -ōris *m* honour, esteem; public office, position, preferment; award, tribute, offering; ornament, beauty; **honōris causā** out of respect; **honōrem praefārī** apologize for a remark

honōrābilis *adj* as a mark of respect

honōrārius *adj* done out of respect, honorary

honōrātē *adv* honourably

honōrātus *adj* esteemed, distinguished; in high office; complimentary

honōrificē *adv* in complimentary terms

honōrificus *adj* complimentary

honōrō, -āre, -āvī, -ātum *vt* to do honour to, embellish

honōrus *adj* complimentary

honōs *etc see* **honor**

hōra, -ae *f* hour; time, season; *(pl)* clock; **in hōrās** hourly; **in hōram vīvere** live from hand to mouth

hōraeum, -ī *nt* pickle

Horātius¹, -ī *m Roman family name (esp the defender of Rome against Porsenna); the lyric poet Horace*

Horātius² *adj see* **Horātius¹**

hordeum, -ī *nt* barley

horia, -ae *f* fishing smack

hornō *adv* this year

hornōtinus *adj* this year's

hornus *adj* this year's

hōrologium, -ī *and* **-iī** *nt* clock

horrendus *adj* fearful, terrible; awesome

horrēns, -entis *pres p of* **horreō** ♦ *adj* bristling, shaggy

horreō, -ēre, -uī *vi* to stand stiff, bristle; to shiver, shudder, tremble ♦ *vt* to dread; to be afraid, be amazed

horrēscō, -ere, horruī *vi* to stand on end, become rough; to begin to quake; to start, be terrified ♦ *vt* to dread

horreum, -ī *nt* barn, granary, store

horribilis *adj* terrifying; amazing

horridē *adv see* **horridus**

horridulus *adj* protruding a little; unkempt; (*fig*) uncouth

horridus *adj* bristling, shaggy, rough, rugged; shivering; (*manners*) rude, uncouth; frightening

horrifer, -ī *adj* chilling; terrifying

horrificē *adv* in awesome manner

horrificō, -āre *vt* to ruffle; to terrify

horrificus *adj* terrifying

horrisonus *adj* dread-sounding

horror, -ōris *m* bristling; shivering, ague; terror, fright, awe, a terror

hōrsum *adv* this way

hortāmen, -inis *nt* encouragement

hortāmentum, -ī *nt* encouragement

hortātiō, -ōnis *f* harangue, encouragement

hortātor, -ōris *m* encourager

hortātus, -ūs *m* encouragement

Hortēnsius, -ī *m* Roman family name (*esp an orator in Cicero's time*)

hortor, -ārī, -ātus *vt* to urge, encourage, exhort, harangue

hortulus, -ī *m* little garden

hortus, -ī *m* garden; (*pl*) park

hospes, -itis *m*, **hospita, -ae** *f* host, hostess; guest, friend; stranger, foreigner ♦ *adj* strange

hospitālis *adj* host's, guest's; hospitable

hospitālitās, -ātis *f* hospitality

hospitāliter *adv* hospitably

hospitium, -ī *and* **-iī** *nt* hospitality, friendship; lodging, inn

hostia, -ae *f* victim, sacrifice

hostiātus *adj* provided with victims

hosticus *adj* hostile; strange ♦ *nt* enemy territory

hostīlis *adj* of the enemy, hostile

hostīliter *adv* in hostile manner

hostīmentum, -ī *nt* recompense

hostiō, -īre *vt* to requite

hostis, -is *m/f* enemy

hūc *adv* hither, here; to this, to such a pitch; **hūc illūc** hither and thither

hui *interj* (*expressing surprise*) ho!, my word!

hūiusmodī such

hūmānē, hūmāniter *adv* humanly; gently, politely

hūmānitās, -ātis *f* human nature, mankind; humanity, kindness, courtesy; culture, refinement

hūmānitus *adv* in accordance with human nature; kindly

hūmānus *adj* human, humane, kind, courteous; cultured, refined, well-educated; **hūmānō māior** superhuman

humātiō, -ōnis *f* burying

hūme-, hūmi- *see* **ūme-, ūmi-**

humilis *adj* low, low-lying, shallow; (*condition*) lowly, humble, poor; (*language*) commonplace; (*mind*) mean, base

humilitās, -ātis *f* low position, smallness, shallowness; lowliness, insignificance; meanness, baseness

humiliter *adv* meanly, humbly

humō, -āre, -āvī, -ātum *vt* to bury

humus, -ī *f* earth, ground; land; **humī** on the ground

hyacinthinus *adj* of the hyacinthus

hyacinthus, -ī *m* iris, lily

Hyades, -um *fpl* Hyads (*a group of stars in Taurus*)

hyaena, -ae *f* hyena

hyalus, -ī *m* glass

Hybla, -ae *f* mountain in Sicily (*famous for bees*)

Hyblaeus *adj see* **Hybla**

hybrida *etc see* **hibrida**

Hydaspēs, -is *m* tributary of river Indus (*now* Jhelum)

Hȳdra, -ae *f* hydra (*a mythical dragon with seven heads*)

hydraulus, -ī *m* water organ

hydria, -ae *f* ewer

Hydrochous, -ī *m* Aquarius

hydrōpicus *adj* suffering from dropsy

hydrōps, -is *m* dropsy

hydrus, -ī *m* serpent

Hylās, -ae *m* a youth loved by Hercules

Hymēn, -enis, Hymenaeus, -ī *m* god of marriage; wedding song; wedding

Hymettius *adj see* **Hymettus**

Hymettus, -ī *m* mountain near Athens (*famous for honey and marble*)

Hypanis, -is *m* river of Sarmatia (*now* Bug)

Hyperboreī, -ōrum *mpl* fabulous people in the far North

Hyperboreus *adj see* **Hyperboreī**

Hyperīōn, -onis *m* father of the Sun; the Sun

hypodidascalus, -ī *m* assistant teacher

hypomnēma, -tis *nt* memorandum

Hyrcānī, -ōrum *mpl* people on the Caspian Sea

Hyrcānus *adj* Hyrcanian

Ii

Iacchus, -ī *m* Bacchus; wine
iaceō, -ēre, -uī *vi* to lie; to be ill, lie dead;
(*places*) to be situated, be flat or low-lying,
be in ruins; (*dress*) to hang loose; (*fig*) to be
inactive, be downhearted; (*things*) to be
dormant, neglected, despised
iaciō, -ere, iēcī, iactum *vt* to throw; to lay,
build; (*seed*) to sow; (*speech*) to cast, let fall,
mention
iactāns, -antis *pres p of* **iactō** ♦ *adj* boastful
iactanter *adv* ostentatiously
iactantia, -ae *f* boasting, ostentation
iactātiō, -ōnis *f* tossing, gesticulation;
boasting, ostentation; ~ **populāris** publicity
iactātus, -ūs *m* waving
iactitō, -āre *vt* to mention, bandy
iactō, -āre, -āvī, -ātum *vt* to throw, scatter; to
shake, toss about; (*mind*) to disquiet; (*ideas*) to
consider, discuss, mention; (*speech*) to boast
of; **sē iactāre** waver, fluctuate; to behave
ostentatiously, be officious
iactūra, -ae *f* throwing overboard; loss,
sacrifice
iactus¹ *ppp of* **iaciō**
iactus², -ūs *m* throwing, throw; **intrā tēlī
iactum** within spear's range
iacuī *perf of* **iaceō**
iaculābilis *adj* missile
iaculātor, -ōris *m* thrower, shooter; light-
armed soldier
iaculātrīx, -īcis *f* huntress
iaculor, -ārī, -ātus *vt* to throw, hurl, shoot; to
throw the javelin; to shoot at, hit; (*fig*) to aim
at, attack
iaculum, -ī *nt* javelin; fishing net
iāien- *etc see* **iēn-**
iam *adv* (*past*) already, by then; (*present*)
now, already; (*future*) directly, very soon;
(*emphasis*) indeed, precisely; (*inference*)
therefore, then surely; (*transition*) moreover,
next; **iam dūdum** for a long time, long
ago; immediately; **iam iam** right now, any
moment now; **non iam** no longer; **iam ...
iam** at one time ... at another; **iam nunc** just
now; **iam prīdem** long ago, for a long time;
iam tum even at that time; **sī iam** supposing
for the purpose of argument
iambēus *adj* iambic
iambus, -ī *m* iambic foot; iambic poetry
Iānālis *adj see* **Iānus**
Iāniculum, -ī *nt* Roman hill across the Tiber

iānitor, -ōris *m* doorkeeper, porter
iānua, -ae *f* door; entrance; (*fig*) key
Iānuārius *adj* of January ♦ *m* January
Iānus, -ī *m* god of gateways and beginnings;
archway, arcade
Iāpetīonidēs, -ae *m* Atlas
Iāpetus, -ī *m a* Titan (*father of Atlas and
Prometheus*)
Iāpyx, -gis *adj* Iapygian; Apulian ♦ *m* west-
north-west wind from Apulia
Iāsōn, -onis *m* Jason (*leader of Argonauts, husband
of Medea*)
Iāsonius *adj see* **Iāsōn**
iaspis, -dis *f* jasper
Ībēr- *etc see* **Hībēr-**
ibi *adv* there; then; in this, at it
ibīdem *adv* in the same place; at that very
moment
ibis, -is *and* **-idis** *f* ibis
Īcarium, -ī *nt* Icarian (Sea)
Īcarius *adj see* **Īcarus**
Īcarus, -ī *m* son of Daedalus (*drowned in the Aegean*)
īcō, -ere, -ī, ictum *vt* to strike; **foedus īcere**
make a treaty
ictericus *adj* jaundiced
ictis, -dis *f* weasel
ictus¹ *ppp of* **īcō**
ictus², -ūs *m* stroke, blow; wound; (*metre*) beat
Īda, -ae, Īdē, -ēs *f* mountain in Crete; mountain
near Troy
Īdaeus *adj* Cretan; Trojan
idcircō *adv* for that reason; for the purpose
īdem, eadem, idem *pron* the same; also,
likewise
identidem *adv* repeatedly, again and again
ideō *adv* therefore, for this reason, that is why
idiōta, -ae *m* ignorant person, layman
īdōlon, -ī *nt* apparition
idōneē *adv see* **idōneus**
idōneus *adj* fit, proper, suitable, sufficient
Īdūs, -uum *fpl* Ides (*the 15th March, May, July,
October, the 13th of other months*)
iēcī *perf of* **iaciō**
iecur, -oris *and* **-inoris** *nt* liver; (*fig*) passion
iecusculum, -ī *nt* small liver
iēiūniōsus *adj* hungry
iēiūnitās, -ātis *f* fasting; (*fig*) meagreness
iēiūnium, -ī *and* **-iī** *nt* fast; hunger; leanness
iēiūnus *adj* fasting, hungry; (*things*) barren,
poor, meagre; (*style*) feeble

99

iēntāculum, -ī nt breakfast

igitur adv therefore, then, so

ignārus adj ignorant, unaware; unknown

ignāvē, ignāviter adv without energy

ignāvia, -ae f idleness, laziness; cowardice

ignāvus adj idle, lazy, listless; cowardly; relaxing

ignēscō, -ere vi to take fire, burn

igneus adj burning, fiery

igniculus, -ī m spark; (fig) fire, vehemence

ignifer, -ī adj fiery

ignigena, -ae m the fireborn (Bacchus)

ignipēs, -edis adj fiery-footed

ignipotēns, -entis adj fire-working (Vulcan)

ignis, -is m fire, a fire; firebrand, lightning; brightness, redness; (fig) passion, love

ignōbilis adj unknown, obscure; low-born

ignōbilitās, -ātis f obscurity; low birth

ignōminia, -ae f dishonour, disgrace

ignōminiōsus adj (person) degraded, disgraced; (things) shameful

ignōrābilis adj unknown

ignōrantia, -ae f ignorance

ignōrātiō, -ōnis f ignorance

ignōrō, -āre, -āvī, -ātum vt to not know, be unacquainted with; to disregard

ignōscō, -scere, -vī, -tum vt, vi to forgive, pardon

ignōtus adj unknown; low-born; ignorant

īlex, -icis f holm oak

Īlia, -ae f mother of Romulus and Remus

īlia, -um ntpl groin; entrails; ~ dūcere become broken-winded

Īliadēs, -adae m son of Ilia; Trojan

Īlias, -dis f the Iliad; a Trojan woman

īlicet adv it's all over, let us go; immediately

īlicō adv on the spot; instantly

īlignus adj of holm oak

Īlīthyia, -ae f Greek goddess of childbirth

Īlium, -ī nt, **Īlion, -ī** nt, **Īlios, -ī** f Troy

Īlius, Īliacus adj Trojan

illā adv that way

illābefactus adj unbroken

illābor, -bī, -psus vi to flow into, fall down

illabōrō, -āre vi to work (at)

illāc adv that way

illacessītus adj unprovoked

illacrimābilis adj unwept; inexorable

illacrimō, -āre, illacrimor, -ārī vi to weep over, lament; to weep

illaesus adj unhurt

illaetābilis adj cheerless

illāpsus ppa of **illābor**

illaqueō, -āre vt to ensnare

illātus ppp of **īnferō**

illaudātus adj wicked

ille, -a, -ud pron, adj that, that one; he, she, it; the famous; the former, the other; **ex illō** since then

illecebra, -ae f attraction, lure, bait, decoy bird

illecebrōsus adj seductive

illectus ppp of **illiciō**

illēctus adj unread

illepidē adv see **illepidus**

illepidus adj inelegant, churlish

illex, -icis m/f lure

illēx, -ēgis adj lawless

illexī perf of **illiciō**

illībātus adj unimpaired

illīberālis adj ungenerous, mean, disobliging

illīberālitās, -ātis f meanness

illīberāliter adv see **illīberālis**

illic, -aec, -ūc pron he, she, it; that

illīc adv there, yonder; in that matter

illiciō, -icere, -exī, -ectum vt to seduce, decoy, mislead

illicitātor, -ōris m sham bidder (at an auction)

illicitus adj unlawful

illīdō, -dere, -sī, -sum vt to strike, dash against

illigō, -āre, -āvī, -ātum vt to fasten on, attach; to connect; to impede, encumber, oblige

illim adv from there

illīmis adj clear

illinc adv from there; on that side

illinō, -inere, -ēvī, -itum vt to smear over, cover, bedaub

illiquefactus adj melted

illīsī perf of **illīdō**

illisus ppp of **illīdō**

illitterātus adj uneducated, uncultured

illitus ppp of **illinō**

illō adv (to) there; to that end

illōtus adj dirty

illūc adv (to) there; to that; to him/her

illūceō, -ēre vi to blaze

illūcēscō, -cēscere, -xī vi to become light, dawn

illūdō, -dere, -sī, -sum vt, vi to play, amuse oneself; to abuse; to jeer at, ridicule

illūminātē adv luminously

illūminō, -āre, -āvī, -ātum vt to light up; to enlighten; to embellish

illūsiō, -ōnis f irony

illūstris adj bright, clear; distinct, manifest; distinguished, illustrious

illūstrō, -āre, -āvī, -ātum vt to illuminate; to make clear, explain; to make famous

illūsus ppp of **illūdō**

illuviēs, -ēī f dirt, filth; floods

Illyria, -ae f, **Illyricum, -cī** nt Illyria

Illyricus, Illyrius adj see **Illyria**

Illyriī, -ōrum mpl people E. of the Adriatic

Ilva, -ae f Italian island (now Elba)

imāginārius adj fancied

imāginātiō, -ōnis f fancy

imāginor, -ārī vt to picture to oneself

imāgō, -inis f likeness, picture, statue; portrait of ancestor; apparition, ghost; echo, mental picture, idea; (fig) semblance, mere shadow; (RHET) comparison

imbēcillē adv faintly

imbēcillitās, -ātis f weakness, helplessness

imbēcillus adj weak, frail; helpless

imbellis adj non-combatant; peaceful; cowardly

imber, -ris *m* rain, heavy shower; water; (*fig*) stream, shower

imberbis, imberbus *adj* beardless

imbibō, -ere, -ī *vt* (*mind*) to conceive; to resolve

imbrex, -icis *f* tile

imbricus *adj* rainy

imbrifer, -ī *adj* rainy

imbuō, -uere, -uī, -ūtum *vt* to wet, steep, dip; (*fig*) to taint, fill; to inspire, accustom, train; to begin, be the first to explore

imitābilis *adj* imitable

imitāmen, -inis *nt* imitation; likeness

imitāmenta, -ōrum *ntpl* pretence

imitātiō, -ōnis *f* imitation

imitātor, -ōris *m*, **imitātrīx, -rīcis** *f* imitator

imitātus *adj* copied

imitor, -ārī, -ātus *vt* to copy, portray; to imitate, act like

immadēscō, -ēscere, -uī *vi* to become wet

immāne *adv* savagely

immānis *adj* enormous, vast; monstrous, savage, frightful

immānitās, -ātis *f* vastness; savageness, barbarism

immānsuētus *adj* wild

immātūritās, -ātis *f* over-eagerness

immātūrus *adj* untimely

immedicābilis *adj* incurable

immemor, -is *adj* unmindful, forgetful, negligent

immemorābilis *adj* indescribable, not worth mentioning

immemorātus *adj* hitherto untold

immēnsitās, -ātis *f* immensity

immēnsum, -ī *nt* infinity, vast extent ♦ *adv* exceedingly

immēnsus *adj* immeasurable, vast, unending

immerēns, -entis *adj* undeserving

immergō, -gere, -sī, -sum *vt* to plunge, immerse

immeritō *adv* unjustly

immeritus *adj* undeserving, innocent; undeserved

immērsābilis *adj* never foundering

immērsus *ppp of* **immergō**

immētātus *adj* unmeasured

immigrō, -āre, -āvī, -ātum *vi* to move (into)

immineō, -ēre, -uī *vi* to overhang, project; to be near, adjoin, impend; to threaten, be a menace to; to long for, grasp at

imminuō, -uere, -uī, -ūtum *vt* to lessen, shorten; to impair; to encroach on, ruin

imminūtiō, -ōnis *f* mutilation; (RHET) understatement

immisceō, -scēre, -scuī, -xtum *vt* to intermingle, blend; **sē immiscēre** join, meddle with

immiserābilis *adj* unpitied

immisericorditer *adv* unmercifully

immisericors, -dis *adj* pitiless

immissiō, -ōnis *f* letting grow

immissus *ppp of* **immittō**

immītis *adj* unripe; severe, inexorable

immittō, -ittere, -īsī, -issum *vt* to let in, put in; to graft on; to let go, let loose, let grow; to launch, throw; to incite, set on

immīxtus *ppp of* **immisceō**

immo *adv* (*correcting preceding words*) no, yes; on the contrary, or rather; ~ **sī** ah, if only

immōbilis *adj* motionless; immovable

immoderātē *adv* extravagantly

immoderātiō, -ōnis *f* excess

immoderātus *adj* limitless; excessive, unbridled

immodestē *adv* extravagantly

immodestia, -ae *f* licence

immodestus *adj* immoderate

immodicē *adv see* **immodicus**

immodicus *adj* excessive, extravagant, unruly

immodulātus *adj* unrhythmical

immolātiō, -ōnis *f* sacrifice

immolātor, -ōris *m* sacrificer

immōlītus *adj* erected

immolō, -āre, -āvī, -ātum *vt* to sacrifice; to slay

immorior, -ī, -tuus *vi* to die upon; to waste away

immorsus *adj* bitten; (*fig*) stimulated

immortālis *adj* immortal, everlasting

immortālitās, -ātis *f* immortality; lasting fame

immortāliter *adv* infinitely

immōtus *adj* motionless, unmoved, immovable

immūgiō, -īre, -iī *vi* to roar (in)

immulgeō, -ēre *vt* to milk

immundus *adj* unclean, dirty

immūniō, -īre, -īvī *vt* to strengthen

immūnis *adj* with no public obligations, untaxed, free from office; exempt, free (from)

immūnitās, -ātis *f* exemption, immunity, privilege

immūnītus *adj* undefended; (*roads*) unmetalled

immurmurō, -āre *vi* to murmur (at)

immūtābilis *adj* unalterable

immūtābilitās, -ātis *f* immutability

immūtātiō, -ōnis *f* exchange; (RHET) metonymy

immūtātus *adj* unchanged

immūtō, -āre, -āvī, -ātum *vt* to change; (*words*) to substitute by metonymy

impācātus *adj* aggressive

impāctus *ppp of* **impingō**

impār, -aris *adj* unequal, uneven, unlike; no match for, inferior; (*metre*) elegiac

imparātus *adj* unprepared, unprovided

impariter *adv* unequally

impāstus *adj* hungry

impatiēns, -entis *adj* unable to endure, impatient

impatienter *adv* intolerably

impatientia, -ae *f* want of endurance

impavidē *adv see* **impavidus**

impavidus *adj* fearless, undaunted

impedīmentum, -ī *nt* hindrance, obstacle; (*pl*) baggage, luggage, supply train

impediō, -īre, -īvī *and* **-iī, -ītum** *vt* to hinder, entangle; to encircle; (*fig*) to embarrass, obstruct, prevent

impedītiō, -ōnis *f* obstruction

impedītus *adj* (MIL) hampered with baggage, in difficulties; (*place*) difficult, impassable; (*mind*) busy, obsessed

impēgī *perf of* **impingō**

impellō, -ellere, -ulī, -ulsum *vt* to strike, drive; to set in motion, impel, shoot; to incite, urge on; (*fig*) to overthrow, ruin

impendeō, -ēre *vi* to overhang; to be imminent, threaten

impendiō *adv* very much

impendium, -ī *and* **-iī** *nt* expense, outlay; interest on a loan

impendō, -endere, -endī, -ēnsum *vt* to weigh out, pay out, spend; (*fig*) to devote

impenetrābilis *adj* impenetrable

impēnsa, -ae *f* expense, outlay

impēnsē *adv* very much; earnestly

impēnsus *ppp of* **impendō** ♦ *adj* (*cost*) high, dear; (*fig*) great, earnest

imperātor, -ōris *m* commander-in-chief, general; emperor; chief, master

imperātōrius *adj* of a general; imperial

imperātum, -ī *nt* order

imperceptus *adj* unknown

impercussus *adj* noiseless

imperditus *adj* not slain

imperfectus *adj* unfinished, imperfect

imperfōssus *adj* not stabbed

imperiōsus *adj* powerful, imperial; tyrannical

imperītē *adv* awkwardly

imperītia, -ae *f* inexperience

imperitō, -āre *vt*, *vi* to rule, command

imperītus *adj* inexperienced, ignorant

imperium, -ī *and* **-iī** *nt* command, order; mastery, sovereignty, power; military command, supreme authority; empire; (*pl*) those in command, the authorities

impermissus *adj* unlawful

imperō, -āre, -āvī, -ātum *vt*, *vi* to order, command; to requisition, demand; to rule, govern, control; to be emperor

imperterritus *adj* undaunted

impertiō, -īre, -īvī *and* **-iī, -ītum** *vt* to share, communicate, impart

imperturbātus *adj* unruffled

impervius *adj* impassable

impetibilis *adj* intolerable

impetis (*gen*) (*abl* **-e**) *m* force; extent

impetrābilis *adj* attainable; successful

impetrātiō, -ōnis *f* favour

impetriō, -īre *vt* to succeed with the auspices

impetrō, -āre, -āvī, -ātum *vt* to achieve; to obtain, secure (*a request*)

impetus, -ūs *m* attack, onset; charge; rapid motion, rush; (*mind*) impulse, passion

impexus *adj* unkempt

impiē *adv* wickedly

impietās, -ātis *f* impiety, disloyalty, unfilial conduct

impiger, -rī *adj* active, energetic

impigrē *adv see* **impiger**

impigritās, -ātis *f* energy

impingō, -ingere, -ēgī, -āctum *vt* to dash, force against; to force upon; (*fig*) to bring against, drive

impiō, -āre *vt* to make sinful

impius *adj* (*to gods*) impious; (*to parents*) undutiful; (*to country*) disloyal; wicked, unscrupulous

implācābilis *adj* implacable

implācābiliter *adv see* **implācābilis**

implācātus *adj* unappeased

implacidus *adj* savage

impleō, -ēre, -ēvī, -ētum *vt* to fill; to satisfy; (*time, number*) to make up, complete; (*duty*) to discharge, fulfil

implexus *adj* entwined; involved

implicātiō, -ōnis *f* entanglement

implicātus *adj* complicated, confused

implicitē *adv* intricately

implicō, -āre, -āvī *and* **-uī, -ātum** *and* **-itum** *vt* to entwine, enfold, clasp; (*fig*) to entangle, involve; to connect closely, join

implōrātiō, -ōnis *f* beseeching

implōrō, -āre, -āvī, -ātum *vt* to invoke, entreat, appeal to

implūmis *adj* unfledged

impluō, -ere *vi* to rain upon

impluvium, -ī *and* **-iī** *nt* roof-opening of the Roman atrium; rain basin in the atrium

impolītē *adv* without ornament

impolītus *adj* unpolished, inelegant

impollūtus *adj* unstained

impōnō, -ōnere, -osuī, -ositum *vt* to put in, lay on, place; to embark; (*fig*) to impose, inflict, assign; to put in charge; (*tax*) to impose; (*with dat*) to impose upon, cheat

importō, -āre, -āvī, -ātum *vt* to bring in, import; (*fig*) to bring upon, introduce

importūnē *adv see* **importūnus**

importūnitās, -ātis *f* insolence, ill nature

importūnus *adj* unsuitable; troublesome; ill-natured, uncivil, bullying

importuōsus *adj* without a harbour

impos, -tis *adj* not master (of)

impositus, impostus *ppp of* **impōnō**

impotēns, -entis *adj* powerless, weak; with no control over; headstrong, violent

impotenter *adv* weakly; violently

impotentia, -ae *f* poverty; want of self-control, violence

impraesentiārum *adv* at present

imprānsus *adj* fasting, without breakfast

imprecor, -ārī *vt* to invoke

impressiō, -ōnis *f* (MIL) thrust, raid; (*mind*) impression; (*speech*) emphasis; (*rhythm*) beat

impressus *ppp of* **imprimō**

imprīmīs *adv* especially

imprimō, -imere, -essī, -essum *vt* to press upon, impress, imprint, stamp

improbātiō, -ōnis *f* blame

improbē *adv* badly, wrongly; persistently

improbitās, -ātis *f* badness, dishonesty

improbō, -āre, -āvī, -ātum *vt* to disapprove, condemn, reject

improbulus *adj* a little presumptuous

improbus *adj* bad, inferior *(in quality)*; wicked, perverse, cruel; unruly, persistent, rebellious

imprōcērus *adj* undersized

imprōdictus *adj* not postponed

imprōmptus *adj* unready, slow

improperātus *adj* lingering

improsper, -ī *adj* unsuccessful

improsperē *adv* unfortunately

imprōvidē *adv see* **imprōvidus**

imprōvidus *adj* unforeseeing, thoughtless

imprōvīsus *adj* unexpected; **imprōvīsō, de imprōvīsō, ex imprōvīsō** unexpectedly

imprūdēns, -entis *adj* unforeseeing, not expecting; ignorant, unaware

imprūdenter *adv* thoughtlessly, unawares

imprūdentia, -ae *f* thoughtlessness; ignorance; aimlessness

impūbēs, -eris *and* **-is** *adj* youthful; chaste

impudens, -entis *adj* shameless, impudent

impudenter *adv see* **impudens**

impudentia, -ae *f* impudence

impudīcitia, -ae *f* lewdness

impudīcus *adj* shameless; immodest

impugnātiō, -ōnis *f* assault

impugnō, -āre, -āvī, -ātum *vt* to attack; *(fig)* to oppose, impugn

impulī *perf of* **impellō**

impulsiō, -ōnis *f* pressure; *(mind)* impulse

impulsor, -ōris *m* instigator

impulsus[1] *ppp of* **impellō**

impulsus[2]**, -ūs** *m* push, pressure, impulse; *(fig)* instigation

impūne *adv* safely, with impunity

impūnitās, -ātis *f* impunity

impūnītē *adv* with impunity

impūnītus *adj* unpunished

impūrātus *adj* vile

impūrē *adv see* **impūrus**

impūritās, -ātis *f* uncleanness

impūrus *adj* unclean; infamous, vile

imputātus *adj* unpruned

imputō, -āre, -āvī, -ātum *vt* to put to one's account; to ascribe, credit, impute

īmulus *adj* little tip of

īmus *adj* lowest, deepest, bottom of; last

in *prep (with abl)* in, on, at; among; in the case of; *(time)* during; *(with acc)* into, on to, to, towards; against; *(time)* for, till; *(purpose)* for; **in armīs** under arms; **in equō** on horseback; **in eō esse ut** be in the position of; be on the point of; **in hōrās** hourly; **in modum** in the manner of; **in rem** of use; **in universum** in general

inaccēssus *adj* unapproachable

inacēscō, -ere *vi* to turn sour

Īnachidēs, -idae *m* Perseus; Epaphus

Īnachis, -idis *f* Io

Īnachius *adj* of Inachus, Argive, Greek

Īnachus, -ī *m first king of Argos*

inadsuētus *adj* unaccustomed

inadūstus *adj* unsinged

inaedificō, -āre, -āvī, -ātum *vt* to build on, erect; to wall up, block up

inaequābilis *adj* uneven

inaequālis *adj* uneven; unequal; capricious

inaequāliter *adv see* **inaequālis**

inaequātus *adj* unequal

inaequō, -āre *vt* to level up

inaestimābilis *adj* incalculable; invaluable; valueless

inaestuō, -āre *vi* to rage in

inamābilis *adj* hateful

inamārēscō, -ere *vi* to become bitter

inambitiōsus *adj* unambitious

inambulātiō, -ōnis *f* walking about

inambulō, -āre *vi* to walk up and down

inamoenus *adj* disagreeable

inanimus *adj* lifeless, inanimate

ināniō, -īre *vt* to make empty

inānis *adj* empty, void; poor, unsubstantial; useless, worthless, vain, idle ♦ *nt (PHILOS)* space; *(fig)* vanity

inānitās, -ātis *f* empty space; inanity

ināniter *adv* idly, vainly

inarātus *adj* fallow

inārdēscō, -dēscere, -sī *vi* to be kindled, flare up

inass- *etc see* **inads-**

inattenuātus *adj* undiminished

inaudāx, -ācis *adj* timorous

inaudiō, -īre *vt* to hear of, learn

inaudītus *adj* unheard of, unusual; without a hearing

inaugurātō *adv* after taking the auspices

inaugurō, -āre *vi* to take auspices ♦ *vt* to consecrate, inaugurate

inaurēs, -ium *fpl* earrings

inaurō, -āre, -āvi, -ātum *vt* to gild; *(fig)* to enrich

inauspicātō *adv* without taking the auspices

inauspicātus *adj* done without auspices

inausus *adj* unattempted

incaeduus *adj* uncut

incalēscō, -ēscere, -uī *vi* to grow hot; *(fig)* to warm, glow

incalfaciō, -ere *vt* to heat

incallidē *adv* unskilfully

incallidus *adj* stupid, simple

incandēscō, -ēscere, -uī *vi* to become hot; to turn white

incānēscō, -ēscere, -uī *vi* to grow grey

incantātus *adj* enchanted

incānus *adj* grey

incassum *adv* in vain

incastīgātus *adj* unrebuked

incautē *adv* negligently

incautus *adj* careless, heedless; unforeseen, unguarded

incēdō, -ēdere, -ēssī, -ēssum *vi* to walk, parade, march; *(MIL)* to advance; *(feelings)* to come upon

incelebrātus *adj* not made known

incēnātus *adj* supperless

incendiārius, -ī *and* **-iī** *m* incendiary

incendium, **-ī** *and* **-iī** *nt* fire, conflagration; heat; (*fig*) fire, vehemence, passion

incendō, **-ere**, **-ī**, **incēnsum** *vt* to set fire to, burn; to light, brighten; (*fig*) to inflame, rouse, incense

incēnsiō, **-ōnis** *f* burning

incēnsus[1] *ppp of* **incendō**

incēnsus[2] *adj* not registered

incēpī *perf of* **incipiō**

inceptiō, **-ōnis** *f* undertaking

inceptō, **-āre** *vt* to begin, attempt

inceptor, **-ōris** *m* originator

inceptum, **-ī** *nt* beginning, undertaking, attempt

inceptus *ppp of* **incipiō**

incērō, **-āre** *vt* to cover with wax

incertō *adv* not for certain

incertus *adj* uncertain, doubtful, unsteady ♦ *nt* uncertainty

incessō, **-ere**, **-īvī** *vt* to attack; (*fig*) to assail

incēssus, **-ūs** *m* gait, pace, tramp; invasion; approach

inceste *adv see* **incestus**[1]

incestō, **-āre** *vt* to pollute, dishonour

incestus[1] *adj* sinful; unchaste, incestuous ♦ *nt* incest

incestus[2], **-ūs** *m* incest

incho- *etc see* **incoh-**

incidō, **-idere**, **-idī**, **-āsum** *vi* to fall upon, fall into; to meet, fall in with, come across; to befall, occur, happen; **in mentem incidere** occur to one

incīdō, **-dere**, **-dī**, **-sum** *vt* to cut open; to cut up; to engrave, inscribe; to interrupt, cut short

incīle, **-is** *nt* ditch

incīlō, **-āre** *vt* to rebuke

incingō, **-gere**, **-xī**, **-ctum** *vt* to gird, wreathe; to surround

incinō, **-ere** *vt* to sing, play

incipiō, **-ipere**, **-ēpī**, **-eptum** *vt*, *vi* to begin

incipissō, **-ere** *vt* to begin

incīsē *adv* in short clauses

incīsim *adv* in short clauses

incīsiō, **-ōnis** *f* clause

incīsum, **-ī** *nt* clause

incīsus *ppp of* **incīdō**

incitāmentum, **-ī** *nt* incentive

incitātē *adv* impetuously

incitātiō, **-ōnis** *f* inciting; rapidity

incitātus *ppp of* **incitō** ♦ *adj* swift, rapid; **equō incitātō** at a gallop

incitō, **-āre**, **-āvī**, **-ātum** *vt* to urge on, rush; to rouse, encourage, excite; to inspire; to increase; **sē incitāre** rush; **currentem incitāre** spur a willing horse

incitus[1] *adj* swift

incitus[2] *adj* immovable; **ad incitās redigere**, **ad incita redigere** bring to a standstill

inclāmō, **-āre** *vt*, *vi* to call out, cry out to; to scold, abuse

inclārēscō, **-ēscere**, **-uī** *vi* to become famous

inclēmēns, **-entis** *adj* severe

inclēmenter *adv* harshly

inclēmentia, **-ae** *f* severity

inclīnātiō, **-ōnis** *f* leaning, slope; (*fig*) tendency, inclination, bias; (*circumstances*) change; (*voice*) modulation

inclīnātus *adj* inclined, prone; falling; (*voice*) deep

inclīnō, **-āre**, **-āvī**, **-ātum** *vt* to bend, turn; to turn back; (*fig*) to incline, direct, transfer; to change ♦ *vi* to bend, sink; (*MIL*) to give way; (*fig*) to change, deteriorate; to incline, tend, turn in favour

inclitus *etc see* **inclutus**

inclūdō, **-dere**, **-sī**, **-sum** *vt* to shut in, keep in, enclose; to obstruct, block; (*fig*) to include; (*time*) to close, end

inclūsiō, **-ōnis** *f* imprisonment

inclūsus *ppp of* **inclūdō**

inclutus *adj* famous, glorious

incoctus[1] *ppp of* **incoquō**

incoctus[2] *adj* uncooked, raw

incōgitābilis *adj* thoughtless

incōgitāns, **-antis** *adj* thoughtless

incōgitantia, **-ae** *f* thoughtlessness

incōgitō, **-āre** *vt* to contrive

incognitus *adj* unknown, unrecognized; (*LAW*) untried

incohātus *adj* unfinished

incohō, **-āre**, **-āvī**, **-ātum** *vt* to begin, start

incola, **-ae** *m/f* inhabitant, resident

incolō, **-ere**, **-uī** *vt* to live in, inhabit ♦ *vi* to live, reside

incolumis *adj* safe and sound, unharmed

incolumitās, **-ātis** *f* safety

incomitātus *adj* unaccompanied

incommendātus *adj* unprotected

incommodē *adv* inconveniently, unfortunately

incommoditās, **-ātis** *f* inconvenience, disadvantage

incommodō, **-āre** *vi* to be inconvenient, annoy

incommodum, **-ī** *nt* inconvenience, disadvantage, misfortune

incommodus *adj* inconvenient, troublesome

incommūtābilis *adj* unchangeable

incompertus *adj* unknown

incompositē *adv see* **incompositus**

incompositus *adj* in disorder, irregular

incōmptus *adj* undressed, inelegant

inconcessus *adj* forbidden

inconciliō, **-āre** *vt* to win over (by guile); trick, inveigle, embarrass

inconcinnus *adj* inartistic, awkward

inconcussus *adj* unshaken, stable

inconditē *adv* confusedly

inconditus *adj* undisciplined, not organized; (*language*) artless

incōnsīderātē *adv see* **incōnsīderātus**

incōnsīderātus *adj* thoughtless, ill-advised

incōnsōlābilis *adj* incurable

incōnstāns, **-antis** *adj* fickle, inconsistent

incōnstanter *adv* inconsistently

incōnstantia, **-ae** *f* fickleness, inconsistency

incōnsultē *adv* indiscreetly

incōnsultū without consulting
incōnsultus *adj* indiscreet, ill-advised; unanswered; not consulted
incōnsūmptus *adj* unconsumed
incontāminātus *adj* untainted
incontentus *adj* untuned
incontinēns, -entis *adj* intemperate
incontinenter *adv* without self-control
incontinentia, -ae *f* lack of self-control
inconveniēns, -entis *adj* ill-matched
incoquō, -quere, -xī, -ctum *vt* to boil; to dye
incorrēctus *adj* unrevised
incorruptē *adv* justly
incorruptus *adj* unspoiled; uncorrupted, genuine
incrēbrēscō, incrēbēscō, -ēscere, -uī *vi* to increase, grow, spread
incrēdibilis *adj* incredible, extraordinary
incrēdibiliter *adv see* **incrēdibilis**
incrēdulus *adj* incredulous
incrēmentum, -ī *nt* growth, increase; addition; offspring
increpitō, -āre *vt* to rebuke; to challenge
increpō, -āre, -uī, -itum *vi* to make a noise, sound; to be noised abroad ♦ *vt* to cause to make a noise; to exclaim against, rebuke
incrēscō, -scere, -vī *vi* to grow in, increase
incrētus *adj* sifted in
incruentātus *adj* unstained with blood
incruentus *adj* bloodless, without bloodshed
incrūstō, -āre *vt* to encrust
incubō, -āre, -uī, -itum *vi* to lie in or on; (*fig*) to brood over
incubuī *perf of* **incubō**; **incumbō**
inculcō, -āre, -āvī, -ātum *vt* to force in; to force upon, impress on
inculpātus *adj* blameless
incultē *adv* uncouthly
incultus¹ *adj* uncultivated; (*fig*) neglected, uneducated, rude
incultus², -ūs *m* neglect, squalor
incumbō, -mbere, -buī, -bitum *vi* to lean, recline on; to fall upon, throw oneself upon; to oppress, lie heavily upon; (*fig*) to devote attention to, take pains with; to incline
incūnābula, -ōrum *ntpl* swaddling clothes; (*fig*) cradle, infancy, birthplace, origin
incūrātus *adj* neglected
incūria, -ae *f* negligence
incūriōsē *adv* carelessly
incūriōsus *adj* careless, indifferent
incurrō, -rrere, -rrī *and* **-curri, -rsum** *vi* to run into, rush, attack; to invade; to meet with, get involved in; (*events*) to occur, coincide
incursiō, -ōnis *f* attack; invasion, raid; collision
incursō, -āre *vt, vi* to run into, assault; to frequently invade; (*fig*) to meet, strike
incursus, -ūs *m* assault, striking; (*mind*) impulse
incurvō, -āre *vt* to bend, crook
incurvus *adj* bent, crooked
incūs, -ūdis *f* anvil
incūsātiō, -ōnis *f* blaming

incūsō, -āre, -āvī, -ātum *vt* to find fault with, accuse
incussī *perf of* **incutiō**
incussus¹, -ūs *ppp of* **incutiō**
incussus², -ūs *m* shock
incustōdītus *adj* unguarded, unconcealed
incūsus *adj* forged
incutiō, -tere, -ssī, -ssum *vt* to strike, dash against; to throw; (*fig*) to strike into, inspire with
indāgātiō, -ōnis *f* search
indāgātor, -ōris *m* explorer
indāgātrīx, -rīcis *f* female explorer
indāgō¹, -āre *vt* to track down; (*fig*) to trace, investigate
indāgō², -inis *f* (*hunt*) drive, encirclement
indaudiō *etc see* **inaudiō**
inde *adv* from there, from that, from them; on that side; from then, ever since; after that, then
indēbitus *adj* not due
indēclīnātus *adj* constant
indecor, -is *adj* dishonourable, a disgrace
indecorē *adv* indecently
indecorō, -āre *vt* to disgrace
indecōrus *adj* unbecoming, unsightly
indēfēnsus *adj* undefended
indēfessus *adj* unwearied, tireless
indēflētus *adj* unwept
indēiectus *adj* undemolished
indēlēbilis *adj* imperishable
indēlībātus *adj* unimpaired
indemnātus *adj* unconvicted
indēplōrātus *adj* unlamented
indēprēnsus *adj* undetected
indeptus *ppa of* **indipīscor**
indēsertus *adj* unforsaken
indēstrictus *adj* unscathed
indētōnsus *adj* unshorn
indēvītātus *adj* unerring
index, -icis *m* forefinger; witness, informer; (*book, art*) title, inscription; (*stone*) touchstone; (*fig*) indication, pointer, sign
India, -iae *f* India
indicātiō, -ōnis *f* value
indīcente mē without my telling
indicium, -ī *and* **-iī** *nt* information, evidence; reward for information; indication, sign, proof; **~ profitērī, ~ offerre** turn King's evidence; **~ postulāre, ~ dare** ask, grant permission to give evidence
indicō, -āre, -āvī, -ātum *vt* to point out; to disclose, betray; to give information, give evidence; to put a price on
indīcō, -īcere, -īxī, -ictum *vt* to declare, proclaim, appoint
indictus¹ *ppp of* **indīcō**
indictus² *adj* not said, unsung; **causā indictā** without a hearing
Indicus *adj see* **India**
indidem *adv* from the same place or thing
indidī *perf of* **indō**
indifferēns, -entis *adj* neither good nor bad
indigena, -ae *m* native ♦ *adj* native

indigēns, -entis adj needy
indigentia, -ae f need; craving
indigeō, -ēre, -uī vi (with abl) to need, want, require; to crave
indiges, -etis m national deity
indīgestus adj confused
indignābundus adj enraged
indignans, -antis adj indignant
indignātiō, -ōnis f indignation
indignē adv unworthily; indignantly
indignitās, -ātis f unworthiness, enormity; insulting treatment; indignation
indignor, -ārī, -ātus vt to be displeased with, be angry at
indignus adj unworthy, undeserving; shameful, severe; undeserved
indigus adj in want
indīligēns, -entis adj careless
indīligenter adv see **indīligēns**
indīligentia, -ae f carelessness
indipīscor, -ī, indeptus vt to obtain, get, reach
indīreptus adj unplundered
indiscrētus adj closely connected, indiscriminate, indistinguishable
indisertē adv without eloquence
indisertus adj not eloquent
indispositus adj disorderly
indissolūbilis adj imperishable
indistinctus adj confused, obscure
inditus ppp of **indō**
indīviduus adj indivisible; inseparable ♦ nt atom
indō, -ere, -idī, -itum vt to put in or on; to introduce; to impart, impose
indocilis adj difficult to teach, hard to learn; untaught
indoctē adv unskilfully
indoctus adj untrained, illiterate, ignorant
indolentia, -ae f freedom from pain
indolēs, -is f nature, character, talents
indolēscō, -ēscere, -uī vi to feel sorry
indomitus adj untamed, wild; ungovernable
indormiō, -īre vi to sleep on; to be careless
indōtātus adj with no dowry; unhonoured; (fig) unadorned
indubitō, -āre vi to begin to doubt
indubius adj undoubted
indūcō, -ūcere, -ūxī, -uctum vt to bring in, lead on; to introduce; to overlay, cover over; (fig) to move, persuade, seduce; (book-keeping) to enter; (dress) to put on; (public show) to exhibit; (writing) to erase; **animum indūcere, in animum indūcere** determine, imagine
inductiō, -ōnis f leading, bringing on; (mind) purpose, intention; (LOGIC) induction
inductus ppp of **indūcō**
indugredior etc see **ingredior**
induī perf of **induō**
indulgēns, -entis pres p of **indulgeō** ♦ adj indulgent, kind
indulgenter adv indulgently
indulgentia, -ae f indulgence, gentleness

indulgeō, -gēre, -sī vi (with dat) to be kind to, indulge, give way to; to indulge in ♦ vt to concede; **sibi indulgēre** take liberties
induō, -uere, -uī, -ūtum vt (dress) to put on; (fig) to assume, entangle
indup- etc see **imp-**
indūrēscō, -ēscere, -uī vi to harden
indūrō, -āre vt to harden
Indus[1], -ī m Indian; Ethiopian; mahout
Indus[2] adj see **India**
industria, -ae f diligence; **dē industriā, ex industriā** on purpose
industriē adv see **industrius**
industrius adj diligent, painstaking
indūtiae, -ārum fpl truce, armistice
indūtus[1] ppp of **induō**
indūtus[2], -us m wearing
induviae, -ārum fpl clothes
indūxī perf of **indūcō**
inēbriō, -āre vt to intoxicate; (fig) to saturate
inedia, -ae f starvation
inēditus adj unpublished
inēlegāns, -antis adj tasteless
inēleganter adv without taste
inēluctābilis adj inescapable
inēmorior, -ī vi to die in
inemptus adj unpurchased
inēnārrābilis adj indescribable
inēnōdābilis adj inexplicable
ineō, -īre, -īvī and **-iī, -itum** vi to go in, come in; to begin ♦ vt to enter; to begin, enter upon, form, undertake; **cōnsilium inīre** form a plan; **grātiam inīre** win favour; **numerum inīre** enumerate; **ratiōnem inīre** calculate, consider, contrive; **suffrāgium inīre** vote; **viam inīre** find out a way
ineptē adv see **ineptus**
ineptia, -ae f stupidity; (pl) nonsense
ineptiō, -īre vi to play the fool
ineptus adj unsuitable; silly, tactless, absurd
inermis, inermus adj unarmed, defenceless; harmless
inerrāns, -antis adj fixed
inerrō, -āre vi to wander about in
iners, -tis adj unskilful; inactive, indolent, timid; insipid
inertia, -ae f lack of skill; idleness, laziness
inērudītus adj uneducated
inescō, -āre vt to entice, deceive
inēvectus adj mounted
inēvītābilis adj inescapable
inexcītus adj peaceful
inexcūsābilis adj with no excuse
inexercitātus adj untrained
inexhaustus adj unexhausted
inexōrābilis adj inexorable; (things) severe
inexperrēctus adj unawakened
inexpertus adj inexperienced; untried
inexpiābilis adj implacable; implacable
inexplēbilis adj insatiable
inexplētus adj incessant
inexplicābilis adj inexplicable; impracticable, unending

inexplōrātō *adv* without making a reconnaissance

inexplōrātus *adj* unreconnoitred

inexpugnābilis *adj* impregnable, safe

inexspectātus *adj* unexpected

inexstinctus *adj* unextinguished; insatiable, imperishable

inexsuperābilis *adj* insurmountable

inextrīcābilis *adj* inextricable

īnfabrē *adv* unskilfully

īnfabricātus *adj* unfashioned

īnfacētus *adj* not witty, crude

īnfācundus *adj* ineloquent

īnfāmia, -ae *f* disgrace, scandal

īnfāmis *adj* infamous, disreputable

īnfāmō, -āre, -āvī, -ātum *vt* to disgrace, bring into disrepute

īnfandus *adj* unspeakable, atrocious

īnfāns, -antis *adj* mute, speechless; young, infant; tongue-tied; childish ♦ *m/f* infant, child

īnfantia, -ae *f* inability to speak; infancy; lack of eloquence

īnfatuō, -āre *vt* to make a fool of

īnfaustus *adj* unlucky

īnfector, -ōris *m* dyer

īnfectus¹ *ppp of* **īnficiō**

īnfectus² *adj* undone, unfinished; rē īnfectā without achieving one's purpose

īnfēcunditās, -ātis *f* infertility

īnfēcundus *adj* unfruitful

īnfēlīcitās, -ātis *f* misfortune

īnfēlīciter *adv see* **īnfēlīx**

īnfēlīcō, -āre *vt* to make unhappy

īnfēlīx, -īcis *adj* unfruitful; unhappy, unlucky

īnfēnsē *adv* aggressively

īnfēnsō, -āre *vt* to make dangerous, make hostile

īnfēnsus *adj* hostile, dangerous

īnferciō, -īre *vt* to cram in

īnferiae, -ārum *fpl* offerings to the dead

īnferior, -ōris *compar of* **īnferus**

īnferius *compar of* **īnfrā**

īnfernē *adv* below

īnfernus *adj* beneath; of the lower world, infernal ♦ *mpl* the shades ♦ *ntpl* the lower world

īnferō, -re, intulī, illātum *vt* to carry in, bring to, put on; to move forward; (*fig*) to introduce, cause; (*book-keeping*) to enter; (LOGIC) to infer; **bellum īnferre** make war (on); **pedem īnferre** advance; **sē īnferre** repair, rush, strut about; **signa īnferre** attack, charge

īnferus (*compar* **īnferior**, *superl* **īnfimus**) *adj* lower, below ♦ *mpl* the dead, the lower world ♦ *compar* lower; later; inferior ♦ *superl* lowest, bottom of; meanest, humblest

īnfervēscō, -vēscere, -buī *vi* to boil

īnfestē *adv* aggressively

īnfestō, -āre *vt* to attack

īnfestus *adj* unsafe; dangerous, aggressive

īnficēt- *see* **īnfacēt-**

īnficiō, -icere, -ēcī, -ectum *vt* to dip, dye, discolour; to taint, infect; (*fig*) to instruct, corrupt, poison

īnfidēlis *adj* faithless

īnfidēlitās, -ātis *f* disloyalty

īnfidēliter *adv* treacherously

īnfidus *adj* unsafe, treacherous

īnfīgō, -gere, -xī, -xum *vt* to thrust, drive in; (*fig*) to impress, imprint

īnfimus *superl of* **īnferus**

īnfindō, -ere *vt* to cut into, plough

īnfīnitās, -ātis *f* boundless extent, infinity

īnfīnītē *adv* without end

īnfīnītiō, -ōnis *f* infinity

īnfīnītus *adj* boundless, endless, infinite; indefinite

īnfirmātiō, -ōnis *f* invalidating, refuting

īnfirmē *adv* feebly

īnfirmitās, -ātis *f* weakness; infirmity, sickness

īnfirmō, -āre *vt* to weaken; to invalidate, refute

īnfirmus *adj* weak, indisposed; weak-minded; (*things*) trivial

īnfit *vi* (*defec*) begins

īnfitiālis *adj* negative

īnfitiās eō deny

īnfitiātiō, -ōnis *f* denial

īnfitiātor, -ōris *m* denier (of a debt)

īnfitior, -ārī, -ātus *vt* to deny, repudiate

īnfīxus *ppp of* **īnfīgō**

īnflammātiō, -ōnis *f* (*fig*) exciting

īnflammō, -āre, -āvī, -ātum *vt* to set on fire, light; (*fig*) to inflame, rouse

īnflātē *adv* pompously

īnflātiō, -ōnis *f* flatulence

īnflātus, -ūs *m* blow; inspiration ♦ *adj* blown up, swollen; (*fig*) puffed up, conceited; (*style*) turgid

īnflectō, -ctere, -xī, -xum *vt* to bend, curve; to change; (*voice*) to modulate; (*fig*) to affect, move

īnflētus *adj* unwept

īnflexiō, -ōnis *f* bending

īnflexus *ppp of* **īnflectō**

īnflīgō, -gere, -xī, -ctum *vt* to dash against, strike; to inflict

īnflō, -āre, -āvī, -ātum *vt* to blow, inflate; (*fig*) to inspire, puff up

īnfluō, -ere, -xī, -xum *vi* to flow in; (*fig*) to stream, pour in

īnfodiō, -odere, -ōdī, -ossum *vt* to dig in, bury

īnfōrmātiō, -ōnis *f* sketch, idea

īnfōrmis *adj* shapeless; hideous

īnfōrmō, -āre, -āvī, -ātum *vt* to shape, fashion; to sketch; to educate

īnfortūnātus *adj* unfortunate

īnfortūnium, -ī and -iī *nt* misfortune

īnfossus *ppp of* **īnfodiō**

īnfrā (*compar* **īnferius**) *adv* underneath, below ♦ *compar* lower down ♦ *prep* (*with acc*) below, beneath, under; later than

īnfrāctiō, -ōnis *f* weakening

īnfrāctus *ppp of* **īnfringō**

īnfragilis *adj* strong

īnfremō, -ere, -uī *vi* to growl

īnfrēnātus¹ *ppp of* īnfrēnō

īnfrēnātus² *adj* without a bridle

īnfrendō, -ere *vi* to gnash

īnfrēnis, -us *adj* unbridled

īnfrēnō, -āre, -āvī, -ātum *vt* to put a bridle on, harness; (*fig*) to curb

īnfrequēns, -entis *adj* not crowded, infrequent; badly attended

īnfrequentia, -ae *f* small number; emptiness

īnfringō, -ingere, -ēgī, -āctum *vt* to break, bruise; (*fig*) to weaken, break down, exhaust

īnfrōns, -ondis *adj* leafless

īnfūcātus *adj* showy

īnfula, -ae *f* woollen band, fillet, badge of honour

īnfumus *etc see* īnfimus

īnfundō, -undere, -ūdī, -ūsum *vt* to pour in or on; to serve; (*fig*) to spread

īnfuscō, -āre *vt* to darken; to spoil, tarnish

īnfūsus *ppp of* īnfundō

ingeminō, -āre *vt* to redouble ♦ *vi* to be redoubled

ingemīscō, -īscere, -uī *vi* to groan, sigh ♦ *vt* to sigh over

ingemō, -ere, -uī *vt, vi* to sigh for, mourn

ingenerō, -āre, -āvī, -ātum *vt* to engender, produce, create

ingeniātus *adj* with a natural talent

ingeniōsē *adv* cleverly

ingeniōsus *adj* talented, clever; (*things*) naturally suited

ingenitus *ppp of* ingignō ♦ *adj* inborn, natural

ingenium, -ī *and* -iī *nt* nature; (*disposition*) bent, character; (*intellect*) ability, talent, genius; (*person*) genius

ingēns, -entis *adj* huge, mighty, great

ingenuē *adv* liberally, frankly

ingenuitās, -ātis *f* noble birth, noble character

ingenuus *adj* native, innate; free-born; noble, frank; delicate

ingerō, -rere, -ssī, -stum *vt* to carry in; to heap on; to throw, hurl; (*fig*) to press, obtrude

ingignō, -ignere, -enuī, -enitum *vt* to engender, implant

inglōrius *adj* inglorious

ingluviēs, -ēī *f* maw; gluttony

ingrātē *adv* unwillingly; ungratefully

ingrātiīs, ingrātīs *adv* against one's will

ingrātus *adj* disagreeable, unwelcome; ungrateful, thankless

ingravēscō, -ere *vi* to grow heavy, become worse, increase

ingravō, -āre *vt* to weigh heavily on; to aggravate

ingredior, -dī, -ssus *vt, vi* to go in, enter; to walk, march; to enter upon, engage in; to commence, begin to speak

ingressiō, -ōnis *f* entrance; beginning; pace

ingressus, -ūs *m* entrance; (*MIL*) inroad; beginning; walking, gait

ingruō, -ere, -ī *vi* to fall upon, assail

inguen, -inis *nt* groin

ingurgitō, -āre *vt* to pour in; sē ingurgitāre gorge oneself; (*fig*) to be absorbed in

ingustātus *adj* untasted

inhabilis *adj* unwieldy, awkward; unfit

inhabitābilis *adj* uninhabitable

inhabitō, -āre *vt* to inhabit

inhaereō, -rēre, -sī, -sum *vi* to stick in, cling to; to adhere, be closely connected with; to be always in

inhaerēscō, -ere *vi* to take hold, cling fast

inhālō, -āre *vt* to breathe on

inhibeō, -ēre, -uī, -itum *vt* to check, restrain, use, practise; inhibēre rēmīs/nāvem back water

inhibitiō, -ōnis *f* backing water

inhiō, -āre *vi* to gape ♦ *vt* to gape at, covet

inhonestē *adv see* inhonestus

inhonestō, -āre *vt* to dishonour

inhonestus *adj* dishonourable, inglorious; ugly

inhonōrātus *adj* unhonoured; unrewarded

inhonōrus *adj* unhonoured; ugly

inhorreō, -ēre, -uī *vt* to stand erect, bristle

inhorrēscō, -ēscere, -uī *vi* to bristle up; to shiver, shudder, tremble

inhospitālis *adj* inhospitable

inhospitālitās, -ātis *f* inhospitality

inhospitus *adj* inhospitable

inhūmānē *adv* uncivilly

inhūmānitās, -ātis *f* barbarity; discourtesy, churlishness, meanness

inhūmāniter *adv* = inhūmānē

inhūmānus *adj* savage, brutal; ill-bred, uncivil, uncultured

inhumātus *adj* unburied

inibi *adv* there, therein; about to happen

īniciō, -icere, -iēcī, -iectum *vt* to throw into, put on; (*fig*) to inspire, cause; (*speech*) to hint, mention; manum īnicere take possession

iniectus, -ūs *m* putting in, throwing over

inimīcē *adv* hostilely

inimīcitia, -ae *f* enmity

inimīcō, -āre *vt* to make enemies

inimīcus *adj* unfriendly, hostile; injurious ♦ *m/f* enemy; inimīcissimus greatest enemy

inīquē *adv* unequally, unjustly

inīquitās, -ātis *f* unevenness; difficulty; injustice, unfair demands

inīquus *adj* unequal, uneven; adverse, unfavourable, injurious; unfair, unjust; excessive; impatient, discontented ♦ *m* enemy

initiō, -āre *vt* to initiate

initium, -ī *and* -iī *nt* beginning; (*pl*) elements, first principles; holy rites, mysteries

initus¹ *ppp of* ineō

initus², -ūs *m* approach; beginning

iniūcundē *adv see* iniūcundus

iniūcunditās, -ātis *f* unpleasantness

iniūcundus *adj* unpleasant

iniungō, -ungere, -ūnxī, -ūnctum *vt* to join, attach; (*fig*) to impose, inflict

iniūrātus *adj* unsworn

iniūria, -ae f wrong, injury, injustice; insult, outrage; severity, revenge; unjust possession; **iniūriā** unjustly

iniūriōsē adv wrongfully

iniūriōsus adj unjust, wrongful; harmful

iniūrius adj wrong, unjust

iniūssū without orders (from)

iniūssus adj unbidden

iniūstē adv see **iniūstus**

iniūstitia, -ae f injustice, severity

iniūstus adj unjust, wrong; excessive, severe

inl- etc see **ill-**

inm- etc see **imm-**

innābilis adj that none may swim

innāscor, -scī, -tus vi to be born in, grow up in

innatō, -āre vt to swim in, float on; to swim, flow into

innātus ppa of **innāscor** ✦ adj innate, natural

innāvigābilis adj unnavigable

innectō, -ctere, -xuī, -xum vt to tie, fasten together, entwine; (fig) to connect; to contrive

innītor, -tī, -xus and **-sus** vi to rest, lean on; to depend

innō, -āre vi to swim in, float on, sail on

innocēns, -entis adj harmless; innocent; upright, unselfish

innocenter adv blamelessly

innocentia, -ae f innocence; integrity, unselfishness

innocuē adv innocently

innocuus adj harmless; innocent; unharmed

innōtēscō, -ēscere, -uī vi to become known

innovō, -āre vt to renew; **sē innovāre** return

innoxius adj harmless, safe; innocent; unharmed

innuba, -ae adj unmarried

innūbilus adj cloudless

innūbō, -bere, -psī vi to marry into

innumerābilis adj countless

innumerābilitās, -ātis f countless number

innumerābiliter adv innumerably

innumerālis adj numberless

innumerus adj countless

innuō, -ere, -ī vi to give a nod

innūpta, -ae adj unmarried

Īnō, -ūs f daughter of Cadmus

inoblītus adj unforgetful

inobrutus adj not overwhelmed

inobservābilis adj unnoticed

inobservātus adj unobserved

inoffēnsus adj without hindrance, uninterrupted

inofficiōsus adj irresponsible; disobliging

inolēns, -entis adj odourless

inolēscō, -scere, -vī vi to grow in

inōminātus adj inauspicious

inopia, -ae f want, scarcity, poverty, helplessness

inopīnāns, -antis adj unaware

inopīnātō adv unexpectedly

inopīnātus adj unexpected; off one's guard

inopīnus adj unexpected

inopiōsus adj in want

inops, -is adj destitute, poor, in need (of); helpless, weak; (speech) poor in ideas

inōrātus adj unpleaded

inōrdinātus adj disordered, irregular

inōrnātus adj unadorned, plain; uncelebrated

Īnōus adj see **Īnō**

inp- etc see **imp-**

inquam vt (defec) to say; (emphatic) I repeat, maintain

inquiēs, -ētis adj restless

inquiētō, -āre vt to unsettle, make difficult

inquiētus adj restless, unsettled

inquilīnus, -ī m inhabitant, tenant

inquinātē adv filthily

inquinātus adj filthy, impure

inquinō, -āre, -āvī, -ātum vt to defile, stain, contaminate

inquīrō, -rere, -sīvī, -sītum vt to search for, inquire into; (LAW) to collect evidence

inquīsītiō, -ōnis f searching, inquiry; (LAW) inquisition

inquīsītor, -ōris m searcher, spy; investigator

inquīsītus¹ ppp of **inquīrō**

inquīsītus² adj not investigated

inr- etc see **irr-**

īnsalūtātus adj ungreeted

īnsānābilis adj incurable

īnsānē adv madly

īnsānia, -ae f madness; folly, mania, poetic rapture

īnsāniō, -īre, -īvī, -ītum vi to be mad, rave; to rage; to be inspired

īnsānitās, -ātis f unhealthiness

īnsānum adv (slang) frightfully

īnsānus adj mad; frantic, furious; outrageous

īnsatiābilis adj insatiable; never cloying

īnsatiābiliter adv see **īnsatiābilis**

īnsatietās, -ātis f insatiateness

īnsaturābilis adj insatiable

īnsaturābiliter adv see **īnsaturābilis**

īnscendō, -endere, -endī, -ēnsum vt, vi to climb up, mount, embark

īnscēnsiō, -ōnis f going on board

īnscēnsus ppp of **īnscendō**

īnsciēns, -entis adj unaware; stupid

īnscienter adv ignorantly

īnscientia, -ae f ignorance, inexperience; neglect

īnscītē adv clumsily

īnscītia, -ae f ignorance, stupidity, inattention

īnscītus adj ignorant, stupid

īnscius adj unaware, ignorant

īnscrībō, -bere, -psī, -ptum vt to write on, inscribe; to ascribe, assign; (book) to entitle; (for sale) to advertise

īnscrīptiō, -ōnis f inscribing, title

īnscrīptus ppp of **īnscrībō**

īnsculpō, -ere, -sī, -tum vt to carve in, engrave on

īnsectātiō, -ōnis f hot pursuit; (words) abusing, persecution

īnsectātor, -ōris m persecutor

īnsector, -ārī, -ātus, īnsectō, -āre *vt* to pursue, attack, criticise

īnsectus *adj* notched

īnsēdābiliter *adv* incessantly

īnsēdī *perf of* **īnsīdō**

īnsenēscō, -ēscere, -uī *vi* to grow old in

īnsēnsilis *adj* imperceptible

īnsepultus *adj* unburied

īnsequēns, -entis *pres p of* **īnsequor ♦** *adj* the following

īnsequor, -quī, -cūtus *vt* to follow, pursue hotly; to proceed; (*time*) to come after, come next; (*fig*) to attack, persecute

īnserō¹, -erere, -ēvī, -itum *vt* to graft; (*fig*) to implant

īnserō², -ere, -uī, -tum *vt* to let in, insert; to introduce, mingle, involve

īnsertō, -āre *vt* to put in

īnsertus *ppp of* **īnserō²**

īnserviō, -īre, -iī, -ītum *vt, vi* to be a slave (to); to be devoted, submissive (to)

īnsessus *ppp of* **īnsīdō**

īnsībilō, -āre *vi* to whistle in

īnsīdeō, -ēre *vi* to sit on or in; to remain fixed ♦ *vt* to hold, occupy

īnsidiae, -ārum *fpl* ambush; (*fig*) trap, trickery

īnsidiātor, -ōris *nt* soldier in ambush; (*fig*) waylayer, plotter

īnsidior, -ārī, -ātus *vi* to lie in ambush; (*with dat*) to lie in wait for, plot against

īnsidiōsē *adv* insidiously

īnsidiōsus *adj* artful, treacherous

īnsīdō, -īdere, -ēdī, -essum *vi* to settle on; (*fig*) to become fixed, rooted in ♦ *vt* to occupy

īnsigne, -is *nt* distinguishing mark, badge, decoration; (*pl*) insignia, honours; (*speech*) purple passages

īnsigniō, -īre *vt* to distinguish

īnsignis *adj* distinguished, conspicuous

īnsignītē *adv* remarkably

īnsilia, -um *ntpl* treadle (*of a loom*)

īnsiliō, -īre, -uī *vi* to jump into or onto

īnsimulātiō, -ōnis *f* accusation

īnsimulō, -āre, -āvī, -ātum *vt* to charge, accuse, allege (*esp falsely*)

īnsincērus *adj* adulterated

īnsinuātiō, -ōnis *f* ingratiating

īnsinuō, -āre, -āvī, -ātum *vt* to bring in, introduce stealthily ♦ *vi* to creep in, worm one's way in, penetrate; **sē īnsinuāre** ingratiate oneself; to make one's way into

īnsipiēns, -entis *adj* senseless, foolish

īnsipienter *adv* foolishly

īnsipientia, -ae *f* folly

īnsistō, -istere, -titī *vi* to stand on, step on; to stand firm, halt, pause; to tread on the heels, press on, pursue; to enter upon, apply oneself to, begin; to persist, continue

īnsitiō, -ōnis *f* grafting; grafting time

īnsitīvus *adj* grafted; (*fig*) spurious

īnsitor, -ōris *m* grafter

īnsitus *ppp of* **īnserō¹ ♦** *adj* innate; incorporated

īnsociābilis *adj* incompatible

īnsōlābiliter *adv* unconsolably

īnsolēns, -entis *adj* unusual, unaccustomed; excessive, extravagant, insolent

īnsolenter *adv* unusually; immoderately, insolently

īnsolentia, -ae *f* inexperience, novelty, strangeness; excess, insolence

īnsolēscō, -ere *vi* to become insolent, elated

īnsolidus *adj* soft

īnsolitus *adj* unaccustomed, unusual

īnsomnia, -ae *f* sleeplessness

īnsomnis *adj* sleepless

īnsomnium, -ī and -iī *nt* dream

īnsonō, -āre, -uī *vi* to resound, sound; to make a noise

īnsōns, -ontis *adj* innocent; harmless

īnsōpītus *adj* sleepless

īnspectō, -āre *vt* to look at

īnspectus *ppp of* **īnspiciō**

īnspērāns, -antis *adj* not expecting

īnspērātus *adj* unexpected; **īnspērātō, ex īnspērātō** unexpectedly

īnspergō, -gere, -sī, -sum *vt* to sprinkle on

īnspiciō, -icere, -exī, -ectum *vt* to look into; to examine, inspect; (*MIL*) to review; (*mind*) to consider, get to know

īnspīcō, -āre *vt* to sharpen

īnspīrō, -āre, -āvī, -ātum *vt, vi* to blow on, breathe into

īnspoliātus *adj* unpillaged

īnspūtō, -āre *vt* to spit on

īnstābilis *adj* unsteady, not firm; (*fig*) inconstant

īnstāns, -antis *pres p of* **īnstō ♦** *adj* present; urgent, threatening

īnstanter *adv* vehemently

īnstantia, -ae *f* presence; vehemence

īnstar *nt* (*indecl*) likeness, appearance; as good as, worth

īnstaurātiō, -ōnis *f* renewal

īnstaurātīvus *adj* renewed

īnstaurō, -āre, -āvī, -ātum *vt* to renew, restore; to celebrate; to requite

īnsternō, -ernere, -rāvī, -rātum *vt* to spread over, cover

īnstīgātor, -ōris *m* instigator

īnstīgātrīx, -rīcis *f* female instigator

īnstīgō, -āre *vt* to goad, incite, instigate

īnstillō, -āre *vt* to drop on, instil

īnstimulātor, -ōris *m* instigator

īnstimulō, -āre *vt* to urge on

īnstinctor, -ōris *m* instigator

īnstinctus¹ *adj* incited, inspired

īnstinctus², -ūs *m* impulse, inspiration

īnstipulor, -ārī, -ātus *vi* to bargain for

īnstita, -ae *f* flounce (*of a lady's tunic*)

īnstitī *perf of* **īnsistō**

īnstitiō, -ōnis *f* stopping

īnstitor, -ōris *m* pedlar

īnstituō, -uere, -uī, -ūtum *vt* to set, implant; to set up, establish, build, appoint; to marshal, arrange, organize; to teach, educate; to undertake, resolve on

īnstitūtiō, -ōnis *f* custom; arrangement; education; (*pl*) principles of education

īnstitūtum, -ī nt way of life, tradition, law; stipulation, agreement; purpose; (pl) principles

īnstō, -āre, -itī vi to stand on or in; to be close, be hard on the heels of, pursue; (events) to approach, impend; (fig) to press on, work hard at; (speech) to insist, urge

īnstrātus ppp of **īnsternō**

īnstrēnuus adj languid, slow

īnstrepō, -ere vi to creak

īnstructiō, -ōnis f building; setting out

īnstructius adv in better style

īnstructor, -ōris m preparer

īnstructus[1] ppp of **īnstruō** ♦ adj provided, equipped; prepared, versed

īnstructus[2], -ūs m equipment

īnstrūmentum, -ī nt tool, instrument; equipment, furniture, stock; (fig) means, provision; dress, embellishment

īnstruō, -ere, -xī, -ctum vt to erect, build up; (MIL) to marshal, array; to equip, provide, prepare; (fig) to teach, train

īnsuāsum, -ī nt a dark colour

īnsuāvis adj disagreeable

īnsūdō, -āre vi to perspire on

īnsuēfactus adj accustomed

īnsuēscō, -scere, -vī, -tum vt to train, accustom ♦ vi to become accustomed

īnsuētus[1] ppp of **īnsuēscō**

īnsuētus[2] adj unaccustomed, unused; unusual

īnsula, -ae f island; block (of houses)

īnsulānus, -ī m islander

īnsulsē adv see **īnsulsus**

īnsulsitās, -ātis f lack of taste, absurdity

īnsulsus adj tasteless, absurd, dull

īnsultō, -āre vt, vi to jump on, leap in; (fig) to exult, taunt, insult

īnsultūra, -ae f jumping on

īnsum, inesse, īnfuī vi to be in or on; to belong to

īnsūmō, -ere, -psī, -ptum vt to spend, devote

īnsuō, -uere, -uī, -ūtum vt to sew in, sew up in

īnsuper adv above, on top; besides, over and above ♦ prep (abl) besides

īnsuperābilis adj unconquerable, impassable

īnsurgō, -gere, -rēxī, -rēctum vi to stand up, rise to; to rise, grow, swell; to rise against

īnsusurrō, -āre vt, vi to whisper

īnsūtus ppp of **īnsuō**

intābēscō, -ēscere, -uī vi to melt away, waste away

intāctilis adj intangible

intāctus adj untouched, intact; untried; undefiled, chaste

intāminātus adj unsullied

intēctus[1] ppp of **integō**

intēctus[2] adj uncovered, unclad; frank

integellus adj fairly whole or pure

integer, -rī adj whole, complete, unimpaired, intact; sound, fresh, new; (mind) unbiased, free; (character) virtuous, pure, upright; (decision) undecided, open; **in integrum restituere** restore to a former state; **ab**

integrō, dē integrō, ex integrō afresh; **integrum est mihi** I am at liberty (to)

integō, -egere, -ēxī, -ēctum vt to cover over; to protect

integrāscō, -ere vi to begin all over again

integrātiō, -ōnis f renewing

integrē adv entirely; honestly; correctly

integritās, -ātis f completeness, soundness; integrity, honesty; (language) correctness

integrō, -āre vt to renew, replenish, repair; (mind) to refresh

integumentum, -ī nt cover, covering, shelter

intellēctus[1] ppp of **intellegō**

intellēctus[2], -ūs m understanding; (word) meaning

intellegēns, -entis pres p of **intellegō** ♦ adj intelligent, a connoisseur

intellegenter adv intelligently

intellegentia, -ae f discernment, understanding; taste

intellegō, -egere, -ēxī, -ēctum vt to understand, perceive, realize; to be a connoisseur

intemerātus adj pure, undefiled

intemperāns, -antis adj immoderate, extravagant; incontinent

intemperanter adv extravagantly

intemperantia, -ae f excess, extravagance; arrogance

intemperātē adv dissolutely

intemperātus adj excessive

intemperiae, -ārum fpl inclemency; madness

intemperiēs, -ēī f inclemency, storm; (fig) fury

intempestīvē adv inopportunely

intempestīvus adj unseasonable, untimely

intempestus adj (night) the dead of; unhealthy

intemptātus adj untried

intendō, -dere, -dī, -tum vt to stretch out, strain, spread; (weapon) to aim; (tent) to pitch; (attention, course) to direct, turn; (fact) to increase, exaggerate; (speech) to maintain; (trouble) to threaten ♦ vi to make for, intend; **animō intendere** purpose; **sē intendere** exert oneself

intentē adv strictly

intentiō, -ōnis f straining, tension; (mind) exertion, attention; (LAW) accusation

intentō, -āre vt to stretch out, aim; (fig) to threaten with, attack

intentus[1] ppp of **intendō** ♦ adj taut; attentive, intent; strict; (speech) vigorous

intentus[2], -ūs m stretching out

intepeō, -ēre vi to be warm

intepēscō, -ēscere, -uī vi to be warmed

inter prep (with acc) between, among, during, in the course of; in spite of; **~ haec** meanwhile; **~ manūs** within reach; **~ nōs** confidentially; **~ sē** mutually, one another; **~ sīcāriōs** in the murder court; **~ viam** on the way

interāmenta, -ōrum ntpl ship's timbers

interaptus adj joined together

interārēscō, -ere vi to wither away

interbibō, -ere *vi* to drink up
interbītō, -ere *vi* to fall through
intercalāris *adj* intercalary
intercalārius *adj* intercalary
intercalō, -āre *vt* to intercalate
intercapēdō, -inis *f* interruption, respite
intercēdō, -ēdere, -ēssī, -ēssum *vi* to come between, intervene; to occur; to become surety; to interfere, obstruct; (*tribune*) to protest, veto
interceptiō, -ōnis *f* taking away
interceptor, -ōris *m* embezzler
interceptus *ppp of* **intercipiō**
intercēssiō, -ōnis *f* (LAW) becoming surety; (*tribune*) veto
intercēssor, -ōris *m* mediator, surety; interposer of the veto; obstructor
intercidō, -ere, -ī *vi* to fall short; to happen in the meantime; to get lost, become obsolete, be forgotten
intercīdō, -dere, -dī, -sum *vt* to cut through, sever
intercinō, -ere *vt* to sing between
intercipiō, -ipere, -ēpi, -eptum *vt* to intercept; to embezzle, steal; to cut off, obstruct
intercīsē *adv* piecemeal
intercīsus *ppp of* **intercīdō**
interclūdō, -dere, -sī, -sum *vt* to cut off, block, shut off, prevent; **animam interclūdere** suffocate
interclūsiō, -ōnis *f* stoppage
interclūsus *ppp of* **interclūdō**
intercolumnium, -ī *and* **-iī** *nt* space between two pillars
intercurrō, -ere *vi* to mingle with; to intercede; to hurry in the meantime
intercursō, -āre *vi* to crisscross; to attack between the lines
intercursus, -ūs *m* intervention
intercus, -tis *adj*: **aqua ~** dropsy
interdīcō, -īcere, -īxī, -ictum *vt, vi* to forbid, interdict; (*praetor*) to make a provisional order; **aquā et ignī interdīcere** banish
interdictiō, -ōnis *f* prohibiting, banishment
interdictum, -ī *nt* prohibition; provisional order (*by a praetor*)
interdiū *adv* by day
interdō, -are *vt* to make at intervals; to distribute; **nōn interdōuim** I wouldn't care
interductus, -ūs *m* punctuation
interdum *adv* now and then, occasionally
intereā *adv* meanwhile, in the meantime; nevertheless
interēmī *perf of* **interimō**
interemptus *ppp of* **interimō**
intereō, -īre, -iī, -itum *vi* to be lost, perish, die
interequitō, -āre *vt, vi* to ride between
interesse *infin of* **intersum**
interfātiō, -ōnis *f* interruption
interfātur, -ārī, -ātus *vi* to interrupt
interfectiō, -ōnis *f* killing
interfector, -ōris *m* murderer
interfectrīx, -rīcis *f* murderess

interfectus *ppp of* **interficiō**
interficiō, -icere, -ēcī, -ectum *vt* to kill, destroy
interfīō, -ierī *vi* to pass away
interfluō, -ere, -xī, -xum *vt, vi* to flow between
interfodiō, -ere *vt* to pierce
interfugiō, -ere *vi* to flee among
interfuī *perf of* **intersum**
interfulgeō, -ēre *vi* to shine amongst
interfūsus *ppp* lying between; marked here and there
interiaceō, -ēre *vi* to lie between
interibi *adv* in the meantime
intericiō, -icere, -iēcī, -iectum *vt* to put amongst or between, interpose, mingle; **annō interiectō** after a year
interiectus, -ūs *m* coming in between; interval
interiī *perf of* **intereō**
interim *adv* meanwhile, in the meantime; sometimes; all the same
interimō, -imere, -ēmī, -emptum *vt* to abolish, destroy, kill
interior, -ōris *adj* inner, interior; nearer, on the near side; secret, private; more intimate, more profound
interitiō, -ōnis *f* ruin
interitus, -ūs *m* destruction, ruin, death
interiūnctus *adj* joined together
interius *adv* inwardly; too short
interlābor, -ī *vi* to glide between
interlegō, -ere *vt* to pick here and there
interlinō, -inere, -ēvī, -itum *vt* to smear in parts; to erase here and there
interloquor, -quī, -cūtus *vi* to interrupt
interlūceō, -cēre, -xī *vi* to shine through, be clearly seen
interlūnia, -ōrum *ntpl* new moon
interluō, -ere *vt* to wash, flow between
intermēnstruus *adj* of the new moon ◆ *nt* new moon
interminātus¹ *ppa* (*occ pass*) *of* **interminor** ◆ *adj* forbidden
interminātus² *adj* endless
interminor, -ārī, -ātus *vi* to threaten; to forbid threateningly
intermisceō, -scēre, -scuī, -xtum *vt* to mix, intermingle
intermissiō, -ōnis *f* interruption
intermittō, -ittere, -īsī, -issum *vt* to break off; to interrupt; to omit, neglect; to allow to elapse ◆ *vi* to cease, pause
intermixtus *ppp of* **intermisceō**
intermorior, -ī, -tuus *vi* to die suddenly
intermortuus *adj* falling unconscious
intermundia, -ōrum *ntpl* space between worlds
intermūrālis *adj* between two walls
internātus *adj* growing among
internecīnus *adj* murderous, of extermination
internecīō, -ōnis *f* massacre, extermination
internecīvus *adj* = **internecīnus**
internectō, -ere *vt* to enclasp

internōdia, **-ōrum** *ntpl* space between joints
internōscō, **-scere**, **-vī**, **-tum** *vt* to distinguish between
internūntia, **-iae** *f* messenger, mediator, go-between
internūntiō, **-āre** *vi* to exchange messages
internūntius, **-ī** *and* **-iī** *m* messenger, mediator, go-between
internus *adj* internal, civil ♦ *ntpl* domestic affairs
interō, **-erere**, **-rīvī**, **-rītum** *vt* to rub in; (*fig*) to concoct
interpellātiō, **-ōnis** *f* interruption
interpellātor, **-ōris** *m* interrupter
interpellō, **-āre**, **-āvī**, **-ātum** *vt* to interrupt; to disturb, obstruct
interpolis *adj* made up
interpolō, **-āre** *vt* to renovate, do up; (*writing*) to falsify
interpōnō, **-ōnere**, **-osuī**, **-ositum** *vt* to put between *or* amongst, insert; (*time*) to allow to elapse; (*person*) to introduce, admit; (*pretext etc*) to put forward, interpose; **fidem interpōnere** pledge one's word; **sē interpōnere** interfere, become involved
interpositiō, **-ōnis** *f* introduction
interpositus¹ *ppp of* **interpōnō**
interpositus², **-ūs** *m* obstruction
interpres, **-tis** *m/f* agent, negotiator; interpreter, explainer, translator
interpretātiō, **-ōnis** *f* interpretation, exposition, meaning
interpretātus *adj* translated
interpretor, **-ārī**, **-ātus** *vt* to interpret, explain, translate, understand
interprimō, **-imere**, **-essī**, **-essum** *vt* to squeeze
interpūnctiō, **-ōnis** *f* punctuation
interpūnctus *adj* well-divided ♦ *ntpl* punctuation
interquiēscō, **-scere**, **-vī** *vi* to rest awhile
interrēgnum, **-ī** *nt* regency, interregnum; interval between consuls
interrēx, **-ēgis** *m* regent; deputy consul
interritus *adj* undaunted, unafraid
interrogātiō, **-ōnis** *f* question; (*LAW*) cross-examination; (*LOGIC*) syllogism
interrogātiuncula, **-ae** *f* short argument
interrogō, **-āre**, **-āvī**, **-ātum** *vt* to ask, put a question; (*LAW*) to cross-examine, bring to trial
interrumpō, **-umpere**, **-ūpī**, **-uptum** *vt* to break up, sever; (*fig*) to break off, interrupt
interruptē *adv* interruptedly
intersaepiō, **-īre**, **-sī**, **-tum** *vt* to shut off, close
interscindō, **-ndere**, **-dī**, **-ssum** *vt* to cut off, break down
interserō¹, **-erere**, **-ēvī**, **-itum** *vt* to plant at intervals
interserō², **-ere**, **-uī**, **-tum** *vt* to interpose
intersitus *ppp of* **interserō¹**
interspīrātiō, **-ōnis** *f* pause for breath
interstinguō, **-guere**, **-ctum** *vt* to mark, spot; to extinguish

interstringō, **-ere** *vt* to strangle
intersum, **-esse**, **-fuī** *vi* to be between; to be amongst, be present at; (*time*) to elapse; **interest** there is a difference; it is of importance, it concerns, it matters; **meā interest** it is important for me
intertextus *adj* interwoven
intertrahō, **-here**, **-xī** *vt* to take away
intertrīmentum, **-ī** *nt* wastage; loss, damage
interturbātiō, **-ōnis** *f* confusion
intervallum, **-ī** *nt* space, distance, interval; (*time*) pause, interval, respite; difference
intervellō, **-ere** *vt* to pluck out; to tear apart
interveniō, **-enīre**, **-ēnī**, **-entum** *vi* to come on the scene, intervene; to interfere (with), interrupt; to happen, occur
interventor, **-ōris** *m* intruder
interventus, **-ūs** *m* appearance, intervention; occurrence
intervertō, **-tere**, **-tī**, **-sum** *vt* to embezzle; to rob, cheat
intervīsō, **-ere**, **-ī**, **-um** *vt* to have a look at, look and see; to visit occasionally
intervolitō, **-āre** *vi* to fly about, amongst
intervomō, **-ere** *vt* to throw up (amongst)
intervortō *vt see* **intervertō**
intestābilis *adj* infamous, wicked
intestātō *adv* without making a will
intestātus *adj* intestate; not convicted by witnesses
intestīnus *adj* internal ♦ *nt*, *ntpl* intestines, entrails
intexō, **-ere**, **-uī**, **-tum** *vt* to inweave, embroider, interlace
intibum, **-ī** *nt* endive
intimē *adv* most intimately, cordially
intimus *adj* innermost; deepest, secret; intimate ♦ *m* most intimate friend
intingō, **intinguō**, **-gere**, **-xī**, **-ctum** *vt* to dip in
intolerābilis *adj* unbearable; irresistible
intolerandus *adj* intolerable
intolerāns, **-antis** *adj* impatient; unbearable
intoleranter *adv* excessively
intolerantia, **-ae** *f* insolence
intonō, **-āre**, **-uī**, **-ātum** *vi* to thunder, thunder out
intōnsus *adj* unshorn, unshaven; long-haired, bearded; uncouth
intorqueō, **-quēre**, **-sī**, **-tum** *vt* to twist, wrap round; to hurl at
intortus *ppp of* **intorqueō** ♦ *adj* twisted, curled; confused
intrā *adv* inside, within ♦ *prep* (*with acc*) inside, within; (*time*) within, during; (*amount*) less than, within the limits of
intrābilis *adj* navigable
intractābilis *adj* formidable
intractātus *adj* not broken in; unattempted
intremīscō, **-īscere**, **-uī** *vi* to begin to shake
intremō, **-ere** *vi* to tremble
intrepidē *adv see* **intrepidus**
intrepidus *adj* calm, brave; undisturbed
intrīcō, **-āre** *vt* to entangle

intrīnsecus *adv* on the inside

intrītus *adj* not worn out

intrīvī *perf of* **interō**

intrō¹ *adv* inside, in

intrō², **-āre**, **-āvī**, **-ātum** *vt*, *vi* to go in, enter; to penetrate

intrōdūcō, **-ūcere**, **-ūxī**, **-uctum** *vt* to bring in, introduce, escort in; to institute

intrōductiō, **-ōnis** *f* bringing in

introeō, **-īre**, **-iī**, **-itum** *vi* to go into, enter

intrōferō, **-ferre**, **-tulī**, **-lātum** *vt* to carry inside

intrōgredior, **-dī**, **-ssus** *vi* to step inside

introitus, **-ūs** *m* entrance; beginning

intrōlātus *ppp of* **intrōferō**

intrōmittō, **-ittere**, **-īsī**, **-issum** *vt* to let in, admit

intrōrsum, **intrōrsus** *adv* inwards, inside

intrōrumpō, **-ere** *vi* to break into

intrōspectō, **-āre** *vt* to look in at

intrōspiciō, **-icere**, **-exī**, **-ectum** *vt* to look inside; to look at, examine

intubum *etc see* **intibum**

intueor, **-ērī**, **-itus** *vt* to look at, watch; to contemplate, consider; to admire

intumēscō, **-ēscere**, **-uī** *vi* to begin to swell, rise; to increase; to become angry

intumulātus *adj* unburied

intuor *etc see* **intueor**

inturbidus *adj* undisturbed; quiet

intus *adv* inside, within, in; from within

intūtus *adj* unsafe; unguarded

inula, **-ae** *f* elecampane

inultus *adj* unavenged; unpunished

inumbrō, **-āre** *vt* to shade; to cover

inundō, **-āre**, **-āvī**, **-ātum** *vt*, *vi* to overflow, flood

inunguō, **-unguere**, **-ūnxī**, **-ūnctum** *vt* to anoint

inurbānē *adv see* **inurbānus**

inurbānus *adj* rustic, unmannerly, unpolished

inurgeō, **-ēre** *vi* to push, butt

inūrō, **-rere**, **-ssī**, **-stum** *vt* to brand; (*fig*) to brand, inflict

inūsitātē *adv* strangely

inūsitātus *adj* unusual, extraordinary

inūstus *ppp of* **inūrō**

inūtilis *adj* useless; harmful

inūtilitās, **-ātis** *f* uselessness, harmfulness

inūtiliter *adv* unprofitably

invādō, **-dere**, **-sī**, **-sum** *vt*, *vi* to get in, make one's way in; to enter upon; to fall upon, attack, invade; to seize, take possession of

invalēscō, **-ēscere**, **-uī** *vi* to grow stronger

invalidus *adj* weak; inadequate

invāsī *perf of* **invādō**

invectiō, **-ōnis** *f* importing; invective

invectus *ppp of* **invehō**

invehō, **-here**, **-xī**, **-ctum** *vt* to carry in, bring in; sē invehere attack

invehor, **-hī**, **-ctus** *vi* to ride, drive, sail in or into, enter; to attack; to inveigh against

invēndibilis *adj* unsaleable

inveniō, **-enīre**, **-ēnī**, **-entum** *vt* to find, come upon; to find out, discover; to invent, contrive; to win, get

inventiō, **-ōnis** *f* invention; (RHET) compiling the subject-matter

inventor, **-ōris** *m* inventor, discoverer

inventrīx, **-rīcis** *f* inventor, discoverer

inventus *ppp of* **inveniō** ♦ *nt* invention, discovery

invenustus *adj* unattractive; unlucky in love

inverēcundus *adj* immodest, shameless

invergō, **-ere** *vt* to pour upon

inversiō, **-ōnis** *f* transposition; irony

inversus *ppp of* **invertō** ♦ *adj* upside down, inside out; perverted

invertō, **-tere**, **-tī**, **-sum** *vt* to turn over, invert; to change, pervert

invesperāscit, **-ere** *vi* it is dusk

investīgātiō, **-ōnis** *f* search

investīgātor, **-ōris** *m* investigator

investīgō, **-āre**, **-āvī**, **-ātum** *vt* to follow the trail of; (*fig*) to track down, find out

inveterāscō, **-scere**, **-vī** *vi* to grow old (in); to become established, fixed, inveterate; to grow obsolete

inveterātiō, **-ōnis** *f* chronic illness

inveterātus *adj* of long standing, inveterate

invexī *perf of* **invehō**

invicem *adv* in turns, alternately; mutually, each other

invictus *adj* unbeaten; unconquerable

invidentia, **-ae** *f* envy

invideō, **-idēre**, **-īdī**, **-īsum** *vt*, *vi* to cast an evil eye on; (*with dat*) to envy, grudge; to begrudge

invidia, **-ae** *f* envy, jealousy, ill-will; unpopularity

invidiōsē *adv* spitefully

invidiōsus *adj* envious, spiteful; enviable; invidious, hateful

invidus *adj* envious, jealous, hostile

invigilō, **-āre** *vi* to be awake over; to watch over, be intent on

inviolābilis *adj* invulnerable; inviolable

inviolātē *adv* inviolately

inviolātus *adj* unhurt; inviolable

invīsitātus *adj* unseen, unknown, strange

invīsō, **-ere**, **-ī**, **-um** *vt* to go and see, visit, have a look at; to inspect

invīsus¹ *adj* hateful, detested; hostile

invīsus² *adj* unseen

invītāmentum, **-ī** *nt* attraction, inducement

invītātiō, **-ōnis** *f* invitation; entertainment

invītātus, **-ūs** *m* invitation

invītē *adv* unwillingly

invītō, **-āre**, **-āvī**, **-ātum** *vt* to invite; to treat, entertain; to summon; to attract, induce

invītus *adj* against one's will, reluctant

invius *adj* trackless, impassable; inaccessible

invocātus¹ *ppp of* **invocō**

invocātus² *adj* unbidden, uninvited

invocō, **-āre**, **-āvī**, **-ātum** *vt* to call upon, invoke; to appeal to; to call

involātus, **-ūs** *m* flight

involitō, **-āre** *vi* to play upon

involō, -āre *vi* to fly at, pounce on, attack
involūcre, -is *nt* napkin
involūcrum, -ī *nt* covering, case
involūtus *ppp of* **involvō** ♦ *adj* complicated
involvō, -vere, -vī, -ūtum *vt* to roll on; to wrap up, envelop, entangle
involvolus, -ī *m* caterpillar
invulnerātus *adj* unwounded
iō *interj* (*joy*) hurrah!; (*pain*) oh!; (*calling*) ho there!
Iōannēs, -is *m* John
iocātiō, -ōnis *f* joke
iocor, -ārī, -ātus *vt, vi* to joke, jest
iocōsē *adv* jestingly
iocōsus *adj* humorous, playful
ioculāris *adj* laughable, funny ♦ *ntpl* jokes
ioculārius *adj* ludicrous
ioculātor, -ōris *m* jester
ioculor, -ārī *vi* to joke
ioculus, -ī *m* a bit of fun
iocus, -ī *m*, **ioca, -ōrum** *ntpl* joke, jest; **extrā iocum** joking apart; **per iocum** for fun
Iōnes, -um *mpl* Ionians
Iōnia, -iae *f* Ionia, *coastal district of Asia Minor*
Iōnium, -ī *nt* Ionian Sea (*W. of Greece*)
Iōnius, Iōnicus *adj* Ionian
iōta *nt indecl* Greek letter I
Iovis *gen of* **Iuppiter**
Īphianassa, -ae *f* Iphigenia
Īphigenīa, -ae *f* daughter of Agamemnon (*who sacrificed her at Aulis to Diana*)
ipse, -a, -um, -īus *pron* self, himself *etc*; in person, for one's own part, of one's own accord, by oneself; just, precisely, very; the master, the host
ipsissimus his very own self; **nunc ipsissimum** right now
īra, -ae *f* anger, rage; object of indignation
īrācundē *adv* angrily
īrācundia, -ae *f* irascibility, quick temper; rage, resentment
īrācundus *adj* irascible, choleric; resentful
īrāscor, -ī *vi* to be angry, get furious
īrātē *adv see* **īrātus**
īrātus *adj* angry, furious
īre *infin of* **eō¹**
Īris, -dis (*acc* **-m**) *f* messenger of the gods; the rainbow
īrōnīa, -ae *f* irony
irrāsus *adj* unshaven
irraucēscō, -cēscere, -sī *vi* to become hoarse
irredivīvus *adj* irreparable
irreligātus *adj* not tied
irreligiōsē *adv see* **irreligiōsus**
irreligiōsus *adj* impious
irremeābilis *adj* from which there is no returning
irreparābilis *adj* irretrievable
irrepertus *adj* undiscovered
irrēpō, -ere, -sī *vi* to steal into, insinuate oneself into
irreprehēnsus *adj* blameless
irrequiētus *adj* restless
irresectus *adj* unpared

irresolūtus *adj* not slackened
irrētiō, -īre, -iī, -ītum *vt* to ensnare, entangle
irretortus *adj* not turned back
irreverentia, -ae *f* disrespect
irrevocābilis *adj* irrevocable; implacable
irrevocātus *adj* without an encore
irrīdeō, -dēre, -sī, -sum *vi* to laugh, joke ♦ *vt* to laugh at, ridicule
irrīdiculē *adv* unwittily
irrīdiculum, -ī *nt* laughing stock
irrigātiō, -ōnis *f* irrigation
irrigō, -āre, -āvī, -ātum *vt* to water, irrigate; to inundate; (*fig*) to shed over, flood, refresh
irriguus *adj* well-watered, swampy; refreshing
irrīsiō, -ōnis *f* ridicule, mockery
irrīsor, -ōris *m* scoffer
irrīsus¹ *ppp of* **irrīdeō**
irrīsus², -ūs *m* derision
irrītābilis *adj* excitable
irrītāmen, -inis *nt* excitement, provocation
irrītātiō, -ōnis *f* incitement, irritation
irrītō, -āre, -āvī, -ātum *vt* to provoke, incite, enrage
irritus *adj* invalid, null and void; useless, vain, ineffective; (*person*) unsuccessful; **ad irritum cadere** come to nothing
irrogātiō, -ōnis *f* imposing
irrogō, -āre *vt* to propose (*a measure*) against; to impose
irrōrō, -āre *vt* to bedew
irrumpō, -umpere, -ūpī, -uptum *vt, vi* to rush in, break in; to intrude, invade
irruō, -ere, -ī *vi* to force a way in, rush in, attack; (*speech*) to make a blunder
irruptiō, -ōnis *f* invasion, raid
irruptus¹ *ppp of* **irrumpō**
irruptus² *adj* unbroken
is, ea, id *pron* he, she, it; this, that, the; such; **nōn is sum quī** I am not the man to; **id** (*with vi*) for this reason; **id quod** what; **ad id** hitherto; for the purpose; besides; **in eō est** it has come to this; one is on the point of; it depends on this
Ismara, -ōrum *ntpl*, **Ismarus, -ī** *m* Mt Ismarus (*in Thrace*)
Ismarius *adj* Thracian
Īsocratēs, -is *m* Athenian orator and teacher of rhetoric
istāc *adv* that way
iste, -a, -ud, -īus *pron* that of yours; (*LAW*) your client, the plaintiff, the defendant; (*contemptuous*) the fellow; that, such
Isthmius *adj* Isthmian ♦ *ntpl* the Isthmian Games
Isthmus, Isthmos, -ī *m* Isthmus of Corinth
istic, -aec, -uc *and* **-oc** *pron* that of yours, that
istīc *adv* there; in this, on this occasion
istinc *adv* from there; of that
istīusmodī such, of that kind
istō, istōc *adv* to you, there, yonder
istōrsum *adv* in that direction
istūc *adv* (to) there, to that

ita *adv* thus, so; as follows; yes; accordingly; **itane** really?; **nōn ita** not so very; **ita ut** just as; **ita … ut** so, to such an extent that; on condition that; only in so far as; **ita … ut nōn** without; **ut … ita** just as … so; although … nevertheless

Ītalī, -ōrum *mpl* Italians

Ītalia, -iae *f* Italy

Ītalicus, Ītalus *adj* Italian

itaque *conj* and so, therefore, accordingly

item *adv* likewise, also

iter, -ineris *nt* way, journey, march; a day's journey or march; route, road, passage; (*fig*) way, course; ~ **mihi est** I have to go to; ~ **dare** grant a right of way; ~ **facere** to journey, march, travel; **ex itinere, in itinere** on the way, on the march; **māgnīs itineribus** by forced marches

iterātiō, -ōnis *f* repetition

iterō, -āre, -āvī, -ātum *vt* to repeat, renew; to plough again

iterum *adv* again, a second time; ~ **atque** ~ repeatedly

Ithaca, -ae, Ithacē, -ēs *f* island W. of Greece (home of Ulysses)

Ithacēnsis, Ithacus *adj* Ithacan

Ithacus, -ī *m* Ulysses

itidem *adv* in the same way, similarly

itiō, -ōnis *f* going

itō, -āre *vi* to go

itus, -ūs *m* going, movement, departure

iuba, -ae *f* mane; crest

Iuba, -ae *m* king of Numidia (supporter of Pompey)

iubar, -is *nt* brightness, light

iubātus *adj* crested

iubeō, -bēre, -ssī, -ssum *vt* to order, command, tell; (*greeting*) to bid; (*MED*) to prescribe; (*POL*) to decree, ratify, appoint

iūcundē *adv* agreeably

iūcunditās, -ātis *f* delight, enjoyment

iūcundus *adj* delightful, pleasing

Iūdaea, -ae *f* Judaea, Palestine

Iūdaeus¹, -ī *m* Jew

Iūdaeus², Iūdaicus *adj* Jewish

iūdex, -icis *m* judge; (*pl*) panel of jurors; (*fig*) critic

iūdicātiō, -ōnis *f* judicial inquiry; opinion

iūdicātum, -ī *nt* judgment, precedent

iūdicātus, -ūs *m* office of judge

iūdiciālis *adj* judicial, forensic

iūdiciārius *adj* judiciary

iūdicium, -ī *and* **-iī** *nt* trial; court of justice; sentence; judgment, opinion; discernment, taste, tact; **in ~ vocāre, iūdiciō arcessere** sue, summon

iūdicō, -āre, -āvī, -ātum *vt* to judge, examine, sentence, condemn; to form an opinion of, decide; to declare

iugālis *adj* yoked together; nuptial

iugātiō, -ōnis *f* training (of a vine)

iūgerum, -ī *nt* a land measure (240 x 120 feet)

iūgis *adj* perpetual, never-failing

iūglāns, -andis *f* walnut tree

iugō, -āre, -āvī, -ātum *vt* to couple, marry

iugōsus *adj* hilly

lugulae, -ārum *fpl* Orion's Belt

iugulō, -āre, -āvī, -ātum *vt* to cut the throat of, kill, murder

iugulus, -ī *m*, **iugulum, -ī** *nt* throat

iugum, -ī *nt* (*animals*) yoke, collar; pair, team; (*MIL*) yoke of subjugation; (*mountain*) ridge, height, summit; (*ASTR*) Libra; (*loom*) crossbeam; (*ship*) thwart; (*fig*) yoke, bond

Iugurtha, -ae *m* king of Numidia (rebel against Rome)

Iugurthīnus *adj see* **Iugurtha**

Iūlēus *adj* of Iulus; of Caesar; of July

Iūlius¹, -ī *m* Roman family name (esp Caesar); (*month*) July

Iūlius², Iūliānus *adj see* **Iūlius¹**

Iūlus, -ī *m* son of Aeneas, Ascanius

iūmentum, -ī *nt* beast of burden, packhorse

iunceus *adj* of rushes; slender

iuncōsus *adj* rushy

iūnctiō, -ōnis *f* union

iūnctūra, -ae *f* joint; combination; relationship

iūnctus *ppp of* **iungō** ✦ *adj* connected, attached

iuncus, -ī *m* rush

iungō, -gere, iūnxī, iūnctum *vt* to join together, unite; to yoke, harness; to mate; (*river*) to span, bridge; (*fig*) to bring together, connect, associate; (*agreement*) to make; (*words*) to compound

iūnior, -ōris *adj* younger

iūniperus, -ī *f* juniper

Iūnius¹, -ī *m* Roman family name; (*month*) June

Iūnius² *adj* of June

Iūnō, -ōnis *f* Roman goddess, wife of Jupiter, patroness of women and marriage

Iūnōnālis *adj see* **Iūnō**

Iūnōnicola, -ae *m/f* worshipper of Juno

Iūnōnigena, -ae *m* Vulcan

Iūnōnius *adj* = **Iūnōnālis**

Iuppiter, Iovis *m* Jupiter (king of the gods, god of sky and weather); ~ **Stygius** Pluto; **sub Iove** in the open air

iūrātor, -ōris *m* sworn judge

iūrecōnsultus *etc see* **iūriscōnsultus**

iūreiūrō, -āre *vi* to swear

iūrepertus *etc see* **iūrisperītus**

iūrgium, -ī *and* **-iī** *nt* quarrel, brawl

iūrgō, -āre *vi* to quarrel, squabble ✦ *vt* to scold

iūridiciālis *adj* of law, juridical

iūriscōnsultus, -ī *m* lawyer

iūrisdictiō, -ōnis *f* administration of justice; authority

iūrisperītus *adj* versed in the law

iūrō, -āre, -āvī, -ātum *vi, vt* to swear, take an oath; to conspire; **in nōmen ~** swear allegiance to; **in verba ~** take a prescribed form of oath; **iūrātus** having sworn, under oath

iūs¹, iūris *nt* broth, soup

iūs², iūris *nt* law, right, justice; law court; jurisdiction, authority; **iūs gentium** international law; **iūs pūblicum** constitutional law; **summum iūs** the strict letter of the law; **iūs dīcere** administer justice; **suī iūris** independent; **iūre** rightly, justly

iūsiūrandum, iūrisiūrandī *nt* oath

iussī *perf of* **iubeō**

iussū *abl m* by order

iussus *ppp of* **iubeō** ♦ *nt* order, command, prescription

iūstē *adv* duly, rightly

iūstificus *adj* just dealing

iūstitia, -ae *f* justice, uprightness, fairness

iūstitium, -ī *and* **-iī** *nt* cessation of legal business

iūstus *adj* just, fair; lawful, right; regular, proper ♦ *nt* right ♦ *ntpl* rights; formalities, obsequies

iūtus *ppp of* **iuvō**

iuvenālis *adj* youthful ♦ *ntpl* youthful games

Iuvenālis, -is *m* Juvenal (*Roman satirist*)

iuvenāliter *adv* vigorously, impetuously

iuvenca, -ae *f* heifer; girl

iuvencus, -ī *m* bullock; young man ♦ *adj* young

iuvenēscō, -ēscere, -uī *vi* to grow up; to grow young again

iuvenīlis *adj* youthful

iuvenīliter *adv see* **iuvenīlis**

iuvenis *adj* young ♦ *m/f* young man or woman (20-45 years), man, warrior

iuvenor, -ārī *vi* to behave indiscreetly

iuventa, -ae *f* youth

iuventās, -ātis *f* youth

iuventūs, -ūtis *f* youth, manhood; men, soldiers

iuvō, -āre, iūvī, iūtum *vt* to help, be of use to; to please, delight; **iuvat mē** I am glad

iuxtā *adv* near by, close; alike, just the same ♦ *prep* (*with acc*) close to, hard by; next to; very like, next door to; **~ ac**, **~ cum**, **~ quam** just the same as

iuxtim *adv* near; equally

īvī *perf of* **eō¹**

Ixīōn, -onis *m* Lapith king (*bound to a revolving wheel in Tartarus*)

Ixīoneus *adj see* **Ixīōn**

Ixīonidae, -ārum *mpl* Centaurs

Ixīonidēs, -ae *m* Pirithous

Jj

J- *see* I-

Kk

Kalendae, **-ārum** Kalends, first day (*of each month*)

Karthāgō *see* **Carthāgō**

labāscō, -ere vi to totter, waver

lābēcula, -ae f aspersion

labefaciō, -facere, -fēcī, -factum (pass **-fīō**) vt to shake; (fig) to weaken, ruin

labefactō, -āre, -āvī, -ātum vt to shake; (fig) to weaken, destroy

labellum, -ī nt lip

lābellum, -ī nt small basin

Laberius, -ī m Roman family name (esp a writer of mimes)

lābēs¹, -is f sinking, fall; ruin, destruction

lābēs², -is f spot, blemish; disgrace, stigma; (person) blot

labia, -iae f lip

Labiēnus, -ī m Roman surname (esp Caesar's officer who went over to Pompey)

labiōsus adj large-lipped

labium, -ī and **-iī** nt lip

labō, -āre vi to totter, be unsteady, give way; to waver, hesitate, collapse

lābor, -bī, -psus vi to slide, glide; to sink, fall; to slip away, pass away; (fig) to fade, decline, perish; to be disappointed, make a mistake

labor, labōs, -ōris m effort, exertion, labour; work, task; hardship, suffering, distress; (ASTR) eclipse

labōrifer, -ī adj sore afflicted

labōriōsē adv laboriously, with difficulty

labōriōsus adj troublesome, difficult; industrious

labōrō, -āre, -āvī, -ātum vi to work, toil, take pains; to suffer, be troubled (with), be in distress; to be anxious, worried ♦ vt to work out, make, produce

labōs etc see **labor**

labrum, -ī nt lip; edge, rim; **primīs labrīs gustāre** acquire a smattering of

lābrum, -ī nt tub, vat; bath

lābrusca, -ae f wild vine

lābruscum, -ī nt wild grape

labyrinthēus adj labyrinthine

labyrinthus, -ī m labyrinth, maze (esp that of Cnossos in Crete)

lac, lactis nt milk

Lacaena, -ae f Spartan woman ♦ adj Spartan

Lacedaemōn, Lacedaemō, -onis (acc **-ona**) f Sparta

Lacedaemonius adj Spartan

lacer, -ī adj torn, mangled, lacerated; tearing

lacerātiō, -ōnis f tearing

lacerna, -ae f cloak (worn in cold weather)

lacernātus adj cloaked

lacerō, -āre, -āvī, -ātum vt to tear, lacerate, mangle; (ship) to wreck; (speech) to slander, abuse; (feeling) to torture, distress; (goods, time) to waste, destroy

lacerta, -ae f lizard; a seafish

lacertōsus adj brawny

lacertus¹, -ī m upper arm, arm; (pl) brawn, muscle

lacertus², -ī m lizard; a sea fish

lacessō, -ere, -īvī and **-iī, -ītum** vt to strike, provoke, challenge; (fig) to incite, exasperate

Lachesis, -is f one of the Fates

lacinia, -ae f flap, corner (of dress)

Lacīnium, -ī nt promontory in S. Italy, with a temple of Juno

Lacīnius adj see **Lacīnium**

Lacō, Lacōn, -ōnis m Spartan; Spartan dog

Lacōnicus adj Spartan ♦ nt sweating bath

lacrima, -ae f tear; (plant) gumdrop

lacrimābilis adj mournful

lacrimābundus adj bursting into tears

lacrimō, -āre, -āvī, -ātum vt, vi to weep, weep for

lacrimōsus adj tearful; lamentable

lacrimula, -ae f tear, crocodile tear

lacrum- etc see **lacrim-**

lactāns, -antis adj giving milk; sucking

lactātiō, -ōnis f allurement

lactēns, -entis adj sucking; milky, juicy

lacteolus adj milk-white

lactēs, -ium fpl guts, small intestines

lactēscō, -ere vi to turn to milk

lacteus adj milky, milk-white

lactō, -āre vt to dupe, wheedle

lactūca, -ae f lettuce

lacūna, -ae f hole, pit; pool, pond; (fig) deficiency

lacūnar, -āris nt panelled ceiling

lacūnō, -āre vt to panel

lacūnōsus adj sunken

lacus, -ūs m vat, tank; lake; reservoir, cistern

laedō, -dere, -sī, -sum vt to hurt, strike, wound; (fig) to offend, annoy, break

Laelius, -ī m Roman family name (esp the friend of Scipio)

laena, -ae f a lined cloak

Lāërtēs, -ae m father of Ulysses

Lāërtiadēs m Ulysses

Lāërtius adj see **Lāërtēs**

laesī perf of **laedō**

laesiō, -ōnis f attack
Laestrygonēs, -um mpl fabulous cannibals of Campania, founders of Formiae
Laestrygonius adj see **Laestrygonēs**
laesus ppp of **laedō**
laetābilis adj joyful
laetē adv gladly
laetificō, -āre vt to gladden
laetificus adj glad, joyful
laetitia, -ae f joy, delight, exuberance
laetor, -ārī, -ātus vi to rejoice, be glad
laetus adj glad, cheerful; delighting (in); pleasing, welcome; (growth) fertile, rich; (style) exuberant
laevē adv awkwardly
laevus adj left; stupid; ill-omened, unfortunate; (AUG) lucky, favourable ♦ f left hand
laganum, -ī nt a kind of oilcake
lagēos, -ī f a Greek vine
lagoena, -ae f flagon
lagōis, -idis f a kind of grouse
lagōna, -ae f flagon
Lāiadēs, -ae m Oedipus
Lāius, -ī m father of Oedipus
lallō, -āre vi to sing a lullaby
lāma, -ae f bog
lamberō, -āre vt to tear to pieces
lambō, -ere, -ī vt to lick, touch; (river) to wash
lāmenta, -ōrum ntpl lamentation
lāmentābilis adj mournful, sorrowful
lāmentārius adj sorrowful
lāmentātiō, -ōnis f weeping, lamentation
lāmentor, -ārī, -ātus vi to weep, lament ♦ vt to weep for, bewail
lamia, -ae f witch
lāmina, lammina, lāmna, -ae f plate, leaf (of metal, wood); blade; coin
lampas, -dis f torch; brightness, day
Lamus, -ī m Laestrygonian king
lāna, -ae f wool
lānārius, -ī and **-iī** m wool-worker
lānātus adj woolly
lancea, -ae f spear, lance
lancinō, -āre vt to tear up; to squander
lāneus adj woollen
languefaciō, -ere vt to make weary
langueō, -ēre vi to be weary, be weak, droop; to be idle, dull
languēscō, -ēscere, -uī vi to grow faint, droop
languidē adv see **languidus**
languidulus adj languid
languidus adj faint, languid, sluggish; listless, feeble
languor, -ōris m faintness, fatigue, weakness; dullness, apathy
laniātus, -ūs m mangling; (mind) anguish
laniēna, -ae f butcher's shop
lānificium, -ī and **-iī** nt wool-working
lānificus adj wool-working
lāniger, -ī adj fleecy ♦ m/f ram, sheep
laniō, -āre, -āvī, -ātum vt to tear to pieces, mangle
lanista, -ae m trainer of gladiators, fencing master; (fig) agitator

lānitium, -ī and **-iī** nt woolgrowing
lanius, -ī and **-iī** m butcher
lanterna, -ae f lamp
lanternārius, -ī and **-iī** m guide
lānūgō, -inis f down, woolliness
Lānuvīnus adj see **Lānuvium**
Lānuvium, -ī nt Latin town on the Appian Way
lānx, lancis f dish, platter; (balance) scale
Lāomedōn, -ontis m king of Troy (father of Priam)
Lāomedontēus adj, **Lāomedontiadēs, -ae** m son of Lāomedōn; (pl) Trojans
Lāomedontius adj Trojan
lapathum, -ī nt, **lapathus, -ī** f sorrel
lapicīda, -ae m stonecutter
lapicīdīnae, -ārum fpl quarries
lapidārius adj stone- (in cpds)
lapidātiō, -ōnis f throwing of stones
lapidātor, -ōris m stone thrower
lapideus adj of stones, stone- (in cpds)
lapidō, -āre vt to stone ♦ vi to rain stones
lapidōsus adj stony; hard as stone
lapillus, -ī m stone, pebble; precious stone, mosaic piece
lapis, -dis m stone; milestone, boundary stone, tombstone; precious stone; marble; auctioneer's stand; (abuse) blockhead; **bis ad eundem lapidem (offendere)** make the same mistake twice; **Juppiter** ~ the Jupiter stone
Lapithae, -ārum and **-um** mpl Lapiths, mythical people of Thessaly
Lapithaeus, -ēius adj see **Lapithae**
lappa, -ae f goosegrass
lāpsiō, -ōnis f tendency
lāpsō, -āre vi to slip, stumble
lāpsus¹ ppa of **lābor**
lāpsus², -ūs m fall, slide, course, flight; error, failure
laqueāria, -ium ntpl panelled ceiling
laqueātus adj panelled, with a panelled ceiling
laqueus, -ī m noose, snare, halter; (fig) trap
Lār, Laris m tutelary deity, household god; hearth, home
lārdum etc see **lāridum**
largē adv plentifully, generously, very much
largificus adj bountiful
largifluus adj copious
largiloquus adj talkative
largior, -īrī, -ītus vt to give freely, lavish; to bestow, confer ♦ vi to give largesse
largitās, -ātis f liberality, abundance
largiter adv = **largē**
largītiō, -ōnis f giving freely, distributing; bribery
largītor, -ōris m liberal giver, dispenser; spendthrift; briber
largus adj copious, ample; liberal, bountiful
lāridum, -ī nt bacon fat
Lārissa, Lārisa, -ae f town in Thessaly
Lārissaeus, -ēnsis adj see **Lārissa**
Lārius, -ī m lake Como
larix, -cis f larch
larva, -ae f ghost; mask
larvātus adj bewitched
lasanum, -ī nt pot

lasārpīcifer, -ī adj producing asafoetida

lascīvia, -ae f playfulness; impudence, lewdness

lascīviō, -īre vi to frolic, frisk; to run wild, be irresponsible

lascīvus adj playful, frisky; impudent, lustful

laserpīcium, -ī and **-iī** nt silphium

lassitūdō, -inis f fatigue, heaviness

lassō, -āre vt to tire, fatigue

lassulus adj rather weary

lassus adj tired, exhausted

lātē adv widely, extensively; **longē lātēque** far and wide, everywhere

latebra, -ae f hiding place, retreat; (fig) loophole, pretext

latebricola, -ae adj low-living

latebrōsē adv in hiding

latebrōsus adj secret, full of coverts; porous

latēns, -entis pres p of **lateō** ♦ adj hidden, secret

latenter adv in secret

lateō, -ēre, -uī vi to lie hid, lurk, skulk; to be in safety, live a retired life; to be unknown, escape notice

later, -is m brick, tile; **laterem lavāre** waste one's time

laterāmen, -inis nt earthenware

laterculus, -ī m small brick, tile; kind of cake

latericius adj of bricks ♦ nt brickwork

lāterna etc see **lanterna**

latēscō, -ere vi to hide oneself

latex, -icis m water; any other liquid

Latiar, -iaris nt festival of Jupiter Latiaris

Latiaris adj Latin

latibulum, -ī nt hiding place, den, lair

lāticlāvius adj with a broad purple stripe ♦ m senator, patrician

lātifundium, -ī and **-iī** nt large estate

Latīnē adv in Latin, into Latin; **~ loquī** speak Latin, speak plainly, speak correctly; **~ reddere** translate into Latin

Latīnitās, -ātis f good Latin, Latinity; Latin rights

Latīnus adj Latin ♦ m legendary king of the Laurentians

lātiō, -ōnis f bringing; proposing

latitō, -āre vi to hide away, lurk, keep out of the way

lātitūdō, -inis f breadth, width; size; broad pronunciation

Latium, -ī nt district of Italy including Rome; Latin rights

Latius = **Latiaris; Latīnus**

Lātōis¹, -idis f Diana

Lātōis², -ius adj see **Lātōis¹**

lātom- etc see **lautum-**

Lātōna, -ae f mother of Apollo and Diana

Lātōnigenae, -ārum pl Apollo and Diana

Lātōnius adj, f Diana

lātor, -ōris m proposer

Lātōus adj of Latona ♦ m Apollo

lātrātor, -ōris m barker

lātrātus, -ūs m barking

lātrō, -āre vi to bark; to rant, roar ♦ vt to bark at; to clamour for

latrō, -ōnis m mercenary soldier; bandit, brigand; (chess) man

latrōcinium, -ī and **-iī** nt highway robbery, piracy

latrōcinor, -āri, -ātus vi to serve as a mercenary; to be a brigand or pirate

latrunculus, -ī m brigand; (chess) man

lātumiae etc see **lautumiae**

lātus¹ ppp of **ferō**

lātus² adj broad, wide; extensive; (pronunciation) broad; (style) diffuse

latus, -eris nt side, flank; lungs; body; **~ dare** expose oneself; **~ tegere** walk beside; **lateris dolor** pleurisy; **ab latere** on the flank

latusculum, -ī nt little side

laudābilis adj praiseworthy

laudābiliter adv laudably

laudātiō, -ōnis f commendation, eulogy; panegyric, testimonial

laudātor, -ōris m, **laudātrīx, -rīcis** f praiser, eulogizer; speaker of a funeral oration

laudātus adj excellent

laudō, -āre, -āvī, -ātum vt to praise, commend, approve; to pronounce a funeral oration over; to quote, name

laurea, -ae f bay tree; crown of bay; triumph

laureātus adj crowned with bay; (despatches) victorious

Laurentēs, -um mpl Laurentians (people of ancient Latium)

Laurentius adj see **Laurentēs**

laureola, -ae f triumph

laureus adj of bay

lauricomus adj bay-covered

lauriger, -ī adj crowned with bay

laurus, -ī f bay tree; bay crown; victory, triumph

laus, laudis f praise, approval; glory, fame; praiseworthy act, merit, worth

lautē adv elegantly, splendidly; excellently

lautia, -ōrum ntpl State banquet

lautitia, -ae f luxury

lautumiae, -ārum fpl stone quarry; prison

lautus ppp of **lavō** ♦ adj neat, elegant, sumptuous; fine, grand, distinguished

lavābrum, -ī nt bath

lavātiō, -ōnis f washing, bath; bathing gear

Lāvīnium, -ī nt town of ancient Latium

Lāvīnius adj see **Lāvīnium**

lavō, -āre, lāvī, lautum, lavātum, lōtum vt to wash, bathe; to wet, soak, wash away

laxāmentum, -ī nt respite, relaxation

laxē adv loosely, freely

laxitās, -ātis f roominess

laxō, -āre, -āvī, -ātum vt to extend, open out; to undo; to slacken; (fig) to release, relieve; to relax, abate ♦ vi (price) to fall off

laxus adj wide, loose, roomy; (time) deferred; (fig) free, easy

lea, -ae f lioness

leaena, -ae f lioness

Lēander, -rī m Hero's lover (who swam the Hellespont)

lebēs, -ētis m basin, pan, cauldron

lectīca, -ae f litter, sedan chair

lectīcārius, -ī and **-iī** m litter-bearer

lectīcula, -ae f small litter; bier

lēctiō, -ōnis f selecting; reading, calling the roll
lectisterniātor, -ōris m arranger of couches
lectisternium, -ī and **-iī** nt religious feast
lēctitō, -āre vt to read frequently
lēctiuncula, -ae f light reading
lēctor, -ōris m reader
lectulus, -ī m couch, bed
lectus, -ī m couch, bed; bier
lēctus ppp of **legō** ♦ adj picked; choice, excellent
Lēda, -ae, Lēdē, -ēs f mother of Castor, Pollux, Helen and Clytemnestra
Lēdaeus adj see **Lēda**
lēgātiō, -ōnis f mission, embassy; members of a mission; (MIL) staff appointment, command of a legion; **lībera ~** free commission to visit provinces; **vōtīva ~** free commission for paying a vow in a province
lēgātor, -ōris m testator
lēgātum, -ī nt legacy, bequest
lēgātus, -ī m delegate, ambassador; deputy, lieutenant; commander (of a legion)
lēgifer, -ī adj law-giving
legiō, -ōnis f legion (up to 6000 men); (pl) troops, army
legiōnārius adj legionary
lēgirupa, -ae, lēgirupiō, -iōnis m lawbreaker
lēgitimē adv lawfully, properly
lēgitimus adj lawful, legal; right, proper
legiuncula, -ae f small legion
legō, -ere, lēgī, lēctum vt to gather, pick; to choose, select; (sail) to furl; (places) to traverse, pass, coast along; (view) to scan; (writing) to read, recite; **senātum legere** call the roll of the senate
lēgō, -āre, -āvī, -ātum vt to send, charge, commission; to appoint as deputy or lieutenant; (will) to leave, bequeath
lēgulēius, -ī and **-iī** m pettifogging lawyer
legūmen, -inis nt pulse, bean
lembus, -ī m pinnace, cutter
Lemnias f Lemnian woman
Lemnicola, -ae m Vulcan
lēmniscātus adj beribboned
lēmniscus, -ī m ribbon (hanging from a victor's crown)
Lēmnius adj see **Lēmnos**
Lēmnos, Lēmnus, -ī f Aegean island, abode of Vulcan
Lemurēs, -um mpl ghosts
lēna, -ae f procuress; seductress
Lēnaeus adj Bacchic ♦ m Bacchus
lēnīmen, -inis nt solace, comfort
lēnīmentum, -ī nt sop
lēniō, -īre, -īvī and **-iī, -ītum** vt to soften, soothe, heal, calm
lēnis adj soft, smooth, mild, gentle, calm
lēnitās, -ātis f softness, smoothness, mildness, tenderness
lēniter adv softly, gently; moderately, half-heartedly
lēnitūdō, -inis f smoothness, mildness
lēnō, -ōnis m pander, brothel keeper; go-between
lēnōcinium, -ī and **-iī** nt pandering; allurement; meretricious ornament

lēnōcinor, -ārī, -ātus vi to pay court to; to promote
lēnōnius adj pander's
lēns, lentis f lentil
lentē adv slowly; calmly, coolly
lentēscō, -ere vi to become sticky, soften; to relax
lentīscifer, -ī adj bearing mastic trees
lentīscus, -ī f mastic tree
lentitūdō, -inis f slowness, dullness, apathy
lentō, -āre vt to bend
lentulus adj rather slow
lentus adj sticky, sluggish; pliant; slow, lasting, lingering; (person) calm, at ease, indifferent
lēnunculus, -ī m skiff
leō, -ōnis m lion
Leōnidās, -ae m Spartan king who fell at Thermopylae
leōnīnus adj lion's
Leontīnī, -ōrum mpl town in Sicily
Leontīnus adj see **Leontīnī**
lepas, -dis f limpet
lepidē adv neatly, charmingly; (reply) very well, splendidly
lepidus adj pleasant, charming, neat, witty
lepōs, lepor, -ōris m pleasantness, charm; wit
lepus, -oris m hare
lepusculus, -ī m young hare
Lerna, -ae, Lernē, -ēs f marsh near Argos (where Hercules killed the Hydra)
Lernaeus adj Lernaean
Lesbias, -iadis f Lesbian woman
Lesbis, Lesbius, Lesbōus, Lesbiacus adj see **Lesbos**
Lesbos, Lesbus, -ī f Aegean island (home of Alcaeus and Sappho)
lētālis adj deadly
Lēthaeus adj of Lethe; infernal; soporific
lēthargicus, -ī m lethargic person
lēthargus, -ī m drowsiness
Lēthē, -ēs f river in the lower world, which caused forgetfulness
lētifer, -ī adj fatal
lētō, -āre vt to kill
lētum, -ī nt death; destruction
Leucadius adj see **Leucas**
Leucas, -dis, Leucadia, -diae f island off W. Greece
Leucothea, -ae, Leucotheē, -ēs f Ino (a sea goddess)
Leuctra, -ōrum ntpl battlefield in Boeotia
Leuctricus adj see **Leuctra**
levāmen, -inis nt alleviation, comfort
levāmentum, -ī nt mitigation, consolation
levātiō, -ōnis f relief; diminishing
lēvī perf of **linō**
leviculus adj rather vain
levidēnsis adj slight
levipēs, -edis adj light-footed
levis adj (weight) light; (MIL) light-armed; (fig) easy, gentle; (importance) slight, trivial; (motion) nimble, fleet; (character) fickle, unreliable
lēvis adj smooth; (youth) beardless, delicate
levisomnus adj light-sleeping
levitās, -ātis f lightness; nimbleness; fickleness, frivolity

lēvitās, -ātis f smoothness; fluency
leviter adv lightly; slightly; easily
levō, -āre vt to lighten, ease; (fig) to alleviate, lessen; to comfort, relieve; to impair; (danger) to avert; **sē levāre** rise
lēvō, -āre vt to smooth, polish
lēvor, -ōris m smoothness
lēx, lēgis f law, statute; bill; rule, principle; contract, condition; **lēgem ferre** propose a bill; **lēgem perferre** carry a motion; **lēge agere** proceed according to law; **sine lēge** out of control
lībāmen, -inis nt offering, libation
lībāmentum, -ī nt offering, libation
lībātiō, -ōnis f libation
lībella, -ae f small coin, as; level; **ad lībellam** exactly; **ex lībellā** sole heir
libellus, -ī m small book; notebook, diary, letter; notice, programme, handbill; petition, complaint; lampoon
libēns, -entis adj willing, glad
libenter adv willingly, with pleasure
liber, -rī m inner bark (of a tree); book; register
Līber, -ī m Italian god of fertility (identified with Bacchus)
līber, -ī adj free, open, unrestricted, undisturbed; (with abl) free from; (speech) frank; (POL) free, not slave, democratic
Lībera, -ae f Proserpine; Ariadne
Līberālia, -ālium ntpl festival of Liber in March
līberālis adj of freedom, of free citizens, gentlemanly, honourable; generous, liberal; handsome
līberālitās, -ātis f courtesy, kindness; generosity; bounty
līberāliter adv courteously, nobly; generously
līberātiō, -ōnis f delivery, freeing; (LAW) acquittal
līberātor, -ōris m liberator, deliverer
līberē adv freely, frankly, boldly
līberī, -ōrum mpl children
līberō, -āre, -āvī, -ātum vt to free, set free, release; to exempt; (LAW) to acquit; (slave) to give freedom to; **fidem līberāre** keep one's promise; **nōmina līberāre** cancel debts
līberta, -ae f freedwoman
lībertās, -ātis f freedom, liberty; status of a freeman; (POL) independence; freedom of speech, outspokenness
lībertīnus adj of a freedman, freed ♦ m freedman ♦ f freedwoman
lībertus, -ī m freedman
libet, lubet, -ēre, -uit and **-itum est** vi (impers) it pleases; **mihi ~** I like; **ut ~** as you please
libīdinōsē adv wilfully
libīdinōsus adj wilful, arbitrary, extravagant; sensual, lustful
libīdō, lubīdō, -inis f desire, passion; wilfulness, caprice; lust
libita, -ōrum ntpl pleasure, fancy
Libitīna, -ae f goddess of burials
lībō, -āre, -āvī, -ātum vt to taste, sip, touch; to pour (a libation), offer; to extract, take out; to impair

lībra, -ae f pound; balance, pair of scales; **ad lībram** of equal size
lībrāmentum, -ī nt level surface, weight (to give balance or movement); (water) fall
lībrāria, -ae f head spinner
lībrāriolus, -ī m copyist
lībrārium, -ī and **-iī** nt bookcase
lībrārius adj of books ♦ m copyist
lībrātus adj level; powerful
lībrīlis adj weighing a pound
lībritor, -ōris m slinger
lībrō, -āre, -āvī, -ātum vt to poise, hold balanced; to swing, hurl
lībum, -ī nt cake
Liburna, -ae f a fast galley, frigate
Liburnī, -ōrum mpl people of Illyria
Liburnus adj Liburnian
Libya, -ae, Libyē, -ēs f Africa
Libycus adj African
Libyes, -um mpl Libyans, people in N. Africa
Libyssus, Libystinus, Libystis adj = **Libycus**
licēns, -entis adj free, bold, unrestricted
licenter adv freely, lawlessly
licentia, -ae f freedom, licence; lawlessness, licentiousness
liceō, -ēre, -uī vi to be for sale, value at
liceor, -ērī, -itus vt, vi to bid (at an auction), bid for
licet, -ēre, -uit and **-itum est** vi (impers) it is permitted, it is lawful; (reply) all right ♦ conj although; **mihi ~** I may
Licinius[1], -ī m Roman family name (esp with surname Crassus)
Licinius[2] adj see **Licinius[1]**
licitātiō, -ōnis f bidding (at a sale)
licitor, -ārī vi to make a bid, bid
licitus adj lawful
līcium, -ī and **-iī** nt thread
līctor, -ōris m lictor (an attendant with fasces preceding a magistrate)
licuī perf of **liceō; liquēscō**
liēn, -ēnis m spleen
ligāmen, -inis nt band, bandage
ligāmentum, -ī nt bandage
Liger, -is m (river) Loire
lignārius, -ī and **-iī** m carpenter
lignātiō, -ōnis f fetching wood
lignātor, -ōris m woodcutter
ligneolus adj wooden
ligneus adj wooden
lignor, -ārī vi to fetch wood
lignum, -ī nt wood, firewood, timber; **in silvam ligna ferre** carry coals to Newcastle
ligō[1], -āre, -āvī, -ātum vt to tie up, bandage; (fig) to unite
ligō[2], -ōnis m mattock, hoe
ligula, -ae f shoestrap
Ligur, -ris m/f Ligurian
Liguria, -riae f district of N.W. Italy
ligūriō, ligurriō, -īre vt to lick; to eat daintily; (fig) to feast on, lust after
ligūrītiō, -ōnis f daintiness
Ligus, -ris m/f Ligurian
Ligusticus, -stīnus adj see **Ligus**

ligustrum, -ī nt privet

līlium, -ī and **-iī** nt lily; (MIL) spiked pit

līma, -ae f file; (fig) revision

līmātius adv more elegantly

līmātulus adj refined

līmāx, -ācis f slug, snail

limbus, -ī m fringe, hem

līmen, -inis nt threshold, lintel; doorway, entrance; house, home; (fig) beginning

līmes, -itis m path between fields, boundary; path, track, way; frontier, boundary line

līmō, -āre, -āvī, -ātum vt to file; (fig) to polish, refine; to file down, investigate carefully; to take away from

līmōsus adj muddy

limpidus adj clear, limpid

līmus¹ adj sidelong, askance

līmus², -ī m mud, slime, dirt

līmus³, -ī m ceremonial apron

līnea, -ae f line, string; plumbline; boundary; **ad līneam, rectā līneā** vertically; **extrēmā līneā amāre** love at a distance

līneāmentum, -ī nt line; feature; outline

līneus adj flaxen, linen

lingō, -ere vt to lick

lingua, -ae f tongue; speech, language; tongue of land; **~ Latīna** Latin

lingula, -ae f tongue of land

līniger, -ī adj linen-clad

linō, -ere, lēvī, litum vt to daub, smear; to overlay; (writing) to rub out; (fig) to befoul

linquō, -ere, līquī vt to leave, quit; to give up, let alone; (pass) to faint, swoon; **linquitur ut** it remains to

linteātus adj canvas

linteō, -ōnis m linen weaver

linter, -ris f boat; trough

linteum, -ī nt linen cloth, canvas; sail

linteus adj linen

lintriculus, -ī m small boat

līnum, -ī nt flax; linen; thread, line, rope; net

Lipara, -ae, Liparē, -ēs f island N. of Sicily (now Lipari)

Liparaeus, -ēnsis adj see **Lipara**

lippiō, -īre vi to have sore eyes

lippitūdō, -inis f inflammation of the eyes

lippus adj blear-eyed, with sore eyes; (fig) blind

liquefaciō, -facere, -fēcī, -factum (pass **-fīō**) vt to melt, dissolve; to decompose; (fig) to enervate

liquēns, -entis adj fluid, clear

liquēscō, -ere, licuī vi to melt; to clear; (fig) to grow soft, waste away

liquet, -ēre, licuit vi (impers) it is clear, it is evident; **nōn ~** not proven

līquī perf of **linquō**

liquidō adv clearly

liquidus adj fluid, liquid, flowing; clear, transparent, pure; (mind) calm, serene ♦ nt liquid water

liquō, -āre vt to melt; to strain

liquor, -ōris m fluidity; liquid, the sea

līquor, -ī vi to flow; (fig) to waste away

Līris, -is m river between Latium and Campania

līs, lītis f quarrel, dispute; lawsuit; matter in dispute; **lītem aestimāre** assess damages

litātiō, -ōnis f favourable sacrifice

lītera etc see **littera**

lītigātor, -ōris m litigant

lītigiōsus adj quarrelsome, contentious; disputed

lītigium, -ī and **-iī** nt quarrel

lītigō, -āre vi to quarrel; to go to law

litō, -āre, -āvī, -ātum vi to offer an acceptable sacrifice, obtain favourable omens; (with dat) to propitiate ♦ vt to offer successfully

lītorālis adj of the shore

lītoreus adj of the shore

littera, -ae f letter (of the alphabet)

litterae, -ārum fpl writing; letter, dispatch; document, ordinance; literature; learning, scholarship; **litterās discere** learn to read and write; **homō trium litterārum** thief (from fur); **sine litterīs** uncultured

litterārius adj of reading and writing

litterātē adv in clear letters; literally

litterātor, -ōris m grammarian

litterātūra, -ae f writing, alphabet

litterātus adj with letters on it, branded; educated, learned

litterula, -ae f small letter; short note; (pl) studies

litūra, -ae f correction, erasure, blot

litus ppp of **linō**

lītus, -oris nt shore, beach, coast; bank; **~ arāre** labour in vain

lituus, -ī m augur's staff; trumpet; (fig) starter

līvēns, -entis pres p of **līveō** ♦ adj bluish, black and blue

līveō, -ēre vi to be black and blue; to envy

līvēscō, -ere vi to turn black and blue

Līviānus adj = **Līvius¹**

līvidulus adj a little jealous

līvidus adj bluish, black and blue; envious, malicious

Līvius¹, -ī Roman family name (esp the first Latin poet); the famous historian, Livy

Līvius² adj see **Līvius¹**

līvor, -ōris m bluish colour; envy, malice

lixa, -ae m sutler, camp-follower

locātiō, -ōnis f leasing; lease, contract

locātōrius adj concerned with leases

locitō, -āre vt to let frequently

locō, -āre, -āvī, -ātum vt to place, put; to give in marriage; to let, lease, hire out; to contract for; (money) to invest

loculus, -ī m little place; (pl) satchel, purse

locuplēs, -ētis adj rich, opulent; reliable, responsible

locuplētō, -āre vt to enrich

locus, -ī (pl **-ī** m and **-a** nt) m place, site, locality, region; (MIL) post; (theatre) seat; (book) passage; (speech) topic, subject, argument; (fig) room, occasion; situation, state; rank, position; **locī** individual spots; **loca** regions, ground; **locī commūnēs** general arguments; **locō** (with gen) instead of; **in locō** opportunely; **eō locī** in the position; **intereā locī** meanwhile

lōcusta, -ae f locust

locūtiō, -ōnis f speech; pronunciation
locūtus ppa of **loquor**
lōdīx, -īcis f blanket
logica, -ōrum ntpl logic
logos, logus, -ī m word; idle talk; witticism
lōlīg- etc see **lollīg-**
lolium, -ī and **-iī** nt darnel
lollīgō, -inis f cuttlefish
lōmentum, -ī nt face cream
Londinium, -ī nt London
longaevus adj aged
longē adv far, far off; (time) long; (compar) by
    far, very much; ~ **esse** be far away, of no avail;
    ~ **latēque** everywhere
longinquitās, -ātis f length; distance; duration
longinquus adj distant, remote; foreign,
    strange; lasting, wearisome; (hope) long
    deferred
longitūdō, -inis f length; duration; **in**
    longitūdinem lengthwise
longiusculus adj rather long
longulē adv rather far
longulus adj rather long
longurius, -ī and **-iī** m long pole
longus adj long; vast; (time) long, protracted,
    tedious; (hope) far-reaching; **longa nāvis**
    warship; **longum est** it would be tedious; **nē**
    longum faciam to cut a long story short
loquācitās, -ātis f talkativeness
loquāciter adv see **loquāx**
loquāculus adj somewhat talkative
loquāx, -ācis adj talkative, chattering
loquella, -ae f language, words
loquor, -quī, cūtus vt, vi to speak, talk, say;
    to talk about, mention; (fig) to indicate; **rēs**
    loquitur ipsa the facts speak for themselves
lōrārius, -ī and **-iī** m flogger
lōrātus adj strapped
lōreus adj of leather strips
lōrīca, -ae f breastplate; parapet
lōrīcātus adj mailed
lōripēs, -edis adj bandylegged
lōrum, -ī nt strap; whip, lash; leather charm;
    (pl) reins
lōtos, lōtus, -ī f lotus
lōtus ppp of **lavō**
lubēns see **libēns**
lubentia, -ae f pleasure
lubet, lubīdō see **libet, libīdō**
lūbricō, -āre vt to make slippery
lūbricus adj slippery, slimy; gliding, fleeting;
    (fig) dangerous, hazardous
Lūca bōs f elephant
Lūcania, -iae f district of S. Italy
Lūcanica f kind of sausage
Lūcanus adj Lucanian ◆ m the epic poet Lucan
lūcar, -āris nt forest tax
lucellum, -ī nt small gain
lūceō, -cēre, -xī vi to shine, be light; (impers)
    to dawn, be daylight; (fig) to shine, be clear;
    meridiē nōn lūcēre (argue) that black is
    white
Lūcerēs, -um mpl a Roman patrician tribe
Lūceria, -iae f town in Apulia

Lūcerīnus adj see **Lūceria**
lucerna, -ae f lamp; (fig) midnight oil
lūcēscō, -ere vi to begin to shine, get light,
    dawn
lūcidē adv clearly
lūcidus adj bright, clear; (fig) lucid
lūcifer, -ī adj light-bringing ◆ m morning star,
    Venus; day
lūcifugus adj shunning the light
Lūcīlius, -ī m Roman family name (esp the first Latin
    satirist)
Lūcīna, -ae f goddess of childbirth
lūcīscō etc see **lūcēscō**
Lucmō, Lucumō, -ōnis m Etruscan prince or
    priest
Lucrētia, -iae f wife of Collatinus, ravished by Tarquin
Lucrētius, -ī m Roman family name (esp the
    philosophic poet)
lucrifuga, -ae m non-profiteer
Lucrīnēnsis adj see **Lucrīnus**
Lucrīnus, -ī m lake near Baiae (famous for oysters)
lucror, -ārī, -ātus vt to gain, win, acquire
lucrōsus adj profitable
lucrum, -ī nt profit, gain; greed; wealth; **lucrī**
    facere gain, get the credit of; **lucrō esse** be of
    advantage; **in lucrīs pōnere** count as gain
luctāmen, -inis nt struggle, exertion
luctātiō, -ōnis f wrestling; fight, contest
luctātor, -ōris m wrestler
lūctificus adj baleful
lūctisonus adj mournful
luctor, -ārī, -ātus vi to wrestle; to struggle, fight
lūctuōsus adj sorrowful, lamentable
lūctus, -ūs m mourning, lamentation;
    mourning (dress)
lūcubrātiō, -ōnis f work by lamplight,
    nocturnal study
lūcubrō, -āre, -āvī, -ātum vi to work by night
    ◆ vt to compose by night
lūculentē adv splendidly, right
lūculenter adv very well
lūculentus adj bright; (fig) brilliant, excellent,
    rich, fine
Lūcullus, -ī m Roman surname (esp the conqueror of
    Mithridates)
lūcus, -ī m grove; wood
lūdia, -ae f woman gladiator
lūdibrium, -ī and **-iī** nt mockery, derision;
    laughing stock; sport, play; **lūdibriō habēre**
    make fun of
lūdibundus adj playful; safely, easily
lūdicer, -rī adj playful; theatrical
lūdicrum, -ī nt public show, play; sport
lūdificātiō, -ōnis f ridicule; tricking
lūdificātor, -ōris m mocker
lūdificō, -āre, lūdificor, -ārī, -ātus vt to make a
    fool of, ridicule; to delude, thwart
lūdiō, -ōnis m actor
lūdius, -ī and **-iī** m actor; gladiator
lūdō, -dere, -sī, -sum vi to play; to sport, frolic;
    to dally, make love ◆ vt to play at; to amuse
    oneself with; to mimic, imitate; to ridicule,
    mock; to delude
lūdus, -ī m game, sport, play; (pl) public
    spectacle, games; school; (fig) child's play; fun,

jest; (love) dalliance; **lūdum dare** humour; **lūdōs facere** put on a public show; make fun of

luella, -ae f atonement

luēs, -is f plague, pest; misfortune

Lugdūnēnsis adj see **Lugdūnum**

Lugdūnum, -ī nt town in S. Gaul (now Lyon)

lūgeō, -gēre, -xī, -ctum vt, vi to mourn; to be in mourning

lūgubris adj mourning; disastrous; (sound) plaintive ♦ ntpl mourning dress

lumbī, -ōrum mpl loins

lumbrīcus, -ī m worm

lūmen, -inis nt light; lamp, torch; day; eye; life; (fig) ornament, glory; clarity

lūmināre, -is nt window

lūminōsus adj brilliant

lūna, -ae f moon; month; crescent

lūnāris adj of the moon

lūnātus adj crescent-shaped

lūnō, -āre vt to bend into a crescent

luō, -ere, -ī vt to pay; to atone for; to avert by expiation

lupa, -ae f she-wolf; prostitute

lupānar, -āris nt brothel

lupātus adj toothed ♦ m, ntpl curb

Lupercal, -ālis nt a grotto sacred to Pan

Lupercālia, -ālium ntpl festival of Pan in February

Lupercus, -ī m Pan; priest of Pan

lupīnum, -ī nt lupin; sham money, counters

lupīnus¹ adj wolf's

lupīnus², -ī m lupin; sham money, counters

lupus, -ī m wolf; (fish) pike; toothed bit; grapnel; ~ **in fābulā** talk of the devil

lūridus adj pale yellow, ghastly pallid

lūror, -ōris m yellowness

lūscinia, -ae f nightingale

luscitiōsus adj purblind

luscus adj one-eyed

lūsiō, -ōnis f play

Lūsitānia, -iae f part of W. Spain (including what is now Portugal)

Lūsitānus adj see **Lūsitānia**

lūsitō, -āre vi to play

lūsor, -ōris m player; humorous writer

lūstrālis adj lustral, propitiatory; quinquennial

lūstrātiō, -ōnis f purification; roving

lūstrō, -āre, -āvī, -ātum vt to purify; (motion) to go round, encircle, traverse; (MIL) to review; (eyes) to scan, survey; (mind) to consider; (light) to illuminate

lustror, -ārī vi to frequent brothels

lustrum, -ī nt den, lair; (pl) wild country; (fig) brothels; debauchery

lūstrum, -ī nt purificatory sacrifice; (time) five years

lūsus¹ ppp of **lūdō**

lūsus², -ūs m play, game, sport; dalliance

lūteolus adj yellow

Lutetia, -ae f town in N. Gaul (now Paris)

luteus adj of clay; muddy, dirty; (fig) vile

lūteus adj yellow, orange

lutitō, -āre vt to throw mud at

lutulentus adj muddy, filthy; (fig) foul

lutum, -ī nt mud, mire; clay

lūtum, -ī nt dyer's weed; yellow

lūx, lūcis f light; daylight; day; life; (fig) public view; glory, encouragement, enlightenment; **lūce** in the daytime; **prīmā lūce** at daybreak; **lūce carentēs** the dead

lūxī perf of **lūceō; lūgeō**

luxor, -ārī vi to live riotously

luxuria, -ae, luxuriēs, -ēī f rankness, profusion; extravagance, luxury

luxuriō, -āre, luxurior, -ārī vi to grow to excess, be luxuriant; (fig) to be exuberant, run riot

luxuriōsē adv voluptuously

luxuriōsus adj luxuriant; excessive, extravagant; voluptuous

luxus, -ūs m excess, debauchery, pomp

Lyaeus, -ī m Bacchus; wine

Lycaeus, -ī m mountain in Arcadia (sacred to Pan)

Lycāōn, -onis m father of Callisto, the Great Bear

Lycāonius adj see **Lycāōn**

Lycēum, Lycīum, -ī nt Aristotle's school at Athens

lychnūchus, -ī m lampstand

lychnus, -ī m lamp

Lycia, -ae f country in S.W. Asia Minor

Lycius adj Lycian

Lyctius adj Cretan

Lycurgus, -ī m Thracian king killed by Bacchus; Spartan lawgiver; Athenian orator

Lȳdia, -iae f country of Asia Minor

Lȳdius adj Lydian; Etruscan

Lȳdus, -ī m Lydian

lympha, -ae f water

lymphāticus adj crazy, frantic

lymphātus adj distracted

Lynceus, -eī m keen-sighted Argonaut

lynx, lyncis m/f lynx

lyra, -ae f lyre; lyric poetry

lyricus adj of the lyre, lyrical

Lysiās, -ae m Athenian orator

Mm

Macedō, -onis _m_ Macedonian
Macedonia _f_ Macedonia
Macedonicus, -onius _adj see_ **Macedonia**
macellum, -ī _nt_ market
maceō, -ēre _vi_ to be lean
macer, -rī _adj_ lean, meagre; poor
māceria, -ae _f_ wall
mācerō, -āre _vt_ to soften; (_body_) to enervate; (_mind_) to distress
macēscō, -ere _vi_ to grow thin
machaera, -ae _f_ sword
machaerophorus, -ī _m_ soldier armed with a sword
Machāōn, -onis _m legendary Greek surgeon_
Machāonius _adj see_ **Machāōn**
māchina, -ae _f_ machine, engine; (_fig_) scheme, trick
māchināmentum, -ī _nt_ engine
māchinātiō, -ōnis _f_ mechanism, machine; (_fig_) contrivance
māchinātor, -ōris _m_ engineer; (_fig_) contriver
māchinor, -ārī, -ātus _vt_ to devise, contrive; (_fig_) to plot, scheme
maciēs, -ēī _f_ leanness, meagreness; poorness
macilentus _adj_ thin
macrēscō, -ere _vi_ to grow thin
macritūdō, -inis _f_ leanness
macrocollum, -ī _nt_ large size of paper
mactābilis _adj_ deadly
mactātus, -ūs _m_ sacrifice
macte blessed; well done!
mactō¹, -āre, -āvī, -ātum _vt_ to sacrifice; to punish, kill
mactō², -āre _vt_ to glorify
macula, -ae _f_ spot, stain; (_net_) mesh; (_fig_) blemish, fault
maculō, -āre, -āvī, -ātum _vt_ to stain, defile
maculōsus _adj_ dappled, mottled; stained, polluted
madefaciō, -facere, -fēcī, -factum (_pass_ **-fīō**) _vt_ to wet, soak
madeō, -ēre _vi_ to be wet, be drenched; to be boiled soft; (_comedy_) to be drunk; (_fig_) to be steeped in
madēscō, -ere _vi_ to get wet, become moist
madidus _adj_ wet, soaked; sodden; drunk
madulsa, -ae _m_ drunkard
Maeander, Maeandros, -rī _m a winding river of Asia Minor_; winding, wandering
Maecēnās, -ātis _m friend of Augustus, patron of poets_
maena, -ae _f_ sprat

Maenala, -ōrum _ntpl mountain range in Arcadia_
Maenalis, -ius _adj_ of Maenalus; Arcadian
Maenalus, Maenalos, -ī _m_ Maenala
Maenas, -dis _f_ Bacchante
Maeniānum _nt_ balcony
Maenius, -ī _m Roman family name_; **Maenia columna** whipping post in the Forum
Maeonia, -ae _f_ Lydia
Maeonidēs, -dae _m_ Homer
Maeonius _adj_ Lydian; Homeric; Etruscan
Maeōticus, Maeōtius _adj_ Scythian, Maeotic
Maeōtis, -dis _f_ Sea of Azov
maereō, -ēre _vi_ to mourn, be sad
maeror, -ōris _m_ mourning, sorrow, sadness
maestiter _adv see_ **maestus**
maestitia, -ae _f_ sadness, melancholy
maestus _adj_ sad, sorrowful; gloomy; mourning
māgālia, -um _ntpl_ huts
mage _etc see_ **magis**
magicus _adj_ magical
magis, mage _adv_ more; eō ~ the more, all the more
magister, -rī _m_ master, chief, director; (_school_) teacher; (_fig_) instigator; ~ **equitum** chief of cavalry, second in command (_to a dictator_); ~ **mōrum** censor; ~ **sacrōrum** chief priest
magisterium, -ī _and_ **-iī** _nt_ presidency, tutorship
magistra, -ae _f_ mistress, instructress
magistrātus, -ūs _m_ magistracy, office; magistrate, official
magnanimitās, -ātis _f_ greatness
magnanimus _adj_ great, brave
Magnēs, -ētis _m_ Magnesian; magnet
Magnēsia _f_ district of Thessaly
Magnēsius, Magnēssus, Magnētis _adj see_ **Magnēsia**
magnidicus _adj_ boastful
magnificē _adv_ grandly; pompously
magnificentia, -ae _f_ greatness, grandeur; pomposity
magnificō, -āre _vt_ to esteem highly
magnificus (_compar_ **-entior**, _superl_ **-entissimus**) _adj_ great, grand, splendid; pompous
magniloquentia, -ae _f_ elevated language; pomposity
magniloquus _adj_ boastful
magnitūdō, -inis _f_ greatness, size, large amount; dignity
magnopere _adv_ greatly, very much
magnus (_compar_ **māior**, _superl_ **māximus**) _adj_ great, large, big, tall; (_voice_) loud; (_age_)

advanced; (*value*) high, dear; (*fig*) grand, noble, important; **avunculus** ~ great-uncle; **magna loquī** boast; **magnī aestimāre** think highly of; **magnī esse** be highly esteemed; **magnō stāre** cost dear; **magnō opere** very much

magus, -ī *m* wise man; magician ◆ *adj* magic

Māia, -ae *f mother of Mercury*

māiestās, -ātis *f* greatness, dignity, majesty; treason; **māiestātem laedere, māiestātem minuere** offend against the sovereignty of; **lēx māiestātis** law against treason

māior, -ōris *compar of* **magnus**; ~ **nātū** older, elder; **in māius crēdere/ferre** exaggerate

māiōrēs, -ōrum *mpl* ancestors

Māius, -ī *m* May ◆ *adj* of May

māiusculus *adj* somewhat greater; a little older

māla, -ae *f* cheek, jaw

malacia, -ae *f* dead calm

malacus *adj* soft

male (*compar* **pēius**, *superl* **pessimē**) *adv* badly, wrongly, unfortunately; not; (*with words having bad sense*) very much; ~ **est animō** I feel ill; ~ **sānus** insane; ~ **dīcere** abuse, curse; ~ **facere** harm

maledicē *adv* abusively

maledictiō, -ōnis *f* abuse

maledictum, -ī *nt* curse

maledicus *adj* scurrilous

malefactum, -ī *nt* wrong

maleficium, -ī *and* **-iī** *nt* misdeed, wrong, mischief

maleficus *adj* wicked ◆ *m* criminal

malesuādus *adj* seductive

malevolēns, -entis *adj* spiteful

malevolentia, -ae *f* ill-will

malevolus *adj* ill-disposed, malicious

mālifer, -ī *adj* apple-growing

malīgnē *adv* spitefully; grudgingly

malīgnitās, -ātis *f* malice; stinginess

malīgnus *adj* unkind, ill-natured, spiteful; stingy; (*soil*) unfruitful; (*fig*) small, scanty

malitia, -ae *f* badness, malice; roguishness

malitiōsē *adv see* **malitiōsus**

malitiōsus *adj* wicked, crafty

maliv- *etc see* **malev-**

mālle *infin of* **mālō**

malleolus, -ī *m* hammer; (*MIL*) fire-brand

malleus, -ī *m* hammer, mallet, maul

mālō, -le, -uī *vt* to prefer; would rather

malobathrum, -ī *nt* an oriental perfume

māluī *perf of* **mālō**

malum, -ī *nt* evil, wrong, harm, misfortune; (*interj*) mischief

mālum, -ī *nt* apple, fruit

malus (*compar* **pēior**, *superl* **pessimus**) *adj* bad, evil, harmful; unlucky; ugly; **ī in malam rem** go to hell!

mālus¹, -ī *f* apple tree

mālus², -ī *m* mast, pole

malva, -ae *f* mallow

Māmers, -tis *m* Mars

Māmertīnī, -ōrum *mpl mercenary troops who occupied Messana*

mamma, -ae *f* breast; teat

mammilla, -ae *f* breast

mānābilis *adj* penetrating

manceps, -ipis *m* purchaser; contractor

mancipium, -ī *and* **-iī** *nt* formal purchase; property; slave

mancipō, -āre *vt* to sell, deliver up

mancup- *etc see* **mancip-**

mancus *adj* crippled

mandātum, -ī *nt* commission, command; (*LAW*) contract

mandātus, -ūs *m* command

mandō¹, -āre, -āvī, -ātum *vt* to entrust, commit; to commission, command

mandō², -ere, -ī, mānsum *vt* to chew, eat, devour

mandra, -ae *f* drove of cattle

mandūcus, -ī *m* masked figure of a glutton

māne *nt* (*indecl*) morning ◆ *adv* in the morning, early

maneō, -ēre, mānsī, mānsum *vi* to remain; to stay, stop; to last, abide, continue ◆ *vt* to wait for, await; **in condiciōne manēre** abide by an agreement

Mānēs, -ium *mpl* ghosts, shades of the dead; the lower world; bodily remains

mangō, -ōnis *m* dealer

manicae, -ārum *fpl* sleeves, gloves; handcuffs

manicātus *adj* with long sleeves

manicula, -ae *f* little hand

manifestō¹, -āre *vt* to disclose

manifestō² *adv* clearly, evidently

manifestus *adj* clear, obvious; convicted, caught

manipl- *etc see* **manipul-**

manipulāris *adj* of a company ◆ *m* private (*in the ranks*); fellow soldier

manipulātim *adv* by companies

manipulus, -ī *m* bundle (*esp of hay*); (*MIL*) company

Manlius¹, -ī *m Roman family name* (*esp the saviour of the Capitol from the Gauls*); a severe disciplinarian

Manlius², Manliānus *adj see* **Manlius¹**

mannus, -ī *m* Gallic horse

mānō, -āre, -āvī, -ātum *vi* to flow, drip, stream; (*fig*) to spread, emanate

mānsī *perf of* **maneō**

mānsiō, -ōnis *f* remaining, stay

mānsitō, -āre *vi* to stay on

mānsuēfaciō, -facere, -fēcī, -factum (*pass* **-fīō**) *vt* to tame

mānsuēscō, -scere, -vī, -tum *vt* to tame ◆ *vi* to grow tame, grow mild

mānsuētē *adv see* **mānsuētus**

mānsuētūdō, -inis *f* tameness; gentleness

mānsuētus *ppp of* **mānsuēscō** ◆ *adj* tame; mild, gentle

mānsus *ppp of* **mandō²**; **maneō**

mantēle, -is *nt* napkin, towel

mantēlum, -ī *nt* cloak

mantica, -ae *f* knapsack

manticinor, -ārī, -ātus *vi* to be a prophet

mantō, -āre *vi* to remain, wait

Mantua, -ae *f birthplace of Vergil in N. Italy*

manuālis *adj* for the hand

manubiae, -ārum *fpl* money from sale of booty

manūbrium, **-ī** *and* **-iī** *nt* handle, haft
manuleātus *adj* with long sleeves
manūmissiō, **-ōnis** *f* emancipation *(of a slave)*
manūmittō, **-ittere**, **-īsī**, **-issum** *vt* to
 emancipate, make free
manupretium, **-ī** *and* **-iī** *nt* pay, wages, reward
manus, **-ūs** *f* hand; corps, band, company;
 (elephant) trunk; *(art)* touch; *(work)* handiwork,
 handwriting; *(war)* force, valour, hand to hand
 fighting; *(fig)* power; ~ **ferrea** grappling iron; **manum**
 dare give up, yield; **manū** artificially; **manū**
 mittere emancipate; **ad manum** at hand;
 in manū obvious; subject; **in manūs venīre**
 come to hand; **in manibus** well known; at
 hand; **in manibus habēre** be engaged on;
 fondle; **per manūs** forcibly; **per manūs**
 trādere hand down
mapālia, **-um** *ntpl* huts
mappa, **-ae** *f* napkin, cloth
Marathōn, **-ōnis** *f* Attic village famous for Persian
 defeat
Marathōnius *adj see* **Marathōn**
Marcellia, **-iōrum** *ntpl* festival of the Marcelli
Marcellus, **-ī** *m* Roman surname *(esp the captor of*
 Syracuse)
marceō, **-ēre** *vi* to droop, be faint
marcēscō, **-ere** *vi* to waste away, grow feeble
Marciānus *adj see* **Marcius**[1]
marcidus *adj* withered; enervated
Marcius[1], **-ī** *m* Roman family name *(esp Ancus, fourth*
 king)
Marcius[2] *adj see* **Marcius**[1]
mare, **-is** *nt* sea; ~ **nostrum** Mediterranean;
 ~ **inferum** Tyrrhenian Sea; ~ **superum**
 Adriatic
Mareōticus *adj* Mareotic; Egyptian
margarīta, **-ae** *f* pearl
marginō, **-āre** *vt* to put a border or kerb on
margō, **-inis** *m/f* edge, border, boundary;
 ~ **cēnae** side dishes
Mariānus *adj see* **Marius**[1]
Marīca, **-ae** *f* nymph of Minturnae
marīnus *adj* of the sea
marītālis *adj* marriage- *(in cpds)*
maritimus *adj* of the sea, maritime, coastal
 ♦ *ntpl* coastal area
marītō, **-āre** *vt* to marry
marītus, **-i** *m* husband ♦ *adj* nuptial
Marius[1], **-ī** *m* Roman family name *(esp the victor over*
 Jugurtha and the Teutons)
Marius[2] *adj see* **Marius**[1]
marmor, **-is** *nt* marble; statue, tablet; sea
marmoreus *adj* of marble; like marble
Marō, **-ōnis** *m* surname of Vergil
marra, **-ae** *f* kind of hoe
Mars, **Martis** *m* god of war, father of Romulus and
 Remus; war, conflict; planet Mars; **aequō Marte**
 on equal terms; **suō Marte** by one's own
 exertions
Marsī, **-ōrum** *mpl* people of central Italy, famous as
 fighters
Marsicus, **Marsus** *adj* Marsian
marsuppium, **-ī** *and* **-iī** *nt* purse
Mārtiālis *adj* of Mars

Mārticola, **-ae** *m* worshipper of Mars
Mārtigena, **-ae** *m* son of Mars
Mārtius *adj* of Mars; of March; warlike
mās, **maris** *m* male, man ♦ *adj* male; manly
māsculus *adj* male, masculine; manly
Masinissa, **-ae** *m* king of Numidia
massa, **-ae** *f* lump, mass
Massicum, **-ī** *nt* Massic wine
Massicus, **-ī** *m* mountain in Campania, famous for
 vines
Massilia, **-ae** *f* Greek colony in Gaul *(now* Marseille)
Massiliēnsis *adj see* **Massilia**
mastīgia, **-ae** *m* scoundrel
mastrūca, **-ae** *f* sheepskin
mastrūcātus *adj* wearing sheepskin
matara, **-ae**, **mataris**, **-is** *f* Celtic javelin
matelliō, **-ōnis** *m* pot
māter, **-ris** *f* mother; **Magna** ~ Cybele
mātercula, **-ae** *f* poor mother
māteria, **-ae**, **māteriēs**, **-ēī** *f* matter,
 substance; wood, timber; *(fig)* subject matter,
 theme; occasion, opportunity; *(person)* ability,
 character
māteriārius, **-ī** *and* **-iī** *m* timber merchant
māteriātus *adj* timbered
māteriēs *etc see* **māteria**
māterior, **-āri** *vi* to fetch wood
māternus *adj* mother's
mātertera, **-ae** *f* aunt *(maternal)*
mathēmaticus, **-ī** *m* mathematician;
 astrologer
mātricīda, **-ae** *m* matricide
mātricīdium, **-ī** *and* **-iī** *nt* a mother's murder
mātrimōnium, **-ī** *and* **-iī** *nt* marriage
mātrimus *adj* whose mother is still alive
mātrōna, **-ae** *f* married woman, matron, lady
mātrōnālis *adj* a married woman's
matula, **-ae** *f* pot
mātūrē *adv* at the right time; early, promptly
mātūrēscō, **-ēscere**, **-uī** *vi* to ripen
mātūritās, **-ātis** *f* ripeness; *(fig)* maturity,
 perfection, height
mātūrō, **-āre**, **-āvī**, **-ātum** *vt* to bring to
 maturity; to hasten, be too hasty with ♦ *vi* to
 make haste
mātūrus *adj* ripe, mature; timely, seasonable;
 early
Mātūta, **-ae** *f* goddess of dawn
mātūtīnus *adj* morning, early
Mauritānia, **-ae** *f* Mauretania *(now* Morocco)
Maurus, **-ī** *m* Moor ♦ *adj* Moorish, African
Maurūsius *adj see* **Maurus**
Māvors, **-tis** *m* Mars
Māvortius *adj see* **Māvors**
maxilla, **-ae** *f* jaw
maximē *adv* most, very much, especially;
 precisely; just; certainly, yes; **cum** ~ just as;
 quam ~ as much as possible
maximitās, **-ātis** *f* great size
maximus *superl of* **magnus**
māxum- *etc see* **māxim-**
māzonomus, **-ī** *m* dish
meāpte my own
meātus, **-ūs** *m* movement, course

mēcastor *interj* by Castor!
mēcum with me
meddix tuticus *m* senior Oscan magistrate
Mēdēa, -ae *f* Colchian wife of Jason, expert in magic
Mēdēis *adj* magical
medentēs, -entum *mpl* doctors
medeor, -ērī *vi* (with dat) to heal, remedy
mediastīnus, -ī *m* drudge
mēdica, -ae *f* lucern (kind of clover)
medicābilis *adj* curable
medicāmen, -inis *nt* drug, medicine; cosmetic; (fig) remedy
medicāmentum, -ī *nt* drug, medicine; potion, poison; (fig) relief; embellishment
medicātus, -ūs *m* charm
medicīna, -ae *f* medicine; cure; (fig) remedy, relief
medicō, -āre, -āvī, -ātum *vt* to cure; to steep, dye
medicor, -ārī *vt, vi* to cure
medicus *adj* healing ♦ *m* doctor
medietās, -ātis *f* mean
medimnum, -ī *nt*, **medimnus, -ī** *m* bushel
mediocris *adj* middling, moderate, average
mediocritās, -ātis *f* mean, moderation; mediocrity
mediocriter *adv* moderately, not particularly; calmly
Mediolānēnsis *adj see* **Mediolānum**
Mediolānum, -ī *nt* town in N. Italy (now Milan)
meditāmentum, -ī *nt* preparation, drill
meditātiō, -ōnis *f* thinking about; preparation, practice
meditātus *adj* studied
mediterrāneus *adj* inland
meditor, -ārī, -ātus *vt, vi* to think over, contemplate, reflect; to practise, study
medius *adj* middle, the middle of; intermediate; intervening; middling, moderate; neutral ♦ *nt* middle; public ♦ *m* mediator; **medium complectī** clasp round the waist; **medium sē gerere** be neutral; **mediō** midway; **mediō temporis** meanwhile; **in medium** for the common good; **in medium prōferre** publish; **dē mediō tollere** do away with; **ē mediō abīre** die, disappear; **in mediō esse** be public; **in mediō positus** open to all; **in mediō relinquere** leave undecided
medius fidius *interj* by Heaven!
medix tuticus *see* **meddix tuticus**
medulla, -ae *f* marrow, pith
medullitus *adv* from the heart
medullula, -ae *f* marrow
Mēdus¹, -ī *m* Mede, Persian
Mēdus² *adj see* **Mēdus¹**
Medūsa, -ae † Gorgon, whose look turned everything to stone
Medūsaeus *adj*: ~ **equus** Pegasus
Megalēnsia, Megalēsia, -um *ntpl* festival of Cybele in April
Megara, -ae *f*, **Megara, -ōrum** *ntpl* town in Greece near the Isthmus
Megarēus, Megarīcus *adj* Megarean
megistānes, -um *mpl* grandees

mehercle, mehercule, mehercules *interj* by Hercules!
mēiō, -ere *vi* to make water
mel, mellis *nt* honey
melancholicus *adj* melancholy
melē *pl of* **melos**
Meleager, Meleagros, -rī *m* prince of Calydon
melicus *adj* musical; lyrical
melilōtos, -ī *f* kind of clover
melimēla, -ōrum *ntpl* honey apples
Mēlīnum, -ī *nt* Melian white
melior, -ōris *adj* better
melisphyllum, -ī *nt* balm
Melita, -ae *f* Malta
Melitēnsis *adj* Maltese
melius *nt of* **melior** ♦ *adv* better
meliusculē *adv* fairly well
meliusculus *adj* rather better
mellifer, -ī *adj* honey-making
mellītus *adj* honeyed; sweet
melos, -ī *nt* tune, song
Melpomenē, -ēs *f* Muse of tragedy
membrāna, -ae *f* skin, membrane, slough; parchment
membrānula, -ae *f* piece of parchment
membrātim *adv* limb by limb; piecemeal; in short sentences
membrum, -ī *nt* limb, member; part, division; clause
mēmet me (emphatic)
meminī, -isse *vi* (with gen) to remember, think of; to mention
Memnōn, -onis *m* Ethiopian king, killed at Troy
Memnonius *adj see* **Memnōn**
memor, -is *adj* mindful, remembering; in memory (of)
memorābilis *adj* memorable, remarkable
memorandus *adj* noteworthy
memorātus¹, -ūs *m* mention
memorātus² *adj* famed
memoria, -ae *f* memory, remembrance; time, lifetime; history; **haec ~** our day; **memoriae prōdere** hand down to posterity; **post hominum memoriam** since the beginning of history
memoriola, -ae *f* weak memory
memoriter *adv* from memory; accurately
memorō, -āre, -āvī, -ātum *vt* to mention, say, speak
Memphis, -is *and* **-idos** *f* town in middle Egypt
Memphītēs, Memphītis, Memphītiticus *adj* of Memphis; Egyptian
Menander, Menandros, -rī *m* Greek writer of comedy
Menandrēus *adj see* **Menander**
menda, -ae *f* fault
mendācium, -ī *and* **-iī** *nt* lie
mendāciunculum, -ī *nt* fib
mendāx, -ācis *adj* lying; deceptive, unreal ♦ *m* liar
mendīcitās, -ātis *f* beggary
mendīcō, -āre, mendīcor, -ārī *vi* to beg, go begging
mendīcus *adj* beggarly, poor ♦ *m* beggar

mendōsē *adv see* **mendōsus**
mendōsus *adj* faulty; wrong, mistaken
mendum, -ī *nt* fault, blunder
Menelāēus *adj see* **Menelāus**
Menelāus, -ī *m brother of Agamemnon, husband of Helen*
Menoetiadēs, -ae *m* Patroclus
mēns, mentis *f* mind, understanding; feelings, heart; idea, plan, purpose; courage; **venit in mentem** it occurs; **mente captus** insane; **eā mente ut** with the intention of
mēnsa, -ae *f* table; meal, course; counter, bank; **secunda ~** dessert
mēnsārius, -ī *and* **-iī** *m* banker
mēnsiō, -ōnis *f* (*metre*) quantity
mēnsis, -is *m* month
mēnsor, -ōris *m* measurer, surveyor
mēnstruālis *adj* for a month
mēnstruus *adj* monthly; for a month ♦ *nt* a month's provisions
mēnsula, -ae *f* little table
mēnsūra, -ae *f* measure, measurement; standard, standing; amount, size, capacity
mēnsus *ppa of* **mētior**
menta, -ae *f* mint
mentiēns, -ientis *m* fallacy
mentiō, -ōnis *f* mention, hint
mentior, -īrī, -ītus *vi* to lie, deceive ♦ *vt* to say falsely; to feign, imitate
mentītus *adj* lying, false
Mentor, -is *m artist in metalwork*; ornamental cup
Mentoreus *adj see* **Mentor**
mentum, -ī *nt* chin
meō, -āre *vi* to go, pass
mephītis, -is *f* noxious vapour, malaria
merācus *adj* pure
mercābilis *adj* buyable
mercātor, -ōris *m* merchant, dealer
mercātūra, -ae *f* commerce; purchase; goods
mercātus, -ūs *m* trade, traffic; market, fair
mercēdula, -ae *f* poor wages, small rent
mercēnārius *adj* hired, mercenary ♦ *m* servant
mercēs, -ēdis *f* pay, wages, fee; bribe; rent; (*fig*) reward, retribution, cost
mercimōnium, -ī *and* **-iī** *nt* wares, goods
mercor, -ārī, -ātus *vt* to trade in, purchase
Mercuriālis *adj see* **Mercurius**
Mercurius, -ī *m messenger of the gods, god of trade, thieves, speech and the lyre*; **stēlla Mercuriī** planet Mercury
merda, -ae *f* dung
merenda, -ae *f* lunch
mereō, -ēre, -uī, mereor, -ērī, -itus *vt, vi* to deserve; to earn, win, acquire; (MIL) to serve; **bene merēre dē** do a service to, serve well; **merēre equō** serve in the cavalry
meretrīcius *adj* a harlot's
meretrīcula, -ae *f* pretty harlot
meretrīx, -īcis *f* harlot
mergae, -ārum *fpl* pitchfork
merges, -itis *f* sheaf
mergō, -gere, -sī, -sum *vt* to dip, immerse, sink; (*fig*) to bury, plunge, drown
mergus, -ī *m* (*bird*) diver

merīdiānus *adj* midday; southerly
merīdiātiō, -ōnis *f* siesta
merīdiēs, -ēī *f* midday, noon; south
merīdiō, -āre *vi* to take a siesta
meritō[1], -āre *vt* to earn
meritō[2] *adv* deservedly
meritōrius *adj* money-earning ♦ *ntpl* lodgings
meritum, -ī *nt* service, kindness, merit; blame
meritus *ppp of* **mereō** ♦ *adj* deserved, just
merops, -is *f* bee-eater
mersī *perf of* **mergō**
mersō, -āre *vt* to immerse, plunge; to overwhelm
mersus *ppp of* **mergō**
merula, -ae *f* blackbird
merum, -ī *nt* neat wine
merus *adj* pure, undiluted; bare, mere
merx, mercis *f* goods, wares
Messalla, -ae *m Roman surname* (*esp* Messalla Corvīnus *Augustan orator, soldier and literary patron*)
Messallīna, -īnae *f wife of emperor Claudius; wife of Nero*
Messāna, -ae *f Sicilian town* (*now* Messina)
messis, -is *f* harvest
messor, -ōris *m* reaper
messōrius *adj* a reaper's
messuī *perf of* **metō**
messus *ppp of* **metō**
mēta, -ae *f pillar at each end of the Circus course; turning point, winning post;* (*fig*) goal, end, limit
metallum, -ī *nt* mine, quarry; metal
mētātor, -ōris *m* surveyor
Metaurus, -ī *m river in Umbria, famous for the defeat of Hasdrubal*
Metellus, -ī *m Roman surname* (*esp the commander against Jugurtha*)
Mēthymna, -ae *f town in Lesbos*
Mēthymnaeus *adj see* **Mēthymna**
mētior, -tīrī, -nsus *vt* to measure, measure out; to traverse; (*fig*) to estimate, judge
metō, -tere, -ssuī, -ssum *vt* to reap, gather; to mow, cut down
mētor, -ārī, -ātus *vt* to measure off, lay out
metrēta, -ae *f liquid measure* (*about 9 gallons*)
metuculōsus *adj* frightful
metuō, -uere, -uī, -ūtum *vt* to fear, be apprehensive
metus, -ūs *m* fear, alarm, anxiety
meus *adj* my, mine
mī *dat of* **ego** ♦ *voc and mpl of* **meus**
mīca, -ae *f* crumb, grain
micō, -āre, -uī *vi* to quiver, flicker, beat, flash, sparkle
Midās, -ae *m Phrygian king whose touch turned everything to gold*
migrātiō, -ōnis *f* removal, change
migrō, -āre, -āvī, -ātum *vi* to remove, change, pass away ♦ *vt* to transport, transgress
mīles, -itis *m* soldier, infantryman; army, troops
Mīlēsius *adj see* **Mīlētus**
Mīlētus, -tī *f town in Asia Minor*
mīlia, -um *ntpl* thousands; **~ passuum** miles

mīliārium, milliārium, -ī *and* **-iī** *nt* milestone
mīlitāris *adj* military, a soldier's
mīlitāriter *adv* in a soldierly fashion
mīlitia, -ae *f* military service, war; the army;
  militiae on service; **domī militiaeque** at
  home and abroad
mīlitō, -āre *vi* to serve, be a soldier
milium, -ī *and* **-iī** *nt* millet
mīlle (*pl* **mīlia**) *num* a thousand; ~ **passūs** a mile
millēnsimus, millēsimus *adj* thousandth
millia *etc see* **mīlia**
milliārium *etc see* **mīliārium**
mīlliēns, milliēs *adv* a thousand times
Milō, -ōnis *m tribune who killed Clodius and was
  defended by Cicero*
Milōniānus *adj see* **Milō**
Miltiadēs, -is *m Athenian general, victor at Marathon*
mīluīnus *adj* resembling a kite; rapacious
mīluus, mīlvus, -ī *m* kite; gurnard
mīma, -ae *f* actress
Mimallonis, -dis *f* Bacchante
mīmicē *adv see* **mīmicus**
mīmicus *adj* farcical
Mimnermus, -ī *m Greek elegiac poet*
mīmula, -ae *f* actress
mīmus, -ī *m* actor; mime, farce
mina, -ae *f Greek silver coin*
mināciter *adv see* **mināx**
minae, -ārum *fpl* threats; (*wall*) pinnacles
minanter *adv* threateningly
minātiō, -ōnis *f* threat
mināx, -ācis *adj* threatening; projecting
Minerva, -ae *f goddess of wisdom and arts, esp
  weaving*; (*fig*) talent, genius; working in wool;
  sūs Minervam "teach your grandmother!"
miniātulus *adj* painted red
miniātus *adj* red-leaded
minimē *adv* least, very little; (*reply*) no, not at all
minimus *adj* least, smallest, very small;
  youngest
miniō, -āre, -āvī, -ātum *vt* to colour red
minister, -rī *m*, **ministra, ministrae** *f*
  attendant, servant; helper, agent, tool
ministerium, -ī *and* **-iī** *nt* service, office, duty;
  retinue
ministrātor, -ōris *m*, **ministrātorrīx,
  ministrātorrīcis** *f* assistant, handmaid
ministrō, -āre *vt* to serve, supply; to manage
minitābundus *adj* threatening
minitor, -ārī, minitō, -āre *vt, vi* to threaten
minium, -ī *and* **-iī** *nt* vermilion, red lead
Mīnōis, -idis *f* Ariadne
Mīnōius, Mīnōus *adj see* **Mīnōs**
minor¹, -ārī, -ātus *vt, vi* to threaten; to project
minor², -ōris *adj* smaller, less, inferior; younger;
  (*pl*) descendants
Mīnōs, -is *m king of Crete, judge in the lower world*
Mīnōtaurus, -ī *m monster of the Cretan labyrinth,
  half bull, half man*
Minturnae, -ārum *fpl town in S. Latium*
Minturnēnsis *adj see* **Minturnae**
minum- *etc see* **minim-**

minuō, -uere, -uī, -ūtum *vt* to make smaller,
  lessen; to chop up; to reduce, weaken ♦ *vi* (*tide*)
  to ebb
minus *nt* = **minor²** ♦ *adv* less; not, not at all; **quō
  ~** (*prevent*) from
minusculus *adj* smallish
minūtal, -ālis *nt* mince
minūtātim *adv* bit by bit
minūtē *adv* in a petty manner
minūtus *ppp of* **minuō** ♦ *adj* small; paltry
mīrābilis *adj* wonderful, extraordinary
mīrābiliter *adv see* **mīrābilis**
mīrābundus *adj* astonished
mīrāculum, -ī *nt* marvel, wonder; amazement
mīrandus *adj* wonderful
mīrātiō, -ōnis *f* wonder
mīrātor, -ōris *m* admirer
mīrātrīx, -īcis *adj* admiring
mīrē *adv see* **mīrus**
mīrificē *adv see* **mīrificus**
mīrificus *adj* wonderful
mirmillō *see* **murmillō**
mīror, -ārī, -ātus *vt* to wonder at, be surprised
  at, admire ♦ *vi* to wonder, be surprised
mīrus *adj* wonderful, strange; **mīrum quam,
  mīrum quantum** extraordinarily
miscellānea, -ōrum *ntpl* (*food*) hotchpotch
misceō, -scēre, -scuī, -xtum *vt* to mix, mingle,
  blend; to join, combine; to confuse, embroil
misellus *adj* poor little
Mīsēnēnsis *adj see* **Mīsēnum**
Mīsēnum, -ī *nt promontory and harbour near Naples*
miser, -ī *adj* wretched, poor, pitiful, sorry
miserābilis *adj* pitiable, sad, plaintive
miserābiliter *adv see* **miserābilis**
miserandus *adj* deplorable
miserātiō, -ōnis *f* pity, compassion, pathos
miserē *adv see* **miser**
misereō, -ēre, -uī, misereor, -ērī, -itus *vt, vi*
  (*with gen*) to pity, sympathize with; **miseret
  mē** I pity, I am sorry
miserēscō, -ere *vi* to feel pity
miseria, -ae *f* misery, trouble, distress
misericordia, -ae *f* pity, sympathy, mercy
misericors, -dis *adj* sympathetic, merciful
miseriter *adv* sadly
miseror, -ārī, -ātus *vt* to deplore; to pity
mīsī *perf of* **mittō**
missa, -ae *f* (ECCL) mass
missilis *adj* missile
missiō, -ōnis *f* sending; release; (MIL) discharge;
  (*gladiators*) quarter; (*events*) end; **sine missiōne**
  to the death
missitō, -āre *vt* to send repeatedly
missus¹ *ppp of* **mittō**
missus², -ūs *m* sending; throwing; ~ **sagittae**
  bowshot
mitella, -ae *f* turban
mītēscō, -ere *vi* to ripen; to grow mild
Mithridātēs, -is *m king of Pontus, defeated by
  Pompey*
Mithridātēus, Mithridāticus *adj see*
  Mithridātēs
mītigātiō, -ōnis *f* soothing

mītigō, -āre, -āvī, -ātum vt to ripen, soften; to calm, pacify

mītis adj ripe, mellow; soft, mild; gentle

mitra, -ae f turban

mittō, -ere, mīsī, missum vt to send, dispatch; to throw, hurl; to let go, dismiss; to emit, utter; (news) to send word; (gift) to bestow; (event) to end; (speech) to omit, stop; **sanguinem mittere** bleed; **ad cēnam mittere** invite to dinner; **missum facere** forgo

mītulus, -ī m mussel

mixtim adv promiscuously

mixtūra, -ae f mingling

Mnēmosynē, -ēs f mother of the Muses

mnēmosynon, -ī nt souvenir

mōbilis adj movable; nimble, fleet; excitable, fickle

mōbilitās, -ātis f agility, rapidity; fickleness

mōbiliter adv rapidly

mōbilitō, -āre vt to make rapid

moderābilis adj moderate

moderāmen, -inis nt control; government

moderanter adv with control

moderātē adv with restraint

moderātim adv gradually

moderātiō, -ōnis f control, government; moderation; rules

moderātor, -ōris m controller, governor

moderātrīx, -īcis f mistress, controller

moderātus adj restrained, orderly

moderor, -ārī, -ātus vt, vi (with dat) to restrain, check; (with acc) to manage, govern, guide

modestē adv with moderation; humbly

modestia, -ae f temperate behaviour, discipline; humility

modestus adj sober, restrained; well-behaved, disciplined; modest, unassuming

modiālis adj holding a peck

modicē adv moderately; slightly

modicus adj moderate; middling, small, mean

modificātus adj measured

modius, -ī and **-iī** m corn measure, peck

modo adv only; at all, in any way; (with imp) just; (time) just now, a moment ago, in a moment ♦ conj if only; **nōn ~** not only; **non ~ ... sed** not only ... but also ...; **~ nōn** all but, almost; **~ ... ~** sometimes ... sometimes; **~ ... tum** at first ... then

modulātē adv melodiously

modulātor, -ōris m musician

modulātus adj played, measured

modulor, -ārī, -ātus vt to modulate, play, sing

modulus, -ī m measure

modus, -ī m measure; size; metre, music; way, method; limit, end; **ēius modī** such; **modō, in modum** like

moecha, -ae f adulteress

moechor, -ārī vi to commit adultery

moechus, -ī m adulterer

moenera etc see **mūnus**

moenia, -um ntpl defences, walls; town, stronghold

moeniō etc see **mūniō**

Moesī, -ōrum mpl people on lower Danube (now Bulgaria)

mola, -ae f millstone, mill; grains of spelt

molāris, -is m millstone; (tooth) molar

mōlēs, -is f mass, bulk, pile; dam, pier, massive structure; (fig) greatness, weight, effort, trouble

molestē adv see **molestus**

molestia, -ae f trouble, annoyance, worry; (style) affectation

molestus adj irksome, annoying; (style) laboured

mōlīmen, -inis nt exertion, labour; importance

mōlīmentum, -ī nt great effort

mōlior, -īrī, -ītus vt to labour at, work, build; to wield, move, heave; to undertake, devise, occasion ♦ vi to exert oneself, struggle

mōlītiō, -ōnis f laborious work

mōlītor, -ōris m builder

mollēscō, -ere vi to soften, become effeminate

molliculus adj tender

molliō, -īre, -īvī, -ītum vt to soften, make supple; to mitigate, make easier; to demoralize

mollis adj soft, supple; tender, gentle; (character) sensitive, weak, unmanly; (poetry) amatory; (opinion) changeable; (slope) easy

molliter adv softly, gently; calmly; voluptuously

mollitia, -ae, mollitiēs, -ēī f softness, suppleness; tenderness, weakness, effeminacy

mollitūdō, -inis f softness; susceptibility

molō, -ere vt to grind

Molossī, -ōrum mpl Molossians, people in Epirus

Molossicus, Molossus adj see **Molossī**

Molossis, -idis f country of the Molossians

Molossus, -ī m Molossian hound

mōly, -os nt a magic herb

mōmen, -inis nt movement, momentum

mōmentum, -ī nt movement; change; (time) short space, moment; (fig) cause, influence, importance; **nullīus mōmentī** unimportant

momordī perf of **mordeō**

Mona, -ae f Isle of Man; Anglesey

monachus, -ī m monk

monēdula, -ae f jackdaw

moneō, -ēre, -uī, -itum vt to remind, advise, warn; to instruct, foretell

monēris, -is f galley with one bank of oars

monērula etc see **monēdula**

monēta, -ae f mint; money; stamp

monīle, -is nt necklace, collar

monim- etc see **monum-**

monitiō, -ōnis f admonishing

monitor, -ōris m admonisher; prompter; teacher

monitum, -ī nt warning; prophecy

monitus, -ūs m admonition; warning

monogrammus adj shadowy

monopodium, -ī and **-iī** nt table with one leg

mōns, montis m mountain

mōnstrātor, -ōris m shower, inventor

mōnstrātus adj distinguished

mōnstrō, -āre, -āvī, -ātum vt to point out, show; to inform, instruct; to appoint; to denounce

mōnstrum, -ī nt portent, marvel; monster

mōnstruōsus adj unnatural

montānus *adj* mountainous, mountain- (*in cpds*), highland
monticola, -ae *m* highlander
montivagus *adj* mountain-roving
montuōsus, montōsus *adj* mountainous
monumentum, -ī *nt* memorial, monument; record
Mopsopius *adj* Athenian
mora¹, -ae *f* delay, pause; hindrance; space of time, sojourn; **moram facere** put off
mora², -ae *f* division of the Spartan army
mōrālis *adj* moral
morātor, -ōris *m* delayer
mōrātus *adj* mannered, of a nature; (*writing*) in character
morbidus *adj* unwholesome
morbus, -ī *m* illness, disease; distress
mordāciter *adv see* **mordāx**
mordāx, -ācis *adj* biting, sharp, pungent; (*fig*) snarling, carking
mordeō, -dēre, momordī, -sum *vt* to bite; to bite into, grip; (*cold*) to nip; (*words*) to sting, hurt, mortify
mordicus *adv* with a bite; (*fig*) doggedly
mōres *pl of* **mōs**
morētum, -ī *nt* salad
moribundus *adj* dying, mortal; deadly
mōrigeror, -ārī, -ātus *vi* (*with dat*) to gratify, humour
mōrigerus *adj* obliging, obedient
morior, -ī, -tuus *vi* to die; to decay, fade
moritūrus *fut p of* **morior**
mōrologus *adj* foolish
moror, -ārī, -ātus *vi* to delay, stay, loiter ♦ *vt* to detain, retard; to entertain; (*with neg*) to heed, object; **nihil morārī, nīl morārī** have no objection to; to not care for; to withdraw a charge against
mōrōsē *adv see* **mōrōsus**
mōrōsitās, -ātis *f* peevishness
mōrōsus *adj* peevish, difficult
Morpheus, -eos *m god of dreams*
mors, mortis *f* death; corpse; **mortem sibi cōnscīscere** commit suicide; **mortis poena** capital punishment
morsiuncula, -ae *f* little kiss
morsus¹ *ppp of* **mordeō ♦** *ntpl* little bits
morsus², -ūs *m* bite; grip; (*fig*) sting, vexation
mortālis *adj* mortal; transient; man-made ♦ *m* human being
mortālitās, -ātis *f* mortality, death
mortārium, -ī *and* **-iī** *nt* mortar
mortifer, -ī *adj* fatal
mortuus *ppa of* **morior ♦** *adj* dead ♦ *m* dead man
mōrum, -ī *nt* blackberry, mulberry
mōrus¹, -ī *f* black mulberry tree
mōrus² *adj* foolish ♦ *m* fool
mōs, mōris *m* nature, manner; humour, mood; custom, practice, law; (*pl*) behaviour, character, morals; **mōs māiōrum** national tradition; **mōrem gerere** oblige, humour; **mōre, in mōrem** like
Mosa, -ae *m* (*river*) Meuse
Mōsēs, -is *m* Moses
mōtiō, -ōnis *f* motion

mōtō, -āre *vt* to keep moving
mōtus¹ *ppp of* **moveō**
mōtus², -ūs *m* movement; dance, gesture; (*mind*) impulse, emotion; (POL) rising, rebellion; **terrae ~** earthquake
movēns, -entis *pres p of* **moveō ♦** *adj* movable ♦ *ntpl* motives
moveō, -ēre, mōvī, mōtum *vt* to move, set in motion; to disturb; to change; to dislodge, expel; to occasion, begin; (*opinion*) to shake; (*mind*) to affect, influence, provoke ♦ *vi* to move; **castra movēre** strike camp; **sē movēre** budge; to dance
mox *adv* presently, soon, later on; next
Mōysēs *see* **Mōsēs**
mūcidus *adj* snivelling; mouldy
Mūcius, -ī *m* Roman family name (*esp Scaevola, who burned his right hand before Porsena*)
mūcrō, -ōnis *m* point, edge; sword
mūcus, -ī *m* mucus
mūgilis, -is *m* mullet
muginor, -ārī *vi* to hesitate
mūgiō, -īre *vi* to bellow, groan
mūgītus, -ūs *m* lowing, roaring
mūla, -ae *f* she-mule
mulceō, -cēre, -sī, -sum *vt* to stroke, caress; to soothe, alleviate, delight
Mulciber, -is *and* **-ī** *m* Vulcan
mulcō, -āre, -āvī, -ātum *vt* to beat, ill-treat, damage
mulctra, -ae *f*, **mulctrārium, -ārī** *and* **-āriī**, **mulctrum, -ī** *nt* milkpail
mulgeō, -ēre, mulsī *vt* to milk
muliebris *adj* woman's, feminine; effeminate
muliebriter *adv* like a woman; effeminately
mulier, -is *f* woman; wife
mulierārius *adj* woman's
muliercula, -ae *f* girl
mulierōsitās, -ātis *f* fondness for women
mulierōsus *adj* fond of women
mūlīnus *adj* mulish
mūliō, -ōnis *m* mule driver
mūliōnius *adj* mule driver's
mullus, -ī *m* red mullet
mulsī *perf of* **mulceō**; **mulgeō**
mulsus¹ *ppp of* **mulceō**
mulsus² *adj* honeyed, sweet ♦ *nt* honey-wine, mead
multa, -ae *f* penalty, fine; loss
multangulus *adj* many-angled
multātīcius *adj* fine- (*in cpds*)
multātiō, -ōnis *f* fining
multēsimus *adj* very small
multicavus *adj* many-holed
multīcia, -ōrum *ntpl* transparent garments
multifāriam *adv* in many places
multifidus *adj* divided into many parts
multifōrmis *adj* of many forms
multiforus *adj* many-holed
multigeneris, multigenus *adj* of many kinds
multiiugis, multiiugus *adj* yoked together; complex
multiloquium, -ī *and* **-iī** *nt* talkativeness
multiloquus *adj* talkative

multimodīs *adv* variously

multiplex, -icis *adj* with many folds, tortuous; many-sided, manifold, various; *(comparison)* far greater; *(character)* fickle, sly

multiplicō, -āre, -āvī, -ātum *vt* to multiply, enlarge

multipotēns, -entis *adj* very powerful

multitūdō, -inis *f* great number, multitude, crowd

multivolus *adj* longing for much

multō¹ *adv* much, far, by far; *(time)* long

multō², -āre, -āvī, -ātum *vt* to punish, fine

multum *adv* much, very, frequently

multus *(compar* **plūs,** *superl* **plūrimus)** *adj* much, many; *(speech)* lengthy, tedious; *(time)* late; **multā nocte** late at night; **nē multa** to cut a long story short

mūlus, -ī *m* mule

Mulvius *adj* Mulvian *(a Tiber bridge above Rome)*

mundānus, -ī *m* world citizen

munditia, -ae, munditiēs, -ēī *f* cleanness; neatness, elegance

mundus¹ *adj* clean, neat, elegant; **in mundō esse** be in readiness

mundus², -ī *m* toilet gear; universe, world, heavens; mankind

mūnerigerulus, -ī *m* bringer of presents

mūnerō, -āre, mūneror, -ārī *vt* to present, reward

mūnia, -ōrum *ntpl* official duties

mūniceps, -ipis *m/f* citizen *(of a municipium),* fellow-citizen

mūnicipālis *adj* provincial

mūnicipium, -ī *and* **-iī** *nt* provincial town, burgh

mūnificē *adv see* **mūnificus**

mūnificentia, -ae *f* liberality

mūnificō, -āre *vt* to treat generously

mūnificus *adj* liberal

mūnīmen, -inis *nt* defence

mūnīmentum, -ī *nt* defencework, protection

mūniō, -īre, -iī, -ītum *vt* to fortify, secure, strengthen; *(road)* to build; *(fig)* to protect

mūnis *adj* ready to oblige

mūnītiō, -ōnis *f* building; fortification; *(river)* bridging

mūnītō, -āre *vt* (road) to open up

mūnītor, -ōris *m* sapper, builder

mūnus, -eris *nt* service, duty; gift; public show; entertainment; tax; *(funeral)* tribute; *(book)* work

mūnusculum, -ī *nt* small present

mūraena, -ae *f* a fish

mūrālis *adj* wall- *(in cpds),* mural, for fighting from or attacking walls

mūrex, -icis *m* purple-fish; purple dye, purple; jagged rock

muria, -ae *f* brine

murmillō, -ōnis *m* kind of gladiator

murmur, -is *nt* murmur, hum, rumbling, roaring

murmurillum, -ī *nt* low murmur

murmurō, -āre *vi* to murmur, rumble; to grumble

murra, -ae *f* myrrh

murreus *adj* perfumed; made of the stone called *murra*

murrina¹, -ae *f* myrrh wine

murrina², -ōrum *ntpl* murrine vases

murt- *etc see* **myrt-**

mūrus, -ī *m* wall; dam; defence

mūs, mūris *m/f* mouse, rat

Mūsa, -ae *f* goddess inspiring an art; poem; *(pl)* studies

mūsaeus *adj* poetic, musical

musca, -ae *f* fly

mūscipula, -ae *f,* **mūscipulum, -ī** *nt* mousetrap

mūscōsus *adj* mossy

mūsculus, -ī *m* mouse; muscle; *(MIL)* shed

mūscus, -ī *m* moss

mūsicē *adv* very pleasantly

mūsicus *adj* of music, of poetry ♦ *m* musician ♦ *f* music, culture ♦ *ntpl* music

mussitō, -āre *vi* to say nothing; to mutter ♦ *vt* to bear in silence

mussō, -āre *vt, vi* to say nothing, brood over; to mutter, murmur

mustāceum, -ī *nt,* **mustāceus, -ī** *m* wedding cake

mustēla, -ae *f* weasel

mustum, -ī *nt* unfermented wine, must; vintage

mūtābilis *adj* changeable, fickle

mūtābilitās, -ātis *f* fickleness

mūtātiō, -ōnis *f* change, alteration; exchange

mutilō, -āre, -āvī, -ātum *vt* to cut off, maim; to diminish

mutilus *adj* maimed

Mutina, -ae *f* town in N. Italy *(now Modena)*

Mutinēnsis *adj see* **Mutina**

mūtiō *etc see* **muttiō**

mūtō, -āre, -āvī, -ātum *vt* to shift; to change, alter; to exchange, barter ♦ *vi* to change; **mūtāta verba** figurative language

muttiō, -īre *vi* to mutter, mumble

mūtuātiō, -ōnis *f* borrowing

mūtuē *adv* mutually, in turns

mūtuitō, -āre *vt* to try to borrow

mūtuō *adv =* **mūtuē**

mūtuor, -ārī, -ātus *vt* to borrow

mūtus *adj* dumb, mute; silent, still

mūtuum, -ī *nt* loan

mūtuus *adj* borrowed, lent; mutual, reciprocal; **mūtuum dare** lend; **mūtuum sūmere** borrow; **mūtuum facere** return like for like

Mycēnae, -ārum *fpl* Agamemnon's capital in S. Greece

Mycēnaeus, Mycēnēnsis *adj see* **Mycēnae**

Mycēnis, -idis *f* Mycenaean woman; Iphigenia

Mygdonius *adj* Phrygian

myoparō, -ōnis *m* pirate galley

myrīca, -ae *f* tamarisk

Myrmidonēs, -um *mpl* followers of Achilles

Myrōn, -ōnis *m* famous Greek sculptor

myropōla, -ae *m* perfumer

myropōlium, -ī *and* **-iī** *nt* perfumer's shop

myrothēcium, -ī *and* **-iī** *nt* perfume-box

myrrh- *etc see* **murr-**

myrtētum, **-ī** *nt* myrtle grove
myrteus *adj* myrtle- (*in cpds*)
Myrtōum mare *sea N.W. of Crete*
myrtum, **-ī** *nt* myrtle-berry
myrtus, **-ī** *and* **-ūs** *f* myrtle
Mȳsia, **-iae** *f country of Asia Minor*
Mȳsius, **Mȳsios** *adj see* **Mȳsia**
mysta, **-ae** *m* priest of mysteries

mystagōgus, **-ī** *m* initiator
mystērium, **-ī** *and* **-iī** *nt* secret religion, mystery; secret
mysticus *adj* mystic
Mytilēnae, **-ārum** *fpl*, **Mytilēnē**, **-es** *f capital of Lesbos*
Mytilēnaeus *adj see* **Mytilēnae**
Mytilēnēnsis *adj see* **Mytilēnae**

Nn

nablium, -ī *and* **-iī** *nt kind of harp*
nactus *ppa of* **nancīscor**
nae *etc see* **nē¹**
naenia *etc see* **nēnia**
Naeviānus *adj see* **Naevius**
Naevius, -ī *m early Latin poet*
naevus, -ī *m mole (on the body)*
Nāias, -adis, Nāis, -dis *f water nymph, Naiad*
Nāicus *adj see* **Nāias**
nam *conj (explaining)* for; *(illustrating)* for example; *(transitional)* now; *(interrog)* but; *(enclitic)* an emphatic particle
namque *conj* for, for indeed, for example
nancīscor, -ī, nactus *and* **nanctus** *vt* to obtain, get; to come upon, find
nānus, -ī *m (with plants)* dwarf
Napaeae, -ārum *fpl* dell nymphs
nāpus, -ī *m* turnip
Narbō, -ōnis *m town in S. Gaul*
Narbōnēnsis *adj see* **Narbō**
narcissus, -ī *m* narcissus
nardus, -ī *f*, **nardum, -ī** *nt* nard, nard oil
nāris, -is *f* nostril; *(pl)* nose; *(fig)* sagacity, scorn
nārrābilis *adj* to be told
nārrātiō, -ōnis *f* narrative
nārrātor, -ōris *m* storyteller, historian
nārrātus, -ūs *m* narrative
nārrō, -āre, -āvī, -ātum *vt* to tell, relate, say; **male nārrāre** bring bad news
narthēcium, -ī *and* **-iī** *nt* medicine chest
nāscor, -scī, -tus *vi* to be born; to originate, grow, be produced
Nāsō, -ōnis *m surname of Ovid*
nassa, -ae *f wicker basket for catching fish; (fig)* snare
nasturtium, -ī *and* **-iī** *nt* cress
nāsus, -ī *m* nose
nāsūtē *adv* sarcastically
nāsūtus *adj* big-nosed; satirical
nāta, -ae *f* daughter
nātālicius *adj* of one's birthday, natal ◆ *ntpl* birthday party
nātālis *adj* of birth, natal ◆ *m* birthday ◆ *mpl* birth, origin
nātātiō, -ōnis *f* swimming
natātor, -ōris *m* swimmer
nātiō, -ōnis *f* tribe, race; breed, class
natis, -is *f (usu pl)* buttocks
nātīvus *adj* created; inborn, native, natural
natō, -āre *vi* to swim, float; to flow, overflow; *(eyes)* to swim, fail; *(fig)* to waver
nātrīx, -īcis *f* watersnake

nātū *abl m* by birth, in age; **grandis ~, māgnō ~** quite old; **māior ~** older; **māximus ~** oldest
nātūra, -ae *f* birth; nature, quality, character; natural order of things; the physical world; *(physics)* element; **rērum ~** Nature
nātūrālis *adj* by birth; by nature, natural
nātūrāliter *adv* by nature
nātus *ppa of* **nāscor** ◆ *m* son ◆ *adj* born, made (for); old, of age; **prō rē nātā, ē rē nātā** under the circumstances, as things are; **annōs vīgintī ~** 20 years old
nauarchus, -ī *m* captain
naucī: nōn ~ esse, nōn ~ facere, nōn ~ habēre to be worthless, consider worthless
nauclēricus *adj* skipper's
nauclērus, -ī *m* skipper
naufragium, -ī *and* **-iī** *nt* shipwreck, wreck; **~ facere** be shipwrecked
naufragus *adj* shipwrecked, wrecked; *(sea)* dangerous to shipping ◆ *m* shipwrecked man; *(fig)* ruined man
naulum, -ī *nt* fare
naumachia, -ae *f* mock sea fight
nausea, -ae *f* seasickness
nauseō, -āre *vi* to be sick; *(fig)* to disgust
nauseola, -ae *f* squeamishness
nauta, nāvita, -ae *m* sailor, mariner
nauticus *adj* nautical, sailors' ◆ *mpl* seamen
nāvālis *adj* naval, of ships ◆ *nt, ntpl* dockyard; rigging
nāvicula, -ae *f* boat
nāviculāria, -ae *f* shipping business
nāviculārius, -ī *and* **-iī** *m* ship-owner
nāvifragus *adj* dangerous
nāvigābilis *adj* navigable
nāvigātiō, -ōnis *f* voyage
nāviger, -ī *adj* ship-carrying
nāvigium, -ī *and* **-iī** *nt* vessel, ship
nāvigō, -āre, -āvī, -ātum *vi* to sail, put to sea ◆ *vt* to sail across, navigate
nāvis, -is *f* ship; **~ longa** warship; **~ mercātōria** merchantman; **~ onerāria** transport; **~ praetōria** flagship; **nāvem dēdūcere** launch; **nāvem solvere** set sail; **nāvem statuere** heave to; **nāvem subdūcere** beach; **nāvibus atque quadrīgīs** with might and main
nāvita *etc see* **nauta**
nāvitās, -ātis *f* energy
nāviter *adv* energetically; absolutely

137

nāvō, -āre vt to perform energetically; **operam nāvāre** be energetic; to come to the assistance (of)

nāvus adj energetic

Naxos, -ī f Aegean island (famous for wines and the story of Ariadne)

nē¹ interj truly, indeed

nē² adv not ◆ conj that not, lest; (fear) that; (purpose) so that … not, to avoid, to prevent

-ne enclitic introducing a question

Neāpolis, -is f Naples

Neāpolītānus adj see **Neāpolis**

nebula, -ae f mist, vapour, cloud

nebulō, -ōnis m idler, good-for-nothing

nebulōsus adj misty, cloudy

nec etc see **neque**

necdum adv and not yet

necessāriē, necessāriō adv of necessity, unavoidably

necessārius adj necessary, inevitable; indispensable; (kin) related ◆ m/f relative ◆ ntpl necessities

necesse adj (indecl) necessary, inevitable; needful

necessitās, -ātis f necessity, compulsion; requirement, want; relationship, connection

necessitūdō, -inis f necessity, need, want; connection; friendship; (pl) relatives

necessum etc see **necesse**

necne adv or not

necnōn adv also, besides

necō, -āre, -āvī, -ātum vt to kill, murder

necopīnāns, -antis adj unaware

necopīnātō adv see **necopīnātus**

necopīnātus adj unexpected

necopīnus adj unexpected; unsuspecting

nectar, -is nt nectar (the drink of the gods)

nectareus adj of nectar

nectō, -ctere, -xī and **-xuī, -xum** vt to tie, fasten, connect; to weave; (fig) to bind, enslave (esp for debt); to contrive, frame

nēcubi conj so that nowhere

nēcunde conj so that from nowhere

nēdum adv much less, much more

nefandus adj abominable, impious

nefāriē adv see **nefārius**

nefārius adj heinous, criminal

nefās nt indecl wickedness, sin, wrong ◆ interj horror!, shame!

nefāstus adj wicked; unlucky; (days) closed to public business

negātiō, -ōnis f denial

negitō, -āre vt to deny, refuse

neglēctiō, -ōnis f neglect

neglēctus¹ ppp of **neglegō**

neglēctus², -ūs m neglecting

neglegēns, -entis pres p of **neglegō** ◆ adj careless, indifferent

neglegenter adv carelessly

neglegentia, -ae f carelessness, neglect, coldness

neglegō, -egere, -ēxī, -ēctum vt to neglect, not care for; to slight, disregard; to overlook

negō, -āre, -āvī, -ātum vt, vi to say no; to say not, deny; to refuse, decline

negōtiālis adj business- (in cpds)

negōtiāns, -antis m businessman

negōtiātiō, -ōnis f banking business

negōtiātor, -ōris m businessman, banker

negōtiolum, -ī nt trivial matter

negōtior, -ārī, -ātus vi to do business, trade

negōtiōsus adj busy

negōtium, -ī and **-iī** nt business, work; trouble; matter, thing; **quid est negōtii?** what is the matter?

Nēlēius adj see **Nēleus¹**

Nēleus¹, -eī m father of Nestor

Nēleus² adj see **Nēleus¹**

Nemea¹, -ae f town in S. Greece, where Hercules killed the lion

Nemea², -ōrum ntpl Nemean Games

Nemeaeus adj Nemean

nēmō, -inis m/f no one, nobody ◆ adj no; ~ **nōn** everybody; **nōn** ~ many; ~ **ūnus** not a soul

nemorālis adj sylvan

nemorēnsis adj of the grove

nemoricultrīx, -īcis f forest dweller

nemorivagus adj forest-roving

nemorōsus adj well-wooded; leafy

nempe adv (confirming) surely, of course, certainly; (in questions) do you mean?

nemus, -ōris nt wood, grove

nēnia, -ae f dirge; incantation; song, nursery rhyme

neō, nēre, nēvī, nētum vt to spin; to weave

Neoptolemus, -ī m Pyrrhus (son of Achilles)

nepa, -ae f scorpion

nepōs, -ōtis m grandson; descendant; spendthrift

nepōtīnus, -ī m little grandson

neptis, -is f granddaughter

Neptūnius adj: ~ **hērōs** Theseus

Neptūnus, -ī m Neptune (god of the sea); sea

nēquam adj (indecl) worthless, bad

nēquāquam adv not at all, by no means

neque, nec adv not ◆ conj and not, but not; neither, nor; ~ … **et** not only not … but also

nequeō, -īre, -īvī, -ītum vi to be unable, cannot

nēquior, nēquissimus compar, superl of **nēquam**

nēquīquam adv fruitlessly, for nothing; without good reason

nēquiter adv worthlessly, wrongly

nēquitia, -ae, nēquitiēs, -ēi f worthlessness, badness

Nērēis, -ēidis f Nereid, sea nymph

Nērēius adj see **Nērēis**

Nēreus, -eī m a sea god; the sea

Nēritius adj of Neritos; Ithacan

Nēritos, -ī m island near Ithaca

Nerō, -ōnis m Roman surname (esp the emperor)

Nerōniānus adj see **Nerō**

nervōsē adv vigorously

nervōsus adj sinewy, vigorous

nervulī, -ōrum mpl energy

nervus, -ī m sinew; string; fetter, prison; (shield) leather; (pl) strength, vigour, energy

nesciō, -īre, -īvī and **-iī, -ītum** vt to not know, be ignorant of; to be unable; ~ **quis**, ~ **quid** somebody, something; ~ **an** probably

nescius *adj* ignorant, unaware; unable; unknown

Nestor, -oris *m Greek leader at Troy (famous for his great age and wisdom)*

neu *etc see* **nēve**

neuter, -rī *adj* neither; neuter

neutiquam *adv* by no means, certainly not

neutrō *adv* neither way

nēve, neu *conj* and not; neither, nor

nēvī *perf of* **neō**

nex, necis *f* murder, death

nexilis *adj* tied together

nexum, -ī *nt* personal enslavement

nexus¹ *ppp of* **nectō**

nexus², -ūs *m* entwining, grip; (LAW) bond, obligation (*esp enslavement for debt*)

nī *adv* not ♦ *conj* if not, unless; that not; **quid nī?** why not?

nīcētērium, -ī *and* **-iī** *nt* prize

nictō, -āre *vi* to wink

nīdāmentum, -ī *nt* nest

nīdor, -ōris *m* steam, smell

nīdulus, -ī *m* little nest

nīdus, -ī *m* nest; (*pl*) nestlings; (*fig*) home

niger, -rī *adj* black, dark; dismal, ill-omened; (*character*) bad

nigrāns, -antis *adj* black, dusky

nigrēscō, -ere *vi* to blacken, grow dark

nigrō, -āre *vi* to be black

nigror, -ōris *m* blackness

nihil, nīl *nt indecl* nothing ♦ *adv* not; ~ **ad nōs** it has nothing to do with us; ~ **est** it's no use; ~ **est quod** there is no reason why; ~ **nisi** nothing but, only; ~ **nōn** everything; **nōn** ~ something

nihilum, -ī *nt* nothing; **nihilī esse** be worthless; **nihilō minus** none the less

nīl, nīlum *see* **nihil, nihilum**

Nīliacus *adj* of the Nile; Egyptian

Nīlus, -ī *m* Nile; conduit

nimbifer, -ī *adj* stormy

nimbōsus *adj* stormy

nimbus, -ī *m* cloud, rain, storm

nimiō *adv* much, far

nīmīrum *adv* certainly, of course

nimis *adv* too much, very much; **nōn** ~ not very

nimium *adv* too, too much; very, very much

nimius *adj* too great, excessive; very great ♦ *nt* excess

ningit, ninguit, -ere *vi* it snows

ninguēs, -ium *fpl* snow

Nioba, -ae, Niobē, -ēs *f daughter of Tantalus (changed to a weeping rock)*

Niobēus *adj see* **Nioba**

Nīreus, -eī *and* **-eos** *m handsomest of the Greeks at Troy*

Nīsaeus, Nīsēius *adj see* **Nīsus**

Nīsēis, -edis *f* Scylla

nisi *conj* if not, unless; except, but

Nīsus, -ī *m father of Scylla*

nīsus¹ *ppa of* **nītor**

nīsus², -ūs *m* pressure, effort; striving, soaring

nītēdula, -ae *f* dormouse

nitēns, -entis *pres p of* **niteō** ♦ *adj* bright; brilliant, beautiful

niteō, -ēre *vi* to shine, gleam; to be sleek, be greasy; to thrive, look beautiful

nitēscō, -ere, nituī *vi* to brighten, shine, glow

nitidē *adv* magnificently

nitidiusculē *adv* rather more finely

nitidiusculus *adj* a little shinier

nitidus *adj* bright, shining; sleek; blooming; smart, spruce; (*speech*) refined

nitor, -ōris *m* brightness, sheen; sleekness, beauty; neatness, elegance

nītor, -tī, -sus *and* **-xus** *vi* to rest on, lean on; to press, stand firmly; to press forward, climb; to exert oneself, strive, labour; to depend on

nitrum, -ī *nt* soda

nivālis *adj* snowy

niveus *adj* of snow, snowy, snow-white

nivōsus *adj* snowy

nix, nivis *f* snow

nīxor, -ārī *vi* to rest on; to struggle

nīxus¹ *ppp of* **nītor**

nīxus², -ūs *m* pressure; labour

nō, nāre, nāvī *vi* to swim, float; to sail, fly

nōbilis *adj* known, noted, famous, notorious; noble, high-born; excellent

nōbilitās, -ātis *f* fame; noble birth; the nobility; excellence

nōbilitō, -āre, -āvī, -ātum *vt* to make famous or notorious

nocēns, -entis *pres p of* **noceō** ♦ *adj* harmful; criminal, guilty

noceō, -ēre, -uī, -itum *vi* (*with dat*) to harm, hurt

nocīvus *adj* injurious

noctifer, -ī *m* evening star

noctilūca, -ae *f* moon

noctivagus *adj* night-wandering

noctū *adv* by night

noctua, -ae *f* owl

noctuābundus *adj* travelling by night

nocturnus *adj* night- (*in cpds*), nocturnal

nōdō, -āre, -āvī, -ātum *vt* to knot, tie

nōdōsus *adj* knotty

nōdus, -ī *m* knot; knob; girdle; (*fig*) bond, difficulty

nōlō, -le, -uī *vt, vi* to not wish, be unwilling, refuse; **nōlī, nōlīte** do not

Nomas, -dis *m/f* nomad; Numidian

nōmen, -inis *nt* name; title; (COMM) demand, debt; (GRAM) noun; (*fig*) reputation, fame; account, pretext; ~ **dare**, ~ **profitērī** enlist; ~ **dēferre** accuse; **nōmina facere** enter the items of a debt

nōmenclātor, -ōris *m slave who told his master the names of people*

nōminātim *adv* by name, one by one

nōminātiō, -ōnis *f* nomination

nōminitō, -āre *vt* to usually name

nōminō, -āre, -āvī, -ātum *vt* to name, call; to mention; to make famous; to nominate; to accuse, denounce

nomisma, -tis *nt* coin

nōn *adv* not; no

Nōnae, -ārum *fpl* Nones (*7th day of March, May, July, October, 5th of other months*)

nōnāgēsimus *adj* ninetieth

nōnāgiēns, nōnāgiēs *adv* ninety times

nōnāgintā *num* ninety

nōnānus *adj* of the ninth legion

nōndum *adv* not yet

nōngentī, -ōrum *num* nine hundred

nonna, -ae *f* nun

nōnne *adv* do not?, is not? *etc;* (*indirect*) whether not

nōnnullus *adj* some

nōnnunquam *adv* sometimes

nōnus *adj* ninth ♦ *f* ninth hour

nōnusdecimus *adj* nineteenth

Nōricum, -ī *nt* country between the Danube and the Alps

Nōricus *adj see* **Nōricum**

nōrma, -ae *f* rule

nōs *pron* we, us; I, me

nōscitō, -āre *vt* to know, recognize; to observe, examine

nōscō, -scere, -vī, -tum *vt* to get to know, learn; to examine; to recognize, allow; (*perf*) to know

nōsmet *pron (emphatic)see* **nōs**

noster, -rī *adj* our, ours; for us; my; (*with names*) my dear, good old ♦ *m* our friend ♦ *mpl* our side, our troops; **nostrī, nostrum** of us

nostrās, -ātis *adj* of our country, native

nota, -ae *f* mark, sign, note; (*writing*) note, letter; (*pl*) memoranda, shorthand, secret writing; (*books*) critical mark, punctuation; (*wine, etc*) brand, quality; (*gesture*) sign; (*fig*) sign, token; (*censor's*) black mark; (*fig*) stigma, disgrace

notābilis *adj* remarkable; notorious

notābiliter *adv* perceptibly

notārius, -ī *and* **-iī** *m* shorthand writer; secretary

notātiō, -ōnis *f* marking; choice; observation; (*censor*) stigmatizing; (*words*) etymology

nōtēscō, -ere, nōtuī *vi* to become known

nothus *adj* bastard; counterfeit

nōtiō, -ōnis *f* (*LAW*) cognisance, investigation; (*PHILOS*) idea

nōtitia, -ae, nōtitiēs, -ēī *f* fame; acquaintance; (*PHILOS*) idea, preconception

notō, -āre, -āvī, -ātum *vt* to mark, write; to denote; to observe; to brand, stigmatize

nōtuī *perf of* **nōtēscō**

Notus, Notos, -ī *m* south wind

nōtus *ppp of* **nōscō** ♦ *adj* known, familiar; notorious ♦ *mpl* acquaintances

novācula, -ae *f* razor

novālis, -is *f,* **novāle, -is** *nt* fallow land; field; crops

novātrīx, -īcis *f* renewer

novē *adv* unusually

novellus *adj* young, fresh, new

novem *num* nine

November, -ris *adj* of November ♦ *m* November

novendecim *num* nineteen

novendiālis *adj* nine days'; on the ninth day

novēnī, -ōrum *adj* in nines; nine

Novēnsilēs, -ium *mpl* new gods

noverca, -ae *f* stepmother

novercālis *adj* stepmother's

nōvī *perf of* **nōscō**

novīcius *adj* new

noviēns, noviēs *adv* nine times

novissimē *adv* lately; last of all

novissimus *adj* latest, last, rear

novitās, -ātis *f* newness, novelty; strangeness

novō, -āre, -āvī, -ātum *vt* to renew, refresh; to change; (*words*) to coin; **rēs novāre** effect a revolution

novus *adj* new, young, fresh, recent; strange, unusual; inexperienced; **~ homō** upstart, first of his family to hold curule office; **novae rēs** revolution; **novae tabulae** cancellation of debts; **quid novī** what news?

nox, noctis *f* night; darkness, obscurity; **nocte, noctū** by night; **dē nocte** during the night

noxa, -ae *f* hurt, harm; offence, guilt; punishment

noxia, -ae *f* harm, damage; guilt, fault

noxius *adj* harmful; guilty

nūbēcula, -ae *f* cloudy look

nūbēs, -is *f* cloud; (*fig*) gloom; veil

nūbifer, -ī *adj* cloud-capped; cloudy

nūbigena, -ae *m* cloudborn, Centaur

nūbilis *adj* marriageable

nūbilus *adj* cloudy; gloomy, sad ♦ *ntpl* clouds

nūbō, -bere, -psī, -ptum *vi* (*women*) to be married

nucleus, -ī *m* nut, kernel

nūdius day since, days ago; **~ tertius** the day before yesterday

nūdō, -āre, -āvī, -ātum *vt* to bare, strip, expose; (*MIL*) to leave exposed; to plunder; (*fig*) to disclose, betray

nūdus *adj* naked, bare; exposed, defenceless; wearing only a tunic; (*fig*) destitute, poor; mere; unembellished, undisguised; **vestīmenta dētrahere nūdō** draw blood from a stone

nūgae, -ārum *fpl* nonsense, trifles; (*person*) waster

nūgātor, -ōris *m* silly creature, liar

nūgātōrius *adj* futile

nūgāx, -ācis *adj* frivolous

nūgor, -ārī, -ātus *vi* to talk nonsense; to cheat

nullus (*gen* **-īus,** *dat* **-ī**) *adj* no, none; not, not at all; non-existent, of no account ♦ *m/f* nobody

num *interrog particle* surely not?; (*indirect*) whether, if

Numa, -ae *m* second king of Rome

nūmen, -inis *nt* nod, will; divine will, power; divinity, god

numerābilis *adj* easy to count

numerātus *adj* in cash ♦ *nt* ready money

numerō¹, -āre, -āvī, -ātum *vt* to count, number; (*money*) to pay out; (*fig*) to reckon, consider as

numerō² *adv* just now, quickly, too soon

numerōsē *adv* rhythmically

numerōsus *adj* populous; rhythmical

numerus, -ī *m* number; many, numbers; (*MIL*) troop; (*fig*) a cipher; (*pl*) mathematics; rank, category, regard; rhythm, metre, verse; **in numerō esse, in numerō habērī** be reckoned as; **nullō numerō** of no account

Numida *adj see* **Numidae**

Numidae, -ārum *mpl* Numidians (*people of N. Africa*)

Numidia, **-iae** *f the country of the Numidians*
Numidicus *adj see* **Numidia**
Numitor, **-ōris** *m king of Alba (grandfather of Romulus)*
nummārius *adj* money- (*in cpds*), financial; mercenary
nummātus *adj* moneyed
nummulī, **-ōrum** *mpl* some money, cash
nummus, **-ī** *m* coin, money, cash; (*Roman coin*) sestertius; (*Greek coin*) two-drachma piece
numnam, **numne** *see* **num**
numquam *adv* never; ~ **nōn** always; **nōn** ~ sometimes
numquid (*question*) do you? does he? *etc*; (*indirect*) whether
nunc *adv* now; at present, nowadays; but as it is; ~ … ~ at one time … at another
nuncupātiō, **-ōnis** *f* pronouncing
nuncupō, **-āre**, **-āvī**, **-ātum** *vt* to call, name; to pronounce formally
nūndinae, **-ārum** *fpl* market day; market; trade
nūndinātiō, **-ōnis** *f* trading
nūndinor, **-ārī** *vi* to trade, traffic; to flock together ♦ *vt* to buy
nūndinum, **-ī** *nt* market time; **trīnum** ~ 17 days
nunq- *etc see* **numq-**
nūntiātiō, **-ōnis** *f* announcing
nūntiō, **-āre**, **-āvī**, **-ātum** *vt* to announce, report, tell

nūntius *adj* informative, speaking ♦ *m* messenger; message, news; injunction; notice of divorce ♦ *nt* message
nūper *adv* recently, lately
nūpsī *perf of* **nūbō**
nūpta, **-ae** *f* bride, wife
nūptiae, **-ārum** *fpl* wedding, marriage
nūptiālis *adj* wedding- (*in cpds*), nuptial
nurus, **-ūs** *f* daughter-in-law; young woman
nūsquam *adv* nowhere; in nothing, for nothing
nūtō, **-āre** *vi* to nod; to sway, totter, falter
nūtrīcius, **-ī** *m* tutor
nūtrīcō, **-āre**, **nūtrīcor**, **-ārī** *vt* to nourish, sustain
nūtrīcula, **-ae** *f* nurse
nūtrīmen, **-inis** *nt* nourishment
nūtrīmentum, **-ī** *nt* nourishment, support
nūtriō, **-īre**, **-īvī**, **-ītum** *vt* to suckle, nourish, rear, nurse
nūtrīx, **-īcis** *f* nurse, foster mother
nūtus, **-ūs** *m* nod; will, command; (*physics*) gravity
nux, **nucis** *f* nut; nut tree, almond tree
Nyctēis, **-idis** *f* Antiopa
nympha, **-ae**, **nymphē**, **-ēs** *f* bride; nymph; water
Nysa, **-ae** *f birthplace of Bacchus*
Nysaeus, **Nysaēis**, **Nysaius** *adj see* **Nysa**

Oo

ō *interj* (*expressing joy, surprise, pain, etc*) oh!; (*with voc*) O!

ob *prep* (*with acc*) in front of; for, on account of, for the sake of; **quam ob rem** accordingly

obaerātus *adj* in debt ♦ *m* debtor

obambulō, -āre *vi* to walk past, prowl about

obarmō, -āre *vt* to arm (*against*)

obarō, -āre *vt* to plough up

obc- *etc see* **occ-**

obdō, -ere, -idī, -itum *vt* to shut; to expose

obdormīscō, -īscere, -īvī *vi* to fall asleep ♦ *vt* to sleep off

obdūcō, -ūcere, -ūxī, -uctum *vt* to draw over, cover; to bring up; (*drink*) to swallow; (*time*) to pass

obductiō, -ōnis *f* veiling

obductō, -āre *vt* to bring as a rival

obductus *ppp of* **obdūcō**

obdūrēscō, -ēscere, -uī *vi* to harden; to become obdurate

obdūrō, -āre *vi* to persist, stand firm

obeō, -īre, -īvī *and* **-iī, -itum** *vi* to go to, meet; to die; (*ASTR*) to set ♦ *vt* to visit, travel over; to survey, go over; to envelop; (*duty*) to engage in, perform; (*time*) to meet; **diem obīre** die; (*LAW*) to appear on the appointed day

obequitō, -āre *vi* to ride up to

oberrō, -āre *vi* to ramble about; to make a mistake

obēsus *adj* fat, plump; coarse

ōbex, -icis *m/f* bolt, bar, barrier

obf- *etc see* **off-**

obg- *etc see* **ogg-**

obhaerēscō, -rēscere, -sī *vi* to stick fast

obiaceō, -ēre *vi* to lie over against

obiciō, -icere, -iēcī, -iectum *vt* to throw to, set before; (*defence*) to put up, throw against; (*fig*) to expose, give up; (*speech*) to taunt, reproach

obiectātiō, -ōnis *f* reproach

obiectō, -āre *vt* to throw against; to expose, sacrifice; to reproach; (*hint*) to let on

obiectus¹ *ppp of* **obiciō** ♦ *adj* opposite, in front of; exposed ♦ *ntpl* accusations

obiectus², -ūs *m* putting in the way, interposing

obīrātus *adj* angered

obiter *adv* on the way; incidentally

obitus¹ *ppp of* **obeō**

obitus², -ūs *m* death, ruin; (*ASTR*) setting; visit

obiūrgātiō, -ōnis *f* reprimand

obiūrgātor, -ōris *m* reprover

obiūrgātōrius *adj* reproachful

obiūrgitō, -āre *vt* to keep on reproaching

obiūrgō, -āre, -āvī, -ātum *vt* to scold, rebuke; to deter by reproof

oblanguēscō, -ēscere, -uī *vi* to become feeble

oblātrātrīx, -īcis *f* nagging woman

oblātus *ppp of* **offerō**

oblectāmentum, -ī *nt* amusement

oblectātiō, -ōnis *f* delight

oblectō, -āre, -āvī, -ātum *vt* to delight, amuse, entertain; to detain; (*time*) to spend pleasantly; **sē oblectāre** enjoy oneself

oblīdō, -dere, -sī, -sum *vt* to crush, strangle

obligātiō, -ōnis *f* pledge

obligō, -āre, -āvī, -ātum *vt* to tie up, bandage; to put under an obligation, embarrass; (*LAW*) to render liable, make guilty; to mortgage

oblimō, -āre *vt* to cover with mud

oblinō, -inere, -ēvī, -itum *vt* to smear over; to defile; (*fig*) to overload

oblīquē *adv* sideways; indirectly

oblīquō, -āre *vt* to turn aside, veer

oblīquus *adj* slanting, downhill; from the side, sideways; (*look*) askance, envious; (*speech*) indirect

oblīsus *ppp of* **oblīdō**

oblitēscō, -ere *vi* to hide away

oblitterō, -āre, -āvī, -ātum *vt* to erase, cancel; (*fig*) to consign to oblivion

oblitus *ppp of* **oblinō**

oblītus *ppa of* **oblīvīscor**

oblīviō, -ōnis *f* oblivion, forgetfulness

oblīviōsus *adj* forgetful

oblīvīscor, -vīscī, -tus *vt, vi* to forget

oblīvium, -ī *and* **-iī** *nt* forgetfulness, oblivion

oblocūtor, -ōris *m* contradicter

oblongus *adj* oblong

obloquor, -quī, -cūtus *vi* to contradict, interrupt; to abuse; (*music*) to accompany

obluctor, -ārī *vi* to struggle against

obmōlior, -īrī *vt* to throw up (*as a defence*)

obmurmurō, -āre *vi* to roar in answer

obmūtēscō, -ēscere, -uī *vi* to become silent; to cease

obnātus *adj* growing on

obnītor, -tī, -xus *vi* to push against, struggle; to stand firm, resist

obnīxē *adv* resolutely

obnīxus *ppa of* **obnītor** ♦ *adj* steadfast

obnoxiē *adv* slavishly

obnoxiōsus *adj* submissive

obnoxius *adj* liable, addicted; culpable; submissive, slavish; under obligation, indebted; exposed (*to danger*)

obnūbō, -bere, -psī, -ptum *vt* to veil, cover

obnūntiātiō, -ōnis *f* announcement of an adverse omen

obnūntiō, -āre *vt* to announce an adverse omen

oboediēns, -entis *pres p of* **oboediō** ♦ *adj* obedient

oboedienter *adv* readily

oboedientia, -ae *f* obedience

oboediō, -īre *vi* to listen; to obey, be subject to

oboleō, -ēre, -uī *vt* to smell of

oborior, -īrī, -tus *vi* to arise, spring up

obp- *etc see* **opp-**

obrēpō, -ere, -sī, -tum *vt, vi* to creep up to, steal upon, surprise; to cheat

obrētiō, -īre *vt* to entangle

obrigēscō, -ēscere, -uī *vi* to stiffen

obrogō, -āre, -āvī, -ātum *vt* to invalidate (*by making a new law*)

obruō, -ere, -ī, -tum *vt* to cover over, bury, sink; to overwhelm, overpower ♦ *vi* to fall to ruin

obrussa, -ae *f* test, touchstone

obrutus *ppp of* **obruō**

obsaepiō, -īre, -sī, -tum *vt* to block, close

obsaturō, -āre *vt* to sate, glut

obscaen- *etc see* **obscen-**

obscēnē *adv* indecently

obscēnitās, -ātis *f* indecency

obscēnus *adj* filthy; indecent; ominous

obscūrātiō, -ōnis *f* darkening, disappearance

obscūrē *adv* secretly

obscūritās, -ātis *f* darkness; (*fig*) uncertainty; (*rank*) lowliness

obscūrō, -āre, -āvī, -ātum *vt* to darken; to conceal, suppress; (*speech*) to obscure; (*pass*) to become obsolete

obscūrus *adj* dark, shady, hidden; (*fig*) obscure, indistinct; unknown, ignoble; (*character*) reserved

obsecrātiō, -ōnis *f* entreaty; public prayer

obsecrō, -āre *vt* to implore, appeal to

obsecundō, -āre *vi* to comply with, back up

obsēdī *perf of* **obsideō**

obsēp- *etc see* **obsaep-**

obsequēns, -entis *pres p of* **obsequor** ♦ *adj* compliant; (*gods*) gracious

obsequenter *adv* compliantly

obsequentia, -ae *f* complaisance

obsequiōsus *adj* complaisant

obsequium, -ī *and* **-iī** *nt* compliance, indulgence; obedience, allegiance

obsequor, -quī, -cūtus *vi* to comply with, yield to, indulge

obserō[1], -āre *vt* to bar, close

obserō[2], -erere, -ēvī, -itum *vt* to sow, plant; to cover thickly

observāns, -antis *pres p of* **observō** ♦ *adj* attentive, respectful

observantia, -ae *f* respect

observātiō, -ōnis *f* watching; caution

observitō, -āre *vt* to observe carefully

observō, -āre, -āvī, -ātum *vt* to watch, watch for; to guard; (*laws*) to keep, comply with; (*person*) to pay respect to

obses, -idis *m/f* hostage; guarantee

obsessiō, -ōnis *f* blockade

obsessor, -ōris *m* frequenter; besieger

obsessus *ppp of* **obsideō**

obsideō, -idēre, -ēdī, -essum *vt* to sit at, frequent; (*MIL*) to blockade, besiege; to block, fill, take up; to guard, watch for ♦ *vi* to sit

obsidiō, -ōnis *f* siege, blockade; (*fig*) imminent danger

obsidium, -ī *and* **-iī** *nt* siege, blockade; hostageship

obsīdō, -ere *vt* to besiege, occupy

obsignātor, -ōris *m* sealer; witness

obsignō, -āre, -āvī, -ātum *vt* to seal up; to sign and seal; (*fig*) to stamp

obsistō, -istere, -titī, -titum *vi* to put oneself in the way, resist

obsitus *ppp of* **obserō[2]**

obsolefīō, -fierī *vi* to wear out, become degraded

obsolēscō, -scere, -vī, -tum *vi* to wear out, become out of date

obsolētius *adv* more shabbily

obsolētus *ppa of* **obsolēscō** ♦ *adj* worn out, shabby; obsolete; (*fig*) ordinary, mean

obsōnātor, -ōris *m* caterer

obsōnātus, -ūs *m* marketing

obsōnium, -ī *and* **-iī** *nt* food eaten with bread (*usu fish*)

obsonō, -āre *vi* to interrupt

obsonō, -āre, obsōnor, -ārī *vi* to cater, buy provisions; to provide a meal

obsorbeō, -ēre *vt* to swallow, bolt

obstantia, -ium *ntpl* obstructions

obstetrīx, -īcis *f* midwife

obstinātē *adv* firmly, obstinately

obstinātiō, -ōnis *f* determination, stubbornness

obstinātus *adj* firm, resolute; stubborn

obstinō, -āre *vi* to be determined, persist

obstipēscō *etc see* **obstupēscō**

obstīpus *adj* bent, bowed, drawn back

obstitī *perf of* **obsistō; obstō**

obstō, -āre, -itī *vi* to stand in the way; to obstruct, prevent

obstrepō, -ere, -uī, -itum *vi* to make a noise; to shout against, cry down, molest ♦ *vt* to drown (*in noise*), fill with noise

obstrictus *ppp of* **obstringō**

obstringō, -ingere, -inxī, -ictum *vt* to bind up, tie round; (*fig*) to confine, hamper; to lay under an obligation

obstructiō, -ōnis *f* barrier

obstructus *ppp of* **obstruō**

obstrūdō, obtrūdō, -dere, -sī, -sum *vt* to force on to; to gulp down

obstruō, -ere, -xī, -ctum *vt* to build up against, block; to shut, hinder

obstupefaciō, -facere, -fēcī, -factum (*pass* **-fīō**) *vt* to astound, paralyse

obstupēscō, -ēscere, -uī *vi* to be astounded, paralysed

obstupidus *adj* stupefied

obsum, -esse, -fuī *vi* to be against, harm

obsuō, -uere, -uī, -ūtum *vt* to sew on, sew up

obsurdēscō, -ēscere, -uī *vi* to grow deaf; to turn a deaf ear

obsūtus *ppp of* **obsuō**

obtegō, -egere, -ēxī, -ēctum *vt* to cover over; to conceal

obtemperātiō, -ōnis *f* obedience

obtemperō, -āre, -āvī, -ātum *vi* (*with dat*) to comply with, obey

obtendō, -dere, -dī, -tum *vt* to spread over, stretch over against; to conceal; to make a pretext of

obtentus¹ *ppp of* **obtendō**; **obtineō**

obtentus², -ūs *m* screen; pretext

obterō, -erere, -rīvī, -rītum *vt* to trample on, crush; to disparage

obtestātiō, -ōnis *f* adjuring; supplication

obtestor, -ārī, -ātus *vt* to call to witness; to entreat

obtexō, -ere, -uī *vt* to overspread

obticeō, -ēre *vi* to be silent

obticēscō, -ēscere, -uī *vi* to be struck dumb

obtigī *perf of* **obtingō**

obtigō *see* **obtegō**

obtineō, -inēre, -inuī, -entum *vt* to hold, possess; to maintain; to gain, obtain ♦ *vi* to prevail, continue

obtingō, -ngere, -gī *vi* to fall to one's lot; to happen

obtorpēscō, -ēscere, -uī *vi* to become numb, lose feeling

obtorqueō, -quēre, -sī, -tum *vt* to twist about, wrench

obtrectātiō, -ōnis *f* disparagement

obtrectātor, -ōris *m* disparager

obtrectō, -āre *vt, vi* to detract, disparage

obtrītus *ppp of* **obterō**

obtrūdō *etc see* **obstrūdō**

obtruncō, -āre *vt* to cut down, slaughter

obtueor, -ērī, -or, -ī *vt* to gaze at, see clearly

obtulī *perf of* **offerō**

obtundō, -undere, -udī, -ūsum *and* **-ūnsum** *vt* to beat, thump; to blunt; (*speech*) to deafen, annoy

obturbō, -āre *vt* to throw into confusion; to bother, distract

obturgēscō, -ere *vi* to swell up

obtūrō, -āre *vt* to stop up, close

obtūsus, obtūnsus *ppp of* **obtundō** ♦ *adj* blunt; (*fig*) dulled, blurred, unfeeling

obtūtus, -ūs *m* gaze

obumbrō, -āre *vt* to shade, darken; (*fig*) to cloak, screen

obuncus *adj* hooked

obūstus *adj* burnt, hardened in fire

obvallātus *adj* fortified

obveniō, -enīre, -ēnī, -entum *vi* to come up; to fall to; to occur

obversor, -ārī *vi* to move about before; (*visions*) to hover

obversus *ppp of* **obvertō** ♦ *adj* turned towards ♦ *mpl* enemy

obvertō, -tere, -tī, -sum *vt* to direct towards, turn against

obviam *adv* to meet, against; ~ **ire** to go to meet

obvius *adj* in the way, to meet; opposite, against; at hand, accessible; exposed

obvolvō, -vere, -vī, -ūtum *vt* to wrap up, muffle up; (*fig*) to cloak

occaecō, -āre, -āvī, -ātum *vt* to blind, obscure, conceal; to benumb

occallēscō, -ēscere, -uī *vi* to grow a thick skin; to become hardened

occanō, -ere *vi* to sound the attack

occāsiō, -ōnis *f* opportunity, convenient time; (*MIL*) surprise

occāsiuncula, -ae *f* opportunity

occāsus, -ūs *m* setting; west; downfall, ruin

occātiō, -ōnis *f* harrowing

occātor, -ōris *m* harrower

occēdō, -ere *vi* to go up to

occentō, -āre *vt, vi* to serenade; to sing a lampoon

occēpī *perf of* **occipiō**

occepsō *archaic fut of* **occipiō**

occeptō, -āre *vt* to begin

occidēns, -entis *pres p of* **occidō** ♦ *m* west

occīdiō, -ōnis *f* massacre; **occīdiōne occīdere** annihilate

occidō, -idere, -idī, -āsum *vi* to fall; to set; to die, perish, be ruined

occīdō, -dere, -dī, -sum *vt* to fell; to cut down, kill; to pester

occiduus *adj* setting; western; failing

occinō, -ere, -uī *vi* to sing inauspiciously

occipiō, -ipere, -ēpī, -eptum *vt, vi* to begin

occipitium, -ī *and* **-iī** *nt* back of the head

occīsiō, -ōnis *f* massacre

occīsor, -ōris *m* killer

occīsus *ppp of* **occīdō**

occlāmitō, -āre *vi* to bawl

occlūdō, -dere, -sī, -sum *vt* to shut up; to stop

occō, -āre *vt* to harrow

occubō, -āre *vi* to lie

occulcō, -āre *vt* to trample down

occulō, -ere, -uī, -tum *vt* to cover over, hide

occultātiō, -ōnis *f* concealment

occultātor, -ōris *m* hider

occultē *adv* secretly

occultō, -āre, -āvī, -ātum *vt* to conceal, secrete

occultus *ppp of* **occulō** ♦ *adj* hidden, secret; (*person*) reserved, secretive ♦ *nt* secret, hiding

occumbō, -mbere, -buī, -bitum *vi* to fall, die

occupātiō, -ōnis *f* taking possession; business; engagement

occupātus *adj* occupied, busy

occupō, -āre, -āvī, -ātum *vt* to take possession of, seize; to occupy, take up; to surprise, anticipate; (*money*) to lend, invest

occurrō, -rere, -rī, -sum *vi* to run up to, meet; to attack; to fall in with; to hurry to; (*fig*) to obviate, counteract; (*words*) to object; (*thought*) to occur, suggest itself

occursātiō, -ōnis *f* fussy welcome

occursō, -āre *vi* to run to meet, meet; to oppose; (*thought*) to occur

occursus, -ūs *m* meeting

Ōceanītis, -ītidis *f* daughter of Ocean
Ōceanus, -ī *m* Ocean, *a stream encircling the earth;*
the Atlantic
ocellus, -ī *m* eye; darling, gem
ōcior, -ōris *adj* quicker, swifter
ōcius *adv* more quickly; sooner, rather; quickly
ocrea, -ae *f* greave
ocreātus *adj* greaved
Octāviānus *adj* of Octavius ♦ *m* Octavian (*a
surname of Augustus*)
Octāvius, -ī *m Roman family name (esp the emperor
Augustus; his father)*
octāvum *adv* for the eighth time
octāvus *adj* eighth ♦ *f* eighth hour
octāvusdecimus *adj* eighteenth
octiēns, octiēs *adv* eight times
octingentēsimus *adj* eight hundredth
octingentī, -ōrum *num* eight hundred
octipēs, -edis *adj* eight-footed
octō *num* eight
Octōber, -ris *adj* of October ♦ *m* October
octōgēnī, -ōrum *adj* eighty each
octōgēsimus *adj* eightieth
octōgiēns, octōgiēs *adv* eighty times
octōgintā *num* eighty
octōiugis *adj* eight together
octōnī, -ōrum *adj* eight at a time, eight each
octōphoros *adj (litter)* carried by eight bearers
octuplicātus *adj* multiplied by eight
octuplus *adj* eightfold
octussis, -is *m* eight asses
oculātus *adj* with eyes; visible; **oculātā diē
vēndere** sell for cash
oculus, -ī *m* eye; sight; *(plant)* bud; *(fig)* darling,
jewel; **oculōs adicere ad** glance at, covet; **ante
oculōs pōnere** imagine; **ex oculīs** out of sight;
esse in oculīs be in view; be a favourite
ōdī, -isse *vt* to hate, dislike
odiōsē *adv see* **odiōsus**
odiōsus *adj* odious, unpleasant
odium, -ī *and* **-iī** *nt* hatred, dislike, displeasure;
insolence; **odiō esse** be hateful, be disliked
odor, odōs, -ōris *m* smell, perfume, stench; *(fig)*
inkling, suggestion
odōrātiō, -ōnis *f* smelling
odōrātus¹ *adj* fragrant, perfumed
odōrātus², -ūs *m* sense of smell; smelling
odōrifer, -ī *adj* fragrant; perfume-producing
odōrō, -āre *vt* to perfume
odōror, -ārī, -ātus *vt* to smell, smell out; *(fig)* to
search out; to aspire to; to get a smattering of
odōrus *adj* fragrant; keen-scented
odōs *etc see* **odor**
Odrysius *adj* Thracian
Odyssēa, -ae *f* Odyssey
Oeagrius *adj* Thracian
Oebalia, -iae *f* Tarentum
Oebalidēs, -idae *m* Castor, Pollux
Oebalis, -idis *f* Helen
Oebalius *adj* Spartan
Oebalus, -ī *m king of Sparta*
Oedipūs, -odis *and* **-ī** *m king of Thebes; solver of
riddles*
oenophorum, -ī *nt* wine basket

Oenopia, -ae *f* Aegina
Oenotria, -ae *f* S.E. Italy
Oenotrius *adj* Italian
oestrus, -ī *m* gadfly; *(fig)* frenzy
Oeta, -ae, Oetē, -ēs *f mountain range in Thessaly,
associated with Hercules*
Oetaeus *adj see* **Oeta**
ofella, -ae *f* morsel
offa, -ae *f* pellet, lump; swelling
offectus *ppp of* **officiō**
offendō, -endere, -endī, -ēnsum *vt* to hit; to
hit on, come upon; to offend, blunder; to take
offence; to fail, come to grief
offēnsa, -ae *f* displeasure, enmity; offence,
injury
offēnsiō, -ōnis *f* stumbling; stumbling
block; misfortune, indisposition; offence,
displeasure
offēnsiuncula, -ae *f* slight displeasure; slight
check
offēnsō, -āre *vt, vi* to dash against
offēnsus¹ *ppp of* **offendō** ♦ *adj* offensive;
displeased ♦ *nt* offence
offēnsus², -ūs *m* shock; offence
offerō, -re, obtulī, oblātum *vt* to present, show;
to bring forward, offer; to expose; to cause,
inflict; **sē offerre** encounter
offerumenta, -ae *f* present
officīna, -ae *f* workshop, factory
officiō, -icere, -ēcī, -ectum *vi* to obstruct; to
interfere with; to hurt, prejudice
officiōsē *adv* courteously
officiōsus *adj* obliging; dutiful
officium, -ī *and* **-iī** *nt* service, attention,
ceremonial; duty, sense of duty; official duty,
function
offigō, -ere *vt* to fasten, drive in
offirmātus *adj* determined
offirmō, -āre *vt, vi* to persevere in
offlectō, -ere *vt* to turn about
offrēnātus *adj* checked
offūcia, -ae *f (cosmetic)* paint; *(fig)* trick
offulgeō, -gēre, -sī *vi* to shine on
offundō, -undere, -ūdī, -ūsum *vt* to pour out to;
to pour over; to spread; to cover, fill
offūsus *ppp of* **offundō**
ogganniō, -īre *vi* to growl at
oggerō, -ere *vt* to bring, give
Ōgygius *adj* Theban
oh *interj (expressing surprise, joy, grief)* oh!
ohē *interj (expressing surfeit)* stop!, enough!
oi *interj (expressing complaint, weeping)* oh!, oh dear!
oiei *interj (lamenting)* oh dear!
Oīleus, -eī *m father of the less famous Ajax*
olea, -ae *f* olive; olive tree
oleāginus *adj* of the olive tree
oleārius *adj* oil- *(in cpds)* ♦ *m* oil seller
oleaster, -rī *m* wild olive
olēns, -entis *pres p of* **oleō** ♦ *adj* fragrant;
stinking, musty
oleō, -ēre, -uī *vt, vi* to smell, smell of; *(fig)* to
betray
oleum, -ī *nt* olive oil, oil; wrestling school; **~ et
operam perdere** waste time and trouble

olfaciō, -facere, -fēcī, -factum vt to smell, scent

olfactō, -āre vt to smell at

olidus adj smelling, rank

ōlim adv once, once upon a time; at the time, at times; for a good while; one day (in the future)

olit- etc see **holit-**

olīva, -ae f olive, olive tree; olive branch, olive staff

olīvētum, -ī nt olive grove

olīvifer, -ī adj olive-bearing

olīvum, -ī nt oil; wrestling school; perfume

olla, -ae f pot, jar

olle, ollus see **ille**

olor, -ōris m swan

olōrīnus adj swan's

olus etc see **holus**

Olympia¹, -ae f site of the Greek games in Elis

Olympia², -ōrum ntpl Olympic Games

Olympiacus adj = **Olympicus**

Olympias, -adis f Olympiad, period of four years

Olympicus, Olympius adj Olympic

Olympionīcēs, -ae m Olympic winner

Olympus, -ī m mountain in N. Greece, abode of the gods; heaven

omāsum, -ī nt tripe; paunch

ōmen, -inis nt omen, sign; solemnity

ōmentum, -ī nt bowels

ōminor, -ārī, -ātus vt to forebode, prophesy

ōmissus ppp of **ōmittō** ◆ adj remiss

ōmittō, -ittere, -īsī, -issum vt to let go; to leave off, give up; to disregard, overlook; (speech) to pass over, omit

omnifer, -ī adj all-sustaining

omnigenus adj of all kinds

omnimodīs adv wholly

omnīnō adv entirely, altogether, at all; in general; (concession) to be sure, yes; (number) in all, just; ~ **nōn** not at all

omniparēns, -entis adj mother of all

omnipotēns, -entis adj almighty

omnis adj all, every, any; every kind of; the whole of ◆ nt the universe ◆ mpl everybody ◆ ntpl everything

omnituēns, -entis adj all-seeing

omnivagus adj roving everywhere

omnivolus adj willing everything

onager, -rī m wild ass

onerārius adj (beast) of burden; (ship) transport

onerō, -āre, -āvī, -ātum vt to load, burden; (fig) to overload, oppress; to aggravate

onerōsus adj heavy, burdensome, irksome

onus, -eris nt load, burden, cargo; (fig) charge, difficulty

onustus adj loaded, burdened; (fig) filled

onyx, -chis m/f onyx; onyx box

opācitās, -ātis f shade

opācō, -āre vt to shade

opācus adj shady; dark

ope abl of **ops**

opella, -ae f light work, small service

opera, -ae f exertion, work; service; care, attention; leisure, time; (person) workman, hired rough; **operam dare** pay attention;

do one's best; **operae pretium** worth while; **operā meā** thanks to me

operārius adj working ◆ m workman

operculum, -ī nt cover, lid

operīmentum, -ī nt covering

operiō, -īre, -uī, -tum vt to cover; to close; (fig) to overwhelm, conceal

operor, -ārī, -ātus vi to work, take pains, be occupied

operōsē adv painstakingly

operōsus adj active, industrious; laborious, elaborate

opertus ppp of **operiō** ◆ adj covered, hidden ◆ nt secret

opēs pl of **ops**

opicus adj barbarous, boorish

opifer, -ī adj helping

opifex, -icis m/f maker; craftsman, artisan

ōpiliō, -ōnis m shepherd

opīmitās, -ātis f abundance

opīmus adj rich, fruitful, fat; copious, sumptuous; (style) overloaded; **spolia opīma** spoils of an enemy commander killed by a Roman general

opīnābilis adj conjectural

opīnātiō, -ōnis f conjecture

opīnātor, -ōris m conjecturer

opīnātus, -ūs m supposition

opīniō, -ōnis f opinion, conjecture, belief; reputation, esteem; rumour; **contrā opīniōnem, praeter opīniōnem** contrary to expectation

opīniōsus adj dogmatic

opīnor, -ārī, -ātus vi to think, suppose, imagine ◆ adj imagined

opiparē adv see **opiparus**

opiparus adj rich, sumptuous

opitulor, -ārī, -ātus vi (with dat) to help

oportet, -ēre, -uit vt (impers) ought, should

oppēdō, -ere vi to insult

opperior, -īrī, -tus vt, vi to wait, wait for

oppetō, -ere, -īvī, -ītum vt to encounter; to die

oppidānus adj provincial ◆ mpl townsfolk

oppidō adv quite, completely, exactly

oppidulum, -ī nt small town

oppidum, -ī nt town

oppignerō, -āre vt to pledge

oppīlō, -āre vt to stop up

oppleō, -ēre, -ēvī, -ētum vt to fill, choke up

oppōnō, -ōnere, -osuī, -ositum vt to put against, set before; to expose; to present; (argument) to adduce, reply, oppose; (property) to pledge, mortgage

opportūnē adv opportunely

opportūnitās, -ātis f suitableness, advantage; good opportunity

opportūnus adj suitable, opportune; useful; exposed

oppositiō, -ōnis f opposing

oppositus¹ ppp of **oppōnō** ◆ adj against, opposite

oppositus², -ūs m opposing

oppressiō, -ōnis f violence; seizure; overthrow

oppressus¹ ppp of **opprimō**

oppressus², -ūs m pressure

opprimō, -imere, -essī, -essum *vt* to press down, crush; to press together, close; to suppress, overwhelm, overthrow; to surprise, seize

opprobrium, -ī *and* **-iī** *nt* reproach, disgrace, scandal

opprobrō, -āre *vt* to taunt

oppsuī *perf of* **oppōnō**

oppugnātiō, -ōnis *f* attack, assault

oppugnātor, -ōris *m* assailant

oppugnō, -āre, -āvī, -ātum *vt* to attack, assault

Ops *goddess of plenty*

ops, opis *f* power, strength; help; (*pl*) resources, wealth

ops- *etc see* **obs-**

optābilis *adj* desirable

optātiō, -ōnis *f* wish

optātus *adj* longed for ♦ *nt* wish; **optātō** according to one's wish

optimās, -ātis *adj* aristocratic ♦ *mpl* the nobility

optimē *adv* best, very well; just in time

optimus *adj* best, very good; excellent; **optimō iūre** deservedly

optiō, -ōnis *f* choice ♦ *m* assistant

optīvus *adj* chosen

optō, -āre, -āvī, -ātum *vt* to choose; to wish for

optum- *etc see* **optim-**

opulēns, -entis *adj* rich

opulentē, -er *adv* sumptuously

opulentia, -ae *f* wealth; power

opulentō, -āre *vt* to enrich

opulentus *adj* rich, sumptuous, powerful

opus, -eris *nt* work, workmanship; (*art*) work, building, book; (*MIL*) siege work; (*colloq*) business; (*with* **esse**) need; **virō ~ est** a man is needed; **māgnō opere** much, greatly

opusculum, -ī *nt* little work

ōra, -ae *f* edge, boundary; coast; country, region; (*NAUT*) hawser

ōrāculum, -ī *nt* oracle, prophecy

ōrātiō, -ōnis *f* speech, language; a speech, oration; eloquence; prose; emperor's message; **ōrātiōnem habēre** deliver a speech

ōrātiuncula, -ae *f* short speech

ōrātor, -ōris *m* speaker, spokesman, orator

ōrātōrius *adj* oratorical

ōrātrīx, -īcis *f* suppliant

ōrātus, -ūs *m* request

orbātor, -ōris *m* bereaver

orbiculātus *adj* round

orbis, -is *m* circle, ring, disc, orbit; world; (*movement*) cycle, rotation; (*style*) rounding off; **~ lacteus** Milky Way; **~ signifer** Zodiac; **~ fortūnae** wheel of Fortune; **~ terrārum** the earth, world; **in orbem cōnsistere** form a circle; **in orbem īre** go the rounds

orbita, -ae *f* rut, track, path

orbitās, -ātis *f* childlessness, orphanhood, widowhood

orbitōsus *adj* full of ruts

orbō, -āre, -āvī, -ātum *vt* to bereave, orphan, make childless

orbus *adj* bereaved, orphan, childless; destitute

orca, -ae *f* vat

orchas, -dis *f* kind of olive

orchēstra, -ae *f* senatorial seats (*in the theatre*)

Orcus, -ī *m* Pluto; the lower world; death

ōrdinārius *adj* regular

ōrdinātim *adv* in order, properly

ōrdinātiō, -ōnis *f* orderly arrangement

ōrdinātus *adj* appointed

ōrdinō, -āre, -āvī, -ātum *vt* to arrange, regulate, set in order

ōrdior, -dīrī, -sus *vt, vi* to begin, undertake

ōrdō, -inis *m* line, row, series; order, regularity, arrangement; (*MIL*) rank, line, company; (*pl*) captains; (*building*) course, layer; (*seats*) row; (*POL*) class, order, station; **ex ōrdine** in order, in one's turn; one after the other; **extrā ōrdinem** irregularly, unusually

Oreās, -dis *f* mountain nymph

Orestēs, -is *and* **-ae** *m son of Agamemnon, whom he avenged by killing his mother*

Orestēus *adj see* **Orestēs**

orexis, -is *f* appetite

organum, -ī *nt* instrument, organ

orgia, -ōrum *ntpl* Bacchic revels; orgies

orichalcum, -ī *nt* copper ore, brass

ōricilla, -ae *f* lobe

oriēns, -entis *pres p of* **orior** ♦ *m* morning; east

orīgō, -inis *f* beginning, source; ancestry, descent; founder

Ōrīōn, -onis *and* **-ōnis** *m mythical hunter and constellation*

orior, -īrī, -tus *vi* to rise; to spring, descend

oriundus *adj* descended, sprung

ōrnāmentum, -ī *nt* equipment, dress; ornament, decoration; distinction, pride of

ōrnātē *adv* elegantly

ōrnātus¹ *ppp of* **ōrnō** ♦ *adj* equipped, furnished; embellished, excellent

ōrnātus², -ūs *m* preparation; dress, equipment; embellishment

ōrnō, -āre, -āvī, -ātum *vt* to fit out, equip, dress, prepare; to adorn, embellish, honour

ornus, -ī *f* manna ash

ōrō, -āre, -āvī, -ātum *vt* to speak, plead; to beg, entreat; to pray

Orontēs, -is *and* **-ī** *m river of Syria*

Orontēus *adj* Syrian

Orpheus, -eī *and* **-eos** (*acc* **-ea**) *m legendary Thracian singer, who went down to Hades for Eurydice*

Orphēus, Orphēicus *adj see* **Orpheus**

ōrsus¹ *ppa of* **ōrdior** ♦ *ntpl* beginning; utterance

ōrsus², -ūs *m* beginning

ortus¹ *ppa of* **orior** ♦ *adj* born, descended

ortus², -ūs *m* rising; east; origin, source

Ortygia, -ae, Ortygiē, -ēs *f* Delos

Ortygius *adj see* **Ortygia**

oryx, -gis *m* gazelle

oryza, -ae *f* rice

os, ossis *nt* bone; (*fig*) very soul

ōs, ōris *nt* mouth; face; entrance, opening; effrontery; **ūnō ōre** unanimously; **in ōre esse** be talked about; **quō ōre redībō** how shall I have the face to go back?

oscen, -inis *m* bird of omen

ōscillum, -ī *nt* little mask

ōscitāns, **-antis** *pres p of* **ōscitō** ♦ *adj* listless, drowsy

ōscitanter *adv* half-heartedly

ōscitō, **-āre**, **ōscitor**, **-ārī** *vi* to yawn, be drowsy

ōsculātiō, **-ōnis** *f* kissing

ōsculor, **-ārī**, **-ātus** *vt* to kiss; to make a fuss of

ōsculum, **-ī** *nt* sweet mouth; kiss

Oscus *adj* Oscan

Osīris, **-is** *and* **-idis** *m Egyptian god, husband of Isis*

Ossa, **-ae** *f mountain in Thessaly*

osseus *adj* bony

ossifraga, **-ae** *f* osprey

ostendō, **-dere**, **-dī**, **-tum** *vt* to hold out, show, display; to expose; to disclose, reveal; (*speech*) to say, make known

ostentātiō, **-ōnis** *f* display; showing off, ostentation; pretence

ostentātor, **-ōris** *m* displayer, boaster

ostentō, **-āre** *vt* to hold out, proffer, exhibit; to show off, boast of; to make known, indicate

ostentum, **-ī** *nt* portent

ostentus¹ *ppp of* **ostendō**

ostentus², **-ūs** *m* display, appearance; proof

Ōstia, **-ae** *f*, **Ōstia**, **-ōrum** *ntpl port at the Tiber mouth*

ōstiārium, **-ī** *and* **-iī** *nt* door tax

ōstiātim *adv* from door to door

Ōstiēnsis *adj see* **Ōstia**

ōstium, **-ī** *and* **-iī** *nt* door; entrance, mouth

ostrea, **-ae** *f* oyster

ostreōsus *adj* rich in oysters

ostreum, **-ī** *nt* oyster

ostrifer, **-ī** *adj* oyster-producing

ostrīnus *adj* purple

ostrum, **-ī** *nt* purple; purple dress *or* coverings

ōsus, **ōsūrus** *ppa and fut p of* **ōdī**

Othō, **-ōnis** *m author of a law giving theatre seats to Equites; Roman emperor after Galba*

Othōniānus *adj see* **Othō**

ōtiolum, **-ī** *nt* bit of leisure

ōtior, **-ārī** *vi* to have a holiday, be idle

ōtiōsē *adv* leisurely; quietly; fearlessly

ōtiōsus *adj* at leisure, free; out of public affairs; neutral, indifferent; quiet, unexcited; (*things*) free, idle ♦ *m* private citizen, civilian

ōtium, **-ī** *and* **-iī** *nt* leisure, time (for), idleness, retirement; peace, quiet

ovātiō, **-ōnis** *f* minor triumph

ovīle, **-is** *nt* sheep fold, goat fold

ovillus *adj* of sheep

ovis, **-is** *f* sheep

ovō, **-āre** *vi* to rejoice; to celebrate a minor triumph

ōvum, **-ī** *nt* egg

Pp

pābulātiō, -ōnis f foraging
pābulātor, -ōris m forager
pābulor, -ārī vi to forage
pābulum, -ī nt food, fodder
pācālis adj of peace
pācātus adj peaceful, tranquil ♦ nt friendly country
Pachӯnum, -ī nt S.E. point of Sicily (now Cape Passaro)
pācifer, -ī adj peace-bringing
pācificātiō, -ōnis f peacemaking
pācificātor, -ōris m peacemaker
pācificātōrius adj peacemaking
pācificō, -āre vi to make a peace ♦ vt to appease
pācificus adj peacemaking
pacīscor, -īscī, -tus vi to make a bargain, agree ♦ vt to stipulate for; to barter
pācō, -āre, -āvī, -ātum vt to pacify, subdue
pactiō, -ōnis f bargain, agreement, contract; collusion; (words) formula
Pactōlus, -ī m river of Lydia (famous for its gold)
pactor, -ōris m negotiator
pactum, -ī nt agreement, contract
pactus ppa of **pacīscor** ♦ adj agreed, settled; betrothed
Pācuvius, -ī m Latin tragic poet
Padus, -ī m (river) Po
paeān, -ānis m healer, epithet of Apollo; hymn of praise, shout of joy; (metre) paeon
paedagōgus, -ī m slave who took children to school
paedor, -ōris m filth
paelex, -icis f mistress, concubine
paelicātus, -ūs m concubinage
Paelignī, -ōrum mpl people of central Italy
Paelignus adj see **Paelignī**
paene adv almost, nearly
paenīnsula, -ae f peninsula
paenitendus adj regrettable
paenitentia, -ae f repentance
paenitet, -ēre, -uit vt, vi (impers) to repent, regret, be sorry; to be dissatisfied; **an ~ is** it not enough?
paenula, -ae f travelling cloak
paenulātus adj wearing a cloak
paeōn, -ōnis m metrical foot of one long and three short syllables
paeōnius adj healing
Paestānus adj see **Paestum**
Paestum, -ī nt town in S. Italy
paetulus adj with a slight cast in the eye
paetus adj with a cast in the eye

pāgānus adj rural ♦ m villager, yokel
pāgātim adv in every village
pāgella, -ae f small page
pāgina, -ae f (book) page, leaf
pāginula, -ae f small page
pāgus, -ī m village, country district; canton
pāla, -ae f spade; (ring) bezel
palaestra, -ae f wrestling school, gymnasium; exercise, wrestling; (RHET) exercise, training
palaestricē adv in gymnastic fashion
palaestricus adj of the wrestling school
palaestrīta, -ae m head of a wrestling school
palam adv openly, publicly, well-known ♦ prep (with abl) in the presence of
Palātīnus adj Palatine; imperial
Palātium, -ī nt Palatine Hill (in Rome); palace
palātum, -ī nt palate; taste, judgment
palea, -ae f chaff
paleāria, -ium ntpl dewlap
Palēs, -is f goddess of shepherds
Palīlis adj of Pales ♦ ntpl festival of Pales
palimpsēstus, -ī m palimpsest
Palinūrus, -ī m pilot of Aeneas; promontory in S. Italy
paliūrus, -ī m Christ's thorn
palla, -ae f woman's robe; tragic costume
Palladium, -dī nt image of Pallas
Palladius adj of Pallas
Pallantēus adj see **Pallas**
Pallas, -dis and **-dos** f Athene, Minerva; oil; olive tree
Pallās, -antis m ancestor or son of Evander
pallēns, -entis pres p of **palleō** ♦ adj pale; greenish
palleō, -ēre, -uī vi to be pale or yellow; to fade; to be anxious
pallēscō, -escere, -uī vi to turn pale, turn yellow
palliātus adj wearing a Greek cloak
pallidulus adj palish
pallidus adj pale, pallid, greenish; in love
palliolum, -ī nt small cloak, cape, hood
pallium, -ī and **-iī** nt coverlet; Greek cloak
pallor, -ōris m paleness, fading; fear
palma, -ae f (hand) palm, hand; (oar) blade; (tree) palm, date; branch; (fig) prize, victory, glory
palmāris adj excellent
palmārius adj prizewinning
palmātus adj palm-embroidered
palmes, -itis m pruned shoot, branch
palmētum, -ī nt palm grove
palmifer, -ī adj palm-bearing**

palmōsus *adj* palm-clad
palmula, -ae *f* oar blade
pālor, -ārī, -ātus *vi* to wander about, straggle
palpātiō, -ōnis *f* flatteries
palpātor, -ōris *m* flatterer
palpebra, -ae *f* eyelid
palpitō, -āre *vi* to throb, writhe
palpō, -āre, palpor, -ārī *vt* to stroke; to coax, flatter
palpus, -ī *m* coaxing
palūdāmentum, -ī *nt* military cloak
palūdātus *adj* in a general's cloak
palūdōsus *adj* marshy
palumbēs, -is *m/f* wood pigeon
pālus, -ī *m* stake, pale
palūs, -ūdis *f* marsh, pool, lake
palūster, -ris *adj* marshy
pampineus *adj* of vineshoots
pampinus, -ī *m* vineshoot
Pān, -ānos (*acc* **-āna**) *m* Greek god of shepherds, hills and woods, esp associated with Arcadia
panacēa, -ae *f* a herb supposed to cure all diseases
Panaetius, -ī *m* Stoic philosopher
Panchāeus, Panchāāius *adj see* **Panchāia**
Panchāia, -iae *f* part of Arabia
panchrēstus *adj* good for everything
pancratium, -i *and* **-iī** *nt* all-in boxing and wrestling match
pandiculor, -āre *vi* to stretch oneself
Pandīōn, -onis *m* king of Athens, father of Procne and Philomela
Pandīonius *adj see* **Pandīōn**
pandō, -ere, -ī, pānsum *and* **passum** *vt* to spread out, stretch, extend; to open; (*fig*) to disclose, explain
pandus *adj* curved, bent
pangō, -ere, panxī *and* **pepigī, pāctum** *vt* to drive in, fasten; to make, compose; to agree, settle
pānicula, -ae *f* tuft
pānicum, -ī *nt* Italian millet
pānis, -is *m* bread, loaf
Pāniscus, -ī *m* little Pan
panniculus, -ī *m* rag
Pannonia, -ae *f* country on the middle Danube
Pannonius *adj see* **Pannonia**
pannōsus *adj* ragged
pannus, -ī *m* piece of cloth, rag, patch
Panormus, -ī *f* town in Sicily (now Palermo)
pānsa *adj* splayfoot
pānsus *ppp of* **pandō**
panthēra, -ae *f* panther
Panthoidēs, -ae *m* Euphorbus
Panthūs, -ī *m* priest of Apollo at Troy
panticēs, -um *mpl* bowels; sausages
panxī *perf of* **pangō**
papae *interj* (*expressing wonder*) ooh!
pāpas, -ae *m* tutor
papāver, -is *nt* poppy
papāvereus *adj see* **papāver**
Paphius *adj see* **Paphos**
Paphos, -ī *f* town in Cyprus, sacred to Venus
pāpiliō, -ōnis *m* butterfly
papilla, -ae *f* teat, nipple; breast

pappus, -ī *m* woolly seed
papula, -ae *f* pimple
papȳrifer, -ī *adj* papyrus-bearing
papȳrum, -ī *nt* papyrus; paper
papȳrus, -ī *m/f* papyrus; paper
pār, paris *adj* equal, like; a match for; proper, right ♦ *m* peer, partner, companion ♦ *nt* pair; **pār parī respondēre** return like for like; **parēs cum paribus facillimē congregantur** birds of a feather flock together; **lūdere pār impār** play at evens and odds
parābilis *adj* easy to get
parasīta, -ae *f* woman parasite
parasītaster, -rī *m* sorry parasite
parasīticus *adj* of a parasite
parasītus, -ī *m* parasite, sponger
parātē *adv* with preparation; carefully; promptly
parātiō, -ōnis *f* trying to get
paratragoedō, -āre *vi* to talk theatrically
parātus¹ *ppp of* **parō** ♦ *adj* ready; equipped; experienced
parātus², -ūs *m* preparation, equipment
Parca, -ae *f* Fate
parcē *adv* frugally; moderately
parcō, -cere, pepercī, -sum *vt, vi* (with dat) to spare, economize; to refrain from, forgo; (with inf) to forbear, stop
parcus *adj* sparing, thrifty; niggardly, scanty; chary
pardus, -ī *m* panther
pārēns, -entis *pres p of* **pāreō** ♦ *adj* obedient ♦ *mpl* subjects
parēns, -entis *m/f* parent, father, mother; ancestor; founder
parentālis *adj* parental ♦ *ntpl* festival in honour of dead ancestors and relatives
parentō, -āre *vi* to sacrifice in honour of dead parents or relatives; to avenge (with the death of another)
pāreō, -ēre, -uī, -itum *vi* to be visible, be evident; (with dat) to obey, submit to, comply with; **pāret** it is proved
pariēs, -etis *m* wall
parietinae, -ārum *fpl* ruins
Parīlia, -ium *ntpl* festival of Pales
parīlis *adj* equal
pariō, -ere, peperī, -tum *vt* to give birth to; to produce, create, cause; to procure
Paris, -idis *m* son of Priam, abductor of Helen
pariter *adv* equally, alike; at the same time, together
paritō, -āre *vt* to get ready
Parius *adj see* **Paros**
parma, -ae *f* shield, buckler
parmātus *adj* armed with a buckler
parmula, -ae *f* little shield
Parnāsis, -idis *adj* Parnassian
Parnāsius *adj* = **Parnāsis**
Parnāsus, -ī *m* Mount Parnassus in central Greece, sacred to the Muses
parō, -āre, -āvī, -ātum *vt* to prepare, get ready, provide; to intend, set about; to procure, get, buy; to arrange
parocha, -ae *f* provision of necessaries (to officials travelling)

parochus, **-ī** *m* purveyor; host
paropsis, **-dis** *f* dish
Paros, **-ī** *f Aegean island (famous for white marble)*
parra, **-ae** *f* owl
Parrhasis, **-idis**, **Parrhasius** *adj* Arcadian
parricīda, **-ae** *m* parricide, assassin; traitor
parricīdium, **-ī** *and* **-iī** *nt* parricide, murder; high treason
pars, **-tis** *f* part, share, fraction; party, side; direction; respect, degree; *(with pl verb)* some; *(pl)* stage part, role; duty, function; **māgna ~** the majority; **māgnam partem** largely; **in eam partem** in that direction, on that side, in that sense; **nullā parte** not at all; **omnī parte** entirely; **ex parte** partly; **ex alterā parte** on the other hand; **ex māgnā parte** to a large extent; **prō parte** to the best of one's ability; **partēs agere** play a part; **duae partēs** two-thirds; **trēs partēs** three-fourths; **multīs partibus** a great deal
parsimōnia, **-ae** *f* thrift, frugality
parthenicē, **-ēs** *f a plant*
Parthenopē, **-ēs** *f old name of Naples*
Parthenopēius *adj see* **Parthenopē**
Parthī, **-ōrum** *mpl* Parthians (Rome's great enemy in the East)
Parthicus, **Parthus** *adj see* **Parthī**
particeps, **-ipis** *adj* sharing, partaking ◆ *m* partner
participō, **-āre** *vt* to share, impart, inform
particula, **-ae** *f* particle
partim *adv* partly, in part; mostly; some ... others
partiō, **-īre**, **-īvī**, **-ītum**, **partior**, **-īrī** *vt* to share, distribute, divide
partītē *adv* methodically
partītiō, **-ōnis** *f* distribution, division
parturiō, **-īre** *vi* to be in labour; *(fig)* to be anxious ◆ *vt* to teem with, be ready to produce; *(mind)* to brood over
partus¹ *ppp of* **pariō** ◆ *ntpl* possessions
partus², **-ūs** *m* birth; young
parum *adv* too little, not enough; not very, scarcely
parumper *adv* for a little while
parvitās, **-ātis** *f* smallness
parvulus, **parvolus** *adj* very small, slight; quite young ◆ *m* child
parvus (*compar* **minor**, *superl* **minimus**) *adj* small, little, slight; *(time)* short; *(age)* young; **parvī esse** be of little value
Pascha, **-ae** *f* Easter
pāscō, **-scere**, **-vī**, **-stum** *vt* to feed, put to graze; to keep, foster; *(fig)* to feast, cherish ◆ *vi* to graze, browse
pāscuus *adj* for pasture ◆ *nt* pasture
Pāsiphaē, **-ēs** *f wife of Minos (mother of the Minotaur)*
passer, **-is** *m* sparrow; *(fish)* plaice; **~ marīnus** ostrich
passerculus, **-ī** *m* little sparrow
passim *adv* here and there, at random; indiscriminately
passum, **-ī** *nt* raisin wine

passus¹ *ppp of* **pandō** ◆ *adj* spread out, dishevelled; dried
passus² *ppa of* **patior**
passus³, **-ūs** *m* step, pace; footstep; **mille passūs** mile; **mīlia passuum** miles
pastillus, **-ī** *m* lozenge
pāstor, **-ōris** *m* shepherd
pāstōrālis *adj* shepherd's, pastoral
pāstōricius, **pāstōrius** *adj* shepherd's
pāstus¹ *ppp of* **pāscō**
pāstus², **-ūs** *m* pasture, food
Patara, **-ae** *f town in Lycia (with oracle of Apollo)*
Pataraeus, **Patareus** *adj see* **Patara**
Patavīnus *adj see* **Patavium**
Patavium, **-ī** *nt birthplace of Livy (now Padua)*
patefaciō, **-facere**, **-fēcī**, **-factum** (*pass* **-fīō**) *vt* to open, open up; to disclose
patefactiō, **-ōnis** *f* disclosing
patefīō *etc see* **patefaciō**
patella, **-ae** *f* small dish, plate
patēns, **-entis** *pres p of* **pateō** ◆ *adj* open, accessible, exposed; broad; evident
patenter *adv* clearly
pateō, **-ēre**, **-uī** *vi* to be open, accessible, exposed; to extend; to be evident, known
pater, **-ris** *m* father; *(pl)* forefathers; senators
patera, **-ae** *f* dish, saucer, bowl
paterfamiliās, **patrisfamiliās** *m* master of the house
paternus *adj* father's, paternal; native
patēscō, **-ere** *vi* to open out; to extend; to become evident
patibilis *adj* endurable; sensitive
patibulātus *adj* pilloried
patibulum, **-ī** *nt* fork-shaped yoke, pillory
patiēns, **-entis** *pres p of* **patior** ◆ *adj* able to endure; patient; unyielding
patienter *adv* patiently
patientia, **-ae** *f* endurance, stamina; forbearance; submissiveness
patina, **-ae** *f* dish, pan
patior, **-tī**, **-ssus** *vt* to suffer, experience; to submit to; to allow, put up with; **facile patī** be well pleased with; **aegrē patī** be displeased with
Patrae, **-ārum** *fpl Greek seaport (now Patras)*
patrātor, **-ōris** *m* doer
patrātus *adj*: **pater ~** officiating priest
Patrēnsis *adj see* **Patrae**
patria, **-ae** *f* native land, native town, home
patricius *adj* patrician ◆ *m* aristocrat
patrimōnium, **-ī** *and* **-iī** *nt* inheritance, patrimony
patrimus *adj* having a father living
patrissō, **-āre** *vi* to take after one's father
patrītus *adj* of one's father
patrius *adj* father's; hereditary, native
patrō, **-āre**, **-āvī**, **-ātum** *vt* to achieve, execute, complete
patrōcinium, **-ī** *and* **-iī** *nt* patronage, advocacy, defence
patrōcinor, **-ārī** *vi* (*with dat*) to defend, support
patrōna, **-ae** *f* patron goddess; protectress, safeguard

patrōnus, -ī *m* patron, protector; (*LAW*) advocate, counsel

patruēlis *adj* cousin's ◆ *m* cousin

patruus, -ī *m* (*paternal*) uncle ◆ *adj* uncle's

patulus *adj* open; spreading, broad

paucitās, -ātis *f* small number, scarcity

pauculus *adj* very few

paucus *adj* few, little ◆ *mpl* a few, the select few ◆ *ntpl* a few words

paulātim *adv* little by little, gradually

paulisper *adv* for a little while

Paullus, -ī *m* = **Paulus**

paulō *adv* a little, somewhat

paululus *adj* very little ◆ *nt* a little bit

paulum *adv* = **paulō**

paulus *adj* little

Paulus, -ī *m* Roman surname (*esp victor of Pydna*)

pauper, -is *adj* poor; meagre ◆ *mpl* the poor

pauperculus *adj* poor

pauperiēs, -ēī *f* poverty

pauperō, -āre *vt* to impoverish; to rob

paupertās, -ātis *f* poverty, moderate means

pausa, -ae *f* stop, end

pauxillātim *adv* bit by bit

pauxillulus *adj* very little

pauxillus *adj* little

pavefactus *adj* frightened

paveō, -ēre, pāvī *vi* to be terrified, quake ◆ *vt* to dread, be scared of

pavēscō, -ere *vt, vi* to become alarmed (at)

pāvī *perf of* **pāscō**

pavidē *adv* in a panic

pavidus *adj* quaking, terrified

pavīmentātus *adj* paved

pavīmentum, -ī *nt* pavement, floor

paviō, -īre *vt* to strike

pavitō, -āre *vi* to be very frightened; to shiver

pāvō, -ōnis *m* peacock

pavor, -ōris *m* terror, panic

pāx, pācis *f* peace; (*gods*) grace; (*mind*) serenity ◆ *interj* enough!; **pāce tuā** by your leave

peccātum, -ī *nt* mistake, fault, sin

peccō, -āre, -āvī, -ātum *vi* to make a mistake, go wrong, offend

pecorōsus *adj* rich in cattle

pecten, -inis *m* comb; (*fish*) scallop; (*loom*) reed; (*lyre*) plectrum

pectō, -ctere, -xī, -xum *vt* to comb

pectus, -oris *nt* breast; heart, feeling; mind, thought

pecū *nt* flock of sheep; (*pl*) pastures

pecuārius *adj* of cattle ◆ *m* cattle breeder ◆ *ntpl* herds

peculātor, -ōris *m* embezzler

peculātus, -ūs *m* embezzlement

peculiāris *adj* one's own; special

peculiātus *adj* provided with money

peculiōsus *adj* with private property

peculium, -ī *and* **-iī** *nt* small savings, private property

pecūnia, -ae *f* property; money

pecūniārius *adj* of money

pecūniōsus *adj* moneyed, well-off

pecus¹, -oris *nt* cattle, herd, flock; animal

pecus², -udis *f* sheep, head of cattle, beast

pedālis *adj* a foot long

pedārius *adj* (*senator*) without full rights

pedes, -itis *m* foot soldier, infantry ◆ *adj* on foot

pedester, -ris *adj* on foot, pedestrian; infantry- (*in cpds*), on land; (*writing*) in prose, prosaic

pedetemptim *adv* step by step, cautiously

pedica, -ae *f* fetter, snare

pedis, -is *m* louse

pedisequa, -ae *f* handmaid

pedisequus, -ī *m* attendant, lackey

peditātus, -ūs *m* infantry

pedum, -ī *nt* crook

Pēgaseus, Pēgasis, -idis *adj* Pegasean

Pēgasus, -ī *m* mythical winged horse (*associated with the Muses*)

pēgma, -tis *nt* bookcase; stage elevator

pēierō, -āre *vi* to perjure oneself

pēior, -ōris *compar of* **malus**

pēius *adv* worse

pelagius *adj* of the sea

pelagus, -ī (*pl -ē*) *nt* sea, open sea

pelamys, -dis *f* young tuna fish

Pelasgī, -ōrum *mpl* Greeks

Pelasgias, Pelasgis, Pelasgus *adj* Grecian

Pēleus, -eī *and* **-eos** (*acc* **-ea**) *m* king of Thessaly (*father of Achilles*)

Peliās, -ae *m* uncle of Jason

Pēlias, Pēliacus, Pēlius *adj see* **Pēlion**

Pēlīdēs, -īdae *m* Achilles; Neoptolemus

Pēlion, -ī *nt* mountain in Thessaly

Pella, -ae, Pellē, -ēs *f* town of Macedonia (*birthplace of Alexander*)

pellācia, -ae *f* attraction

Pellaeus *adj* of Pella; Alexandrian; Egyptian

pellāx, -ācis *adj* seductive

pellēctiō, -ōnis *f* reading through

pellectus *ppp of* **pelliciō**

pellegō *etc see* **perlegō**

pelliciō, -icere, -exī, -ectum *vt* to entice, inveigle

pellicula, -ae *f* skin, fleece

pelliō, -ōnis *m* furrier

pellis, -is *f* skin, hide; leather, felt; tent

pellītus *adj* wearing skins, with leather coats

pellō, -ere, pepulī, pulsum *vt* to push, knock, drive; to drive off, rout, expel; (*lyre*) to play; (*mind*) to touch, affect; (*feeling*) to banish

pellūc- *etc see* **perlūc-**

Pelopēis, Pelopēias, Pelopēius, Pelopēus *adj see* **Pelops**

Pelopidae, -idārum *mpl* house of Pelops

Peloponnēsiacus, -ius *adj see* **Peloponnēsus**

Peloponnēsus, -ī *f* Peloponnese, S. Greece

Pelops, -is *m* son of Tantalus (*grandfather of Agamemnon*)

pelōris, -idis *f* a large mussel

pelta, -ae *f* light shield

peltastae, -ārum *mpl* peltasts

peltātus *adj* armed with the pelta

Pēlūsiacus *adj see* **Pēlūsium**

Pēlūsium, -ī *nt* Egyptian town at the E. mouth of the Nile

Pēlūsius *adj see* **Pēlūsium**

pelvis, -is *f* basin

penārius *adj* provision- (*in cpds*)

Penātēs, -ium *mpl* spirits of the larder, household gods; home

penātiger, -ī *adj* carrying his home gods

pendeō, -ēre, pependī *vi* to hang; to overhang, hover; to hang down, be flabby; (*fig*) to depend; to gaze, listen attentively; (*mind*) to be in suspense, be undecided

pendō, -ere, pependī, pēnsum *vt* to weigh; to pay; (*fig*) to ponder, value ♦ *vi* to weigh

pendulus *adj* hanging; in doubt

Pēnēis, Pēnēius *adj see* **Pēnēus**

Pēnelopē, -ēs, Pēnelopa, -ae *f wife of Ulysses (famed for her constancy)*

Pēnelopēus *adj see* **Pēnelopē**

penes *prep* (*with acc*) in the power or possession of; in the house of, with

penetrābilis *adj* penetrable; piercing

penetrālis *adj* penetrating; inner, inmost ♦ *ntpl* inner room, interior, sanctuary; remote parts

penetrō, -āre, -āvī, -ātum *vt, vi* to put into, penetrate, enter

Pēnēus, -ī *m chief river of Thessaly*

pēnicillus, -ī *m* painter's brush, pencil

pēniculus, -ī *m* brush; sponge

pēnis, -is *m* penis

penitē *adj* inwardly

penitus *adv* inside, deep within; deeply, from the depths; utterly, thoroughly

penna, pinna, -ae *f* feather, wing; flight

pennātus *adj* winged

penniger, -ī *adj* feathered

pennipotēns, -entis *adj* winged

pennula, -ae *f* little wing

pēnsilis *adj* hanging, pendent

pēnsiō, -ōnis *f* payment, instalment

pēnsitō, -āre *vt* to pay; to consider

pēnsō, -āre, -āvī, -ātum *vt* to weight out; to compensate, repay; to consider, judge

pēnsum, -ī *nt* spinner's work; task, duty; weight, value; **pēnsī esse** bc of importance; **pēnsī habēre** care at all about

pēnsus *ppp of* **pendō**

pentēris, -is *f* quinquereme

Pentheus, -eī *and* **-eos** *m king of Thebes (killed by Bacchantes)*

pēnūria, -ae *f* want, need

penus, -ūs *and* **-ī** *m/f,* **penum, -ī** *nt,* **penus, -oris** *nt* provisions, store of food

pependī *perf of* **pendeō; pendō**

pepercī *perf of* **parcō**

peperī *perf of* **pariō**

pepigī *perf of* **pangō**

peplum, -ī *nt,* **peplus, -ī** *m* state robe of Athena

pepulī *perf of* **pellō**

per *prep* (*with acc: space*) through, all over; (: *time*) throughout, during; (: *means*) by, by means of; (: *cause*) by reason of, for the sake of; **per īram** in anger; **per manūs** from hand to hand; **per mē** as far as I am concerned; **per vim** forcibly; **per ego tē deōs ōrō** in Heaven's name I beg you

pēra, -ae *f* bag

perabsurdus *adj* very absurd

peraccommodātus *adj* very convenient

perācer, -ris *adj* very sharp

peracerbus *adj* very sour

peracēscō, -ēscere, -uī *vi* to get vexed

perāctiō, -ōnis *f* last act

perāctus *ppp of* **peragō**

peracūtē *adv* very acutely

peracūtus *adj* very sharp, very clear

peradulēscēns, -entis *adj* very young

peraequē *adv* quite equally, uniformly

peragitātus *adj* harried

peragō, -agere, -ēgī, -āctum *vt* to carry through, complete; to pass through, pierce; to disturb; (LAW) to prosecute to a conviction; (*words*) to go over, describe

peragrātiō, -ōnis *f* travelling

peragrō, -āre, -āvī, -ātum *vt* to travel through, traverse

peramāns, -antis *adj* very fond

peramanter *adv* devotedly

perambulō, -āre *vt* to walk through, traverse

peramoenus *adj* very pleasant

peramplus *adj* very large

perangustē *adv see* **perangustus**

perangustus *adj* very narrow

perantīquus *adj* very old

perappositus *adj* very suitable

perarduus *adj* very difficult

perargūtus *adj* very witty

perarō, -āre *vt* to furrow; to write (*on wax*)

perattentē *adv see* **perattentus**

perattentus *adj* very attentive

peraudiendus *adj* to be heard to the end

perbacchor, -ārī *vt* to carouse through

perbeātus *adj* very happy

perbellē *adv* very nicely

perbene *adv* very well

perbenevolus *adj* very friendly

perbenignē *adv* very kindly

perbibō, -ere, -ī *vt* to drink up, imbibe

perbītō, -ere *vi* to perish

perblandus *adj* very charming

perbonus *adj* very good

perbrevis *adj* very short

perbreviter *adv* very briefly

perca, -ae *f* perch

percalefactus *adj* quite hot

percalēscō, -ēscere, -uī *vi* to become quite hot

percallēscō, -ēscere, -uī *vi* to become quite hardened ♦ *vt* to become thoroughly versed in

percārus *adj* very dear

percautus *adj* very cautious

percelebrō, -āre *vt* to talk much of

perceler, -is *adj* very quick

perceleriter *adv see* **perceler**

percellō, -ellere, -ulī, -ulsum *vt* to knock down, upset; to strike; (*fig*) to ruin, overthrow; to discourage, unnerve

percēnseō, -ēre, -uī *vt* to count over; (*place*) to travel through; (*fig*) to review

perceptiō, -ōnis *f* harvesting; understanding, idea

perceptus *ppp of* **percipiō**

percieō, -iēre, -iō, -īre *vt* to rouse, excite

percipiō, -ipere, -ēpī, -eptum *vt* to take, get hold of; to gather in; *(senses)* to feel; *(mind)* to learn, grasp, understand
percitus *ppp of* **percieō** ♦ *adj* roused, excited; excitable
percoctus *ppp of* **percoquō**
percolō¹, -āre *vt* to filter through
percolō², -olere, -oluī, -ultum *vt* to embellish; to honour
percōmis *adj* very friendly
percommodē *adv* very conveniently
percommodus *adj* very suitable
percontātiō, -ōnis *f* asking questions
percontātor, -ōris *m* inquisitive person
percontor, -ārī, -ātus *vt* to question, inquire
percontumāx, -ācis *adj* very obstinate
percoquō, -quere, -xī, -ctum *vt* to cook thoroughly, heat, scorch, ripen
percrēbēscō, percrēbrēscō, -ēscere, -uī *vi* to be spread abroad
percrepō, -āre, -uī *vi* to resound
perculī *perf of* **percellō**
perculsus *ppp of* **percellō**
percultus *ppp of* **percolō²**
percunct- *etc see* **percont-**
percupidus *adj* very fond
percupiō, -ere *vi* to wish very much
percūriōsus *adj* very inquisitive
percūrō, -āre *vt* to heal completely
percurrō, -rrere, -currī *and* **-rrī, -rsum** *vt* to run through, hurry over; *(fig)* to run over, look over ♦ *vi* to run along; to pass
percursātiō, -ōnis *f* travelling through
percursiō, -ōnis *f* running over
percursō, -āre *vi* to rove about
percursus *ppp of* **percurrō**
percussiō, -ōnis *f* beating; *(fingers)* snapping; *(music)* time
percussor, -ōris *m* assassin
percussus¹ *ppp of* **percutiō**
percussus², -ūs *m* striking
percutiō, -tere, -ssī, -ssum *vt* to strike, beat; to strike through, kill; *(feeling)* to shock, impress, move; *(colloq)* to trick
perdēlīrus *adj* quite crazy
perdidī *perf of* **perdō**
perdifficilis *adj* very difficult
perdifficiliter *adv* with great difficulty
perdignus *adj* most worthy
perdīligēns, -entis *adj* very diligent
perdīligenter *adv see* **perdīligēns**
perdiscō, -scere, -dicī *vt* to learn by heart
perdisertē *adv* very eloquently
perditē *adv* desperately; recklessly
perditor, -ōris *m* destroyer
perditus *ppp of* **perdō** ♦ *adj* desperate, ruined; abandoned, profligate
perdiū *adv* for a very long time
perdiūturnus *adj* protracted
perdīves, -itis *adj* very rich
perdīx, -īcis *m/f* partridge
perdō, -ere, -idī, -itum *vt* to destroy, ruin; to squander, waste; to lose; **dī tē perduint** curse you!

perdoceō, -ēre, -uī, -tum *vt* to teach thoroughly
perdolēscō, -ēscere, -uī *vi* to take it to heart
perdomō, -āre, -uī, -itum *vt* to subjugate, tame completely
perdormīscō, -ere *vi* to sleep on
perdūcō, -ūcere, -ūxī, -uctum *vt* to bring, guide to; to induce, seduce; to spread over; to prolong, continue
perductō, -āre *vt* to guide
perductor, -ōris *m* guide; pander
perductus *ppp of* **perdūcō**
perduelliō, -ōnis *f* treason
perduellis, -is *m* enemy
perduim *archaic subj of* **perdō**
perdūrō, -āre *vi* to endure, hold out
peredō, -edere, -ēdī, -ēsum *vt* to consume, devour
peregrē *adv* away from home, abroad; from abroad
peregrīnābundus *adj* travelling
peregrīnātiō, -ōnis *f* living abroad, travel
peregrīnātor, -ōris *m* traveller
peregrīnitās, -ātis *f* foreign manners
peregrīnor, -ārī, -ātus *vi* to be abroad, travel; to be a stranger
peregrīnus *adj* foreign, strange ♦ *m* foreigner, alien
perēlegāns, -antis *adj* very polished
perēleganter *adv* in a very polished manner
perēloquēns, -entis *adj* very eloquent
perēmī *perf of* **perimō**
peremnia, -ium *ntpl* auspices taken on crossing a river
peremptus *ppp of* **perimō**
perendiē *adv* the day after tomorrow
perendinus *adj* (*the day*) after tomorrow
perennis *adj* perpetual, unfailing
perennitās, -ātis *f* continuance
perennō, -āre *vi* to last a long time
pereō, -īre, -iī, -itum *vi* to be lost, pass away, perish, die; *(fig)* to be wasted, be in love, be undone
perequitō, -āre *vt, vi* to ride up and down
pererrō, -āre, -āvī, -ātum *vt* to roam over, cover
perērudītus *adj* very learned
perēsus *ppp of* **peredō**
perexcelsus *adj* very high
perexiguē *adv* very meagrely
perexiguus *adj* very small, very short
perfacētē *adv* very wittily
perfacētus *adj* very witty
perfacilē *adv* very easily
perfacilis *adj* very easy; very courteous
perfamiliāris *adj* very intimate ♦ *m* very close friend
perfectē *adv* fully
perfectiō, -ōnis *f* completion, perfection
perfector, -ōris *m* perfecter
perfectus *ppp of* **perficiō** ♦ *adj* complete, perfect
perferō, -ferre, -tulī, -lātum *vt* to carry through, bring, convey; to bear, endure, put up with; *(work)* to finish, bring to completion; *(LAW)* to get passed; *(message)* to bring news

perficiō, -icere, -ēcī, -ectum *vt* to carry out, finish, complete; to perfect; to cause, make
perficus *adj* perfecting
perfidēlis *adj* very loyal
perfidia, -ae *f* treachery, dishonesty
perfidiōsē *adv see* **perfidiōsus**
perfidiōsus *adj* treacherous, dishonest
perfidus *adj* treacherous, faithless
perfīgō, -gere, -xī, -xum *vt* to pierce
perflābilis *adj* that can be blown through
perflāgitiōsus *adj* very wicked
perflō, -āre *vt* to blow through, blow over
perfluctuō, -āre *vt* to flood through
perfluō, -ere, -xī *vi* to run out, leak
perfodiō, -odere, -ōdī, -ossum *vt* to dig through, excavate, pierce
perforō, -āre, -āvī, -ātum *vt* to bore through, pierce
perfortiter *adv* very bravely
perfossor, -ōris *m:* ~ **parietum** burglar
perfossus *ppp of* **perfodiō**
perfrāctus *ppp of* **perfringō**
perfrēgī *perf of* **perfringō**
perfremō, -ere *vi* to snort along
perfrequēns, -entis *adj* much frequented
perfricō, -āre, -uī, -tum *and* **-ātum** *vt* to rub all over; ōs **perfricāre** to put on a bold face
perfrīgefaciō, -ere *vt* to make shudder
perfrīgēscō, -gēscere, -xī *vi* to catch a bad cold
perfrīgidus *adj* very cold
perfringō, -ingere, -ēgī, -āctum *vt* to break through, fracture, wreck; (*fig*) to violate; to affect powerfully
perfrīxī *perf of* **perfrīgēscō**
perfrūctus *ppa of* **perfruor**
perfruor, -uī, -ūctus *vi* (*with abl*) to enjoy to the full; to fulfil
perfuga, -ae *m* deserter
perfugiō, -ugere, -ūgī *vi* to flee for refuge, desert to
perfugium, -ī *and* **-iī** *nt* refuge, shelter
perfūnctiō, -ōnis *f* performing
perfūnctus *ppa of* **perfungor**
perfundō, -undere, -ūdī, -ūsum *vt* to pour over, drench, besprinkle; to dye; (*fig*) to flood, fill
perfungor, -gī, perfūnctus *vi* (*with abl*) to perform, discharge; to undergo
perfurō, -ere *vi* to rage furiously
perfūsus *ppp of* **perfundō**
Pergama, -ōrum *ntpl* Troy
Pergamēnus *adj see* **Pergama**
Pergameus *adj* Trojan
Pergamum, -ī *nt* town in Mysia (*famous for its library*)
pergaudeō, -ēre *vi* to be very glad
pergō, -gere, -rēxī, -rēctum *vi* to proceed, go on, continue ♦ *vt* to go on with, continue
pergraecor, -ārī *vi* to have a good time
pergrandis *adj* very large; very old
pergraphicus *adj* very artful
pergrātus *adj* very pleasant
pergravis *adj* very weighty
pergraviter *adv* very seriously
pergula, -ae *f* balcony; school; brothel
perhibeō, -ēre, -uī, -itum *vt* to assert, call, cite

perhīlum *adv* very little
perhonōrificē *adv* very respectfully
perhonōrificus *adj* very complimentary
perhorrēscō, -ēscere, -uī *vi* to shiver, tremble violently ♦ *vt* to have a horror of
perhorridus *adj* quite horrible
perhūmāniter *adv see* **perhūmānus**
perhūmānus *adj* very polite
Periclēs, -is *and* **-ī** *m* famous Athenian statesman and orator
perīclitātiō, -ōnis *f* experiment
perīclitor, -ārī, -ātus *vt* to test, try; to risk, endanger ♦ *vi* to attempt, venture; to run a risk, be in danger
perīculōsē *adv see* **perīculōsus**
perīculōsus *adj* dangerous, hazardous
perīculum, perīclum, -ī *nt* danger, risk; trial, attempt; (*LAW*) lawsuit, writ
peridōneus *adj* very suitable
periī *perf of* **pereō**
perillūstris *adj* very notable; highly honoured
perimbēcillus *adj* very weak
perimō, -imere, -ēmī, -emptum *vt* to destroy, prevent, kill
perincommodē *adv see* **perincommodus**
perincommodus *adj* very inconvenient
perinde *adv* just as, exactly as
perindulgēns, -entis *adj* very tender
perinfirmus *adj* very feeble
peringeniōsus *adj* very clever
perinīquus *adj* very unfair; very discontented
perinsignis *adj* very conspicuous
perinvītus *adj* very unwilling
periodus, -ī *f* sentence, period
Peripatēticī, -ōrum *mpl* Peripatetics (*followers of Aristotle*)
peripetasmata, -um *ntpl* curtains
perīrātus *adj* very angry
periscelis, -dis *f* anklet
peristrōma, -atis *nt* coverlet
peristylum, -ī *nt* colonnade, peristyle
perītē *adv* expertly
perītia, -ae *f* practical knowledge, skill
perītus *adj* experienced, skilled, expert
periūcundē *adv see* **periūcundus**
periūcundus *adj* very enjoyable
periūrium, -ī *and* **-iī** *nt* perjury
periūrō *see* **pēierō**
periūrus *adj* perjured, lying
perlābor, -bī, -psus *vi* to glide along or through, move on
perlaetus *adj* very glad
perlāpsus *ppa of* **perlābor**
perlātē *adv* very extensively
perlateō, -ēre *vi* to lie quite hidden
perlātus *ppp of* **perferō**
perlegō, -egere, -ēgī, -ēctum *vt* to survey; to read through
perlevis *adj* very slight
perleviter *adv see* **perlevis**
perlibēns, -entis *adj* very willing
perlibenter *adv see* **perlibēns**
perlīberālis *adj* very genteel
perlīberāliter *adv* very liberally

perlibet, -ēre vi (impers) (I) should very much like

perliciō etc see **pelliciō**

perlitō, -āre, -āvī, -ātum vi to sacrifice with auspicious results

perlongē adv very far

perlongus adj very long, very tedious

perlub- etc see **perlib-**

perlūceō, -cēre, -xī vi to shine through, be transparent; (fig) to be quite intelligible

perlūcidulus adj transparent

perlūcidus adj transparent; very bright

perlūctuōsus adj very mournful

perluō, -ere vt to wash thoroughly; (pass) to bathe

perlūstrō, -āre vt to traverse; (fig) to survey

permāgnus adj very big, very great

permānanter adv by flowing through

permānāscō, -ere vi to penetrate

permaneō, -anēre, -ānsī, -ānsum vi to last, persist, endure to the end

permānō, -āre, -āvī, -ātum vi to flow or ooze through, penetrate

permānsiō, -ōnis f continuing, persisting

permarīnus adj of seafaring

permātūrēscō, -ēscere, -uī vi to ripen fully

permediocris adj very moderate

permēnsus ppa of **permētior**

permeō, -āre vt, vi to pass through, penetrate

permētior, -tīrī, -nsus vt to measure out; to traverse

permīrus adj very wonderful

permisceō, -scēre, -scuī, -xtum vt to mingle, intermingle; to throw into confusion

permissiō, -ōnis f unconditional surrender; permission

permissus¹ ppp of **permittō**

permissus², -ūs m leave, permission

permitiālis adj destructive

permitiēs, -ēī f ruin

permittō, -ittere, -īsī, -issum vt to let go, let pass; to hurl; to give up, entrust, concede; to allow, permit

permixtē adv see **permixtus**

permixtiō, -ōnis f mixture; disturbance

permixtus ppp of **permisceō** ◆ adj promiscuous, disordered

permodestus adj very moderate

permolestē adv with much annoyance

permolestus adj very troublesome

permōtiō, -ōnis f excitement; emotion

permōtus ppp of **permoveō**

permoveō, -ovēre, -ōvī, -ōtum vt to stir violently; (fig) to influence, induce; to excite, move deeply

permulceō, -cēre, -sī, -sum vt to stroke, caress; (fig) to charm, flatter; to soothe, appease

permulsus ppp of **permulceō**

permultus adj very much, very many

permūniō, -īre, -īvī, -ītum vt to finish fortifying; to fortify strongly

permūtātiō, -ōnis f change, exchange

permūtō, -āre, -āvī, -ātum vt to change completely; to exchange; (money) to remit by bill of exchange

perna, -ae f ham

pernecessārius adj very necessary; very closely related

pernecesse adj indispensable

pernegō, -āre vi to deny flatly

perniciābilis adj ruinous

perniciēs, -ēī f destruction, ruin, death

perniciōsē adv see **perniciōsus**

perniciōsus adj ruinous

pernicitās, -ātis f agility, swiftness

perniciter adv nimbly

pernimius adj much too much

pernīx, -īcis adj nimble, agile, swift

pernōbilis adj very famous

pernoctō, -āre vi to stay all night

pernōscō, -scere, -vī, -tum vt to examine thoroughly; to become fully acquainted with, know thoroughly

pernōtēscō, -ēscere, -uī vi to become generally known

pernōtus ppp of **pernōscō**

pernox, -octis adj all night long

pernumerō, -āre vt to count up

pērō, -ōnis m rawhide boot

perobscūrus adj very obscure

perodiōsus adj very troublesome

perofficiōsē adv very attentively

peroleō, -ēre vi to give off a strong smell

peropportūnē adv very opportunely

peropportūnus adj very timely

peroptātō adv very much to one's wish

peropus est it is most essential

perōrātiō, -ōnis f peroration

perōrnātus adj very ornate

perōrnō, -āre vt to give great distinction to

perōrō, -āre, -āvī, -ātum vt to plead at length; (speech) to bring to a close; to conclude

perōsus adj detesting

perpācō, -āre vt to quieten completely

perparcē adv very stingily

perparvulus adj very tiny

perparvus adj very small

perpāstus adj well fed

perpauculus adj very very few

perpaucus adj very little, very few

perpaulum, -ī nt a very little

perpauper, -is adj very poor

perpauxillum, -ī nt a very little

perpellō, -ellere, -ulī, -ulsum vt to urge, force, influence

perpendiculum, -ī nt plumbline; **ad ~** perpendicularly

perpendō, -endere, -endī, -ēnsum vt to weigh carefully, judge

perperam adv wrongly, falsely

perpes, -etis adj continuous

perpessiō, -ōnis f suffering, enduring

perpessus ppa of **perpetior**

perpetior, -tī, -ssus vt to endure patiently, allow

perpetrō, -āre, -āvī, -ātum vt to perform, carry out

perpetuitās, -ātis f continuity, uninterrupted duration

perpetuō¹ *adv* without interruption, forever, utterly

perpetuō², **-āre** *vt* to perpetuate, preserve

perpetuus *adj* continuous, entire; universal; **in perpetuum** forever

perplaceō, **-ēre** *vi* to please greatly

perplexē *adv* obscurely

perplexor, **-ārī** *vi* to cause confusion

perplexus *adj* confused, intricate, obscure

perplicātus *adj* interlaced

perpluō, **-ere** *vi* to let the rain through, leak

perpoliō, **-īre**, **-īvī**, **-ītum** *vt* to polish thoroughly

perpolītus *adj* finished, refined

perpopulor, **-ārī**, **-ātus** *vt* to ravage completely

perpōtātiō, **-ōnis** *f* drinking bout

perpōtō, **-āre** *vi* to drink continuously ♦ *vt* to drink off

perprimō, **-ere** *vt* to lie on

perpugnāx, **-ācis** *adj* very pugnacious

perpulcher, **-rī** *adj* very beautiful

perpulī *perf of* **perpellō**

perpūrgō, **-āre**, **-āvī**, **-ātum** *vt* to make quite clean; to explain

perpusillus *adj* very little

perquam *adv* very, extremely

perquīrō, **-rere**, **-sīvī**, **-sītum** *vt* to search for, inquire after; to examine carefully

perquīsītius *adv* more accurately

perrārō *adv* very seldom

perrārus *adj* very uncommon

perreconditus *adj* very abstruse

perrēpō, **-ere** *vt* to crawl over

perrēptō, **-āre**, **-āvī**, **-ātum** *vt*, *vi* to creep about or through

perrēxī *perf of* **pergō**

perrīdiculē *adv see* **perrīdiculus**

perrīdiculus *adj* very laughable

perrogātiō, **-ōnis** *f* passing (*of a law*)

perrogō, **-āre** *vt* to ask one after another

perrumpō, **-umpere**, **-ūpī**, **-uptum** *vt*, *vi* to break through, force a way through; (*fig*) to break down

perruptus *ppp of* **perrumpō**

Persae, **-ārum** *mpl* Persians

persaepe *adv* very often

persalsē *adv see* **persalsus**

persalsus *adj* very witty

persalūtātiō, **-ōnis** *f* greeting everyone in turn

persalūtō, **-āre** *vt* to greet in turn

persanctē *adv* most solemnly

persapiēns, **-entis** *adj* very wise

persapienter *adv see* **persapiēns**

perscienter *adv* very discreetly

perscindō, **-ndere**, **-dī**, **-ssum** *vt* to tear apart

perscītus *adj* very smart

perscrībō, **-bere**, **-psī**, **-ptum** *vt* to write in full; to describe, report; (*record*) to enter; (*money*) to make over in writing

perscrīptiō, **-ōnis** *f* entry; assignment

perscrīptor, **-ōris** *m* writer

perscrīptus *ppp of* **perscrībō**

perscrūtor, **-ārī**, **-ātus** *vt* to search, examine thoroughly

persecō, **-āre**, **-uī**, **-tum** *vt* to dissect; to do away with

persector, **-ārī** *vt* to investigate

persecūtiō, **-ōnis** *f* (LAW) prosecution

persecūtus *ppa of* **persequor**

persedeō, **-edēre**, **-ēdī**, **-essum** *vi* to remain sitting

persegnis *adj* very slow

Persēius *adj see* **Perseus**

persentiō, **-entīre**, **-ēnsī** *vt* to see clearly; to feel deeply

persentīscō, **-ere** *vi* to begin to see; to begin to feel

Persephonē, **-ēs** *f* Proserpine

persequor, **-quī**, **-cūtus** *vt* to follow all the way; to pursue, chase, hunt after; to overtake; (*pattern*) to be a follower of, copy; (*enemy*) to proceed against, take revenge on; (*action*) to perform, carry out; (*words*) to write down, describe

Persēs¹, **-ae** *m* last king of Macedonia

Persēs², **-ae** *m* Persian

Perseus, **-eī** *and* **-eos** (*acc* **-ea**) *m* son of Danaë (killer of Medusa, rescuer of Andromeda)

Persēus *adj see* **Perseus**

persevērāns, **-antis** *pres p of* **persevērō** ♦ *adj* persistent

persevēranter *adv see* **persevērāns**

persevērantia, **-ae** *f* persistence

persevērō, **-āre**, **-āvī**, **-ātum** *vi* to persist ♦ *vt* to persist in

persevērus *adj* very strict

Persicum *nt* peach

Persicus *adj* Persian; of Perses

persīdō, **-īdere**, **-ēdī**, **-essum** *vi* to sink down into

persignō, **-āre** *vt* to record

persimilis *adj* very like

persimplex, **-icis** *adj* very simple

Persis, **-idis** *f* Persia

persistō, **-istere**, **-titī** *vi* to persist

persōlus *adj* one and only

persolūtus *ppp of* **persolvō**

persolvō, **-vere**, **-vī**, **-ūtum** *vt* to pay, pay up; to explain

persōna, **-ae** *f* mask; character, part; person, personality

persōnātus *adj* masked; in an assumed character

personō, **-āre**, **-uī**, **-itum** *vi* to resound, ring (with); to play ♦ *vt* to make resound; to cry aloud

perspectē *adv* intelligently

perspectō, **-āre** *vt* to have a look through

perspectus *ppp of* **perspiciō** ♦ *adj* well-known

perspeculor, **-ārī** *vt* to reconnoitre

perspergō, **-gere**, **-sī**, **-sum** *vt* to besprinkle

perspicāx, **-ācis** *adj* sharp, shrewd

perspicientia, **-ae** *f* full understanding

perspiciō, **-icere**, **-exī**, **-ectum** *vt* to see through; to examine, observe

perspicuē *adv* clearly

perspicuitās, **-ātis** *f* clarity

perspicuus *adj* transparent; clear, evident

persternō, -ernere, -rāvī, -rātum vt to pave all over

perstimulō, -āre vt to rouse violently

perstitī perf of **persistō; perstō**

perstō, -āre, -itī, -ātum vi to stand fast; to last; to continue, persist

perstrātus ppp of **persternō**

perstrepō, -ere vi to make a lot of noise

perstrictus ppp of **perstringō**

perstringō, -ingere, -inxī, -ictum vt to graze, touch lightly; (words) to touch on, belittle, censure; (senses) to dull, deaden

perstudiōsē adv very eagerly

perstudiōsus adj very fond

persuādeō, -dēre, -sī, -sum vi (with dat) to convince, persuade; **persuāsum habeō, mihi persuāsum est** I am convinced

persuāsiō, -ōnis f convincing

persuāsus, -ūs m persuasion

persubtīlis adj very fine

persultō, -āre vt, vi to prance about, frisk over

pertaedet, -dēre, -sum est vt (impers) to be weary of, be sick of

pertegō, -egere, -ēxī, -ēctum vt to cover over

pertemptō, -āre vt to test carefully; to consider well; to pervade, seize

pertendō, -ere, -ī vi to push on, persist ♦ vt to go on with

pertenuis adj very small, very slight

perterebrō, -āre vt to bore through

pertergeō, -gēre, -sī, -sum vt to wipe over; to touch lightly

perterrefaciō, -ere vt to scare thoroughly

perterreō, -ēre, -uī, -itum vt to frighten thoroughly

perterricrepus adj with a terrifying crash

perterritus adj terrified

pertexō, -ere, -uī, -tum vt to accomplish

pertica, -ae f pole, staff

pertimefactus adj very frightened

pertimēscō, -ēscere, -uī vt, vi to be very alarmed, be very afraid of

pertinācia, -ae f perseverance, stubbornness

pertināciter adv see **pertināx**

pertināx, -ācis adj very tenacious; unyielding, stubborn

pertineō, -ēre, -uī vi to extend, reach; to tend, lead to, concern; to apply, pertain, belong; **quod pertinet ad** as far as concerns

pertingō, -ere vi to extend

pertolerō, -āre vt to endure to the end

pertorqueō, -ēre vt to distort

pertractātē adv in a hackneyed fashion

pertractātiō, -ōnis f handling

pertractō, -āre vt to handle, feel all over; (fig) to treat, study

pertractus ppp of **pertrahō**

pertrahō, -here, -xī, -ctum vt to drag across, take forcibly; to entice

pertrect- etc see **pertract-**

pertristis adj very sad, very morose

pertulī perf of **perferō**

pertumultuōsē adv very excitedly

pertundō, -undere, -udī, -ūsum vt to perforate

perturbātē adv in confusion

perturbātiō, -ōnis f confusion, disturbance; emotion

perturbātrīx, -īcis f disturber

perturbātus ppp of **perturbō** ♦ adj troubled; alarmed

perturbō, -āre, -āvī, -ātum vt to throw into disorder, upset, alarm

perturpis adj scandalous

pertūsus ppp of **pertundō** ♦ adj in holes, leaky

perungō, -ungere, -ūnxī, -ūnctum vt to smear all over

perurbānus adj very refined; over-fine

perūrō, -rere, -ssi, -stum vt to burn up, scorch; to inflame, chafe; to freeze, nip

Perusia, -iae f Etruscan town (now Perugia)

Perusīnus adj see **Perusia**

perūstus ppp of **perūrō**

perūtilis adj very useful

pervādō, -dere, -sī, -sum vt, vi to pass through, spread through; to penetrate, reach

pervagātus adj widespread, well-known; general

pervagor, -ārī, -ātus vi to range, rove about; to extend, spread ♦ vt to pervade

pervagus adj roving

pervariē adv very diversely

pervastō, -āre, -āvī, -ātum vt to devastate

pervāsus ppp of **pervādō**

pervectus ppp of **pervehō**

pervehō, -here, -xī, -ctum vt to carry, convey, bring through; (pass) to ride, drive, sail through; to attain

pervellō, -ere, -ī vt to pull, twitch, pinch; to stimulate; to disparage

perveniō, -enīre, -ēnī, -entum vi to come to, arrive, reach; to attain to

pervēnor, -ārī vi to chase through

perversē adv perversely

perversitās, -ātis f perverseness

perversus, pervorsus ppp of **pervertō** ♦ adj awry, squint; wrong, perverse

pervertō, -tere, -tī, -sum vt to overturn, upset; to overthrow, undo; (speech) to confute

pervesperī adv very late

pervestīgātiō, -ōnis f thorough search

pervestīgō, -āre, -āvī, -ātum vt to track down; to investigate

pervetus, -eris adj very old

pervetustus adj antiquated

pervicācia, -ae f obstinacy; firmness

pervicāciter adv see **pervicāx**

pervicāx, -ācis adj obstinate, wilful; dogged

pervictus ppp of **pervincō**

pervideō, -idēre, -īdī, -īsum vt to look over, survey; to consider; to discern

pervigeō, -ēre, -uī vi to continue to flourish

pervigil, -is adj awake, watchful

pervigilātiō, -ōnis f vigil

pervigilium, -ī and -iī nt vigil

pervigilō, -āre, -āvī, -ātum vt, vi to stay awake all night, keep vigil

pervīlis adj very cheap

pervincō, -incere, -īcī, -ictum vt, vi to conquer completely; to outdo, surpass; to prevail upon, effect; (*argument*) to carry a point, maintain, prove

pervius *adj* passable, accessible

pervīvō, -ere *vi* to survive

pervolgō *etc see* **pervulgō**

pervolitō, -āre *vt, vi* to fly about

pervolō¹, -āre, -āvī, -ātum *vt, vi* to fly through or over, fly to

pervolō², -elle, -oluī *vi* to wish very much

pervolūtō, -āre *vt* (*books*) to read through

pervolvō, -vere, -vī, -ūtum *vt* to tumble about; (*book*) to read through; (*pass*) to be very busy (with)

pervor- *etc see* **perver-**

pervulgātus *adj* very common

pervulgō, -āre, -āvī, -ātum *vt* to make public, impart; to haunt

pēs, pedis *m* foot; (*length*) foot; (*verse*) foot, metre; (*sailrope*) sheet; **pedem cōnferre** come to close quarters; **pedem referre** go back; **ante pedēs** self-evident; **pedibus** on foot, by land; **pedibus īre in sententiam** take sides; **pedibus aequīs** (NAUT) with the wind right aft; **servus ā pedibus** footman

pessimē *superl of* **male**

pessimus *superl of* **malus**

pessulus, -ī *m* bolt

pessum *adv* to the ground, to the bottom; ~ **dare** put an end to, ruin, destroy; ~ **īre** sink, perish

pestifer, -ī *adj* pestilential; baleful, destructive

pestilēns, -entis *adj* unhealthy; destructive

pestilentia, -ae *f* plague, pest; unhealthiness

pestilitās, -ātis *f* plague

pestis, -is *f* plague, pest; ruin, destruction

petasātus *adj* wearing the petasus

petasunculus, -ī *m* small leg of pork

petasus, -ī *m* broadbrimmed hat

petessō, -ere *vt* to be eager for

petītiō, -ōnis *f* thrust, attack; request, application; (*office*) candidature, standing for; (LAW) civil suit, right of claim

petītor, -ōris *m* candidate; plaintiff

petīturiō, -īre *vt* to long to be a candidate

petītus¹ *ppp of* **petō**

petītus², -ūs *m* falling to

petō, -ere, -īvī and -iī, -ītum *vt* to aim at, attack; (*place*) to make for, go to; to seek, look for, demand, ask; to go and fetch; (LAW) to sue; (*love*) to court; (*office*) to stand for

petorritum, -ī *nt* carriage

petrō, -ōnis *m* yokel

Petrōnius, -ī *m* arbiter of fashion under Nero

petulāns, -antis *adj* pert, impudent, lascivious

petulanter *adv see* **petulāns**

petulantia, -ae *f* pertness, impudence

petulcus *adj* butting

pexus *ppp of* **pectō**

Phaeāces, -cum *mpl fabulous islanders in the Odyssey*

Phaeācius, Phaeācus, Phaeax *adj* Phaeacian

Phaedra, -ae *f stepmother of Hippolytus*

Phaedrus, -ī *m pupil of Socrates; writer of Latin fables*

Phaethōn, -ontis *m son of the Sun (killed while driving his father's chariot)*

Phaethonteus *adj see* **Phaethōn**

Phaethontiades, -um *fpl sisters of Phaethon*

phalangae, -ārum *fpl* wooden rollers

phalangītae, -ārum *mpl* soldiers of a phalanx

phalanx, -gis *f* phalanx; troops, battle order

Phalaris, -dis *m tyrant of Agrigentum*

phalerae, -ārum *fpl* medallions, badges; (*horse*) trappings

phalerātus *adj* wearing medallions; ornamented

Phalēreus, -icus *adj see* **Phalērum**

Phalērum, -ī *nt harbour of Athens*

pharetra, -ae *f* quiver

pharetrātus *adj* wearing a quiver

Pharius *adj see* **Pharus**

pharmaceutria, -ae *f* sorceress

pharmacopōla, -ae *m* quack doctor

Pharsālicus, -ius *adj see* **Pharsālus**

Pharsālus, Pharsālos, -ī *f town in Thessaly (where Caesar defeated Pompey)*

Pharus, Pharos, -ī *f island off Alexandria with a famous lighthouse;* lighthouse

phasēlus, -ī *m/f* French bean; (*boat*) pinnace

Phāsiacus *adj* Colchian

Phāsiānus, -āna *m/f* pheasant

Phāsis¹, -dis *and* **-dos** *m river of Colchis*

Phāsis² *adj see* **Phāsis¹**

phasma, -tis *nt* ghost

Pherae, -ārum *fpl town in Thessaly (home of Admetus)*

Pheraeus *adj see* **Pherae**

phiala, -ae *f* saucer

Phīdiacus *adj see* **Phīdiās**

Phīdiās, -ae *m famous Athenian sculptor*

philēma, -tis *nt* kiss

Philippēus *adj see* **Philippus**

Philippī, -ōrum *mpl town in Macedonia (where Brutus and Cassius were defeated)*

Philippicae *fpl Cicero's speeches against Antony*

Philippicus *adj see* **Philippus**

Philippus, -ī *m king of Macedonia; gold coin*

philitia, phīditia, -ōrum *ntpl* public meals at Sparta

Philō, Philōn, -ōnis *m Academic philosopher (teacher of Cicero)*

Philoctētēs, -ae *m Greek archer who gave Hercules poisoned arrows*

philologia, -ae *f* study of literature

philologus *adj* scholarly, literary

Philomēla, -ae *f sister of Procne;* nightingale

philosophē *adv see* **philosophus**

philosophia, -ae *f* philosophy

philosophor, -ārī, -ātus *vi* to philosophize

philosophus, -ī *m* philosopher ◆ *adj* philosophical

philtrum, -ī *nt* love potion

philyra, -ae *f* inner bark of the lime tree

phīmus, -ī *m* dice box

Phlegethōn, -ontis *m a river of Hades*

Phlegethontis *adj see* **Phlegethōn**

Phlīāsius *adj see* **Phlīūs**

Phlīūs, -ūntis *f town in Peloponnese*

phōca, -ae *f* seal

Phōcaicus *adj see* **Phōcis**

Phōcēus *adj see* **Phōcis**

Phōcis, -idis f country of central Greece
Phōcius adj see **Phōcis**
Phoebas, -adis f prophetess
Phoebē, -ēs f Diana, the moon
Phoebēius, -ēus adj see **Phoebus**
Phoebigena, -ae m son of Phoebus, Aesculapius
Phoebus, -ī m Apollo; the sun
Phoenīcē, -cēs f Phoenicia
Phoenīces, -cum mpl Phoenicians
phoenīcopterus, -ī m flamingo
Phoenīssus adj Phoenician ♦ f Dido
phoenīx, -īcis m phoenix
Phoenīx, -īcis m friend of Achilles
Phorcis, -idos = **Phorcynis**
Phorcus, -ī m son of Neptune (father of Medusa)
Phorcynis, -ynidos f Medusa
Phraātēs, -ae m king of Parthia
phrenēsis, -is f delirium
phrenēticus adj mad, delirious
Phrixēus adj see **Phrixus**
Phrixus, -ī m Helle's brother (who took the ram with the golden fleece to Colchis)
Phryges, -um mpl Phrygians; Trojans
Phrygia, -iae f Phrygia (country of Asia Minor); Troy
Phrygius adj Phrygian, Trojan
Phthīa, -ae f home of Achilles in Thessaly
Phthīōta, -ōtēs, -ōtae m native of Phthia
phthisis f consumption
Phthīus adj see **Phthīa**
phy interj bah!
phylaca, -ae f prison
phylarchus, -ī m chieftain
physica, -ae, physicē, -ēs f physics
physicē adv scientifically
physicus adj of physics, natural ♦ m natural philosopher ♦ ntpl physics
physiognōmōn, -onis m physiognomist
physiologia, -ae f natural philosophy, science
piābilis adj expiable
piāculāris adj atoning ♦ ntpl sin offerings
piāculum, -ī nt sin offering; victim; atonement, punishment; sin, guilt
piāmen, -inis nt atonement
pīca, -ae f magpie
picāria, -ae f pitch hut
picea, -ae f pine
Picēns, -entis adj = **Picēnus**
Picēnum, -ēnī nt Picenum
Picēnus adj of Picenum in E. Italy
piceus adj pitch black; of pitch
pictor, -ōris m painter
pictūra, -ae f painting; picture
pictūrātus adj painted; embroidered
pictus ppp of **pingō** ♦ adj coloured, tattooed; (style) ornate; (fear) unreal
pīcus, -ī m woodpecker
piē adv religiously, dutifully
Pīeris, -dis f Muse
Pīerius adj of the Muses, poetic
pietās, -ātis f sense of duty (to gods, family, country), piety, filial affection, love, patriotism
piger, -rī adj reluctant, slack, slow; numbing, dull

piget, -ēre, -uit vt (impers) to be annoyed, dislike; to regret, repent
pigmentārius, -ī and **-iī** m dealer in paints
pigmentum, -ī nt paint, cosmetic; (style) colouring
pignerātor, -ōris m mortgagee
pignerō, -āre vt to pawn, mortgage
pigneror, -ārī, -ātus vt to claim, accept
pignus, -oris and **-eris** nt pledge, pawn, security; wager, stake; (fig) assurance, token; (pl) children, dear ones
pigritia, -ae, pigritiēs, -ēī f sluggishness, indolence
pigrō, -āre, pigror, -ārī vi to be slow, be slack
pila, -ae f ball, ball game
pīla¹, -ae f mortar
pīla², -ae f pillar; pier
pīlānus, -ī m soldier of the third line
pīlātus adj armed with javelins
pīlentum, -ī nt carriage
pilleātus adj wearing the felt cap
pilleolus, -ī m skullcap
pilleum, -ī nt, **pilleus, -ī** m felt cap presented to freed slaves; (fig) liberty
pilōsus adj hairy
pīlum, -ī nt javelin
pilus, -ī m hair; a whit
pīlus, -ī m division of triarii; **prīmus** ~ chief centurion
Pimplēa, -ae, Pimplēis, -idis f Muse
Pimplēus adj of the Muses
Pindaricus adj see **Pindarus**
Pindarus, -ī m Pindar (Greek lyric poet)
Pindus, -ī m mountain range in Thessaly
pīnētum, -ī nt pine wood
pīneus adj pine- (in cpds)
pingō, -ere, pinxī, pictum vt to paint, embroider; to colour; (fig) to embellish, decorate
pinguēscō, -ere vi to grow fat, become fertile
pinguis adj fat, rich, fertile; (mind) gross, dull; (ease) comfortable, calm; (weather) thick ♦ nt grease
pīnifer, -ī, pīniger, -ī adj pine-clad
pinna, -ae f feather; wing, arrow; battlement; (fish) fin
pinnātus adj feathered, winged
pinniger, -ī adj winged; finny
pinnipēs, -edis adj wing-footed
pinnirapus, -ī m plume-snatcher
pinnula, -ae f little wing
pīnotērēs, -ae m hermit crab
pīnsō, -ere vt to beat, pound
pīnus, -ūs and **-ī** f stone pine, Scots fir; ship, torch, wreath
pinxī perf of **pingō**
piō, -āre vt to propitiate, worship; to atone for, avert; to avenge
piper, -is nt pepper
pīpilō, -āre vi to chirp
Pīraea, -ōrum ntpl Piraeus (main port of Athens)
Pīraeeus, Pīraeus, -ī m main port of Athens
Pīraeus adj see **Pīraeeus**
pīrāta, -ae m pirate

pīrāticus *adj* pirate ◆ *f* piracy
Pīrēnē, -ēs *f spring in Corinth*
Pīrēnis, -idis *adj see* **Pīrēnē**
Pīrithous, -ī *m king of the Lapiths*
pirum, -ī *nt* pear
pirus, -ī *f* pear tree
Pīsa, -ae *f Greek town near the Olympic Games site*
Pīsae, -ārum *fpl town in Etruria (now Pisa)*
Pīsaeus *adj see* **Pīsae**
Pīsānus *adj see* **Pīsae**
piscārius *adj* fish- (in cpds), fishing- (in cpds)
piscātor, -ōris *m* fisherman
piscātōrius *adj* fishing- (in cpds)
piscātus, -ūs *m* fishing; fish; catch, haul
pisciculus, -ī *m* little fish
piscīna, -ae *f* fishpond; swimming pool
piscīnārius, -ī *and* **-iī** *m* person keen on fish
  ponds
piscis, -is *m* fish; (ASTR) Pisces
piscor, -ārī, -ātus *vi* to fish
piscōsus *adj* full of fish
pisculentus *adj* full of fish
Pīsistratidae, -idārum *mpl* sons of Pisistratus
Pīsistratus, -ī *m tyrant of Athens*
pistillum, -ī *nt* pestle
pistor, -ōris *m* miller; baker
pistrilla, -ae *f* little mortar
pistrīnum, -ī *nt* mill, bakery; drudgery
pistris, -is, pistrīx, -īcis *f* sea monster, whale;
  swift ship
pithēcium, -ī *and* **-iī** *nt* little ape
pītuīta, -ae *f* phlegm; catarrh, cold in the head
pītuītōsus *adj* phlegmatic
pius *adj* dutiful, conscientious; godly, holy;
  filial, affectionate; patriotic; good, upright
  ◆ *mpl* the blessed dead
pix, picis *f* pitch
plācābilis *adj* easily appeased
plācābilitās, -ātis *f* readiness to condone
plācāmen, -inis, plācāmentum, -ī *nt* peace-
  offering
plācātē *adv* calmly
plācātiō, -ōnis *f* propitiating
plācātus *ppp of* **plācō** ◆ *adj* calm, quiet,
  reconciled
placenta, -ae *f* cake
Placentia, -iae *f town in N. Italy (now Piacenza)*
Placentīnus *adj see* **Placentia**
placeō, -ēre, -uī, -itum *vi (with dat)* to please,
  satisfy; **placet** it seems good, it is agreed,
  resolved; **mihi ~** I am pleased with myself
placidē *adv* peacefully, gently
placidus *adj* calm, quiet, gentle
placitum, -ī *nt* belief
placitus *ppa of* **placeō** ◆ *adj* pleasing; agreed on
plācō, -āre, -āvī, -ātum *vt* to calm, appease,
  reconcile
plaga¹, -ae *f* region, zone
plaga², -ae *f* hunting net, snare, trap
plāga, -ae *f* blow, stroke, wound
plagiārius, -ī *and* **-iī** *m* plunderer, kidnapper
plāgigerulus *adj* much flogged
plāgōsus *adj* fond of punishing
plagula, -ae *f* curtain

planctus, -ūs *m* beating the breast,
  lamentation
plānē *adv* plainly, clearly; completely, quite;
  certainly
plangō, -gere, -xī, -ctum *vt, vi* to beat noisily; to
  beat in grief; to lament loudly, bewail
plangor, -ōris *m* beating; loud lamentation
plānipēs, -edis *m* ballet dancer
plānitās, -ātis *f* perspicuity
plānitiēs, -ēī, plānitia, -ae *f* level ground, plain
planta, -ae *f* shoot, slip; sole, foot
plantāria, -ium *ntpl* slips, young trees
planus, -ī *m* impostor
plānus *adj* level, flat; plain, clear ◆ *nt* level
  ground; **dē plānō** easily
platalea, -ae *f* spoonbill
platea, -ae *f* street
Platō, -ōnis *m* Plato (founder of the Academic school
  of philosophy)
Platōnicus *adj see* **Platō**
plaudō, -dere, -sī, -sum *vt* to clap, beat, stamp
  ◆ *vi* to clap, applaud; to approve, be pleased
  with
plausibilis *adj* praiseworthy
plausor, -ōris *m* applauder
plaustrum, -ī *nt* wagon, cart; (ASTR) Great Bear;
  ~ percellere upset the applecart
plausus¹ *ppp of* **plaudō**
plausus², -ūs *m* flapping; clapping, applause
Plautīnus *adj see* **Plautus**
Plautus, -ī *m early Latin comic poet*
plēbēcula, -ae *f* rabble
plēbēius *adj* plebeian; common, low
plēbicola, -ae *m* friend of the people
plēbīscītum, -ī *nt* decree of the people
plēbs, plēbēs, -is *f* common people, plebeians;
  lower classes, masses
plēctō, -ere *vt* to punish
plēctrum, -ī *nt* plectrum; lyre, lyric poetry
Plēias, -dis *f* Pleiad; (pl) the Seven Sisters
plēnē *adv* fully, entirely
plēnus *adj* full, filled; (fig) sated; (age) mature;
  (amount) complete; (body) stout, plump; (female)
  pregnant; (matter) solid; (style) copious; (voice)
  loud; **ad plēnum** abundantly
plērumque *adv* generally, mostly
plērusque *adj* a large part, most; (pl) the
  majority, the most; very many
plexus *adj* plaited, interwoven
Plīas *see* **Plēias**
plicātrīx, -īcis *f* clothes folder
plicō, -āre, -āvī *and* **-uī, -ātum** *and* **-itum** *vt* to
  fold, coil
Plīnius, -ī *m Roman family name (esp Pliny the Elder,
  who died in the eruption of Vesuvius); Pliny the Younger,
  writer of letters*
plōrātus, -ūs *m* wailing
plōrō, -āre, -āvī, -ātum *vi* to wail, lament ◆ *vt* to
  weep for, bewail
plōstellum, -ī *nt* cart
ploxenum, -ī *nt* cart box
pluit, -ere, -it *vi (impers)* it is raining
plūma, -ae *f* soft feather, down
plumbeus *adj* of lead; (fig) heavy, dull, worthless

plumbum, **-ī** *nt* lead; bullet, pipe, ruler; ~ **album** tin

plŭmeus *adj* down, downy

plŭmipēs, **-edis** *adj* feather-footed

plŭmōsus *adj* feathered

plŭrimus *superl of* **multus**

plŭs, **-ūris** *compar of* **multus** ♦ *adv* more

plŭsculus *adj* a little more

pluteus, **-ī** *m* shelter, penthouse; parapet; couch; bookcase

Plŭtō, **-ōnis** *m king of the lower world*

Plŭtōnius *adj see* **Plŭtō**

pluvia, **-ae** *f* rain

pluviālis *adj* rainy

pluvius *adj* rainy, rain- (*in cpds*)

pōcillum, **-ī** *nt* small cup

pōculum, **-ī** *nt* cup; drink, potion

podagra, **-ae** *f* gout

podagrōsus *adj* gouty

podium, **-ī** *and* **-iī** *nt* balcony

poēma, **-tis** *nt* poem

poena, **-ae** *f* penalty, punishment; **poenas dare** to be punished

Poenī, **-ōrum** *mpl* Carthaginians

Poenus, **Pŭnicus** *adj* Punic

poēsis, **-is** *f* poetry, poem

poēta, **-ae** *m* poet

poēticē *adv* poetically

poēticus *adj* poetic ♦ *f* poetry

poētria, **-ae** *f* poetess

pol *interj* by Pollux!, truly

polenta, **-ae** *f* pearl barley

poliō, **-īre**, **-īvī**, **-ītum** *vt* to polish; to improve, put in good order

polītē *adv* elegantly

polītīa, **-ae** *f* Plato's Republic

politicus *adj* political

polītus *adj* polished, refined, cultured

pollen, **-inis** *nt* fine flour, meal

pollēns, **-entis** *pres p of* **polleō** ♦ *adj* powerful, strong

pollentia, **-ae** *f* power

polleō, **-ēre** *vi* to be strong, be powerful

pollex, **-icis** *m* thumb

polliceor, **-ērī**, **-itus** *vt* to promise, offer

pollicitātiō, **-ōnis** *f* promise

pollicitor, **-ārī**, **-ātus** *vt* to promise

pollicitum, **-ī** *nt* promise

Polliō, **-ōnis** *m* Roman surname (*esp C. Asinius, soldier, statesman and literary patron under Augustus*)

pollis, **-inis** *m/f see* **pollen**

pollūcibiliter *adv* sumptuously

pollūctus *adj* offered up ♦ *nt* offering

polluō, **-uere**, **-uī**, **-ūtum** *vt* to defile, pollute, dishonour

Pollūx, **-ūcis** *m* twin brother of Castor (*famous as a boxer*)

polus, **-ī** *m* pole, North pole; sky

Polyhymnia, **-ae** *f* a Muse

Polyphēmus, **-ī** *m* one-eyed Cyclops

pōlypus, **-ī** *m* polypus

pōmārium, **-ī** *and* **-iī** *nt* orchard

pōmārius, **-ī** *and* **-iī** *m* fruiterer

pōmerīdiānus *adj* afternoon

pōmērium, **-ī** *and* **-iī** *nt* free space round the city boundary

pōmifer, **-ī** *adj* fruitful

pōmoerium *see* **pōmērium**

pōmōsus *adj* full of fruit

pompa, **-ae** *f* procession; retinue, train; ostentation

Pompeiānus *adj see* **Pompeiī**

Pompeiī, **-ōrum** *mpl* Campanian town buried by an eruption of Vesuvius

Pompeius¹, **-ī** *m* Roman family name (*esp Pompey the Great*)

Pompeius², **-ānus** *adj see* **Pompeius¹**

Pompilius¹, **-ī** *m* Numa (*second king of Rome*)

Pompilius² *adj see* **Pompilius¹**

Pomptīnus *adj* Pomptine (*name of marshy district in S. Latium*)

pōmum, **-ī** *nt* fruit; fruit tree

pōmus, **-ī** *f* fruit tree

ponderō, **-āre** *vt* to weigh; to consider, reflect on

ponderōsus *adj* heavy, weighty

pondō *adv* in weight; pounds

pondus, **-eris** *nt* weight; mass, burden; (*fig*) importance, authority; (*character*) firmness; (*pl*) balance

pōne *adv* behind

pōnō, **-ere**, **posuī**, **positum** *vt* to put, place, lay, set; to lay down, lay aside; (*fig*) to regard, reckon; (*art*) to make, build; (*camp*) to pitch; (*corpse*) to lay out, bury; (*example*) to take; (*food*) to serve; (*hair*) to arrange; (*hope*) to base, stake; (*hypothesis*) to suppose, assume; (*institution*) to lay down, ordain; (*money*) to invest; (*sea*) to calm; (*theme*) to propose; (*time*) to spend, devote; (*tree*) to plant; (*wager*) to put down ♦ *vi* (*wind*) to abate

pōns, **pontis** *m* bridge; drawbridge; (*ship*) gangway, deck

ponticulus, **-ī** *m* small bridge

Ponticus *adj see* **Pontus**

pontifex, **-icis** *m* high priest, pontiff

pontificālis *adj* pontifical

pontificātus, **-ūs** *m* high priesthood

pontificius *adj* pontiff's

pontō, **-ōnis** *m* ferryboat

Pontus, **-ī** *m* Black Sea; kingdom of Mithridates in Asia Minor

pontus, **-ī** *m* sea

popa, **-ae** *m* minor priest

popanum, **-ī** *nt* sacrificial cake

popellus, **-ī** *m* mob

popīna, **-ae** *f* eating house, restaurant

popīnō, **-ōnis** *m* glutton

popl- *etc see* **pŭbl-**

poples, **-itis** *m* knee

poposcī *perf of* **poscō**

poppysma, **-tis** *nt* clicking of the tongue

populābilis *adj* destroyable

populābundus *adj* ravaging

populāris *adj* of, from, for the people; popular, democratic; native ♦ *m* fellow countryman ♦ *mpl* the people's party, the democrats

populāritās, **-ātis** *f* courting popular favour

populāriter *adv* vulgarly; democratically

populātiō, -ōnis *f* plundering; plunder
populātor, -ōris *m* ravager
pōpuleus *adj* poplar- *(in cpds)*
pōpulifer, -ī *adj* rich in poplars
populor, -ārī, -ātus, populō, -āre *vt* to ravage, plunder; to destroy, ruin
populus, -ī *m* people, nation; populace, the public; large crowds; district
pōpulus, -ī *f* poplar tree
porca, -ae *f* sow
porcella, -ae *f*, **porcellus, -ī** *m* little pig
porcīna, -ae *f* pork
porcīnārius, -ī *and* **-iī** *m* pork seller
Porcius¹, -ī *m family name of Cato*
Porcius² *adj see* **Porcius¹**
porculus, -ī *m* porker
porcus, -ī *m* pig, hog
porgō *etc see* **porrigō**
Porphyriōn, -ōnis *m a Giant*
porrēctiō, -ōnis *f* extending
porrēctus *ppp of* **porrigō** ✦ *adj* long, protracted; dead
porrēxī *perf of* **porrigō**
porriciō, -ere *vt* to make an offering of; **inter caesa et porrēcta** at the eleventh hour
porrigō, -igere, -ēxī, -ēctum *vt* to stretch, spread out, extend; to offer, hold out
porrīgō, -inis *f* scurf, dandruff
porrō *adv* forward, a long way off; *(time)* in future, long ago; *(sequence)* next, moreover, in turn
porrum, -ī *nt* leek
Porsena, Porsenna, Porsinna, -ae *f king of Clusium in Etruria*
porta, -ae *f* gate; entrance, outlet
portātiō, -ōnis *f* carrying
portendō, -dere, -dī, -tum *vt* to denote, predict
portentificus *adj* marvellous
portentōsus *adj* unnatural
portentum, -ī *nt* omen, unnatural happening; monstrosity, monster; *(story)* marvel
porthmeus, -eī *and* **-eos** *m* ferryman
porticula, -ae *f* small gallery
porticus, -ūs *m* portico, colonnade; *(MIL)* gallery; *(PHILOS)* Stoicism
portiō, -ōnis *f* share, instalment; **prō portiōne** proportionally
portitor¹, -ōris *m* customs officer
portitor², -ōris *m* ferryman
portō, -āre, -āvī, -ātum *vt* to carry, convey, bring
portōrium, -ī *and* **-iī** *nt* customs duty, tax
portula, -ae *f* small gate
portuōsus *adj* well-off for harbours
portus, -ūs *m* harbour, port; *(fig)* safety, haven
pōsca, -ae *f* a vinegar drink
poscō, -ere, poposcī *vt* to ask, require, demand; to call on
Posīdōnius, -ī *m Stoic philosopher (teacher of Cicero)*
positiō, -ōnis *f* position, climate
positor, -ōris *m* builder
positūra, -ae *f* position; formation

positus *ppp of* **pōnō** ✦ *adj* situated
posse *infin of* **possum**
possēdī *perf of* **possideō; possīdō**
possessiō, -ōnis *f* seizing; occupation; possession, property
possessiuncula, -ae *f* small estate
possessor, -ōris *m* occupier, possessor
possessus *ppp of* **possideō; possīdō**
possideō, -idēre, -ēdī, -essum *vt* to hold, occupy; to have, possess
possīdō, -īdere, -ēdī, -essum *vt* to take possession of
possum, -sse, -tuī *vi* to be able, can; to have power, avail
post *adv (place)* behind; *(time)* after; *(sequence)* next *prep (with acc)* behind; after, since; **paulō ~** soon after; **~ urbem conditam** since the foundation of the city
posteā *adv* afterwards, thereafter; next, then; **~ quam** *conj* after
posterior, -ōris *adj* later, next; inferior, less important
posteritās, -ātis *f* posterity, the future
posterius *adv* later
posterus *adj* next, following ✦ *mpl* posterity
postferō, -re *vt* to put after, sacrifice
postgenitī, -ōrum *mpl* later generations
posthabeō, -ēre, -uī, -itum *vt* to put after, neglect
posthāc *adv* hereafter, in future
postibi *adv* then, after that
postīculum, -ī *nt* small back building
postīcus *adj* back- *(in cpds)*, hind- *(in cpds)* ✦ *nt* back door
postideā *adv* after that
postillā *adv* afterwards
postis, -is *m* doorpost, door
postlīminium, -ī *and* **-iī** *nt* right of recovery
postmerīdiānus *adj* in the afternoon
postmodo, postmodum *adv* shortly, presently
postpōnō, -ōnere, -osuī, -ositum *vt* to put after, disregard
postputō, -āre *vt* to consider less important
postquam *conj* after, when
postrēmō *adv* finally
postrēmus *adj* last, rear; lowest, worst
postrīdiē *adv* next day, the day after
postscaenium, -ī *and* **-iī** *nt* behind the scenes
postscrībō, -ere *vt* to write after
postulātiō, -ōnis *f* demand, claim; complaint
postulātum, -ī *nt* demand, claim
postulātus, -ūs *m* claim
postulō, -āre, -āvī, -ātum *vt* to demand, claim; *(LAW)* to summon, prosecute; to apply for a writ *(to prosecute)*
postumus *adj* last, last-born
postus *etc see* **positus**
posuī *perf of* **pōnō**
pōtātiō, -ōnis *f* drinking
pōtātor, -ōris *m* toper
pote *etc see* **potis**
potēns, -entis *adj* able, capable; powerful, strong, potent; master of, ruling over; successful in carrying out

potentātus, **-ūs** *m* political power
potenter *adv* powerfully; competently
potentia, **-ae** *f* power, force, efficacy; tyranny
potērium, **-ī** *and* **-iī** *nt* goblet
potesse *archaic infin of* **possum**
potestās, **-ātis** *f* power, ability; control,
    sovereignty, authority; opportunity,
    permission; (*person*) magistrate; (*things*)
    property; **potestātem suī facere** allow access
    to oneself
potin can (you)?, is it possible?
potiō, **-īre** *vt* to put into the power of
pōtiō, **-ōnis** *f* drink, draught, philtre
potior[1], **-īrī**, **-ītus** *vi* (*with gen and abl*) to take
    possession of, get hold of, acquire; to be
    master of
potior[2], **-ōris** *adj* better, preferable
potis *adj* (*indecl*) able; possible
potissimum *adv* especially
potissimus *adj* chief, most important
pōtitō, **-āre** *vt* to drink much
potius *adv* rather, more
pōtō, **-āre**, **-āvī**, **-ātum** *and* **-um** *vt* to drink
pōtor, **-ōris** *m* drinker
pōtrīx, **-īcis** *f* woman tippler
potuī *perf of* **possum**
pōtulenta, **-ōrum** *ntpl* drinks
pōtus[1] *ppp of* **pōtō** ♦ *adj* drunk
pōtus[2], **-ūs** *m* drink
prae *adv* in front, before; in comparison ♦ *prep*
    (*with abl*) in front of; compared with; (*cause*)
    because of, for; **~ sē** openly; **~ sē ferre** display;
    ~ manū to hand
praeacūtus *adj* pointed
praealtus *adj* very high, very deep
praebeō, **-ēre**, **-uī**, **-itum** *vt* to hold out,
    proffer; to give, supply; to show, represent; **sē**
    praebēre behave, prove
praebibō, **-ere**, **-ī** *vt* to toast
praebitor, **-ōris** *m* purveyor
praecalidus *adj* very hot
praecānus *adj* prematurely grey
praecautus *ppp of* **praecaveō**
praecaveō, **-avēre**, **-āvī**, **-autum** *vt* to guard
    against ♦ *vi* to beware, take precautions
praecēdō, **-dere**, **-ssī**, **-ssum** *vt* to go before; to
    surpass ♦ *vi* to lead the way; to excel
praecellō, **-ere** *vi* to excel, be distinguished
    ♦ *vt* to surpass
praecelsus *adj* very high
praecentiō, **-ōnis** *f* prelude
praecentō, **-āre** *vi* to sing an incantation for
praeceps, **-ipitis** *adj* head first, headlong;
    going down, precipitous; rapid, violent,
    hasty; inclined (to); dangerous ♦ *nt* edge of
    an abyss, precipice; danger ♦ *adv* headlong;
    into danger
praeceptiō, **-ōnis** *f* previous notion; precept
praeceptor, **-ōris** *m* teacher
praeceptrīx, **-rīcis** *f* teacher
praeceptum, **-ī** *nt* maxim, precept; order
praeceptus *ppp of* **praecipiō**
praecerpō, **-ere**, **-sī**, **-tum** *vt* to gather
    prematurely; to forestall

praecīdō, **-dere**, **-dī**, **-sum** *vt* to cut off,
    damage; (*fig*) to cut short, put an end to
praecinctus *ppp of* **praecingō**
praecingō, **-ingere**, **-inxī**, **-inctum** *vt* to gird
    in front; to surround
praecinō, **-inere**, **-inuī**, **-entum** *vt* to play
    before; to chant a spell ♦ *vt* to predict
praecipiō, **-ipere**, **-ēpī**, **-ēptum** *vt* to take
    beforehand, get in advance; to anticipate; to
    teach, admonish, order
praecipitanter *adv* at full speed
praecipitem *acc of* **praeceps**
praecipitō, **-āre**, **-āvī**, **-ātum** *vt* to throw
    down, throw away, hasten; (*fig*) to remove,
    carry away, ruin ♦ *vi* to rush headlong, fall;
    to be hasty
praecipuē *adv* especially, chiefly
praecipuus *adj* special; principal,
    outstanding
praecīsē *adv* briefly, absolutely
praecīsus *ppp of* **praecīdō** ♦ *adj* steep
praeclārē *adv* very clearly; excellently
praeclārus *adj* very bright; beautiful,
    splendid; distinguished, noble
praeclūdō, **-dere**, **-sī**, **-sum** *vt* to close, shut
    against; to close to, impede
praecō, **-ōnis** *m* crier, herald; auctioneer
praecōgitō, **-āre** *vt* to premeditate
praecognitus *adj* foreseen
praecolō, **-olere**, **-oluī**, **-ultum** *vt* to cultivate
    early
praecompositus *adj* studied
praecōnium, **-ī** *and* **-iī** *nt* office of a crier;
    advertisement; commendation
praecōnius *adj* of a public crier
praecōnsūmō, **-ere**, **-ptum** *vt* to use up
    beforehand
praecontrectō, **-āre** *vt* to consider
    beforehand
praecordia, **-ōrum** *ntpl* midriff; stomach;
    breast, heart; mind
praecorrumpō, **-umpere**, **-ūpī**, **-uptum** *vt* to
    bribe beforehand
praecox, **-cis** *adj* early, premature
praecultus *ppp of* **praecolō**
praecurrentia, **-ium** *ntpl* antecedents
praecurrō, **-rrere**, **-currī** *and* **-rrī**, **-rsum** *vi*
    to hurry on before, precede; to excel ♦ *vt* to
    anticipate; to surpass
praecursiō, **-ōnis** *f* previous occurrence; (*RHET*)
    preparation
praecursor, **-ōris** *m* advance guard; scout
praecutiō, **-ere** *vt* to brandish before
praeda, **-ae** *f* booty, plunder; (*animal*) prey;
    (*fig*) gain
praedābundus *adj* plundering
praedamnō, **-āre** *vt* to condemn beforehand
praedatiō, **-ōnis** *f* plundering
praedātor, **-ōris** *m* plunderer
praedātōrius *adj* marauding
praedēlassō, **-āre** *vt* to weaken beforehand
praedēstinō, **-āre** *vt* to predetermine
praediātor, **-ōris** *m* buyer of landed estates
praediātōrius *adj* relating to the sale of
    estates

praedicābilis *adj* laudatory

praedicātiō, -ōnis *f* proclamation; commendation

praedicātor, -ōris *m* eulogist

praedicō, -āre, -āvī, -ātum *vt* to proclaim, make public; to declare; to praise, boast

praedīcō, -īcere, -īxī, -ictum *vt* to mention beforehand, prearrange; to foretell; to warn, command

praedictiō, -ōnis *f* foretelling

praedictum, -ī *nt* prediction; command; prearrangement

praedictus *ppp of* **praedīcō**

praediolum, -ī *nt* small estate

praediscō, -ere *vt* to learn beforehand

praedispositus *adj* arranged beforehand

praeditus *adj* endowed, provided

praedium, -ī *and* **-iī** *nt* estate

praedīves, -itis *adj* very rich

praedō, -ōnis *m* robber, pirate

praedor, -ārī, -ātus *vt, vi* to plunder, rob; (*fig*) to profit

praedūcō, -ūcere, -ūxī, -uctum *vt* to draw in front

praedulcis *adj* very sweet

praedūrus *adj* very hard, very tough

praeēmineō, -ēre *vt* to surpass

praeeō, -īre, -īvī *and* **-iī, -itum** *vi* to lead the way, go first; (*formula*) to dictate, recite first ◆ *vt* to precede, outstrip

praeesse *infin of* **praesum**

praefātiō, -ōnis *f* formula; preface

praefātus *ppa of* **praefor**

praefectūra, -ae *f* superintendence; governorship; *Italian town governed by Roman edicts*, prefecture; district, province

praefectus *ppp of* **praeficiō** ◆ *m* overseer, director, governor, commander; ~ **classis** admiral; ~ **legiōnis** colonel; ~ **urbis** *or* **urbī** city prefect (*of Rome*)

praeferō, -ferre, -tulī, -lātum *vt* to carry in front, hold out; to prefer; to show, display; to anticipate; (*pass*) to hurry past, outflank

praeferōx, -ōcis *adj* very impetuous, very insolent

praefervidus *adj* very hot

praefestīnō, -āre *vi* to be too hasty; to hurry past

praefica, -ae *f* hired mourner

praeficiō, -icere, -ēcī, -ectum *vt* to put in charge, give command over

praefidēns, -entis *adj* over-confident

praefīgō, -gere, -xī, -xum *vt* to fasten in front, set up before; to tip, point; to transfix

praefīniō, -īre, -īvī *and* **-iī, -ītum** *vt* to determine, prescribe

praefiscinē, -ī *adv* without offence

praeflōrō, -āre *vt* to tarnish

praefluō, -ere *vt, vi* to flow past

praefocō, -āre *vt* to choke

praefodiō, -odere, -ōdī *vt* to dig in front of; to bury beforehand

praefor, -ārī, -ātus *vt, vi* to say in advance, preface; to pray beforehand; to predict

praefrāctē *adv* resolutely

praefrāctus *ppp of* **praefringō** ◆ *adj* abrupt; stern

praefrīgidus *adj* very cold

praefringō, -ingere, -ēgī, -āctum *vt* to break off, shiver

praefuī *perf of* **praesum**

praefulciō, -cīre, -sī, -tum *vt* to prop up; to use as a prop

praefulgeō, -ulgēre, -ulsī *vt* to shine conspicuously; to outshine

praegelidus *adj* very cold

praegestiō, -īre *vi* to be very eager

praegnāns, -antis *adj* pregnant; full

praegracilis *adj* very slim

praegrandis *adj* very large, very great

praegravis *adj* very heavy; very wearisome

praegravō, -āre *vt* to weigh down; to eclipse

praegredior, -dī, -ssus *vt, vi* to go before; to go past; to surpass

praegressiō, -ōnis *f* precession, precedence

praegustātor, -ōris *m* taster

praegustō, -āre *vt* to taste beforehand

praehibeō, -ēre *vt* to offer, give

praeiaceō, -ēre *vt* to lie in front of

praeiūdicium, -ī *and* **-iī** *nt* precedent, example; prejudgment

praeiūdicō, -āre, -āvī, -ātum *vt* to prejudge, decide beforehand

praeiuvō, -āre *vt* to give previous assistance to

praelabor, -bī, -psus *vt, vi* to move past, move along

praelambō, -ere *vt* to lick first

praelātus *ppp of* **praeferō**

praelegō, -ere *vt* to coast along

praeligō, -āre *vt* to bind, tie up

praelongus *adj* very long, very tall

praeloquor, -quī, -cūtus *vt* to speak first

praelūceō, -cēre, -xī *vi* to light, shine; to outshine

praelūstris *adj* very magnificent

praemandāta *ntpl* warrant of arrest

praemandō, -āre, -āvī, -ātum *vt* to bespeak

praemātūrē *adv* too soon

praemātūrus *adj* too early, premature

praemedicātus *adj* protected by charms

praemeditātiō, -ōnis *f* thinking over the future

praemeditātus *adj* premeditated

praemeditor, -ārī, -ātus *vt* to think over, practise

praemetuenter *adv* anxiously

praemetuō, -ere *vi* to be anxious ◆ *vt* to fear the future

praemissus *ppp of* **praemittō**

praemittō, -ittere, -īsī, -issum *vt* to send in advance

praemium, -ī *and* **-iī** *nt* prize, reward

praemolestia, -ae *f* apprehension

praemōlior, -īrī *vt* to prepare thoroughly

praemoneō, -ēre, -uī, -itum *vt* to forewarn, foreshadow

praemonitus, -ūs *m* premonition

praemōnstrātor, -ōris *m* guide**

praemōnstrō, **-āre** vt to guide; to predict
praemordeō, **-ēre** vt to bite off; to pilfer
praemorior, **-ī**, **-tuus** vi to die too soon
praemūniō, **-īre**, **-īvī**, **-ītum** vt to fortify, strengthen, secure
praemūnītiō, **-ōnis** f (RHET) preparation
praenārrō, **-āre** vt to tell beforehand
praenatō, **-āre** vt to flow past
Praeneste, **-is** nt/f Latin town (now Palestrina)
Praenestīnus adj see **Praeneste**
praeniteō, **-ēre**, **-uī** vi to seem more attractive
praenōmen, **-inis** nt first name
praenōscō, **-ere** vt to foreknow
praenōtiō, **-ōnis** f preconceived idea
praenūbilus adj very gloomy
praenūntia, **-iae** f harbinger
praenūntiō, **-āre** vt to foretell
praenūntius, **-ī** and **-iī** m harbinger
praeoccupō, **-āre**, **-āvī**, **-ātum** vt to take first, anticipate
praeolit mihi I get a hint of
praeoptō, **-āre**, **-āvī**, **-ātum** vt to choose rather, prefer
praepandō, **-ere** vt to spread out; to expound
praeparātiō, **-ōnis** f preparation
praeparō, **-āre**, **-āvī**, **-ātum** vt to prepare, prepare for; **ex praeparātō** by arrangement
praepediō, **-īre**, **-īvī**, **-ītum** vt to shackle, tether; to hamper
praependeō, **-ēre** vi to hang down in front
praepes, **-etis** adj swift, winged; of good omen ◆ f bird
praepilātus adj tipped with a ball
praepinguis adj very rich
praepolleō, **-ēre** vi to be very powerful, be superior
praeponderō, **-āre** vt to outweigh
praepōnō, **-ōnere**, **-osuī**, **-ositum** vt to put first, place in front; to put in charge, appoint commander; to prefer
praeportō, **-āre** vt to carry before
praepositiō, **-ōnis** f preference; (GRAM) preposition
praepositus ppp of **praepōnō** ◆ m overseer, commander
praepossum, **-sse**, **-tuī** vi to gain the upper hand
praeposterē adv the wrong way round
praeposterus adj inverted, perverted; absurd
praepotēns, **-entis** adj very powerful
praeproperanter adv too hastily
praeproperē adv too hastily
praeproperus adj overhasty, rash
praepūtium, **-ī** and **-iī** nt foreskin
praequam adv compared with
praequestus adj complaining beforehand
praeradiō, **-āre** vt to outshine
praerapidus adj very swift
praereptus ppp of **praeripiō**
praerigēscō, **-ēscere**, **-uī** vi to become very stiff
praeripiō, **-ipere**, **-ipuī**, **-eptum** vt to take before, forestall; to carry off prematurely; to frustrate

praerōdō, **-dere**, **-sum** vt to bite the end of, nibble off
praerogātīva, **-ae** f tribe or century with the first vote, the first vote; previous election; omen, sure token
praerogātīvus adj voting first
praerōsus ppp of **praerōdō**
praerumpō, **-umpere**, **-ūpī**, **-uptum** vt to break off
praeruptus ppp of **praerumpō** ◆ adj steep, abrupt; headstrong
praes, **-aedis** m surety; property of a surety
praesaep- etc see **praesēp-**
praesāgiō, **-īre** vt to have a presentiment of, forebode
praesāgītiō, **-ōnis** f foreboding
praesāgium, **-ī** and **-iī** nt presentiment; prediction
praesāgus adj foreboding, prophetic
praesciō, **-īre**, **-iī** vt to know before
praescīscō, **-ere** vt to find out beforehand
praescius adj foreknowing
praescrībō, **-bere**, **-psī**, **-ptum** vt to write first; to direct, command; to dictate, describe; to put forward as a pretext
praescrīptiō, **-ōnis** f preface, heading; order, rule; pretext
praescrīptum, **-ī** nt order, rule
praescrīptus ppp of **praescrībō**
praesecō, **-āre**, **-uī**, **-tum** and **-ātum** vt to cut off, pare
praesēns, **-entis** adj present, in person; (things) immediate, ready, prompt; (mind) resolute; (gods) propitious ◆ ntpl present state of affairs; **in ~** for the present; **~ in rē praesentī** on the spot
praesēnsiō, **-ōnis** f foreboding; preconception
praesēnsus ppp of **praesentiō**
praesentārius adj instant, ready
praesentia, **-ae** f presence; effectiveness
praesentiō, **-entīre**, **-ēnsī**, **-ēnsum** vt to presage, have a foreboding of
praesēpe, **-is** nt, **praesēpēs**, **-is** f stable, fold, pen; hovel; hive
praesēpiō, **-īre**, **-sī**, **-tum** vt to barricade
praesēpis f = **praesēpe**
praesertim adv especially
praeserviō, **-īre** vi to serve as a slave
praeses, **-idis** m guardian, protector; chief, ruler
praesideō, **-idēre**, **-ēdī** vi to guard, defend; to preside over, direct
praesidiārius adj garrison-
praesidium, **-ī** and **-iī** nt defence, protection; support, assistance; guard, garrison, convoy; defended position, entrenchment
praesignificō, **-āre** vt to foreshadow
praesignis adj conspicuous
praesonō, **-āre**, **-uī** vi to sound before
praespargō, **-ere** vt to strew before
praestābilis adj outstanding; preferable
praestāns, **-antis** pres p of **praestō²** ◆ adj outstanding, pre-eminent
praestantia, **-ae** f pre-eminence
praestes, **-itis** adj presiding, guardian

praestīgiae, -ārum *fpl* illusion, sleight of hand

praestīgiātor, -ōris *m*, **praestīgiātrīx, -rīcis** *f* conjurer, cheat

praestinō, -āre *vt* to buy

praestitī *perf of* **praestō²**

praestituō, -uere, -uī, -ūtum *vt* to prearrange, prescribe

praestitus *ppp of* **praestō²**

praestō¹ *adv* at hand, ready

praestō², -āre, -itī, -itum *and* **-ātum** *vi* to be outstanding, be superior; (*impers*) it is better ♦ *vt* to excel; to be responsible for, answer for; (*duty*) to discharge, perform; (*quality*) to show, prove; (*things*) to give, offer, provide; **sē praestāre** behave, prove

praestōlor, -ārī, -ātus *vt, vi* to wait for, expect

praestrictus *ppp of* **praestringō**

praestringō, -ingere, -inxī, -ictum *vt* to squeeze; to blunt, dull; (*eyes*) to dazzle

praestruō, -ere, -xī, -ctum *vt* to block up; to build beforehand

praesul, -is *m/f* public dancer

praesultātor, -ōris *m* public dancer

praesultō, -āre *vi* to dance before

praesum, -esse, -fuī *vi* (*with dat*) to be at the head of, be in command of; to take the lead; to protect

praesūmō, -ere, -psī, -ptum *vt* to take first; to anticipate; to take for granted

praesūtus *adj* sewn over at the point

praetemptō, -āre *vt* to feel for, grope for; to test in advance

praetendō, -dere, -dī, -tum *vt* to hold out, put before, spread in front of; to give as an excuse, allege

praetentō *etc see* **praetemptō**

praetentus *ppp of* **praetendō** ♦ *adj* lying over against

praetepeō, -ēre, -uī *vi* to glow before

praeter *adv* beyond; excepting ♦ *prep* (*with acc*) past, along; except, besides; beyond, more than, in addition to, contrary to

praeteragō, -ere *vt* to drive past

praeterbītō, -ere *vt, vi* to pass by

praeterdūcō, -ere *vt* to lead past

praetereā *adv* besides; moreover; henceforth

praetereō, -īre, -iī, -itum *vi* to go past ♦ *vt* to pass, overtake; to escape, escape the notice of; to omit, leave out, forget, neglect; to reject, exclude; to surpass; to transgress

praeterequitāns, -antis *adj* riding past

praeterfluō, -ere *vt, vi* to flow past

praetergredior, -dī, -ssus *vt* to pass, march past; to surpass

praeterhāc *adv* further, more

praeteritus *ppp of* **praetereō** ♦ *adj* past, gone by ♦ *ntpl* the past

praeterlābor, -bī, -psus *vt* to flow past, move past ♦ *vi* to slip away

praeterlātus *adj* driving, flying past

praetermeō, -āre *vi* to pass by

praetermissiō, -ōnis *f* omission, passing over

praetermittō, -ittere, -īsī, -issum *vt* to let pass; to omit, neglect; to make no mention of; to overlook

praeterquam *adv* except, besides

praetervectiō, -ōnis *f* passing by

praetervehor, -hī, -ctus *vt, vi* to ride past, sail past; to march past; to pass by, pass over

praetervolō, -āre *vt, vi* to fly past; to escape

praetexō, -ere, -uī, -tum *vt* to border, fringe; to adorn; to pretend, disguise

praetextātus *adj* wearing the toga praetexta, under age

praetextus¹ *ppp of* **praetexō** ♦ *adj* wearing the toga praetexta ♦ *f* toga with a purple border; Roman tragedy ♦ *nt* pretext

praetextus², -ūs *m* splendour; pretence

praetimeō, -ēre *vi* to be afraid in advance

praetinctus *adj* dipped beforehand

praetor, -ōris *m* chief magistrate, commander; praetor; propraetor, governor

praetōriānus *adj* of the emperor's bodyguard

praetōrium, -ī *and* **-iī** *nt* general's tent, camp headquarters; governor's residence; council of war; palace, grand building; emperor's bodyguard

praetōrius *adj* praetor's, praetorian; of a propraetor; of the emperor's bodyguard ♦ *m* ex-praetor; **praetōria cohors** bodyguard of general *or* emperor; **porta praetōria** camp gate facing the enemy

praetorqueō, -ēre *vt* to strangle first

praetrepidāns, -antis *adj* very impatient

praetruncō, -āre *vt* to cut off

praetulī *perf of* **praeferō**

praetūra, -ae *f* praetorship

praeumbrāns, -antis *adj* obscuring

praeūstus *adj* hardened at the point; frostbitten

praeut *adv* compared with

praevaleō, -ēre, -uī *vi* to be very powerful, have most influence, prevail

praevalidus *adj* very strong, very powerful; too strong

praevāricātiō, -ōnis *f* collusion

praevāricātor, -ōris *m* advocate guilty of collusion

praevāricor, -ārī, -ātus *vi* (*with dat*) to favour by collusion

praevehor, -hī, -ctus *vi* to ride, fly in front, flow past

praeveniō, -enīre, -ēnī, -entum *vt, vi* to come before; to anticipate, prevent

praeverrō, -ere *vt* to sweep before

praevertō, -ere, -ī, **praevertor, -ī** *vt* to put first, prefer; to turn to first, attend first to; to outstrip; to anticipate, frustrate, prepossess

praevideō, -idēre, -īdī, -īsum *vt* to foresee

praevitiō, -āre *vt* to taint beforehand

praevius *adj* leading the way

praevolō, -āre *vi* to fly in front

pragmaticus *adj* of affairs ♦ *m* legal expert

prandeō, -ēre, -ī *vi* to take lunch ♦ *vt* to eat

prandium, -ī *and* **-iī** *nt* lunch

prānsor, -ōris *m* guest at lunch

prānsus *adj* having lunched, fed

prasinus *adj* green
prātēnsis *adj* meadow (*in cpds*)
prātulum, -ī *nt* small meadow
prātum, -ī *nt* meadow; grass
prāvē *adv* wrongly, badly
prāvitās, -ātis *f* irregularity; perverseness, depravity
prāvus *adj* crooked, deformed; perverse, bad, wicked
Prāxitelēs, -is *m* famous Greek sculptor
Prāxitelius *adj see* **Prāxitelēs**
precāriō *adv* by request
precārius *adj* obtained by entreaty
precātiō, -ōnis *f* prayer
precātor, -ōris *m* intercessor
preces *pl of* **prex**
preciae, -ārum *fpl* kind of vine
precor, -ārī, -ātus *vt, vi* to pray, beg, entreat; to wish (well), curse
prehendō, -endere, -endī, -ēnsum *vt* to take hold of, catch; to seize, detain; to surprise; (*eye*) to take in; (*mind*) to grasp
prehēnsō *etc see* **prēnsō**
prehēnsus *ppp of* **prehendō**
prēlum, -ī *nt* wine press, oil press
premō, -mere, -ssī, -ssum *vt* to press, squeeze; to press together, compress; (*eyes*) to close; (*reins*) to tighten; (*trees*) to prune; to press upon, lie, sit, stand on, cover, conceal, surpass; to press hard on, follow closely; (*coast*) to hug; to press down, lower, burden; (*fig*) to overcome, rule; (*words*) to disparage; to press in, sink, stamp, plant; to press back, repress, check, stop
prendō *etc see* **prehendō**
prēnsātiō, -ōnis *f* canvassing
prēnsō, prehēnsō, -āre, -āvī, -ātum *vt* to clutch at, take hold of, buttonhole
prēnsus *ppp of* **prehendō**
presbyter, -ī *m* (ECCL) elder
pressē *adv* concisely, accurately, simply
pressī *perf of* **premō**
pressiō, -ōnis *f* fulcrum
pressō, -āre *vt* to press
pressus¹ *ppp of* **premō** ◆ *adj* (*style*) concise, compressed; (*pace*) slow; (*voice*) subdued
pressus², -ūs *m* pressure
prēster, -ēris *m* waterspout
pretiōsē *adv* expensively
pretiōsus *adj* valuable, expensive; extravagant
pretium, -ī *and* **-iī** *nt* price, value; worth; money, fee, reward; **māgnī pretiī, in pretiō** valuable; **operae** ~ worth while
prex, -ecis *f* request, entreaty; prayer; good wish; curse
Priamēis, -ēidis *f* Cassandra
Priamēius *adj see* **Priamus**
Priamidēs, -idae *m* son of Priam
Priamus, -ī *m* king of Troy
Priāpus, -ī *m* god of fertility and of gardens
prīdem *adv* long ago, long
prīdiē *adv* the day before
prīmaevus *adj* youthful
prīmānī, -ōrum *mpl* soldiers of the 1st legion

prīmārius *adj* principal, first-rate
prīmigenus *adj* original
prīmipīlāris, -is *m* chief centurion
prīmipīlus, -ī *m* chief centurion
prīmitiae, -ārum *fpl* first fruits
prīmitus *adv* originally
prīmō *adv* at first; firstly
prīmōrdium, -ī *and* **-iī** *nt* beginning; **prīmōrdia rērum** atoms
prīmōris *adj* first, foremost, tip of; principal ◆ *mpl* nobles; (MIL) front line
prīmulum *adv* first
prīmulus *adv* very first
prīmum *adv* first, to begin with, in the first place; for the first time; **cum** ~, **ubi** ~, **ut** ~ as soon as; **quam** ~ as soon as possible; ~ **dum** in the first place
prīmus *adj* first, foremost, tip of; earliest; principal, most eminent; ~ **veniō** I am the first to come; **prima lux** dawn, daylight; **prīmō mēnse** at the beginning of the month; **prīmīs digitīs** with the fingertips; **prīmās agere** play the leading part; **prīmās dare** give first place to; **in prīmīs** in the front line; especially
prīnceps, -ipis *adj* first, in front, chief, most eminent ◆ *m* leader, chief; first citizen, emperor; (MIL) company, captain, captaincy ◆ *pl* (MIL) the second line
prīncipālis *adj* original; chief; the emperor's
prīncipātus, -ūs *m* first place; post of commander-in-chief; emperorship
prīncipiālis *adj* from the beginning
prīncipium, -ī *and* **-iī** *nt* beginning, origin; first to vote ◆ *pl* first principles; (MIL) front line; camp headquarters
prior, -ōris (*nt* **-us**) *adj* former, previous, first; better, preferable ◆ *mpl* forefathers
prīscē *adv* strictly
prīscus *adj* former, ancient, old-fashioned
prīstinus *adj* former, original; of yesterday
prius *adv* previously, before; in former times; ~ **quam** before, sooner than
prīvātim *adv* individually, privately; at home
prīvātiō, -ōnis *f* removal
prīvātus *adj* individual, private; not in public office ◆ *m* private citizen
Prīvernās, -ātis *adj see* **Prīvernum**
Prīvernum, -ī *nt* old Latin town
prīvīgna, -ae *f* stepdaughter
prīvīgnus, -ī *m* stepson; (*pl*) stepchildren
prīvilēgium, -ī *and* **-iī** *nt* law in favour of or against an individual
prīvō, -āre, -āvī, -ātum *vt* to deprive, rob; to free
prīvus *adj* single, one each; own, private
prō¹ *adv* (*with* **ut** *and* **quam**) in proportion (as) ◆ *prep* (*with abl*) in front of, on the front of; for, on behalf of, instead of, in return for; as, as good as; according to, in proportion to, by virtue of; **prō eō ac** just as; **prō eō quod** just because; **prō eō quantum, prō eō ut** in proportion as
prō² *interj* (*expressing wonder or sorrow*) O!, alas!

proăgorus, **-ī** m chief magistrate (*in Sicilian towns*)
proavītus adj ancestral
proavus, **-ī** m great-grandfather, ancestor
probābilis adj laudable; credible, probable
probābilitās, **-ātis** f credibility
probābiliter adv credibly
probātiō, **-ōnis** f approval; testing
probātor, **-ōris** m approver
probātus adj tried, excellent; acceptable
probē adv well, properly; thoroughly, well done!
probitās, **-ātis** f goodness, honesty
probō, **-āre**, **-āvī**, **-ātum** vt to approve, approve of; to appraise; to recommend; to prove, show
probrōsus adj abusive; disgraceful
probrum, **-ī** nt abuse, reproach; disgrace; infamy, unchastity
probus adj good, excellent; honest, upright
procācitās, **-ātis** f impudence
procāciter adv insolently
procāx, **-ācis** adj bold, forward, insolent
prōcēdō, **-ēdere**, **-essī**, **-essum** vi to go forward, advance; to go out, come forth; (*time*) to go on, continue; (*fig*) to make progress, get on; (*events*) to turn out, succeed
procella, **-ae** f hurricane, storm; (MIL) charge
procellōsus adj stormy
procer, **-is** m chief, noble, prince
prōcēritās, **-ātis** f height; length
prōcērus adj tall; long
prōcessiō, **-ōnis** f advance
prōcessus, **-ūs** m advance, progress
prōcidō, **-ere**, **-ī** vi to fall forwards, fall down
prōcinctus, **-ūs** m readiness (*for action*)
prōclāmātor, **-ōris** m bawler
prōclāmō, **-āre** vi to cry out
prōclīnātus adj tottering
prōclīnō, **-āre** vt to bend
prōclīvē adv downwards; easily
prōclīvis, **prōclīvus** adj downhill, steep; (*mind*) prone, willing; (*act*) easy; **in prōclīvī** easy
prōclīvitās, **-ātis** f descent; tendency
prōclīvus etc see **prōclīvis**
Procnē, **-ēs** f wife of Tereus (*changed to a swallow*); swallow
prōcōnsul, **-is** m proconsul, governor
prōcōnsulāris adj proconsular
prōcōnsulātus, **-ūs** m proconsulship
prōcrāstinātiō, **-ōnis** f procrastination
prōcrāstinō, **-āre** vt to put off from day to day
prōcreātiō, **-ōnis** f begetting
prōcreātor, **-ōris** m creator, parent
prōcreātrīx, **-īcis** f mother
prōcreō, **-āre** vt to beget, produce
prōcrēscō, **-ere** vi to be produced, grow up
Procrūstēs, **-ae** m Attic highwayman (*who tortured victims on a bed*)
prōcubō, **-āre** vi to lie on the ground
prōcūdō, **-dere**, **-dī**, **-sum** vt to forge; to produce
procul adv at a distance, far, from afar
prōculcō, **-āre** vt to trample down

prōcumbō, **-mbere**, **-buī**, **-bitum** vi to fall forwards, bend over; to sink down, be broken down
prōcūrātiō, **-ōnis** f management; (*religion*) expiation
prōcūrātor, **-ōris** m administrator, financial agent; (*province*) governor
prōcūrātrīx, **-īcis** f governess
prōcūrō, **-āre**, **-āvī**, **-ātum** vt to take care of, manage; to expiate ◆ vi to be a procurator
prōcurrō, **-rrere**, **-currī** and **-rrī**, **-rsum** vi to rush forward; to jut out
prōcursātiō, **-ōnis** f charge
prōcursātor, **-ōris** m skirmisher
prōcursō, **-āre** vi to make a sally
prōcursus, **-ūs** m charge
prōcurvus adj curving forwards
procus¹, **-ī** m nobleman
procus², **-ī** m wooer, suitor
Procyōn, **-ōnis** m Lesser Dog Star
prōdeambulō, **-āre** vi to go out for a walk
prōdeō, **-īre**, **-iī**, **-itum** vi to come out, come forward, appear; to go ahead, advance; to project
prōdesse infin of **prōsum**
prōdīcō, **-īcere**, **-īxī**, **-ictum** vt to appoint, adjourn
prōdictātor, **-ōris** m vice-dictator
prōdigē adv extravagantly
prōdigentia, **-ae** f profusion
prōdigiāliter adv unnaturally
prōdigiōsus adj unnatural, marvellous
prōdigium, **-ī** and **-iī** nt portent; unnatural deed; monster
prōdigō, **-igere**, **-ēgī**, **-āctum** vt to squander
prōdigus adj wasteful; lavish, generous
prōditiō, **-ōnis** f betrayal
prōditor, **-ōris** m traitor
prōditus ppp of **prōdō**
prōdō, **-ere**, **-idī**, **-itum** vt to bring forth, produce; to make known, publish; to betray, give up; (*tradition*) to hand down
prōdoceō, **-ēre** vt to preach
prodromus, **-ī** m forerunner
prōdūcō, **-ūcere**, **-ūxī**, **-uctum** vt to bring forward, bring out; to conduct; to drag in front; to draw out, extend; (*acting*) to perform; (*child*) to beget, bring up; (*fact*) to bring to light; (*innovation*) to introduce; (*rank*) to promote; (*slave*) to put up for sale; (*time*) to prolong, protract, put off; (*tree*) to cultivate; (*vowel*) to lengthen
prōductē adv long
prōductiō, **-ōnis** f lengthening
prōductō, **-āre** vt to spin out
prōductus ppp of **prōdūcō** ◆ adj lengthened, long
proēgmenon, **-ī** nt a preferred thing
proeliātor, **-ōris** m fighter
proelior, **-ārī**, **-ātus** vi to fight, join battle
proelium, **-ī** and **-iī** nt battle, conflict
profānō, **-āre** vt to desecrate
profānus adj unholy, common; impious; ill-omened
profātus ppa of **profor**

profectiō, -ōnis f departure; source
profectō adv really, certainly
profectus ppa of **proficīscor**
prŏfectus¹ ppp of **prŏficiō**
prŏfectus², -ūs m growth, progress, profit
prōferō, -ferre, -tulī, -lātum vt to bring forward, forth or out; to extend, enlarge; (time) to prolong, defer; (instance) to mention, quote; (knowledge) to publish, reveal; **pedem prōferre** proceed; **signa prōferre** advance
professiō, -ōnis f declaration; public register; profession
professor, -ōris m teacher
professōrius adj authoritative
professus ppa of **profiteor**
profēstus adj not holiday, working
prŏficiō, -icere, -ēcī, -ectum vi to make progress, profit; to be of use
proficīscor, -icīscī, -ectus vi to set out, start; to originate, proceed
profiteor, -itērī, -essus vt to declare, profess; to make an official return of; to promise, volunteer
prōflīgātor, -ōris m spendthrift
prōflīgātus adj dissolute
prōflīgō, -āre, -āvī, -ātum vt to dash to the ground; to destroy, overthrow; to bring almost to an end; to degrade
prōflō, -āre vt to breathe out
prōfluēns, -entis pres p of **prōfluō** ♦ adj flowing; fluent ♦ f running water
prōfluenter adv easily
prōfluentia, -ae f fluency
prōfluō, -ere, -xī vi to flow on, flow out; (fig) to proceed
prōfluvium, -ī and **-iī** nt flowing
profor, -ārī, -ātus vi to speak, give utterance
profugiō, -ugere, -ūgī vi to flee, escape; to take refuge (with) ♦ vt to flee from
profugus adj fugitive; exiled; nomadic
prōfuī perf of **prōsum**
profundō, -undere, -ūdī, -ūsum vt to pour out, shed; to bring forth, produce; to prostrate; to squander; **sē profundere** burst forth, rush out
profundus adj deep, vast, high; infernal; (fig) profound, immoderate ♦ nt depths, abyss
profūsē adv in disorder, extravagantly
profūsus ppp of **profundō** ♦ adj lavish; excessive
prōgener, -ī m grandson-in-law
prōgenerō, -āre vt to beget
prōgeniēs, -ēī f descent; offspring, descendants
prōgenitor, -ōris m ancestor
prōgignō, -ignere, -enuī, -enitum vt to beget, produce
prōgnātus adj born, descended ♦ m son, descendant
Prognē see **Procnē**
prognōstica, -ōrum ntpl weather signs
prōgredior, -dī, -ssus vi to go forward, advance; to go out
prōgressiō, -ōnis f advancing, increase; (RHET) climax

prōgressus¹ ppa of **prōgredior**
prōgressus², -ūs m advance, progress; (events) march
prōh interj see **prō²**
prohibeō, -ēre, -uī, -itum vt to hinder, prevent; to keep away, protect; to forbid
prohibitiō, -ōnis f forbidding
prōiciō, -icere, -iēcī, -iectum vt to throw down, fling forwards; to banish; (building) to make project; (fig) to discard, renounce; to forsake; (words) to blurt out; (time) to defer; **sē prōicere** rush forward, run into danger; to fall prostrate
prōiectiō, -ōnis f forward stretch
prōiectus¹ ppp of **prōiciō** ♦ adj projecting, prominent; abject, useless; downcast; addicted (to)
prōiectus², -ūs m jutting out
proinde, proin adv consequently, therefore; just (as)
prōlābor, -bī, -psus vi to slide, move forward; to fall down; (fig) to go on, come to; to slip out; to fail, fall, sink into ruin
prōlāpsiō, -ōnis f falling
prōlāpsus ppa of **prōlābor**
prōlātiō, -ōnis f extension; postponement; adducing
prōlātō, -āre vt to extend; to postpone
prōlātus ppp of **prōferō**
prōlectō, -āre vt to entice
prōlēs, -is f offspring; child; descendants, race
prōlētārius, -ī and **-iī** m citizen of the lowest class
prōliciō, -cere, -xī vt to entice
prōlixē adv fully, copiously, willingly
prōlixus adj long, wide, spreading; (person) obliging; (circumstances) favourable
prōlogus, -ī m prologue
prōloquor, -quī, -cūtus vt to speak out
prōlubium, -ī and **-iī** nt inclination
prōlūdō, -dere, -sī, -sum vi to practise
prōluō, -uere, -uī, -ūtum vt to wash out, wash away
prōlūsiō, -ōnis f prelude
prōluviēs, -ēī f flood; excrement
prōmereō, -ēre, -uī, prōmereor, -ērī, -itus vt to deserve, earn
prōmeritum, -ī nt desert, merit, guilt
Promētheus, -eī and **-eos** m demigod who stole fire from the gods
Promēthēus adj see **Promētheus**
prōminēns, -entis pres p of **prōmineō** ♦ adj projecting ♦ nt headland, spur
prōmineō, -ēre, -uī vi to jut out, overhang; to extend
prōmiscam, prōmiscamē, prōmiscuē adv indiscriminately
prōmiscuus, prōmiscus adj indiscriminate, in common; ordinary; open to all
prōmīsī perf of **prōmittō**
prōmissiō, -ōnis f promise
prōmissor, -ōris m promiser
prōmissum, -ī nt promise
prōmissus ppp of **prōmittō** ♦ adj long

prōmittō, -ittere, -īsī, -issum *vt* to let grow; to promise, give promise of

prōmō, -ere, -psī, -ptum *vt* to bring out, produce; to disclose

prōmont- *etc see* **prōmunt-**

prōmontorium, -ī *and* **-iī** *nt* headland, promontory, ridge

prōmōtus *ppp of* **prōmoveō** ♦ *ntpl* preferable things

prōmoveō, -ovēre, -ōvī, -ōtum *vt* to move forward, advance; to enlarge; to postpone; to disclose

prōmpsī *perf of* **prōmō**

prōmptē *adv* readily; easily

prōmptō, -āre *vt* to distribute

prōmptū *abl m:* **in ~** at hand, in readiness; obvious, in evidence; easy

prōmptus *ppp of* **prōmō** ♦ *adj* at hand, ready; prompt, resolute; easy

prōmulgātiō, -ōnis *f* promulgating

prōmulgō, -āre, -āvī, -ātum *vt* to make public, publish

prōmulsis, -idis *f* hors d'oeuvre

prōmus, -ī *m* cellarer, butler

prōmūtuus *adj* as a loan in advance

prōnepōs, -ōtis *m* great-grandson

pronoea, -ae *f* providence

prōnōmen, -inis *nt* pronoun

prōnuba, -ae *f* matron attending a bride

prōnūntiātiō, -ōnis *f* declaration; (RHET) delivery; (LOGIC) proposition

prōnūntiātor, -ōris *m* narrator

prōnūntiātum, -ātī *nt* proposition

prōnūntiō, -āre, -āvī, -ātum *vt* to declare publicly, announce; to recite, deliver; to narrate; to nominate

prōnurus, -ūs *f* granddaughter-in-law

prōnus *adj* leaning forward; headlong, downwards; sloping, sinking; (*fig*) inclined, disposed, favourable; easy

prooemium, -ī *and* **-iī** *nt* prelude, preface

propāgātiō, -ōnis *f* propagating; extension

propāgātor, -ōris *m* enlarger

propāgō¹, -āre, -āvī, -ātum *vt* to propagate; to extend; to prolong

propāgō², -inis *f* (*plant*) layer, slip; (*men*) offspring, posterity

prōpalam *adv* openly, known

prōpatulum, -ī *nt* open space

prōpatulus *adj* open

prope *adv* (*compar* **propius**, *superl* **proximē**) near; nearly ♦ *prep* (*with acc*) near, not far from

propediem *adv* very soon

prōpellō, -ellere, -ulī, -ulsum *vt* to drive, push forward, impel; to drive away, keep off

propemodum, propemodo *adv* almost

prōpendeō, -endēre, -endī, -ēnsum *vi* to hang down; to preponderate; to be disposed (to)

prōpēnsē *adv* willingly

prōpēnsiō, -ōnis *f* inclination

prōpēnsus *adj* inclining; inclined, well-disposed; important

properanter *adv* hastily, quickly

properantia, -ae *f* haste

properātiō, -ōnis *f* haste

properātō *adv* quickly

properātus *adj* speedy

properē *adv* quickly

properipēs, -edis *adj* swiftfooted

properō, -āre, -āvī, -ātum *vt* to hasten, do with haste ♦ *vi* to make haste, hurry

Propertius, -ī *m* Latin elegiac poet

properus *adj* quick, hurrying

prōpexus *adj* combed forward

prōpīnō, -āre *vt* to drink as a toast; to pass on (*a cup*)

propinquitās, -ātis *f* nearness; relationship, friendship

propinquō, -āre *vi* to approach ♦ *vt* to hasten

propinquus *adj* near, neighbouring; related ♦ *m/f* relation ♦ *nt* neighbourhood

propior, -ōris *adj* nearer; more closely related, more like; (*time*) more recent

propitiō, -āre *vt* to appease

propitius *adj* favourable, gracious

propius *adv* nearer, more closely

propōla, -ae *f* retailer

prōpolluō, -ere *vt* to defile further

prōpōnō, -ōnere, -osuī, -ositum *vt* to set forth, display; to publish, declare; to propose, resolve; to imagine; to expose; (LOGIC) to state the first premise; **ante oculōs prōpōnere** picture to oneself

Propontiacus *adj see* **Propontis**

Propontis, -idis *and* **-idos** *f* Sea of Marmora

prōporrō *adv* furthermore; utterly

prōportiō, -ōnis *f* symmetry, analogy

prōpositiō, -ōnis *f* purpose; theme; (LOGIC) first premise

prōpositum, -ī *nt* plan, purpose; theme; (LOGIC) first premise

prōpositus *ppp of* **prōpōnō**

prōpraetor, -ōris *m* propraetor, governor; vice-praetor

propriē *adv* properly, strictly; particularly

proprietās, -ātis *f* peculiarity, property

prōprītim *adv* properly

proprius *adj* one's own, peculiar; personal, characteristic; permanent; (*words*) literal, regular

propter *adv* near by ♦ *prep* (*with acc*) near, beside; on account of; by means of

proptereā *adv* therefore

prōpudium, -ī *and* **-iī** *nt* shameful act; villain

prōpugnāculum, -ī *nt* bulwark, tower; defence

prōpugnātiō, -ōnis *f* defence

prōpugnātor, -ōris *m* defender, champion

prōpugnō, -āre *vi* to make a sortie; to fight in defence

prōpulsātiō, -ōnis *f* repulse

prōpulsō, -āre, -āvī, -ātum *vt* to repel, avert

prōpulsus *ppp of* **prōpellō**

Propylaea, -ōrum *ntpl* gateway to the Acropolis of Athens

prō quaestōre *m* proquaestor

prōquam *conj* according as

prōra, -ae *f* prow, bows; ship

prōrēpō, -ere, -sī, -tum *vi* to crawl out

prōrēta, -ae *m* man at the prow

prōreus, -eī *m* man at the prow

prōripiō, -ipere, -ipuī, -eptum *vt* to drag out; to hurry away; **sē prōripere** rush out, run away

prōrogātiō, -ōnis *f* extension; deferring

prōrogō, -āre, -āvī, -ātum *vt* to extend, prolong, continue; to defer

prōrsum *adv* forwards; absolutely

prōrsus *adv* forwards; absolutely; in short

prōrumpō, -umpere, -ūpī, -uptum *vt* to fling out; (*pass*) to rush forth ♦ *vi* to break out, burst forth

prōruō, -ere, -ī, -tum *vt* to throw down, demolish ♦ *vi* to rush forth

prōruptus *ppp of* **prōrumpō**

prōsāpia, -ae *f* lineage

proscaenium, -ī *and* **-iī** *nt* stage

proscindō, -ndere, -dī, -ssum *vt* to plough up; (*fig*) to revile

prōscrībō, -bere, -psī, -ptum *vt* to publish in writing; to advertise; to confiscate; to proscribe, outlaw

prōscrīptiō, -ōnis *f* advertisement; proscription

prōscrīpturiō, -īre *vi* to want to have a proscription

prōscrīptus *ppp of* **prōscrībō** ♦ *m* outlaw

prōsecō, -āre, -uī, -tum *vt* to cut off (*for sacrifice*)

prōsēminō, -āre *vt* to scatter; to propagate

prōsentiō, -entīre, -ēnsī *vt* to see beforehand

prōsequor, -quī, -cūtus *vt* to attend, escort; to pursue, attack; to honour (with); (*words*) to proceed with, continue

Proserpina, -ae *f* Proserpine (*daughter of Ceres and wife of Pluto*)

proseucha, -ae *f* place of prayer

prōsiliō, -īre, -uī *vi* to jump up, spring forward; to burst out, spurt

prōsocer, -ī *m* wife's grandfather

prōspectō, -āre *vt* to look out at, view; to look forward to, await; (*place*) to look towards

prōspectus[1] *ppp of* **prōspiciō**

prōspectus[2], -ūs *m* sight, view, prospect; gaze

prōspeculor, -ārī *vi* to look out, reconnoitre ♦ *vt* to watch for

prosper, prosperus *adj* favourable, successful

prosperē *adv see* **prosper**

prosperitās, -ātis *f* good fortune

prosperō, -āre *vt* to make successful, prosper

prosperus *etc see* **prosper**

prōspicientia, -ae *f* foresight

prōspiciō, -icere, -exī, -ectum *vi* to look out, watch; to see to, take precautions ♦ *vt* to descry, watch for; to foresee; to provide; (*place*) to command a view of

prōsternō, -ernere, -rāvī, -rātum *vt* to throw in front, prostrate; to overthrow, ruin; **sē prōsternere** fall prostrate; to demean oneself

prōstibulum, -ī *nt* prostitute

prōstituō, -uere, -uī, -ūtum *vt* to put up for sale, prostitute

prōstō, -āre, -itī *vi* to project; to be on sale; to prostitute oneself

prōstrātus *ppp of* **prōsternō**

prōsubigō, -ere *vt* to dig up

prōsum, -desse, -fuī *vi* (*with dat*) to be useful to, benefit

Prōtagorās, -ae *m Greek sophist (native of Abdera)*

prōtēctus *ppp of* **prōtegō**

prōtegō, -egere, -ēxī, -ēctum *vt* to cover over, put a projecting roof on; (*fig*) to shield, protect

prōtēlō, -āre *vt* to drive off

prōtēlum, -ī *nt* team of oxen; (*fig*) succession

prōtendō, -dere, -dī, -tum *vt* to stretch out, extend

prōtentus *ppp of* **prōtendō**

prōterō, -erere, -rīvī, -rītum *vt* to trample down, crush; to overthrow

prōterreō, -ēre, -uī, -itum *vt* to scare away

protervē *adv* insolently; boldly

protervitās, -ātis *f* forwardness, insolence

protervus *adj* forward, insolent, violent

Prōtesilāēus *adj see* **Prōtesilāus**

Prōtesilāus, -ī *m* first Greek killed at Troy

Prōteus, -eī *and* **-eos** *m seagod with power to assume many forms*

prothȳmē *adv* gladly

prōtinam *adv* immediately

prōtinus *adv* forward, onward; continuously; right away, forthwith

prōtollō, -ere *vt* to stretch out; to put off

prōtractus *ppp of* **prōtrahō**

prōtrahō, -here, -xī, -ctum *vt* to draw on (to); to drag out; to bring to light, reveal

prōtrītus *ppp of* **prōterō**

prōtrūdō, -dere, -sī, -sum *vt* to thrust forward, push out; to postpone

prōtulī *perf of* **prōferō**

prōturbō, -āre, -āvī, -ātum *vt* to drive off; to overthrow

prout *conj* according as

prōvectus *ppp of* **prōvehō** ♦ *adj* advanced

prōvehō, -here, -xī, -ctum *vt* to carry along, transport; to promote, advance, bring to; (*speech*) to prolong; (*pass*) to drive, ride, sail on

prōveniō, -enīre, -ēnī, -entum *vi* to come out, appear; to arise, grow; to go on, prosper, succeed

prōventus, -ūs *m* increase; result, success

prōverbium, -ī *and* **-iī** *nt* saying, proverb

prōvidēns, -entis *pres p of* **prōvideō** ♦ *adj* prudent

prōvidenter *adv* with foresight

prōvidentia, -ae *f* foresight, forethought

prōvideō, -idēre, -īdī, -īsum *vi* to see ahead; to take care, make provision ♦ *vt* to foresee; to look after, provide for; to obviate

prōvidus *adj* foreseeing, cautious, prudent; provident

prōvincia, -ae *f* sphere of action, duty, province

prōvinciālis *adj* provincial ♦ *mpl* provincials

prōvīsiō, -ōnis *f* foresight; precaution

prōvīsō[1] *adv* with forethought

prōvīsō[2], -ere *vi* to go and see

prōvīsor, -ōris *m* foreseer; provider
prōvīsus[1] *ppp of* **prōvideō**
prōvīsus[2], **-ūs** *m* looking forward; foreseeing; providing, providence
prōvīvō, -vere, -xī *vi* to live on
prōvocātiō, -ōnis *f* challenge; appeal
prōvocātor, -ōris *m kind of gladiator*
prōvocō, -āre, -āvī, -ātum *vt* to challenge, call out; to provoke; to bring about ◆ *vi* to appeal
prōvolō, -āre *vi* to fly out, rush out
prōvolvō, -vere, -vī, -ūtum *vt* to roll forward, tumble over; (*pass*) to fall down, humble oneself, be ruined; **sē prōvolvere** wallow
prōvomō, -ere *vt* to belch forth
proximē *adv* next, nearest; (*time*) just before or after; (*with acc*) next to, very close to, very like
proximitās, -ātis *f* nearness; near relationship; similarity
proximus *adj* nearest, next; (*time*) previous, last, following, next; most akin, most like ◆ *m* next of kin ◆ *nt* next door
proxum- *etc see* **proxim-**
prūdēns, -entis *adj* foreseeing, aware; wise, prudent, circumspect; skilled, versed (in)
prūdenter *adv* prudently; skilfully
prūdentia, -ae *f* prudence, discretion; knowledge
pruīna, -ae *f* hoar frost
pruīnōsus *adj* frosty
prūna, -ae *f* live coal
prūnitius *adj* of plum tree wood
prūnum, -ī *nt* plum
prūnus, -ī *f* plum tree
prūriō, -īre *vi* to itch
prytanēum, -ī *nt* Greek town hall
prytanis, -is *m* Greek chief magistrate
psallō, -ere *vi* to play the lyre or lute
psaltērium, -ī *and* **-iī** *nt kind of lute*
psaltria, -ae *f* girl musician
psecas, -adis *f slave who perfumed the ladies' hair*
psēphisma, -tis *nt* decree of the people
Pseudocatō, -ōnis *m* sham Cato
pseudomenos, -ī *m* sophistical argument
pseudothyrum, -ī *nt* back door
psithius *adj* psithian (*kind of Greek vine*)
psittacus, -ī *m* parrot
psychomantēum, psychomantīum, -ī *nt* place of necromancy
-pte *enclitic* (*to pronouns*) self, own
ptisanārium, -ī *and* **-iī** *nt* gruel
Ptolemaeēus, Ptolemaeus *adj see* **Ptolemaeus**
Ptolemaeus, -ī *m* Ptolemy (*name of Egyptian kings*)
pūbēns, -entis *adj* full-grown; (*plant*) juicy
pūbertās, -ātis *f* manhood; signs of puberty
pūbēs[1], **pūber, -eris** *adj* grown up, adult; (*plant*) downy
pūbēs[2], **-is** *f* hair at age of puberty; groin; youth, men, people
pūbēscō, -ēscere, -uī *vi* to grow to manhood, become mature; to become clothed
pūblicānus *adj* of public revenue ◆ *m* tax farmer

pūblicātiō, -ōnis *f* confiscation
pūblicē *adv* by or for the State, at the public expense; all together
pūblicitus *adv* at the public expense; in public
pūblicō, -āre, -āvī, -ātum *vt* to confiscate; to make public
Pūblicola, -ae *m* P. Valerius (*an early Roman consul*)
pūblicum, -ī *nt* State revenue; State territory; public
pūblicus *adj* of the State, public, common ◆ *m* public official; **pūblica causa** criminal trial; **rēs pūblica** the State; **dē pūblicō** at the public expense; **in pūblicō** in public
Publius, -ī *m* Roman first name
pudendus *adj* shameful
pudēns, -entis *adj* bashful, modest
pudenter *adv* modestly
pudet, -ēre, -uit *and* **-itum est** *vt impers* to shame, be ashamed
pudibundus *adj* modest
pudīcē *adv see* **pudīcus**
pudīcitia, -ae *f* modesty, chastity
pudīcus *adj* modest, chaste
pudor, -ōris *m* shame, modesty, sense of honour; disgrace
puella, -ae *f* girl; sweetheart, young wife
puellāris *adj* girlish, youthful
puellula, -ae *f* little girl
puellus, -ī *m* little boy
puer, -ī *m* boy, child; son; slave
puerīlis *adj* boyish, child's; childish, trivial
puerīliter *adv* like a child; childishly
pueritia, -ae *f* childhood, youth
puerperium, -ī *and* **-iī** *nt* childbirth
puerperus *adj* to help childbirth ◆ *f* woman in labour
puertia *etc see* **pueritia**
puerulus, -ī *m* little boy, slave
pugil, -is *m* boxer
pugilātiō, -iōnis *f*, **pugilātus, -ūs** *m* boxing
pugillāris *adj* that can be held in the hand ◆ *mpl, ntpl* writing tablets
pugillātōrius *adj*: **follis ~** punchball
pugiō, -ōnis *m* dirk, dagger
pugiunculus, -ī *m* small dagger
pugna, -ae *f* fight, battle
pugnācitās, -ātis *f* fondness for a fight
pugnāciter *adv* aggressively
pugnāculum, -ī *nt* fortress
pugnātor, -ōris *m* fighter
pugnāx, -ācis *adj* fond of a fight, aggressive; obstinate
pugneus *adj* with the fist
pugnō, -āre, -āvī, -ātum *vi* to fight; to disagree; to struggle; **sēcum pugnāre** be inconsistent; **pugnātum est** the battle was fought
pugnus, -ī *m* fist
pulchellus *adj* pretty little
pulcher, -rī *adj* beautiful, handsome; fine, glorious
pulchrē *adv* excellently; well done!
pulchritūdō, -inis *f* beauty, excellence
pūlēium, pūlegium, -ī *and* **-iī** *nt* pennyroyal

pūlex, -icis *m* flea

pullārius, -ī *and* -iī *m* keeper of the sacred chickens

pullātus *adj* dressed in black

pullulō, -āre *vi* to sprout

pullus¹, -ī *m* young (*of animals*), chicken

pullus² *adj* dark-grey; mournful ♦ *nt* dark grey clothes

pulmentārium, -ārī *and* -āriī, pulmentum, -ī *nt* relish; food

pulmō, -ōnis *m* lung

pulmōneus *adj* of the lungs

pulpa, -ae *f* fleshy part

pulpāmentum, -ī *nt* titbits

pulpitum, -ī *nt* platform, stage

puls, pultis *f* porridge

pulsātiō, -ōnis *f* beating

pulsō, -āre, -āvī, -ātum *vt* to batter, knock, strike

pulsus¹ *ppp of* pellō

pulsus², -ūs *m* push, beat, blow; impulse

pultiphagus, -ī *m* porridge eater

pultō, -āre *vt* to beat, knock at

pulvereus *adj* of dust, dusty, fine as dust; raising dust

pulverulentus *adj* dusty; laborious

pulvillus, -ī *m* small cushion

pulvīnar, -āris *nt* sacred couch; seat of honour

pulvīnus, -ī *m* cushion, pillow

pulvis, -eris *m* dust, powder; arena; effort

pulvisculus, -ī *m* fine dust

pūmex, -icis *m* pumice stone; stone, rock

pūmiceus *adj* of soft stone

pūmicō, -āre *vt* to smooth with pumice stone

pūmiliō, -ōnis *m/f* person of small stature

pūnctim *adv* with the point

pūnctum, -ī *nt* point, dot; vote; (*time*) moment; (*speech*) short section

pūnctus *ppp of* pungō

pungō, -ere, pupugī, pūnctum *vt* to prick, sting, pierce; (*fig*) to vex

Pūnicānus *adj* in the Carthaginian style

Pūnicē *adv* in Punic

pūniceus *adj* reddish, purple

Pūnicum, -ī *nt* pomegranate

Pūnicus *adj* Punic, Carthaginian; purple-red

pūniō, poeniō, -īre, pūnior, -īrī *vt* to punish; to avenge

pūnītor, -ōris *m* avenger

pūpa, -ae *f* doll

pūpilla, -ae *f* ward; (*eye*) pupil

pūpillāris *adj* of a ward, of an orphan

pūpillus, -ī *m* orphan, ward

puppis, -is *f* after part of a ship, stern; ship

pupugī *perf of* pungō

pūpula, -ae *f* (*eye*) pupil

pūpulus, -ī *m* little boy

pūrē *adv* cleanly, brightly; plainly, simply, purely, chastely

pūrgāmen, -inis *nt* sweepings, dirt; means of expiation

pūrgāmentum, -ī *nt* refuse, dirt

pūrgātiō, -ōnis *f* purging; justification

pūrgō, -āre, -āvī, -ātum *vt* to cleanse, purge, clear away; to exculpate, justify; to purify

pūriter *adv* cleanly, purely

purpura, -ae *f* purple-fish, purple; purple cloth; finery, royalty

purpurātus *adj* wearing purple ♦ *m* courtier

purpureus *adj* red, purple, black; wearing purple; bright, radiant

purpurissum, -ī *nt* kind of rouge

pūrus *adj* clear, unadulterated, free from obstruction or admixture; pure, clean; plain, unadorned; (*moral*) pure, chaste ♦ *nt* clear sky

pūs, pūris *nt* pus; (*fig*) malice

pusillus *adj* very little; petty, paltry

pūsiō, -ōnis *m* little boy

pūstula, -ae *f* pimple, blister

putāmen, -inis *nt* peeling, shell, husk

putātiō, -ōnis *f* pruning

putātor, -ōris *m* pruner

puteal, -ālis *nt* low wall round a well or sacred place

puteālis *adj* well- (*in cpds*)

pūteō, -ēre *vi* to stink

Puteolānus *adj see* Puteolī

Puteolī, -ōrum *mpl* town on the Campanian coast

puter, putris, -ris *adj* rotten, decaying; crumbling, flabby

putēscō, -ēscere, -uī *vi* to become rotten

puteus, -ī *m* well; pit

pūtidē *adv see* pūtidus

pūtidiusculus *adj* somewhat nauseating

pūtidus *adj* rotten, stinking; (*speech*) affected, nauseating

putō, -āre, -āvī, -ātum *vt* to think, suppose; to think over; to reckon, count; (*money*) to settle; (*tree*) to prune

pūtor, -ōris *m* stench

putrefaciō, -facere, -fēcī, -factum *vt* to make rotten; to make crumble

putrēscō, -ere *vi* to rot, moulder

putridus *adj* rotten, decayed; withered

putris *etc see* puter

putus¹ *adj* perfectly pure

putus², -ī *m* boy

pycta, pyctēs, -ae *m* boxer

Pydna, -ae *f* town in Macedonia

Pydnaeus *adj see* Pydna

pȳga, -ae *f* buttocks

Pygmaeus *adj* Pygmy

Pyladēs, -ae *and* -is *m* friend of Orestes

Pyladēus *adj see* Pyladēs

Pylae, -ārum *fpl* Thermopylae

Pylaicus *adj see* Pylae

Pylius *adj see* Pylos

Pylos, -ī *f* Pylus (*Peloponnesian town, home of Nestor*)

pyra, -ae *f* funeral pyre

Pȳramaeus *adj see* Pȳramus

pȳramis, -idis *f* pyramid

Pȳramus, -ī *m* lover of Thisbe

Pȳrēnē, -ēs *f* Pyrenees

pyrethrum, **-ī** *nt* Spanish camomile
Pyrgēnsis *adj see* **Pyrgī**
Pyrgī, **-ōrum** *mpl ancient town in Etruria*
pyrŏpus, **-ī** *m* bronze
Pyrrha, **-ae**, **Pyrrhē**, **-ēs** *f* wife of Deucalion
Pyrrhaeus *adj see* **Pyrrha**
Pyrrhō, **-ōnis** *m* Greek philosopher (*founder of the Sceptics*)
Pyrrhŏnēus *adj see* **Pyrrhō**
Pyrrhus, **-ī** *m* son of Achilles; king of Epirus, enemy of Rome

Pȳthagorās, **-ae** *m* Greek philosopher who founded a school in S. Italy
Pȳthagorēus, **-icus** *adj* Pythagorean
Pȳthius, **Pȳthicus** *adj* Pythian, Delphic ◆ *m* Apollo ◆ *f* priestess of Apollo ◆ *ntpl* Pythian Games
Pȳthō, **-ūs** *f* Delphi
Pȳthōn, **-ōnis** *m serpent killed by Apollo*
pȳtisma, **-tis** *nt* what is spat out
pȳtissō, **-āre** *vi* to spit out wine
pyxis, **-dis** *f* small box, toilet box

Qq

quā *adv* where, which way; whereby; as far as; partly ... partly

quācumque *adv* wherever; anyhow

quādam: ~ **tenus** *adv* only so far

quadra, -ae *f* square; morsel; table

quadrāgēnī, -ōrum *adj* forty each

quadrāgēsimus *adj* fortieth ♦ *f* 2.5 per cent tax

quadrāgiēns, quadrāgiēs *adv* forty times

quadrāgintā *num* forty

quadrāns, -antis *m* quarter; *(coin)* quarter as

quadrantārius *adj* of a quarter

quadrātum, -ī *nt* square; *(ASTR)* quadrature

quadrātus *ppp of* **quadrō** ♦ *adj* square; **quadrātō agmine** in battle order

quadrīduum, -ī *nt* four days

quadriennium, -ī *and* **-iī** *nt* four years

quadrifāriam *adv* in four parts

quadrifidus *adj* split in four

quadrīgae, -ārum *fpl* team of four; chariot

quadrīgārius, -ī *and* **-iī** *m* chariot racer

quadrīgātus *adj* stamped with a chariot

quadrīgulae, -ārum *fpl* little four horse team

quadriiugī, -ōrum *mpl* team of four

quadriiugis, quadriiugus *adj* of a team of four

quadrilībris *adj* weighing four pounds

quadrīmulus *adj* four years old

quadrīmus *adj* four years old

quadringēnārius *adj* of four hundred each

quadringēnī, -ōrum *adj* four hundred each

quadringentēsimus *adj* four-hundredth

quadringentī, -ōrum *num* four hundred

quadringentiēns, quadringentiēs *adv* four hundred times

quadripertītus *adj* fourfold

quadrirēmis, -is *f* quadrireme

quadrivium, -ī *and* **-iī** *nt* crossroads

quadrō, -āre *vt* to make square; to complete ♦ *vi* to square, fit, agree

quadrum, -i *nt* square

quadrupedāns, -antis *adj* galloping

quadrupēs, -edis *adj* four-footed, on all fours ♦ *m/f* quadruped

quadruplātor, -ōris *m* informer, twister

quadruplex, -icis *adj* four-fold

quadruplum, -ī *nt* four times as much

quaeritō, -āre *vt* to search diligently for; to earn *(a living)*; to keep on asking

quaerō, -rere, -sīvī *and* **-siī, -sītum** *vt* to look for, search for; to seek, try to get; to acquire, earn; *(plan)* to think out, work out; *(question)* to ask, make inquiries; *(LAW)* to investigate; *(with inf)* to try, wish; **quid quaeris?** in short; **sī quaeris/ quaerimus** to tell the truth

quaesītiō, -ōnis *f* inquisition

quaesītor, -ōris *m* investigator, judge

quaesītus *ppp of* **quaerō** ♦ *adj* special; far-fetched ♦ *nt* question ♦ *ntpl* gains

quaesīvī *perf of* **quaerō**

quaesō, -ere *vt* to ask, beg

quaesticulus, -ī *m* slight profit

quaestiō, -ōnis *f* seeking, questioning; investigation, research; criminal trial; court; **servum in quaestiōnem ferre** take a slave for questioning by torture; **quaestiōnēs perpetuae** standing courts

quaestiuncula, -ae *f* trifling question

quaestor, -ōris *m* quaestor, treasury official

quaestōrius *adj* of a quaestor ♦ *m* ex-quaestor ♦ *nt* quaestor's tent *or* residence

quaestuōsus *adj* lucrative, productive; money-making; wealthy

quaestūra, -ae *f* quaestorship; public money

quaestus, -ūs *m* profit, advantage; money-making, occupation; **quaestuī habēre** make money out of; **quaestum facere** make a living

quālibet *adv* anywhere; anyhow

quālis *adj* *(interrog)* what kind of?; *(rel)* such as, even as

quāliscumque *adj* of whatever kind; any, whatever

quāliscunque *adj* = **quāliscumque**

quālitās, -ātis *f* quality, nature

quāliter *adv* just as

quālubet *adv* anywhere; anyhow

quālus, -ī *m* wicker basket

quam *adv* *(interrog, excl)* how?, how much?; *(comparison)* as, than; *(with superl)* as ... as possible; *(emphatic)* very; **dīmidium ~ quod** half of what; **quīntō diē ~** four days after

quamdiū *adv* how long?; as long as

quamlibet, quamlubet *adv* as much as you like, however

quamobrem *adv* *(interrog)* why?; *(rel)* why ♦ *conj* therefore

quamquam *conj* although; and yet

quamvīs *adv* however, ever so ♦ *conj* however much, although

quānam *adv* what way

quandō *adv* *(interrog)* when?; *(rel)* when; *(with sī, nē, num)* ever ♦ *conj* when; since

quandōcumque, quandocunque *adv* whenever, as often as; some day

quandōque *adv* whenever; some day ◆ *conj* seeing that
quandō quidem *conj* seeing that, since
quanquam *etc see* **quamquam**
quantillus *adj* how little, how much
quantopere *adv* how much; (*after* **tantopere**) as
quantulus *adj* how little, how small
quantuluscumque *adj* however small, however trifling
quantum *adv* how much; as much as; **quantumcumque** as much as ever; **quantumlibet** however much; **quantumvīs** as much as you like; although
quantus *adj* how great; so great as, such as; **quantī** how dear, how highly; **quantō** (*with comp*) how much; the; **in quantum** as far as
quantuscumque *adj* however great, whatever size
quantuslibet *adj* as great as you like
quantus quantus *adj* however great
quantusvīs *adj* however great
quāpropter *adv* why; and therefore
quāquā *adv* whatever way
quārē *adv* how, why; whereby; and therefore
quartadecumānī, -ōrum *mpl* men of the fourteenth legion
quartānus *adj* every four days ◆ *f* quartan fever ◆ *mpl* men of the fourth legion
quartārius, -ī *and* **-iī** *m* quarter pint
quartus *adj* fourth; **quartum/quartō** for the fourth time
quartusdecimus *adj* fourteenth
quasi *adv* as if; as it were; (*numbers*) about
quasillus, -ī *m*, **quasillum, -ī** *nt* wool basket
quassātiō, -ōnis *f* shaking
quassō, -āre, -āvī, -ātum *vt* to shake, toss; to shatter, damage
quassus *ppp of* **quatiō** ◆ *adj* broken
quatefaciō, -facere, -fēcī *vt* to shake, give a jolt to
quātenus *adv* (*interrog*) how far?; how long?; (*rel*) as far as; in so far as, since
quater *adv* four times; ~ **deciēs** fourteen times
quaternī, -ōrum *adj* four each, in fours
quatiō, -tere, -ssī, -ssum *vt* to shake, disturb, brandish; to strike, shatter; (*fig*) to agitate, harass
quattuor *num* four
quattuordecim *num* fourteen
quattuorvirātus, -ūs *m* membership of quattuorviri
quattuorvirī, -ōrum *mpl* board of four officials
-que *conj* and; both ... and; (*after neg*) but
quemadmodum *adv* (*interrog*) how?; (*rel*) just as
queō, -īre, -īvī *and* **-iī, -itum** *vi* to be able, can
quercētum, -ī *nt* oak forest
querceus *adj* of oak
quercus, -ūs *f* oak; garland of oak leaves; acorn
querēla, querella, -ae *f* complaint; plaintive sound
queribundus *adj* complaining
querimōnia, -ae *f* complaint; elegy
queritor, -ārī *vi* to complain much
quernus *adj* oak- (*in cpds*)

queror, -rī, -stus *vt, vi* to complain, lament; (*birds*) to sing
querquetulānus *adj* of oakwoods
querulus *adj* complaining; plaintive, warbling
questus¹ *ppa of* **queror**
questus², -ūs *m* complaint, lament
quī¹, quae, quod *pron* (*interrog*) what?, which?; (*rel*) who, which, that; what; and this, he *etc*; (*with* **sī, nisi, nē, num**) any
quī² *adv* (*interrog*) how?; (*rel*) with which, whereby; (*indef*) somehow; (*excl*) indeed
quia *conj* because; **quianam** why?
quicquam *nt see* **quisquam**
quicque *nt see* **quisque**
quicquid *nt see* **quisquis**
quīcum with whom, with which
quīcumque, quīcunque *pron* whoever, whatever, all that; every possible
quid *nt see* **quis** ◆ *adv* why?
quīdam, quaedam, quoddam *pron* a certain, a sort of, a ...
quiddam *nt* something
quidem *adv* (*emphatic*) in fact; (*qualifying*) at any rate; (*conceding*) it is true; (*alluding*) for instance; **nē ... ~** not even
quidlibet *nt* anything
quidnam *nt see* **quisnam**
quidnī *adv* why not?
quidpiam *nt see* **quispiam**
quidquam *nt see* **quisquam**
quidquid *nt see* **quisquis**
quiēs, -ētis *f* rest, peace, quiet; sleep, dream, death; neutrality; lair
quiēscō, -scere, -vī, -tum *vi* to rest, keep quiet; to be at peace, keep neutral; to sleep; (*with acc and infin*) to stand by and see; (*with inf*) to cease
quiētē *adv* peacefully, quietly
quiētus *ppa of* **quiēscō** ◆ *adj* at rest; peaceful, neutral; calm, quiet, asleep
quīlibet, quaelibet, quodlibet *pron* any, anyone at all
quīn *adv* (*interrog*) why not?; (*correcting*) indeed, rather ◆ *conj* who not; but that, but, without; (*preventing*) from; (*doubting*) that
quīnam, quaenam, quodnam *pron* which?, what?
Quīnct- *etc see* **Quīnt-**
quīncūnx, -ūncis *m* five-twelfths; number five on a dice; **in quīncūncem dispositī** arranged in oblique lines
quīndeciēns, quīndeciēs *adv* fifteen times
quīndecim *num* fifteen; ~ **prīmī** fifteen chief magistrates
quīndecimvirālis *adj* of the council of fifteen
quīndecimvirī, -ōrum *mpl* council of fifteen
quīngēnī, -ōrum *adj* five hundred each
quīngentēsimus *adj* five-hundredth
quīngentī, -ōrum *num* five hundred
quīngentiēns, quīngentiēs *adv* five hundred times
quīnī, -ōrum *adj* five each; five; ~ **dēnī** fifteen each; ~ **vīcēnī** twenty-five each
quīnquāgēnī, -ōrum *adj* fifty each
quīnquāgēsimus *adj* fiftieth ◆ *f* 2 per cent tax
quīnquāgintā *num* fifty

Quīnquātria, -iōrum *and* **-ium** *ntpl festival of Minerva*

Quīnquātrūs, -uum *fpl festival of Minerva*

quīnque *num* five

quīnquennālis *adj* quinquennial; lasting five years

quīnquennis *adj* five years old; quinquennial

quīnquennium, -ī *and* **-iī** *nt* five years

quīnquēpartītus *adj* fivefold

quīnqueprīmī, -ōrum *mpl* five leading men

quīnquerēmis *adj* five-banked ♦ *f* quinquereme

quīnquevirātus, -ūs *m* membership of the board of five

quīnquevirī, -ōrum *mpl* board of five

quīnquiēns, quīnquiēs *adv* five times

quīnquiplicō, -āre *vt* to multiply by five

quīntadecimānī, -ōrum *mpl* men of the fifteenth legion

quīntānus *adj* of the fifth ♦ *f street in a camp between the 5th and 6th maniples* ♦ *mpl* men of the fifth legion

Quīntiliānus, -ī *m* Quintilian (*famous teacher of rhetoric in Rome*)

Quīntīlis *adj* of July

quīntum, quīntō *adv* for the fifth time

Quīntus, -ī *m* Roman first name

quīntus *adj* fifth

quīntusdecimus *adj* fifteenth

quippe *adv* (*affirming*) certainly, of course ♦ *conj* (*explaining*) for in fact, because, since; ~ **quī** since I, he *etc*

quippiam *etc see* **quispiam**

quippinī *adv* certainly

Quirīnālis *adj* of Romulus; Quirinal (hill)

Quirīnus, -ī *m* Romulus ♦ *adj* of Romulus

Quirīs, -ītis *m* inhabitant of Cures; Roman citizen; citizen

quirītātiō, -ōnis *f* shriek

Quirītēs *mpl* inhabitants of Cures; Roman citizens

quirītō, -āre *vi* to cry out, wail

quis, quid *pron* who?, what?; (*indef*) anyone, anything

quīs *poetic dat pl and abl pl of* **quī**

quisnam, quaenam, quidnam *pron* who?, what?

quispiam, quaepiam, quodpiam *and* **quidpiam** *pron* some, someone, something

quisquam, quaequam, quicquam *and* **quidquam** *pron* any, anyone, anything; **nec** ~ and no one

quisque, quaeque, quodque *pron* each, every, every one; **quidque, quicque** everything; **decimus** ~ every tenth; **optimus** ~ all the best; **prīmus** ~ the first possible

quisquiliae, -ārum *fpl* refuse, rubbish

quisquis, quaequae, quodquod, quidquid *and* **quicquid** *pron* whoever, whatever, all

quīvīs, quaevīs, quodvīs, quidvīs *pron* any you please, anyone, anything

quīvīscumque, quaevīscumque, quodvīscumque *pron* any whatsoever

quō *adv* (*interrog*) where?; whither?; for what purpose?, what for?; (*rel*) where, to which (place), to whom; (*with comp*) the (more); (*with* **sī**) anywhere ♦ *conj* (*with subj*) in order that; **nōn quō** not that

quoad *adv* how far?; how long? ♦ *conj* as far as, as long as; until

quōcircā *conj* therefore

quōcumque *adv* whithersoever

quod *conj* as for, in that, that; because; why; ~ **sī** but if

quōdam modo *adv* in a way

quoi *old dat form of* **quī**

quōius *old gen form of* **quī**

quōlibet *adv* anywhere, in any direction

quom *etc conj see* **cum²**

quōminus *conj* that not; (*preventing*) from

quōmodo *adv* (*interrog*) how?; (*rel*) just as; **quōmodocumque** howsoever; **quōmodonam** how?

quōnam *adv* where, where to?

quondam *adv* once, formerly; sometimes; (*fut*) one day

quōniam *conj* since, seeing that

quōpiam *adv* anywhere

quōquam *adv* anywhere

quoque *adv* also, too

quōquō *adv* to whatever place, wherever

quōquō modo *adv* howsoever

quōquō versus, quōquō versum *adv* in every direction

quōrsus, quōrsum *adv* where to?, in what direction?; what for?, to what end?

quot *adj* how many; as many as, every

quotannīs *adv* every year

quotcumque *adj* however many

quotēnī, -ōrum *adj* how many

quotīd- *etc see* **cottīd-**

quotiēns, quotiēs *adv* how often?; (*rel*) as often as

quotiēnscumque *adv* however often

quotquot *adj* however many

quotumus *adj* which number?, what date?

quotus *adj* what number, how many; ~ **quisque** how few; **quota hōra** what time

quotuscumque *adj* whatever number, however big

quōusque *adv* how long, till when; how far

quōvīs *adv* anywhere

quum *etc conj see* **cum²**

Rr

rabidē *adv* furiously
rabidus *adj* raving, mad; impetuous
rabiēs, (*acc* **-em**, *abl* **-ē**) *f* madness, rage, fury
rabiō, -ere *vi* to rave
rabiōsē *adv* wildly
rabiōsulus *adj* somewhat rabid
rabiōsus *adj* furious, mad
rabula, -ae *m* wrangling lawyer
racēmifer, -ī *adj* clustered
racēmus, -ī *m* stalk of a cluster; bunch of grapes; grape
radiātus *adj* radiant
rādīcitus *adv* by the roots; utterly
rādīcula, -ae *f* small root
radiō, -āre *vt* to irradiate ◆ *vi* to radiate, shine
radius, -ī *and* **-iī** *m* stick, rod; (*light*) beam, ray; (*loom*) shuttle; (MATH) rod for drawing figures, radius of a circle; (*plant*) long olive; (*wheel*) spoke
rādīx, -īcis *f* root; radish; (*hill*) foot; (*fig*) foundation, origin
rādō, -dere, -sī, -sum *vt* to scrape, shave, scratch; to erase; to touch in passing, graze, pass along
raeda, -ae *f* four-wheeled carriage
raedārius, -ī *and* **-iī** *m* driver
Raetī, -ōrum *mpl Alpine people between Italy and Germany*
Raetia, -iae *f country of the Raetī*
Raeticus, Raetius, Raetus *adj see* **Raetia**
rāmālia, -ium *ntpl* twigs, brushwood
rāmentum, -ī *nt* shavings, chips
rāmeus *adj* of branches
rāmex, -icis *m* rupture, blood vessels of the lungs
Ramnēnsēs, Ramnēs, -ium *mpl one of the original Roman tribes; a century of equites*
rāmōsus *adj* branching
rāmulus, -ī *m* twig, sprig
rāmus, -ī *m* branch, bough
rāna, -ae *f* frog; frogfish
rancēns, -entis *adj* putrid
rancidulus *adj* rancid
rancidus *adj* rank, rancid; disgusting
rānunculus, -ī *m* tadpole
rapācida, -ae *m* son of a thief
rapācitās, -ātis *f* greed
rapāx, -ācis *adj* greedy, grasping, ravenous
raphanus, -ī *m* radish
rapidē *adv* swiftly, hurriedly
rapiditās, -ātis *f* rapidity

rapidus *adj* tearing, devouring; swift, rapid; hasty, impetuous
rapīna, -ae *f* pillage, robbery; booty, prey
rapiō, -ere, -uī, -tum *vt* to tear, snatch, carry off; to seize, plunder; to hurry, seize quickly
raptim *adv* hastily, violently
raptiō, -ōnis *f* abduction
raptō, -āre, -āvī, -ātum *vt* to seize and carry off, drag away, move quickly; to plunder, lay waste; (*passion*) to agitate
raptor, -ōris *m* plunderer, robber, ravisher
raptus¹ *ppp of* **rapiō** ◆ *nt* plunder
raptus², -ūs *m* carrying off, abduction; plundering
rāpulum, -ī *nt* small turnip
rāpum, -ī *nt* turnip
rārēfaciō, -facere, -fēcī, -factum (*pass* **-fīō**) *vt* to rarefy
rārēscō, -ere *vi* to become rarefied, grow thin; to open out
rāritās, -ātis *f* porousness, open texture; thinness, fewness
rārō, rārē *adv* seldom
rārus *adj* porous, open in texture; thin, scanty; scattered, straggling, here and there; (MIL) in open order; few, infrequent; uncommon, rare
rāsī *perf of* **rādō**
rāsilis *adj* smooth, polished
rāstrum, -ī *nt* hoe, mattock
rāsus *ppp of* **rādō**
ratiō, -ōnis *f* 1. (*reckoning of*) account, calculation; list, register; affair, business 2. (*relation*) respect, consideration; procedure, method, system, way, kind 3. (*reason*) reasoning, thought; cause, motive; science, knowledge, philosophy; ~ **atque ūsus** theory and practice; ~ **est** it is reasonable; **Stōicōrum** ~ Stoicism; **ratiōnem dūcere, ratiōnem inīre** calculate; **ratiōnem habēre** take account of, have to do with, consider; **ratiōnem reddere** give an account of; **cum ratiōne** reasonably; **meae ratiōnēs** my interests; **ā ratiōnibus** accountant
ratiōcinātiō, -ōnis *f* reasoning; syllogism
ratiōcinātīvus *adj* syllogistic
ratiōcinātor, -ōris *m* accountant
ratiōcinor, -ārī, -ātus *vt, vi* to calculate; to consider; to argue, infer
ratiōnālis *adj* rational; syllogistic
ratis, -is *f* raft; boat

ratiuncula, -ae f small calculation; slight reason; petty syllogism

ratus ppa of **reor ◆** adj fixed, settled, sure; valid; **prō ratā (parte)** proportionally; **ratum dūcere, ratum facere, ratum habēre** ratify

raucisonus adj hoarse

raucus adj hoarse; harsh, strident

raudus, -eris nt copper coin

raudusculum, -ī nt bit of money

Ravenna, -ae f port in N.E. Italy

Ravennās, -ātis adj see **Ravenna**

rāvis (acc **-im**) f hoarseness

rāvus adj grey, tawny

rea, -ae f defendant, culprit

reāpse adv in fact, actually

Reāte, -is nt ancient Sabine town

Reātīnus adj see **Reāte**

rebellātiō, -ōnis f revolt

rebellātrīx, -īcis adj rebellious

rebelliō, -ōnis f revolt

rebellis adj rebellious ◆ mpl rebels

rebellium, -ī and **-iī** nt revolt

rebellō, -āre vi to revolt

rebītō, -ere vi to return

reboō, -āre vi to re-echo ◆ vt to make resound

recalcitrō, -āre vi to kick back

recaleō, -ēre vi to be warm again

recalēscō, -ere vi to grow warm again

recalfaciō, -facere, -fēcī vt to warm again

recalvus adj bald in front

recandēscō, -ēscere, -uī vi to whiten (in response); to glow

recantō, -āre, -āvī, -ātum vt to recant; to charm away

reccidī perf of **recidō**

recēdō, -ēdere, -essī, -essum vi to move back, withdraw, depart; (place) to recede; (head) to be severed

recellō, -ere vi to spring back

recēns, -entis adj fresh, young, recent; (writer) modern; (with **ab**) immediately after ◆ adv newly, just

recēnseō, -ēre, -uī, -um vt to count; to review

recēnsiō, -ōnis f revision

recēnsus ppp of **recēnseō**

recēpī perf of **recipiō**

receptāculum, -ī nt receptacle, reservoir; refuge, shelter

receptō, -āre vt to take back; to admit, harbour; to tug hard at

receptor, -ōris m (male) receiver, shelterer

receptrīx, -īcis f (female) receiver, shelterer

receptum, -ī nt obligation

receptus¹ ppp of **recipiō**

receptus², -ūs m withdrawal; retreat; return; refuge; **receptuī canere** sound the retreat

recessī perf of **recēdō**

recessim adv backwards

recessus, -ūs m retreat, departure; recess, secluded spot; (tide) ebb

recidīvus adj resurrected; recurring

recidō, -idere, -cidī, -āsum vi to fall back; to recoil, relapse; (fig) to fall, descend

recīdō, -dere, -dī, -sum vt to cut back, cut off

recingō, -gere, -ctum vt to ungird, loose

recinō, -ere vt, vi to re-echo, repeat; to sound a warning

reciper- etc see **recuper-**

recipiō, -ipere, -ēpī, -eptum vt to take back, retake; to get back, regain, rescue; to accept, admit; (MIL) to occupy; (duty) to undertake; (promise) to pledge, guarantee; **sē recipere** withdraw, retreat; **nōmen recipere** receive notice of a prosecution

reciprocō, -āre vt to move to and fro; (ship) to bring round to another tack; (proposition) to reverse ◆ vi (tide) to rise and fall

reciprocus adj ebbing

recīsus ppp of **recīdō**

recitātiō, -ōnis f reading aloud, recital

recitātor, -ōris m reader, reciter

recitō, -āre, -āvī, -ātum vt to read out, recite

reclāmātiō, -ōnis f outcry (of disapproval)

reclāmitō, -āre vi to cry out against

reclāmō, -āre vi to cry out, protest; to reverberate

reclīnis adj leaning back

reclīnō, -āre, -āvī, -ātum vt to lean back

reclūdō, -dere, -sī, -sum vt to open up; to disclose

reclūsus ppp of **reclūdō**

recoctus ppp of **recoquō**

recōgitō, -āre vi to think over, reflect

recognitiō, -ōnis f review

recognōscō, -ōscere, -ōvī, -itum vt to recollect; to examine, review

recolligō, -igere, -ēgī, -ēctum vt to gather up; (fig) to recover, reconcile

recolō, -olere, -oluī, -ultum vt to recultivate; to resume; to reflect on, contemplate; to revisit

recomminīscor, -ī vi to recollect

recompositus adj rearranged

reconciliātiō, -ōnis f restoration, reconciliation

reconciliō, -āre, -āvī, -ātum vt to win back again, restore, reconcile

reconcinnō, -āre vt to repair

reconditus ppp of **recondō ◆** adj hidden, secluded; abstruse, profound; (disposition) reserved

recondō, -ere, -idī, -itum vt to store away, stow; to hide away, bury

reconflō, -āre vt to rekindle

recoquō, -quere, -xī, -ctum vt to cook again, boil again; to forge again, recast; (fig) to rejuvenate

recordātiō, -ōnis f recollection

recordor, -ārī, -ātus vt, vi to recall, remember; to ponder over

recreō, -āre, -āvī, -ātum vt to remake, reproduce; to revive, refresh

recrepō, -āre vt, vi to ring, re-echo

recrēscō, -scere, -vī vi to grow again

recrūdēscō, -ēscere, -uī vi (wound) to open again; (war) to break out again

rēctā adv straight forward, right on

rēctē *adv* straight; correctly, properly, well; quite; (*colloq*) good, all right, no thank you

rēctiō, -ōnis *f* government

rēctor, -ōris *m* guide, driver, helmsman; governor, master

rēctum, -ī *nt* right, virtue

rēctus *ppp of* **regō** ♦ *adj* straight; upright, steep; right, correct, proper; (*moral*) good, virtuous

recubō, -āre *vi* to lie, recline

recultus *ppp of* **recolō**

recumbō, -mbere, -buī *vi* to lie down, recline; to fall, sink down

recuperātiō, -ōnis *f* recovery

recuperātor, -ōris *m* recapturer; (*pl*) *board of justices who tried civil cases requiring a quick decision, esp cases involving foreigners*

recuperātōrius *adj* of the recuperatores

recuperō, -āre, -āvī, -ātum *vt* to get back, recover, recapture

recūrō, -āre *vt* to restore

recurrō, -ere, -ī *vi* to run back; to return, recur; to revert

recursō, -āre *vi* to keep coming back, keep recurring

recursus, -ūs *m* return, retreat

recurvō, -āre *vt* to bend back, curve

recurvus *adj* bent, curved

recūsātiō, -ōnis *f* refusal, declining; (*LAW*) objection, counterplea

recūsō, -āre, -āvī, -ātum *vt* to refuse, decline, be reluctant; (*LAW*) to object, plead in defence

recussus *adj* reverberating

redāctus *ppp of* **redigō**

redambulō, -āre *vi* to come back

redamō, -āre *vt* to love in return

redārdēscō, -ere *vi* to blaze up again

redarguō, -ere, -ī *vt* to refute, contradict

redauspicō, -āre *vi* to take auspices for going back

redditus *ppp of* **reddō**

reddō, -ere, -idī, -itum *vt* to give back, return, restore; to give in response, repay; to give up, deliver, pay; (*copy*) to represent, reproduce; (*speech*) to report, repeat, recite, reply; to translate; (*with adj*) to make; **iūdicium reddere** fix the date for a trial; **iūs reddere** administer justice

redēgī *perf of* **redigō**

redēmī *perf of* **redimō**

redemptiō, -ōnis *f* ransoming; bribing; (*revenue*) farming

redemptō, -āre *vt* to ransom

redemptor, -ōris *m* contractor

redemptūra, -ae *f* contracting

redemptus *ppp of* **redimō**

redeō, -īre, -iī, -itum *vi* to go back, come back, return; (*speech*) to revert; (*money*) to come in; (*circumstances*) to be reduced to, come to

redhālō, -āre *vt* to exhale

redhibeō, -ēre *vt* to take back

redigō, -igere, -ēgī, -āctum *vt* to drive back, bring back; (*money*) to collect, raise; (*to a*

condition) to reduce, bring; (*number*) to reduce; **ad irritum redigere** make useless

rediī *perf of* **redeō**

redimīculum, -ī *nt* band

redimiō, -īre, -iī, -ītum *vt* to bind, crown, encircle

redimō, -imere, -ēmī, -emptum *vt* to buy back; to ransom, redeem; to release, rescue; (*good*) to procure; (*evil*) to avert; (*fault*) to make amends for; (*COMM*) to undertake by contract, hire

redintegrō, -āre, -āvī, -ātum *vt* to restore, renew, refresh

redipīscor, -ī *vt* to get back

reditiō, -ōnis *f* returning

reditus, -ūs *m* return, returning; (*money*) revenue

redivīvus *adj* renovated

redoleō, -ēre, -uī *vi* to give out a smell ♦ *vt* to smell of, smack of

redomitus *adj* broken in again

redōnō, -āre *vt* to restore; to give up

redūcō, -ūcere, -ūxī, -uctum *vt* to draw back; to lead back, bring back; to escort home; to marry again; (*troops*) to withdraw; (*fig*) to restore; (*to a condition*) to make into

reductiō, -ōnis *f* restoration

reductor, -ōris *m* man who brings back

reductus *ppp of* **redūcō** ♦ *adj* secluded, aloof

reduncus *adj* curved back

redundantia, -ae *f* extravagance

redundō, -āre, -āvī, -ātum *vi* to overflow; to abound, be in excess; (*fig*) to stream

reduvia, -ae *f* hangnail

redux, -cis *adj* (*gods*) who brings back; (*men*) brought back, returned

refectus *ppp of* **reficiō**

refellō, -ere, -ī *vt* to disprove, rebut

referciō, -cīre, -sī, -tum *vt* to stuff, cram, choke full

referiō, -īre *vt* to hit back; to reflect

referō, -ferre, -ttulī, -lātum *vt* to bring back, carry back; to give back, pay back, repay; to repeat, renew; (*authority*) to refer to, trace back to; (*blame, credit*) to ascribe; (*likeness*) to reproduce, resemble; (*memory*) to recall; (*news*) to report, mention; (*opinion*) to reckon amongst; (*record*) to enter; (*senate*) to lay before, move; (*speech*) to reply, say in answer; **grātiam referre** be grateful, requite; **pedem referre, gradum referre** return; retreat; **ratiōnēs referre** present an account; **sē referre** return

rēfert, -ferre, -tulit *vi* (*impers*) it is of importance, it matters, it concerns; **meā ~** it matters to me

refertus *ppp of* **referciō** ♦ *adj* crammed, full

referveō, -ēre *vi* to boil over

refervēscō, -ere *vi* to bubble up

reficiō, -icere, -ēcī, -ectum *vt* to repair, restore; (*body, mind*) to refresh, revive; (*money*) to get back, get in return; (*POL*) to re-elect

refīgō, -gere, -xī, -xum *vt* to unfasten, take down; (*fig*) to annul

refingō, -ere vt to remake
refixus ppp of **refigō**
reflāgitō, -āre vt to demand back
reflātus, -ūs m contrary wind
reflectō, -ctere, -xī, -xum vt to bend back, turn back; (fig) to bring back ♦ vi to give way
reflexus ppp of **reflectō**
reflō, -āre, -āvī, -ātum vi to blow contrary ♦ vt to breathe out again
refluō, -ere vi to flow back, overflow
refluus adj ebbing
reformīdō, -āre vt to dread; to shun in fear
refōrmō, -āre vt to reshape
refōtus ppp of **refoveō**
refoveō, -ovēre, -ōvī, -ōtum vt to refresh, revive
refrāctāriolus adj rather stubborn
refrāctus ppp of **refringō**
refrāgor, -ārī, -ātus vi (with dat) to oppose, thwart
refrēgī perf of **refringō**
refrēnō, -āre vt to curb, restrain
refricō, -āre, -uī, -ātum vt to scratch open; to reopen, renew ♦ vi to break out again
refrīgerātiō, -ōnis f coolness
refrīgerō, -āre, -āvī, -ātum vi to cool, cool off; (fig) to flag
refrīgēscō, -gēscere, -xī vi to grow cold; (fig) to flag, grow stale
refringō, -ingere, -ēgī, -āctum vt to break open; to break off; (fig) to break, check
refrīxī perf of **refrīgēscō**
refugiō, -ugere, -ūgī vi to run back, flee, shrink ♦ vt to run away from, shun
refugium, -ī and **-iī** nt refuge
refugus adj fugitive, receding
refulgeō, -gēre, -sī vi to flash back, reflect light
refundō, -undere, -ūdī, -ūsum vt to pour back, pour out; (pass) to overflow
refūsus ppp of **refundō**
refūtātiō, -ōnis f refutation
refūtātus, -ūs m refutation
refūtō, -āre, -āvī, -ātum vt to check, repress; to refute, disprove
rēgālis adj king's, royal, regal
rēgāliter adv magnificently; tyrannically
regerō, -rere, -ssī, -stum vt to carry back, throw back
rēgia, -ae f palace; court; (camp) royal tent; (town) capital
rēgiē adv regally; imperiously
rēgificus adj magnificent
regignō, -ere vt to reproduce
Rēgillānus, Rēgillēnsis adj see **Rēgillus**
Rēgillus, -ī m Sabine town; lake in Latium (scene of a Roman victory over the Latins)
regimen, -inis nt guiding, steering; rudder; rule, command, government; ruler
rēgīna, -ae f queen, noblewoman
Rēgīnus adj see **Rēgium**
regiō, -ōnis f direction, line; boundary line; quarter, region; district, ward, territory; (fig)

sphere, province; **ē regiōne** in a straight line; (with gen) exactly opposite
regiōnātim adv by districts
Rēgium, -ī and **-iī** nt town in extreme S. of Italy (now Reggio)
rēgius adj king's, kingly, royal; princely, magnificent
reglūtinō, -āre vt to unstick
rēgnātor, -ōris m ruler
rēgnātrīx, -īcis adj imperial
rēgnō, -āre, -āvī, -ātum vi to be king, rule, reign; to be supreme, lord it; (things) to prevail, predominate ♦ vt to rule over
rēgnum, -ī nt kingship, monarchy; sovereignty, supremacy; despotism; kingdom; domain
regō, -ere, rēxī, rēctum vt to keep straight, guide, steer; to manage, direct; to control, rule, govern; **regere fīnēs** (law) mark out the limits
regredior, -dī, -ssus vi to go back, come back, return; (MIL) to retire
regressus[1] ppa of **regredior**
regressus[2], -ūs m return; retreat
rēgula, -ae f rule, ruler; stick, board; (fig) rule, pattern, standard
rēgulus, -ī m petty king, chieftain; prince
Rēgulus, -ī m Roman consul taken prisoner by the Carthaginians
regustō, -āre vt to taste again
rēiciō, -icere, -iēcī, -iectum vt to throw back, throw over the shoulder, throw off; to drive back, repel; to cast off, reject; to reject with contempt, scorn; (jurymen) to challenge, refuse; (matter for discussion) to refer; (time) to postpone; **sē rēicere** fling oneself
rēiectāneus adj to be rejected
rēiectiō, -ōnis f rejection; (LAW) challenging
rēiectō, -āre vt to throw back
rēiectus ppp of **rēiciō**
relābor, -bī, -psus vi to glide back, sink back, fall back
relanguēscō, -ēscere, -ī vi to faint; to weaken
relātiō, -ōnis f (LAW) retorting; (pl) magistrate's report; (RHET) repetition
relātor, -ōris m proposer of a motion
relātus[1] ppp of **referō**
relātus[2], -ūs m official report; recital
relaxātiō, -ōnis f easing
relaxō, -āre, -āvī, -ātum vt to loosen, open out; (fig) to release, ease, relax, cheer
relēctus ppp of **relegō**
relēgātiō, -ōnis f banishment
relegō, -egere, -ēgī, -ēctum vt to gather up; (place) to traverse, sail over again; (speech) to go over again, reread
relēgō, -āre, -āvī, -ātum vt to send away, send out of the way; to banish; (fig) to reject; to refer, ascribe
relentēscō, -ere vi to slacken off
relēvī perf of **relinō**
relevō, -āre, -āvī, -ātum vt to lift up; to lighten; (fig) to relieve, ease, comfort
relictiō, -ōnis f abandoning

relictus *ppp of* **relinquō**
rēlicuus *etc see* **reliquus**
religātiō, -ōnis *f* tying up
rēligiō, -ōnis *f* religious scruple, reverence,
awe; religion; superstition; scruples,
conscientiousness; holiness, sanctity (*in
anything*); object of veneration, sacred place;
religious ceremony, observance
rēligiōsē *adv* devoutly; scrupulously,
conscientiously
rēligiōsus *adj* devout, religious; superstitious;
involving religious difficulty; scrupulous,
conscientious; (*objects*) holy, sacred
religō, -āre, -āvī, -ātum *vt* to tie up, fasten
behind; (*ship*) to make fast, moor; (*fig*) to bind
relinō, -inere, -ēvī *vt* to unseal
relinquō, -inquere, -īquī, -ictum *vt* to leave,
leave behind; to bequeath; to abandon,
forsake; (*argument*) to allow; (*pass*) to remain
rēliquiae, -ārum *fpl* leavings, remainder,
relics
reliquus *adj* remaining, left; (*time*)
subsequent, future; (*debt*) outstanding
♦ *nt* remainder, rest; arrears ♦ *mpl* the rest;
reliquum est it remains, the next point is;
reliquī facere leave behind, leave over, omit;
in reliquum for the future
rell- *etc see* **rel-**
relūceō, -cēre, -xī *vi* to blaze
relūcēscō, -cēscere, -xī *vi* to become bright
again
reluctor, -ārī, -ātus *vi* to struggle against,
resist
remaneō, -anēre, -ānsī *vi* to remain behind;
to remain, continue, endure
remānō, -āre *vi* to flow back
remānsiō, -ōnis *f* remaining behind
remedium, -ī *and* **-iī** *nt* cure, remedy, medicine
remēnsus *ppa of* **remētior**
remeō, -āre *vi* to come back, go back, return
remētior, -tīrī, -nsus *vt* to measure again; to
go back over
rēmex, -igis *m* rower, oarsman
Rēmī, -ōrum *mpl* people of Gaul (*in region of what is
now* Rheims)
rēmigātiō, -ōnis *f* rowing
rēmigium, -ī *and* **-iī** *nt* rowing; oars; oarsmen
rēmigō, -āre *vi* to row
remigrō, -āre *vi* to move back, return (home)
reminīscor, -ī *vt*, *vi* (*usu gen*) to remember, call
to mind
remīsceō, -scēre, -scuī, -xtum *vt* to mix up,
mingle
remissē *adv* mildly, gently
remissiō, -ōnis *f* release; (*tension*) slackening,
relaxing; (*payment*) remission; (*mind*)
slackness, mildness, relaxation; (*illness*)
abating
remissus *ppp of* **remittō** ♦ *adj* slack; negligent;
mild, indulgent, cheerful
remittō, -ittere, -īsī, -issum *vt* to let go back,
send back, release; to slacken, loosen, relax;
to emit, produce; (*mind*) to relax, relieve;
(*notion*) to discard, give up; (*offence, penalty*) to

let off, remit; (*right*) to resign, sacrifice; (*sound*)
to give back ♦ *vi* to abate
remixtus *ppp of* **remisceō**
remōlior, -īrī, -ītus *vt* to heave back
remollēscō, -ere *vi* to become soft again, be
softened
remolliō, -īre *vt* to weaken
remora, -ae *f* hindrance
remorāmina, -um *ntpl* hindrances
remordeō, -dēre, -dī, -sum *vt* (*fig*) to worry,
torment
remoror, -ārī, -ātus *vi* to linger, stay behind
♦ *vt* to hinder, delay, defer
remorsus *ppp of* **remordeō**
remōtē *adv* far
remōtiō, -ōnis *f* removing
remōtus *ppp of* **removeō** ♦ *adj* distant, remote;
secluded; (*fig*) far removed, free from
removeō, -ovēre, -ōvī, -ōtum *vt* to move
back, withdraw, set aside; to subtract
remūgiō, -īre *vi* to bellow in answer, re-echo
remulceō, -cēre, -sī *vt* to stroke; (*tail*) to droop
remulcum, -ī *nt* towrope
remūnerātiō, -ōnis *f* recompense, reward
remūneror, -ārī, -ātus *vt* to repay, reward
remurmurō, -āre *vi* to murmur in answer
Remus, -ī *m* brother of Romulus
rēmus, -ī *m* oar
renārrō, -āre *vt* to tell over again
renāscor, -scī, -tus *vi* to be born again; to
grow, spring up again
renātus *ppa of* **renāscor**
renāvigō, -āre *vi* to sail back
reneō, -ēre *vt* to unspin, undo
rēnēs, -um *mpl* kidneys
renīdeō, -ēre *vi* to shine back, be bright; to be
cheerful, smile, laugh
renīdēscō, -ere *vi* to reflect the gleam of
renītor, -ī *vi* to struggle, resist
renō, -āre *vi* to swim back
rēnō, -ōnis *m* fur
renōdō, -āre *vt* to tie back in a knot
renovāmen, -inis *nt* new condition
renovātiō, -ōnis *f* renewal; compound
interest
renovō, -āre, -āvī, -ātum *vt* to renew, restore;
to repair, revive, refresh; (*speech*) to repeat;
faenus renovāre take compound interest
renumerō, -āre *vt* to pay back
renūntiātiō, -ōnis *f* report, announcement
renūntiō, -āre, -āvī, -ātum *vt* to report, bring
back word; to announce, make an official
statement; (*election*) to declare elected, return;
(*duty*) to refuse, call off, renounce
renūntius, -ī *and* **-iī** *m* reporter
renuō, -ere, -ī *vt*, *vi* to deny, decline, refuse
renūtō, -āre *vi* to refuse firmly
reor, rērī, ratus *vi* to think, suppose
repāgula, -ōrum *ntpl* (*door*) bolts, bars
repandus *adj* curving back, turned up
reparābilis *adj* retrievable
reparcō, -ere *vi* to be sparing with, refrain

reparō, -āre, -āvī, -ātum vt to retrieve, recover; to restore, repair; to purchase; (mind, body) to refresh; (troops) to recruit

repastinātiō, -ōnis f digging up again

repellō, -ellere, -pulī, -ulsum vt to push back, drive back, repulse; to remove, reject

rependō, -endere, -endī, -ēnsum vt to return by weight; to pay, repay; to requite, compensate

repēns, -entis adj sudden; new

repēnsus ppp of **rependō**

repentē adv suddenly

repentīnō adv suddenly

repentīnus adj sudden, hasty; upstart

repercō etc see **reparcō**

repercussus¹ ppp of **repercutiō**

repercussus², -ūs m reflection, echo

repercutiō, -tere, -ssī, -ssum vt to make rebound, reflect, echo

reperiō, -īre, repperī, -tum vt to find, find out; to get, procure; to discover, ascertain; to devise, invent

repertor, -ōris m discoverer, inventor, author

repertus ppp of **reperiō** ♦ ntpl discoveries

repetītiō, -ōnis f repetition; (RHET) anaphora

repetītor, -ōris m reclaimer

repetītus ppp of **repetō** ♦ adj: **altē/longē** ~ far-fetched

repetō, -ere, -īvī and **-iī, -ītum** vt to go back to, revisit; to fetch back, take back; (MIL) to attack again; (action, speech) to resume, repeat; (memory) to recall, think over; (origin) to trace, derive; (right) to claim, demand back; **rēs repetere** demand satisfaction; reclaim one's property; **pecūniae repetundae** extortion

repetundae, -ārum fpl extortion (by a provincial governor)

repexus adj combed

repleō, -ēre, -ēvī, -ētum vt to fill up, refill; to replenish, make good, complete; to satiate, fill to overflowing

replētus adj full

replicātiō, -ōnis f rolling up

replicō, -āre vt to roll back, unroll, unfold

rēpō, -ere, -sī, -tum vi to creep, crawl

repōnō, -ōnere, -osuī, -ositum vt to put back, replace, restore; to bend back; to put (in the proper place); (performance) to repeat; (something received) to repay; (store) to lay up, put away; (task) to lay aside, put down; (hope) to place, rest; (with **prō**) substitute; **in numerō repōnere, in numerum repōnere** count, reckon among

reportō, -āre, -āvī, -ātum vt to bring back, carry back; (prize) to win, carry off; (words) to report

reposcō, -ere vt to demand back; to claim, require

repositus ppp of **repōnō** ♦ adj remote

repostor, -ōris m restorer

repostus etc see **repositus**

repōtia, -ōrum ntpl second drinking

repperī perf of **reperiō**

reppulī perf of **repellō**

repraesentātiō, -ōnis f vivid presentation; (COMM) cash payment

repraesentō, -āre, -āvī, -ātum vt to exhibit, reproduce; to do at once, hasten; (COMM) to pay cash

reprehendō, -endere, -endī, -ēnsum vt to hold back, catch, restrain; to hold fast, retain; to blame, rebuke, censure; to refute

reprehēnsiō, -ōnis f check; blame, reprimand, refutation

reprehēnsō, -āre vt to keep holding back

reprehēnsor, -ōris m censurer, critic, reviser

reprehēnsus ppp of **reprehendō**

reprendō etc see **reprehendō**

repressor, -ōris m restrainer

repressus ppp of **reprimō**

reprimō, -imere, -essī, -essum vt to keep back, force back; to check, restrain, suppress

reprōmissiō, -ōnis f counterpromise

reprōmittō, -ittere, -īsī, -issum vt to promise in return, engage oneself

rēptō, -āre vi to creep about, crawl along

repudiātiō, -ōnis f rejection

repudiō, -āre, -āvī, -ātum vt to reject, refuse, scorn; (wife) to divorce

repudium, -ī and **-iī** nt divorce; repudiation

repuerāscō, -ere vi to become a child again; to behave like a child

repugnanter adv reluctantly

repugnantia, -ium ntpl contradictions

repugnō, -āre, -āvī, -ātum vi to oppose, resist; to disagree, be inconsistent

repulsa, -ae f refusal, denial, repulse; (election) rebuff

repulsō, -āre vi to throb, reverberate

repulsus¹ ppp of **repellō**

repulsus², -ūs m (light) reflection; (sound) echoing

repungō, -ere vt to prod again

repūrgō, -āre, -āvī, -ātum vt to clear again, cleanse again; to purge away

reputātiō, -ōnis f pondering over

reputō, -āre, -āvī, -ātum vt to count back; to think over, consider

requiēs, -ētis f rest, relaxation, repose

requiēscō, -scere, -vī, -tum vi to rest, find rest; to cease ♦ vt to stay

requiētus adj rested, refreshed

requīritō, -āre vt to keep asking after

requīrō, -rere, -sīvī and **-siī, -sītum** vt to search for, look for; to ask, inquire after; (with **ex** or **ab**) to question; to need, want, call for; to miss, look in vain for

requīsītus ppp of **requīrō**

rēs, reī f thing, object; circumstance, case, matter, affair; business, transaction; fact, truth, reality; possessions, wealth, money; advantage, interest; (LAW) case; (MIL) campaign, operations; (POL) politics, power, the State; (writing) subject matter, story, history; **rēs mihi est tēcum** I have to do with you; **rēs dīvīna** sacrifice; **rēs mīlitāris** war; **rēs pūblica** public affairs, politics, the State, republic; **rēs rūstica** agriculture; **rem**

facere get rich; **rem gerere** wage war, fight; **ad rem** to the point, to the purpose; **in rem** usefully; **ob rem** to the purpose; **ob eam rem** therefore; **ī in malam rem** go to the devil!; **contrā rem pūblicam** unconstitutionally; ē **rē pūblicā** constitutionally; **rē vērā** in fact, actually; **eā rē** for that reason; **tuā rē, ex tuā rē** to your advantage; **ab rē** unhelpfully; ē **rē (nātā)** as things are; **prō rē** according to circumstances; **rēs adversae** failure, adversity; **rēs dubiae** danger; **rēs gestae** achievements, career; **rēs novae** revolution; **rēs prosperae, rēs secundae** success, prosperity; **rērum māximus** greatest in the world; **rērum scrīptor** historian

resacrō *etc see* **resecrō**

resaeviō, -īre *vi* to rage again

resalūtō, -āre *vt* to greet in return

resānēscō, -ēscere, -uī *vi* to heal up again

resarciō, -cīre, -tum *vt* to patch up, repair

rescindō, -ndere, -dī, -ssum *vt* to cut back, cut open, break down; to open up; (*law, agreement*) to repeal, annul

rescīscō, -īscere, -īvī *and* **-iī, -ītum** *vt* to find out, learn

rescissus *ppp of* **rescindō**

rescrībō, -bere, -psī, -ptum *vt* to write back, reply; to rewrite, revise; (*emperors*) to give a decision; (*MIL*) to transfer, re-enlist; (*money*) to place to one's credit, pay back

rescrīptus *ppp of* **rescrībō** ♦ *nt* imperial rescript

resecō, -āre, -uī, -tum *vt* to cut back, cut short; to curtail; **ad vīvum resecāre** cut to the quick

resecrō, -āre *vt* to pray again; to free from a curse

resectus *ppp of* **resecō**

resecūtus *ppa of* **resequor**

resēdī *perf of* **resideō; resīdō**

resēminō, -āre *vt* to reproduce

resequor, -quī, -cūtus *vt* to answer

reserō, -āre, -āvī, -ātum *vt* to unbar, unlock; to disclose

reservō, -āre, -āvī, -ātum *vt* to keep back, reserve; to preserve, save

reses, -idis *adj* remaining; inactive; idle; calm

resideō, -idēre, -ēdī *vi* to remain behind; to be idle, be listless; (*fig*) to remain, rest

resīdō, -īdere, -ēdī *vi* to sit down, sink down, settle; to subside; (*fig*) to abate, calm down

residuus *adj* remaining, left over; (*money*) outstanding

resignō, -āre *vt* to unseal, open; (*fig*) to reveal; (*COMM*) to cancel, pay back

resiliō, -īre, -uī *vi* to spring back; to recoil, rebound, shrink

resīmus *adj* turned up

rēsīna, -ae *f* resin

rēsīnātus *adj* smeared with resin

resipiō, -ere *vt* to savour of, smack of

resipīscō, -īscere, -iī *and* **-uī** *vi* to come to one's senses

resistō, -istere, -titī *vi* to stand still, stop, halt; to resist, oppose; to rise again

resolūtus *ppp of* **resolvō**

resolvō, -vere, -vī, -ūtum *vt* to unfasten, loosen, open, release; to melt, dissolve; to relax; (*debt*) to pay up; (*difficulty*) to banish, dispel; (*tax*) to abolish; (*words*) to explain

resonābilis *adj* answering

resonō, -āre *vi* to resound, re-echo ♦ *vt* to echo the sound of; to make resound

resonus *adj* echoing

resorbeō, -ēre *vt* to suck back, swallow again

respectō, -āre *vi* to look back; to gaze about, watch ♦ *vt* to look back at, look for; to have regard for

respectus¹ *ppp of* **respiciō**

respectus², -ūs *m* looking back; refuge; respect, regard

respergō, -gere, -sī, -sum *vt* to besprinkle, splash

respersiō, -ōnis *f* sprinkling

respersus *ppp of* **respergō**

respiciō, -icere, -exī, -ectum *vt* to look back at, see behind; (*help*) to look to; (*care*) to have regard for, consider, respect ♦ *vi* to look back, look

respīrāmen, -inis *nt* windpipe

respīrātiō, -ōnis *f* breathing; exhalation; taking breath, pause

respīrātus, -ūs *m* inhaling

respīrō, -āre, -āvī, -ātum *vt, vi* to breathe, blow back; to breathe again, revive; (*things*) to abate

resplendeō, -ēre *vi* to flash back, shine brightly

respondeō, -ondēre, -ondī, -ōnsum *vt* to answer, reply; (*lawyer, priest, oracle*) to advise, give a response; (*law court*) to appear; (*pledge*) to promise in return; (*things*) to correspond, agree, match; **pār parī respondēre** return like for like, give tit for tat

respōnsiō, -ōnis *f* answering; refutation

respōnsitō, -āre *vi* to give advice

respōnsō, -āre *vt, vi* to answer back; to defy

respōnsor, -ōris *m* answerer

respōnsum, -ī *nt* answer, reply; response, opinion, oracle

rēspūblica, reīpūblicae *f* public affairs, politics, the State, republic

respuō, -ere, -ī *vt* to spit out, eject; to reject, refuse

restagnō, -āre *vi* to overflow; to be flooded

restaurō, -āre *vt* to repair, rebuild

resticula, -ae *f* rope, cord

restinctiō, -ōnis *f* quenching

restinctus *ppp of* **restinguō**

restinguō, -guere, -xī, -ctum *vt* to extinguish, quench; (*fig*) to destroy

restiō, -ōnis *m* rope maker

restipulātiō, -ōnis *f* counterobligation

restipulor, -ārī *vt* to stipulate in return

restis, -is *f* rope

restitī *perf of* **resistō; restō**

restitō, -āre *vi* to stay behind, hesitate

restituō, -uere, -uī, -ūtum *vt* to replace, restore; to rebuild, renew; to give back, return; (*to a condition*) to reinstate; (*decision*) to quash, reverse; (*character*) to reform

restitūtiō, -ōnis f restoration; reinstating

restitūtor, -ōris m restorer

restitūtus ppp of **restituō**

restō, -āre, -itī vi to stand firm; to resist; to remain, be left; to be in store (for); **quod restat** for the future

restrictē adv sparingly; strictly

restrictus ppp of **restringō** ♦ adj tight, short; niggardly; severe

restringō, -ngere, -nxī, -ctum vt to draw back tightly, bind fast; (*teeth*) to bare; (*fig*) to check

resultō, -āre vi to rebound; to re-echo

resūmō, -ere, -psī, -ptum vt to take up again, get back, resume

resupīnō, -āre vt to turn back, throw on one's back

resupīnus adj lying back, face upwards

resurgō, -gere, -rēxī, -rēctum vi to rise again, revive

resuscitō, -āre vt to revive

retardātiō, -ōnis f hindering

retardō, -āre, -āvī, -ātum vt to retard, detain, check

rēte, -is nt net; (*fig*) snare

retēctus ppp of **retegō**

retegō, -egere, -ēxī, -ēctum vt to uncover, open; to reveal

retemptō, -āre vt to try again

retendō, -endere, -endī, -entum and **-ēnsum** vt to slacken, relax

retēnsus ppp of **retendō**

retentiō, -ōnis f holding back

retentō¹ etc see **retemptō**

retentō², -āre vt to keep back, hold fast

retentus ppp of **retendō**; **retineō**

retēxī perf of **retegō**

retexō, -ere, -uī, -tum vt to unravel; (*fig*) to break up, cancel; to renew

rētiārius, -ī and **-iī** m net-fighter

reticentia, -ae f saying nothing; pause

reticeō, -ēre, -uī vi to be silent, say nothing ♦ vt to keep secret

rēticulum, -ī nt small net, hairnet; network bag

retināculum, -ī nt tether, hawser

retinēns, -entis pres p of **retineō** ♦ adj tenacious, observant

retinentia, -ae f memory

retineō, -inēre, -inuī, -entum vt to hold back, detain, restrain; to keep, retain, preserve

retinniō, -īre vi to ring

retonō, -āre vi to thunder in answer

retorqueō, -quēre, -sī, -tum vt to turn back, twist

retorridus adj dried up, wizened

retortus ppp of **retorqueō**

retractātiō, -ōnis f hesitation

retractō, -āre, -āvī, -ātum vt to rehandle, take up again; to reconsider, revise; to withdraw ♦ vi to draw back, hesitate

retractus ppp of **retrahō** ♦ adj remote

retrahō, -here, -xī, -ctum vt to draw back, drag back; to withdraw, remove

retrectō etc see **retractō**

retribuō, -uere, -uī, -ūtum vt to restore, repay

retrō adv back, backwards, behind; (*time*) back, past

retrōrsum adv backwards, behind; in reverse order

retrūdō, -dere, -sum vt to push back; to withdraw

rettulī perf of **referō**

retundō, -undere, -udī and **-tudī, -ūsum** and **-ūnsum** vt to blunt; (*fig*) to check, weaken

retūnsus, retūsus ppp of **retundō** ♦ adj blunt, dull

reus, -ī m the accused, defendant; guarantor, debtor, one responsible; culprit, criminal; **vōtī ~** one who has had a prayer granted

revalēscō, -ēscere, -uī vi to recover

revehō, -here, -xī, -ctum vt to carry back, bring back; (*pass*) to ride, drive, sail back

revellō, -ellere, -ellī, -ulsum (-olsum) vt to pull out, tear off; to remove

revēlō, -āre vt to unveil, uncover

reveniō, -enīre, -ēnī, -entum vi to come back, return

rēvērā adv in fact, actually

reverendus adj venerable, awe-inspiring

reverēns, -entis pres p of **revereor** ♦ adj respectful, reverent

reverenter adv respectfully

reverentia, -ae f respect, reverence, awe

revereor, -ērī, -itus vt to stand in awe of; to respect, revere

reversiō, revorsiō, -ōnis f turning back; recurrence

reversus ppa of **revertor**

revertō, -ere, -ī, revertor, -tī, -sus vi to turn back, return; to revert

revexī perf of **revehō**

revictus ppp of **revincō**

revinciō, -cīre, -xī, -ctum vt to tie back, bind fast

revincō, -incere, -īcī, -ictum vt to conquer, repress; (*words*) to refute, convict

revinctus ppp of **revinciō**

revirēscō, -ēscere, -uī vi to grow green again; to be rejuvenated; to grow strong again; flourish again

revīsō, -ere vt, vi to come back to, revisit

revīvēscō, -vīscō, -vīscere, -xī vi to come to life again, revive

revocābilis adj revocable

revocāmen, -inis nt recall

revocātiō, -ōnis f recalling; (*word*) withdrawing

revocō, -āre, -āvī, -ātum vt to call back, recall; (*action*) to revoke; (*former state*) to recover, regain; (*growth*) to check; (*guest*) to invite in return; (*judgment*) to apply, refer; (*law*) to summon again; (*performer*) to encore; (*troops*) to withdraw

revolō, -āre vi to fly back

revolsus etc see **revulsus**

revolūbilis *adj* that may be rolled back
revolūtus *ppp of* **revolvō**
revolvō, -vere, -vī, -ūtum *vt* to roll back, unroll, unwind; (*speech*) to relate, repeat; (*thought*) to think over; (*writing*) to read over; (*pass*) to revolve, return, come round
revomō, -ere, -uī *vt* to disgorge
revor- *etc see* **rever-**
revulsus *ppp of* **revellō**
rēx, rēgis *m* king; tyrant, despot; leader; patron, rich man
rēxī *perf of* **regō**
Rhadamanthus, -ī *m judge in the lower world*
Rhaeti *etc see* **Raetī**
Rhamnūs, -ūntis *f town in Attica (famous for its statue of Nemesis)*
Rhamnūsis, -ūsidis *f* Nemesis
Rhamnūsius *adj see* **Rhamnūs**
rhapsōdia, -ae *f* a book of Homer
Rhea, -ae *f* Cybele
Rhea Silvia, Rheae Silviae *f mother of Romulus and Remus*
Rhēgium *etc see* **Rēgium**
Rhēnānus *adj* Rhenish
rhēnō *etc see* **rēnō**
Rhēnus, -ī *m* Rhine
Rhēsus, -ī *m Thracian king (killed at Troy)*
rhētor, -oris *m* teacher of rhetoric; orator
rhētorica, -ae, rhētoricē, -ēs *f* art of oratory, rhetoric
rhētoricē *adv* rhetorically, in an oratorical manner
rhētoricī, -ōrum *mpl* teachers of rhetoric
rhētoricus *adj* rhetorical, on rhetoric
rhīnocerōs, -ōtis *m* rhinoceros
rhō *nt indecl* (Greek letter) rho
Rhodanus, -ī *m* Rhone
Rhodius *adj see* **Rhodos**
Rhodopē, -ēs *f mountain range in Thrace*
Rhodopēius *adj* Thracian
Rhodos, Rhodus, -ī *f* (island) of Rhodes
Rhoetēum, -ī *nt promontory on the Dardanelles (near Troy)*
Rhoetēus *adj* Trojan
rhombus, -ī *m* magician's circle; (*fish*) turbot
rhomphaea, -ae *f* long barbarian javelin
rhythmicus, -ī *m* teacher of prose rhythm
rhythmos, rhythmus, -i *m* rhythm, symmetry
rīca, -ae *f* sacrificial veil
rīcinium, -ī *and* **-iī** *nt* small cloak with hood
rictum, -ī *nt,* **rictus, -ūs** *m* open mouth, gaping jaws
rīdeō, -dēre, -sī, -sum *vi* to laugh, smile ♦ *vt* to laugh at, smile at; to ridicule
rīdibundus *adj* laughing
rīdiculāria, -ium *ntpl* jokes
rīdiculē *adv* jokingly; absurdly
rīdiculus *adj* amusing, funny; ridiculous, silly ♦ *m* jester ♦ *nt* joke
rigēns, -entis *pres p of* **rigeō** ♦ *adj* stiff, rigid, frozen
rigeō, -ēre *vi* to be stiff

rigēscō, -ēscere, -uī *vi* to stiffen, harden; to bristle
rigidē *adv* rigorously
rigidus *adj* stiff, rigid, hard; (*fig*) hardy, strict, inflexible
rigō, -āre *vt* to water, moisten, bedew; to convey (*water*)
rigor, -ōris *m* stiffness, hardness; numbness, cold; strictness, severity
riguī *perf of* **rigēscō**
riguus *adj* irrigating; watered
rīma, -ae *f* crack, chink
rīmor, -ārī, -ātus *vt* to tear open; to search for, probe, examine; to find out
rīmōsus *adj* cracked, leaky
ringor, -ī *vi* to snarl
rīpa, -ae *f* river bank; shore
Rīphaeī, -ōrum *mpl mountain range in N. Scythia*
Rīphaeus *adj see* **Rīphaeī**
rīpula, -ae *f* riverbank
riscus, -ī *m* trunk, chest
rīsī *perf of* **rīdeō**
rīsor, -ōris *m* scoffer
rīsus, -ūs *m* laughter, laugh; laughing stock
rīte *adv* with the proper formality or ritual; duly, properly, rightly; in the usual manner; fortunately
rītus, -ūs *m* ritual, ceremony; custom, usage; **rītū** after the manner of
rīvālis, -is *m* rival in love
rīvālitās, -ātis *f* rivalry in love
rīvulus, -ī *m* brook
rīvus, -ī *m* stream, brook; **ē rīvō flūmina māgna facere** make a mountain of a molehill
rixa, -ae *f* quarrel, brawl, fight
rixor, -ārī, -ātus *vi* to quarrel, brawl, squabble
rōbīginōsus *adj* rusty
rōbīgō, -inis *f* rust; blight, mould, mildew
rōboreus *adj* of oak
rōborō, -āre *vt* to strengthen, invigorate
rōbur, -oris *nt* oak; hard wood; prison, dungeon (*at Rome*); (*fig*) strength, hardness, vigour; best part, élite, flower
rōbustus *adj* of oak; strong, hard; robust, mature
rōdō, -dere, -sī, -sum *vt* to gnaw; (*rust*) to corrode; (*words*) to slander
rogālis *adj* of a pyre
rogātiō, -ōnis *f* proposal, motion, bill; request; (RHET) question
rogātiuncula, -ae *f* unimportant bill; question
rogātor, -ōris *m* proposer; polling clerk
rogātus, -ūs *m* request
rogitō, -āre *vt* to ask for, inquire eagerly
rogō, -āre, -āvī, -ātum *vt* to ask, ask for; (*bill*) to propose, move; (*candidate*) to put up for election; **lēgem rogāre** introduce a bill; **populum rogāre** introduce a bill; **magistrātum populum rogāre** nominate for election to an office; **militēs sacrāmentō rogāre** administer the oath to the troops; **mālō emere quam rogāre** I'd rather buy it than borrow it

rogus, **-ī** *m* funeral pyre

Rōma, **-ae** *f* Rome

Rōmānus *adj* Roman

Rōmuleus, **Rōmulus** *adj* of Romulus; Roman

Rōmulidae, **-idārum** *mpl* the Romans

Rōmulus, **-ī** *m* founder and first king of Rome

rōrāriī, **-ōrum** *mpl* skirmishers

rōridus *adj* dewy

rōrifer, **-ī** *adj* dew-bringing

rōrō, **-āre** *vi* to distil dew; to drip, trickle ♦ *vt* to bedew, wet

rōs, **rōris** *m* dew; moisture, water; (*plant*) rosemary; **rōs marīnus** rosemary

rosa, **-ae** *f* rose; rose bush

rosāria, **-ōrum** *ntpl* rose garden

rōscidus *adj* dewy; wet

Roscius¹, **-ī** *m*: L. ~ Othō *tribune in 67 BC, whose law reserved theatre seats for the equites*; Q. ~ Gallus *famous actor defended by Cicero*; Sex. ~ *of Ameria, defended by Cicero*

Roscius², **-iānus** *adj see* **Roscius¹**

rosētum, **-ī** *nt* rosebed

roseus *adj* rosy; of roses

rōsī *perf of* **rōdō**

rōstrātus *adj* beaked, curved; **columna rōstrāta** *column commemorating a naval victory*

rōstrum, **-ī** *nt* (*bird*) beak, bill; (*animal*) snout, muzzle; (*ship*) beak, end of prow; (*pl*) *orators' platform in the Forum*

rōsus *ppp of* **rōdō**

rota, **-ae** *f* wheel; potter's wheel, torture wheel; car, disc

rotō, **-āre**, **-āvī**, **-ātum** *vt* to turn, whirl, roll; (*pass*) to revolve

rotundē *adv* elegantly

rotundō, **-āre** *vt* to round off

rotundus *adj* round, circular, spherical; (*style*) well-turned, smooth

rubefaciō, **-facere**, **-fēcī**, **-factum** *vt* to redden

rubēns, **-entis** *pres p of* **rubeō** ♦ *adj* red; blushing

rubeō, **-ēre** *vi* to be red; to blush

ruber, **-rī** *adj* red; **mare rubrum** Red Sea; Persian Gulf; **ōceanus ~** Indian Ocean; **Saxa rubra** *stone quarries between Rome and Veii*

rubēscō, **-ēscere**, **-uī** *vi* to redden, blush

rubēta¹, **-ae** *f* toad

rubēta², **-ōrum** *ntpl* bramble bushes

rubeus *adj* of bramble

Rubicō, **-ōnis** *m* stream marking the frontier between Italy and Gaul

rubicundulus *adj* reddish

rubicundus *adj* red, ruddy

rūbīg- *etc see* **rōbīg-**

rubor, **-ōris** *m* redness; blush; bashfulness; shame

rubrīca, **-ae** *f* red earth, red ochre

rubuī *perf of* **rubēscō**

rubus, **-ī** *m* bramble bush; bramble, blackberry

ructō, **-āre**, **ructor**, **-ārī** *vt*, *vi* to belch

ructus, **-us** *m* belching

rudēns, **-entis** *pres p of* **rudō** ♦ *m* rope; (*pl*) rigging

Rudiae, **-iārum** *fpl town in E. Italy (birthplace of Ennius)*

rudiārius, **-ī** *and* **-iī** *m* retired gladiator

rudīmentum, **-ī** *nt* first attempt, beginning

Rudīnus *adj see* **Rudiae**

rudis¹ *adj* unwrought, unworked, raw; coarse, rough, badly-made; (*age*) new, young; (*person*) uncultured, unskilled, clumsy; ignorant (of), inexperienced (in)

rudis², **-is** *f* stick, rod; foil (*for fighting practice*); (*fig*) discharge

rudō, **-ere**, **-īvī**, **-ītum** *vi* to roar, bellow, bray; to creak

rūdus¹, **-eris** *nt* rubble, rubbish; piece of copper

rūdus², **-eris** *nt* copper coin

Rūfulī, **-ōrum** *mpl* military tribunes (*chosen by the general*)

rūfulus *adj* red-headed

rūfus *adj* red, red-haired

rūga, **-ae** *f* wrinkle, crease

rūgō, **-āre** *vi* to become creased

rūgōsus *adj* wrinkled, shrivelled, corrugated

ruī *perf of* **ruō**

ruīna, **-ae** *f* fall, downfall; collapse, falling in; debris, ruins; destruction, disaster, ruin (*fig*)

ruīnōsus *adj* collapsing; ruined

rumex, **-icis** *f* sorrel

rūmificō, **-āre** *vt* to report

Rūmīna, **-ae** *f goddess of nursing mothers*; **fīcus Rūmīnālis** *the fig tree of Romulus and Remus (under which the she-wolf suckled them)*

rūminātiō, **-ōnis** *f* chewing the cud; (*fig*) ruminating

rūminō, **-āre** *vt*, *vi* to chew the cud

rūmor, **-ōris** *m* noise, cheering; rumour, hearsay; public opinion; reputation

rumpia *etc see* **rhomphaea**

rumpō, **-ere**, **rūpī**, **ruptum** *vt* to break, burst, tear; to break down, burst through; (*activity*) to interrupt; (*agreement*) to violate, annul; (*delay*) to put an end to; (*voice*) to give vent to; (*way*) to force through

rūmusculī, **-ōrum** *mpl* gossip

rūna, **-ae** *f* dart

runcō, **-āre** *vt* to weed

ruō, **-ere**, **-ī**, **-tum** *vi* to fall down, tumble; to rush, run, hurry; to come to ruin ♦ *vt* to dash down, hurl to the ground; to throw up, turn up

rūpēs, **-is** *f* rock, cliff

rūpī *perf of* **rumpō**

ruptor, **-ōris** *m* violator

ruptus *ppp of* **rumpō**

rūricola, **-ae** *adj* rural, country- (*in cpds*)

rūrigena, **-ae** *m* countryman

rūrsus, **rūrsum**, **rūsum** *adv* back, backwards; on the contrary, in return; again

rūs, **rūris** *nt* the country, countryside; estate, farm; **rūs** to the country; **rūrī** in the country; **rūre** from the country

ruscum, **-ī** *nt* butcher's-broom

russus *adj* red

rūsticānus *adj* country- (*in cpds*), rustic
rūsticātiō, -ōnis *f* country life
rūsticē *adv* in a countrified manner, awkwardly
rūsticitās, -ātis *f* country manners, rusticity
rūsticor, -ārī *vi* to live in the country
rūsticulus, -ī *m* yokel
rūsticus *adj* country- (*in cpds*), rural, rough, clownish ♦ *m* countryman
rūsum *see* **rūrsus**
rūta, -ae *f* (*herb*) rue; (*fig*) unpleasantness

ruta caesa *ntpl* minerals and timber on an estate
rutilō, -āre *vt* to colour red ♦ *vi* to glow red
rutilus *adj* red, auburn
rutrum, -ī *nt* spade, shovel, trowel
rŭtula, -ae *f* little piece of rue
Rutulī, -ōrum *mpl* ancient Latin people
Rutulus *adj* Rutulian
Rutupiae, -iārum *fpl* seaport in Kent (now Richborough)
Rutupīnus *adj see* **Rutupiae**
rutus *ppp of* **ruō**

Ss

Saba, -ae f *town in Arabia Felix*
Sabaeus *adj see* **Saba**
Sabāzia, -iōrum *ntpl festival of Bacchus*
Sabāzius, -ī m *Bacchus*
sabbata, -ōrum *ntpl* Sabbath, Jewish holiday
Sabellus¹, -ī m *Sabine, Samnite*
Sabellus², -icus *adj see* **Sabellus¹**
Sabīnī, -ōrum *mpl* Sabines *(a people of central Italy)*
Sabīnus *adj* Sabine ◆ f Sabine woman ◆ *nt*
  Sabine estate; Sabine wine; **herba Sabīna**
  savin *(a kind of juniper)*
Sabrīna, -ae f *(river)* Severn
saburra, -ae f *sand, ballast*
Sacae, -ārum *mpl tribe of Scythians*
saccipērium, -ī and -iī *nt purse-pocket*
saccō, -āre *vt* to strain, filter
sacculus, -ī m *little bag, purse*
saccus, -ī m *bag, purse, wallet*
sacellum, -ī *nt chapel*
sacer, -rī *adj* sacred, holy; devoted for sacrifice,
  forfeited; accursed, criminal, infamous; **Mōns
  ~** hill to which the Roman plebs seceded; **Via sacra**
  street from the Forum to the Capitol
sacerdōs, -ōtis m/f *priest, priestess*
sacerdōtium, -ī and -iī *nt priesthood*
sacrāmentum, -ī *nt deposit made by parties to a
  lawsuit; civil lawsuit, dispute; (MIL) oath of
  allegiance, engagement*
sacrārium, -ī and -iī *nt shrine, chapel*
sacrātus *adj* holy, hallowed; **sacrāta lēx** *a law
  whose violation was punished by devotion to the infernal
  gods*
sacricola, -ae m/f *sacrificing priest or priestess*
sacrifer, -ī *adj carrying holy things*
sacrificālis *adj sacrificial*
sacrificātiō, -ōnis f *sacrificing*
sacrificium, -ī and -iī *nt sacrifice*
sacrificō, -āre *vt, vi to sacrifice*
sacrificulus, -i m *sacrificing priest;* **rēx ~** high
  priest
sacrificus *adj sacrificial*
sacrilēgium, -ī and -iī *nt sacrilege*
sacrilegus *adj* sacrilegious; profane, wicked ◆ m
  temple-robber
sacrō, -āre, -āvī, -ātum *vt* to consecrate; to
  doom, curse; to devote, dedicate; to make
  inviolable; *(poetry)* to immortalize
sacrōsanctus *adj inviolable, sacrosanct*
sacruficō *etc see* **sacrificō**
sacrum, -rī *nt* holy thing, sacred vessel;
  shrine; offering, victim; rite; *(pl)* sacrifice,

worship, religion; **sacra facere** sacrifice;
inter ~ saxumque with one's back to the wall;
hērēditās sine sacrīs *a gift with no awkward
  obligations*
saeclum *etc see* **saeculum**
saeculāris *adj* centenary; *(ECCL)* secular, pagan
saeculum, -ī *nt* generation, lifetime, age; the
  age, the times; century; **in saecula** *(ECCL)* for
  ever
saepe *adv* often, frequently
saepe numerō *adv* very often
saepēs, -is f *hedge, fence*
saepīmentum, -ī *nt enclosure*
saepiō, -īre, -sī, -tum *vt* to hedge round, fence
  in, enclose; *(fig)* to shelter, protect
saeptus *ppp of* **saepiō** ◆ *nt* fence, wall; stake,
  pale; *(sheep)* fold; *(Rome)* voting area in the Campus
  Martius
saeta, -ae f *hair, bristle*
saetiger, -ī *adj bristly*
saetōsus *adj bristly, hairy*
saevē, saeviter *adv* fiercely, cruelly
saevidicus *adj furious*
saeviō, -īre, -iī, -ītum *vi* to rage, rave
saevitia, -ae f *rage; ferocity, cruelty*
saevus *adj* raging, fierce; cruel, barbarous
sāga, -ae f *fortune teller*
sagācitās, -ātis f *(dogs)* keen scent; *(mind)*
  shrewdness
sagāciter *adv* keenly; shrewdly
sagātus *adj wearing a soldier's cloak*
sagāx, -ācis *adj (senses)* keen, keen-scented;
  (mind) quick, shrewd
sagīna, -ae f *stuffing, fattening; food, rich food;
  fatted animal*
sagīnō, -āre *vt* to cram, fatten; to feed, feast
sāgiō, -īre *vi* to perceive keenly
sagitta, -ae f *arrow*
sagittārius, -ī and -iī m *archer*
sagittifer, -ī *adj armed with arrows*
sagmen, -inis *nt* tuft of sacred herbs *(used as a
  mark of inviolability)*
sagulum, -ī *nt short military cloak*
sagum, -ī *nt* military cloak; woollen mantle
Saguntīnus *adj see* **Saguntum**
Saguntum, -ī *nt*, **Saguntus, -ī, Saguntos, -ī** f
  town in E. Spain
sāgus *adj prophetic*
sāl, salis m *salt; brine, sea; (fig)* shrewdness, wit,
  humour, witticism; good taste
salacō, -ōnis m *swaggerer*

Salamīnius adj see **Salamīs**
Salamīs, -īnis f Greek island near Athens; town in Cyprus
salapūtium, -ī and **-iī** nt manikin
salārius adj salt- (in cpds) ♦ nt allowance, salary
salāx, -ācis adj lustful, salacious
salebra, -ae f roughness, rut
Saliāris adj of the Salii; sumptuous
salictum, -ī nt willow plantation
salientēs, -ium fpl springs
salignus adj of willow
Saliī, -ōrum mpl priests of Mars
salillum, -ī nt little saltcellar
salīnae, -ārum fpl saltworks
salīnum, -ī nt saltcellar
saliō, -īre, -uī, -tum vi to leap, spring; to throb
saliunca, -ae f Celtic nard
salīva, -ae f saliva, spittle; taste
salix, -icis f willow
Sallustiānus adj see **Sallustius**
Sallustius, -ī m Sallust (Roman historian); his wealthy grand-nephew
Salmōneus, -eos m son of Aeolus (punished in Tartarus for imitating lightning)
Salmōnis, -idis f his daughter Tyro
salsāmentum, -ī nt brine, pickle; salted fish
salsē adv wittily
salsus adj salted; salt, briny; (fig) witty
saltātiō, -ōnis f dancing, dance
saltātor, -ōris m dancer
saltātōrius adj dancing- (in cpds)
saltātrīx, -īcis f dancer
saltātus, -ūs m dance
saltem adv at least, at all events; **nōn** ~ not even
saltō, -āre vt, vi to dance
saltuōsus adj wooded
saltus¹, -ūs m leap, bound
saltus², -ūs m woodland pasture, glade; pass, ravine
salūber adj see **salūbris**
salūbris adj health-giving, wholesome; healthy, sound
salūbritās, -ātis f healthiness; health
salūbriter adv wholesomely; beneficially
saluī perf of **saliō**
salum, -ī nt sea, high sea
salūs, -ūtis f health; welfare, life; safety; good wish, greeting; **salūtem dīcere** greet; bid farewell
salūtāris adj wholesome, healthy; beneficial; ~ **littera** letter A (for absolvō = acquittal)
salūtāriter adv beneficially
salūtātiō, -ōnis f greeting; formal morning visit, levee
salūtātor, -ōris m morning caller; male courtier
salūtātrīx, -īcis f morning caller; female courtier
salūtifer, -ī adj health-giving
salūtigerulus adj carrying greetings
salūtō, -āre, -āvī, -ātum vt to greet, salute, wish well; to call on, pay respects to
salvē¹ adv well, in good health; all right
salvē² impv of **salveō**

salveō, -ēre vi to be well, be in good health; **salvē, salvētō, salvēte** hail!, good day!, goodbye!; **salvēre iubeō** I bid good day
salvus, salvos adj safe, alive, intact, well; without violating; all right; ~ **sīs** good day to you!; **salva rēs est** all is well; **salvā lēge** without breaking the law
Samaous adj see **Samē**
Samarobrīva, -ae f Belgian town (now Amiens)
sambūca, -ae f harp
sambūcistria, -ae f harpist
Samē, -ēs f old name of the Greek island Cephalonia
Samius adj Samian ♦ ntpl Samian pottery
Samnīs, -ītis adj Samnite
Samnium, -ī and **-iī** nt district of central Italy
Samos, Samus, -ī f Aegean island off Asia Minor (famous for its pottery and as the birthplace of Pythagoras)
Samothrāces, -um mpl Samothracians
Samothrācia, -iae, Samothrāca, -ae f Samothrace (island in the N. Aegean)
Samothrācius adj see **Samothrācia**
sānābilis adj curable
sānātiō, -ōnis f healing
sanciō, -īre, -xī, -ctum vt to make sacred or inviolable; to ordain, ratify; to enact a punishment against
sanctimōnia, -ae f sanctity; chastity
sanctiō, -ōnis f decree, penalty for violating a law
sanctitās, -ātis f sacredness; integrity, chastity
sanctitūdō, -inis f sacredness
sānctō adv solemnly, religiously
sānctor, -ōris m enacter
sanctus ppp of **sanciō** ♦ adj sacred, inviolable; holy, venerable; pious, virtuous, chaste
sandaligerula, -ae f sandalbearer
sandalium, -ī and **-iī** nt sandal, slipper
sandapila, -ae f common bier
sandȳx, -ȳcis f scarlet
sānē adv sensibly; (intensive) very, doubtless; (ironical) to be sure, of course; (concessive) of course, indeed; (in answer) certainly, surely; (with impv) then, if you please; ~ **quam** very much; **haud** ~ not so very, not quite
sanguen etc see **sanguis**
sanguināns, -antis adj bloodthirsty
sanguinārius adj bloodthirsty
sanguineus adj bloody, of blood; blood-red
sanguinolentus adj bloody; blood-red; sanguinary
sanguis, -inis m blood, bloodshed; descent, family; offspring; (fig) strength, life; **sanguinem dare** shed one's blood; **sanguinem mittere** let blood
saniēs (acc **-em**, abl **-ē**) f diseased blood, matter; venom
sānitās, -ātis f (body) health, sound condition; (mind) sound sense, sanity; (style) correctness, purity
sanna, -ae f grimace, mocking
sanniō, -ōnis m clown
sānō, -āre, -āvī, -ātum vt to cure, heal; (fig) to remedy, relieve
Sanquālis avis f osprey

sānus *adj* (*body*) sound, healthy; (*mind*) sane, sensible; (*style*) correct; **male ~** mad, inspired; **sānun es?** are you in your senses?

sanxī *perf of* **sanciō**

sapa, **-ae** *f* new wine

sapiēns, **-entis** *pres p of* **sapiō** ♦ *adj* wise, discreet ♦ *m* wise man, philosopher; man of taste

sapienter *adv* wisely, sensibly

sapientia, **-ae** *f* wisdom, discernment; philosophy; knowledge

sapiō, **-ere**, **-īvī** *and* **-uī** *vi* to have a flavour or taste; to have sense, be wise ♦ *vt* to taste of, smell of, smack of; to understand

sapor, **-ōris** *m* taste, flavour; (*food*) delicacy; (*fig*) taste, refinement

Sapphicus *adj see* **Sapphō**

Sapphō, **-ūs** *f* famous Greek lyric poetess, native of Lesbos

sarcina, **-ae** *f* bundle, burden; (MIL) pack

sarcinārius *adj* baggage- (*in cpds*)

sarcinātor, **-ōris** *m* patcher

sarcinula, **-ae** *f* little pack

sarciō, **-cīre**, **-sī**, **-tum** *vt* to patch, mend, repair

sarcophagus, **-ī** *m* sepulchre

sarculum, **-ī** *nt* light hoe

Sardēs, **Sardis**, **-ium** *fpl* Sardis (*capital of Lydia*)

Sardiānus *adj see* **Sardēs**

Sardinia, **-iniae** *f* (island of) Sardinia

sardonyx, **-chis** *f* sardonyx

Sardus, **Sardōus**, **Sardiniēnsis** *adj see* **Sardinia**

sariō, **-īre**, **-īvī** *and* **-uī** *vt* to hoe, weed

sarīsa, **-ae** *f* Macedonian lance

sarīsophorus, **-ī** *m* Macedonian lancer

Sarmatae, **-ārum** *mpl* Sarmatians (*a people of S.E. Russia*)

Sarmaticus, **-is** *adj see* **Sarmatae**

sarmentum, **-ī** *nt* twigs, brushwood

Sarpēdōn, **-onis** *m* king of Lycia

Sarra, **-ae** *f* Tyre

sarrācum, **-ī** *nt* cart

Sarrānus *adj* Tyrian

sarriō *etc see* **sariō**

sarsī *perf of* **sarciō**

sartāgō, **-inis** *f* frying pan

sartor, **-ōris** *m* hoer, weeder

sartus *ppp of* **sarciō**

sat *etc see* **satis**

satagō, **-ere** *vi* to have one's hands full, be in trouble; to bustle about, fuss

satelles, **-itis** *m/f* attendant, follower; assistant, accomplice

satiās, **-ātis** *f* sufficiency; satiety

satietās, **-ātis** *f* sufficiency; satiety

satin, **satine** *see* **satisne**

satiō¹, **-āre**, **-āvī**, **-ātum** *vt* to satisfy, appease; to fill, saturate; to glut, cloy, disgust

satiō², **-ōnis** *f* sowing, planting; (*pl*) fields

satis, **sat** *adj* enough, sufficient ♦ *adv* enough, sufficiently; tolerably, fairly, quite; **~ accipiō** take sufficient bail; **~ agō**, **~ agitō** have one's hands full, be harassed; **~ dō** offer sufficient bail; **~ faciō** satisfy; give satisfaction, make amends; (*creditor*) pay

satisdatiō, **-ōnis** *f* giving security

satisdō *see* **satis**

satisfaciō *see* **satis**

satisfactiō, **-ōnis** *f* amends, apology

satisne *adv* quite, really

satius *compar of* **satis**; better, preferable

sator, **-ōris** *m* sower, planter; father; promoter

satrapēs, **-is** *m* satrap (*Persian governor*)

satur, **-ī** *adj* filled, sated; (*fig*) rich

satura, **-ae** *f* mixed dish; medley; (*poem*) satire; **per saturam** confusingly

saturēia, **-ōrum** *ntpl* (*plant*) savory

saturitās, **-ātis** *f* repletion; fulness, plenty

Saturnālia, **-ium** *and* **-iōrum** *ntpl* festival of Saturn in December

Saturnia, **-iae** *f* Juno

Saturnīnus, **-ī** *m* revolutionary tribune in 103 and 100 B.C.

Saturnius *adj see* **Saturnus**

Saturnus, **-ī** *m* Saturn (*god of sowing, ruler of the Golden Age*); (*the planet*) Saturn

saturō, **-āre**, **-āvī**, **-ātum** *vt* to fill, glut, satisfy; to disgust

satus¹ *ppp of* **serō¹** ♦ *m* son ♦ *f* daughter ♦ *ntpl* crops

satus², **-ūs** *m* sowing, planting; begetting

satyriscus, **-ī** *m* little satyr

satyrus, **-ī** *m* satyr

sauciātiō, **-ōnis** *f* wounding

sauciō, **-āre** *vt* to wound, hurt

saucius *adj* wounded, hurt; ill, stricken

Sauromatae *etc see* **Sarmatae**

sāviātiō, **-ōnis** *f* kissing

sāviolum, **-ī** *nt* sweet kiss

sāvior, **-ārī** *vt* to kiss

sāvium, **-ī** *and* **-iī** *nt* kiss

saxātilis *adj* rock- (*in cpds*)

saxētum, **-ī** *nt* rocky place

saxeus *adj* of rock, rocky

saxificus *adj* petrifying

saxōsus *adj* rocky, stony

saxulum, **-ī** *nt* small rock

saxum, **-ī** *nt* rock, boulder; the Tarpeian Rock

scaber, **-rī** *adj* rough, scurfy; mangy, itchy

scabiēs (*acc* **-em**, *abl* **-ē**) *f* roughness, scurf; mange, itch

scabillum, **-ī** *nt* stool; a castanet played with the foot

scabō, **-ere**, **scābī** *vt* to scratch

Scaea porta, **Scaeae portae** *f* the west gate of Troy

scaena, **-ae** *f* stage, stage setting; (*fig*) limelight, public life; outward appearance, pretext

scaenālis *adj* theatrical

scaenicus *adj* stage- (*in cpds*), theatrical ♦ *m* actor

Scaevola, **-ae** *m* early Roman who burned his hand off before Porsenna; famous jurist of Cicero's day

scaevus *adj* on the left; perverse ♦ *f* omen

scālae, **-ārum** *fpl* steps, ladder, stairs

scalmus, **-ī** *m* tholepin

scalpellum, **-ī** *nt* scalpel, lancet

scalpō, **-ere**, **-sī**, **-tum** *vt* to carve, engrave; to scratch

scalprum, **-ī** *nt* knife, penknife; chisel

scalpurriō, **-īre** *vi* to scratch

Scamander, **-rī** *m* river of Troy (*also called Xanthus*)

scammōnea, **-ae** *f* (*plant*) scammony

scamnum, -ī *nt* bench, stool; throne

scandō, -ere *vt, vi* to climb, mount

scapha, -ae *f* boat, skiff

scaphium, -ī *and* **-iī** *nt* a boat-shaped cup

scapulae, -ārum *fpl* shoulder blades; shoulders

scāpus, -ī *m* shaft; (*loom*) yarnbeam

scarus, -ī *m* (*fish*) scar

scatebra, -ae *f* gushing water

scateō, -ēre, scatō, -ere *vi* to bubble up, gush out; (*fig*) to abound, swarm

scatūrīginēs, -um *fpl* springs

scatūriō, -īre *vi* to gush out; (*fig*) to be full of

scaurus *adj* large-ankled

scelerātē *adv* wickedly

scelerātus *adj* desecrated; wicked, infamous, accursed; pernicious

scelerō, -āre *vt* to desecrate

scelerōsus *adj* vicious, accursed

scelestē *adv* wickedly

scelestus *adj* wicked, villainous, accursed; unlucky

scelus, -eris *nt* wickedness, crime, sin; (*person*) scoundrel; (*event*) calamity

scēn- *etc see* **scaen-**

scēptrifer, -ī *adj* sceptered

scēptrum, -ī *nt* staff, sceptre; kingship, power

scēptūchus, -ī *m* sceptre-bearer

scheda *etc see* **scida**

schēma, -ae *f* form, figure, style

Schoenēis, -ēidis *f* Atalanta

Schoenēius *adj see* **Schoenēis**

Schoeneus, -eī *m* father of Atalanta

schoenobatēs, -ae *m* rope dancer

schola, -ae *f* learned discussion, dissertation; school; sect, followers

scholasticus *adj* of a school ♦ *m* rhetorician

scida, -ae *f* sheet of paper

sciēns, -entis *pres p of* **sciō** ♦ *adj* knowing, purposely; versed in, acquainted with

scienter *adv* expertly

scientia, -ae *f* knowledge, skill

scīlicet *adv* evidently, of course; (*concessive*) no doubt; (*ironical*) I suppose, of course

scilla *etc see* **squilla**

scindō, -ndere, -dī, -ssum *vt* to cut open, tear apart, split, break down; to divide, part

scintilla, -ae *f* spark

scintillō, -āre *vi* to sparkle

scintillula, -ae *f* little spark

sciō, -īre, -īvī, -ītum *vt* to know; to have skill in; (*with inf*) to know how to; **quod sciam** as far as I know; **scītō** you may be sure

Scīpiadēs, -ae *m* Scipio

scīpiō, -ōnis *m* staff

Scīpiō, -ōnis *m famous Roman family name (esp the conqueror of Hannibal Africanus); Aemilianus (destroyer of Carthage and patron of literature)*

scirpeus *adj* rush (*in cpds*) ♦ *f* wickerwork frame

scirpiculus, -ī *m* rush basket

scirpus, -ī *m* bulrush

scīscitor, -ārī, -ātus, scīscitō, -āre *vt* to inquire; to question

scīscō, -scere, -vī, -tum *vt* to inquire, learn; (*POL*) to approve, decree, appoint

scissus *ppp of* **scindō** ♦ *adj* split; (*voice*) harsh

scītāmenta, -ōrum *ntpl* dainties

scītē *adv* cleverly, tastefully

scītor, -ārī, -ātus *vt, vi* to inquire; to consult

scītulus *adj* neat, smart

scītum, -ī *nt* decree, statute

scītus¹ *ppp of* **sciō; scīscō** ♦ *adj* clever, shrewd, skilled; (*words*) sensible, witty; (*appearance*) fine, smart

scītus², -ūs *m* decree

sciūrus, -ī *m* squirrel

scīvī *perf of* **sciō; scīscō**

scobis, -is *f* sawdust, filings

scomber, -rī *m* mackerel

scōpae, -ārum *fpl* broom

Scōpās, -ae *m famous Greek sculptor*

scopulōsus *adj* rocky

scopulus, -ī *m* rock, crag, promontory; (*fig*) danger

scorpiō, -ōnis, scorpius, -ī, scorpios, -ī *m* scorpion; (*MIL*) a kind of catapult

scortātor, -ōris *m* fornicator

scorteus *adj* of leather

scortor, -ārī *vi* to associate with harlots

scortum, -ī *nt* harlot, prostitute

screātor, -ōris *m* one who clears his throat noisily

screātus, -ūs *m* clearing the throat

scrība, -ae *m* clerk, writer

scrībō, -bere, -psī, -ptum *vt* to write, draw; to write down, describe; (*document*) to draw up; (*LAW*) to designate; (*MIL*) to enlist

scrīnium, -ī *and* **-iī** *nt* book box, lettercase

scrīptiō, -ōnis *f* writing; composition; text

scrīptitō, -āre, -āvī, -ātum *vt* to write regularly, compose

scrīptor, -ōris *m* writer, author; secretary; **rērum** ~ historian

scrīptula, -ōrum *ntpl* lines of a squared board

scrīptum, -ī *nt* writing, book, work; (*LAW*) ordinance; **duōdecim scrīpta** Twelve Lines (*a game played on a squared board*)

scrīptūra, -ae *f* writing; composition; document; (*POL*) tax on public pastures; (*will*) provision

scrīptus¹ *ppp of* **scrībō**

scrīptus², -ūs *m* clerkship

scrīpulum, -ī *nt* small weight, scruple

scrobis, -is *f* ditch, trench; grave

scrōfa, -ae *f* breeding sow

scrōfipāscus, -ī *m* pig breeder

scrūpeus *adj* stony, rough

scrūpōsus *adj* rocky, jagged

scrūpulōsus *adj* stony, rough; (*fig*) precise

scrūpulum *etc see* **scrīpulum**

scrūpulus, -ī *m* small sharp stone; (*fig*) uneasiness, doubt, scruple

scrūpus, -ī *m* sharp stone; (*fig*) uneasiness

scrūta, -ōrum *ntpl* trash

scrūtor, -ārī, -ātus *vt* to search, probe into, examine; to find out

sculpō, -ere, -sī, -tum *vt* to carve, engrave

sculpōneae, -ārum *fpl* clogs

sculptilis *adj* carved

sculptor, -ōris *m* sculptor
sculptus *ppp of* **sculpō**
scurra, -ae *m* jester; dandy
scurrīlis *adj* jeering
scurrīlitās, -ātis *f* scurrility
scurror, -ārī *vi* to play the fool
scūtāle, -is *nt* sling strap
scūtātus *adj* carrying a shield
scutella, -ae *f* bowl
scutica, -ae *f* whip
scutra, -ae *f* flat dish
scutula¹, -ae *f* small dish
scutula² *f* wooden roller; secret letter
scutulāta, -ae *f* a checked garment
scūtulum, -ī *nt* small shield
scūtum, -ī *nt* shield
Scylla, -ae *f* dangerous rock or sea monster (in the Straits of Messina)
Scyllaeus *adj see* **Scylla**
scymnus, -ī *m* cub
scyphus, -ī *m* wine cup
Scyrius, -ias *adj see* **Scyros**
Scyros, Scyrus, -ī *f Aegean island near Euboea*
scytala *see* **scutula²**
Scytha, Scythēs, -ae *m* Scythian
Scythia, -iae *f* Scythia (*country N.E. of the Black Sea*)
Scythicus *adj* Scythian
Scythis, -idis *f* Scythian woman
sē *pron* himself, herself, itself, themselves; one another; **apud sē** at home; in his senses; **inter sē** mutually
sēbum, -ī *nt* tallow, suet, grease
sēcēdō, -ēdere, -essī, -essum *vi* to withdraw, retire; to revolt, secede
sēcernō, -ernere, -rēvī, -rētum *vt* to separate, set apart; to dissociate; to distinguish
sēcessiō, -ōnis *f* withdrawal; secession
sēcessus, -ūs *m* retirement, solitude; retreat, recess
sēclūdō, -dere, -sī, -sum *vt* to shut off, seclude; to separate, remove
sēclūsus *ppp of* **sēclūdō** ♦ *adj* remote
secō, -āre, -uī, -tum *vt* to cut; to injure; to divide; (*MED*) to operate on; (*motion*) to pass through; (*dispute*) to decide
sēcrētiō, -ōnis *f* separation
sēcrētō *adv* apart, in private, in secret
sēcrētum, -ī *nt* privacy, secrecy; retreat, remote place; secret, mystery
sēcrētus *ppp of* **sēcernō** ♦ *adj* separate; solitary, remote; secret, private
secta, -ae *f* path; method, way of life; (*POL*) party; (*PHILOS*) school
sectārius *adj* leading
sectātor, -ōris *m* follower, adherent
sectilis *adj* cut; for cutting
sectiō, -ōnis *f* auctioning of confiscated goods
sector¹, -ōris *m* cutter; buyer at a public sale
sector², -ārī, -ātus *vt* to follow regularly, attend; to chase, hunt
sectūra, -ae *f* digging
sectus *ppp of* **secō**
sēcubitus, -ūs *m* lying alone

sēcubō, -āre, -uī *vi* to sleep by oneself; to live alone
secuī *perf of* **secō**
sēcul- *etc see* **saecul-**
sēcum with himself *etc*
secundānī, -ōrum *mpl* men of the second legion
secundārius *adj* second-rate
secundō¹ *adv* secondly
secundō², -āre *vt* to favour, make prosper
secundum *prep* (*place*) behind, along; (*time*) after; (*rank*) next to; (*agreement*) according to, in favour of ♦ *adv* behind
secundus *adj* following, next, second; inferior; favourable, propitious, fortunate ♦ *fpl* (*play*) subsidiary part; (*fig*) second fiddle ♦ *ntpl* success, good fortune; **secundō flūmine** downstream; **rēs secundae** prosperity, success
secūricula, -ae *f* little axe
secūrifer, -ī *adj* armed with an axe
secūriger, -ī *adj* armed with an axe
secūris, -is *f* axe; (*fig*) death blow; (*POL*) authority, supreme power
sēcūritās, -ātis *f* freedom from anxiety, composure; negligence; safety, feeling of security
sēcūrus *adj* untroubled, unconcerned; carefree, cheerful; careless
secus¹ *nt* (*indecl*) sex
secus² *adv* otherwise, differently; badly; **nōn ~** even so
secūtor, -ōris *m* pursuer
sed *conj* but; but also, but in fact
sēdātē *adv* calmly
sēdātiō, -ōnis *f* calming
sēdātus *ppp of* **sēdō** ♦ *adj* calm, quiet, composed
sēdecim *num* sixteen
sēdēcula, -ae *f* low stool
sedentārius *adj* sitting
sedeō, -ēre, sēdī, sessum *vi* to sit; (*army*) to be encamped, blockade; (*magistrates*) to be in session; (*clothes*) to suit, fit; (*places*) to be low-lying; (*heavy things*) to settle, subside; (*weapons*) to stick fast; (*inactivity*) to be idle; (*thought*) to be firmly resolved
sēdēs, -is *f* seat, chair; abode, home; site, ground, foundation
sēdī *perf of* **sedeō**
sedīle, -is *nt* seat, chair
sēditiō, -ōnis *f* insurrection, mutiny
sēditiōsē *adv* seditiously
sēditiōsus *adj* mutinous, factious; quarrelsome; troubled
sēdō, -āre, -āvī, -ātum *vt* to calm, allay, lull
sēdūcō, -ūcere, -ūxī, -uctum *vt* to take away, withdraw; to divide
sēductiō, -ōnis *f* taking sides
sēductus *ppp of* **sēdūcō** ♦ *adj* remote
sēdulitās, -ātis *f* earnestness, assiduity; officiousness
sēdulō *adv* busily, diligently; purposely
sēdulus *adj* busy, diligent, assiduous; officious
seges, -itis *f* cornfield; crop
Segesta, -ae *f town in N.W. Sicily*

Segestānus *adj see* **Segesta**
segmentātus *adj* flounced
segmentum, -ī *nt* brocade
segne, segniter *adv* slowly, lazily
segnipēs, -edis *adj* slow of foot
segnis *adj* slow, sluggish, lazy
segnitia, -ae, segnitiēs (*acc* -**em**, *abl* -**ē**) *f* slowness, sluggishness, sloth
sēgregō, -āre, -āvī, -ātum *vt* to separate, put apart; to dissociate
sēiugātus *adj* separated
sēiugis, -is *m* chariot and six
sēiūnctim *adv* separately
sēiūnctiō, -ōnis *f* separation
sēiūnctus *ppp of* **sēiungō**
sēiungō, -gere, sēiūnxī, sēiūnctum *vt* to separate, part
sēlēctiō, -ōnis *f* choice
sēlēctus *ppp of* **sēligō**
Seleucus, -ī *m* king of Syria
sēlībra, -ae *f* half pound
sēligō, -igere, -ēgī, -ēctum *vt* to choose, select
sella, -ae *f* seat, chair, stool, sedan chair; ~ **cūrūlis** *chair of office for higher magistrates*
sellisternia, -ōrum *ntpl* sacred banquets to goddesses
sellula, -ae *f* stool; sedan chair
sellulārius, -ī *and* -**iī** *m* mechanic
sēmanimus *etc see* **sēmianimis**
semel *adv* once; once for all; first; ever; ~ **atque iterum** again and again; ~ **aut iterum** once or twice
Semelē, -ēs *f* mother of Bacchus
Semelēius *adj see* **Semelē**
sēmen, -inis *nt* seed; (*plant*) seedling; slip; (*men*) race, child; (*physics*) particle; (*fig*) origin, instigator
sēmentifer, -ī *adj* fruitful
sēmentis, -is *f* sowing, planting; young corn
sēmentīvus *adj* of seed time
sēmermis *etc see* **sēmiermis**
sēmēstris *adj* half-yearly, for six months
sēmēsus *adj* half-eaten
sēmet *pron* self, selves
sēmiadapertus *adj* half-open
sēmianimis, -us *adj* half-dead
sēmiapertus *adj* half-open
sēmibōs, -ovis *adj* half-ox
sēmicaper, -rī *adj* half-goat
sēmicremātus, sēmicremus *adj* half-burned
sēmicubitālis *adj* half a cubit long
sēmideus *adj* half-divine ♦ *m* demigod
sēmidoctus *adj* half-taught
sēmiermis, -us *adj* half-armed
sēmiēsus *adj* half-eaten
sēmifactus *adj* half-finished
sēmifer, -ī *adj* half-beast; half-savage
sēmigermānus *adj* half-German
sēmigravis *adj* half-overcome
sēmigrō, -āre *vi* to go away
sēmihiāns, -antis *adj* half-opened
sēmihomō, -inis *m* half-man, half-human
sēmihōra, -ae *f* half an hour
sēmilacer, -ī *adj* half-mangled

sēmilautus *adj* half-washed
sēmilīber, -ī *adj* half-free
sēmilixa, -ae *m* not much better than a camp follower
sēmimarīnus *adj* half in the sea
sēmimās, -āris *m* hermaphrodite ♦ *adj* castrated
sēmimortuus *adj* half-dead
sēminārium, -ī *and* -**iī** *nt* nursery, seed plot
sēminātor, -ōris *m* originator
sēminecis *adj* half-dead
sēminium, -ī *and* -**iī** *nt* procreation; breed
sēminō, -āre *vt* to sow; to produce; to beget
sēminūdus *adj* half-naked; almost unarmed
sēmipāgānus *adj* half-rustic
sēmiplēnus *adj* half-full, half-manned
sēmiputātus *adj* half-pruned
Semīramis, -is *and* -**idis** *f* queen of Assyria
Semīramius *adj see* **Semīramis**
sēmirāsus *adj* half-shaven
sēmireductus *adj* half turned back
sēmirefectus *adj* half-repaired
sēmirutus *adj* half-demolished, half in ruins
sēmis, -issis *m* (*coin*) half an as; (*interest*) 1/2 per cent per month (*i.e. 6 per cent per annum*); (*area*) half an acre
sēmisepultus *adj* half-buried
sēmisomnus *adj* half-asleep
sēmisupīnus *adj* half lying back
sēmita, -ae *f* path, way
sēmitālis *adj* of byways
sēmitārius *adj* frequenting byways
sēmiūst- *etc see* **sēmūst-**
sēmivir, -ī *adj* half-man; emasculated; unmanly
sēmivīvus *adj* half-dead
sēmodius, -ī *and* -**iī** *m* half a peck
sēmōtus *ppp of* **sēmoveō** ♦ *adj* remote; distinct
sēmoveō, -ovēre, -ōvī, -ōtum *vt* to put aside, separate
semper *adv* always, ever, every time
sempiternus *adj* everlasting, lifelong
Semprōnius¹, -ī *m* Roman family name (*esp the Gracchi*)
Semprōnius², -iānus *adj see* **Semprōnius¹**
sēmūncia, -ae *f* half an ounce; a twenty-fourth
sēmūnciārius *adj* (*interest*) at the rate of one twenty-fourth
sēmūstulātus *adj* half-burned
sēmūstus *adj* half-burned
senāculum, -ī *nt* open air meeting place (*of the Senate*)
sēnāriolus, -ī *m* little trimeter
sēnārius, -ī *and* -**iī** *m* (iambic) trimeter
senātor, -ōris *m* senator
senātōrius *adj* senatorial, in the Senate
senātus, -ūs *m* Senate; meeting of the Senate
senātūscōnsultum, -ī *nt* decree of the Senate
Seneca, -ae *m* Stoic philosopher, tutor of Nero
senecta, -ae *f* old age
senectus *adj* old, aged
senectūs, -ūtis *f* old age; old men
seneō, -ēre *vi* to be old
senēscō, -ēscere, -uī *vi* to grow old; (*fig*) to weaken, wane, pine away

195

senex, **-is** (*compar* **-ior**) *adj* old (*over 45*) ♦ *m/f* old man, old woman

sēnī, **-ōrum** *adj* six each, in sixes; six; ~ **dēnī** sixteen each

senīlis *adj* of an old person, senile

sēniō, **-ōnis** *m* number six on a dice

senior *compar of* **senex**

senium, **-ī** *and* **-iī** *nt* weakness of age, decline; affliction; peevishness

Senonēs, **-um** *mpl* tribe of S. Gaul

sēnsī *perf of* **sentiō**

sēnsifer, **-ī** *adj* sensory

sēnsilis *adj* having sensation

sēnsim *adv* tentatively, gradually

sēnsus¹ *ppp of* **sentiō** ♦ *ntpl* thoughts

sēnsus², **-ūs** *m* (*body*) feeling, sensation, sense; (*intellect*) understanding, judgment, thought; (*emotion*) sentiment, attitude, frame of mind; (*language*) meaning, purport, sentence; **commūnis** ~ universal human feelings, human sympathy, social instinct

sententia, **-ae** *f* opinion, judgment; purpose, will; (*LAW*) verdict, sentence; (*POL*) vote, decision; (*language*) meaning, sentence, maxim, epigram; **meā sententiā** in my opinion; **dē meā sententiā** in accordance with my wishes; **ex meā sententiā** to my liking; **ex animī meī sententiā** to the best of my knowledge and belief; **in sententiam pedibus īre** support a motion

sententiola, **-ae** *f* phrase

sententiōsē *adv* pointedly

sententiōsus *adj* pithy

senticētum, **-ī** *nt* thornbrake

sentīna, **-ae** *f* bilge water; (*fig*) dregs, scum

sentiō, **-īre**, **sēnsī**, **sēnsum** *vt* (*senses*) to feel, see, perceive; (*circumstances*) to experience, undergo; (*mind*) to observe, understand; (*opinion*) to think, judge; (*LAW*) to vote, decide

sentis, **-is** *m* thorn, brier

sentīscō, **-ere** *vt* to begin to perceive

sentus *adj* thorny; untidy

senuī *perf of* **senēscō**

seorsum, **seorsus** *adv* apart, differently

sēparābilis *adj* separable

sēparātim *adv* apart, separately

sēparātiō, **-ōnis** *f* separation, severing

sēparātius *adv* less closely

sēparātus *adj* separate, different

sēparō, **-āre**, **-āvī**, **-ātum** *vt* to part, separate, divide; to distinguish

sepeliō, **-elīre**, **-elīvī** *and* **-eliī**, **-ultum** *vt* to bury; (*fig*) to overwhelm, overcome

sēpia, **-ae** *f* cuttlefish

Sēplasia, **-ae** *f* street in Capua where perfumes were sold

sēpōnō, **-ōnere**, **-osuī**, **-ositum** *vt* to put aside, pick out; to reserve; to banish; to appropriate; to separate

sēpositus *ppp of* **sēpōnō** ♦ *adj* remote; distinct, choice

sēpse *pron* oneself

septem *num* seven

September, **-ris** *m* September ♦ *adj* of September

septemdecim *etc see* **septendecim**

septemfluus *adj* with seven streams

septemgeminus *adj* sevenfold

septemplex, **-icis** *adj* sevenfold

septemtriō *etc see* **septentriō**

septemvirālis *adj* of the septemviri ♦ *mpl* the septemviri

septemvirātus, **-ūs** *m* office of septemvir

septemvirī, **-ōrum** *mpl* board of seven officials

septēnārius, **-ī** *and* **-iī** *m* verse of seven feet

septendecim *num* seventeen

septēnī, **-ōrum** *adj* seven each, in sevens

septentriō, **-ōnis** *m*, **septentriōnēs**, **-ōnum** *mpl* Great Bear, Little Bear; north; north wind

septentriōnālis *adj* northern ♦ *ntpl* northern regions

septiēns, **septiēs** *adv* seven times

septimānī, **-ōrum** *mpl* men of the seventh legion

septimum *adv* for the seventh time

septimus *adj* seventh

septimus decimus seventeenth

septingentēsimus *adj* seven hundredth

septingentī, **-ōrum** *adj* seven hundred

septuāgēsimus *adj* seventieth

septuāgintā *adj* seventy

septuennis *adj* seven years old

septumus *adj see* **septimus**

septūnx, **-ūncis** *m* seven ounces, seven-twelfths

sepulcrālis *adj* funeral

sepulcrētum, **-ī** *nt* cemetery

sepulcrum, **-ī** *nt* grave, tomb

sepultūra, **-ae** *f* burial, funeral

sepultus *ppp of* **sepeliō**

Sequāna, **-ae** *f* (river) Seine

Sequānī, **-ōrum** *mpl* people of N. Gaul

sequāx, **-ācis** *adj* pursuing, following

sequens, **-entis** *pres p of* **sequor** ♦ *adj* following, next

sequester, **-rī** *and* **-ris** *m* trustee; agent, mediator

sequestrum, **-rī** *nt* deposit

sēquius *compar of* **secus**²; otherwise; **nihilō** ~ nonetheless

sequor, **-quī**, **-cūtus** *vt*, *vi* to follow; to accompany, go with; (*time*) to come after, come next, ensue; (*enemy*) to pursue; (*objective*) to make for, aim at; (*pulling*) to come away easily; (*share, gift*) to go to, come to; (*words*) to come naturally

sera, **-ae** *f* door bolt, bar

Serāpēum, **-ēī** *nt* temple of Serapis

Serāpis, **-is** *and* **-idis** *m* chief Egyptian god

serēnitās, **-ātis** *f* fair weather

serēnō, **-āre** *vt* to clear up, brighten up

serēnus *adj* fair, clear; (*wind*) fair-weather; (*fig*) cheerful, happy ♦ *nt* clear sky, fair weather

Sērēs, **-um** *mpl* Chinese

serēscō, **-ere** *vi* to dry off

sēria, **-ae** *f* tall jar

sērica, **-ōrum** *ntpl* silks

Sēricus *adj* Chinese; silk

seriēs (*acc* **-em**, *abl* **-ē**) *f* row, sequence, succession
sēriō *adv* in earnest, seriously
sēriola, -ae *f* small jar
Serīphius *adj see* **Serīphus**
Serīphus, Serīphos, -ī *f Aegean island*
sērius¹ *adj* earnest, serious
sērius² *compar of* **sērō**
sermō, -ōnis *m* conversation, talk; learned discussion, discourse; common talk, rumour; language, style; everyday language, prose; (*pl*) Satires (*of Horace*)
sermōcinor, -ārī *vi* to converse
sermunculus, -ī *m* gossip, rumour
serō¹, -ere, sēvī, -satum *vt* to sow, plant; (*fig*) to produce, sow the seeds of
serō², -ere, -tum *vt* to sew, join, wreathe; (*fig*) to compose, devise, engage in
sērō (*compar* **-ius**) *adv* late; too late
serpēns, -entis *m/f* snake, serpent; (*constellation*) Draco
serpentigena, -ae *m* offspring of a serpent
serpentipēs, -edis *adj* serpent-footed
serperastra, -ōrum *ntpl* splints
serpō, -ere, -sī, -tum *vi* to creep, crawl; (*fig*) to spread slowly
serpyllum, -ī *nt* wild thyme
serra, -ae *f* saw
serrācum *etc see* **sarrācum**
serrātus *adj* serrated, notched
serrula, -ae *f* small saw
Sertōriānus *adj see* **Sertōrius**
Sertōrius, -ī *m commander under Marius, who held out against Sulla in Spain*
sertus *ppp of* **serō²** ♦ *ntpl* garlands
serum, -ī *nt* whey, serum
sērum, -ī *nt* late hour
sērus *adj* late; too late; **sērā nocte** late at night
serva, -ae *f* maidservant, slave
servābilis *adj* that can be saved
servātor, -ōris *m* deliverer; watcher
servātrīx, -īcis *f* deliverer
servīlis *adj* of slaves, servile
servīliter *adv* slavishly
Servīlius¹, -ī *m Roman family name of many consuls*
Servīlius², -ānus *adj see* **Servīlius¹**
serviō, -īre, -īvī *and* **-iī, -ītum** *vi* to be a slave; (*with dat*) to serve, be of use to, be good for; (*property*) to be mortgaged
servitium, -ī *and* **-iī** *nt* slavery, servitude; slaves
servitūdō, -inis *f* slavery
servitūs, -ūtis *f* slavery, service; slaves; (*property*) liability
Servius, -ī *m sixth king of Rome; famous jurist of Cicero's day*
servō, -āre, -āvī, -ātum *vt* to save, rescue; to keep, preserve, retain; to store, reserve; to watch, observe, guard; (*place*) to remain in
servolus, -ī *m* young slave
servos, -ī *m see* **servus**
servula, -ae *f* servant girl
servulus, -ī *m* young slave
servus, -ī *m* slave, servant ♦ *adj* slavish, serving; (*property*) liable to a burden
sescēnāris *adj* a year and a half old

sescēnī, -ōrum *adj* six hundred each
sescentēsimus *adj* six hundredth
sescentī, -ōrum *num* six hundred; *an indefinitely large number*
sescentiēns, sescentiēs *adv* six hundred times
sēsē *etc see* **sē**
seselis, -is *f* (*plant*) seseli
sesqui *adv* one and a half times
sesquialter, -ī *adj* one and a half
sesquimodius, -ī *and* **-iī** *m* a peck and a half
sesquioctāvus *adj* of nine to eight
sesquiopus, -eris *nt* a day and a half's work
sesquipedālis *adj* a foot and a half
sesquipēs, -edis *m* a foot and a half
sesquiplāga, -ae *f* a blow and a half
sesquiplex, -icis *adj* one and a half times
sesquitertius *adj* of four to three
sessilis *adj* for sitting on
sessiō, -ōnis *f* sitting; seat; session; loitering
sessitō, -āre, -āvī *vi* to sit regularly
sessiuncula, -ae *f* small meeting
sessor, -ōris *m* spectator; resident
sēstertium, -ī *nt* 1000 sesterces; **dēna sēstertia** 10,000 sesterces; **centēna mīlia ~** 100,000 sesterces; **deciēns ~** 1,000,000 sesterces
sēstertius, -ī *and* **-iī** *m* sesterce (*a silver coin*)
Sestius¹, -ī *m tribune defended by Cicero*
Sestius², -iānus *adj* of Sestius
Sestos, Sestus, -ī *f town on Dardanelles (home of Hero)*
Sestus *adj see* **Sestos**
sēt- *etc see* **saet-**
Sētia, -iae *f town in S. Latium (famous for wine)*
Sētiaīnus *adj see* **Sētia**
sētius *compar of* **secus²**
seu *etc see* **sīve**
sevērē *adv* sternly, severely
sevēritās, -ātis *f* strictness, austerity
sevērus *adj* strict, stern; severe, austere; grim, terrible
sēvī *perf of* **serō¹**
sēvocō, -āre *vt* to call aside; to withdraw, remove
sēvum *etc see* **sēbum**
sex *num* six
sexāgēnārius *adj* sixty years old
sexāgēnī, -ōrum *adj* sixty each
sexāgēsimus *adj* sixtieth
sexāgiēns, sexāgiēs *adv* sixty times
sexāgintā *num* sixty
sexangulus *adj* hexagonal
sexcēn- *etc see* **sescēn-**
sexcēnārius *adj* of six hundred
sexennis *adj* six years old, after six years
sexennium, -ī *and* **-iī** *nt* six years
sexiēns, sexiēs *adv* six times
sexprīmī, -ōrum *mpl* a provincial town council
sextadecimānī, -ōrum *mpl* men of the sixteenth legion
sextāns, -antis *m* a sixth; (*coin, weight*) a sixth of an as
sextārius, -ī *and* **-iī** *m* pint
Sextīlis, -is *m* August ♦ *adj* of August

sextula, -ae f a sixth of an ounce

sextum adv for the sixth time

sextus adj sixth; ~ **decimus** sixteenth

sexus, -ūs m sex

sī conj if; if only; to see if; **sī forte** in the hope that; **sī iam** assuming for the moment; **sī minus** if not; **sī quandō** whenever; **sī quidem** if indeed; since; **sī quis** if anyone, whoever; **mīrum sī** surprising that; **quod sī** and if, but if

sībila, -ōrum ntpl whistle, hissing

sībilō, -āre vi to hiss, whistle ♦ vt to hiss at

sībilus¹, -ī m whistle, hissing

sībilus² adj hissing

Sibulla, Sibylla, -ae f prophetess, Sibyl

Sibyllīnus adj see **Sibulla**

sīc adv so, thus, this way, as follows; as one is, as things are; on this condition; yes

sīca, -ae f dagger

Sicānī, -ōrum mpl ancient people of Italy (later of Sicily)

Sicānia, -iae f Sicily

Sicānus, -ius adj Sicanian, Sicilian

sīcārius, -ī and **-iī** m assassin, murderer

siccē adv (speech) firmly

siccitās, -ātis f dryness, drought; (body) firmness; (style) dullness

siccō, -āre, -āvī, -ātum vt to dry; to drain, exhaust; (sore) to heal up

siccoculus adj dry-eyed

siccus adj dry; thirsty, sober; (body) firm, healthy; (argument) solid, sound; (style) flat, dull ♦ nt dry land

Sicilia, -ae f Sicily

sicilicula, -ae f little sickle

Siciliēnsis, Sicilis, -dis adj Sicilian

sīcine is this how?

sīcubi adv if anywhere, wheresoever

Siculus adj Sicilian

sīcunde adv if from anywhere

sīcut, sīcutī adv just as, as in fact; (comparison) like, as; (example) as for instance; (with subj) as if

Sicyōn, -ōnis f town in N. Peloponnese

Sicyōnius adj see **Sicyōn**

sīdereus adj starry; (fig) radiant

Sidicīnī, -ōrum mpl people of Campania

Sidicīnus adj see **Sidicīnī**

sīdō, -ere, -ī vi to sit down, settle; to sink, subside; to stick fast

Sīdōn, -ōnis f famous Phoenician town

Sīdōnis, -ōnidis adj Phoenician ♦ f Europa; Dido

Sīdōnius adj Sidonian, Phoenician

sīdus, -eris nt constellation; heavenly body, star; season, climate, weather; destiny; (pl) sky; (fig) fame, glory

siem archaic subj of **sum**

Sigambrī etc see **Sugambrī**

Sīgēum, -ī nt promontory near Troy

Sīgēus, -ius adj Sigean

sigilla, -ōrum ntpl little figures; seal

sigillātus adj decorated with little figures

signātor, -ōris m witness (to a document)

signifer, -ī adj with constellations; ~ **orbis** Zodiac ♦ m (MIL) standard-bearer

significanter adv pointedly, tellingly

significātiō, -ōnis f indication, signal, token; sign of approval; (RHET) emphasis; (word) meaning

significō, -āre, -āvī, -ātum vt to indicate, show; to betoken, portend; (word) to mean

signō, -āre, -āvī, -ātum vt to mark, stamp, print; (document) to seal; (money) to coin, mint; (fig) to impress, designate, note

signum, -ī nt mark, sign, token; (MIL) standard; signal, password; (art) design, statue; (document) seal; (ASTR) constellation; **signa cōnferre** join battle; **signa cōnstituere** halt; **signa convertere** wheel about; **signa ferre** move camp; attack; **signa īnferre** attack; **signa prōferre** advance; **signa sequī** march in order; **ab signīs discēdere** leave the ranks; **sub signīs īre** march in order

Sīla, -ae f forest in extreme S. Italy

sīlānus, -ī m fountain, jet of water

silēns, -entis pres p of **sileō** ♦ adj still, silent ♦ mpl the dead

silentium, -ī and **-iī** nt stillness, silence; (fig) standstill, inaction

Sīlēnus, -ī m old and drunken companion of Bacchus

sileō, -ēre, -uī vi to be still, be silent; to cease ♦ vt to say nothing about

siler, -is nt willow

silēscō, -ere vi to calm down, fall silent

silex, -icis m flint, hard stone; rock

silicernium, -ī and **-iī** nt funeral feast

sīlīgō, -inis f winter wheat; fine flour

siliqua, -ae f pod, husk; (pl) pulse

sillybus, -ī m label bearing a book's title

Silurēs, -um mpl British tribe in S. Wales

silūrus, -ī m sheatfish

sīlus adj snub-nosed

silva, -ae f wood, forest; plantation, shrubbery; (plant) flowering stem; (LIT) material

Silvānus, -ī m god of uncultivated land

silvēscō, -ere vi to run to wood

silvestris adj wooded, forest- (in cpds), pastoral

silvicola, -ae m/f sylvan

silvicultrīx, -īcis adj living in the woods

silvifragus adj tree-breaking

silvōsus adj woody

sīmia, -ae f ape

simile, -is nt comparison, parallel

similis adj like, similar; ~ **atque** like what; **vērī ~** probable

similiter adv similarly

similitūdō, -inis f likeness, resemblance; imitation; analogy; monotony; (RHET) simile

sīmiolus, -ī m monkey

simītū adv at the same time, together

sīmius, -ī and **-iī** m ape

Simoīs, -entis m river of Troy

Simōnidēs, -is m Greek lyric poet of Ceos (famous for dirges)

Simōnidēus adj see **Simōnidēs**

simplex, -icis adj single, simple; natural, straightforward; (character) frank, sincere

simplicitās, -ātis f singleness; frankness, innocence

simpliciter adv simply, naturally; frankly

simplum, -ī nt simple sum

simpulum, -ī *nt* small ladle; **excitāre fluctūs in simpulō** raise a storm in a teacup
simpuvium, -ī *and* **-iī** *nt* libation bowl
simul *adv* at the same time, together, at once; likewise, also; both ... and; **~ ac, ~ atque, ~ ut** as soon as ♦ *conj* as soon as
simulācrum, -ī *nt* likeness, image, portrait, statue; phantom, ghost; (*writing*) symbol; (*fig*) semblance, shadow
simulāmen, -inis *nt* copy
simulāns, -antis *pres p of* **simulō** ♦ *adj* imitative
simulātē *adv* deceitfully
simulātiō, -ōnis *f* pretence, shamming, hypocrisy
simulātor, -ōris *m* imitator; pretender, hypocrite
simulatque *conj* as soon as
simulō, -āre, -āvī, -ātum *vt* to imitate, represent; to impersonate; to pretend, counterfeit
simultās, -ātis *f* feud, quarrel
sīmulus *adj* snub-nosed
sīmus *adj* snub-nosed
sīn *conj* but if; **sīn aliter, sīn minus** but if not
sināpi, -is *nt*, **sinapis, -is** *f* mustard
sincērē *adv* honestly
sincēritās, -ātis *f* integrity
sincērus *adj* clean, whole, genuine; (*fig*) pure, sound, honest
sincipitāmentum, -ī *nt* half a head
sinciput, -itis *nt* half a head; brain
sine *prep* (*with abl*) without, -less (*in cpds*)
singillātim *adv* singly, one by one
singulāris *adj* one at a time, single, sole; unique, extraordinary
singulāriter *adv* separately; extremely
singulārius *adj* single
singulī, -ōrum *adj* one each, single, one
singultim *adv* in sobs
singultō, -āre *vi* to sob, gasp, gurgle ♦ *vt* to gasp out
singultus, -ūs *m* sob, gasp, death rattle
singulus *etc see* **singulī**
sinister, -rī *adj* left; (*fig*) perverse, unfavourable; (*Roman auspices*) lucky; (*Greek auspices*) unlucky
sinistra, -rae *f* left hand, left-hand side
sinistrē *adv* badly
sinistrōrsus, -um *adv* to the left
sinō, -ere, sīvī, situm *vt* to let, allow; to let be; **nē dī sīrint** God forbid!
Sinōpē, -ēs *f* Greek colony on the Black Sea
Sinōpēnsis, -eus *adj see* **Sinōpē**
Sinuessa, -ae *f* town on the borders of Latium and Campania
Sinuessānus *adj see* **Sinuessa**
sīnum *etc see* **sīnus**
sinuō, -āre, -āvī, -ātum *vt* to wind, curve
sinuōsus *adj* winding, curved
sinus, -ūs *m* curve, fold; (*fishing*) net; (GEOG) bay, gulf, valley; (*hair*) curl; (*ship*) sail; (*toga*) fold, pocket, purse; (*person*) bosom; (*fig*) protection, love, heart, hiding place; **in sinū gaudēre** be secretly glad
sīnus, -ī *m* large cup
sīparium, -ī *and* **-iī** *nt* act curtain

sīphō, -ōnis *m* siphon; fire engine
sīquandō *adv* if ever
sīquī, sīquis *pron* if any, if anyone, whoever
sīquidem *adv* if in fact ♦ *conj* since
sirempse *adj* the same
Sīrēn, -ēnis *f* Siren
sīris, sīrit *perf subj of* **sinō**
Sīrius, -ī *m* Dog Star ♦ *adj* of Sirius
sirpe, -is *nt* silphium
sīrus, -ī *m* corn pit
sīs *adv* (*for* **sī vīs**) please
sistō, -ere, stitī, statum *vt* to place, set, plant; (LAW) to produce in court; (*monument*) to set up; (*movement*) to stop, arrest, check ♦ *vi* to stand, rest; (LAW) to appear in court; (*movement*) to stand still, stop, stand firm; **sē sistere** appear, present oneself; **tūtum sistere** see safe; **vadimōnium sistere** duly appear in court; **sistī nōn potest** the situation is desperate
sistrum, -ī *nt* Egyptian rattle, cymbal
sisymbrium, -ī *and* **-iī** *nt* fragrant herb (*perhaps mint*)
Sīsyphides, -idae *m* Ulysses
Sīsyphius *adj see* **Sīsyphus**
Sīsyphus, -ī *m* criminal condemned in Hades to roll a rock repeatedly up a hill
sitella, -ae *f* lottery urn
Sīthonis, -idis *adj* Thracian
Sīthonius *adj* Thracian
sitīculōsus *adj* thirsty, dry
sitiēns, -entis *pres p of* **sitiō** ♦ *adj* thirsty, dry; parching; (*fig*) eager
sitienter *adv* eagerly
sitiō, -īre *vi* to be thirsty; to be parched ♦ *vt* to thirst for, covet
sitis, -is *f* thirst; drought
sittybus *etc see* **sillybus**
situla, -ae *f* bucket
situs¹ *ppp of* **sinō** ♦ *adj* situated, lying; founded; (*fig*) dependent
situs², -ūs *m* situation, site; structure; neglect, squalor, mould; (*mind*) dullness
sīve *conj* or if, or; whether ... or
sīvī *perf of* **sinō**
smaragdus, -ī *m/f* emerald
smīlax, -acis *f* bindweed
Smintheus, -eī *m* Apollo
Smyrna, -ae *f* Ionian town in Asia Minor
Smyrnaeus *adj see* **Smyrna**
sobol- *etc see* **subol-**
sobriē *adv* temperately; sensibly
sobrīna, -ae *f* cousin (*on the mother's side*)
sobrīnus, -ī *m* cousin (*on the mother's side*)
sobrius *adj* sober; temperate, moderate; (*mind*) sane, sensible
soccus, -ī *m* slipper (*esp the sock worn by actors in comedy*); comedy
socer, -ī *m* father-in-law
sociābilis *adj* compatible
sociālis *adj* of allies, confederate; conjugal
sociāliter *adv* sociably
sociennus, -ī *m* friend
societās, -ātis *f* fellowship, association; alliance

socio, -āre, -āvi, -ātum *vt* to unite, associate, share

sociofraudus, -ī *m* deceiver of friends

socius *adj* associated, allied ♦ *m* friend, companion; partner, ally

sōcordia, -ae *f* indolence, apathy; folly

sōcordius *adv* more carelessly, lazily

sōcors, -dis *adj* lazy, apathetic; stupid

Sōcratēs, -is *m* famous Athenian philosopher

Sōcraticus *adj* of Socrates, Socratic ♦ *mpl* the followers of Socrates

socrus, -ūs *f* mother-in-law

sodalicium, -ī *and* **-iī** *nt* fellowship; secret society

sodalicius *adj* of fellowship

sodalis, -is *m/f* companion, friend; member of a society, accomplice

sodalitās, -ātis *f* companionship, friendship; society, club; secret society

sodalitius *etc see* **sodalicius**

sodēs *adv* please

sōl, sōlis *m* sun; sunlight, sun's heat; (*poetry*) day; (*myth*) Sun god; **sōl oriēns, sōlis ortus** east; **sōl occidēns, sōlis occāsus** west

sōlāciolum, -ī *nt* a grain of comfort

sōlācium, -ī *and* **-iī** *nt* comfort, consolation, relief

sōlāmen, -inis *nt* solace, relief

sōlāris *adj* of the sun

sōlārium, -ī *and* **-iī** *nt* sundial; clock; balcony, terrace

sōlātium *etc see* **sōlācium**

sōlātor, -ōris *m* consoler

soldūriī, -ōrum *mpl* retainers

soldus *etc see* **solidus**

solea, -ae *f* sandal, shoe; fetter; (*fish*) sole

soleārius, -ī *and* **-iī** *m* sandal maker

soleātus *adj* wearing sandals

soleō, -ēre, -itus *vi* to be accustomed, be in the habit, usually do; **ut solēre** as usual

solidē *adv* for certain

soliditās, -ātis *f* solidity

solidō, -āre *vt* to make firm, strengthen

solidus *adj* solid, firm, dense; whole, complete; (*fig*) sound, genuine, substantial ♦ *nt* solid matter, firm ground

sōliferreum, -ī *nt* an all-iron javelin

sōlistimus *adj* (*AUG*) most favourable

sōlitārius *adj* solitary, lonely

sōlitūdō, -inis *f* solitariness, loneliness; destitution; (*place*) desert

solitus *ppa of* **soleō** ♦ *adj* usual, customary ♦ *nt* custom; **plūs solitō** more than usual

solium, -ī *and* **-iī** *nt* seat, throne; tub; (*fig*) rule

sōlivagus *adj* going by oneself; single

sollemne, -is *nt* religious rite, festival; usage, practice

sollemnis *adj* annual, regular; religious, solemn; usual, ordinary

sollemniter *adv* solemnly

sollers, -tis *adj* skilled, clever, expert; ingenious

sollerter *adv* cleverly

sollertia, -ae *f* skill, ingenuity

sollicitātiō, -ōnis *f* inciting

sollicitō, -āre, -āvī, -ātum *vt* to stir up, disturb; to trouble, distress, molest; to rouse, urge, incite, tempt, tamper with

sollicitūdō, -inis *f* uneasiness, anxiety

sollicitus *adj* agitated, disturbed; (*mind*) troubled, worried, alarmed; (*things*) anxious, careful; (*cause*) disquieting

solliferreum *etc see* **sōliferreum**

sollistimus *etc see* **sōlistimus**

soloecismus, -ī *m* grammatical mistake

Solōn, -ōnis *m* famous Athenian lawgiver

sōlor, -ārī, -ātus *vt* to comfort, console; to relieve, ease

sōlstitiālis *adj* of the summer solstice; midsummer

sōlstitium, -ī *and* **-iī** *nt* summer solstice; midsummer, summer heat

solum, -ī *nt* ground, floor, bottom; soil, land, country; (*foot*) sole; (*fig*) basis; **solō aequāre** raze to the ground

sōlum *adv* only, merely

sōlus (*gen* **-īus**, *dat* **-ī**) *see* **vicis** ♦ *adj* only, alone; lonely, forsaken; (*place*) lonely, deserted

solūtē *adv* loosely, freely, carelessly, weakly, fluently

solūtiō, -ōnis *f* loosening; payment

solūtus *ppp of* **solvō** ♦ *adj* loose, free; (*from distraction*) at ease, at leisure, merry; (*from obligation*) exempt; (*from restraint*) free, independent, unprejudiced; (*moral*) lax, weak, insolent; (*language*) prose, unrhythmical; (*speaker*) fluent; **ōrātiō solūta, verba solūta** prose

solvō, -vere, -vī, -ūtum *vt* to loosen, undo; to free, release, acquit, exempt; to dissolve, break up, separate; to relax, slacken, weaken; to cancel, remove, destroy; to solve, explain; to pay, fulfil; (*argument*) to refute; (*discipline*) to undermine; (*feelings*) to get rid of; (*hair*) to let down; (*letter*) to open; (*sail*) to unfurl; (*siege*) to raise; (*troops*) to dismiss ♦ *vi* to set sail; to pay; **nāvem solvere** set sail; **poenās solvere** be punished; **praesēns solvere** pay cash; **rem solvere** pay; **sacrāmentō solvere** discharge; **solvendō esse** be solvent

Solyma, -ōrum *ntpl* Jerusalem

Solymus *adj* of the Jews

somniculōsē *adv* sleepily

somniculōsus *adj* sleepy

somnifer, -ī *adj* soporific; fatal

somniō, -āre *vt* to dream, dream about; to talk nonsense

somnium, -ī *and* **-iī** *nt* dream; nonsense, fancy

somnus, -ī *m* sleep; sloth

sonābilis *adj* noisy

sonipēs, -edis *m* steed

sonitus, -ūs *m* sound, noise

sonivius *adj* noisy

sonō, -āre, -uī, -itum *vi* to sound, make a noise ♦ *vt* to utter, speak, celebrate; to sound like

sonor, -ōris *m* sound, noise

sonōrus *adj* noisy, loud

sōns, sontis *adj* guilty

sonticus *adj* critical; important

sonus, -ī *m* sound, noise; (*fig*) tone

sophistēs, -ae m sophist
Sophoclēs, -is m famous Greek tragic poet
Sophoclēus adj of Sophocles, Sophoclean
sophus adj wise
sōpiō, -īre, -īvī, -ītum vt to put to sleep; (fig) to calm, lull
sopor, -ōris m sleep; apathy
sopōrifer, -ī adj soporific, drowsy
sopōrō, -āre vt to lull to sleep; to make soporific
sopōrus adj drowsy
Sōracte, -is nt mountain in S. Etruria
sorbeō, -ēre, -uī vt to suck, swallow; (fig) to endure
sorbillō, -āre vt to sip
sorbitiō, -ōnis f drink, broth
sorbum, -ī nt service berry
sorbus, -ī f service tree
sordeō, -ēre vi to be dirty, be sordid; to seem shabby; to be of no account
sordēs, -is f dirt, squalor, shabbiness; mourning; meanness; vulgarity; (people) rabble
sordēscō, -ere vi to become dirty
sordidātus adj shabbily dressed, in mourning
sordidē adv meanly, vulgarly
sordidulus adj soiled, shabby
sordidus adj dirty, squalid, shabby; in mourning; poor, mean; base, vile
sōrex, -icis m shrewmouse
sōricīnus adj of the shrewmouse
sōrītēs, -ae m chain syllogism
soror, -ōris f sister
sorōricīda, -ae m murderer of a sister
sorōrius adj of a sister
sors, sortis f lot; allotted duty; oracle, prophecy; fate, fortune; (money) capital, principal
sōrsum etc see **seorsum**
sortilegus adj prophetic ♦ m soothsayer
sortior, -īrī, -ītus vi to draw or cast lots ♦ vt to draw lots for, allot, obtain by lot; to distribute, share; to choose; to receive
sortītiō, -ōnis f drawing lots, choosing by lot
sortītus' ppa of **sortior** ♦ adj assigned, allotted; sortītō by lot
sortītus², -ūs m drawing lots
Sosius, -ī m Roman family name (esp two brothers Sosii, famous booksellers in Rome)
sōspes, -itis adj safe and sound, unhurt; favourable, lucky
sōspita, -ae f saviour
sōspitālis adj beneficial
sōspitō, -āre vt to preserve, prosper
sōtēr, -ēris m saviour
spādīx, -īcis adj chestnut-brown
spadō, -ōnis m eunuch
spargō, -gere, -sī, -sum vt to throw, scatter, sprinkle; to strew, spot, moisten; to disperse, spread abroad
sparsus ppp of **spargō** ♦ adj freckled
Sparta, -ae, Spartē, -ēs f famous Greek city
Spartacus, -ī m gladiator who led a revolt against Rome
Spartānus, -icus adj Spartan
Spartiātēs, -iātae m Spartan
spartum, -ī nt Spanish broom

sparulus, -ī m bream
sparus, -ī m hunting spear
spatha, -ae f broadsword
spatior, -ārī, -ātus vi to walk; to spread
spatiōsē adv greatly; after a time
spatiōsus adj roomy, ample, large; (time) prolonged
spatium, -ī and **-iī** nt space, room, extent; (between points) distance; (open space) square, walk, promenade; (race) lap, track, course; (time) period, interval; (opportunity) time, leisure; (metre) quantity
speciēs, -ēī f seeing, sight; appearance, form, outline; (thing seen) sight; (mind) idea; (in sleep) vision, apparition; (fair show) beauty, splendour; (false show) pretence, pretext; (classification) species; **in speciem** for the sake of appearances; like; **per speciem** under the pretence; **sub speciē** under the cloak
specillum, -ī nt probe
specimen, -inis nt sign, evidence, proof; pattern, ideal
speciōsē adv handsomely
speciōsus adj showy, beautiful; specious, plausible
spectābilis adj visible; notable, remarkable
spectāclum, spectāculum, -ī nt sight, spectacle; public show, play; theatre, seats
spectāmen, -inis nt proof
spectātiō, -ōnis f looking; testing
spectātor, -ōris m onlooker, observer, spectator; critic
spectātrīx, -īcis f observer
spectātus ppp of **spectō** ♦ adj tried, proved; worthy, excellent
spectiō, -ōnis f the right to take auspices
spectō, -āre, -āvī, -ātum vt to look at, observe, watch; (place) to face; (aim) to look to, bear in mind, contemplate, tend towards; (judging) to examine, test
spectrum, -ī nt spectre
specula, -ae f watchtower, lookout; height
spēcula, -ae f slight hope
speculābundus adj on the lookout
speculāris adj transparent ♦ ntpl window
speculātor, -ōris m explorer, investigator; (MIL) spy, scout
speculātōrius adj for spying, scouting ♦ f spy boat
speculātrīx, -īcis f watcher
speculor, -ārī, -ātus vt to spy out, watch for, observe
speculum, -ī nt mirror
specus, -ūs m, nt cave; hollow, chasm
spēlaeum, -ī nt cave, den
spēlunca, -ae f cave, den
spērābilis adj to be hoped for
spērāta, -ātae f bride
Sperchēis, -idis adj see **Sperchēus**
Sperchēus, Sperchēos, -ī m river in Thessaly
spernō, -ere, sprēvī, sprētum vt to remove, reject, scorn
spērō, -āre, -āvī, -ātum vt to hope, hope for, expect; to trust; to look forward to

spēs, **speī** f hope, expectation; **praeter spem** unexpectedly; **spē dēiectus** disappointed

Speusippus, **-ī** m successor of Plato in the Academy

sphaera, **-ae** f ball, globe, sphere

Sphinx, **-ingis** f fabulous monster near Thebes

spīca, **-ae** f (grain) ear; (plant) tuft; (ASTR) brightest star in Virgo

spīceus adj of ears of corn

spīculum, **-ī** nt point, sting; dart, arrow

spīna, **-ae** f thorn; prickle; fish bone; spine, back; (pl) difficulties, subtleties

spīnētum, **-ī** nt thorn hedge

spīneus adj of thorns

spīnifer, **-ī** adj prickly

spīnōsus adj thorny, prickly; (style) difficult

spintēr, **-ēris** nt elastic bracelet

spīnus, **-ī** f blackthorn, sloe

spīra, **-ae** f coil; twisted band

spīrābilis adj breathable, life-giving

spīrāculum, **-ī** nt vent

spīrāmentum, **-ī** nt vent, pore; breathing space

spīritus, **-ūs** m breath, breathing; breeze, air; inspiration; character, spirit, courage, arrogance

spīrō, **-āre**, **-āvī**, **-ātum** vi to breathe, blow; to be alive; to be inspired ◆ vt to emit, exhale; (fig) to breathe, express

spissātus adj condensed

spissē adv closely; slowly

spissēscō, **-ere** vi to thicken

spissus adj thick, compact, crowded; slow; (fig) difficult

splendeō, **-ēre** vi to be bright, shine; to be illustrious

splendēscō, **-ere** vi to become bright

splendidē adv brilliantly, magnificently, nobly

splendidus adj bright, brilliant, glittering; (sound) clear; (dress, house) magnificent; (person) illustrious; (appearance) showy

splendor, **-ōris** m brightness, lustre; magnificence; clearness; nobility

spoliātiō, **-ōnis** f plundering

spoliātor, **-ōris** m robber

spoliātrīx, **-īcis** f robber

spoliō, **-āre**, **-āvī**, **-ātum** vt to strip; to rob, plunder

spolium, **-ī** and **-iī** nt (beast) skin; (enemy) spoils, booty

sponda, **-ae** f bed frame; bed, couch

spondālium, **-ī** and **-iī** nt hymn accompanied by the flute

spondeō, **-ēre**, **spopondī**, **spōnsum** vt to promise, pledge, vow; (LAW) to go bail for; (marriage) to betroth

spondēus, **-ī** m spondee

spongia, **-ae** f sponge; coat of mail

spōnsa, **-ae** f fiancée, bride

spōnsālia, **-ium** ntpl engagement

spōnsiō, **-ōnis** f promise, guarantee; (LAW) agreement that the loser in a suit pays the winner a sum; bet

spōnsor, **-ōris** m guarantor, surety

spōnsus¹ ppp of **spondeō** ◆ m fiancé, bridegroom ◆ nt agreement, covenant

spōnsus², **-ūs** m contract, surety

sponte f (abl) voluntarily, of one's own accord; unaided, by oneself; spontaneously

spopondī perf of **spondeō**

sportella, **-ae** f fruit basket

sportula, **-ae** f small basket; gift to clients, dole

sprētiō, **-ōnis** f contempt

sprētor, **-ōris** m despiser

sprētus ppp of **spernō**

sprēvī perf of **spernō**

spūma, **-ae** f foam, froth

spūmēscō, **-ere** vi to become frothy

spūmeus adj foaming, frothy

spūmifer, **-ī** adj foaming

spūmiger, **-ī** adj foaming

spūmō, **-āre** vi to foam, froth

spūmōsus adj foaming

spuō, **-uere**, **-uī**, **-ūtum** vi to spit ◆ vt to spit out

spurcē adv obscenely

spurcidicus adj obscene

spurcificus adj obscene

spurcitia, **-ae**, **spurcitiēs**, **-ēī** f filth, smut

spurcō, **-āre** vt to befoul

spurcus adj filthy, nasty, foul

spūtātilicus adj despicable

spūtātor, **-ōris** m spitter

spūtō, **-āre** vt to spit out

spūtum, **-ī** nt spit, spittle

squāleō, **-ēre**, **-uī** vi to be rough, stiff, clotted; to be parched; to be neglected, squalid, filthy; to be in mourning

squālidē adv rudely

squālidus adj rough, scaly; neglected, squalid, filthy; (speech) unpolished

squālor, **-ōris** m roughness; filth, squalor

squāma, **-ae** f scale; scale armour

squāmeus adj scaly

squāmifer, **-ī** adj scaly

squāmiger, **-ī** adj scaly ◆ mpl fishes

squāmōsus adj scaly

squilla, **-ae** f prawn, shrimp

st interj sh!

stabilīmentum, **-ī** nt support

stabiliō, **-īre** vt to make stable; to establish

stabilis adj firm, steady; (fig) steadfast, unfailing

stabilitās, **-ātis** f firmness, steadiness, reliability

stabulō, **-āre** vt to house, stable ◆ vi to have a stall

stabulum, **-ī** nt stall, stable, steading; lodging, cottage; brothel

stacta, **-ae** f myrrh oil

stadium, **-ī** and **-iī** nt stade, furlong; racetrack

Stagīra, **-ōrum** ntpl town in Macedonia (birthplace of Aristotle)

Stagīrītēs, **-ītae** m Aristotle

stagnō, **-āre** vi to form pools; to be inundated ◆ vt to flood

stagnum, **-ī** nt standing water, pool, swamp; waters

stāmen, -inis *nt* warp; thread; (*instrument*) string; (*priest*) fillet

stāmineus *adj* full of threads

stata *adj*: Stata māter Vesta

statārius *adj* standing, stationary, steady; calm ♦ *f* refined comedy ♦ *mpl* actors in this comedy

statēra, -ae *f* scales

statim *adv* steadily; at once, immediately; ~ ut as soon as

statiō, -ōnis *f* standing still; station, post, residence; (*pl*) sentries; (NAUT) anchorage

Statius, -ī *m* Caecilius (*early writer of comedy*), Papinius (*epic and lyric poet of the Silver Age*)

statīvus *adj* stationary ♦ *ntpl* standing camp

Stator, -ōris *m* the Stayer (*epithet of Jupiter*)

stator, -ōris *m* attendant, orderly

statua, -ae *f* statue

statūmen, -inis *nt* (*ship*) rib

statuō, -uere, -uī, -ūtum *vt* to set up, place; to bring to a stop; to establish, constitute; to determine, appoint; to decide, settle; to decree, prescribe; (*with inf*) to resolve, propose; (*with acc and infin*) to judge, consider, conclude; (*army*) to draw up; (*monument*) to erect; (*price*) to fix; (*sentence*) to pass; (*tent*) to pitch; (*town*) to build; **condiciōnem statuere** dictate (to); **fīnem statuere** put an end (to); **iūs statuere** lay down a principle; **modum statuere** impose restrictions; **apud animum statuere** make up one's mind; **dē sē statuere** commit suicide; **gravius statuere in** deal severely with

statūra, -ae *f* height, stature

status¹ *ppp of* sistō ♦ *adj* appointed, due

status², -ūs *m* posture, attitude; position; (*social*) standing, status, circumstances; (POL) situation, state, form of government; (*nature*) condition; **reī pūblicae ~** the political situation; constitution; **dē statū movēre** dislodge

statūtus *ppp of* statuō

stega, -ae *f* deck

stēliō *see* stēlliō

stēlla, -ae *f* star; ~ **errāns** planet

stēllāns, -antis *adj* starry

stēllātus *adj* starred; set in the sky

stēllifer, -ī *adj* starry

stēlliger, -ī *adj* starry

stēlliō, -ōnis *m* newt

stemma, -tis *nt* pedigree

stercoreus *adj* filthy

stercorō, -āre *vt* to manure

stercus, -oris *nt* dung

sterilis *adj* barren, sterile; bare, empty; unprofitable, fruitless

sterilitās, -ātis *f* barrenness

sternāx, -ācis *adj* bucking

sternō, -ere, strāvī, strātum *vt* to spread, cover, strew; to smooth, level; to stretch out, extend; to throw to the ground, prostrate; to overthrow; (*bed*) to make; (*horse*) to saddle; (*road*) to pave

sternūmentum, -ī *nt* sneezing

sternuō, -ere, -ī *vt, vi* to sneeze

Steropē, -ēs *f a Pleiad*

sterquilīnium, -ī *and* -**iī, sterquilīnum, -ī** *nt* dung heap

stertō, -ere, -uī *vi* to snore

Stēsichorus, -ī *m Greek lyric poet*

stetī *perf of* stō

Sthenelēius, Sthenelēis, ēidis *adj see* Sthenelus

Sthenelus, -ī *m father of Eurystheus; father of Cycnus*

stigma, -tis *nt* brand

stigmatiās, -ae *m* branded slave

stilla, -ae *f* drop

stillicidium, -ī *and* -**iī** *nt* dripping water, rainwater from the eaves

stillō, -āre, -āvī, -ātum *vi* to drip, trickle ♦ *vt* to let fall in drops, distil

stilus, -ī *m* stake; pen; (*fig*) writing, composition, style; **stilum vertere** erase

stimulātiō, -ōnis *f* incentive

stimulātrīx, -īcis *f* provocative woman

stimuleus *adj* smarting

stimulō, -āre, -āvī, -ātum *vt* to goad; to trouble, torment; to rouse, spur on, excite

stimulus, -ī *m* goad; (MIL) stake; (*pain*) sting, pang; (*incentive*) spur, stimulus

stinguō, -ere *vt* to extinguish

stīpātiō, -ōnis *f* crowd, retinue

stīpātor, -ōris *m* attendant; (*pl*) retinue, bodyguard

stīpendiārius *adj* tributary, liable to a money tax; (MIL) receiving pay ♦ *mpl* tributary peoples

stīpendium, -ī *and* -**iī** *nt* tax, tribute; soldier's pay; military service, campaign; ~ **merēre**, ~ **merērī** serve; ~ **ēmerērī** complete one's period of service

stīpes, -itis *m* log, trunk; tree; (*insult*) blockhead

stīpō, -āre, -āvī, -ātum *vt* to press, pack together; to cram, stuff full; to crowd round, accompany in a body

stips, stipis *f* donation, contribution

stipula, -ae *f* stalk, blade, stubble; reed

stipulātiō, -ōnis *f* promise, bargain

stipulātiuncula, -ae *f* slight stipulation

stipulātus *adj* promised

stipulor, -ārī *vt, vi* to demand a formal promise, bargain, stipulate

stīria, -ae *f* icicle

stirpēs *etc see* stirps

stirpitus *adv* thoroughly

stirps, -is *f* lower trunk and roots, stock; plant, shoot; family, lineage, progeny; origin; **ab stirpe** utterly

stīva, -ae *f* plough handle

stlattārius *adj* seaborne

stō, -āre, stetī, statum *vi* to stand; to remain in position, stand firm; to be conspicuous; (*fig*) to persist, continue; (*battle*) to go on; (*hair*) to stand on end; (NAUT) to ride at anchor; (*play*) to be successful; (*price*) to cost; (*with* **ab, cum, prō**) to be on the side of, support; (*with* **in**) to rest, depend on; (*with* **per**) to be the fault of; **stat sententia** one's mind is made up; **per**

Āfrānium stetit quŏminus dīmicārētur
thanks to Afranius there was no battle

Stŏicē *adv* like a Stoic

Stŏicus *adj* Stoic ♦ *m* Stoic philosopher ♦ *ntpl* Stoicism

stola, -ae *f* long robe (*esp worn by matrons*)

stolidē *adv* stupidly

stolidus *adj* dull, stupid

stomachor, -ārī, -ātus *vi* to be vexed, be annoyed

stomachōsē *adv see* **stomachōsus**

stomachōsus *adj* angry, irritable

stomachus, -ī *m* gullet; stomach; taste, liking; dislike, irritation, chagrin

stŏrea, storia, -ae *f* rush mat, rope mat

strabō, -ōnis *m* squinter

strāgēs, -is *f* heap, confused mass; havoc, massacre

strāgulus *adj* covering ♦ *nt* bedspread, rug

strāmen, -inis *nt* straw, litter

strāmentum, -ī *nt* straw, thatch; straw bed; covering, rug

strāmineus *adj* straw-thatched

strangulō, -āre, -āvī, -ātum *vt* to throttle, choke

strangūria, -ae *f* difficult discharge of urine

stratēgēma, -tis *nt* a piece of generalship, stratagem

stratēgus, -ī *m* commander, president

stratiōticus *adj* military

strātum, -ī *nt* coverlet, blanket; bed, couch; horsecloth, saddle; pavement

strātus *ppp of* **sternō** ♦ *adj* prostrate

strāvī *perf of* **sternō**

strēnuē *adv* energetically, quickly

strēnuitās, -ātis *f* energy, briskness

strēnuus *adj* brisk, energetic, busy; restless

strepitō, -āre *vi* to make a noise, rattle, rustle

strepitus, -ūs *m* din, clatter, crashing, rumbling; sound

strepō, -ere, -uī *vi* to make a noise, clang, roar, rumble, rustle *etc* ♦ *vt* to bawl out

striāta, -ae *f* scallop

strictim *adv* superficially, cursorily

strictūra, -ae *f* mass of metal

strictus *ppp of* **stringō** ♦ *adj* close, tight

strīdeō, -ēre, -ī, strīdō, -ere, -ī *vi* to creak, hiss, shriek, whistle

strīdor, -ōris *m* creaking, hissing, grating

strīdulus *adj* creaking, hissing, whistling

strigilis *f* scraper, strigil

strigō, -āre *vi* to stop, jib

strīgōsus *adj* thin, scraggy; (*style*) insipid

stringō, -ngere, -nxī, -ctum *vt* to draw together, draw tight; to touch, graze; to cut off, prune, trim; (*sword*) to draw; (*mind*) to affect, pain

stringor, -ōris *m* twinge

strix, -igis *f* screech owl

stropha, -ae *f* trick

Strophades, -um *fpl* islands off S. Greece

strophiārius, -ī *and* **-iī** *m* maker of breastbands

strophium, -ī *and* **-iī** *nt* breastband; headband

structor, -ōris *m* mason, carpenter; (*at table*) server, carver

structūra, -ae *f* construction, structure; works

structus *ppp of* **struō**

struēs, -is *f* heap, pile

struix, -icis *f* heap, pile

strūma, -ae *f* tumour

strūmōsus *adj* scrofulous

struō, -ere, -xī, -ctum *vt* to pile up; to build, erect; to arrange in order; to make, prepare; to cause, contrive, plot

strūtheus *adj* sparrow- (*in cpds*)

strūthiocamēlus, -ī *m* ostrich

Strȳmōn, -onis *m river between Macedonia and Thrace (now Struma)*

Strȳmonius *adj* Strymonian, Thracian

studeō, -ēre, -uī *vi* (*usu with dat*) to be keen, be diligent, apply oneself to; to study; (*person*) to be a supporter of

studiōsē *adv* eagerly, diligently

studiōsus *adj* (*usu with gen*) keen on, fond of, partial to; studious ♦ *m* student

studium, -ī *and* **-iī** *nt* enthusiasm, application, inclination; fondness; affection; party spirit, partisanship; study, literary work

stultē *adv* foolishly

stultiloquentia, -ae *f* foolish talk

stultiloquium, -ī *and* **-iī** *nt* foolish talk

stultitia, -ae *f* folly, silliness

stultividus *adj* simple-sighted

stultus *adj* foolish, silly ♦ *m* fool

stupefaciō, -facere, -fēcī, -factum (*pass* **-fīō**) *vt* to stun, astound

stupeō, -ēre, -uī *vi* to be stunned, be astonished; to be brought to a standstill ♦ *vt* to marvel at

stupēscō, -ere *vi* to become amazed

stŭpeus *etc see* **stuppeus**

stupiditās, -ātis *f* senselessness

stupidus *adj* senseless, astounded; dull, stupid

stupor, -ōris *m* numbness, bewilderment; dullness, stupidity

stuppa, -ae *f* tow

stuppeus *adj* of tow

stuprō, -āre, -āvī, -ātum *vt* to defile; to ravish

stuprum, -ī *nt* debauchery, unchastity

sturnus, -ī *m* starling

Stygius *adj* of the lower world, Stygian

stylus *etc see* **stilus**

Stymphalicus, Stymphalicius, Stymphalicis *adj* Stymphalian

Stymphalum, -ī *nt,* **Stymphalus, -ī** *m district of Arcadia (famous for birds of prey killed by Hercules)*

Styx, -ygis *and* **-ygos** *f river of Hades*

Styxius *adj see* **Styx**

suādēla, -ae *f* persuasion

suādeō, -dēre, -sī, -sum *vi* (*with dat*) to advise, urge, recommend

suāsiō, -ōnis *f* speaking in favour (of a proposal), *persuasive type of oratory*

suāsor, -ōris *m* adviser; advocate

suāsus¹ *ppp of* **suādeō**

suāsus², -ūs *m* advice

suāveolēns, -entis *adj* fragrant

suāviātiō *etc see* **sāviātiō**

suāvidicus *adj* charming
suāviloquēns, -entis *adj* charming
suāviloquentia, -ae *f* charm of speech
suāvior *etc see* **sāvior**
suāvis *adj* sweet, pleasant, delightful
suāvitās, -ātis *f* sweetness, pleasantness, charm
suāviter *adv see* **suāvis**
suāvium *etc see* **sāvium**
sub *prep* 1. (*with abl*) (*place*) under, beneath; (*hills, walls*) at the foot of, close to; (*time*) during, at; (*order*) next to; (*rule*) under, in the reign of 2. (*with acc*) (*place*) under, along under; (*hills, walls*) up to, to; (*time*) up to, just before, just after; **sub ictum venīre** come within range; **sub manum** to hand
subabsurdē *adv see* **subabsurdus**
subabsurdus *adj* somewhat absurd
subaccūsō, -āre *vt* to find some fault with
subāctiō, -ōnis *f* working (*the soil*)
subāctus *ppp of* **subigō**
subadroganter *adv* a little conceitedly
subagrestis *adj* rather boorish
subalāris *adj* carried under the arms
subamārus *adj* rather bitter
subaquilus *adj* brownish
subauscultō, -āre *vt, vi* to listen secretly, eavesdrop
subbasilicānus, -ī *m* lounger
subblandior, -īrī *vi* (*with dat*) to flirt with
subc- *etc see* **succ-**
subdidī *perf of* **subdō**
subdifficilis *adj* rather difficult
subdiffīdō, -ere *vi* to be a little doubtful
subditīcius *adj* sham
subditīvus *adj* sham
subditus *ppp of* **subdō** ♦ *adj* spurious
subdō, -ere, -idī, -itum *vt* to put under, plunge into; to subdue; to substitute, forge
subdoceō, -ēre *vt* to teach as an assistant
subdolē *adv* slily
subdolus *adj* sly, crafty, underhand
subdubitō, -āre *vi* to be a little undecided
subdūcō, -ūcere, -ūxī, -uctum *vt* to pull up, raise; to withdraw, remove; to take away secretly, steal; (*account*) to balance; (*ship*) to haul up, beach; **sē subdūcere** steal away, disappear
subductiō, -ōnis *f* (*ship*) hauling up; (*thought*) reckoning
subductus *ppp of* **subdūcō**
subedō, -esse, -ēdī *vt* to wear away underneath
subēgī *perf of* **subigō**
subeō, -īre, -iī, -itum *vi* to go under, go in; to come up to, climb, advance; to come immediately after; to come to the assistance; to come as a substitute, succeed; to come secretly, steal in; to come to mind, suggest itself ♦ *vt* to enter, plunge into; to climb; to approach, attack; to take the place of; to steal into; to submit to, undergo, suffer; (*mind*) to occur to
sūber, -is *nt* cork tree; cork
subesse *infin of* **subsum**

subf- *etc see* **suff-**
subg- *etc see* **sugg-**
subhorridus *adj* somewhat uncouth
subiaceō, -ēre, -uī *vi* to lie under, be close (to); to be connected (with)
subiciō, -icere, -iēcī, -iectum *vt* to put under, bring under; to bring up, throw up; to bring near; to submit, subject, expose; to subordinate, deal with under; to append, add on, answer; to adduce, suggest; to substitute; to forge, suborn; **sē subicere** grow up
subiectē *adv* submissively
subiectiō, -ōnis *f* laying under; forging
subiectō, -āre *vt* to lay under, put to; to throw up
subiector, -ōris *m* forger
subiectus *ppp of* **subiciō** ♦ *adj* neighbouring, bordering; subject, exposed
subigitātiō, -ōnis *f* lewdness
subigitō, -āre *vt* to behave improperly to
subigō, -igere, -ēgī, -āctum *vt* to bring up to; to impel, compel; to subdue, conquer; (*animal*) to tame, break in; (*blade*) to sharpen; (*boat*) to row, propel; (*cooking*) to knead; (*earth*) to turn up, dig; (*mind*) to train
subiī *perf of* **subeō**
subimpudēns, -entis *adj* rather impertinent
subinānis *adj* rather empty
subinde *adv* immediately after; repeatedly
subīnsulsus *adj* rather insipid
subinvideō, -ēre *vi* to be a little envious of
subinvīsus *adj* somewhat odious
subinvītō, -āre *vt* to invite vaguely
subīrāscor, -scī, -tus *vi* to be rather angry
subīrātus *adj* rather angry
subitārius *adj* sudden, emergency (*in cpds*)
subitō *adv* suddenly
subitus *ppp of* **subeō** ♦ *adj* sudden, unexpected; (*man*) rash; (*troops*) hastily raised ♦ *nt* surprise, emergency
subiūnctus *ppp of* **subiungō**
subiungō, -ungere, -ūnxī, -ūnctum *vt* to harness; to add, affix; to subordinate, subdue
sublābor, -bī, -psus *vi* to sink down; to glide away
sublāpsus *ppa of* **sublābor**
sublātē *adv* loftily
sublātiō, -ōnis *f* elevation
sublātus *ppp of* **tollō** ♦ *adj* elated
sublectō, -āre *vt* to coax
sublēctus *ppp of* **sublegō**
sublegō, -egere, -ēgī, -ēctum *vt* to gather up; to substitute; (*child*) to kidnap; (*talk*) to overhear
sublestus *adj* slight
sublevātiō, -ōnis *f* alleviation
sublevō, -āre, -āvī, -ātum *vt* to lift up, hold up; to support, encourage; to lighten, alleviate
sublica, -ae *f* pile, palisade
sublicius *adj* on piles
subligāculum, -ī, subligar, -āris *nt* loincloth
subligō, -āre *vt* to fasten on
sublīmē *adv* aloft, in the air

sublīmis *adj* high, raised high, lifted up; (*character*) eminent, aspiring; (*language*) lofty, elevated

sublīmitās, -ātis *f* loftiness

sublīmus *etc see* **sublīmis**

sublingiō, -ōnis *m* scullion

sublinō, -inere, -ēvī, -itum *vt*: **ōs sublinere** to fool, bamboozle

sublitus *ppp of* **sublinō**

sublūceō, -ēre *vi* to glimmer

subluō, -ere *vt* (*river*) to flow past the foot of

sublūstris *adj* faintly luminous

sublūtus *ppp of* **subluō**

subm- *etc see* **summ-**

subnātus *adj* growing up underneath

subnectō, -ctere, -xuī, -xum *vt* to tie under, fasten to

subnegō, -āre *vt* to half refuse

subnexus *ppp of* **subnectō**

subniger, -rī *adj* darkish

subnīxus, subnīsus *adj* supported, resting (on); relying (on)

subnuba, -ae *f* rival

subnūbilus *adj* overcast

subō, -āre *vi* to be in heat

subobscēnus *adj* rather indecent

subobscūrus *adj* somewhat obscure

subodiōsus *adj* rather odious

suboffendō, -ere *vi* to give some offence

subolēs, -is *f* offspring, children

subolēscō, -ere *vi* to grow up

subolet, -ēre *vi* (*impers*) there is a faint scent; **~ mihi** I detect, have an inkling

suborior, -īrī *vi* to spring up in succession

subōrnō, -āre, -āvī, -ātum *vt* to fit out, equip; to instigate secretly, suborn

subortus, -ūs *m* rising up repeatedly

subp- *etc see* **supp-**

subrancidus *adj* slightly tainted

subraucus *adj* rather hoarse

subrēctus *ppp of* **subrigō**

subrēmigō, -āre *vi* to paddle under (*water*)

subrēpō, -ere, -sī, -tum *vi* to creep along, steal up to

subreptus *ppp of* **subripiō**

subrīdeō, -dēre, -sī *vi* to smile

subrīdiculē *adv* rather funnily

subrigō, -igere, -ēxī, -ēctum *vt* to lift, raise

subringor, -ī *vi* to make a wry face, be rather vexed

subripiō, -ipere, -ipuī *and* **-upuī, -eptum** *vt* to take away secretly, steal

subrogō, -āre *vt* to propose as successor

subrōstrānī, -ōrum *mpl* idlers

subrubeō, -ēre *vi* to blush slightly

subrūfus *adj* ginger-haired

subruō, -ere, -ī, -tum *vt* to undermine, demolish

subrūsticus *adj* rather countrified

subrutus *ppp of* **subruō**

subscrībō, -bere, -psī, -ptum *vt* to write underneath; (*document*) to sign, subscribe; (*censor*) to set down; (LAW) to add to an indictment, prosecute; (*fig*) to record; (*with dat*) to assent to, approve

subscrīptiō, -ōnis *f* inscription underneath; signature; (*censor*) noting down; (LAW) subscription (*to an indictment*); register

subscrīptor, -ōris *m* subscriber (*to an indictment*)

subscrīptus *ppp of* **subscrībō**

subsecīvus *etc see* **subsicīvus**

subsecō, -āre, -uī, -ctum *vt* to cut off, clip

subsēdī *perf of* **subsīdō**

subsellium, -ī *and* **-iī** *nt* bench, seat; (LAW) the bench, the court

subsentiō, -entīre, -ēnsī *vt* to have an inkling of

subsequor, -quī, -cūtus *vt, vi* to follow closely; to support; to imitate

subserviō, -īre *vi* to be a slave; (*fig*) to comply (with)

subsicīvus *adj* left over; (*time*) spare; (*work*) overtime

subsidiārius *adj* in reserve ♦ *mpl* reserves

subsidium, -ī *and* **-iī** *nt* reserve ranks, reserve troops; relief, aid, assistance

subsīdō, -īdere, -ēdī, -essum *vi* to sit down, crouch, squat; to sink down, settle, subside; (*ambush*) to lie in wait; (*residence*) to stay, settle ♦ *vt* to lie in wait for

subsignānus *adj* special reserve (troops)

subsignō, -āre *vt* to register; to guarantee

subsiliō, -īre, -uī *vi* to leap up

subsistō, -istere, -titī *vi* to stand still, make a stand; to stop, halt; to remain, continue, hold out; (*with dat*) to resist ♦ *vt* to withstand

subsortior, -īrī, -ītus *vt* to choose as a substitute by lot

subsortītiō, -ōnis *f* choosing of substitutes by lot

substantia, -ae *f* means, wealth

substernō, -ernere, -rāvī, -rātum *vt* to scatter under, spread under; (*fig*) to put at one's service

substitī *perf of* **subsistō**

substituō, -uere, -uī, -ūtum *vt* to put next; to substitute; (*idea*) to present, imagine

substitūtus *ppp of* **substituō**

substō, -āre *vi* to hold out

substrātus *ppp of* **substernō**

substrictus *ppp of* **substringō** ♦ *adj* narrow, tight

substringō, -ngere, -nxī, -ctum *vt* to bind up; to draw close; to check

substructiō, -ōnis *f* foundation

substruō, -ere, -xī, -ctum *vt* to lay, pave

subsultō, -āre *vi* to jump up

subsum, -esse *vi* to be underneath; to be close to, be at hand; (*fig*) to underlie, be latent in

subsūtus *adj* fringed at the bottom

subtēmen, -inis *nt* woof; thread

subter *adv* below, underneath ♦ *prep* (*with acc and abl*) beneath; close up to

subterdūcō, -cere, -xī *vt* to withdraw secretly

subterfugiō, -ugere, -ūgī *vt* to escape from, evade

subterlābor, -ī *vt, vi* to flow past under; to slip away

subterrāneus *adj* underground

subtexō, -ere, -uī, -tum *vt* to weave in; to veil, obscure

subtīlis *adj* slender, fine; *(senses)* delicate, nice; *(judgment)* discriminating, precise; *(style)* plain, direct

subtīlitās, -ātis *f* fineness; *(judgment)* acuteness, exactness; *(style)* plainness, directness

subtīliter *adv* finely; accurately; simply

subtimeō, -ēre *vt* to be a little afraid of

subtractus *ppp of* **subtrahō**

subtrahō, -here, -xī, -ctum *vt* to draw away from underneath; to take away secretly; to withdraw, remove

subtristis *adj* rather sad

subturpiculus *adj* a little bit mean

subturpis *adj* rather mean

subtus *adv* below, underneath

subtūsus *adj* slightly bruised

subūcula, -ae *f* shirt, vest

sūbula, -ae *f* awl

subulcus, -ī *m* swineherd

Subūra, -ae *f a disreputable quarter of Rome*

Subūrānus *adj see* **Subūra**

suburbānitās, -ātis *f* nearness to Rome

suburbānus *adj* near Rome ♦ *nt* villa near Rome ♦ *mpl* inhabitants of the towns near Rome

suburbium, -ī *and* **-iī** *nt* suburb

suburgeō, -ēre *vt* to drive close (to)

subvectiō, -ōnis *f* transport

subvectō, -āre *vt* to carry up regularly

subvectus[1] *ppp of* **subvehō**

subvectus[2]**, -ūs** *m* transport

subvehō, -here, -xī, -ctum *vt* to carry up, transport upstream

subveniō, -enīre, -ēnī, -entum *vi* *(with dat)* to come to the assistance of, relieve, reinforce

subventō, -āre *vi* *(with dat)* to come quickly to help

subvereor, -ērī *vi* to be a little afraid

subversor, -ōris *m* subverter

subversus *ppp of* **subvertō**

subvertō, -tere, -tī, -sum *vt* to turn upside down, upset; to overthrow, subvert

subvexī *perf of* **subvehō**

subvexus *adj* sloping upwards

subvolō, -āre *vi* to fly upwards

subvolvō, -ere *vt* to roll uphill

subvortō *etc see* **subvertō**

succavus *adj* hollow underneath

succēdō, -ēdere, -essī, -essum *vt, vi* *(with dat)* to go under, pass into, take on; *(with dat, acc, in)* to go up, climb; *(with dat, acc, ad, sub)* to march on, advance to; *(with dat, in)* to come to take the place of, relieve; *(with dat, in, ad)* to follow after, succeed, succeed to; *(result)* to turn out, be successful

succendō, -endere, -endī, -ēnsum *vt* to set fire to, kindle; *(fig)* to fire, inflame

succēnseō *etc see* **suscēnseō**

succēnsus *ppp of* **succendō**

succenturiātus *adj* in reserve

succenturiō, -ōnis *m* under-centurion

successī *perf of* **succēdō**

successiō, -ōnis *f* succession

successor, -ōris *m* successor

successus[1] *ppp of* **succēdō**

successus[2]**, -ūs** *m* advance uphill; result, success

succīdia, -ae *f* leg or side of meat, flitch

succidō, -ere, -ī *vi* to sink, give way

succīdō, -dere, -dī, -sum *vt* to cut off, mow down

succiduus *adj* sinking, failing

succinctus *ppp of* **succingō**

succingō, -gere, -xī, -ctum *vt* to gird up, tuck up; to equip, arm

succingulum, -ī *nt* girdle

succinō, -ere *vi* to chime in

succīsus *ppp of* **succīdō**

succlāmātiō, -ōnis *f* shouting, barracking

succlāmō, -āre, -āvī, -ātum *vt* to shout after, interrupt with shouting

succontumēliōsē *adv* somewhat insolently

succrēscō, -ere *vi* to grow up from or to

succrispus *adj* rather curly

succumbō, -mbere, -buī, -bitum *vi* to fall, sink under; to submit, surrender

succurrō, -rere, -rī, -sum *vi* to come quickly up; to run to the help of, succour; *(idea)* to occur

succus *etc see* **sūcus**

succussus, -ūs *m* shaking

succustōs, -ōdis *m* assistant keeper

succutiō, -tere, -ssī, -ssum *vt* to toss up

sūcidus *adj* juicy, fresh, plump

sūcinum, -ī *nt* amber

sūctus *ppp of* **sūgō**

sucula[1]**, -ae** *f* winch, windlass

sucula[2]**, -ae** *f* piglet; *(pl)* the Hyads

sūcus, -ī *m* juice, sap; medicine, potion; taste, flavour; *(fig)* strength, vigour, life

sūdārium, -ī *and* **-iī** *nt* handkerchief

sūdātōrius *adj* for sweating ♦ *nt* sweating bath

sudis, -is *f* stake, pile, pike, spike

sūdō, -āre, -āvī, -ātum *vi* to sweat, perspire; to be drenched with; to work hard ♦ *vt* to exude

sūdor, -ōris *m* sweat, perspiration; moisture; hard work, exertion

sudus *adj* cloudless, clear ♦ *nt* fine weather

sueō, -ēre *vi* to be accustomed

suēscō, -scere, -vī, -tum *vi* to be accustomed ♦ *vt* to accustom

Suessa, -ae *f town in Latium*

Suessiōnēs, -um *mpl people of Gaul (near what is now Soissons)*

suētus *ppp of* **suēscō** ♦ *adj* accustomed; usual

Suēvī, -ōrum *mpl people of N.E. Germany*

sūfes, -etis *m chief magistrate of Carthage*

suffarcinātus *adj* stuffed full

suffectus *ppp of* **sufficiō** ♦ *adj* *(consul)* appointed to fill a vacancy during the regular term of office

sufferō, -re *vt* to support, undergo, endure

suffes *etc see* **sūfes**

sufficiō, -icere, -ēcī, -ectum vt to dye, tinge; to supply, provide; to appoint in place of (another), substitute ♦ vi to be adequate, suffice

suffigō, -gere, -xī, -xum vt to fasten underneath, nail on

suffīmen, -inis nt, **suffīmentum, -ī** nt incense

suffiō, -īre vt to fumigate, perfume

suffīxus ppp of **suffigō**

sufflāmen, -inis nt brake

sufflō, -āre vt to blow up; to puff up

suffocō, -āre vt to choke, stifle

suffodiō, -odere, -ōdī, -ossum vt to stab; to dig under, undermine

suffossus ppp of **suffodiō**

suffrāgātiō, -ōnis f voting for, support

suffrāgātor, -ōris m voter, supporter

suffrāgātōrius adj supporting a candidate

suffrāgium, -ī and **-iī** nt vote, ballot; right of suffrage; (fig) judgment, approval; ~ **ferre** vote

suffrāgor, -ārī, -ātus vi to vote for; to support, favour

suffringō, -ere vt to break

suffugiō, -ugere, -ūgī vi to run for shelter ♦ vt to elude

suffugium, -ī and **-iī** nt shelter, refuge

suffulciō, -cīre, -sī, -tum vt to prop up, support

suffundō, -undere, -ūdī, -ūsum vt to pour in; to suffuse, fill; to tinge, colour; (blush) to overspread

suffūror, -ārī vi to filch

suffuscus adj darkish

suffūsus ppp of **suffundō**

Sugambrī, -ōrum mpl people of N.W. Germany

suggerō, -rere, -ssī, -stum vt to bring up to, supply; to add on, put next

suggestum, -ī nt platform

suggestus¹ ppp of **suggerō**

suggestus², -ūs m platform, stage

suggrandis adj rather large

suggredior, -dī, -ssus vi to come up close, approach ♦ vt to attack

sūgillātiō, -ōnis f affronting

sūgillātus adj bruised; insulted

sūgō, -gere, -xī, -ctum vt to suck

suī gen of **sē**

suī² perf of **suō**

suillus adj of pigs

sulcō, -āre vt to furrow, plough

sulcus, -ī m furrow; trench; track

sulfur, -uris n sulphur

Sulla, -ae m famous Roman dictator

Sullānus adj see **Sulla**

sullātūriō, -īre vi to hanker after being a Sulla

Sulmō, -ōnis m town in E. Italy (birthplace of Ovid)

Sulmōnēnsis adj see **Sulmō**

sultis adv please

sum, esse, fuī vi to be, exist; **sum ab** belong to; **sum ad** be designed for; **sum ex** consist of; **est, sunt** there is, are; **est mihi** I have; **mihi tēcum nīl est** I have nothing to do with you; **est quod** something; there is a reason for; **est ubi** sometimes; **est ut** it is possible that;

est (with gen) to belong to, be the duty of, be characteristic of; (with inf) it is possible, it is permissible; **sunt quī** some; **fuit Ilium** Troy is no more

sūmen, -inis nt udder, teat; sow

summa, -ae f main part, chief point, main issue; gist, summary; sum, amount, the whole; supreme power; ~ **rērum** the general interest, the whole responsibility; ~ **summārum** the universe; **ad summam** in short, in fact; in conclusion; **in summā** in all; after all

Summānus, -ī m god of nocturnal thunderbolts

summās, -ātis adj high-born, eminent

summātim adv cursorily, summarily

summātus, -ūs m sovereignty

summē adv in the highest degree, extremely

summergō, -gere, -sī, -sum vt to plunge under, sink

summersus ppp of **summergō**

sumministrō, -āre, -āvī, -ātum vt to provide, furnish

summissē adv softly; humbly, modestly

summissiō, -ōnis f lowering

summissus ppp of **summittō** ♦ adj low; (voice) low, calm; (character) mean, grovelling, submissive, humble

summittō, -ittere, -īsī, -issum vt (growth) to send up, raise, rear; to despatch, supply; to let down, lower, reduce, moderate; to supersede; to send secretly; **animum summittere** submit; **sē summittere** condescend

summoleste adv with some annoyance

summolestus adj a little annoying

summoneō, -ēre, -uī vt to drop a hint to

summōrōsus adj rather peevish

summōtor, -ōris m clearer

summōtus ppp of **summoveō**

summoveō, -ovēre, -ōvī, -ōtum vt to move away, drive off; to clear away (to make room), withdraw, remove, banish; (fig) to dispel

summum¹, -ī nt top, surface

summum² adv at the most

summus adj highest, the top of, the surface of; last, the end of; (fig) utmost, greatest, most important; (person) distinguished, excellent ♦ m head of the table

summūtō, -āre vt to substitute

sūmō, -ere, -psī, -ptum vt to take, take up; to assume, arrogate; (action) to undertake; (argument) to assume, take for granted; (dress) to put on; (punishment) to exact; (for a purpose) to use, spend

sūmptiō, -ōnis f assumption

sūmptuārius adj sumptuary

sūmptuōsē adv see **sūmptuōsus**

sūmptuōsus adj expensive, lavish, extravagant

sūmptus¹ ppp of **sūmō**

sūmptus², -ūs m expense, cost

Sūnium, -ī and **-iī** nt S.E. promontory of Attica

suō, suere, suī, sūtum vt to sew, stitch, join together

suōmet, suōpte abl of **suus**

suovetaurīlia, -ium *ntpl* sacrifice of a pig, sheep and bull

supellex, -ectilis *f* furniture, goods, outfit

super¹ *etc adj see* **superus**

super² *adv* above, on the top; besides, moreover; left, remaining ♦ *prep (with abl)* upon, above; concerning; besides; *(time)* at; *(with acc)* over, above, on; beyond; besides, over and above

superā *etc see* **suprā**

superābilis *adj* surmountable, conquerable

superaddō, -ere, -itum *vt* to add over and above

superāns, -antis *pres p of* **superō** ♦ *adj* predominant

superātor, -ōris *m* conqueror

superbē *adv* arrogantly, despotically

superbia, -ae *f* arrogance, insolence, tyranny; pride, lofty spirit

superbiloquentia, -ae *f* arrogant speech

superbiō, -īre *vi* to be arrogant, take a pride in; to be superb

superbus *adj* arrogant, insolent, overbearing; fastidious; superb, magnificent

supercilium, -ī *and* **-iī** *nt* eyebrow; *(hill)* brow, ridge; *(fig)* arrogance

superēmineō, -ēre *vt* to overtop

superesse *infin of* **supersum**

superficiēs, -ēī *f* surface; *(LAW)* a building *(esp on another's land)*

superfīō, -ierī *vi* to be left over

superfīxus *adj* fixed on top

superfluō, -ere *vi* to overflow

superfuī *perf of* **supersum**

superfundō, -undere, -ūdī, -ūsum *vt, vi* to pour over, shower; *(pass)* to overflow, spread out

superfūsus *ppp of* **superfundō**

supergredior, -dī, -ssus *vt* to surpass

superiaciō, -iacere, -iēcī, -iectum *and* **-iactum** *vt* to throw over, overspread; to overtop; *(fig)* to exaggerate

superiectus *ppp of* **superiaciō**

superimmineō, -ēre *vi* to overhang

superimpendēns, -entis *adj* overhanging

superimpōnō, -ōnere, -osuī, -ositum *vt* to place on top

superimpositus *ppp of* **superimpōnō**

superincidēns, -entis *adj* falling from above

superincubāns, -antis *adj* lying upon

superincumbō, -ere *vi* to fling oneself down upon

superingerō, -ere *vt* to pour down

superiniciō, -icere, -iēcī, -iectum *vt* to throw upon, put on top

superiniectus *ppp of* **superiniciō**

superīnsternō, -ere *vt* to lay over

superior, -ōris *adj* higher, upper; *(time, order)* preceding, previous, former; *(age)* older; *(battle)* victorious, stronger; *(quality)* superior, greater

superlātiō, -ōnis *f* exaggeration

superlātus *adj* exaggerated

supernē *adv* at the top, from above

supernus *adj* upper; celestial

superō, -āre, -āvī, -ātum *vi* to rise above, overtop; to have the upper hand; to be in excess, be abundant; to be left over, survive ♦ *vt* to pass over, surmount, go beyond; to surpass, outdo; *(MIL)* to overcome, conquer; *(NAUT)* to sail past, double

superobruō, -ere *vt* to overwhelm

superpendēns, -entis *adj* overhanging

superpōnō, -ōnere, -osuī, -ositum *vt* to place upon; to put in charge of

superpositus *ppp of* **superpōnō**

superscandō, -ere *vt* to climb over

supersedeō, -edēre, -ēdī, -essum *vi* to forbear, desist from

superstes, -itis *adj* standing over; surviving

superstitiō, -ōnis *f* awful fear, superstition

superstitiōsē *adv* superstitiously; scrupulously

superstitiōsus *adj* superstitious; prophetic

superstō, -āre *vt, vi* to stand over, stand on

superstrātus *adj* spread over

superstruō, -ere, -xī, -ctum *vt* to build on top

supersum, -esse, -fuī *vi* to be left, remain; to survive; to be in abundance, be sufficient; to be in excess

supertegō, -ere *vt* to cover over

superurgēns, -entis *adj* pressing from above

superus *(compar* **-ior,** *superl* **suprēmus** *and* **summus)** *adj* upper, above ♦ *mpl* the gods above; the living ♦ *ntpl* the heavenly bodies; higher places; **mare superum** Adriatic Sea

supervacāneus *adj* extra, superfluous

supervacuus *adj* superfluous, pointless

supervādō, -ere *vt* to climb over, surmount

supervehor, -hī, -ctus *vt* to ride past, sail past

superveniō, -enīre, -ēnī, -entum *vt* to overtake, come on top of ♦ *vi* to come on the scene, arrive unexpectedly

superventus, -ūs *m* arrival

supervolitō, -āre *vt* to fly over

supervolō, -āre *vt, vi* to fly over

supīnō, -āre, -āvī, -ātum *vt* to upturn, lay on its back

supīnus *adj* lying back, face up; sloping, on a slope; backwards; *(mind)* indolent, careless

suppāctus *ppp of* **suppingō**

suppaenitet, -ēre *vt impers* to be a little sorry

suppalpor, -ārī *vi* to coax gently

suppār, -aris *adj* nearly equal

supparasītor, -ārī *vi* to flatter gently

supparus, -ī *m,* **supparum, -ī** *nt* woman's linen garment; topsail

suppeditātiō, -ōnis *f* abundance

suppeditō, -āre, -āvī, -ātum *vi* to be at hand, be in full supply, be sufficient; to be rich in ♦ *vt* to supply, furnish

suppēdō, -ere *vi* to break wind quietly

suppetiae, -ārum *fpl* assistance

suppetior, -ārī, -ātus *vi* to come to the assistance of

suppetō, -ere, -īvī *and* **-iī, -ītum** *vi* to be available, be in store; to be equal to, suffice for

suppīlō, -āre *vt* to steal

suppingō, -ingere, -āctum vt to fasten underneath

supplantō, -āre vt to trip up

supplēmentum, -ī nt full complement; reinforcements

suppleō, -ēre vt to fill up, make good, make up to the full complement

supplex, -icis adj suppliant, in entreaty

supplicātiō, -ōnis f day of prayer, public thanksgiving

suppliciter adv in supplication

supplicium, -ī and **-iī** nt prayer, entreaty; sacrifice; punishment, execution, suffering; **suppliciō afficere** execute

supplicō, -āre, -āvī, -ātum vi (with dat) to entreat, pray to, worship

supplōdō, -dere, -sī vt to stamp

supplōsiō, -ōnis f stamping

suppōnō, -ōnere, -osuī, -ositum vt to put under, apply; to subject; to add on; to substitute, falsify

supportō, -āre vt to bring up, transport

supposittcius adj spurious

suppositiō, -ōnis f substitution

suppositus ppp of **suppōnō**

supposuī perf of **suppōnō**

suppressiō, -ōnis f embezzlement

suppressus ppp of **supprimō ◆** adj (voice) low

supprimō, -imere, -essī, -essum vt to sink; to restrain, detain, put a stop to; to keep secret, suppress

supprōmus, -ī m underbutler

suppudet, -ēre vt impers to be a little ashamed

suppūrō, -āre vi to fester

suppus adj head downwards

supputō, -āre vt to count up

suprā adv above, up on top; (time) earlier, previously; (amount) more; **~ quam** beyond what ◆ prep (with acc) over, above; beyond; (time) before; (amount) more than, over

suprāscandō, -ere vt to surmount

suprēmum adv for the last time

suprēmus adj highest; last, latest; greatest; supreme ◆ ntpl moment of death; funeral rites; testament

sūra, -ae f calf (of the leg)

sūrculus, -ī m twig, shoot; graft; slip

surdaster, -rī adj rather deaf

surditās, -ātis f deafness

surdus adj deaf; silent

surēna, -ae m grand vizier (of the Parthians)

surgō, -ere, surrēxī, surrēctum vi to rise, get up, stand up; to arise, spring up, grow

surpere etc = **surripere**

surr- etc see **subr-**

surrēxī perf of **surgō**

surrupticius adj stolen

surrupuī perf of **subripiō**

sūrsum, sūrsus adv upwards, up, high up; **~ deōrsum** up and down

sūs, suis m/f pig, boar, hog, sow

Sūsa, -ōrum ntpl ancient Persian capital

suscēnseō, -ēre, -uī vi to be angry, be irritated

susceptiō, -ōnis f undertaking

susceptus ppp of **suscipiō**

suscipiō, -ipere, -ēpī, -eptum vt to take up, undertake; to receive, catch; (child) to acknowledge; to beget; to take under one's protection

suscitō, -āre, -āvī, -ātum vt to lift, raise; to stir, rouse, awaken; to encourage, excite

suspectō, -āre vt, vi to look up at, watch; to suspect, mistrust

suspectus¹ ppp of **suspiciō ◆** adj suspected, suspicious

suspectus², -ūs m looking up; esteem

suspendium, -ī and **-iī** nt hanging

suspendō, -endere, -endī, -ēnsum vt to hang, hang up; (death) to hang; (building) to support; (mind) to keep in suspense; (movement) to check, interrupt; (pass) to depend

suspēnsus ppp of **suspendō ◆** adj raised, hanging, poised; with a light touch; (fig) in suspense, uncertain, anxious; dependent; **suspēnsō gradū** on tiptoe

suspicāx, -ācis adj suspicious

suspiciō, -icere, -exī, -ectum vt to look up at, look up to; to admire, respect; to mistrust

suspiciō, -ōnis f mistrust, suspicion

suspiciōsē adv suspiciously

suspiciōsus adj suspicious

suspicor, -ārī, -ātus vt to suspect; to surmise, suppose

suspīrātus, -ūs m sigh

suspīritus, -ūs m deep breath, difficult breathing; sigh

suspīrium, -ī and **-iī** nt deep breath, sigh

suspīrō, -āre, -āvī, -ātum vi to sigh ◆ vt to sigh for; to exclaim with a sigh

susque dēque adv up and down

sustentāculum, -ī nt prop

sustentātiō, -ōnis f forbearance

sustentō, -āre, -āvī, -ātum vt to hold up, support; (fig) to uphold, uplift; (food, means) to sustain, support; (enemy) to check, hold; (trouble) to suffer; (event) to hold back, postpone

sustineō, -inēre, -inuī, -entum vt to hold up, support; to check, control; (fig) to uphold, maintain; (food, means) to sustain, support; (trouble) to bear, suffer, withstand; (event) to put off

sustollō, -ere vt to lift up, raise; to destroy

sustulī perf of **tollō**

susurrātor, -ōris m whisperer

susurrō, -āre vt, vi to murmur, buzz, whisper

susurrus¹, -ūs m murmuring, whispering

susurrus² adj whispering

sūtēla, -ae f trick

sūtilis adj sewn

sūtor, -ōris m shoemaker; **~ nē suprā crepidam** let the cobbler stick to his last

sūtōrius adj shoemaker's; ex-cobbler

sūtrīnus adj shoemaker's

sūtūra, -ae f seam

sūtus ppp of **suō**

suus adj his, her, its, their; one's own, proper, due, right ◆ mpl one's own troops, friends, followers etc ◆ nt one's own property

Sybaris, -is f town in E. Italy (noted for its debauchery)

Sybarīta, **-ītae** *m* Sybarite
Sychaeus, **-ī** *m husband of Dido*
sycophanta, **-ae** *m* slanderer, cheat, sycophant
sycophantia, **-ae** *f* deceit
sycophantiōsē *adv* deceitfully
sycophantor, **-ārī** *vi* to cheat
Syēnē, **-ēs** *f town in S. Egypt (now Aswan)*
syllaba, **-ae** *f* syllable
syllabātim *adv* syllable by syllable
symbola, **-ae** *f* contribution
symbolus, **-ī** *m* token, symbol
symphōnia, **-ae** *f* concord, harmony
symphōniacus *adj* choir *(in cpds)*
Symplēgades, **-um** *fpl clashing rocks in the Black Sea*
synedrus, **-ī** *m* senator *(in Macedonia)*
Synephēbī, **-ōrum** *mpl* Youths Together *(comedy by Caecilius)*

syngrapha, **-ae** *f* promissory note
syngraphus, **-ī** *m* written contract; passport, pass
Synnada, **-ōrum** *ntpl town in Phrygia (famous for marble)*
Synnadēnsis *adj see* **Synnada**
synodūs, **-ontis** *m* bream
synthesis, **-is** *f* dinner service; suit of clothes; dressing gown
Syphāx, **-ācis** *m king of Numidia*
Syrācūsae, **-ārum** *fpl* Syracuse
Syrācūsānus, **Syrācūsānius**, **Syrācosius** *adj* Syracusan
Syria, **-iae** *f country at the E. end of the Mediterranean*
Syrius, **Syriacus**, **Syriscus** *adj* Syrian
syrma, **-ae** *f* robe with a train; *(fig)* tragedy
Syrtis, **-is** *f Gulf of Sidra in N. Africa*; sandbank

Tt

tabella, -ae f small board, sill; writing tablet, voting tablet, votive tablet; picture; (pl) writing, records, dispatches

tabellārius adj about voting ♦ m courier

tābeō, -ēre vi to waste away; to be wet

taberna, -ae f cottage; shop; inn; (circus) stalls

tabernāculum, -ī nt tent; ~ **capere** choose a site (for auspices)

tabernāriī, -ōrum mpl shopkeepers

tābēs, -is f wasting away, decaying, melting; putrefaction; plague, disease

tābēscō, -ēscere, -uī vi to waste away, melt, decay; (fig) to pine, languish

tābidulus adj consuming

tābidus adj melting, decaying; pining; corrupting, infectious

tābificus adj melting, wasting

tabula, -ae f board, plank; writing tablet; votive tablet; map; picture; auction; (pl) account books, records, lists, will; ~ **Sullae** Sulla's proscriptions; **XII tabulae** Twelve Tables of Roman laws; **tabulae novae** cancellation of debts

tabulārium, -ī and **-iī** nt archives

tabulātiō, -ōnis f flooring, storey

tabulātum, -ī nt flooring, storey; (trees) layer, row

tābum, -ī nt decaying matter; disease, plague

taceō, -ēre, -uī, -itum vi to be silent, say nothing; to be still, be hushed ♦ vt to say nothing about, not speak of

tacitē adv silently; secretly

taciturnitās, -ātis f silence, taciturnity

taciturnus adj silent, quiet

Tacitus, -ī m famous Roman historian

tacitus ppp of **taceō** ♦ adj silent, mute, quiet; secret, unmentioned; tacit, implied; **per tacitum** quietly

tāctilis adj tangible

tāctiō, -ōnis f touching; sense of touch

tāctus¹ ppp of **tangō**

tāctus², -ūs m touch, handling, sense of touch; influence

taeda, -ae f pitch pine, pinewood; torch; plank; (fig) wedding

taedet, -ēre, -uit and **-aesum est** vt (impers) to be weary (of), loathe

taedifer, -ī adj torch-bearing

taedium, -ī and **-iī** nt weariness, loathing

Taenaridēs, -idae m Spartan (esp Hyacinthus)

Taenarius, -is adj of Taenarus; Spartan

Taenarum, -ī nt, **Taenaron, -ī** nt, **Taenarus, -ī** m/f, **Taenaros, -ī** m/f town and promontory in S. Greece (now Matapan), lower world

taenia, -ae f hairband, ribbon

taesum est perf of **taedet**

taeter, -rī adj foul, hideous, repulsive

taetrē adv hideously

taetricus see **tetricus**

tagāx, -ācis adj light-fingered

Tagus, -ī m river of Lusitania (now Tagus)

tālāris adj reaching to the ankles ♦ ntpl winged sandals; a garment reaching to the ankles

tālārius adj of dice

Talāsius, -ī and **-iī** m god of weddings; wedding cry

tālea, -ae f rod, stake

talentum, -ī nt talent, a Greek weight about 25.4kg; a large sum of money (esp the Attic talent of 60 minae)

tāliō, -ōnis f retaliation in kind

tālis adj such; the following

talpa, -ae f mole

tālus, -ī m ankle; heel; (pl) knuckle bones, oblong dice

tam adv so, so much, so very

tamdiū adv so long, as long

tamen adv however, nevertheless, all the same

Tāmesis, -is, Tāmesa, -ae m Thames

tametsī conj although

tamquam adv as, just as, just like ♦ conj as if

Tanagra, -ae f town in Boeotia

Tanais, -is m river in Sarmatia (now Don)

Tanaquil, -ilis f wife of the elder Tarquin

tandem adv at last, at length, finally; (question) just

tangō, -ere, tetigī, tāctum vt to touch, handle; (food) to taste; (with force) to hit, strike; (with liquid) to sprinkle; (mind) to affect, move; (place) to reach; to border on; (task) to take in hand; (by trick) to take in, fool; (in words) to touch on, mention; **dē caelō tāctus** struck by lightning

tanquam see **tamquam**

Tantaleus adj see **Tantalus**

Tantalidēs, -idae m Pelops, Atreus, Thyestes or Agamemnon

Tantalis, -idis f Niobe or Hermione

Tantalus, -ī m father of Pelops (condemned to hunger and thirst in Tartarus, or to the threat of an overhanging rock)

tantillus adj so little, so small

tantisper adv so long, just for a moment

tantopere *adv* so much
tantulus *adj* so little, so small
tantum *adv* so much, so, as; only, merely; ~ **modo** only; ~ **nōn** all but, almost; ~ **quod** only just
tantummodo *adv* only
tantundem *adv* just as much, just so much
tantus *adj* so great; so little ♦ *nt* so much; so little; **tantī esse** be worth so much, be so dear, be so important; **tantō** so much, so far; (*with comp*) so much the; **tantō opere** so much; **in tantum** to such an extent; **tria tanta** three times as much
tantusdem *adj* just so great
tapēta, -ae *m*, **tapētia, -ium** *ntpl* carpet, tapestry, hangings
Taprobanē, -ēs *f* Ceylon
tardē *adv* slowly, tardily
tardēscō, -ere *vi* to become slow, falter
tardipēs, -edis *adj* limping
tarditās, -ātis *f* slowness, tardiness; (*mind*) dullness
tardiusculus *adj* rather slow
tardō, -āre, -āvī, -ātum *vt* to retard, impede ♦ *vi* to delay, go slow
tardus *adj* slow, tardy, late; (*mind*) dull; (*speech*) deliberate
Tarentīnus *adj* Tarentine
Tarentum, -ī *nt* town in S. Italy (*now* Taranto)
tarmes, -itis *m* woodworm
Tarpēius *adj* Tarpeian; **mōns** ~ *the Tarpeian Rock on the Capitoline Hill from which criminals were thrown*
tarpezīta, -ae *m* banker
Tarquiniēnsis *adj* of Tarquinii
Tarquiniī, -iōrum *mpl* ancient town in Etruria
Tarquinius[1] *adj* of Tarquin
Tarquinius[2]**, -ī** *m* Tarquin (*esp Priscus, the fifth king of Rome, and Superbus, the last king*)
Tarracīna, -ae *f*, **Tarracīnae, -ārum** *fpl* town in Latium
Tarracō, -ōnis *f* town in Spain (*now* Tarragona)
Tarracōnēnsis *adj see* **Tarracō**
Tarsēnsis *adj see* **Tarsus**
Tarsus, -ī *f* capital of Cilicia
Tartareus *adj* infernal
Tartarus, -ī *m*, **Tartaros, -ī** *m*, **Tartara, -ōrum** *ntpl* Tartarus, the lower world (*esp the part reserved for criminals*)
tat *interj* hallo there!
Tatius[1]**, -ī** *m* Sabine king (*who ruled jointly with Romulus*)
Tatius[2] *adj see* **Tatius**[1]
Taum, -ī *nt* Firth of Tay
taureus *adj* bull's ♦ *f* whip of bull's hide
Taurī, -ōrum *mpl* Thracians of the Crimea
tauriformis *adj* bull-shaped
Taurīnī, -ōrum *mpl* people of N. Italy (*near what is now* Turin)
taurīnus *adj* bull's
Tauromenītānus *adj see* **Tauromenium**
Tauromenium, -ī *and* **-iī** *nt* town in E. Sicily
taurus, -ī *m* bull
Taurus, -ī *m* mountain range in S.E. Asia Minor
taxātiō, -ōnis *f* valuing
taxeus *adj* of yews

taxillus, -ī *m* small dice
taxō, -āre *vt* to value, estimate
taxus, -ī *f* yew
Tāygeta, -ōrum *ntpl*, **Tāygetus, -ī** *m* mountain range in S. Greece
Tāygetē, -ēs *f* a Pleiad
tē *acc and abl of* **tū**
-te *suffix for* **tū**
Teānēnsis *adj see* **Teānum**
Teānum, -ī *nt* town in Apulia; town in Campania
techina, -ae *f* trick
Tecmessa, -ae *f* wife of Ajax
tēctor, -ōris *m* plasterer
tēctōriolum, -ī *nt* a little plaster
tēctōrium, -ī *and* **-iī** *nt* plaster, stucco
tēctōrius *adj* of a plasterer
tēctum, -ī *nt* roof, ceiling, canopy; house, dwelling, shelter
tēctus *ppp of* **tegō** ♦ *adj* hidden; secret, reserved, close
tēcum with you
Tegea, -ae *f* town in Arcadia
Tegeaeus *adj* Arcadian ♦ *m* the god Pan ♦ *f* Atalanta
Tegeātae, -ātārum *mpl* Tegeans
teges, -etis *f* mat
tegillum, -ī *nt* hood, cowl
tegimen, -inis *nt* covering
tegimentum, -ī *nt* covering
tegmen- *etc see* **tegim-**
tegō, -ere, tēxī, -tēctum *vt* to cover; to hide, conceal; to protect, defend; to bury; **latus tegere** walk by the side of
tēgula, -ae *f* tile; (*pl*) tiled roof
tegum- *etc see* **tegim-**
Tēius *adj* of Teos
tēla, -ae *f* web; warp; yarnbeam, loom; (*fig*) plan
Telamōn, -ōnis *m* father of Ajax
Tēlegonus, -ī *m* son of Ulysses and Circe
Tēlemachus, -ī *m* son of Ulysses and Penelope
Tēlephus, -ī *m* king of Mysia (*wounded by Achilles' spear*)
tellūs, -ūris *f* the earth; earth, ground; land, country
tēlum, -ī *nt* weapon, missile; javelin, sword; (*fig*) shaft, dart
temerārius *adj* accidental; rash, thoughtless
temerē *adv* by chance, at random; rashly, thoughtlessly; **nōn** ~ not for nothing; not easily; hardly ever
temeritās, -ātis *f* chance, rashness, thoughtlessness
temerō, -āre, -āvī, -ātum *vt* to desecrate, disgrace
tēmētum, -ī *nt* wine, alcohol
temnō, -ere *vt* to slight, despise
tēmō, -ōnis *m* beam (*of plough or carriage*); (ASTR) the Plough
Tempē *ntpl* famous valley in Thessaly
temperāmentum, -ī *nt* moderation, compromise
temperāns, -antis *pres p of* **temperō** ♦ *adj* moderate, temperate
temperanter *adv* with moderation
temperantia, -ae *f* moderation, self-control

temperātē *adv* with moderation

temperātiō, -ōnis *f* proper mixture, composition, constitution; organizing power

temperātor, -ōris *m* organizer

temperātus *ppp of* **temperō ♦** *adj* moderate, sober

temperī *adv* in time, at the right time

temperiēs, -ēī *f* due proportion; temperature, mildness

temperō, -āre, -āvī, -ātum *vt* to mix in due proportion, blend, temper; to regulate, moderate, tune; to govern, rule ♦ *vi* to be moderate, forbear, abstain; (*with dat*) to spare, be lenient to

tempestās, -ātis *f* time, season, period; weather; storm; (*fig*) storm, shower

tempestīvē *adv* at the right time, appropriately

tempestīvitās, -ātis *f* seasonableness

tempestīvus *adj* timely, seasonable, appropriate; ripe, mature; early

templum, -ī *nt* space marked off for taking auspices; open space, region, quarter; sanctuary; temple

temporārius *adj* for the time, temporary

temptābundus *adj* making repeated attempts

temptāmentum, -ī *nt* trial, attempt, proof

temptāmina, -um *ntpl* attempts, essays

temptātiō, -ōnis *f* trial, proof; attack

temptātor, -ōris *m* assailant

temptō, -āre, -āvī, -ātum *vt* to feel, test by touching; to make an attempt on, attack; to try, essay, attempt; to try to influence, tamper with, tempt, incite; **vēnās temptāre** feel the pulse

tempus, -oris *nt* time; right time, opportunity; danger, emergency, circumstance; (*head*) temple; (*verse*) unit of metre; (*verb*) tense; **tempore** at the right time, in time; **ad ~** at the right time; for the moment; **ante ~** too soon; **ex tempore** on the spur of the moment; to suit the circumstances; **in tempore** in time; **in ~** temporarily; **per ~** just in time; **prō tempore** to suit the occasion

tēmulentus *adj* intoxicated

tenācitās, -ātis *f* firm grip; stinginess

tenāciter *adv* tightly, firmly

tenāx, -ācis *adj* gripping, tenacious; sticky; (*fig*) firm, persistent; stubborn; stingy

tendicula, -ae *f* little snare

tendō, -ere, tetendī, tentum *and* **tēnsum** *vt* to stretch, spread; to strain; (*arrow*) to aim, shoot; (*bow*) to bend; (*course*) to direct; (*lyre*) to tune; (*tent*) to pitch; (*time*) to prolong; (*trap*) to lay ♦ *vi* to encamp; to go, proceed; to aim, tend; (*with inf*) to endeavour, exert oneself

tenebrae, -ārum *fpl* darkness, night; unconsciousness; death, blindness; (*place*) dungeon, haunt, the lower world; (*fig*) ignorance, obscurity

tenebricōsus *adj* gloomy

tenebrōsus *adj* dark, gloomy

Tenedius *adj see* **Tenedos**

Tenedos, Tenedus, -ī *f* Aegean island near Troy

tenellulus *adj* dainty little

teneō, -ēre, -uī *vt* to hold, keep; to possess, occupy, be master of; to attain, acquire; (*argument*) to maintain, insist; (*category*) to comprise; (*goal*) to make for; (*interest*) to fascinate; (*LAW*) to bind, be binding on; (*mind*) to grasp, understand, remember; (*movement*) to hold back, restrain ♦ *vi* to hold on, last, persist; (*rumour*) to prevail; **cursum tenēre** keep on one's course; **sē tenēre** remain; to refrain

tener, -ī *adj* tender, delicate; young, weak; effeminate; (*poet*) erotic

tenerāscō, -ere *vi* to grow weak

tenerē *adv* softly

teneritās, -ātis *f* weakness

tenor, -ōris *m* steady course; **ūnō tenōre** without a break, uniformly

tēnsa, -ae *f* carriage bearing the images of the gods in procession

tēnsus *ppp of* **tendō ♦** *adj* strained

tentā- *etc see* **temptā-**

tentīgō, -inis *f* lust

tentō *etc see* **temptō**

tentōrium, -ī *and* **-iī** *nt* tent

tentus *ppp of* **tendō**

tenuiculus *adj* paltry

tenuis *adj* thin, fine; small, shallow; (*air*) rarefied; (*water*) clear; (*condition*) poor, mean, insignificant; (*style*) refined, direct, precise

tenuitās, -ātis *f* thinness, fineness; poverty, insignificance; (*style*) precision

tenuiter *adv* thinly; poorly; with precision; superficially

tenuō, -āre, -āvī, -ātum *vt* to make thin, attenuate, rarefy; to lessen, reduce

tenus *prep* (*with gen or abl*) as far as, up to, down to; **verbō ~** in name, nominally

Teos, -ī *f* town on coast of Asia Minor (*birthplace of Anacreon*)

tepefaciō, -facere, -fēcī, -factum *vt* to warm

tepeō, -ēre *vi* to be warm, be lukewarm; (*fig*) to be in love

tepēscō, -ēscere, -uī *vi* to grow warm; to become lukewarm, cool off

tepidus *adj* warm, lukewarm

tepor, -ōris *m* warmth; coolness

ter *adv* three times, thrice

terdeciēns, terdeciēs *adv* thirteen times

terebinthus, -ī *f* turpentine tree

terebra, -ae *f* gimlet

terebrō, -āre *vt* to bore

terēdō, -inis *f* grub

Terentia, -iae *f* Cicero's wife

Terentius[1], -ī *m* Roman family name (*esp the comic poet Terence*)

Terentius[2], -iānus *adj see* **Terentius[1]**

teres, -etis *adj* rounded (*esp cylindrical*), smooth, shapely; (*fig*) polished, elegant

Tēreus, -eī *and* **-eos** *m* king of Thrace (*husband of Procne, father of Itys*)

tergeminus *adj* threefold, triple

tergeō, -gēre, -sī, -sum *vt* to wipe off, scour, clean; to rub up, burnish

terginum, -ī *nt* rawhide

tergiversātiō, -ōnis *f* refusal, subterfuge

tergiversor, -ārī, -ātus *vi* to hedge, boggle, be evasive

tergō *etc see* **tergeō**

tergum, -ī *nt* back; rear; (*land*) ridge; (*water*) surface; (*meat*) chine; (*skin*) hide, leather, *anything made of leather;* **terga vertere** take to flight; **ā tergō** behind, in the rear

tergus, -oris *see* **tergum**

termes, -itis *m* branch

Terminālia, -ium *ntpl Festival of the god of Boundaries*

terminātiō, -ōnis *f* decision; (*words*) clausula

terminō, -āre, -āvī, -ātum *vt* to set bounds to, limit; to define, determine; to end

terminus, -ī *m* boundary line, limit, bound; god of boundaries

ternī, -ōrum *adj* three each; three

terō, -ere, -trīvī, trītum *vt* to rub, crush, grind; to smooth, sharpen; to wear away, use up; (*road*) to frequent; (*time*) to waste; (*word*) to make commonplace

Terpsichorē, -ēs *f Muse of dancing*

terra, -ae *f* dry land, earth, ground, soil; land, country; **orbis terrārum** the world; **ubi terrārum** where in the world

terrēnus *adj* of earth; terrestrial, land- (*in cpds*) ◆ *nt* land

terreō, -ēre, -uī, -itum *vt* to frighten, terrify; to scare away; to deter

terrestris *adj* earthly, on earth, land- (*in cpds*)

terribilis *adj* terrifying, dreadful

terricula, -ōrum *ntpl* scare, bogy

terrificō, -āre *vt* to terrify

terrificus *adj* alarming, formidable

terrigena, -ae *m* earth-born

terriloquus *adj* alarming

territō, -āre *vt* to frighten, intimidate

territōrium, -ī *and* **-iī** *nt* territory

territus *adj* terrified

terror, -ōris *m* fright, alarm, terror; a terror

tersī *perf of* **tergeō**

tersus *ppp of* **tergeō** ◆ *adj* clean; neat, terse

tertiadecimānī, -ōrum *mpl* men of the thirteenth legion

tertiānus *adj* recurring every second day ◆ *f* a fever ◆ *mpl* men of the third legion

tertiō *adv* for the third time; thirdly

tertium *adv* for the third time

tertius *adj* third; **~ decimus (decumus)** thirteenth

terūncius, -ī *and* **-iī** *m* quarter-as; a fourth; (*fig*) farthing

tesqua, tesca, -ōrum *ntpl* waste ground, desert

tessella, -ae *f* cube of mosaic stone

tessera, -ae *f* cube, dice; (MIL) password; token (*for mutual recognition of friends*); ticket (*for doles*)

tesserārius, -ī *and* **-iī** *m* officer of the watch

testa, -ae *f* brick, tile; (*earthenware*) pot, jug, sherd; (*fish*) shell, shellfish

testāmentārius *adj* testamentary ◆ *m* forger of wills

testāmentum, -ī *nt* will, testament

testātiō, -ōnis *f* calling to witness

testātus *ppa of* **testor** ◆ *adj* public

testiculus, -ī *m* testicle

testificātiō, -ōnis *f* giving evidence, evidence

testificor, -ārī, -ātus *vt* to give evidence, vouch for; to make public, bring to light; to call to witness

testimōnium, -ī *and* **-iī** *nt* evidence, testimony; proof

testis¹, -is *m/f* witness; eyewitness

testis², -is *m* testicle

testor, -ārī, -ātus *vt* to give evidence, testify; to prove, vouch for; to call to witness, appeal to ◆ *vi* to make a will

testū (*abl* **-ū**) *nt* earthenware lid, pot

testūdineus *adj* of tortoiseshell, tortoise- (*in cpds*)

testūdō, -inis *f* tortoise; tortoiseshell; lyre, lute; (MIL) shelter for besiegers, covering of shields; (*building*) vault

testum, -i *nt* earthenware lid, pot

tēte *emphatic acc of* **tū**

tetendī *perf of* **tendō**

tēter *etc see* **taeter**

Tēthys, -os *f sea goddess;* the sea

tetigī *perf of* **tangō**

tetrachmum, tetradrachmum, -ī *nt* four drachmas

tetraō, -ōnis *m* blackcock, grouse or capercaillie

tetrarchēs, -ae *m* tetrarch, ruler

tetrarchia, -ae *f* tetrarchy

tetricus *adj* gloomy, sour

tetulī *archaic perf of* **ferō**

Teucer, -rī *m* son of Telamon of Salamis; son-in-law of Dardanus

Teucrī, -rōrum *mpl* Trojans

Teucria, -riae *f* Troy

Teutonī, -ōrum, Teutones, -um *mpl* Teutons (*a German people*)

Teutonicus *adj* Teutonic, German

tēxī *perf of* **tegō**

texō, -ere, -uī, -tum *vt* to weave; to plait; to build, make; (*fig*) to compose, contrive

textilis *adj* woven ◆ *nt* fabric

textor, -ōris *m* weaver

textrīnum, -ī *nt* weaving; shipyard

textūra, -ae *f* web, fabric

textus¹ *ppp of* **texō** ◆ *nt* web, fabric

textus², -ūs *m* texture

texuī *perf of* **texō**

Thāis, -idis *f an Athenian courtesan*

thalamus, -ī *m* room, bedroom; marriage bed; marriage

thalassicus *adj* sea-green

thalassinus *adj* sea-green

Thalēs, -is *and* **-ētis** *m early Greek philosopher (one of the seven wise men)*

Thalia, -ae *f Muse of comedy*

thallus, -ī *m* green bough

Thamyrās, -ae *m* blinded Thracian poet

Thapsitānus *adj see* **Thapsus**

Thapsus, Thapsos, -ī *f town in N. Africa (scene of Caesar's victory)*

Thasius *adj see* **Thasus**

Thasus, Thasos, -ī *f Greek island in N. Aegean*

Thaumantias, -dis *f* Iris

theātrālis *adj* of the theatre, in the theatre

theãtrum, **-ĩ** *nt* theatre; audience; *(fig)* theatre, stage

Thēbae, **-ārum** *fpl* Thebes *(capital of Boeotia)*; *town in Upper Egypt*

Thēbais, **-aidis** *f* Theban woman; *epic poem by Statius*

Thēbānus *adj* Theban

thēca, **-ae** *f* case, envelope

Themis, **-dis** *f* goddess of justice

Themistoclēs, **-ĩ** *and* **-is** *m* famous Athenian statesman

Themistoclēus *adj see* **Themistoclēs**

thēnsaurārius *adj* of treasure

thēnsaurus *see* **thēsaurus**

theologus, **-ĩ** *m* theologian

Theophrastus, **-ĩ** *m* Greek philosopher *(successor to Aristotle)*

Theopompēus, **-ĩnus** *adj see* **Theopompus**

Theopompus, **-ĩ** *m* Greek historian

thermae, **-ārum** *fpl* warm baths

Thermōdōn, **-ontis** *m* river of Pontus *(where the Amazons lived)*

Thermōdontēus, **-ontiacus** *adj* Amazonian

thermopŏlium *nt* restaurant serving warm drinks

thermōpotō, **-āre** *vt* to refresh with warm drinks

Thermopylae, **-ārum** *fpl* famous Greek pass defended by Leonidas

thēsaurus, **-ĩ** *m* treasure, store; storehouse, treasury

Thēseus, **-eĩ** *and* **-eos** *m* Greek hero *(king of Athens)*

Thēsēus, **-ēius** *adj* of Theseus, Athenian

Thēsĩdēs, **-ĩdae** *m* Hippolytus; *(pl)* Athenians

Thespiae, **-ārum** *fpl* Boeotian town near Helicon

Thespiēnsis, **Thespias**, **-adis** *adj* Thespian

Thespis, **-is** *m* traditional founder of Greek tragedy

Thessalia, **-iae** *f* Thessaly *(district of N. Greece)*

Thessalicus, **Thessalus**, **Thessalis**, **-idis** *adj* Thessalian

Thetis, **-idis** *and* **-idos** *f* sea nymph *(mother of Achilles)*; the sea

thiasus, **-ĩ** *m* Bacchic dance

Thoantēus *adj see* **Thoãs**

Thoãs, **-antis** *m* king of Crimea *(killed by Orestes)*, king of Lemnos *(father of Hypsipyle)*

tholus, **-ĩ** *m* rotunda

thōrãx, **-ācis** *m* breastplate

Thrãca, **-ae**, **Thrãcē**, **-ēs**, **Thrãcia**, **-iae** *f* Thrace

Thracius, **Thrēicius** *adj* Thracian

Thrasea, **-ae** *m* Stoic philosopher under Nero

Thrasymachus, **-ĩ** *m* Greek sophist

Thrãx, **-ācis** *m* Thracian; kind of gladiator

Thrēssa, **-ae**, **Thrēissa**, **-ae** *f* Thracian woman

Thrēx, **-ēcis** *m* kind of gladiator

Thūcydidēs, **-is** *m* famous Greek historian

Thūcydidius *adj* Thucydidean

Thūlē, **-ēs** *f* island in the extreme N. *(perhaps Shetland)*

thunnus *see* **thynnus**

thūr, **-is** *nt* = **tūs**

Thūriĩ, **-iōrum** *mpl* town in S. Italy

Thūrĩnus *adj see* **Thūriĩ**

thũs *see* **tũs**

thỹa, **thỹia**, **-ae** *f* citrus tree

Thybris, **-is** *and* **-idis** *m* (river) Tiber

Thyestēs, **-ae** *m* brother of Atreus *(whose son's flesh he served up to him to eat)*

Thyestēus *adj see* **Thyestēs**

Thyestiadēs, **-iadae** *m* Aegisthus

Thyias, **Thỹas**, **-adis** *f* Bacchante

Thỹlē *see* **Thūlē**

thymbra, **-ae** *f* savory

thymum, **-ĩ** *nt* garden thyme

Thỹnia, **-iae** *f* Bithynia

thynnus, **-ĩ** *m* tuna

Thỹnus, **Thỹniacus**, **Thỹnias** *adj* Bithynian

Thyōneus, **-eĩ** *m* Bacchus

thyrsus, **-ĩ** *m* Bacchic wand

tiãra, **-ae** *f*, **tiãrãs**, **-ae** *m* turban

Tiberiānus *adj see* **Tiberius**

Tiberĩnus', **Tiberĩnis** *adj see* **Tiberis**

Tiberĩnus², **-ĩnĩ** *m* Tiber

Tiberis, **Tibris**, **-is** *m* (river) Tiber

Tiberius, **-ĩ** *m* Roman praenomen *(esp the second emperor)*

tibi *dat of* **tũ**

tĩbia, **-ae** *f* shinbone; pipe, flute

tĩbĩcen, **-inis** *m* flute player; pillar

tĩbĩcina, **-ae** *f* flute player

tĩbĩcinium, **-ĩ** *and* **-iĩ** *nt* flute playing

Tibullus, **-ĩ** *m* Latin elegiac poet

Tĩbur, **-is** *nt* town on the river Anio *(now* Tivoli*)*

Tĩburs, **-tis**, **Tĩburtĩnus**, **Tĩburnus** *adj* Tiburtine

Tĩcĩnus, **-ĩ** *m* tributary of the river Po

Tigellĩnus, **-ĩ** *m* favourite of Nero

tigillum, **-ĩ** *nt* small log, small beam

tignārius *adj* working in wood; **faber** ~ carpenter

tignum, **-ĩ** *nt* timber, trunk, log

Tigrãnēs, **-is** *m* king of Armenia

tigris, **-is** *and* **-idis** *f* tiger

tĩlia, **-ae** *f* lime tree

Tĩmaeus, **-ĩ** *m* Sicilian historian; Pythagorean philosopher; a dialogue of Plato

timefactus *adj* frightened

timeō, **-ēre**, **-uĩ** *vt*, *vi* to fear, be afraid

timidē *adv* timidly

timiditãs, **-ãtis** *f* timidity, cowardice

timidus *adj* timid, cowardly

timor, **-ōris** *m* fear, alarm; a terror

tinctilis *adj* dipped in

tinctus *ppp of* **tingō**

tinea, **-ae** *f* moth, bookworm

tingō, **-gere**, **-xĩ**, **-ctum** *vt* to dip, soak; to dye, colour; *(fig)* to imbue

tinnĩmentum, **-ĩ** *nt* ringing noise

tinniō, **-ĩre** *vt*, *vi* to ring, tinkle

tinnĩtus, **-ũs** *m* ringing, jingle

tinnulus *adj* ringing, jingling

tintinnãbulum, **-ĩ** *nt* bell

tintinō, **-ãre** *vi* to ring

tĩnus, **-ĩ** *m* a shrub, laurustinus

tinxĩ *perf of* **tingō**

Tĩphys, **-os** *m* helmsman of the Argo

tippula, **-ae** *f* water spider

Tīresiās, -ae m blind soothsayer of Thebes
Tīridātēs, -ae m king of Armenia
tīrō, -ōnis m recruit, beginner
Tīrō, -ōnis m Cicero's freedman secretary
tīrōcinium, -ī and **-iī** nt first campaign; recruits; (fig) first attempt, inexperience
Tīrōniānus adj see **Tīrō**
tīrunculus, -ī m young beginner
Tīryns, -this f ancient town in S.E. Greece (home of Hercules)
Tīrynthius adj of Tiryns, of Hercules ♦ m Hercules
tis archaic gen of **tū**
Tīsiphonē, -ēs f a Fury
Tīsiphonēus adj guilty
Tītān, -ānis, Tītānus, -ānī m Titan (an ancient race of gods); the sun
Tītānius, Tītāniacus, Tītānis adj see **Tītān**
Tīthōnius adj see **Tīthōnus**
Tīthōnus, -ī m consort of Aurora (granted immortality without youth)
tītillātiō, -ōnis f tickling
tītillō, -āre vt to tickle
titubanter adv falteringly
titubātiō, -ōnis f staggering
titubō, -āre vi to stagger, totter; to stammer; to waver, falter
titulus, -ī m inscription, label, notice; title of honour; fame; pretext
Tityos, -ī m giant punished in Tartarus
Tmōlus, -ī m mountain in Lydia
toculiō, -ōnis m usurer
tōfus, -ī m tufa
toga, -ae f toga (dress of the Roman citizen); (fig) peace; ~ **candida** dress of election candidates; ~ **picta** ceremonial dress of a victor in triumph; ~ **praetexta** purple-edged toga of magistrates and children; ~ **pūra, ~ virīlis** plain toga of manhood
togātus adj wearing the toga ♦ m Roman citizen; client ♦ f drama on a Roman theme
togula, -ae f small toga
tolerābilis adj bearable, tolerable; patient
tolerābiliter adv patiently
tolerāns, -antis pres p of **tolerō** ♦ adj patient
toleranter adv patiently
tolerantia, -ae f endurance
tolerātiō, -ōnis f enduring
tolerātus adj tolerable
tolerō, -āre, -āvī, -ātum vt to bear, endure; to support, sustain
tollēnō, -ōnis m crane, derrick, lift
tollō, -ere, sustulī, sublātum vt to lift, raise; to take away, remove; to do away with, abolish, destroy; (anchor) to weigh; (child) to acknowledge, bring up; (mind) to elevate, excite, cheer; (passenger) to take on board; **signa tollere** decamp
Tolōsa, -ae f Toulouse
Tolōsānus adj see **Tolōsa**
tolūtim adv at a trot
tomāculum, -ī nt sausage
tōmentum, -ī nt stuffing, padding
Tomis, -is f town on the Black Sea (to which Ovid was exiled)
Tomītānus adj see **Tomis**

Tonāns, -antis m Thunderer (epithet of Jupiter)
tondeō, -ēre, totondī, tōnsum vt to shear, clip, shave; to crop, reap, mow; to graze, browse on; (fig) to fleece, rob
tonitrālis adj thunderous
tonitrus, -ūs m, **tonitrua, -uōrum** ntpl thunder
tonō, -āre, -uī vi to thunder ♦ vt to thunder out
tōnsa, -ae f oar
tōnsillae, -ārum fpl tonsils
tōnsor, -ōris m barber
tōnsōrius adj for shaving
tōnstrīcula, -ae f barber girl
tōnstrīna, -ae f barber's shop
tōnstrīx, -īcis f woman barber
tōnsūra, -ae f shearing, clipping
tōnsus¹ ppp of **tondeō**
tōnsus², -ūs m coiffure
tōphus see **tōfus**
topiārius adj of ornamental gardening ♦ m topiarist ♦ f topiary
topicē, -ēs f the art of finding topics
toral, -ālis nt valance
torcular, -āris, torcularium, -ī nt press
toreuma, -tis nt embossed work, relief
tormentum, -ī nt windlass, torsion catapult, artillery; shot; rack, torture; (fig) torment, anguish
tormina, -um ntpl colic
torminōsus adj subject to colic
tornō, -āre, -āvī, -ātum vt to turn (in a lathe), round off
tornus, -ī m lathe
torōsus adj muscular
torpēdō, -inis f numbness, lethargy; (fish) electric ray
torpeō, -ēre vi to be stiff, be numb; to be stupefied
torpēscō, -ēscere, -uī vi to grow stiff, numb, listless
torpidus adj benumbed
torpor, -ōris m numbness, torpor, listlessness
torquātus adj wearing a neckchain
Torquātus, -ī m surname of Manlius
torqueō, -quēre, -sī, -tum vt to turn, twist, bend, wind; (missile) to whirl, hurl, brandish; (body) to rack, torture; (mind) to torment
torquēs, torquis, -is m/f neckchain, necklace, collar
torrēns, -entis pres p of **torreō** ♦ adj scorching, hot; rushing, rapid ♦ m torrent
torreō, -ēre, -uī, tostum vt to parch, scorch, roast
torrēscō, -ere vi to become parched
torridus adj parched, dried up; frostbitten
torris, -is m brand, firebrand
torsī perf of **torqueō**
tortē adv awry
tortilis adj twisted, winding
tortor¹, -ārī vi to writhe
tortor², -ōris m torturer, executioner
tortuōsus adj winding; (fig) complicated
tortus¹ ppp of **torqueō** ♦ adj crooked; complicated
tortus², -ūs m twisting, writhing

torulus, -ī m tuft (of hair)

torus, -ī m knot, bulge; muscle, brawn; couch, bed; (earth) bank, mound; (language) ornament

torvitās, -ātis f wildness, grimness

torvus adj wild, grim, fierce

tostus ppp of **torreō**

tot adj (indecl) so many, as many

totidem adj (indecl) just as many, the same number of

totiēns, totiēs adv so often, as often

totondī perf of **tondeō**

tōtus (gen **-īus**, dat **-ī**) adj entire, the whole, all; entirely, completely taken up with; **ex tōtō** totally; **in tōtō** on the whole

toxicum, -ī nt poison

trabālis adj for beams; **clāvus ~** large nail

trabea, -ae f ceremonial robe

trabeātus adj wearing a ceremonial robe

trabs, -abis f beam, timber; tree; ship; roof

Trāchīn, -īnis f town in Thessaly (where Hercules cremated himself)

Trāchīnius adj see **Trāchīn**

tractābilis adj manageable, tractable

tractātiō, -ōnis f handling, treatment

tractātus, -ūs m handling

tractim adv slowly, little by little

tractō, -āre, -āvī, -ātum vt to maul; to handle, deal with, manage; (activity) to conduct, perform; (person) to treat; (subject) to discuss, consider

tractus¹ ppp of **trahō ♦** adj fluent

tractus², -ūs m dragging, pulling, drawing; train, track; (place) extent, region, district; (movement) course; (time) lapse; (word) drawling

trādidī perf of **trādō**

trāditiō, -ōnis f surrender; handing down

trāditor, -ōris m traitor

trāditus ppp of **trādō**

trādō, -ere, -idī, -itum vt to hand over, deliver, surrender; to commit, entrust; to betray; to bequeath, hand down; (narrative) to relate, record; (teaching) to propound; **sē trādere** surrender, devote oneself

trādūcō, trānsdūcō, -ūcere, -ūxī, -uctum vt to bring across, lead over, transport across; to transfer; to parade, make an exhibition of (in public); (time) to pass, spend

trāductiō, -ōnis f transference; (time) passage; (word) metonymy

trāductor, -ōris m transferrer

trāductus ppp of **trādūcō**

trādux, -ucis m vine layer

tragicē adv dramatically

tragicōmoedia, -ae f tragicomedy

tragicus adj of tragedy, tragic; in the tragic manner, lofty; terrible, tragic ♦ m writer of tragedy

tragoedia, -ae f tragedy; (fig) bombast

tragoedus, -ī m tragic actor

trāgula, -ae f kind of javelin

trahea, -ae f sledge

trahō, -here, -xī, -ctum vt to draw, drag, pull, take with one; to pull out, lengthen; to draw together, contract; to carry off, plunder; (liquid) to drink, draw; (money) to squander; (wool) to

spin; (fig) to attract; (appearance) to take on; (consequence) to derive, get; (praise, blame) to ascribe, refer; (thought) to ponder; (time) to spin out

trāiciō, -icere, -iēcī, -iectum vt to throw across, shoot across; (troops) to get across, transport; (with weapon) to pierce, stab; (river, etc) to cross; (fig) to transfer ♦ vi to cross

trāiectiō, -ōnis f crossing, passage; (fig) transferring; (RHET) exaggeration; (words) transposition

trāiectus¹ ppp of **trāiciō**

trāiectus², -ūs m crossing, passage

trālāt- etc see **trānslāt-**

Trallēs, -ium fpl town in Lydia

Trālliānus adj see **Trallēs**

trālūceō etc see **trānslūceō**

trāma, -ae f woof, web

trāmes, -itis m footpath, path

trāmittō etc see **trānsmittō**

trānatō etc see **trānsnatō**

trānō, -āre, -āvī, -ātum vt, vi to swim across; (air) to fly through

tranquillē adv quietly

tranquillitās, -ātis f quietness, calm; (fig) peace, quiet

tranquillō, -āre vt to calm

tranquillus adj quiet, calm ♦ nt calm sea

trāns prep (with acc) across, over, beyond

trānsabeō, -īre, -iī vt to pierce

trānsāctor, -ōris m manager

trānsāctus ppp of **trānsigō**

trānsadigō, -ere vt to drive through, pierce

Trānsalpīnus adj Transalpine

trānscendō, trānsscendō, -endere, -endī, -ēnsum vt, vi to pass over, surmount; to overstep, surpass, transgress

trānscrībō, trānsscrībō, -bere, -psī, -ptum vt to copy out; (fig) to make over, transfer

trānscurrō, -rere, -rī, -sum vt, vi to run across, run past, traverse

trānscursus, -ūs m running through; (speech) cursory remark

trānsd- etc see **trānsd-**

trānsēgī perf of **trānsigō**

trānsenna, -ae f net, snare; trellis, latticework

trānseō, -īre, -iī, -itum vt, vi to pass over, cross over; to pass along or through; to pass by; to outstrip, surpass, overstep; (change) to turn into; (speech) to mention briefly, leave out, pass on; (time) to pass, pass away

trānsferō, -ferre, -tulī, -lātum vt to bring across, transport, transfer; (change) to transform; (language) to translate; (RHET) to use figuratively; (time) to postpone; (writing) to copy

trānsfīgō, -gere, -xī, -xum vt to pierce; to thrust through

trānsfīxus ppp of **trānsfīgō**

trānsfodiō, -odere, -ōdī, -ossum vt to run through, stab

trānsfōrmis adj changed in shape

trānsfōrmō, -āre vt to change in shape

trānsfossus ppp of **trānsfodiō**

trānsfuga, -ae m/f deserter

trānsfugiō, -ugere, -ūgī vi to desert, come over

trānsfugium, **-ī** *and* **-iī** *nt* desertion
trānsfundō, **-undere**, **-ūdī**, **-ūsum** *vt* to decant, transfuse
trānsfūsiō, **-ōnis** *f* transmigration
trānsfūsus *ppp of* **trānsfundō**
trānsgredior, **-dī**, **-ssus** *vt*, *vi* to step across, cross over, cross; to pass on; to exceed
trānsgressiō, **-ōnis** *f* passage; (*words*) transposition
trānsgressus¹ *ppa of* **trānsgredior**
trānsgressus², **-ūs** *m* crossing
trānsiciō *etc see* **trāiciō**
trānsigō, **-igere**, **-ēgī**, **-āctum** *vt* to carry through, complete, finish; (*difference*) to settle; (*time*) to pass, spend; (*with* **cum**) to put an end to; (*with weapon*) to stab
trānsiī *perf of* **trānseō**
trānsiliō, **trānssiliō**, **-īre**, **-uī** *vi* to jump across ♦ *vt* to leap over; (*fig*) to skip, disregard; to exceed
trānsitiō, **-ōnis** *f* passage; desertion; (*disease*) infection
trānsitō, **-āre** *vi* to pass through
trānsitus¹ *ppp of* **trānseō**
trānsitus², **-ūs** *m* passing over, passage; desertion; passing by; transition
trānslātīcius, **trālātīcius** *adj* traditional, customary, common
trānslātiō, **trālātiō**, **-ōnis** *f* transporting, transferring; (*language*) metaphor
trānslātīvus *adj* transferable
trānslātor, **-ōris** *m* transferrer
trānslātus *ppp of* **trānsferō**
trānslegō, **-ere** *vt* to read through
trānslūceō, **-ēre** *vi* to be reflected; to shine through
trānsmarīnus *adj* overseas
trānsmeō, **-āre** *vi* to cross
trānsmigrō, **-āre** *vi* to emigrate
trānsmissiō, **-ōnis** *f* crossing
trānsmissus¹ *ppp of* **trānsmittō**
trānsmissus², **-ūs** *m* crossing
trānsmittō, **-ittere**, **-īsī**, **-issum** *vt* to send across, put across; to let pass through; to transfer, entrust, devote; to give up, pass over; (*place*) to cross over, go through, pass ♦ *vi* to cross
trānsmontānus *adj* beyond the mountains
trānsmoveō, **-ovēre**, **-ōvī**, **-ōtum** *vt* to move, transfer
trānsmūtō, **-āre** *vt* to shift
trānsnatō, **trānatō**, **-āre** *vi* to swim across ♦ *vt* to swim
trānsnō *etc see* **trānō**
Trānspadānus *adj* north of the Po
trānspectus, **-ūs** *m* view
trānspiciō, **-ere** *vt* to look through
trānspōnō, **-ōnere**, **-osuī**, **-ositum** *vt* to transfer
trānsportō, **-āre** *vt* to carry across, transport, remove
trānspositus *ppp of* **trānspōnō**
Trānsrhēnānus *adj* east of the Rhine
trānss- *etc see* **trāns-**
Trānstiberīnus *adj* across the Tiber

trānstineō, **-ēre** *vi* to get through
trānstrum, **-ī** *nt* thwart
trānstulī *perf of* **trānsferō**
trānsultō, **-āre** *vi* to jump across
trānsūtus *adj* pierced
trānsvectiō, **-ōnis** *f* crossing
trānsvectus *ppp of* **trānsvehō**
trānsvehō, **-here**, **-xī**, **-ctum** *vt* to carry across, transport
trānsvehor, **-hī**, **-ctus** *vi* to cross, pass over; (*parade*) to ride past; (*time*) to elapse
trānsverberō, **-āre** *vt* to pierce through, wound
trānsversus, **trāversus** *adj* lying across, crosswise, transverse; **digitum trānsversum** a finger's breadth; **dē trānsversō** unexpectedly; **ex trānsversō** sideways
trānsvolitō, **-āre** *vt* to fly through
trānsvolō, **-āre** *vt*, *vi* to fly across, fly through; to move rapidly across; to fly past, disregard
trānsvorsus *etc see* **trānsversus**
trapētus, **-ī** *m* olive mill, oil mill
trapezīta *etc see* **tarpezīta**
Trapezūs, **-ūntis** *f* Black Sea town (*now* Trabzon)
Trasumennus, **Trasimēnus**, **-ī** *m* lake in Etruria (*where Hannibal defeated the Romans*)
trāv- *see* **trānsv-**
trāvectiō *etc see* **trānsvectiō**
traxī *perf of* **trahō**
trecēnī, **-ōrum** *adj* three hundred each
trecentēsimus *adj* three-hundredth
trecentī, **-ōrum** *num* three hundred
trecentiēns, **trecentiēs** *adv* three hundred times
trechedīpna, **-ōrum** *ntpl* dinner shoes (*of parasites*)
tredecim *num* thirteen
tremebundus *adj* trembling
tremefaciō, **-facere**, **-fēcī**, **-factum** *vt* to shake
tremendus *adj* formidable, terrible
tremēscō, **tremīscō**, **-ere** *vi* to begin to shake ♦ *vt* to be afraid of
tremō, **-ere**, **-uī** *vi* to tremble, quake, quiver ♦ *vt* to tremble at, dread
tremor, **-ōris** *m* shaking, quiver, tremor; earthquake
tremulus *adj* trembling, shivering
trepidanter *adv* with agitation
trepidātiō, **-ōnis** *f* agitation, alarm, consternation
trepidē *adv* hastily, in confusion
trepidō, **-āre**, **-āvī**, **-ātum** *vi* to be agitated, bustle about, hurry; to be alarmed; to flicker, quiver ♦ *vt* to start at
trepidus *adj* restless, anxious, alarmed; alarming, perilous
trēs, **trium** *num* three
trēssis, **-is** *m* three asses
trēsvirī, **triumvirōrum** *mpl* three commissioners, triumvirs
Trēverī, **-ōrum** *mpl* people of E. Gaul (*about what is now* Trier)
Trēvericus *adj see* **Trēverī**
triangulum, **-ī** *nt* triangle
triangulus *adj* triangular

triāriī, -ōrum *mpl* the third line (*in Roman battle order*), the reserves

tribuārius *adj* of the tribes

tribūlis, -is *m* fellow tribesman

trībulum, -ī *nt* threshing sledge

tribulus, -ī *m* star thistle

tribūnal, -ālis *nt* platform; judgment seat; camp platform, cenotaph

tribūnātus, -ūs *m* tribuneship, rank of tribune

tribūnicius *adj* of a tribune ✦ *m* ex-tribune

tribūnus, -ī *m* tribune; ~ **plēbis** tribune of the people, *a magistrate who defended the rights of the plebeians*; ~ **mīlitum** *or* **mīlitāris** military tribune, *an officer under the legatus*; **tribūnī aerāriī** paymasters

tribuō, -uere, -uī, -ūtum *vt* to assign, allot; to give, bestow, pay; to concede, allow; to ascribe, attribute; (*subject*) to divide; (*time*) to devote

tribus, -ūs *m* tribe

tribūtārius *adj*: **tribūtāriae tabellae** letters of credit

tribūtim *adv* by tribes

tribūtiō, -ōnis *f* distribution

tribūtum, -ī *nt* contribution, tribute, tax

tribūtus¹ *ppp of* **tribuō**

tribūtus² *adj* arranged by tribes

trīcae, -ārum *fpl* nonsense; tricks, vexations

trīcēnī, -ōrum *adj* thirty each, in thirties

triceps, -ipitis *adj* three-headed

trīcēsimus *adj* thirtieth

trichila, -ae *f* arbour, summerhouse

trīciēns, trīciēs *adv* thirty times

trīclīnium, -ī *and* **-iī** *nt* dining couch; dining room

trīcō, -ōnis *m* mischief-maker

trīcor, -ārī *vi* to make mischief, play tricks

tricorpor, -is *adj* three-bodied

tricuspis, -idis *adj* three-pointed

tridēns, -entis *adj* three-pronged ✦ *m* trident

tridentifer, -ī *adj* trident-wielding

tridentiger, -i *adj* trident-wielding

triduum, -ī *nt* three days

triennia, -ium *ntpl* a triennial festival

triennium, -ī *and* **-iī** *nt* three years

triēns, -entis *m* a third; (*coin*) a third of an as; (*measure*) a third of a pint

trientābulum, -ī *nt* land given by the State as a third of a debt

trientius *adj* sold for a third

triērarchus, -ī *m* captain of a trireme

triēris, -is *f* trireme

trietēricus *adj* triennial ✦ *ntpl* festival of Bacchus

trietēris, -idis *f* three years; a triennial festival

trifāriam *adv* in three parts, in three places

trifaux, -aucis *adj* three-throated

trifidus *adj* three-forked

trifōrmis *adj* triple

trifūr, -ūris *m* archthief

trifurcifer, -ī *m* hardened criminal

trigeminus *adj* threefold, triple ✦ *mpl* triplets

trīgintā *num* thirty

trigōn, -ōnis *m* a ball game

trilībris *adj* three-pound

trilinguis *adj* three-tongued

trilīx, -icis *adj* three-ply, three-stranded

trimēstris *adj* of three months

trimetrus, -ī *m* trimeter

trīmus *adj* three years old

Trīnacria, -iae *f* Sicily

Trīnacrius, Trīnacris, -idis *adj* Sicilian

trīnī, -ōrum *adj* three each, in threes; triple

Trinobantēs, -um *mpl* British tribe in East Anglia

trinōdis *adj* three-knotted

triōbolus, -ī *m* half-a-drachma

Triōnēs, -um *mpl* the Plough; the Little Bear

tripartītō *adv* in or into three parts

tripartītus, tripertītus *adj* divided into three parts

tripectorus *adj* three-bodied

tripedālis *adj* three-foot

tripert- *etc see* **tripart-**

tripēs, -edis *adj* three-legged

triplex, -icis *adj* triple, threefold ✦ *nt* three times as much ✦ *mpl* three-leaved writing tablet

triplus *adj* triple

Triptolemus, -ī *m* inventor of agriculture, judge in Hades

tripudiō, -āre *vi* to dance

tripudium, -ī *and* **-iī** *nt* ceremonial dance, dance; *a favourable omen* (*when the sacred chickens ate greedily*)

tripūs, -odis *f* tripod; the Delphic oracle

triquetrus *adj* triangular; Sicilian

trirēmis *adj* with three banks of oars ✦ *f* trireme

trīs *etc see* **trēs**

triscurria, -ōrum *ntpl* sheer fooling

tristē *adv* sadly; severely

tristiculus *adj* rather sad

tristificus *adj* ominous

tristimōnia, -ae *f* sadness

tristis *adj* sad, glum, melancholy; gloomy, sombre, dismal; (*taste*) bitter; (*smell*) offensive; (*temper*) severe, sullen, ill-humoured

tristitia, -ae *f* sadness, sorrow, melancholy; moroseness, severity

tristitiēs, -ēī *f* sorrow

trisulcus *adj* three-forked

tritavus, -ī *m* great-great-great-grandfather

trīticeus *adj* of wheat, wheaten

trīticum, -ī *nt* wheat

Trītōn, -ōnis *m* sea god (son of Neptune); African lake (*where Minerva was born*)

Trītōnius, -ōniacus, -ōnis *adj* of Lake Triton, of Minerva ✦ *f* Minerva

trītūra, -ae *f* threshing

trītus¹ *ppp of* **terō** ✦ *adj* well-worn; (*judgment*) expert; (*language*) commonplace, trite

trītus², -ūs *m* rubbing, friction

triumphālis *adj* triumphal ✦ *ntpl* insignia of a triumph

triumphō, -āre, -āvī, -ātum *vi* to celebrate a triumph; to triumph, exult ✦ *vt* to triumph over, win by conquest

triumphus, -ī *m* triumphal procession, victory parade; triumph, victory

triumvir, -ī *m* commissioner, triumvir; mayor (*of a provincial town*)

triumvirālis *adj* triumviral

triumvirātus, -ūs m office of triumvir, triumvirate

triumvirī, -ōrum mpl three commissioners, triumvirs

trivenēfica, -ae f old witch

trīvī perf of **terō**

Trivia, -ae f Diana

triviālis adj common, popular

trivium, -ī and -iī nt crossroads; public street

trivius adj of the crossroads

Trōas, -adis f the district of Troy, Troad; Trojan woman ♦ adj Trojan

trochaeus, -ī m trochee; tribrach

trochlea, -ae f block and tackle

trochus, -ī m hoop

Trōglodytae, -ārum mpl cave dwellers of Ethiopia

Trōia, -ae f Troy

Trōilus, -ī m son of Priam

Trōiugena, -ae m/f Trojan; Roman

Trōius, Trōiānus, Trōicus adj Trojan

tropaeum, -ī nt victory memorial, trophy; victory; memorial, token

Trōs, -ōis m king of Phrygia; Trojan

trucīdātiō, -ōnis f butchery

trucīdō, -āre, -āvī, -ātum vt to slaughter, massacre

truculentē adv see **truculentus**

truculentia, -ae f ferocity, inclemency

truculentus adj ferocious, grim, wild

trudis, -is f pike

trūdō, -dere, -sī, -sum vt to push, thrust, drive; (buds) to put forth

trulla, -ae f ladle, scoop; washbasin

truncō, -āre, -āvī, -ātum vt to lop off, maim, mutilate

truncus, -ī m (tree) trunk, bole; (human) trunk, body; (abuse) blockhead ♦ adj maimed, broken, stripped (of); defective

trūsī perf of **trūdō**

trūsitō, -āre vt to keep pushing

trūsus ppp of **trūdō**

trutina, -ae f balance, scales

trux, -ucis adj savage, grim, wild

trȳgōnus, -ī m stingray

tū pron you, thou

tuātim adv in your usual fashion

tuba, -ae f trumpet, war trumpet

tuber, -is f kind of apple tree

tūber, -is nt swelling, lump; (food) truffle

tubicen, -inis m trumpeter

tubilūstria, -ōrum ntpl festival of trumpets

tuburcinor, -ārī vi to gobble up, guzzle

tubus, -ī m pipe

tuditō, -āre vt to strike repeatedly

tueor, -ērī, -itus and -tūtus vt to see, watch, look; to guard, protect, keep

tugurium, -ī and -iī nt hut, cottage

tuitiō, -ōnis f defence

tuitus ppa of **tueor**

tulī perf of **ferō**

Tulliānum, -ī nt State dungeon of Rome

Tulliānus adj see **Tullius**

Tulliola, -ae f little Tullia (Cicero's daughter)

Tullius, -ī and -iī m Roman family name (esp the sixth king), the orator Cicero

Tullus, -ī m third king of Rome

tum adv (time) then, at that time; (sequence) then, next ♦ conj moreover, besides; **tum ... tum** at one time ... at another; **tum ... cum** at the time when, whenever; **cum ... tum** not only ... but; **tum dēmum** only then; **tum ipsum** even then; **tum māximē** just then; **tum vērō** then more than ever

tumefaciō, -facere, -fēcī, -factum vt to make swell; (fig) to puff up

tumeō, -ēre vi to swell, be swollen; (emotion) to be excited; (pride) to be puffed up; (language) to be turgid

tumēscō, -ēscere, -uī vi to begin to swell, swell up

tumidus adj swollen, swelling; (emotion) excited, enraged; (pride) puffed up; (language) bombastic

tumor, -ōris m swelling, bulge; hillock; (fig) commotion, excitement

tumulō, -āre vt to bury

tumulōsus adj hilly

tumultuārius adj hasty; (troops) emergency

tumultuātiō, -ōnis f commotion

tumultuō, -āre, tumultuor, -ārī vi to make a commotion, be in an uproar

tumultuōsē adv see **tumultuōsus**

tumultuōsus adj uproarious, excited, turbulent

tumultus, -ūs m commotion, uproar, disturbance; (MIL) rising, revolt, civil war; (weather) storm; (mind) disorder

tumulus, -ī m mound, hill; burial mound, barrow

tunc adv (time) then, at that time; (sequence) then, next; ~ **dēmum** only then; ~ **quoque** then too; even so

tundō, -ere, tutudī, tūnsum and tūsum vt to beat, thump, hammer; (grain) to pound; (speech) to din, importune

Tūnēs, -ētis m Tunis

tunica, -ae f tunic; (fig) skin, husk

tunicātus adj wearing a tunic

tunicula, -ae f little tunic

tūnsus ppp of **tundō**

tuor etc see **tueor**

turba, -ae f disorder, riot, disturbance; brawl, quarrel; crowd, mob, troop, number

turbāmenta, -ōrum ntpl propaganda

turbātē adv in confusion

turbātiō, -ōnis f confusion

turbātor, -ōris m agitator

turbātus ppp of **turbō¹** ♦ adj troubled, disorderly

turbellae, -ārum fpl stir, row

turben etc see **turbō²**

turbidē adv in disorder

turbidus adj confused, wild, boisterous; (water) troubled, muddy; (fig) disorderly, troubled, alarmed, dangerous

turbineus adj conical

turbō¹, -āre, -āvī, -ātum vt to disturb, throw into confusion; (water) to trouble, make muddy

turbō², **-inis** *m* whirl, spiral, rotation; reel, whorl, spindle; (*toy*) top; (*wind*) tornado, whirlwind; (*fig*) storm

turbulentē, turbulenter *adv* wildly

turbulentus *adj* agitated, confused, boisterous, stormy; troublemaking, seditious

turdus, -ī *m* thrush

tūreus *adj* of incense

turgeō, -gēre, -sī *vi* to swell, be swollen; (*speech*) to be bombastic

turgēscō, -ere *vi* to swell up, begin to swell; (*fig*) to become enraged

turgidulus *adj* poor swollen

turgidus *adj* swollen, distended; bombastic

tūribulum, -ī *nt* censer

tūricremus *adj* incense-burning

tūrifer, -ī *adj* incense-producing

tūrilegus *adj* incense-gathering

turma, -ae *f* troop, squadron (*of cavalry*); crowd

turmālis *adj* of a troop; equestrian

turmātim *adv* troop by troop

Turnus, -ī *m* Rutulian king (*chief opponent of Aeneas*)

turpiculus *adj* ugly little; slightly indecent

turpificātus *adj* debased

turpilucricupidus *adj* fond of filthy lucre

turpis *adj* ugly, deformed, unsightly; base, disgraceful ◆ *nt* disgrace

turpiter *adv* repulsively; shamefully

turpitūdō, -inis *f* deformity; disgrace, infamy

turpō, -āre *vt* to disfigure, soil

turriger, -ī *adj* turreted

turris, -is *f* tower, turret; siege tower; (*elephant*) howdah; (*fig*) mansion

turrītus *adj* turreted; castellated; towering

tursī *perf of* **turgeō**

turtur, -is *m* turtledove

tūs, tūris *nt* incense, frankincense

Tusculānēnsis *adj* at Tusculum

Tusculānum, -ānī *nt* villa at Tusculum (*esp Cicero's*)

Tusculānus *adj* Tusculan

Tusculum, -ī *nt* Latin town near Rome

tūsculum, -ī *nt* a little incense

Tusculus *adj* Tusculan

Tuscus *adj* Etruscan

tussiō, -īre *vi* to cough, have a cough

tussis, -is *f* cough

tūsus *ppp of* **tundō**

tūtāmen, -inis *nt* defence

tūtāmentum, -ī *nt* protection

tūte *emphatic form of* **tū**

tūtē *adv* safely, in safety

tūtēla, -ae *f* keeping, charge, protection; (*of minors*) guardianship, wardship; (*person*) watcher, guardian; ward, charge

tūtemet *emphatic form of* **tū**

tūtor¹, -ārī, -ātus, tūtō, -āre *vt* to watch, guard, protect; to guard against

tūtor², -ōris *m* protector; (*LAW*) guardian

tutudī *perf of* **tundō**

tūtus *ppp of* **tueor** ◆ *adj* safe, secure; cautious ◆ *nt* safety

tuus *adj* your, yours, thy, thine; your own, your proper; of you

Tȳdeus, -eī *and* **-eos** *m* father of Diomedes

Tȳdīdēs, -īdae *m* Diomedes

tympanotrība, -ae *m* timbrel player

tympanum, typanum, -ī *nt* drum, timbrel (*esp of the priests of Cybele*); (*mechanism*) wheel

Tyndareus, -eī *m* king of Sparta (*husband of Leda*)

Tyndaridae, -idārum *mpl* Castor and Pollux

Tyndaris, -idis *f* Helen; Clytemnestra

Typhōeus, -eos *m* giant under Etna

Typhōius, -is *adj see* **Typhōeus**

typus, -ī *m* figure

tyrannicē *adv see* **tyrannicus**

tyrannicīda, -ae *m* tyrannicide

tyrannicus *adj* tyrannical

tyrannis, -idis *f* despotism, tyranny

tyrannoctonus, -ī *m* tyrannicide

tyrannus, -ī *m* ruler, king; despot, tyrant

Tyrās, -ae *m* (river) Dniester

Tyrius *adj* Tyrian, Phoenician, Carthaginian; purple

tȳrotarīchos, -ī *m* dish of salt fish and cheese

Tyrrhēnia, -iae *f* Etruria

Tyrrhēnus *adj* Etruscan, Tyrrhenian

Tyrtaeus, -ī *m* Spartan war poet

Tyrus, Tyros, -ī *f* Tyre (*famous Phoenician seaport*)

Uu

ūber¹, -is *nt* breast, teat; (*fig*) richness
ūber², -is *adj* fertile, plentiful, rich (in); (*language*)
full, copious
ūberius (*superl* **-rime**) *compar* more fully, more
copiously
ūbertās, -ātis *f* richness, plenty, fertility
ūbertim *adv* copiously
ubī *adv* (*interrog*) where; (*rel*) where, in which,
with whom; when
ubīcumque *adv* wherever; everywhere
Ubiī, -ōrum *mpl* German tribe on the lower Rhine
ubīnam *adv* where (in fact)?
ubīquāque *adv* everywhere
ubīque *adv* everywhere, anywhere
ubiubī *adv* wherever
ubīvīs *adv* anywhere
ūdus *adj* wet, damp
ulcerō, -āre *vt* to make sore, wound
ulcerōsus *adj* full of sores; wounded
ulcīscor, -ī, ultus *vt* to take vengeance on,
punish; to take vengeance for, avenge
ulcus, -eris *nt* sore, ulcer; ~ **tangere** touch on a
delicate subject
ūlīgō, -inis *f* moisture, marshiness
Ulixēs, -is *m* Ulysses, Odysseus (*king of Ithaca, hero
of Homer's Odyssey*)
ullus (*gen* **-īus**, *dat* **-ī**) *adj* any
ulmeus *adj* of elm
ulmus, -ī *f* elm; (*pl*) elm rods
ulna, -ae *f* elbow; arm; (*measure*) ell
ulterior, -ōris *compar* farther, beyond, more
remote
ulterius *compar of* **ultrā**
ultimus *superl* farthest, most remote, the end
of; (*time*) earliest, latest, last; (*degree*) extreme,
greatest, lowest ♦ *ntpl* the end; **ultimum** for
the last time; **ad ultimum** finally
ultiō, -ōnis *f* vengeance, revenge
ultor, -ōris *m* avenger, punisher
ultrā *adv* beyond, farther, besides ♦ *prep* (*with acc*)
beyond, on the far side of; (*time*) past; (*degree*)
over and above
ultrīx, -īcis *adj* avenging
ultrō *adv* on the other side, away; besides; of
one's own accord, unasked, voluntarily
ultrō tribūta *ntpl* State expenditure for public
works
ultus *ppa of* **ulcīscor**
ulula, -ae *f* screech owl
ululātus, -ūs *m* wailing, shrieking, yells,
whoops

ululō, -āre, -āvī, -ātum *vi* to shriek, yell, howl
♦ *vt* to cry out to
ulva, -ae *f* sedge
umbella, -ae *f* parasol
Umber, -rī *adj* Umbrian ♦ *m* Umbrian dog
umbilīcus, -ī *m* navel; (*fig*) centre; (*book*) roller
end; (*sea*) cockle or pebble
umbō, -ōnis *m* boss (*of a shield*); elbow
umbra, -ae *f* shadow, shade; (*dead*) ghost; (*diner*)
uninvited guest; (*fish*) grayling; (*painting*)
shade; (*place*) shelter, school, study; (*unreality*)
semblance, mere shadow
umbrāculum, -ī *nt* arbour; school; parasol
umbrāticola, -ae *m* lounger
umbrāticus *adj* fond of idling; in retirement
umbrātilis *adj* in retirement, private, academic
Umbria, -riae *f* Umbria (*district of central Italy*)
umbrifer, -ī *adj* shady
umbrō, -āre *vt* to shade
umbrōsus *adj* shady
ūmectō, -āre *vt* to wet, water
ūmectus *adj* damp, wet
ūmeō *vi* to be damp, be wet
umerus, -ī *m* upper arm, shoulder
ūmēscō, -ere *vi* to become damp, get wet
ūmidē *adv* with damp
ūmidulus *adj* dampish
ūmidus *adj* wet, damp, dank, moist
ūmor, -ōris *m* liquid, fluid, moisture
umquam, unquam *adv* ever, at any time
ūnā *adv* together
ūnanimāns, -antis *adj* in full agreement
ūnanimitās, -ātis *f* concord
ūnanimus *adj* of one accord, harmonious
ūncia, -ae *f* a twelfth; (*weight*) ounce; (*length*)
inch
ūnciārius *adj* of a twelfth; (*interest*) 8 $^1/_3$ per cent
ūnciātim *adv* little by little
uncīnātus *adj* barbed
ūnciola, -ae *f* a mere twelfth
ūnctiō, -ōnis *f* anointing
ūnctitō, -āre *vt* to anoint regularly
ūnctiusculus *adj* rather too unctuous
ūnctor, -ōris *m* anointer
ūnctūra, -ae *f* anointing (*of the dead*)
ūnctus *ppp of* **ungō** ♦ *adj* oiled; greasy, resinous;
(*fig*) rich, sumptuous ♦ *nt* sumptuous dinner
uncus¹, -ī *m* hook, grappling-iron
**uncus² ** *adj* hooked, crooked, barbed
unda, -ae *f* wave, water; (*fig*) stream, surge

unde *adv* from where, whence; from whom, from which; ~ **petitur** the defendant; ~ **unde** from wherever; somehow or other

ūndeciēns, ūndeciēs *adv* eleven times

ūndecim *num* eleven

ūndecimus *adj* eleventh

undecumque *adv* from wherever

ūndēnī, -ōrum *adj* eleven each, eleven

ūndēnōnāgintā *num* eighty-nine

ūndeoctōgintā *num* seventy-nine

ūndēquadrāgintā *num* thirty-nine

ūndēquīnquāgēsimus *adj* forty-ninth

ūndēquīnquāgintā *num* forty-nine

ūndēsexāgintā *num* fifty-nine

ūndētrīcēsimus *adj* twenty-ninth

ūndēvīcēsimānī, -ōrum *mpl* men of the nineteenth legion

ūndēvīcēsimus *adj* nineteenth

ūndēvīgintī *num* nineteen

undique *adv* from every side, on all sides, everywhere; completely

undisonus *adj* sea-roaring

undō, -āre *vi* to surge; (*fig*) to roll, undulate

undōsus *adj* billowy

ūnetvīcēsimānī, -ōrum *mpl* men of the twenty-first legion

ūnetvīcēsimus *adj* twenty-first

ungō, unguō, -gere, ūnxī, ūnctum *vt* to anoint, smear, grease

unguen, -inis *nt* fat, grease, ointment

unguentārius, -ī *and* **-iī** *m* perfumer

unguentātus *adj* perfumed

unguentum, -ī *nt* ointment, perfume

unguiculus, -ī *m* fingernail

unguis, -is *m* nail (*of finger or toe*); claw, talon, hoof; **ad unguem** with perfect finish; **trānsversum unguem** a hair's breadth; **dē tenerō unguī** from earliest childhood

ungula, -ae *f* hoof, talon, claw

unguō *etc see* **ungō**

ūnicē *adv* solely, extraordinarily

ūnicolor, -ōris *adj* all one colour

ūnicus *adj* one and only, sole; unparalleled, unique

ūnifōrmis *adj* simple

ūnigena, -ae *adj* only-begotten; of the same parentage

ūnimanus *adj* with only one hand

ūniō, -ōnis *m* a single large pearl

ūniter *adv* together in one

ūniversālis *adj* general

ūniversē *adv* in general

ūniversitās, -ātis *f* the whole; the universe

ūniversus *adj* all taken together, entire, general ♦ *mpl* the community as a whole ♦ *nt* the universe; **in ūniversum** in general

unquam *etc see* **umquam**

ūnus *num* one ♦ *adj* sole, single, only; one and the same; the outstanding one; an individual; ~ **et alter** one or two; ~ **quisque** every single one; **nēmō** ~ not a single one; **ad ūnum** to a man

ūnxī *perf of* **ungō**

ūpiliō, -ōnis *m* shepherd

upupa, -ae *f* hoopoe; crowbar

Ūrania, -ae, Ūraniē, -ēs *f Muse of astronomy*

urbānē *adv* politely; wittily, elegantly

urbānitās, -ātis *f* city life; refinement, politeness; wit

urbānus *adj* town (*in cpds*), city (*in cpds*); refined, polite; witty, humorous; impertinent ♦ *m* townsman

urbicapus, -ī *m* taker of cities

urbs, urbis *f* city; Rome

urceolus, -ī *m* jug

urceus, -ī *m* pitcher, ewer

ūrēdō, -inis *f* blight

urgeō, -gēre, -sī *vt, vi* to force on, push forward; to press hard on, pursue closely; to crowd, hem in; to burden, oppress; (*argument*) to press, urge; (*work, etc*) to urge on, ply hard, follow up

ūrīna, -ae *f* urine

ūrīnātor, -ōris *m* diver

urna, -ae *f* water jar, urn; voting urn, lottery urn, cinerary urn, money jar

urnula, -ae *f* small urn

ūrō, -ere, ūssī, ūstum *vt* to burn; to scorch, parch; (*cold*) to nip; (*MED*) to cauterize; (*rubbing*) to chafe, hurt; (*passion*) to fire, inflame; (*vexation*) to annoy, oppress

ursa, -ae *f* she-bear, bear; (*ASTR*) Great Bear, Lesser Bear

ursī *perf of* **urgeō**

ursīnus *adj* bear's

ursus, -ī *m* bear

urtīca, -ae *f* nettle

ūrus, -ī *m* wild ox

Usipetēs, -etum, Usipetiī, -iōrum *mpl German tribe on the Rhine*

ūsitātē *adv* in the usual manner

ūsitātus *adj* usual, familiar

uspiam *adv* anywhere, somewhere

usquam *adv* anywhere; in any way, at all

usque *adv* all the way (to, from), right on, right up to; (*time*) all the time, as long as, continuously; (*degree*) even, as much as; ~ **quāque** everywhere; every moment; on every occasion

ūssī *perf of* **ūrō**

ūstor, -ōris *m* cremator

ūstulō, -āre *vt* to burn

ūstus *ppp of* **ūrō**

ūsūcapiō¹, -apere, -ēpī, -aptum *vt* to acquire ownership of, take over

ūsūcapiō², -ōnis *f* ownership by use or possession

ūsūra, -ae *f* use, enjoyment; interest, usury

ūsūrārius *adj* for use and enjoyment; paying interest

ūsurpātiō, -ōnis *f* making use (of)

ūsurpō, -āre, -āvī, -ātum *vt* to make use of, employ, exercise; (*LAW*) to take possession of, enter upon; (*senses*) to perceive, make contact with; (*word*) to call by, speak of

ūsus¹ *ppa of* **ūtor**

ūsus², -ūs *m* use, enjoyment, practice; experience, skill; usage, custom; intercourse, familiarity; usefulness, benefit, advantage; need, necessity; ~ **est**, ~ **venit** there is need (of);

ūsuī esse, **ex ūsū esse** be of use, be of service; **ūsū venīre** happen; **~ et frūctus** use and enjoyment, usufruct

ut, **utī** *adv* how; *(rel)* as; *(explaining)* considering how, according as; *(place)* where; **ut in ōrātōre** for an orator ♦ *conj* **1**. *(with indic: manner)* as; *(: concessive)* while, though; *(: time)* when, as soon as **2**. *(with subj: expressing the idea of a verb)* that, to; *(: purpose)* so that, to; *(: causal)* seeing that; *(: concessive)* granted that, although; *(: result)* that, so that; *(: fear)* that not; **ut ... ita** while ... nevertheless; **ut nōn** without; **ut quī** seeing that I, he *etc*; **ut quisque māximē** the more

utcumque, **utcunque** *adv* however; whenever; one way or another

ūtēnsilis *adj* of use ♦ *ntpl* necessaries

uter *(gen* **-rīus**, *dat* **-rī)**, **-ra**, **-rum** *pron* which *(of two)*, the one that; one or the other

ūter, **-ris** *m* bag, skin, bottle

utercumque, **utracumque**, **utrumcumque** *pron* whichever (of two)

uterlibet, **utralibet**, **utrumlibet** *pron* whichever (of the two) you please, either one

uterque, **utraque**, **utrumque** *pron* each *(of two)*, either, both

uterum, **-ī** *nt*, **uterus**, **-ī** *m* womb; child; belly

utervīs, **utravīs**, **utrumvīs** *pron* whichever (of two) you please; either

utī *etc see* **ut**

ūtī *infin of* **ūtor**

ūtibilis *adj* useful, serviceable

Utica, **-ae** *f town near Carthage (where Cato committed suicide)*

Uticēnsis *adj see* **Utica**

ūtilis *adj* useful, expedient, profitable; fit (for)

ūtilitās, **-ātis** *f* usefulness, expediency, advantage

ūtiliter *adv* usefully, advantageously

utinam *adv* I wish!, would that!, if only!

utique *adv* at least, by all means, especially

ūtor, **ūtī**, **ūsus** *vi (with abl)* to use, employ; to possess, enjoy; to practise, experience; *(person)* to be on intimate terms with, find; **ūtendum rogāre** borrow

utpote *adv* inasmuch as, as being

ūtrārius, **-ī** *and* **-iī** *m* watercarrier

ūtriculārius, **-ī** *and* **-iī** *m* bagpiper

utrimque, **utrinque** *adv* on both sides, on either side

utrō *adv* in which direction

utrobīque *see* **utrubīque**

utrōque *adv* in both directions, both ways

utrubī *adv* on which side

utrubīque *adv* on both sides, on either side

utrum *adv* whether

utut *adv* however

ūva, **-ae** *f* grape, bunch of grapes; vine; cluster

ūvēscō, **-ere** *vi* to become wet

ūvidulus *adj* moist

ūvidus *adj* wet, damp; drunken

uxor, **-ōris** *f* wife

uxorcula, **-ae** *f* little wife

uxōrius *adj* of a wife; fond of his wife

Vv

vacāns, -antis *pres p of* **vacō** ♦ *adj* unoccupied; (*woman*) single

vacātiō, -ōnis *f* freedom, exemption; exemption from military service; payment for exemption from service

vacca, -ae *f* cow

vaccīnium, -ī *and* **-iī** *nt* hyacinth

vaccula, -ae *f* heifer

vacēfiō, -ierī *vi* to become empty

vacillō, -āre *vi* to stagger, totter; to waver, be unreliable

vacīvē *adv* at leisure

vacīvitās, -ātis *f* want

vacīvus *adj* empty, free

vacō, -āre, -āvī, -ātum *vi* to be empty, vacant, unoccupied; to be free, aloof (from); to have time for, devote one's time to; **vacat** there is time

vacuātus *adj* empty

vacuēfaciō, -facere, -fēcī, -factum *vt* to empty, clear

vacuitās, -ātis *f* freedom, exemption; vacancy

vacuus *adj* empty, void, wanting; vacant; free (from), clear; disengaged, at leisure; (*value*) worthless; (*woman*) single ♦ *nt* void, space

vadimōnium, -ī *and* **-iī** *nt* bail, security; ~ **sistere** appear in court; ~ **dēserere** default

vādō, -ere *vi* to go, go on, make one's way

vador, -ārī, -ātus *vt* to bind over by bail

vadōsus *adj* shallow

vadum, -ī *nt* shoal, shallow, ford; water, sea; bottom

vae *interj* woe!, alas!

vafer, -rī *adj* crafty, subtle

vafrē *adv* artfully

vagē *adv* far afield

vāgīna, -ae *f* sheath, scabbard; (*grain*) husk

vāgiō, -īre *vi* to cry

vāgītus, -ūs *m* crying, bleating

vagor, -ārī, -ātus *vi* to wander, rove, go far afield; (*fig*) to spread

vāgor, -ōris *m* cry

vagus *adj* wandering, unsettled; (*fig*) fickle, wavering, vague

vah *interj* (*expressing surprise, joy, anger*) oh!, ah!

valdē *adv* greatly, intensely; very

valē, valēte *interj* goodbye, farewell

valēns, -entis *pres p of* **valeō** ♦ *adj* strong, powerful, vigorous; well, healthy

valenter *adv* strongly

valentulus *adj* strong

valeō, -ēre, -uī, -itum *vi* to be strong; to be able, have the power (to); to be well, fit, healthy; (*fig*) to be powerful, effective, valid; (*force*) to prevail; (*money*) to be worth; (*word*) to mean; **valēre apud** have influence over, carry weight with; **valēre iubeō** say goodbye to; **valē dīcō** say goodbye; **valeās** away with you!

valēscō, -ere *vi* to grow strong, thrive

valētūdinārium, -ī *and* **-iī** *nt* hospital

valētūdō, -inis *f* state of health, health; illness

valgus *adj* bow-legged

validē *adv* powerfully, very

validus *adj* strong, powerful, able; sound, healthy; effective

vallāris *adj* (*decoration*) for scaling a rampart

vallēs, vallis, -is *f* valley

vallō, -āre, -āvī, -ātum *vt* to palisade, entrench, fortify

vallum, -ī *nt* rampart, palisade, entrenchment

vallus, -ī *m* stake; palisade, rampart; (*comb*) tooth

valvae, -ārum *fpl* folding door

vānēscō, -ere *vi* to disappear, pass away

vānidicus, -ī *m* liar

vāniloquentia, -ae *f* idle talk

vāniloquus *adj* untruthful; boastful

vānitās, -ātis *f* emptiness; falsehood, worthlessness, fickleness; vanity

vānitūdō, -inis *f* falsehood

vannus, -ī *f* winnowing fan

vānus *adj* empty; idle, useless, groundless; false, untruthful, unreliable; conceited

vapidus *adj* spoilt, corrupt

vapor, -ōris *m* steam, vapour; heat

vapōrārium, -ī *and* **-iī** *nt* steam pipe

vapōrō, -āre *vt* to steam, fumigate, heat ♦ *vi* to burn

vappa, -ae *f* wine that has gone flat; (*person*) good-for-nothing

vāpulō, -āre *vi* to be flogged, beaten; to be defeated

variantia, -ae *f* diversity

variātiō, -ōnis *f* difference

vāricō, -āre *vi* to straddle

vāricōsus *adj* varicose

vāricus *adj* with feet wide apart

variē *adv* diversely, with varying success

varietās, -ātis *f* difference, diversity

variō, -āre, -āvī, -ātum *vt* to diversify, variegate; to make different, change, vary ♦ *vi* to change colour; to differ, vary

varius *adj* coloured, spotted, variegated; diverse, changeable, various; *(ability)* versatile; *(character)* fickle

Varius, -ī *m* epic poet *(friend of Vergil and Horace)*

varix, -icis *f* varicose vein

Varrō, -ōnis *m* consul defeated at Cannae; antiquarian writer of Cicero's day

Varrōniānus *adj see* **Varrō**

vārus *adj* knock-kneed; crooked; contrary

vas, vadis *m* surety, bail

vās, vāsis *nt*, **vāsa, -ōrum** *ntpl* vessel, dish; utensil, implement; *(MIL)* baggage

vāsārium, -ī *and* **-iī** *nt* furnishing allowance *(of a governor)*

vāsculārius, -ī *and* **-iī** *m* metalworker

vāsculum, -ī *nt* small dish

vastātiō, -ōnis *f* ravaging

vastātor, -ōris *m* ravager

vastē *adv (size)* enormously; *(speech)* coarsely

vastificus *adj* ravaging

vastitās, -ātis *f* desolation, desert; devastation, destruction

vastitiēs, -ēī *f* ruin

vastō, -āre, -āvī, -ātum *vt* to make desolate, denude; to lay waste, ravage

vastus *adj* empty, desolate, uncultivated; ravaged, devastated; *(appearance)* uncouth, rude; *(size)* enormous, vast

vāsum *etc see* **vās**

vātēs, -is *m/f* prophet, prophetess; poet, bard

Vāticānus *adj* Vatican *(hill on right bank of Tiber)*

vāticinātiō, -ōnis *f* prophesying, prediction

vāticinātor, -ōris *m* prophet

vāticinor, -ārī, -ātus *vt, vi* to prophesy; to celebrate in verse; to rave, rant

vāticinus *adj* prophetic

-ve *conj* or; either ... or

vēcordia, -ae *f* senselessness; insanity

vēcors, -dis *adj* senseless, foolish, mad

vectīgal, -ālis *nt* tax, honorarium *(to a magistrate)*; income

vectiō, -ōnis *f* transport

vectis, -is *m* lever, crowbar; *(door)* bolt, bar

Vectis, -is *f* Isle of Wight

vectō, -āre *vt* to carry; *(pass)* to ride

vector, -ōris *m* carrier; passenger, rider

vectōrius *adj* transport *(in cpds)*

vectūra, -ae *f* transport; *(payment)* carriage, fare

vectus *ppp of* **vehō**

Vediovis, -is = **Vēiovis**

vegetus *adj* lively, sprightly

vēgrandis *adj* small

vehemēns, -entis *adj* impetuous, violent; powerful, strong

vehementer *adv* violently, eagerly; powerfully, very much

vehementia, -ae *f* vehemence

vehiculum, -ī *nt* carriage, cart; *(sea)* vessel

vehō, -here, -xī, -ctum *vt* to carry, convey; *(pass)* to ride, sail, drive

Vēiēns, -entis, Vēientānus, Vēius *adj see* **Vēiī**

Vēiī, -ōrum *mpl* ancient town in S. Etruria

Vēiovis, -is *m* ancient Roman god *(anti-Jupiter)*

vel *conj* or, or perhaps; or rather; or else; either ... or ◆ *adv* even, if you like; perhaps; for instance; **vel māximus** the very greatest

Vēlābrum, -ī *nt* low ground between Capitol and Palatine hills

vēlāmen, -inis *nt* covering, garment

vēlāmentum, -ī *nt* curtain; *(pl)* draped olive branches carried by suppliants

vēlārium, -ī *and* **-iī** *nt* awning

vēlātī, -ōrum *mpl* supernumerary troops

vēles, -itis *m* light-armed soldier, skirmisher

vēlifer, -ī *adj* carrying sail

vēlificātiō, -ōnis *f* sailing

vēlificō, -āre *vi* to sail ◆ *vt* to sail through

vēlificor, -ārī *vi* to sail; *(with dat)* to make an effort to obtain

Velīnus, -ī *m* a Sabine lake

vēlitāris *adj* of the light-armed troops

vēlitātiō, -ōnis *f* skirmishing

vēlitēs *pl of* **vēles**

vēlitor, -ārī *vi* to skirmish

vēlivolus *adj* sail-winged

velle *infin of* **volō²**

vellicō, -āre *vt* to pinch, pluck, twitch; *(speech)* to taunt, disparage

vellō, -ere, vellī *and* **vulsī, vulsum** *vt* to pluck, pull, pick; to pluck out, tear up

vellus, -eris *nt* fleece, pelt; wool; fleecy clouds

vēlō, -āre, -āvī, -ātum *vt* to cover up, clothe, veil; *(fig)* to conceal

vēlōcitās, -ātis *f* speed, rapidity

vēlōciter *adv* rapidly

vēlōx, -ōcis *adj* fast, quick, rapid

vēlum, -ī *nt* sail; curtain, awning; **rēmis vēlīsque** with might and main; **vēla dare** set sail

velut, velutī *adv* as, just as; for instance; just as if

vēmēns *etc see* **vehemēns**

vēna, -ae *f* vein, artery; vein of metal; water course; *(fig)* innermost nature of feelings, talent, strength; **vēnās temptāre** feel the pulse; **vēnās tenēre** have one's finger on the pulse *(of)*

vēnābulum, -ī *nt* hunting spear

Venāfrānus *adj see* **Venāfrum**

Venāfrum, -ī *nt* Samnite town famous for olive oil

vēnālicius *adj* for sale ◆ *m* slave dealer

vēnālis *adj* for sale; bribable ◆ *m* slave offered for sale

vēnāticus *adj* hunting- *(in cpds)*

vēnātiō, -ōnis *f* hunting; a hunt; public show of fighting wild beasts; game

vēnātor, -ōris *m* hunter

vēnātōrius *adj* hunter's

vēnātrīx, -īcis *f* huntress

vēnātūra, -ae *f* hunting

vēnātus, -ūs *m* hunting

vēndibilis *adj* saleable; *(fig)* popular

vēnditātiō, -ōnis *f* showing off, advertising

vēnditātor, -ōris *m* braggart

vēnditiō, -ōnis *f* sale

vēnditō, -āre *vt* to try to sell; to praise up, advertise; **sē vēnditāre** ingratiate oneself *(with)*

vēnditor, -ōris *m* seller

vēndō (*pass* **vēneō**), **-ere**, **-idī**, **-itum** *vt* to sell; to betray; to praise up

venēficium, -ī *and* **-iī** *nt* poisoning; sorcery

venēficus *adj* poisonous; magic ◆ *m* sorcerer ◆ *f* sorceress

venēnātus *adj* poisonous; magic

venēnifer, -ī *adj* poisonous

venēnō, -āre *vt* to poison

venēnum, -ī *nt* drug, potion; dye; poison; magic charm; (*fig*) mischief; charm

vēneō, -īre, -iī, -itum *vi* to be sold

venerābilis *adj* honoured, venerable

venerābundus *adj* reverent

venerātiō, -ōnis *f* respect, reverence

venerātor, -ōris *m* reverencer

Venereus, Venerius *adj* of Venus ◆ *m* highest throw (*at dice*)

veneror, -ārī, -ātus *vt* to worship, revere, pray to; to honour, respect; to ask for, entreat

Venetia, -iae *f* district of the Veneti

Veneticus *adj see* **Venetia**

Venetus *adj* Venetian; (*colour*) blue

vēnī *perf of* **veniō**

venia, -ae *f* indulgence, favour, kindness; permission, leave; pardon, forgiveness; **bonā tuā veniā** by your leave; **bonā veniā audīre** give a fair hearing

vēniī *perf of* **vēneō**

veniō, -īre, vēnī, ventum *vi* to come; (*fig*) to fall into, incur, go as far as; **in amīcitiam venīre** make friends (with); **in spem venīre** entertain hopes

vēnor, -ārī, -ātus *vt, vi* to hunt, chase

venter, -ris *m* stomach, belly; womb, unborn child

ventilātor, -ōris *m* juggler

ventilō, -āre *vt* to fan, wave, agitate

ventiō, -ōnis *f* coming

ventitō, -āre *vi* to keep coming, come regularly

ventōsus *adj* windy; like the wind; fickle; conceited

ventriculus, -ī *m* belly; (*heart*) ventricle

ventriōsus *adj* pot-bellied

ventulus, -ī *m* breeze

ventus, -ī *m* wind

vēnūcula, -ae *f* kind of grape

vēnum, vēnō for sale

vēnumdō, vēnundō, -āre, -edī, -atum *vt* to sell, put up for sale

Venus, -eris *f* goddess of love; planet Venus; highest throw (*at dice*)

venus, -eris *f* charm, beauty; love, mating

Venusia, -iae *f* town in Apulia (*birthplace of Horace*)

Venusīnus *adj see* **Venusia**

venustās, -ātis *f* charm, beauty

venustē *adv* charmingly

venustulus *adj* charming little

venustus *adj* charming, attractive, beautiful

vēpallidus *adj* very pale

veprēcula, -ae *f* little brier bush

veprēs, -is *m* thornbush, bramblebush

vēr, vēris *nt* spring; **vēr sacrum** offerings of firstlings

vērātrum, -ī *nt* hellebore

vērāx, -ācis *adj* truthful

verbēna, -ae *f* vervain; (*pl*) sacred boughs carried by heralds or priests

verber, -is *nt* lash, scourge; (*missile*) strap; (*pl*) flogging, strokes

verberābilis *adj* deserving a flogging

verberātiō, -ōnis *f* punishment

verbereus *adj* deserving a flogging

verberō¹, -āre, -āvī, -ātum *vt* to flog, beat, lash

verberō², -ōnis *m* scoundrel

verbōsē *adv* verbosely

verbōsus *adj* wordy

verbum, -ī *nt* word; saying, expression; (GRAM) verb; (*pl*) language, talk; **~ ē verbō, ~ dē verbō, ~ prō verbō** literally; **ad ~** word for word; **verbī causā (grātiā)** for instance; **verbō** orally; briefly; **verba dare** cheat, fool; **verba facere** talk; **meīs verbīs** in my name

vērē *adv* really, truly, correctly

verēcundē *adv see* **verēcundus**

verēcundia, -ae *f* modesty, shyness; reverence, dread; shame

verēcundor, -ārī *vi* to be bashful, feel shy

verēcundus *adj* modest, shy, bashful

verendus *adj* venerable

vereor, -ērī, -itus *vt, vi* to fear, be afraid; to revere, respect

verētrum, -ī *nt* the private parts

Vergiliae, -ārum *fpl* the Pleiads

Vergilius, -ī *m* Vergil, Virgil (*famous epic poet*)

vergō, -ere *vt* to turn, incline ◆ *vi* to turn, incline, decline; (*place*) to face

vēridicus *adj* truthful

vērī similis *adj* probable

vērī similitūdō, -inis *f* probability

vēritās, -ātis *f* truth, truthfulness; reality, real life; (*character*) integrity; (*language*) etymology

veritus *ppa of* **vereor**

vermiculātus *adj* inlaid with wavy lines, mosaic

vermiculus, -ī *m* grub

vermina, -um *ntpl* stomach pains

vermis, -is *m* worm

verna, -ae *f* slave born in his master's home

vernāculus *adj* of home-born slaves; native

vernīlis *adj* slavish; (*remark*) smart

vernīliter *adv* slavishly

vernō, -āre *vi* to bloom, be spring-like; to be young

vernula, -ae *f* young home-born slave; native

vērnus *adj* of spring

vērō *adv* in fact, assuredly; (*confirming*) certainly, yes; (*climax*) indeed; (*adversative*) but in fact; **minimē ~** certainly not

Vērōna, -ae *f* town in N. Italy (*birthplace of Catullus*)

Vērōnēnsis *adj see* **Vērōna**

verpus, -ī *m* circumcised man

Verrēs, -is *m* praetor prosecuted by Cicero

verrēs, -is *m* boar

verrīnus *adj* boar's, pork (*in cpds*)

Verrius, Verrīnus *adj see* **Verrēs**

verrō, -rere, -rī, -sum *vt* to sweep, scour; to sweep away, carry off

verrūca, -ae *f* wart; (*fig*) slight blemish

verrūcōsus *adj* warty

verruncō, -āre *vi* to turn out successfully
versābundus *adj* rotating
versātilis *adj* revolving; versatile
versicolor, -ōris *adj* of changing or various colours
versiculus, -ī *m* short line; *(pl)* unpretentious verses
versificātor, -ōris *m* versifier
versipellis *adj* of changed appearance; crafty ♦ *m* werewolf
versō, -āre, -āvī, -ātum *vt* to keep turning, wind, twist; *(fig)* to upset, disturb, ruin; *(mind)* to ponder, consider
versor, -ārī, -ātus *vi* to live, be, be situated; to be engaged (in), be busy (with)
versum *adv* turned, in the direction
versūra, -ae *f* borrowing to pay a debt; loan
versus¹ *ppp of* **vertō** ♦ *adv* turned, in the direction
versus², -ūs *m* line, row; verse; *(dance)* step
versūtē *adv* craftily
versūtiae, -ārum *fpl* tricks
versūtiloquus *adj* sly
versūtus *adj* clever; crafty, deceitful
vertex, -icis *m* whirlpool, eddy; whirlwind; crown of the head, head; top, summit; *(sky)* pole
verticōsus *adj* eddying, swirling
vertīgō, -inis *f* turning round; dizziness
vertō, -tere, -tī, -sum *vt* to turn; to turn over, invert; to turn round; to turn into, change, exchange; *(cause)* to ascribe, impute; *(language)* to translate; *(war)* to overthrow, destroy; *(pass)* to be (in), be engaged (in) ♦ *vi* to turn; to change; to turn out; **in fugam vertere** put to flight; **terga vertere** flee; **solum vertere** emigrate; **vitiō vertere** blame; **annō vertente** in the course of a year
Vertumnus, -ī *m* god of seasons
verū, -ūs *nt* spit; javelin
vērum¹ *adv* truly, yes; but actually; but, yet; **~ tamen** nevertheless
vērum², -ī *nt* truth, reality; right; **vērī similis** probable
vērus *adj* true, real, actual; truthful; right, reasonable
verūtum, -ī *nt* javelin
verūtus *adj* armed with the javelin
vervēx, -ēcis *m* wether
vēsānia, -ae *f* madness
vēsāniēns, -entis *adj* raging
vēsānus *adj* mad, insane; furious, raging
vescor, -ī *vi* (with abl) to feed, eat; to enjoy
vescus *adj* little, feeble; corroding
vēsīca, -ae *f* bladder; purse; football
vēsīcula, -ae *f* small bladder, blister
vespa, -ae *f* wasp
Vespasiānus, -ī *m* Roman emperor
vesper, -is *and* **-ī** *m* evening; supper; evening star; west; **vespere, vesperī** in the evening
vespera, -ae *f* evening
vesperāscō, -ere *vi* to become evening, get late
vespertīliō, -ōnis *m* bat
vespertīnus *adj* evening (in cpds), in the evening; western

vesperūgō, -inis *f* evening star
Vesta, -ae *f* Roman goddess of the hearth
Vestālis *adj* Vestal ♦ *f* virgin priestess of Vesta
vester, -rī *adj* your, yours
vestibulum, -ī *nt* forecourt, entrance
vestīgium, -ī *and* **-iī** *nt* footstep, footprint, track; *(fig)* trace, sign, vestige; *(time)* moment, instant; **ē vestīgiō** instantly
vestīgō, -āre, -āvī, -ātum *vt* to track, trace, search for, discover
vestīmentum, -ī *nt* clothes
vestiō, -īre, -iī, -ītum *vt* to clothe, dress; to cover, adorn
vestipica, -ae *f* wardrobe woman
vestis, -is *f* clothes, dress; coverlet, tapestry, blanket; *(snake)* slough; **vestem mūtāre** change one's clothes; go into mourning
vestispica *etc see* **vestipica**
vestītus, -ūs *m* clothes, dress; covering; **mūtāre vestītum** go into mourning; **redīre ad suum vestītum** come out of mourning
Vesuvius, -ī *m* (the volcano) Vesuvius
veterānus *adj* veteran
veterāscō, -scere, -vī *vi* to grow old
veterātor, -ōris *m* expert, old hand; sly fox
veterātōriē *adv see* **veterātōrius**
veterātōrius *adj* crafty
veterīnus *adj* of burden ♦ *f and ntpl* beasts of burden
veternōsus *adj* lethargic, drowsy
veternus, -ī *m* lethargy, drowsiness
vetitus *ppp of* **vetō** ♦ *nt* prohibition
vetō, -āre, -uī, -itum *vt* to forbid, prohibit, oppose; *(tribune)* to protest
vetulus *adj* little old, poor old
vetus, -eris *adj* old, former ♦ *mpl* the ancients ♦ *fpl* the old shops (in the Forum) ♦ *ntpl* antiquity, tradition
vetustās, -ātis *f* age, long standing; antiquity; great age, future age
vetustus *adj* old, ancient; old-fashioned
vexāmen, -inis *nt* shaking
vexātiō, -ōnis *f* shaking; trouble, distress
vexātor, -ōris *m* troubler, opponent
vexī *perf of* **vehō**
vexillārius, -ī *and* **-iī** *m* standard-bearer, ensign; *(pl)* special reserve of veterans
vexillum, -ī *nt* standard, flag; company, troop; **~ prōpōnere** hoist the signal for battle
vexō, -āre, -āvī, -ātum *vt* to shake, toss, trouble, distress, injure, attack
via, -ae *f* road, street, way; journey, march; passage; *(fig)* way, method, fashion; the right way; **viā** properly; **inter viās** on the way
viālis *adj* of the highways
viārius *adj* for the upkeep of roads
viāticātus *adj* provided with travelling money
viāticus *adj* for a journey ♦ *nt* travelling allowance; *(MIL)* prizemoney, savings
viātor, -ōris *m* traveller; *(LAW)* summoner
vībīx, -īcis *f* weal
vibrō, -āre, -āvī, -ātum *vt* to wave, shake, brandish, hurl, launch ♦ *vi* to shake, quiver, vibrate; to shimmer, sparkle
vīburnum, -ī *nt* wayfaring-tree or guelder rose

229

vīcānus *adj* village (*in cpds*) ◆ *mpl* villagers

Vica Pota, **Vicae Potae** *f* goddess of victory

vicārius *adj* substituted ◆ *m* substitute, proxy; underslave

vīcātim *adv* from street to street; in villages

vice (*with gen*) on account of; like

vicem in turn; (*with gen*) instead of; on account of; like; **tuam ~** on your account

vīcēnārius *adj* of twenty

vīcēnī, **-ōrum** *adj* twenty each, in twenties

vicēs *pl of* **vicis**

vīcēsimānī, **-ōrum** *mpl* men of the twentieth legion

vīcēsimārius *adj* derived from the 5 per cent tax

vīcēsimus *adj* twentieth ◆ *f* a 5 per cent tax

vīcī *perf of* **vincō**

vicia, **-ae** *f* vetch

vīciēns, **vīciēs** *adv* twenty times

vīcīnālis *adj* neighbouring

vīcīnia, **-ae** *f* neighbourhood, nearness

vīcīnitās, **-ātis** *f* neighbourhood, nearness

vīcīnus *adj* neighbouring, nearby; similar, kindred ◆ *m/f* neighbour ◆ *nt* neighbourhood

vicis *gen* (*acc* **-em**, *abl* **-e**) *f* interchange, alternation, succession; recompense, retaliation; fortune, changing conditions; duty, function, place; **in vicem** in turn, mutually

vicissim *adv* in turn, again

vicissitūdō, **-inis** *f* interchange, alternation

victima, **-ae** *f* victim, sacrifice

victimārius, **-ī** *and* **-iī** *m* assistant at sacrifices

vīctitō, **-āre** *vi* to live, subsist

victor, **-ōris** *m* conqueror, victor, winner ◆ *adj* victorious

victōria, **-ae** *f* victory

victōriātus, **-ūs** *m* silver coin stamped with Victory

Victōriola, **-ae** *f* little statue of Victory

victrīx, **-īcis** *f* conqueror ◆ *adj* victorious

victus *ppp of* **vincō**

vīctus, **-ūs** *m* sustenance, livelihood; way of life

vīculus, **-ī** *m* hamlet

vīcus, **-ī** *m* (*city*) quarter, street; (*country*) village, estate

vidēlicet *adv* clearly, evidently; (*ironical*) of course; (*explaining*) namely

videō, **-ēre**, **vīdī**, **vīsum** *vt* to see, look at; (*mind*) to observe, be aware, know; to consider, think over; to see to, look out for; to live to see; (*pass*) to seem, appear; to seem right, be thought proper; **mē vidē** rely on me; **vīderit** let him see to it; **mihi videor esse** I think I am; **sī (tibi) vidētur** if you like

viduāta *adj* widowed

viduitās, **-ātis** *f* bereavement, want; widowhood

vīdulus, **-ī** *m* trunk, box

viduō, **-āre** *vt* to bereave

viduus *adj* bereft, bereaved; unmarried; (*with abl*) without ◆ *f* widow; spinster

Vienna, **-ae** *f* town in Gaul on the Rhone (now Vienne)

viētus *adj* shrivelled

vigeō, **-ēre**, **-uī** *vi* to thrive, flourish

vigēscō, **-ere** *vi* to begin to flourish, become lively

vīgēsimus *etc see* **vīcēsimus**

vigil, **-is** *adj* awake, watching, alert ◆ *m* watchman, sentinel; (*pl*) the watch, police

vigilāns, **-antis** *pres p of* **vigilō** ◆ *adj* watchful

vigilanter *adv* vigilantly

vigilantia, **-ae** *f* wakefulness; vigilance

vigilāx, **-ācis** *adj* watchful

vigilia, **-ae** *f* lying awake, sleeplessness; keeping watch, guard; a watch; the watch, sentries; vigil; vigilance

vigilō, **-āre**, **-āvī**, **-ātum** *vi* to remain awake; to keep watch; to be vigilant ◆ *vt* to spend awake, make while awake at night

vīgintī *num* twenty

vīgintīvirātus, **-ūs** *m* membership of a board of twenty

vīgintīvirī, **-ōrum** *mpl* a board or commission of twenty men

vigor, **-ōris** *m* energy, vigour

vīlica, **-ae** *f* wife of a steward

vīlicō, **-āre** *vi* to be an overseer

vīlicus, **-ī** *m* overseer, manager of an estate, steward

vīlis *adj* cheap; worthless, poor, mean, common

vīlitās, **-ātis** *f* cheapness, low price; worthlessness

vīliter *adv* cheaply

vīlla, **-ae** *f* country house, villa

vīllic- *etc see* **vīlic-**

villōsus *adj* hairy, shaggy

vīllula, **-ae** *f* small villa

vīllum, **-ī** *nt* a drop of wine

villus, **-ī** *m* hair, fleece; (*cloth*) nap

vīmen, **-inis** *nt* osier; basket

vīmentum, **-ī** *nt* osier

Vīminālis *adj* Viminal (hill of Rome)

vīmineus *adj* of osiers, wicker

vīnāceus *adj* grape- (*in cpds*)

Vīnālia, **-ium** *ntpl* Wine festival

vīnārius *adj* of wine, wine (*in cpds*) ◆ *m* vintner ◆ *nt* wine flask

vincibilis *adj* easily won

vinciō, **-īre**, **-xī**, **-ctum** *vt* to bind, fetter; to encircle; (*fig*) to confine, restrain, envelop, attach

vinclum *nt see* **vinculum**

vincō, **-ere**, **vīcī**, **victum** *vt* to conquer, defeat, subdue; to win, prevail, be successful; (*fig*) to surpass, excel; (*argument*) to convince, refute, prove conclusively; (*life*) to outlive

vinctus *ppp of* **vinciō**

vinculum, **-ī** *nt* bond, fetter, chain; (*pl*) prison

vīndēmia, **-ae** *f* vintage, grape harvest

vīndēmiātor, **-ōris** *m* vintager

vīndēmiola, **-ae** *f* small vintage

Vīndēmitor, **-ōris** *m* the Vintager (*a star in Virgo*)

vindex, **-icis** *m* champion, protector; liberator; avenger ◆ *adj* avenging

vindicātiō, **-ōnis** *f* punishment of offences

vindiciae, **-ārum** *fpl* legal claim; **vindiciās ab lībertāte in servitūtem dare** condemn a free person to slavery

vindicō, -āre, -āvī, -ātum *vt* to lay claim to; to claim, appropriate; to liberate, protect, champion; to avenge, punish; **in lībertātem vindicāre** emancipate

vindicta, -ae *f* rod used in manumitting a slave; defence, deliverance; revenge, punishment

vīnea, -ae *f* vineyard; vine; (MIL) penthouse (*for besiegers*)

vīnētum, -ī *nt* vineyard

vīnitor, -ōris *m* vine-dresser

vinnulus *adj* delightful

vīnolentia, -ae *f* wine drinking

vīnolentus *adj* drunk

vīnōsus *adj* fond of wine, drunken

vīnum, -ī *nt* wine

vinxī *perf of* **vinciō**

viola, -ae *f* violet; stock

violābilis *adj* vulnerable

violāceus *adj* violet

violārium, -ī *and* **-iī** *nt* violet bed

violārius, -ī *and* **-iī** *m* dyer of violet

violātiō, -ōnis *f* desecration

violātor, -ōris *m* violator, desecrator

violēns, -entis *adj* raging, vehement

violenter *adv* violently, furiously

violentia, -ae *f* violence, impetuosity

violentus *adj* violent, impetuous, boisterous

violō, -āre, -āvī, -ātum *vt* to do violence to, outrage, violate; (*agreement*) to break

vīpera, -ae *f* viper, adder, snake

vīpereus *adj* snake's, serpent's

vīperīnus *adj* snake's, serpent's

vir, virī *m* man; grown man; brave man, hero; husband; (MIL) footsoldier

virāgō, -inis *f* heroine, warrior maid

virecta, -ōrum *ntpl* grassy sward

vireō, -ēre, -uī *vi* to be green; (*fig*) to be fresh, flourish

vīrēs *pl of* **vīs¹**

virēscō, -ere *vi* to grow green

virga, -ae *f* twig; graft; rod, staff, walking stick, wand; (*colour*) stripe

virgātor, -ōris *m* flogger

virgātus *adj* made of osiers; striped

virgētum, -ī *nt* thicket of osiers

virgeus *adj* of brushwood

virgidēmia, -ae *f* crop of flogging

virginālis *adj* maidenly, of maids

virginārius *adj* of maids

virgineus *adj* maidenly, virgin, of virgins

virginitās, -ātis *f* maidenhood

virgō, -inis *f* maid, virgin; young woman, girl; (*constellation*) Virgo; *a Roman aqueduct*

virgula, -ae *f* wand

virgulta, -ōrum *ntpl* thicket, shrubbery; cuttings, slips

virguncula, -ae *f* little girl

viridāns, -antis *adj* green

viridārium, -ī *and* **-iī** *nt* plantation, garden

viridis *adj* green; fresh, young, youthful ◆ *ntpl* greenery

viriditās, -ātis *f* verdure, greenness; freshness

viridor, -ārī *vi* to become green

virīlis *adj* male, masculine; man's, adult; manly, brave, bold; ~ **pars** one's individual part or duty; **prō virīlī parte, prō virīlī portiōne** to the best of one's ability

virīlitās, -ātis *f* manhood

virīliter *adv* manfully

virītim *adv* individually, separately

vīrōsus *adj* slimy; rank

virtūs, -ūtis *f* manhood, full powers; strength, courage, ability, worth; (MIL) valour, prowess, heroism; (*moral*) virtue; (*things*) excellence, worth

vīrus, -ī *nt* slime; poison; offensive smell; salt taste

vīs¹ (*acc* **vim**, *abl* **vī**, *pl* **vīrēs**) *f* power, force, strength; violence, assault; quantity, amount; (*mind*) energy, vigour; (*word*) meaning, import; (*pl*) strength; (MIL) troops; **per vim** forcibly; **dē vī damnārī** be convicted of assault; **prō vīribus** with all one's might

vīs² *2nd pers of* **volō²**

viscātus *adj* limed

viscerātiō, -ōnis *f* public distribution of meat

viscō, -āre *vt* to make sticky

viscum, -ī *nt* mistletoe; bird lime

viscus, -eris (*pl* **-era, -erum**) *nt* internal organs; flesh; womb, child; (*fig*) heart, bowels

vīsendus *adj* worth seeing

vīsiō, -ōnis *f* apparition; idea

vīsitō, -āre *vt* to see often; to visit

vīsō, -ere, -ī, -um *vt* to look at, survey; to see to; to go and see, visit

Visurgis, -is *m* (*river*) Weser

vīsus¹ *ppp of* **videō** ◆ *nt* vision

vīsus², -ūs *m* sight, the faculty of seeing; a sight, vision

vīta, -ae *f* life, livelihood; way of life; career, biography

vītābilis *adj* undesirable

vītābundus *adj* avoiding, taking evasive action

vītālis *adj* of life, vital ◆ *nt* subsistence ◆ *ntpl* vitals

vītāliter *adv* with life

vītātiō, -ōnis *f* avoidance

Vitellius¹, -ī *m* Roman emperor in AD 69

Vitellius², -iānus *adj see* **Vitellius¹**

vitellus, -ī *m* little calf; (*egg*) yolk

vīteus *adj* of the vine

vīticula, -ae *f* little vine

vītigenus *adj* produced from the vine

vitilēna, -ae *f* procuress

vitiō, -āre, -āvī, -ātum *vt* to spoil, corrupt, violate; to falsify

vitiōsē *adv* badly, defectively

vitiōsitās, -ātis *f* vice

vitiōsus *adj* faulty, corrupt; wicked, depraved; ~ **cōnsul** *a consul whose election had a religious flaw in it*

vītis, -is *f* vine; vine branch, centurion's staff, centurionship

vītisator, -ōris *m* vine planter

vitium, -ī *and* **-iī** *nt* fault, flaw, defect; (*moral*) failing, offence, vice; (*religion*) flaw in the auspices

vītō, -āre, -āvī, -ātum *vt* to avoid, evade, shun

vītor, -ōris *m* basket maker, cooper
vitreus *adj* of glass; glassy ♦ *ntpl* glassware
vītricus, -ī *m* stepfather
vitrum, -ī *nt* glass; woad
vitta, -ae *f* headband, sacrificial fillet
vittātus *adj* wearing a fillet
vitula, -ae *f* (*of cow*) calf
vitulīnus *adj* of veal ♦ *f* veal
vītulor, -ārī *vi* to hold a celebration
vitulus, -ī *m* calf; foal; ~ marīnus seal
vituperābilis *adj* blameworthy
vituperātiō, -ōnis *f* blame, censure; scandalous conduct
vituperātor, -ōris *m* critic
vituperō, -āre *vt* to find fault with, disparage; (*omen*) to spoil
vīvārium, -ī *and* -iī *nt* fishpond, game preserve
vīvātus *adj* animated
vīvāx, -ācis *adj* long-lived; lasting; (*sulphur*) inflammable
vīvēscō, -ere *vi* to grow, become active
vīvidus *adj* full of life; (*art*) true to life, vivid; (*mind*) lively
vīvirādīx, -īcis *f* a rooted cutting, layer
vīvīscō *etc see* vīvēscō
vīvō, -vere, -xī, -ctum *vi* to live, be alive; to enjoy life; (*fame*) to last, be remembered; (*with abl*) to live on; vīve farewell!; vīxērunt they are dead
vīvus *adj* alive, living; (*light*) burning; (*rock*) natural; (*water*) running; vīvō videntīque before his very eyes; mē vīvō as long as I live, in my lifetime; ad vīvum resecāre cut to the quick; dē vīvō dētrahere take out of capital
vix *adv* with difficulty, hardly, scarcely
vixdum *adv* hardly, as yet
vīxī *perf of* vīvō
vocābulum, -ī *nt* name, designation; (GRAM) noun
vōcālis *adj* speaking, singing, tuneful ♦ *f* vowel
vocāmen, -inis *nt* name
vocātiō, -ōnis *f* invitation; (LAW) summons
vocātus, -ūs *m* summons, call
vōciferātiō, -ōnis *f* loud cry, outcry
vōciferor, -ārī *vt* to cry out loud, shout
vocitō, -āre, -āvī, -ātum *vt* to usually call; to shout
vocīvus *etc see* vacīvus
vocō, -āre, -āvī, -ātum *vt* to call, summon; to call, name; (*gods*) to call upon; (*guest*) to invite; (MIL) to challenge; (*fig*) to bring (*into some condition or plight*); vocāre dē name after; in dubium vocāre call in question; in iūdicium vocāre call to account
vōcula, -ae *f* weak voice; soft tone; gossip
volaema *ntpl* kind of large pear
Volaterrae, -ārum *fpl* old Etruscan town (*now* Volterra)
Volaterrānus *adj see* Volaterrae
volāticus *adj* winged; fleeting, inconstant
volātilis *adj* winged; swift; fleeting
volātus, -ūs *m* flight
Volcānius *adj see* Volcānus
Volcānus, -ī *m* Vulcan (*god of fire*), fire

volēns, -entis *pres p of* volō² ♦ *adj* willing, glad, favourable; mihi volentī est it is acceptable to me
volg- *etc see* vulg-
volitō, -āre *vi* to fly about, flutter; to hurry, move quickly; (*fig*) to hover, soar; to get excited
voln- *etc see* vuln-
volō¹, -āre, -āvī, -ātum *vi* to fly; to speed
volō², velle, voluī *vt* to wish, want; to be willing; to will, purpose, determine; (*opinion*) to hold, maintain; (*word, action*) to mean; ~ dīcere I mean; bene velle like; male velle dislike; ōrātum tē ~ I beg you; paucīs tē ~ a word with you!; numquid vīs (*before leaving*) is there anything else?; quid sibi vult? what does he mean?; what is he driving at?; velim faciās please do it; vellem fēcissēs I wish you had done it
volōnēs, -um *mpl* volunteers
volpēs *etc see* vulpēs
Volscī, -ōrum *mpl* people in S. Latium
Volscus *adj* Volscian
volsella, -ae *f* tweezers
volsus *ppp of* vellō
volt *old 3rd pers sg of* volō²
voltis *old 2nd pers pl of* volō²
Voltumna, -ae *f* patron goddess of Etruria
voltus *etc see* vultus
volūbilis *adj* spinning, revolving; (*fortune*) fickle; (*speech*) fluent
volūbilitās, -ātis *f* whirling motion; roundness; fluency; inconstancy
volūbiliter *adv* fluently
volucer, -ris *adj* winged; flying, swift; fleeting
volucris, -is *f* bird; insect
volūmen, -inis *nt* roll, book; coil, eddy, fold
voluntārius *adj* voluntary ♦ *mpl* volunteers
voluntās, -ātis *f* will, wish, inclination; attitude, goodwill; last will, testament; suā voluntāte of one's own accord; ad voluntātem with the consent (of)
volup *adv* agreeably, to one's satisfaction
voluptābilis *adj* agreeable
voluptās, -ātis *f* pleasure, enjoyment; (*pl*) entertainments, sports
voluptuārius *adj* pleasureable, agreeable; voluptuous
volūtābrum, -ī *nt* wallowing place
volūtātiō, -ōnis *f* wallowing
volūtō, -āre *vt* to roll about, turn over; (*mind*) to occupy, engross; (*thought*) to ponder, think over; (*pass*) to wallow, flounder
volūtus *ppp of* volvō
volva, -ae *f* womb; (*dish*) sow's womb
volvō, -vere, -vī, -ūtum *vt* to roll, turn round; to roll along; (*air*) to breathe; (*book*) to open; (*circle*) to form; (*thought*) to ponder, reflect on; (*time*) to roll on; (*trouble*) to undergo; (*pass*) to roll, revolve ♦ *vi* to revolve, elapse
vōmer, -eris *m* ploughshare
vomica, -ae *f* sore, ulcer, abscess, boil
vōmis *etc see* vōmer
vomitiō, -ōnis *f* vomiting
vomitus, -ūs *m* vomiting, vomit

vomō, -ere, -uī, -itum vt to vomit, throw up; to emit, discharge
vorāgō, -inis f abyss, chasm, depth
vorāx, -ācis adj greedy, ravenous; consuming
vorō, -āre, -āvī, -ātum vt to swallow, devour; (sea) to swallow up; (reading) to devour
vors-, vort- see **vers-, vert-** etc
vōs pron you
Vosegus, -ī m Vosges (mountains)
voster etc see **vester**
vōtīvus adj votive, promised in a vow
votō etc see **vetō**
vōtum, -ī nt vow, prayer; votive offering; wish, longing; **vōtī damnārī** have one's prayer granted
vōtus ppp of **voveō**
voveō, -ēre, vōvī, vōtum vt to vow, promise solemnly; to dedicate; to wish
vōx, vōcis f voice; sound, cry, call; word, saying, expression; accent; **unā vōce** unanimously
Vulcānus see **Volcānus**
vulgāris adj common, general
vulgāriter adv in the common fashion
vulgātor, -ōris m betrayer
vulgātus adj common; generally known, notorious
vulgivagus adj roving; inconstant

vulgō¹ adv publicly, commonly, usually, everywhere
vulgō², -āre, -āvī, -ātum vt to make common, spread; to publish, divulge, broadcast; to prostitute; to level down
vulgus, -ī nt (occ m) the mass of the people, the public; crowd, herd; rabble, populace
vulnerātiō, -ōnis f wounding, injury
vulnerō, -āre, -āvī, -ātum vt to wound, hurt; to damage
vulnificus adj wounding, dangerous
vulnus, -eris nt wound, injury; (things) damage, hole; (fig) blow, misfortune, pain
vulpēcula, -ae f little fox
vulpēs, -is f fox; (fig) cunning
vulsī perf of **vellō**
vulsus ppp of **vellō**
vulticulus, -ī m a mere look (from)
vultum etc see **vultus**
vultuōsus adj affected
vultur, -is m vulture
vulturius, -ī and **-iī** m vulture, bird of prey; (dice) an unlucky throw
Vulturnus, -ī m river in Campania
vultus, -ūs m look, expression (esp in the eyes); face; (things) appearance
vulva etc see **volva**

Xx

Xanthippē, -ēs *f wife of Socrates*
Xanthus, -ī *m river of Troy (identified with Scamander); river of Lycia*
xenium, -ī *and* **-iī** *nt present*
Xenocratēs, -is *m disciple of Plato*
Xenophanēs, -is *m early Greek philosopher*
Xenophōn, -ontis *m famous Greek historian*

Xenophontēus *adj see* **Xenophōn**
xērampelinae, -ārum *fpl* dark-coloured clothes
Xerxēs, -is *m Persian king defeated at Salamis*
xiphiās, -ae *m swordfish*
xystum, -ī *nt,* **xystus, -ī** *m* open colonnade, walk, avenue

Zz

Zacynthius *adj see* **Zacynthus**
Zacynthus, **Zacynthos**, **-ī** *f island off W. Greece (now* Zante*)*
Zama, **-ae** *f town in Numidia (where Scipio defeated Hannibal)*
Zamēnsis *adj see* **Zama**
zāmia, **-ae** *f* harm
Zanclaeus, **Zanclēius** *adj see* **Zanclē**
Zanclē, **-ēs** *f old name of Messana*
zēlotypus *adj* jealous
Zēnō, **Zēnōn**, **-ōnis** *m founder of Stoicism; a philosopher of Elea; an Epicurean teacher of Cicero*
Zephyrītis, **-idis** *f* Arsinoe (*queen of Egypt*)

Zephyrus, **-ī** *m* west wind, zephyr; wind
Zēthus, **-ī** *m brother of Amphion*
Zeuxis, **-is** *and* **-idis** *m famous Greek painter*
zmaragdus *etc see* **smaragdus**
Zmyrna *etc see* **Smyrna**
zōdiacus, **-ī** *m* zodiac
zōna, **-ae** *f* belt, girdle; (GEOG) zone; (ASTR) Orion's Belt
zōnārius *adj* of belts; **sector** ~ cutpurse ♦ *m* belt maker
zōnula, **-ae** *f* little belt
zōthēca, **-ae** *f* private room
zōthēcula, **-ae** *f* cubicle

ROMAN LIFE AND CULTURE

KEY EVENTS IN ROMAN HISTORY

B.C.

753	Foundation of Rome. Romulus became first king.
600-510	Rome ruled by Etruscan kings.
510	Expulsion of Tarquin and republic established.
507	Consecration of Temple of Jupiter on Capitol.
451	Code of Twelve Tables laid basis of Roman law.
390	Gauls sacked Rome.
367	Lex Liciniae Sextiae; plebeians allowed to be consul.
354	Treaty with Samnites.
343-341	First Samnite war; Romans occupied northern Campania.
340-338	Latin War; separate treaties made with Latins.
327-304	Second Samnite war; Rome increased influence in southern Italy.
321	Samnites defeated Romans at Caudine Forks; truce.
312	Appian Way, first Roman road, built.
298-290	Third Samnite war; Rome now all-powerful in southern Italy.
287	Hortensian Law; People's Assembly became a law-making body.
282-272	Wars with Tarentum and King Pyrrhus of Epirus.
270	Whole peninsula under Roman power.
264-241	First Punic war; Rome defended Greek cities in Sicily.
260	Fleet built; first naval victory at Mylae against Carthaginians.
241	Roman victory over Carthage secured Sicily, source of corn supply.
226	River Ebro treaty; Carthage should not cross into northern Spain.
218-201	Second Punic war against Hannibal.
216	Rome defeated at Battle of Cannae.
214-205	First Macedonian war with Philip V.
202	Scipio defeated Hannibal at Zama.
201	Peace concluded with Carthage; Rome now controlled the western Mediterranean.
200-196	Second Macedonian war; freedom of Greece proclaimed.
172-168	Third Macedonian war; Perseus crushed at Pydna.
148	Macedonia became a Roman province.
146	Carthage destroyed; Corinth destroyed.
133	Tiberius Gracchus became tribune; his assassination caused class conflict.
123-122	Gaius Gracchus carried out political/economic reforms.
121	Gaius was killed.
111-105	Marius and Sulla conducted war against Jugurtha of Numidia.
91-89	Social war between Rome and allies.
89-85	War with Mithridates VI of Pontus.
83-82	Civil war between Sulla and Marius; Sulla captured Rome.
81-79	Sulla, dictator, restored constitution, introduced reforms.
78	Death of Sulla.

77-72	Pompey fought Sertorius in Spain.
73-71	Spartacus' slave revolt.
70	Pompey and Crassus joint consuls; tribunes restored.
67	End of war against Mithridates; pirates controlled by Pompey.
63	Cicero suppressed Catiline's conspiracy.
60	First Triumvirate (Caesar, Pompey, Crassus) was formed.
58-51	Caesar conquered Gaul.
53	Battle of Carrhae; Rome defeated by Parthians; Crassus killed.
49	Caesar crossed Rubicon; civil war with Pompey began.
48	Pompey defeated by Caesar at Pharsalus; Caesar became dictator.
44	Caesar assassinated; Antony sought revenge against conspirators.
43	Second Triumvirate (Antony, Octavian, Lepidus).
42	Battle of Philippi; Triumvirate defeated Brutus and Cassius.
41-40	Antony and Octavian divided territory.
33-32	Rupture between Antony and Octavian.
31	Battle of Actium; Octavian defeated Antony and Cleopatra at sea.
27	Octavian returned powers to Senate; received name Augustus.
18	Julian laws promoted morality, condemned adultery, regulated divorce.
12	Augustus became Pontifex Maximus, head of state religion.
2	Augustus became 'pater patriae', father of his country; apex of his power.

A.D.

4	Tiberius adopted as Augustus' heir.
6	Annexation of Judaea.
9	Varus' three legions destroyed in Germany.
14	Death of Augustus.
14-37	Tiberius emperor; efficient administrator but unpopular.
14-16	Germanicus' successful campaign in Germany.
19	Germanicus died mysteriously; funeral at Antioch.
21-22	Sejanus organized Praetorian Guard.
26-31	Sejanus powerful in Rome; executed in 31.
37-41	Caligula emperor; cruel and tyrannical, was murdered by a tribune.
41-54	Claudius emperor; conquered Britain; showed political judgement.
57-68	Nero emperor; great fire (64); Christians persecuted.
68-69	Year of four emperors - Galba, Otho, Vitellius, Vespasian.
69-79	Vespasian began Flavian dynasty. Colosseum built.
70	Titus, Vespasian's son, captured Jerusalem, destroyed the Temple.
79-81	Titus emperor. Vesuvius erupted (79), Pompeii destroyed.
81-96	Domitian emperor. Border built in Germany; period ended in terror.
96-98	Nerva emperor after Domitian's assassination.
98-117	Trajan emperor - conqueror of Dacia and Parthian empire.
117-138	Hadrian, cultured traveller, soldier and administrator of empire.
122	Hadrian's Wall built between Solway and Tyne.
138-161	Antoninus Pius emperor; orderly, peaceful rule.
141-143	Antonine's Wall built between Forth and Clyde.
161-180	Marcus Aurelius emperor; Commodus, his son, shared power (177-180).

162	War with Parthia.
175-180	War against Germans on the Danube.
180-192	Commodus emperor.
193-211	Septimius Severus became emperor after crisis; died in Britain.
	Authorized special benefits for army.
211-217	Deterioration under criminal rule of Caracalla.
212	All free men of the empire became citizens.
284-305	Diocletian and Maximian co-emperors, empire divided into 12 dioceses.
	Prices imposed throughout empire.
303	Christians persecuted by Diocletian.
312	Constantine's victory at Milvian Bridge gave him Rome.
313	Edict of Milan ended persecution of Christians.
324	Constantine became sole emperor.
325	Council of Nicaea made Christianity religion of the empire.
330	Constantine made Byzantium seat of government; renamed it Constantinople.
337	Constantine died a Christian, trying to reorganize the empire.
379-395	Emperor Theodosius kept empire formally intact.
410	Alaric and Goths captured and destroyed Rome.

GOVERNMENT AND ADMINISTRATION

Republic

There was no written constitution. The Republic evolved from the struggle between the Senate and the People - Senatus Populusque Romanus - SPQR.

The Senate (Senatus)
This was the governing body, largely in the hands of the nobles (nobiles) or patricians (patricii).

- it prepared proposals to bring before the people
- it passed decrees (senatus consulta)
- it dealt with emergencies
- it controlled finances and building contracts
- it appointed magistrates to provinces
- it directed foreign relations
- it supervised state religion

The People (Populus)
The resolutions of the people, plebiscita, could have the force of law, but the Senate was allowed greater control. There were four assemblies:

- comitia curiata   formal duties
- comitia centuriata   elected magistrates
- comitia tributa   elected lesser magistrates
- comitia plebis   passed plebiscita

The Knights (Equites)
A third element, or class, emerged (originally from Rome's cavalry) to engage in trade and finance. These businessmen acquired more political influence and became wealthy. By the time of Cicero, they could enter the Senate. Cicero tried to reconcile the three classes, **senatores**, **equites** and **plebs** by his **concordia ordinum** (harmony of the classes).

Magistrates (Magistratus)
A magistrate was an official elected annually by the people. Offices were held in a strict order - cursus honorum. After ten years' military service, a young man could begin on the lowest rung of the ladder as follows:

Age	Office	Number	Duties
28	**Quaestor**	(8)	• administered finance maintained public records
30	**Aedile**	(4)	• maintained roads, water supply organized games and festivals
33(39)	**Praetor**	(6)	• civil judge could introduce laws
39(43)	**Consul**	(2)	• commanded army conducted elections presided over Senate carried out its decrees

Other magistrates:

Tribune (10) • defended plebs' rights
(tribunus   had right of veto
plebis)

Censor (2) • conducted census (every 5 years)
                 conducted purification
                 revised roll of senators

Dictator (1) • ruled in crisis (maximum of 6 months)
                   conducted military and domestic matters

Imperium (supreme power) was held by consuls and praetors and dictators.

Potestas (power to enforce laws) was held by all magistrates.

Lictores (lictors *or* officials) carried **fasces** (bundles of rods) in front of consuls, praetors and dictators as a sign of their authority.

ORGANIZATION OF THE ARMY

Empire

At the time of Augustus there were 28 **legions** (later 25), each legion consisting of approximately 5000 infantrymen, trained for close combat. It was organized as follows:

Legio	Legion	5000 men
10 Cohortes	Cohorts	500 men
6 Centuriae	Centuries	80/100 men

Officers		
	Legatus	legionary commander
6	Tribuni Militum	tribunes
60	Centuriones	centurions (from ranks), in charge of centuries

Recruitment	Citizens
Length of service	20/25 years
Duties	Offensive in important battles, repelling invasion *etc*
Pay	250/300 denarii per day
On retirement	Land or cash bounty

Additional **auxiliary forces** were recruited to help the legions. Particularly necessary were cavalry, drawn from all parts of the Empire, slingers, bowmen, etc. Infantrymen were often recruited locally and formed cohorts of about 500 men.

Auxilia	Auxiliaries	
Ala	Cavalry unit	500 men approx.
16 Turmae	turmae	32 men
Cohors	Infantry unit	500 men

Officers	
Decurio	Decurion (cavalry officer)
Recruitment	Non-citizens
Length of service	25 years
Duties	Frontier skirmishes, occupation, assisting legions
Pay	100 denarii per day
On retirement	Citizenship for self/family

The **Praetorian Guard** was the Emperor's special bodyguard. Three cohorts were based in Rome, six more in nearby towns.

Praetorium	Praetorian Guard	4500 men
9 Cohortes	cohorts	500 men

Officers	
2 Praefecti Praetorio	praetorian prefects
Recruitment	Citizens (Italy)
Length of service	16 years
Duties	Preserving emperor's power and safety
Pay	1000 denarii per day
On retirement	5000 denarii

FAMILY TREE

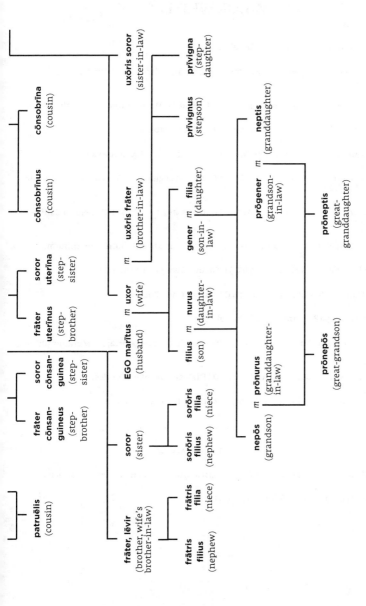

Note: This is the Family Tree of the man designated EGO in the fourth generation from the end.

9

MAJOR WRITERS

ENNIUS (Quintus Ennius: b 239 B.C.) **Annales**.

PLAUTUS (Titus Maccus *or* Maccius Plautus: b 254 B.C.) **Amphitruo**; the **Aulularia**; the **Menaechmi** and **Miles Gloriosus**.

TERENCE (Publius Terentius Afer: c.190 - c.159 B.C.) **Andria**; **Mother-in-law**; **Phormio**.

LUCRETIUS (Titus Lucretius Carus: 94 - 55B.C.) **De Rerum Natura**.

CATULLUS (Gaius Valerius Catullus: c.84 - c.54 B.C.) Lyric poetry; **Ave atque vale**.

CICERO (Marcus Tullius Cicero: b 106 B.C.) **Pro Caelio**; **De Legibus**; the **Tusculan Disputations**; **De Officiis**; **Philippics**.

JULIUS CAESAR (Gaius Julius Caesar: b c.102 B.C. and assassinated in 44 B.C.) **Bellum Gallicum**; **Bellum Civile**.

SALLUST (Gaius Sallustius Crispus: 86 - 35 B.C.) **Bellum Catilinae**; **Bellum Iugurthinum**.

VIRGIL (Publius Vergilius Maro: 70 - 19 B.C.) **Eclogues**; **Georgics**; the **Aeneid**.

HORACE (Quintus Horatius Flaccus: b 65 B.C.) **Satires**; **Odes**; **Epistles**.

LIVY (Titus Livius: 59 B.C. - 17A.D.) **Ab Urbe Condita**.

OVID (Publius Ovidius Naso: 43B.C. - 17 A.D.) the **Heroides**, **Ars Amatoria**; the **Metamorphoses**; **Tristia**.

SENECA (Lucius Annaeus Seneca: 4 B.C. - 65 A.D.) **Dialogi**; **Epistolae Morales**.

QUINTILIAN (Marcus Fabius Quintilianus: c.35 - c.95 A.D.) **Institutio Oratorio**.

MARTIAL (Marcus Valerius Martialis: 40 - 104 A.D.) the **Epigrams**.

JUVENAL (Decimus Iunius Iuvenalis: c.60 - c.140 A.D.) **Satires**.

TACITUS (Cornelius Tacitus: c.55 - c.120 A.D.) **Agricola**; **Germania**; **Histories**; the **Annals**.

PLINY (Gaius Plinius Secundus: b 61 *or* 62 A.D.) **Letters**.

GEOGRAPHICAL NAMES

The following list of geographical names and their adjectives includes both ancient and medieval Latin forms. The former are printed in Roman type, the latter in Italics. Medieval place names tend to have a variety of Latin forms, but only one has been selected in each case; occasionally both the ancient and the medieval forms have been given. Modern names which have a ready made Latin form (*e.g.* America) have been omitted, and many names not included in this selection can be easily Latinized on the analogy of those which do appear.

Aachen	*Aquīsgrānum nt*	*adj Aquīsgrānēnsis*
Aberdeen	*Aberdōnia f*	*adj Aberdōnēnsis*
Abergavenny	Gobannium *nt*	
Aberystwith	*Aberistyvium nt*	
Adige, *River*	Athesis *m*	
Adriatic	Mare superum *nt*	*adj* Hadriāticus
Aegean	Mare Aegaeum *nt*	*adj* Aegaeus
Afghanistan	Ariāna *f*	*adj* Ariānus
Africa	Libya *f*,	*adj* Libycus,
	Africa *f*	Africānus
Agrigento	Agrigentum *nt*	*adj* Agrigentīnus
Aisne, *River*	Axona *m*	
Aix-en-Provence	Aquae Sextiae *fpl*	*adj Aquēnsis*
Aix-la-Chapelle	*Aquīsgrānum nt*	*adj Aquisgrānēnsis*
Aix-les-Bains	Aquae Grātiānae *fpl*	
Ajaccio	*Adiacium nt*	*adj Adiacēnsis*
Aldborough	Isurium *(nt)*	
	Brigantum	
Alexandria	Alexandrēa,	*adj* Alexandrīnus
	Alexandrīa *f*	
Algiers	*Algerium nt*	*adj Algerīnus*
Alps	Alpēs *fpl*	*adj* Alpīnus
Alsace	*Alsatia f*	
Amalfi	*Amalphis f*	*adj* Amalphitānus
Ambleside	Galava *f*	
Amiens	*Ambiānum nt*	*adj Ambiānēnsis*
Amsterdam	*Amstelodamum nt*	*adj Amstelodamēnsis*
Ancaster	Causennae *fpl*	
Angers	*Andegāvum nt*	*adj* Andegāvēnsis
Anglesey	Mona *f*	
Aniene, *River*	Aniō *m*	*adj* Aniēnus
Anjou	Andegāvēnsis ager *m*	
Ankara	Ancyra *f*	*adj* Ancyrānus
Antibes	Antipolis *f*	*adj* Antipolītānus
Antioch	Antiochīa *f*	*adj* Antiochēnus
Antwerp	*Antwerpium nt*	*adj Antwerpiēnsis*
Anzio	Antium *nt*	*adj* Antīās, Antiānus
Aosta	Augusta Praetōria *f*	
Apennines	Mōns Apennīnus *m*	

Aragon	*Aragōnia f*	
Archangel	*Archangelopolis f*	
Ardennes	*Arduenna f*	
Arezzo	*Ārētium nt*	*adj* Ārētinus
Argenteuil	*Argentōlium nt*	
Argyll	*Argadia f*	
Aries	*Arelās f*	*adj* Arelātēnsis
Armagh	*Armācha f*	*adj* Armāchānus
Arno, *River*	*Arnus m*	*adj* Arniēnsis
Arras	*Atrebatēs mpl*	*adj* Atrebatēnsis
Artois	*Atrebatēs mpl*	
Assisi	*Assīsium nt*	*adj* Assīsiēnsis
Athens	*Athēnae fpl*	*adj* Athēniēnsis
Atlantic	*Mare Atlanticum nt*	
Augsburg	*Augusta (f) Vindelicōrum*	*adj* Augustānus
Autun	*Augustodūnum nt*	*adj* Augustodūnēnsis
Auvergne	*Arvernī mpl*	*adj* Arvernus
Aventine	*Aventīnus m*	
Avignon	*Aveniō f*	*adj* Aveniōnēnsis
Avon, *River*	*Auvona m*	
Babylon	*Babylōn f*	*adj* Babylōnius
Baden-Baden	*Aquae Aurēliae fpl*	
Balearic Islands	*Baliārēs Insulae fpl*	*adj* Baliāricus
Balkh	*Bactra ntpl*	*adj* Bactriānus
Baltic	*Balticum Mare nt*	
Bangor	*Bangertium nt*	*adj* Bangertiēnsis
Barcelona	*Barcinō f*	*adj* Barcinōnēnsis
Bari	*Bārium nt*	*adj* Bārēnsis
Basle	*Basilēa f*	*adj* Basilēēnsis
Basques	*Vasconēs mpl*	*adj* Vasconicus
Bath	*Aquae (fpl) Sulis*	
Bayeux	*Augustodūrum nt*	
Bayreuth	*Barūthum nt*	
Beauvais	*Bellovacī mpl*	*adj* Bellovacēnsis
Beirut	*Bērȳtus f*	*adj* Bērȳtius
Belgium	*Belgae mpl*	*adj* Belgicus
Bergen	*Bergae fpl*	
Berlin	*Berolīnum nt*	*adj* Berolīnēnsis
Berne	*Vērona f*	
Berwick	*Barvīcum nt*	
Besançon	*Vesontiō m*	*adj* Bisuntīnus
Black Sea	*Pontus (Euxīnus) m*	*adj* Ponticus
Bobbio	*Bobbium nt*	*adj* Bobbiēnsis
Bohemia	*Boiohaemī mpl*	
Bologna	*Bonōnia f*	*adj* Bonōniēnsis
Bonn	*Bonna f*	
Bordeaux	*Burdigala f*	*adj* Burdigalēnsis
Boulogne	*Bonōnia f*	*adj* Bononiēnsis
Bourges	*Avāricum nt*	*adj* Avāricensis

Brabant	Brabantia f	
Braganza	Brigantia f	adj Brigantiēnsis
Brancaster	Branodūnum nt	
Brandenburg	Brandenburgia f	adj Brandenburgēnsis
Bremen	Brēma f	adj Brēmēnsis
Breslau	Bratislavia f	adj Bratislaviēnsis
Brindisi	Brundisium nt	adj Brundisīnus
Bristol	Bristolium nt	adj Bristoliēnsis
Britain	Britannia f	adj Britannicus
Brittany	Armoricae fpl	
Bruges	Brugae fpl	adj Brugēnsis
Brunswick	Brunsvīcum nt	adj Brunsvīcēnsis
Brussels	Bruxellae fpl	adj Bruxellēnsis
Bucharest	Bucarestum nt	adj Bucarestiēnsis
Burgos	Burgī mpl	adj Burgitānus
Burgundy	Burgundiōnēs mpl	
Cadiz	Gādēs fpl	adj Gāditānus
Caen	Cadomum nt	adj Cadomēnsis
Caerleon	Isca f	
Caermarthen	Maridūnum nt	
Caernarvon	Segontium nt	
Caerwent	Venta (f) Silurum	
Cagliari	Caralis f	adj Caralītānus
Cairo	Cairus f	
Calais	Calētum nt	adj Calētanus
Cambrai	Camerācum nt	adj Camerācēnsis
Cambridge	Cantabrigia f	adj Cantabrigiēnsis
Campagna	Campānia f	adj Campānus
Cannes	Canoē f	
Canterbury	Durovernum nt, Cantuāria f	adj Cantuāriēnsis
Capri	Capreae fpl	adj Capreēnsis
Cardigan	Ceretica f	
Carlisle	Luguvallium nt	
Cartagena	Carthāgō Nova f	
Carthage	Carthāgō f	adj Carthāginiēnsis
Caspian Sea	Mare Caspium nt	
Cevennes	Gebenna f	adj Gebennicus
Ceylon	Tāprobanē f	
Champagne	Campānia f	adj Campānicus
Chartres	Carnūtēs mpl	adj Carnōtēnus
Chelmsford	Caesaromagus m	
Cherbourg	Caesaris burgus m	
Chester	Deva f	
Chichester	Rēgnum nt	
China	Sēres mpl	adj Sēricus
Cirencester	Corinium (nt) Dobunōrum	
Clairvaux	Clāra Vallis f	adj Clāravallēnsis
Clermont	Nemossus f	

Cluny	Clīniacum nt	adj Clīniacēnsis
Clyde, River	Clōta f	
Colchester	Camulodūnum nt	
Cologne	Colōnia Agrippīna f	adj Colōniēnsis
Como, Lake	Lārius m	adj Lārius
Constance, Lake	Lacus Brigantīnus m	
Copenhagen	Hafnia f	
Corbridge	Corstopitum nt	
Cordoba	Corduba f	adj Cordubēnsis
Corfu	Corcȳra f	adj Corcȳraeus
Corinth	Corinthus f	adj Corinthius
Cork	Corcagia f	adj Corcagiēnsis
Cornwall	Cornubia f	
Cracow	Cracovia f	adj Cracoviēnsis
Crete	Crēta f	adj Crētēnsis, Crēticus
Cumberland	Cumbria f	
Cyprus	Cyprus f	adj Cyprius
Cyrene	Cȳrēnae fpl	adj Cȳrēnaicus
Damascus	Damascus f	adj Damascēnus
Danube, River	(lower) Ister m,	
	(upper) Dānuvius m	
Dardanelles	Hellēspontus m	adj Hellespontius
Dee, River	Deva f	
Denmark	Dānia f	adj Dānicus
Derby	Derventiō m	
Devon	Devōnia f	
Dijon	Diviō f	adj Diviōnēnsis
Dneiper, River	Borysthenēs m	
Dneister, River	Danaster m	
Don, River (Russian)	Tanais m	
Doncaster	Dānum nt	
Dorchester	Durnovāria f	
Douro, River	Durius m	
Dover	Dubrī mpl	
Dover, Straits of	Fretum Gallicum nt	
Dresden	Dresda f	adj Dresdēnsis
Dublin	Dublīnum nt	adj Dublīnēnsis
Dumbarton	Britannodūnum nt	
Dundee	Taodūnum nt	
Dunstable	Durocobrīvae fpl	
Durham	Dunelmum nt	adj Dunelmēnsis
Ebro, River	Hibērus m	
Eden, River	Itūna f	
Edinburgh	Edinburgum nt	adj Edinburgēnsis
Egypt	Aegyptus f	adj Aegyptius
Elba	Ilva f	
Elbe, River	Albis m	
England	Anglia f	adj Anglicus
Etna	Aetna f	adj Aetnaeus
Europe	Eurōpa	adj Eurōpaeus

Exeter	Isca (f) Dumnoniōrum	
Fiesole	Faesulae *fpl*	*adj* Faesulānus
Flanders	Menapiī *mpl*	
Florence	Flōrentia *f*	*adj* Flōrentīnus
Fontainebleau	*Bellofontānum nt*	
Forth, *River*	Bodotria *f*	
France	Gallia *f*	*adj* Gallicus
Frankfurt	*Francofurtum nt*	
Frejus	Forum (*nt*) Iūliī	*adj* Foroiūliēnsis
Friesland	Frīsiī *mpl*	*adj* Frīsius
Gallipoli	*Callipolis f*	*adj* Callipolitānus
Galloway	*Gallovidia f*	
Ganges	Gangēs *m*	*adj* Gangēticus
Garda, *Lake*	Bēnācus *m*	
Garonne, *River*	Garumna *f*	
Gaul	Gallia *f*	*adj* Gallicus
Gdansk	*Gedānum m*	
Geneva	Genāva *f*	*adj* Genāvēnsis
Geneva, *Lake*	Lemannus lacus *m*	
Genoa	Genua *f*	*adj* Genuēnsis
Germany	Germānia *f*	*adj* Germānicus
Ghent	*Gandavum nt*	*adj* Gandavēnsis
Gibraltar	Calpē *f*	*adj* Calpētānus
Gibraltar, *Straits of*	Fretum Gāditānum *nt*	
Glasgow	Glasgua *f*	*adj* Glasguēnsis
Gloucester	Glēvum *nt*	
Gothenburg	*Gothoburgum nt*	
Graz	*Graecium nt*	
Greece	Graecia *f*	*adj* Graecus
Greenwich	*Grenovīcum nt*	
Grenoble	Grātiānopolis *f*	
Groningen	*Groninga f*	
Guadalquivir, *River*	Baetis *m*	
Guadiana, *River*	Anas *m*	
Guernsey	*Sarnia f*	
Hague, *The*	Haga (f) Comitis	
Halle	Halla *f*	*adj* Hallēnsis
Hamadān	Ecbatana *ntpl*	
Hamburg	*Hamburgum nt*	*adj* Hamburgēnsis
Hanover	Hannovera *f*	
Harwich	*Harvīcum nt*	
Havre	Grātiae Portus *m*	
Hebrides	Ebūdae Insulae *fpl*	
Hexham	Axelodūnum *nt*	
Holland	Batāvī *mpl*	*adj* Batāvus
Ibiza	Ebusus *f*	*adj* Ebusitānus
Ilkley	Olicāna *f*	
Inn, *River*	Aenus *m*	
Ipswich	*Gippevīcum nt*	
Ireland	Hibernia *f*	*adj* Hibernicus

Isar, *River*	Isara *f*	
Istanbul	Bӯzantium *nt*	*adj* Bӯzantīnus
Italy	Italia *f*	*adj* Italicus
Jersey	Caesarea *f*	
Jerusalem	Hierosolyma *ntpl*	*adj* Hierosolymītānus
Jutland	Chersonnēsus	
	Cimbrica *f*	
Karlsbad	*Aquae Carolīnae fpl*	
Kent	Cantium *nt*	
Kiel	*Chilonium nt*	
Koblenz	Cōnfluentēs *mpl*	
Lancaster	*Lancastria f*	
Lanchester	Longovicium *nt*	
Land's End	Bolerium	
	Prōmunturium *nt*	
Lausanne	Lausonium *nt*	*adj* Lausoniēnsis
Lebanon	Libanus *m*	
Leeds	*Ledesia f*	
Leicester	Ratae (*fpl*) Coritānōrum	
Leiden	Lugdūnum (*nt*) Batāvōrum	
Leipsig	*Lipsia f*	*adj* Lipsiēnsis
Lērida	Ilerda *f*	*adj* Ilerdēnsis
Lichfield	*Etocētum nt*	
Limoges	Augustorītum *nt*	
Lincoln	Lindum *nt*	
Lisbon	Olisīpō *m*	*adj* Olisīpōnēnsis
Lizard Point	Damnonium	
	Prōmunturium *nt*	
Loire, *River*	Liger *m*	*adj* Ligericus
Lombardy	*Langobardia f*	
London	Londinium *nt*	*adj* Londiniēnsis
Lorraine	*Lōthāringia f*	
Lucerne	*Lūceria f*	*adj* Lūcernēnsis
Lund	Londinium (*nt*)	
	Gothōrum	
Lyons	Lugdūnum *nt*	*adj* Lugdūnēnsis
Madrid	*Matrītum nt*	*adj* Matrītēnsis
Maggiore, *Lake*	Verbannus *m*	
Main, *River*	Moenus *m*	
Mainz	Mogontiacum *nt*	
Majorca	Baliāris Māior *f*	
Malta	Melita *f*	
Man, *Isle of*	Monapi *f*	
Manchester	*Mancunium nt*	
Marmara, *Sea of*	Propontis *f*	
Marne, *River*	*Māterna f*	
Marseilles	Massilia *f*	*adj* Massiliēnsis
Matapan	Taenarum *nt*	*adj* Taenarius

Mediterranean	Mare internum *nt*	
Melun	Melodūnum *nt*	
Mérida	Ēmerita *f*	*adj* Ēmeritēnsis
Messina	Messāna *f*	*adj* Messānius
Metz	Dīvodūrum *nt*	
Meuse, *River*	Mosa *f*	
Milan	Mediōlānum *nt*	*adj* Mediōlānēnsis
Minorca	Baliāris Minor *f*	
Modena	Mutina *f*	*adj* Mutinensis
Mons	Montēs *mpl*	
Monte Cassino	Casīnum *nt*	*adj* Casīnās
Moray	*Moravia f*	
Morocco	Maurētānia *f*	*adj* Maurus
Moscow	*Moscovia f*	
Moselle, *River*	Mosella *f*	
Munich	*Monacum nt*	*adj Monacēnsis*
Nantes	Namnētēs *mpl*	
Naples	Neāpolis *f*	*adj* Neāpolītānus
Neckar, *River*	Nīcer *m*	
Newcastle	Pōns (*m*) Aeliī,	*adj Novocastrēnsis*
	Novum Castrum *nt*	
Nice	Nīcaea *f*	*adj* Nicaeēnsis
Nile, *River*	Nīlus *m*	*adj* Nīlōticus
Nîmes	Nemausus *f*	*adj* Nemausēnsis
Norway	*Norvēgia f*	*adj Norvēgiānus*
Norwich	*Nordovīcum nt*	
Oder, *River*	Viadrus *m*	
Oporto	Portus Calēnsis *m*	
Orange	Arausiō *f*	
Orkneys	Orcades *fpl*	
Orléans	*Aurēliānum nt*	*adj Aurēliānēnsis*
Oudenarde	*Aldenarda f*	
Oxford	*Oxonia f*	*adj Oxoniēnsis*
Padua	Patavium *nt*	*adj* Patavīnus
Palermo	Panormus *m*	*adj* Panormitānus
Paris	Lutetia *f*, Parīsiī *mpl*	*adj Parīsiēnsis*
Patras	Patrae *fpl*	*adj* Patrēnsis
Persian Gulf	Mare Rubrum *nt*	
Piacenza	Placentia *f*	*adj* Placentīnus
Po, *River*	Padus	*adj* Padānus
Poitiers	Limōnum *nt*	
Poland	*Polōnia f*	
Portsmouth	Māgnus Portus *m*	
Portugal	Lūsitānia *f*	
Pozzuoli	Puteolī *mpl*	*adj* Puteolānus
Prague	*Prāga f*	*adj Prāgēnsis*
Provence	Prōvincia *f*	
Pyrenees	Pȳrēnaeī montēs *mpl*	

Red Sea	Sinus Arābicus *m*	
Rheims	Dūrocortorum *nt*	
Rhine, *River*	Rhēnus *m*	*adj* Rhēnānus
Rhodes	Rhodos *f*	*adj* Rhodius
Rhône, *River*	Rhodanus *m*	
Richborough	Rutupiae *fpl*	*adj* Rutupīnus
Rimini	Arīminum	*adj* Arīminēnsis
Rochester	Dūrobrīvae *fpl*	
Rome	Rōma *f*	*adj* Rōmānus
Rotterdam	Roterodamum *nt*	*adj* Roterodamēnsis
Rouen	Rothomagus *f*	*adj* Rothomagēnsis
Saar, *River*	Sangona *f*	
Salisbury	Sarisberia *f*	
Salzburg	Iuvāvum *nt*	*adj* Salisburgēnsis
Saône, *River*	Arar *m*	
Savoy	Sabaudia *f*	
Scheidt, *River*	Scaldis *m*	
Schleswig	*Slesvīcum nt*	
Scilly Isles	Cassiterides *fpl*	
Scotland	Calēdonia *f*	*adj* Calēdonius
Seine, *River*	Sēquana *f*	
Severn, *River*	Sabrīna *f*	
Seville	Hīspalis *f*	*adj* Hispalēnsis
Shrewsbury	Salōpia *f*	
Sicily	Sicilia *f*	*adj* Siculus
Sidra, *Gulf of*	Syrtis (māior) *f*	
Silchester	Callēva (*f*) Atrebatum	
Soissons	Augusta (*f*) Suessiōnum	
Solway Firth	Itūna (*f*) aestuarium	
Somme, *River*	Samara *f*	
Spain	Hispānia *f*	*adj* Hispānus
St.Albans	Verulamium *nt*	
St.Andrews	*Andreopolis f*	
St. Bernard	(*Great*) Mōns Pennīnus *m*, (*Little*) Alpis Grāia *f*	
St. Gallen	Sangallanēse coenobium *nt*	*adj* Sangallēnsis
St. Gotthard	Alpēs summae *fpl*	
St.Moritz	Agaunum *nt*	*adj* Agaunēnsis
Strasbourg	Argentorātus *f*	*adj* Argentorātēnsis
Swabia	Suēvia *f*	*adj* Suēvicus
Sweden	*Suēcia f*	*adj* Suēcicus
Switzerland	Helvētia *f*	*adj* Helvēticus
Syracuse	Syrācūsae *fpl*	*adj* Syrācūsānus
Tangier	Tingī *f*	*adj* Tingitānus
Taranto	Tarentum *nt*	*adj* Tarentīnus
Tarragona	Tarracō *f*	*adj* Tarracōnēnsis
Tay, *River*	Taus *m*	
Thames, *River*	Tamesis *m*	

Thebes	Thēbae *fpl*	*adj* Thēbānus
Tiber, *River*	Tiberis *m*	*adj* Tiberīnus
Tivoli	Tībur *nt*	*adj* Tīburtīnus
Toledo	Tolētum *nt*	*adj* Tolētanus
Toulon	Tolōna *f*	*adj* Tolōnēnsis
Toulouse	Tolōsa *f*	*adj* Tolōsānus
Tours	Caesarodūnum *nt*	
Trèves, Trier	Augusta (*f*) Treverōrum	
Trieste	Tergeste *nt*	*adj* Tergestīnus
Tripoli	Tripolis *f*	*adj* Tripolitānus
Tunis	Tūnēs *f*	*adj* Tūnētānus
Turin	Augusta (*f*) Taurīnōrum	*adj* Taurīnus
Tuscany	Etrūria *f*	*adj* Etrūscus
Tyrrhenian Sea	Mare īnferum *nt*	
Utrecht	Ultrāiectum *nt*	*adj* Ultrāiēctensis
Vardar, *River*	Axius *m*	
Venice	Venetī *mpl*, Venetiae *fpl*	*adj* Venetus
Verdun	Virodūnum *nt*	*adj* Virodūnēnsis
Versailles	Versāliae *fpl*	*adj* Versāliēnsis
Vichy	Aquae (*fpl*) Sōlis	
Vienna	Vindobona *f*	*adj* Vindobonēnsis
Vosges	Vosegus *m*	
Wales	Cambria *f*	
Wallsend	Segedūnum *nt*	
Warsaw	Varsavia *f*	*adj* Varsaviēnsis
Wash, *The*	Metaris (*m*) aestuārium	
Wear, *River*	Vedra *f*	
Weser, *River*	Visurgis *m*	
Westminster	Westmonastērium *nt*	*adj* Westmonastēriēnsis
Wiesbaden	Mattiacum *nt*	*adj* Mattiacus
Wight, *Isle of*	Vectis *f*	
Winchester	Venta (*f*) Belgārum	
Worcester	Vigornia *f*	
Worms	Vormatia *f*	
Wroxeter	Viroconium *nt*	
York	Eborācum *nt*	*adj* Eborācēnsis
Zuider Zee	Flēvō *m*	
Zurich	Turicum *nt*	*adj* Tigurīnus

NUMERALS

	Cardinal		Ordinal	
1	ūnus	I	prīmus	1st
2	duo	II	secundus, alter	2nd
3	trēs	III	tertius	3rd
4	quattuor	IV	quārtus	4th
5	quīque	V	quīntus	5th
6	sex	VI	sextus	6th
7	septem	VII	septimus	7th
8	octō	VIII	octāvus	8th
9	novem	IX	nōnus	9th
10	decem	X	decimus	10th
11	undecim	XI	undecimus	11th
12	duodecim	XII	duodecimus	12th
13	tredecim	XIII	tertius decimus	13th
14	quattuordecim	XIV	quārtus decimus	14th
15	quīndecim	XV	quīntus decimus	15th
16	sēdecim	XVI	sextus decimus	16th
17	septendecim	XVII	septimus decimus	17th
18	duodēvīgintī	XVIII	duodēvīcēsimus	18th
19	ūndēvīgintī	XIX	ūndēvīcēsimus	19th
20	vīgintī	XX	vīcēsimus	20th
21	vīgintī ūnus	XXI	vīcēsimus prīmus	21st
28	duodētrīgintā	XXVIII	duodētrīcēsimus	28th
29	ūndētrīgintā	XXIX	ūndētrīcēsimus	29th
30	trīgintā	XXX	trīcēsimus	30th
40	quadrāgintā	XL	quadrāgēsimus	40th
50	quīnquāgintā	L	quīnquāgēsimus	50th
60	sexāgintā	LX	sexāgēsimus	60th
70	septuāgintā	LXX	septuāgēsimus	70th
80	octōgintā	LXXX	octōgēsimus	80th
90	nōnāgintā	XC	nōnāgēsimus	90th
100	centum	C	centēsimus	100th
101	centum et ūnus	CI	centēsimus prīmus	101st
122	centum vīgintī duo	CXXII	centēsimus vīcēsimus alter	122nd
200	ducentī	CC	ducentēsimus	200th
300	trecentī	CCC	trecentēsimus	300th
400	quadringentī	CCCC	quadringentēsimus	400th
500	quīngentī	D	quīngentēsimus	500th
600	sēscentī	DC	sēscentēsimus	600th
700	septingentī	DCC	septingentēsimus	700th
800	octingentī	DCCC	octingentēsimus	800th
900	nōngentī	DCCCC	nōngentēsimus	900th
1000	mīlle	M	mīllēsimus	1000th
1001	mīlle et ūnus	MI	mīllēsimus prīmus	1001st
1102	mīlle centum duo	MCII	mīllēsimus centēsimus alter	1102nd
3000	tria mīlia	MMM	ter mīllēsimus	3000th
5000	quīnque mīlia	IƆƆ	quīnquiēs mīllēsimus	5000th
10,000	decem mīlia	CCIƆƆ	deciēs mīllēsimus	10,000th
100,000	centum mīlia	CCCIƆƆƆ	centiēs mīllēsimus	100,000th
1,000,000	deciēs centēna mīlia	CCCCIƆƆƆƆ	deciēs centiēs mīllēsimus	1,000,000th

NUMERALS

	Distributive		Adverb	
1	singulī	I	semel	1st
2	bīnī	II	bis	2nd
3	ternī (trīnī)	III	ter	3rd
4	quaternī	IV	quater	4th
5	quīnī	V	quīnquiēs	5th
6	sēnī	VI	sexiēs	6th
7	septēnī	VII	septiēs	7th
8	octōnī	VIII	octiēs	8th
9	novēnī	IX	noviēs	9th
10	dēnī	X	deciēs	10th
11	undēnī	XI	undeciēs	11th
12	duodēnī	XII	duodeciēs	12th
13	ternī dēnī	XIII	ter deciēs	13th
14	quaternī dēnī	XIV	quattuordeciēs	14th
15	quīnī dēnī	XV	quīndeciēs	15th
16	sēnī dēnī	XVI	sēdeciēs	16th
17	septēnī dēnī	XVII	septiēs deciēs	17th
18	duodēvīcēnī	XVIII	duodēviciēs	18th
19	undēvīcēnī	XIX	ūndēvīciēs	19th
20	vīcēnī	XX	vīciēs	20th
21	vīcēnī singulī	XXI	semel et vīciēs	21st
28	duodētrīcēnī	XXVIII	duodētrīciēs	28th
29	ūndētrīcēnī	XXIX	ūndētrīciēs	29th
30	trīcēnī	XXX	trīciēs	30th
40	quadrāgēnī	XL	quadrāgiēs	40th
50	quīnquāgēnī	L	quīnquāgiēs	50th
60	sexāgēnī	LX	sexāgiēs	60th
70	septuāgēnī	LXX	septuāgiēs	70th
80	octōgēnī	LXXX	octōgiēs	80th
90	nōnagēnī	XC	nōnāgiēs	90th
100	centēnī	C	centiēs	100th
101	centēnī singulī	CI	semel et centiēs	101st
122	centēnī vīcēnī bīnī	CXXII	centiēs vīciēs bis	122nd
200	ducēnī	CC	ducentiēs	200th
300	trecēnī	CCC	trecentiēs	300th
400	quadringēnī	CCCC	quadringentiēs	400th
500	quīngēnī	D	quīngentiēs	500th
600	sexcēnī	DC	sexcentiēs	600th
700	septingēnī	DCC	septingentiēs	700th
800	octingēnī	DCCC	octingentiēs	800th
900	nōngēnī	DCCCC	nōngentiēs	900th
1000	singula mīlia	M	mīlliēs	1000th
1001	singula mīlia singulī	MI	semel et mīlliēs	1001st
1102	singula mīlia centēnī bīnī	MCII	mīlliēs centiēs bis	1102nd
3000	trīna mīlia	MMM	ter mīlliēs	3000th
5000	quīna mīlia	IↃↃ	quīnquiēs mīlliēs	5000th
10,000	dēna mīlia	CCIↃↃ	deciēs mīlliēs	10,000th
100,000	centēna mīlia	CCCIↃↃↃ	centiēs mīlliēs	100,000th
1,000,000	deciēs centēna mīlia	CCCCIↃↃↃↃ	mīlliēs mīlliēs	1,000,000th

DATES

MONTHS

Three days of the month have special names:

Kalendae the 1st.

Nōnae the 5th of most months, but the 7th of March, May, July and October.

> "In March, July, October, May,
> The Nones are on the 7th day."

Idūs the 13th of most months, but the 15th of March, May, July and October.

If the date is one of these three days, it is expressed in the ablative, with the adjective of the month in agreement, *e.g.*

1stJanuary, **Kalendīs Iānuāriīs**, usually abbreviated **Kal. Ian.**

The day immediately before any of these three is expressed by **prīdiē** with the accusative, *e.g.*

4th February, **prīdiē Nōnās Februāriās**, usually abbreviated **prid. Non. Feb.**

All other dates are expressed as so many days before the next named day, and in reckoning the interval both the date and the named day are counted, *e.g.* the 11th is the 5th day before the 15th.

The formula is all in the accusative, beginning with the words **ante diem**, *e.g.* 11th March, **ante diem quintum Idūs Martiās**, usually abbreviated **a.d. V Id. Mar.**

The following selection of dates for April and May should be a sufficient guide to the dates of any month in the year:-

APRIL		MAY
Kal.Apr.	1	Kal. Mai.
a.d. IV Non. Apr.	2	a.d. VI Non. Mai.
a.d. III Non. Apr.	3	a.d. V Non. Mai.
prid. Non. Apr.	4	a.d. IV Non. Mai.
Non. Apr.	5	a.d. III Non. Mai.
a.d. VIII Id. Apr.	6	prid. Non. Mai.
a.d. VII ld. Apr.	7	Non. Mai.
a.d. VI Id. Apr.	8	a.d. VIII Id. Mai.
a.d. V ld. Apr.	9	a.d. VII Id. Mai.
a.d. IV Id. Apr.	10	a.d. VI ld. Mai.
a.d. III Id. Apr.	11	a.d. V Id. Mai.
prid. Id. Apr.	12	a.d. IV Id. Mai.
ld. Apr.	13	a.d. III Id. Mai.
a.d. XVIII Kal. Mai.	14	prid. Id. Mai.
a.d. XVII Kal. Mai.	15	Id. Mai.
a.d. XVI Kal. Mai.	16	a.d. XVII Kal. Iun.

a.d. XV Kal. Mai.	**17**	a.d.XVI Kal. Iun.
a.d. XII Kal. Mai.	**20**	a.d. XIII Kal. Iun.
a.d. VII Kal. Mai.	**25**	a.d. VIII Kal. Iun.
prid. Kal. Mai.	**30**	a.d. III Kal. Iun.
-	**31**	prid. Kal. Iun.

YEARS

A year is denoted either by giving the names of the consuls or by reckoning the number of years from the traditional date of the foundation of Rome, 753 B.C. (A date B.C. should be subtracted from 754, a date A.D. should be added to 753.)

E.g. "In the year 218 B.C.," *either* P. Cornelio Scipione Ti. Sempronio Longo coss. *or* a. u. c. DXXXVI.

MEASURES

Length

12 ūnciae	=	1 pēs
5 pedēs	=	1 passus
125 passūs	=	1 stadium
8 stadia	=	mīlle passūs

The Roman mile was about 1.48km.

Area

100 pedēs quadrātī	=	1 scrīpulum
144 scrīpula	=	1 āctus quadrātus
2 āctūs quadrātī	=	1 iugerum
2 iugera	=	1 hērēdium
100 hērēdia	=	1 centuria

The **iugerum** was about 2529.28 square metres.

Capacity

	4 cochleāria	=	1 cyathus
	12 cyathī	=	1 sextārius
(liquid)	6 sextāriī	=	1 congius
	8 congiī	=	1 amphora
	20 amphorae	=	1 culleus
(dry)	8 sextāriī	=	1 sēmodius
	2 sēmodiī	=	1 modius

The **sextārius** was about half a litre, the **modius** about 9 litres.

Weight

4 scrīpula	=	1 sextula
6 sextulae	=	1 ūncia
12 ūnciae	=	1 lībra

The Roman lb. was about 326 g, and the **ūncia** was therefore about 27 g. The twelfths of the **lībra** have the following names, which are also used to denote fractions generally, *e.g.* **hērēs ex triente**, heir to a third of an estate.

$\frac{1}{12}$	ūncia	$\frac{5}{12}$	quīncūnx	$\frac{3}{4}$	dōdrāns
$\frac{1}{6}$	sextāns	$\frac{1}{2}$	sēmis	$\frac{5}{6}$	dextāns
$\frac{1}{4}$	quadrāns	$\frac{7}{12}$	septūnx	$\frac{11}{12}$	deūnx
$\frac{1}{3}$	triēns	$\frac{2}{3}$	bēs		

MONEY

Roman

$2\frac{1}{2}$ assēs	=	1 sēstertius (or nummus)
4 sēstertii	=	1 dēnārius
25 dēnāriī	=	1 aureus

The sesterce is represented by a symbol for $2\frac{1}{2}$, properly **II S(ēmis)**, usually standardized in the form HS. The *ntpl* **sēstertia** with the distributive numeral denotes thousands of sesterces, and the numeral adverb with the *gen pl* **sēstertium** (understanding **centena milia**) means hundred thousands, *e.g.*

10,000 sesterces	=	dēna sēstertia	=	HS $\bar{\text{X}}$
1,000,000 sesterces	=	deciēs sēstertium	=	HS I$\bar{\text{X}}$I

Greek

100 drachumae	=	1 mina
60 minae	=	1 talentum

MONEY

Roman

Greek

LATIN VERSE

QUANTITY

Both vowels and syllables in Latin may be described as long or short. A long vowel or syllable is one on which the voice dwells for a longer time than on a short one, in much the same way as a minim is long compared with a crotchet in musical notation.

A syllable is long if the vowel in it is either long in itself or followed by two or more consonants. The letter **x** counts as a double consonant, the letter **h** not at all, and the following pairs of consonants occurring in the same word after a short vowel do not necessarily make the syllable long:

br, cr, dr, fr, gr, pr, tr; fl, gl, pl.

A syllable is short if its vowel is a short one and not followed by two or more consonants (except for the groups noted in the preceding paragraph).

Examples: In **dūcō** both the vowels are long ("by nature") and therefore the two syllables are long.

In **deus** both the vowels are short, neither is followed by more than one consonant, and therefore the two syllables are short; but if a word beginning with a consonant follows, then the syllable **-us** will become long.

In **adsunt** both the vowels are short, but they are both followed by two consonants, and the two syllables are therefore "long by position".

This long or short characteristic of Latin vowels and syllables is called "quantity." To determine the quantities of vowels no general rules can be given, and some of them are now not known for certain. The vowel quantities of words will have to be learned when the words are learned, or else looked up when the need arises. In final syllables, however, there is a certain regularity to be found, and the following table shows the commonest of these:

ENDING

	Long	Short
-a	*1st decl abl sing*	*1st decl nom and voc sing*
	1st conj impv sing	*all nom and acc ntpl*
	numerals and most adverbs	**ita, quia**
-e	*5th decl abl sing*	*all other noun and verb endings*
	2nd conj impv sing	
	most adverbs	**bene, male**
	Greek nouns	*enclitics*

-i	*all endings, except*	**quasi, nisi**: *and sometimes* **mihi, tibi, sibi, ibi, ubi**
-o	*all endings, except*	*sometimes iambic words, esp* **cito, duo, ego, homo, modo, puto, rogo, scio**
-u	*all endings*	
-as	*all endings, except*	*Greek nouns*
-es	*all endings, except*	*3rd dec/ nom sing with short* **-e-** *in stem* **es** *(be) and compounds* **penes**
-is	*1st and 2nd decl dat and abl pl 3rd decl acc pl 4th conj 2nd pers sing* **vīs, sīs, velīs**	*all others*
-os	*all endings, except*	*2nd dec/ nom sing* **os** *(bone)* **compos, impos**
-us	*3rd dec/ nom sing with long* **-u-** *in stem 4th dec/ gen sing and nom and acc pl*	*all others*

METRES

Latin Verse is a pattern of long and short syllables, grouped together in "feet" or in lyric lines.

FEET

The commonest feet employed in Latin metres are:

Anapaest	(short-short-long)	˘ ˘ —
Dactyl	(long-short-short)	— ˘ ˘
Iambus	(short-long)	˘ —
Proceleusmatic	(short-short-short-short)	˘ ˘ ˘ ˘
Spondee	(long-long)	— —
Tribrach	(short-short-short)	˘ ˘ ˘
Trochee	(long-short)	— ˘

CAESURA AND DIAERESIS

The longer lines usually have a regular break near the middle, occurring either in the middle of a foot (**Caesura**) or at the end of a foot (**Diaeresis**). This break need not imply a pause in the sense of the words, but merely the end of a word, provided that it does not go too closely with the word following, as in the case of a preposition before a noun. See examples on pages 30-35 where the caesura is marked †, and the diaeresis //.

ELISION

A vowel or a vowel followed by **m** at the end of a word ("open vowel") is regularly elided before a vowel at the beginning of the next word in the same line. In reciting, the elided syllable should not be dropped entirely, but slurred into the following vowel. An open vowel at the end of a line does not elide before a vowel at the beginning of the next line.

FINAL SYLLABLES

Where the metre requires the final syllable in a line to be long, this syllable may in fact be a short one. This position in the line is commonly called a **syllaba anceps**, and marked down as being either long or short. It is perhaps better to regard this syllable, when the vowel is short, as long by position, since metrical length is a matter of duration, and the end of a line calls naturally for a slight pause in reading, even if the sense runs on to the next line. In the metrical schemes which follow, a long final syllable should be understood in this sense: it may in itself be a short one.

Latin metres fall into three fairly distinct categories, associated with three different genres of verse:

1. *Dactylic*
2. *Iambic and Trochaic*
3. *Lyric*

DACTYLIC VERSE

The Dactylic metres are the **Hexameter** and the **Pentameter**. The Hexameter is the medium of epic, didactic and pastoral poetry, of satires and epistles, and other examples of occasional verse. In conjunction with the Pentameter it forms the **Elegiac Couplet**, the metre most commonly used for love poetry, occasional pieces, and the epigram.

Dactylic Hexameter

The first four feet may be either **dactyls** or **spondees**, the 5th is regularly a dactyl, the 6th always a spondee. In Virgil and later poets the last word is either disyllabic or trisyllabic. A **Caesura** normally occurs in either the 3rd or the 4th foot, and pastoral poetry often has the "**Bucolic Diaeresis**" at the end of the 4th foot. In Virgilian and later usage there is a tendency for words and feet to overlap in the first four feet and to coincide in the last two. Similarly in the first part of the line the metrical ictus and the normal accent of the spoken word tend to fall on different syllables, whereas they regularly coincide in the last two feet.

Example:

Clāss(em) āp|tēnt tăcĭ|tī † sŏcĭ|ōsqu(e) ād |lītŏră| tōrquēnt

(*Virgil, Aen.* 4, 289)

Occasional lines will be found in the poets, which deliberately violate the above rules for the sake of obtaining some special effect,

pēr cō|nūbĭă| nōstrā,† pĕr| īncēp|tōs hȳmĕ|nāeōs

(*Aen.* 4, 316)

The above echoes Greek hexameter, where the final word is Greek and has four syllables, and the caesura comes between the two short syllables of the dactyl in the 3rd foot:

cūm sŏcĭ|īs nā|tōqŭe† pĕ|nātĭ bŭs| ēt māg|nīs dīs

(*Aen.* 3, 12)

Note the solemn, archaic touch, suggesting a line of Ennius, where the 5th foot is a spondee, and the last word is monosyllabic.

pārtŭrĭ|ēnt mōn|tēs, ˈnā| sēctūr| rīdĭcŭ|lūs mūs

(Hor, A. P. 139)

The monosyllabic ending, above, creates a comic effect.

Dactylic Pentameter

This line has two equal parts of 2½ feet each. The two feet in the first part may be either **dactyls** or **spondees**, those in the second part are always dactylic. The two half-feet are long (though the final syllable may be a short one), and there is always a diaeresis between the two parts of the line. In Ovid and later poets the last word in the line is regularly disyllabic.

Example:

Aēnē|ān ănĭ|mō // nōxquĕ dĭ|ēsquĕ rĕ|fērt

(Ovid, Her. 7, 26)

SCANSION

The following procedure may assist beginners to scan a normal hexameter or pentameter correctly :-

1. Mark off elisions.
2. Mark the first syllable long, and (Hexameter) the last five dactyl and spondee, or (Pentameter) the last seven syllables, two dactyls and a long syllable.
3. Mark all diphthongs long.
4. Mark all syllables that are long by position, omitting any doubtful cases.
5. Mark any other syllables known to be long.
6. Mark any syllables known to be short.
7. Fill in the few (if any) remaining syllables, and identify the principal caesura.
8. Read the line aloud.

IAMBIC AND TROCHAIC VERSE

The Iambic and Trochaic metres occur mainly in dramatic verse, but some are found elsewhere, as in the lyrics of Catullus and Horace. The principal Iambic metres are the **Senarius**, the **Septenarius**, and the **Octonarius**; the principal Trochaic metres are the Septenarius and Octonarius.

Iambic Senarius

Basically this line consists of six iambic feet, but in practice such a line is very rare.

Example:

Phăsēl|lŭs īl|lĕ quēm| vĭdē|tĭs, hōs|pĭtēs

(*Cat.* 4,1)

In drama the last foot is always iambic, and the 5th regularly a spondee. The **spondee** is also very common in the first four feet, the **dactyl** and the **tribrach** are frequent, occasionally the **anapaest** is found, and, more rarely, the **proceleusmatic**. There is usually a **caesura** in either the third or the fourth foot.

Example:

Ĭn hāc| hăbĭtās|sĕ plătĕ|ā dīc|tūmst Chrȳ|sĭdēm

(*Ter, And.* 796)

Iambic Septenarius

This line consists of seven and a half feet, basically iambic, but allowing the same variations as in the Senarius. The 4th foot is regularly an Iambus, and is usually followed by a diaeresis: this is an aid to identifying the line.

Example:

N(am) īdcīr|c(o) āccēr|sōr nūp|tĭās| quŏd m(i) ād|părā|rī sēn|sīt

(*Ter, And.*690)

Iambic Octonarius

This line has eight iambic feet, with the same variations as in the other iambic lines. The 4th and 8th feet are regularly iambic, and a diaeresis follows the 4th foot.

Example:

Cūrā|bĭtūr.| sēd pătĕr| ădēst.| căvĕt(e) ēs|sĕ trīs|tēm sēn|tĭāt

(*Ter, And.*403)

Trochaic Septenarius

Apart from drama, this line is common in popular verses, and comes into its own in later Latin poetry. It consists of seven and a half **trochees**, but in practice only the seventh foot is regularly trochaic, while the others may be **spondee, dactyl, tribrach**, or (more rarely) **anapaest**. There is usually a diaeresis after the 4th foot.

Example:

Crās ă|mēt quī| nūnqu(am) ă|māvīt,| quīqu(e) ă|māvīt| crās ă|mēt

(*Pervigilium Veneris*)

Trochaic Octonarius

This is a line of eight trochees, allowing the same variations as above. There is a diaeresis after the 4th foot.

Example:

Prōin tū| sōllĭcĭ|tūdĭn|(em) īstām| fālsām| quāe t(e) ēx|crŭcĭăt| mīttās

(*Ter, Heaut.* 177)

LYRIC VERSE

In most lyric metres the line is not to be subdivided into feet, but is itself the unit of scansion, and has a fixed number of syllables. The commonest, which are those used by Catullus and Horace, are the **Hendecasyllabic**, the **Asclepiads**, the **Glyconic** and the **Pherecratic**, which occur either singly or in combinations to form either couplets or stanzas of four lines. Beside these groupings there are the **Alcaic** and **Sapphic** stanzas. Elisions occur much more rarely than in the other metres.

Hendecasyllabic

This is Catullus's favourite line. It consists of eleven syllables in the following pattern:

_ _ _ ˘ ˘_ ˘_ ˘_ _

Either the first or the second syllable may occasionally be short, and there is usually a caesura after the 5th syllable.

Example:

Vīvāmūs, mĕă Lēsbĭ(a), ātqu(e) ămēmūs

(*Cat.* 5, 1)

33

Asclepiads

There are two Asclepiad lines, of which the **Lesser** is by far the commoner. It has twelve syllables, in the following pattern with a caesura after the 6th syllable:

$$- - - \; \smile\smile\; - \; \| \; - \; \smile\smile\; - \; \smile\; -$$

Mǣcēnās, ǎtǎvīs' ēdǐtě rēgǐbūs

(Hor, Od. I, 1, 1)

The **Greater Asclepiad** is formed by adding a **choriambus** $- \smile\smile -$ after the 6th syllable with a **diaeresis** both before and after it.

Example:

Nūllām, Vārě, sǎcrā vītě priĭs sēvěrĭs ārbǒrēm

(Hor, Od. I, 18, 1)

Glyconic

The **Glyconic** occurs by itself in Catullus, but more usually it is found in combination with the **Lesser Asclepiad** or the **Pherecratic**. It consists of eight syllables ($- - - \smile\smile - \smile -$), so that it is like a Lesser Asclepiad minus the choriambus. It has no regular caesura.

Example:

Dōnēc grātǔs ěrām tǐbī

(Hor, Od. III, 9, 1)

Pherecratic

The **Pherecratic** is a Glyconic minus the second last (short) syllable. It is found only in combination with other lines.

Example:

Sūspēndīssě pǒtēntī

(Hor, Od. I, 5, 11)

Alcaic Stanza

The **Alcaic stanza** has four lines, of which the first two have the same pattern $-- \breve{} --- \breve{} \breve{} - \breve{} -$. In these there is a regular caesura after the 5th syllable. The third line is $-- \breve{} --- \breve{} --$ and the 4th $- \breve{} \breve{} - \breve{} \breve{} - \breve{} --$. Neither of the last two lines has a regular break in it.

Example:

> Nūnc ēst bĭbēndūm,† nūnc pĕdĕ lībĕrō
> pūlsāndă tēllūs, †nūnc Sălĭărĭbūs
> ōrnārĕ pūlvīnār dĕōrūm
> tēmpŭs ĕrāt dăpĭbūs, sŏdālēs.

$\hfill$ (*Hor, Od.* I.37, 1-4)

Sapphic Stanza

The **Sapphic stanza** also has four lines, of which the first three are the same: $- \breve{} --- \breve{}\ \breve{} - \breve{} -\ -$. As in the Alcaic there is a **caesura** after the 5th syllable. The last line is a short **Adonic** $- \breve{}\ \breve{} --$

Example:

> Īntĕgēr vītāe † scĕlĕrīsquĕ pūrūs
> nōn ĕgēt Māurīs † iăcūlīs nĕqu(e) ārcū
> nēc vĕnēnātīs † grăvĭdā săgīttīs,
> Fūscĕ, phărētrā.

$\hfill$ (*Hor, Od.* I. 22, 1-4)

LATIN PHRASES USED IN ENGLISH

What follows is a list of some of the Latin phrases used in English today.

ab initio	from the beginning.
ab ovo	(lit: from the egg) from the beginning.
absit omen	(lit: may the (evil) omen be absent) may the presentiment not become real or take place.
ab urbe condita	(used in dates) from the foundation of the city (*i.e. from the foundation of Rome in 753 B.C.*).
A.D.	abbr for **anno Domini**.
ad hoc	(lit: for this) for a particular purpose only: **an ad hoc committee; an ad hoc decision**.
ad hominem	(lit: according to the person) **1** directed against a person rather than against his or her arguments. **2** based on or appealing to emotion rather than reason.
ad infinitum	without end; endlessly; to infinity.
ad interim	for the meantime; for the present: **ad interim measures**.
ad-lib	(abbr for **ad libitum**) • *adj* improvised; impromptu • *adv* without restraint; freely; as one pleases • *vb* to improvise and deliver without preparation.
ad libitum	(lit: according to pleasure) as one pleases.
ad majorem Dei gloriam	for the greater glory of God (*the Jesuit motto*).
ad nauseam	(lit: to (the point of) nausea) to a disgusting extent.
ad rem	(lit: to the matter) to the point; without digression: **to reply ad rem; an ad rem discussion**.
advocatus diaboli	devil's advocate.
ad valorem	(lit: according to value) in proportion to the estimated value of the goods taxed.
aet.	(abbr for **aetatis**) at the age of.
Agnus Dei	Lamb of God.
alma mater	(lit: nurturing mother) one's former university, college or school.
alter ego	(lit: other self) **1** a second self. **2** a very close and intimate friend.
a.m.	abbr for **ante meridiem**.
AMDG	abbr for **ad majorem Dei gloriam**.
amor patriae	love of one's country; patriotism.
an.	(abbr for **anno**) in the year.
anno Domini	in the year of our Lord.
anno urbis conditae	in the year of the foundation of the city (*i.e. of Rome in 753 B.C., used in dates*)
anno regni	in the year of the reign (of).

annus mirabilis	(lit: wonderful year) a year of wonders.
antebellum	(lit: before the war) of or during the period before a war, especially the American Civil War.
ante meridiem	before noon.
ante-mortem	before death (*esp in legal or medical contexts*).
a.p.	(abbr for **ante prandium**) before a meal (*in prescriptions*).
apparatus criticus	(lit: critical apparatus) textual notes (*list of variant readings, etc., relating to a document, especially in a scholarly edition of a text*).
aq.	abbr for **aqua**.
aqua vitae	(lit: water of life) brandy.
a.r.	abbr for **anno regni**.
arbiter elegantiae *or* elegantiarum	judge in a matter of taste.
arcus senilis	(lit: senile bow) opaque circle around the cornea of the eye (*often seen in elderly people*).
argumentum ad hominem	(lit:argument according to the person: *Logic*) **1** fallacious argument that attacks not an opponent's beliefs but his motives or character. **2** argument that shows an opponent's statement to be inconsistent with his other beliefs.
ars longa vita brevis	art is long, life is short.
AUC	abbr for: **1 ab urbe condita. 2 anno urbis conditae.**
aut vincere aut mori	death or victory.
aurora australis	the southern lights.
aurora borealis	the northern lights.
ave	**1** hail! **2** farewell!
ave atque vale	hail and farewell!
Ave Maria	Hail Mary.
beatae memoriae	of blessed memory.
Beata Virgo	the Blessed Virgin.
Beata Virgo Maria	the Blessed Virgin Mary.
b.i.d	(abbr for **bis in die**) twice a day (*in prescriptions*).
bis dat, qui cito dat	the person who gives promptly gives twice.
BV	abbr for **Beata Virgo**.
c,ca	abbr for **circa**.
camera obscura	(lit: dark chamber) camera obscura.
carpe diem	(lit: seize the day) enjoy the pleasures of the moment, without concern for the future.
casus belli	(lit: occasion of war) **1** an event or act used to justify a war. **2** the immediate cause of a quarrel.
caveat emptor	let the buyer beware.
cetera desunt	the rest is missing.

ceteris paribus	other things being equal.
circa	around.
Codex Juris Canonici	(lit: book of canon law) the official code of canon law (*in the Roman Catholic Church*).
cogito, ergo sum	I think, therefore I am (*the basis of Descartes' philosophy*).
compos mentis	of sound mind; sane.
coram populo	in the presence of the people; openly.
corpus delicti	(lit: the body of the crime: LAW) the body of facts that constitute an offence.
Corpus Juris Canonici	(lit: body of canon law) the official compilation of canon law (*in the Roman Catholic Church*).
Corpus Juris Civilis	(lit: body of civil law) the body of Roman or civil law.
corrigenda	things to be corrected.
corpus vile	(lit: worthless body) person or thing fit only to be the object of an experiment.
culpa	1 (*LAW*) an act of neglect. 2 (*gen*) a fault; sin; guilt.
cum grano salis	with a grain of salt; not too literally.
cum laude	(*chiefly US*) with praise (*the lowest of three designations for above-average achievement in examinations*).
curriculum vitae	(lit: the course of one's life) curriculum vitae.
de facto	*adv* in fact • *adj* existing in fact.
de gustibus non est disputandum	there is no arguing about tastes.
de jure	according to law; by right; legally.
de mortuis nil nisi bonum	say nothing but good of the dead.
de novo	anew.
Deo gratias	thanks be to God.
Deo Optimo Maximo	to God, the best, the Greatest.
Deo volente	God willing.
de profundis	out of the depths of misery or dejection.
deus ex machina	(lit: the god from the machine) 1 (in ancient Greek and Roman drama) a god introduced into a play to resolve the plot. 2 any unlikely or artificial device serving this purpose.
Dies Irae	(lit: the day of wrath) 1 a famous Latin hymn of the 13th century, describing the Last Judgment. It is used in the Mass for the dead. 2 a musical setting of this hymn, usually part of a setting of the Requiem.
disjecta membra	the scattered remains.
DOM	abbr for **Deo Optimo Maximo.**
dramatis personae	(lit: the persons of the drama) the list of characters in a drama.

Ecce Homo	behold the man (*the words of Pontius Pilate to Christ's accusers [John 19:5]*).
editio princeps	(lit: the first edition) the first printed edition of a work.
e.g., eg	abbr for **exempli gratia**.
emeritus	retired from office.
e pluribus unum	one out of many (*motto of USA*).
ER	**1** (abbr for **Elizabeth Regina**) Queen Elizabeth; **2** (abbr for **Eduardus Rex**) King Edward.
errare est humanum	to err is human.
erratum (*pl* errata)	error.
et seq.	(abbr for **et sequens**) and the following.
et seqq.	(abbr for **et sequentia**) and those that follow.
ex	(lit: out of, from) **1** (FINANCE) not participating in; excluding;without: **ex bonus; ex dividend; ex rights**. **2** (COMMERCE) without charge to the buyer until removed from: **ex quay; ex ship; ex works**.
ex cathedra	(lit: from the chair) **1** with authority. **2** defined by the pope as infallibly true, to be accepted by all Roman Catholics.
exeat	(lit: let him or her go out) formal leave of absence.
exempli gratia	for example.
exeunt	they go out (*used as a stage direction*).
exeunt omnes	they all go out (*used as a stage direction*).
exit	he or she goes out (*used as a stage direction*).
ex libris	(lit: from the books (of)) from the collection or library of.
ex officio	by right of position or office.
ex parte	(LAW) on behalf of one side or party only (*of an application in a judicial proceeding*): **an ex parte injunction**.
ex post facto	having retrospective effect: **an ex post facto law**.
ex silentio	(lit: from silence) based on a lack of evidence to the contrary (*of a theory, assumption etc*).
extempore	(lit: instantaneously) without planning or preparation; impromptu.
ex voto	*adv, adj* in accordance with a vow • *n* offering made in fulfilment of a vow.
facile princeps	(lit: easily first) an obvious leader.
fecit (*abbr* fec)	(he or she) made it (*used formerly on works of art next to the artist's name*).
felo de se	suicide.
festina lente	more haste, less speed.
fiat lux	let there be light.
Fidei Defensor	defender of the faith.

fidus Achates	(lit: faithful Achates) faithful friend or companion (*the name of the faithful companion of Aeneas in Virgil's Aeneid*).
floruit	(he or she) flourished (*used to indicate the period when a historical figure, whose birth and death dates are unknown, was most active*).
fons et origo	the source and origin.
genius loci	(lit: genius of the place) **1** the guardian spirit of a place. **2** the special atmosphere of a particular place.
Gloria in Excelsis Deo	(lit: glory to God in the highest) **1** the Greater Doxology, beginning in Latin with these words. **2** a musical setting of this.
Gloria Patri	(lit: glory to the father) **1** the Lesser Doxology, beginning in Latin with these words. **2** a musical setting of this.
hinc illae lacrimae	hence those tears.
HJ	(abbr for **hic jacet**) here lies (*on gravestones*).
HJS	(abbr for **hic jacet sepultus**) here lies buried (*on gravestones*).
horrible dictu	horrible to relate.
ibid.	abbr for **ibidem**.
ibidem	in the same place (*in annotations, bibliographies, etc., when referring to a book, article, chapter, or page previously cited*).
id est	that is (to say); in other words.
idem	the same (*used to refer to an article, chapter, etc., previously cited*).
i.e.	abbr for **id est**.
ign.	abbr for **ignotus**.
ignoratio elenchi	(lit: an ignorance of proof: *Logic*) **1** a purported refutation of a proposition that does not in fact prove it false but merely establishes a related but strictly irrelevant proposition. **2** the fallacy of arguing in this way.
ignotum per ignotius	(lit: the unknown by means of the more unknown) an explanation that is obscurer than the thing to be explained.
ignotus	unknown.
ignis fatuus	will o' the wisp.
Imp.	**1** (abbr for **Imperator**) Emperor; **2** (abbr for **Imperatrix**) Empress.
in absentia	in one's absence; in the absence of: **he was condemned in absentia**.
in aeternum	forever; eternally.
in articulo mortis	at the point of death.

in camera	(lit: in the chamber) in private.
in extenso	at full length.
in extremis	(lit: in the furthest reaches) 1 in extremity; in dire straits. 2 at the point of death.
infra	below.
infra dig	(abbr for **infra dignitatem**) beneath one's dignity.
in loco parentis	in place of a parent (*said of a person acting in a parental capacity*).
in medias res	(lit: into the midst of things) in or into the middle of events or a narrative.
in memoriam	in memory of; as a memorial to (*used in obituaries, epitaphs etc*).
in perpetuum	forever
in personam	(lit: against the person) directed against a specific person or persons (LAW: *of a judicial act*).
in propria persona	in person; personally.
in rem	(lit: against the matter) directed against property rather than against a specific person (LAW: *of a judicial act*).
in rerum natura	in the nature of things.
INRI	(lit: Jesus of Nazareth, King of the Jews) abbr for **Iesus Nazarenus Rex Iudaeorum** (*the inscription placed over Christ's head during the Crucifixion*).
in situ	(lit: in position) in the natural, original, or appropriate position.
inter alia	among other things.
inter alios	among other people.
inter vivos	(LAW) between living people: **an inter vivos gift**.
in toto	totally; entirely; completely.
in utero	within the womb.
in vacuo	in a vacuum.
in vino veritas	in wine there is truth.
in vitro	(lit: in glass) made to occur outside the body of the organism in an artificial environment (*of biological processes or reactions*): **in vitro fertilization**.
in vivo	(lit: in a living (thing)) occurring or carried out in the living organism (*of biological processes or experiments*).
ipse dixit	(lit: he himself said it) an arbitrary and unsupported assertion.
ipsissima verba	the very words.
ipso facto	by the fact itself.
i.q.	(lit: the same as) abbr for **idem quod**.
lapsus linguae	a slip of the tongue
lc	(abbr for (**in**) **loco citato**) in the place cited.

lex loci	the law of the place.
lex non scripta	the unwritten law; common law.
lex scripta	the written law; statute law.
lex talionis	the law of revenge or retaliation.
loc. cit.	(abbr for (**in**) **loco citato**) in the place cited (*in textual annotation*).
magna cum laude	(chiefly *U.S.*) with great praise (*the second of three designations for above-average achievement in examinations*).
magnum opus	a great work of art or literature (*especially the greatest single work of an artist*).
mala fide	undertaken in bad faith.
mare clausum	(lit: closed sea: LAW) a sea coming under the jurisdiction of one nation and closed to all others.
mare liberum	(lit: free sea: LAW) a sea open to navigation by shipping of all nations.
mare nostrum	(lit: our sea) the Mediterranean.
mater	mother (*often used facetiously*).
mater dolorosa	(lit: sorrowful mother) the Virgin Mary sorrowing for the dead Christ (*especially as depicted in art*).
materfamilias	(lit:mother of family) the mother of a family or the female head of a family.
materia medica	(lit: medical matter) **1** the branch of medical science concerned with the study of drugs used in the treatment of disease. **2** the drugs used in the treatment of disease.
mea culpa	(lit: my fault) an acknowledgement of guilt.
memento mori	(lit: remember you must die) an object, such as a skull, intended to remind people of the inevitability of death.
mens sana in corpore sano	a healthy mind in a healthy body.
mens rea	(lit: guilty mind: LAW) a criminal intention or knowledge that an act is wrong.
miles gloriosus	a braggart soldier (*especially as a stock figure in comedy*).
mirabile dictu	wonderful to relate.
mittimus	(lit: we send) a warrant of commitment to prison or a command to a jailer directing him to hold someone in prison.
modus operandi	procedure; method of operating; manner of working.
modus ponens	(lit: mood that affirms) the principle that whenever a conditional statement and its antecedent are given to be true its consequent may be validly inferred.

modus tollens	(lit: mood that denies) the principle that whenever a conditional statement and the negation of its consequent are given to be true, the negation of its antecedent may be validly inferred.
modus vivendi	(lit: way of living) a working arrangement between conflicting interests; practical compromise.
motu proprio	(lit: of his own accord) an administrative papal bull.
multum in parvo	much in a small space.
mutatis mutandis	with the necessary changes.
NB, N.B., nb, n.b.	(abbr for **nota bene**) note well.
nem. con.	(abbr for **nemine contradicente**) no-one contradicting; unanimously.
nemo me impune lacessit	no-one provokes me with impunity.
ne plus ultra	(lit: not more beyond) the extreme or perfect point or state.
nihil	nil; nothing.
nihil obstat	there is no obstacle.
nil desperandum	(lit: nothing to be despaired of) never despair.
nisi prius	(lit: unless previously) **1** *in England* (a) a direction that a case be brought up to Westminster for trial before a single judge and jury. (b) the writ giving this direction. **2** *in the US* a court where civil actions are tried by a single judge sitting with a jury as distinguished from an appellate court.
nolens volens	whether willing or unwilling.
noli me tangere	(lit: do not touch me) a warning against interfering with or against touching a person or thing.
nolle prosequi	(lit: do not pursue) an entry made on the court record when the plaintiff in a civil suit or prosecutor in a criminal prosecution undertakes not to continue the action or prosecution.
nolo contendere	(lit: I do not wish to contend) a plea made by a defendant to a criminal charge having the same effect in those proceedings as a plea of guilty but not precluding him from denying the charge in a subsequent action.
non compos mentis	(lit: not in control of one's mind) mentally incapable of managing one's own affairs; of unsound mind; insane.
non prosequitur	(lit: he does not proceed) a judgment in favour of a defendant when the plaintiff failed to take the necessary steps in an action within the time allowed.
non sequitur	(lit: it does not follow) **1** (*gen*) a statement having little or no relevance to what preceded it. **2** (*Logic*) a conclusion that does not follow from the premises.
nulli secundus	second to none

numen	(lit: divine power) **1** (*especially in ancient Roman religion*) a deity or spirit presiding over a thing or place. **2** a guiding principle, force, or spirit.
Nunc Dimittis	(lit: now let depart) **1** the Canticle of Simeon (*Luke 2:29-32*). **2** a musical setting of this.
ob.	**1** abbr for **obiit**. **2** (abbr for **obiter**) incidentally; in passing.
obiit	he or she died (*on gravestones*).
obiter dictum	(lit: something said in passing) **1** (*LAW*) an observation by a judge on some point of law not directly in issue in the case before him and thus neither requiring his decision nor serving as a precedent, but nevertheless of persuasive authority. **2** any comment, remark, or observation made in passing.
obscurum per obscurius	(lit: the obscure by means of the more obscure) an explanation that is obscurer than the thing to be explained.
omnium-gatherum	(*often facetious*) a miscellaneous collection; assortment.
onus probandi	(*LAW*) the burden of proof.
op. cit.	(abbr of **opere citato**) in the work cited.
opus anglicanum	(lit: English work) fine embroidery (*especially of church vestments*).
ora pro nobis	pray for us.
o tempora! o mores!	oh the times! oh the customs!
p.a.	abbr of **per annum**.
pace	by leave of; with due deference to (*used to acknowledge politely someone who disagrees with the speaker or writer*).
pari passu	with equal speed or progress; equably (*often used to refer to the right of creditors to receive assets from the same source without one taking precedence*).
passim	here and there; throughout (*used to indicate that what is referred to occurs frequently in the work cited*).
paterfamilias	(lit: father of the family) **1** the male head of a household. **2** the head of a household having authority over its members.
pax vobiscum	peace be with you.
peccavi	(lit: I have sinned) a confession of guilt.
peculium	(lit: property) property that a father or master allowed his child or slave to hold as his own.
per annum	every year; year by year.
per ardua ad astra	through difficulties to the stars (*motto of the RAF*).
per capita	(lit: according to heads) of or for each person.
per contra	on the contrary

per diem	(lit: for the day) **1** every day; by the day. **2** an allowance for daily expenses, usually those incurred while working.
per mensem	every month; by the month.
per pro	(abbr for **per procurationem**) by delegation to; through the agency of (*used when signing documents on behalf of someone else*).
persona grata	an acceptable person (*especially a diplomat acceptable to the government of the country to which he is sent*).
persona non grata	unacceptable or unwelcome person.
petitio principii	(lit: an assumption at the beginning: *Logic*) a form of fallacious reasoning in which the conclusion has been assumed in the premises; begging the question.
pia mater	(lit: pious mother) the innermost of the three membranes that cover the brain and spinal cord.
pinxit	(he or she) painted this (*used formerly on works of art next to the artist's name*).
p.m., P.M., pm, PM	abbr for **1** **post meridiem** **2** **postmortem**.
post-bellum	(lit: after war) of or during the period after a war, especially the American Civil War.
post hoc	(lit: after this: *Logic*) the fallacy of assuming that temporal succession is evidence of causal relation.
post hoc, ergo propter hoc	after this, therefore because of this (*a fallacy of reasoning*).
post meridiem	afternoon.
postmortem	(lit: after death) *n* **1** dissection and examination of a dead body to determine the cause of death. **2** analysis or study of a recently completed event • *adj* occurring after death.
pp	abbr for **1** **per pro**. **2** **post prandium** after a meal (*in prescriptions*).
PPS	(lit: after postscript; abbr for **post postscriptum**) additional postscript.
pr	(abbr for: **per rectum**) through the rectum (*in prescriptions*).
prima facie	at a first view
primum mobile	(lit: first moving (thing)) prime mover.
primus inter pares	first among equals.
prn	(abbr for **pro re nata**) as the situation demands, as needed (*in prescriptions*).
pro forma	(lit: for form's sake) **1** prescribing a set form or procedure. **2** performed in a set manner.
pro patria	for one's country
pro rata	in proportion.
pro tempore	for the time being.
proxime accessit	(lit: he or she came next) the runner-up.

q.e.	(abbr for **quod est**) which is.
QED	abbr for **quod erat demonstrandum**.
QEF	abbr for **quod erat faciendum**.
quid pro quo	(lit: something for something) **1** a reciprocal exchange. **2** something given in compensation, especially an advantage or object given in exchange for another.
quis custodiet ipsos custodes?	who will guard the guards?
q.l.	(abbr for **quantum libet**) as much as you please (*in prescriptions*).
qm	(abbr for **quaque mane**) every morning (*in prescriptions*).
qn	(abbr for **quaque nocte**) every night (*in prescriptions*).
quod erat demonstrandum	which was to be proved.
quod erat faciendum	which was to be done.
quot homines, tot sententie	there are as many opinions as there are people.
quo vadis?	whither goest thou?
qqv	abbr for **quae vide**) which (words, items etc) see (*denoting a cross reference to more than one item*).
qs	(abbr for **quantum sufficit**) as much as will suffice (*in prescriptions*).
qv	(abbr for **quod vide**) which (word, item etc) see (*denoting a cross reference*).
rara avis	(lit: rare bird) an unusual, uncommon or exceptional person or thing.
reductio ad absurdum	(lit: reduction to the absurd) **1** a method of disproving a proposition by showing that its inevitable consequences would be absurd. **2** a method of indirectly proving a proposition by assuming its negation to be true and showing that this leads to an absurdity. **3** application of a principle or a proposed principle to an instance in which it is absurd.
requiescat	(lit: may he or she rest) a prayer for the repose of the souls of the dead.
requiescat in pace	may he or she rest in peace.
res gestae	(lit: things done) **1** things done or accomplished; achievements. **2** (*LAW*) incidental facts and circumstances that are admissible in evidence because they introduce or explain the matter in issue.
res ipsa loquitur	(*LAW*) the thing or matter speaks for itself.
res judicata	(*LAW*) a matter already adjudicated upon that cannot be raised again.
res publica	(lit: the public thing) the state, republic, or commonwealth.

resurgam	I shall rise again.
RI	**1** (abbr for **Regina et Imperatrix**) Queen and Empress. **2** (abbr for **Rex et Imperator**) King and Emperor.
rigor mortis	(lit: rigidity of death) the stiffness of joints and muscular rigidity of a dead body.
RIP	abbr for **requiescat** or **requiescant in pace**.
risus sardonicus	(lit: sardonic laugh) fixed contraction of the facial muscles resulting in a peculiar distorted grin, caused especially by tetanus.
sanctum sanctorum	(lit: holy of holies) **1** (*Bible*) the holy of holies. **2** (*often facetious*) an especially private place.
sartor resartus	the tailor patched.
schola cantorum	(lit: school of singers) a choir or choir school maintained by a church.
scire facias	(lit: cause (him) to know) **1** (*LAW*, rare) a judicial writ founded upon some record, such as a judgement, letters patent, etc., requiring the person against whom it is brought to show cause why the record should not be enforced or annulled. **2** a proceeding begun by the issue of such a writ.
semper fidelis	always faithful.
semper idem	always the same.
seq.	(abbr for **sequens**) the following (one).
seqq.	(abbr for **sequentia**) the following (ones).
seriatim	in order.
sic	thus (*often used to call attention to some quoted mistake*).
sic itur ad astra	such is the way to the stars.
sic transit gloria mundi	so passes the glory of the world.
si monumentum requiris, circumspice	if you seek (his) monument, look around you (*inscription on the architect Sir Christopher Wren's tomb in St Paul's Cathedral*).
sine die	without a day.
sine prole	(*LAW*) without issue.
sine qua non	(lit: without which not) an indispensable condition or requirement.
sl	(abbr for **sine loco**) without place (*of publication*).
sp	abbr for **sine prole**.
spiritus asper	rough breathing.
spiritus lenis	smooth breathing.
SPQR	(abbr for **Senatus Populusque Romanus**) the Senate and People of Rome.
sq.	(abbr for **sequens**) the following (one).
sqq.	(abbr for **sequentia**) the following (ones).

Stabat Mater	(lit: the mother was standing) **1** a Latin hymn, probably of the 13th century, commemorating the sorrows of the Virgin Mary at the crucifixion and used in the Mass and various other services. **2** a musical setting of this hymn.
status quo	(lit: the state in which) the existing state of affairs.
stet	let it stand.
sub judice	before a court of law or a judge; under judicial consideration.
sub rosa	(lit: under the rose) secretly.
sub voce	under the word.
sui generis	(lit: of its own kind) unique.
sui juris	(lit: of one's own right) (*LAW*) of full age and not under disability; legally competent to manage one's own affairs; independent.
summa cum laude	(*chiefly U.S.*) with the utmost praise (*the highest of three designations for above-average achievement in examinations. In Britain it is sometimes used to designate a first-class honours degree*).
summum bonum	the principle of goodness in which all moral values are included or from which they are derived; highest or supreme good.
suo jure	(*chiefly LAW*) in one's own right.
suo loco	(*chiefly LAW*) in a person or thing's own or rightful place.
supra	above.
sursum corda	lift up your hearts (to God).
sv	abbr for **sub voce**.
tabula rasa	(lit: a scraped tablet) **1** the mind in its uninformed original state. **2** an opportunity for a fresh start; clean slate.
taedium vitae	(lit: weariness of life) the feeling that life is boring and dull.
Te Deum	(lit: Thee, God) **1** an ancient Latin hymn in rhythmic prose, sung or recited at matins in the Roman Catholic Church and in English translation at morning prayer in the Church of England and used by both churches as an expression of thanksgiving on special occasions. **2** a musical setting of this hymn. **3** a service of thanksgiving in which the recital of this hymn forms a central part.
te igitur	(lit: Thee, therefore: *Roman Catholic Church*) the first prayer of the canon of the Mass.
tempore	in the time of.
tempus fugit	time flies.
terminus ad quem	(lit: the end to which) the aim or terminal point.
terminus a quo	(lit: the end from which) the starting point; beginning.

terra firma	the solid earth; firm ground.
terra incognita	an unexplored or unknown land, region or area for study.
tertium quid	a third something.
t.i.d.	(abbr for **ter in die**) three times a day (*in prescriptions*).
tu quoque	you likewise (*a retort made by a person accused of a crime implying that the accuser is also guilty of the same crime*).
uberrima fides	utmost good faith.
ubique	everywhere.
ubi supra	where (mentioned or cited) above.
ultima Thule	(lit: the most distant Thule) **1** the utmost boundary or limit. **2** a remote goal or aim.
ultra vires	beyond one's powers.
una voce	with one voice.
urbi et orbi	(*Roman Catholic Church*) to the city and the world (*a phrase qualifying the solemn papal blessing*).
ut dict.	(abbr for **ut dictum**) as directed.
ut infra	as below.
ut supra	as above.
v.	abbr for **1 verso. 2 versus. 3 vide**.
vade in pace	go in peace.
vade mecum	(lit: go with me) a handbook or other aid carried on the person for immediate use when needed.
vae victis	woe to the conquered!
vale	farewell!
veni, vidi, vici	I came, I saw, I conquered.
venire facias	(lit: you must make come: *LAW*) a writ directing a sheriff to summon suitable persons to form a jury.
verbatim et litteratim	word for word and letter for letter.
verb. sap.	(abbr for **verbum sapienti sat est**) a word is enough to the wise.
verso	**1** the back of a sheet of printed paper. **2** the side of a coin opposite to the obverse; reverse.
versus	**1** against; in opposition to. **2** as opposed to; in contrast with.
via	by way of.
via media	a middle course.
vice	in the place of; instead of; as a substitute for.
vice versa	the other way round.
vide	see.
videlicet	namely; to wit.

vi et armis	(lit: by force and arms) a kind of trespass accompanied by force and violence.
VIR	(abbr for **Victoria lmperatrix Regina**) Victoria, Empress and Queen.
virginibus puerisque	for maidens and youths.
vis inertiae	the power of inertia.
viva voce	(lit: with living voice) *adv, adj* by word of mouth • *n* an oral examination.
viz.	abbr for **videlicet**.
vl	(abbr for **varia lecto**) variant reading.
volente Deo	God willing.
vox populi	the voice of the people; popular or public opinion.
vox populi, vox Dei	the voice of the people is the voice of God.
VR	(abbr for **Victoria Regina**) Queen Victoria.
VRI	(abbr for **Victoria Regina et Imperatrix**) Victoria, Queen and Empress.

ENGLISH – LATIN

Aa

a, an *art* not translated; (*a certain*) quīdam; **twice a day** bis in diē; **four acres a man** quaterna in singulōs iūgera
aback *adv*: **taken ~** dēprehēnsus
abaft *adv* in puppī ♦ *prep* post, pōne
abandon *vt* relinquere; (*wilfully*) dērelinquere, dēserere; (*to danger*) ōbicere; (*to pleasure*) dēdere; (*plan*) abicere; **~ hope** spem abicere
abandoned *adj* perditus
abase *vt* dēprimere; **~ oneself** sē prōsternere
abash *vt* perturbāre; rubōrem incutere (*dat*)
abate *vt* minuere, imminuere; (*a portion*) remittere ♦ *vi* (*fever*) dēcēdere; (*passion*) dēfervēscere; (*price*) laxāre; (*storm*) cadere
abatement *n* remissiō *f*, dēminūtiō *f*
abbess *n* abbātissa *f*
abbey *n* abbātia *f*
abbot *n* abbās *m*
abbreviate *vt* imminuere
abbreviation *n* (*writing*) nota *f*
abdicate *vt* sē abdicāre (*abl*)
abdication *n* abdicātiō *f*
abduct *vt* abripere
abduction *n* raptus *m*
aberration *n* error *m*
abet *vt* adiuvāre, adesse (*dat*), favēre (*dat*)
abettor *n* adiūtor *m*, minister *m*, fautor *m*, socius *m*
abeyance *n*: **in ~** intermissus; **be in ~** iacēre
abhor *vt* ōdisse, invīsum habēre
abhorrence *n* odium *nt*
abhorrent *adj*: **~ to** aliēnus ab
abide *vi* (*dwell*) habitāre; (*tarry*) commorārī; (*last*) dūrāre; **~ by** *vt fus* stāre (*abl*), perstāre in (*abl*)
abiding *adj* perpetuus, diūturnus
ability *n* (*to do*) facultās *f*, potestās *f*; (*physical*) vīrēs *fpl*; (*mental*) ingenium *nt*; **to the best of my ~** prō meā parte, prō virīlī parte
abject *adj* abiectus, contemptus; (*downcast*) dēmissus
abjectly *adv* humiliter, dēmissē
abjure *vt* ēiūrāre
ablative *n* ablātīvus *m*
ablaze *adj* flāgrāns, ardēns
able *adj* perītus, doctus; **be ~** posse, valēre
able-bodied *adj* rōbustus
ablution *n* lavātiō *f*
ably *adv* perītē, doctē
abnegation *n* abstinentia *f*
abnormal *adj* inūsitātus; (*excess*) immodicus
abnormally *adv* inūsitātē, praeter mōrem

aboard *adv* in nāvī; **go ~** nāvem cōnscendere; **put ~** impōnere
abode *n* domicilium *nt*, sēdes *f*
abolish *vt* tollere, ē mediō tollere, abolēre; (*LAW*) abrogāre
abolition *n* dissolūtiō *f*; (*LAW*) abrogātiō *f*
abominable *adj* dētestābilis, nefārius
abominably *adv* nefāriē, foedē
abominate *vt* dētestārī
abomination *n* odium *nt*; (*thing*) nefas *nt*
aboriginal *adj* prīscus
aborigines *n* aborīginēs *mpl*
abortion *n* abortus *m*
abortive *adj* abortīvus; (*fig*) inritus; **be ~** ad inritum redigī
abound *vi* abundāre, superesse; **~ in** abundāre (*abl*), adfluere (*abl*)
abounding *adj* abundāns, adfluēns; cōpiōsus ab
about *adv* (*place*) *usu expressed by compound verbs*; (*number*) circiter, ferē, fermē ♦ *prep* (*place*) circā, circum (*acc*); (*number*) circā, ad (*acc*); (*time*) sub (*acc*); (*concerning*) dē (*abl*); **~ to die** moritūrus; **I am ~ to go** in eō est ut eam
above *adv* suprā; **from ~** dēsuper; **over and ~** īnsuper ♦ *prep* suprā (*acc*); (*motion*) super (*acc*); (*rest*) super (*abl*); **be ~** (*conduct*) indignārī
abreast *adv* (*ships*) aequātīs prōrīs; **walk ~ of** latus tegere (*dat*)
abridge *vt* contrahere, compendī facere
abridgement *n* epitomē *f*
abroad *adv* peregrē; (*out of doors*) forīs; **be ~** peregrīnārī; **from ~** peregrē
abrogate *vt* dissolvere; (*LAW*) abrogāre
abrupt *adj* subitus, repentīnus; (*speech*) concīsus
abscess *n* vomica *f*
abscond *vi* aufugere
absence *n* absentia *f*; **in my ~** mē absente; **leave of ~** commeātus *m*
absent *adj* absēns; **be ~** abesse; **~ oneself** *vi* deesse, nōn adesse
absent-minded *adj* immemor, parum attentus
absolute *adj* absolūtus, perfectus; (*not limited*) īnfīnītus; (*not relative*) simplex; **~ power** rēgnum *nt*, dominātiō *m*; **~ ruler** rēx
absolutely *adv* absolūtē, omnīnō
absolution *n* venia *f*
absolve *vt* absolvere, exsolvere; (*from punishment*) condōnāre
absorb *vt* bibere, absorbēre; (*fig*) distringere; **I am absorbed in** tōtus sum in (*abl*)
absorbent *adj* bibulus

abstain vi abstinēre, sē abstinēre; (*from violence*) temperāre
abstemious adj sobrius
abstinence n abstinentia f, continentia f
abstinent adj abstinēns, sobrius
abstract adj mente perceptus, cōgitātiōne comprehēnsus ♦ n epitomē f ♦ vt abstrahere, dēmere
abstraction n (*idea*) nōtiō f; (*inattention*) animus parum attentus
abstruse adj reconditus, obscūrus, abstrūsus
absurd adj ineptus, absurdus
absurdity n ineptiae fpl, insulsitās f
absurdly adv ineptē, absurdē
abundance n cōpia f, abundantia f; **there is ~ of** abundē est (*gen*)
abundant adj cōpiōsus, abundāns, largus; **be ~** abundāre
abundantly adv abundē, abundanter, adfātim
abuse vt abūtī (*abl*); (*words*) maledīcere (*dat*) ♦ n probra ntpl, maledicta ntpl, convīcium nt, contumēlia f
abusive adj maledicus, contumēliōsus
abut vi adiacēre; **abutting on** cōnfīnis (*dat*), fīnitimus (*dat*)
abysmal adj profundus
abyss n profundum nt, vorāgō f; (*water*) gurges m; (*fig*) barathrum nt
academic adj scholasticus; (*style*) umbrātilis; (*sect*) Acadēmicus
academy n schola f; (*Plato's*) Acadēmīa f
accede vi adsentīrī; **~ to** accipere
accelerate vt, vi adcelerāre, festīnāre; (*process*) mātūrāre
accent n vōx f; (*intonation*) sonus m; (*mark*) apex m ♦ vt (*syllable*) acuere; (*word*) sonum admovēre (*dat*)
accentuate vt exprimere
accept vt accipere
acceptable adj acceptus, grātus, probābilis; **be ~** placēre
acceptation n significātiō f
access n aditus m; (*addition*) accessiō f; (*illness*) impetus m
accessary n socius m, particeps m
accessible adj (*person*) adfābilis, facilis; **be ~** (*place*) patēre; (*person*) facilem sē praebēre
accession n (*addition*) accessiō f; (*king's*) initium rēgnī
accident n cāsus m, calamitās f
accidental adj fortuītus
accidentally adv cāsū, fortuītō
acclaim vt adclāmāre
acclamation n clāmor m, studium nt
acclimatize vt aliēnō caelō adsuēfacere
accommodate vt accommodāre, aptāre; (*lodging*) hospitium parāre (*dat*); **~ oneself to** mōrigerārī (*dat*)
accommodating adj facilis
accommodation n hospitium nt
accompany vt comitārī; (*courtesy*) prōsequī; (*to Forum*) dēdūcere; (*music*) concinere (*dat*)
accomplice n socius m, particeps m, cōnscius m
accomplish vt efficere, perficere, patrāre
accomplished adj doctus, perītus

accomplishment n effectus m, perfectiō f, fīnis m; **accomplishments** pl artēs fpl
accord vi inter sē congruere, cōnsentīre ♦ vt dare, praebēre, praestāre ♦ n cōnsēnsus m, concordia f; (*music*) concentus m; **of one's own ~** suā sponte, ultrō; **with one ~** unā vōce
accordance n: **in ~ with** ex, ē (*abl*), secundum (*acc*)
according adv: **~ to** ex, ē (*abl*), secundum (*acc*); (*proportion*) prō (*abl*); **~ as** prōut
accordingly adv itaque, igitur, ergō
accost vt appellāre, adloquī, compellāre
account n ratiō f; (*story*) nārrātiō f, expositiō f; **on ~ of** ob (*acc*); propter (*acc*), causā (*gen*); **be of no ~** (*person*) nihilī aestimārī, nēquam esse; **on that ~** idcircō, ideō; **on your ~** tuā grātiā, tuō nōmine; **give an ~** ratiōnem reddere; **present an ~** ratiōnem referre; **take ~ of** ratiōnem habēre (*gen*); **put down to my ~** mihī expēnsum ferre; **the accounts balance** ratiō cōnstat/convenit ♦ vi: **~ for** ratiōnēs reddere, adferre (*cūr*); **that accounts for it** haec causa est, (*proverb*)hinc illae lacrimae
accountable adj reus; **I am ~ for** mihi ratiō reddenda est (*gen*)
accountant n ā ratiōnibus, ratiōcinātor m
account book n tabulae fpl; cōdex acceptī et expēnsī
accoutred adj īnstructus, ōrnātus
accoutrements n ōrnāmenta ntpl, arma ntpl
accredited adj pūblicā auctōritate missus
accretion n accessiō f
accrue vi (*addition*) cēdere; (*advantage*) redundāre
accumulate vt cumulāre, congerere, coacervāre ♦ vi crēscere, cumulārī
accumulation n cumulus m, acervus m
accuracy n cūra f; (*writing*) subtīlitās f
accurate adj (*work*) exāctus, subtīlis; (*worker*) dīligēns
accurately adv subtīliter, ad amussim, dīligenter
accursed adj sacer; (*fig*) exsecrātus, scelestus
accusation n (*act*) accūsātiō f; (*charge*) crīmen nt; (*unfair*) īnsimulātiō f; (*false*) calumnia f; **bring an ~ against** accūsāre; (*to a magistrate*) nōmen dēferre (*gen*)
accusative n (*case*) accūsātīvus m
accuse vt accūsāre, crīminārī, reum facere; (*falsely*) īnsimulāre; **the accused** reus; (*said by prosecutor*) iste
accuser n accūsātor m; (*civil suit*) petītor m; (*informer*) dēlātor m
accustom vt adsuēfacere; **~ oneself** adsuēscere, consuēscere
accustomed adj adsuētus; **be ~** solēre; **become ~** adsuēscere, consuēscere
ace n ūniō f; **I was within an ace of going** minimum āfuit quin īrem
acerbity n acerbitās f
ache n dolor m ♦ vi dolēre
achieve vt cōnficere, patrāre; (*win*) cōnsequī, adsequī
achievement n factum nt, rēs gesta
acid adj acidus
acknowledge vt (*fact*) agnōscere; (*fault*) fatērī, cōnfitērī; (*child*) tollere; (*service*) grātias agere

prō *(abl)*; **I have to ~ your letter of 1st March**
accēpī litterās tuās Kal. Mart. datās
acknowledgement *n* cōnfessiō *f*; grātia *f*
acme *n* fastīgium *nt*, flōs *m*
aconite *n* aconītum *nt*
acorn *n* glāns *f*
acoustics *n* rēs audītōria *f*
acquaint *vt* certiōrem facere, docēre; **~ oneself
with** cognōscere; **acquainted with** gnārus
(gen), perītus *(gen)*
acquaintance *n (with fact)* cognitiō *f*, scientia *f*;
(with person) familiāritās *f*, ūsus *m*; *(person)* nōtus
m, familiāris *m*
acquiesce *vi (assent)* adquiēscere; *(submit)* aequō
animō patī
acquiescence *n*: **with your ~** tē nōn adversante,
pāce tuā
acquire *vt* adquīrere, adipīscī, cōnsequī;
nanciscī
acquirements *n* artēs *fpl*
acquisition *n (act)* comparātiō *f*, quaestus *m*;
(thing) quaesītum *nt*
acquisitive *adj* quaestuōsus
acquit *vt* absolvere; **~ oneself** sē praestāre,
officiō fungī
acquittal *n* absolūtiō *f*
acre *n* iūgerum *nt*
acrid *adj* asper, ācer
acrimonious *adj* acerbus, truculentus
acrimony *n* acerbitās *f*
acrobat *n* fūnambulus *m*
acropolis *n* arx *f*
across *adv* trānsversus ♦ *prep* trāns *(acc)*
act *n* factum *nt*, facinus *nt*; *(play)* āctus *m*; *(POL)*
āctum *nt*, senātus cōnsultum *nt*, dēcrētum *nt*; **I
was in the act of saying** in eō erat ut dīcerem;
caught in the act dēprehēnsus ♦ *vi* facere,
agere; *(conduct)* sē gerere; *(stage)* histriōnem
esse, partēs agere; *(pretence)* simulāre ♦ *vt*: **act a
part** partēs agere, persōnam sustinēre; **act the
part of** agere; **act as** esse, munere fungī *(gen)*;
act upon *(instructions)* exsequī
action *n (doing)* āctiō *f*; *(deed)* factum *nt*, facinus
nt; *(legal)* āctiō *f*, līs *f*; *(MIL)* proelium *nt*; *(of play)*
āctiō *f*; *(of speaker)* gestus *m*; **bring an ~ against**
lītem intendere, āctiōnem īnstituere *(dat)*; **be
in ~** agere, rem gerere; *(MIL)* pugnāre, in aciē
dīmicāre; **man of ~** vir strēnuus
active *adj* impiger, strēnuus, sēdulus, nāvus
actively *adv* impigrē, strēnuē, nāviter
activity *n (motion)* mōtus *m*; *(energy)* industria *f*,
sēdulitās *f*
actor *n* histriō *m*; *(in comedy)* cōmoedus *m*; *(in
tragedy)* tragoedus *m*
actress *n* mīma *f*
actual *adj* vērus, ipse
actually *adv* rē vērā
actuate *vt* movēre, incitāre
acumen *n* acūmen *nt*, ingenī aciēs, argūtiae *fpl*
acute *adj* acūtus, ācer; *(pain)* ācer; *(speech)*
argūtus, subtīlis
acutely *adv* acūtē, ācriter, argūtē
acuteness *n (mind)* acūmen *nt*, aciēs *f*, subtīlitas
f
adage *n* prōverbium *nt*
adamant *n* adamās *m* ♦ *adj* obstinātus

adamantine *adj* adamantinus
adapt *vt* accommodāre
adaptable *adj* flexibilis, facile accommodandus
adaptation *n* accommodātiō *f*
add *vt* addere, adicere, adiungere; **be added**
accēdere
adder *n* vīpera *f*
addicted *adj* dēditus
addition *n* adiūnctiō *f*, accessiō *f*;
additāmentum *nt*, incrēmentum *nt*; **in
~** īnsuper, praetereā; **in ~ to** praeter *(acc)*
additional *adj* novus, adiūnctus
addled *adj (egg)* inritus; *(brain)* inānis
address *vt* compellāre, alloquī; *(crowd)*
cōntiōnem habēre apud *(acc)*; *(letter)* īnscrībere;
~ oneself *(to action)* accingī ♦ *n* adloquium *nt*;
(public) cōntiō *f*, ōrātiō *f*; *(letter)* īnscrīptiō *f*
adduce *vt (argument)* adferre; *(witness)* prōdūcere
adept *adj* perītus
adequate *adj* idōneus, dignus, pār; **be
~** sufficere
adequately *adv* satis, ut pār est
adhere *vi* haerēre, adhaerēre; **~ to** inhaerēre
(dat), inhaerēscere in *(abl)*; *(agreement)* manēre,
stāre in *(abl)*
adherent *n* adsectātor *m*; *(of party)* fautor *m*; *(of
person)* cliēns *m*
adhesive *adj* tenax
adieu *interj* valē, valēte; **bid ~ to** valēre iubēre
adjacent *adj* fīnitimus, vīcīnus; **be ~ to** adiacēre
(dat)
adjoin *vi* adiacēre *(dat)*
adjoining *adj* fīnitimus, adiūnctus; proximus
adjourn *vt (short time)* differre; *(longer time)*
prōferre; *(case)* ampliāre ♦ *vi* rem differre,
prōferre
adjournment *n* dīlātiō *f*, prōlātiō *f*
adjudge *vt* addīcere, adiūdicāre
adjudicate *vi* dēcernere
adjudicator *n* arbiter *m*
adjunct *n* appendix *f*, accessiō *f*
adjure *vt* obtestārī, obsecrāre
adjust *vt (adapt)* accommodāre; *(put in order)*
compōnere
adjutant *n (MIL)* optiō *m*; *(civil)* adiūtor *m*
administer *vt* administrāre, gerere; *(justice)*
reddere; *(oath to)* iūreiūrandō adigere; *(medicine)*
dare, adhibēre
administration *n* administrātiō *f*
administrator *n* administrātor *m*, prōcūrātor *m*
admirable *adj* admīrābilis, ēgregius
admirably *adv* ēgregiē
admiral *n* praefectus classis; **admiral's ship**
nāvis praetōria
admiralty *n* praefectī classium
admiration *n* admīrātiō *f*, laus *f*
admire *vt* admīrārī; mīrārī
admirer *n* laudātor *m*; amātor *m*
admissible *adj* aequus
admission *n (entrance)* aditus *m*; *(of guilt etc)*
cōnfessiō *f*
admit *vt (let in)* admittere, recipere, accipere; *(to
membership)* adscīscere; *(argument)* concēdere;
(fault) fatērī; **~ of** patī, recipere
admittedly *adv* sānē
admonish *vt* admonēre, commonēre, hortārī

admonition n admonitiō f
ado n negōtium nt; **make much ado about nothing** fluctūs in simpulō excitāre; **without more ado** prōtinus, sine morā
adolescence n prīma adulēscentia f
adolescent adj adulēscēns ♦ n adulēscentulus m
adopt vt (person) adoptāre; (custom) adscīscere; **~ a plan** consilium capere
adoption n (person) adoptiō f; (custom) adsūmptiō f; **by ~** adoptīvus
adoptive adj adoptīvus
adorable adj amābilis, venustus
adorably adv venustē
adoration n (of gods) cultus m; (of kings) venerātiō f; (love) amor m
adore vt (worship) venerārī; (love) adamāre
adorn vt ōrnāre, exōrnāre, decorāre
adornment n ōrnāmentum nt, decus nt; ōrnātus m
adrift adj fluctuāns; **be ~** fluctuāre
adroit adj sollers, callidus
adroitly adv callidē, scītē
adroitness n sollertia f, calliditās f
adulation n adūlātiō f, adsentātiō f
adulatory adj blandus
adult adj adultus
adulterate vt corrumpere, adulterāre
adulterer n adulter m
adulteress n adultera f
adulterous adj incestus
adultery n adulterium nt; **commit ~** adulterāre
adults npl pūberēs mpl
adumbrate vt adumbrāre
advance vt prōmovēre; (a cause) fovēre; (money) crēdere; (opinion) dīcere; (to honours) prōvehere; (time) mātūrāre ♦ vi prōcēdere, prōgredī, adventāre; (MIL) signa prōferre, pedem īnferre; (progress) prōficere; (walk) incēdere; **~ to the attack** signa īnferre ♦ n prōgressus m, prōcessus m; (attack) impetus m; (money) mūtuae pecūniae; **in ~** mātūrius; **fix in ~** praefīnīre; **get in ~** praecipere
advanced adj prōvectus; **well ~** (task) adfectus
advancement n (POL) honōs m
advantage n (benefit) commodum nt, bonum nt, ūsus m; (of place or time) opportūnitās f; (profit) fructus m; (superiority) praestantia f; **it is an ~** bono est; **be of ~ to** prōdesse (dat), ūsuī esse (dat); **to your ~** in rem tuam; **it is to your ~** tibi expedit, tuā interest; **take ~ of** (circumstances) ūtī; (person) dēcipere, fallere; **have an ~ over** praestāre (dat); **be seen to ~** māximē placēre
advantageous adj ūtilis, opportūnus
advantageously adv ūtiliter, opportūnē
advent n adventus m
adventitious adj fortuītus
adventure n (exploit) facinus memorābile nt; (hazard) perīculum nt
adventurer n vir audāx m; (social) parasītus m
adventurous adj audāx
adversary n adversārius m, hostis m
adverse adj adversus, contrārius, inimīcus
adversely adv contrāriē, inimīcē, male
adversity n rēs adversae fpl, calamitās f
advert vi: **~ to** attingere
advertise vt prōscrībere; vēnditāre

advertisement n prōscrīptiō f, libellus m
advice n cōnsilium nt; (POL) auctōritās f; (legal) respōnsum nt; **ask ~ of** cōnsulere; **on the ~ of** Sulla auctōre Sullā
advisable adj ūtilis, operae pretium
advise vt monēre, suādēre (dat), cēnsēre (dat); **~ against** dissuādēre
advisedly adv cōnsultō
adviser n auctor m, suāsor m
advocacy n patrōcinium nt
advocate n patrōnus m, causidicus m; (supporter) auctor m; **be an ~** causam dīcere ♦ vt suādēre, cēnsēre
adze n ascia f
aedile n aedīlis m
aedile's adj aedīlicius
aedileship n aedīlitās f
aegis n aegis f; (fig) praesidium nt
Aeneid n Aenēis f
aerial adj āerius
aesthetic adj pulchritūdinis amāns, artificiōsus
afar adv procul; **from ~** procul
affability n cōmitās f, facilitās f, bonitās f
affable adj cōmis, facilis, commodus
affably adv cōmiter
affair n negōtium nt, rēs f
affect vt afficere, movēre, commovēre; (concern) attingere; (pretence) simulāre
affectation n simulātiō f; (RHET) adfectātiō f; (in diction) īnsolentia f; quaesīta ntpl
affected adj (style) molestus, pūtidus
affectedly adv pūtidē
affecting adj miserābilis
affection n amor m, cāritās f, studium nt; (family) pietās f
affectionate adj amāns, pius
affectionately adv amanter, piē
affiance vt spondēre
affidavit n testimōnium nt
affinity n affīnitās f, cognātiō f
affirm vt adfirmāre, adsevērāre
affirmation n adfirmātiō f
affirmative adj: **I reply in the ~** āiō
affix vt adfīgere, adiungere
afflict vt adflīctāre, angere, vexāre; affligere
affliction n miseria f, dolor m, rēs adversae fpl
affluence n cōpia f, opēs fpl
affluent adj dīves, opulentus, locuplēs
afford vt praebēre, dare; **I cannot ~** rēs mihi nōn suppetit ad
affray n rixa f, pugna f
affright vt terrēre ♦ n terror m, pavor m
affront vt offendere, contumēliam dīcere (dat) ♦ n iniūria f, contumēlia f
afield adv forīs; **far ~** peregrē
afloat adj natāns; **be ~** natāre
afoot adv pedibus; **be ~** gerī
aforesaid adj suprā dictus
afraid adj timidus; **be ~ of** timēre, metuere; verērī
afresh adv dēnuō, dē integrō
Africa n Africa f
aft adv in puppī, puppim versus
after adj posterior ♦ adv posthāc, posteā; **the day ~** postrīdiē ♦ conj postquam; **the day ~** postrīdiē

quam ♦ *prep* post *(acc)*; *(in rank)* secundum *(acc)*; *(in imitation)* ad *(acc)*, dē *(abl)*; ~ **all** tamen, dēnique; ~ **reading the book** librō lēctō; **one thing ~ another** aliud ex aliō; **immediately ~** statim ab

aftermath *n* ēventus *m*

afternoon *n*: **in the ~** post merīdiem ♦ *adj* postmerīdiānus

afterthought *n* posterior cōgitātiō *f*

afterwards *adv* post, posteā, deinde

again *adv* rūrsus, iterum; ~ **and ~** etiam atque etiam, identidem; **once ~** dēnuō; *(new point in a speech)* quid?

against *prep* contrā *(acc)*, adversus *(acc)*, in *(acc)*; ~ **the stream** adversō flūmine; ~ **one's will** invitus

agape *adj* hiāns

age *n* *(life)* aetās *f*; *(epoch)* aetās *f*, saeculum *nt*; **old age** senectūs *f*; **he is of age** suī iūris est; **he is eight years of age** octō annōs nātus est, nōnum annum agit; **of the same age** aequālis

aged *adj* senex, aetāte prōvectus; *(things)* antīquus

agency *n* opera *f*; **through the ~ of** per *(acc)*

agent *n* āctor *m*, prōcūrātor *m*; *(in crime)* minister *m*

aggrandize *vt* augēre, amplificāre

aggrandizement *n* amplificātiō *f*

aggravate *vt* *(wound)* exulcerāre; *(distress)* augēre; **become aggravated** ingravēscere

aggravating *adj* molestus

aggregate *n* summa *f*

aggression *n* incursiō *f*, iniūria *f*

aggressive *adj* ferōx

aggressiveness *n* ferōcitās *f*

aggressor *n* oppugnātor *m*

aggrieved *adj* īrātus; **be ~** indignārī

aghast *adj* attonitus, stupefactus; **stand ~** obstupēscere

agile *adj* pernix, vēlōx

agility *n* pernīcitās *f*

agitate *vt* agitāre; *(mind)* commovēre, perturbāre

agitation *n* commōtiō *f*, perturbātiō *f*, trepidātiō *f*; *(POL)* tumultus *m*

agitator *n* turbātor *m*, concitātor *m*

aglow *adj* fervidus ♦ *adv*: **be ~** fervēre

ago *adv* abhinc *(acc)*; **three days ago** abhinc trēs diēs; **long ago** antīquitus, iamprīdem, iamdūdum; **a short time ago** dūdum

agog *adj* sollicitus, ērēctus

agonize *vt* cruciāre, torquēre

agonizing *adj* horribilis

agony *n* cruciātus *m*, dolor *m*

agrarian *adj* agrārius; ~ **party** agrāriī *mpl*

agree *vi* *(together)* cōnsentīre, congruere; *(with)* adsentīrī *(dat)*, sentīre cum; *(bargain)* pacīscī; *(facts)* cōnstāre, convenīre; *(food)* facilem esse ad concoquendum; ~ **upon** cōnstituere, compōnere; **it is agreed** constat (inter omnes)

agreeable *adj* grātus, commodus, acceptus

agreeableness *n* dulcēdō *f*, iūcunditas *f*

agreeably *adv* iūcundē

agreement *n* *(together)* cōnsēnsus *m*, concordia *f*; *(with)* adsēnsus *m*; *(pact)* pactiō *f*, conventum

nt, foedus *nt*; **according to** ~ compāctō, ex compositō; **be in** ~ cōnsentīre, congruere

agricultural *adj* rūsticus, agrestis

agriculture *n* rēs rūstica *f*, agrī cultūra *f*

aground *adv*: **be ~** sīdere; **run ~** in lītus ēicī, offendere

ague *n* horror *m*, febris *f*

ahead *adv* ante; **go ~** anteīre, praeīre; **go-ahead** *adj* impiger; **ships in line ~** agmen nāvium

aid *vt* adiuvāre, succurrere *(dat)*, subvenīre *(dat)* ♦ *n* auxilium *nt*, subsidium *nt*

aide-de-camp *n* optiō *m*

ail *vt* dolēre ♦ *vi* aegrōtāre, labōrāre, languēre

ailing *adj* aeger, īnfirmus

ailment *n* morbus *m*, valētūdō *f*

aim *vt* intendere; **aim at** petere; *(fig)* adfectāre, spectāre, sequī; *(with verb)* id agere ut ♦ *n* fīnis *m*, prōpositum *nt*

aimless *adj* inānis, vānus

aimlessly *adv* sine ratiōne

aimlessness *n* vānitās *f*

air *n* āēr *m*; *(breeze)* aura *f*; *(look)* vultus *m*, speciēs *f*; *(tune)* modus *m*; **in the open air** sub dīvō; **airs** fastus *m*; **give oneself airs** sē iactāre

airily *adv* hilarē

airy *adj* *(of air)* āerius; *(light)* tenuis; *(place)* apertus; *(manner)* hilaris

aisle *n* āla *f*

ajar *adj* sēmiapertus

akin *adj* cōnsanguineus, cognātus

alacrity *n* alacritās *f*

alarm *n* terror *m*, formīdō *f*, trepidātiō *f*; *(sound)* clāmor *m*; **sound an** ~ ad arma conclāmāre; **give the ~** increpāre; **be in a state of ~** trepidāre ♦ *vt* terrēre, perterrēre, perturbāre

alarming *adj* formīdolōsus

alas *interj* heu

albeit *conj* etsī, etiamsī

alcove *n* zōthēca *f*

alder *n* alnus *f*

alderman *n* decuriō *m*

ale *n* cervīsia *f*

alehouse *n* caupōna *f*, taberna *f*

alert *adj* prōmptus, alacer, vegetus

alertness *n* alacritās *f*

alien *adj* externus; ~ **to** abhorrēns ab ♦ *n* peregrīnus *m*

alienate *vt* aliēnāre, abaliēnāre, āvertere, āvocāre

alienation *n* aliēnātiō *f*

alight *adj*: **be ~** ārdēre; **set ~** accendere ♦ *vi* *(from horse)* dēscendere, dēsilīre; *(bird)* īnsīdere

alike *adj* pār, similis ♦ *adv* aequē, pariter

alive *adj* vīvus; **be ~** vīvere

all *adj* omnis; *(together)* ūniversus, cūnctus; *(whole)* tōtus; **all but** paene; **all for** studiōsus *(gen)*; **all in** cōnfectus; **all of** tōtus; **all over with** āctum dē *(abl)*; **all the best men** optimus quisque; **all the more** eō plūs, tantō plūs; **at all** ullō modō, quid; **it is all up with** actum est dē *(abl)*; **not at all** haudquāquam ♦ *n* fortūnae *fpl*

allay *vt* sēdāre, mītigāre, lēnīre

allegation *n* adfirmātiō *f*; *(charge)* īnsimulātiō *f*

allege *vt* adfirmāre, praetendere; *(in excuse)* excūsāre

allegiance n fidēs f; **owe ~ to** in fidē esse (gen); **swear ~ to** in verba iūrāre (gen)
allegory n allēgoria f, immūtāta ōrātiō f
alleviate vt mītigāre, adlevāre, sublevāre
alleviation n levātiō f, levāmentum nt
alley n (garden) xystus m; (town) angiportus m
alliance n societās f, foedus nt
allied adj foederātus, socius; (friends) coniūnctus
alligator n crocodīlus m
allocate vt adsignāre, impertīre
allot vt adsignāre, distribuere; **be allotted** obtingere
allotment n (land) adsignātiō f
allow vt sinere, permittere (dat), concēdere (dat), patī; (admit) fatērī, concēdere; (approve) comprobāre; **it is allowed** licet (dat + infin); **for** vt ratiōnem habēre (gen)
allowance n venia f, indulgentia f; (pay) stīpendium nt; (food) cibāria ntpl; (for travel) viāticum nt; **make ~ for** indulgēre (dat), ignōscere (dat), excusāre
alloy n admixtum nt
all right adj rēctē; **it is all right** bene est
allude vi: **~ to** dēsignāre, attingere, significāre
allure vt adlicere, pellicere
allurement n blanditia f, blandīmentum nt, illecebra f
alluring adj blandus
alluringly adv blandē
allusion n mentiō f, indicium nt
alluvial adj: **~ land** adluviō f
ally n socius m ♦ vt sociāre, coniungere
almanac n fāstī mpl
almighty adj omnipotēns
almond n (nut) amygdalum nt; (tree) amygdala f
almost adv paene, ferē, fermē, propemodum
alms n stipem (no nom) f
aloe n aloē f
aloft adj sublīmis ♦ adv sublīmē
alone adj sōlus, sōlitārius, ūnus ♦ adv sōlum
along prep secundum (acc), praeter (acc) ♦ adv porrō; **all ~** iamdūdum, ab initiō; **~ with** unā cum (abl)
alongside adv: **bring ~** adpellere; **come ~** ad crepīdinem accēdere
aloof adv procul; **stand ~** sē removēre ♦ adj sēmōtus
aloofness n sōlitūdō f, sēcessus m
aloud adv clārē, māgnā vōce
alphabet n elementa ntpl
Alps n Alpēs fpl
already adv iam
also adv etiam, et, quoque; īdem
altar n āra f
alter vt mūtāre, commūtāre; (order) invertere
alteration n mūtātiō f, commūtātiō f
altercation n altercātiō f, iūrgium nt
alternate adj alternus ♦ vt variāre
alternately adv invicem
alternation n vicem (no nom) f, vicissitūdō f
alternative adj alter, alius ♦ n optiō f
although conj quamquam (+indic), etsī/etiamsī (+ cond clause); quamvīs (subj)
altitude n altitūdō f
altogether adv omnīnō; (emphasis) plānē, prōrsus

altruism n beneficentia f
alum n alūmen nt
always adv semper
amalgamate vt miscēre, coniungere
amalgamation n coniūnctiō f, temperātiō f
amanuensis n librārius m
amass vt cumulāre, coacervāre
amateur n idiōta m
amatory adj amātōrius
amaze vt obstupefacere; attonāre; **be amazed** obstupēscere
amazement n stupor m; **in ~** attonitus, stupefactus
ambassador n lēgātus m
amber n sūcinum nt
ambidextrous adj utrīusque manūs compos
ambiguity n ambiguitās f; (RHET) amphibolia f
ambiguous adj ambiguus, anceps, dubius
ambiguously adv ambiguē
ambition n glōria f, laudis studium
ambitious adj glōriae cupidus, laudis avidus
amble vi ambulāre
ambrosia n ambrosia f
ambrosial adj ambrosius
ambuscade n īnsidiae fpl
ambush n īnsidiae fpl ♦ vt īnsidiārī (dat)
ameliorate vt corrigere, meliōrem reddere
amelioration n prōfectus m
amenable adj facilis, docilis
amend vt corrigere, ēmendāre
amendment n ēmendātiō f
amends n (apology) satisfactiō f; **make ~ for** expiāre; **make ~ to** satisfacere (dat)
amenity n (scenery) amoenitās f; (comfort) commodum nt
amethyst n amethystus f
amiability n benignitās f, suāvitās f
amiable adj benignus, suāvis
amiably adv benignē, suāviter
amicable adj amīcus, cōmis
amicably adv amīcē, cōmiter
amid, amidst prep inter (acc)
amiss adv perperam, secus, incommodē; **take ~ aegrē** ferre
amity n amīcitia f
ammunition n tēla ntpl
amnesty n venia f
among, amongst prep inter (acc), apud (acc)
amorous adj amātōrius, amāns
amorously adv cum amōre
amount vi: **~ to** efficere; (fig) esse ♦ n summa f
amours n amōrēs mpl
amphibious adj anceps
amphitheatre n amphitheātrum nt
ample adj amplus, satis
amplification n amplificātiō f
amplify vt amplificāre
amplitude n amplitūdō f, cōpia f
amputate vt secāre, amputāre
amuck adv: **run ~** bacchārī
amulet n amulētum nt
amuse vt dēlectāre, oblectāre
amusement n oblectāmentum nt, dēlectātiō f; **for ~** animī causā
amusing adj rīdiculus, facētus
an indef art see **a**

anaemic *adj* exsanguis
analogous *adj* similis
analogy *n* prōportiō *f*, comparātiō *f*
analyse *vt* excutere, perscrūtārī
analysis *n* explicātiō *f*
anapaest *n* anapaestus *m*
anarchical *adj* sēditiōsus
anarchy *n* reī pūblicae perturbātiō, lēgēs nullae *fpl*, licentia *f*
anathema *n* exsecrātiō *f*; (*object*) pestis *f*
ancestor *n* proavus *m*; **ancestors** *pl* māiōrēs *mpl*
ancestral *adj* patrius
ancestry *n* genus *nt*, orīgō *f*
anchor *n* ancora *f*; **lie at ~** in ancorīs stāre; **weigh ~** ancoram tollere ♦ *vi* ancoram iacere
anchorage *n* statiō *f*
ancient *adj* antīquus, prīscus, vetustus; **~ history, ~ world** antīquitās *f*; **from/in ~ times** antīquitus; **the ancients** veterēs
and *conj* et, atque, ac, -que; **and ... not** nec, neque; **and so** itaque
anecdote *n* fābella *f*
anent *prep* dē (*abl*)
anew *adv* dēnuō, ab integrō
angel *n* angelus *m*
angelic *adj* angelicus; (*fig*) dīvīnus, eximius
anger *n* īra *f* ♦ *vt* inrītāre
angle *n* angulus *m* ♦ *vi* hāmō piscārī
angler *n* piscātor *m*
Anglesey *n* Mona *f*
angrily *adv* īrātē
angry *adj* īrātus; **be ~** īrāscī (*dat*)
anguish *n* cruciātus *m*, dolor *m*; (*mind*) angor *m*
angular *adj* angulātus
animal *n* animal *nt*; (*domestic*) pecus *f*; (*wild*) fera *f*
animate *vt* animāre
animated *adj* excitātus, vegetus
animation *n* ārdor *m*, alacritās *f*
animosity *n* invidia *f*, inimīcitia *f*
ankle *n* tālus *m*
annalist *n* annālium scrīptor
annals *n* annālēs *mpl*
annex *vt* addere
annexation *n* adiectiō *f*
annihilate *vt* dēlēre, exstinguere, perimere
annihilation *n* exstinctiō *f*, interneciō *f*
anniversary *n* diēs anniversārius; (*public*) sollemne *nt*
annotate *vt* adnotāre
annotation *n* adnotātiō *f*
announce *vt* nūntiāre; (*officially*) dēnūntiāre, prōnūntiāre; (*election result*) renūntiāre
announcement *n* (*official*) dēnūntiātiō *f*; (*news*) nūntius *m*
announcer *n* nūntius *m*
annoy *vt* inrītāre, vexāre; **be annoyed with** aegrē ferre
annoyance *n* molestia *f*, vexātiō *f*; (*felt*) dolor *m*
annoying *adj* molestus
annual *adj* annuus, anniversārius
annually *adv* quotannīs
annuity *n* annua *ntpl*
annul *vt* abrogāre, dissolvere, tollere
annulment *n* abrogātiō *f*
anoint *vt* ungere, illinere
anomalous *adj* novus

anomaly *n* novitās *f*
anon *adv* mox
anonymous *adj* incertī auctōris
anonymously *adv* sine nōmine
another *adj* alius; (*second*) alter; **of ~** aliēnus; **one after ~** alius ex aliō; **one ~** inter sē, alius alium; **in ~ place** alibī; **to ~ place** aliō; **in ~ way** aliter; **at ~ time** aliās
answer *vt* respondēre (*dat*); (*by letter*) rescrībere (*dat*); (*agree*) respondēre, congruere; **~ a charge** crīmen dēfendere; **~ for** *vt* (*surety*) praestāre; (*account*) ratiōnem referre; (*substitute*) īnstar esse (*gen*) ♦ *n* respōnsum *nt*; (*to a charge*) dēfēnsiō *f*; **~ to the name of** vocārī; **give an ~** respondēre
answerable *adj* reus; **I am ~ for ...** ratiō mihī reddenda est ... (*gen*)
ant *n* formīca *f*
antagonism *n* simultās *f*, inimīcitia *f*
antagonist *n* adversārius *m*, hostis *m*
antarctic *adj* antarcticus
antecedent *adj* antecēdēns, prior
antediluvian *adj* prīscus, horridus, Deucaliōnēus
antelope *n* dorcas *f*
anterior *adj* prior
anteroom *n* vestibulum *nt*
anthology *n* excerpta *ntpl*; **make an ~** excerpere
anthropology *n* rēs hūmānae *fpl*
anticipate *vt* (*expect*) exspectāre; (*forestall*) antevenīre, occupāre; (*in thought*) animō praecipere
anticipation *n* exspectātiō *f*, spēs *f*; praesūmptiō *f*
antics *n* gestus *m*, ineptiae *fpl*
anticyclone *n* serēnitās *f*
antidote *n* remedium *nt*, medicāmen *nt*
antipathy *n* fastīdium *nt*, odium *nt*; (*things*) repugnantia *f*
antiphonal *adj* alternus
antiphony *n* alterna *ntpl*
antipodes *n* contrāria pars terrae
antiquarian *adj* historicus
antiquary *n* antīquārius *m*
antiquated *adj* prīscus, obsolētus
antique *adj* antīquus, prīscus
antiquity *n* antīquitās *f*, vetustas *f*, veterēs *mpl*
antithesis *n* contentiō *f*, contrārium *nt*
antlers *n* cornua *ntpl*
anvil *n* incūs *f*
anxiety *n* sollicitūdō *f*, metus *m*, cūra *f*; anxietās *f*
anxious *adj* sollicitus, anxius; avidus, cupidus
any *adj* ullus; (*interrog*) ecquī; (*after sī, nisī, num, nē*) quī; (*indef*) quīvīs, quīlibet; **hardly any** nullus ferē; **any further** longius; **any longer** (*of time*) diutius
anybody *pron* aliquis; (*indef*) quīvīs, quīlibet; (*after sī, nisī, num, nē*) quis; (*interrog*) ecquis, numquis; (*after neg*) quisquam; **hardly ~** nēmō ferē
anyhow *adv* ullō modō, quōquō modō
anyone *pron see* **anybody**
anything *pron* aliquid; quidvīs, quidlibet; (*interrog*) ecquid, numquid; (*after neg*) quicquam; (*after sī, nisī, num, nē*) quid; **hardly ~** nihil ferē

anywhere adv usquam, ubīvīs
apace adv citō, celeriter
apart adv seōrsum, sēparātim ♦ adj dīversus;
    be six feet ~ sex pedēs distāre; **set ~** sēpōnere;
    stand ~ distāre; **joking ~** remōtō iocō; **~ from**
    praeter (acc)
apartment n cubiculum nt, conclāve nt
apathetic adj lentus, languidus, ignāvus
apathy n lentitūdō f, languor m, ignāvia f
ape n sīmia f ♦ vt imitārī
aperture n hiātus m, forāmen nt, rīma f
apex n fastīgium nt
aphorism n sententia f
apiary n alveārium nt
apiece adv in singulōs; **two ~** bīnī
aplomb n cōnfidentia f
apocryphal adj commentīcius
apologetic adj cōnfitēns, veniam petēns
apologize vi veniam petere, sē excūsāre
apology n excūsātiō f
apoplectic adj apoplēcticus
apoplexy n apoplēxis f
apostle n apostolus m
apothecary n medicāmentārius m
appal vt perterrēre, cōnsternere
appalling adj dīrus
apparatus n īnstrūmenta ntpl, ōrnāmenta ntpl
apparel n vestis f, vestīmenta ntpl
apparent adj manifestus, apertus, ēvidēns
apparently adv speciē, ut vidētur
apparition n vīsum nt, speciēs f
appeal vi (to magistrate) appellāre; (to people)
    prōvocāre ad; (to gods) invocāre, testārī; (to
    senses) placēre (dat) ♦ n appellātiō f, prōvocātiō
    f, testātiō f
appear vi (in sight) apparēre; (in court) sistī; (in
    public) prōdīre; (at a place) adesse, advenīre;
    (seem) vidērī
appearance n (coming) adventus m; (look)
    aspectus m, faciēs f; (semblance) speciēs f; (thing)
    vīsum nt; **for the sake of appearances** in
    speciem; (formula) dicis causā; **make one's**
    ~ prōcēdere, prōdīre
appeasable adj plācābilis
appease vt plācāre, lēnīre, mītigāre, sēdāre
appeasement n plācātiō f; (of enemy) pācificātiō
    f
appellant n appellātor m
appellation n nōmen nt
append vt adiungere, subicere
appendage n appendix f, adiūnctum nt
appertain vi pertinēre
appetite n adpetītus m; (for food) fāmēs f
applaud vt plaudere; (fig) laudāre
applause n plausus m; (fig) adsēnsiō f,
    adprobātiō f
apple n pōmum nt; mālum nt; **~ tree** mālus f;
    ~ of my eye ocellus meus; **upset the ~ cart**
    plaustrum percellere
appliance n māchina f, īnstrūmentum nt
applicable adj aptus, commodus; **be ~** pertinēre
applicant n petītor m
application n (work) industria f; (mental)
    intentiō f; (asking) petītiō f; (MED) fōmentum nt
apply vt adhibēre, admovēre; (use) ūtī (abl);
    ~ oneself to sē adplicāre, incumbere in (acc)

♦ vi pertinēre; (to a person) adīre (acc); (for office)
    petere
appoint vt (magistrate) creāre, facere,
    cōnstituere; (commander) praeficere; (guardian,
    heir) īnstituere; (time) dīcere, statuere; (for a
    purpose) dēstināre; (to office) creāre
appointment n cōnstitūtum nt; (duty)
    mandātum nt; (office) magistrātus m; **have an**
    ~ with cōnstitūtum habēre cum; **keep an ~** ad
    cōnstitūtum venīre
apportion vt dispertīre, dīvīdere; (land)
    adsignāre
apposite adj aptus, appositus
appraisal n aestimātiō f
appraise vt aestimāre
appreciable adj haud exiguus
appreciate vt aestimāre
appreciation n aestimātiō f
apprehend vt (person) comprehendere; (idea)
    intellegere, mente comprehendere; (fear)
    metuere, timēre
apprehension n comprehēnsiō f; metus m,
    formīdō f
apprehensive adj anxius, sollicitus; **be ~ of**
    metuere
apprentice n discipulus m, tīrō m
apprenticeship n tīrōcinium nt
apprise vt docēre, certiōrem facere
approach vt appropinquāre ad (acc), accēdere
    ad; (person) adīre ♦ vi (time) adpropinquāre;
    (season) appetere ♦ n (act) accessus m, aditus m;
    (time) adpropinquātiō f; (way) aditus m; **make**
    approaches to adīre ad, ambīre, petere
approachable adj (place) patēns; (person) facilis
approbation n adprobātiō f, adsēnsiō f
appropriate adj aptus, idōneus, proprius ♦ vt
    adscīscere, adsūmere
appropriately adv aptē, commodē
approval n adprobātiō f, adsēnsus m, favor m
approve vt, vi adprobāre, comprobāre, adsentīrī
    (dat); (LAW) scīscere
approved adj probātus, spectātus
approximate adj propinquus ♦ vi: **~ to** accēdere
    ad
approximately adv prope, propemodum;
    (number) ad (acc)
appurtenances n īnstrūmenta ntpl, apparātus
    m
apricot n armēniacum nt; **~ tree** armēniaca f
April n mēnsis Aprīlis m; **of ~** Aprīlis
apron n operīmentum nt
apropos of prep quod attinet ad
apse n apsis f
apt adj aptus, idōneus; (pupil) docilis, prōmptus;
    apt to prōnus, prōclīvis ad; **be apt to** solēre
aptitude n ingenium nt, facultās f
aptly adv aptē
aquarium n piscīna f
aquatic adj aquātilis
aqueduct n aquae ductus m
aquiline adj (nose) aduncus
arable land n arvum nt
arbiter n arbiter m
arbitrarily adv ad libīdinem, licenter
arbitrary adj libīdinōsus (act); (ruler) superbus
arbitrate vi dīiūdicāre, disceptāre

arbitration *n* arbitrium *nt*, dīiūdicātiō *f*
arbitrator *n* arbiter *m*, disceptātor *m*
arbour *n* umbrāculum *nt*
arbutus *n* arbutus *f*
arc *n* arcus *m*
arcade *n* porticus *f*
arch *n* fornix *m*, arcus *m* ♦ *vt* arcuāre ♦ *adj*
lascīvus, vafer
archaeologist *n* antīquitātis investīgātor *m*
archaeology *n* antīquitātis investīgātiō *f*
archaic *adj* prīscus
archaism *n* verbum obsolētum *nt*
archbishop *n* archiepiscopus *m*
arched *adj* fornicātus
archer *n* sagittārius *m*
archery *n* sagittāriōrum ars *f*
architect *n* architectus *m*
architecture *n* architectūra *f*
architrave *n* epistylium *nt*
archives *n* tabulae (pūblicae) *fpl*
arctic *adj* arcticus, septentriōnālis ♦ *n*
septentriōnēs *mpl*
ardent *adj* ārdēns, fervidus, vehemēns
ardently *adv* ārdenter, ācriter, vehementer
ardour *n* ārdor *m*, fervor *m*
arduous *adj* difficilis, arduus
area *n* regiō *f*; (MATH) superficiēs *f*
arena *n* harēna *f*
argonaut *n* argonauta *m*
argosy *n* onerāria *f*
argue *vi* (*discuss*) disserere, disceptāre; (*dispute*)
ambigere; disputāre; (*reason*) argūmentārī ♦ *vt*
(*prove*) arguere
argument *n* (*discussion*) contrōversia *f*,
disputātiō *f*; (*reason*) ratiō *f*; (*proof, theme*)
argūmentum *nt*
argumentation *n* argūmentātiō *f*
argumentative *adj* lītigiōsus
aria *n* canticum *nt*
arid *adj* āridus, siccus
aright *adv* rectē, vērē
arise *vi* orīrī, coorīrī, exsistere; ~ **from** nāscī ex,
proficīscī ab
aristocracy *n* optimātēs *mpl*, nōbilēs *mpl*; (*govt*)
optimātium dominātus *m*
aristocrat *n* optimās *m*
aristocratic *adj* patricius, generōsus
arithmetic *n* numerī *mpl*, arithmētica *ntpl*
ark *n* arca *f*
arm *n* bracchium *nt*; (*upper*) lacertus *m*; (*sea*)
sinus *m*; (*weapon*) tēlum *nt* ♦ *vt* armāre ♦ *vi* arma
capere
armament *n* bellī apparātus *m*; cōpiae *fpl*
armed *adj* (*men*) armātus; **light-armed troops**
levis armātūra *f*, vēlitēs *mpl*
armistice *n* indutiae *fpl*
armlet *n* armilla *f*
armour *n* arma *ntpl*; (*kind of*) armātūra *f*
armourer *n* (armōrum) faber *m*
armoury *n* armāmentārium *nt*
armpit *n* āla *f*
arms *npl* (MIL) arma *ntpl*; **by force of** ~ vī et armīs;
under ~ in armīs
army *n* exercitus *m*; (*in battle*) aciēs *f*; (*on march*)
agmen *nt*
aroma *n* odor *m*

aromatic *adj* frāgrāns
around *adv* circum, circā ♦ *prep* circum (*acc*)
arouse *vt* suscitāre, ērigere, excitāre
arraign *vt* accūsāre
arrange *vt* (*in order*) compōnere, ōrdināre,
dīgerere, dispōnere; (*agree*) pacīscī; ~ **a truce**
indūtias compōnere
arrangement *n* ōrdō *m*, collocātiō *f*, dispositiō *f*;
pactum *nt*, cōnstitūtum *nt*
arrant *adj* summus
array *n* vestis *f*, habitus *m*; (MIL) aciēs *f* ♦ *vt*
vestīre, exōrnāre; (MIL) īnstruere
arrears *n* residuae pecūniae *fpl*, reliqua *ntpl*
arrest *vt* comprehendere, adripere; (*attention*)
in sē convertere; (*movement*) morārī, tardāre ♦ *n*
comprehēnsiō *f*
arrival *n* adventus *m*
arrive *vi* advenīre ('*ad*' + *acc*), pervenīre ('*ad*' + *acc*)
arrogance *n* superbia *f*, adrogantia *f*, fastus *m*
arrogant *adj* superbus, adrogāns
arrogantly *adv* superbē, adroganter
arrogate *vt* adrogāre
arrow *n* sagitta *f*
arsenal *n* armāmentārium *nt*
arson *n* incēnsiōnis crīmen *nt*
art *n* ars *f*, artificium *nt*; **fine arts** ingenuae
artēs
artery *n* artēria *f*
artful *adj* callidus, vafer, astūtus
artfully *adv* callidē, astūtē
artfulness *n* astūtia *f*, dolus *m*
artichoke *n* cinara *f*
article *n* rēs *f*, merx *f*; (*clause*) caput *nt*; (*term*)
condiciō *f*
articulate *adj* explānātus, distinctus ♦ *vt*
explānāre, exprimere
articulately *adv* explānātē, clārē
articulation *n* prōnūntiātiō *f*
artifice *n* ars *f*, artificium *nt*, dolus *m*
artificer *n* artifex *m*, opifex *m*, faber *m*
artificial *adj* (*work*) artificiōsus; (*appearance*)
fūcātus
artificially *adv* arte, manū
artillery *n* tormenta *ntpl*
artisan *n* faber *m*, opifex *m*
artist *n* artifex *m*; pictor *m*
artistic *adj* artificiōsus, ēlegāns
artistically *adv* artificiōsē, ēleganter
artless *adj* (*work*) inconditus; (*person*) simplex
artlessly *adv* inconditē; simpliciter, sine dolō
artlessness *n* simplicitās *f*
as *adv* (*before adj, adv*) tam; (*after* **aequus, īdem,
similis**) ac, atque; (*correlative*) quam, quālis,
quantus ♦ *conj* (*compar*) ut (+ *indic*), sīcut, velut,
quemadmodum; (*cause*) cum (+ *indic*), quōniam,
quippe quī; (*time*) dum, ut ♦ *relat pron* quī, quae,
quod (*subj*); **as being** utpote; **as follows** ita; **as
for** quod attinet ad; **as if** quasī, tamquam si,
velut; (*while*) *usu expressed by pres part*; **as it were**
ut ita dīcam; **as yet** adhūc; **as soon as** simul
ac/atque (+ *perf indic*); **as ... as possible** quam (+
superl) ♦ *n* (*coin*) as *m*
ascend *vt, vi* ascendere
ascendancy *n* praestantia *f*, auctōritās *f*
ascendant *adj* surgēns, potēns; **be in the**
~ praestāre

9

ascent n ascēnsus m; (slope) clīvus m
ascertain vt comperīre, cognōscere
ascetic adj nimis abstinēns, austērus
asceticism n dūritia f
ascribe vt adscrībere, attribuere, adsignāre
ash n (tree) fraxinus f ♦ adj fraxineus
ashamed adj: **I am** ~ pudet mē; ~ **of** pudet (+ acc of person, + gen of thing)
ashen adj pallidus
ashes n cinis m
ashore adv (motion) in lītus; (rest) in lītore; **go** ~ ēgredī
Asia n Asia f
aside adv sēparatim, sē- (in cpd)
ask vt (question) rogāre, quaerere; (request) petere, poscere; (beg, entreat) orāre; **ask for** vt petere; rogāre; scīscitārī; percontārī
askance adv oblīquē; **look** ~ **at** līmīs oculīs aspicere, invidēre (dat)
askew adv prāvē
aslant adv oblīquē
asleep adj sōpītus; **be** ~ dormīre; **fall** ~ obdormīre, somnum inīre
asp n aspis f
asparagus n asparagus m
aspect n (place) aspectus m; (person) vultus m; (circumstances) status m; **have a southern** ~ ad merīdiem spectāre; **there is another** ~ **to the matter** aliter sē rēs habet
aspen n pōpulus f
asperity n acerbitās f
asperse vt maledīcere (dat), calumniārī
aspersion n calumnia f; **cast aspersions on** calumniārī, īnfāmiā aspergere
asphalt n bitūmen nt
asphyxia n strangulātiō f
asphyxiate vt strangulāre
aspirant n petītor m
aspirate n (GRAM) aspīrātiō f
aspiration n spēs f; (POL) ambitiō f
aspire vi: ~ **to** adfectāre, petere, spērāre, contendere
ass n asinus m, asellus m; (fig) stultus
assail vt oppugnāre, adorīrī, aggredī
assailable adj expugnābilis
assailant n oppugnātor m
assassin n sīcārius m, percussor m
assassinate vt interficere, occīdere, iugulāre
assassination n caedēs f, parricidium nt
assault vt oppugnāre, adorīrī, aggredī; (speech) invehī in (acc) ♦ n impetus m, oppugnātiō f; (personal) vīs f
assay vt (metal) spectāre; temptāre, cōnārī
assemble vt convocāre, congregāre, cōgere ♦ vi convenīre, congregārī
assembly n coetus m, conventus m; (plebs) concilium nt; (Roman people) comitia ntpl; (troops) cōntiō f; (things) congeriēs f
assent vi adsentīrī, adnuere ♦ n adsēnsus m
assert vt adfirmāre, adsevērāre, dīcere
assertion n adfirmātiō f, adsevērātiō f, dictum nt, sententia f
assess vt cēnsēre, aestimāre; ~ **damages** lītem aestimāre
assessment n cēnsus m, aestimātiō f
assessor n cēnsor m; (assistant) cōnsessor m

assets n bona ntpl
assiduity n dīligentia f, sēdulitās f, industria f
assiduous adj dīligēns, sēdulus, industrius
assign vt tribuere, attribuere; (land) adsignāre; (in writing) perscrībere; (task) dēlēgāre; (reason) adferre
assignation n cōnstitūtum nt
assignment n adsignātiō f, perscrīptiō f; (task) mūnus nt, pēnsum nt
assimilate vt aequāre; (food) concoquere; (knowledge) concipere
assist vt adiuvāre, succurrere (dat), adesse (dat)
assistance n auxilium nt, opem (no nom) f; **come to the** ~ **of** subvenīre (dat); **be of** ~ **to** auxiliō esse (dat)
assistant n adiūtor m, minister m
assize n conventus m; **hold assizes** conventūs agere
associate vt cōnsociāre, coniungere ♦ vi rem inter sē cōnsociāre; ~ **with** familiāriter ūtī (abl) ♦ n socius m, sodālis m
association n societās f; (club) sodālitās f
assort vt dīgerere, dispōnere ♦ vi congruere
assortment n (of goods) variae mercēs fpl
assuage vt lēnīre, mītigāre, sēdāre
assume vt (for oneself) adsūmere, adrogāre; (hypothesis) pōnere; (office) inīre
assumption n (hypothesis) sūmptiō f, positum nt
assurance n (given) fidēs f, pignus nt; (felt) fīdūcia f; (boldness) cōnfidentia f
assure vt cōnfirmāre, prōmittere (dat)
assured adj (person) fīdēns; (fact) explōrātus, certus
assuredly adv certō, certē, profectō, sānē
astern adv ā puppī; (movement) retrō; ~ **of** post
asthma n anhēlitus m
astonish vt obstupefacere; attonāre
astonished adj attonitus, stupefactus; **be** ~ **at** admīrārī
astonishing adj mīrificus, mīrus
astonishment n stupor m, admīrātiō f
astound vt obstupefacere
astray adj vagus; **go** ~ errāre, aberrāre, deerrāre
astride adj vāricus
astrologer n Chaldaeus m, mathēmaticus m
astrology n Chaldaeōrum dīvīnātiō f
astronomer n astrologus m
astronomy n astrologia f
astute adj callidus, vafer
astuteness n calliditās f
asunder adv sēparātim, dis- (in cpd)
asylum n asylum nt
at prep in (abl), ad (acc); (time) usu expressed by abl; (towns, small islands) locative; **at the house of** apud (acc); **at all events** saltem; see also **dawn**, **hand**, **house** etc
atheism n deōs esse negāre
atheist n atheos m; **be an** ~ deōs esse negāre
Athenian adj Atheniensis
Athens n Athenae fpl; **at/from** ~ Athenis; **to** ~ Athenas
athirst adj sitiens; (fig) avidus
athlete n athlēta m
athletic adj rōbustus, lacertōsus
athletics n athlētica ntpl
athwart prep trāns (acc)

atlas n orbis terrārum dēscrīptiō f
atmosphere n āēr m
atom n atomus f, corpus indīviduum nt
atone vi: ~ **for** expiāre
atonement n expiātiō f, piāculum nt
atrocious adj immānis, nefārius, scelestus
atrociously adv nefāriē, scelestē
atrociousness n immānitās f
atrocity n nefas nt, scelus nt, flāgitium nt
atrophy vi marcēscere
attach vt adiungere, adfīgere, illigāre; (word)
    subicere; **attached to** amāns (gen)
attachment n vinculum nt; amor m, studium nt
attack vt oppugnāre, adorīrī, aggredī; impetum
    facere in (acc); (speech) īnsequī, invehī in
    (acc); (disease) ingruere in (acc) ◆ n impetus m,
    oppugnātiō f, incursus m
attacker n oppugnātor m
attain vt adsequī, adipīscī, cōnsequī; ~ **to**
    pervenīre ad
attainable adj impetrābilis, in prōmptū
attainder n: **bill of** ~ prīvilēgium nt
attainment n adeptiō f
attainments npl doctrīna f, ērudītiō f
attaint vt māiestātis condemnāre
attempt vt cōnārī, temptāre; (with effort) mōlīrī
    ◆ n cōnātus m, inceptum nt; (risk) perīculum nt;
    first attempts rudīmenta ntpl
attend vt (meeting) adesse (dat), interesse (dat);
    (person) prōsequī, comitārī; (master) appārēre
    (dat); (invalid) cūrāre ◆ vi animum advertere,
    animum attendere; ~ **to** (task) adcūrāre; ~ **upon**
    prōsequī, adsectārī; ~ **the lectures of** audīre;
    not ~ aliud agere; ~ **first to** praevertere (dat);
    well attended frequēns; **thinly attended**
    īnfrequēns
attendance n (courtesy) adsectātiō f; (MED)
    cūrātiō f; (service) apparitiō f; **constant**
    ~ adsiduitās f; **full** ~ frequentia f; **poor**
    ~ īnfrequentia f; **dance** ~ **on** haerēre (dat)
attendant n famulus m, minister m; (on
    candidate) sectātor m; (on nobleman) adsectātor m;
    (on magistrate) apparitor m
attention n animadversiō f, animī attentiō f;
    (to work) cūra f; (respect) observantia f; **attract**
    ~ digitō mōnstrārī; **call** ~ **to** indicāre; **pay** ~ **to**
    animadvertere, observāre; ratiōnem habēre
    (gen); **attention!** hōc age!
attentive adj intentus; (to work) dīligēns
attentively adv intentē, dīligenter
attenuate vt attenuāre
attest vt cōnfirmāre, testārī
attestation n testificātiō f
attestor n testis m
attic n cēnāculum nt
attire vt vestīre ◆ n vestis f, habitus m
attitude n (body) gestus m, status m, habitus m;
    (mind) ratiō f
attorney n āctor m; advocātus m
attract vt trahere, attrahere, adlicere
attraction n vīs attrahendī; illecebra f,
    invītāmentum nt
attractive adj suāvis, venustus, lepidus
attractively adv suāviter, vēnustē, lepidē
attractiveness n venustās f, lepōs m

attribute vt tribuere, attribuere, adsignāre ◆ n
    proprium nt
attrition n attrītus m
attune vt modulārī
auburn adj flāvus
auction n auctiō f; (public) hasta f; **hold an**
    ~ auctiōnem facere; **sell by** ~ sub hastā
    vēndere
auctioneer n praecō m
audacious adj audāx; protervus
audaciously adv audācter, protervē
audacity n audācia f, temeritās f
audible adj: **be** ~ exaudīrī posse
audibly adv clārā vōce
audience n audītōrēs mpl; (interview) aditus m;
    give an ~ **to** admittere
audit vt īnspicere ◆ n ratiōnum īnspectiō f
auditorium n cavea f
auditory adj audītōrius
auger n terebra f
augment vt augēre, adaugēre ◆ vi crēscere,
    augērī
augmentation n incrēmentum nt
augur n augur m; **augur's staff** lituus m ◆ vi
    augurārī; (fig) portendere
augural adj augurālis
augurship n augurātus m
augury n augurium nt, auspicium nt; ōmen
    nt; **take auguries** augurārī; **after taking**
    auguries augurātō
August n mēnsis Augustus, Sextīlis; **of**
    ~ Sextīlis
august adj augustus
aunt n (paternal) amita f; (maternal) mātertera f
auspices n auspicium nt; **take** ~ auspicārī;
    after taking ~ auspicātō; **without taking**
    ~ inauspicātō
auspicious adj faustus, fēlīx
auspiciously adv fēlīciter, prosperē
austere adj austērus, sevērus, dūrus
austerely adv sevērē
austerity n sevēritās f, dūritia f
authentic adj vērus, certus
authenticate vt recognōscere
authenticity n auctōritās f, fidēs f
author n auctor m, inventor m; scrīptor m
authoress n auctor f
authoritative adj fīdus; imperiōsus
authority n auctōritās f, potestās f, iūs nt; (MIL)
    imperium nt; (LIT) auctor m, scrīptor m; **enforce**
    ~ iūs suum exsequī; **have great** ~ multum
    pollēre; **on Caesar's** ~ auctōre Caesare; **an** ~ **on**
    perītus (gen)
authorize vt potestātem facere (dat), mandāre;
    (LAW) sancīre
autobiography n dē vītā suā scrīptus liber m
autocracy n imperium singulāre nt, tyrannis f
autocrat n tyrannus m, dominus m
autocratic adj imperiōsus
autograph n manus f, chīrographum nt
automatic adj necessārius
automatically adv necessāriō
autonomous adj līber
autonomy n lībertās f
autumn n auctumnus m
autumnal adj auctumnālis

auxiliaries *npl* auxilia *ntpl*, auxiliāriī *mpl*
auxiliary *adj* auxiliāris ♦ *n* adiūtor *m*; ~ **forces** auxilia *ntpl*; novae copiae *fpl*
avail *vi* valēre ♦ *vt* prōdesse *(dat)*; ~ **oneself of** ūtī *(abl)* ♦ *n* ūsus *m*; **of no** ~ frustrā
available *adj* ad manum, in prōmptū
avalanche *n* montis ruīna *f*
avarice *n* avāritia *f*, cupīditās *f*
avaricious *adj* avārus, cupidus
avariciously *adv* avārē
avenge *vt* ulcīscī *(abl)*, vindicāre
avenger *n* ultor *m*, vindex *m*
avenue *n* xystus *m*; *(fig)* aditus *m*, iānua *f*
aver *vt* adfirmāre, adsevērāre
average *n* medium *nt*; **on the** ~ ferē
averse *adj* āversus *(abl)*; **be** ~ **to** abhorrēre ab
aversion *n* odium *nt*, fastīdium *nt*
avert *vt* arcēre, dēpellere; *(by prayer)* dēprecārī
aviary *n* aviārium *nt*
avid *adj* avidus
avidity *n* aviditās *f*
avidly *adv* avidē
avoid *vt* vītāre, fugere, dēclīnāre; *(battle)* dētrectāre
avoidance *n* fuga *f*, dēclīnātiō *f*
avow *vt* fatērī, cōnfitērī
avowal *n* cōnfessiō *f*
avowed *adj* apertus
avowedly *adv* apertē, palam
await *vt* exspectāre; *(future)* manēre

awake *vt* suscitāre, exsuscitāre ♦ *vi* expergīscī ♦ *adj* vigil
awaken *vt* exsuscitāre
award *vt* tribuere; *(LAW)* adiūdicāre ♦ *n (decision)* arbitrium *nt*, iūdicium *nt*; *(thing)* praemium *nt*
aware *adj* gnārus; conscius *(gen)*; **be** ~ scīre; **become** ~ **of** percipere
away *adv* ā-, ab- *(in cpd)*; **be** ~ abesse ab *(abl)*; **far** ~ procul, longē; **make** ~ **with** dē mediō tollere
awe *n* formīdō *f*, reverentia *f*, rēligiō *f*; **stand in awe of** verērī; *(gods)* venerārī
awe-struck *adj* stupidus
awful *adj* terribilis, formīdolōsus, dīrus
awfully *adv* formīdolōsē
awhile *adv* aliquamdiū, aliquantisper, parumper
awkward *adj* incallidus, inconcinnus; *(to handle)* inhabilis; *(fig)* molestus
awkwardly *adv* incallidē, imperītē
awkwardness *n* imperītia *f*, īnscītia *f*
awl *n* sūbula *f*
awning *n* vēlum *nt*
awry *adj* prāvus, dissidēns
axe *n* secūris *f*
axiom *n* prōnūntiātum *nt*, sententia *f*
axiomatic *adj* ēvidēns, manifestus
axis *n* axis *m*
axle *n* axis *m*
aye *adv* semper; **for aye** in aeternum
azure *adj* caeruleus

Bb

baa *vi* bālāre ♦ *n* bālātus *m*
babble *vi* garrīre, blaterāre
babbler *n* garrulus *m*
babbling *adj* garrulus
babe *n* īnfāns *m/f*
babel *n* dissonae vōcēs *fpl*
baboon *n* sīmia *f*
baby *n* īnfāns *m/f*
Bacchanalian *adj* Bacchicus
Bacchante *n* Baccha *f*
bachelor *n* caelebs *m*; *(degree)* baccalaureus *m*
back *n* tergum *nt*; *(animal)* dorsum *nt*; *(head)*
occipitium *nt*; **at one's ~** ā tergō; **behind one's**
~ *(fig)* clam *(acc)*; **put one's ~ up** stomachum
movēre *(dat)*; **turn one's ~ on** sē āvertere ab
♦ *adj* āversus, postīcus ♦ *adv* retrō, retrōrsum,
re- *(in cpd)* ♦ *vt* obsecundāre *(dat)*, adesse *(dat)*;
~ water inhibēre rēmīs, inhibēre nāvem ♦ *vi*:
~ out dētrectāre, dēfugere
backbite *vt* obtrectāre *(dat)*, maledīcere *(dat)*
backbone *n* spīna *f*
backdoor *n* postīcum *nt*
backer *n* fautor *m*
background *n* recessus *m*, umbra *f*
backing *n* fidēs *f*, favor *m*
backslide *vi* dēscīscere
backward *adj* āversus; *(slow)* tardus; *(late)* sērus
backwardness *n* tardītās *f*, pigritia *f*
backwards *adv* retrō, retrōrsum
bacon *n* lārdum *nt*
bad *adj* malus, prāvus, improbus, turpis; **go bad**
corrumpī; **be bad for** obesse *(dat)*, nocēre *(dat)*
badge *n* īnsigne *nt*, īnfula *f*
badger *n* mēles *f* ♦ *vt* sollicitāre
badly *adv* male, prāvē, improbē, turpiter
badness *n* prāvitās *f*, nēquitia *f*, improbitās *f*
baffle *vt* ēlūdere, fallere, frustrārī
bag *n* saccus *m*, folliculus *m*; **handbag** mantica *f*
bagatelle *n* nūgae *fpl*, floccus *m*
baggage *n* impedīmenta *ntpl*, vāsa *ntpl*, sarcinae
fpl; **~ train** impedīmenta *ntpl*; **without**
~ expedītus
bail *n* vadimōnium *nt*; *(person)* vas *m*; **become**
~ for spondēre prō *(abl)*; **accept ~ for** vadārī;
keep one's ~ vadimōnium obīre ♦ *vt* spondēre
prō *(abl)*
bailiff *n* (POL) apparitor *m*; *(private)* vīlicus *m*
bait *n* esca *f*, illecebra *f* ♦ *vt* lacessere
bake *vt* coquere, torrēre
bakehouse *n* pistrīna *f*
baker *n* pistor *m*
bakery *n* pistrīna *f*

balance *n* *(scales)* lībra *f*, trutina *f*; *(equilibrium)*
lībrāmentum *nt*; *(money)* reliqua *ntpl* ♦ *vt* lībrāre;
(fig) compēnsāre; **the account balances** ratiō
cōnstat
balance sheet *n* ratiō acceptī et expēnsī
balcony *n* podium *nt*, Maeniānum *nt*
bald *adj* calvus; *(style)* āridus, iēiūnus
baldness *n* calvitium *nt*; *(style)* iēiūnitās *f*
bale *n* fascis *m*; **~ out** *vt* exhaurīre
baleful *adj* fūnestus, perniciōsus, tristis
balk *n* tignum *nt* ♦ *vt* frustrārī, dēcipere
ball *n* globus *m*; *(play)* pila *f*; *(wool)* glomus *nt*;
(dance) saltātiō *f*
ballad *n* carmen *nt*
ballast *n* saburra *f*
ballet *n* saltātiō *f*
ballot *n* suffrāgium *nt*
ballot box urna *f*
balm *n* unguentum *nt*; *(fig)* sōlātium *nt*
balmy *adj* lēnis, suāvis
balsam *n* balsamum *nt*
balustrade *n* cancellī *mpl*
bamboozle *vt* cōnfundere
ban *vt* interdīcere *(dat)*, vetāre ♦ *n* interdictum *nt*
banal *adj* trītus
banana *n* ariēna *f*; *(tree)* pāla *f*
band *n* vinculum *nt*, redimīculum *nt*; *(head)*
īnfula *f*; *(men)* caterva *f*, manus *f*, grex *f* ♦ *vi*:
~ together cōnsociārī
bandage *n* fascia *f*, īnfula *f* ♦ *vt* obligāre,
adligāre
bandbox *n*: **out of a ~** *(fig)* dē capsulā
bandeau *n* redimīculum *nt*
bandit *n* latrō *m*
bandy *vt* iactāre; **~ words** altercārī ♦ *adj* vārus
bane *n* venēnum *nt*, pestis *f*, perniciēs *f*
baneful *adj* perniciōsus, pestifer
bang *vt* pulsāre ♦ *n* fragor *m*
bangle *n* armilla *f*
banish *vt* pellere, expellere, ēicere; (LAW) aquā
et ignī interdīcere *(dat)*; *(temporarily)* relēgāre;
(feeling) abstergēre
banishment *n* *(act)* aquae et ignis interdictiō *f*;
relēgātiō *f*; *(state)* exsilium *nt*, fuga *f*
bank *n* *(earth)* agger *m*; *(river)* rīpa *f*; *(money)*
argentāria *f*
banker *n* argentārius *m*; *(public)* mēnsārius *m*
bankrupt *adj*: **be ~** solvendō nōn esse; **declare**
oneself ~ bonam cōpiam ēiūrāre; **go**
~ dēcoquere ♦ *n* dēcoctor *m*
banner *n* vexillum *nt*

banquet n cēna f, epulae fpl; convīvium nt; (religious) daps f ✦ vi epulārī

banter n cavillātiō f ✦ vi cavillārī

baptism n baptisma nt

baptize vt baptizāre

bar n (door) sera f; (gate) claustrum nt; (metal) later m; (wood) asser m; (lever) vectis m; (obstacle) impedīmentum nt; (law-court) cancellī mpl; (barristers) advocātī mpl; (profession) forum nt; **of the bar** forēnsis; **practise at the bar** causās agere ✦ vt (door) obserāre; (way) obstāre (dat), interclūdere, prohibēre; (exception) excipere, exclūdere

barb n acūleus m, dēns m, hāmus m

barbarian n barbarus m ✦ adj barbarus

barbarism n barbaria f

barbarity n saevitia f, ferōcia f, immānitās f, inhūmānitās f

barbarous adj barbarus, saevus, immānis, inhūmānus

barbarously adv barbarē, inhūmānē

barbed adj hāmātus

barber n tōnsor m; **barber's shop** tōnstrīna f

bard n vātēs m/f; (Gallic) bardus m

bare adj nūdus; (mere) merus; **lay ~** nūdāre, aperīre, dētegere ✦ vt nūdāre

barefaced adj impudēns

barefoot adj nūdis pedibus

bare-headed adj capite aperto

barely adv vix

bargain n pactum nt, foedus nt; **make a ~** pacīscī; **make a bad ~** male emere; **into the ~** grātiīs ✦ vi pacīscī

barge n linter f

bark n cortex m; (dog) lātrātus m; (ship) nāvis f, ratis f ✦ vi lātrāre

barking n latratus m

barley n hordeum nt; **of ~** hordeāceus

barn n horreum nt

barrack vt obstrepere (dat)

barracks n castra ntpl

barrel n cūpa f; ligneum vās nt

barren adj sterilis

barrenness n sterilitās f

barricade n claustrum nt, mūnīmentum nt ✦ vt obsaepīre, obstruere; **~ off** intersaepīre

barrier n impedīmentum nt, claustra ntpl; (racecourse) carcer nt

barrister n advocātus m, patrōnus m, causidicus m

barrow n ferculum nt; (mound) tumulus m

barter vt mūtāre ✦ vi mercēs mūtāre ✦ n mūtātiō f, commercium nt

base adj turpis, vīlis; (birth) humilis, ignōbilis; (coin) adulterīnus ✦ n fundāmentum nt; (statue) basis f; (hill) rādīcēs fpl; (MIL) castra ntpl

baseless adj falsus, inānis

basely adv turpiter

basement n basis f; (storey) īmum tabulātum nt

baseness n turpitūdō f

bashful adj pudīcus, verēcundus

bashfully adv verēcundē

bashfulness n pudor m, verēcundia f

basic adj prīmus

basin n alveolus m, pelvis f; **washbasin** aquālis m

basis n fundāmentum nt

bask vi aprīcārī

basket n corbis f, fiscus m; (for bread) canistrum nt; (for wool) quasillum nt

basking n aprīcātiō f

bas-relief n toreuma nt

bass adj (voice) gravis

bastard adj nothus

bastion n prōpugnāculum nt

bat n vespertiliō m; (games) clāva f

batch n numerus m

Bath n Aquae Sulis fpl

bath n balneum nt; (utensil) lābrum nt, lavātiō f; **Turkish ~** Lacōnicum nt; **cold ~** frīgidārium nt; **hot ~** calidārium nt; **~ superintendent** balneātor m ✦ vt lavāre

bathe vt lavāre ✦ vi lavārī, perluī

bathroom n balneāria ntpl

baths n (public baths) balneae fpl

batman n cālō m

baton n virga f, scīpiō m

battalion n cohors f

batter vt quassāre, pulsāre, verberāre

battering ram n ariēs m

battery n (assault) vīs f

battle n pugna f, proelium nt, certāmen nt; **a ~ was fought** pugnatum est; **pitched ~** iūstum proelium; **line of ~** aciēs f; **drawn ~** anceps proelium ✦ vi pugnāre, contendere; **~ order** aciēs f

battle-axe n bipennis f

battlefield, battle-line n aciēs f

battlement n pinna f

bawl vt vōciferārī, clāmitāre

bay n (sea) sinus m; (tree) laurus f, laurea f; **of bay** laureus; **at bay** interclūsus ✦ adj (colour) spādīx ✦ vi (dog) lātrāre

be vi esse; (circumstances) versārī; (condition) sē habēre; **be at** adesse (dat); **be amongst** interesse (dat); **be in** inesse (dat); **consul-to-be** cōnsul dēsignātus; **how are you?** quid agis?; **so be it** estō; see also **absent**, **here** etc

beach n lītus nt, acta f ✦ vt (ship) subdūcere

beacon n ignis m

bead n pilula f

beadle n apparitor m

beak n rōstrum nt

beaked adj rōstrātus

beaker n cantharus m, scyphus m

beam n (wood) trabs f, tignum nt; (balance) iugum nt; (light) radius m; (ship) latus nt; **on the ~** ā latere ✦ vi fulgēre; (person) adrīdēre

beaming adj hilaris

bean n faba f

bear n ursus m, ursa f; **Great Bear** septentriōnēs mpl, Arctos f; **Little Bear** septentriō minor m, Cynosūra f; **bear's** ursīnus ✦ vt (carry) ferre, portāre; (endure) ferre, tolerāre, patī; (produce) ferre, fundere; (child) parere; **~ down upon** appropinquāre; **~ off** ferre; **~ out** vt arguere; **~ up** vi; **~ up under** obsistere (dat), sustinēre; **~ upon** innītī (dat); (refer) pertinēre ad; **~ with** vt indulgēre (dat); **~ oneself** sē gerere; **I cannot ~ to** addūcī nōn possum ut

bearable adj tolerābilis

beard n barba f ✦ vt ultrō lacessere

bearded *adj* barbātus
beardless *adj* imberbis
bearer *n* bāiulus *m*; (*letter*) tabellārius *m*; (*litter*) lectīcārius *m*; (*news*) nūntius *m*
bearing *n* (*person*) gestus *m*, vultus *m*; (*direction*) regiō *f*; **have no ~ on** nihil pertinēre ad; **I have lost my bearings** ubi sim nesciō
beast *n* bestia *f*; (*large*) bēlua *f*; (*wild*) fera *f*; (*domestic*) pecus *f*
beastliness *n* foeditās *f*, stuprum *nt*
beastly *adj* foedus
beast of burden *n* iūmentum *nt*
beat *n* ictus *m*; (*heart*) palpitātiō *f*; (*music*) percussiō *f*; (*oars, pulse*) pulsus *m* ◆ *vt* ferīre, percutere, pulsāre; (*the body in grief*) plangere; (*punish*) caedere; (*whip*) verberāre; (*conquer*) vincere, superāre ◆ *vi* palpitāre, micāre; **~ back** repellere; **~ in** perfringere; **~ out** excutere; (*metal*) extundere; **~ a retreat** receptui canere; **~ about the bush** circuitiōne ūtī; **be beaten** vāpulāre; **dead ~** cōnfectus
beating *n* verbera *ntpl*; (*defeat*) clādēs *f*; (*time*) percussiō *f*; **get a ~** vāpulāre
beatitude *n* beātitūdō *f*, fēlīcitās *f*
beau *n* nitidus homō *m*; (*lover*) amāns *m*
beauteous *adj* pulcher, fōrmōsus
beautiful *adj* pulcher, fōrmōsus; (*looks*) decōrus; (*scenery*) amoenus
beautifully *adv* pulchrē
beautify *vt* exōrnāre, decorāre
beauty *n* fōrma *f*, pulchritūdō *f*, amoenitās *f*
beaver *n* castor *m*, fiber *m*; (*helmet*) buccula *f*
becalmed *adj* ventō dēstitūtus
because *conj* quod, quia, quōniam (*+ indic*); quippe quī; **~ of** propter (*acc*)
beck *n* nūtus *m*
beckon *vt* innuere, vocāre
become *vi* fierī; **what will ~ of me?** quid me fiet? ◆ *vt* decēre, convenīre in (*acc*)
becoming *adj* decēns, decōrus
becomingly *adv* decōrē, convenienter
bed *n* cubīle *nt*, lectus *m*, lectulus *m*; **go to bed** cubitum īre; **make a bed** lectum sternere; **be bedridden** lectō tenērī; **camp bed** grabātus *m*; **flowerbed** pulvīnus *m*; **marriage bed** lectus geniālis *m*; **riverbed** alveus *m*
bedaub *vt* illinere, oblinere
bedclothes *n* strāgula *ntpl*
bedding *n* strāgula *ntpl*
bedeck *vt* ōrnāre, exōrnāre
bedew *vt* inrōrāre
bedim *vt* obscūrāre
bedpost *n* fulcrum *nt*
bedraggled *adj* sordidus, madidus
bedroom *n* cubiculum *nt*
bedstead *n* sponda *f*
bee *n* apis *f*; **queen bee** rēx *m*
beech *n* fāgus *f* ◆ *adj* fāginus
beef *n* būbula *f*
beehive *n* alvus *f*
beekeeper *n* apiārius *m*
beer *n* cervīsia *f*, fermentum *nt*
beet *n* bēta *f*
beetle *n* (*insect*) scarabaeus *m*; (*implement*) fistūca *f*
beetling *adj* imminēns, mināx

befall *vi*, *vt* accidere, ēvenīre (*dat*); (*good*) contingere (*dat*)
befit *vt* decēre, convenīre in (*acc*)
before *adv* ante, anteā, antehāc ◆ *prep* ante (*acc*); (*place*) prō (*abl*); (*presence*) apud (*acc*), cōram (*abl*) ◆ *conj* antequam, priusquam
beforehand *adv* ante, anteā; prae (*in cpd*)
befoul *vt* inquināre, foedāre
befriend *vt* favēre (*dat*), adiuvāre; (*in trouble*) adesse (*dat*)
beg *vt* ōrāre, obsecrāre, precārī, poscere ab, petere ab; **beg for** petere ◆ *vi* mendīcāre
beget *vt* gignere, prōcreāre, generāre
begetter *n* generātor *m*, creātor *m*
beggar *n* mendīcus *m*
beggarly *adj* mendīcus, indigēns
beggary *n* mendīcitās *f*, indigentia *f*
begin *vi*, *vt* incipere, coepisse; (*speech*) exōrdīrī; (*plan*) īnstituere, incohāre; (*time*) inīre; **~ with** incipere ab
beginning *n* initium *nt*, prīncipium *nt*, exōrdium *nt*, inceptiō *f*; (*learning*) rudīmenta *ntpl*, elementa *ntpl*; (*origin*) orīgō *f*, fōns *m*; **at the ~ of spring** ineunte vēre
begone *interj* apage, tē āmovē
begotten *adj* genitus, nātus
begrudge *vt* invidēre (*dat*)
beguile *vt* dēcipere, fallere
behalf *n*: **on ~ of** prō (*abl*); **on my ~** meō nōmine
behave *vi* sē gerere, sē praebēre (*with adj*); **well behaved** bene mōrātus
behaviour *n* mōrēs *mpl*
behead *vt* dētruncāre, secūrī percutere
behest *n* iūssum *nt*
behind *adv* pōne, post, ā tergō ◆ *prep* post (*acc*), pōne (*acc*)
behindhand *adv* sērō; **be ~** parum prōficere
behold *vt* aspicere, cōnspicere, intuērī ◆ *interj* ecce, ēn
beholden *adj* obnoxius, obstrictus, obligātus
behoof *n* ūsus *m*
behove *vt* oportēre
being *n* (*life*) animātiō *f*; (*nature*) nātūra *f*; (*person*) homō *m/f*
bejewelled *adj* gemmeus, gemmātus
belabour *vt* verberāre, caedere
belated *adj* sērus
belch *vi* ructāre, ēructāre
beldam *n* anus *f*
beleaguer *vt* obsidēre, circumsedēre
belie *vt* abhorrēre ab, repugnāre
belief *n* fidēs *f*, opīniō *f*; (*opinion*) sententia *f*; **to the best of my ~** ex animī meī sententiā; **past ~** incrēdibilis
believe *vt*, *vi* (*thing*) crēdere; (*person*) crēdere (*dat*); (*suppose*) crēdere, putāre, arbitrārī, opīnārī; **~ in gods** deōs esse crēdere; **make ~** simulāre
believer *n* deōrum cultor *m*; Christiānus *m*
belike *adv* fortasse
belittle *vt* obtrectāre
bell *n* tintinnābulum *nt*; (*public*) campāna *f*
belle *n* fōrmōsa *f*, pulchra *f*
belles-lettres *n* litterae *fpl*
bellicose *adj* ferōx
belligerent *adj* bellī particeps
bellow *vi* rūdere, mūgīre ◆ *n* mūgītus *m*

bellows n follis m

belly n abdōmen nt, venter m; (sail) sinus m ♦ vi tumēre

belong vi esse (gen), proprium esse (gen), inesse (dat); (concern) attinēre, pertinēre

belongings n bona ntpl

beloved adj cārus, dīlectus, grātus

below adv īnfrā, subter ♦ adj īnferus ♦ prep īnfrā (acc), sub (abl, acc)

belt n zōna f; (sword) balteus m

bemoan vt dēplōrāre, lāmentārī

bemused adj stupefactus, stupidus

bench n subsellium nt; (rowing) trānstrum nt; (LAW) iūdicēs mpl; **seat on the ~** iūdicātus m

bend vt flectere, curvāre, inclīnāre; (bow) intendere; (course) tendere, flectere; (mind) intendere ♦ vi sē īnflectere; (person) sē dēmittere; **~ back** reflectere; **~ down** vi dēflectere; sē dēmittere ♦ n flexus m, ānfrāctus m

beneath adv subter ♦ prep sub (acc or abl)

benediction n bonae precēs fpl

benedictory adj faustus

benefaction n beneficium nt, dōnum nt

benefactor n patrōnus m; **be a ~** bene merērī (dē)

beneficence n beneficentia f, līberālitās f

beneficent adj beneficus

beneficial adj ūtilis, salūbris

benefit n beneficium nt; (derived) fructus m; **have the ~ of** fruī (abl) ♦ vt prōdesse (dat), usuī esse (dat)

benevolence n benevolentia f, benignitās f

benevolent adj benevolus, benignus

benevolently adv benevolē, benignē

benighted adj nocte oppressus; (fig) ignārus, indoctus

benign adj benignus, cōmis

bent n (mind) inclīnātiō f, ingenium nt ♦ adj curvus, flexus; (mind) attentus; **be ~ on** studēre (dat)

benumb vt stupefacere

benumbed adj stupefactus, torpidus; **be ~ torpēre**

bequeath vt lēgāre

bequest n lēgātum nt

bereave vt orbāre, prīvāre

bereavement n damnum nt

bereft adj orbus, orbātus, prīvātus

berry n bāca f

berth n statiō f; **give a wide ~ to** dēvītāre

beryl n bēryllus m

beseech vt implōrāre, ōrāre, obsecrāre

beset vt obsidēre, circumsedēre

beside prep ad (acc), apud (acc); (close) iuxtā (acc); **~ the point** nihil ad rem; **be ~ oneself** nōn esse apud sē

besides adv praetereā, accēdit quod; (in addition) īnsuper ♦ prep praeter (acc)

besiege vt obsidēre, circumsedēre

besieger n obsessor m

besmear vt illinere

besmirch vt maculāre

besom n scōpae fpl

besotted adj stupidus

bespatter vt aspergere

bespeak vt (order) imperāre; (denote) significāre

besprinkle vt aspergere

best adj optimus; **the ~ part** māior pars ♦ n flōs m, rōbur nt; **do one's ~** prō virīlī parte agere; **do one's ~ to** operam dare ut; **have the ~ of it** vincere; **make the ~ of** (a situation) aequō animō accipere; **to the ~ of one's ability** prō virīlī parte; **to the ~ of my knowledge** quod sciam ♦ adv optimē

bestial adj foedus

bestir vt movēre; **~ oneself** expergīscī

bestow vt dōnāre, tribuere, dare, cōnferre

bestride vt (horse) sedēre in (abl)

bet n pignus nt ♦ vt oppōnere ♦ vi pignore contendere

betake vt cōnferre, recipere; **~ oneself** sē cōnferre

bethink vt: **~ oneself** sē colligere; **~ oneself of** respicere

betide vi accidere, ēvenīre

betoken vt significāre; (foretell) portendere

betray vt prōdere, trādere; (feelings) arguere; **without betraying one's trust** salvā fidē

betrayal n prōditiō f

betrayer n prōditor m; (informer) index m

betroth vt spondēre, dēspondēre

betrothal n spōnsālia ntpl

better adj melior; **it is ~ to** praestat (inf); **get the ~ of** vincere, superāre; **I am ~** (in health) melius est mihī; **I had ~ go** praestat īre; **get ~ convalēscere**; **think ~ of** sententiam mūtāre dē ♦ adv melius ♦ vt corrigere; **~ oneself** prōficere

betterment n prōfectus m

between prep inter (acc)

beverage n pōtiō f

bevy n manus f, grex f

bewail vt dēflēre, lāmentārī, dēplōrāre

beware vt cavēre

bewilder vt cōnfundere, perturbāre

bewildered adj attonitus

bewilderment n perturbātiō f, admīrātiō f

bewitch vt fascināre; (fig) dēlēnīre

beyond adv ultrā, suprā ♦ prep ultrā (acc), extrā (acc); (motion) trāns (acc); (amount) ultrā, suprā (acc); **go/pass ~** excēdere, ēgredī

bezel n pāla f

bias n inclīnātiō f; (party) favor m ♦ vt inclīnāre

biassed adj prōpēnsior

bibber n pōtor m, pōtātor m

Bible n litterae sacrae fpl

bibulous adj bibulus

bicephalous adj biceps

bicker vi altercārī, iūrgāre

bid vt iubēre; (guest) vocāre, invītāre ♦ vi (at auction) licērī; **bid for** licērī; **bid good day** salvēre iubēre; **he bids fair to make progress** spēs est eum prōfecturum esse

biddable adj docilis

bidding n iussum nt; (auction) licitātiō f

bide vt manēre, opperīrī

biennial adj biennālis

bier n ferculum nt

bifurcate vi sē scindere

bifurcation n (road) trivium nt

big *adj* māgnus, grandis, amplus; (*with child*) gravida; **very big** permāgnus; **talk big** glōriārī
bight *n* sinus *m*
bigness *n* māgnitūdō *f*, amplitūdō *f*
bigot *n* nimis obstinātus fautor *m*
bigoted *adj* contumāx
bigotry *n* contumācia *f*, nimia obstinātiō *f*
bile *n* bīlis *f*, fel *nt*
bilgewater *n* sentīna *f*
bilk *vt* fraudāre
bill *n* (*bird*) rōstrum *nt*; (*implement*) falx *f*; (LAW) rogātiō *f*, lēx *f*; (*money*) syngrapha *f*; (*notice*) libellus *m*, titulus *m*; **introduce a ~** populum rogāre, lēgem ferre; **carry a ~** lēgem perferre
billet *n* hospitium *nt* ♦ *vt* in hospitia dīvidere
billhook *n* falx *f*
billow *n* fluctus *m*
billowy *adj* undōsus
billy goat *n* caper *m*
bin *n* lacus *m*
bind *vt* adligāre, dēligāre, vincīre; (*by oath*) adigere; (*by obligation*) obligāre, obstringere; (*wound*) obligāre; **~ fast** dēvincīre; **~ together** conligāre; **~ over** *vt* vadārī
binding *n* compāgēs *f* ♦ *adj* (LAW) ratus; **it is ~ on** oportet
bindweed *n* convolvulus *m*
biographer *n* vītae nārrātor *m*
biography *n* vīta *f*
bipartite *adj* bipartītus
biped *n* bipēs *m*
birch *n* bētula *f*; (*flogging*) virgae ulmeae *fpl*
bird *n* avis *f*; **birds of a feather** parēs cum paribus facillimē congregantur; **kill two birds with one stone** ūnō saltū duōs aprōs capere, dē eādem fidēliā duōs parietēs dealbāre; **bird's-eye view of** dēspectus in (*acc*)
birdcatcher *n* auceps *m*
birdlime *n* viscum *nt*
birth *n* (*act*) partus *m*; (*origin*) genus *nt*; **low ~** ignōbilitās *f*; **high ~** nōbilitās *f*; **by ~** nātū, ortū
birthday *n* nātālis *m*
birthday party *n* nātālicia *ntpl*
birthplace *n* locus nātālis *m*; (*fig*) incūnābula *ntpl*
birthright *n* patrimōnium *nt*
bisect *vt* dīvidere
bishop *n* epīscopus *m*
bison *n* ūrus *m*
bit *n* pars *f*; (*food*) frustum *nt*; (*broken off*) fragmentum *nt*; (*horse*) frēnum *nt*; **bit by bit** minūtātim; **a bit** *adv* aliquantulum; **a bit sad** tristior
bitch *n* (*dog*) canis *f*
bite *vt* mordēre; (*frost*) ūrere ♦ *n* morsus *m*; **with a ~** mordicus
biting *adj* mordāx
bitter *adj* (*taste*) acerbus, amārus; (*words*) asper
bitterly *adv* acerbē, asperē
bittern *n* būtiō *m*, ardea *f*
bitterness *n* acerbitās *f*
bitumen *n* bitūmen *nt*
bivouac *n* excubiae *fpl* ♦ *vi* excubāre
bizarre *adj* īnsolēns
blab *vt*, *vi* garrīre, effūtīre

black *adj* (*dull*) āter; (*glossy*) niger; (*dirt*) sordidus; (*eye*) līvidus; (*looks*) trux; **~ and blue** līvidus ♦ *n* ātrum *nt*, nigrum *nt*; **dressed in ~** ātrātus; (*in mourning*) sordidātus
blackberry *n* mōrum *nt*
blackbird *n* merula *f*
blacken *vt* nigrāre, nigrum reddere; (*character*) īnfāmāre, obtrectāre (*dat*)
blackguard *n* scelestus, scelerātus *m*
blacking *n* ātrāmentum *nt*
blacklist *n* prōscrīptiō *f*
black magic *n* magicae artēs *fpl*
blackmail *n* minae *fpl* ♦ *vt* minīs cōgere
black mark *n* nota *f*
blacksmith *n* faber *m*
bladder *n* vēsīca *f*
blade *n* (*grass*) herba *f*; (*oar*) palma *f*; (*sword*) lāmina *f*
blame *vt* reprehendere, culpāre; **I am to ~** reus sum ♦ *n* reprehēnsiō *f*, culpa *f*
blameless *adj* innocēns
blamelessly *adv* innocenter
blamelessness *n* innocentia *f*, integritās *f*
blameworthy *adj* accūsābilis, nocēns
blanch *vi* exalbēscere, pallēscere
bland *adj* mītis, lēnis
blandishment *n* blanditiae *fpl*
blank *adj* vacuus, pūrus; (*look*) stolidus
blanket *n* lōdīx *f*; **wet ~** nimium sevērus
blare *vi* canere, strīdere ♦ *n* clangor *m*, strīdor *m*
blarney *n* lēnōcinium *nt*
blaspheme *vi* maledīcere
blasphemous *adj* maledicus, impius
blasphemy *n* maledicta *ntpl*, impietās *f*
blast *n* flātus *m*, īnflātus *m* ♦ *vt* discutere, discutere; (*crops*) rōbīgine adficere
blatant *adj* raucus
blaze *n* flamma *f*, ignis *m*, fulgor *m* ♦ *vi* flāgrāre, ārdēre, fulgēre; **~ up** exārdēscere ♦ *vt*: **~ abroad** pervulgāre
blazon *vt* prōmulgāre
bleach *vt* candidum reddere
bleak *adj* dēsertus, tristis, inamoenus
bleary-eyed *adj* lippus
bleat *vi* bālāre ♦ *n* bālātus *m*
bleed *vi* sanguinem fundere ♦ *vt* sanguinem mittere (*dat*); **my heart bleeds** animus mihī dolet
bleeding *adj* crūdus, sanguineus ♦ *n* sanguinis missiō *f*
blemish *n* macula *f*, vitium *nt* ♦ *vt* maculāre, foedāre
blend *vt* miscēre, immiscēre, admiscēre ♦ *n* coniūnctiō *f*
bless *vt* beāre; laudāre; (ECCL) benedīcere; **~ with** augēre (*abl*); **~ my soul!** ita mē dī ament!
blessed *adj* beātus, fortūnātus; (*emperors*) dīvus
blessing *n* (*thing*) commodum *nt*, bonum *nt*; (ECCL) benedictiō *f*
blight *n* rōbīgō *f*, ūrēdō *f* ♦ *vt* rōbīgine adficere; (*fig*) nocēre (*dat*)
blind *adj* caecus; (*in one eye*) luscus; (*fig*) ignārus, stultus; (*alley*) nōn pervius; (*forces*) necessārius; **turn a ~ eye to** cōnīvēre in (*abl*) ♦ *vt* excaecāre, caecāre; (*fig*) occaecāre; (*with light*) praestringere
blindfold *adj* capite obvolūtō

blindly *adv* temerē
blindness *n* caecitās *f*; *(fig)* temeritās *f*, īnsipientia *f*
blink *vi* nictāre
bliss *n* fēlīcitās *f*, laetitia *f*
blissful *adj* fēlīx, beātus, laetus
blissfully *adv* fēlīciter, beātē
blister *n* pustula *f*
blithe *adj* hilaris, laetus
blithely *adv* hilare, laetē
blizzard *n* hiems *f*
bloated *adj* tumidus, turgidus
blob *n* gutta *f*, particula *f*
block *n* *(wood)* stīpes *m*, caudex *m*; *(stone)* massa *f*; *(houses)* īnsula *f*; ~ **letter** quadrāta littera; **stumbling** ~ offēnsiō *f* ♦ *vt* claudere, obstruere, interclūdere; ~ **the way** obstāre
blockade *n* obsidiō *f*; **raise a** ~ obsidiōnem solvere ♦ *vt* obsidēre, interclūdere
blockhead *n* caudex *m*, bārō *m*, truncus *m*
blockhouse *n* castellum *nt*
blond *adj* flāvus
blood *n* sanguis *m*; *(shed)* cruor *m*; *(murder)* caedēs *f*; *(kin)* genus *nt*; **let** ~ sanguinem mittere; **staunch** ~ sanguinem supprimere; **bad** ~ simultās *f*; **in cold** ~ cōnsultō; **own flesh and** ~ cōnsanguineus
bloodless *adj* exsanguis; *(victory)* incruentus
bloodshed *n* caedēs *f*
bloodshot *adj* sanguineus
bloodstained *adj* cruentus
bloodsucker *n* hirūdō *f*
bloodthirsty *adj* sanguinārius
blood vessel *n* vēna *f*
bloody *adj* cruentus
bloom *n* flōs *m*; **in** ~ flōrēns ♦ *vi* flōrēre, flōrēscere, vigēre
blooming *adj* flōrēns, flōridus
blossom *n* flōs *m* ♦ *vi* efflōrēscere, flōrēre
blot *n* macula *f*; *(erasure)* litūra *f* ♦ *vt* maculāre; ~ **out** dēlēre, oblitterāre
blotch *n* macula *f*
blotched *adj* maculōsus
blow *vt, vi* *(wind)* flāre; *(breath)* adflāre, anhēlāre; *(instrument)* canere; *(flower)* efflōrēscere; *(nose)* ēmungere; ~ **out** *vi* exstinguere; ~ **over** *vi* *(storm)* cadere, *(fig)* abīre; ~ **up** *vt* īnflāre; *(destroy)* discutere, disturbāre ♦ *n* ictus *m*; *(on the cheek)* alapa *f*; *(fig)* plāga *f*; *(misfortune)* calamitās *f*; **aim a** ~ **at** petere; **come to blows** ad manūs venīre
blowy *adj* ventōsus
bludgeon *n* fustis *m*
blue *adj* caeruleus; **black and** ~ līvidus; **true** ~ fīdissimus; ~ **blood** nōbilitās *f*
bluff *n* rūpēs *f*, prōmontōrium *nt* ♦ *adj* inurbānus ♦ *vt* fallere, dēcipere, verba dare *(dat)*, impōnere *(dat)*
blunder *vi* errāre, offendere ♦ *n* error *m*, errātum *nt*; *(in writing)* mendum *nt*
blunt *adj* hebes; *(manners)* horridus, rūsticus, inurbānus; **be** ~ hebēre ♦ *vt* hebetāre, obtundere, retundere
bluntly *adv* līberius, plānē et apertē
blur *n* macula *f* ♦ *vt* obscūrāre
blurt *vt*: ~ **out** ēmittere
blush *vi* rubēre, ērubēscere ♦ *n* rubor *m*

bluster *vi* dēclāmitāre, lātrāre
boa *n* boa *f*
Boadicea *n* Boudicca *f*
boar *n* verrēs *m*; *(wild)* aper *m*
board *n* tabula *f*; *(table)* mēnsa *f*; *(food)* vīctus *m*; *(committee)* concilium *nt*; *(judicial)* quaestiō *f*; *(of ten men)* decemvirī *mpl*; *(gaming)* abacus *m*, alveus *m*; **on** ~ in nāvī; **go on** ~ in nāvem cōnscendere; **go by the** ~ intercidere, perīre; **above** ~ sine fraude ♦ *vt* *(building)* contabulāre; *(ship)* cōnscendere; *(person)* vīctum praebēre *(dat)* ♦ *vi*: ~ **with** dēvertere ad
boarder *n* hospes *m*
boast *vi* glōriārī, sē iactāre; ~ **of** glōriārī dē *(abl)* ♦ *n* glōria *f*, glōriātiō *f*, iactātiō *f*
boastful *adj* glōriōsus
boastfully *adv* glōriōsē
boasting *n* glōriātiō *f* ♦ *adj* glōriōsus
boat *n* linter *f*, scapha *f*, cymba *f*; *(ship)* nāvis *f*; **be in the same** ~ *(fig)* in eādem nāvī esse
boatman *n* nauta *m*
boatswain *n* hortātor *m*
bobbin *n* fūsus *m*
bode *vt* portendere, praesāgīre
bodiless *adj* sine corpore
bodily *adj* corporeus
bodkin *n* acus *f*
body *n* corpus *nt*; *(dead)* cadāver *nt*; *(small)* corpusculum *nt*; *(person)* homō *m/f*; *(of people)* globus *m*, numerus *m*; *(of troops)* manus *f*, caterva *f*; *(of cavalry)* turma *f*; *(of officials)* collēgium *nt*; *(heavenly)* astrum *nt*; **in a** ~ ūniversī, frequentēs
bodyguard *n* custōs *m*, stīpātōrēs *mpl*; *(emperor's)* praetōriānī *mpl*
bog *n* palūs *f*
bogey *n* mōnstrum *nt*
boggle *vi* tergiversārī, haesitāre
boggy *adj* palūster
bogus *adj* falsus, fictus
Bohemian *adj* līberior, solūtior, libīdinōsus
boil *vt* coquere; *(liquid)* fervefacere; ~ **down** dēcoquere ♦ *vi* fervēre, effervēscere; *(sea)* exaestuāre; *(passion)* exārdēscere, aestuāre; ~ **over** effervēscere ♦ *n* *(MED)* fūrunculus *m*
boiler *n* cortīna *f*
boiling *adj* *(hot)* fervēns
boisterous *adj* *(person)* turbulentus, vehemēns; *(sea)* turbidus, agitātus; *(weather)* procellōsus, violentus
boisterously *adv* turbidē, turbulentē
boisterousness *n* tumultus *m*, violentia *f*
bold *adj* audāx, fortis, intrepidus; *(impudent)* impudēns, protervus; *(language)* līber; *(headland)* prōminēns; **make** ~ audēre
boldly *adv* audācter, fortiter, intrepidē; impudenter
boldness *n* audācia *f*, cōnfidentia *f*; impudentia *f*, petulantia *f*; *(speech)* lībertās *f*
bolster *n* pulvīnus *m* ♦ *vt*: ~ **up** sustinēre, cōnfirmāre
bolt *n* *(door)* claustrum *nt*, pessulus *m*, sera *f*; *(missile)* tēlum *nt*, sagitta *f*; *(lightning)* fulmen *nt*; **make a** ~ **for it** sē prōripere, aufugere; **a** ~ **from the blue** rēs subita, rēs inopīnāta ♦ *vt* *(door)* obserāre, obdere

bombard *vt* tormentīs verberāre; (*fig*) lacessere
bombast *n* ampullae *fpl*
bombastic *adj* tumidus, īnflātus; **be ~** ampullārī
bond *n* vinculum *nt*, catēna *f*, compes *f*; (*of union*) cōpula *f*, iugum *nt*, nōdus *m*; (*document*) syngrapha *f*; (*agreement*) foedus *nt* ♦ *adj* servus, addictus
bondage *n* servitūs *f*, famulātus *m*
bone *n* os *nt*; (*fish*) spīna *f* ♦ *vt* exossāre
boneless *adj* exos
bonfire *n* ignis festus *m*
bonhomie *n* festīvitās *f*
bon mot *n* dictum *nt*, sententia *f*
bonny *adj* pulcher, bellus
bony *adj* osseus
boo *vt* explōdere
book *n* liber *m*; (*small*) libellus *m*; (*scroll*) volūmen *nt*; (*modern form*) cōdex *m*; **books** (COMM) rationēs *fpl*, tabulae *fpl*; **bring to ~** in iūdicium vocāre
bookbinder *n* glūtinātor *m*
bookcase *n* librārium *nt*, pēgma *nt*
bookish *adj* litterārum studiōsus
book-keeper *n* āctuārius *m*
bookseller *n* librārius *m*, bibliopōla *m*
bookshop *n* bibliothēca *f*, librāria taberna *f*
bookworm *n* tinea *f*
boom *n* (*spar*) longurius *m*; (*harbour*) ōbex *m/f* ♦ *vi* resonāre
boon *n* bonum *nt*, beneficium *nt*, dōnum *nt* ♦ *adj* festīvus; **~ companion** sodālis *m*, compōtor *m*
boor *n* agrestis *m*, rūsticus *m*
boorish *adj* agrestis, rūsticus, inurbānus
boorishly *adv* rūsticē
boost *vt* efferre; (*wares*) vēnditāre
boot *n* calceus *m*; (MIL) caliga *f*; (*rustic*) pērō *m*; (*tragic*) cothurnus *m* ♦ *vi* prōdesse; **to ~** īnsuper, praetereā
booted *adj* calceātus, caligātus
booth *n* taberna *f*
bootless *adj* inūtilis, vānus
bootlessly *adv* frustrā
booty *n* praeda *f*, spolia *ntpl*
border *n* ōra *f*, margō *f*; (*country*) fīnis *m*; (*dress*) limbus *m* ♦ *vt* praetexere, margināre; fīnīre ♦ *vi*: **~ on** adiacēre (*dat*), imminēre (*dat*), attingere; (*fig*) fīnitimum esse (*dat*)
bordering *adj* fīnitimus
bore *vt* perforāre, perterebrāre; (*person*) obtundere, fatīgāre; **~ out** exterebrāre ♦ *n* terebra *f*; (*hole*) forāmen *nt*; (*person*) homō importūnus *m*, ineptus *m*
boredom *n* lassitūdō *f*
borer *n* terebra *f*
born *adj* nātus; **be ~** nāscī
borough *n* mūnicipium *nt*
borrow *vt* mūtuārī
borrowed *adj* mūtuus; (*fig*) aliēnus
borrowing *n* mūtuātiō *f*; (*to pay a debt*) versūra *f*
bosky *adj* nemorōsus
bosom *n* sinus *m*; (*fig*) gremium *nt*; **~ friend** familiāris *m/f*, sodālis *m*; **be a ~ friend of** ab latere esse (*gen*)
boss *n* bulla *f*; (*shield*) umbō *m*
botanist *n* herbārius *m*
botany *n* herbāria *f*

botch *vt* male sarcīre, male gerere
both *pron* ambō, uterque (*gen* **utriusque** *each of two*) ♦ *adv*: **~ ... and** et ... et, cum ... tum
bother *n* negōtium *nt* ♦ *vt* vexāre, molestus esse (*dat*) ♦ *vi* operam dare
bothersome *adj* molestus
bottle *n* lagoena *f*, amphora *f* ♦ *vt* (*wine*) diffundere
bottom *n* fundus *m*; (*ground*) solum *nt*; (*ship*) carīna *f*; **the ~ of** īmus; **be at the ~ of** (*cause*) auctōrem esse; **go to the ~** pessum īre, perīre; **send to the ~** pessum dare; **from the ~** funditus, ab īnfimō
bottomless *adj* profundus, fundō carēns
bottommost *adj* īnfimus
bough *n* rāmus *m*
boulder *n* saxum *nt*
boulevard *n* platea *f*
bounce *vi* salīre, resultāre
bound *n* fīnis *m*, modus *m*, terminus *m*; (*leap*) saltus *m*; **set bounds to** modum facere (*dat*) ♦ *vt* fīnīre, dēfīnīre, termināre ♦ *vi* salīre, saltāre ♦ *adj* adligātus, obligātus, obstrictus; **be ~ to** (*duty*) dēbēre; **it is ~ to happen** necesse est ēveniat; **be ~ for** tendere in (*acc*); **be stormbound** tempestāte tenērī
boundaries *npl* fīnes *mpl*
boundary *n* fīnis *m*; (*of fields*) terminus *m*; (*fortified*) līmes *m*; **~ stone** terminus *m*
boundless *adj* immēnsus, īnfīnītus
boundlessness *n* īnfīnitās *f*, immēnsum *nt*
bounteous *adj see* **bountiful**
bounteously *adv* largē, līberāliter, cōpiōsē
bountiful *adj* largus, līberālis, benignus
bounty *n* largitās *f*, līberālitās *f*; (*store*) cōpia *f*
bouquet *n* corollārium *nt*; (*of wine*) flōs *m*
bourn *n* fīnis *m*
bout *n* certāmen *nt*; (*drinking*) cōmissātiō *f*
bovine *adj* būbulus; (*fig*) stolidus
bow *n* arcus *m*; (*ship*) prōra *f*; (*courtesy*) salūtātiō *f*; **have two strings to one's bow** duplicī spē ūtī; **rainbow** arcus *m* ♦ *vt* flectere, inclīnāre ♦ *vi* caput dēmittere
bowels *n* alvus *f*; (*fig*) viscera *ntpl*
bower *n* umbrāculum *nt*, trichila *f*
bowl *n* (*cooking*) catīnus *m*; (*drinking*) calix *m*; (*mixing wine*) crātēra *f*; (*ball*) pila *f* ♦ *vt* volvere; **~ over** prōruere
bow-legged *adj* valgus
bowler *n* (*game*) dator *m*
bowstring *n* nervus *m*
box *n* arca *f*, capsa *f*; (*for clothes*) cista *f*; (*for medicine*) pyxis *f*; (*for perfume*) alabaster *m*; (*tree*) buxus *f*; (*wood*) buxum *nt*; (*blow on ears*) alapa *f* ♦ *vt* inclūdere; **box the ears of** alapam dūcere (*dat*), colaphōs īnfringere (*dat*) ♦ *vi* (*fight*) pugnīs certāre
boxer *n* pugil *m*
boxing *n* pugilātiō *f*
boxing glove *n* caestus *m*
boy *n* puer *m*; **become a boy again** repuerāscere
boycott *vt* repudiāre
boyhood *n* pueritia *f*; **from ~** ā puerō
boyish *adj* puerīlis
boyishly *adv* puerīliter

brace n (building) fībula f; (strap) fascia f; (pair) pār nt ♦ vt adligāre; (strengthen) firmāre

bracelet n armilla f

bracing adj (air) salūbris

bracken n filix f

bracket n uncus m

brackish adj amārus

bradawl n terebra f

brag vi glōriārī, sē iactāre

braggart n glōriōsus m

braid vt nectere

brain n cerebrum nt; ingenium nt

brainless adj sōcors, stultus

brainy adj ingeniōsus

brake n (wood) dūmētum nt; (on wheel) sufflāmen nt

bramble n rubus m

bran n furfur nt

branch n rāmus m; (kind) genus nt ♦ vi: ~ out rāmōs porrigere

branching adj rāmōsus

brand n (fire) torris m, fax f; (mark) nota f; (sword) ēnsis m; (variety) genus nt ♦ vt (mark) inūrere; (stigma) notāre; ~ new recēns

brandish vt vibrare

brass n orichalcum nt

bravado n ferōcitās f; out of ~ per speciem ferōcitātis

brave adj fortis, ācer ♦ vt adīre, patī

bravely adv fortiter, ācriter

bravery n fortitūdō f, virtūs f

bravo interj bene, euge, macte

brawl n rixa f, iūrgium nt ♦ vi rixārī

brawn n lacertī mpl

brawny adj lacertōsus, rōbūstus

bray vi rūdere

brazen adj aēneus; (fig) impudēns

brazier n foculus m

breach n (in wall) ruīna f; (of friendship) dissēnsiō f ♦ vt perfringere; ~ of trust mala fidēs; commit a ~ of promise prōmissīs nōn stāre

breach of the peace n iūrgium nt, tumultus m

bread n pānis m

breadth n lātitūdō f; in ~ in lātitūdinem (acc)

break vt frangere, perfringere; ~ down vt īnfringere, dīruere; ~ in vt (animal) domāre; ~ into pieces dīrumpere; ~ off vt abrumpere, dēfringere; (action) dīrimere; ~ open effringere, solvere; ~ through vt interrumpere; ~ up vt dissolvere, interrumpere; ~ one's word fidem fallere, violāre; without breaking the law salvīs lēgibus ♦ vi rumpī, frangī; (day) illūcēscere; (strength) dēficere; ~ off vi dēsinere; ~ into intrāre; ~ out vi ērumpere; (sore) recrūdēscere; (trouble) exārdēscere; ~ up vi dīlābī, dissolvī; (meeting) dīmittī; ~ through vi inrumpere; ~ with dissidēre ab ♦ n intermissiō f, intervallum nt

breakable adj fragilis

breakage n frāctum nt

breakdown n (activity) mora f; (health) dēbilitās f

breaker n fluctus m

breakfast n ientāculum nt, prandium nt ♦ vi ientāre, prandēre

breakwater n mōlēs f

bream n sparulus m

breast n pectus nt; (woman's) mamma f; make a clean ~ of cōnfitērī

breastplate n lōrīca f

breastwork n lōrīca f, pluteus m

breath n spīritus m, anima f; (bad) hālitus m; (quick) anhēlitus m; (of wind) aura f, adflātus m; below one's ~ mussitāns; catch one's ~ obstipēscere; hold one's ~ animam comprimere, continēre; take a ~ spīritum dūcere; take one's ~ away exanimāre; waste one's ~ operam perdere; out of ~ exanimātus

breathable adj spīrābilis

breathe vt, vi spīrāre, respīrāre; (quickly) anhēlāre; ~ again respīrāre; ~ in vi spīritum dūcere; ~ out vt, vi exspīrāre, exhālāre; ~ upon īnspīrāre (dat), adflāre (dat); ~ one's last animam agere, efflāre

breathing n hālitus m, respīrātiō f

breathing space n respīrātiō f

breathless adj exanimātus

breeches n brācae fpl

breed n genus nt ♦ vt generāre, prōcreāre; (raise) ēducāre, alere; (fig) adferre, efficere; well-bred generōsus

breeder n (animal) mātrix f; (man) generātor m; (fig) nūtrix f

breeding n (act) fētūra f; (manners) mōrēs mpl; good ~ hūmānitās f

breeze n aura f, flātus m

breezy adj ventōsus; (manner) hilaris

brevity n brevitās f

brew vt coquere ♦ vi (fig) parārī, imminēre

bribe vt corrumpere ♦ vi largīrī ♦ n pecūnia f, mercēs f

briber n corruptor m, largītor m

bribery n ambitus m, largītiō f

brick n later m ♦ adj latericius

brickwork n latericium nt

bridal adj nūptiālis; (bed) geniālis ♦ n nūptiae fpl

bride n nūpta f

bridegroom n marītus m

bridge n pōns m ♦ vt pontem impōnere (dat)

bridle n frēnum nt ♦ vt frēnāre, īnfrēnāre

brief adj brevis; to be ~ nē longum sit, nē multa

briefly adv breviter, paucīs verbīs

briefness n brevitās f

brier n veprēs m, sentis m

brig n liburna f

brigade n legiō f; (cavalry) turma f

brigadier n lēgātus m

brigand n latrō m, praedō m

brigandage n latrōcinium nt

bright adj clārus, lūculentus; (sky) serēnus; (intellect) ingeniōsus; (manner) hilaris, laetus; be ~ lūcēre, splendēre

brighten vt illūstrāre; laetificāre ♦ vi lūcēscere; (person) hilarem fierī

brightly adv clārē

brightness n fulgor m, candor m; (sky) serēnitās f

brilliance n splendor m, fulgor m; (style) nitor m, lūmen nt, īnsignia ntpl

brilliant adj clārus, illūstris, splendidus; (fig) īnsignis, praeclārus, lūculentus

brilliantly adv splendidē, praeclārē, lūculentē

brim n lābrum nt, margō f; fill to the ~ explēre

brimstone n sulfur nt

brindled *adj* varius
brine *n* salsāmentum *nt*
bring *vt* ferre; *(person)* dūcere; *(charge)* intendere;
    (to a place) adferre, addūcere, advehere, dēferre;
    (to a destination) perdūcere; *(to a worse state)*
    redigere; ~ **about** *vt* efficere; ~ **before** dēferre
    ad, referre ad; ~ **back** *vt (thing)* referre; *(person)*
    redūcere; ~ **down** *vt* dēdūcere, dēferre; ~ **forth**
    (from store) dēprōmere; *(child)* parere; *(crops)*
    ferre, ēdere; ~ **forward** *vt (for discussion)* iactāre,
    iacere; *(reason)* adferre; ~ **home** *(bride)* dēdūcere;
    (in triumph) dēportāre; ~ **home to** pervincere;
    ~ **in** *vt* invehere, indūcere, intrōdūcere;
    (import) importāre; *(revenue)* reddere; ~ **off** *vt*
    (success) reportāre; ~ **on** īnferre, importāre;
    (stage) indūcere; ~ **out** *vt* efferre; *(book)* ēdere;
    (play) dare; *(talent)* ēlicere; ~ **over** perdūcere,
    trādūcere; ~ **to bear** adferre; ~ **to light** nūdāre,
    dētegere; ~ **to pass** perficere, peragere;
    ~ **to shore** ad litus appellere; ~ **together**
    contrahere, cōgere; *(enemies)* conciliāre; ~ **up** *vt*
    (child) ēducāre, tollere; *(troops)* admovēre; *(topic)*
    prōferre; ~ **upon oneself** sibī cōnscīscere, sibī
    contrahere
brink *n* ōra *f*, margō *f*
briny *adj* salsus
brisk *adj* alacer, vegetus, ācer
briskly *adv* ācriter
briskness *n* alacritās *f*
bristle *n* sēta *f* ♦ *vi* horrēre, horrēscere
bristly *adj* horridus, hirsūtus
Britain *n* Britannia *f*
Britons *n* Britannī *mpl*
brittle *adj* fragilis
broach *vt (topic)* in medium prōferre
broad *adj* lātus; *(accent)* lātus; *(joke)* inurbānus;
    (daylight) multus
broadcast *vt* dissēmināre
broaden *vt* dīlātāre
broadly *adv* lātē
broadsword *n* gladius *m*
brocade *n* Attalica *ntpl*
brochure *n* libellus *m*
brogue *n* pērō *m*
broil *n* rixa *f*, iūrgium *nt* ♦ *vt* torrēre
broiling *adj* torridus
broken *adj* frāctus; *(fig)* cōnfectus; *(speech)*
    īnfrāctus
broken-hearted *adj* dolōre cōnfectus
broker *n* īnstitor *m*
bronze *n* aes *nt* ♦ *adj* aēneus, aerātus
brooch *n* fībula *f*
brood *n* fētus *m*; *(fig)* gēns *f* ♦ *vi* incubāre *(dat)*;
    (fig) incubāre *(dat)*, fovēre; ~ **over** meditārī
brook *n* rīvus *m* ♦ *vt* ferre, patī
brooklet *n* rīvulus *m*
broom *n (plant)* genista *f*; *(brush)* scōpae *fpl*
broth *n* iūs *nt*
brother *n* frāter *m*; *(full)* germānus *m*
brotherhood *n* frāternitās *f*
brother-in-law *n* lēvir *m*, uxōris frāter *m*, sorōris
    marītus *m*
brotherly *adj* frāternus
brow *n* frōns *f*; *(eye)* supercilium *nt*; *(hill)* dorsum
    nt
browbeat *vt* obiūrgāre, exagitāre

brown *adj* fulvus, spādīx; *(skin)* adūstus
browse *vi* pāscī, dēpāscī
bruise *vt* atterere, frangere, contundere ♦ *n*
    vulnus *nt*
bruit *vt* pervulgāre
brunt *n* vīs *f*; **bear the ~ of** exhaurīre
brush *n* pēniculus *m*; *(artist's)* pēnicillus *m*;
    (quarrel) rixa *f* ♦ *vt* verrere, dētergēre; *(teeth)*
    dēfricāre; ~ **aside** *vt* aspernārī, neglegere; ~ **up**
    vt (fig) excolere
brushwood *n* virgulta *ntpl*; *(for cutting)* sarmenta
    ntpl
brusque *adj* parum cōmis
brutal *adj* atrōx, saevus, inhūmānus
brutality *n* atrōcitās *f*, saevitia *f*
brutally *adv* atrōciter, inhūmānē
brute *n* bēlua *f*, bestia *f*
brutish *adj* stolidus
bubble *n* bulla *f* ♦ *vi* bullāre; ~ **over** effervēscere;
    ~ **up** scatēre
buccaneer *n* praedō *m*, pīrāta *m*
buck *n* cervus *m* ♦ *vi* exsultāre
bucket *n* situla *f*, fidēlia *f*
buckle *n* fībula *f* ♦ *vt* fībulā nectere; ~ **to** accingī
buckler *n* parma *f*
buckram *n* carbasus *m*
bucolic *adj* agrestis
bucolics *n* būcolica *ntpl*
bud *n* gemma *f*, flōsculus *m* ♦ *vi* gemmāre
budge *vi* movērī, cēdere
budget *n* pūblicae pecūniae ratiō *f* ♦ *vi*: ~ **for**
    prōvidēre *(dat)*
buff *adj* lūteus
buffalo *n* ūrus *m*
buffet *n (blow)* alapa *f*; *(fig)* plāga *f*; *(sideboard)*
    abacus *m* ♦ *vt* iactāre, tundere
buffoon *n* scurra *m*, balatrō *m*
buffoonery *n* scurrilitās *f*
bug *n* cīmex *m*
bugbear *n* terricula *ntpl*, terror *m*
bugle *n* būcina *f*
bugler *n* būcinātor *m*
build *vt* aedificāre, struere; *(bridge)* facere; *(road)*
    mūnīre; ~ **on** *vt (add)* adstruere; *(hopes)* pōnere;
    ~ **on sand** in aquā fundāmenta pōnere; ~ **up**
    vt exstruere; *(to block)* inaedificāre; *(knowledge)*
    īnstruere; ~ **castles in the air** spem inānem
    pāscere ♦ *n* statūra *f*
builder *n* aedificātor *m*, structor *m*
building *n (act)* aedificātiō *f*; *(structure)*
    aedificium *nt*
bulb *n* bulbus *m*
bulge *vi* tumēre, tumēscere, prōminēre ♦ *n*
    tuberculum *nt*; *(of land)* locus prōminēns *m*
bulk *n* māgnitūdō *f*, amplitūdō *f*; *(mass)* mōlēs *f*;
    (most) plērīque, māior pars
bulky *adj* amplus, grandis
bull *n* taurus *m*; **bull's** taurīnus; **take the ~ by**
    the horns rem fortiter adgredī
bulldog *n* Molossus *m*
bullet *n* glāns *f*
bulletin *n* libellus *m*
bullion *n* aurum īnfectum *nt*, argentum
    īnfectum *nt*
bullock *n* iuvencus *m*

bully n obiūrgātor m, patruus m ♦ vt obiūrgāre, exagitāre

bulrush n scirpus m

bulwark n prōpugnāculum nt; (fig) arx f

bump n (swelling) tuber nt, tuberculum nt; (knock) ictus m ♦ vi: ~ **against** offendere

bumper n plēnum pōculum nt ♦ adj plēnus, māximus

bumpkin n rūsticus m

bumptious adj adrogāns

bunch n fasciculus m; (of berries) racēmus m

bundle n fascis m; (of hay) manipulus m ♦ vt obligāre

bung n obtūrāmentum nt ♦ vt obtūrāre

bungle vt male gerere

bunk n lectus m, lectulus m

buoy n cortex m ♦ vt sublevāre

buoyancy n levitās f

buoyant adj levis; (fig) hilaris

bur n lappa f

burden n onus nt; **beast of** ~ iūmentum nt ♦ vt onerāre; **be a** ~ oneri esse

burdensome adj gravis, molestus

bureau n scrīnium nt

burgeon vi gemmāre

burgess n mūniceps m

burgh n mūnicipium nt

burgher n mūniceps m

burglar n fūr m

burglary n fūrtum nt

burial n fūnes nt, humātiō f, sepultūra f

burin n caelum nt

burlesque n imitātiō f ♦ vt per iocum imitārī

burly adj crassus

burn vt incendere, ūrere; (to ashes) cremāre ♦ vi ārdēre, flāgrāre; ~ **up** ambūrere, combūrere, exūrere; **be burned down** dēflāgrāre; ~ **out** vi exstinguī; ~ **the midnight oil** lūcubrāre ♦ n (MED) ambūstum nt

burning adj igneus

burnish vt polīre

burrow n cuniculus m ♦ vi dēfodere

burst vt rumpere, dīrumpere ♦ vi rumpī, dīrumpī; ~ **in** inrumpere; ~ **into tears** in lacrimās effundī; ~ **open** refringere; ~ **out** ērumpere, prōrumpere; ~ **out laughing** cachinnum tollere; ~ **through** perrumpere per (acc); ~ **upon** offerrī (dat), invādere ♦ n ēruptiō f; (noise) fragor m; ~ **of applause** clāmōrēs mpl; **with a** ~ **of speed** citātō gradū, citātō equō

bury vt sepelīre, humāre; (ceremony) efferre; (hiding) condere; (things) dēfodere; (fig) obruere; ~ **the hatchet** amīcitiam reconciliāre

bush n frutex m; dūmus m; **beat about the** ~ circuitiōne ūtī

bushel n medimnus m

bushy adj fruticōsus; (thick) dēnsus; (hair) hirsūtus

busily adv strēnuē, impigrē

business n negōtium nt; (occupation) ars f, quaestus m; (public life) forum nt; (matter) rēs f; **it is your** ~ tuum est; **make it one's** ~ ut; **you have no** ~ **to** nōn tē decet (inf); **mind one's own** ~ suum negōtium agere; ~ **days** diēs fāstī mpl

businessman negōtiātor m

buskin n cothurnus m

bust n imāgō f

bustle vi trepidāre, festīnāre; ~ **about** discurrere

busy adj negōtiōsus, occupātus; (active) operōsus, impiger, strēnuus; ~ **in** occupātus (abl); ~ **on** intentus (dat); **keep** ~ vt exercēre; ~ **oneself with** pertractāre, studēre (dat)

busybody n: **be a** ~ aliēnīs negōtīs sē immiscēre

but conj sed, at; (2nd place) autem, tamen ♦ adv modo ♦ prep praeter (acc); **nothing but** nihil nisī; **but that, but what** quīn; **not but what** nihilōminus

butcher n lanius m ♦ vt trucīdāre

butcher's shop n laniēna f

butchery n strāgēs f, occīdiō f

butler n prōmus m

butt n (cask) cadus m; (of ridicule) lūdibrium nt ♦ vi arietāre; ~ **in** interpellāre

butter n būtyrum nt

butterfly n pāpiliō m

buttock n clūnis m/f

button n bulla f

buttonhole vt (fig) dētinēre, prēnsāre

buttress n antērides fpl ♦ vt fulcīre

buxom adj nitidus

buy vt emere; **buy provisions** obsonāre; **buy back** vt redimere; **buy off** vt redimere; **buy up** vt coemere

buyer n emptor m; (at auctions) manceps m

buzz n strīdor m, susurrus m ♦ vi strīdere, susurrāre

buzzard n būteō m

by prep (near) ad (acc), apud (acc); prope (acc); (along) secundum (acc); (past) praeter (acc); (agent) a, ab (abl); (instrument) abl; (time) ante (acc); (oath) per (acc) ♦ adv prope, iuxtā; **by and by** mox; **be by** adesse, adstāre; **by force of arms** vī et armīs; **by land and sea** terrā marique

bygone adj praeteritus

bystander n arbiter m ♦ pl circumstantēs mpl

byway n dēverticulum nt, trāmes m, sēmita f

byword n prōverbium nt

Cc

cabal n factiō f
cabbage n brassica f, caulis m
cabin n casa f; (ship) cubiculum nt
cabinet n armārium nt
cable n fūnis m; (anchor) ancorāle nt
cache n thēsaurus m
cachet n nota f
cackle vi strepere n, strepitus m, clangor m
cacophonous adj dissonus
cacophony n vōcēs dissonae fpl
cadaverous adj cadāverōsus
cadence n clausula numerōsa f, numerus m
cadet n (son) nātū minor; (MIL) contubernālis m
cage n cavea f ♦ vt inclūdere
caitiff n ignāvus m
cajole vt blandīrī, dēlēnīre
cake n placenta f
calamitous adj exitiōsus, calamitōsus
calamity n calamitās f, malum nt; (MIL) clādēs f
calculate vt ratiōnem dūcere, inīre
calculation n ratiō f
calculator n ratiōcinātor m
calendar n fāstī mpl
calends n Kalendae fpl
calf n (animal) vitulus m, vitula f; (leg) sūra f
calibre n (fig) ingenium nt, auctōritās f
call vt vocāre; (name) appellāre, nōmināre;
  (aloud) clāmāre; (to a place) advocāre, convocāre;
  ~ **aside** sēvocāre; ~ **down** (curse) dētestārī; ~ **for**
  vt postulāre, requīrere; ~ **forth** ēvocāre, excīre,
  ēlicere; ~ **in** vt advocāre; ~ **together** convocāre;
  ~ **on** vt (for help) implōrāre; (visit) salūtāre; ~ **off**
  vt āvocāre, revocāre; ~ **out** vi exclāmāre; ~ **up**
  (dead) excitāre, ēlicere; (MIL) ēvocāre ♦ n vōx f,
  clāmor m; (summons) invītātiō f; (visit) salūtātiō f
caller n salūtātor m
calling n ars f, quaestus m
callous adj dūrus; **become ~** obdūrēscere
callow adj rudis
calm adj tranquillus, placidus; (mind) aequus
  ♦ vi: ~ **down** (fig) dēfervēscere ♦ vt sēdāre,
  tranquillāre ♦ n tranquillitās f; **dead ~** (at sea)
  malacia f
calmly adv tranquillē, placidē; aequō animō
calumniate vt obtrectāre, crīminārī; (falsely)
  calumniārī
calumniator n obtrectātor m
calumny n opprobria ntpl, obtrectātiō f
calve vi parere

cambric n linteum nt
camel n camēlus m
camouflage n dissimulātiō f ♦ vt dissimulāre
camp n castra ntpl; **summer ~** aestīva ntpl;
  winter ~ hīberna ntpl; **in ~** sub pellibus; **pitch**
  ~ castra pōnere; **strike ~** castra movēre ♦ adj
  castrēnsis ♦ vi tendere
campaign n stīpendium nt, bellum nt; (rapid)
  expedītiō f ♦ vi bellum gerere, stīpendium
  merēre
campaigner n mīles m; **old ~** veterānus m; (fig)
  veterātor m
campbed n grabātus m
camp followers n lixae mpl
can¹ n hirnea f
can² vi posse (inf); (know how) scīre
canaille n vulgus nt, plebs f
canal n fossa nāvigābilis f, eurīpus m
cancel vt indūcere, abrogāre
cancellation n (writing) litūra f; (LAW) abrogātiō f
cancer n cancer m; (fig) carcinōma nt, ulcus nt
cancerous adj (fig) ulcerōsus
candelabrum n candēlābrum nt
candid adj ingenuus, apertus, līber, simplex
candidate n petītor m; **be a ~ for** petere
candidature n petītiō f
candidly adv ingenuē
candle n candēla f
candlestick n candēlābrum nt
candour n ingenuitās f, simplicitās f, lībertās f
cane n (reed) harundō f; (for walking, punishing)
  virga f ♦ vt verberāre
canine adj canīnus
canister n capsula f
canker n (plants) rōbīgō f; (fig) aerūgō f,
  carcinōma nt ♦ vt corrumpere
Cannae n Cannae fpl
cannibal n anthrōpophagus m
cannon n tormentum nt
cannot nōn posse, nequīre; **I ~ help but …**
  facere nōn possum quīn … (subj), nōn possum
  nōn … (inf)
canny adj prūdens, prōvidus, cautus,
  circumspectus
canoe n linter f
canon n nōrma f, rēgula f; (ECCL) canonicus m
canopy n aulaeum nt
cant n fūcus m, fūcāta verba ntpl ♦ vi oblīquāre
cantankerous adj importūnus

cantankerousness n importūnitās f
canter n lēnis cursus m ♦ vi lēniter currere
canticle n canticum nt
canto n carmen nt
canton n pāgus m
canvas n carbasus m, linteum nt ♦ adj carbaseus; under ~ sub pellibus
canvass vi ambīre ♦ vt prēnsāre, circumīre
canvassing n ambitus m, ambitiō f
cap n pilleus m; (priest's) galērus m, apex m
capability n facultās f, potestās f
capable adj capāx, doctus, perītus
capably adv bene, doctē
capacious adj capāx, amplus
capacity n capācitās f, amplitūdō f; (mind) ingenium nt
caparison n ephippium nt
cape n (GEOG) prōmontōrium nt; (dress) chlamys f
caper vi saltāre; (animal) lascīvīre ♦ n saltus m
capering n lascivia f
capital adj (chief) praecipuus, prīnceps; (excellent) ēgregius; (LAW) capitālis; **convict of a ~ offence** capitis damnāre ♦ n (town) caput nt; (money) sors f; (class) negōtiātōrēs mpl; **make ~ out of** ūtī (abl)
capitalist n faenerātor m
capital punishment n capitis supplicum nt
capitation tax n capitum exāctiō f
Capitol n Capitolium nt
capitulate vi sē dēdere; **troops who have capitulated** dēditīciī mpl
capitulation n dēditiō f
capon n capō m
caprice n libīdō f, incōnstantia f
capricious adj incōnstāns, levis
capriciously adv incōnstanter, leviter
capriciousness n incōnstantia f, libīdō f
capsize vt ēvertere ♦ vi ēvertī
captain n dux m, praefectus m, prīnceps m; (MIL) centuriō m; (naval) nāvarchus m; (of merchant ship) magister m ♦ vt praeesse (dat), dūcere
captaincy n centuriātus m
caption n caput nt
captious adj mōrōsus; (question) captiōsus
captiously adv mōrōsē
captiousness n mōrōsitās f
captivate vt capere, dēlēnīre, adlicere
captive n captīvus m
captivity n captīvitās f, vincula ntpl
captor n (by storm) expugnātor m; victor m
capture n (by storm) expugnātiō f ♦ vt capere
car n currus m
caravan n commeātus m
carbuncle n (MED) fūrunculus m; (stone) acaustus m
carcass n cadāver nt
card n charta f; (ticket) tessera f; (wool) pecten nt ♦ vt pectere
cardamom n amōmum nt
cardinal adj praecipuus; **~ point** cardō m ♦ n (ECCL) cardinālis
care n cūra f; (anxiety) sollicitūdō f; (attention) dīligentia f; (charge) custōdia f; **take ~** cavēre; **take ~ of** cūrāre ♦ vi cūrāre; **~ for** vt (look after) cūrāre; (like) amāre; **I don't ~** nīl moror; **I couldn't ~ less about …** floccī nōn faciō …,

pendō; **I don't ~ about** mittō, nihil moror; **for all I ~** per mē
career n curriculum nt; (POL) cursus honōrum; (completed) rēs gestae fpl ♦ vi ruere, volāre
carefree adj sēcūrus
careful adj (cautious) cautus; (attentive) dīligēns, attentus; (work) accūrātus
carefully adv cautē; dīligenter, attentē; accūrātē
careless adj incautus, neglegēns
carelessly adv incautē, neglegenter
carelessness n incūria f, neglegentia f
caress vt fovēre, blandīrī ♦ n blandīmentum nt, amplexus m
cargo n onus nt
caricature n (picture) gryllus m; (fig) imāgō dētorta f ♦ vt dētorquēre
carmine n coccum nt ♦ adj coccineus
carnage n strāgēs f, caedēs f
carnal adj corporeus; (pleasure) libīdinōsus
carnival n fēriae fpl
carol n carmen nt ♦ vi cantāre
carouse vi perpōtāre, cōmissārī ♦ n cōmissātiō f
carp vi obtrectāre; **~ at** carpere, rōdere
carpenter n faber m, lignārius m
carpet n tapēte nt
carriage n (conveying) vectūra f; (vehicle) vehiculum nt; (for journeys) raeda f, petorritum nt; (for town) carpentum nt, pīlentum nt; (deportment) gestus m, incessus m; **~ and pair** bīgae fpl; **~ and four** quadrīgae fpl
carrier n vector m; (porter) bāiulus m; **letter ~** tabellārius m
carrion n cadāver nt
carrot n carōta f
carry vt portāre, vehere, ferre, gerere; (LAW) perferre; (by assault) expugnāre; **~ away** auferre, āvehere; (by force) rapere; (with emotion) efferre; **~ all before one** ēvincere; **~ along** (building) dūcere; **~ back** reportāre; revehere, referre; **~ down** dēportāre, dēvehere; **~ in** invehere, intrōferre; **~ off** auferre, asportāre, āvehere; (by force) abripere, ēripere; (prize) ferre, reportāre; (success) bene gerere; **~ on** vt gerere; (profession) exercēre; **~ out** vi efferre, ēgerere, ēvehere; (task) exsequī; **~ out an undertaking** rem suscipere; **~ over** trānsportāre, trānsferre; **~ the day** vincere; **~ one's point** pervincere; **~ through** perferre; **~ to** adferre, advehere; **~ up** subvehere ♦ vi (sound) audīrī; **~ on** vi pergere; (flirt) lascīvīre
cart n plaustrum nt; carrus nt; **put the ~ before the horse** praeposterum dīcere ♦ vt plaustrō vehere
Carthage n Carthāgō, Carthāginis f
Carthaginian adj Carthāginiēnsis; Pūnicus; **the Carthaginians** Poenī mpl
carthorse n iūmentum nt
carve vt sculpere; (on surface) caelāre; (meat) secāre; **~ out** exsculpere
carver n caelātor m
carving n caelātūra f
cascade n cataracta m
case n (instance) exemplum nt, rēs f; (legal) āctiō f, līs f, causa f; (plight) tempus nt; (GRAM) cāsus m; (receptacle) thēca f, involucrum nt; **in ~** sī; (to prevent) nē; **in any ~** utut est rēs; **in that ~** ergō; **such is the ~** sic sē rēs habet; **civil**

~ causa prīvāta; **criminal** ~ causa pūblica; **win a** ~ causam, lītem obtinēre; **lose a** ~ causam, lītem āmittere
casement n fenestra f
cash n nummī mpl; (ready) numerātum nt, praesēns pecūnia f; **pay** ~ ex arcā absolvere, repraesentāre
cash box n arca f
cashier n dispēnsātor m ✦ vt (MIL) exauctōrāre
cash payment n repraesentātiō f
cask n cūpa f
casket n arcula f, pyxis f
casque n galea f, cassis f
cast vt iacere; (account) inīre; (eyes) conicere; (lots) conicere; (covering) exuere; (metal) fundere; ~ **ashore** ēicere; ~ **away** prōicere; ~ **down** dēicere; (humble) abicere; ~ **in one's teeth** exprobrāre; ~ **lots** sortīrī; ~ **off** vi abicere, exuere; ~ **out** prōicere, ēicere, pellere ✦ n iactus m; (moulding) typus m, fōrma f; **with a ~ in the eye** paetus
castanet n crotalum nt
castaway n ēiectus m
caste n ōrdō m
castigate vt animadvertere, castīgāre
castigation n animadversiō f, castīgātiō f
castle n arx f, castellum nt
castrate vt castrāre
casual adj fortuītus; (person) neglegēns
casually adv temerē
casualty n īnfortūnium nt ✦ pl: **casualties** occīsī mpl
casuist n sophistēs m
cat n fēlēs f
cataclysm n dīluvium nt, ruīna f
catalogue n index m
catapult n catapulta f, ballista f
cataract n cataracta f
catarrh n gravēdō f; **liable to** ~ gravēdinōsus
catastrophe n calamitās f, ruīna f
catastrophic adj calamitōsus, exitiōsus
catch vt capere, dēprehendere, excipere; (disease) contrahere, nancīscī; (fire) concipere, comprehendere; (meaning) intellegere; ~ **at** captāre; ~ **out** vi dēprehendere; ~ **up with** adsequī; ~ **birds** aucupārī; ~ **fish** piscārī ✦ n bolus m
categorical adj (statement) plānus
categorically adv sine exceptiōne
category n numerus m, genus nt
cater vi obsōnāre
cateran n praedātor m
caterer n obsōnātor m
caterpillar n ērūca f
caterwaul vi ululāre
catgut n chorda f
catharsis n pūrgātiō f
cathedral n aedēs f
catholic adj generālis
catkin n iūlus m
cattle n (collectively) pecus nt; (singly) pecus f; (for plough) armenta ntpl
cattle breeder n pecuārius m
cattle market n forum boārium nt
cattle thief n abāctor m
cauldron n cortīna f

cause n causa f; (person) auctor m; (LAW) causa f; (party) partēs fpl; **give** ~ **for** māteriam dare (gen); **make common** ~ **with** facere cum, stāre ab; **plead a** ~ causam dīcere; **in the** ~ **of** prō (abl); **without** ~ iniūriā ✦ vt efficere ut (subj), facere, facessere (with 'ut'), cūrāre (with gerundive); (feelings) movēre, inicere, ciēre
causeless adj vānus, sine causā
causeway n agger m
caustic adj (fig) mordāx
cauterize vt adūrere
caution n (wariness) cautiō f, prūdentia f; (warning) monitum nt ✦ vt monēre, admonēre
cautious adj cautus, prōvidus, prūdēns
cautiously adv cautē, prūdenter
cavalcade n pompa f
cavalier n eques m ✦ adj adrogāns
cavalierly adv adroganter
cavalry n equitēs mpl, equitātus m ✦ adj equester; **troop of** ~ turma f
cavalryman n eques m
cave n spēlunca f, caverna f; antrum nt; ~ **in** vi concidere, conlābī
cavern n spēlunca f, caverna f
cavil vi cavillārī; ~ **at** carpere, cavillārī ✦ n captiō f, cavillātiō f
cavity n caverna f, cavum nt
cavort vi saltāre
caw vi cornīcārī
cease vi dēsinere, dēsistere
ceaseless adj adsiduus, perpetuus
ceaselessly adv adsiduē, perpetuō
cedar n cedrus f ✦ adj cedrinus
cede vt cēdere, concēdere
ceiling n tēctum nt; (panelled) lacūnar nt, laqueārium nt
celebrate vt (rite) celebrāre, agitāre; (in crowds) frequentāre; (person, theme) laudāre, celebrāre, dīcere
celebrated adj praeclārus, illūstris, nōtus; **the** ~ **ille**
celebration n celebrātiō f; (rite) sollemne nt
celebrity n celebritās f, fāma f; (person) vir illūstris
celerity n celeritās f, vēlōcitās f
celery n apium nt
celestial adj caelestis; dīvīnus
celibacy n caelibātus m
celibate n caelebs m
cell n cella f
cellar n cella f
cement n ferrūmen nt ✦ vt coagmentāre
cemetery n sepulchrētum nt
cenotaph n tumulus honōrārius, tumulus inānis m
censer n tūribulum nt, acerra f
censor n cēnsor m ✦ vt cēnsēre
censorious adj cēnsōrius, obtrectātor
censorship n cēnsūra f
censure n reprehēnsiō f, animadversiō f; (censor's) nota f ✦ vt reprehendere, animadvertere, increpāre; notāre
census n cēnsus m
cent n: **one per** ~ centēsima f; **12 per** ~ **per annum** centēsima f (ie monthly)
centaur n centaurus m

centaury n (plant) centaurēum nt
centenarian n centum annōs nātus m, nāta f
centenary n centēsimus annus m
centesimal adj centēsimus
central adj medius
centralize vt in ūnum locum cōnferre; (power) ad ūnum dēferre
centre n centrum nt, media pars f; **the ~ of** medius
centuple adj centuplex
centurion n centuriō m
century n (MIL) centuria f; (time) saeculum nt
ceramic adj fictilis
cereal n frūmentum nt
ceremonial adj sollemnis ♦ n rītus m
ceremonious adj (rite) sollemnis; (person) officiōsus
ceremoniously adv sollemniter; officiōsē
ceremony n caerimōnia f, rītus m; (politeness) officium nt; (pomp) apparātus m; **master of ceremonies** dēsignātor m
cerise n coccum nt ♦ adj coccineus
certain adj (sure) certus; (future) explōrātus; **a ~** quīdam, quaedam, quoddam; **be ~** (know) prō certō scīre/habēre
certainly adv certē, certō, sine dubiō; (yes) ita, māximē; (concessive) quidem
certainty n (thing) certum nt; (belief) fidēs f; **for a ~** prō certō, explōrātē; **regard as a ~** prō explōrātō habēre
certificate n testimōnium nt
certify vt (writing) recognōscere; (fact) adfirmāre, testificārī
cessation n fīnis m; (from labour) quiēs f; (temporary) intermissiō f; (of hostilities) indutiae fpl
chafe vt ūrere; (fig) inrītāre ♦ vi stomachārī
chaff n palea f ♦ vt lūdere
chaffinch n fringilla f
chagrin n dolor m, stomachus m ♦ vt stomachum facere (dat), sollicitāre
chain n catēna f; (for neck) torquis m; (sequence) seriēs f; **chains** pl vincula ntpl ♦ vt vincīre
chair n sella f; (of office) sella curūlis f; (sedan) sella gestātōria f, lectīca f; (teacher's) cathedra f
chairman n (at meeting) magister m; (of debate) disceptātor m
chalet n casa f
chalice n calix m
chalk n crēta f
chalky adj crētōsus
challenge n prōvocātiō f ♦ vt prōvocāre, lacessere; (statement) in dubium vocāre; (fig) invītāre, dēposcere
challenger n prōvocātor m
chamber n conclāve nt; (bed) cubiculum nt; (bridal) thalamus m; (parliament) cūria f
chamberlain n cubiculārius m
chambermaid n serva f, ancilla f
chameleon n chamaeleōn f
chamois n rūpicapra f
champ vt mandere
champion n prōpugnātor m, patrōnus m; (winner) victor m ♦ vt favēre (dat), adesse (dat)
chance n fors f, fortūna f, cāsus m; (opportunity) occāsiō f; potestās f, facultās f; (prospect) spēs f;

game of ~ ālea f; **by ~** cāsū, fortuītō; **have an eye to the main ~** forō ūtī; **on the ~ of** sī forte ♦ adj fortuītus ♦ vi accidere, ēvenīre; **it chanced that ...** accidit ut ... (subj); **~ upon** incidere in, invenīre ♦ vt periclitārī
chancel n absis f
chancellor n cancellārius m
chancy adj dubius, perīculōsus
chandelier n candēlābrum nt
chandler n candēlārum propōla m
change n mūtātiō f, commūtātiō f, permūtātiō f; (POL) rēs novae fpl; (alternation) vicēs fpl, vicissitūdō f; (money) nummī minōrēs mpl ♦ vt mūtāre, commūtāre, permūtāre ♦ vi mūtārī; **~ hands** abaliēnarī; **~ places** ōrdinem permūtāre, inter sē loca permūtāre
changeable adj incōnstāns, mūtābilis
changeableness n incōnstantia f, mūtābilitās f
changeful adj varius
changeless adj cōnstāns, immūtābilis
changeling adj subditus m
channel n canālis m; (sea) fretum nt; (irrigation) rīvus m; (groove) sulcus m
chant vt cantāre, canere ♦ n cantus m
chaos n chaos nt; (fig) perturbātiō f
chaotic adj perturbātus
chap n rīma f; (man) homō m
chapel n sacellum nt, aedicula f
chaplain n diāconus m
chaplet n corōna f, sertum nt
chaps n (animal) mālae fpl
chapter n caput nt
char vt ambūrere
character n (inborn) indolēs f, ingenium nt, nātūra f; (moral) mōrēs mpl; (reputation) existimātiō f; (kind) genus nt; (mark) signum nt, littera f; (THEAT) persōna f, partēs fpl; **sustain a ~** persōnam gerere; **I know his ~** sciō quālis sit
characteristic adj proprius ♦ n proprium nt
characteristically adv suō mōre
characterize vt dēscrībere; proprium esse (gen)
charcoal n carbō m
charge n (LAW) accūsātiō f, crīmen nt; (MIL) impetus m, dēcursus m; (cost) impēnsa f; (task) mandātum nt, onus nt; (trust) cūra f, tūtēla f; **bring a ~ against** lītem intendere (dat); **entertain a ~ against** nōmen recipere (gen); **give in ~** in custōdiam trādere; **put in ~ of** praeficere (acc, dat); **be in ~ of** praeesse (dat) ♦ vt (LAW) accūsāre; (falsely) īnsimulāre; (MIL) incurrere in (acc), signa īnferre in (acc), impetum facere in (acc); (duty) mandāre; (cost) ferre, īnferre; (empty space) complēre; (trust) committere; (speech) hortārī; **~ to the account of** expēnsum ferre (dat)
chargeable adj obnoxius
charger n (dish) lānx f; (horse) equus m
charily adv cautē, parcē
chariot n currus m; (races) quadrīgae fpl; (war) essedum nt
charioteer n aurīga m; (war) essedārius m
charitable adj benevolus, benignus
charitably adv benevolē, benignē
charity n amor m, benignitās f; līberālitās f
charlatan n planus m

charm n (spell) carmen nt; (amulet) bulla f; (fig) blanditiae fpl, dulcēdō f, illecebra f; (beauty) venus f, lepōs m ♦ vt (magic) fascināre; (delight) dēlectāre, dēlēnīre

charming adj venustus, lepidus; (speech) blandus; (scenery) amoenus

charmingly adv venustē, blandē

chart n tabula f

charter n diplōma nt ♦ vt condūcere

chary adj (cautious) cautus; (sparing) parcus

chase vt fugāre; (hunt) vēnārī; (pursue) persequī, īnsequī; (engrave) caelāre; ~ away pellere, abigere ♦ n vēnātus m, vēnātiō f; (pursuit) īnsectātiō f

chaser n (in metal) caelātor m

chasm n hiātus m

chaste adj castus, pudīcus; (style) pūrus

chasten vt castīgāre, corrigere

chastener n castīgātor m, corrēctor m

chastise vt castīgāre, animadvertere

chastisement n castīgātiō f, poena f

chastity n castitās f, pudīcitia f

chat vi colloquī, sermōcinārī ♦ n sermō m, colloquium nt

chatelaine n domina f

chattels n bona ntpl, rēs mancipī

chatter vi garrīre; (teeth) crepitāre ♦ n garrulitās f, loquācitās f

chatterbox n lingulāca m/f

chatterer n garrulus m, loquāx m

chattering adj garrulus, loquāx ♦ n garrulitās f, loquācitās f; (teeth) crepitus m

cheap adj vīlis; **hold** ~ parvī aestimāre; **buy** ~ bene emere

cheapen vt pretium minuere (gen)

cheaply adv vīliter, parvō pretiō

cheapness n vīlitās f

cheat vt dēcipere, fraudāre, dēfraudāre, frustrārī ♦ n fraudātor m

check vt cohibēre, coercēre; (movement) impedīre, inhibēre; (rebuke) reprehendere; (test) probāre ♦ n impedīmentum nt, mora f; (MIL) offēnsiō f; (rebuke) reprehēnsiō f; (test) probātiō f; (ticket) tessera f

checkmate n incitae calcēs fpl ♦ vt ad incitās redigere

cheek n gena f; (impudence) ōs nt; **cheeks** pl mālae fpl; **how have you the** ~ **to say?** quō ōre dīcis?

cheekbone n maxilla f

cheeky adj impudēns

cheep vi pīpilāre

cheer vt hilarāre, exhilarāre; hortārī; (in sorrow) cōnsōlārī ♦ vi clāmāre, adclāmāre; ~ **up!** bonō animō es! ♦ n (shout) clāmor m, plausus m; (food) hospitium nt; (mind) animus m

cheerful adj alacer, hilaris, laetus

cheerfully adv hilare, laetē

cheerfulness n hilaritās f

cheerily adv hilare

cheerless adj tristis, maestus

cheerlessly adv triste

cheery adj hilaris

cheese n cāseus m

chef n coquus m

cheque n perscrīptiō f, syngrapha f

chequer vt variāre

chequered adj varius; (mosaic) tessellātus

cherish vt fovēre, colere

cherry n (fruit) cerasum nt; (tree) cerasus f

chess n latrunculī mpl

chessboard n abacus m

chest n (box) arca f, arcula f; (body) pectus nt; ~ **of drawers** armārium nt

chestnut n castanea f ♦ adj (colour) spādīx

chevalier n eques m

chevaux-de-frise n ēricius m

chew vt mandere

chic adj expolītus, concinnus

chicanery n (LAW) calumnia f; (fig) dolus m

chick n pullus m

chicken n pullus m; **don't count your chickens before they're hatched** adhūc tua messis in herbā est

chicken-hearted adj timidus, ignāvus

chick-pea n cicer nt

chide vt reprehendere, increpāre, obiūrgāre

chief n prīnceps m, dux m ♦ adj praecipuus, prīmus; ~ **point** caput nt

chief command n summa imperiī

chiefly adv in prīmīs, praesertim, potissimum

chieftain n prīnceps m, rēgulus m

chilblain n perniō m

child n īnfāns m/f; puer m, puerulus m, puella f; fīlius m, fīlia f; **child's play** lūdus m

childbed n puerperium nt

childbirth n partus m

childhood n pueritia f; **from** ~ ā puerō

childish adj puerīlis

childishly adv puerīliter

childless adj orbus

childlessness n orbitās f

childlike adj puerīlis

children npl līberī mpl

chill n frīgus nt ♦ adj frīgidus ♦ vt refrīgerāre

chilly adj frīgidus, frīgidior

chime vi sonāre, canere; ~ **in** interpellāre; (fig) cōnsonāre ♦ n sonus m

chimera n chimaera f; (fig) somnium nt

chimerical adj commentīcius

chimney n camīnus m

chin n mentum nt

china n fictilia ntpl

chink n rīma f; (sound) tinnītus m ♦ vi crepāre, tinnīre

chip n assula f, fragmentum nt ♦ vt dolāre

chirp vi pīpilāre

chirpy adj hilaris

chisel n scalprum nt, scalpellum nt ♦ vt sculpere

chit n (child) pūsiō m, puerulus m

chitchat n sermunculī mpl

chitterlings n hillae fpl

chivalrous adj generōsus

chivalry n virtūs f; (men) iuventūs f; (class) equitēs mpl

chive n caepe nt

chock n cuneus m

chock-full adj refertus

choice n dēlēctus m, ēlēctiō f; (of alternatives) optiō f ♦ adj lēctus, eximius, exquīsītus

choiceness n ēlegantia f, praestantia f

choir n chorus m

choke vt suffocāre; (emotion) reprimere; (passage) obstruere

choler n bīlis f; (anger) īra f, stomachus m

choleric adj īrācundus

choose vt legere, ēligere, dēligere; (alternative) optāre; (for office) dēsignāre; (with infin) velle, mālle

chop vt concīdere; ~ **off** praecīdere ♦ n (meat) offa f

chopper n secūris f

choppy adj (sea) asper

choral adj symphōniacus

chord n (string) nervus m, chorda f

chortle vi cachinnāre

chorus n (singers) chorus m; (song) concentus m, symphōnia f; **in** ~ ūnā vōce

christen vt baptizāre

Christian adj Christiānus

Christianity n Christiānismus m

chronic adj inveterātus; **become** ~ inveterāscere

chronicle n annālēs mpl, ācta pūblica ntpl ♦ vt in annālēs referre

chronicler n annālium scrīptor m

chronological adj: **in** ~ **order** servātō temporum ōrdine; **make a** ~ **error** temporibus errāre

chronology n temporum ratiō f, temporum ōrdō m

chronometer n hōrologium nt

chubby adj pinguis

chuck vt conicere; ~ **out** extrūdere

chuckle vi rīdēre ♦ n rīsus m

chum n sodālis m

church n ecclēsia f

churl n rūsticus m

churlish adj difficilis, importūnus; avārus

churlishly adv rūsticē, avārē

churlishness n mōrōsitās f, avāritia f

chute n (motion) lāpsus m; (place) dēclīve nt

cicada n cicāda f

cincture n cingulum nt

cinder n cinis m

cipher n numerus m, nihil nt; (code) notae fpl; **in** ~ per notās

circle n orbis m, circulus m, gyrus m; **form a** ~ **in orbem cōnsistere** ♦ vi sē circumagere, circumīre

circlet n īnfula f

circuit n ambitus m, circuitus m; (assizes) conventus m

circuitous adj longus; **a** ~ **route** circuitus m; (speech) ambāgēs fpl

circular adj rotundus

circulate vt (news) pervulgāre ♦ vi circumagī; (news) circumferrī, percrēbrēscere

circulation n ambitus m; **be in** ~ in manibus esse; **go out of** ~ obsolēscere

circumcise vt circumcīdere

circumference n ambitus m

circumlocution n ambāgēs fpl, circuitiō f

circumnavigate vt circumvehī

circumscribe vt circumscrībere; (restrict) coercēre, fīnīre

circumspect adj cautus, prūdēns

circumspection n cautiō f, prūdentia f, circumspectiō f

circumspectly adv cautē, prūdenter

circumstance n rēs f; **circumstances** rērum status m; (wealth) rēs f; **as circumstances arise** ē rē nātā; **under the circumstances** cum haec ita sint, essent; **under no circumstances** nēquāquam

circumstantial adj adventīcius; (detailed) accūrātus; ~ **evidence** coniectūra f

circumstantially adv accūrātē, subtīliter

circumvallation n circummūnītiō f

circumvent vt circumvenīre, fallere

circus n circus m

cistern n lacus m, cisterna f

citadel n arx f

citation n (LAW) vocātiō f; (mention) commemorātiō f

cite vt in iūs vocāre; (quote) commemorāre, prōferre

citizen n cīvis m/f; (of provincial town) mūniceps m; **fellow** ~ cīvis m/f; **Roman citizens** Quirītes mpl ♦ adj cīvīlis, cīvicus

citizenship n cīvitās f; **deprived of** ~ capite dēminūtus; **loss of** ~ capitis dēminūtiō f

citron n (fruit) citrum nt; (tree) citrus f

city n urbs f, oppidum nt

civic adj cīvīlis, cīvicus

civil adj (of citizens) cīvīlis; (war) cīvīlis, intestīnus, domesticus; (manners) urbānus, cōmis, officiōsus; (lawsuit) prīvātus

civilian n togātus m

civility n urbānitās f, cōmitās f; (act) officium nt

civilization n exculta hominum vīta f, cultus atque hūmānitās

civilize vt excolere, expolīre, ad hūmānum cultum dēdūcere

civil war n bellum cīvīle, bellum domesticum, bellum intestīnum

clad adj vestītus

claim vt (for oneself) adrogāre, adserere; (something due) poscere, postulāre, vindicāre; (at law) petere; (statement) adfirmāre ♦ n postulātiō f, postulātum nt; (at law) petītiō f, vindiciae fpl

claimant n petītor m

clam n chāma f

clamber vi scandere

clammy adj ūmidus, lentus

clamorous adj vōciferāns

clamour n strepitus m, clāmōrēs mpl ♦ vi: ~ **against** obstrepere (dat)

clamp n cōnfībula f

clan n gēns f

clandestine adj fūrtīvus

clandestinely adv clam, fūrtim

clang n clangor m, crepitus m ♦ vi increpāre

clangour n clangor m

clank n crepitus m ♦ vi crepitāre

clansman n gentīlis m

clap vi plaudere, applaudere; ~ **eyes on** cōnspicere; ~ **in prison** in vincula conicere ♦ n plausus m; (thunder) fragor m

clapper n plausor m

claptrap n iactātiō f

claque n plausōrēs mpl, operae fpl

clarify vt pūrgāre; (knowledge) illūstrāre ♦ vi liquēre

clarinet n tībia f

clarion n lituus m, cornū nt

clarity n perspicuitās f

clash n concursus m; (sound) strepitus m, crepitus m; (fig) discrepantia f ♦ vi concurrere; (sound) increpāre; (fig) discrepāre ♦ vt conflīgere

clasp n fībula f; (embrace) amplexus m ♦ vt implicāre; amplectī, complectī; ~ **together** interiungere

class n (POL) ōrdō m, classis f; (kind) genus nt; (school) classis f ♦ vt dēscrībere; ~ **as** in numerō (gen pl) referre, repōnere, habēre

classic n scrīptor classicus m

classical adj classicus; ~ **literature** litterae Graecae et Rōmānae

classics npl scrīptōrēs Graecī et Rōmānī

classify vt dēscrībere, in ōrdinem redigere

class-mate n condiscipulus m

clatter n crepitus m ♦ vi increpāre

clause n (GRAM) incīsum nt, membrum nt; (LAW) caput nt; (will) ēlogium nt; **in short clauses** incīsim

claw n unguis m, ungula f ♦ vt unguibus lacerāre

clay n argilla f; **made of ~** fictilis

clayey adj argillāceus

claymore n gladius m

clean adj mundus; (fig) pūrus, castus; ~ **slate** novae tabulae fpl; **make a ~ sweep of** omnia tollere; **show a ~ pair of heels** sē in pedēs conicere; **my hands are ~** innocēns sum ♦ adv prōrsus, tōtus ♦ vt pūrgāre

cleanliness n munditia f

cleanly adj mundus, nitidus ♦ adv mundē, pūrē

cleanse vt pūrgāre, abluere, dētergēre

clear adj clārus; (liquid) līmpidus; (space) apertus, pūrus; (sound) clārus; (weather) serēnus; (fact) manifestus, perspicuus; (language) illūstris, dīlūcidus; (conscience) rēctus, innocēns; **it is ~** liquet; ~ **of** līber (abl), expers (gen); **be ~ about** rēctē intellegere; **keep ~ of** ēvītāre; **the coast is ~** arbitrī absunt ♦ vt (of obstacles) expedīre, pūrgāre; (of a charge) absolvere; (self) pūrgāre; (profit) lucrārī; ~ **away** āmovēre, tollere; ~ **off** vt (debt) solvere, exsolvere ♦ vi facessere; ~ **out** ēluere, dētergēre; ~ **up** vt (difficulty) illūstrāre, ēnōdāre, explicāre ♦ vi (weather) disserēnāscere

clearance n pūrgātiō f; (space) intervallum nt

clearing n (in forest) lūcus m

clearly adv clārē; manifestē, apertē, perspicuē; (with clause) vidēlicet

clearness n clāritās f; (weather) serēnitās f; (mind) acūmen nt; (style) perspicuitās f

clear-sighted adj sagāx, perspicāx

cleavage n discidium nt

cleave vt (cut) findere, discindere ♦ vi (cling) ~ **to** haerēre (dat), adhaerēre (dat)

cleaver n dolabra f

cleft n rīma f, hiātus m ♦ adj fissus, discissus

clemency n clēmentia f, indulgentia f; **with ~** clēmenter

clement adj clēmēns, misericors

clench vt (nail) retundere; (hand) comprimere

clerk n scrība m; (of court) lēctor m

clever adj callidus, ingeniōsus, doctus, astūtus

cleverly adv doctē, callidē, ingeniōsē

cleverness nt calliditās f, sollertia f

clew n glomus nt

cliché n verbum trītum nt

client n cliēns m/f; (lawyer's) cōnsultor m; **body of clients** clientēla f

clientele n clientēla f

cliff n rūpēs f, scopulus m

climate n caelum nt

climax n (RHET) gradātiō f; (fig) culmen nt

climb vt, vi scandere, ascendere; ~ **down** dēscendere ♦ n ascēnsus m

climber n scandēns m

clime n caelum nt, plāga f

clinch vt cōnfirmāre

cling vi adhaerēre; ~ **together** cohaerere

clink vi tinnīre ♦ n tinnītus m

clip vt tondēre; praecīdere

clippers n forfex f

clique n factiō f

cloak n (rain) lacerna f; (travel) paenula f; (MIL) sagum nt; palūdāmentum nt; (Greek) pallium nt; (fig) involūcrum nt; (pretext) speciēs f ♦ vt tegere, dissimulāre

clock n hōrologium nt; (sun) sōlārium nt; (water) clepsydra f; **ten o'clock** quarta hōra

clockwise adv dextrōvorsum, dextrōrsum

clod n glaeba f

clog n (shoe) sculpōnea f; (fig) impedīmentum nt ♦ vt impedīre

cloister n porticus f

cloistered adj (fig) umbrātilis

close¹ adj (shut) clausus; (tight) artus; (narrow) angustus; (near) propinquus; (compact) refertus, dēnsus; (stingy) parcus; (secret) obscūrus; (weather) crassus; ~ **together** dēnsus, refertus; **at ~ quarters** comminus; **be ~ at hand** īnstāre; **keep ~ to** adhaerēre; ~ **to** prope (acc), iuxtā (acc) ♦ adv prope, iuxtā ♦ n angiportus m

close² vt claudere, operīre; (finish) perficere, fīnīre, conclūdere, termināre; (ranks) dēnsāre ♦ vi claudī; conclūdī, termināri; (time) exīre; (wound) coīre; (speech) perōrāre; ~ **with** (fight) manum cōnserere, signa cōnferre; (deal) pacīscī; (offer) accipere ♦ n fīnis m, terminus m; (action) exitus m; (sentence) conclūsiō f; **at the ~ of summer** aestāte exeunte

closely adv prope; (attending) attentē; (associating) coniūnctē; **follow ~** īnstāre (dat)

closeness n propinquitās f; (weather) gravitās f, crassitūdō f; (with money) parsimōnia f; (friends) coniūnctiō f; (manner) cautiō f

closet n cubiculum nt, cella f ♦ vt inclūdere

clot n (blood) concrētus sanguis m ♦ vi concrēscere

cloth n textile nt; (piece) pannus m; (linen) linteum nt; (covering) strāgulum nt

clothe vt vestīre

clothes n vestis f, vestītus m, vestīmenta ntpl

clothier n vestiārius m

clothing n vestis f, vestītus m, vestīmenta ntpl

clotted adj concrētus

cloud n nūbēs f; (storm) nimbus m; (dust) globus m; (disfavour) invidia f ♦ vt nūbibus obdūcere; (fig) obscūrāre

clouded adj obnūbilus

cloudiness n nūbilum nt

cloudless adj pūrus, serēnus

cloudy adj obnūbilus

clout *n* pannus *m*
cloven *adj* (*hoof*) bifidus
clover *n* trifolium *nt*
clown *n* (*boor*) rūsticus *m*; (*comic*) scurra *m*
clownish *adj* rūsticus, inurbānus
clownishness *n* rūsticitās *f*
cloy *vt* satiāre
cloying *adj* pūtidus
club *n* (*stick*) fustis *m*, clāva *f*; (*society*) sodālitās *f*;
  ~ together *vi* in commūne cōnsulere, pecūniās
  cōnferre
club-footed *adj* scaurus
cluck *vi* singultīre ♦ *n* singultus *m*
clue *n* indicium *nt*, vestīgium *nt*
clump *n* massa *f*; (*earth*) glaeba *f*; (*trees*) arbustum
  nt; (*willows*) salictum *nt*
clumsily *adv* ineptē, inēleganter; inconditē,
  īnfabrē
clumsiness *n* īnscītia *f*
clumsy *adj* (*person*) inconcinnus, ineptus; (*thing*)
  inhabilis; (*work*) inconditus
cluster *n* cumulus *m*; (*grapes*) racēmus *m*; (*people*)
  corōna *f* ♦ *vi* congregārī
clutch *vt* prehendere, adripere; ~ at captāre
  nt, comprehēnsiō *f*; from one's clutches ē
  manibus; in one's clutches in potestāte
clutter *n* turba *f* ♦ *vt* impedīre, obstruere
coach *n* currus *m*, raeda *f*, pīlentum *nt*; (*trainer*)
  magister *m* ♦ *vt* ēdocēre, praecipere (*dat*)
coachman *n* aurīga *m*, raedārius *m*
coagulate *vt* cōgere ♦ *vi* concrēscere
coagulation *n* concrētiō *f*
coal *n* carbō *m*; carry coals to Newcastle in
  silvam ligna ferre
coalesce *vi* coīre, coalēscere
coalition *n* coitiō *f*, cōnspīrātiō *f*
coarse *adj* (*quality*) crassus; (*manners*) rūsticus,
  inurbānus; (*speech*) īnfacētus
coarsely *adv* inurbānē, inēleganter
coarseness *n* crassitūdō *f*; rūsticitās *f*
coast *n* lītus *nt*, ōra maritima *f* ♦ *vi*: ~ along
  legere, praetervehī
coastal *adj* lītorālis, maritimus
coastline *n* lītus *nt*
coat *n* pallium *nt*; (*animals*) pellis *f* ♦ *vt* indūcere,
  inlinere
coating *n* corium *nt*
coax *vt* blandīrī, dēlēnīre
coaxing *adj* blandus ♦ *n* blanditiae *fpl*
cob *n* (*horse*) mannus *m*; (*swan*) cygnus *m*
cobble *n* lapis *m* ♦ *vt* sarcīre
cobbler *n* sūtor *m*
cobweb *n* arāneum *nt*
cock *n* gallus *m*, gallus gallīnāceus *m*; (*other birds*)
  mās *m*; (*tap*) epitonium *nt*; (*hay*) acervus *m*
cockatrice *n* basiliscus *m*
cockchafer *n* scarabaeus *m*
cockcrow *n* gallī cantus *m* ♦ *vt* ērigere
cockerel *n* pullus *m*
cockroach *n* blatta *f*
cocksure *adj* cōnfīdēns
cod *n* callarias *m*
coddle *vt* indulgēre (*dat*), permulcēre
code *n* fōrmula *f*; (*secret*) notae *fpl*
codicil *n* cōdicillī *mpl*
codify *vt* in ōrdinem redigere

coequal *adj* aequālis
coerce *vt* cōgere
coercion *n* vīs *f*
coffer *n* arca *f*, cista *f*; (*public*) fiscus *m*
coffin *n* arca *f*
cog *n* dēns *m*
cogency *n* vīs *f*, pondus *nt*
cogent *adj* gravis, validus
cogitate *vi* cōgitāre, meditārī
cogitation *n* cōgitātiō *f*; meditātiō *f*
cognate *adj* cognātus
cognition *n* cognitiō *f*
cognizance *n* cognitiō *f*; take ~ of cognōscere
cognizant *adj* gnārus
cohabit *vi* cōnsuēscere
cohabitation *n* cōnsuētūdō *f*
coheir *n* cohērēs *m/f*
cohere *vi* cohaerēre; (*statement*) congruere
coherence *n* coniūnctiō *f*; (*fig*) convenientia *f*
coherent *adj* congruēns
cohesion *n* coagmentātiō *f*
cohesive *adj* tenāx
cohort *n* cohors *f*
coil *n* spīra *f* ♦ *vt* glomerāre
coin *n* nummus *m* ♦ *vt* cūdere; (*fig*) fingere
coinage *n* monēta *f*; (*fig*) fictum *nt*
coincide *vi* concurrere; (*opinion*) cōnsentīre
coincidence *n* concursus *m*; cōnsēnsus *m*; by
  a ~ cāsū
coincidental *adj* fortuītus
coiner *n* (*of money*) signātor *m*
col *n* iugum *nt*
colander *n* cōlum *nt*
cold *adj* frīgidus; (*icy*) gelidus; very ~ perfrīgidus;
  be ~, feel ~ algēre, frīgēre; get ~ algēscere,
  frīgēscere ♦ *n* frīgus *nt*; (*felt*) algor *m*; (*malady*)
  gravēdō *f*; catch ~ algēscere, frīgus colligere;
  catch a ~ gravēdinem contrahere; have a
  ~ gravēdine labōrāre
coldish *adj* frīgidulus, frīgidior
coldly *adv* (*manner*) sine studiō
coldness *n* frīgus *nt*, algor *m*
cold water *n* frīgida *f*
colic *n* tormina *ntpl*
collar *n* collāre *nt*
collarbone *n* iugulum *nt*
collate *vt* cōnferre, comparāre
collateral *adj* adiūnctus; (*evidence*)
  cōnsentāneus
collation *n* collātiō *f*; (*meal*) prandium *nt*,
  merenda *f*
colleague *n* collēga *m*
collect *vt* colligere, cōgere, congerere; (*persons*)
  congregāre, convocāre; (*taxes*) exigere;
  (*something due*) recipere; ~ oneself animum
  colligere; cool and collected aequō animō ♦ *vi*
  convenīre, congregārī
collection *n* (*persons*) coetus *m*, conventus *m*;
  (*things*) congeriēs *f*; (*money*) exāctiō *f*
collective *adj* commūnis
collectively *adv* commūniter
collector *n* (*of taxes*) exāctor *m*
college *n* collēgium *nt*
collide *vi* concurrere, cōnflīctārī
collier *n* carbōnārius *m*
collision *n* concursus *m*

collocation *n* collocātiō *f*
collop *n* offa *f*
colloquial *adj* cottīdiānus
colloquy *n* sermō *m*, colloquium *nt*
collude *vi* praevāricārī
collusion *n* praevāricātiō *f*
collusive *adj* praevāricātor
colonel *n* lēgātus *m*
colonial *adj* colōnicus ♦ *n* colōnus *m*
colonist *n* colōnus *m*
colonization *n* dēductiō *f*
colonize *vt* colōniam dēdūcere, cōnstituere in *(acc)*
colonnade *n* porticus *f*
colony *n* colōnia *f*
colossal *adj* ingēns, vastus
colossus *n* colossus *m*
colour *n* color *m*; *(paint)* pigmentum *nt*; *(artificial)* fūcus *m*; *(complexion)* color *m*; *(pretext)* speciēs *f*; **take on a ~** colōrem dūcere; **under ~ of** per speciem *(gen)*; **local ~** māteria dē regiōne sūmpta ♦ *vt* colōrāre; *(dye)* īnficere, fūcāre; *(fig)* praetendere *(dat)* ♦ *vi* rubēre, ērubēscere
colourable *adj* speciōsus
coloured *adj* *(naturally)* colōrātus; *(artificially)* fūcātus
colourful *adj* fūcōsus, varius
colouring *n* pigmentum *nt*; *(dye)* fūcus *m*
colourless *adj* perlūcidus; *(person)* pallidus; *(fig)* īnsulsus
colours *n* *(MIL)* signum *nt*, vexillum *nt*; *(POL)* partēs *fpl*; **sail under false ~** aliēnō nōmine ūtī; **with flying ~** māximā cum glōriā
colour sergeant *n* signifer *m*
colt *n* equuleus *m*, equulus *m*
coltsfoot *n* farfarus *m*
column *n* columna *f*; *(MIL)* agmen *nt*
coma *n* sopor *m*
comb *n* pecten *m*; *(bird)* crista *f*; *(loom)* pecten *m*; *(honey)* favus *m* ♦ *vt* pectere
combat *n* pugna *f*, proelium *nt*, certāmen *nt* ♦ *vi* pugnāre, dīmicāre, certāre ♦ *vt* pugnāre cum *(abl)*, obsistere *(dat)*
combatant *n* pugnātor *m* ♦ *adj* pugnāns; **non-combatant** imbellis
combative *adj* ferōx, pugnāx
combination *n* coniūnctiō *f*, cōnfūsiō *f*; *(persons)* cōnspīrātiō *f*; *(illegal)* coniūrātiō *f*
combine *vt* coniungere, iungere ♦ *vi* coīre, coniungī ♦ *n* societās *f*
combustible *adj* ignī obnoxius
combustion *n* dēflāgrātiō *f*, incendium *nt*
come *vi* venīre, advenīre; *(after a journey)* dēvenīre; *(interj)* age!; **how comes it that ...?** quī fit ut ...?; **~ across** *vi* invenīre, offendere; **~ after** sequī, excipere, succēdere *(dat)*; **~ again** revenīre, redīre; **~ away** *vi* abscēdere; *(when pulled)* sequī; **~ back** *vi* revenīre, redīre; regredī; **~ between** intervenīre, intercēdere; **~ down** *vi* dēvenīre, dēscendere; *(from the past)* trādī, prōdī; **~ forward** *vi* prōcēdere, prōdīre; **~ from** *vi* *(origin)* dēfluere; **~ in** *vi* inīre, introīre; ingredī; *(revenue)* redīre; **~ near** accēdere ad *(acc)*, appropinquāre *(dat)*; **~ nearer and nearer** adventāre; **~ of** *vi* *(family)* ortum esse ab, ex *(abl)*; **~ off** *vi* ēvādere, discēdere; **~ on** *vi* prōcēdere; *(progress)* prōficere;

(interj) age, agite; **~ on the scene** intervenīre, supervenīre, adesse; **~ out** *vi* exīre, ēgredī; *(hair, teeth)* cadere; *(flower)* flōrēscere; *(book)* ēdī; **~ over** *vi* trānsīre; *(feeling)* subīre, occupāre; **~ to** *vi* advenīre ad, in *(acc)*; *(person)* adīre; *(amount)* efficere; **~ to the help of** subvenīre *(dat)*; succurrere *(dat)*; **~ to nought** ad nihilum recidere; **~ to pass** ēvenīre, fierī; **~ together** convenīre, coīre; **~ up** *vi* subīre, succēdere; *(growth)* prōvenīre; **~ upon** *vt* invenīre; **he is coming to** animus eī redit
comedian *n* *(actor)* cōmoedus *m*; *(writer)* cōmicus *m*
comedienne *n* mīma *f*
comedy *n* cōmoedia *f*
comeliness *n* decor *m*, decōrum *nt*
comely *adj* decōrus, pulcher
comestibles *n* vīctus *m*
comet *n* comētēs *m*
comfort *vt* sōlārī, cōnsōlārī, adlevāre ♦ *n* sōlācium *nt*, cōnsōlātiō *f*
comfortable *adj* commodus; **make oneself ~** corpus cūrāre
comfortably *adv* commodē
comforter *n* cōnsōlātor *m*
comfortless *adj* incommodus; **be ~** sōlātiō carēre
comforts *npl* commoda *ntpl*
comic *adj* cōmicus; facētus ♦ *n* scurra *m*
comical *adj* facētus, rīdiculus
coming *adj* futūrus ♦ *n* adventus *m*
comity *n* cōmitās *f*
command *vt* iubēre *(+ acc and infin)*, imperāre *(dat and ut + subj)*; dūcere; *(feelings)* regere; *(resources)* fruī *(abl)*; *(view)* prōspectāre ♦ *n* *(MIL)* imperium *nt*; *(sphere)* prōvincia *f*; *(order)* imperium *nt*, iussum *nt*, mandātum *nt*; **be in ~ of** praeesse *(dat)*; **put in ~ of** praeficere *(dat)*; **~ of language** fācundia *f*
commandant *n* praefectus *m*
commandeer *vt* pūblicāre
commander *n* dux *m*, praefectus *m*
commander in chief *n* imperātor *m*
commandment *n* mandātum *nt*
commemorate *vt* celebrāre, memoriae trādere
commemoration *n* celebrātiō *f*
commence *vt* incipere, exōrdīrī, initium facere *(gen)*
commencement *n* initium *nt*, exōrdium *nt*, prīncipium *nt*
commend *vt* laudāre; *(recommend)* commendāre; *(entrust)* mandāre; **~ oneself** sē probāre
commendable *adj* laudābilis, probābilis
commendation *n* laus *f*, commendātiō *f*
commendatory *adj* commendātīcius
commensurable *adj* pār
commensurate *adj* congruēns, conveniēns
comment *vi* dīcere, scrībere; **~ on** interpretārī; *(with notes)* adnotāre ♦ *n* dictum *nt*, sententia *f*
commentary *n* commentāriī *mpl*
commentator *n* interpres *m*
commerce *n* mercātūra *f*, commercium *nt*; **engage in ~** mercātūrās facere, negōtiārī
commercial dealings *npl* commercium *nt*
commercial traveller *n* īnstitor *m*
commination *n* minae *fpl*

comminatory *adj* mināx
commingle *vt* intermiscēre
commiserate *vt* miserērī (*gen*)
commiseration *n* misericordia *f*; (RHET)
commiserātiō *f*
commissariat *n* rēs frūmentāria *f*, commeātus
m; (*staff*) frūmentāriī *mpl*
commissary *n* lēgātus *m*; reī frūmentāriae
praefectus *m*
commission *n* (*charge*) mandātum *nt*; (*persons*)
triumvirī *mpl*, decemvirī *mpl*; (*abroad*) lēgātiō *f*;
get a ~ (MIL) tribūnum fierī; **standing ~** (LAW)
quaestiō perpetua *f* ♦ *vt* mandāre, adlēgāre
commissioner *n* lēgātus *m*; **three**
commissioners triumvirī *mpl*; **ten**
commissioners decemvirī *mpl*
commit *vt* (*charge*) committere, mandāre; (*crime*)
admittere; (*to prison*) conicere; (*to an undertaking*)
obligāre, obstringere; **~ to memory** memoriae
trādere; **~ to writing** litterīs mandāre; **~ an**
error errāre; **~ a theft** fūrtum facere; *see also*
suicide
commitment *n* mūnus *nt*, officium *nt*
committee *n* dēlēctī *mpl*
commodious *adj* capāx
commodity *n* merx *f*, rēs *f*
commodore *n* praefectus classis *m*
common *adj* (*for all*) commūnis; (*ordinary*)
vulgāris, cottīdiānus; (*repeated*) frequēns,
crēber; (*inferior*) nēquam ♦ *n* compāscuus
ager *m*, prātum *nt*; **~ man** homō plēbēius *m*;
~ soldier gregārius mīles *m*
commonalty *n* plēbs *f*
commoner *n* homō plēbēius *m*
common law *n* mōs māiōrum *m*
commonly *adv* ferē, vulgō
common people *n* plēbs *f*, vulgus *nt*
commonplace *n* trītum prōverbium *nt*; (RHET)
locus commūnis *m* ♦ *adj* vulgāris, trītus
commons *npl* plēbs *f*; (*food*) diāria *ntpl*
common sense *n* prūdentia *f*
commonwealth *n* cīvitās *f*, rēs pūblica *f*
commotion *n* perturbātiō *f*, tumultus *m*; **cause**
a ~ tumultuārī
communal *adj* commūnis
commune *n* pāgus *m* ♦ *vi* colloquī, sermōnēs
cōnferre
communicate *vt* commūnicāre; (*information*)
nūntiāre, patefacere ♦ *vi*: **~ with** commūnicāre
(*dat*), commercium habēre (*gen*), agere cum
(*abl*)
communication *n* (*dealings*) commercium *nt*;
(*information*) litterae *fpl*, nūntius *m*; (*passage*)
commeātus *m*; **cut off the communications**
of interclūdere
communicative *adj* loquāx
communion *n* societās *f*
communiqué *n* litterae *fpl*, praedicātiō *f*
communism *n* bonōrum aequātiō *f*
community *n* cīvitās *f*, commūne *nt*;
(*participation*) commūniō *f*
commutation *n* mūtātiō *f*
commute *vt* mūtāre, commūtāre
compact *n* foedus *nt*, conventum *nt* ♦ *adj* dēnsus
♦ *vt* dēnsāre

companion *n* socius *m*, comes *m/f*; (*intimate*)
sodālis *m*; (*at school*) condiscipulus *m*; (*in army*)
commīlitō *m*, contubernālis *m*
companionable *adj* facilis, commodus
companionship *n* sodālitās *f*, cōnsuētūdō *f*;
(MIL) contubernium *nt*
company *n* societās *f*, cōnsuētūdō *f*; (*gathering*)
coetus *m*, conventus *m*; (*guests*) cēnantēs *mpl*;
(*commercial*) societās *f*; (*magistrates*) collēgium *nt*;
(MIL) manipulus *m*; (THEAT) grex *m*, caterva *f*; **~ of**
ten decuria *f*
comparable *adj* comparābilis, similis
comparative *adj* māgnus, sī cum aliīs
cōnfertur
comparatively *adv* ut in tālī tempore, ut in
eā regiōne, ut est captus hominum; **~ few**
perpaucī, nullus ferē
compare *vt* comparāre, cōnferre; **compared**
with ad (*acc*)
comparison *n* comparātiō *f*, collātiō *f*; (RHET)
similitūdō *f*; **in ~ with** prō (*abl*)
compartment *n* cella *f*, pars *f*
compass *n* ambitus *m*, spatium *nt*, modus *m*;
pair of compasses circinus *m* ♦ *vt* circumdare,
cingere; (*attain*) cōnsequī
compassion *n* misericordia *f*
compassionate *adj* misericors, clēmēns
compassionately *adv* clēmenter
compatibility *n* convenientia *f*
compatible *adj* congruēns, conveniēns; **be**
~ congruere
compatibly *adv* congruenter, convenienter
compatriot *n* cīvis *m*, populāris *m*
compeer *n* pār *m*; aequālis *m*
compel *vt* cōgere
compendious *adj* brevis
compendiously *adv* summātim
compendium *n* epitomē *f*
compensate *vt* compēnsāre, satisfacere (*dat*)
compensation *n* compēnsātiō *f*; pretium *nt*,
poena *f*
compete *vi* certāre, contendere
competence *n* facultās *f*; (LAW) iūs *nt*; (*money*)
quod sufficit
competent *adj* perītus, satis doctus, capāx;
(*witness*) locuplēs; **it is ~** licet
competition *n* certāmen *nt*, contentiō *f*
competitor *n* competītor *m*, aemulus *m*
compilation *n* collectānea *ntpl*, liber *m*
compile *vt* compōnere
compiler *n* scrīptor *m*
complacency *n* amor suī *m*
complacent *adj* suī contentus
complain *vi* querī, conquerī; **~ of** (*person*) nōmen
dēferre (*gen*)
complainant *n* accūsātor *m*, petītor *m*
complaint *n* questus *m*, querimōnia *f*; (LAW)
crīmen *nt*; (MED) morbus *m*, valētūdō *f*
complaisance *n* cōmitās *f*, obsequium *nt*,
indulgentia *f*
complaisant *adj* cōmis, officiōsus, facilis
complement *n* complēmentum *nt*; numerus
suus *m*; **make up the ~ of** complēre
complete *vt* (*amount, time*) complēre, explēre;
(*work*) cōnficere, perficere, absolvere, peragere

♦ *adj* perfectus, absolūtus, integer; (*victory*) iūstus; (*amount*) explētus

completely *adv* funditus, omnīnō, absolūtē, plānē; penitus

completeness *n* integritās *f*; (*perfection*) perfectiō *f*

completion *n* (*process*) absolūtiō *f*, cōnfectiō *f*; (*end*) fīnis *m*; **bring to** ~ absolvere

complex *adj* implicātus, multiplex

complexion *n* color *m*

complexity *n* implicātiō *f*

compliance *n* accommodātiō *f*, obsequium *nt*, obtemperātiō *f*

compliant *adj* obsequēns, facilis

complicate *vt* implicāre, impedīre

complicated *adj* implicātus, involūtus, impedītus

complication *n* implicātiō *f*

complicity *n* cōnscientia *f*

compliment *n* blandīmentum *nt*, honōs *m* ♦ *vt* blandīrī, laudāre; ~ **on** grātulārī (*dat*) dē (*abl*)

complimentary *adj* honōrificus, blandus

compliments *npl* (*as greeting*) salūs *f*

comply *vi* obsequī (*dat*), obtemperāre (*dat*); mōrem gerere (*dat*), mōrigerārī (*dat*)

component *n* elementum *nt*, pars *f*

comport *vt* gerere

compose *vt* (*art*) compōnere, condere, pangere; (*whole*) efficere, cōnflāre; (*quarrel*) compōnere, dīrimere; (*disturbance*) sēdāre; **be composed of** cōnsistere ex (*abl*), cōnstāre ex (*abl*)

composed *adj* tranquillus, placidus

composer *n* auctor *m*, scrīptor *m*

composite *adj* multiplex

composition *n* (*process*) compositiō *f*, scrīptūra *f*; (*product*) opus *nt*, poēma *nt*, carmen *nt*; (*quality*) structūra *f*

composure *n* sēcūritās *f*, aequus animus *m*; (*face*) tranquillitās *f*

compound *vt* miscēre; (*words*) duplicāre, iungere ♦ *vi* (*agree*) pacīscī ♦ *adj* compositus ♦ *n* (*word*) iūnctum verbum *nt*; (*area*) saeptum *nt*

compound interest *n* anatocismus *m*

comprehend *vt* intellegere, comprehendere; (*include*) continēre, complectī

comprehensible *adj* perspicuus

comprehension *n* intellegentia *f*, comprehēnsiō *f*

comprehensive *adj* capāx; **be** ~ **lātē** patēre, multa complectī

compress *vt* comprimere, coartāre ♦ *n* fōmentum *nt*

compression *n* compressus *m*

comprise *vt* continēre, complectī, comprehendere

compromise *n* (*by one side*) accommodātiō *f*; (*by both sides*) comprōmissum *nt* ♦ *vi* comprōmittere ♦ *vt* implicāre, in suspiciōnem vocāre; **be compromised** in suspiciōnem venīre

comptroller *n* moderātor *m*

compulsion *n* necessitās *f*, vīs *f*; **under** ~ coāctus

compulsory *adj* necesse, lēge imperātus; **use** ~ **measures** vim adhibēre

compunction *n* paenitentia *f*

computation *n* ratiō *f*

compute *vt* computāre, ratiōnem dūcere

comrade *n* socius *m*, contubernālis *m*

comradeship *n* contubernium *nt*

concatenation *n* seriēs *f*

concave *adj* concavus

conceal *vt* cēlāre, abdere, abscondere; (*fact*) dissimulāre

concealment *n* occultātiō *f*; (*place*) latebrae *fpl*; (*of facts*) dissimulātiō *f*; **be in** ~ latēre, latitāre; **go into** ~ dēlitēscere

concede *vt* concēdere

conceit *n* (*idea*) nōtiō *f*; (*wit*) facētiae *fpl*; (*pride*) superbia *f*, adrogantia *f*, vānitās *f*

conceited *adj* glōriōsus, adrogāns

conceitedness *n* adrogantia *f*, vānitās *f*

conceive *vt* concipere, comprehendere, intellegere

concentrate *vt* (*in one place*) cōgere, congregāre; (*attention*) intendere, dēfīgere

concentrated *adj* dēnsus

concentration *n* animī intentiō *f*

concept *n* nōtiō *f*

conception *n* conceptus *m*; (*mind*) intellegentia *f*, īnfōrmātiō *f*; (*idea*) nōtiō *f*, cōgitātiō *f*, cōnsilium *nt*

concern *vt* (*refer*) attinēre ad (*acc*), interesse (*gen*); (*worry*) sollicitāre; **it concerns me** meā rēfert, meā interest; **as far as I am concerned** per mē ♦ *n* rēs *f*, negōtium *nt*; (*importance*) mōmentum *nt*; (*worry*) sollicitūdō *f*, cūra *f*; (*regret*) dolor *m*

concerned *adj* sollicitus, anxius; **be** ~ dolēre; **be** ~ **about** molestē ferre

concerning *prep* dē (*abl*)

concernment *n* sollicitūdō *f*

concert *n* (*music*) concentus *m*; (*agreement*) cōnsēnsus *m*; **in** ~ ex compositō, ūnō animō ♦ *vt* compōnere; (*plan*) inīre

concession *n* concessiō *f*; **by the** ~ **of** concessū (*gen*); **make a** ~ concēdere, tribuere

conciliate *vt* conciliāre

conciliation *n* conciliātiō *f*

conciliator *n* arbiter *m*

conciliatory *adj* pācificus

concise *adj* brevis; (*style*) dēnsus

concisely *adv* breviter

conciseness *n* brevitās *f*

conclave *n* sēcrētus cōnsessus *m*

conclude *vt* (*end*) termināre, fīnīre, cōnficere; (*settle*) facere, compōnere, pangere; (*infer*) īnferre, colligere

conclusion *n* (*end*) fīnis *m*; (*of action*) exitus *m*; (*of speech*) perōrātiō *f*; (*inference*) coniectūra *f*; (*decision*) placitum *nt*, sententia *f*; **in** ~ dēnique; **try conclusions with** contendere cum

conclusive *adj* certus, manifestus, gravis

conclusively *adv* sine dubiō

concoct *vt* coquere; (*fig*) cōnflāre

concoction *n* (*fig*) māchinātiō *f*

concomitant *adj* adiūnctus

concord *n* concordia *f*; (*music*) harmonia *f*

concordant *adj* concors

concordat *n* pactum *nt*, foedus *nt*

concourse *n* frequentia *f*, celebrātiō *f*; (*moving*) concursus *m*

concrete *adj* concrētus; **in the** ~ rē

concretion *n* concrētiō *f*

concubine n concubīna f
concupiscence n libīdō f
concur vi (time) concurrere; (opinion) cōnsentīre, adsentīre
concurrence n (time) concursus m; (opinion) cōnsēnsus m
concurrent adj (time) aequālis; (opinion) cōnsentāneus; **be ~** concurrere, cōnsentīre
concurrently adv simul, ūnā
concussion n ictus m
condemn vt damnāre, condemnāre; (disapprove) improbāre; **~ to death** capitis damnāre; **~ for treason** dē māiestāte damnāre
condemnation n damnātiō f; condemnātiō f
condemnatory adj damnātōrius
condense vt dēnsāre; (words) premere
condescend vi dēscendere, sē submittere
condescending adj cōmis
condescension n cōmitās f
condiment n condīmentum nt
condition n (of body) habitus m; (external) status m, condiciō f, rēs f; (in society) locus m, fortūna f; (of agreement) condiciō f, lēx f; **conditions of sale** mancipī lēx f; **on ~ that** eā condicione ut (subj); **in ~** (animals) nitidus ♦ vt fōrmāre, regere
conditional adj: **the assistance is ~ on** eā condiciōne succurritur ut (subj)
conditionally adv sub condiciōne
conditioned adj (character) mōrātus
condole vi: **~ with** cōnsōlārī
condolence n cōnsōlātiō f
condonation n venia f
condone vt condōnāre, ignōscere (dat)
conduce vi condūcere (ad), prōficere (ad)
conducive adj ūtilis, accommodātus
conduct vt dūcere; (escort) dēdūcere; (to a place) addūcere, perdūcere; (business) gerere, administrāre; (self) gerere ♦ n mōrēs mpl; (past) vīta f, facta ntpl; (business) administrātiō f; **safe ~** praesidium nt
conductor n dux m, ductor m
conduit n canālis m, aquae ductus m
cone n cōnus m
coney n cunīculus m
confabulate vi colloquī
confection n cuppēdō f
confectioner n cuppēdinārius m
confectionery n dulcia ntpl
confederacy n foederātae cīvitātēs fpl, societās f
confederate adj foederātus ♦ n socius m ♦ vi coniūrāre, foedus facere
confederation n societās f
confer vt cōnferre, tribuere ♦ vi colloquī, sermōnem cōnferre; **~ about** agere dē (abl)
conference n colloquium nt, congressus m
conferment n dōnātiō f
confess vt fatērī, cōnfitērī
confessedly adv manifestō
confession n cōnfessiō f
confidant n cōnscius m
confide vi fīdere (dat), cōnfīdere (dat) ♦ vt crēdere, committere
confidence n fidēs f, fīdūcia f; **have ~ in** fīdere (dat), cōnfīdere (dat); **inspire ~ in** fidem facere (dat); **tell in ~** tūtīs auribus dēpōnere

confident adj fīdens; **~ in** frētus (abl); **be ~ that** certō scīre, prō certō habēre
confidential adj arcānus, intimus
confidentially adv inter nōs
confidently adv fīdenter
confiding adj crēdulus
configuration n figūra f, fōrma f
confine vt (prison) inclūdere, in vincula conicere; (limit) termināre, circumscrībere; (restrain) coercēre, cohibēre; (to bed) dētinēre; **be confined** (women) parturīre
confinement n custōdia f, vincula ntpl, inclūsiō f; (women) puerperium nt
confines n fīnēs mpl
confirm vt (strength) corrōborāre, firmāre; (decision) sancīre, ratum facere; (fact) adfirmāre, comprobāre
confirmation n cōnfirmātiō f, adfirmātiō f
confirmed adj ratus
confiscate vt pūblicāre
confiscation n pūblicātiō f
conflagration n incendium nt, dēflāgrātiō f
conflict n (physical) concursus m; (hostile) certāmen nt, proelium nt; (verbal) contentiō f, contrōversia f; (contradiction) repugnantia f, discrepantia f ♦ vi inter sē repugnāre
conflicting adj contrārius
confluence n cōnfluēns m
confluent adj cōnfluēns
conform vt accommodāre ♦ vi sē cōnfōrmāre (ad), obsequī (dat), mōrem gerere (dat)
conformable adj accommodātus, conveniēns
conformably adv convenienter
conformation n structūra f, cōnfōrmātiō f
conformity n convenientia f, cōnsēnsus m
confound vt (mix) cōnfundere, permiscēre; (amaze) obstupefacere; (thwart) frustrārī; (suppress) opprimere, obruere; **~ you!** dī tē perduint
confounded adj miser, sacer, nefandus
confoundedly adv mīrum quantum nefāriē
confraternity n frāternitās f
confront vt sē oppōnere (dat), obviam īre (dat), sē cōram offerre
confuse vt permiscēre, perturbāre
confused adj perturbātus
confusedly adv perturbātē, prōmiscuē
confusion n perturbātiō f; (shame) rubor m
confutation n refūtātiō f
confute vt refūtāre, redarguere, convincere
congé n commeātus m
congeal vt congelāre, dūrāre ♦ vi concrēscere
congealed adj concrētus
congenial adj concors, congruēns, iūcundus
congeniality n concordia f, mōrum similitūdō f
congenital adj nātīvus
conger n conger m
congested adj refertus, dēnsus; (with people) frequentissimus
congestion n congeriēs f; frequentia f
conglomerate vt glomerāre
conglomeration n congeriēs f, cumulus m
congratulate vt grātulārī (dat)
congratulation n grātulātiō f
congratulatory adj grātulābundus

congregate vt congregāre, cōgere ♦ vi
convenīre, congregārī
congregation n conventus m, coetus m
congress n conventus m, cōnsessus m,
concilium nt; senātus m
congruence n convenientia f
congruent adj conveniēns, congruēns
congruently adv convenienter, congruenter
congruous adj see **congruent**
conical adj turbinātus
coniferous adj cōnifer
conjectural adj opīnābilis
conjecturally adv coniectūrā
conjecture n coniectūra f ♦ vt conicere, augurārī
conjoin vt coniungere
conjoint adj coniūnctus
conjointly adv coniūnctē, ūnā
conjugal adj coniugālis
conjugate vt dēclīnāre
conjugation n (GRAM) dēclīnātiō f
conjunct adj coniūnctus
conjunction n coniūnctiō f, concursus m
conjure vt (entreat) obtestārī, obsecrāre; (spirits)
ēlicere, ciēre ♦ vi praestigiīs ūtī
conjurer n praestigiātor m
conjuring n praestigiae fpl
connate adj innātus, nātūrā īnsitus
connect vt iungere, coniungere, cōpulāre,
connectere
connected adj coniūnctus; (unbroken) continēns;
(by marriage) adfīnis; **be ~ with** contingere; **be
closely ~ with** inhaerēre (dat), cohaerēre cum
(abl)
connectedly adv coniūnctē, continenter
connection n coniūnctiō f, contextus m, seriēs
f; (kin) necessitūdō f; (by marriage) adfīnitās f;
~ between ... and ... ratiō (gen) ... cum ... (abl); **I
have no ~ with you** nīl mihī tēcum est
connivance n venia f, dissimulātiō f
connive vi conīvēre in (abl), dissimulāre
connoisseur n intellegēns m
connotation n vīs f, significātiō f
connote vt significāre
connubial adj coniugālis
conquer vt vincere, superāre
conquerable adj superābilis, expugnābilis
conqueror n victor m
conquest n victōria f; (town) expugnātiō f; (prize)
praemium nt, praeda f; **the ~ of Greece** Graecia
capta
conscience n cōnscientia f; **guilty ~** mala
cōnscientia; **have a clear ~** nullīus culpae sibi
cōnscium esse; **have no ~** nullam rēligiōnem
habēre
conscientious adj probus, rēligiōsus
conscientiously adv bonā fidē, rēligiōsē
conscientiousness n fidēs f, rēligiō f
conscious adj sibī cōnscius; (aware) gnārus;
(physically) mentis compos; **be ~** sentīre
consciously adv sciēns
consciousness n animus m; (of action)
cōnscientia f; **he lost ~** animus eum relīquit
conscript n tīrō m ♦ vt cōnscrībere
conscription n dēlēctus m; (of wealth) pūblicātiō
f

consecrate vt dēdicāre, cōnsecrāre; (self)
dēvovēre
consecrated adj sacer
consecration n dēdicātiō f, cōnsecrātiō f; (self)
dēvōtiō f
consecutive adj dēinceps, continuus
consecutively adv dēinceps, ōrdine
consensus n cōnsēnsus m
consent vi adsentīre (dat), adnuere (inf);
(together) cōnsentīre ♦ n (one side) adsēnsus
m; (all) cōnsēnsus m; **by common ~** omnium
cōnsēnsū
consequence n ēventus m, exitus m; (LOGIC)
conclūsiō f; (importance) mōmentum nt,
auctōritās f; **it is of ~ interest**; **what will be the
~ of?** quō ēvādet?
consequent adj cōnsequēns
consequential adj cōnsentāneus; (person)
adrogāns
consequently adv itaque, igitur, proptereā
conservation n cōnservātiō f
conservative adj reī pūblicae cōnservandae
studiōsus; (estimate) mediōcris; **~ party**
optimātēs mpl
conservator n custōs m, cōnservātor m
conserve vt cōnservāre, servāre
consider vt cōnsīderāre, contemplārī; (reflect)
sēcum volūtāre, meditarī, dēlīberāre, cōgitāre;
(deem) habēre, dūcere; (respect) respicere,
observāre
considerable adj aliquantus, nōnnullus; (person)
illūstris
considerably adv aliquantum; (with compar)
aliquantō, multō
considerate adj hūmānus, benignus
considerately adv hūmānē, benignē
consideration n cōnsīderātiō f, contemplātiō
f, dēlīberātiō f; (respect) respectus m, ratiō f;
(importance) mōmentum nt; (reason) ratiō f; (pay)
pretium nt; **for a ~** mercēde, datā mercēde; **in
~ of** propter (acc), prō (abl); **on no ~** nēquāquam;
with ~ cōnsultō; **without ~** temerē; **take into
~** ad cōnsilium dēferre; **show ~ for** respectum
habēre (gen)
considered adj (reasons) exquīsītus
considering prep prō (abl), propter (acc) ♦ conj ut,
quōniam
consign vt mandāre, committere
consist vi cōnstāre; **~ in** cōnstāre ex (abl),
continērī (abl), positum esse in (abl); **~ with**
congruere (dat), convenīre (dat)
consistence n firmitās f
consistency n cōnstantia f
consistent adj cōnstāns; (with) cōnsentāneus,
cōngruens; (of movement) aequābilis; **be
~** cohaerēre
consistently adv cōnstanter
consolable adj cōnsōlābilis
consolation n cōnsōlātiō f; (thing) sōlācium nt
consolatory adj cōnsōlātōrius
console vt cōnsōlārī
consoler n cōnsōlātor m
consolidate vt (liquid) cōgere; (strength)
corrōborāre; (gains) obtinēre ♦ vi concrēscere
consolidation n concrētiō f; cōnfirmātiō f
consonance n concentus m

consonant adj cōnsonus, haud absonus ♦ n cōnsonāns f
consort n cōnsors m/f, socius m; (married) coniunx m/f ♦ vi: ~ **with** familiāriter ūtī (abl), coniūnctissimē vīvere cum (abl)
conspectus n summārium nt
conspicuous adj ēminēns, īnsignis, manifestus; **be ~** ēminēre
conspicuously adv manifestō, palam, ante oculōs
conspiracy n coniūrātiō f
conspirator n coniūrātus m
conspire vi coniūrāre; (for good) cōnspīrāre
constable n lictor m
constancy n cōnstantia f, firmitās f; **with ~** cōnstanter
constant adj cōnstāns; (faithful) fīdus, fidēlis; (continuous) adsiduus
constantly adv adsiduē, saepe, crēbrō
constellation n sīdus nt
consternation n trepidātiō f, pavor m; **throw into ~** perterrēre, cōnsternere
constituency n suffrāgātōrēs mpl
constituent adj: **~ part** elementum nt ♦ n (voter) suffrāgātor m
constitute vt creāre, cōnstituere; esse
constitution n nātūra f, status m; (body) habitus m; (POL) cīvitātis fōrma f, reī pūblicae status m, lēgēs fpl
constitutional adj lēgitimus, iūstus
constitutionally adv ē rē pūblicā
constrain vt cōgere
constraint n vīs f; **under ~** coāctus; **without ~** suā sponte
constrict vt comprimere, cōnstringere
constriction n contractiō f
construct vt aedificāre, exstruere
construction n aedificātiō f; (method) structūra f; (meaning) interpretātiō f; **put a wrong ~ on** in malam partem interpretārī
construe vt interpretārī
consul n cōnsul m; **~ elect** cōnsul dēsignātus; **ex-consul** cōnsulāris m
consular adj cōnsulāris
consulship n cōnsulātus m; **stand for the ~** cōnsulātum petere; **hold the ~** cōnsulātum gerere; **in my ~** mē cōnsule
consult vt cōnsulere; **~ the interests of** cōnsulere (dat) ♦ vi dēlīberāre, cōnsiliārī
consultation n (asking) cōnsultātiō f; (discussion) dēlīberātiō f
consume vt cōnsūmere, absūmere; (food) edere
consumer n cōnsūmptor m
consummate adj summus, perfectus ♦ vt perficere, absolvere
consummation n absolūtiō f; fīnis m, ēventus m
consumption n cōnsūmptiō f; (disease) tābēs f, phthisis f
consumptive adj pulmōnārius
contact n tāctus m, contāgiō f; **come in ~ with** contingere
contagion n contāgiō f
contagious adj tābificus; **be ~** contāgiīs vulgārī
contain vt capere, continēre; (self) cohibēre
container n vās nt
contaminate vt contāmināre, īnficere

contamination n contāgiō f, lābēs f
contemplate vt contemplārī, intuērī; (action) in animō habēre; (prospect) spectāre
contemplation n contemplātiō f; (thought) cōgitātiō f
contemplative adj cōgitāns, meditāns; **in a ~ mood** cōgitātiōnī dēditus
contemporaneous adj aequālis
contemporaneously adv simul
contemporary adj aequālis
contempt n contemptiō f; **be an object of ~** contemptuī esse; **treat with ~** contemptum habēre, conculcāre
contemptible adj contemnendus, abiectus, vīlis
contemptuous adj fastīdiōsus
contemptuously adv contemptim, fastīdiōsē
contend vi certāre, contendere; (in battle) dīmicāre, pugnāre; (in words) adfirmāre, adsevērāre
contending adj contrārius
content adj contentus ♦ n aequus animus m ♦ vt placēre (dat), satisfacere (dat); **be contented** satis habēre
contentedly adv aequō animō
contention n certāmen nt; contrōversia f; (opinion) sententia f
contentious adj pugnāx, lītigiōsus
contentiously adv pugnāciter
contentiousness n contrōversiae studium nt
contentment n aequus animus m
contents n quod inest, quae insunt; (of speech) argūmentum nt
conterminous adj adfīnis
contest n certāmen nt, contentiō f ♦ vt (LAW) lēge agere dē (abl); (office) petere; (dispute) repugnāre (dat), resistere (dat)
contestable adj contrōversus
contestant n petītor m, aemulus m
context n contextus m
contiguity n vīcīnia f, propinquitās f
contiguous adj vīcīnus, adiacēns; **be ~ to** adiacēre (dat), contingere
continence n continentia f, abstinentia f
continent adj continēns, abstinēns ♦ n continēns f
continently adv continenter, abstinenter
contingency n cāsus m, rēs f
contingent adj fortuītus ♦ n (MIL) numerus m
continual adj adsiduus, perpetuus
continually adv adsiduē, semper
continuance n perpetuitās f, adsiduitās f
continuation n continuātiō f; (of a command) prōrogātiō f; (of a story) reliqua pars f
continue vt continuāre; (time) prōdūcere; (command) prōrogāre ♦ vi (action) pergere; (time) manēre; (endurance) perstāre, dūrāre; **~ to** imperf indic
continuity n continuātiō f; (of speech) perpetuitās f
continuous adj continuus, continēns, perpetuus
continuously adv perpetuō, continenter
contort vt contorquēre, dētorquēre
contortion n distortiō f
contour n fōrma f

contraband adj interdictus, vetitus
contract n pactum nt, mandātum nt,
conventum nt; (POL) foedus nt; **trial for a
breach of** ~ mandātī iūdicium nt ♦ vt (narrow)
contrahere, addūcere; (short) dēminuere;
(illness) contrahere; (agreement) pacīscī; (for work)
locāre; (to do work) condūcere ♦ vi pacīscī
contraction n contractiō f; (word) compendium
nt
contractor n redemptor m, conductor m
contradict vt (person) contrādīcere (dat),
refrāgārī (dat); (statement) īnfitiās īre (dat); (self)
repugnāre (dat)
contradiction n repugnantia f, īnfitiae fpl
contradictory adj repugnāns, contrārius; **be**
~ inter sē repugnāre
contradistinction n oppositiō f
contraption n māchina f
contrariety n repugnantia f
contrariwise adv ē contrāriō
contrary adj contrārius, adversus; (person)
difficilis, mōrōsus; ~ **to** contrā (acc), praeter
(acc); ~ **to expectations** praeter opiniōnem ♦ n
contrārium nt; **on the** ~ ē contrāriō, contrā;
(retort) immo
contrast n discrepantia f ♦ vt comparāre,
oppōnere ♦ vi discrepāre
contravene vt (LAW) violāre; (statement)
contrādīcere (dat)
contravention n violātiō f
contribute vt cōnferre, adferre, contribuere ♦ vi:
~ **towards** cōnferre ad (acc), adiuvāre; ~ **to the
cost** impēnsās cōnferre
contribution n conlātiō f; (money) stipem (no
nom) f
contributor n quī cōnfert
contributory adj adiūnctus
contrite adj paenitēns
contrition n paenitentia f
contrivance n māchinātiō f, excōgitātiō f;
(thing) māchina f; (idea) cōnsilium nt; (deceit)
dolus m
contrive vt māchinārī, excōgitāre, struere; (to
do) efficere ut
contriver n māchinātor m, artifex m, auctor m
control n (restraint) frēnum nt; (power) moderātiō
f, potestās f, imperium nt; **have ~ of** praeesse
(dat); **out of** ~ impotēns ♦ vt moderārī (dat),
imperāre (dat)
controller n moderātor m
controversial adj concertātōrius
controversy n contrōversia f, disceptātiō f
controvert vt redarguere, impugnāre, in
dubium vocāre
contumacious adj contumāx, pervicāx
contumaciously adv contumāciter,
pervicāciter
contumacy n contumācia f, pervicācia f
contusion n sūgillātiō f
conundrum n aenigma nt
convalesce vi convalēscere
convalescence n melior valētūdō f
convalescent adj convalēscēns
convene vt convocāre
convenience n opportūnitās f, commoditās
f; (thing) commodum nt; **at your** ~ commodō tuō

convenient adj idōneus, commodus,
opportūnus; **be** ~ convenīre; **very**
~ percommodus
conveniently adv opportūnē, commodē
convention n (meeting) conventus m; (agreement)
conventum nt; (custom) mōs m, iūsta ntpl
conventional adj iūstus, solitus
conventionality n mōs m, cōnsuētūdō f
converge vi in medium vergere, in eundem
locum tendere
conversant adj perītus, doctus, exercitātus; **be**
~ **with** versārī in (abl)
conversation n sermō m, colloquium nt
converse n sermō m, colloquium nt; (opposite)
contrārium nt ♦ vi colloquī, sermōnem cōnferre
♦ adj contrārius
conversely adv ē contrāriō, contrā
conversion n mūtātiō f; (moral) mōrum
ēmendātiō f
convert vt mūtāre, convertere; (to an opinion)
dēdūcere ♦ n discipulus m
convertible adj commūtābilis
convex adj convexus
convexity n convexum nt
convey vt vehere, portāre, convehere; (property)
abaliēnāre; (knowledge) commūnicāre;
(meaning) significāre; ~ **across** trānsmittere,
trādūcere, trānsvehere; ~ **away** auferre,
āvehere; ~ **down** dēvehere, dēportāre; ~ **into**
importāre, invehere; ~ **to** advehere, adferre;
~ **up** subvehere
conveyance n vehiculum nt; (property)
abaliēnātiō f
convict vt (prove guilty) convincere; (sentence)
damnāre ♦ n reus m
conviction n (LAW) damnātiō f; (argument)
persuāsiō f; (belief) fidēs f; **carry** ~ fidem facere;
have a ~ persuāsum habēre
convince vt persuādēre (dat); **I am firmly
convinced** mihi persuāsum habeō
convincing adj (argument) gravis; (evidence)
manifestus
convincingly adv manifestō
convivial adj convīvalis, festīvus
conviviality n festīvitās f
convocation n conventus m
convoke vt convocāre
convolution n spīra f
convoy n praesidium nt ♦ vt prōsequī
convulse vt agitāre; **be convulsed with
laughter** sē in cachinnōs effundere
convulsion n (MED) convulsiō f; (POL) tumultus m
convulsive adj spasticus
coo vi gemere
cook vt coquere ♦ n coquus m
cookery n ars coquīnāria f
cool adj frīgidus; (conduct) impudens; (mind)
impavidus, lentus ♦ n frīgus nt ♦ vt refrīgerāre;
(passion) restinguere, sēdāre ♦ vi refrīgēscere,
refrīgerārī, dēfervēscere
coolly adv aequō animō; impudenter
coolness n frīgus nt; (mind) aequus animus m;
impudentia f
coop n hara f; (barrel) cūpa f ♦ vt inclūdere
co-operate vi operam cōnferre; ~ **with**
adiuvāre, socius esse (gen)

co-operation n cōnsociātiō f; auxilium nt, opera f
co-operative adj (person) officiōsus
co-operator n socius m
co-opt vt cooptāre
coot n fulica f
copartner n socius m
copartnership n societās f
cope vi: ~ with contendere cum (abl); able to ~ with pār (dat); **unable to ~ with** impār (dat)
copier n librārius m
coping n fastīgium nt
copious adj cōpiōsus, largus, plēnus, abundāns
copiously adv cōpiōsē, abundanter
copiousness n cōpia f, ūbertās f
copper n aes nt ♦ adj aēneus
coppersmith n faber aerārius m
coppice, copse n dūmētum nt, virgultum nt
copy n exemplar nt ♦ vt imitārī; (writing) exscrībere, trānscrībere
copyist n librārius m
coracle n linter f
coral n cūrālium nt
cord n fūniculus m
cordage n fūnēs mpl
cordial adj cōmis, festīvus, amīcus; (greetings) multus
cordiality n cōmitās f, studium nt
cordially adv cōmiter, libenter, ex animō
cordon n corōna f
core n (fig) nucleus m
cork n sūber nt; (bark) cortex m
corn n frūmentum nt ♦ adj frūmentārius; (on the foot) clāvus m; **price of ~** annōna f
corndealer n frūmentārius m
cornel n (tree) cornus f
corner n angulus m
cornet n cornū nt
cornfield n seges f
cornice n corōna f
coronet n diadēma nt
corporal adj corporeus
corporal punishment n verbera ntpl
corporation n collēgium nt; (civic) magistrātūs mpl
corporeal adj corporeus
corps n manus f
corpse n cadāver nt
corpulence n obēsum corpus nt
corpulent adj obēsus, pinguis
corpuscle n corpusculum nt
corral n praesēpe nt
correct vt corrigere, ēmendāre; (person) castīgāre ♦ adj vērus; (language) integer; (style) ēmendātus
correction n ēmendātiō f; (moral) corrēctiō f; (punishment) castīgātiō f
correctly adv bene, vērē
correctness n (fact) vēritās f; (language) integritās f; (moral) probitās f
corrector n ēmendātor m, corrēctor m
correspond vi (agree) respondēre (dat), congruere (dat); (by letter) inter sē scrībere
correspondence n similitūdō f; epistulae fpl
correspondent n epistulārum scrīptor m
corresponding adj pār
correspondingly adv pariter

corridor n porticus f
corrigible adj ēmendābilis
corroborate vt cōnfirmāre
corroboration n cōnfirmātiō f
corrode vt ērōdere, edere
corrosive adj edāx
corrugate vt rūgāre
corrugated adj rūgōsus
corrupt vt corrumpere, dēprāvāre; (text) vitiāre ♦ adj corruptus, vitiātus; (person) prāvus, vēnālis; (text) vitiātus
corrupter n corruptor m
corruptible adj (matter) dissolūbilis; (person) vēnālis
corruption n (of matter) corruptiō f; (moral) corruptēla f, dēprāvātiō f; (bribery) ambitus m
corsair n pīrāta m
cortège n pompa f
coruscate vi fulgēre
coruscation n fulgor m
Corybant n Corybas m
Corybantic adj Corybantius
cosmetic n medicāmen nt
cosmic adj mundānus
cosmopolitan adj mundānus
cosmos n mundus m
cost vt emī, stāre (dat); **it ~ me dear** māgnō mihi stetit, male ēmī; **it ~ me a talent** talentō mihi stetit, talentō ēmī; **it ~ me my freedom** lībertātem perdidī ♦ n pretium nt, impēnsa f; **~ of living** annōna f; **to your ~** incommodō tuō, dētrīmentō tuō; **at the ~ of one's reputation** violātā fāmā, nōn salvā existimātiōne; **I sell at ~ price** quantī ēmī vēndō
costliness n sūmptus m; cāritās f
costly adj cārus; (furnishings) lautus, sūmptuōsus
costume n habitus m
cosy adj commodus
cot n lectulus m
cote n columbārium nt
cottage n casa f, tugurium nt
cottager n rūsticus m
cotton n (tree) gossympinus f; (cloth) xylinum nt
couch n lectus m ♦ vi recumbere ♦ vt (lance) intendere; (words) exprimere, reddere
cough n tussis f ♦ vi tussīre
council n concilium nt; (small) cōnsilium nt
councillor n (town) dēcuriō m
counsel n (debate) cōnsultātiō f; (advice) cōnsilium nt; (LAW) advocātus m, patrōnus m; **take ~** cōnsiliārī, dēlīberāre; **take ~ of** cōnsulere ♦ vt suādēre (dat), monēre
counsellor n cōnsiliārius m
count vt numerāre, computāre; **~ as** dūcere, habēre; **~ amongst** pōnere in (abl); **~ up** vt ēnumerāre; **~ upon** cōnfidere (dat); **be counted among** in numerō esse (gen) ♦ vi aestimārī, habērī ♦ n ratiō f; (in indictment) caput nt; (title) comes m
countenance n faciēs f, vultus m, ōs nt; (fig) favor m; **put out of ~** conturbāre ♦ vt favēre (dat), indulgēre (dat)
counter n (for counting) calculus m; (for play) tessera f; (shop) mēnsa f ♦ adj contrārius ♦ adv contrā, obviam ♦ vt obsistere (dat), respondēre (dat)

counteract vt obsistere (dat), adversārī (dat); (malady) medērī (dat)
counterattack vt in vicem oppugnāre, adgredī
counterattraction n altera illecebra f
counterbalance vt compēnsāre, exaequāre
counterclockwise adv sinistrōrsus
counterfeit adj falsus, fūcātus, adsimulātus, fictus ♦ vt fingere, simulāre, imitārī
countermand vt renūntiāre
counterpane n lōdīx f, strāgulum nt
counterpart n pār m/f/nt
counterpoise n aequum pondus nt ♦ vt compēnsāre, exaequāre
countersign n (MIL) tessera f
counting table n abacus m
countless adj innumerābilis
countrified adj agrestis, rūsticus
country n (region) regiō f, terra f; (territory) fīnēs mpl; (native) patria f; (not town) rūs nt; (open) agrī mpl; **of our ~** nostrās; **live in the ~** rūsticārī; **living in the ~** rūsticātiō f
country house n vīlla f
countryman n agricola m; **fellow ~** populāris m, cīvis m
countryside n agrī mpl, rus nt
couple n pār nt; **a ~ of** duo ♦ vt cōpulare, coniungere
couplet n distichon nt
courage n fortitūdō f, animus m; (MIL) virtūs f; **have the ~ to** audēre; **lose ~** animōs dēmittere; **take ~** bonō animō esse
courageous adj fortis, ācer; audāx
courageously adv fortiter, ācriter
courier n tabellārius m
course n (movement) cursus m; (route) iter nt; (sequence) seriēs f; (career) dēcursus; (for races) stadium nt, circus m; (of dinner) ferculum nt; (of stones) ōrdō m; (of water) lāpsus m; **of ~** certē, sānē, scīlicet; **as a matter of ~** continuō; **in due ~** mox; **in the ~ of** inter (acc), in (abl); **keep on one's ~** cursum tenēre; **be driven off one's ~** dēicī; **second ~** secunda mēnsa
court n (space) ārea f; (of house) ātrium nt; (of king) aula f; (suite) cohors f, comitēs mpl; (LAW) iūdicium nt, iūdicēs mpl; **pay ~ to** ambīre, īnservīre (dat); **hold a ~** forum agere; **bring into ~** in iūs vocāre ♦ vt colere, ambīre; (danger) sē offerre (dat); (woman) petere
courteous adj cōmis, urbānus, hūmānus
courteously adv cōmiter, urbānē
courtesan n meretrīx f
courtesy n (quality) cōmitās f, hūmānitās f; (act) officium nt
courtier n aulicus m; **courtiers** pl aula f
courtly adj officiōsus
cousin n cōnsobrīnus m, cōnsobrīna f
cove n sinus m
covenant n foedus nt, pactum nt ♦ vi pacīscī
cover vt tegere, operīre; (hide) vēlāre; (march) claudere; **~ over** obdūcere; **~ up** vi obtegere ♦ n integumentum nt, operculum nt; (shelter) latebrae fpl, suffugium nt; (pretence) speciēs f; **under ~ of** sub (abl), sub speciē (gen); **take ~** dēlitēscere
covering n integumentum nt, involucrum nt, operculum nt; (of couch) strāgulum nt

coverlet n lōdīx f
covert adj occultus; (language) oblīquus ♦ n latebra f, perfugium nt; (thicket) dūmētum nt
covertly adv occultē, sēcrētō
covet vt concupīscere, expetere
covetous adj avidus, cupidus
covetously adv avidē, cupidē
covetousness n aviditās f, cupiditās f
covey n grex f
cow n vacca f ♦ vt terrēre
coward n ignāvus m
cowardice n ignāvia f
cowardly adj ignāvus
cower vi subsīdere
cowherd n bubulcus m
cowl n cucullus m
coxswain n rēctor m
coy adj pudens, verēcundus
coyly adv pudenter, modestē
coyness n pudor m, verēcundia f
cozen vt fallere, dēcipere
crab n cancer m
crabbed adj mōrōsus, difficilis
crack n (chink) rīma f; (sound) crepitus m ♦ vt findere, frangere; (whip) crepitāre (abl) ♦ vi (open) fatīscere; (sound) crepāre, crepitāre
crackle vi crepitāre
crackling n crepitus m
cradle n cūnae fpl; (fig) incūnābula ntpl
craft n ars f; (deceit) dolus m; (boat) nāvigium nt
craftily adv callidē, sollerter; dolōsē
craftsman n artifex m, faber m
craftsmanship n ars f, artificium nt
crafty adj callidus, sollers; dolōsus
crag n rūpēs f, scopulus m
cram vt farcīre, refercīre; (with food) sagīnāre
cramp n convulsiō f; (tool) cōnfībula f ♦ vt coercēre, coartāre
crane n (bird) grus f; (machine) māchina f, trochlea f
crank n uncus m; (person) ineptus m
crannied adj rīmōsus
cranny n rīma f
crash n (fall) ruīna f; (noise) fragor m ♦ vi ruere; strepere
crass adj crassus; **~ stupidity** mera stultitia
crate n crātēs fpl
crater n crātēr m
cravat n focāle nt
crave vt (desire) concupīscere, adpetere, exoptāre; (request) ōrāre, obsecrāre
craven adj ignāvus
craving n cupīdō f, dēsīderium nt, adpetītiō f
crawl vi (animal) serpere; (person) rēpere
crayfish n commarus m
craze n libīdō f ♦ vt mentem aliēnāre
craziness n dēmentia f
crazy adj dēmēns, fatuus
creak vi crepāre
creaking n crepitus m
cream n spūma lactis f; (fig) flōs m
crease n rūga f ♦ vt rūgāre
create vt creāre, facere, gignere
creation n (process) fabricātiō f; (result) opus nt; (human) hominēs mpl

creative adj (nature) creātrīx; (mind) inventor, inventrīx
creator n creātor m, auctor m, opifex m
creature n animal nt; (person) homō m/f
credence n fidēs f
credentials n litterae commendātīciae fpl; (fig) auctōritās f
credibility n fidēs f; (source) auctōritās f
credible adj crēdibilis; (witness) locuplēs
credit n (belief) fidēs f; (repute) existimātiō f; (character) auctōritās f, grātia f; (COMM) fidēs f; **be a ~ to** decus esse (gen); **it is to your ~** tibī laudī est; **give ~ for** laudem tribuere (gen); **have ~** fidē stāre ♦ vt crēdere (dat); (with money) acceptum referre (dat)
creditable adj honestus, laudābilis
creditably adv honestē, cum laude
creditor n crēditor m
credulity n crēdulitās f
credulous adj crēdulus
creed n dogma nt
creek n sinus m
creel n vīdulus m
creep vi (animal) serpere; (person) rēpere; (flesh) horrēre
cremate vt cremāre
crescent n lūna f
crescent-shaped adj lūnātus
cress n nasturtium nt
crest n crista f
crested adj cristātus
crestfallen adj dēmissus
crevasse n hiātus m
crevice n rīma f
crew n nautae mpl, rēmigēs mpl, grex f, turba f
crib n (cot) lectulus m; (manger) praesēpe nt
cricket n gryllus m
crier n praecō m
crime n scelus nt, facinus nt, flāgitium nt
criminal adj scelestus, facinorōsus, flāgitiōsus ♦ n reus m
criminality n scelus nt
criminally adv scelestē, flāgitiōsē
crimson n coccum nt ♦ adj coccineus
cringe vi adūlārī, adsentārī
crinkle n rūga f
cripple vt dēbilitāre, mūtilāre; (fig) frangere
crisis n discrīmen nt
crisp adj fragilis; (manner) alacer; (hair) crispus
crisscross adj in quīncūncem dispositus
criterion n index m, indicium nt; **take as a ~** referre ad (acc)
critic n iūdex m; (literary) criticus, grammaticus m; (adverse) castīgātor m
critical adj (mind) accūrātus, ēlegāns; (blame) cēnsōrius, sevērus; (danger) perīculōsus, dubius; **~ moment** discrīmen nt
critically adv accūrātē, ēleganter; sevērē; cum perīculō
criticism n iūdicium nt; (adverse) reprehēnsiō f
criticize vt iūdicāre; reprehendere, castīgāre
croak vi (raven) crōcīre; (frog) coaxāre
croaking n cantus m ♦ adj raucus
crock n olla f

crockery n fictilia ntpl
crocodile n crocodīlus m; **weep ~ tears** lacrimās cōnfingere
crocus n crocus m
croft n agellus m
crone n anus f
crony n sodālis m
crook n pedum nt ♦ vt incurvāre
crooked adj incurvus, aduncus; (deformed) prāvus; (winding) flexuōsus; (morally) perversus
crookedly adv perversē, prāvē
crookedness n prāvitās f
croon vt, vi cantāre
crop n (grain) seges f, messis f; (tree) fructus m; (bird) ingluviēs f ♦ vt (reap) metere; (graze) carpere, tondēre; **~ up** vi intervenīre
cross n (mark) decussis m; (torture) crux f ♦ adj trānsversus, oblīquus; (person) acerbus, īrātus ♦ vt trānsīre; (water) trāicere; (mountain) trānscendere; superāre; (enemy) obstāre (dat), frustrārī; **~ out** vt (writing) expungere ♦ vi trānsīre; **~ over** (on foot) trānsgredī; (by sea) trānsmittere
crossbar n iugum nt
crossbow n scorpiō m
cross-examination n interrogātiō f
cross-examine vt interrogāre, percontārī
cross-grained adj (fig) mōrōsus
crossing n trānsitus m; (on water) trāiectus m
cross purpose n: **be at cross purposes** dīversa spectāre
cross-question vt interrogāre
crossroads n quadrivium nt
crosswise adv ex trānsversō; **divide ~** decussāre
crotchety adj mōrōsus, difficilis
crouch vi subsīdere, sē submittere
crow n cornīx f; **as the ~ flies** rēctā regiōne ♦ vi cantāre; (fig) exsultāre, gestīre
crowbar n vectis m
crowd n turba f, concursus m, frequentia f; (small) grex m; multitūdō f; **in crowds** gregātim ♦ vi frequentāre, celebrāre ♦ vt (place) complēre; (person) stīpāre
crowded adj frequēns
crown n corōna f; (royal) diadēma nt; (of head) vertex m; (fig) apex m, flōs m; **the ~ of** summus ♦ vt corōnāre; (fig) cumulāre, fastīgium impōnere (dat)
crucial adj gravissimus, māximī mōmentī; **~ moment** discrīmen nt
crucifixion n crucis supplicium nt
crucify vt crucī suffīgere
crude adj crūdus; (style) dūrus, inconcinnus
crudely adv dūrē, asperē
crudity n asperitās f
cruel adj crūdēlis, saevus, atrōx
cruelly adv crūdēliter, atrōciter
cruelty n crūdēlitās f, saevitia f, atrōcitās f
cruise n nāvigātiō f ♦ vi nāvigāre
cruiser n speculātōria nāvis f
crumb n mīca f
crumble vi corruere, putrem fierī ♦ vt putrefacere, friāre
crumbling adj putris

crumple *vt* rūgāre
crunch *vt* dentibus frangere
crupper *n* postilēna *f*
crush *vt* frangere, contundere, obterere; *(fig)*
 adflīgere, opprimere, obruere ♦ *n* turba *f*,
 frequentia *f*
crust *n* crusta *f*; *(bread)* frustum *nt*
crusty *adj* *(fig)* stomachōsus
crutch *n* baculum *nt*
cry *vt, vi* clāmāre, clāmitāre; *(weep)* flēre;
 (infant) vāgīre; **cry down** dētrectāre; **cry
 out** exclāmāre, vōciferārī; **cry out against**
 adclāmāre, reclāmāre; **cry up** laudāre,
 vēnditāre ♦ *n* clāmor *m*, vōx *f*; *(child's)* vāgītus *m*;
 (of grief) plōrātus *m*
cryptic *adj* arcānus
crystal *n* crystallum *nt* ♦ *adj* crystallinus
cub *n* catulus *m*
cube *n* cubus *m*
cubit *n* cubitum *nt*
cuckoo *n* coccyx *m*
cucumber *n* cucumis *m*
cud *n*: **chew the cud** rūminārī
cudgel *n* fustis *m* ♦ *vt* verberāre
cue *n* signum *nt*, indicium *nt*
cuff *n* *(blow)* alapa *f*
cuirass *n* lōrīca *f*
culinary *adj* coquīnārius
cull *vt* legere, carpere, dēlībāre
culminate *vi* ad summum fastīgium venīre
culmination *n* fastīgium *nt*
culpability *n* culpa *f*, noxa *f*
culpable *adj* nocēns
culprit *n* reus *m*
cultivate *vt* *(land)* colere, subigere; *(mind)*
 excolere; *(interest)* fovēre, studēre *(dat)*
cultivation *n* cultus *m*, cultūra *f*
cultivator *n* cultor *m*, agricola *m*
cultural *adj* hūmānior
culture *n* hūmānitās *f*, bonae artēs *fpl*
cultured *adj* doctus, litterātus
culvert *n* cloāca *f*
cumber *vt* impedīre, obesse *(dat)*; *(load)* onerāre
cumbersome *adj* molestus, gravis
cumulative *adj* alius ex aliō; **be ~** cumulārī
cuneiform *adj* cuneātus
cunning *adj* callidus, astūtus ♦ *n* ars *f*, astūtia *f*,
 calliditās *f*
cunningly *adv* callidē, astūtē
cup *n* pōculum *nt*; **drink the cup of** *(fig)*
 exanclāre, exhaurīre; **in one's cups** ēbrius,
 pōtus
cupboard *n* armārium *nt*
Cupid *n* Cupīdō *m*, Amor *m*
cupidity *n* avāritia *f*
cupola *n* tholus *m*
cupping glass *n* cucurbita *f*
cur *n* canis *m*
curable *adj* sānābilis
curative *adj* salūbris
curator *n* custōs *m*
curb *vt* frēnāre, īnfrēnāre; *(fig)* coercēre,
 cohibēre ♦ *n* frēnum *nt*
curdle *vt* cōgere ♦ *vi* concrēscere

curds *n* concrētum lac *nt*
cure *vt* sānāre, medērī *(dat)* ♦ *n* remedium *nt*;
 (process) sānātiō *f*
curio *n* dēliciae *fpl*
curiosity *n* studium *nt*; *(thing)* mīrāculum *nt*
curious *adj* *(inquisitive)* cūriōsus, cupidus; *(artistic)*
 ēlābōrātus; *(strange)* mīrus, novus
curiously *adv* cūriōsē; summā arte; mīrum in
 modum
curl *n* *(natural)* cirrus *m*; *(artificial)* cincinnus *m* ♦ *vt*
 (hair) crispāre ♦ *vi* *(smoke)* volvī
curling irons *n* calamistrī *mpl*
curly *adj* crispus
currency *n* *(coin)* monēta *f*; *(use)* ūsus *m*; **gain
 ~** *(rumour)* percrēbrēscere
current *adj* vulgātus, ūsitātus; *(time)* hīc ♦ *n*
 flūmen *nt*; **with the ~** secundō flūmine;
 against the ~ adversō flūmine
currently *adv* vulgō
curriculum *n* īnstitūtiō *f*
curry *vt* *(favour)* aucupārī
curse *n* exsecrātiō *f*, maledictum *nt*; *(formula)*
 exsecrābile carmen *nt*; *(fig)* pestis *f*; **curses** *interj*
 malum! ♦ *vt* exsecrārī, maledīcere *(dat)*
cursed *adj* exsecrātus, sacer; scelestus
cursorily *adv* breviter, strictim
cursory *adj* brevis
curt *adj* brevis
curtail *vt* minuere, contrahere
curtailment *n* dēminūtiō *f*, contractiō *f*
curtain *n* aulaeum *nt* ♦ *vt* vēlāre
curule *adj* curūlis
curve *n* flexus *m*, arcus *m* ♦ *vt* flectere, incurvāre,
 arcuāre
cushion *n* pulvīnus *m*
custodian *n* custōs *m*
custody *n* custōdia *f*, tūtēla *f*; *(prison)* carcer *m*;
 hold in ~ custōdīre
custom *n* mōs *m*, cōnsuētūdō *f*; *(national)*
 īnstitūtum *nt*; **customs** *pl* portōria *ntpl*
customarily *adv* plērumque, dē mōre, vulgō
customary *adj* solitus, ūsitātus; *(rite)* sollemnis;
 it is ~ mōs est
customer *n* emptor *m*
customs officer *n* portitor *m*
cut *vt* secāre, caedere, scindere; *(corn)* metere;
 (branch) amputāre; *(acquaintance)* āversārī;
 (hair) dētondēre; **cut away** abscindere,
 resecāre; **cut down** rescindere, caedere,
 succīdere; **cut into** incīdere; **cut off** *vt*
 abscīdere, praecīdere; *(exclude)* exclūdere;
 (intercept) interclūdere, intercipere; *(head)*
 abscindere; **cut out** *vt* excīdere, exsecāre;
 (omit) ōmittere; **cut out for** aptus ad, nātus
 ad *(acc)*; **cut round** circumcīdere; **cut short**
 praecīdere; *(speech)* incīdere, interrumpere;
 cut through intercīdere; **cut up** *vt* concīdere
 ♦ *n* vulnus *nt*
cutlass *n* gladius *m*
cutlery *n* cultrī *mpl*
cutter *n* sector *m*; *(boat)* lembus *m*
cutthroat *n* sīcārius *m*
cutting *n* *(plant)* propāgō *f* ♦ *adj* acūtus; *(fig)*
 acerbus, mordāx

cuttlefish n sēpia f
cyclamen n baccar nt
cycle n orbis m
cyclone n turbō f
cylinder n cylindrus m
cymbal n cymbalum nt

cynic n (PHILOS) cynicus m
cynical adj mordāx, acerbus
cynically adv mordāciter, acerbē
cynicism n acerbitās f
cynosure n cynosūra f
cypress n cypressus f

Dd

dabble *vi*: ~ **in** gustāre, leviter attingere
dactyl *n* dactylus *m*
dactylic *adj* dactylicus
dagger *n* sīca *f*, pugiō *f*
daily *adj* diūrnus, cottīdiānus ♦ *adv* cottīdiē, in
  diēs
daintily *adv* molliter, concinnē; fastīdiōsē
daintiness *n* munditia *f*, concinnitās *f*;
  (*squeamish*) fastīdium *nt*
dainty *adj* mundus, concinnus, mollis;
  fastīdiōsus; **dainties** *npl* cuppēdia *ntpl*
dais *n* suggestus *m*
daisy *n* bellis *f*
dale *n* vallis *f*
dalliance *n* lascīvia *f*
dally *vi* lūdere; morārī
dam *n* mōlēs *f*, agger *m*; (*animal*) māter *f* ♦ *vt*
  obstruere, exaggerāre
damage *n* damnum *nt*, dētrīmentum *nt*,
  malum *nt*; (*inflicted*) iniūria *f*; (*LAW*) damnum *nt*;
  assess damages lītem aestimāre ♦ *vt* laedere,
  nocēre (*dat*); (*by evidence*) laedere; (*reputation*)
  violāre
damageable *adj* fragilis
dame *n* mātrōna *f*, domina *f*
damn *vt* damnāre, exsecrārī
damnable *adj* dētestābilis, improbus
damnably *adv* improbē
damnation *n* malum *nt*
damp *adj* ūmidus ♦ *n* ūmor *m* ♦ *vt* madefacere;
  (*enthusiasm*) restinguere, dēmittere
damsel *n* puella *f*, virgō *f*
damson *n* Damascēnum *nt*
dance *vi* saltāre ♦ *n* saltātiō *f*; (*religious*)
  tripudium *nt*
dancer *n* saltātor *m*, saltātrīx *f*
dandruff *n* porrīgō *f*
dandy *n* dēlicātus *m*
danger *n* perīculum *nt*, discrīmen *nt*
dangerous *adj* perīculōsus, dubius; (*in attack*)
  īnfestus
dangerously *adv* perīculōsē
dangle *vt* suspendere ♦ *vi* pendēre
dank *adj* ūmidus
dapper *adj* concinnus, nitidus
dapple *vt* variāre, distinguere
dappled *adj* maculōsus, distinctus
dare *vt* audēre; (*challenge*) prōvocāre; **I ~ say** haud
  sciō an
daring *n* audācia *f* ♦ *adj* audāx
daringly *adv* audācter

dark *adj* obscūrus, opācus; (*colour*) fuscus, āter;
  (*fig*) obscūrus; **it is getting ~** advesperāscit;
  keep ~ silēre ♦ *n* tenebrae *fpl*; (*mist*) cālīgō *f*;
  keep in the ~ cēlāre
darken *vt* obscūrāre, occaecāre
darkish *adj* subobscūrus
darkling *adj* obscūrus
darkness *n* tenebrae *fpl*; (*mist*) cālīgō *f*
darksome *adj* obscūrus
darling *adj* cārus, dīlēctus ♦ *n* dēliciae *fpl*,
  voluptās *f*
darn *vt* resarcīre
darnel *n* lolium *nt*
dart *n* tēlum *nt*; iaculum *nt* ♦ *vi* ēmicāre, sē
  conicere ♦ *vt* iaculārī, iacere
dash *vt* adflīgere; (*hope*) frangere; ~ **against**
  illīdere, incutere; ~ **down** dēturbāre; ~ **out**
  ēlīdere; ~ **to pieces** discutere; ~ **to the ground**
  prōsternere ♦ *vi* currere, sē incitāre, ruere ♦ *n*
  impetus *m*; (*quality*) ferōcia *f*
dashing *adj* ferōx, animōsus
dastardly *adj* ignāvus
date *n* (*fruit*) palmula *f*; (*time*) tempus *nt*, diēs *m*;
  out of ~ obsolētus; **become out of ~** exolēscere;
  to ~ adhūc; **be up to ~** praesentī mōre ūtī ♦ *vt*
  (*letter*) diem adscrībere; (*past event*) repetere ♦ *vi*
  initium capere
dative *n* datīvus *m*
daub *vt* inlinere
daughter *n* fīlia *f*; (*little*) fīliola *f*
daughter-in-law *n* nurus *f*
daunt *vt* terrēre, perterrēre
dauntless *adj* impavidus, intrepidus
dauntlessly *adv* impavidē, intrepidē
dawdle *vi* cessāre, cunctārī
dawdler *n* cunctātor *m*
dawn *n* aurōra *f*, dīlūculum *nt*; (*fig*) orīgō *f*,
  prima lux *f*; **at ~** prīmā lūce ♦ *vi* dīlūcēscere;
  day dawns diēs illūcēscit; **it dawns upon me**
  mente concipiō
day *n* diēs *m/f*; (*period*) aetās *f*; **day about** alternīs
  diēbus; **day by day** in diēs; cottīdiē; **by day**
  (*adj*) diūrnus; (*adv*) interdiū; **during the day**
  interdiū; **every day** cottīdiē; **from day to day**
  in diēs, diem dē diē; **late in the day** multō
  diē; **next day** postrīdiē; **one day/some day**
  ōlim; **the day after** (*adv*) postrīdiē; (*conj*)
  postrīdiē quam; **the day after tomorrow**
  perendiē; **the day before** (*adv*) prīdiē; (*conj*)
  prīdiē quam; **the day before yesterday** nūdius
  tertius; **the present day** haec aetās; **time of
  day** hōra; **twice a day** bis (in) diē; **days of old**

praeteritum tempus; **days to come** posteritās; **better days** rēs prosperae; **evil days** rēs adversae; **three days** trīduum *nt*; **two days** biduum *nt*; **win the day** vincere
daybook *n* adversāria *ntpl*
daybreak *n* aurōra *f*, prīma lūx *f*
daylight *n* diēs *m*; **become ~** illūcēscere
daystar *n* lūcifer *m*
daytime *n* diēs *m*; **in the ~** interdiū
daze *vt* obstupefacere ♦ *n* stupor *m*
dazzle *vt* praestringere
dazzling *adj* splendidus, nitēns
deacon *n* diāconus *m*
deaconess *n* diāconissa *f*
dead *adj* mortuus; (*in battle*) occīsus; (LIT) frīgidus; (*place*) iners, sōlitarius; (*senses*) hebes; **~ of night** nox intempesta *f*; **be ~ to** nōn sentīre; **in ~ earnest** sēriō ac vērō; **rise from the ~** revīvīscere ♦ *adv* prōrsus, omnīnō
dead beat *adj* cōnfectus
dead body *n* cadāver *m*
dead calm *n* malacia *f*
dead certainty *n* rēs certissima
deaden *vt* (*senses*) hebetāre, obtundere; (*pain*) restinguere
deadlock *n* incitae *fpl*; **reach a ~** ad incitās redigī
dead loss *n* mera iactūra
deadly *adj* fūnestus, exitiōsus, exitiābilis; (*enmity*) implācābilis; (*pain*) acerbissimus
dead weight *n* mōlēs *f*
deaf *adj* surdus; **become ~** obsurdēscere; **be ~ to** nōn audīre, obdūrēscere contrā
deafen *vt* (*with noise*) obtundere
deafness *n* surditās *f*
deal *n* (*amount*) cōpia *f*; **a good ~** aliquantum *nt*, bona pars *f*; (*wood*) abiēs *f* ♦ *adj* abiēgnus ♦ *vt* (*blow*) dare, īnflīgere; (*share*) dīvidere, partīrī ♦ *vi* agere, negōtiārī; **~ with** (*person*) agere cum (*abl*); (*matter*) tractāre
dealer *n* (*wholesale*) negōtiātor *m*, mercātor *m*; (*retail*) caupō *m*
dealings *n* commercium *nt*, negōtium *nt*, rēs *f*
dean *n* decānus *m*
dear *adj* (*love*) cārus, grātus; (*cost*) cārus, pretiōsus; **my ~ Quintus** mī Quīnte; (*beginning of letter from Marcus*) Marcus Quintō salūtem; **~ me!** (*sorrow*) hei!; (*surprise*) ehem!; **buy ~** male emere; **sell ~** bene vēndere
dearly *adv* (*love*) valdē, ārdenter; (*value*) magnī
dearness *n* cāritās *f*
dearth *n* inopia *f*, pēnūria *f*
death *n* mors *f*; (*natural*) obitus *m*; (*violent*) nex *f*, interitus *m*; **condemn to ~** capitis damnāre; **put to ~** interficere; **give the ~ blow to** interimere
deathbed *n*: **on one's ~** moriēns, moribundus
deathless *adj* immortālis
deathly *adj* pallidus
debar *vt* prohibēre, exclūdere
debase *vt* dēprāvāre, corrumpere; (*coin*) adulterāre; (*self*) prōsternere, dēmittere
debasement *n* dēdecus *nt*; (*coin*) adulterium *nt*
debatable *adj* ambiguus, dubius
debate *vt* disputāre, disceptāre ♦ *n* contrōversia *f*, disceptātiō *f*, altercātiō *f*
debater *n* disputātor *m*

debauch *vt* corrumpere, pellicere ♦ *n* cōmissātiō *f*
debauched *adj* perditus, prāvus
debauchee *n* cōmissātor *m*
debaucher *n* corruptor *m*
debauchery *n* luxuria *f*, stuprum *nt*
debilitate *vt* dēbilitāre
debility *n* īnfirmitās *f*
debit *n* expēnsum *nt* ♦ *vt* in expēnsum referre
debonair *adj* urbānus, cōmis
debouch *vi* exīre
debris *n* rūdus *nt*
debt *n* aes aliēnum *nt*; (*booked*) nōmen *nt*; (*fig*) dēbitum *nt*; **be in ~** in aere aliēnō esse; **pay off ~** aes aliēnum persolvere; **run up ~** aes aliēnum contrahere; **collect debts** nōmina exigere; **abolition of debts** novae tabulae *fpl*
debtor *n* dēbitor *m*
decade *n* decem annī *mpl*
decadence *n* occāsus *m*
decadent *adj* dēgener, dēterior
decamp *vi* (MIL) castra movēre; (*fig*) discēdere, aufugere
decant *vt* dēfundere, diffundere
decanter *n* lagoena *f*
decapitate *vt* dētruncāre
decay *vi* dīlābī, perīre, putrēscere; (*fig*) tābēscere, senēscere ♦ *n* ruīna *f*, lāpsus *m*; (*fig*) occāsus *m*, dēfectiō *f*
deceased *adj* mortuus
deceit *n* fraus *f*, fallācia *f*, dolus *m*
deceitful *adj* fallāx, fraudulentus, dolōsus
deceitfully *adv* fallāciter, dolōsē
deceive *vt* dēcipere, fallere, circumvenīre, fraudāre
deceiver *n* fraudātor *m*
December *n* mēnsis December *m*; **of ~** December
decemvir *n* decemvir *m*; **of the decemvirs** decemvirālis
decemvirate *n* decemvirātus *m*
decency *n* honestum *nt*, decōrum *nt*, pudor *m*
decent *adj* honestus, pudēns
decently *adv* honestē, pudenter
deception *n* fraus *f*, fallācia *f*
deceptive *adj* fallāx, fraudulentus
decide *vt*, *vi* (*dispute*) diiūdicāre, dēcernere, dīrimere; **~ to do** statuere, cōnstituere (*inf*); **I have decided** mihī certum est; **~ the issue** dēcernere
decided *adj* certus, firmus
decidedly *adv* certē, plānē
deciduous *adj* cadūcus
decimate *vt* decimum quemque occīdere
decipher *vt* expedīre, ēnōdāre
decision *n* (*of judge*) iūdicium *nt*; (*of council*) dēcrētum *nt*; (*of senate*) auctōritās *f*; (*of referee*) arbitrium *nt*; (*personal*) sententia *f*; (*quality*) cōnstantia *f*
decisive *adj* certus; **~ moment** discrīmen *nt*
decisively *adv* sine dubiō
deck *vt* ōrnāre, exōrnāre ♦ *n* (*ship*) pōns *m*; **with a ~** cōnstrātus
decked *adj* ōrnātus; (*ship*) cōnstrātus
declaim *vt*, *vi* dēclāmāre, prōnūntiāre
declamation *n* dēclāmātiō *f*

declamatory *adj* dēclāmātōrius
declaration *n* affirmātiō *f*, adsevērātiō *f*;
  (*formal*) prōfessiō *f*; (*of war*) dēnūntiātiō *f*
declare *vt* affirmāre, adsevērāre; (*secret*) aperīre,
  expōnere; (*proclamation*) dēnūntiāre, ēdīcere;
  (*property in census*) dēdicāre; (*war*) indīcere
declension *n* dēclīnātiō *f*
declination *n* dēclīnātiō *f*
decline *n* (*slope*) dēclīve *nt*, dēiectus *m*; (*of age*)
  senium *nt*; (*of power*) dēfectiō *f*; (*of nation*)
  occāsus *m* ◆ *vi* inclīnāre, occidere; (*fig*) ruere,
  dēlābī, dēgenerāre ◆ *vt* dētrectāre, recūsare;
  (*GRAM*) dēclīnāre
decode *vt* expedīre, ēnōdāre
decompose *vt* dissolvere ◆ *vi* putrēscere
decomposed *adj* putridus
decomposition *n* dissolūtiō *f*
decorate *vt* ōrnāre, decorāre
decoration *n* ōrnāmentum *nt*; (*medal*) īnsigne *nt*
decorous *adj* pudēns, modestus, decōrus
decorously *adv* pudenter, modestē
decorum *n* pudor *m*, honestum *nt*
decoy *n* illecebra *f* ◆ *vt* adlicere, inescāre
decrease *n* dēminūtiō *f*, dēcessiō *f* ◆ *vt*
  dēminuere, extenuāre ◆ *vi* dēcrēscere
decree *n* (*of magistrate*) dēcrētum *nt*, ēdictum
  nt; (*of senate*) cōnsultum *nt*, auctōritās *f*; (*of
  people*) scītum *nt* ◆ *vt* ēdīcere, dēcernere; (*people*)
  scīscere, iubēre; **the senate decrees** placet
  senātuī
decrepit *adj* īnfirmus, dēbilis, dēcrepitus
decrepitude *n* īnfirmitās *f*, dēbilitās *f*
decry *vt* obtrectāre, reprehendere
decurion *n* decuriō *m*
dedicate *vt* dēdicāre, cōnsecrāre; (*life*) dēvovēre
dedication *n* dēdicātiō *f*; dēvōtiō *f*
dedicatory *adj* commendātīcius
deduce *vt* colligere, conclūdere
deduct *vt* dēmere, dētrahere
deduction *n* (*inference*) conclūsiō *f*, cōnsequēns
  nt; (*subtraction*) dēductiō *f*, dēminūtiō *f*
deed factum *nt*, facinus *nt*; gestum *nt*; (*legal*)
  tabulae *fpl*; **deeds** *pl* rēs gestae *fpl*
deem *vt* dūcere, cēnsēre, habēre
deep *adj* altus, profundus; (*discussion*) abstrūsus;
  (*sleep*) artus; (*sound*) gravis; (*width*) lātus; **three**
  ~ (*MIL*) ternī in lātitūdinem ◆ *n* altum *nt*
deepen *vt* dēfodere, altiōrem reddere; (*fig*)
  augēre ◆ *vi* altiōrem fierī; (*fig*) crēscere
deepest *adj* īmus
deeply *adv* altē, graviter; (*inside*) penitus; **very**
  ~ valdē, vehementer
deep-seated *adj* (*fig*) inveterātus
deer *n* cervus *m*, cerva *f*; (*fallow*) dāma *f*
deface *vt* dēfōrmāre, foedāre
defaced *adj* dēfōrmis
defacement *n* dēfōrmitās *f*
defalcation *n* peculātus *m*
defamation *n* calumnia *f*, opprobrium *nt*
defamatory *adj* contumēliōsus, probrōsus
defame *vt* īnfāmāre, obtrectāre, calumniārī
default *vi* dēesse; (*money*) nōn solvere ◆ *n*
  dēfectiō *f*, culpa *f*; **let judgment go by**
  ~ vadimōnium dēserere, nōn respondēre
defaulter *n* reus *m*

defeat *vt* vincere, superāre; (*completely*)
  dēvincere; (*plan*) frustrārī, disicere ◆ *n* clādēs
  f; (*at election*) repulsa *f*, offēnsiō *f*; (*of plan*)
  frustrātiō *f*
defeatism *n* patientia *f*
defeatist *n* imbellis *m*
defect *n* vitium *nt*
defection *n* dēfectiō *f*, sēditiō *f*
defective *adj* mancus, vitiōsus
defence *n* praesidium *nt*, tūtēla *f*; patrōcinium
  nt; (*speech*) dēfēnsiō *f*; **speak in** ~ dēfendere
defenceless *adj* inermis, indēfēnsus; **leave**
  ~ nūdāre
defences *npl* mūnīmenta *ntpl*, mūnītiōnēs *fpl*
defend *vt* dēfendere, tuērī, custōdīre
defendant *n* reus *m*
defender *n* dēfēnsor *m*, prōpugnātor *m*; (*LAW*)
  patrōnus *m*
defensible *adj* iūstus
defensive *adj* dēfēnsiōnis causā; **be on the** ~ sē
  dēfendere
defensively *adv* dēfendendō
defer *vt* differre, prōlātāre ◆ *vi* mōrem gerere
  (*dat*); **I** ~ **to you in this** hōc tibī tribuō
deference *n* obsequium *nt*, observantia *f*; **show**
  ~ **to** observāre, īnservīre (*dat*)
deferential *adj* observāns, officiōsus
deferment *n* dīlatiō *f*, prōlātiō *f*
defiance *n* ferōcia *f*, minae *fpl*
defiant *adj* ferōx, mināx
defiantly *adv* ferōciter, mināciter
deficiency *n* vitium *nt*; (*lack*) pēnūria *f*, inopia *f*
deficient *adj* vitiōsus, inops; **be** ~ dēesse,
  dēficere
deficit *n* lacūna *f*
defile *n* faucēs *fpl*, angustiae *fpl* ◆ *vt* inquināre,
  contāmināre
defilement *n* sordēs *f*, foedītās *f*
define *vt* (*limits*) fīnīre, dēfīnīre, termināre;
  (*meaning*) explicāre
definite *adj* certus, dēfīnītus
definitely *adv* dēfīnītē; prōrsus
definition *n* dēfīnītiō *f*, explicātiō *f*
definitive *adj* dēfīnītīvus
deflate *vt* laxāre
deflect *vt* dēdūcere, dēclīnāre ◆ *vi* dēflectere,
  dēgredī
deflection *n* dēclīnātiō *f*, flexus *m*
deform *vt* dēfōrmāre
deformed *adj* dēfōrmis, distortus
deformity *n* dēfōrmitās *f*, prāvitās *f*
defraud *vt* fraudāre, dēfraudāre
defrauder *n* fraudātor *m*
defray *vt* solvere, suppeditāre
deft *adj* habilis
deftly *adv* habiliter
defunct *adj* mortuus
defy *vt* contemnere, spernere, adversārī (*dat*);
  (*challenge*) prōvocāre, lacessere
degeneracy *n* dēprāvātiō *f*
degenerate *adj* dēgener ◆ *vi* dēgenerāre,
  dēscīscere
degradation *n* īnfāmia *f*, ignōminia *f*, nota *f*
degrade *vt* notāre, abicere, (*from office*) movēre
degrading *adj* turpis, indignus

degree *n* gradus; (*social*) locus *m*; **in some ~** aliquā ex parte; **by degrees** gradātim, sēnsim
deification *n* apotheōsis *f*
deified *adj* (*emperor*) dīvus
deify *vt* cōnsecrāre, inter deōs referre
deign *vi* dignārī
deity *n* deus *m*
dejected *adj* adflīctus, dēmissus
dejectedly *adv* animō dēmissō
dejection *n* maestitia *f*
delay *vt* dēmorārī, dētinēre, retardāre ♦ *vi* cunctārī, cessāre ♦ *n* mora *f*, cunctātiō *f*
delayer *n* morātor *m*, cunctātor *m*
delectable *adj* iūcundus, amoenus
delegate *vt* lēgāre, mandāre, committere ♦ *n* lēgātus *m*
delegation *n* lēgātiō *f*, lēgātī *mpl*
delete *vt* dēlēre
deleterious *adj* perniciōsus, noxius
deletion *n* (*writing*) litūra *f*
deliberate *vi* dēlīberāre, cōnsulere ♦ *adj* (*act*) cōnsīderātus; (*intention*) certus; (*manner*) cōnsīderātus; (*speech*) lentus
deliberately *adv* dē industriā
deliberation *n* dēlīberātiō *f*
deliberative *adj* dēlīberātīvus
delicacy *n* (*judgment*) subtīlitās *f*, ēlegantia *f*; (*manners*) mollitia *f*, luxus *m*; (*health*) valētūdō *f*; (*food*) cuppēdia *ntpl*
delicate *adj* mollis; (*health*) īnfirmus; (*shape*) gracilis; (*feelings*) hūmānus
delicately *adv* molliter; hūmānē
delicious *adj* suāvis, lautus
delight *n* voluptās *f*, gaudium *nt*, dēlectātiō *f* ♦ *vt* dēlectāre, oblectāre, iuvāre ♦ *vi* gaudēre, dēlectārī
delightful *adj* iūcundus, dulcis, festīvus; (*scenery*) amoenus
delightfully *adv* iūcundē, suāviter
delimitation *n* dēfīnītiō *f*
delineate *vt* dēscrībere, dēpingere
delineation *n* dēscrīptiō *f*
delinquency *n* culpa *f*, dēlictum *nt*, noxa *f*
delinquent *n* nocēns *m/f*, reus *m*
delirious *adj* dēlīrus, āmēns, furiōsus; **be ~** furere, dēlīrāre
delirium *n* furor *m*, āmentia *f*
deliver *vt* (*from*) līberāre, exsolvere, ēripere; (*blow*) intendere; (*message*) referre; (*speech*) habēre; **~ to** dēferre, trādere, dare; **~ up** dēdere, trādere; **be delivered of** parere
deliverance *n* līberātiō *f*
deliverer *n* līberātor *m*
delivery *n* (*of things due*) trāditiō *f*; (*of speech*) āctiō *f*, prōnūntiātiō *f*; (*of child*) partus *m*
dell *n* convallis *f*
Delphi *n* Delphī *mpl*
delude *vt* dēcipere, frustrārī, dēlūdere
deluge *n* ēluviō *f* ♦ *vt* inundāre
delusion *n* error *m*, fraus *f*
delusive *adj* fallāx, inānis
delve *vt* fodere
demagogue *n* plēbicola *m*
demand *vt* poscere, postulāre, imperāre; (*urgently*) flāgitāre, poscere; (*thing due*) exigere; (*answer*) quaerere; **~ back** repetere ♦ *n* postulātiō *f*, postulātum *nt*
demarcation *n* līmes *m*
demean *vt* (*self*) dēmittere
demeanour *n* gestus *m*, mōs *m*, habitus *m*
demented *adj* dēmēns, furiōsus
demerit *n* culpa *f*, vitium *nt*
demesne *n* fundus *m*
demigod *n* hērōs *m*
demise *n* obitus *m* ♦ *vt* lēgāre
democracy *n* cīvitās populāris *f*
democrat *n* homō populāris *m/f*
democratic *adj* populāris
demolish *vt* dēmōlīrī, dīruere, dēstruere; (*argument*) discutere
demolition *n* ruīna *f*, ēversiō *f*
demon *n* daemōn *m*
demonstrate *vt* (*show*) mōnstrāre, ostendere, indicāre; (*prove*) dēmōnstrāre
demonstration *n* exemplum *nt*; (*proof*) dēmōnstrātiō *f*
demonstrative *adj* (*manner*) vehemēns; (RHET) dēmōnstrātīvus
demoralization *n* corruptiō *f*, dēprāvātiō *f*
demoralize *vt* corrumpere, dēprāvāre, labefactāre
demote *vt* locō movēre
demur *vi* gravārī, recūsāre ♦ *n* mora *f*, dubitātiō *f*
demure *adj* modestus, verēcundus
demurely *adv* modestē, verēcundē
demureness *n* modestia *f*, verēcundia *f*, pudor *m*
demurrer *n* (LAW) exceptiō *f*
den *n* latibulum *nt*, latebra *f*; (*of vice*) lustrum *nt*
denarius *n* dēnārius *m*
denial *n* īnfitiātiō *f*, negātiō *f*
denigrate *vt* obtrectāre, calumniārī
denizen *n* incola *m/f*
denominate *vt* nōmināre, appellāre
denomination *n* nōmen *nt*; (*religious*) secta *f*
denote *vt* notāre, significāre
denouement *n* exitus *m*
denounce *vt* dēferre, incūsāre
denouncer *n* dēlātor *m*
dense *adj* dēnsus; (*crowd*) frequēns; (*person*) stolidus
density *n* crassitūdō *f*; (*crowd*) frequentia *f*
dent *n* nota *f*
dentate *adj* dentātus
denture *n* dentēs *mpl*
denudation *n* spoliātiō *f*
denude *vt* spoliāre, nūdāre
denunciation *n* (*report*) indicium *nt*, dēlātiō *f*; (*threat*) minae *fpl*
deny *vt* īnfitiārī, īnfitiās īre, negāre, abnuere; (*on oath*) abiūrāre; **~ oneself** genium dēfraudāre
depart *vi* discēdere (*abl*), abīre, exīre, ēgredī
department *n* (*district*) regiō *f*, pars *f*; (*duty*) prōvincia *f*, mūnus *nt*
departure *n* discessus *m*, abitus *m*, dīgressus *m*, exitus *m*; (*change*) mūtātiō *f*; (*death*) obitus *m*
depend *vi* pendēre; (*be dependent*) pendēre ex (*abl*), nītī (*abl*); (*rely*) fīdere, cōnfīdere; **depending on** frētus (*abl*)
dependable *adj* fīdus

dependant n cliēns m/f
dependence n clientēla f; (reliance) fīdūcia f
dependency n prōvincia f
dependent adj subiectus, obnoxius
depict vt dēscrībere, dēpingere; (to the life) expingere
deplete vt dēminuere
depletion n dēminūtiō f
deplorable adj turpis, nefandus, pessimus
deplorably adv turpiter, pessimē, miserē
deplore vt dēplōrāre, dēflēre, conquerī
deploy vt explicāre; instruere, dispōnere
depopulate vt vastāre, nūdāre
depopulation n vastātiō f, sōlitūdō f
deport vt (banish) dēportāre; (self) gerere
deportation n exsilium nt
deportment n gestus m, habitus m
depose vt dēmovēre, dēpellere; (evidence) testārī
deposit n fīdūcia f, dēpositum nt ♦ vt dēpōnere, mandāre
depositary n sequester m
deposition n (LAW) testimōnium nt, indicium nt
depository n apothēca f
depot n (for arms) armāmentārium nt; (for trade) emporium nt
deprave vt dēprāvāre, corrumpere
depraved adj prāvus
depravity n dēprāvātiō f, turpitūdō f
deprecate vt abōminārī, dēprecārī
deprecation n dēprecātiō f
depreciate vt obtrectāre, dētrectāre
depreciation n obtrectātiō f; (price) vīlitās f
depredation n praedātiō f, dīreptiō f
depress vt dēprimere; (mind) adflīgere, frangere; **be depressed** iacēre, animum dēspondēre
depressing adj maestus, tristis
depression n (place) cavum nt; (mind) tristitia f, sollicitūdō f
deprivation n prīvātiō f, spoliātiō f
deprive vt prīvāre, spoliāre
depth n altitūdō f; (place) profundum nt, gurges m
deputation n lēgātiō f, lēgātī mpl
depute vt lēgāre, mandāre
deputy n lēgātus m; (substitute) vicārius m
derange vt conturbāre
deranged adj īnsānus, mente captus
derangement n perturbātiō f; (mind) īnsānia f, dēmentia f
derelict adj dēsertus
dereliction n (of duty) neglegentia f
deride vt dērīdēre, inlūdere
derision n rīsus m, irrīsiō f
derisive adj mordāx
derivation n orīgō f
derive vt dūcere, trahere; (advantage) capere, parāre; (pleasure) dēcerpere, percipere; **be derived** dēfluere
derogate vi dērogāre, dētrahere; ~ **from** imminuere, obtrectāre
derogation n imminūtiō f, obtrectātiō f
derogatory adj indignus; ~ **remarks** obtrectātiō f
derrick n trochlea f
descant vt disserere ♦ n cantus m

descend vi dēscendere; (water) dēlābī; (from heaven) dēlābī; (by inheritance) pervenīre, prōdī; (morally) dēlābī, sē dēmittere; **be descended from** orīrī ex (abl)
descendant n prōgeniēs f; **descendants** pl minōrēs mpl, posterī mpl
descent n dēscensus m; (slope) clīvus m, dēiectus m; (birth) genus nt; (hostile) dēcursus m, incursiō f; **make a ~ upon** inrumpere in (acc), incursāre in (acc)
describe vt dēscrībere; (tell) nārrāre; (portray) dēpingere, exprimere
description n dēscrīptiō f; (tale) nārrātiō f; (kind) genus nt
descry vt cernere, cōnspicere, prōspectāre
desecrate vt prōfānāre, exaugurāre
desecration n exaugurātiō f, violātiō f
desert vt dēserere, dērelinquere, dēstituere ♦ vi dēscīscere, dēficere ♦ adj dēsertus, sōlitārius ♦ n (place) sōlitūdō f, loca dēserta ntpl; (merit) meritum nt
deserted adj dēsertus
deserter n dēsertor m; (MIL) trānsfuga m
desertion n dēfectiō f, trānsfugium nt
deserve vt merērī; dignus esse quī (subj); ~ **well of** bene merērī dē (abl)
deserved adj meritus
deservedly adv meritō
deserving adj dignus
desiccate vt siccāre
design n (drawing) adumbrātiō f; (plan) cōnsilium nt, prōpositum nt; **by ~** cōnsultō ♦ vt adumbrāre, in animō habēre
designate vt dēsignāre, mōnstrāre; (as heir) scrībere; (as official) dēsignāre ♦ adj dēsignātus
designation n nōmen nt, titulus m
designedly adv dē industriā, cōnsultō
designer n auctor m, inventor m
designing adj vafer, dolōsus
desirable adj optābilis, expetendus, grātus
desire n cupiditās f; studium nt; (uncontrolled) libīdō f; (natural) adpetītiō f ♦ vt cupere; (much) exoptāre, expetere; (command) iubēre
desirous adj cupidus, avidus, studiōsus
desist vi dēsistere
desk n scrīnium nt
desolate adj dēsertus, sōlitārius; (place) vastus ♦ vt vastāre
desolation n sōlitūdō f, vastitās f; (process) vastātiō f
despair vi dēspērāre dē (abl), animum dēspondēre ♦ n dēspērātiō f
despairingly adv dēspēranter
despatch see dispatch
desperado n homō dēspērātus m
desperate adj (hopeless) dēspērātus; (wicked) perditus; (dangerous) perīculōsus
desperately adv dēspēranter
desperation n dēspērātiō f
despicable adj dēspectus, abiectus, turpis
despicably adv turpiter
despise vt contemnere, dēspicere, spernere
despiser n contemptor m
despite n malevolentia f, odium nt
despoil vt spoliāre, nūdāre
despoiler n spoliātor m, praedātor m

despond vi animum dēspondēre, dēspērāre
despondency n dēspērātiō f
despondent adj abiectus, adflīctus, dēmissus;
  be ~ animum dēspondēre
despondently adv animō dēmissō
despot n dominus m, rēx m
despotic adj imperiōsus, superbus
despotically adv superbē
despotism n dominātiō f, superbia f, rēgnum nt
dessert n secunda mēnsa f
destination n fīnis m
destine vt dēstināre, dēsignāre; **destined to be**
  futūrus
destiny n fātum nt; **of** ~ fātālis
destitute adj inops, pauper, prīvātus; ~ **of**
  expers (gen)
destitution n inopia f, egestās f
destroy vt dēlēre, ēvertere, dīrimere, perdere
destroyer n ēversor m
destructible adj fragilis
destruction n exitium nt, ēversiō f, excidium nt
destructive adj exitiābilis, perniciōsus
destructively adv perniciōsē
desuetude n dēsuētūdō f
desultorily adv carptim
desultory adj varius, incōnstāns
detach vt abiungere, sēiungere, āmovēre,
  sēparāre
detachment n (MIL) manus f, cohors f; (mind)
  integer animus m, līber animus
detail n: **in** ~ singillātim ♦ vt exsequī; **details** pl
  singula ntpl
detain vt dēmorārī, dētinēre, distinēre, morārī
detect vt dēprehendere, patefacere
detection n dēprehēnsiō f
detective n inquīsītor m
detention n retentiō f; (prison) vincula ntpl
deter vt dēterrēre, absterrēre, impedīre
deteriorate vi dēgenerāre
deterioration n dēprāvātiō f, lāpsus m
determinate adj certus, fīnītus
determination n obstinātiō f, cōnstantia f;
  (intention) prōpositum nt, sententia f
determine vt (fix) fīnīre; (decide) statuere,
  cōnstituere
determined adj obstinātus; (thing) certus; **I am**
  ~ **to** mihī certum est (inf)
determinedly adv cōnstanter
deterrent n: **act as a** ~ **to** dēterrēre
detest vt ōdisse, dētestārī
detestable adj dētestābilis, odiōsus
detestation n odium nt, invidia f
dethrone vt rēgnō dēpellere
detour n circuitus m; **make a** ~ iter flectere; (MIL)
  agmen circumdūcere
detract vi: ~ **from** dērogāre, dētrahere
detraction n obtrectātiō f
detractor n obtrectātor m, invidus m
detriment n damnum nt, dētrīmentum nt
detrimental adj damnōsus; **be** ~ **to** dētrīmentō
  esse (dat)
devastate vt vastāre, populārī
devastation n vastātiō f, populātiō f; (state)
  vastitās f
develop vt ēvolvere, explicāre; (person) ēducāre,
  alere ♦ vi crēscere; ~ **into** ēvādere in (acc)

development n explicātiō f; (of men) ēducātiō f;
  (of resources) cultus m; (of events) exitus m
deviate vi dēcēdere dē viā, aberrāre, dēclīnāre;
  (speech) dēgredī
deviation n dēclīnātiō f; (from truth) error m; (in
  speech) dīgressus m
device n (plan) cōnsilium nt; (machine) māchina f;
  (emblem) īnsigne nt
devil n diabolus m; **go to the** ~ abī in malam
  crucem!; **talk of the** ~ lupus in fābulā!
devilish adj scelestus, impius
devil-may-care adj praeceps, lascīvus
devilment n malitia f
devilry n magicae artēs fpl
devious adj dēvius, errābundus
devise vt excōgitāre, commentārī, fingere
devoid adj vacuus, expers; **be** ~ **of** carēre (abl)
devolve vi obtingere, obvenīre ♦ vt dēferre,
  committere
devote vt dēdicāre; (attention) dēdere, trādere;
  (life) dēvovēre
devoted adj dēditus, studiōsus; (victim) dēvōtus,
  sacer; **be** ~ **to** studēre (dat), incumbere (dat)
devotee n cultor m
devotion n amor m, studium nt; rēligiō f
devour vt dēvorāre, cōnsūmere; (fig) haurīre
devout adj pius, rēligiōsus
devoutly adv piē, rēligiōsē
dew n rōs m
dewy adj rōscidus
dexterity n ars f, sollertia f
dexterous adj sollers, habilis
dexterously adv sollerter, habiliter
diabolical adj scelestus, nefārius
diadem n diadēma nt
diagnose vt discernere, diiūdicāre
diagnosis n iūdicium nt
diagonal adj oblīquus
diagram n fōrma f
dial n sōlārium nt
dialect n dialectus f, sermō m
dialectic n ars disserendī f, dialecticē f ♦ adj
  dialecticus
dialectician n dialecticus m
dialogue n dialogus m, colloquium nt
diameter n diametros f
diamond n adamās m
diaphanous adj perlūcidus
diaphragm n praecordia ntpl
diary n ephēmeris f
diatribe n convīcium nt
dice n tālus m, tessera f; **game of** ~ ālea f
dictate vt dictāre ♦ n praeceptum nt; **dictates of**
  nature nātūrae iūdicia ntpl
dictation n dictāta ntpl; (fig) arbitrium nt
dictator n dictātor m; **dictator's** dictātōrius
dictatorial adj imperiōsus, superbus
dictatorship n dictātūra f
diction n (enunciation) ēlocūtiō f; (words) ōrātiō f
dictionary n verbōrum thēsaurus m
die n signum nt; **the die is cast** iacta ālea est ♦ vi
  morī, perīre, obīre; (in battle) cadere, occumbere;
  die off dēmorī; **die out** ēmorī; **be dying to**
  exoptāre
diet n (food) diaeta f; (meeting) conventus m
differ vi differre, discrepāre, dissentīre

difference n discrepantia f, dissimilitūdō f; (of opinion) dissēnsiō f; **there is a** ~ interest
different adj dīversus, varius, dissimilis; ~ **from** alius ... ac; **in** ~ **directions** dīversī; **they say** ~ **things** alius aliud dīcit
differentiate vt discernere
differently adv dīversē, variē, alius aliter; ~ **from** aliter ... ac
difficult adj difficilis, arduus; **very** ~ perdifficilis, perarduus
difficulty n difficultās f, labor m, negōtium nt; **with** ~ difficulter, aegrē, vix; **be in** ~ labōrāre
diffidence n diffīdentia f; (shyness) pudor m; **with** ~ modestē
diffident adj diffīdēns; (shy) modestus, verēcundus
diffidently adv modestē
diffuse vt diffundere, dispergere; **be diffused** diffluere ♦ adj fūsus, diffūsus, cōpiōsus
diffusely adv diffūsē, cōpiōsē
diffuseness n cōpia f
dig vt fodere; dūcere; (nudge) fodicāre; **dig up** vt effodere, ēruere
digest vt coquere, concoquere ♦ n summārium nt
digestion n concoctiō f; **with a bad** ~ crūdus
digger n fossor m
dignified adj gravis, augustus
dignify vt honōrāre, honestāre
dignity n gravitās f, māiestās f, amplitūdō f
digress vi dēvertere, dīgredī, dēclīnāre
digression n dēclīnātiō f, dīgressus m
dike n (ditch) fossa f; (mound) agger m
dilapidated adj ruīnōsus
dilapidation n ruīna f
dilate vt dīlātāre; (speech) plūra dīcere
dilatorily adv tardē, cunctanter
dilatoriness n mora f, cunctātiō f
dilatory adj tardus, lentus, segnis
dilemma n nōdus m, angustiae fpl; **be in a** ~ haerēre; **be on the horns of a** ~ auribus tenēre lupum
diligence n dīligentia f, industria f, cūra f
diligent adj dīligēns, industrius, sēdulus
diligently adv dīligenter, sēdulō
dill n anēthum nt
dilly-dally vi cessāre
dilute vt dīluere, temperāre
dim adj obscūrus; (fig) hebes ♦ vt obscūrāre; hebetāre
dimension n modus m; **dimensions** pl amplitūdō f, māgnitūdō f
diminish vt minuere, imminuere, extenuāre, īnfringere ♦ vi dēcrēscere
diminution n imminūtiō f, dēminūtiō f
diminutive adj parvulus, exiguus ♦ n (word) dēminūtum nt
diminutiveness n exiguitās f
dimly adv obscūrē
dimness n tenebrae fpl, cālīgō f
dimple n gelasīnus m
din n fragor m, strepitus m; **make a din** strepere ♦ vt obtundere
dine vi cēnāre
diner n convīva m
dinghy n scapha f

dingy adj sordidus; (colour) fuscus
dining room n cēnātiō f
dinner n cēna f
dinner party convīvium nt
dint n ictus m; **by** ~ **of** per (acc)
dip vt imbuere, mergere ♦ vi mergī; **dip into** (study) perstringere
diploma n diplōma nt
diplomacy n (embassy) lēgātiō f; (tact) iūdicium nt, sagācitās f
diplomat n lēgātus m
diplomatic adj sagāx, circumspectus
diptych n tabellae fpl
dire adj dīrus, horridus
direct vt regere, dīrigere; (attention) attendere, admovēre, advertere; (course) tendere; (business) administrāre, moderārī; (letter) īnscrībere; (order) imperāre (dat), iubēre; (to a place) viam mōnstrāre (dat); (weapon) intendere ♦ adj rēctus, dīrēctus; (person) simplex; (language) apertus ♦ adv rēctā
direction n (of going) cursus m, iter nt; (of looking) pars f, regiō f; (control) administrātiō f, regimen nt; (order) praeceptum nt, iussum nt; **in the** ~ **of Rome** Rōmam versus; **in all directions** passim, undique; **in both directions** utrōque
directly adv (place) rēctā; (time) prōtinus, continuō, statim; (language) apertē ♦ conj simulac
directness n (fig) simplicitās f
director n dux m, gubernātor m, moderātor m
dirge n nēnia f
dirk n pūgiō m
dirt n sordēs f; (mud) lūtum nt
dirty adj sordidus, foedus; (speech) inquinātus ♦ vt foedāre, inquināre
disability n vitium nt
disable vt dēbilitāre, imminuere
disabled adj mutilus, dēbilis
disabuse vt errōrem dēmere (dat)
disaccustom vt dēsuēfacere
disadvantage n incommodum nt, dētrīmentum nt; **it is a** ~ dētrīmentō est
disadvantageous adj incommodus, inīquus
disadvantageously adv incommodē
disaffected adj aliēnātus, sēditiōsus
disaffection n aliēnātiō f, sēditiō f
disagree vi discrepāre, dissentīre, dissidēre
disagreeable adj molestus, incommodus, iniūcundus
disagreeably adv molestē, incommodē
disagreement n discordia f, dissēnsiō f, discrepantia f
disallow vt improbāre, abnuere, vetāre
disappear vi dēperīre, perīre, abīre, diffugere, ēvānēscere
disappearance n dēcessiō f, fuga f
disappoint vt dēcipere, spē dēicere, frustrārī; **be disappointed in a hope** ā spē dēcidere, dē spē dēicī
disappointment n frustrātiō f, malum nt
disapprobation n reprehēnsiō f, improbātiō f
disapproval n improbātiō f
disapprove vt, vi improbāre, reprehendere
disarm vt exarmāre, dearmāre; (fig) mītigāre
disarrange vt turbāre, cōnfundere

disarranged *adj* incompositus
disarrangement *n* turbātiō *f*
disarray *n* perturbātiō *f* ◆ *vt* perturbāre
disaster *n* calamitās *f*, cāsus *m*; (MIL) clādēs *f*
disastrous *adj* īnfēlīx, exitiōsus, calamitōsus
disavow *vt* diffitērī, īnfitiārī
disavowal *n* īnfitiātiō *f*
disband *vt* dīmittere
disbelief *n* diffīdentia *f*, suspiciō *f*
disbelieve *vt* diffīdere (*dat*)
disburden *vt* exonerāre
disburse *vt* ērogāre, expendere
disbursement *n* impēnsa *f*
disc *n* orbis *m*
discard *vt* mittere, pōnere, prōicere
discern *vt* cōnspicere, dīspicere, cernere; (*fig*) intellegere
discernment *n* iūdicium *nt*, intellegentia *f*, sagācitās *f*
discharge *vt* (*load*) exonerāre; (*debt*) exsolvere; (*duty*) fungī (*abl*), exsequī; (*officer*) exauctōrāre; (*troops*) missōs facere, dīmittere; (*weapon*) iacere, iaculārī; (*prisoner*) absolvere; (*from body*) ēdere, reddere ◆ *vi* (*river*) effundī, īnfluere ◆ *n* (*bodily*) dēfluxiō *f*; (MIL) missiō *f*, dīmissiō *f*; (*of a duty*) perfūnctiō *f*
disciple *n* discipulus *m*
discipline *n* (MIL) modestia *f*; (*punishment*) castīgātiō *f*; (*study*) disciplīna *f* ◆ *vt* coercēre, castīgāre
disciplined *adj* modestus
disclaim *vt* renūntiāre, repudiāre, rēicere
disclaimer *n* repudiātiō *f*
disclose *vt* aperīre, patefacere, indicāre
disclosure *n* indicium *nt*
discoloration *n* dēcolōrātiō *f*
discolour *vt* dēcolōrāre
discoloured *adj* dēcolor
discomfit *vt* vincere, conturbāre, dēprehendere
discomfiture *n* clādēs *f*; (POL) repulsa *f*
discomfort *n* molestia *f*, incommodum *nt*
disconcert *vt* conturbāre, percellere
disconcerting *adj* molestus
disconnect *vt* abiungere, sēiungere
disconnected *adj* dissolūtus, abruptus
disconnectedly *adv* dissolūtē
disconsolate *adj* maestus, dēmissus
disconsolately *adv* animō dēmissō
discontent *n* offēnsiō *f*, fastīdium *nt*, taedium *nt*
discontented *adj* invidus, fastīdiōsus, parum contentus
discontentedly *adv* invītus, inīquō animō
discontinuance *n* intermissiō *f*
discontinue *vt* intermittere ◆ *vi* dēsistere, dēsinere
discord *n* discordia *f*; (*music*) dissonum *nt*
discordance *n* discrepantia *f*, dissēnsiō *f*
discordant *adj* discors, discrepāns; (*music*) dissonus, absonus
discount *vt* dētrahere; (*fig*) praetermittere ◆ *n* dēcessiō *f*; **be at a ~** iacēre
discountenance *vt* improbāre
discourage *vt* dēhortārī, dēterrēre; **be discouraged** animum dēmittere, animō dēficere

discouragement *n* animī abiectiō *f*; (*cause*) incommodum *nt*
discourse *n* sermō *m*; (*lecture*) ōrātiō *f* ◆ *vi* conloquī, disserere, disputāre
discourteous *adj* inurbānus, asper, inhūmānus
discourteously *adv* inhūmānē, rūsticē
discourtesy *n* inhūmānitās *f*, acerbitās *f*
discover *vt* (*find*) invenīre, reperīre; (*detect*) dēprehendere; (*reveal*) aperīre, patefacere; (*learn*) cognōscere
discoverer *n* inventor *m*
discovery *n* inventum *nt*
discredit *vt* notāre, fidem imminuere (*gen*) ◆ *n* invidia *f*, lābēs *f*; **be in ~** iacēre
discreditable *adj* inhonestus, turpis
discreditably *adv* inhonestē, turpiter
discreet *adj* prūdēns, sagāx, cautus
discreetly *adv* prūdenter, sagāciter, cautē
discrepancy *n* discrepantia *f*, dissēnsiō *f*
discretion *n* prūdentia *f*; (*tact*) iūdicium *nt*; (*power*) arbitrium *nt*, arbitrātus *m*; **at your ~** arbitrātū tuō; **surrender at ~** in dēditiōnem venīre, sine ullā pactiōne sē tradere; **years of ~** adulta aetās *f*
discretionary *adj* līber
discriminate *vt, vi* discernere, internōscere, distinguere
discriminating *adj* perspicāx, sagāx
discrimination *n* discrīmen *nt*, iūdicium *nt*
discursive *adj* vagus, loquāx; **be ~** excurrere
discuss *vt* agere, disputāre, disceptāre dē (*abl*); **~ terms of peace** dē pāce agere
discussion *n* disceptātiō *f*, disputātiō *f*
disdain *vt* contemnere, aspernārī, fastīdīre ◆ *n* contemptiō *f*, fastīdium *nt*
disdainful *adj* fastīdiōsus, superbus
disdainfully *adv* fastīdiōsē, superbē
disease *n* morbus *m*; pestilentia *f*
diseased *adj* aeger, aegrōtus
disembark *vi* ē nave ēgredī ◆ *vt* mīlitēs etc ē nāve expōnere
disembarkation *n* ēgressus *m*
disembodied *adj* sine corpore
disembowel *vt* exenterāre
disencumber *vt* exonerāre
disengage *vt* expedīre, līberāre; (*mind*) abstrahere, abdūcere
disengaged *adj* vacuus, ōtiōsus
disentangle *vt* expedīre, explicāre, exsolvere
disfavour *n* invidia *f*
disfigure *vt* dēfōrmāre, foedāre
disfigured *adj* dēfōrmis
disfigurement *n* dēfōrmātiō *f*
disfranchise *vt* cīvitātem adimere (*dat*)
disfranchised *adj* capite dēminūtus
disfranchisement *n* capitis dēminūtiō *f*
disgorge *vt* ēvomere
disgrace *n* dēdecus *nt*, ignōminia *f*, īnfāmia *f* ◆ *vt* dēdecorāre, dēdecorī esse (*dat*)
disgraceful *adj* ignōminiōsus, flāgitiōsus, turpis; **~ thing** flāgitium *nt*
disgracefully *adv* turpiter, flāgitiōsē
disgruntled *adj* mōrōsus, invidus
disguise *n* integumentum *nt*; (*fig*) speciēs *f*, simulātiō *f*; **in ~** mūtātā veste ◆ *vt* obtegere,

involvere; *(fact)* dissimulāre; ~ **oneself** vestem mūtāre

disgust *vt* displicēre *(dat)*, fastīdium movēre *(dat)*; **be disgusted** stomachārī; **I am disgusted** mē taedet, mē piget ♦ *n* fastīdium *nt*, taedium *nt*

disgusting *adj* taeter, foedus, dēfōrmis

disgustingly *adv* foedē

dish *n* lanx *f*; *(course)* ferculum *nt*

dishearten *vt* percellere; **be disheartened** animō dēficere, animum dēmittere

dishevelled *adj* solūtus, passus

dishonest *adj* perfidus, inīquus, improbus

dishonestly *adv* improbē, dolō malō

dishonesty *n* mala fidēs *f*, perfidia *f*, fraus *f*

dishonour *n* dēdecus *nt*, ignōminia *f*, turpitūdō *f* ♦ *vt* dēdecorāre

dishonourable *adj* ignōminiōsus, indecōrus, turpis

dishonourably *adv* turpiter, inhonestē

disillusion *vt* errōrem adimere *(dat)*

disinclination *n* odium *nt*

disinclined *adj* invītus, āversus

disinfect *vt* pūrgāre

disingenuous *adj* dolōsus, fallāx

disingenuously *adv* dolōsē

disinherit *vt* abdicāre, exhērēdāre

disinherited *adj* exhērēs

disintegrate *vt* dissolvere ♦ *vi* dīlābī, dissolvī

disinter *vt* effodere, ēruere

disinterested *adj* grātuītus, favōris expers

disinterestedly *adv* sine favōre

disinterestedness *n* innocentia *f*, integritās *f*

disjoin *vt* sēiungere

disjointed *adj* parum cohaerēns

disk *n* orbis *m*

dislike *n* odium *nt*, offēnsiō *f*, invidia *f* ♦ *vt* ōdisse; **I ~** mihī displicet, mē piget *(gen)*

dislocate *vt* extorquēre

dislocated *adj* luxus

dislodge *vt* dēmovēre, dēicere, dēpellere, dētrūdere

disloyal *adj* īnfīdus, īnfidēlis; *(to gods, kin, country)* impius

disloyally *adv* īnfidēliter

disloyalty *n* perfidia *f*, īnfidēlitās *f*; impietās *f*

dismal *adj* fūnestus, maestus

dismally *adv* miserē

dismantle *vt* nūdāre; *(building)* dīruere

dismay *n* pavor *m*, formīdō *f* ♦ *vt* terrēre, perturbāre

dismember *vt* discerpere

dismiss *vt* dīmittere; *(troops)* missōs facere; *(from service)* exauctōrāre; *(fear)* mittere, pōnere

dismissal *n* missiō *f*, dīmissiō *f*

dismount *vi* dēgredī, (ex equō) dēscendere

disobedience *n* contumācia *f*

disobedient *adj* contumāx

disobediently *adv* contrā iūssa

disobey *vt* nōn pārēre *(dat)*, aspernārī

disoblige *vt* displicēre *(dat)*, offendere

disobliging *adj* inofficiōsus, difficilis

disobligingly *adv* contrā officium

disorder *n* turba *f*, cōnfūsiō *f*; *(MED)* morbus *m*; *(POL)* mōtus *m*, tumultus *m* ♦ *vt* turbāre, miscēre, sollicitāre

disorderly *adj* immodestus, inōrdinātus, incompositus; *(POL)* turbulentus, sēditiōsus; **in a ~ manner** nullō ōrdine, temerē

disorganize *vt* dissolvere, perturbāre

disown *vt* *(statement)* īnfitiārī; *(thing)* abnuere, repudiāre; *(heir)* abdicāre

disparage *vt* obtrectāre, dētrectāre

disparagement *n* obtrectātiō *f*, probrum *nt*

disparager *n* obtrectātor *m*, dētrectātor *m*

disparate *adj* dispār

disparity *n* discrepantia *f*, dissimilitūdō *f*

dispassionate *adj* studiī expers

dispassionately *adv* sine īrā et studiō

dispatch *vt* mittere, dīmittere; *(finish)* absolvere, perficere; *(kill)* interficere ♦ *n* *(letter)* litterae *fpl*; *(speed)* celeritās *f*

dispel *vt* dispellere, discutere

dispensation *n* *(distribution)* partītiō *f*; *(exemption)* venia *f*; *(of heaven)* sors *f*; **by divine ~** dīvīnitus

dispense *vt* dispertīrī, dīvidere ♦ *vi*: **~ with** ōmittere, praetermittere, repudiāre

dispersal *n* dīmissiō *f*, diffugium *nt*

disperse *vt* dispergere, dissipāre, dīsicere ♦ *vi* diffugere, dīlābī

dispirited *adj* dēmissō animō; **be ~** animō dēficere, animum dēmittere

displace *vt* locō movēre

display *n* ostentātiō *f*, iactātiō *f*; **for ~** per speciem ♦ *vt* exhibēre, ostendere, praestāre, sē ferre

displease *vt* displicēre *(dat)*, offendere; **be displeased** aegrē ferre, stomachārī, indignārī

displeasing *adj* ingrātus, odiōsus

displeasure *n* invidia *f*, offēnsiō *f*, odium *nt*

disport *vt*: **~ oneself** lūdere

disposal *n* *(sale)* vēnditiō *f*; *(power)* arbitrium *nt*

dispose *vt* *(troops)* dispōnere; *(mind)* inclīnāre, addūcere ♦ *vi*: **~ of** abaliēnāre, vēndere; *(get rid)* tollere; *(argument)* refellere

disposed *adj* adfectus, inclīnātus, prōnus; **well ~** benevolus, bonō animō

disposition *n* animus *m*, adfectiō *f*, ingenium *nt*, nātūra *f*; *(of troops)* dispositiō *f*

dispossess *vt* dētrūdere, spoliāre

disproportion *n* inconcinnitās *f*

disproportionate *adj* impār, inconcinnus

disproportionately *adv* inaequāliter

disprove *vt* refūtāre, redarguere, refellere

disputable *adj* dubius, ambiguus

disputation *n* disputātiō *f*

dispute *n* altercātiō *f*, contrōversia *f*; *(violent)* iūrgium *nt*; **beyond ~** certissimus ♦ *vi* altercārī, certāre, rixārī ♦ *vt* negāre, in dubium vocāre

disqualification *n* impedīmentum *nt*

disqualify *vt* impedīre

disquiet *n* sollicitūdō *f* ♦ *vt* sollicitāre

disquisition *n* disputātiō *f*

disregard *n* neglegentia *f*, contemptiō *f* ♦ *vt* neglegere, contemnere, ōmittere

disrepair *n* vitium *nt*; **in ~** male sartus

disreputable *adj* inhonestus, īnfāmis

disrepute *n* īnfāmia *f*

disrespect *n* neglegentia *f*, contumācia *f*

disrespectful *adj* contumāx, īnsolēns

disrespectfully *adv* īnsolenter

disrobe vt nūdāre, vestem exuere (dat) ♦ vi
  vestem exuere
disrupt vt dīrumpere, dīvellere
disruption n discidium nt
dissatisfaction n molestia f, aegritūdō f, dolor
  m
dissatisfied adj parum contentus; I am ~ with
  ... mē taedet (gen) ...
dissect vt incīdere; (fig) investīgāre
dissemble vt, vi dissimulāre; mentīrī
dissembler n simulātor m
disseminate vt dīvulgāre, dissēmināre
dissension n discordia f, dissēnsiō f; (violent)
  iūrgium nt
dissent vi dissentīre, dissidēre ♦ n dissēnsiō f
dissertation n disputātiō f
disservice n iniūria f, incommodum nt
dissident adj discors
dissimilar adj dispār, dissimilis
dissimilarity n discrepantia f, dissimilitūdō f
dissimulation n dissimulātiō f
dissipate vt dissipāre, diffundere, disperdere
dissipated adj dissolūtus, lascīvus, luxuriōsus
dissipation n dissipātiō f; (vice) luxuria f,
  licentia f
dissociate vt dissociāre, sēiungere
dissociation n sēparātiō f, discidium nt
dissoluble adj dissolūbilis
dissolute adj dissolūtus, perditus, libīdinōsus
dissolutely adv libīdinōsē, luxuriōsē
dissoluteness n luxuria f
dissolution n dissolūtiō f, discidium nt
dissolve vt dissolvere; (ice) liquefacere; (meeting)
  dīmittere; (contract) dīrimere ♦ vi liquēscere;
  (fig) solvī
dissonance n dissonum nt
dissonant adj dissonus
dissuade vt dissuādēre (dat), dēhortārī
dissuasion n dissuāsiō f
distaff n colus f
distance n intervallum nt, spatium nt; (long way)
  longinquitās f; at a ~ (far) longē; (within sight)
  procul; (fight) ēminus; at a ~ of ... spatiō (gen) ...;
  within striking ~ intrā iactum tēlī
distant adj longinquus; (measure) distāns; (person)
  parum familiāris; be ~ abesse (abl)
distaste n fastīdium nt
distasteful adj molestus, iniūcundus
distemper n morbus m
distend vt distendere
distil vt, vi stillāre
distinct adj (different) dīversus; (separate)
  distinctus; (clear) clārus, argūtus; (marked)
  distinctus; (sure) certus; (well-drawn) expressus
distinction n discrīmen nt; (dissimilarity)
  discrepantia f; (public status) amplitūdō f;
  (honour) honōs m, decus nt; (mark) īnsigne nt;
  there is a ~ interest; without ~ prōmiscuē
distinctive adj proprius, īnsignītus
distinctively adv propriē, īnsignītē
distinctly adv clārē, distinctē, certē, expressē
distinguish vt distinguere, internōscere,
  dīiūdicāre, discernere; (honour) decorāre,
  ōrnāre; ~ oneself ēminēre
distinguished adj īnsignis, praeclārus,
  ēgregius, amplissimus

distort vt dētorquēre; (fig) dēprāvāre
distorted adj distortus
distortion n distortiō f; dēprāvātiō f
distract vt distrahere, distinēre, āvocāre; (mind)
  aliēnāre
distracted adj āmēns, īnsānus
distraction n (state) indīligentia f; (cause)
  invītāmentum nt; (madness) furor m, dēmentia
  f; to ~ efflīctim
distraught adj āmēns, dēmēns
distress n labor m, dolor m, aegrimōnia f,
  aerumna f; be in ~ labōrāre ♦ vt adflīgere,
  sollicitāre
distressed adj adflīctus, sollicitus; be ~ at rem
  etc aegrē ferre
distressing adj tristis, miser, acerbus
distribute vt distribuere, dīvidere, dispertīre
distribution n partītiō f, distribūtiō f
district n regiō f, pars f
distrust n diffīdentia f ♦ vt diffīdere (dat), nōn
  crēdere (dat)
distrustful adj diffīdēns
distrustfully adv diffīdenter
disturb vt perturbāre, conturbāre; commovēre;
  (mind) sollicitāre
disturbance n turba f, perturbātiō f; (POL) mōtus
  m, tumultus m
disturber n turbātor m
disunion n discordia f, discidium nt
disunite vt dissociāre, sēiungere
disuse n dēsuētūdō f; fall into ~ obsolēscere
disused adj dēsuētus, obsolētus
disyllabic adj disyllabus
ditch n fossa f, scrobis m
dithyrambic adj dithyrambicus
dittany n dictamnum nt
ditty n carmen nt, cantilēna f
diurnal adj diūrnus
divan n lectus m, lectulus m
dive vi dēmergī
diver n ūrīnātor m
diverge vi dēvertere, dīgredī; (road) sē scindere;
  (opinions) discrepāre
divergence n dīgressiō f, discrepantia f
divers adj complūrēs
diverse adj varius, dīversus
diversify vt variāre
diversion n (of water) dērīvātiō f; (of thought)
  āvocātiō f; (to amuse) oblectāmentum nt; create
  a ~ (MIL) hostēs dīstringere; for a ~ animī causā
diversity n varietās f, discrepantia f
divert vt dēflectere, āvertere; (attention)
  āvocāre, abstrahere; (water) dērīvāre; (to amuse)
  oblectāre, placēre (dat)
diverting adj iūcundus; (remark) facētus
divest vt exuere, nūdāre; ~ oneself of (fig)
  pōnere, mittere
divide vt dīvidere; (troops) dīdūcere; ~ among
  partīrī, distribuere; ~ from sēparāre ab,
  sēiungere ab; ~ out dispertīrī, dīvidere ♦ vi
  discēdere, sē scindere; (senate) in sententiam
  īre; be divided (opinions) discrepāre
divination n dīvīnātiō f; (from birds) augurium nt;
  (from entrails) haruspicium nt
divine adj dīvīnus ♦ vt dīvīnāre, augurārī,
  hariolārī; by ~ intervention dīvīnitus

divinely *adv* dīvīnē
diviner *n* dīvīnus *m*, augur *m*, haruspex *m*
divinity *n* (*status*) dīvīnitās *f*; (*god*) deus *m*, dea *f*
divisible *adj* dīviduus
division *n* (*process*) dīvīsiō *f*, partītiō *f*; (*variance*) discordia *f*, dissēnsiō *f*; (*section*) pars *f*; (*grade*) classis *f*; (*of army*) legiō *f*; (*of time*) discrīmen *nt*; (*in senate*) discessiō *f*
divorce *n* dīvortium *nt*, repudium *nt* ◆ *vt* (*wife*) nūntium mittere (*dat*); (*things*) dīvellere, sēparāre
divulge *vt* aperīre, patefacere, ēvulgāre, ēdere
dizziness *n* vertīgō *f*
dizzy *adj* vertīginōsus; (*fig*) attonitus
do *vt* facere, agere; (*duty*) fungī (*abl*); (*wrong*) admittere; **do away with** *vt* tollere; (*kill*) interimere; **do one's best to** id agere ut (*subj*); **do without** repudiāre; **do not ... nolī/ nolīte** (*inf*); **how do you do?** quid agis?; **I have nothing to do with you** mihī tēcum nihil est commercī; **it has nothing to do with me** nihil est ad mē; **that will do** iam satis est; **be done** fierī; **have done with** dēfungī (*abl*)
docile *adj* docilis
docility *n* docilitās *f*
dock *n* (*ships*) nāvāle *nt*; (*LAW*) cancellī *mpl* ◆ *vt* praecīdere
dockyard *n* nāvālia *ntpl*
doctor *n* medicus *m*; (*univ*) doctor *m* ◆ *vt* cūrāre
doctrine *n* dogma *nt*, dēcrētum *nt*; (*system*) ratiō *f*
document *n* litterae *fpl*, tabula *f*
dodge *vt* dēclīnāre, ēvādere ◆ *n* dolus *m*
doe *n* cerva *f*
doer *n* āctor *m*, auctor *m*
doff *vt* exuere
dog *n* canis *m/f*; **dog star** Canīcula *f*; **dog's** canīnus ◆ *vt* īnsequī, īnstāre (*dat*)
dogged *adj* pertināx
doggedly *adv* pertināciter
dogma *n* dogma *nt*, praeceptum *nt*
dogmatic *adj* adrogāns
dogmatically *adv* adroganter
doing *n* factum *nt*
dole *n* sportula *f* ◆ *vt*: **~ out** dispertīrī, dīvidere
doleful *adj* lūgubris, flēbilis, maestus
dolefully *adv* flēbiliter
dolefulness *n* maestitia *f*, miseria *f*
doll *n* pūpa *f*
dolorous *adj* lūgubris, maestus
dolour *n* maestitia *f*, dolor *m*
dolphin *n* delphīnus *m*
dolt *n* stīpes *m*, caudex *m*
domain *n* ager *m*; (*king's*) rēgnum *nt*
dome *n* tholus *m*, testūdō *f*
domestic *adj* domesticus, familiāris; (*animal*) mānsuētus ◆ *n* famulus *m*, servus *m*, famula *f*, ancilla *f*; **domestics** *pl* familia *f*
domesticate *vt* mānsuēfacere
domesticated *adj* mānsuētus
domesticity *n* larēs suī *mpl*
domicile *n* domicilium *nt*, domus *f*
dominant *adj* superior, praepotēns
dominate *vt* dominārī in (*acc*), imperāre (*dat*); (*view*) dēspectāre
domination *n* dominātiō *f*, dominātus *m*
domineer *vi* dominārī, rēgnāre

dominion *n* imperium *nt*, rēgnum *nt*
don *vt* induere ◆ *n* scholasticus *m*
donate *vt* dōnāre
donation *n* dōnum *nt*
donkey *n* asellus *m*
donor *n* dōnātor *m*
doom *n* fātum *nt* ◆ *vt* damnāre
door *n* (*front*) iānua *f*; (*back*) postīcum *nt*; (*double*) forēs *fpl*; **folding doors** valvae *fpl*; **out of doors** forīs; (*to*) forās; **next ~ to** iuxtā (*acc*)
doorkeeper *n* iānitor *m*
doorpost *n* postis *m*
doorway *n* ōstium *nt*
dormant *adj* sōpītus; **lie ~** iacēre
dormitory *n* cubiculum *nt*
dormouse *n* glīs *m*
dose *n* pōculum *nt*
dot *n* pūnctum *nt*
dotage *n* senium *nt*
dotard *n* senex dēlīrus *m*
dote *vi* dēsipere; **~ upon** dēamāre
doting *adj* dēsipiēns, peramāns
dotingly *adv* perditē
double *adj* duplex; (*amount*) duplus; (*meaning*) ambiguus ◆ *n* duplum *nt* ◆ *vt* duplicāre; (*promontory*) superāre; (*fold*) complicāre ◆ *vi* duplicārī; (*MIL*) currere
double-dealer *n* fraudātor *m*
double-dealing *adj* fallāx, dolōsus ◆ *n* fraus *f*, dolus *m*
doublet *n* tunica *f*
doubly *adv* bis, dupliciter
doubt *n* dubium *nt*; (*hesitancy*) dubitātiō *f*; (*distrust*) suspiciō *f*; **give one the benefit of the ~** innocentem habēre; **no ~** sānē; **I do not ~ that ...** nōn dubito quīn ... (*subj*); **there is no ~ that ...** nōn dubium est quīn ... (*subj*) ◆ *vt* dubitāre; (*distrust*) diffīdere (*dat*), suspicārī
doubtful *adj* dubius, incertus; (*result*) anceps; (*word*) ambiguus
doubtfully *adv* dubiē; (*hesitation*) dubitanter
doubtless *adv* scīlicet, nīmīrum
doughty *adj* fortis, strēnuus
dove *n* columba *f*
dovecote *n* columbārium *nt*
dowdy *adj* inconcinnus
dower *n* dōs *f* ◆ *vt* dōtāre
dowerless *adj* indōtātus
down *n* plūmae *fpl*, lānūgō *f*; (*thistle*) pappus *m* ◆ *adv* deōrsum; **be ~** iacēre; **~ with!** perea(n)t; **up and ~** sūrsum deōrsum ◆ *prep* dē (*abl*); **~ from** dē (*abl*)
downcast *adj* dēmissus, maestus
downfall *n* ruīna *f*; (*fig*) occāsus *m*
downhearted *adj* dēmissus, frāctus animī
downhill *adj* dēclīvis; (*fig*) prōclīvis ◆ *adv* in praeceps
downpour *n* imber *m*
downright *adj* dīrēctus; (*intensive*) merus
downstream *adv* secundō flūmine
downtrodden *adj* subiectus, oppressus
downward *adj* dēclīvis, prōclīvis
downwards *adv* deōrsum
downy *adj* plūmeus
dowry *n* dōs *f*
doyen *n* pater *m*

doze vi dormītāre
dozen n duodecim
drab adj sordidior
drachma n drachma f
draft n (writing) exemplum nt; (MIL) dīlēctus m; (money) syngrapha f; (literary) silva f ✦ vt scrībere; (MIL) mittere
drag vt trahere ✦ vi (time) trahī; ~ **on** vi (war) prōdūcere ✦ n harpagō m; (fig) impedīmentum nt
dragnet n ēverriculum nt
dragon n drācō m
dragoon n eques m
drain n cloāca f ✦ vt (water) dērīvāre; (land) siccāre; (drink) exhaurīre; (resources) exhaurīre
drainage n dērīvātiō f
drake n anas m
drama n fābula f; **the** ~ scaena f
dramatic adj scaenicus
dramatist n fābulārum scrīptor m
dramatize vt ad scaenam compōnere
drape vt vēlāre
drapery n vestīmenta ntpl
drastic adj vehemēns, efficāx
draught n (air) aura f; (drink) haustus m; (net) bolus m
draughts n latrunculī mpl
draw vt dūcere, trahere; (bow) addūcere; (inference) colligere; (picture) scrībere, pingere; (sword) stringere, dēstringere; (tooth) eximere; (water) haurīre; ~ **aside** sēdūcere; ~ **away** āvocāre; ~ **back** vt retrahere ✦ vi recēdere; ~ **near** adpropinquāre; ~ **off** dētrahere; (water) dērīvāre; ~ **out** vt ēdūcere; (lengthen) prōdūcere; ~ **over** obdūcere; ~ **taut** addūcere; ~ **together** contrahere; ~ **up** vt (MIL) īnstruere; (document) scrībere
drawback n scrūpulus m; **this was the only** ~ hōc ūnum dēfuit
drawing n dēscrīptiō f; (art) graphicē f
drawing room n sellāria f
drawings npl līneāmenta ntpl
drawl vi lentē dīcere
drawling adj lentus in dīcendō
dray n plaustrum nt
dread n formīdō f, pavor m, horror m ✦ adj dīrus ✦ vt expavēscere, extimēscere, formīdāre
dreadful adj terribilis, horribilis, formīdolōsus, dīrus
dreadfully adv vehementer, atrōciter
dream n somnium nt ✦ vt, vi somniāre
dreamy adj somniculōsus
dreariness n (place) vastitās f; (mind) tristitia f
dreary adj (place) vastus; (person) tristis
dregs n faex f; (of oil) amurca f; **drain to the** ~ exhaurīre
drench vt perfundere
dress n vestis f, vestītus m, vestīmenta ntpl; (style) habitus m ✦ vt vestīre; (wound) cūrāre; (tree) amputāre ✦ vi induī; ~ **up** vi vestum induere
dressing n (MED) fōmentum nt
drift n (motion) mōtus m; (snow) agger m; (language) vīs f; **I see the** ~ **of your speech** videō quōrsum ōrātiō tua tendat ✦ vi fluitāre; (fig) lābī, ferrī
drill n terebra f; (MIL) exercitātiō f ✦ vt (hole) terebrāre; (MIL) exercēre; (pupil) īnstruere

drink vt, vi bibere, pōtāre; ~ **a health** propīnāre, Graecō mōre bibere; ~ **deep of** exhaurīre; ~ **in** haurīre; ~ **up** ēpōtāre ✦ n pōtiō f
drinkable adj pōtulentus
drinker n pōtor m
drinking bout n pōtātiō f
drip vi stillāre, dēstillāre
drive vt agere; (force) cōgere; ~ **away** abigere; (fig) pellere, prōpulsāre; ~ **back** repellere; ~ **home** dēfīgere; ~ **in/into** īnfīgere in (acc); (flock) cōgere in (acc); ~ **off** dēpellere; ~ **out** exigere, expellere, exturbāre; ~ **through** trānsfīgere ✦ vi vehī; ~ **away** āvehī; ~ **back** revehī; ~ **in** invehī; ~ **on** vt impellere; ~ **round** circumvehī; ~ **past** praetervehī; **what are you driving at?** quōrsum tua spectat ōrātiō? ✦ n gestātiō f
drivel vi dēlīrāre
drivelling adj dēlīrus, ineptus ✦ n ineptiae fpl
driver n aurīga m; rēctor m
drizzle vi rōrāre
droll adj facētus, ioculāris
drollery n facētiae fpl
dromedary n dromas m
drone n (bee) fūcus m; (sound) bombus m ✦ vi fremere
droop vi dēmittī; (flower) languēscere; (mind) animum dēmittere
drooping adj languidus
drop n gutta f ✦ vi cadere; (liquid) stillāre ✦ vt mittere; (anchor) iacere; (hint) ēmittere; (liquid) īnstillāre; (work) dēsistere ab (abl) ✦ vi: ~ **behind** cessāre; ~ **in** vi vīsere, supervenīre; ~ **out** excidere
dross n scōria f; (fig) faex f
drought n siccitās f
drouth n sitis f
drove n grex f
drover n bubulcus m
drown vt mergere, obruere; (noise) obscūrāre ✦ vi aquā perīre
drowse vi dormītāre
drowsily adv somniculōsē
drowsiness n sopor m
drowsy adj sēmisomnus, somniculōsus
drub vt pulsāre, verberāre
drudge n mediastīnus m ✦ vi labōrāre
drudgery n labor m
drug n medicāmentum nt ✦ vt medicāre
Druids n Druidae, Druidēs mpl
drum n tympanum nt; (container) urna f
drummer n tympanista m
drunk adj pōtus, ēbrius, tēmulentus
drunkard n ēbriōsus m
drunken adj ēbriōsus, tēmulentus
drunkenness n ēbrietās f
dry adj siccus, āridus; (thirst) sitiēns; (speech) āridus, frīgidus; (joke) facētus; **be dry** ārēre ✦ vt siccāre ✦ vi ārēscere; **dry up** exārēscere
dryad n dryas f
dry rot n rōbīgō f
dual adj duplex
duality n duplex nātūra f
dubiety n dubium nt
dubious adj dubius, incertus; (meaning) ambiguus
dubiously adv dubiē; ambiguē

duck *n* anas *f* ♦ *vt* dēmergere ♦ *vi* dēmergī, sē dēmittere
duckling *n* anaticula *f*
duct *n* ductus *m*
dudgeon *n* dolor *m*, stomachus *m*
due *adj* dēbitus, meritus, iūstus; **be due** dēbērī; **it is due to me that ... not** per mē stat quōminus *(subj)*; **be due to** orīrī ex, fierī *(abl)* ♦ *n* iūs *nt*, dēbitum *nt*; *(tax)* vectīgal *nt*; *(harbour)* portōrium *nt*; **give every man his due** suum cuīque tribuere ♦ *adv* rēctā; **due to** ob *(acc)*, propter *(acc)*
duel *n* certāmen *nt*
dug *n* ūber *nt*
duke *n* dux *m*
dulcet *adj* dulcis
dull *adj* hebes; *(weather)* subnūbilus; *(language)* frīgidus; *(mind)* tardus; **be ~** hebēre; **become ~** hebēscere ♦ *vt* hebetāre, obtundere, retundere
dullard *n* stolidus *m*
dulness *n* *(mind)* tarditās *f*, stultitia *f*
duly *adv* rītē, ut pār est
dumb *adj* mūtus; **be struck ~** obmūtēscere
dun *n* flāgitātor *m* ♦ *vt* flāgitāre ♦ *adj* fuscus
dunce *n* bārō *m*
dune *n* tumulus *m*
dung *n* fimus *m*
dungeon *n* carcer *m*, rōbur *nt*
dupe *vt* dēlūdere, fallere ♦ *n* crēdulus *m*
duplicate *n* exemplar *nt* ♦ *vt* duplicāre
duplicity *n* fraus *f*, perfidia *f*
durability *n* firmitās *f*, firmitūdō *f*
durable *adj* firmus, perpetuus

durably *adv* firmē
duration *n* spatium *nt*; *(long)* diūturnitās *f*
duress *n* vīs *f*
during *prep* inter *(acc)*, per *(acc)*
dusk *n* crepusculum *nt*, vesper *m*; **at ~** prīmā nocte, prīmīs tenebrīs
dusky *adj* fuscus
dust *n* pulvis *m*; **throw ~ in the eyes of** tenebrās offundere *(dat)* ♦ *vt* dētergēre
dusty *adj* pulverulentus
dutiful *adj* pius, officiōsus
dutifully *adv* piē, officiōsē
dutifulness *n* pietās *f*
duty *n* *(moral)* officium *nt*; *(task)* mūnus *nt*; *(tax)* vectīgal *nt*; **be on ~** *(MIL)* statiōnem agere, excubāre; **do one's ~** officiō fungī; **do ~ for** *(person)* in locum sufficī *(gen)*; *(thing)* adhibērī prō *(abl)*; **it is my ~** dēbeō, mē oportet, meum est; **it is the ~ of a commander** ducis est; **sense of ~** pietās *f*
duty call *n* salūtātiō *f*
duty-free *adj* immūnis
dwarf *n* *(of plant)* nānus *m*
dwell *vi* habitāre; **~ in** incolere; **~ upon** *(theme)* commorārī in *(abl)*
dweller *n* incola *m*
dwelling *n* domus *f*, domicilium *nt*; *(place)* sēdēs *f*
dwindle *vi* dēcrēscere, extenuārī
dye *n* fūcus *m*, color *m* ♦ *vt* īnficere, fūcāre
dyer *n* īnfector *m*
dying *adj* moribundus, moriēns
dynasty *n* domus *(rēgia)* *f*
dyspepsia *n* crūditās *f*

Ee

each *adj, pron* quisque; (*of two*) uterque; ~ **other**
inter sē; **one** ~ singulī; ~ **year** quotannīs

eager *adj* avidus, cupidus, alācer; ~ **for** avidus
(*gen*)

eagerly *adv* avidē, cupidē, ācriter

eagerness *n* cupīdō *f*, ārdor *m*, studium *nt*;
alacritās *f*

eagle *n* aquila *f*

ear *n* auris *f*; (*of corn*) spīca *f*; **give ear** aurem
praebēre, auscultāre; **go in at one ear and
out at the other** surdīs auribus nārrārī; **prick
up one's ears** aurēs ērigere; **with long ears**
aurītus

earl *n* comes *m*

earlier *adv* ante; anteā

early *adj* (*in season*) mātūrus; (*in day*) mātūtīnus;
(*at beginning*) prīmus; (*in history*) antīquus ♦ *adv*
(*in day*) māne; (*before time*) mātūrē, temperī; ~ **in
life** ab ineunte aetāte

earn *vt* merērī, cōnsequī; ~ **a living** vīctum
quaerere, quaestum facere

earnest *adj* (*serious*) sērius; (*eager*) ācer, sēdulus
♦ *n* pignus *nt*; (*money*) arrabō *m*; **in** ~ sēdulō,
ēnīxē

earnestly *adv* sēriō, graviter, sēdulō

earnestness *n* gravitās *f*, studium *nt*

earnings *n* quaestus *m*

earring *n* elenchus *m*

earth *n* (*planet*) tellūs *f*; (*inhabited*) orbis terrārum
m; (*land*) terra *f*; (*soil*) solum *nt*, humus *f*; (*fox's*)
latibulum *nt*; **where on earth?** ubī gentium?;
of the ~ terrestris

earthen *adj* (*ware*) fictilis; (*mound*) terrēnus

earthenware *n* fictilia *ntpl* ♦ *adj* fictilis

earthly *adj* terrestris

earthquake *n* terrae mōtus *m*

earthwork *n* agger *m*

earthy *adj* terrēnus

ease *n* facilitās *f*; (*leisure*) ōtium *nt*; **at** ~ ōtiōsus;
(*in mind*) sēcūrus; **ill at** ~ sollicitus ♦ *vt* laxāre,
relevāre; (*pain*) mītigāre

easily *adv* facile; (*gladly*) libenter; (*at leisure*)
ōtiōsē; **not** ~ nōn temerē

easiness *n* facilitās *f*

east *n* Oriēns *m*, sōlis ortus *m*; ~ **wind** eurus *m*

Easter *n* Pascha *f*

easterly, eastern *adj* orientālis

eastward *adv* ad orientem

easy *adj* facilis; (*manner*) adfābilis, facilis; (*mind*)
sēcūrus; (*speech*) expedītus; (*discipline*) remissus;
~ **circumstances** dīvitiae *fpl*, abundantia *f*

eat *vt* edere; cōnsūmere; vescī (*abl*); **eat away**
rōdere; **eat up** exedere

eatable *adj* esculentus

eating *n* cibus *m*

eaves *n* suggrunda *f*

eavesdropper *n* sermōnis auceps *m*

ebb *n* dēcessus *m*, recessus *m*; **at ebbtide**
minuente aestū; **be at a low ebb** (*fig*) iacēre ♦ *vi*
recēdere

ebony *n* ebenus *f*

ebullient *adj* fervēns

ebullition *n* fervor *m*

eccentric *adj* īnsolēns

eccentricity *n* īnsolentia *f*

echo *n* imāgō *f* ♦ *vt, vi* resonāre

eclipse *n* dēfectus *m*, dēfectiō *f* ♦ *vt* obscūrāre; **be
eclipsed** dēficere, labōrāre

eclogue *n* ecloga *f*

economic *adj* quaestuōsus, sine iactūrā

economical *adj* (*person*) frūgī, parcus

economically *adv* nūllā iactūrā factā

economics *n* reī familiāris dispēnsātiō *f*

economize *vi* parcere

economy *n* frūgālitās *f*

ecstasy *n* alacritās *f*, furor *m*

ecstatic *adj* gaudiō ēlātus

eddy *n* vertex *m* ♦ *vi* volūtārī

edge *n* ōra *f*, margō *f*; (*of dish*) labrum *nt*; (*of blade*)
aciēs *f*; **take the** ~ **off** obtundere; **on** ~ (*fig*)
suspēnsō animō ♦ *vt* (*garment*) praetexere;
(*blade*) acuere ♦ *vi*: ~ **in** sē īnsinuāre

edging *n* limbus *m*

edible *adj* esculentus

edict *n* ēdictum *nt*, dēcrētum *nt*

edification *n* ērudītiō *f*

edifice *n* aedificium *nt*

edify *vt* ērudīre

edit *vt* recognōscere, recēnsēre

edition *n* ēditiō *f*

educate *vt* ērudīre, īnfōrmāre; ~ **in** īnstituere
ad (*acc*)

education *n* doctrīna *f*; (*process*) īnstitūtiō *f*

eel *n* anguilla *f*

eerie *adj* mōnstruōsus

efface *vt* dēlēre, tollere

effect *n* (*result*) ēventus *m*; (*impression*) vīs *f*,
effectus *m*; (*show*) iactātiō *f*; **effects** *pl* bona *ntpl*;
for ~ iactātiōnis causā; **in** ~ rē vērā; **to this**
~ in hanc sententiam; **without** ~ inritus ♦ *vt*
efficere, facere, patrāre

effective *adj* valēns, validus; (RHET) gravis,
ōrnātus

effectively *adv* validē, graviter, ōrnātē
effectiveness *n* vīs *f*
effectual *adj* efficāx, idōneus
effectually *adv* efficāciter
effectuate *vt* efficere, cōnsequī
effeminacy *n* mollitiēs *f*
effeminate *adj* mollis, effēminātus
effeminately *adv* molliter, effēminātē
effervesce *vi* effervēscere
effete *adj* effētus
efficacious *adj* efficāx
efficaciously *adv* efficāciter
efficacy *n* vīs *f*
efficiency *n* virtūs *f*, perītia *f*
efficient *adj* capāx, perītus; (LOGIC) efficiēns
efficiently *adv* perītē, bene
effigy *n* simulācrum *nt*, effigiēs *f*
effloresce *vi* flōrēscere
efflorescence *n* (fig) flōs *m*
effluvium *n* hālitus *m*
effort *n* opera *f*, cōnātus *m*; (of mind) intentiō *f*;
   make an ~ ēnītī
effrontery *n* audācia *f*, impudentia *f*
effusive *adj* officiōsus
egg *n* ōvum *nt*; **lay an egg** ōvum parere ♦ *vt*
   impellere, īnstīgāre
egoism *n* amor suī *m*
egoist *n* suī amāns *m*
egotism *n* iactātiō *f*
egotist *n* glōriōsus *m*
egregious *adj* singulāris
egress *n* exitus *m*
eight *num* octō; **~ each** octōnī; **~ times** octiēns
eighteen *num* duodēvīgintī
eighteenth *adj* duodēvīcēsimus
eighth *adj* octāvus
eight hundred *num* octingentī
eight hundredth *adj* octingentēsimus
eightieth *adj* octōgēsimus
eighty *num* octōgintā; **~ each** octōgēnī; **~ times**
   octōgiēns
either *pron* alteruter, uterlibet, utervīs ♦ *conj* aut,
   vel; **~ ... or** aut, vel ... vel
ejaculation *n* clāmor *m*
eject *vt* ēicere, expellere
ejection *n* expulsiō *f*
eke *vt*: **eke out** parcendō prōdūcere
elaborate *vt* ēlabōrāre ♦ *adj* ēlabōrātus,
   exquīsītus
elaborately *adv* summō labōre, exquīsītē
elan *n* ferōcia *f*
elapse *vi* abīre, intercēdere; **allow to**
   ~ intermittere; **a year has elapsed since** annus
   est cum (+ *indic*)
elated *adj* ēlātus; **be ~** efferrī
elation *n* laetitia *f*
elbow *n* cubitum *nt*
elder *adj* nātū māior, senior ♦ *n* (tree) sambūcus *f*
elderly *adj* aetāte prōvectus
elders *npl* patrēs *mpl*
eldest *adj* nātū māximus
elecampane *n* inula *f*
elect *vt* ēligere, dēligere; (magistrate) creāre;
   (colleague) cooptāre ♦ *adj* dēsignātus; (special)
   lēctus
election *n* (POL) comitia *ntpl*

electioneering *n* ambitiō *f*
elector *n* suffrāgātor *m*
elegance *n* ēlegantia *f*, lepōs *m*, munditia *f*,
   concinnitās *f*
elegant *adj* ēlegāns, concinnus, nitidus
elegantly *adv* ēleganter, concinnē
elegiac *adj*: **~ verse** elegī *mpl*, versūs alternī *mpl*
elegy *n* elegīa *f*
element *n* elementum *nt*; **elements** *pl* initia
   ntpl, prīncipia *ntpl*; **out of one's ~** peregrīnus
elementary *adj* prīmus
elephant *n* elephantus *m*, elephas *m*
elevate *vt* efferre, ērigere
elevated *adj* ēditus, altus
elevation *n* altitūdō *f*; (style) ēlātiō *f*
eleven *num* ūndecim; **~ each** ūndēnī; **~ times**
   ūndeciēns
eleventh *adj* ūndecimus
elf *n* deus *m*
elicit *vt* ēlicere; (with effort) ēruere
elide *vt* ēlīdere
eligible *adj* idōneus, aptus
eliminate *vt* tollere, āmovēre
elite *n* flōs *m*, rōbur *nt*
elk *n* alcēs *f*
ell *n* ulna *f*
ellipse *n* (RHET) dētractiō *f*; (oval) ōvum *nt*
elm *n* ulmus *f* ♦ *adj* ulmeus
elocution *n* prōnūntiātiō *f*
elongate *vt* prōdūcere
elope *vi* aufugere
eloquence *n* ēloquentia *f*; (natural) fācundia *f*,
   dīcendī vīs *f*
eloquent *adj* ēloquēns; (natural) fācundus;
   (fluent) disertus
eloquently *adv* fācundē, disertē
else *adv* aliōquī, aliter ♦ *adj* alius; **or ~** aliōquī;
   who ~ quis alius
elsewhere *adv* alibī; **~ to** aliō
elucidate *vt* ēnōdāre, illūstrāre
elucidation *n* ēnōdātiō *f*, explicātiō *f*
elude *vt* ēvītāre, frustrārī, fallere
elusive *adj* fallāx
emaciated *adj* macer
emaciation *n* maciēs *f*
emanate *vi* mānāre; (fig) ēmānāre, orīrī
emanation *n* exhālātiō *f*
emancipate *vt* ēmancipāre, manū mittere,
   līberāre
emancipation *n* lībertās *f*
emasculate *vt* ēnervāre, dēlumbāre
embalm *vt* condīre
embankment *n* agger *m*, mōlēs *f*
embargo *n* interdictum *nt*
embark *vi* cōnscendere, nāvem cōnscendere;
   ~ upon (fig) ingredī ♦ *vt* impōnere
embarkation *n* cōnscēnsiō *f*
embarrass *vt* (by confusing) perturbāre;
   (by obstructing) impedīre; (by revealing)
   dēprehendere; **be embarrassed** haerēre
embarrassing *adj* incommodus, intempestīvus
embarrassment *n* (in speech) haesitātiō *f*; (in
   mind) sollicitūdō *f*; (in business) angustiae *fpl*,
   difficultās *f*; (cause) molestia *f*, impedīmentum
   nt
embassy *n* lēgātiō *f*

embedded *adj* dēfixus
embellish *vt* adōrnāre, exōrnāre, decorāre
embellishment *n* decus *nt*, exōrnātiō *f*,
　ōrnāmentum *nt*
embers *n* cinis *m*, favilla *f*
embezzle *vt* peculārī, dēpeculārī
embezzlement *n* peculātus *m*
embezzler *n* peculātor *m*
embitter *vt* exacerbāre
emblazon *vt* īnsignīre
emblem *n* īnsigne *nt*
embodiment *n* exemplar *nt*
embody *vt* repraesentāre; (MIL) cōnscrībere
embolden *vt* cōnfirmāre; ~ **the hearts of**
　animōs cōnfirmāre
emboss *vt* imprimere, caelāre
embrace *vt* amplectī, complectī; (*items*)
　continēre, comprehendere; (*party*) sequī;
　(*opportunity*) adripere ♦ *n* amplexus *m*,
　complexus *m*
embroider *vt* acū pingere
embroidery *n* vestis picta *f*
embroil *vt* miscēre, implicāre
emend *vt* ēmendāre, corrigere
emendation *n* ēmendātiō *f*, correctiō *f*
emerald *n* smaragdus *m*
emerge *vi* ēmergere, exsistere; ēgredī
emergency *n* tempus *nt*, discrīmen *nt* ♦ *adj*
　subitārius
emigrate *vi* migrāre, ēmigrāre
emigration *n* migrātiō *f*
eminence *n* (*ground*) tumulus *m*, locus ēditus *m*;
　(*rank*) praestantia *f*, amplitūdō *f*
eminent *adj* ēgregius, ēminēns, īnsignis,
　amplus
eminently *adv* ēgregiē, prae cēterīs, in prīmīs
emissary *n* lēgātus *m*
emit *vt* ēmittere
emolument *n* lucrum *nt*, ēmolumentum *nt*
emotion *n* animī mōtus *m*, commōtiō *f*,
　adfectus *m*
emotional *adj* (*person*) mōbilis; (*speech*)
　flexanimus
emperor *n* prīnceps *m*, imperātor *m*
emphasis *n* pondus *nt*; (*words*) impressiō *f*
emphasize *vt* exprimere
emphatic *adj* gravis
emphatically *adv* adsevēranter, vehementer
empire *n* imperium *nt*
employ *vt* ūtī (*abl*); (*for purpose*) adhibēre; (*person*)
　exercēre
employed *adj* occupātus
employees *npl* operae *fpl*
employer *n* redemptor *m*
employment *n* (*act*) ūsus *m*; (*work*) quaestus *m*
empower *vt* permittere (*dat*), potestātem facere
　(*dat*)
emptiness *n* inānitās *f*
empty *adj* inānis, vacuus; (*fig*) vānus, inritus ♦ *vt*
　exhaurīre, exinānīre ♦ *vi* (*river*) īnfluere
emulate *vt* aemulārī
emulation *n* aemulātiō *f*
emulous *adj* aemulus
emulously *adv* certātim
enable *vt* potestātem facere (*dat*); efficere ut
　(*subj*)

enact *vt* dēcernere, ēdīcere, scīscere; (*part*) agere
enactment *n* dēcrētum *nt*, lēx *f*
enamoured *adj* amāns; **be ~ of** dēamāre
encamp *vi* castra pōnere, tendere
encampment *n* castra *ntpl*
encase *vt* inclūdere
enchant *vt* fascināre; (*fig*) dēlectāre
enchantment *n* fascinātiō *f*; blandīmentum *nt*
enchantress *n* sāga *f*
encircle *vt* cingere, circumdare, amplectī
enclose *vt* inclūdere, saepīre
enclosure *n* saeptum *nt*, māceria *f*
encompass *vt* cingere, circumdare, amplectī
encounter *vt* obviam īre (*dat*), occurrere (*dat*); (*in*
　battle) concurrere cum (*abl*), congredī cum ♦ *n*
　occursus *m*, concursus *m*
encourage *vt* cōnfirmāre, (co)hortārī,
　sublevāre, favēre (*dat*)
encouragement *n* hortātiō *f*, favor *m*, auxilium
　nt
encroach *vi* invādere; ~ **upon** occupāre; (*fig*)
　imminuere
encrust *vt* incrustāre
encumber *vt* impedīre, onerāre
encumbrance *n* impedīmentum *nt*, onus *nt*
end *n* fīnis *m*; (*aim*) prōpositum *nt*; (*of action*)
　ēventus *m*, exitus *m*; (*of speech*) perōrātiō *f*;
　end to end continuī; **at a loose end** vacuus,
　ōtiōsus; **for two days on end** biduum
　continenter; **in the end** dēnique; **the end of**
　extrēmus; (*time*) exāctus; **put an end to** fīnem
　facere (*dat*), fīnem impōnere (*dat*); **to the end**
　that eō cōnsiliō ut (*subj*); **to what end?** quō?,
　quōrsum? ♦ *vt* fīnīre, cōnficere; (*mutual dealings*)
　dīrimere ♦ *vi* dēsinere; (*event*) ēvādere; (*sentence*)
　cadere; (*speech*) perōrāre; (*time*) exīre; **end up as**
　ēvādere; **end with** dēsinere in (*acc*)
endanger *vt* perīclitārī, in discrīmen addūcere
endear *vt* dēvincīre
endearing *adj* blandus
endearment *n* blanditiae *fpl*
endeavour *vt* cōnārī, ēnītī ♦ *n* cōnātus *m*
ending *n* fīnis *m*, exitus *m*
endive *n* intubum *nt*
endless *adj* īnfīnītus; (*time*) aeternus, perpetuus
endlessly *adv* sine fīne, īnfīnītē
endorse *vt* ratum facere
endow *vt* dōnāre, īnstruere
endowed *adj* praeditus (*abl*)
endowment *n* dōnum *nt*
endurance *n* patientia *f*
endure *vi* dūrāre, permanēre ♦ *vt* ferre, tolerāre,
　patī
enemy *n* (*public*) hostis *m*, hostēs *mpl*; (*private*)
　inimīcus *m*; **greatest ~** inimīcissimus *m*;
　~ territory hosticum *nt*
energetic *adj* impiger, nāvus, strēnuus; (*style*)
　nervōsus
energetically *adv* impigrē, nāviter, strēnuē
energy *n* impigritās *f*, vigor *m*, incitātiō *f*; (*mind*)
　contentiō *f*; (*style*) nervī *mpl*
enervate *vt* ēnervāre, ēmollīre
enervation *n* languor *m*
enfeeble *vt* īnfirmāre, dēbilitāre
enfold *vt* involvere, complectī
enforce *vt* (LAW) exsequī; (*argument*) cōnfirmāre

enfranchise vt cīvitāte dōnāre; (slave) manū mittere

engage vt (affection) dēvincīre; (attention) distinēre, occupāre; (enemy) manum cōnserere cum (abl); (hire) condūcere; (promise) spondēre, recipere; ~ **the enemy** proelium cum hostibus committere; **be engaged in** versārī in (abl) ♦ vi: ~ **in** ingredī, suscipere

engagement n (COMM) occupātiō f; (MIL) pugna f, certāmen nt; (agreement) spōnsiō f; **keep an** ~ fidem praestāre; **break an** ~ fidem fallere; **I have an** ~ **at your house** prōmīsī ad tē

engaging adj blandus

engender vt ingenerāre, ingignere

engine n māchina f

engineer n māchinātor m ♦ vt mōlīrī

engraft vt īnserere

engrave vt īnsculpere, incīdere, caelāre

engraver n sculptor m, caelātor m

engraving n sculptūra f, caelātūra f

engross vt dīstringere, occupāre; **engrossed in** tōtus in (abl)

engulf vt dēvorāre, obruere

enhance vt amplificāre, augēre, exaggerāre

enigma n aenigma nt, ambāgēs fpl

enigmatic adj ambiguus, obscūrus

enigmatically adv per ambāgēs, ambiguē

enjoin vt imperāre (dat), iniungere (dat)

enjoy vt fruī (abl); (advantage) ūtī (abl); (pleasure) percipere, dēcerpere; ~ **oneself** dēlectārī, geniō indulgēre

enjoyable adj iūcundus

enjoyment n fructus m; dēlectātiō f, voluptās f

enlarge vt augēre, amplificāre, dīlātāre; (territory) prōpāgāre; ~ **upon** amplificāre

enlargement n amplificātiō f, prōlātiō f

enlighten vt inlūstrāre; docēre, ērudīre

enlightenment n ērudītiō f, hūmānitās f

enlist vt scrībere, cōnscrībere; (sympathy) conciliāre ♦ vi nōmen dare

enliven vt excitāre

enmesh vt impedīre, implicāre

enmity n inimīcitia f, simultās f

ennoble vt honestāre, excolere

ennui n taedium nt

enormity n immānitās f; (deed) scelus nt, nefās nt

enormous adj immānis, ingēns

enormously adv immēnsum

enough adj satis (indecl, gen) ♦ adv satis; **more than** ~ satis superque; **I have had** ~ **of** ... mē taedet (gen) ...

enquire vi quaerere, percontārī; ~ **into** cognōscere, inquīrere in (acc)

enquiry n percontātiō f; (legal) quaestiō f

enrage vt inrītāre, incendere

enrapture vt dēlectāre

enrich vt dītāre, locuplētāre; ~ **with** augēre (abl)

enrol vt adscrībere, cōnscrībere ♦ vi nōmen dare

enshrine vt dēdicāre; (fig) sacrāre

enshroud vt involvere

ensign n signum nt, īnsigne nt; (officer) signifer m

enslave vt in servitūtem redigere

enslavement n servitūs f

ensnare vt dēcipere, inlaqueāre, inrētīre

ensue vi īnsequī

ensure vt praestāre; ~ **that** efficere ut (subj)

entail vt adferre

entangle vt impedīre, implicāre, inrētīre

entanglement n implicātiō f

enter vi inīre, ingredī, intrāre; (riding) invehī; ~ **into** introīre in (acc); ~ **upon** inīre, ingredī ♦ vt (place) intrāre; (account) ferre, indūcere; (mind) subīre

enterprise n inceptum nt; (character) prōmptus animus m

enterprising adj prōmptus, strēnuus

entertain vt (guest) invītāre, excipere; (state of mind) habēre, concipere; (to amuse) oblectāre

entertainer n acroāma nt

entertainment n hospitium nt; oblectāmentum nt; acroāma nt

enthral vt capere

enthusiasm n studium nt, fervor m; ~ **for** studium nt (gen)

enthusiastic adj studiōsus, fervidus

enthusiastically adv summō studiō

entice vt inlicere, ēlicere, invītāre

enticement n illecebra f, lēnōcinium nt

entire adj integer, tōtus, ūniversus

entirely adv omnīnō, funditus, penitus

entitle vt (book) īnscrībere; **be entitled to** merērī, dignum esse quī (subj), iūs habēre (gen)

entity n rēs f

entomb vt humāre, sepelīre

entrails n intestīna ntpl, exta ntpl

entrance n aditus m, introitus m; (act) ingressiō f; (of house) vestibulum nt; (of harbour) ōstium nt ♦ vt fascināre, cōnsōpīre, capere

entreat vt implōrāre, obsecrāre; (successfully) exōrāre

entreaty n precēs fpl

entrenchment n mūnītiō f

entrust vt committere, crēdere, mandāre; (for keeping) dēpōnere

entry n introitus m, aditus m; **make an** ~ (book) in tabulās referre

entwine vt implicāre, involvere

enumerate vt numerāre, dīnumerāre

enunciate vt ēdīcere; (word) exprimere

envelop vt implicāre, involvere

envelope n involucrum nt

enviable adj beātus

envious adj invidus, invidiōsus

enviously adv invidiōsē

environment n vīcīnia f; **our** ~ ea in quibus versāmur

envoy n lēgātus m

envy n invidia f ♦ vt invidēre (dat)

enwrap vt involvere

ephemeral adj brevis

ephor n ephorus m

epic adj epicus ♦ n epos nt

epicure n dēlicātus m

epigram n sententia f; (poem) epigramma nt

epilepsy n morbus comitiālis m

epilogue n epilogus m

episode n ēventum nt

epistle n epistula f, litterae fpl

epitaph n epigramma nt, titulus m

epithet n adsūmptum nt

epitome n epitomē f
epoch n saeculum nt
equable adj aequālis; (temper) aequus
equal adj aequus, pār; **be ~ to** aequāre; (task) sufficere (dat) ♦ n pār m/f ♦ vt aequāre, adaequāre
equality n aequālitās f
equalize vt adaequāre, exaequāre
equally adv aequē, pariter
equanimity n aequus animus m
equate vt aequāre
equator n aequinoctiālis circulus m
equestrian adj equester
equidistant adj: **be ~** aequō spatiō abesse, idem distāre
equilibrium n lībrāmentum nt
equine adj equīnus
equinoctial adj aequinoctiālis
equinox n aequinoctium nt
equip vt armāre, īnstruere, ōrnāre
equipment n arma ntpl, īnstrūmenta ntpl, adparātus m
equipoise n lībrāmentum nt
equitable adj aequus, iūstus
equitably adv iūstē, aequē
equity n aequum nt, aequitās f
equivalent adj pār, īdem īnstar (gen)
equivocal adj anceps, ambiguus
equivocally adv ambiguē
equivocate vi tergiversārī
era n saeculum nt
eradicate vt ēvellere, exstirpāre
erase vt dēlēre, indūcere
erasure n litūra f
ere conj priusquam
erect vt ērigere; (building) exstruere; (statute) pōnere ♦ adj ērēctus
erection n (process) exstructiō f; (product) aedificium nt
erode vt rōdere
erotic adj amātōrius
err vi errāre, peccāre
errand n mandātum nt
errant adj vagus
erratic adj incōnstāns
erroneous adj falsus
erroneously adv falsō, perperam
error n error m; (moral) peccātum nt; (writing) mendum nt
erudite adj doctus
erudition n doctrīna f, ērudītiō f
erupt vi ērumpere
eruption n ēruptiō f
escapade n ausum nt
escape vi effugere, ēvādere ♦ vt fugere, ēvītāre; (memory) excidere ex (abl); **~ the notice of** fallere, praeterīre ♦ n effugium nt, fuga f; **way of ~** effugium nt
eschew vt vītāre
escort n praesidium nt; (private) dēductor m ♦ vt comitārī, prōsequī; (out of respect) dēdūcere
especial adj praecipuus
especially adv praecipuē, praesertim, māximē, in prīmīs
espionage n inquīsītiō f
espouse vt (wife) dūcere; (cause) fovēre

espy vt cōnspicere, cōnspicārī
essay n cōnātus m; (test) perīculum nt; (LIT) libellus m ♦ vt cōnārī, incipere
essence n vīs f, nātūra f
essential adj necesse, necessārius
essentially adv necessāriō
establish vt īnstituere, condere; (firmly) stabilīre
established adj firmus, certus; **be ~** cōnstāre; **become ~** (custom) inveterāscere
establishment n (act) cōnstitūtiō f; (domestic) familia f
estate n fundus m, rūs nt; (in money) rēs f; (rank) ōrdō m
esteem vt aestimāre, respicere ♦ n grātia f, opīniō f
estimable adj optimus
estimate vt aestimāre, ratiōnem inīre (gen) ♦ n aestimātiō f, iūdicium nt
estimation n opīniō f, sententia f
estrange vt aliēnāre, abaliēnāre
estrangement n aliēnātiō f, discidium nt
estuary n aestuārium nt
eternal adj aeternus, perennis
eternally adv semper, aeternum
eternity n aeternitās f
etesian winds n etēsiae fpl
ether n (sky) aethēr m
ethereal adj aetherius, caelestis
ethic, ethical adj mōrālis
ethics n mōrēs mpl, officia ntpl
Etruscan n Etruscus m ♦ adj Etruscus
etymology n verbōrum notātiō f
eulogist n laudātor m
eulogize vt laudāre, conlaudāre
eulogy n laudātiō f
eunuch n eunūchus m
euphony n sonus m
evacuate vt (place) exinānīre; (people) dēdūcere
evacuation n discessiō f
evade vt dēclīnāre, dēvītāre, ēlūdere
evaporate vt exhālāre ♦ vi exhālārī
evaporation n exhālātiō f
evasion n tergiversātiō f
evasive adj ambiguus
eve n vesper m; (before festival) pervigilium nt; **on the eve of** prīdiē (gen)
even adj aequus, aequālis; (number) pār ♦ adv et, etiam; (tentative) vel; **~ if** etsī, etiamsī; tametsī; **~ more** etiam magis; **~ so** nihilōminus; **~ yet** etiamnum; **not ~ ...** nē quidem ♦ vt aequāre
evening n vesper m ♦ adj vespertīnus; **~ is drawing on** invesperāscit; **in the ~** vesperī
evening star n Vesper m, Hesperus m
evenly adv aequāliter, aequābiliter
evenness n aequālitās f, aequābilitās f
event n ēventum nt; (outcome) ēventus m
eventide n vespertīnum tempus nt
eventuality n cāsus m
eventually adv mox, aliquandō, tandem
ever adv unquam; (after sī, nisī, num, nē) quandō; (always) semper; (after interrog) -nam, tandem; ever so nimium, nimium quantum; **best ~** omnium optimus; **for ~** in aeternum
everlasting adj aeternus, perpetuus, immortālis
evermore adv semper, in aeternum

every *adj* quisque, omnis; ~ **four years** quintō
quōque annō; ~ **now and then** interdum; **in**
~ **direction** passim, undique; ~ **other day**
alternis diebus; ~ **day** cottīdiē ◆ *adj* cottīdiānus
everybody *pron* quisque, omnēs *mpl*; ~ **agrees**
inter omnēs constat; ~ **knows** nēmō est quīn
sciat
everyday *adj* cottīdiānus
everyone *pron see* **everybody**
everything omnia *ntpl*; **your health is** ~ **to me**
meā māximē interest tē valēre
everywhere *adv* ubīque, passim
evict *vt* dēicere, dētrūdere
eviction *n* dēiectiō *f*
evidence *n* testimōnium *nt*, indicium *nt*; (*person*)
testis *m/f*; (*proof*) argūmentum *nt*; **on the** ~ **of**
fidē (*gen*); **collect** ~ **against** inquīrere in (*acc*);
turn King's ~ indicium profitērī
evident *adj* manifestus, ēvidēns, clārus; **it is**
~ appāret
evidently *adv* manifestō, clārē
evil *adj* malus, improbus, scelerātus
evildoer *n* scelerātus *m*, maleficus *m*
evil eye *n* fascinum *nt*, malum *nt*, improbitās *f*
evil-minded *adj* malevolus
evince *vt* praestāre
evoke *vt* ēvocāre, ēlicere
evolution *n* seriēs *f*, prōgressus *m*; (MIL) dēcursus
m, dēcursiō *f*
evolve *vt* explicāre, ēvolvere ◆ *vi* crēscere
ewe *n* ovis *f*
ewer *n* hydria *f*
exacerbate *vt* exacerbāre, exasperāre
exact *vt* exigere ◆ *adj* accūrātus; (*person*) dīligēns;
(*number*) exāctus
exaction *n* exāctiō *f*
exactly *adv* accūrātē; (*reply*) ita prōrsus; ~ **as**
perinde que
exactness *n* cūra *f*, dīligentia *f*
exaggerate *vt* augēre, in māius extollere
exalt *vt* efferre, extollere; laudāre
exaltation *n* ēlātiō *f*
examination *n* inquīsītiō *f*, scrūtātiō *f*; (*of*
witness) interrogātiō *f*; (*test*) probātiō *f*
examine *vt* investīgāre, scrūtārī; īnspicere;
(*witness*) interrogāre; (*case*) quaerere dē (*abl*);
(*candidate*) probāre
examiner *n* scrūtātor *m*
example *n* exemplum *nt*, documentum *nt*; **for**
~ exemplī grātiā; **make an** ~ **of** animadvertere
in (*acc*); **I am an** ~ exemplō sum
exasperate *vt* exacerbāre, inrītāre
exasperation *n* inrītātiō *f*
excavate *vt* fodere
excavation *n* fossiō *f*
excavator *n* fossor *m*
exceed *vt* excēdere, superāre
exceedingly *adv* nimis, valdē, nimium
quantum
excel *vt* praestāre (*dat*), exsuperāre ◆ *vi* excellere
excellence *n* praestantia *f*, virtūs *f*
excellent *adj* ēgregius, praestāns, optimus
excellently *adv* ēgregiē, praeclārē
except *vt* excipere ◆ *prep* praeter (*acc*) ◆ *adv* nisī
◆ *conj* praeterquam, nisī quod

exception *n* exceptiō *f*; **make an** ~ **of** excipere;
take ~ **to** gravārī quod; **with the** ~ **of** praeter
(*acc*)
exceptional *adj* ēgregius, eximius
exceptionally *adv* ēgregiē, eximiē
excerpt *vt* excerpere ◆ *n* excerptum *nt*
excess *n* immoderātiō *f*, intemperantia *f* ◆ *adj*
supervacāneus; **be in** ~ superesse
excessive *adj* immoderātus, immodestus,
nimius
excessively *adv* immodicē, nimis
exchange *vt* mūtāre, permūtāre ◆ *n* permūtātiō
f; (*of currencies*) collybus *m*
exchequer *n* aerārium *nt*; (*emperor's*) fiscus *m*
excise *n* vectīgālia *ntpl* ◆ *vt* excīdere
excision *n* excīsiō *f*
excitable *adj* mōbilis
excite *vt* excitāre, concitāre; (*to action*) incitāre,
incendere; (*to hope*) ērigere, exacuere; (*emotion*)
movēre, commovēre
excitement *n* commōtiō *f*
exclaim *vt* exclāmāre; ~ **against** adclāmāre (*dat*)
exclamation *n* clāmor *m*, exclāmātiō *f*
exclude *vt* exclūdere
exclusion *n* exclūsiō *f*
exclusive *adj* proprius
exclusively *adv* sōlum
excogitate *vt* excōgitāre
excrescence *n* tūber *nt*
excruciating *adj* acerbissimus
exculpate *vt* pūrgāre, absolvere
excursion *n* iter *nt*; (MIL) excursiō *f*
excuse *n* excūsātiō *f*; (*false*) speciēs *f* ◆ *vt*
excūsāre, ignōscere (*dat*); (*something due*)
remittere; **plead in** ~ excūsāre; **put forward as**
an ~ praetendere
execrable *adj* dētestābilis, sacer, nefārius
execrate *vt* dētestārī, exsecrārī
execration *n* dētestātiō *f*, exsecrātiō *f*
execute *vt* efficere, patrāre, exsequī; suppliciō
afficere; (*behead*) secūrī percutere
execution *n* effectus *m*; (*penalty*) supplicium *nt*,
mors *f*
executioner *n* carnifex *m*
exemplar *n* exemplum *nt*
exempt *adj* immūnis, līber ◆ *vt* līberāre
exemption *n* (*from tax*) immūnitās *f*; (*from service*)
vacātiō *f*
exercise *n* exercitātiō *f*, ūsus *m*; (*school*) dictāta
ntpl ◆ *vt* exercēre, ūtī (*abl*); (*mind*) acuere
exert *vt* extendere, intendere, ūtī (*abl*); ~ **oneself**
mōlīrī, ēnītī, sē intendere
exertion *n* mōlīmentum *nt*; (*mind*) intentiō *f*
exhalation *n* exhālātiō *f*, vapor *m*
exhale *vt* exhālāre, exspīrāre
exhaust *vt* exhaurīre; (*tire*) dēfatīgāre, cōnficere
exhaustion *n* dēfatīgātiō *f*
exhaustive *adj* plēnus
exhibit *vt* exhibēre, ostendere, expōnere; (*on*
stage) ēdere
exhibition *n* expositiō *f*, ostentātiō *f*
exhilarate *vt* exhilarāre
exhort *vt* hortārī, cohortārī
exhortation *n* hortātiō *f*, hortāmen *nt*
exhume *vt* ēruere
exigency *n* necessitās *f*

exile n exsilium nt, fuga f; (temporary) relēgātiō f; (person) exsul m; **live in ~** exsulāre ♦ vt in exsilium pellere, dēportāre; (temporarily) relēgāre
exist vi esse
existence n vīta f
exit n exitus m, ēgressus m
exodus n discessus m
exonerate vt absolvere
exorbitant adj nimius, immoderātus
exotic adj peregrīnus
expand vt extendere, dīlātāre
expanse n spatium nt, lātitūdō f
expatiate vi: **~ upon** amplificāre
expatriate vt extermināre ♦ n extorris m
expect vt exspectāre, spērāre
expectancy, expectation n spēs f, exspectātiō f; opīniō f
expediency n ūtile nt, ūtilitās f
expedient adj ūtilis, commodus; **it is ~** expedit ♦ n modus m, ratiō f
expediently adv commodē
expedite vt mātūrāre
expedition n (MIL) expedītiō f
expeditious adj prōmptus, celer
expeditiously adv celeriter
expel vt pellere, expellere, ēicere
expend vt impendere, expendere
expenditure n impēnsae fpl, sūmptus m
expense n impēnsae fpl, impendia ntpl; **at my ~** meō sūmptū; **at the public ~** dē pūblicō
expensive adj cārus, pretiōsus; (furnishings) lautus
expensively adv sūmptuōsē, māgnō pretiō
experience n ūsus m, experientia f ♦ vt experīrī, patī
experienced adj perītus, expertus (gen)
experiment n experīmentum nt ♦ vi: **~ with** experīrī
expert adj perītus, sciēns
expertly adv perītē, scienter
expertness n perītia f
expiate vt expiāre, lūere
expiation n (act) expiātiō f; (penalty) piāculum nt
expiatory adj piāculāris
expiration n (breath) exspīrātiō f; (time) exitus m
expire vi exspīrāre; (die) animam agere, animam efflāre; (time) exīre
expiry n exitus m, fīnis m
explain vt explicāre, expōnere, explānāre, interpretārī; (lucidly) ēnōdāre; (in detail) ēdisserere
explanation n explicātiō f, ēnōdātiō f, interpretātiō f
explicit adj expressus, apertus
explicitly adv apertē
explode vt discutere ♦ vi dīrumpī
exploit n factum nt, ausum nt; **exploits** pl rēs gestae fpl ♦ vt ūtī (abl), fruī (abl)
explore vt, vi explōrāre, scrūtārī
explorer n explōrātor m
explosion n fragor m
exponent n interpres m, auctor m
export vt exportāre ♦ n exportātiō f
exportation n exportātiō f

expose vt dētegere, dēnūdāre, patefacere; (child) expōnere; (to danger) obicere; (MIL) nūdāre; (for sale) prōpōnere; **~ oneself** se obicere
exposed adj apertus, obnoxius
exposition n explicātiō f, interpretātiō f
expostulate vi expostulāre, conquerī
expostulation n expostulātiō f
exposure n (of child) expositiō f; (of guilt) dēprehēnsiō f; (to hardship) patientia f
expound vt expōnere, interpretārī
expounder n interpres m
express vt (in words) exprimere, dēclārāre, ēloquī; (in art) effingere ♦ adj expressus; (speed) celerrimus
expression n significātiō f; (word) vōx f, verbum nt; (face) vultus m
expressive adj significāns; **~ of** index (gen); **be very ~** māximam vim habēre
expressively adv significanter
expressiveness n vīs f
expressly adv plānē
expulsion n expulsiō f, ēiectiō f
expurgate vt pūrgāre
exquisite adj ēlegāns, exquīsītus, eximius; (judgment) subtīlis
exquisitely adv ēleganter, exquīsītē
ex-service adj ēmeritus
extant adj superstes; **be ~** exstāre
extempore adv ex tempore, subitō ♦ adj extemporālis
extemporize vi subita dīcere
extend vt extendere, dīlātāre; (hand) porrigere; (line) dūcere; (office) prōrogāre; (territory) propāgāre ♦ vi patēre, porrigī; **~ into** incurrere in (acc)
extension n prōductiō f, prōlātiō f; (of office) prōrogātiō f; (of territory) propāgātiō f; (extra) incrēmentum nt
extensive adj effūsus, amplus, lātus
extensively adv lātē
extent n spatium nt, amplitūdō f; **to a large ~** māgnā ex parte; **to some ~** aliquā ex parte; **to this ~** hāctenus; **to such an ~** adeō
extenuate vt levāre, mītigāre
exterior adj externus, exterior ♦ n speciēs f
exterminate vt occīdiōne occīdere, interimere
extermination n occīdiō f, interneciō f
external adj externus
externally adv extrīnsecus
extinct adj mortuus; (custom) obsolētus
extinction n exstinctiō f, interitus m
extinguish vt exstinguere, restinguere
extinguisher n exstinctor m
extirpate vt exstirpāre, excīdere
extol vt laudāre, laudibus efferre
extort vt extorquēre, exprimere
extortion n (offence) rēs repetundae fpl
extortionate adj inīquus, rapāx
extra adv īnsuper, praetereā ♦ adj additus
extract vt excerpere, extrahere ♦ n: **make extracts** excerpere
extraction n ēvulsiō f; (descent) genus nt
extraneous adj adventīcius, aliēnus
extraordinarily adv mīrificē, eximiē
extraordinary adj extraōrdinārius; (strange) mīrus, novus; (outstanding) eximius, īnsignis

extravagance *n* intemperantia *f*; *(language)* immoderātiō *f*, luxuria *f*; *(spending)* sūmptus *m*
extravagant *adj* immoderātus, immodestus; *(spending)* sūmptuōsus, prōdigus
extreme *adj* extrēmus, ultimus
extremely *adv* valdē, vehementer
extremity *n* extrēmum *nt*, fīnis *m*; *(distress)* angustiae *fpl*; **the ~ of** extrēmus
extricate *vt* expedīre, absolvere; **~ oneself** ēmergere
exuberance *n* ūbertās *f*, luxuria *f*
exuberant *adj* ūber, laetus, luxuriōsus
exuberantly *adv* ūbertim
exude *vt* exsūdāre ♦ *vi* mānāre
exult *vi* exsultārī, laetārī, gestīre
exultant *adj* laetus
exultantly *adv* laetē
exultation *n* laetitia *f*
eye *n* oculus *m*; *(needle)* forāmen *nt*; **cast eyes on** oculōs conicere in *(acc)*; **have an eye to** spectāre; **in your eyes** iūdice tē; **keep one's eyes on** oculōs dēfigere in *(abl)*; **lose an eye** alterō oculō capī; **see eye to eye** cōnsentīre; **set eyes on** cōnspicere; **shut one's eyes to** cōnīvēre in *(abl)*; **take one's eyes off** oculōs dēicere ab *(abl)*; **up to the eyes in** tōtus in *(abl)*; **with a cast in the eye** paetus; **with sore eyes** lippus; **sore eyes** lippitūdō *f*; **with one's own eyes** cōram; **with one's eyes open** sciēns ♦ *vt* intuērī, aspicere
eyeball *n* pūpula *f*
eyebrow *n* supercilium *nt*
eyelash *n* palpebrae pilus *m*
eyelid *n* palpebra *f*
eyeshot *n* oculōrum coniectus *m*
eyesight *n* aciēs *f*, oculī *mpl*
eyesore *n* turpe *nt*; **it is an ~ to me** oculī meī dolent
eye tooth *n* dēns canīnus *m*
eyewash *n* sycophantia *f*
eyewitness *n* arbiter *m*; **be an ~ of** interesse *(dat)*

Ff

fable *n* fābula *f*, apologus *m*
fabled *adj* fābulōsus
fabric *n* (*built*) structūra *f*; (*woven*) textile *nt*
fabricate *vt* fabricārī; (*fig*) comminīscī, fingere
fabricated *adj* commentīcius
fabrication *n* (*process*) fabricātiō *f*; (*thing*) commentum *nt*
fabricator *n* auctor *m*
fabulous *adj* commentīcius, fictus
fabulously *adv* incrēdibiliter
facade *n* frōns *f*
face *n* faciēs *f*, ōs *nt*; (*aspect*) aspectus *m*; (*impudence*) ōs *nt*; ~ **to** ~ cōram; **how shall I have the** ~ **to go back?** quō ōre redībō?; **on the** ~ **of it** ad speciem, prīmō aspectū; **put a bold** ~ **on** fortēm sē praebēre; **save** ~ factum pūrgāre; **set one's** ~ **against** adversārī (*dat*) ♦ *vt* spectāre ad (*acc*); (*danger*) obviam īre (*dat*), sē oppōnere (*dat*) ♦ *vi* (*place*) spectāre, vergere; ~ **about** (*MIL*) signa convertere
facetious *adj* facētus, salsus
facetiously *adv* facētē, salsē
facetiousness *n* facētiae *fpl*, salēs *mpl*
facile *adj* facilis
facilitate *vt* expedīre
facilities *npl* opportūnitās *f*
facility *n* facilitās *f*
facing *adj* adversus ♦ *prep* exadversus (*acc*)
facsimile *n* exemplār *nt*
fact *n* rēs *f*, vērum *nt*; **as a matter of** ~ enimvērō; **the** ~ **that** quod; **in** ~ rē vērā ♦ *conj* etenim; (*climax*) dēnique
faction *n* factiō *f*
factious *adj* factiōsus, sēditiōsus
factiously *adv* sēditiōsē
factor *n* prōcūrātor *m*
factory *n* officīna *f*
faculty *n* facultās *f*, vīs *f*
fad *n* libīdō *f*
fade *vi* dēflōrēscere, marcēscere
faded *adj* marcidus
faggot *n* (*twigs*) sarmentum *nt*
fail *vi* dēficere, dēesse; (*fig*) cadere, dēcidere; (*in business*) forō cēdere; ~ **to** nōn posse; ~ **to come** nōn venīre ♦ *vt* dēficere, dēstituere
failing *n* culpa *f*, vitium *nt*
failure *n* (*of supply*) dēfectiō *f*; (*in action*) offēnsiō *f*; (*at election*) repulsa *f*
fain *adv* libenter
faint *adj* (*body*) languidus, dēfessus; (*impression*) hebes, levis; (*courage*) timidus; (*colour*) pallidus;

be ~ languēre; hebēre ♦ *vi* intermorī, animō linquī; **I feel** ~ animō male est
faint-hearted *adj* animō dēmissus; timidus
faintly *adv* languidē; leviter
faintness *n* dēfectiō *f*, languor *m*; levitās *f*
fair *adj* (*appearance*) pulcher, fōrmōsus; (*hair*) flāvus; (*skin*) candidus; (*weather*) serēnus; (*wind*) secundus; (*copy*) pūrus; (*dealings*) aequus; (*speech*) speciōsus, blandus; (*ability*) mediocris; (*reputation*) bonus ♦ *n* nūndinae *fpl*; ~ **and square** sine fūcō ac fallāciīs
fairly *adv* iūre, iūstē; mediocriter
fairness *n* aequitās *f*
fair play *n* aequum et bonum *nt*
fairy *n* nympha *f*
faith *n* fidēs *f*; **in good** ~ bonā fidē
faithful *adj* fidēlis, fīdus
faithfully *adv* fidēliter
faithfulness *n* fidēlitās *f*
faithless *adj* īnfidēlis, īnfīdus, perfidus
faithlessly *adv* īnfidēliter
faithlessness *n* īnfidēlitās *f*
fake *vt* simulāre
falchion *n* falx *f*
falcon *n* falcō *m*
fall *vi* cadere; (*gently*) lābī; (*morally*) prōlābī; (*dead*) concidere, occidere; (*fortress*) expugnārī, capī; ~ **at** accidere; ~ **away** dēficere, dēscīscere; ~ **back** recidere; (*MIL*) pedem referre; ~ **between** intercidere; ~ **behind** cessāre; ~ **by the way** intercidere; ~ **down** dēcidere, dēlābī; (*building*) ruere, corruere; ~ **due** cadere; ~ **flat** sē prōsternere; (*speech*) frīgēre; ~ **forward** prōlābī; ~ **foul of** incurrere in (*acc*); ~ **headlong** sē praecipitāre; ~ **in**, ~ **into** incidere; ~ **in with** occurrere (*dat*); ~ **off** dēcidere; (*fig*) dēscīscere; ~ **on** incumbere in (*acc*), incidere in (*acc*); ~ **out** excidere; (*event*) ēvenīre; (*hair*) dēfluere; ~ **short of** deesse ab; ~ **to** (*by lot*) obtingere, obvenīre (*dat*); ~ **to the ground** (*case*) iacēre; ~ **upon** invādere, ingruere in (*acc*); (*one's neck*) in collum invādere ♦ *n* cāsus *m*; (*building*) ruīna *f*; (*moral*) lāpsus *m*; (*season*) autumnus *m*; **the** ~ **of Capua** Capua capta
fallacious *adj* captiōsus, fallāx
fallaciously *adv* fallāciter
fallacy *n* captiō *f*
fallible *adj*: **be** ~ errāre solēre
fallow *adj* (*land*) novālis ♦ *n* novāle *nt*; **lie** ~ cessāre
false *adj* falsus, fictus

falsehood *n* falsum *nt*, mendācium *nt*; **tell a ~** mentīrī
falsely *adv* falsō
falsify *vt* vitiāre, interlinere
falter *vi* (speech) haesitāre; (gait) titubāre
faltering *adj* (speech) īnfrāctus; (gait) titubāns ♦ *n* haesitātiō *f*
fame *n* fāma *f*, glōria *f*, nōmen *nt*
famed *adj* illūstris, praeclārus
familiar *adj* (friend) intimus; (fact) nōtus; (manner) cōmis; **~ spirit** genius *m*; **be ~ with** nōvisse; **be on ~ terms with** familiāriter ūtī (abl)
familiarity *n* ūsus *m*, cōnsuētūdō *f*
familiarize *vt* adsuēfacere
familiarly *adv* familiāriter
family *n* domus *f*, gēns *f* ♦ *adj* domesticus, familiāris; **~ property** rēs familiāris *f*
famine *n* famēs *f*
famished *adj* famēlicus
famous *adj* illūstris, praeclārus, nōbilis; **make ~** nōbilitāre; **the ~** ille
fan *n* flābellum *nt*; (winnowing) vannus *f* ♦ *vt* ventilāre; **fan the flames of** (fig) īnflammāre
fanatic *n* (religious) fānāticus *m*
fanciful *adj* (person) incōnstāns; (idea) commentīcius
fancy *n* (faculty) mēns *f*; (idea) opīnātiō *f*; (caprice) libīdō *f*; **take a ~ to** amāre incipere; **~ oneself** se amāre ♦ *vt* animō fingere, imāginārī, sibi prōpōnere; **~ you thinking …!** tē crēdere …! ♦ *adj* dēlicātus
fancy-free *adj* sēcūrus, vacuus
fang *n* dēns *m*
fantastic *adj* commentīcius, mōnstruōsus
fantasy *n* imāginātiō *f*; (contemptuous) somnium *nt*
far *adj* longinquus ♦ *adv* longē, procul; (with compar) multō; **be far from** longē abesse ab; **be not far from doing** haud multum abest quin (subj); **by far** longē; **how far?** quātenus?, quoūsque?; **so far** hāctenus, eātenus; (limited) quādam tenus; **thus far** hāctenus; **far and wide** lātē; **far be it from me to say** equidem dīcere nōlim; **far from thinking … I** adeō nōn crēdō … ut; **as far as** prep tenus (abl) ♦ adv ūsque ♦ conj quātenus; (know) quod
farce *n* mīmus *m*
farcical *adj* rīdiculus
fare *vi* sē habēre, agere ♦ *n* vectūra *f*; (boat) naulum *nt*; (food) cibus *m*
farewell *interj* valē, valēte; **say ~ to** valēre iubēre
far-fetched *adj* quaesītus, arcessītus, altē repetītus
farm *n* fundus *m*, praedium *nt* ♦ *vt* (soil) colere; (taxes) redimere; **~ out** locāre
farmer *n* agricola *m*; (of taxes) pūblicānus *m*
farming *n* agrīcultūra *f*
farrow *vt* parere ♦ *n* fētus *m*
far-sighted *adj* prōvidus, prūdēns
farther *adv* longius, ultrā ♦ *adj* ulterior
farthest *adj* ultimus, extrēmus ♦ *adv* longissimē
fasces *n* fascēs *mpl*
fascinate *vt* dēlēnīre, capere
fascination *n* dulcēdō *f*, dēlēnīmenta *ntpl*, lēnōcinia *ntpl*

fashion *n* mōs *m*, ūsus *m*; (manner) modus *m*, ratiō *f*; (shape) fōrma *f* ♦ *vt* fingere, fōrmāre; **after the ~ of** rītū (gen); **come into ~** in mōrem venīre; **go out of ~** obsolēscere
fashionable *adj* ēlegāns; **it is ~** mōris est
fashionably *adv* ēleganter
fast *adj* (firm) firmus; (quick) celer; **make ~** dēligāre ♦ *adv* firmē; celeriter; **be ~ asleep** artē dormīre ♦ *vi* iēiūnus esse, cibō abstinēre ♦ *n* iēiūnium *nt*
fasten *vt* fīgere, ligāre; **~ down** dēfīgere; **~ on** inligāre; **~ to** adligāre; **~ together** conligāre, cōnfīgere
fastening *n* iūnctūra *f*
fastidious *adj* dēlicātus, ēlegāns
fastidiously *adv* fastīdiōsē
fastidiousness *n* fastīdium *nt*
fasting *n* iēiūnium *nt*, inedia *f* ♦ *adj* iēiūnus
fastness *n* arx *f*, castellum *nt*
fat *adj* pinguis, opīmus, obēsus; **grow fat** pinguēscere ♦ *n* adeps *m/f*
fatal *adj* (deadly) fūnestus, exitiābilis; (fated) fātālis
fatality *n* fātum *nt*, cāsus *m*
fatally *adv*: **be ~ wounded** vulnere perīre
fate *n* fātum *nt*, fortūna *f*, sors *f*
fated *adj* fātālis
fateful *adj* fātālis; fūnestus
Fates *npl* (goddesses) Parcae *fpl*
father *n* pater *m*; (fig) auctor *m* ♦ *vt* gignere; **~ upon** addīcere, tribuere
father-in-law *n* socer *m*
fatherland *n* patria *f*
fatherless *adj* orbus
fatherly *adj* paternus
fathom *n* sex pedēs *mpl* ♦ *vt* (fig) exputāre
fathomless *adj* profundus
fatigue *n* fatīgātiō *f*, dēfatīgātiō *f* ♦ *vt* fatīgāre, dēfatīgāre
fatness *n* pinguitūdō *f*
fatten *vt* sagīnāre
fatty *adj* pinguis
fatuity *n* īnsulsitās *f*, ineptiae *fpl*
fatuous *adj* fatuus, īnsulsus, ineptus
fault *n* culpa *f*, vitium *nt*; (written) mendum *nt*; **count as a ~** vitiō vertere; **find ~ with** incūsāre; **it is not your ~ that …** nōn per tē stat quōminus (subj)
faultily *adv* vitiōsē, mendōsē
faultiness *n* vitium *nt*
faultless *adj* ēmendātus, integer
faultlessly *adv* ēmendātē
faulty *adj* vitiōsus, mendōsus
faun *n* faunus *m*
fauna *n* animālia *ntpl*
favour *n* grātia *f*, favor *m*; (done) beneficium *nt*; **win ~ with** grātiam inīre apud; **by your ~** bonā veniā tuā ♦ *vt* favēre (dat), indulgēre (dat)
favourable *adj* faustus, prosperus, secundus
favourably *adv* faustē, fēlīciter, benignē
favourite *adj* dīlectus, grātissimus ♦ *n* dēliciae *fpl*
favouritism *n* indulgentia *f*, studium *nt*
fawn *n* hinnuleus *m* ♦ *adj* (colour) gilvus ♦ *vi*: **~ upon** adūlārī
fawning *adj* blandus ♦ *n* adūlātiō *f*

fear n timor m, metus m, formīdō f ✦ vt timēre, metuere, formīdāre, verērī; **fearing that** veritus ne (+ imperf subj)
fearful adj timidus; horrendus, terribilis, formīdolōsus
fearfully adv timidē; formīdolōsē
fearless adj impavidus, intrepidus
fearlessly adv impavidē, intrepidē
fearlessness n fīdentia f, audācia f
fearsome adj formīdolōsus
feasible adj: **it is** ~ fierī potest
feast n epulae fpl; (private) convīvium nt; (public) epulum nt; (religious) daps f; (festival) festus diēs m ✦ vi epulārī, convīvārī; (fig) pāscī ✦ vt: ~ **one's eyes on** oculōs pāscere (abl)
feat n factum nt, facinus nt
feather n penna f; (downy) plūma f; **birds of a** ~ **flock together** parēs cum paribus facillimē congregantur
feathered adj pennātus
feathery adj plūmeus
feature n līneāmentum nt; (fig) proprium nt
February n mēnsis Februārius m; **of** ~ Februārius
federal adj sociālis, foederātus
federate vi societātem facere
federated adj foederātus
federation n societās f, foederātae cīvitātēs fpl
fee n honōs m, mercēs f
feeble adj imbēcillus, īnfirmus, dēbilis
feebleness n imbēcillitās f, īnfirmitās f
feebly adv īnfirmē
feed vt alere, pāscere ✦ vi pāscī; ~ **on** vescī (abl) ✦ n pābulum nt
feel vt sentīre; (with hand) tractāre, tangere; (emotion) capere, adficī (abl); (opinion) cēnsēre, sentīre; ~ **one's way** pedetemptim prōgredī ✦ vi sentīre; **I** ~ **glad** gaudeō; ~ **sure** prō certō habēre
feeling n sēnsus m, tāctus m; (mind) animus m, adfectus m; (pity) misericordia f; **good** ~ voluntās f; **bad** ~ invidia f
feign vt simulāre, fingere
feignedly adv simulātē, fictē
feint n simulātiō f
felicitate vt grātulārī (dat)
felicitation n grātulātiō f
felicitous adj fēlīx, aptus
felicity n fēlīcitās f
feline adj fēlīnus
fell vt (tree) succīdere; (enemy) sternere, caedere ✦ adj dīrus, crūdēlis, atrōx ✦ n mōns m; (skin) pellis f
fellow n socius m, aequālis m; (contemptuous) homō m
fellow citizen n cīvis m/f
fellow countryman n cīvis m/f, populāris m/f
fellow feeling n misericordia f
fellowship n societās f, sodālitās f
fellow slave n cōnservus m
fellow soldier n commīlitō m
fellow student n condiscipulus m
felon n nocēns m
felonious adj scelestus, scelerātus
felony n scelus nt, noxa f
felt n coāctum nt
female adj muliebris ✦ n fēmina f

feminine adj muliebris
fen n palūs f
fence n saepēs f; **sit on the** ~ quiēscere, medium sē gerere ✦ vt saepīre; ~ **off** intersaepīre ✦ vi bātuere, rudibus lūdere
fencing n rudium lūdus m; ~ **master** lānista m
fend vt arcēre ✦ vi prōvidēre
fennel n ferula f
fenny adj palūster
ferment n fermentum nt; (fig) aestus m ✦ vt fermentāre; (fig) excitāre, accendere ✦ vi fervēre
fermentation n fervor m
fern n filix f
ferocious adj ferōx, saevus, truculentus
ferociously adv truculentē
ferocity n ferōcitās f, saevitia f
ferret n viverra m ✦ vt: ~ **out** rīmārī, ēruere
ferry n trāiectus m; (boat) cymba f, pontō m ✦ vt trānsvehere
ferryman n portitor m
fertile adj fertilis, fēcundus
fertility n fertilitās f, fēcunditās f
fertilize vt fēcundāre, laetificāre
fervent adj fervidus, ārdēns
fervently adv ārdenter
fervid adj fervidus
fervour n ārdor m, fervor m
festal adj festus
fester vi exulcerārī
festival n diēs festus m, sollemne nt
festive adj (time) festus; (person) festīvus
festivity n hilaritās f; (event) sollemne nt
festoon n sertum nt ✦ vt corōnāre
fetch vt arcessere, addūcere; (price) vēnīre (gen); ~ **out** dēprōmere; ~ **water** aquārī
fetching adj lepidus, blandus
fetid adj foetidus, pūtidus
fetter n compēs f, vinculum m ✦ vt compedēs inicere (dat), vincīre; (fig) impedīre
fettle n habitus m, animus m
feud n simultās f, inimīcitia f
fever n febris f
feverish adj febrīculōsus; (fig) sollicitus
few adj paucī; **very few** perpaucī; **how few?** quotus quisque?
fewness n paucitās f
fiancé n spōnsus m
fiasco n calamitās f; **be a** ~ frīgēre
fiat n ēdictum nt
fibre n fibra f
fickle adj incōnstāns, levis, mōbilis
fickleness n incōnstantia f, levitās f, mōbilitās f
fiction n fābula f, commentum nt
fictitious adj fictus, falsus, commentīcius; (character) persōnātus
fictitiously adv fictē
fidelity n fidēlitās f, fidēs f
fidget vi sollicitārī
field n ager m; (ploughed) arvum nt; (of grain) seges f; (MIL) campus m, aciēs f; (scope) campus m, locus m; **in the** ~ (MIL) mīlitiae; **hold the** ~ vincere, praevalēre; ~ **of vision** cōnspectus m
fiend n diabolus m
fiendish adj nefārius, improbus
fierce adj saevus, ācer, atrōx; (look) torvus
fiercely adv ācriter, atrōciter, saevē

fierceness – fittingly

fierceness n saevitia f, atrōcitās f
fieriness n ārdor m, fervor m
fiery adj igneus, flammeus; (fig) ārdēns, fervidus
fife n tībia f
fifteen num quīndecim; ~ **each** quīndēnī; ~ **times** quīndeciēns
fifteenth adj quīntus decimus
fifth adj quīntus ♦ n quīnta pars f
fiftieth adj quīnquāgēsimus
fifty num quīnquāgintā
fig n fīcus f; (tree) fīcus f; **of fig** fīculnus; **not care a fig for** floccī nōn facere
fight n pugna f, proelium nt ♦ vi pugnāre, dīmicāre; ~ **it out** dēcernere, dēcertāre; ~ **to the end** dēpugnāre ♦ vt (battle) committere; (enemy) pugnāre cum (abl)
fighter n pugnātor m
fighting n dīmicātiō f
figment n commentum nt
figurative adj trānslātus; **in ~ language** trānslātīs per similitūdinem verbīs; **use figuratively** trānsferre
figure n figūra f, fōrma f; (in art) signum nt; (of speech) figūra f, trānslātiō f; (pl, on pottery) sigilla ntpl ♦ vt figūrāre, fōrmāre; (art) fingere, effingere; ~ **to oneself** sibi prōpōnere
figured adj sigillātus
figurehead n (of ship) īnsigne nt
filament n fibra f
filch vt fūrārī, surripere
file n (tool) līma f; (line) ōrdō m, agmen nt; (of papers) fasciculus m; **files** pl tabulae fpl; **in single ~** simplicī ōrdine; **the rank and ~** gregāriī mīlitēs ♦ vt līmāre
filial adj pius
filigree n diatrēta ntpl
fill vt implēre, explēre, complēre; (office) fungī (abl); ~ **up** supplēre
fillet n īnfula f, vitta f ♦ vt (fish) exossāre
fillip n stimulus m
filly n equula f
film n membrāna f
filter n cōlum nt ♦ vt dēliquāre ♦ vi percōlārī
filth n sordēs f, caenum nt
filthily adv foedē, inquinātē
filthiness n foeditās f, impūritās f
filthy adj foedus, impūrus; (speech) inquinātus
fin n pinna f
final adj ultimus, postrēmus, extrēmus
finally adv dēnique, tandem, postrēmō
finance n rēs nummāria f; (state) vectīgālia ntpl
financial adj aerārius
financier n faenerātor m
finch n fringilla f
find vt invenīre, reperīre; (supplies) parāre; (verdict) iūdicāre; (pleasure) capere; ~ **fault with** incūsāre; ~ **guilty** damnāre; ~ **out** comperīre, cognōscere
finder n inventor m
finding n iūdicium nt, sententia f
fine n (LAW) multa f, damnum nt; **in ~** dēnique ♦ vt multāre ♦ adj (thin) tenuis, subtīlis; (refined) ēlegāns, mundus, decōrus; (beautiful) pulcher, venustus; (showy) speciōsus; (of weather) serēnus
finely adv pulchrē, ēleganter, subtīliter

fineness n tenuitās f; ēlegantia f; pulchritūdō f; speciēs f; serēnitās f
finery n ōrnātus m, munditiae fpl
finesse n astūtia f, ars f, argūtiae fpl
finger n digitus m; **a finger's breadth** trānsversus digitus; **not lift a ~** (in effort) nē manum quidem vertere ♦ vt pertractāre
fingertips npl extrēmī digitī
finish n fīnis m; (art) perfectiō f ♦ vt fīnīre, perficere; cōnficere; (with art) perficere, expolīre ♦ vi dēsinere; ~ **off** transigere, peragere, absolvere
finishing post n mēta f
finishing touch n manus extrēma
finite adj circumscrīptus
fir n abiēs f; **of fir** abiēgnus
fire n ignis m; (conflagration) incendium nt; (in hearth) focus m; (fig) ārdor m, calor m, impetus m; **be on ~** ārdēre, flagrāre; **catch ~** flammam concipere, ignem comprehendere; **set on ~** accendere, incendere ♦ vt incendere; (fig) īnflammāre; (missile) iaculārī
firebrand n fax f
fire brigade n vigilēs mpl
fireplace n focus m
fireside n focus m
firewood n lignum nt
firm n societās f ♦ adj firmus, stabilis; (mind) cōnstāns; **stand ~** perstāre
firmament n caelum nt
firmly adv firmē, cōnstanter
firmness n firmitās f, firmitūdō f; cōnstantia f
first adj prīmus, prīnceps; (of two) prior ♦ adv prīmum; **at ~** prīmō, prīncipiō; **at ~ hand** ipse, ab ipsō; **come in ~** vincere; **give ~ aid to** ad tempus medērī (dat); **I was the ~ to see** prīmus vīdī
first-class adj classicus
first fruits npl prīmitiae fpl
firstly adv prīmum
first-rate adj eximius, lūculentus
firth n aestuārium nt, fretum nt
fiscal adj vectīgālis, aerārius
fish n piscis m ♦ vi piscārī; (fig) expiscārī
fisher, fisherman n piscātor m
fishing n piscātus m ♦ adj piscātōrius
fishing-rod n harundō f
fish market n forum piscārium nt
fishmonger n piscārius m
fish pond n piscīna f
fissile adj fissilis
fissure n rīma f
fist n pugnus m
fit n (MED) convulsiō f; (of anger, illness) impetus m; **by fits and starts** temerē, carptim ♦ vt aptāre, accommodāre; (dress) sedēre (dat); **fit out** armāre, īnstruere ♦ adj aptus, idōneus, dignus; **I see fit to** mihi vidētur; **fit for** aptus ad (acc)
fitful adj dubius, incōnstāns
fitfully adv incōnstanter
fitly adv dignē, aptē
fitness n convenientia f
fitting n adparātus m, īnstrūmentum nt ♦ adj idōneus, dignus; **it is ~** convenit, decet
fittingly adv dignē, convenienter

67

five *num* quīnque; ~ **each** quīnī; ~ **times**
quīnquiēns; ~ **years** quīnquennium *nt*,
lūstrum *nt*; ~ **sixths** quīnque partēs
five hundred *num* quīngentī; **five hundred**
each quīngēnī; **five hundred times**
quīngentiēns
five hundredth *adj* quīngentēsimus
fix *vt* fīgere; (*time*) dīcere, cōnstituere; (*decision*)
statuere ♦ *n* angustiae *fpl*; **put in a fix**
dēprehendere
fixed *adj* fixus; (*attention*) intentus; (*decision*)
certus; (*star*) inerrāns; **be firmly ~ in** īnsidēre
(*dat*)
fixedly *adv* intentē
fixity *n* stabilitās *f*; (*of purpose*) cōnstantia *f*
fixtures *npl* adfīxa *ntpl*
flabbergast *vt* obstupefacere
flabbiness *n* mollitia *f*
flabby *adj* flaccidus, mollis
flag *n* vexillum *nt*; ~ **officer** praefectus classis *m*
♦ *vi* flaccēre, flaccēscere, languēscere
flagellate *vt* verberāre
flagon *n* lagoena *f*
flagrant *adj* manifestus; flāgitiōsus
flagrantly *adv* flāgitiōsē
flagship *n* nāvis imperātōria *f*
flail *n* fūstis *m*
flair *n* iūdicium *nt*
flake *n* squāma *f*; **flakes** *pl* (*snow*) nix *f*
flame *n* flamma *f* ♦ *vi* flagrāre, exārdēscere
flaming *adj* flammeus
flamingo *n* phoenīcopterus *m*
flank *n* latus *nt*; cornū *nt*; **on the ~** ab latere, ad
latus ♦ *vt* latus tegere (*gen*)
flap *n* flābellum *nt*; (*dress*) lacinia *f* ♦ *vt* plaudere
(*abl*)
flare *n* flamma *f*, fulgor *m* ♦ *vi* exārdēscere,
flagrāre
flash *n* fulgor *m*; (*lightning*) fulgur *nt*; (*time*)
mōmentum *nt* ♦ *vi* fulgēre; (*motion*) micāre
flashy *adj* speciōsus
flask *n* ampulla *f*
flat *adj* plānus; (*ground*) aequus; (*on back*) supīnus;
(*on face*) prōnus; (*music*) gravis; (*style*) āridus,
frīgidus; **fall ~** (*fig*) frīgēre ♦ *n* (*land*) plānitiēs *f*;
(*sea*) vadum *nt*; (*house*) tabulātum *nt*
flatly *adv* prōrsus
flatness *n* plānitiēs *f*
flatten *vt* aequāre, complānāre
flatter *vt* adūlārī (*dat*), adsentārī (*dat*), blandīrī
(*dat*)
flatterer *n* adsentātor *m*
flattering *adj* blandus
flatteringly *adv* blandē
flattery *n* adūlātiō *f*, adsentātiō *f*, blanditiae *fpl*
flatulence *n* īnflātiō *f*
flatulent *adj* īnflātus
flaunt *vt* iactāre ♦ *vi* iactāre, glōriārī
flaunting *n* iactātiō *f* ♦ *adj* glōriōsus
flauntingly *adv* glōriōsē
flautist *n* tībīcen *m*
flavour *n* gustātus *m*, sapor *m* ♦ *vt* imbuere,
condīre
flavouring *n* condītiō *f*
flavourless *adj* īnsulsus
flaw *n* vitium *nt*

flawless *adj* ēmendātus
flax *n* līnum *nt*
flaxen *adj* flāvus
flay *vt* dēglūbere
flea *n* pūlex *m*
fleck *n* macula *f* ♦ *vt* variāre
fledged *adj* pennātus
flee *vi* fugere, effugere; (*for refuge*) cōnfugere
fleece *n* vellus *nt* ♦ *vt* tondēre; (*fig*) spoliāre
fleecy *adj* lāneus
fleet *n* classis *f* ♦ *adj* vēlōx, celer
fleeting *adj* fugāx
fleetness *n* vēlōcitās *f*, celeritās *f*
flesh *n* cārō *f*; (*fig*) corpus *nt*; **in the ~** vīvus; **one's**
own ~ and blood cōnsanguineus; **put on**
~ pinguēscere
fleshiness *n* corpus *nt*
fleshliness *n* libīdō *f*
fleshly *adj* libīdinōsus
fleshy *adj* pinguis
flexibility *n* lentitia *f*
flexible *adj* flexibilis, lentus
flicker *vi* coruscāre
flickering *adj* tremulus
flight *n* (*flying*) volātus *m*; (*fleeing*) fuga *f*; (*steps*)
scāla *f*; **put to ~** fugāre, in fugam conicere; **take**
to ~ sē in fugam dare, terga vertere
flightiness *n* mōbilitās *f*
flighty *adj* mōbilis, incōnstāns
flimsy *adj* tenuis, pertenuis
flinch *vi* recēdere
fling *vt* iacere, conicere; (*missile*) intorquēre;
~ **away** abicere, prōicere; ~ **open** patefacere;
~ **in one's teeth** obicere (*dat*); ~ **to the ground**
prōsternere ♦ *vi* sē incitāre ♦ *n* iactus *m*
flint *n* silex *m*
flinty *adj* siliceus
flippancy *n* lascīvia *f*
flippant *adj* lascīvus, protervus
flippantly *adv* petulanter
flirt *vi* lūdere, lascīvīre ♦ *n* lascīvus *m*, lascīva *f*
flit *vi* volitāre
flitch *n* succīdia *f*
float *vi* innāre, fluitāre; (*in air*) volitāre; ~ **down**
dēfluere
flock *n* grex *m*; (*wool*) floccus *m* ♦ *vi* concurrere,
congregārī, cōnfluere; ~ **in** adfluere
flog *vt* verberāre, virgīs caedere
flogging *n* verbera *ntpl*
flood *n* (*deluge*) ēluviō *f*; (*river*) torrēns *m*; (*tide*)
accessus *m*; (*fig*) flūmen *nt* ♦ *vt* inundāre
floodgate *n* cataracta *f*
floor *n* solum *nt*; (*paved*) pavīmentum *nt*; (*storey*)
tabulātum *nt*; (*threshing*) ārea *f* ♦ *vt* contabulāre;
be floored (*in argument*) iacēre
flora *n* herbae *fpl*
floral *adj* flōreus
florid *adj* flōridus
flotilla *n* classicula *f*
flounce *vi* sē conicere ♦ *n* īnstita *f*
flounder *vi* volutāre; (*in speech*) haesitāre
flour *n* fārīna *f*
flourish *vi* flōrēre, vigēre ♦ *vt* vibrāre, iactāre ♦ *n*
(RHET) calamistrī *mpl*; (*music*) clangor *m*
flout *vt* aspernārī, inlūdere (*dat*)

flow vi fluere, mānāre; (tide) accēdere; ~ **back**
recēdere; ~ **between** interfluere; ~ **down**
dēfluere; ~ **into** īnfluere in (acc); ~ **out**
prōfluere, ēmānāre; ~ **past** praeterfluere;
~ **through** permānāre; ~ **together** cōnfluere;
~ **towards** adfluere ♦ n flūmen nt, cursus m;
(tide) accessus m; (words) flūmen nt
flower n flōs m, flōsculus m ♦ vi flōrēre, flōrēscere
floweret n flōsculus m
flowery adj flōridus
flowing adj prōfluēns; ~ **with** abundāns (abl)
flowingly adv prōfluenter
flown adj īnflātus
fluctuate vi aestuāre, fluctuāre
fluctuating adj incōnstāns, incertus
fluctuation n aestus m, dubitātiō f
fluency n fācundia f, verbōrum cōpia f
fluent adj disertus, prōfluēns
fluently adv disertē, prōfluenter
fluid adj liquidus ♦ n liquor m
fluidity n liquor m
fluke n (anchor) dēns m; (luck) fortuītum nt
flurry n trepidātiō f ♦ vt sollicitāre, turbāre
flush n rubor m; **in the first** ~ **of victory** victōriā
ēlātus ♦ vi ērubēscere ♦ adj (full) abundāns;
(level) aequus
fluster n trepidātiō f ♦ vt turbāre, sollicitāre
flute n tībia f; **play the** ~ tībiā canere
fluted adj striātus
flutter n tremor m; (fig) trepidātiō f ♦ vi (heart)
palpitāre; (mind) trepidāre; (bird) volitāre
fluvial adj fluviātilis
flux n fluxus m; **be in a state of** ~ fluere
fly n musca f ♦ vi volāre; (flee) fugere; **fly apart**
dissilīre; **fly at** involāre in (acc); **fly away**
āvolāre; **fly from** fugere; **fly in the face of**
obviam īre (dat); **fly out** ēvolāre; **fly to** advolāre
ad (acc); **fly up** ēvolāre, subvolāre; **let fly at**
immittere in (acc)
flying adj volucer, volātilis; (time) fugāx
foal n equuleus m, equulus m ♦ vt parere
foam n spūma f ♦ vi spūmāre; (with rage) saevīre
foaming adj spūmeus
focus vt (mind) intendere
fodder n pābulum nt
foe n hostis m; (private) inimīcus m
fog n cālīgō f, nebula f
foggy adj cālīginōsus, nebulōsus
foible n vitium nt
foil n (metal) lāmina f; (sword) rudis f ♦ vt ēlūdere,
ad inritum redigere
foist vt inculcāre, interpōnere
fold n sinus m; (sheep) ovīle nt ♦ vt plicāre,
complicāre; (hands) comprimere; (sheep)
inclūdere; ~ **back** replicāre; ~ **over** plicāre;
~ **together** complicāre; ~ **up in** involvere in
(abl)
folding doors npl valvae fpl
foliage n frondēs fpl
folk n hominēs mpl ♦ adj patrius
follow vt sequī; (calling) facere; (candidate)
adsectārī; (enemy) īnsequī; (example) imitārī;
(instructions) pārēre (dat); (predecessor) succēdere
(dat); (road) pergere; (speaker) intellegere;
~ **closely** īnsequī; ~ **hard on the heels of**
īnsequī, īnsistere (dat), īnstāre (dat); ~ **out**

exsequī; ~ **to the grave** exsequī; ~ **up** subsequī,
īnsistere (dat) ♦ vi (time) īnsequī; (inference) sequī;
as follows ita, in hunc modum
follower n comes m; (of candidate) adsectātor m;
(of model) imitātor m; (of teacher) audītor m
following adj tālis; īnsequēns, proximus,
posterus; **on the** ~ **day** postrīdiē, postero diē,
proximo diē ♦ n adsectātōrēs mpl
folly n stultitia f, dēmentia f, īnsipientia f
foment vt fovēre; (fig) augēre
fond adj amāns, studiōsus; ineptus; **be** ~ **of**
amāre
fondle vt fovēre, mulcēre
fondly adv amanter, ineptē
food n cibus m; (fig) pābulum nt
fool n stultus m, ineptus m; (jester) scurra
m; **make a** ~ **of** ludibriō habēre; **play the**
~ dēsipere ♦ vt dēcipere, lūdere; ~ **away**
disperdere ♦ vi dēsipere
foolery n ineptiae fpl, nūgae fpl
foolhardy adj temerārius
foolish adj stultus, ineptus, īnsipiēns
foolishly adv stultē, ineptē
foolishness n stultitia f, īnsipientia f
foot n pēs m; (MIL) peditātus m; **a** ~ **long** pedālis;
on ~ pedes; **set** ~ **on** īnsistere (dat); **set on**
~ īnstituere; **the** ~ **of** īmus ♦ vt (bill) solvere
football n follis m
footing n locus m, status m; **keep one's**
~ īnsistere; **on an equal** ~ ex aequō
footman n pedisequus m
footpad n grassātor m
footpath n sēmita f, trāmes m
footprint n vestīgium nt
foot soldier n pedes m
footstep n vestīgium nt; **follow in the**
footsteps of vestīgiīs ingredī (gen)
foppish adj dēlicātus
for prep (advantage) dat; (duration) acc; (after noun)
gen; (price) abl; (behalf) prō (abl); (cause) propter
(acc), causā (gen); (after neg) prae (abl); (feelings)
erga (acc); (lieu) prō (abl); (purpose) ad, in (acc);
(time fixed) in (acc) ♦ conj namque; nam (1st word),
enim (2nd word); (with pron) quippe quī; **for a**
long time diū; **for some time** aliquamdiū
forage n pābulum nt ♦ vi pābulārī, frūmentārī
forager n pābulātor m, frūmentātor m
foraging n pābulātiō f, frūmentātiō f
forasmuch as conj quōniam
foray n incursiō f
forbear vi parcere (dat), supersedēre (inf)
forbearance n venia f, indulgentia f
forbears n māiōrēs mpl
forbid vt vetāre (+ acc and infin), interdīcere (dat
and 'quominus' and subj); **Heaven** ~ !, dī meliōra!
forbidding adj tristis
force n vīs f; (band of men) manus m; **by** ~ **of**
arms vī et armis ♦ vt cōgere, impellere;
(way) rumpere, mōlīrī; (growth) festīnāre;
~ **an engagement** hostes proeliārī cogere;
~ **down** dētrūdere; ~ **out** extrūdere, expellere,
exturbāre; ~ **upon** inculcāre; ~ **a way in**
intrōrumpere, inrumpere
forced adj (march) māgnus; (style) quaesītus;
~ **march** māgnum iter
forceful adj validus

forceps n forceps m/f
forces npl (MIL) cōpiae fpl
forcible adj validus; (fig) gravis
forcibly adv vī, violenter; (fig) graviter
ford n vadum nt ♦ vt vadō trānsīre
fore adj prior; **to the ~** praestō ♦ adv: **~ and aft** in
  longitūdinem
forearm n bracchium nt ♦ vt: **be forearmed**
  praecavēre
forebode vt ōminārī, portendere; praesentīre
foreboding n praesēnsiō f; ōmen nt
forecast n praedictiō f ♦ vt praedīcere, prōvidēre
forecourt n vestibulum nt
forefathers n māiōrēs mpl
forefinger n index m
foreground n ēminentia ntpl
forehead n frōns f
foreign adj peregrīnus, externus; (goods)
  adventīcius; **~ to** aliēnus ab; **~ ways**
  peregrīnitās f
foreigner n peregrīnus m, advena m
foreknow vt praenōscere
foreknowledge n prōvidentia f
foreland n prōmontōrium nt
foremost adj prīmus, prīnceps
forenoon n antemerīdiānum tempus nt
forensic adj forēnsis
forerunner n praenūntius m
foresee vt praevidēre
foreshadow vt praemonēre
foresight n prōvidentia f
forest n silva f
forestall vt occupāre, antevenīre
forester n silvicola m
foretaste vt praegustāre
foretell vt praedīcere, vāticinārī
forethought n prōvidentia f
forewarn vt praemonēre
foreword n praefātiō f
forfeit n multa f, damnum nt ♦ vt āmittere,
  perdere, multārī (abl); (bail) dēserere
forfeiture n damnum nt
forgather vi congregārī, convenīre
forge n fornāx f ♦ vt fabricārī, excūdere;
  (document) subicere; (will) suppōnere; (signature)
  imitārī; (money) adulterīnōs nummōs
  percutere
forged adj falsus, adulterīnus, commentīcius
forger n (of will) subiector m
forgery n falsum nt, commentum nt
forget vt oblīvīscī (gen); (thing learnt) dēdiscere; **be**
  forgotten memoriā cadere, ex animō effluere
forgetful adj immemor; (by habit) oblīviōsus
forgetfulness n oblīviō f
forgive vt ignōscere (dat), veniam dare (dat)
forgiveness n venia f
forgo vt dīmittere, renūntiāre; (rights) dēcēdere
  dē iūre
fork n furca f; (small) furcula f; (road) trivium nt
forlorn adj inops, dēstitūtus, exspēs
form n fōrma f, figūra f; (of procedure) fōrmula
  f; (condition) vigor m; (etiquette) mōs m; (seat)
  scamnum nt; (school) schola f; (hare's) latibulum
  nt ♦ vt fōrmāre, fingere, efficere; (MIL) īnstruere;
  (plan) inīre, capere
formal adj iūstus; (rite) sollemnis

formality n iūsta ntpl, rītus m; **as a ~** dicis causā;
  with due ~ rītē
formally adv rītē
formation n fōrma f, figūra f; (process)
  cōnfōrmātiō f; **in ~** (MIL) īnstructus
former adj prior, prīstinus, vetus; **the ~** ille
formerly adv anteā, ōlim, quondam
formidable adj formīdolōsus
formidably adv formīdolōsē
formula n fōrmula f; (dictated) praefātiō f
formulate vt compōnere
forsake vt dērelinquere, dēstituere, dēserere
forswear vt pēierāre, abiūrāre
fort n castellum nt
forth adv forās; (time) posthāc
forthwith adv extemplō, statim, prōtinus
fortieth adj quadrāgēsimus
fortification n (process) mūnītiō f; (place)
  mūnīmentum nt, arx f
fortify vt mūnīre, ēmūnīre, commūnīre; (fig)
  cōnfirmāre
fortitude n fortitūdō f
fortnight n quīndecim diēs mpl
fortnightly adv quīntō decimō quōque diē
fortress n arx f, castellum nt
fortuitous adj fortuītus
fortuitously adv fortuītō, cāsū
fortunate adj fēlīx, fortūnātus
fortunately adv fēlīciter, bene
fortune n fortūna f, fors f; (wealth) rēs f, dīvitiae
  fpl; **good ~** fēlīcitās f, secundae rēs fpl; **bad**
  ~ adversae rēs fpl; **make one's ~** rem facere, rem
  quaerere; **tell fortunes** hariolārī
fortune-hunter n captātor m
fortune-teller n hariolus m, sāga f
forty num quadrāgintā; **~ each** quadrāgēnī;
  ~ times quadrāgiēns
forum n forum nt
forward adj (person) protervus, audāx; (fruit)
  praecox ♦ adv porrō, ante; **bring ~** prōferre;
  come ~ prōdīre ♦ vt (letter) perferre; (cause)
  adiuvāre, favēre (dat)
forwardness n audācia f, alacritās f
forwards adv porrō, prōrsus; **backwards and**
  ~ rursum prōrsum, hūc illūc
fosse n fossa f
foster vt alere, nūtrīre; (fig) fovēre
foster child n alumnus m, alumna f
foster father n altor m, ēducātor m
foster mother n altrīx f, nūtrīx f
foul adj foedus; (speech) inquinātus; **fall ~ of**
  inruere in (acc)
foully adv foedē, inquinātē
foul-mouthed adj maledicus
foulness n foed+ tās f
found vt condere, fundāre, īnstituere; (metal)
  fundere
foundation n fundāmenta ntpl
founder n fundātor m, conditor m ♦ vi submergī,
  naufragium facere
foundling n expositīcius m, expositīcia f
fount n fōns m
fountain n fōns m
fountainhead n fōns m, orīgō f

four *num* quattuor *(indecl)*; ~ **each** quaternī;
~ **times** quater; ~ **days** quadriduum *nt*; ~ **years**
quadriennium *nt*
fourfold *adj* quadruplex ♦ *adv* quadrifāriam
four hundred *num* quadringentī; **four hundred
each** quadringēnī; **four hundred times**
quadringentiēns
four hundredth *adj* quadringentēsimus
fourteen *num* quattuordecim; ~ **each** quaternī
dēnī; ~ **times** quater deciēns
fourteenth *adj* quartus decimus
fourth *adj* quartus ♦ *n* quadrāns *m*; **three
fourths** dōdrāns *m*, trēs partēs *fpl*
fowl *n* avis *f*; gallīna *f*
fowler *n* auceps *m*
fox *n* vulpes *f*; **fox's** vulpīnus
foxy *adj* astūtus, vafer
fracas *n* rīxa *f*
fraction *n* pars *f*
fractious *adj* difficilis
fracture *n* frāctum os *nt* ♦ *vt* frangere
fragile *adj* fragilis
fragility *n* fragilitās *f*
fragment *n* fragmentum *nt*
fragrance *n* odor *m*
fragrant *adj* suāvis
fragrantly *adv* suāviter
frail *adj* fragilis, īnfirmus, dēbilis
frailty *n* dēbilitās *f*; *(moral)* error *m*
frame *vt* fabricārī, fingere, effingere; *(document)*
compōnere ♦ *n* fōrma *f*; *(of mind)* adfectiō *f*,
habitus *m*; **in a ~ of mind** animātus
framer *n* fabricātor *m*, opifex *m*; *(of law)* lātor *m*
framework *n* compāgēs *f*
franchise *n* suffrāgium *nt*, cīvitās *f*
frank *adj* ingenuus, apertus; *(speech)* līber
frankincense *n* tūs *nt*
frankly *adv* ingenuē, apertē; līberē
frankness *n* ingenuitās *f*; *(speech)* lībertās *f*
frantic *adj* furēns, furiōsus, dēlīrus
frantically *adv* furenter
fraternal *adj* frāternus
fraternally *adv* frāternē
fraternity *n* frāternitās *f*; *(society)* sodālitās *f*;
(guild) collēgium *nt*
fraternize *vi* amīcitiam iungere
fratricide *n* frātricīda *m*; *(act)* frātris
parricīdium *nt*
fraud *n* fraus *f*, dolus *m*, falsum *nt*; *(criminal)*
dolus malus *m*
fraudulence *n* fraus *f*
fraudulent *adj* fraudulentus, dolōsus
fraudulently *adv* dolōsē, dolō malō
fraught *adj* plēnus
fray *n* pugna *f*, rīxa *f* ♦ *vt* terere
freak *n* mōnstrum *nt*; *(caprice)* libīdō *f*
freckle *n* lentīgō *f*
freckly *adj* lentīginōsus
free *adj* līber; *(disengaged)* vacuus; *(generous)*
līberālis; *(from cost)* grātuītus; *(from duty)*
immūnis; *(from encumbrance)* expedītus; **be
~ from** vacāre *(abl)*; **I am still ~ to** integrum est
mihī *(inf)*; **set ~** absolvere, līberāre; *(slave)* manū
mittere ♦ *adv* grātīs, grātuītō ♦ *vt* līberāre,
expedīre, exsolvere
freebooter *n* praedō *m*

freeborn *adj* ingenuus
freedman *n* lībertus *m*
freedom *n* lībertās *f*; *(from duty)* immūnitās *f*
freehold *n* praedium līberum *nt* ♦ *adj* immūnis
freely *adv* līberē; *(lavishly)* cōpiōsē, largē; *(frankly)*
apertē; *(voluntarily)* ultrō, suā sponte
freeman *n* cīvis *m*
free will *n* voluntās *f*; **of one's own free will** suā
sponte
freeze *vt* gelāre, glaciāre ♦ *vi* concrēscere
freezing *adj* gelidus; **it is ~** gelat
freight *n* vectūra *f*; *(cargo)* onus *nt* ♦ *vt* onerāre
freighter *n* nāvis onerāria *f*
frenzied *adj* furēns, furiōsus, fānāticus
frenzy *n* furor *m*, īnsania *f*
frequency *n* adsiduitās *f*
frequent *adj* frequēns, crēber ♦ *vt* frequentāre,
commeāre in *(acc)*
frequently *adv* saepe, saepenumerō, frequenter
fresh *adj* *(new)* recēns, novus; *(vigorous)* integer;
(water) dulcis; *(wind)* ācer
freshen *vt* renovāre ♦ *vi* *(wind)* incrēbrēscere
freshly *adv* recenter
freshman *n* tīrō *m*
freshness *n* novitās *f*, viriditās *f*
fret *vi* maerēre, angī ♦ *vt* sollicitāre
fretful *adj* mōrōsus, querulus
fretfulness *n* mōrōsitās *f*
fretted *adj* laqueātus
friable *adj* puter
friction *n* trītus *m*
friend *n* amīcus *m*, familiāris *m/f*, hospes *m*,
sodālis *m*; **make friends with** sē cōnferre ad
amīcitiam *(gen)*
friendless *adj* sine amīcīs
friendliness *n* cōmitās *f*, officium *nt*
friendly *adj* cōmis, facilis, benīgnus; **on ~ terms**
familiāriter
friendship *n* amīcitia *f*, familiāritās *f*
frigate *n* liburna *f*
fright *n* horror *m*, pavor *m*, terror *m*; **take
~** extimēscere, expavēscere
frighten *vt* terrēre, exterrēre, perterrēre; **~ away**
absterrēre; **~ off** dēterrēre; **~ the life out of**
exanimāre
frightful *adj* horribilis, immānis; *(look)* taeter
frightfully *adv* foedē
frigid *adj* frīgidus
frigidity *n* frīgus *nt*
frill *n* fimbriae *fpl*; *(RHET)* calamistrī *mpl*
fringe *n* fimbriae *fpl*
frisk *vi* lascīvīre, exsultāre
frisky *adj* lascīvus
fritter *vt*: ~ **away** dissipāre; *(time)* extrahere
frivolity *n* levitās *f*
frivolous *adj* levis, inānis
frivolously *adv* ināniter
fro *adv*: **to and fro** hūc illūc
frock *n* stola *f*
frog *n* rāna *f*
frolic *n* lūdus *m* ♦ *vi* lūdere, lascīvīre
frolicsome *adj* lascīvus, hilaris
from *prep* ab *(abl)*, ā *before consonants*; *(out)* ē, ex
(abl); *(cause)* propter *(acc)*; *(prevention)* quōminus,
quīn; ~ **all directions** undique

front n frōns f; **in ~ ā** fronte, adversus; **in ~ of**
pro (abl)
frontier n līmes m, cōnfīnia ntpl; **frontiers** fīnes
mpl
front line n prima aciēs
frost n gelū nt
frostbitten adj: **be ~ vī** frīgoris ambūrī
frosty adj gelidus, glaciālis
froth n spūma f ♦ vi spūmās agere
frothy adj spūmeus
froward adj contumāx
frown n frontis contractiō f ♦ vi frontem
contrahere
frozen adj glaciālis
fructify vt fēcundāre
frugal adj parcus, frūgī
frugality n frūgālitās f, parsimōnia f
frugally adv parcē, frūgāliter
fruit n fructus m; (tree) māla ntpl; (berry) bāca f; (fig)
fructus m; **fruits** pl (of earth) frūgēs fpl
fruiterer n pōmārius m
fruitful adj fēcundus, fructuōsus
fruitfully adv ferāciter
fruitfulness n fēcunditās f, ūbertās f
fruition n fructus m
fruitless adj inūtilis, vānus
fruitlessly adv nēquīquam, frustrā
fruit tree n pōmum nt
frustrate vt frustrārī, ad inritum redigere
frustration n frustrātiō f
fry vt frīgere
frying pan n sartāgō f; **out of the frying pan
into the fire** incidit in Scyllam quī vult vītāre
Charybdim
fuel n fōmes m
fugitive adj fugitīvus ♦ n fugitīvus m, trānsfuga
m; (from abroad) extorris m
fulfil vt (duty) explēre, implēre; (promise)
praestāre; (order) exsequī, perficere
fulfilment n absolūtiō f
full adj plēnus (abl), refertus, explētus; (entire)
integer; (amount) solidus; (brother) germānus;
(measure) iūstus; (meeting) frequēns; (style)
cōpiōsus; **at ~ length** porrēctus; **at ~ speed**
citātō gradū, citātō equō
fuller n fullō m
full-grown adj adultus
full moon n lūna plēna
fullness n (style) cōpia f; (time) mātūritās f
fully adv plēnē, penitus, funditus
fulminate vi intonāre
fulsome adj fastīdiōsus, pūtidus
fumble vi haesitāre

fume n fūmus m, hālitus m ♦ vi stomachārī
fumigate vt suffīre
fun n iocus m, lūdus m; **for fun** animī causā;
make fun of inlūdere, dēlūdere, lūdibriō
habēre
function n officium nt, mūnus nt
fund n cōpia f
fundamental adj prīmus ♦ n prīncipium nt,
elementum nt
funds npl sors f, pecūniae fpl
funeral n fūnus nt, exsequiae fpl ♦ adj fūnebris
funeral pile n rogus m
funeral pyre n rogus m
funeral rites npl exsequiae fpl, īnferiae fpl
funereal adj fūnebria, lūgubris
funnel n īnfundibulum nt
funny adj ioculāris, rīdiculus
fur n pellis m
furbelow n īnstita f
furbish vt expolīre; **~ up** interpolāre
Furies npl Furiae fpl
furious adj saevus, vehemēns, perīrātus
furiously adv furenter, saevē, vehementer
furl vt (sail) legere
furlong n stadium nt
furlough n commeātus m
furnace n fornāx f
furnish vt praebēre, suppeditāre; (equip)
īnstruere, ōrnāre
furniture n supellex f
furrow n sulcus m ♦ vt sulcāre
furry adj villōsus
further adj ulterior ♦ adv ultrā, porrō; amplius
♦ vt adiuvāre, cōnsulere (dat)
furtherance n prōgressus m; (means)
īnstrūmentum nt
furthermore adv praetereā, porrō
furthest adj ultimus ♦ adv longissimē
furtive adj fūrtīvus, clandestīnus
furtively adv clam, fūrtim
fury n furor m, saevitia f; īra f
fuse vt fundere; (together) coniungere
fusion n coniūnctiō f
fuss n importūnitās f, querimōnia f ♦ vi
conquerī, sollicitārī
fussy adj importūnus, incommodus
fusty adj mūcidus
futile adj inānis, inūtilis, futilis
futility n vānitās f, futilitās f
future adj futūrus, posterus ♦ n posterum
nt, reliquum nt; **in ~** posthāc; **for the ~** in
posterum
futurity n posterum tempus nt, posteritās f

Gg

gabble *vi* garrīre
gable *n* fastīgium *nt*
gadfly *n* tabānus *m*
gag *vt* ōs praeligāre (*dat*), ōs obvolvere (*dat*)
gage *n* pignus *nt*
gaiety *n* laetitia *f*, hilaritās *f*, festīvitās *f*
gaily *adv* hilare, festīve
gain *n* lucrum *nt*, quaestus *m* ♦ *vt* comparāre; adipīscī; (*profit*) lucrārī; (*thing*) parāre, cōnsequī, capere; (*case*) vincere; (*place*) pervenīre ad; (*possession of*) potīrī (*gen*); (*victory*) reportāre; ~ **over** conciliāre; ~ **ground** incrēbrēscere; ~ **possession of** potior (*abl*); ~ **the upper hand** rem obtinēre
gainful *adj* quaestuōsus
gainsay *vt* contrādīcere (*dat*)
gait *n* incessus *m*, ingressiō *f*
gaiters *n* ocreae *fpl*
gala *n* diēs festus *m*
galaxy *n* circulus lacteus *m*
gale *n* ventus *m*
gall *n* fel *nt*, bīlis *m* ♦ *vt* ūrere
gallant *adj* fortis, audāx; (*courteous*) officiōsus
gallantly *adv* fortiter; officiōsē
gallantry *n* virtūs *f*; urbānitās *f*
gall bladder *n* fel *nt*
gallery *n* porticus *f*
galley *n* nāvis āctuāria *f*; (*cook's*) culīna *f*
galling *adj* amārus, mordāx
gallon *n* congius *m*
gallop *n* cursus *m*; **at the ~** citātō equō, admissō equō ♦ *vi* admissō equō currere
gallows *n* īnfēlīx arbor *m*, furca *f*
gallows bird *n* furcifer *m*
galore *adv* adfatim
gamble *n* ālea *f* ♦ *vi* āleā lūdere
gambler *n* āleātor *m*
gambling *n* ālea *f*
gambol *n* lūsus *m* ♦ *vi* lūdere, lascīvīre, exsultāre
game *n* lūdus *m*; (*with dice*) ālea *f*; (*hunt*) praeda *f*; **play the ~** rēctē facere; **public games** lūdī *mpl*; **Olympic games** Olympia *ntpl*; **the game's up** āctum est ♦ *adj* animōsus
gamester *n* āleātor *m*
gammon *n* perna *f*
gander *n* ānser *m*
gang *n* grex *m*, caterva *f*
gangster *n* grassātor *m*
gangway *n* forus *m*
gaol *n* carcer *m*
gaoler *n* custōs *m*
gap *n* hiātus *m*, lacūna *f*

gape *vi* hiāre, inhiāre; (*opening*) dēhiscere
garb *n* habitus *m*, amictus *m* ♦ *vt* amicīre
garbage *n* quisquiliae *fpl*
garden *n* hortus *m*; (*public*) hortī *mpl*
gardener *n* hortulānus *m*; (*ornamental*) topiārius *m*
gardening *n* hortī cultūra *f*; (*ornamental*) topiāria *f*
gargle *vi* gargarissāre
garish *adj* speciōsus, fūcātus
garland *n* sertum *nt*, corōna *f* ♦ *vt* corōnāre
garlic *n* ālium *nt*
garment *n* vestis *f*, vestīmentum *nt*
garnish *vt* ōrnāre, decorāre
garret *n* cēnāculum *nt*
garrison *n* praesidium *nt*, dēfēnsōrēs *mpl* ♦ *vt* praesidiō mūnīre, praesidium collocāre in (*abl*)
garrotte *vt* laqueō gulam frangere (*dat*)
garrulity *n* garrulitās *f*
garrulous *adj* garrulus, loquāx
gas *n* vapor *m*
gash *n* vulnus *nt* ♦ *vt* caedere, lacerāre
gasp *n* anhēlitus *m*, singultus *m* ♦ *vi* anhēlāre
gastronomy *n* gula *f*
gate *n* porta *f*
gather *vt* colligere, cōgere; (*fruit*) legere; (*inference*) colligere, conicere ♦ *vi* congregārī
gathering *n* conventus *m*, coetus *m*
gauche *adj* inconcinnus, illepidus
gaudily *adv* splendidē, speciōsē
gaudy *adj* speciōsus, fūcātus, lautus
gauge *n* modulus *m* ♦ *vt* mētīrī
Gaul *n* Gallia *f*; (*person*) Gallus *m*
gaunt *adj* macer
gauntlet *n* manica *f*
gauze *n* Coa *ntpl*
gay *adj* hilaris, festīvus, laetus
gaze *vi* intuērī; ~ **at** intuērī, adspectāre, contemplārī
gazelle *n* oryx *m*
gazette *n* ācta diūrna *ntpl*, ācta pūblica *ntpl*
gear *n* īnstrūmenta *ntpl*; (*ship's*) armāmenta *ntpl*
gelding *n* cantērius *m*
gelid *adj* gelidus
gem *n* gemma *f*
gender *n* genus *nt*
genealogical *adj* dē stirpe
genealogical table *n* stemma *nt*
genealogist *n* geneālogus *m*
genealogy *n* geneālogia *f*

general *adj* generālis, ūniversus; (*usual*) vulgāris, commūnis; **in ~** omnīnō ♦ *n* dux *m*, imperātor *m*; **general's tent** praetorium *nt*

generalissimo *n* imperātor *m*

generality *n* vulgus *nt*, plērīque *mpl*

generalize *vi* ūniversē loquī

generally *adv* ferē, plērumque; (*discuss*) īnfīnītē

generalship *n* ductus *m*

generate *vt* gignere, generāre

generation *n* aetās *f*, saeculum *nt*

generic *adj* generālis

generically *adv* genere

generosity *n* līberālitās *f*, largitās *f*

generous *adj* līberālis, largus, benīgnus

generously *adv* līberāliter, largē, benīgnē

genesis *n* orīgō *f*, prīncipium *nt*

genial *adj* cōmis, hilaris

geniality *n* cōmitās *f*, hilaritās *f*

genially *adv* cōmiter, hilare

genitive *n* genitīvus *m*

genius *n* (*deity*) genius *m*; (*talent*) ingenium *nt*, indolēs *f*; **of ~** ingeniōsus

genre *n* genus *nt*

genteel *adj* urbānus, polītus

gentility *n* urbānitās *f*, ēlegantia *f*

gentle *adj* (*birth*) ingenuus; (*manner*) hūmānus, indulgēns, mītis; (*slope*) lēnis, mollis; (*thing*) placidus, lēnis

gentleman *n* vir *m*, ingenuus *m*, vir honestus *m*

gentlemanly *adj* ingenuus, līberālis, honestus

gentleness *n* hūmānitās *f*, indulgentia *f*, lēnitās *f*

gentlewoman *n* ingenua *f*, mulier honesta *f*

gently *adv* lēniter, molliter, placidē

gentry *n* ingenuī *mpl*, optimātēs *mpl*; (*contempt*) hominēs *mpl*

genuine *adj* vērus, germānus, sincērus

genuinely *adv* germānē, sincērē

genuineness *n* fidēs *f*

geographical *adj* geōgraphicus; **~ position** situs *m*

geography *n* geōgraphia *f*

geometrical *adj* geōmetricus

geometry *n* geōmetria *f*

Georgics *n* Geōrgica *ntpl*

germ *n* germen *nt*, sēmen *nt*

germane *adj* adfīnis

germinate *vi* gemmāre

gesticulate *vi* sē iactāre, gestū ūtī

gesticulation *n* gestus *m*

gesture *n* gestus *m*, mōtus *m*

get *vt* adipīscī, nancīscī, parāre; (*malady*) contrahere; (*request*) impetrāre; (*return*) capere; (*reward*) ferre; **get sth done** cūrāre (*with gerundive*); **get sb to do** persuādēre (*dat*), addūcere; **get by heart** ēdiscere; **get in** repōnere; **get the better of** superāre; **go and get** arcessere ♦ *vi* fierī; **get about** (*rumour*) palam fierī, percrēbrēscere; **get away** effugere; **get at** (*intent*) spectāre; **get behind** cessāre; **get off** absolvī; **get on** prōficere; **get out** effugere, ēvādere; **get out of hand** lascīvīre; **get out of the way** dē viā dēcēdere; **get ready** parāre; **get rid of** abicere, tollere; **get to** pervenīre ad; **get to know** cognōscere; **get together** congregārī; **get up** exsurgere

get-up *n* ōrnātus *m*

ghastliness *n* pallor *m*

ghastly *adj* pallidus; (*sight*) taeter

ghost *n* larva *f*, īdōlon *nt*; **ghosts** *pl* mānēs *mpl*; **give up the ~** animam agere, efflāre

giant *n* Gigas *m*

gibberish *n* barbaricus sermō *m*

gibbet *n* furca *f*

gibe *vi* inrīdēre

giddiness *n* vertīgō *f*

giddy *adj* vertīginōsus; (*fig*) levis

gift *n* dōnum *nt*; (*small*) mūnusculum *nt*; **gifts** *pl* (*mind*) ingenium *nt*

gifted *adj* ingeniōsus

gig *n* cisium *nt*

gigantic *adj* ingēns, immānis

gild *vt* inaurāre

gill *n* (*measure*) quartārius *m*; (*fish*) branchia *f*

gilt *adj* aurātus

gimlet *n* terebra *f*

gin *n* pedica *f*, laqueus *m*

ginger *n* zingiberī *nt*

gingerly *adv* pedetemptim

giraffe *n* camēlopardālis *f*

gird *vt* circumdare; **~ on** accingere; **~ oneself** cingī; **~ up** succingere

girder *n* tignum *nt*

girdle *n* cingulus *m* ♦ *vt* cingere

girl *n* puella *f*, virgō *f*

girlhood *n* aetās puellāris *f*

girlish *adj* puellāris

girth *n* ambitus *m*, amplitūdō *f*

gist *n* firmāmentum *nt*

give *vt* dare, dōnāre, tribuere; (*thing due*) reddere; **~ away** largīrī; (*bride*) in matrimōnium collocāre; (*secret*) prōdere; **~ back** reddere, restituere; **~ birth (to)** pārere; **~ in** (*name*) profiterī; **~ off** ēmittere; **~ out** (*orders*) ēdere; (*sound*) ēmittere; **~ thanks** gratias agere; **~ up** dēdere, trādere; (*hope of*) dēspērāre; (*rights*) dēcēdere dē, renūntiāre; **~ way** cēdere; (MIL) inclīnāre ♦ *vi* labāre; **~ in** sē victum fatērī; (MIL) manūs dare; **~ out** (*fail*) dēficere; (*pretend*) ferre; **~ up** dēsistere; **~ way** cēdere

giver *n* dator *m*

glacial *adj* glaciālis

glad *adj* laetus, alacer, hilaris; **be ~** gaudēre

gladden *vt* exhilārāre, oblectāre

glade *n* saltus *m*

gladiator *n* gladiātor *m*

gladiatorial *adj* gladiātōrius; **present a ~ show** gladiātōrēs dare

gladly *adv* laetē, libenter

gladness *n* laetitia *f*, alacritās *f*, gaudium *nt*

glamorous *adj* venustus

glamour *n* venustās *f*

glance *n* aspectus *m* ♦ *vi* oculōs conicere; **~ at** aspicere; (*fig*) attingere, perstringere; **~ off** stringere

glare *n* fulgor *m* ♦ *vi* fulgēre; **~ at** torvīs oculīs intuērī

glaring *adj* (*look*) torvus; (*fault*) manifestus; **be ~** ante pedēs positum esse

glass *n* vitrum *nt*; (*mirror*) speculum *nt*

glassy *adj* vitreus

glaze *vt* vitrō obdūcere

gleam n fulgor m, lūx f ◆ vi fulgēre, lūcēre
gleaming adj splendidus, nitidus
glean vi spīcās legere
gleaning n spīcilegium nt
glebe n fundus m
glee n hilaritās f, gaudium nt
gleeful adj hilaris, festīvus, laetus
gleefully adv hilare, laetē
glen n vallis f
glib adj prōfluēns, fācundus
glibly adv prōfluenter
glide n lāpsus m ◆ vi lābī; ~ **away** ēlābī
glimmer vi sublūcēre ◆ n: a ~ **of hope** spēcula f
glimpse n aspectus m ◆ vt cōnspicārī
glint vi renīdēre
glisten vi fulgēre, nitēre
glitter vi micāre
gloaming n crepusculum nt
gloat vi: ~ **over** inhiāre, animō haurīre, oculōs
   pāscere (abl)
globe n globus m, sphaera f; (inhabited) orbis
   terrārum m
globular adj globōsus
globule n globulus m, pilula f
gloom n tenebrae fpl; tristitia f
gloomy adj tenebricōsus; tristis, dēmissus
glorify vt illūstrāre, extollere, laudāre
glorious adj illūstris, praeclārus, splendidus
gloriously adv praeclārē, splendidē
glory n laus f, glōria f, decus nt ◆ vi glōriārī, sē
   iactāre
gloss n nitor m ◆ vt: ~ **over** (fig) dissimulāre
glossy adj nitidus
glove n manica f
glow n (light) lūmen nt; (heat) ārdor m; (passion)
   calor m ◆ vi lūcēre, ārdēre, calēre, candēre
glowing adj candēns, ārdēns, calidus
glue n glūten nt ◆ vt glūtināre
glum adj tristis, maestus
glut vt explēre, saturāre ◆ n satietās f,
   abundantia f
glutton n gāneō m, helluō m
gluttonous adj edāx, vorāx, avidus
gluttony n gula f, edācitās f
gnarled adj nōdōsus
gnash vt, vi frendere; ~ **one's teeth** dentibus
   frendere
gnat n culex m
gnaw vt rōdere; ~ **away** ērōdere
gnawing adj mordāx
go vi īre, vādere; (depart) abīre, discēdere; (event)
   ēvādere; (mechanism) movērī; **go about** incipere,
   adgredī; **go after** īnsequī; **go away** abīre,
   discēdere; **go back** redīre, regredī; **go before**
   anteīre, praeīre; **go by** praeterīre; (rule) sequī,
   ūtī (abl); **go down** dēscendere; (storm) cadere;
   (star) occidere; **go for** petere; **go forward**
   prōgredī; **go in** intrāre, ingredī; **go in for**
   (profession) facere, exercēre; **go off** abīre; **go on**
   pergere; (event) agī; **go out** exīre, ēgredī; (fire)
   extinguī; **go over** trānsīre; (to enemy) dēscīscere;
   (preparation) meditārī; (reading) legere; (work done)
   retractāre; **go round** circumīre, ambīre; **go**
   through percurrere; penetrāre; (suffer) perferre;
   go to adīre, petere; **go up** ascendere; **go to the**
   help of subvenīre (dat); **go to meet** obviam īre;

go with comitārī; **go without** carēre (abl), sē
   abstinēre (abl) ◆ n vīs f, ācrimōnia f
goad n stimulus m ◆ vt irrītāre; pungere; (fig)
   stimulāre
go-ahead adj impiger
goal n fīnis m, mēta f
goat n caper m, capra f
gobble vt dēvorāre
go-between n internūntius m, internūntia f;
   (bribery) sequester m
goblet n pōculum nt, scyphus m
god n deus m
goddess n dea f
godhead n dīvīnitās f, nūmen nt
godless adj impius
godlike adj dīvīnus
godliness n pietās f, rēligiō f
godly adj pius
godsend n quasi caelō dēmissus
going n itiō f; (way) iter nt; (departure) profectiō f,
   discessus m
goitre n strūma nt
gold n aurum nt ◆ adj aureus
golden adj aureus; (hair) flāvus
gold leaf n bractea f
goldmine n aurāria f
goldsmith n aurārius m, aurifex m
good adj bonus, probus; (fit) idōneus, aptus;
   (considerable) magnus; ~ **day!** salvē, salvēte!;
   ~ **looks** fōrma f, pulchritūdō f; ~ **nature**
   facilitās f, cōmitās f ◆ n bonum nt, commodum
   nt; **do** ~ **to** prōdesse (dat); **make** ~ supplēre,
   praestāre; **seem** ~ vidērī ◆ interj bene
goodbye interj valē, valēte; **say** ~ **to** valēre iubēre
good-for-nothing adj nēquam
good-humoured adj cōmis
good-looking adj pulcher
goodly adj pulcher; (size) amplus
good nature n facilitās f, cōmitās f
good-natured adj facilis, benīgnus, benevolus
goodness n bonitās f; (character) virtūs f,
   probitās f, pietās f
goods npl bona ntpl, rēs f; (for sale) merx f
good-tempered adj mītis, lēnis
goodwill n benevolentia f, favor m, grātia f
goose n ānser m/f
goose flesh n horror m
gore n cruor m ◆ vt cornibus cōnfodere
gorge n faucēs fpl, gula f; (GEOG) angustiae fpl ◆ vt:
   ~ **oneself** sē ingurgitāre
gorgeous adj lautus, splendidus
gorgeously adv lautē, splendidē
gorgeousness n lautitia f
gormandize vi helluārī
gory adj cruentus
gospel n ēvangelium nt
gossip n (talk) sermunculus m, rūmusculus m,
   fāma f; (person) lingulāca f ◆ vi garrīre
gouge vt ēruere
gourd n cucurbita f
gourmand n helluō m, gāneō m
gout n podagra f, articulāris morbus m
gouty adj arthrīticus
govern vt (subjects) regere; (state) administrāre,
   gubernāre; (emotion) moderārī (dat), cohibēre
governess n ēducātrīx f

government n gubernātiō f, administrātiō f; (*men*) magistrātūs mpl
governor n gubernātor m, moderātor m; (*province*) prōcōnsul m, prōcūrātor m
gown n (*men*) toga f; (*women*) stola f
grab vt adripere, corripere
grace n grātia f, lepōs m, decor m; (*favour*) grātia f, venia f; (*of gods*) pāx f; **be in the good graces of** in grātiā esse apud (*acc*); **with a bad ~** invītus ◆ vt decorāre, ōrnāre
graceful adj decōrus, venustus, lepidus
gracefully adv venustē, lepidē
graceless adj illepidus, impudēns
gracious adj benīgnus, prōpitius, misericors
graciously adv benīgnē, līberāliter
graciousness n benīgnitās f, līberālitās f
gradation n gradus m
grade n gradus m
gradient n clīvus m
gradual adj lēnis
gradually adv gradātim, sēnsim, paulātim
graft n surculus m; (*POL*) ambitus m ◆ vt īnserere
grafting n īnsitiō f
grain n frūmentum nt; (*seed*) grānum nt; **against the ~** invītā Minervā
grammar n grammatica f
grammarian n grammaticus m
granary n horreum nt
grand adj (*person*) amplus, illūstris, ēgregius; (*way of life*) lautus, māgnificus; (*language*) grandis, sublīmis
granddaughter n neptis f; **great ~** prōneptis f
grandeur n māiestās f, māgnificentia f; (*style*) granditās f
grandfather n avus m; **great ~** proavus m; **great-great-grandfather** abavus m; **of a ~** avītus
grandiloquence n māgniloquentia f
grandiloquent adj grandiloquus, tumidus
grandiose adj māgnificus
grandmother n avia f; **great ~** proavia f
grandson n nepōs m; **great ~** prōnepōs m
grant vt dare, concēdere, tribuere; (*admit*) fatērī ◆ n concessiō f
grape n ūva f
graphic adj expressus; **give a ~ account of** ante oculōs pōnere, oculīs subicere
grapnel n manus ferrea f, harpagō f
grapple vi luctārī
grappling iron n manus ferrea f
grasp vt prēnsāre, comprehendere; (*with mind*) complectī, adsequī, percipere, intellegere; **~ at** captāre, adpetere ◆ n manus f, comprehēnsiō f; (*mind*) captus m
grasping adj avārus, rapāx
grass n herba f
grasshopper n gryllus m
grassy adj herbōsus; herbidus
grate n focus m ◆ vt atterere; **~ upon** offendere
grateful adj grātus; **feel ~** grātiam habēre
gratefully adv grātē
gratification n voluptās f
gratify vt mōrem gerere (*dat*), mōrigerārī (*dat*), grātificārī (*dat*)
gratifying adj iūcundus
gratis adv grātuītō, grātīs
gratitude n grātia f; **show ~** grātiam referre

gratuitous adj grātuītus
gratuitously adv grātuītō
gratuity n stips f; (*MIL*) dōnātīvum nt
grave n sepulchrum nt ◆ adj gravis, austērus ◆ vt scalpere
gravel n glārea f
gravely adv graviter, sevērē
gravitate vi vergere
gravity n (*person*) sevēritās f, tristitia f; (*circumstances*) gravitās f, mōmentum nt; (*physics*) nūtus m; **by force of ~** nūtū suō
gray adj rāvus; (*hair*) cānus
graze vi pāscī ◆ vt (*cattle*) pāscere; (*by touch*) stringere
grazing n pāstus m
grease n arvīna f ◆ vt ungere
greasy adj pinguis, ūnctus
great adj māgnus, grandis, ingēns, amplus; (*fame*) īnsignis, praeclārus; **as ~ as ... tantus ... quantus**; **~ deal** plūrimum; **~ many** plūrimī; **how ~** quantus; **very ~** permāgnus
greatcoat n lacerna f
greatest adj māximus
greatly adv multum, māgnopere
greave n ocrea f
greed n avāritia f
greedily adv avārē, cupidē
greedy adj avārus, cupidus; avidus
Greek adj Graecus
green adj viridis; (*unripe*) crūdus; **be ~** virēre
greenness n viriditās f
greens n olus nt
greet vt salūtāre
greeting n salūs f, salūtātiō f
grey adj rāvus; (*hair*) cānus
greyhound n vertagus m
grief n dolor m, maeror m, lūctus m; **come to ~ perīre**
grievance n querimōnia f; iniūria f
grieve vi dolēre, maerēre, lūgēre
grievous adj tristis, lūctuōsus; molestus, gravis, acerbus
grievously adv graviter, valdē
grim adj trux, truculentus; atrōx
grimace n ōris dēprāvātiō f; **make a ~ ōs dūcere**
grime n sordēs f, lutum nt
grimy adj sordidus, lutulentus
grin n rīsus m ◆ vi adrīdēre
grind vt contundere; (*corn*) molere; (*blade*) acuere; **~ down** (*fig*) opprimere
grindstone n cōs f
grip vt comprehendere, arripere ◆ n comprehēnsiō f; **come to grips with** in complexum venīre (*gen*)
gripe n tormina ntpl
grisly adj horridus, dīrus
grist n (*fig*) ēmolumentum nt
grit n harēna f
groan n gemitus m ◆ vi gemere, ingemere
groin n inguen nt
groom n agāsō m
groove n canālis m, stria f
grope vi praetentāre
gross adj crassus, pinguis; (*morally*) turpis, foedus
grossly adv foedē, turpiter; (*very*) valdē

grossness *n* crassitūdō *f*; turpitūdō *f*
grotto *n* spēlunca *f*, antrum *nt*
ground *n* (*bottom*) solum *nt*; (*earth*) terra *f*, humus *f*; (*cause*) ratiō *f*, causa *f*; (*sediment*) faex *f*; **on the ~** humī; **on the grounds that** quod (*subj*); **to the ~** humum; **gain ~** prōficere; (*rumour*) incrēbrēscere; **lose ~** cēdere; (*MIL*) inclīnāre ◆ *vt* īnstituere ◆ *vi* (*ship*) sīdere
grounding *n* īnstitūtiō *f*
groundless *adj* vānus, inānis
groundlessly *adv* frustrā, temerē
grounds *n* faex *f*; (*property*) praedium *nt*; (*reason*) causa *f*; **have good ~ for doing** nōn sine causā faciō, iūstīs dē causīs faciō
groundwork *n* fundāmentum *nt*
group *n* globus *m*, circulus *m* ◆ *vt* dispōnere
grouse *n* (*bird*) tetraō *m*; (*complaint*) querēla *f* ◆ *vi* querī
grove *n* nemus *nt*, lūcus *m*
grovel *vi* serpere, sē prōsternere, sē advolvere
grovelling *adj* humilis, abiectus
grow *vi* crēscere, glīscere; (*spread*) percrēbrēscere; (*become*) fierī; **~ old** (con)senēscere; **~ up** adolēscere, pūbēscere; **let ~** (*hair*) prōmittere ◆ *vt* (*crops*) colere; (*beard*) dēmittere
growl *n* fremitus *m* ◆ *vi* fremere
grown-up *adj* adultus, grandis
growth *n* incrēmentum *nt*, auctus *m*
grub *n* vermiculus *m*
grudge *n* invidia *f* ◆ *vt* invidēre (*dat*); (*thing*) gravārī
grudgingly *adv* invītus, gravātē
gruesome *adj* taeter
gruff *adj* acerbus, asper
grumble *vi* querī, mussāre ◆ *n* querēla *f*
grumpy *adj* mōrōsus, querulus
grunt *n* grunnītus *m* ◆ *vi* grunnīre
guarantee *n* (*money*) spōnsiō *f*; (*promise*) fidēs *f*; (*person*) praes *m* ◆ *vt* spondēre, praestāre
guarantor *n* spōnsor *m*
guard *n* custōdia *f*, praesidium *nt*; (*person*) custōs *m*; **on ~** in statiōne; **be on one's ~** cavēre; **keep ~** statiōnem agere; **off one's ~** imprūdēns, inopīnāns; **be taken off one's ~** dē gradū dēicī ◆ *vt* custōdīre, dēfendere; (*keep*) cōnservāre; **~ against** cavēre
guarded *adj* cautus
guardedly *adv* cautē

guardhouse *n* custōdia *f*
guardian *n* custōs *m*; (*of minors*) tūtor *m*
guardianship *n* custōdia *f*, tūtēla *f*
guardian spirit *n* genius *m*
gudgeon *n* gōbius *m*
guerdon *n* praemium *nt*, mercēs *f*
guess *n* coniectūra *f* ◆ *vt* dīvīnāre, conicere
guest *n* hospes *m*, hospita *f*; (*at dinner*) convīva *m*; **uninvited ~** umbra *f*; **guest's** hospitālis
guffaw *n* cachinnus *m* ◆ *vi* cachinnāre
guidance *n* moderātiō *f*; **under the ~ of God** dūcente deō
guide *n* dux *m*, ductor *m*; (*in policy*) auctor *m* ◆ *vt* dūcere; (*steer*) regere; (*control*) moderārī
guild *n* collēgium *nt*
guile *n* dolus *m*, fraus *f*
guileful *adj* dolōsus, fraudulentus
guilefully *adv* dolosē
guileless *adj* simplex, innocēns
guilelessly *adv* sine fraude
guilt *n* culpa *f*, scelus *nt*
guiltless *adj* innocēns, īnsōns
guiltlessly *adv* integrē
guilty *adj* nocēns, sōns; **find ~** damnāre
guise *n* speciēs *f*
guitar *n* fidēs *fpl*; **play the ~** fidibus canere
gulf *n* sinus *m*; (*chasm*) hiātus *m*
gull *n* mergus *m* ◆ *vt* dēcipere
gullet *n* gula *f*, guttur *nt*
gullible *adj* crēdulus
gulp *vt* dēvorāre, haurīre
gum *n* gummī *nt*; (*mouth*) gingīva *f*
gumption *n* prūdentia *f*
gurgle *vi* singultāre
gush *vi* sē prōfundere, ēmicāre ◆ *n* scatūrīginēs *fpl*
gust *n* flāmen *nt*, impetus *m*
gusto *n* studium *nt*
gusty *adj* ventōsus
gut *n* intestīnum *nt* ◆ *vt* exenterāre; (*fig*) extergēre
gutter *n* canālis *m*
guzzle *vi* sē ingurgitāre
gymnasium *n* gymnasium *nt*, palaestra *f*; **head of a ~** gymnasiarchus *m*
gymnastic *adj* gymnicus; **gymnastics** *pl* palaestra *f*
gyrate *vi* volvī

Hh

habit n mōs m, cōnsuētūdō f; (dress) habitus m, vestītus m; **be in the ~ of** solēre

habitable adj habitābilis

habitation n domus f, domicilium nt; (place) sēdēs f

habitual adj ūsitātus

habitually adv ex mōre, persaepe

habituate vt adsuēfacere, īnsuēscere

hack vt caedere, concīdere ♦ n (horse) caballus m

hackneyed adj trītus

Hades n īnferī mpl

haft n manubrium nt

hag n anus f

haggard adj ferus

haggle vi altercārī

hail n grandō f ♦ vi: **it hails** grandinat ♦ vt salūtāre, adclāmāre ♦ interj avē, avēte; salvē, salvēte; **I ~ from Rome** Rōma mihi patria est

hair n capillus m; crīnis m; (single) pīlus m; (animals) sēta f, villus nt; **deviate a hair's breadth from** trānsversum digitum discēdere ab; **split hairs** cavillārī

hairdresser n tōnsor m

hairless adj (head) calvus; (body) glaber

hairpin n crīnāle nt

hairsplitting adj captiōsus ♦ n cavillātiō f

hairy adj pīlōsus

halberd n bipennis f

halcyon n alcēdō f; **~ days** alcēdōnia ntpl

hale adj validus, rōbustus ♦ vt trahere, rapere

half n dīmidium nt, dīmidia pars f ♦ adj dīmidius, dīmidiātus; **~ as much again** sesquī; **well begun is ~ done** dīmidium factī quī coepit habet

half-asleep adj sēmisomnus

half-baked adj (fig) rudis

half-dead adj sēmianimis, sēmivīvus

half-full adj sēmiplēnus

half-hearted adj incūriōsus, sōcors

half-heartedly adv sine studiō

half-hour n sēmihōra f

half-moon n lūna dīmidiāta f

half-open adj sēmiapertus

half pound n sēlībra f

half-way adj medius; **~ up the hill** in mediō colle

half-yearly adj sēmestris

hall n ātrium nt; (public) exedra f

hallo interj heus

hallow vt sacrāre

hallucination n error m, somnium nt

halo n corōna f

halt vi īnsistere, cōnsistere ♦ vt sistere ♦ n: **come to a ~** cōnsistere, agmen cōnstituere ♦ adj claudus

halter n capistrum nt; (fig) laqueus m

halve vt bipartīre

ham n perna f

hamlet n vīcus m

hammer n malleus m ♦ vt tundere; **~ out** excūdere

hamper n corbis f ♦ vt impedīre; (with debt) obstringere

hamstring vt poplitem succīdere (dat)

hand n manus f; **left ~** laeva f, sinistra f; **right ~** dextra f; **an old ~** veterātor m; **at ~** praestō, ad manum; **be at ~** adesse; **at first ~** ipse; **at second ~** ab aliō; **on the one ~ … on the other** et … et, quidem … at; **near at ~** in expedītō, inibī; **the matter in ~** quod nunc īnstat, quae in manibus sunt; **get out of ~** lascīvīre; **have a ~ in** interesse (dat); **have one's hands full** satis agere; **lay hands on** manum adferre, inicere (dat); **live from ~ to mouth** ad hōram vīvere; **pass from ~ to ~** per manūs trādere; **take in ~** suscipere; **hands** pl (workmen) operae fpl ♦ vt trādere, porrigere; **~ down** trādere, prōdere; **~ over** dēferre, reddere

handbill n libellus m

handbook n ars f

handcuffs n manicae fpl

handful n manipulus m

handicap n impedīmentum nt

handicraft n artificium nt, ars operōsa f

handily adv habiliter

handiness n habilitās f; commoditās f

handiwork n opus nt, manus f

handkerchief n sūdārium nt

handle n (cup) ānsa f; (knife) manubrium nt; (fig) ānsa f, occāsiō f ♦ vt tractāre

handling n tractātiō f

handmaid n famula f

handsome adj fōrmōsus, pulcher; (gift) līberālis

handsomely adv pulchrē; līberāliter

handsomeness n pulchritūdō f, fōrma f

hand-to-hand adv: **fight ~** manum cōnserere, comminus pugnāre

handwriting n manus f

handy adj (to use) habilis; (near) praestō

hang vt suspendere; (head) dēmittere; (wall) vestīre ♦ vi pendēre; **~ back** gravārī, dubitāre; **~ down** dēpendēre; **~ on to** haerēre (dat); **~ over** imminēre (dat), impendēre (dat); **go and be hanged** abī in malam crucem!

hanger-on n cliēns m/f, assecla m/f
hanging n (death) suspendium nt; **hangings** pl
  aulaea ntpl ♦ adj pendulus
hangman n carnifex m
hanker vi: ~ **after** appetere, exoptāre
hap n fors f
haphazard adj fortuītus
hapless adj miser, īnfēlīx
haply adv fortasse
happen vi accidere, ēvenīre, contingere; (become)
  fierī; **as usually happens** ut fit; ~ **upon**
  incidere in (acc); **it happens that** accidit ut
  (subj)
happily adv fēlīciter, beātē, bene
happiness n fēlīcitās f
happy adj fēlīx, beātus; laetus; (in some respect)
  fortūnātus
harangue n cōntiō f ♦ vt cōntiōnārī apud (acc),
  hortārī
harass vt vexāre, lacessere, exagitāre, sollicitāre
harassing adj molestus
harbinger n praenūntius m
harbour n portus m ♦ vt recipere
harbour dues n portōria ntpl
hard adj dūrus; (circumstances) asper, inīquus;
  (task) difficilis, arduus; ~ **of hearing** surdaster;
  grow ~ dūrēscere ♦ adv sēdulō, valdē; ~ **by**
  prope, iuxtā; **I am** ~ **put to it to do** aegerrimē
  faciō
hard cash n praesēns pecūnia f
harden vt dūrāre ♦ vi dūrēscere; (fig)
  obdūrēscere; **become hardened** obdūrēscere
hard-fought adj atrōx
hard-hearted adj crūdēlis, dūrus, inhūmānus
hardihood n audācia f
hardily adv sevērē
hardiness n rōbur nt; dūritia f
hardly adv vix, aegrē; (severely) dūriter, acerbē;
  ~ **any** nullus ferē
hardness n dūritia f; (fig) asperitās f, inīquitās f;
  (difficulty) difficultās f; ~ **of hearing** surditās f
hard-pressed adj: **be** ~ labōrāre
hardship n labor m, malum nt, iniūria f
hard-working adj industrius, nāvus, sēdulus
hardy adj dūrus, rōbustus, sevērus
hare n lepus m
hark interj auscultā, auscultāte ♦ vi: ~ **back to**
  repetere
harm n iniūria f, damnum nt, malum nt,
  dētrīmentum nt; **come to** ~ dētrīmentum
  capere, accipere ♦ vt laedere, nocēre (dat)
harmful adj damnōsus, noxius
harmfully adv male
harmless adj innocēns
harmlessly adv innocenter; (escape) salvus,
  incolumis, inviolātus
harmonious adj cōnsonus, canōrus; (fig)
  concors; (things) congruēns
harmoniously adv modulātē; concorditer;
  convenienter
harmonize vi concinere, cōnsentīre, congruere
harmony n concentus m; (fig) concordia f,
  cōnsēnsus m
harness n arma ntpl ♦ vt īnfrēnāre, iungere
harp n fidēs fpl; **play the** ~ fidibus canere ♦ vi:
  ~ **on** (fig) cantāre, dictitāre; **be always harping**
  on the same thing cantilēnam eandem
  canere
harpist n fidicen m, fidicina f
harpoon n iaculum nt
harpy n Harpyia f
harrow n rāstrum nt ♦ vt occāre
harrower n occātor m
harrowing adj horrendus
harry vt vexāre, dīripere
harsh adj dūrus, acerbus, asper; (person)
  inclēmēns, sevērus
harshly adv acerbē, asperē; sevērē
harshness n acerbitās f, asperitās f; crūdēlitās f
hart n cervus m
harvest n messis f ♦ vt metere, dēmetere
harvester n messor m
hash n farrāgō f ♦ vt comminuere
haste n festīnātiō f, properātiō f; **in**
  ~ festīnanter; **in hot** ~ incitātus; **make**
  ~ festīnāre
hasten vt mātūrāre, adcelerāre ♦ vi festīnāre,
  properāre, mātūrāre
hastily adv properē, raptim; temerē, incōnsulte;
  īrācundē
hastiness n temeritās f; (temper) īrācundia f
hasty adj properus, celer; (action) incōnsultus,
  temerārius; (temper) īrācundus, ācer; **over**
  ~ praeproperus
hat n petasus m
hatch vt exclūdere, parere
hatchet n dolābra f
hate n odium nt, invidia f ♦ vt ōdisse
hated adj: **to be** ~ (by sb) odiō esse (dat)
hateful adj odiōsus, invīsus
hatefully adv odiōsē
hatred n odium nt
haughtily adv adroganter, superbē, insolenter
haughtiness n fastus m, adrogantia f, superbia f
haughty adj adrogāns, superbus, īnsolēns
haul vt trahere ♦ n bolus m
haulage n vectūra f
haulm n culmus m
haunch n femur nt
haunt vt frequentāre ♦ n locus m; (animals)
  lustrum nt
have vt habēre, tenēre; (get done) cūrāre (with
  gerundive); **I** ~ **a house** est mihī domus; **I** ~ **to**
  go mihī abeundum est; ~ **it out with** rem
  dēcernere cum; ~ **on** gerere, gestāre, induī;
  I had better go melius est īre, praestat īre; **I had**
  rather mālim, māllem
haven n portus m; (fig) perfugium nt
havoc n exitium nt, vastātiō f, ruīna f
hawk n accipiter m ♦ vt (wares) circumferre
hawker n īnstitor m
hay n faenum nt; **make hay while the sun**
  shines forō ūtī
hazard n perīculum nt, discrīmen nt, ālea f ♦ vt
  perīclitārī, in āleam dare
hazardous adj perīculōsus
haze n nebula f
hazel n corylus f
hazy adj nebulōsus; (fig) incertus
he pron hic, ille, is
head n caput nt; (person) dux m, prīnceps
  m; (composition) caput nt; (mind) animus m,

ingenium *nt*; ~ **over heels** cernuus; **off one's**
~ dēmēns; **be at the** ~ **of** dūcere, praeesse (*dat*);
come to a ~ caput facere; (*fig*) in discrīmen
addūcī; **give one his** ~ indulgēre (*dat*), habēnās
immittere (*dat*); **keep one's** ~ praesentī animō
ūtī; **lose one's** ~ suī compotem nōn esse; **shake
one's** ~ abnuere ◆ *vt* dūcere, praeesse (*dat*); ~ **off**
intercipere ◆ *vi* (*in a direction*) tendere
headache *n* capitis dolor *m*
headfirst *adj* praeceps
heading *n* caput *nt*
headland *n* prōmontōrium *nt*
headlong *adj* praeceps ◆ *adv* in praeceps; **rush**
~ sē praecipitāre
headquarters *n* (*MIL*) praetōrium *nt*
headship *n* prīncipātus *m*
headsman *n* carnifex *m*
headstrong *adj* impotēns, pervicāx
headway *n* prōfectus *m*
heady *adj* incōnsultus; (*wine*) vehemēns
heal *vt* sānāre, medērī (*dat*) ◆ *vi* sānēscere; ~ **over**
obdūcī
healer *n* medicus *m*
healing *adj* salūbris
health *n* valētūdō *f*, salūs *f*; **state of** ~ valētūdō *f*;
ill ~ valētūdō *f*; **be in good** ~ valēre; **drink the**
~ **of** propīnāre (*dat*)
healthful *adj* salūbris
healthiness *n* sānitās *f*
healthy *adj* sānus, integer; (*conditions*) salūber
heap *n* acervus *m*, cumulus *m*; **in heaps**
acervātim ◆ *vt* acervāre; ~ **together** congerere;
~ **up** adcumulāre, coacervāre, congerere
hear *vt* audīre; (*case*) cognōscere; ~ **clearly**
exaudīre; ~ **in secret** inaudīre
hearer *n* audītor *m*
hearing *n* (*sense*) audītus *m*; (*act*) audītiō *f*; (*of
case*) cognitiō *f*; **get a** ~ sibī audientiam facere;
hard of ~ surdaster; **without a** ~ indictā causā
hearken *vi* auscultāre
hearsay *n* fāma *f*, rūmor *m*
heart *n* cor *nt*; (*emotion*) animus *m*, pectus *nt*;
(*courage*) animus *m*; (*interior*) viscera *ntpl*; **by**
~ memoriā, memoriter; **learn by** ~ ēdiscere;
the ~ **of the matter** rēs ipsa; **lose** ~ animum
dēspondēre; **take to** ~ graviter ferre
heartache *n* dolor *m*, angor *m*
heartbroken *adj* animī frāctus, aeger; **be**
~ animō labōrāre
heartburning *n* invidia *f*
heartfelt *adj* sincērus
hearth *n* focus *m*; ~ **and home** ārae et focī
heartily *adv* vehementer, valdē
heartiness *n* studium *nt*, vigor *m*
heartless *adj* dūrus, inhūmānus, crūdēlis
heartlessly *adv* inhūmānē
heartlessness *n* inhūmānitās *f*, crūdēlitās *f*
hearty *adj* studiōsus, vehemēns; (*health*)
rōbustus; (*feeling*) sincērus
heat *n* ārdor *m*, calor *m*; (*emotion*) ārdor *m*, aestus
m; (*race*) missus *m* ◆ *vt* calefacere, fervefacere;
(*fig*) accendere; **become heated** incalēscere
heatedly *adv* ferventer, ārdenter
heath *n* inculta loca *ntpl*
heathcock *n* attagēn *m*
heathen *n* pāgānus *m*

heather *n* erīcē *f*
heave *vt* tollere; (*missile*) conicere; (*sigh*) dūcere
◆ *vi* tumēre, fluctuāre
heaven *n* caelum *nt*, dī *mpl*; ~ **forbid!** dī meliōra;
from ~ dīvīnitus; **in heaven's name** prō
deum fidem!; **be in seventh** ~ digitō caelum
attingere
heavenly *adj* caelestis, dīvīnus
heavily *adv* graviter
heaviness *n* gravitās *f*, pondus *nt*; (*of spirit*)
maestitia *f*
heavy *adj* gravis; (*air*) crassus; (*spirit*) maestus;
(*shower*) māgnus, dēnsus
heckle *vt* interpellāre
heckler *n* interpellātor *m*
hectic *adj* violēns, ācer, fervidus
hector *vt* obstrepere (*dat*)
hedge *n* saepēs *f* ◆ *vt* saepīre; ~ **off** intersaepīre
◆ *vi* tergiversārī
hedgehog *n* echīnus *m*, ēricius *m*
heed *vt* cūrāre, respicere ◆ *n* cūra *f*, opera *f*; **pay**
~ animum attendere; **take** ~ cavēre
heedful *adj* attentus, cautus, dīligēns
heedfully *adv* attentē, cautē
heedfulness *n* cūra *f*, dīligentia *f*
heedless *adj* incautus, immemor, neglegēns
heedlessly *adv* incautē, neglegenter, temerē
heedlessness *n* neglegentia *f*
heel *n* calx *f*; **take to one's heels** sē in pedēs
conicere ◆ *vi* sē inclīnāre
hegemony *n* prīncipātus *m*
heifer *n* būcula *f*
height *n* altitūdō *f*; (*person*) prōcēritās *f*; (*hill*)
collis *m*, iugum *nt*; (*fig*) fastīgium *nt*; **the** ~ **of**
summus
heighten *vt* augēre, exaggerāre
heinous *adj* atrōx, nefārius
heinously *adv* atrōciter, nefāriē
heinousness *n* atrōcitās *f*
heir *n* hērēs *m*; **sole** ~ hērēs ex asse
heiress *n* hērēs *f*
heirship *n* hērēditās *f*
hell *n* Tartarus *m*, īnfernī *mpl*
hellish *adj* īnfernus, scelestus
helm *n* gubernāculum *nt*, clāvus *m*
helmet *n* galea *f*
helmsman *n* gubernātor *m*
helots *n* Hīlōtae *mpl*
help *n* auxilium *nt*, subsidium *nt*; **I am a**
~ auxiliō sum ◆ *vt* iuvāre (*acc*), auxiliārī,
subvenīre (*dat*), succurrere (*dat*) ◆ *vi* prōdesse;
I cannot ~ facere nōn possum quīn (*subj*); **it**
can't be helped fierī nōn potest aliter; **so** ~ **me**
God ita me dī ament
helper *n* adiūtor *m*, adiūtrix *f*
helpful *adj* ūtilis; **be** ~ **to** auxiliō esse (*dat*)
helpless *adj* inops
helplessness *n* inopia *f*
hem *n* ōra *f*, limbus *m* ◆ *vt*: **hem in** interclūdere,
circumsedēre
hemlock *n* cicūta *f*
hemp *n* cannabis *f*
hen *n* gallīna *f*
hence *adv* hinc; (*consequence*) igitur, ideō
henceforth, **henceforward** *adv* dehinc,
posthāc, ex hōc tempore

her *adj* suus, ēius
herald *n* praecō *m*; (POL) fētiālis *m* ◆ *vt* praenūntiāre
herb *n* herba *f*, olus *nt*
herbage *n* herbae *fpl*
herd *n* pecus *nt*; grex *f*, armentum *nt* ◆ *vi* congregārī
herdsman *n* pāstor *m*
here *adv* hīc; **be ~** adesse; **~ and there** passim; **~ ... there** alibī ... alibī; **from ~** hinc; **~ is ...** ecce (*acc*) ...
hereabouts *adv* hīc ferē
hereafter *adv* posthāc, posteā
hereat *adv* hīc
hereby *adv* ex hōc, hinc
hereditary *adj* hērēditārius, patrius
heredity *n* genus *nt*
herein *adv* hīc
hereinafter *adv* īnfrā
hereof *adv* ēius reī
hereupon *adv* hīc, quō factō
herewith *adv* cum hōc, ūnā
heritable *adj* hērēditārius
heritage *n* hērēditās *f*
hermaphrodite *n* androgynus *m*
hermit *n* homō sōlitārius *m*
hero *n* vir fortissimus *m*; (*demigod*) hērōs *m*
heroic *adj* fortissimus, māgnanimus; (*epic*) hērōicus; (*verse*) hērōus
heroically *adv* fortissimē, audācissimē
heroism *n* virtūs *f*, fortitūdō *f*
heron *n* ardea *f*
hers *pron* suus, ēius
herself *pron* ipsa *f*; (*reflexive*) sē
hesitancy *n* dubitātiō *f*
hesitant *adj* incertus, dubius
hesitate *vi* dubitāre, haesitāre
hesitating *adj* dubius
hesitatingly *adv* cunctanter
hesitation *n* dubitātiō *f*; **with ~** dubitanter
heterogeneous *adj* dīversus, aliēnigenus
hew *vt* dolāre, caedere; **hew down** excīdere, interscindere
hexameter *n* hexameter *m*
heyday *n* flōs *m*
hiatus *n* hiātus *m*
hiccup *n* singultus *m* ◆ *vi* singultīre
hide *vt* cēlāre, abdere, abscondere, occultāre; **~ away** abstrūdere; **~ from** cēlāre (*acc*) ◆ *vi* sē abdere, latēre; **~ away** dēlitēscere ◆ *n* pellis *f*, corium *nt*
hideous *adj* foedus, dēfōrmis, turpis
hideously *adv* foedē
hideousness *n* foeditās *f*, dēfōrmitās *f*
hiding *n* (*place*) latebra *f*
hierarchy *n* ōrdinēs *mpl*
high *adj* altus, excelsus; (*ground*) ēditus; (*pitch*) acūtus; (*rank*) amplus; (*price*) cārus; (*tide*) māximus; (*wind*) māgnus; **~ living** luxuria *f*; **~ treason** māiestās *f*; **~ and mighty** superbus; **on ~** sublīmis ◆ *adv* altē
highborn *adj* nōbilis, generōsus
high-class *adj* (*goods*) lautus
high-flown *adj* īnflātus, tumidus
high-handed *adj* superbus, īnsolēns
high-handedly *adv* superbē, licenter

high-handedness *n* licentia *f*, superbia *f*
highland *adj* montānus
highlander *n* montānus *m*
highlands *npl* montāna *ntpl*
highly *adv* (*value*) māgnī; (*intensity*) valdē
highly-strung *adj* trepidus
high-minded *adj* generōsus
high-spirited *adj* ferōx, animōsus
highway *n* via *f*
highwayman *n* grassātor *m*, latrō *m*
hilarious *adj* festīvus, hilaris
hilariously *adv* festīvē, hilare
hilarity *n* festīvitās *f*, hilaritās *f*
hill *n* collis *m*, mōns *m*; (*slope*) clīvus *m*
hillock *n* tumulus *m*
hilly *adj* montuōsus, clīvōsus
hilt *n* manubrium *nt*, capulus *m*
himself *pron* ipse; (*reflexive*) sē
hind *n* cerva *f*
hinder *vt* impedīre, obstāre (*dat*), morārī
hindmost *adj* postrēmus; (*in column*) novissimus
hindrance *n* impedīmentum *nt*, mora *f*
hinge *n* cardō *f*
hint *n* indicium *nt*, suspiciō *f*; **throw out a ~** inicere ◆ *vt* subicere, significāre
hip *n* coxendīx *f*
hippodrome *n* spatium *nt*
hire *vt* condūcere; **~ out** locāre ◆ *n* conductiō *f*, locātiō *f*; (*wages*) mercēs *f*
hired *adj* mercennārius, conductus
hireling *n* mercennārius *m*
hirsute *adj* hirsūtus
his *adj* suus, ēius
hiss *vi* sībilāre ◆ *vt*: **~ off stage** explōdere, exsībilāre ◆ *n* sībilus *m*
historian *n* historicus *m*, rērum scrīptor *m*
historical *adj* historicus
history *n* historia *f*; **the ~ of Rome** rēs Rōmānae *fpl*; **since the beginning of ~** post hominum memoriam; **ancient ~** antīquitās *f*
histrionic *adj* scaenicus
hit *n* ictus *m*, plāga *f*; **a hit!** (*in duel*) habet! ◆ *vt* ferīre, icere, percutere; **hit against** offendere; **hit upon** invenīre
hitch *n* mora *f* ◆ *vt* implicāre; **~ up** succingere
hither *adv* hūc; **~ and thither** hūc illūc ◆ *adj* citerior
hitherto *adv* adhūc, hāctenus, hūcusque
hive *n* alveārium *nt*
hoar *adj* cānus ◆ *n* pruīna *f*
hoard *n* thēsaurus *m*, acervus *m* ◆ *vt* condere, recondere
hoarfrost *n* pruīna *f*
hoarse *adj* raucus, fuscus
hoarsely *adv* raucā vōce
hoary *adj* cānus
hoax *n* fraus *f*, fallācia *f*, lūdus *m* ◆ *vt* dēcipere, fallere
hobble *vi* claudicāre
hobby *n* studium *nt*
hob-nob *vi* familiāriter ūtī (*abl*)
hocus-pocus *n* trīcae *fpl*
hoe *n* sarculum *nt* ◆ *vt* sarrīre
hog *n* sūs *m*, porcus *m*; **hog's** porcīnus
hogshead *n* dōlium *nt*
hoist *vt* tollere; (*sail*) vēla dare

hold n (grasp) comprehēnsiō f; (power) potestās f; (ship) alveus m; **gain a ~ over** obstringere, sibi dēvincīre; **get ~ of** potīrī (abl); **keep ~ of** retinēre; **lose ~ of** ōmittere; **take ~ of** prehendere, comprehendere ♦ vt tenēre, habēre; (possession) obtinēre, possidēre; (office) gerere, fungī (abl); (capacity) capere; (meeting) habēre; **~ a meeting** concilium habēre; **~ one's own with** parem esse (dat); **~ over** differre, prōlātāre; **~ water** (fig) stāre ♦ vi manēre, dūrāre; (opinion) dūcere, existimāre, adfirmāre; **~ back** vt retinēre, inhibēre ♦ vi gravārī, dubitāre; **~ cheap** parvī facere; **~ fast** retinere, amplectī ♦ vi haerēre; **~ good** valēre; **~ out** vt porrigere, extendere; (hope) ostendere ♦ vi dūrāre, perstāre; **~ together** cohaerēre; **~ up** tollere; (falling) sustinēre; (movement) obstāre (dat), morārī; **~ with** adsentīre (dat)

holdfast n fībula f

holding n (land) agellus m

hole n forāmen nt, cavum nt; **make a ~ in** pertundere, perforāre

holiday n ōtium nt; festus diēs m; **on ~** fēriātus; **holidays** pl fēriae fpl

holily adv sānctē

holiness n sānctitās f

hollow adj cavus, concavus; (fig) inānis, vānus ♦ n cavum nt, caverna f ♦ vt excavāre

hollowness n (fig) vānitās f

holly n aquifolium nt

holy adj sanctus

homage n observantia f, venerātiō f; **pay ~ to** venerārī, colere

home n domus f; (town, country) patria f; **at ~** domī; **from ~** domō ♦ adj domesticus ♦ adv domum

homeless adj profugus

homely adj simplex, rūsticus; (speech) plēbēius

homestead n fundus m

homewards adv domum

homicide n (act) homicīdium nt, caedēs f; (person) homicīda m

homily n sermō m

homogeneous adj aequābilis

homologous adj cōnsimilis

hone n cōs f ♦ vt acuere

honest adj probus, frūgī, integer

honestly adv probē, integrē

honesty n probitās f, fidēs f

honey n mel nt

honeycomb n favus m

honeyed adj mellītus, mulsus

honorarium n stips f

honorary adj honōrārius

honour n honōs m; (repute) honestās f; existimātiō f; (chastity) pudor m; (trust) fidēs f; (rank) dignitās f; (award) decus nt, īnsigne nt; (respect) observantia f ♦ vt honōrāre, decorāre; (respect) observāre, colere; **do ~ to** honestāre

honourable adj honestus, probus; (rank) illūstris, praeclārus

honourably adv honestē

hood n cucullus m

hoodwink vt verba dare (dat)

hoof n ungula f

hook n uncus m, hāmus m ♦ vt hāmō capere

hooked adj aduncus, hāmātus

hoop n circulus m; (toy) trochus m

hoot vi obstrepere; **~ off** (stage) explōdere

hop n saltus m; **catch on the hop** in ipsō articulō opprimere ♦ vi salīre

hope n spēs f; **in the ~ that** sī forte; **give up ~** spem dēpōnere, dēspērāre; **past ~** dēspērātus; **entertain hopes** spem habēre ♦ vt spērāre

hopeful adj bonae speī; **be ~** aliquam spem habēre

hopefully adv nōn sine spē

hopeless adj dēspērātus

hopelessly adv dēspēranter

hopelessness n dēspērātiō f

horde n multitūdō f

horizon n fīniēns m

horizontal adj aequus, lībrātus

horizontally adv ad lībram

horn n cornū nt; (shepherd's) būcina f

horned adj corniger

hornet n crabrō m; **stir up a hornet's nest** crabrōnēs inrītāre

horny adj corneus

horoscope n sīdus nātālicium nt

horrible adj horrendus, horribilis, dīrus, foedus

horribly adv foedē

horrid adj horribilis

horrify vt terrēre, perterrēre

horror n horror m, terror m; odium nt

horse n equus m; (cavalry) equitēs mpl; **flog a dead ~** asellum currere docēre; **spur a willing ~** currentem incitāre; **horse's** equīnus

horseback n: **ride on ~** in equō vehī; **fight on ~** ex equō pugnāre

horseman n eques m

horseradish n armoracia f

horse soldier n eques m

horticulture n hortōrum cultus m

hospitable adj hospitālis

hospitably adv hospitāliter

hospital n valētūdinārium nt

hospitality n hospitālitās f, hospitium nt

host n hospes m; (inn) caupō m; (number) multitūdō f; (MIL) exercitus m

hostage n obses m/f

hostelry n taberna f, dēversōrium nt

hostile adj hostīlis, īnfēnsus, inimīcus; īnfestus; **in a ~ manner** īnfēnsē, hostīliter, inimīcē

hostility n inimīcitia f; **hostilities** pl bellum nt

hot adj calidus, fervidus, aestuōsus; (boiling) fervēns; (fig) ārdēns; **be hot** calēre, fervēre, ārdēre; **get hot** calēscere

hotch-potch n farrāgō f

hotel n dēversōrium nt

hot-headed adj ārdēns, temerārius, praeceps

hotly adv ārdenter, ācriter

hot-tempered adj īrācundus

hot water n calida f

hound n canis m ♦ vt īnstāre (dat)

hour n hōra f

hourly adv in hōrās

house n domus f, aedēs fpl; (country) vīlla f; (family) domus f, gēns f; **at the ~ of** apud (acc); **full ~** frequēns senātus, frequēns theātrum ♦ vt hospitiō accipere, recipere; (things) condere

household n familia f, domus f ♦ adj familiāris, domesticus
householder n paterfamiliās m, dominus m
housekeeping n reī familiāris cūra f
housemaid n ancilla f
housetop n fastīgium nt
housewife n māterfamiliās f, domina f
housing n hospitium nt; (horse) ōrnāmenta ntpl
hovel n gurgustium nt
hover vi pendēre; (fig) impendēre
how adv (interrog) quemadmodum; quōmodō, quō pactō; (excl) quam; **how great/big/large** quantus; **how long** (time) quamdiū; **how many** quot; **how much** quantum; **how often** quotiēns
howbeit adv tamen
however adv tamen; autem, nihilōminus; utcumque, quōquō modō; ~ **much** quamvīs, quantumvīs; ~ **great** quantuscumque
howl n ululātus m ♦ vi ululāre; (wind) fremere
howsoever adv utcumque
hub n axis m
hubbub n tumultus m
huckster n īnstitor m, propōla m
huddle n turba f ♦ vi congregārī
hue n color m; **hue and cry** clāmor m
huff n offēnsiō f ♦ vt offendere
hug n complexus m ♦ vt complectī
huge adj ingēns, immānis, immēnsus, vastus
hugely adv vehementer
hugeness n immānitās f
hulk n alveus m
hull n alveus m
hum n murmur nt, fremitus m ♦ vi murmurāre, fremere
human adj hūmānus
human being n homō m/f
humane adj hūmānus, misericors
humanely adv hūmānē, hūmāniter
humanism n litterae fpl
humanist n homō litterātus m
humanity n hūmānitās f; misericordia f
humanize vt excolere
humanly adv hūmānitus
human nature n hūmānitās f
humble adj humilis, modestus ♦ vt dēprimere; (oneself) summittere
humbleness n humilitās f
humbly adv summissē, modestē
humbug n trīcae fpl
humdrum adj vulgāris; (style) pedester
humid adj ūmidus, madidus; **be** ~ madēre
humidity n ūmor m
humiliate vt dēprimere, dēdecorāre
humiliation n dēdecus nt
humility n modestia f, animus summissus m
humorist n homō facētus m
humorous adj facētus, ioculāris, rīdiculus
humorously adv facētē
humour n facētiae fpl; (disposition) ingenium nt; (mood) libīdō f; **be in a bad** ~ sibī displicēre ♦ vt indulgēre (dat), mōrem gerere (dat), mōrigerārī (dat)

hump n gibbus m
hunchback n gibber m
hundred num centum; ~ **each** centēnī; ~ **times** centiēns
hundredth adj centēsimus
hundredweight n centumpondium nt
hunger n famēs f ♦ vi ēsurīre
hungrily adv avidē
hungry adj ēsuriēns, iēiūnus, avidus; **be** ~ ēsurīre
hunt n vēnātiō f, vēnātus m ♦ vt vēnārī, indāgāre, exagitāre
hunter n vēnātor m
hunting n vēnātiō f; (fig) aucupium nt
hunting spear n vēnābulum nt
huntress n vēnātrix f
huntsman n vēnātor m
hurdle n crātēs f; (obstacle) obex m/f
hurl vt conicere, ingerere, iaculārī, iācere
hurly-burly n turba f, tumultus m
hurrah interj euax, iō
hurricane n procella f
hurried adj praeproperus, praeceps, trepidus
hurriedly adv properātō, cursim, festīnanter
hurry vt adcelerāre, mātūrāre ♦ vi festīnāre, properāre; ~ **along** vt rapere; ~ **away** vi discēdere, properāre; ~ **about** vi discurrere; ~ **on** vt mātūrāre; ~ **up** vi properāre ♦ n festīnātiō f; **in a** ~ festīnanter, raptim
hurt n iniūria f, damnum nt; vulnus nt ♦ vt laedere, nocēre (dat); **it hurts** dolet
hurtful adj nocēns, damnōsus
hurtfully adv nocenter, damnōsē
hurtle vi volāre; sē praecipitāre
husband n vir m, marītus m ♦ vt parcere (dat)
husbandry n agrī cultūra f; (economy) parsimōnia f
hush n silentium nt ♦ vt silentium facere (dat), lēnīre ♦ vi tacēre, silēre; ~ **up** comprimere, cēlāre ♦ interj st!
hushed adj tacitus
husk n folliculus m, siliqua f ♦ vt dēglūbāre
husky adj fuscus, raucus
hustle vt trūdere, īnstāre (dat)
hut n casa f, tugurium nt
hutch n cavea f
hyacinth n hyacinthus m
hybrid n hibrida m/f
hydra n hydra f
hyena n hyaena f
hygiene n salūbritās f
hygienic adj salūbris
hymeneal adj nūptiālis
hymn n carmen nt ♦ vt canere
hyperbole n superlātiō f
hypercritical adj Aristarchus m
hypocaust n hypocaustum nt
hypocrisy n simulātiō f, dissimulātiō f
hypocrite n simulātor m, dissimulātor m
hypocritical adj simulātus, fictus
hypothesis n positum nt, sūmptiō f, coniectūra f
hypothetical adj sūmptus

I i

I *pron* ego
iambic *adj* iambēus
iambus *n* iambus *m*
ice *n* glaciēs *f*
icicle *n* stīria *f*
icon *n* simulacrum *nt*
icy *adj* glaciālis, gelidus
idea *n* nōtiō *f*, nōtitia *f*, imāgō *f*; *(Platonic)* fōrma
f; *(expressed)* sententia *f*; **conceive the ~ of**
īnfōrmāre; **with the ~ that** eō cōnsiliō ut *(subj)*
ideal *adj* animō comprehēnsus; *(perfect)*
perfectus, optimus ◆ *n* specimen *nt*, speciēs *f*,
exemplar *nt*
identical *adj* īdem, cōnsimilis
identify *vt* agnōscere
identity *n*: **establish the ~ of** cognōscere quis sit
Ides *n* Idūs *fpl*
idiocy *n* animī imbēcillitās *f*
idiom *n* proprium *nt*, sermō *m*
idiomatic *adj* proprius
idiomatically *adv* sermōne suō, sermōne
propriō
idiosyncrasy *n* proprium *nt*, libīdō *f*
idiot *n* excors *m*
idiotic *adj* fatuus, stultus
idiotically *adv* stultē, ineptē
idle *adj* ignāvus, dēses, iners; *(unoccupied)* ōtiōsus,
vacuus; *(useless)* inānis, vānus; **be ~** cessāre,
dēsidēre; **lie ~** *(money)* iacēre ◆ *vi* cessāre
idleness *n* ignāvia *f*, dēsidia *f*, inertia *f*; ōtium *nt*
idler *n* cessātor *m*
idly *adv* ignāvē; ōtiōsē; frustrā, nēquīquam
idol *n* simulacrum *nt*; *(person)* dēliciae *fpl*
idolater *n* falsōrum deōrum cultor *m*
idolatry *n* falsōrum deōrum cultus *m*
idolize *vt* venerārī
idyll *n* carmen Theocrītēum *nt*
if *conj* sī; *(interrog)* num, utrum; **if anyone** sī quis;
if ever sī quandō; **if not** nisī; **if only** dum,
dummodo; **if … or** sīve … sīve; **as if** quasi,
velut; **but if** sīn, quodsī; **even if** etiamsī
igneous *adj* igneus
ignite *vt* accendere, incendere ◆ *vi* ignem
concipere
ignoble *adj* *(birth)* ignōbilis; *(repute)* illīberālis,
turpis
ignominious *adj* ignōminiōsus, īnfāmis, turpis
ignominiously *adv* turpiter
ignominy *n* ignōminia *f*, īnfāmia *f*, dēdecus *nt*
ignoramus *n* idiōta *m*, indoctus *m*
ignorance *n* īnscītia *f*, ignōrātiō *f*

ignorant *adj* ignārus, indoctus; *(of something)*
īnscītus, rudis; *(unaware)* īnscius; **be ~ of**
nescīre, ignōrāre
ignorantly *adv* īnscienter, īnscītē, indoctē
ignore *vt* praetermittere
ilex *n* īlex *f*
Iliad *n* Ilias *f*
ill *adj* aeger, aegrōtus, invalidus; *(evil)* malus; **be
ill** aegrōtāre; **fall ill** in morbum incidere; **ill at
ease** sollicitus ◆ *adv* male, improbē ◆ *n* malum
nt, incommodum *nt*, aerumna *f*, damnum *nt*
ill-advised *adj* incōnsultus
ill-bred *adj* agrestis, inurbānus
ill-disposed *adj* malevolus, invidus
illegal *adj* illicitus, vetitus
illegally *adv* contrā lēgēs
ill-fated *adj* īnfēlīx
ill-favoured *adj* turpis
ill-gotten *adj* male partus
ill-health *n* valētūdō *f*
illicit *adj* vetitus
illimitable *adj* īnfīnītus
illiteracy *n* litterārum īnscītia *f*
illiterate *adj* illitterātus, inērudītus
ill-natured *adj* malevolus, malignus
illness *n* morbus *m*, valētūdō *f*
illogical *adj* absurdus
ill-omened *adj* dīrus, īnfaustus
ill-starred *adj* īnfēlīx
ill-tempered *adj* īrācundus, amārus,
stomachōsus
ill-timed *adj* immātūrus, intempestīvus
ill-treat *vt* malefacere *(dat)*
illuminate *vt* illūmināre, illūstrāre
illumination *n* lūmina *ntpl*
illusion *n* error *m*, somnium *nt*
illusive, illusory *adj* fallāx
illustrate *vt* illūstrāre; *(with instances)* exemplō
cōnfirmāre
illustration *n* exemplum *nt*
illustrious *adj* illūstris, īnsignis, praeclārus
illustriously *adv* praeclārē
ill will *n* invidia *f*
image *n* imāgō *f*, effigiēs *f*; *(idol)* simulacrum *nt*;
(verbal) figūra *f*, similitūdō *f*
imagery *n* figūrae *fpl*
imaginary *adj* commentīcius, fictus
imagination *n* cōgitātiō *f*, opīnātiō *f*
imaginative *adj* ingeniōsus
imagine *vt* animō fingere, animum indūcere,
ante oculōs pōnere; *(think)* opīnārī, arbitrārī

imbecile *adj* animō imbēcillus, fatuus, mente captus
imbecility *n* animī imbēcillitās *f*
imbibe *vt* adbibere; (*fig*) imbuī (*abl*)
imbrue *vt* īnficere
imbue *vt* imbuere, īnficere, tingere
imitable *adj* imitābilis
imitate *vt* imitārī
imitation *n* imitātiō *f*; (*copy*) imāgō *f*
imitator *n* imitātor *m*, imitātrix *f*, aemulātor *m*
immaculate *adj* integer, ēmendātus
immaculately *adv* integrē, sine vitiō
immaterial *adj* indifferēns
immature *adj* immātūrus
immeasurable *adj* immēnsus, īnfīnītus
immediate *adj* īnstāns, praesēns; (*neighbour*) proximus
immediately *adv* statim, extemplō, cōnfestim
immemorial *adj* antīquissimus; **from time ~** post hominum memoriam
immense *adj* immēnsus, immānis, ingēns, vastus
immensely *adv* vehementer
immensity *n* immēnsum *nt*, māgnitūdō *f*
immerse *vt* immergere, mergere
immigrant *n* advena *m*
immigrate *vi* migrāre
imminent *adj* īnstāns, praesēns; **be ~** imminēre, impendēre
immobile *adj* fīxus, immōbilis
immoderate *adj* immoderātus, immodestus
immoderately *adv* immoderātē, immodestē
immodest *adj* impudīcus, inverēcundus
immolate *vt* immolāre
immoral *adj* prāvus, corruptus, turpis
immorality *n* corruptī mōrēs *mpl*, turpitūdō *f*
immorally *adv* prāvē, turpiter
immortal *adj* immortālis, aeternus
immortality *n* immortālitās *f*
immortalize *vt* in astra tollere
immortally *adv* aeternum
immovable *adj* fīxus, immōbilis
immune *adj* immūnis, vacuus
immunity *n* immūnitās *f*, vacātiō *f*
immure *vt* inclūdere
immutability *n* immūtābilitās *f*
immutable *adj* immūtābilis
imp *n* puer improbus *m*
impact *n* ictus *m*, incussus *m*
impair *vt* imminuere, corrumpere
impale *vt* induere, īnfīgere
impalpable *adj* tenuissimus
impart *vt* impertīre, commūnicāre; (*courage*) addere
impartial *adj* aequus, medius
impartiality *n* aequābilitās *f*
impartially *adv* sine favōre
impassable *adj* invius; (*mountains*) inexsuperābilis; (*fig*) inexplicābilis
impasse *n* mora *f*, incitae *fpl*
impassioned *adj* ārdēns, fervidus
impassive *adj* rigidus, sēnsū carēns
impatience *n* aviditās *f*; (*of anything*) impatientia *f*
impatient *adj* trepidus, avidus; impatiēns
impatiently *adv* aegrē

impeach *vt* diem dīcere (*dat*), accūsāre
impeachment *n* accūsātiō *f*, crīmen *nt*
impeccable *adj* ēmendātus
impecunious *adj* pauper
impede *vt* impedīre, obstāre (*dat*)
impediment *n* impedīmentum *nt*
impel *vt* impellere, incitāre
impend *vi* impendēre, imminēre, īnstāre
impenetrable *adj* impenetrābilis; (*country*) invius, impervius
impenitent *adj*: **I am ~** nīl mē paenitet
imperative *adj* necessārius
imperceptible *adj* tenuissimus, obscurus
imperceptibly *adv* sēnsim
imperfect *adj* imperfectus, vitiōsus
imperfection *n* vitium *nt*
imperfectly *adv* vitiōsē
imperial *adj* imperātōrius, rēgius
imperil *vt* in discrīmen addūcere, labefactāre
imperious *adj* imperiōsus, superbus
imperiously *adv* superbē
imperishable *adj* immortālis, aeternus
impersonate *vt* partēs agere (*gen*)
impertinence *n* importūnitās *f*, protervitās *f*
impertinent *adj* importūnus, protervus, ineptus
impertinently *adv* importūnē, ineptē, protervē
imperturbable *adj* immōtus, gravis
impervious *adj* impervius, impenetrābilis
impetuosity *n* ārdor *m*, violentia *f*, vīs *f*
impetuous *adj* violēns, fervidus, effrēnātus
impetuously *adv* effrēnātē
impetus *n* impetus *m*
impiety *n* impietās *f*
impinge *vi* incidere
impious *adj* impius, profānus; **it is ~** nefas est
impiously *adv* impiē
impish *adj* improbus
implacable *adj* implācābilis, inexōrābilis, dūrus
implacably *adv* dūrē
implant *vt* īnserere, ingignere
implement *n* īnstrūmentum *nt* ♦ *vt* implēre, exsequī
implicate *vt* implicāre, impedīre
implication *n* indicium *nt*
implicit *adj* tacitus; absolūtus
implicitly *adv* absconditē; (*trust*) omnīnō, summā fidē
implore *vt* implōrāre, obsecrāre
imply *vt* significāre, continēre; **be implied** inesse
impolite *adj* inurbānus, illepidus
impolitely *adv* inurbānē
impolitic *adj* incōnsultus, imprūdēns
imponderable *adj* levissimus
import *vt* importāre, invehere; (*mean*) velle ♦ *n* significātiō *f*
importance *n* gravitās *f*, mōmentum *nt*; (*rank*) dignitās *f*, amplitūdō *f*, auctōritās *f*; **it is of great ~ to me** meā māgnī rēfert
important *adj* gravis, magnī mōmentī; **it is ~** interest (*gen*), rēfert; **more ~**, **most ~** antīquior, antīquissimus
importation *n* invectiō *f*
imports *npl* importātīcia *ntpl*

importunate *adj* molestus
importune *vt* flāgitāre, īnstāre (*dat*)
impose *vt* impōnere; (*by order*) indīcere,
iniungere; ~ **upon** illūdere, fraudāre, abūtī (*abl*)
imposing *adj* māgnificus, lautus
imposition *n* fraus *f*; (*tax*) tribūtum *nt*
impossible *adj*: **it is** ~ fierī nōn potest
impost *n* tribūtum *nt*, vectīgal *nt*
impostor *n* planus *m*, fraudātor *m*
imposture *n* fraus *f*, fallācia *f*
impotence *n* īnfirmitās *f*
impotent *adj* īnfirmus, dēbilis; (*with rage*)
impotēns
impotently *adv* frustrā; (*rage*) impotenter
impound *vt* inclūdere; (*confiscate*) pūblicāre
impoverish *vt* in inopiam redigere
impracticable *adj*: **be** ~ fierī nōn posse
imprecate *vt* exsecrārī
imprecation *n* exsecrātiō *f*
impregnable *adj* inexpugnābilis
impregnate *vt* imbuere, īnficere
impress *vt* imprimere; (*on mind*) īnfīgere; (*person*)
permovēre; (*MIL*) invītum scrībere
impression *n* (*copy*) exemplar *nt*; (*mark*) signum
nt; (*feeling*) impulsiō *f*; (*belief*) opīnātiō *f*; **make
an ~ of** exprimere; **make an ~ on** commovēre;
have the ~ opīnārī
impressionable *adj* crēdulus
impressive *adj* gravis
impressively *adv* graviter
impressiveness *n* gravitās *f*
imprint *n* impressiō *f*, signum *nt* ◆ *vt* imprimere;
(*on mind*) īnfīgere, inūrere
imprison *vt* inclūdere, in vincula conicere
imprisonment *n* custōdia *f*, vincula *ntpl*
improbable *adj* incrēdibilis, haud vērīsimilis
impromptu *adv* ex tempore
improper *adj* indecōrus, ineptus
improperly *adv* prāvē, perperam
impropriety *n* culpa *f*, offēnsa *f*
improve *vt* ēmendāre, corrigere; (*mind*) excolere
◆ *vi* prōficere, meliōrem fierī
improvement *n* ēmendātiō *f*, prōfectus *m*
improvident *adj* imprōvidus; (*with money*)
prōdigus
improvidently *adv* imprōvidē, prōdigē
improvise *vt* ex tempore compōnere, excōgitāre
imprudence *n* imprūdentia *f*
imprudent *adj* imprūdēns
imprudently *adv* imprūdenter
impudence *n* impudentia *f*, audācia *f*
impudent *adj* impudēns, audāx
impudently *adv* impudenter, protervē
impugn *vt* impugnāre, in dubium vocāre
impulse *n* impetus *m*, impulsus *m*
impulsive *adj* praeceps, violentus
impulsively *adv* impetū quōdam animī
impulsiveness *n* impetus *m*, violentia *f*
impunity *n* impūnitās *f*; **with** ~ impūne
impure *adj* impūrus, incestus, inquinātus
impurely *adv* impūrē, incestē, inquinātē
impurity *n* impūritās *f*, sordēs *fpl*
imputation *n* crīmen *nt*
impute *vt* attribuere, adsignāre; ~ **as a fault**
vitiō vertere

in *prep* in (*abl*); (*with motion*) in (*acc*); (*authors*) apud
(*acc*); (*time*) *abl*; **in doing this** dum hoc faciō; **in
my youth** adulēscēns; **in that** quod ◆ *adv* (*rest*)
intrā; (*motion*) intrō
inaccessible *adj* inaccessus
inaccuracy *n* neglegentia *f*, incūria *f*; (*error*)
mendum *nt*
inaccurate *adj* parum dīligēns, neglegēns
inaccurately *adv* neglegenter
inaction *n* inertia *f*
inactive *adj* iners, quiētus; **be** ~ cessāre
inactivity *n* inertia *f*, ōtium *nt*
inadequate *adj* impār, parum idōneus
inadequately *adv* parum
inadvertency *n* imprūdentia *f*
inadvertent *adj* imprūdēns
inadvertently *adv* imprūdenter
inane *adj* inānis, vānus; ineptus, stultus
inanely *adv* ineptē
inanimate *adj* inanimus
inanity *n* ineptiae *fpl*, stultitia *f*
inapplicable *adj*: **be** ~ nōn valēre
inappropriate *adj* aliēnus, parum aptus
inarticulate *adj* īnfāns
inartistic *adj* sine arte, dūrus, inēlegāns
inasmuch as *conj* quōniam, cum (*subj*)
inattention *n* incūria *f*, neglegentia *f*
inattentive *adj* neglegēns
inattentively *adv* neglegenter
inaudible *adj*: **be** ~ audīrī nōn posse
inaugurate *vt* inaugurāre, cōnsecrāre
inauguration *n* cōnsecrātiō *f*
inauspicious *adj* īnfaustus, īnfēlix
inauspiciously *adv* malīs ōminibus
inborn *adj* innātus
incalculable *adj* inaestimābilis
incantation *n* carmen *nt*
incapable *adj* inhabilis, indocilis; **be** ~ nōn
posse
incapacitate *vt* dēbilitāre
incapacity *n* inertia *f*, īnscītia *f*
incarcerate *vt* inclūdere, in vincula conicere
incarnate *adj* hūmānā speciē indūtus
incautious *adj* incautus, temerārius
incautiously *adv* incautē
incendiary *adj* incendiārius
incense *n* tūs *nt* ◆ *vt* inrītāre, stomachum
movēre (*dat*); **be incensed** stomachārī
incentive *n* incitāmentum *nt*, stimulus *m*
inception *n* initium *nt*, exōrdium *nt*
incessant *adj* adsiduus
incessantly *adv* adsiduē
incest *n* incestus *m*
inch *n* digitus *m*, ūncia *f*
incident *n* ēventum *nt*, cāsus *m*, rēs *f*
incidental *adj* fortuītus
incidentally *adv* cāsū
incipient *adj* prīmus
incisive *adj* ācer
incite *vt* īnstīgāre, impellere, hortārī, incitāre
incitement *n* invītāmentum *nt*, stimulus *m*
inciter *n* īnstimulātor *m*
incivility *n* importūnitās *f*, inhūmānitās *f*
inclemency *n* (*weather*) intemperiēs *f*
inclement *adj* asper, tristis

inclination *n* inclīnātiō *f*, animus *m*, libīdō *f*;
  (slope) clīvus *m*
incline *vt* inclīnāre; *(person)* indūcere ♦ *vi*
  inclīnāre, incumbere; ~ **towards** sē adclīnāre
  ♦ *n* adclīvitās *f*, clīvus *m*
inclined *adj* inclīnātus, prōpēnsus; **I am** ~ **to**
  think haud sciō an
include *vt* inclūdere, continēre, complectī
incognito *adv* clam
incoherent *adj* interruptus; **be** ~ nōn cohaerēre
income *n* fructus *m*, mercēs *f*
incommensurate *adj* dispār
incommode *vt* molestiam adferre *(dat)*
incomparable *adj* singulāris, eximius
incompatibility *n* discrepantia *f*, repugnantia *f*
incompatible *adj* īnsociābilis, repugnāns; **be**
  ~ **with** dissidēre ab, repugnāre *(dat)*
incompetence *n* inertia *f*, īnscītia *f*
incompetent *adj* iners, īnscītus
incomplete *adj* imperfectus
incomprehensible *adj* incrēdibilis
inconceivable *adj* incrēdibilis
inconclusive *adj* inānis
incongruous *adj* absonus, aliēnus
inconsiderable *adj* exiguus
inconsiderate *adj* imprōvidus, incōnsultus
inconsistency *n* discrepantia *f*, incōnstantia *f*
inconsistent *adj* incōnstāns; **be** ~ discrepāre; **be**
  ~ **with** abhorrēre ab, repugnāre *(dat)*
inconsistently *adv* incōnstanter
inconsolable *adj* nōn cōnsōlābilis
inconspicuous *adj* obscūrus; **be** ~ latēre
inconstancy *n* incōnstantia *f*, levitās *f*
inconstant *adj* incōnstāns, levis, mōbilis
inconstantly *adv* incōnstanter
incontestable *adj* certus
incontinence *n* incontinentia *f*
incontinent *adj* intemperāns
inconvenience *n* incommodum *nt* ♦ *vt*
  incommodāre
inconvenient *adj* incommodus
inconveniently *adv* incommodē
incorporate *vt* īnserere, adiungere
incorrect *adj* falsus; **be** ~ nōn cōnstāre
incorrectly *adv* falsō, perperam
incorrigible *adj* improbus, perditus
incorruptibility *n* integritās *f*
incorruptible *adj* incorruptus
increase *n* incrēmentum *nt*, additāmentum *nt*,
  auctus *m* ♦ *vt* augēre, amplificāre ♦ *vi* crēscere,
  incrēscere
increasingly *adv* magis magisque
incredible *adj* incrēdibilis
incredibly *adv* incrēdibiliter
incredulous *adj* incrēdulus
increment *n* incrēmentum *nt*
incriminate *vt* crīminārī
inculcate *vt* inculcāre, īnfīgere
incumbent *adj*: **it is** ~ **on** oportet
incur *vt* subīre; *(guilt)* admittere
incurable *adj* īnsānābilis
incursion *n* incursiō *f*
indebted *adj* obnoxius; **be** ~ dēbēre
indecency *n* obscēnitās *f*
indecent *adj* obscēnus, impudīcus
indecently *adv* obscēnē

indecision *n* dubitātiō *f*
indecisive *adj* anceps, dubius; **the battle is**
  ~ ancipitī Marte pugnātur
indecisively *adv* incertō ēventū
indecorous *adj* indecōrus
indeed *adv* profectō, sānē; *(concessive)* quidem;
  (interrog) itane vērō?; *(reply)* certē, vērō; *(with pron)*
  dēmum; *(with adj, adv, conj)* adeō
indefatigable *adj* impiger
indefensible *adj*: **be** ~ dēfendī nōn posse; *(belief)*
  tenērī nōn posse; *(offence)* excūsārī nōn posse
indefinite *adj* incertus, ambiguus, īnfīnītus
indefinitely *adv* ambiguē; *(time)* in incertum
indelicate *adj* pūtidus, indecōrus
independence *n* lībertās *f*
independent *adj* līber, suī iūris
indescribable *adj* inēnārrābilis
indestructible *adj* perennis
indeterminate *adj* incertus
index *n* index *m*
indicate *vt* indicāre, significāre
indication *n* indicium *nt*, signum *nt*
indict *vt* diem dīcere *(dat)*, accūsāre, nōmen
  dēferre *(gen)*
indictment *n* accūsātiō *f*
indifference *n* neglegentia *f*, languor *m*
indifferent *adj* *(manner)* neglegēns, frīgidus,
  sēcūrus; *(quality)* mediocris
indifferently *adv* neglegenter; mediocriter;
  (without distinction) promiscuē, sine discrīmine
indigence *n* indigentia *f*, egestās *f*
indigenous *adj* indigena
indigent *adj* indigēns, egēnus
indigestible *adj* crūdus
indigestion *n* crūditās *f*
indignant *adj* indignābundus, īrātus; **be**
  ~ indignārī
indignantly *adv* īrātē
indignation *n* indignātiō *f*, dolor *m*
indignity *n* contumēlia *f*, indignitās *f*
indigo *n* Indicum *nt*
indirect *adj* oblīquus
indirectly *adv* oblīquē, per ambāgēs
indirectness *n* ambāgēs *fpl*
indiscipline *n* lascīvia *f*, licentia *f*
indiscreet *adj* incōnsultus, imprūdēns
indiscreetly *adv* incōnsultē, imprūdenter
indiscretion *n* imprūdentia *f*; *(act)* culpa *f*
indiscriminate *adj* prōmiscuus
indiscriminately *adv* prōmiscuē, sine
  discrīmine
indispensable *adj* necesse, necessārius
indisposed *adj* īnfirmus, aegrōtus; *(will)*
  āversus, aliēnātus; **be** ~ aegrōtāre; abhorrēre,
  aliēnārī
indisposition *n* īnfirmitās *f*, valētūdō *f*
indisputable *adj* certus, manifestus
indisputably *adv* certē, sine dubiō
indissoluble *adj* indissolūbilis
indistinct *adj* obscūrus, obtūsus; *(speaker)* balbus
indistinctly *adv* obscūrē; **pronounce**
  ~ opprimere; **speak** ~ balbutīre
individual *adj* proprius ♦ *n* homō *m/f*, prīvātus
  m; **individuals** *pl* singulī *mpl*
individuality *n* proprium *nt*
individually *adv* singulātim, prīvātim

indivisible *adj* indīviduus
indolence *n* dēsidia *f*, ignāvia *f*, inertia *f*
indolent *adj* dēses, ignāvus, iners
indolently *adv* ignāvē
indomitable *adj* indomitus
indoor *adj* umbrātilis
indoors *adv* intus; (*motion*) intrā
indubitable *adj* certus
indubitably *adv* sine dubiō
induce *vt* indūcere, addūcere, persuādēre (*dat*)
inducement *n* illecebra *f*, praemium *nt*
induction *n* (LOGIC) inductiō *f*
indulge *vt* indulgēre (*dat*)
indulgence *n* indulgentia *f*, venia *f*; (*favour*) grātia *f*
indulgent *adj* indulgēns, lēnis
indulgently *adv* indulgenter
industrious *adj* industrius, impiger, dīligēns
industriously *adv* industriē
industry *n* industria *f*, dīligentia *f*, labor *m*
inebriated *adj* ēbrius
inebriation *n* ēbrietās *f*
ineffable *adj* eximius
ineffective *adj* inūtilis, invalidus
ineffectively *adv* ināniter
ineffectual *adj* inritus
inefficient *adj* īnscītus, parum strēnuus
inelegant *adj* inēlegāns, inconcinnus
inelegantly *adv* inēleganter
inept *adj* ineptus
ineptly *adv* ineptē
inequality *n* dissimilitūdō *f*, inīquitās *f*
inert *adj* iners, sōcors, immōbilis
inertia *n* inertia *f*
inertly *adv* tardē, lentē
inestimable *adj* inaestimābilis
inevitable *adj* necessārius
inevitably *adv* necessāriō
inexact *adj* parum subtīlis
inexhaustible *adj* perennis
inexorable *adj* inexōrābilis
inexpediency *n* inūtilitās *f*, incommodum *nt*
inexpedient *adj* inūtilis; **it is ~** nōn expedit
inexpensive *adj* vīlis
inexperience *n* imperītia *f*, īnscītia *f*
inexperienced *adj* imperītus, rudis, īnscītus
inexpert *adj* imperītus
inexpiable *adj* inexpiābilis
inexplicable *adj* inexplicābilis, inēnōdābilis
inexpressible *adj* inēnārrābilis
inextricable *adj* inexplicābilis
infallible *adj* certus, errōris expers
infamous *adj* īnfāmis, flāgitiōsus
infamously *adv* flāgitiōsē
infamy *n* īnfāmia *f*, flāgitium *nt*, dēdecus *nt*
infancy *n* īnfantia *f*; (*fig*) incūnābula *ntpl*
infant *n* īnfāns *m/f*
infantile *adj* puerīlis
infantry *n* peditēs *mpl*, peditātus *m*
infantryman *n* pedes *m*
infatuate *vt* īnfatuāre
infatuated *adj* dēmēns
infatuation *n* dēmentia *f*
infect *vt* īnficere
infection *n* contāgiō *f*
infer *vt* īnferre, colligere

inference *n* conclūsiō *f*
inferior *adj* (*position*) īnferior; (*quality*) dēterior
infernal *adj* īnfernus
infest *vt* frequentāre
infidel *adj* impius
infidelity *n* perfīdia *f*, īnfidēlitās *f*
infiltrate *vi* sē īnsinuāre
infinite *adj* īnfīnītus, immēnsus
infinitely *adv* longē, immēnsum
infinitesimal *adj* minimus
infinity *n* īnfīnitās *f*
infirm *adj* īnfirmus, invalidus
infirmary *n* valētūdinārium *nt*
infirmity *n* morbus *m*
inflame *vt* accendere, incendere, īnflammāre; **be inflamed** exārdēscere
inflammation *n* (MED) īnflātiō *f*
inflate *vt* īnflāre
inflated *adj* (*fig*) īnflātus, tumidus
inflexible *adj* rigidus
inflexion *n* (GRAM) flexūra *f*; (*voice*) flexiō *f*
inflict *vt* īnflīgere, incutere; (*burden*) impōnere; (*penalty*) sūmere; **be inflicted with** labōrāre ex
infliction *n* poena *f*; malum *nt*
influence *n* (*physical*) impulsiō *f*, mōmentum *nt*; (*moral*) auctōritās *f*; (*partial*) grātia *f*; **have ~ valēre**; **have great ~ with** plūrimum posse apud; **under the ~ of** īnstinctus (*abl*) ♦ *vt* impellere, movēre, addūcere
influential *adj* gravis, potēns; grātiōsus
influenza *n* gravēdō *f*
inform *vt* docēre, certiōrem facere; **~ against** nōmen dēferre (*gen*)
informant *n* index *m*, auctor *m*
information *n* indicium *nt*, nūntius *m*
informer *n* index *m*, dēlātor *m*; **turn ~** indicium profitērī
infrequent *adj* rārus
infrequently *adv* rārō
infringe *vt* violāre, imminuere
infringement *n* violātiō *f*
infuriate *vt* efferāre
infuriated *adj* furibundus
infuse *vt* īnfundere; (*fig*) inicere
ingenious *adj* ingeniōsus, callidus; (*thing*) artificiōsus
ingeniously *adv* callidē, summā arte
ingenuity *n* ars *f*, artificium *nt*, acūmen *nt*
ingenuous *adj* ingenuus, simplex
ingenuously *adv* ingenuē, simpliciter
ingenuousness *n* ingenuitās *f*
ingle *n* focus *m*
inglorious *adj* inglōrius, ignōbilis, inhonestus
ingloriously *adv* sine glōriā, inhonestē
ingot *n* later *m*
ingrained *adj* īnsitus
ingratiate *vt*: **~ oneself with** grātiam inīre ab, sē īnsinuāre in familiāritātem (*gen*); **~ oneself into** sē īnsinuāre in (*acc*)
ingratitude *n* ingrātus animus *m*
ingredient *n* pars *f*
inhabit *vt* incolere, habitāre in (*abl*)
inhabitable *adj* habitābilis
inhabitant *n* incola *m/f*
inhale *vt* haurīre
inharmonious *adj* dissonus

inherent *adj* īnsitus; **be ~ in** inhaerēre *(dat)*, inesse *(dat)*
inherently *adv* nātūrā
inherit *vt* excipere
inheritance *n* hērēditās *f*, patrimōnium *nt*; **divide an ~** herctum ciēre; **come into an ~** hērēditātem adīre
inheritor *n* hērēs *m/f*
inhibit *vt* prohibēre, inhibēre
inhospitable *adj* inhospitālis
inhuman *adj* inhūmānus, immānis, crūdēlis
inhumanity *n* inhūmānitās *f*, crūdēlitās *f*
inhumanly *adv* inhūmānē, crūdēliter
inimical *adj* inimīcus
inimitable *adj* singulāris, eximius
iniquitous *adj* inīquus, improbus, nefārius
iniquity *n* scelus *nt*, flāgitium *nt*
initial *adj* prīmus
initiate *vt* initiāre; *(with knowledge)* imbuere
initiative *n* initium *nt*; **take the ~** initium capere, facere; occupāre *(inf)*
inject *vt* inicere
injudicious *adj* incōnsultus, imprūdēns
injunction *n* iussum *nt*, praeceptum *nt*
injure *vt* laedere, nocēre *(dat)*
injurious *adj* damnōsus, nocēns
injury *n* iniūria *f*, damnum *nt*; *(bodily)* vulnus *nt*
injustice *n* iniūria *f*, inīquitās *f*
ink *n* ātrāmentum *nt*
inkling *n* audītiō *f*, suspiciō *f*
inland *adj* mediterrāneus; **further ~** interior
inlay *vt* īnserere
inlet *n* sinus *m*, aestuārium *nt*
inly *adv* penitus
inmate *n* inquilīnus *m*
inmost *adj* intimus
inn *n* dēversōrium *nt*; caupōna *f*, taberna *f*
innate *adj* innātus, īnsitus
inner *adj* interior
innermost *adj* intimus
innkeeper *n* caupō *m*
innocence *n* innocentia *f*
innocent *adj* innocēns, īnsōns; *(character)* integer, castus
innocently *adv* innocenter, integrē, castē
innocuous *adj* innoxius
innovate *vt* novāre
innovation *n* novum *nt*, nova rēs *f*
innovator *n* novārum rērum auctor *m*
innuendo *n* verbum inversum *nt*
innumerable *adj* innumerābilis
inoffensive *adj* innocēns
inoffensively *adv* innocenter
inopportune *adj* intempestīvus
inopportunely *adv* intempestīvē
inordinate *adj* immodicus, immoderātus
inordinately *adv* immoderātē
inquest *n* quaestiō *f*; **hold an ~ on** quaerere dē
inquire *vi* exquīrere, rogāre; **~ into** inquīrere in *(acc)*, investigāre
inquiry *n* quaestiō *f*, investīgātiō *f*; *(asking)* interrogātiō *f*; **make ~** exquīrere; **make inquiries about** inquīrere in *(acc)*; **hold an ~ on** quaerere dē, quaestiōnem īnstituere dē
inquisition *n* inquīsītiō *f*
inquisitive *adj* cūriōsus

inquisitiveness *n* cūriōsitās *f*
inquisitor *n* inquīsītor *m*
inroad *n* incursiō *f*, impressiō *f*; **make an ~** incursāre
insane *adj* īnsānus, mente captus; **be ~** īnsānīre
insanity *n* īnsānia *f*, dēmentia *f*
insatiable *adj* īnsatiābilis, inexplēbilis, īnsaturābilis
insatiably *adv* īnsaturābiliter
inscribe *vt* īnscrībere
inscription *n* epigramma *nt*; *(written)* īnscrīptiō *f*
inscrutable *adj* obscūrus
insect *n* bestiola *f*
insecure *adj* īnstabilis, intūtus
insecurity *n* perīcula *ntpl*
insensate *adj* ineptus, stultus
insensible *adj* torpidus; *(fig)* dūrus
insensitive *adj* dūrus
inseparable *adj* coniūnctus; **be the ~ companion of** ab latere esse *(gen)*
inseparably *adv* coniūnctē
insert *vt* īnserere, immittere, interpōnere
insertion *n* interpositiō *f*
inshore *adv* prope lītus
inside *adv* intus; *(motion)* intrō ♦ *adj* interior ♦ *n* pars *f* interior ♦ *prep* intrā *(acc)*; **get right ~ sē** īnsinuāre in *(acc)*; **turn ~ out** excutere; **on the ~** interior
insidious *adj* īnsidiōsus, subdolus
insidiously *adv* īnsidiōsē
insight *n* intellegentia *f*, cognitiō *f*
insignia *n* īnsignia *ntpl*
insignificance *n* levitās *f*
insignificant *adj* levis, exiguus, nullīus mōmentī; *(position)* humilis
insincere *adj* simulātus, fūcōsus
insincerely *adv* simulātē
insincerity *n* simulātiō *f*, fraus *f*
insinuate *vt* īnsinuāre; *(hint)* significāre ♦ *vi* sē īnsinuāre
insinuating *adj* blandus
insinuation *n* ambigua verba *ntpl*
insipid *adj* īnsulsus, frīgidus
insipidity *n* īnsulsitās *f*
insist *vi* īnstāre; **~ on** postulāre
insistence *n* pertinācia *f*
insistent *adj* pertināx
insolence *n* īnsolentia *f*, contumācia *f*, superbia *f*
insolent *adj* īnsolēns, contumāx, superbus
insolently *adv* īnsolenter
insoluble *adj* inexplicābilis
insolvency *n* reī familiāris naufragium *nt*
insolvent *adj*: **be ~** solvendō nōn esse
inspect *vt* īnspicere; *(MIL)* recēnsēre
inspection *n* cognitiō *f*; *(MIL)* recēnsiō *f*
inspector *n* cūrātor *m*
inspiration *n* adflātus *m*, īnstinctus *m*
inspire *vt* īnstinguere, incendere
instability *n* mōbilitās *f*
install *vt* inaugurāre
instalment *n* pēnsiō *f*
instance *n* exemplum *nt*; **for ~** exemplī causā, grātiā; **at the ~** admonitū; **at my ~** mē auctōre ♦ *vt* memorāre

instant adj īnstāns, praesēns ♦ n temporis pūnctum nt, mōmentum nt
instantaneous adj praesēns
instantaneously adv continuō, īlicō
instantly adv īlicō, extemplō
instead of prep prō (abl), locō (gen); (with verb) nōn ... sed
instigate vt īnstigāre, impellere
instigation n impulsus m, stimulus m; auctōritās f; **at my ~** mē auctōre
instigator n īnstimulātor m, auctor m
instil vt imbuere, adspīrāre, inicere
instinct n nātūra f, ingenium nt, sēnsus m
instinctive adj nātūrālis
instinctively adv nātūrā, ingeniō suō
institute vt īnstituere, inaugurāre
institution n īnstitūtum nt; societās f
instruct vt docēre, īnstituere, īnstruere; ērudīre; (order) praecipere (dat)
instruction n doctrīna f, disciplīna f; praeceptum nt; **give instructions** dēnūntiāre, praecipere
instructor n doctor m, praeceptor m
instructress n magistra f
instrument n īnstrūmentum nt; (music) fidēs fpl; (legal) tabulae fpl
instrumental adj ūtilis
instrumentalist n fidicen m, fidicina f
instrumentality n opera f
insubordinate adj turbulentus, sēditiōsus
insubordination n intemperantia f, licentia f
insufferable adj intolerandus, intolerābilis
insufficiency n inopia f
insufficient adj minor; **be ~** nōn sufficere
insufficiently adv parum
insulate vt sēgregāre
insult n iniūria f, contumēlia f, probrum nt ♦ vt maledīcere (dat), contumēliam impōnere (dat)
insulting adj contumēliōsus
insultingly adv contumēliōsē
insuperable adj inexsuperābilis
insupportable adj intolerandus, intolerābilis
insurance n cautiō f
insure vi cavēre
insurgent n rebellis m
insurmountable adj inexsuperābilis
insurrection n mōtus m, sēditiō f
intact adj integer, intāctus, incolumis
integrity n integritās f, innocentia f, fidēs f
intellect n ingenium nt, mēns f, animus m
intellectual adj ingeniōsus
intelligence n intellegentia f, acūmen nt; (MIL) nūntius m
intelligent adj ingeniōsus, sapiēns, argūtus
intelligently adv ingeniōsē, sapienter, satis acūtē
intelligible adj perspicuus, apertus
intemperance n intemperantia f, licentia f
intemperate adj intemperāns, intemperātus
intemperately adv intemperanter
intend vt (with inf) in animō habēre, velle; (with object) dēstināre
intense adj ācer, nimius
intensely adv valdē, nimium
intensify vt augēre, amplificāre; **be intensified** ingravēscere

intensity n vīs f
intensive adj ācer, multus, adsiduus
intensively adv summō studiō
intent adj ērēctus, intentus; **be ~ on** animum intendere in (acc) ♦ n cōnsilium nt; **with ~** cōnsultō
intention n cōnsilium nt, prōpositum nt; **it is my ~** mihī in animō est; **with the ~ of** eā mente, eō cōnsiliō ut (subj)
intentionally adv cōnsultō, dē industriā
inter vt humāre
intercalary adj intercalāris
intercalate vt intercalāre
intercede vi intercēdere, dēprecārī
intercept vt excipere, intercipere; (cut off) interclūdere
intercession n dēprecātiō f; (tribune's) intercessiō f
intercessor n dēprecātor m
interchange vt permūtāre ♦ n permūtātiō f, vicissitūdō f
intercourse n commercium nt, ūsus m, cōnsuētūdō f
interdict n interdictum nt ♦ vt interdīcere (dat), vetāre
interest n (advantage) commodum nt; (study) studium nt; (money) faenus nt, ūsūra f; **compound ~** anatocismus m; **rate of ~** faenus nt; **~ at 12 per cent (per annum)** centēsimae fpl; **it is of ~** interest; **it is in my interests** meā interest; **consult the interests of** cōnsulere (dat); **take an ~ in** animum intendere (dat) ♦ vt dēlectāre, capere; (audience) tenēre; **~ oneself in** studēre (dat)
interested adj attentus; (for gain) ambitiōsus
interesting adj iūcundus, novus
interfere vi intervenīre; (with) sē interpōnere (dat), sē admiscēre ad; (hinder) officere (dat)
interference n interventus m, intercessiō f
interim n: **in the ~** interim, intereā
interior adj interior ♦ n pars interior f; (country) interiōra ntpl
interject vt exclāmāre
interjection n interiectiō f
interlace vt intexere
interlard vt variāre
interlock vt implicāre
interloper n interpellātor m
interlude n embolium nt
intermarriage n cōnūbium nt
intermediary adj medius ♦ n internūntius m
intermediate adj medius
interment n humātiō f
interminable adj sempiternus, longus
intermingle vt intermiscēre ♦ vi sē immiscēre
intermission n intercapēdō f, intermissiō f
intermittent adj interruptus
intermittently adv interdum
intern vt inclūdere
internal adj internus; (POL) domesticus
internally adv intus, domī
international adj: **~ law** iūs gentium
internecine adj internecīvus
interplay n vicēs fpl
interpolate vt interpolāre
interpose vt interpōnere ♦ vi intercēdere

interposition n intercessiō f
interpret vt interpretārī
interpretation n interpretātiō f
interpreter n interpres m/f
interrogate vt interrogāre, percontārī
interrogation n interrogātiō f, percontātiō f
interrupt vt (action) intercipere; (speaker)
   interpellāre; (talk) dirimere; (continuity)
   intermittere
interrupter n interpellātor m
interruption n interpellātiō f; intermissiō f
intersect vt dīvidere, secāre
intersperse vt distinguere
interstice n rīma f
intertwine vt intexere, implicāre
interval n intervallum nt, spatium nt; after an
   ~ spatiō interpositō; after an ~ of a year annō
   interiectō; at intervals interdum; at frequent
   intervals identidem; leave an ~ intermittere
intervene vt intercēdere, intervenīre
intervention n intercessiō f, interventus m; by
   the ~ of intercursū (gen)
interview n colloquium nt, aditus m ♦ vt
   convenīre
interweave vt implicāre, intexere
intestate adj intestātus ♦ adv intestātō
intestine adj intestīnus; (POL) domesticus ♦ npl
   intestīna ntpl; (victim's) exta ntpl
intimacy n familiāritās f
intimate adj familiāris; be an ~ friend of ab
   latere esse (gen); a very ~ friend perfamiliāris
   m/f ♦ vt dēnūntiāre
intimately adv familiāriter
intimation n dēnūntiātiō f; (hint) indicium nt
intimidate vt minārī (dat), terrōrem inicere (dat)
intimidation n metus m, minae fpl
into prep in (acc), intrā (acc)
intolerable adj intolerandus, intolerābilis
intolerably adv intoleranter
intolerance n impatientia f
intolerant adj impatiēns, intolerāns
intonation n sonus m, flexiō f
intone vt cantāre
intoxicate vt ēbrium reddere
intoxicated adj ēbrius
intoxication n ēbrietās f
intractable adj indocilis, difficilis
intransigent adj obstinātus
intrepid adj intrepidus, impavidus
intrepidity n audācia f, fortitūdō f
intricacy n implicātiō f
intricate adj implicātus, involūtus
intricately adv implicitē
intrigue n factiō f, artēs fpl, fallācia f ♦ vi
   māchinārī, fallāciīs ūtī
intriguing adj factiōsus; blandus
intrinsic adj vērus, innātus
intrinsically adv per sē
introduce vt indūcere, īnferre, importāre;
   (acquaintance) commendāre; (custom) īnstituere
introduction n exōrdium nt, prooemium nt;
   (of person) commendātiō f; letter of ~ litterae
   commendātīciae fpl
intrude vi sē interpōnere, intervenīre
intruder n interpellātor m, advena m; (fig)
   aliēnus m

intrusion n interpellātiō f
intuition n sēnsus m, cognitiō f
inundate vt inundāre
inundation n ēluviō f
inure vt dūrāre, adsuēfacere
invade vt invādere
invalid adj aeger, dēbilis; (null) inritus
invalidate vt infirmāre
invaluable adj inaestimābilis
invariable adj cōnstāns, immūtābilis
invariably adv semper
invasion n incursiō f
invective n convīcium nt
inveigh vi: ~ against invehī in (acc), īnsectārī
inveigle vt illicere, pellicere
invent vt fingere, comminīscī, invenīre
invention n inventum nt; (faculty) inventiō f
inventor n inventor m, auctor m
inverse adj inversus
inversely adv inversō ōrdine
invert vt invertere
invest vt (in office) inaugurāre; (MIL) obsidēre,
   circumsedēre; (money) locāre
investigate vt investīgāre, indāgāre; (case)
   cognōscere
investigation n investīgātiō f, indāgātiō f; (case)
   cognitiō f
investment n (MIL) obsessiō f; (money) locāta
   pecūnia f
inveterate adj inveterātus, vetus; become
   ~ inveterāscere
invidious adj invidiōsus
invidiously adv invidiōsē
invigorate vt recreāre, reficere
invincible adj invictus
inviolable adj inviolātus; (person) sacrōsanctus
inviolably adv inviolātē
inviolate adj integer
invisible adj caecus; be ~ vidērī nōn posse
invitation n invītātiō f; at the ~ of invītātū (gen)
invite vt invītāre, vocāre
inviting adj suāvis, blandus
invitingly adv blandē, suāviter
invocation n testātiō f
invoke vt invocāre, testārī
involuntarily adv īnscienter, invītus
involuntary adj coāctus
involve vt implicāre, involvere; be involved in
   inligārī (abl)
invulnerable adj inviolābilis; be ~ vulnerārī
   nōn posse
inward adj interior
inwardly adv intus
inwards adv intrōrsus
inweave vt intexere
inwrought adj intextus
irascibility n īrācundia f
irascible adj īrācundus
irate adj īrātus
ire n īra f
iris n hyacinthus m
irk vt incommodāre; I am irked mē piget
irksome adj molestus
irksomeness n molestia f
iron n ferrum nt; of ~ ferreus ♦ adj ferreus

ironical *adj* inversus
ironically *adv* inversīs verbīs
iron mine *n* ferrāria *f*
ironmonger *n* negōtiātor ferrārius *m*
ironmongery *n* ferrāmenta *ntpl*
iron ore *n* ferrum īnfectum *nt*
iron-tipped *adj* ferrātus
irony *n* illūsiō *f*, verbōrum inversiō *f*,
  dissimulātiō *f*
irradiate *vt* illūstrāre
irrational *adj* absurdus, ratiōnis expers; (*animal*)
  brūtus
irrationally *adv* absurdē, sine ratiōne
irreconcilable *adj* repugnāns, īnsociābilis
irrefutable *adj* certus, invictus
irregular *adj* incompositus; (*ground*) inaequālis;
  (*meeting*) extraōrdinārius; (*troops*) tumultuārius
irregularity *n* inaequālitās *f*; (*conduct*) prāvitās *f*,
  licentia *f*; (*election*) vitium *nt*
irregularly *adv* nullō ōrdine; (*elected*) vitiō
irrelevant *adj* aliēnus
irreligion *n* impietās *f*
irreligious *adj* impius
irremediable *adj* īnsānābilis
irreparable *adj* inrevocābilis
irreproachable *adj* integer, innocēns
irresistible *adj* invictus
irresolute *adj* dubius, anceps
irresolutely *adv* dubitanter
irresolution *n* dubitātiō *f*
irresponsibility *n* licentia *f*
irresponsible *adj* lascīvus, levis
irretrievable *adj* inrevocābilis

irreverence *n* impietās *f*
irreverent *adj* impius
irreverently *adv* impiē
irrevocable *adj* inrevocābilis
irrigate *vt* inrigāre
irrigation *n* inrigātiō *f*
irritability *n* īrācundia *f*
irritable *adj* īrācundus
irritate *vt* inrītāre, stomachum movēre (*dat*)
irritation *n* īrācundia *f*, stomachus *m*
island *n* īnsula *f*
islander *n* īnsulānus *m*
isle *n* īnsula *f*
isolate *vt* sēgregāre, sēparāre
isolation *n* sōlitūdō *f*
issue *n* (*result*) ēventus *m*, exitus *m*; (*children*)
  prōlēs *f*; (*question*) rēs *f*; (*book*) ēditiō *f*; **decide
  the ~** dēcernere, dēcertāre; **the point at ~** quā
  dē rē agitur ♦ *vt* distribuere; (*book*) ēdere;
  (*announcement*) prōmulgāre; (*coin*) ērogāre ♦ *vi*
  ēgredī, ēmānāre; (*result*) ēvādere, ēvenīre
isthmus *n* isthmus *m*
it *pron* hōc, id
itch *n* (*disease*) scabiēs *f*; (*fig*) cacoēthes *nt* ♦ *vi*
  prūrīre
item *n* nōmen *nt*, rēs *f*
iterate *vt* iterāre
itinerant *adj* vāgus, circumforāneus
itinerary *n* iter *nt*
its *adj* suus, ēius
itself *pron* ipse, ipsa, ipsum
ivory *n* ebur *nt* ♦ *adj* eburneus
ivy *n* hedera *f*

jabber *vi* blaterāre
jackdaw *n* grāculus *m*
jaded *adj* dēfessus, fatīgātus
jagged *adj* serrātus
jail *n* carcer *m*
jailer *n* custōs *m*, carcerārius *m*
jam *vt* comprimere; *(way)* obstruere
jamb *n* postis *m*
jangle *vi* crepitāre; rixārī
janitor *n* iānitor *m*
January *n* mēnsis Iānuārius *m*; **of ~** Iānuārius
jar *n* urna *f*; *(for wine)* amphora *f*; *(for water)* hydria *f*; *(sound)* offēnsa *f*; *(quarrel)* rixa *f* ◆ *vi* offendere
jasper *n* iaspis *f*
jaundice *n* morbus arquātus
jaundiced *adj* ictericus
jaunt *n*: **take a ~** excurrere
jauntily *adv* hilare, festīvē
jauntiness *n* hilaritās *f*
jaunty *adj* hilaris, festīvus
javelin *n* iaculum *nt*, pīlum *nt*; **throw the ~** iaculārī
jaw *n* māla *f*; **jaws** *pl* faucēs *fpl*
jay *n* grāculus *m*
jealous *adj* invidus; **be ~ of** invidēre *(dat)*
jealousy *n* invidia *f*
jeer *n* irrīsiō *f* ◆ *vi* irrīdēre; **~ at** illūdere
jejune *adj* iēiūnus, exīlis
jeopardize *vt* in perīculum addūcere
jeopardy *n* perīculum *nt*
jerk *n* subitus mōtus *m*
jest *n* iocus *m*
jester *n* scurra *m*
jet *n* *(mineral)* gagātēs *m*; *(of water)* saltus *m* ◆ *vi* salīre
jetsam *n* ēiectāmenta *ntpl*
jettison *vt* ēicere
jetty *n* mōlēs *f*
Jew *n* Iūdaeus *m*
jewel *n* gemma *f*
Jewish *adj* Iūdaicus
jig *n* tripudium *nt*
jilt *vt* repudiāre
jingle *n* nēnia *f* ◆ *vi* crepitāre, tinnīre
job *n* opus *nt*
jocose *adj see* **jocular**
jocular *adj* facētus, ioculāris
jocularity *n* facētiae *fpl*
jocularly *adv* facētē, per iocum
jocund *adj* hilaris, festīvus
jog *vt* fodicāre; *(fig)* stimulāre ◆ *vi* ambulāre

join *vt* iungere, coniungere, cōpulāre ◆ *vi* coniungī, sē coniungere; **~ in** interesse *(dat)*, sē immiscēre *(dat)*; **~ battle with** proelium committere *(abl)*
joiner *n* faber *m*
joint *adj* commūnis ◆ *n* commissūra *f*; *(of body)* articulus *m*, nōdus *m*; **~ by ~** articulātim
jointed *adj* geniculātus
joint-heir *n* cohērēs *m/f*
jointly *adv* ūnā, coniūnctē
joist *n* tignum *nt*
joke *n* iocus *m* ◆ *vi* iocārī, lūdere
joking *n* iocus *m*; **~ apart** remōtō iocō
jokingly *adv* per iocum
jollity *n* hilaritās *f*, festīvitās *f*
jolly *adj* hilaris, festīvus
jolt *vt* iactāre
jolting *n* iactātiō *f*
jostle *vt* agitāre, offendere
jot *n* minimum *nt*; **not a jot** nihil; **not care a jot** nōn floccī facere
journal *n* ācta diūrna *ntpl*
journey *n* iter *nt*
journeyman *n* opifex *m*
Jove *n* Iuppiter *m*
jovial *adj* hilaris
joviality *n* hilaritās *f*
jovially *adv* hilare
jowl *n* māla *f*; **cheek by ~** iuxtā
joy *n* gaudium *nt*, laetitia *f*, alacritās *f*
joyful *adj* laetus, hilaris
joyfully *adv* laetē, hilare
joyfulness *n* gaudium *nt*, laetitia *f*
joyless *adj* tristis, maestus
joyous *adj see* **joyful**
joyously *adv see* **joyfully**
jubilant *adj* laetus, gaudiō exsultāns
judge *n* iūdex *m*, arbiter *m* ◆ *vt* iūdicāre; *(think)* exīstimāre, cēnsēre; **~ between** diiūdicāre
judgeship *n* iūdicātus *m*
judgment *n* iūdicium *nt*, arbitrium *nt*; *(opinion)* sententia *f*; *(punishment)* poena *f*; *(wisdom)* iūdicium *nt*; **in my ~** meō animō, meō arbitrātū; **pass ~ on** statuere dē; **sit in ~** iūdicium exercēre
judgment seat *n* tribūnal *nt*
judicature *n* iūrisdictiō *f*; *(men)* iūdicēs *mpl*
judicial *adj* iūdiciālis; *(LAW)* iūdiciārius
judiciary *n* iūdicēs *mpl*
judicious *adj* prūdēns, cōnsīderātus
judiciously *adv* prūdenter

jug *n* hydria *f*, urceus *m*
juggler *n* praestigiātor *m*
juggling *n* praestīgiae *fpl*
juice *n* liquor *m*, sūcus *m*
juicy *adj* sūcī plēnus
July *n* mēnsis Quīnctīlis, Iūlius *m*; **of**
~ Quīnctīlis, Iūlius
jumble *n* congeriēs *f* ♦ *vt* cōnfundere
jump *n* saltus *m* ♦ *vi* salīre; ~ **across** transilīre;
~ **at** (*opportunity*) captāre, adripere, amplecti;
~ **down** dēsilīre; ~ **on to** īnsilīre in (*acc*)
junction *n* coniūnctiō *f*
juncture *n* tempus *nt*
June *n* mēnsis Iūnius; **of** ~ Iūnius
junior *adj* iūnior, nātū minor
juniper *n* iūniperus *f*
Juno *n* Iūnō, Iūnōnis *f*
Jupiter *n* Iuppiter, Iovis *m*
juridical *adj* iūdiciārius
jurisconsult *n* iūriscōnsultus *m*
jurisdiction *n* iūrisdictiō *f*, diciō *f*; **exercise** ~ iūs
dīcere

jurisprudence *n* iūrisprūdentia *f*
jurist *n* iūriscōnsultus *m*
juror *n* iūdex *m*
jury *n* iūdicēs *mpl*
just *adj* iūstus, aequus ♦ *adv* (*exactly*) prōrsus;
(*only*) modo; (*time*) commodum, modo; (*with
adv*) dēmum, dēnique; (*with pron*) adeō dēmum,
ipse; ~ **as** (*comparison*) aequē ac, perinde ac,
quemadmodum; sīcut; ~ **before** (*time*) cum
māximē, sub (*acc*); ~ **now** modo, nunc; ~ **so** ita
prōrsus, sānē; **only** ~ vix
justice *n* iūstitia *f*, aequitās *f*, iūs *nt*; (*person*)
praetor *m*; **administer** ~ iūs reddere
justiciary *n* praetor *m*
justifiable *adj* iūstus
justifiably *adv* iūre
justification *n* pūrgātiō *f*, excūsātiō *f*
justify *vt* excūsāre, pūrgāre
justly *adv* iūstē, aequē; iūre, meritō
jut *vi* prōminēre, excurrere
jutting *adj* prōiectus
juvenile *adj* iuvenīlis, puerīlis

Kk

keel *n* carīna *f*
keen *adj* ācer; (*mind*) acūtus, argūtus; (*sense*) sagāx; (*pain*) acerbus; **I am ~ on** studeō
keenly *adv* ācriter, sagāciter, acūtē, acerbē
keenness *n* (*scent*) sagācitās *f*; (*sight*) aciēs *f*; (*pain*) acerbitās *f*; (*eagerness*) studium *nt*, ārdor *m*
keep *vt* servāre, tenēre, habēre; (*celebrate*) agere, celebrāre; (*guard*) custōdīre; (*obey*) observāre; (*preserve*) cōnservāre; (*rear*) alere, pāscere; (*store*) condere; **~ apart** distinēre; **~ away** arcēre; **~ back** dētinēre, reservāre; **~ down** comprimere; (*exuberance*) dēpāscere; **~ in** cohibēre, claudere; **~ in with** grātiam sequī (*gen*); **~ off** arcēre, dēfendere; **~ one's word** fidem praestāre; **~ one's hands off** manūs abstinēre; **~ house** domī sē retinēre; **~ secret** cēlāre; **~ together** continēre; **~ up** sustinēre, cōnservāre; **~ up with** subsequī; **~ waiting** dēmorārī ♦ *vi* dūrāre, manēre ♦ *n* arx *f*
keeper *n* custōs *m*
keeping *n* custōdia *f*; **in ~ with** prō (*abl*); **be in ~ with** convenīre (*dat*)
keg *n* cadus *m*
ken *n* cōnspectus *m*
kennel *n* stabulum *nt*
kerb *n* crepīdō *f*
kernel *n* grānum *nt*, nucleus *m*
kettle *n* lebēs *f*
key *n* clāvis *f*; (*fig*) claustra *ntpl*, iānua *f*; **key position** cardō *m*
kick *vi* calcitrāre ♦ *vt* calce ferīre
kid *n* haedus *m*
kidnap *vt* surripere
kidnapper *n* plagiārius *m*
kidney *n* rēn *m*
kidney bean *n* phasēlus *m*
kid's *adj* haedīnus
kill *vt* interficere, interimere; (*in battle*) occīdere; (*murder*) necāre, iugulāre; (*time*) perdere
killer *n* interfector *m*
kiln *n* fornāx *f*
kin *n* cognātī *mpl*, propinquī *mpl*; **next of kin** proximī *mpl*
kind *adj* bonus, benīgnus, benevolus, cōmis ♦ *n* genus *nt*; **of such a ~** tālis; **what ~ of** quālis
kindle *vt* incendere, succendere, īnflammāre
kindliness *n* cōmitās *f*, hūmānitās *f*
kindling *n* (*fuel*) fōmes *m*
kindly *adv* benīgnē
kindness *n* benīgnitās *f*, benevolentia *f*; (*act*) beneficium *nt*, officium *nt*, grātia *f*

kindred *n* necessitūdō *f*, cognātiō *f*; propinquī *mpl*, cognātī *mpl* ♦ *adj* cognātus, adfīnis
king *n* rēx *m*
kingdom *n* rēgnum *nt*
kingfisher *n* alcēdō *f*
kingly *adj* rēgius, rēgālis
kingship *n* rēgnum *nt*
kink *n* vitium *nt*
kinsfolk *n* cognātī *mpl*, necessāriī *mpl*
kinsman *n* cognātus *m*, propinquus *m*, necessārius *m*
kinswoman *n* cognāta *f*, propinqua *f*, necessāria *f*
kismet *n* fātum *nt*
kiss *n* ōsculum *nt* ♦ *vt* ōsculārī
kit *n* (MIL) sarcina *f*
kitchen *n* culīna *f*
kitchen garden *n* hortus *m*
kite *n* mīluus *m*
kite's *adj* mīluīnus
knack *n* calliditās *f*, artificium *nt*; **have the ~ of** callēre
knapsack *n* sarcina *f*
knave *n* veterātor *m*
knavish *adj* improbus
knavishly *adv* improbē
knead *vt* depsere, subigere
knee *n* genū *nt*
kneel *vi* genibus nītī
knife *n* culter *m*; (*surgeon's*) scalprum *nt*
knight *n* eques *m* ♦ *vt* in ōrdinem equestrem recipere
knighthood *n* ōrdō equester *m*
knightly *adj* equester
knit *vt* texere; (*brow*) contrahere
knob *n* bulla *f*
knock *vt* ferīre, percutere; **~ at** pulsāre; **~ against** offendere; **~ down** dēicere, adflīgere; (*at auction*) addīcere; **~ off** dēcutere; (*work*) dēsistere ab; **~ out** ēlīdere, excutere; (*unconscious*) exanimāre; (*fig*) dēvincere; **~ up** suscitāre ♦ *n* pulsus *m*, ictus *m*
knock-kneed *adj* vārus
knoll *n* tumulus *m*
knot *n* nōdus *m* ♦ *vt* nectere
knotty *adj* nōdōsus; **~ point** nōdus *m*
know *vt* scīre; (*person*) nōvisse; **~ all about** explōrātum habēre; **~ again** agnōscere; **~ how to** scīre; **not ~** ignōrāre, nescīre; **let me ~** fac sciam, fac mē certiōrem; **get to ~** cognōscere ♦ *n*: **in the ~** cōnscius

knowing *adj* prūdēns, callidus
knowingly *adv* cōnsultō, sciēns
knowledge *n* scientia *f*, doctrīna *f*; (*practical*)
   experientia *f*; (*of something*) cognitiō *f*
knowledgeable *adj* gnārus, doctus

known *adj* nōtus; **make ~** dēclārāre
knuckle *n* articulus *m*
knuckle bone *n* tālus *m*
kowtow *vi* adulārī
kudos *n* glōria *f*, laus *f*

label *n* titulus *m* ◆ *vt* titulō īnscrībere
laboratory *n* officīna *f*
laborious *adj* labōriōsus, operōsus
laboriously *adv* operōsē
laboriousness *n* labor *m*
labour *n* labor *m*, opera *f*; (*work done*) opus *nt*; (*work allotted*) pēnsum *nt*; (*workmen*) operae *fpl*; **be in** ~ parturīre ◆ *vi* labōrāre, ēnītī; ~ **at** ēlabōrāre; ~ **under a delusion** errōre fallī
laboured *adj* adfectātus
labourer *n* operārius *m*; **labourers** *pl* operae *fpl*
labyrinth *n* labyrinthus *m*
lace *n* texta rēticulāta *ntpl*; (*shoe*) ligula *f* ◆ *vt* nectere
lacerate *vt* lacerāre
laceration *n* lacerātiō *f*
lack *n* inopia *f*, dēfectiō *f* ◆ *vt* egēre (*abl*), carēre (*abl*)
lackey *n* pedisequus *m*
laconic *adj* brevis
laconically *adv* ūnō verbō, paucīs verbīs
lacuna *n* lacūna *f*
lad *n* puer *m*
ladder *n* scāla *f*
lade *vt* onerāre
laden *adj* onustus, onerātus
lading *n* onus *nt*
ladle *n* trulla *f*
lady *n* domina *f*, mātrōna *f*, mulier *f*
ladylike *adj* līberālis, honestus
lag *vi* cessāre
lagoon *n* stagnum *nt*
lair *n* latibulum *nt*
lake *n* lacus *m*
lamb *n* agnus *m*; (*flesh*) agnīna *f*; **ewe** ~ agna *f*
lame *adj* claudus; (*argument*) inānis; **be** ~ claudicāre
lameness *n* claudicātiō *f*
lament *n* lāmentātiō *f*, lāmentum *nt* ◆ *vt* lūgēre, lāmentārī; (*regret*) dēplōrāre
lamentable *adj* lāmentābilis, miserābilis
lamentably *adv* miserābiliter
lamentation *n* lāmentātiō *f*
lamp *n* lucerna *f*, lychnus *m*
lampoon *n* satura *f* ◆ *vt* carmine dēstringere
lance *n* hasta *f*, lancea *f*
lancer *n* hastātus *m*
lancet *n* scalpellum *nt*
land *n* terra *f*; (*country*) terra *f*, regiō *f*; (*territory*) fīnēs *mpl*; (*native*) patria *f*; (*property*) praedium *nt*, ager *m*; (*soil*) solum *nt* ◆ *vt* expōnere ◆ *vi* ē nāve ēgredī ◆ *adj* terrēnus, terrestris

landfall *n* adpulsus *m*
landing place *n* ēgressus *m*
landlady *n* caupōna *f*
landlord *n* dominus *m*; (*inn*) caupō *m*
landmark *n* lapis *m*; **be a** ~ ēminēre
landscape *n* agrōrum prōspectus *m*
landslide *n* terrae lābēs *f*, lāpsus *m*
landwards *adv* terram versus
lane *n* (*country*) sēmita *f*; (*town*) angiportus *m*
language *n* lingua *f*; (*style*) ōrātiō *f*, sermō *m*; (*diction*) verba *ntpl*; **bad** ~ maledicta *ntpl*
languid *adj* languidus, remissus
languidly *adv* languidē
languish *vi* languēre, languēscere; (*with disease*) tābēscere
languor *n* languor *m*
lank, lanky *adj* exīlis, gracilis
lantern *n* lanterna *f*, lucerna *f*
lap *n* gremium *nt*, sinus *m* ◆ *vt* lambere; (*cover*) involvere
lapse *n* (*time*) lāpsus *m*; (*mistake*) errātum *nt*; **after the** ~ **of a year** interiectō annō ◆ *vi* lābī; (*agreement*) inritum fierī; (*property*) revertī
larceny *n* fūrtum *nt*
larch *n* larix *f* ◆ *adj* larignus
lard *n* adeps *m/f*
larder *n* cella penāria *f*
large *adj* māgnus, grandis, amplus; **at** ~ solūtus; **very** ~ permāgnus; **as** ~ **as** ... tantus ... quantus
largely *adv* plērumque
largesse *n* largitiō *f*; (*MIL*) dōnātivum *nt*; (*civil*) congiārium *nt*; **give** ~ largīrī
lark *n* alauda *f*
lascivious *adj* libīdinōsus
lasciviously *adv* libīdinōsē
lasciviousness *n* libīdō *f*
lash *n* flagellum *nt*, lōrum *nt*; (*eye*) cilium *nt* ◆ *vt* verberāre; (*tie*) adligāre; (*with words*) castīgāre
lashing *n* verbera *ntpl*
lass *n* puella *f*
lassitude *n* languor *m*
last *adj* ultimus, postrēmus, suprēmus; (*in line*) novissimus; (*preceding*) proximus; **at** ~ tandem, dēmum, dēnique; **for the** ~ **time** postrēmum ◆ *n* fōrma *f*; **let the cobbler stick to his** ~ nē sūtor suprā crepidam ◆ *vi* dūrāre, permanēre
lasting *adj* diūtinus, diūturnus
lastly *adv* postrēmō, dēnique
latch *n* pessulus *m*
latchet *n* corrigia *f*
late *adj* sērus; (*date*) recēns; (*dead*) dēmortuus; (*emperor*) dīvus; ~ **at night** multā nocte; **till** ~ **in**

the day ad multum diem ♦ adv sērō; too ~ sērō; too ~ to sērius quam quī (subj); of ~ nūper

lately adv nūper

latent adj occultus, latitāns

later adj posterior ♦ adv posteā, posthāc, mox

latest adj novissimus

lath n tigillum nt

lathe n tornus m

lather n spūma f

Latin adj Latīnus; **speak ~** Latīnē loquī; **understand ~** Latīnē scīre; **translate into ~** Latīnē reddere; **in ~** Latīnē

Latinity n Latīnitās f

latitude n (CEOG) caelum nt; (scope) lībertās f, licentia f

latter adj posterior; **the ~** hīc

latterly adv nūper

lattice n trānsenna f

laud n laus f ♦ vt laudāre

laudable adj laudābilis, laude dignus

laudatory adj honōrificus

laugh n rīsus m; (loud) cachinnus m ♦ vi rīdēre, cachinnāre; **~ at** (joke) rīdēre; (person) dērīdēre; **~ up one's sleeve** in sinū gaudēre

laughable adj rīdiculus

laughing stock n lūdibrium nt

laughter n rīsus m

launch vt (missile) contorquēre; (ship) dēdūcere; **~ an attack impetum dare** ♦ vi: **~ out into** ingredī in (acc) ♦ n celōx f, lembus m

laureate adj laureātus

laurel n laurus m ♦ adj laureus

lave vt lavāre

lavish adj prōdigus, largus ♦ vt largīrī, profundere

lavishly adv prōdigē, effūsē

lavishness n largitās f

law n lēx f; (system) iūs nt; (divine) fās nt; **civil law** iūs cīvīle; **constitutional law** iūs pūblicum; **international law** iūs gentium; **go to law** lēge agere, lītigāre; **break the law** lēges violāre; **pass a law** (magistrate) lēgem perferre; (people) lēgem iubēre

law-abiding adj bene mōrātus

law court n iūdicium nt; (building) basilica f

lawful adj lēgitimus; (morally) fās

lawfully adv lēgitimē, lēge

lawgiver n lēgum scrīptor m

lawless adj exlēx

lawlessly adv licenter

lawlessness n licentia f

lawn n prātulum nt

law-suit n līs f, āctiō f

lawyer n iūriscōnsultus m, causidicus m

lax adj dissolūtus, remissus

laxity n dissolūtiō f

lay adj (ECCL) lāicus ♦ vt pōnere, locāre; (ambush) collocāre, tendere; (disorder) sēdāre; (egg) parere; (foundation) iacere; (hands) inīcere; (plan) capere, inīre; (trap) tendere; (wager) facere; **lay aside** pōnere; (in store) repōnere; **lay by** repōnere; **lay down** dēpōnere; (rule) statuere; **lay hold of** prehendere, adripere; **lay in** condere; **lay a motion before** referre ad; **lay on** impōnere; **lay open** patefacere; (to attack) nūdāre; **lay out** (money) impendere, ērogāre; (camp)

mētārī; **lay siege to** obsidēre; **lay to heart** in pectus dēmittere; **lay up** recondere; **lay upon** iniungere, impōnere; **lay violent hands on** vim adferre, adhibēre (dat); **whatever they could lay hands on** quod cuīque in manum vēnisset; **lay waste** vastāre ♦ n carmen nt, melos nt

layer n corium nt; (stones) ōrdō m; (plant) propāgō f

layout n dēsignātiō f

laze vi ōtiārī

lazily adv ignāvē, ōtiōsē

laziness n ignāvia f, dēsidia f, pigritia f

lazy adj ignāvus, dēsidiōsus, piger

lea n prātum nt

lead¹ vt dūcere; (life) agere; (wall) perdūcere; (water) dērīvāre; **~ across** tradūcere; **~ around** circumdūcere; **~ astray** in errōrem indūcere; **~ away** abdūcere; **~ back** redūcere; **~ down** dēdūcere; **~ in** intrōdūcere; **~ on** addūcere; **~ out** ēdūcere; **~ over** tradūcere; **~ the way** dūcere, praeīre; **~ up to** tendere ad, spectāre ad; **the road leads ...** via fert ...

lead² n plumbum nt ♦ adj plumbeus

leaden adj (colour) līvidus

leader n dux m, ductor m

leadership n ductus m

leading adj prīmus, prīnceps, praecipuus

leaf n folium nt, frōns f; (paper) scheda f; **put forth leaves** frondēscere

leaflet n libellus m

leafy adj frondōsus

league n foedus nt, societās f; (distance) tria mīlia passuum ♦ vi coniūrāre, foedus facere

leagued adj foederātus

leak n rīma f ♦ vi mānāre, rīmās agere

leaky adj rīmōsus

lean adj macer, exīlis, gracilis ♦ vi nītī; **~ back** sē reclīnāre; **~ on** innītī in (abl), incumbere (dat); **~ over** inclīnāre

leaning n prōpēnsiō f ♦ adj inclīnātus

leanness n gracilitās f, maciēs f

leap n saltus m ♦ vi salīre; (for joy) exsultāre; **~ down** dēsilīre; **~ on to** īnsilīre in (acc)

leap year n annus bissextilis m

learn vt discere; (news) accipere, audīre; (by heart) ēdiscere; (discover) cognōscere

learned adj doctus, ērudītus, litterātus

learnedly adv doctē

learner n tīrō m, discipulus m

learning n doctrīna f, ērudītiō f, litterae fpl

lease n (taken) conductiō f; (given) locātiō f ♦ vt condūcere; locāre

leash n cōpula f

least adj minimus ♦ adv minimē; **at ~** saltem; **to say the ~** ut levissimē dīcam; **not in the ~** haudquāquam

leather n corium nt, alūta f

leathery adj lentus

leave n (of absence) commeātus m; (permission) potestās f, venia f; **ask ~** veniam petere; **give ~** potestātem facere; **obtain ~** impetrāre; **by your ~** pace tuā, bonā tuā veniā ♦ vt relinquere, dēserere; (legacy) lēgāre; **~ alone** nōn tangere, manum abstinēre ab; **~ behind** relinquere; **~ in the lurch** dēstituere, dērelinquere; **~ off** dēsinere, dēsistere ab; (temporarily)

intermittere; (*garment*) pōnere; ~ **out** praetermittere, ōmittere ♦ *vi* discēdere ab (*abl*), abīre
leaven *n* fermentum *nt*
leavings *n* rēliquiae *fpl*
lecherous *adj* salāx
lecture *n* acroāsis *f*, audītiō *f* ♦ *vi* docēre, scholam habēre
lecturer *n* doctor *m*
lecture room *n* audītōrium *nt*
ledge *n* līmen *nt*
ledger *n* cōdex acceptī et expēnsī
lee *n* pars ā ventō tūta
leech *n* hirūdō *f*
leek *n* porrum *nt*
leer *vi* līmīs oculīs intuērī
lees *n* faex *f*; (*of oil*) amurca *f*
left *adj* sinister, laevus ♦ *n* sinistra *f*, laeva *f*; **on the** ~ ā laevā, ad laevam, ā sinistrā
leg *n* crūs *nt*; (*of table*) pēs *m*
legacy *n* lēgātum *nt*; ~ **hunter** captātor *m*
legal *adj* lēgitimus
legalize *vt* sancīre
legally *adv* secundum lēgēs, lēge
legate *n* lēgātus *m*
legation *n* lēgātiō *f*
legend *n* fābula *f*; (*inscription*) titulus *m*
legendary *adj* fābulōsus
legerdemain *n* praestīgiae *fpl*
legging *n* ocrea *f*
legible *adj* clārus
legion *n* legiō *f*; **men of the 10th** ~ decumānī *mpl*
legionary *n* legiōnārius *m*
legislate *vi* lēgēs scrībere, lēgēs facere
legislation *n* lēgēs *fpl*, lēgēs scrībendae
legislator *n* lēgum scrīptor *m*
legitimate *adj* lēgitimus
legitimately *adv* lēgitimē
leisure *n* ōtium *nt*; **at** ~ ōtiōsus, vacuus; **have** ~ **for** vacāre (*dat*)
leisured *adj* ōtiōsus
leisurely *adj* lentus
lend *vt* commodāre, mūtuum dare; (*at interest*) faenerārī; (*ear*) aurēs praebēre, admovēre; ~ **a ready ear** aurēs patefacere; ~ **assistance** opem ferre
length *n* longitūdō *f*; (*time*) diūturnitās *f*; **at** ~ tandem, dēmum, dēnique; (*speech*) cōpiōsē
lengthen *vt* extendere; (*time*) prōtrahere; (*sound*) prōdūcere
lengthwise *adv* in longitūdinem
lengthy *adj* longus, prōlixus
leniency *n* clēmentia *f*
lenient *adj* clēmēns, mītis
leniently *adv* clēmenter
lentil *n* lēns *f*
leonine *adj* leōnīnus
leopard *n* pardus *m*
less *adj* minor ♦ *adv* minus; ~ **than** (*num*) intrā (*acc*); **much** ~, **still** ~ nēdum
lessee *n* conductor *m*
lessen *vt* minuere, imminuere, dēminuere ♦ *vi* dēcrēscere
lesson *n* documentum *nt*; **be a** ~ **to** documentō esse (*dat*); **lessons** *pl* dictāta *ntpl*; **give lessons** scholās habēre; **give lessons in** docēre

lessor *n* locātor *m*
lest *conj* nē (*subj*)
let *vt* (*allow*) sinere; (*lease*) locāre; (*imper*) fac; **let alone** ōmittere; (*mention*) nē dīcam; **let blood** sanguinem mittere; **let down** dēmittere; **let fall** ā manibus mittere; (*word*) ēmittere; **let fly** ēmittere; **let go** mittere, āmittere; (*ship*) solvere; **let in** admittere; **let loose** solvere; **let off** absolvere, ignōscere (*dat*); **let oneself go** geniō indulgēre; **let out** ēmittere; **let slip** āmittere, ōmittere
lethal *adj* mortifer
lethargic *adj* veternōsus
lethargy *n* veternus *m*
letter *n* epistula *f*, litterae *fpl*; (*of alphabet*) littera *f*; **the** ~ **of the law** scrīptum *nt*; **to the** ~ ad praescrīptum; **by** ~ per litterās; **letters** (*learning*) litterae *fpl*; **man of letters** scrīptor *m*
lettered *adj* litterātus
lettuce *n* lactūca *f*
levee *n* salūtātiō *f*
level *adj* aequus, plānus ♦ *n* plānitiēs *f*; (*instrument*) lībra *f*; **do one's** ~ **best** prō virīlī parte agere; **put on a** ~ **with** exaequāre cum ♦ *vt* aequāre, adaequāre, inaequāre; (*to the ground*) solō aequāre, sternere; (*weapon*) intendere
level-headed *adj* prūdēns
levelled *adj* (*weapon*) īnfestus
lever *n* vectis *m*
levity *n* levitās *f*; (*fun*) iocī *mpl*, facētiae *fpl*
levy *vt* (*troops*) scrībere; (*tax*) exigere ♦ *n* dīlectus *m*
lewd *adj* impudīcus
lewdness *n* impudīcitia *f*
liable *adj* obnoxius; **render** ~ obligāre
liaison *n* cōnsuētūdō *f*
liar *n* mendāx *m*
libel *n* probrum *nt*, calumnia *f* ♦ *vt* calumniārī
libellous *adj* probrōsus, fāmōsus
liberal *adj* līberālis; (*in giving*) largus, benīgnus; ~ **education** bonae artēs *fpl*
liberality *n* līberālitās *f*, largitās *f*
liberally *adv* līberāliter, largē, benīgnē
liberate *vt* līberāre; (*slave*) manū mittere
liberation *n* līberātiō *f*
liberator *n* līberātor *m*
libertine *n* libīdinōsus *m*
liberty *n* lībertās *f*; (*excess*) licentia *f*; **I am at** ~ **to** mihī licet (*inf*); **I am still at** ~ **to** integrum est mihī (*inf*); **take a** ~ **with** licentius ūtī (*abl*), familiārius sē gerere in (*acc*)
libidinous *adj* libīdinōsus
librarian *n* librārius *m*
library *n* bibliothēca *f*
licence *n* (*permission*) potestās *f*; (*excess*) licentia *f*
license *vt* potestātem dare (*dat*)
licentious *adj* dissolūtus
licentiousness *n* libīdō *f*, licentia *f*
lick *vt* lambere; mulcēre
lictor *n* lictor *m*
lid *n* operculum *nt*
lie *n* mendācium *nt*; **give the lie to** redarguere; **tell a lie** mentīrī ♦ *vi* mentīrī; **lie down** iacēre; (*place*) situm esse; (*consist*) continērī; **as far as in me lies** quantum in mē est; **lie at anchor**

stāre; **lie between** interiacēre; **lie down**
cubāre, discumbere; **lie heavy on** premere;
lie hid latēre; **lie in wait** īnsidiārī; **lie low**
dissimulāre; **lie on** incumbere (dat); **lie open**
patēre; hiāre
lien n nexus m
lieu n: **in ~ of** locō (gen)
lieutenant n decuriō m; legātus m
life n vīta f; (in danger) salūs f, caput nt; (biography)
vīta f; (breath) anima f; (RHET) sanguis m; (time)
aetās f; **come to ~ again** revīvīscere; **draw to
the ~** exprimere; **for ~** aetātem; **matter of
~ and death** capitāle nt; **prime of ~** flōs aetātis;
way of ~ mōrēs mpl
lifeblood n sanguis m
life-giving adj almus, vītalis
lifeguard n custōs m; (emperor's) praetōriānus m
lifeless adj exanimis; (style) exsanguis
lifelike adj expressus
lifelong adj perpetuus
lifetime n aetās f
lift vt tollere, sublevāre; **~ up** efferre, attollere
light n lūx f, lūmen nt; (painting) lūmen nt; **bring
to ~** in lūcem prōferre; **see in a favourable ~** in
meliōrem partem interpretārī; **throw ~ on**
lūmen adhibēre (dat) ♦ vt accendere, incendere;
(illuminate) illūstrāre, illūmināre; **be lit up**
collūcēre ♦ vi: **~ upon** invenīre, offendere ♦ adj
illūstris; (movement) agilis; (weight) levis; **grow
~** illūcēscere, dīlūcēscere; **make ~ of** parvī
pendere
light-armed adj expedītus
lighten vi fulgurāre ♦ vt levāre
lighter n linter f
light-fingered adj tagāx
light-footed adj celer, pernīx
light-headed adj levis, volāticus
light-hearted adj hilaris, laetus
lightly adv leviter; pernīciter
lightness n levitās f
lightning n fulgur nt; (striking) fulmen nt; **be hit
by ~** dē caelō percutī; **of ~** fulgurālis
like adj similis, pār; **~ this** ad hunc modum ♦ adv
similiter, sīcut, rītū (gen) ♦ vt amāre; **I ~ mihī**
placet, mē iuvat; **I ~ to** libet (inf); **I don't ~** nīl
moror, mihī displicet; **look ~** similem esse,
referre
likelihood n vērī similitūdō f
likely adj vērī similis ♦ adv sānē
liken vt comparāre, aequiperāre
likeness n imāgō f, īnstar nt, similitūdō f
likewise adv item; (also) etiam
liking n libīdō f, grātia f; **to one's ~** ex sententiā
lily n līlium nt
limb n membrum nt, artus m
lime n calx f; (tree) tilia f
limelight n celebritās f; **enjoy the ~** mōnstrārī
digitō
limestone n calx f
limit n fīnis m, terminus m, modus m; **mark
the limits of** dētermināre ♦ vt fīnīre, dēfinīre,
termināre; (restrict) circumscrībere
limitation n modus m
limp adj mollis, flaccidus ♦ vi claudicāre
limpid adj limpidus
linden n tilia f

line n līnea f; (battle) aciēs f; (limit) modus m;
(outline) līneāmentum nt; (writing) versus m; **in
a straight ~ ē** regiōne; **~ of march** agmen nt;
read between the lines dissimulātā dispicere;
ship of the ~ nāvis longa; **write a ~** pauca
scrībere ♦ vt (street) saepīre
lineage n genus nt, stirps f
lineal adj (descent) gentīlis
lineaments n līneāmenta ntpl, ōris ductūs mpl
linen n linteum nt ♦ adj linteus
liner n nāvis f
linger vi cunctārī, cessāre, dēmorārī
lingering adj tardus ♦ n cunctātiō f
linguist n: **be a ~** complūrēs linguās callēre
link n ānulus m; (fig) nexus m, vinculum nt ♦ vt
coniungere
lintel n līmen superum nt
lion n leō m; **lion's** leōnīnus; **lion's share** māior
pars
lioness n leaena f
lip n lābrum nt; **be on everyone's lips** in ōre
omnium hominum esse, per omnium ōra ferrī
lip service n: **pay lip service to** verbō tenus
obsequī (dat)
liquefy vt liquefacere
liquid adj liquidus ♦ n liquor m
liquidate vt persolvere
liquor n liquor m; vīnum nt
lisp vi balbūtīre
lisping adj blaesus
lissom adj agilis
list n index m, tabula f; (ship) inclīnātiō f
♦ vt scrībere ♦ vi (lean) sē inclīnāre; (listen)
auscultāre; (wish) cupere
listen vi auscultāre; **~ to** auscultāre, audīre
listener n audītor m, auscultātor m
listless adj languidus
listlessness n languor m
literally adv ad verbum
literary adj (man) litterātus; **~ pursuits** litterae
fpl, studia ntpl
literature n litterae fpl
lithe adj mollis, agilis
litigant n lītigātor m
litigate vi lītigāre
litigation n līs f
litigious adj lītigiōsus
litter n (carriage) lectīca f; (brood) fētus m; (straw)
strāmentum nt; (mess) strāgēs f ♦ vt sternere;
(young) parere
little adj parvus, exiguus; (time) brevis; **very
~** perexiguus, minimus; **~ boy** puerulus m ♦ n
paulum nt, aliquantulum nt; **for a ~** paulisper,
parumper; **~ or nothing** vix quicquam ♦ adv
paulum, nōnnihil; (with comp) paulō; **~ by
~** paulātim, sēnsim, gradātim; **think ~ of** parvī
aestimāre; **too ~** parum (gen)
littleness n exiguitās f
littoral n lītus nt
live vi vīvere, vītam agere; (dwell) habitāre;
~ down (reproach) ēluere; **~ on** (food) vescī (abl)
♦ adj vīvus
livelihood n vīctus m
liveliness n alacritās f, hilaritās f
livelong adj tōtus
lively adj alacer, hilaris

liven vt exhilarāre
liver n iecur nt
livery n vestis famulāris f
livid adj līvidus; **be ~** līvēre
living adj vīvus ♦ n vīctus m; (earning) quaestus m
lizard n lacerta f
lo interj ecce
load n onus nt ♦ vt onerāre
loaf n pānis m ♦ vi grassārī
loafer n grassātor m
loam n lutum nt
loan n mūtuum nt, mūtua pecūnia f
loathe vt fastīdīre, ōdisse
loathing n fastīdium nt
loathsome adj odiōsus, taeter
lobby n vestibulum nt
lobe n fibra f
lobster n astacus m
local adj indigena, locī
locality n locus m
locate vt reperīre; **be located** situm esse
location n situs m
loch n lacus m
lock n (door) sera f; (hair) coma f ♦ vt obserāre
locomotion n mōtus m
locust n locusta f
lodge n casa f ♦ vi dēversārī ♦ vt īnfīgere; (complaint) dēferre
lodger n inquilīnus m
lodging n hospitium nt, dēversōrium nt
loft n cēnāculum nt
loftiness n altitūdō f, sublīmitās f
lofty adj excelsus, sublīmis
log n stīpes m; (fuel) lignum nt
loggerhead n: **be at loggerheads** rixārī
logic n dialecticē f
logical adj dialecticus, ratiōne frētus
logically adv ex ratiōne
logician n dialecticus m
loin n lumbus m
loiter vi grassārī, cessāre
loiterer n grassātor m, cessātor m
loll vi recumbere
lone adj sōlus, sōlitārius
loneliness n sōlitūdō f
lonely, lonesome adj sōlitārius
long adj longus; (hair) prōmissus; (syllable) prōductus; (time) longus, diūturnus; **in the ~ run** aliquandō; **for a ~ time** diū; **to make a ~ story short** nē longum sit, nē longum faciam ♦ adv diū; **~ ago** iamprīdem, iamdūdum; **as ~ as** (conj) dum; **before ~** mox; **for ~** diū; **how ~** quamdiū, quōusque; **I have ~ been wishing** iam prīdem cupiō; **not ~ after** haud multō post; **any longer** (time) diūtius; (distance) longius; **no longer** nōn iam ♦ vi: **~ for** dēsīderāre, exoptāre, expetere; **~ to** gestīre
longevity n vīvācitās f
longing n dēsīderium nt, cupīdō f ♦ adj avidus
longingly adv avidē
longitudinally adv in longitūdinem
long-lived adj vīvāx
long-suffering adj patiēns
long-winded adj verbōsus, longus
longwise adv in longitūdinem

look n aspectus m; (expression) vultus m ♦ vi aspicere; (seem) vidērī, speciem praebēre; **~ about** circumspicere; **~ after** prōvidēre (dat), cūrāre; **~ at** spectāre ad (acc), aspicere, intuērī; (with mind) contemplārī; **~ back** respicere; **~ down on** dēspectāre; (fig) dēspicere; **~ for** quaerere, petere; **~ forward to** exspectāre; **~ here** heus tu, ehodum; **~ into** īnspicere, intrōspicere; **~ out** prōspicere; (beware) cavēre; **~ round** circumspicere; **~ through** perspicere; **~ to** ratiōnem habēre (gen); (leader) spem pōnere in (abl); **~ up** suspicere; **~ up to** suspicere; **~ upon** habēre
looker-on n arbiter m
lookout n (place) specula f; (man) vigil m, excubiae fpl
looks npl speciēs f; **good ~** fōrma f, pulchritūdō f
loom n tēla f ♦ vi in cōnspectum sē dare
loop n orbis m, sinus m
loophole n fenestra f
loose adj laxus, solūtus, remissus; (morally) dissolūtus; **let ~** on immittere in (acc) ♦ vt (undo) solvere; (slacken) laxāre
loosely adv solūtē, remissē
loosen vt (re)solvere; (structure) labefacere
looseness n dissolūtiō f, dissolūtī mōrēs mpl
loot n praeda f, rapīna f
lop vt amputāre
lopsided adj inaequālis
loquacious adj loquāx
loquacity n loquācitās f
lord n dominus m ♦ vi: **~ it** dominārī
lordliness n superbia f
lordly adj superbus; (rank) nōbilis
lordship n dominātiō f, imperium nt
lore n litterae fpl, doctrīna f
lose vt āmittere, perdere; **~ an eye** alterō oculō capī; **~ heart** animum dēspondēre; **~ one's way** deerrāre ♦ vi (in contest) vincī
loss n damnum nt, dētrīmentum nt; **be at a ~** haerēre, haesitāre; **suffer ~** damnum accipere, facere; **losses** (in battle) caesī mpl
lost adj āmissus, absēns; **be ~** perīre, interīre; **give up for ~** dēplōrāre
lot n sors f; **be assigned by lot** sorte obvenīre; **draw a lot** sortem dūcere; **draw lots for** sortīrī; **a lot of** multus, plūrimus
loth adj invītus
lottery n sortēs fpl; (fig) ālea f
lotus n lōtos f
loud adj clārus, māgnus
loudly adv māgnā vōce
loudness n māgna vōx f
lounge vi ōtiārī
louse n pedis m/f
lout n agrestis m
lovable adj amābilis
love n amor m; **be hopelessly in ~** dēperīre; **fall in ~ with** adamāre ♦ vt amāre, dīligere; **I ~ to** mē iuvat (inf)
love affair n amor m
loveless adj amōre carēns
loveliness n grātia f, venustās f
lovely adj pulcher, amābilis, venustus
love poem n carmen amātōrium nt
lover n amāns m, amātor m

lovesick *adj* amōre aeger
loving *adj* amāns
lovingly *adv* amanter
low *adj* humilis; (*birth*) ignōbilis; (*price*) vīlis; (*sound*) gravis; (*spirits*) dēmissus; (*voice*) dēmissus; **at low water** aestūs dēcessū; **be low** iacēre; **lay low** interficere ♦ *vi* mūgīre
lower *adj* īnferior; **the ~ world** īnferī *mpl*; **of the ~ world** īnfernus ♦ *adv* īnferius ♦ *vt* dēmittere, dēprimere ♦ *vi* (*cloud*) obscūrārī, minārī
lowering *adj* mināx
lowest *adj* īnfimus, īmus
lowing *n* mūgītus *m*
lowland *adj* campestris
lowlands *n* campī *mpl*
lowliness *n* humilitās *f*
lowly *adj* humilis, obscūrus
low-lying *adj* dēmisssus; **be ~** sedēre
lowness *n* humilitās *f*; (*spirit*) tristitia *f*
loyal *adj* fidēlis, fīdus; (*citizen*) bonus
loyally *adv* fidēliter
loyalty *n* fidēs *f*, fidēlitās *f*
lubricate *vt* ungere
lucid *adj* clārus, perspicuus
lucidity *n* perspicuitās *f*
lucidly *adv* clārē, perspicuē
luck *n* fortūna *f*, fors *f*; **good ~** fēlicitās *f*; **bad ~** īnfortūnium *nt*
luckily *adv* fēlīciter, faustē, prosperē
luckless *adj* īnfēlīx
lucky *adj* fēlīx, fortūnātus; (*omen*) faustus
lucrative *adj* quaestuōsus
lucre *n* lucrum *nt*, quaestus *m*
lucubration *n* lūcubrātiō *f*
ludicrous *adj* rīdiculus
ludicrously *adv* rīdiculē
lug *vt* trahere
luggage *n* impedīmenta *ntpl*, sarcina *f*
lugubrious *adj* lūgubris, maestus
lukewarm *adj* tepidus; (*fig*) segnis, neglegēns; **be ~** tepēre
lukewarmly *adv* segniter, neglegenter

lukewarmness *n* tepor *m*; (*fig*) neglegentia *f*, incūria *f*
lull *vt* sōpīre; (*storm*) sēdāre ♦ *n* intermissiō *f*
lumber *n* scrūta *ntpl*
luminary *n* lūmen *nt*, astrum *nt*
luminous *adj* lūcidus, illūstris
lump *n* massa *f*; (*on body*) tuber *nt*
lumpish *adj* hebes, crassus, stolidus
lunacy *n* īnsānia *f*
lunar *adj* lūnāris
lunatic *n* īnsānus *m*
lunch *n* prandium *nt* ♦ *vi* prandēre
lung *n* pulmō *m*; (*pl*, RHET) latera *ntpl*
lunge *n* ictus *m* ♦ *vi* prōsilīre
lurch *n*: **leave in the ~** dērelinquere, dēstituere ♦ *vi* titubāre
lure *n* esca *f* ♦ *vt* allicere, illicere, ēlicere
lurid *adj* lūridus
lurk *vi* latēre, latitāre, dēlitēscere
luscious *adj* praedulcis
lush *adj* luxuriōsus
lust *n* libīdō *f* ♦ *vi* libīdine flagrāre, concupīscere
lustful *adj* libīdinōsus
lustily *adv* validē, strēnuē
lustiness *n* vigor *m*, nervī *mpl*
lustration *n* lūstrum *nt*
lustre *n* fulgor *m*, splendor *m*
lustrous *adj* illūstris
lusty *adj* validus, lacertōsus
lute *n* cithara *f*, fidēs *fpl*
lute player *n* citharista *m*, citharistria *f*, fidicen *m*, fidicina *f*
luxuriance *n* luxuria *f*
luxuriant *adj* luxuriōsus
luxuriate *vi* luxuriārī
luxuries *npl* lautitiae *fpl*
luxurious *adj* luxuriōsus, sūmptuōsus, lautus
luxuriously *adv* sūmptuōsē, lautē
luxury *n* luxuria *f*, luxus *m*
lynx *n* lynx *m/f*; **lynx-eyed** lyncēus
lyre *n* lyra *f*, fidēs *fpl*; **play the ~** fidibus canere
lyric *adj* lyricus ♦ *n* carmen *nt*
lyrist *n* fidicen *m*, fidicina *f*

Mm

mace *n* scīpiō *m*
machination *n* dolus *m*
machine *n* māchina *f*
mackerel *n* scomber *m*
mad *adj* īnsānus, furiōsus, vēcors, dēmēns; **be mad** īnsānīre, furere
madam *n* domina *f*
madden *vt* furiāre, mentem aliēnāre *(dat)*
madly *adv* īnsānē, furiōsē, dēmenter
madness *n* īnsānia *f*, furor *m*, dēmentia *f*; *(animals)* rabiēs *f*
maelstrom *n* vertex *m*
magazine *n* horreum *nt*, apothēca *f*
maggot *n* vermiculus *m*
magic *adj* magicus ♦ *n* magicae artēs *fpl*
magician *n* magus *m*, veneficus *m*
magistracy *n* magistrātus *m*
magistrate *n* magistrātus *m*
magnanimity *n* māgnanimitās *f*, līberalitās *f*
magnanimous *adj* generōsus, līberālis, māgnanimus
magnet *n* magnēs *m*
magnificence *n* māgnificentia *f*, adparātus *m*
magnificent *adj* māgnificus, amplus, splendidus
magnificently *adv* māgnificē, amplē, splendidē
magnify *vt* amplificāre, exaggerāre
magnitude *n* māgnitūdō *f*
magpie *n* pīca *f*
maid *n* virgō *f*; *(servant)* ancilla *f*
maiden *n* virgō *f*
maidenhood *n* virginitās *f*
maidenly *adj* virginālis
mail *n* *(armour)* lōrīca *f*; *(letters)* epistulae *fpl*
maim *vt* mutilāre
maimed *adj* mancus
main *adj* prīnceps, prīmus; **~ point** caput *nt* ♦ *n* *(sea)* altum *nt*, pelagus *nt*; **with might and ~** manibus pedibusque, omnibus nervīs
mainland *n* continēns *f*
mainly *adv* praecipuē, plērumque
maintain *vt* *(keep)* tenēre, servāre; *(keep up)* sustinēre; *(keep alive)* alere, sustentāre; *(argue)* adfirmāre, dēfendere
maintenance *n* *(food)* alimentum *nt*
majestic *adj* augustus, māgnificus
majestically *adv* augustē
majesty *n* māiestās *f*
major *adj* māior
majority *n* māior pars *f*, plērīque; **have attained one's ~** suī iūris esse

make *vt* facere, fingere; *(appointment)* creāre; *(bed)* sternere; *(cope)* superāre; *(compulsion)* cōgere; *(consequence)* efficere; *(craft)* fabricārī; *(harbour)* capere; *(living)* quaerere; *(sum)* efficere; *(with adj)* reddere; *(with verb)* cōgere; **~ away with** tollere, interimere; **~ good** supplēre, resarcīre; **~ light of** parvī facere; **~ one's way** iter facere; **~ much of** māgnī aestimāre, multum tribuere *(dat)*; **~ for** petere; **~ out** arguere; **~ over** dēlēgāre, trānsferre; **~ ready** parāre; **~ a speech** ōrātiōnem habēre; **~ a truce** indutiās compōnere; **~ war on** bellum inferre; **~ up** *(loss)* supplēre; *(total)* efficere; *(story)* fingere; **be made** fierī
make-believe *n* simulātiō *f*
maker *n* fabricātor *m*, auctor *m*
make-up *n* medicāmina *ntpl*
maladministration *n* *(charge)* repetundae *fpl*
malady *n* morbus *m*
malcontent *adj* novārum rērum cupidus
male *adj* mās, māsculus
malefactor *n* nocēns *m*, reus *m*
malevolence *n* malevolentia *f*
malevolent *adj* malevolus, malignus
malevolently *adv* malignē
malformation *n* dēprāvātiō *f*
malice *n* invidia *f*, malevolentia *f*; **bear ~ towards** invidēre *(dat)*
malicious *adj* invidiōsus, malevolus, malignus
maliciously *adv* malignē
malign *adj* malignus, invidiōsus ♦ *vt* obtrectāre
malignant *adj* malevolus
maligner *n* obtrectātor *m*
malignity *n* malevolentia *f*
malleable *adj* ductilis
mallet *n* malleus *m*
mallow *n* malva *f*
malpractices *n* dēlicta *ntpl*
maltreat *vt* laedere, vexāre
malversation *n* pecūlātus *m*
man *n* *(human being)* homō *m/f*; *(male)* vir *m*; *(MIL)* mīles *m*; *(chess)* latrunculus *m*; **to a man** omnēs ad ūnum; **man who** is quī; **old man** senex *m*; **young man** adulēscēns *m*; **man of war** nāvis longa *f* ♦ *vt* *(ship)* complēre; *(walls)* praesidiō firmāre
manacle *n* manicae *fpl* ♦ *vt* manicās inicere *(dat)*
manage *vt* efficere, gerere, gubernāre, administrāre; *(horse)* moderārī; *(with verb)* posse
manageable *adj* tractābilis, habilis
management *n* administrātiō *f*, cūra *f*; *(finance)* dispēnsātiō *f*

manager n administrātor m, moderātor m; dispēnsātor m
mandate n mandātum nt
mane n iuba f
manful adj virīlis, fortis
manfully adv virīliter, fortiter
manger n praesēpe nt
mangle vt dīlaniāre, lacerāre
mangy adj scaber
manhood n pūbertās f, toga virīlis f
mania n īnsānia f
maniac n furiōsus m
manifest adj manifestus, apertus, clārus ♦ vt dēclārāre, aperīre
manifestation n speciēs f
manifestly adv manifestō, apertē
manifesto n ēdictum nt
manifold adj multiplex, varius
manikin n homunciō m, homunculus m
manipulate vt tractāre
manipulation n tractātiō f
mankind n hominēs mpl, genus hūmānum nt
manliness n virtūs f
manly adj fortis, virīlis
manner n modus m, ratiō f; (custom) mōs m, ūsus m; **manners** pl mōrēs mpl; **after the ~ of** rītū, mōre (gen); **good manners** hūmānitās f, modestia f
mannered adj mōrātus
mannerism n mōs m
mannerly adj bene mōrātus, urbānus
manoeuvre n (MIL) dēcursus m, dēcursiō f; (fig) dolus m ♦ vi dēcurrere; (fig) māchinārī
manor n praedium nt
mansion n domus f
manslaughter n homicīdium nt
mantle n pallium nt; (women's) palla f
manual adj: ~ **labour** opera f ♦ n libellus m, ars f
manufacture n fabrica f ♦ vt fabricārī
manumission n manūmissiō f
manumit vt manū mittere, ēmancipāre
manure n fimus m, stercus nt ♦ vt stercorāre
manuscript n liber m, cōdex m
many adj multi; **as ~ as** tot ... quot; **how many?** quot?; **so ~** tot; **in ~ places** multifāriam; **a good ~** complūrēs; **too ~** nimis multī; **the ~** vulgus nt; **very ~** permultī, plūrimī
map n tabula f ♦ vt: **map out** dēscrībere, dēsignāre
maple n acer nt ♦ adj acernus
mar vt corrumpere, dēfōrmāre
marauder n praedātor m, dēpopulātor m
marble n marmor nt ♦ adj marmoreus
March n mēnsis Martius m; **of ~** Martius
march n iter nt; **line of ~** agmen nt; **by forced marches** māgnīs itineribus; **on the ~** ex itinere, in itinere; **quick ~** plēnō gradū; **a regular day's ~** iter iūstum nt ♦ vi contendere, iter facere, incēdere, īre; **~ out** exīre; **~ on** signa prōferre, prōgredī ♦ vt dūcere; **~ out** ēdūcere; **~ in** intrōdūcere
mare n equa f
margin n margō f; (fig) discrīmen nt
marigold n caltha f
marine adj marīnus ♦ n mīles classicus m
mariner n nauta m

marital adj marītus
maritime adj maritimus
marjoram n amāracus m
mark n nota f; (of distinction) īnsigne nt; (target) scopos m; (trace) vestīgium nt; **beside the ~** nihil ad rem; **it is the ~ of a wise man to** sapientis est (inf); **be wide of the ~** errāre ♦ vt notāre, dēsignāre; (observe) animadvertere, animum attendere; ~ **out** (site) mētārī, dēsignāre; (for purpose) dēnotāre
marked adj īnsignis, manifestus
markedly adv manifestō
marker n index m
market n macellum nt; ~ **day** nūndinae fpl; ~ **town** emporium nt; **cattle ~** forum boārium nt; **fish ~** forum piscārium nt
marketable adj vēndibilis
marketplace n forum nt
market prices npl annōna f
market town n emporium nt
marking n macula f
maroon vt dērelinquere
marriage n mātrimōnium nt, coniugium nt; (ceremony) nūptiae fpl; **give in ~** collocāre; ~ **bed** lectus geniālis m
marriageable adj nūbilis
marrow n medulla f
marry vt (a wife) dūcere, in mātrimōnium dūcere; (a husband) nūbere (dat)
marsh n palūs f
marshal n imperātor m ♦ vt īnstruere
marshy adj palūster
mart n forum nt
marten n mēlēs f
martial adj bellicōsus, ferōx
martyr n dēvōtus m; (ECCL) martyr m/f
marvel n mīrāculum nt, portentum nt ♦ vi mīrārī; ~ **at** admīrārī
marvellous adj mīrus, mīrificus, mīrābilis
marvellously adv mīrē, mīrum quantum
masculine adj mās, virīlis
mash n farrāgō f ♦ vt commiscēre, contundere
mask n persōna f ♦ vt persōnam induere (dat); (fig) dissimulāre
mason n structor m
masonry n lapidēs mpl, caementum nt
masquerade n simulātiō f ♦ vi vestem mūtāre; ~ **as** speciem sibi induere (gen), persōnam ferre (gen)
mass n mōlēs f; (of small things) congeriēs f; (of people) multitūdō f; (ECCL) missa f; **the masses** vulgus nt, plēbs f ♦ vt congerere, coacervāre
massacre n strāgēs f, caedēs f, interneciō f ♦ vt trucīdāre
massive adj ingēns, solidus
massiveness n mōlēs f, soliditās f
mast n mālus m
master n dominus m; (school) magister m; **be ~ of** dominārī in (abl); (skill) perītum esse (gen); **become ~ of** potīrī (abl); **be one's own ~** suī iūris esse; **not ~ of** impotēns (gen); **a past ~** veterātor m ♦ vt dēvincere; (skill) ēdiscere; (passion) continēre
masterful adj imperiōsus
masterly adj doctus, perītus
masterpiece n praeclārum opus nt

mastery n dominātiō f, imperium nt, arbitrium nt
masticate vt mandere
mastiff n Molossus m
mat n storea f
match n (person) pār m/f; (marriage) nūptiae fpl; (contest) certāmen nt; **a ~ for** pār (dat); **no ~ for** impār (dat) ◆ vt exaequāre, adaequāre ◆ vi congruere
matchless adj singulāris, ūnicus
mate n socius m; (married) coniunx m/f ◆ vi coniungī
material adj corporeus; (significant) haud levis ◆ n māteriēs f; (literary) silva f
materialize vi ēvenīre
materially adv māgnopere
maternal adj māternus
mathematical adj mathēmaticus
mathematician n mathēmaticus m, geōmetrēs m
mathematics n ars mathēmatica f, numerī mpl
matin adj mātūtīnus
matricide n (act) mātricīdium nt; (person) mātricīda m
matrimony n mātrimōnium nt
matrix n fōrma f
matron n mātrōna f
matter n māteria f, corpus nt; (affair) rēs f; (MED) pūs nt; **what is the ~ with you?** quid tibī est? ◆ vi: **it matters** interest, rēfert
matting n storea f
mattock n dolābra f
mattress n culcita f
mature adj mātūrus; (age) adultus ◆ vi mātūrēscere
maturity n mātūritās f; (age) adulta aetās f
maul n fistūca f ◆ vt contundere, dīlaniāre
maw n ingluviēs f
mawkish adj pūtidus
mawkishly adv pūtidē
maxim n dictum nt, praeceptum nt, sententia f
maximum adj quam māximus, quam plūrimus
May n mēnsis Māius m; **of May** Māius
may vi posse; **I may** licet mihī
mayor n praefectus m
maze n labyrinthus m
mead n (drink) mulsum nt; (land) prātum nt
meagre adj exīlis, iēiūnus
meagrely adv exīliter, iēiūnē
meagreness n exīlitās f
meal n (flour) farīna f; (repast) cibus m
mealy-mouthed adj blandiloquus
mean adj humilis, abiectus; (birth) ignōbilis; (average) medius, mediocris ◆ n modus m, mediocritās f ◆ vt dīcere, significāre; (word) valēre; (intent) velle, in animō habēre
meander vi sinuōsō cursū fluere
meaning n significātiō f, vīs f, sententia f; **what is the ~ of?** quid sibī vult?, quōrsum spectat?
meanly adv abiectē, humiliter
meanness n humilitās f; (conduct) illīberālitās f, avāritia f
means n īnstrūmentum nt; (of doing) facultās f; (wealth) opēs fpl; **by ~ of** per (acc); **by all ~ māximē**; **by no ~** nūllō modō, haudquāquam; **of small ~** pauper

meantime, meanwhile adv intereā, interim
measles n boa f
measure n modus m, mēnsūra f; (rhythm) numerī mpl; (plan) cōnsilium nt; (LAW) rogātiō f, lēx f; **beyond ~** nimium; **in some ~** aliquā ex parte; **take measures** cōnsulere; **take the ~ of** quālis sit cognōscere; **without ~** immoderātē ◆ vt mētīrī; **~ out** dīmētīrī; (land) mētārī
measured adj moderātus
measureless adj īnfīnītus, immēnsus
measurement n mēnsūra f
meat n carō f
mechanic n opifex m, faber m
mechanical adj mēchanicus
mechanical device māchinātiō f
mechanics n māchinālis scientia f
mechanism n māchinātiō f
medal n īnsigne nt
meddle vi sē interpōnere
meddlesome adj cūriōsus
Medes n Mēdī mpl
mediate vi intercēdere; **~ between** compōnere, conciliāre
mediator n intercessor m, dēprecātor m
medical adj medicus
medicate vt medicāre
medicinal adj medicus, salūbris
medicine n (art) medicīna f; (drug) medicāmentum nt
medicine chest n narthēcium nt
mediocre adj mediocris
mediocrity n mediocritās f
meditate vi meditārī, cōgitāre, sēcum volūtāre
meditation n cōgitātiō f, meditātiō f
medium n internūntius m; (means) modus m ◆ adj mediocris
medley n farrāgō f
meek adj mītis, placidus
meekly adv summissō animō
meet adj idōneus, aptus ◆ n conventus m ◆ vi convenīre ◆ vt obviam īre (dat), occurrere (dat); (fig) obīre; **~ with** invenīre, excipere
meeting n cōnsilium nt, conventus m
melancholic adj melancholicus
melancholy n ātra bīlis f; tristitia f, maestitia f ◆ adj tristis, maestus
mêlée n turba f, concursus m
mellow adj mītis; (wine) lēnis; **become ~** mītēscere; **make ~** mītigāre
mellowness n mātūritās f
melodious adj canōrus, numerōsus
melodiously adv numerōsē
melody n melos nt, modī mpl
melt vt liquefacere, dissolvere; (fig) movēre ◆ vi liquēscere, dissolvī; (fig) commovērī; **~ away** dēliquēscere
member n membrum nt; (person) socius m
membrane n membrāna f
memento n monumentum nt
memoir n commentārius m
memorable adj memorābilis, commemorābilis
memorandum n hypomnēma nt
memorial n monumentum nt
memorize vt ēdiscere
memory n memoria f; **from ~** memoriter

menace *n* minae *fpl* ◆ *vt* minārī, minitārī;
(*things*) imminēre (*dat*)
menacing *adj* mināx
menacingly *adv* mināciter
menage *n* familia *f*
mend *vt* sarcīre, reficere ◆ *vi* meliōrem fierī;
(*health*) convalēscere
mendacious *adj* mendāx
mendacity *n* mendācium *nt*
mendicant *n* mendīcus *m*
mendicity *n* mendīcitās *f*
menial *adj* servīlis, famulāris ◆ *n* servus *m*,
famulus *m*
menstrual *adj* mēnstruus
mensuration *n* mētiendī ratiō *f*
mental *adj* cōgitātiōnis, mentis
mentality *n* animī adfectus *m*, mēns *f*
mentally *adv* cōgitātiōne, mente
mention *n* mentiō *f* ◆ *vt* memorāre, mentiōnem
facere (*gen*); (*casually*) inicere; (*briefly*) attingere;
omit to ~ praetermittere
mentor *n* auctor *m*, praeceptor *m*
mercantile *adj* mercātōrius
mercenary *adj* mercennārius, vēnālis ◆ *n*
mercennārius mīles *m*
merchandise *n* mercēs *fpl*
merchant *n* mercātor *m*
merchantman *n* nāvis onerāria *f*
merchant ship *n* nāvis onerāria *f*
merciful *adj* misericors, clēmens
mercifully *adv* clēmenter
merciless *adj* immisericors, inclēmens,
inhūmānus
mercilessly *adv* inhūmānē
mercurial *adj* hilaris
mercy *n* misericordia *f*, clēmentia *f*, venia *f*; **at
the ~ of** obnoxius (*dat*), in manū (*gen*)
mere *n* lacus *m* ◆ *adj* merus, ipse
merely *adv* sōlum, tantum, dumtaxat
meretricious *adj* meretricius; ~ **attractions**
lēnōcinia *ntpl*
merge *vt* cōnfundere ◆ *vi* cōnfundī
meridian *n* merīdiēs *m* ◆ *adj* merīdiānus
merit *n* meritum *nt*, virtūs *f* ◆ *vt* merērī
meritorious *adj* laudābilis
meritoriously *adv* optimē
mermaid *n* nympha *f*
merrily *adv* hilare, festīvē
merriment *n* hilaritās *f*, festīvitās *f*
merry *adj* hilaris, festīvus; **make ~** lūdere
merrymaking *n* lūdus *m*, festīvitās *f*
mesh *n* macula *f*
mess *n* (*dirt*) sordēs *f*, squālor *m*; (*trouble*) turba *f*;
(*food*) cibus *m*; (MIL) contubernālēs *mpl*
message *n* nūntius *m*
messenger *n* nūntius *m*
messmate *n* contubernālis *m*
metal *n* metallum *nt* ◆ *adj* ferreus, aereus
metamorphose *vt* mūtāre, trānsfōrmāre
metamorphosis *n* mūtātiō *f*
metaphor *n* trānslātiō *f*
metaphorical *adj* trānslātus
metaphorically *adv* per trānslātiōnem
metaphysics *n* dialectica *ntpl*
mete *vt* mētīrī
meteor *n* fax caelestis *f*

meteorology *n* prognōstica *ntpl*
methinks *vi*: ~ **I am** mihī videor esse
method *n* ratiō *f*, modus *m*
methodical *adj* dispositus; (*person*) dīligēns
methodically *adv* dispositē
meticulous *adj* accūrātus
meticulously *adv* accūrātē
meticulousness *n* cūra *f*
metonymy *n* immūtātiō *f*
metre *n* numerī *mpl*, modī *mpl*
metropolis *n* urbs *f*
mettle *n* ferōcitās *f*, virtūs *f*
mettlesome *adj* ferōx, animōsus
mew *n* (*bird*) larus *m*; **mews** *pl* stabula *ntpl* ◆ *vi*
vāgīre
miasma *n* hālitus *m*
mid *adj* medius ◆ *prep* inter (*acc*)
midday *n* merīdiēs *m* ◆ *adj* merīdiānus
middle *adj* medius ◆ *n* medium *nt*; **in the
~** medius, in mediō; **~ of** medius
middling *adj* mediocris
midge *n* culex *m*
midget *n* (*offensive*) pūmiliō *m/f*
midland *adj* mediterrāneus
midnight *n* media nox *f*
midriff *n* praecordia *ntpl*
midst *n* medium *nt*; **in the ~** medius; **in the ~ of**
inter (*acc*); **through the ~ of** per medium
midsummer *n* sōlstitium *nt* ◆ *adj* sōlstitiālis
midway *adv* medius
midwife *n* obstetrix *f*
midwinter *n* brūma *f* ◆ *adj* brūmālis
mien *n* aspectus *m*, vultus *m*
might *n* vīs *f*, potentia *f*; **with ~ and main**
omnibus nervīs, manibus pedibusque
mightily *adv* valdē, magnopere
mighty *adj* ingēns, validus
migrate *vi* abīre, migrāre
migration *n* peregrīnātiō *f*
migratory *adj* advena
mild *adj* mītis, lēnis, clēmēns
mildew *n* rōbīgō *f*
mildly *adv* lēniter, clēmenter
mildness *n* clēmentia *f*, mānsuētūdō *f*; (*weather*)
caelī indulgentia *f*
mile *n* mīlle passūs *mpl*; **miles** *pl* mīlia passuum
milestone *n* lapis *m*, mīliārium *nt*
militant *adj* ferōx
military *adj* mīlitāris ◆ *n* mīlitēs *mpl*
military service *n* mīlitia *f*
militate *vi*: ~ **against** repugnāre (*dat*), facere
contrā (*acc*)
militia *n* mīlitēs *mpl*
milk *n* lac *nt* ◆ *vt* mulgēre
milk pail *n* mulctra *f*
milky *adj* lacteus
mill *n* pistrīnum *nt*
milled *adj* (*coin*) serrātus
millennium *n* mīlle annī *mpl*
miller *n* pistor *m*
millet *n* mīlium *nt*
million *num* deciēs centēna mīlia *ntpl*
millionaire *n* rēx *m*
millstone *n* mola *f*, molāris *m*
mime *n* mīmus *m*
mimic *n* imitātor *m*, imitātrīx *f* ◆ *vt* imitārī

mimicry n imitātiō f
minatory adj mināx
mince vt concīdere; **not ~ words** plānē
apertēque dīcere ♦ n minūtal nt
mind n mēns f, animus m, ingenium nt; (opinion)
sententia f; (memory) memoria f; **be in one's
right ~** mentis suae esse; **be of the same
~** eadem sentīre; **be out of one's ~** īnsanīre;
bear in ~ meminisse (gen), memorem esse (gen);
call to ~ memoriā repetere, recordārī; **have
a ~ to** libet; **have in ~** in animō habēre; **put
one's ~ to** animum applicāre ad (acc); **make up
one's ~** animum indūcere, animō obstināre,
statuere; **put in ~ of** admonēre (gen); **speak
one's ~** sententiam suam aperīre; **to one's ~** ex
sententiā ♦ vt cūrāre, attendere; **~ one's own
business** suum negōtium agere ♦ vi gravārī; **I
don't ~** nīl moror; **never ~** mitte
minded adj animātus
mindful adj memor
mine n metallum nt; (MIL) cuniculus m; (fig)
thēsaurus m ♦ vi fodere; (MIL) cuniculum agere
♦ pron meus
miner n fossor m
mineral n metallum nt
mingle vt miscēre, commiscēre ♦ vi sē
immiscēre
miniature n minima pictūra f
minimize vt dētrectāre
minimum n minimum nt ♦ adj quam minimus
minion n cliēns m/f, dēlicātus m
minister n administer m ♦ vi ministrāre, servīre
ministry n mūnus nt, officium nt
minor adj minor ♦ n pupillus m, pupilla f
minority n minor pars f; **in one's ~** nōndum
suī iūris
Minotaur n Mīnōtaurus m
minstrel n fidicen m
minstrelsy n cantus m
mint n (plant) menta f; (money) Monēta f ♦ vt
cūdere
minute¹ n temporis mōmentum nt
minute² adj minūtus, exiguus, subtīlis
minutely adv subtīliter
minuteness n exiguitās f, subtīlitas f
minutiae n singula ntpl
minx n lascīva f
miracle n mīrāculum nt, mōnstrum nt
miraculous adj mīrus, mīrābilis
miraculously adv dīvīnitus
mirage n falsa speciēs f
mire n lutum nt
mirror n speculum nt ♦ vt reddere
mirth n hilaritās f, laetitia f
mirthful adj hilaris, laetus
mirthfully adv hilare, laetē
miry adj lutulentus
misadventure n īnfortūnium nt, cāsus m
misapply vt abūtī (abl); (words) invertere
misapprehend vt male intellegere
misapprehension n error m
misappropriate vt intervertere
misbegotten adj nothus
misbehave vi male sē gerere
miscalculate vi errāre, fallī
miscalculation n error m

miscall vt maledīcere (dat)
miscarriage n abortus m; (fig) error m
miscarry vi aborīrī; (fig) cadere, inritum esse
miscellaneous adj prōmiscuus, varius
miscellany n farrāgō f
mischance n īnfortūnium nt
mischief n malum nt, facinus nt, maleficīum nt;
(children) lascīvia f
mischievous adj improbus, maleficus; lascīvus
misconceive vt male intellegere
misconception n error m
misconduct n dēlictum nt, culpa f
misconstruction n prāva interpretātiō f
misconstrue vt male interpretārī
miscreant n scelerātus m
misdeed n maleficium nt, dēlictum nt
misdemeanour n peccātum nt, culpa f
miser n avārus m
miserable adj miser, īnfēlīx; **make oneself ~** sē
cruciāre
miserably adv miserē
miserliness n avāritia f
miserly adj avārus
misery n miseria f, aerumna f
misfortune n malum nt, īnfortūnium nt,
incommodum nt, rēs adversae fpl
misgiving n suspiciō f, cūra f; **have misgivings**
parum cōnfīdere
misgovern vt male regere
misgovernment n prāva administrātiō f
misguide vt fallere, dēcipere
misguided adj dēmēns
mishap n īnfortūnium nt
misinform vt falsa docēre
misinterpret vt male interpretārī
misinterpretation n prāva interpretātiō f
misjudge vt male iūdicāre
mislay vt āmittere
mislead vt dēcipere, indūcere, auferre
mismanage vt male gerere
misnomer n falsum nōmen nt
misogyny n mulierum odium nt
misplace vt in aliēnō locō collocāre
misplaced adj (fig) vānus
misprint n mendum nt
mispronounce vt prāvē appellāre
misquote vt perperam prōferre
misrepresent vt dētorquēre, invertere; (person)
calumniārī
misrepresentation n calumnia f
misrule n prāva administrātiō f
miss vt (aim) aberrāre (abl); (loss) requīrere,
dēsīderāre; (notice) praetermittere ♦ n error m;
(girl) virgō f
misshapen adj distortus, dēfōrmis
missile n tēlum nt
missing adj absēns; **be ~** dēesse, dēsīderārī
mission n lēgātiō f
missive n litterae fpl
misspend vt perdere, dissipāre
misstatement n falsum nt, mendācium nt
mist n nebula f, cālīgō f
mistake n error m; (writing) mendum nt; **full of
mistakes** mendōsus ♦ vt: **~ for** habēre prō (abl);
be mistaken errāre, fallī
mistletoe n viscum nt

mistranslate vt prāvē reddere
mistress n domina f; (school) magistra f; (lover) amīca f
mistrust n diffīdentia f, suspiciō f ♦ vt diffīdere (dat)
mistrustful adj diffīdēns
mistrustfully adv diffīdenter
misty adj nebulōsus
misunderstand vt male intellegere ♦ vi errāre
misunderstanding n error m; (quarrel) discidium nt
misuse n malus ūsus m ♦ vt abūtī (abl)
mite n parvulus m; (insect) vermiculus m
mitigate vt mītigāre, lēnīre
mitigation n mītigātiō f
mix vt miscēre; **mix in** admiscēre; **mix together** commiscēre; **get mixed up with** admiscērī cum, sē interpōnere (dat)
mixed adj prōmiscuus
mixture n (act) temperātiō f; (state) dīversitās f
mnemonic n artificium memoriae nt
moan n gemitus m ♦ vi gemere
moat n fossa f
mob n vulgus nt, turba f ♦ vt circumfundī in (acc)
mobile adj mōbilis, agilis
mobility n mōbilitās f, agilitās f
mobilize vt (MIL) ēvocāre
mock vt irrīdēre, lūdibriō habēre, lūdificārī; (ape) imitārī; ~ **at** inlūdere ♦ n lūdibrium nt ♦ adj simulātus, fictus
mocker n dērīsor m
mockery n lūdibrium nt, irrīsus m
mode n modus m, ratiō f
model n exemplar nt, exemplum nt ♦ vt fingere
modeller n fictor m
moderate adj (size) modicus; (conduct) moderātus ♦ vt temperāre; (emotion) temperāre (dat) ♦ vi mītigārī
moderately adv modicē, moderātē, mediocriter
moderation n moderātiō f, modus m; (mean) mediocritās f
moderator n praefectus m
modern adj recēns
modernity n haec aetās f
modest adj pudīcus, verēcundus
modestly adv verēcundē, pudenter
modesty n pudor m, verēcundia f
modicum n paullulum nt, aliquantulum nt
modification n mūtātiō f
modify vt immūtāre; (LAW) derogāre aliquid dē
modulate vt (voice) īnflectere
modulation n flexiō f, inclīnātiō f
moiety n dīmidia pars f
moist adj ūmidus
moisten vt ūmectāre, rigāre
moisture n ūmor m
molar n genuīnus m
mole n (animal) talpa f; (on skin) naevus m; (pier) mōlēs f
molecule n corpusculum nt
molehill n: **make a mountain out of a ~** ē rīvō flūmina māgna facere, arcem facere ē cloācā
molest vt sollicitāre, vexāre
molestation n vexātiō f
mollify vt mollīre, lēnīre
molten adj liquefactus

moment n temporis mōmentum nt, temporis pūnctum nt; **for a ~** parumper; **in a ~** iam; **without a moment's delay** nullā interpositā morā; **be of great ~** māgnō mōmentō esse; **it is of ~** interest
momentary adj brevis
momentous adj gravis, māgnī mōmentī
momentum n impetus m
monarch n rēx m, tyrannus m
monarchical adj rēgius
monarchy n rēgnum nt
monastery n monastērium nt
monetary adj pecūniārius
money n pecūnia f; (cash) nummī mpl; **for ~** mercēde; **ready ~** nummī, praesēns pecūnia; **make ~** rem facere, quaestum facere
moneybag n fiscus m
moneyed adj nummātus, pecūniōsus
moneylender n faenerātor m
moneymaking n quaestus m
mongoose n ichneumōn m
mongrel n (dog) hibrida m
monitor n admonitor m
monk n monachus m
monkey n sīmia f
monograph n libellus m
monologue n ōrātiō f
monopolize vt absorbēre, sibī vindicāre
monopoly n arbitrium nt
monosyllabic adj monosyllabus
monosyllable n monosyllabum nt
monotonous adj aequābilis
monotony n taedium nt
monster n mōnstrum nt, portentum nt, bēlua f
monstrosity n mōnstrum nt
monstrous adj immānis, mōnstruōsus; improbus
month n mēnsis m
monthly adj mēnstruus
monument n monumentum nt
monumental adj ingēns
mood n adfectiō f, adfectus m, animus m; (GRAM) modus m; **I am in the ~ for** libet (inf)
moody adj mōrōsus, tristis
moon n lūna f; **new ~** interlūnium nt
moonlight n: **by ~** ad lūnam
moonshine n somnia ntpl
moonstruck adj lūnāticus
moor vt religāre ♦ n tesqua ntpl
moorings n ancorae fpl
moot n conventus m; **it is a ~ point** discrepat ♦ vt iactāre
mop n pēniculus m ♦ vt dētergēre
mope vi maerēre
moral adj honestus, probus; (opposed to physical) animī; (PHILOS) mōrālis ♦ n documentum nt
morale n animus m; **~ is low** iacet animus
morality n bonī mōrēs mpl, virtūs f
moralize vi dē officiīs disserere
morally adv honestē
morals npl mōrēs mpl
morass n palūs f
moratorium n mora f
morbid adj aeger
mordant adj mordāx

more *adj* plūs, pluris *(in sg + gen, in pl + adj)* ◆ *adv* plūs, magis, amplius; *(extra)* ultrā; ~ **than** amplius quam; ~ **than three feet** amplius trēs pedēs; ~ **and** ~ magis magisque; **never** ~ immo; ~ **or less** ferē; **no** ~ *(time)* nōn diūtius, nunquam posteā

moreover *adv* tamen, autem, praettereā

moribund *adj* moribundus

morning *n* māne *nt*; **early in the** ~ bene māne; **this** ~ hodiē māne; **good** ~ salvē ◆ *adj* mātūtīnus

morning call *n* salūtātiō *f*

morning watch *n* (NAUT) tertia vigilia *f*

moron *n* *(offensive)* sōcors *m*

morose *adj* acerbus, tristis

moroseness *n* acerbitās *f*, tristitia *f*

morrow *n* posterus diēs *m*; **on the** ~ posterō diē, postrīdiē

morsel *n* offa *f*

mortal *adj* mortālis, hūmānus; *(wound)* mortifer ◆ *n* mortālis *m/f*, homō *m/f*; **poor** ~ homunculus *m*

mortality *n* mortālitās *f*; *(death)* mors *f*; **the** ~ **was high** plūrimī periērunt

mortally *adv*: **be** ~ **wounded** mortiferum vulnus accipere

mortar *n* mortārium *nt*

mortgage *n* pignus *nt*, fīdūcia *f* ◆ *vt* obligāre

mortification *n* dolor *m*, angor *m*

mortified *adj*: **be** ~ **at** aegrē ferre

mortify *vt* mordēre, vexāre; *(lust)* coercēre ◆ *vi* putrēscere

mortise *vt* immittere

mosaic *n* emblēma *nt*, lapillī *mpl* ◆ *adj* tessellātus

mosquito *n* culex *m*

mosquito net *n* cōnōpēum *nt*

moss *n* muscus *m*

mossy *adj* muscōsus

most *adj* plūrimus, plērusque; **for the** ~ **part** māximam partem ◆ *adv* māximē, plūrimum

mostly *adv* plērumque, ferē

mote *n* corpusculum *nt*

moth *n* tinea *f*

mother *n* māter *f*; **of a** ~ māternus

mother-in-law *n* socrus *f*

motherless *adj* mātre orbus

motherly *adj* māternus

mother tongue *n* patrius sermō *m*

mother wit *n* Minerva *f*

motif *n* argūmentum *nt*

motion *n* mōtus *m*; *(for law)* rogātiō *f*; *(in debate)* sententia *f*; **propose a** ~ ferre; **set in** ~ movēre ◆ *vt* innuere

motionless *adj* immōbilis

motive *n* causa *f*, ratiō *f*; **I know your** ~ **in asking** sciō cūr rogēs

motley *adj* versicolor, varius

mottled *adj* maculōsus

motto *n* sententia *f*

mould *n* fōrma *f*; *(soil)* humus *f*; *(fungus)* mūcor *m* ◆ *vt* fingere, fōrmāre

moulder *vi* putrēscere ◆ *n* fictor *m*

mouldering *adj* puter

mouldiness *n* situs *m*

mouldy *adj* mūcidus

moult *vi* pennas exuere

mound *n* agger *m*, tumulus *m*

mount *n* mōns *m*; *(horse)* equus *m* ◆ *vt* scandere, cōnscendere, ascendere ◆ *vi* ascendere; ~ **up** ēscendere

mountain *n* mōns *m*

mountaineer *n* montānus *m*

mountainous *adj* montuōsus

mourn *vi* maerēre, lūgēre ◆ *vt* dēflēre, lūgēre

mourner *n* plōrātor *m*; *(hired)* praefica *f*

mournful *adj* *(cause)* lūctuōsus, acerbus; *(sound)* lūgubris, maestus

mournfully *adv* maestē

mourning *n* maeror *nt*, lūctus *m*; *(dress)* sordēs *fpl*; **in** ~ fūnestus; **be in** ~ lūgere; **put on** ~ vestem mūtāre, sordēs suscipere; **wearing** ~ ātrātus

mouse *n* mūs *m*

mousetrap *n* mūscipulum *nt*

mouth *n* ōs *nt*; *(river)* ōstium *nt*

mouthful *n* bucca *f*

mouthpiece *n* interpres *m*

movable *adj* mōbilis; **movables** *npl* rēs *fpl*, suppellex *f*

move *vt* movēre; *(emotion)* commovēre; ~ **backwards and forwards** reciprocāre; ~ **out of the way** dēmovēre; ~ **up** admovēre ◆ *vi* movērī; *(residence)* dēmigrāre; *(proposal)* ferre, cēnsēre; ~ **into** immigrāre in *(acc)*; ~ **on** prōgredī

movement *n* mōtus *m*; *(process)* cursus *m*; *(society)* societās *f*

mover *n* auctor *m*

moving *adj* flēbilis, flexanimus

mow *vt* secāre, dēmetere

mower *n* faenisex *m*

much *adj* multus ◆ *adv* multum; *(with compar)* multō; **as** ~ **as** tantum quantum; **so** ~ tantum; *(with verbs)* adeo; ~ **less** nēdum; **too** ~ nimis ◆ *n* multum *nt*

muck *n* stercus *nt*

mud *n* lutum *nt*

muddle *n* turba *f* ◆ *vt* turbāre

muffle *vt* involvere; ~ **up** obvolvere

muffled *adj* surdus

mug *n* pōculum *nt*

mulberry *n* mōrum *nt*; *(tree)* mōrus *f*

mule *n* mūlus *m*

muleteer *n* mūliō *m*

mulish *adj* obstinātus

mullet *n* mullus *m*

multifarious *adj* multiplex, varius

multiform *adj* multifōrmis

multiply *vt* multiplicāre ◆ *vi* crēscere

multitude *n* multitūdō *f*

multitudinous *adj* crēberrimus

mumble *vt* *(words)* opprimere ◆ *vi* murmurāre

munch *vt* mandūcāre

mundane *adj* terrestris

municipal *adj* mūnicipālis

municipality *n* mūnicipium *nt*

munificence *n* largitās *f*

munificent *adj* largus, mūnificus

munificently *adv* mūnificē

munitions *n* bellī adparātus *m*

mural *adj* mūrālis

murder n parricīdium nt, caedēs f; **charge with**
~ inter sīcāriōs accūsāre; **trial for** ~ quaestiō
inter sīcāriōs ♦ vt interficere, iūgulāre, necāre
murderer n sīcārius m, homicīda m, parricīda m,
percussor m
murderess n interfectrīx f
murderous adj cruentus
murky adj tenebrōsus
murmur n murmur nt; (angry) fremitus m ♦ vi
murmurāre; fremere
murmuring n admurmurātiō f
muscle n torus m
muscular adj lacertōsus
muse vi meditārī ♦ n Mūsa f
mushroom n fungus m, bōlētus m
music n (art) mūsica f; (sound) cantus m, modī mpl
musical adj (person) mūsicus; (sound) canōrus
musician n mūsicus m; (strings) fidicen m; (wind)
tībīcen m
muslin n sindōn f
must n (wine) mustum nt ♦ vi dēbēre; **I** ~ **go** mē
oportet īre, mihī eundum est
mustard n sināpi nt
muster vt convocāre, cōgere; (review) recēnsēre
♦ vi convenīre, coīre ♦ n conventus m; (review)
recēnsiō f
muster roll n album nt
mustiness n situs m
musty adj mūcidus
mutability n incōnstantia f
mutable adj incōnstāns, mūtābilis

mute adj mūtus
mutilate vt mūtilāre, truncāre
mutilated adj mūtilus, truncus
mutilation n lacerātiō f
mutineer n sēditiōsus m
mutinous adj sēditiōsus
mutiny n sēditiō f ♦ vi sēditiōnem facere
mutter vi mussitāre
mutton n carō ovilla f
mutual adj mūtuus
mutually adv mūtuō, inter sē
muzzle n ōs nt, rōstrum nt; (guard) fiscella f ♦ vt
fiscellā capistrāre
my adj meus
myriad n decem mīlia; (any large no.) sēscentī
myrmidon n satelles m
myrrh n murra f
myrtle n myrtus f ♦ adj myrteus
myrtle grove n myrtētum nt
myself pron ipse, egomet; (reflexive) mē
mysterious adj arcānus, occultus
mysteriously adv occultē
mystery n arcānum nt; (rites) mystēria ntpl; (fig)
latebra f
mystic adj mysticus
mystical adj mysticus
mystification n fraus f, ambāgēs fpl
mystify vt fraudāre, cōnfundere
myth n fābula f
mythical adj fābulōsus
mythology n fābulae fpl

Nn

nabob *n* rēx *m*
nadir *n* fundus *m*
nag *n* caballus *m* ♦ *vt* obiūrgītāre
naiad *n* nāias *f*
nail *n* clāvus *m*; *(finger)* unguis *m*; **hit the ~ on the head** rem acū tangere ♦ *vt* clāvīs adfīgere
naive *adj* simplex
naively *adv* simpliciter
naiveté *n* simplicitās *f*
naked *adj* nūdus
nakedly *adv* apertē
name *n* nōmen *nt*; *(repute)* existimātiō *f*; *(term)* vocābulum *nt*; **by ~** nōmine; **have a bad ~** male audīre; **have a good ~** bene audīre; **in the ~ of** verbīs *(gen)*; *(oath)* per ♦ *vt* appellāre, vocāre, nōmināre; *(appoint)* dīcere
nameless *adj* nōminis expers, sine nōmine
namely *adv* nempe, dīcō
namesake *n* gentīlis *m/f*
nanny goat *n* capra *f*
nap *n* brevis somnus *m*; *(cloth)* villus *nt*
napkin *n* linteum *nt*
narcissus *n* narcissus *m*
narcotic *adj* somnifer
nard *n* nardus *f*
narrate *vt* nārrāre, ēnārrāre
narration *n* nārrātiō *f*
narrative *n* fābula *f*
narrator *n* nārrātor *m*
narrow *adj* angustus ♦ *vt* coartāre ♦ *vi* coartārī
narrowly *adv* aegrē, vix
narrowness *n* angustiae *fpl*
narrows *n* angustiae *fpl*
nasal *adj* nārium
nascent *adj* nāscēns
nastily *adv* foedē
nastiness *n* foedītās *f*
nasty *adj* foedus, taeter, impūrus
natal *adj* nātālis
nation *n* populus *m*; *(foreign)* gēns *f*
national *adj* pūblicus, cīvīlis; *(affairs)* domesticus
nationality *n* cīvitās *f*
native *adj* indigena; *(speech)* patrius ♦ *n* incola *m*, indigena *m/f*
native land *n* patria *f*
nativity *n* ortus *m*
natural *adj* nātūrālis; *(innate)* nātīvus, genuīnus, īnsitus
naturalization *n* cīvitās *f*
naturalize *vt* cīvitāte dōnāre

naturalized *adj* *(person)* cīvitāte dōnātus; *(thing)* īnsitus
naturally *adv* nātūrāliter, secundum nātūram; *(of course)* scīlicet, certē
nature *n* nātūra *f*; rērum nātūra *f*; *(character)* indolēs *f*, ingenium *nt*; *(species)* genus *nt*; **course of ~** nātūra *f*; **I know the ~ of** sciō quālis sit
naught *n* nihil *nt*; **set at ~** parvī facere
naughty *adj* improbus
nausea *n* nausea *f*; *(fig)* fastīdium *nt*
nauseate *vt* fastīdium movēre *(dat)*; **be nauseated with** fastīdīre
nauseous *adj* taeter
nautical *adj* nauticus, maritimus
naval *adj* nāvālis
navel *n* umbilīcus *m*
navigable *adj* nāvigābilis
navigate *vt*, *vi* nāvigāre
navigation *n* rēs nautica *f*; *(sailing)* nāvigātiō *f*
navigator *n* nauta *m*, gubernātor *m*
navy *n* classis *f*, cōpiae nāvālēs *fpl*
nay *adv* nōn; **nay more** immo
near *adv* prope ♦ *adj* propinquus ♦ *prep* prope *(acc)*, ad *(acc)*; **lie ~** adiacēre *(dat)* ♦ *vt* adpropinquāre *(dat)*
nearby *adj* iuxtā
nearer *adj* propior
nearest *adj* proximus
nearly *adv* paene, prope, fermē
neat *adj* nitidus, mundus, concinnus; *(wine)* pūrus
neatly *adv* mundē, concinnē
neatness *n* munditia *f*
nebulous *adj* nebulōsus; *(fig)* incertus
necessaries *n* rēs ad vīvendum necessāriae *fpl*
necessarily *adv* necessāriō, necesse
necessary *adj* necessārius, necesse; **it is ~** oportet *(+ acc and infin or gerundive of vt)*
necessitate *vt* cōgere *(inf)*, efficere ut *(subj)*
necessitous *adj* egēnus, pauper
necessity *n* necessitās *f*; *(thing)* rēs necessāria *f*; *(want)* paupertās *f*, egestās *f*
neck *n* collum *nt*
neckcloth *n* fōcāle *nt*
necklace *n* monīle *nt*, torquis *m*
nectar *n* nectar *nt*
need *n* *(necessity)* necessitās *f*; *(want)* egestās *f*, inopia *f*, indigentia *f*; **there is ~ of** opus est *(abl)*; **there is no ~ to** nihil est quod, cūr *(subj)* ♦ *vt* egēre *(abl)*, carēre, indigēre *(abl)*; **I ~** opus est mihī *(abl)*
needful *adj* necessārius

needle n acus f
needless adj vānus, inūtilis
needlessly adv frustrā, sine causā
needs adv necesse ♦ npl necessitātēs fpl
needy adj egēns, inops, pauper
nefarious adj nefārius, scelestus
negation n negātiō f, īnfitiātiō f
negative adj negāns ♦ n negātiō f; **answer in the ~** negāre ♦ vt vetāre, contrādīcere (dat)
neglect n neglegentia f, incūria f; (of duty) dērelictiō f ♦ vt neglegere, ōmittere
neglectful adj neglegēns, immemor
negligence n neglegentia f, incūria f
negligent adj neglegēns, indīligēns
negligently adv neglegenter, indīligenter
negligible adj levissimus, minimī mōmentī
negotiate vi agere dē ♦ vt (deal) peragere; (difficulty) superāre
negotiation n āctiō f, pactum nt
negotiator n lēgātus m, conciliātor m
negro n (offensive) Aethiops m
neigh vi hinnīre
neighbour n vīcīnus m, fīnitimus m
neighbourhood n vīcīnia f, vīcīnitās f
neighbouring adj vīcīnus, fīnitimus, propinquus
neighbourly adj hūmānus, amīcus
neighing n hinnītus m
neither adv neque, nec; nēve, neu ♦ pron neuter ♦ adj neuter, neutra, neutrum (like alter); **neither... nor** nec/neque ... nec/neque
neophyte n tīrō m
nephew n frātris fīlius m, sorōris fīlius m
Nereid n Nērēis f
nerve n nervus m; (fig) audācia f; **nerves** pl pavor m, trepidātiō f; **have the ~ to** audēre ♦ vt cōnfirmāre
nervous adj diffīdēns, sollicitus, trepidus
nervously adv trepidē
nervousness n sollicitūdō f, diffīdentia f
nest n nīdus m ♦ vi nīdificāre
nestle vi recubāre
nestling n pullus m
net n rēte nt ♦ vt inrētīre
nether adj īnferior
nethermost adj īnfimus, īmus
netting n rēticulum nt
nettle n urtīca f ♦ vt inrītāre, ūrere
neuter adj neuter
neutral adj medius; **be ~** neutrī partī sē adiungere, medium sē gerere
neutralize vt compēnsāre
never adv nunquam
nevertheless adv nihilōminus, at tamen
new adj novus, integer, recēns
newcomer n advena m/f
newfangled adj novus, inaudītus
newly adv nūper, modo
newness n novitās f
news n nūntius m; **what news?** quid novī?; **~ was brought that** nūntiātum est (+ acc and infin)
newspaper n ācta diūrna/pūblica ntpl
newt n lacerta f

next adj proximus; (time) īnsequēns ♦ adv dēinde, deinceps; **~ day** postrīdiē; **~ to** iuxtā; **come ~ to** excipere
nibble vi rōdere
nice adj bellus, dulcis; (exact) accūrātus; (particular) fastīdiōsus
nicely adv bellē, probē
nicety n subtīlitās f
niche n aedicula f
nick n: **in the ~ of time** in ipsō articulō temporis
nickname n cognōmen nt
niece n frātris fīlia f, sorōris fīlia f
niggardliness n illīberālitās f, avāritia f
niggardly adj illīberālis, parcus, avārus
nigh adv prope
night n nox f; **by ~** noctū; **all ~** pernox; **spend the ~** pernoctāre; **be awake all ~** pervigilāre ♦ adj nocturnus
night bird n noctua f
nightfall n prīmae tenebrae fpl; **at ~** sub noctem
nightingale n luscinia f
nightly adj nocturnus ♦ adv noctū
nightmare n incubus m
night work n lūcubrātiō f
nimble adj agilis, pernīx
nimbleness n agilitās f, pernīcitās f; (mind) argūtiae fpl
nimbly adv pernīciter
nine num novem; **~ each** novēnī; **~ times** noviēns; **~ days'** novendiālis
nine hundred num nōngentī
nine hundredth adj nōngentēsimus
nineteen num ūndēvīgintī; **~ each** ūndēvīcēnī; **~ times** deciēns et noviēns
nineteenth adj ūndēvīcēsimus
ninetieth adj nōnāgēsimus
ninety num nōnāgintā; **~ each** nōnāgēnī; **~ times** nōnāgiēns
ninth adj nōnus
nip vt vellicāre; (frost) ūrere
nippers n forceps m
nipple n papilla f
no adv nōn; (correcting) immo; **say no** negāre ♦ adj nullus
nobility n nōbilitās f; (persons) optimātēs mpl, nōbilēs mpl
noble adj nōbilis; (birth) generōsus; (appearance) decōrus
nobleman n prīnceps m, optimās m
nobly adv nōbiliter, praeclārē
nobody n nēmō m
nocturnal adj nocturnus
nod n nūtus m ♦ vi nūtāre; (sign) adnuere; (sleep) dormītāre
noddle n caput nt
node n nōdus m
noise n strepitus m, sonitus m; (loud) fragor m; **make a ~** increpāre, strepere ♦ vt: **~ abroad** ēvulgāre; **be noised abroad** percrēbrēscere
noiseless adj tacitus
noiselessly adv tacitē
noisily adv cum strepitū
noisome adj taeter, gravis
noisy adj clāmōsus
nomadic adj vagus
nomenclature n vocābula ntpl

nominally *adv* nōmine, verbō
nominate *vt* nōmināre, dīcere; (*in writing*) scrībere
nomination *n* nōminātiō *f*
nominative *adj* nōminātīvus
nominee *n* nōminātus *m*
nonappearance *n* absentia *f*
nonce *n*: for the ~ semel
nonchalance *n* aequus animus *m*
nonchalantly *adv* aequō animō
noncombatant *adj* imbellis
noncommittal *adj* circumspectus
nondescript *adj* īnsolitus
none *adj* nullus ♦ *pron* nēmō *m*
nonentity *n* nihil *nt*, nullus *m*
nones *n* Nōnae *fpl*
nonexistent *adj* quī nōn est
nonplus *vt* ad incitās redigere
nonresistance *n* patientia *f*
nonsense *n* nūgae *fpl*, ineptiae *fpl*
nonsensical *adj* ineptus, absurdus
nook *n* angulus *m*
noon *n* merīdiēs *m* ♦ *adj* merīdiānus
no one *pron* nēmō *m*
noose *n* laqueus *m*
nor *adv* neque, nec; nēve, neu
norm *n* nōrma *f*
normal *adj* solitus
normally *adv* plērumque
north *n* septentriōnēs *mpl* ♦ *adj* septentriōnālis
northeast *adv* inter septentriōnēs et orientem
northerly *adj* septentriōnālis
northern *adj* septentriōnālis
North Pole *n* arctos *f*
northwards *adv* ad septentriōnēs versus
northwest *adv* inter septentriōnēs et occidentem ♦ *adj*: ~ **wind** Cōrus *m*
north wind *n* aquilō *m*
nose *n* nāsus *m*, nārēs *fpl*; **blow the ~** ēmungere; **lead by the ~** labiīs ductāre ♦ *vi* scrūtārī
nostril *n* nāris *f*
not *adv* nōn, haud; **not at all** haudquāquam; **not as if** nōn quod, nōn quō; **not but what** nōn quīn; **not even** nē ... quidem; **not so very** nōn ita; **not that** nōn quō; **and not** neque; **does not**, **did not** (*interrog*) nonne; **if ... not** nisi; **that not** (*purpose*) nē; (*fear*) nē nōn; **not long after** haud multō post; **not only ... but also** non modo/solum ... sed etiam; **not yet** nōndum
notability *n* vir praeclārus *m*
notable *adj* insignis, īnsignītus, memorābilis
notably *adv* īnsignītē
notary *n* scrība *m*
notation *n* notae *fpl*
notch *n* incīsūra *f* ♦ *vt* incīdere
note *n* (*mark*) nota *f*; (*comment*) adnotātiō *f*; (*letter*) litterulae *fpl*; (*sound*) vōx *f*; **make a ~ of** in commentāriōs referre ♦ *vt* notāre; (*observe*) animadvertere
notebook *n* pugillārēs *mpl*
noted *adj* insignis, praeclārus, nōtus
noteworthy *adj* memorābilis
nothing *n* nihil, nīl *nt*; ~ **but** merus, nīl nisi; **come to ~** in inritum cadere; **for ~** frustrā; (*gift*) grātīs, grātuītō; **good for ~** nēquam; **think ~ of** nihilī facere

notice *n* (*official*) prōscrīptiō *f*; (*private*) libellus *m*; **attract ~** cōnspicī; **escape ~** latēre; **escape the ~ of** fallere; **give ~ of** dēnūntiāre; **take ~ of** animadvertere ♦ *vt* animadvertere, cōnspicere
noticeable *adj* cōnspicuus, insignis
noticeably *adv* īnsignītē
notification *n* dēnūntiātiō *f*
notify *vt* (*event*) dēnūntiāre, indicāre; (*person*) renūntiāre (*dat*), certiōrem facere
notion *n* nōtiō *f*, īnfōrmātiō *f*; suspiciō *f*
notoriety *n* īnfāmia *f*
notorious *adj* fāmōsus, īnfāmis; (*thing*) manifestus
notoriously *adv* manifestō
notwithstanding *adv* nihilōminus, tamen ♦ *prep*: ~ **the danger** in tantō discrīmine
nought *n* nihil, nīl *nt*
noun *n* nōmen *nt*
nourish *vt* alere, nūtrīre
nourisher *n* altor *m*, altrīx *f*
nourishment *n* cibus *m*, alimenta *ntpl*
novel *adj* novus, inaudītus ♦ *n* fābella *f*
novelty *n* rēs nova *f*; novitās *f*, īnsolentia *f*
November *n* mēnsis November *m*; **of** ~ November
novice *n* tīrō *m*
now *adv* nunc; (*past*) iam; **now and then** interdum; **just now** nunc; (*lately*) dūdum, modo; **now ... now** modo ... modo ♦ *conj* at, autem
nowadays *adv* nunc, hodiē
nowhere *adv* nusquam
nowise *adv* nullō modō, haudquāquam
noxious *adj* nocēns, noxius
nuance *n* color *m*
nucleus *n* sēmen *nt*
nude *adj* nūdus
nudge *vt* fodicāre
nudity *n* nūdātum corpus *nt*
nugget *n* massa *f*
nuisance *n* malum *nt*, incommodum *nt*
null *adj* inritus
nullify *vt* inritum facere; (*LAW*) abrogāre
numb *adj* torpēns, torpidus; **be ~** torpēre; **become ~** torpēscere
number *n* numerus *m*; **a ~ of** complūrēs, aliquot; **a great ~** multitūdō *f*, frequentia *f*; **a small ~** īnfrequentia *f*; **in large numbers** frequentēs ♦ *vt* numerāre, ēnumerāre
numberless *adj* innumerābilis
numbness *n* torpor *m*
numerous *adj* frequēns, crēber, plūrimī
nun *n* monacha *f*
nuptial *adj* nūptiālis
nuptials *n* nūptiae *fpl*
nurse *n* nūtrix *f* ♦ *vt* (*child*) nūtrīre; (*sick*) cūrāre; (*fig*) fovēre
nursery *n* (*children*) cubiculum *nt*; (*plants*) sēminārium *nt*
nursling *n* alumnus *m*, alumna *f*
nurture *n* ēducātiō *f*
nut *n* nux *f*
nutrition *n* alimenta *ntpl*
nutritious *adj* salūbris
nutshell *n* putāmen *nt*
nut tree *n* nux *f*
nymph *n* nympha *f*

Oo

O *interj* ō!
oaf *n* agrestis *m*
oak *n* quercus *f*; *(evergreen)* īlex *f*; *(timber)* rōbur *nt* ◆ *adj* quernus, īlignus, rōboreus; **oak forest** quercētum *nt*
oakum *n* stuppa *f*
oar *n* rēmus *m*
oarsman *n* rēmex *m*
oaten *adj* avēnāceus
oath *n* iūsiūrandum *nt*; *(MIL)* sacrāmentum *nt*; *(imprecation)* exsecrātiō *f*; **false ~** periūrium *nt*; **take an ~** iūrāre; **take an ~ of allegiance to** in verba iūrāre *(gen)*
oats *n* avēna *f*
obduracy *n* obstinātus animus *m*
obdurate *adj* obstinātus, pervicāx
obdurately *adv* obstinātē
obedience *n* oboedientia *f*, obsequium *nt*
obedient *adj* oboediēns, obsequēns; **be ~ to** pārēre *(dat)*, obtemperāre *(dat)*, obsequī *(dat)*
obediently *adv* oboedienter
obeisance *n* obsequium *nt*; **make ~ to** adōrāre
obelisk *n* obeliscus *m*
obese *adj* obēsus, pinguis
obesity *n* obēsitās *f*, pinguitūdō *f*
obey *vt* pārēre *(dat)*, obtemperāre *(dat)*, oboedīre *(dat)*; **~ orders** dictō pārēre
obituary *n* mortēs *fpl*
object *n* rēs *f*; *(aim)* fīnis *m*, prōpositum *nt*; **be an ~ of hate** odiō esse; **with what ~** quō cōnsiliō ◆ *vi* recūsāre, gravārī; **but, it is objected at** enim; **~ to** improbāre
objection *n* recūsātiō *f*, mora *f*; **I have no ~** nīl moror
objectionable *adj* invīsus, iniūcundus
objective *adj* externus ◆ *n* prōpositum *nt*, fīnis *m*
objurgate *vt* obiūrgāre, culpāre
oblation *n* dōnum *nt*
obligation *n* *(legal)* dēbitum *nt*; *(moral)* officium *nt*; **lay under an ~** obligāre, obstringere
obligatory *adj* dēbitus, necessārius
oblige *vt* *(force)* cōgere; *(contract)* obligāre, obstringere; *(compliance)* mōrem gerere *(dat)*, mōrigerārī *(dat)*; **I am obliged to** *(action)* dēbeō *(inf)*; *(person)* amāre, grātiam habēre *(dat)*
obliging *adj* cōmis, officiōsus
obligingly *adv* cōmiter, officiōsē
oblique *adj* oblīquus
obliquely *adv* oblīquē
obliquity *n* *(moral)* prāvitās *f*
obliterate *vt* dēlēre, oblitterāre
obliteration *n* litūra *f*

oblivion *n* oblīviō *f*
oblivious *adj* oblīviōsus, immemor
oblong *adj* oblongus
obloquy *n* vītuperātiō *f*, opprobrium *nt*
obnoxious *adj* invīsus
obscene *adj* obscaenus, impūrus
obscenity *n* obscaenitās *f*, impūritās *f*
obscure *adj* obscūrus, caecus ◆ *vt* obscūrāre, officere *(dat)*
obscurely *adv* obscūrē; *(speech)* per ambāgēs
obscurity *n* obscūritās *f*; *(speech)* ambāgēs *fpl*
obsequies *n* exsequiae *fpl*
obsequious *adj* officiōsus, ambitiōsus
obsequiously *adv* officiōsē
obsequiousness *n* adsentātiō *f*
observance *n* observantia *f*; *(rite)* rītus *m*
observant *adj* attentus, dīligēns
observation *n* observātiō *f*, animadversiō *f*; *(remark)* dictum *nt*
observe *vt* animadvertere, contemplārī; *(see)* cernere, cōnspicere; *(remark)* dīcere; *(adhere to)* cōnservāre, observāre
observer *n* spectātor *m*, contemplātor *m*
obsess *vt* occupāre; **I am obsessed by** tōtus sum in *(abl)*
obsession *n* studium *nt*
obsolescent *adj*: **be ~** obsolēscere
obsolete *adj* obsolētus; **become ~** exolēscere
obstacle *n* impedīmentum *nt*, mora *f*
obstinacy *n* pertinācia *f*, obstinātus animus *m*
obstinate *adj* pertināx, obstinātus
obstinately *adv* obstinātō animō
obstreperous *adj* clāmōsus, ferus
obstruct *vt* impedīre, obstruere, obstāre *(dat)*; *(POL)* intercēdere *(dat)*; *(fig)* officere *(dat)*
obstruction *n* impedīmentum *nt*; *(POL)* intercessiō *f*
obstructionist *n* intercessor *m*
obtain *vt* adipīscī, nancīscī, cōnsequī; comparāre; *(by request)* impetrāre ◆ *vi* tenēre, obtinēre
obtrude *vi* sē inculcāre ◆ *vt* ingerere
obtrusive *adj* importūnus, molestus
obtuse *adj* hebes, stolidus
obtusely *adv* stolidē
obtuseness *n* stupor *m*
obverse *adj* obversus
obviate *vt* tollere, praevertere
obvious *adj* ēvidēns, manifestus, apertus; **it is ~** appāret
obviously *adv* ēvidenter, apertē, manifestō

occasion n occāsiō f, locus m; (reason) causa f ♦ vt movēre, facessere, auctōrem esse (gen)
occasional adj fortuītus
occasionally adv interdum, nōnnunquam
occidental adj occidentālis
occult adj arcānus
occupancy n possessiō f
occupant n habitātor m, possessor m
occupation n quaestus m, occupātiō f
occupier n possessor m
occupy vt possidēre; (MIL) occupāre; (space) complēre; (attention) distinēre, occupāre
occur vi ēvenīre, accidere; (to mind) occurrere, in mentem venīre
occurrence n ēventum nt; rēs f
ocean n mare nt, ōceanus m
October n mēnsis Octōber m; of ~ Octōber
ocular adj oculōrum; **give ~ proof of** ante oculōs pōnere, videntī dēmōnstrāre
odd adj (number) impār; (moment) subsecīvus; (appearance) novus, īnsolitus
oddity n novitās f; (person) homō rīdiculus m
oddly adv mīrum in modum
odds n praestantia f; **be at ~ with** dissidēre cum; **the ~ are against us** imparēs sumus; **the ~ are in our favour** superiōrēs sumus
ode n carmen nt
odious adj invīsus, odiōsus
odium n invidia f
odorous adj odōrātus
odour n odor m
of prep gen; (origin) ex, dē; (cause) abl; **all of us** nōs omnēs; **the city of Rome** urbs Rōma
off adv procul; (prefix) ab-; **off and on** interdum; **off with you** aufer tē; **come off** ēvādere; **well off** beātus; **well off for** abundāns (abl)
offal n quisquiliae fpl
offence n offēnsiō f; (legal) dēlictum nt; **commit an ~** dēlinquere
offend vt laedere, offendere; **be offended** aegrē ferre ♦ vi delinquere; **~ against** peccāre in (acc), violāre
offender n reus m
offensive adj odiōsus; (smell) gravis; (language) contumēliōsus; **take the ~** bellum īnferre
offensively adv odiōsē; graviter
offer vt offerre, dare, praebēre; (hand) porrigere; (violence) adferre; (honour) dēferre; (with verb) profitērī, pollicērī ♦ n condiciō f; **~ for sale** venditāre
offering n dōnum nt; (to the dead) īnferiae fpl
off-hand adj neglegēns, incūriōsus
office n (POL) magistrātus m, mūnus nt, honōs m; (kindness) officium nt; (place) mēnsa f
officer n praefectus m; lēgātus m
official adj pūblicus ♦ n adiūtor m, minister m
officially adv pūblicē
officiate vi operārī, officiō fungī
officious adj molestus
officiously adv molestē
officiousness n occursātiō f
offing n: **in the ~** procul
offset vt compēnsāre
offspring n prōgeniēs f, līberī mpl; (animal) fētus m

often adv saepe, saepenumerō; **as ~ as** quotiēns; totiēs … quotiēs; **how often?** quotiēns?; **so ~** totiēns; **very ~** persaepe
ogle vi: **~ at** līmīs oculīs intuērī
ogre n mōnstrum nt
oh interj (joy, surprise) ōh!; (sorrow) prō!
oil n oleum nt ♦ vt ungere
oily adj oleōsus
ointment n unguentum nt
old adj (person) senex; (thing) vetus; (ancient) antīquus, prīscus; **old age** senectūs f; **be ten years old** decem annōs habēre; **ten years old** decem annōs nātus; **two years old** bīmus; **good old** antīquus; **good old days** antīquitās f; **grow old** senēscere; **of old** quondam
olden adj prīscus, prīstinus
older adj nātū māior, senior
oldest adj nātū māximus
old-fashioned adj antīquus, obsolētus
old man n senex m
oldness n vetustās f
old woman n anus f
oligarchy n paucōrum dominātiō f, optimātium factiō f
olive n olea f; **~ orchard** olīvētum nt
Olympiad n Olympias f
Olympic adj Olympicus; **win an ~ victory** Olympia vincere
Olympic Games n Olympia ntpl
omen n ōmen nt, auspicium nt; **announce a bad ~** obnūntiāre; **obtain favourable omens** litāre
ominous adj īnfaustus, mināx
omission n praetermissiō f, neglegentia f
omit vt ōmittere, praetermittere
omnipotence n īnfīnīta potestās f
omnipotent adj omnipotēns
on prep (place) in (abl), in- (prefix); (time) abl; (coast of) ad (acc); (subject) dē (abl); (side) ab (abl) ♦ adv porrō, usque; **and so on** ac deinceps; **on hearing the news** nūntiō acceptō; **on equal terms** (in battle) aequō Marte; **on the following day** posterō/ proximō diē, postrīdiē; **on this side of** citrā (acc)
once adv semel; (past) ōlim, quondam; **at ~** extemplō, statim; (together) simul; **for ~** aliquandō; **~ and for all** semel; **~ more** dēnuō, iterum; **~ upon a time** ōlim, quondam
one num ūnus ♦ pron quīdam; (of two) alter, altera, alterum; **one and the same** ūnus; **one another** inter sē, alius alium; **one or the other** alteruter; **one day** ōlim; **one each** singulī; **one would have thought** crēderēs; **be one of** in numerō esse (gen); **be at one** idem sentīre; **it is all one** nihil interest; **the one** alter, hic; **this is the one** hōc illud est
one-eyed adj luscus
oneness n ūnitās f
onerous adj gravis
oneself pron ipse; (reflexive) sē
one-sided adj inaequālis, inīquus
onion n caepe nt
onlooker n spectātor m
only adj ūnus, sōlus; (son) ūnicus ♦ adv sōlum, tantum, modo; (with clause) nōn nisi, nīl nisi, nihil aliud quam; (time) dēmum; **if ~** sī modo; (wish) utinam

onrush n incursus m
onset n impetus m
onslaught n incursus m; **make an ~ on** (words) invehī in (acc)
onto prep in (acc)
onus n officium nt
onward, onwards adv porrō
onyx n onyx m
ooze vi mānāre, stillāre
opaque adj haud perlūcidus
open adj apertus; (wide) patēns, hiāns; (ground) pūrus, apertus; (question) integer; **lie ~** patēre; **stand ~** hiāre; **throw ~** adaperīre, patefacere; **it is ~ to me to** mihī integrum est (inf); **while the question is still ~ rē** integrā ♦ vt aperīre, patefacere; (book) ēvolvere; (letter) resolvere; (speech) exōrdīrī; (with ceremony) inaugurāre; (will) resignāre ♦ vi aperīrī, hiscere; (sore) recrūdēscere; **~ out** extendere, pandere; **~ up** (country) aperīre
open air n: **in the open air** sub dīvō
open-handed adj largus, mūnificus
open-handedness n largitās f
open-hearted adj ingenuus
opening n forāmen nt, hiātus m; (ceremony) cōnsecrātiō f; (opportunity) occāsiō f, ānsa f ♦ adj prīmus
openly adv palam, apertē
open-mouthed adj: **stand ~ at** inhiāre
operate vi rem gerere ♦ vt movēre
operation n opus nt, āctiō f; (MED) sectiō f
operative adj efficāx
ophthalmia n lippitūdō f
opiate adj somnifer
opine vi opīnārī, existimāre
opinion n sententia f; (of person) existimātio f; **public ~** fāma f; **in my ~** meō iūdiciō, meō animō
opponent n adversārius m, hostis m
opportune adj opportūnus, tempestīvus
opportunely adv opportūnē
opportunity n occāsiō f; (to act) facultās f; potestās f
oppose vt (barrier) obicere; (contrast) oppōnere ♦ vi adversārī (dat), resistere (dat), obstāre (dat); **be opposed to** adversārī (dat); (opinion) dīversum esse ab
opposite adj (facing) adversus; (contrary) contrārius, dīversus ♦ prep contrā (acc), adversus (acc); **directly ~ ē** regiōne (gen) ♦ adv ex adversō
opposition n repugnantia f; (party) factiō adversa f
oppress vt opprimere, adflīgere; (burden) premere, onerāre
oppression n iniūria f, servitūs f
oppressive adj gravis, inīquus; **become more ~** ingravēscere
oppressor n tyrannus m
opprobrious adj turpis
opprobriously adv turpiter
opprobrium n dēdecus nt, ignōminia f
optical adj oculōrum
optical illusion n oculōrum lūdibrium nt
optimism n spēs f

option n optiō f, arbitrium nt; **I have no ~** nōn est arbitriī meī
optional adj: **it is ~ for you** optiō tua est
opulence n opēs fpl, cōpia f
opulent adj dīves, cōpiōsus
or conj aut, vel, -ve; (after utrum) an; **or else** aliōquīn; **or not** (direct) annōn; (indirect) necne
oracle n ōrāculum nt
oracular adj fātidicus; (fig) obscūrus
oral adj: **give an ~ message** vōce nūntiāre
orally adv vōce, verbīs
oration n ōrātiō f
orator n ōrātor m
oratorical adj ōrātōrius
oratory n ēloquentia f, rhētoricē f; (for prayer) sacellum nt; **of ~** dīcendī, ōrātōrius
orb n orbis m
orbit n orbis m, ambitus m
orchard n pōmārium nt
ordain vt ēdīcere, sancīre
ordeal n labor m
order n (arrangement) ōrdō m; (class) ōrdō m; (battle) aciēs f; (command) iussum nt, imperium nt; (money) perscrīptiō f; **in ~** dispositus; (succession) deinceps; **in ~ that/to** ut (subj); **in ~ that not** nē (subj); **put in ~** dispōnere, ōrdināre; **by ~ of** iussū (gen); **out of ~** incompositus; **without orders from** iniussū (gen) ♦ vt (arrange) dispōnere, ōrdināre; (command) iubēre (+ acc and infin), imperāre (dat and 'ut' + subj or 'nē' + subj)
orderly adj ōrdinātus; (conduct) modestus ♦ n accēnsus m
ordinance n ēdictum nt, institūtum nt
ordinarily adv plērumque, ferē
ordinary adj ūsitātus, solitus, cottīdiānus
ordnance n tormenta ntpl
ordure n stercus m
ore n aes nt; **iron ore** ferrum īnfectum nt
Oread n (myth) Oreas f
organ n (bodily) membrum nt; (musical) organum nt, hydraulus m
organic adj nātūrālis
organically adv nātūrā
organization n ōrdinātiō f, structūra f
organize vt ōrdināre, īnstituere, adparāre
orgies n orgia ntpl
orgy n cōmissātiō f
orient n oriēns m
oriental adj Asiāticus
orifice n ōstium nt
origin n orīgō f, prīncipium nt; (source) fōns m; (birth) genus nt
original adj prīmus, prīstinus; (LIT) proprius ♦ n exemplar nt
originally adv prīncipiō, antīquitus
originate vt īnstituere, auctōrem esse (gen) ♦ vi exorīrī; **~ in** innāscī in (abl), initium dūcere ab
originator n auctor m
orisons n precēs fpl
ornament n ōrnāmentum nt; (fig) decus nt ♦ vt ōrnāre, decorāre; **I am ~** ornamentō sum
ornamental adj decōrus; **be ~** decorī esse
ornamentally adv ōrnātē
ornate adj ōrnātus
ornately adv ōrnātē
orphan n orbus m, orba f

orphaned *adj* orbātus
orthodox *adj* antīquus
orthography *n* orthographia *f*
oscillate *vi* reciprocāre
osculate *vt* ōsculārī
osier *n* vīmen *nt* ◆ *adj* vīmineus
osprey *n* haliaeetos *m*
ostensible *adj* speciōsus
ostensibly *adv* per speciem
ostentation *n* iactātiō *f*, ostentātiō *f*
ostentatious *adj* glōriōsus, ambitiōsus
ostentatiously *adv* glōriōsē
ostler *n* agāsō *m*
ostrich *n* strūthiocamēlus *m*
other *adj* alius; *(of two)* alter; **one or the**
  ~ alteruter; **every ~ year** tertiō quōque annō; **on**
  the ~ side of ultrā *(acc)*; **of others** aliēnus
otherwise *adv* aliter; *(if not)* aliōquī
otter *n* lutra *f*
ought *vi* dēbēre (*+ infin or gerundive of vt*); **I ~ mē**
  oportet; **I ~ to have said** dēbuī dīcere
ounce *n* ūncia *f*; **two ounces** sextāns *m*; **three**
  ounces quadrāns *m*; **four ounces** triēns *m*;
  five ounces quīncūnx *m*; **six ounces** sēmis *m*;
  seven ounces septūnx *m*; **eight ounces** bēs *m*;
  nine ounces dōdrāns *m*; **ten ounces** dextāns
  m; **eleven ounces** deūnx *m*
our *adj* noster
ourselves *pron* ipsī; *(reflexive)* nōs
oust *vt* extrūdere, ēicere
out *adv (rest)* forīs; *(motion)* forās; **out of** dē, ē/ex
  (abl); *(cause)* propter *(acc)*; *(beyond)* extrā, ultrā
  (acc); **be out** *(book)* in manibus esse; *(calculation)*
  errāre; *(fire)* exstinctum esse; *(secret)* palam esse
outbreak *n* initium *nt*, ēruptiō *f*
outburst *n* ēruptiō *f*
outcast *n* profugus *m*
outcome *n* ēventus *m*, exitus *m*
outcry *n* clāmor *m*, adclāmātiō *f*; **raise an**
  ~ against obstrepere *(dat)*
outdistance *vt* praevertere
outdo *vt* superāre
outdoor *adj* sub dīvō
outer *adj* exterior
outermost *adj* extrēmus
outfit *n* īnstrūmenta *ntpl*; vestīmenta *ntpl*
outflank *vt* circumīre
outgrow *vt* excēdere ex
outing *n* excursiō *f*
outlandish *adj* barbarus
outlaw *n* prōscrīptus *m* ◆ *vt* prōscrībere, aquā et
  ignī interdīcere *(dat)*
outlawry *n* aquae et ignis interdictiō *f*
outlay *n* impēnsa *f*, sūmptus *m*
outlet *n* ēmissārium *nt*, exitus *m*
outline *n* ductus *m*, adumbrātiō *f* ◆ *vt*
  adumbrāre
outlive *vt* superesse *(dat)*
outlook *n* prōspectus *m*
outlying *adj* longinquus, exterior
outnumber *vt* numerō superiōrēs esse,
  multitūdine superāre
out-of-doors *adv* forīs
outpost *n* statiō *f*
outpouring *n* effūsiō *f*
output *n* fructus *m*

outrage *n* flāgitium *nt*, iniūria *f* ◆ *vt* laedere,
  violāre
outrageous *adj* flāgitiōsus, indignus
outrageously *adv* flāgitiōsē
outrider *n* praecursor *m*
outright *adv* penitus, prōrsus; semel
outrun *vt* praevertere
outset *n* initium *nt*
outshine *vt* praelūcēre *(dat)*
outside *adj* externus ◆ *adv* extrā, forīs; *(motion*
  to) forās; **~ in** inversus; **from ~** extrīnsecus
  ◆ *n* exterior pars *f*; *(show)* speciēs *f*; **at**
  the ~ summum, ad summum; **on the**
  ~ extrīnsecus ◆ *prep* extrā *(acc)*
outsider *n* aliēnus *m*; *(POL)* novus homō *m*
outskirts *n* suburbānus ager *m*; **on the**
  ~ suburbānus
outspoken *adj* līber
outspokenness *n* lībertās *f*
outspread *adj* patulus
outstanding *adj* ēgregius, īnsignis, singulāris;
  (debt) residuus
outstep *vt* excēdere
outstretched *adj* passus, porrēctus, extentus
outstrip *vt* praevertere
outvote *vt* suffrāgiīs superāre
outward *adj* externus; **~ form** speciēs *f* ◆ *adv*
  domō, forās
outweigh *vt* praeponderāre
outwit *vt* dēcipere, circumvenīre
outwork *n* prōpugnāculum *nt*, bracchium *nt*
outworn *adj* exolētus
oval *adj* ōvātus ◆ *n* ōvum *nt*
ovation *n* *(triumph)* ovātiō *f*; **receive an ~** cum
  laudibus excipī
oven *n* furnus *m*, fornāx *f*
over *prep (above)* super *(abl)*, suprā *(acc)*; *(across)*
  super *(acc)*; *(extent)* per *(acc)*; *(time)* inter *(acc)*;
  ~ and above super *(acc)*, praeter *(acc)*; **all ~** per;
  ~ against adversus *(acc)* ◆ *adv* suprā; *(excess)*
  nimis; *(done)* cōnfectus; **~ again** dēnuō; **~ and**
  above īnsuper; **~ and ~** identidem; **be left**
  ~ superesse, restāre; **it is all ~ with** āctum est
  dē
overall *adj* tōtus ◆ *adv* ubīque, passim
overawe *vt* formīdinem inicere *(dat)*
overbalance *vi* titubāre
overbearing *adj* superbus
overboard *adv* ē nāvī, in mare; **throw**
  ~ excutere, iactāre
overbold *adj* importūnus
overburden *vt* praegravāre
overcast *adj* nūbilus
overcoat *n* paenula *f*, lacerna *f*
overcome *vt* superāre, vincere
overconfidence *n* cōnfīdentia *f*
overconfident *adj* cōnfīdēns
overdo *vt* modum excēdere in *(abl)*
overdone *adj (style)* pūtidus
overdraw *vt (style)* exaggerāre
overdue *adj (money)* residuus
overestimate *vt* māiōris aestimāre
overflow *n* ēluviō *f* ◆ *vi* abundāre, redundāre ◆ *vt*
  inundāre
overgrown *adj* obsitus; **be ~** luxuriāre
overhang *vt*, *vi* impendēre, imminēre *(dat)*

overhaul *vt* reficere
overhead *adv* īnsuper
overhear *vt* excipere, auscultāre
overjoyed *adj* nimiō gaudiō ēlātus
overladen *adj* praegravātus
overland *adv* terrā
overlap *vt* implicāre
overlay *vt* indūcere
overload *vt* (*fig*) obruere
overlook *vt* (*place*) dēspectāre, imminēre
  (*dat*); (*knowledge*) ignōrāre; (*notice*) neglegere,
  praetermittere; (*fault*) ignōscere (*dat*)
overlord *n* dominus *m*
overmaster *vt* dēvincere
overmuch *adv* nimis, plūs aequō
overnight *adj* nocturnus ◆ *adv* noctū
overpower *vt* superāre, domāre, obruere,
  opprimere
overpraise *vt* in māius extollere
overrate *vt* māiōris aestimāre
overreach *vt* circumvenīre
overriding *adj* praecipuus
overrule *vt* rescindere
overrun *vt* pervagārī; (*fig*) obsidēre
oversea *adj* trānsmarīnus
oversee *vt* praeesse (*dat*)
overseer *n* cūrātor *m*, custōs *m*
overset *vt* ēvertere
overshadow *vt* officere (*dat*)
overshoot *vt* excēdere
oversight *n* neglegentia *f*
overspread *vt* offendere (*dat*), obdūcere

overstep *vt* excēdere
overt *adj* apertus
overtake *vt* cōnsequī; (*surprise*) opprimere,
  dēprehendere
overtax *vt* (*fig*) abūtī (*abl*)
overthrow *vt* ēvertere; (*destroy*) prōflīgāre,
  dēbellāre ◆ *n* ēversiō *f*, ruīna *f*
overtly *adv* palam
overtop *vt* superāre
overture *n* exōrdium *nt*; **make overtures to**
  temptāre, agere cum, lēgātōs mittere ad
overturn *vt* ēvertere
overweening *adj* superbus, adrogāns, īnsolēns
overwhelm *vt* obruere, dēmergere, opprimere
overwhelming *adj* īnsignis, vehementissimus
overwhelmingly *adv* mīrum quantum
overwork *vi* plūs aequō labōrāre ◆ *vt* cōnficere
  ◆ *n* immodicus labor *m*
overwrought *adj* (*emotion*) ēlātus; (*style*)
  ēlabōrātus
owe *vt* dēbēre
owing *adj*: **be ~** dēbērī; **~ to** (*person*) per; (*cause*) ob/
  propter (*acc*)
owl *n* būbō *m*; ulula *f*
own *adj* proprius; **my own** meus; **have of one's**
  own domī habēre; **hold one's own** parem esse
  ◆ *vt* possidēre, habēre; (*admit*) fatērī, cōnfitērī
owner *n* dominus *m*, possessor *m*
ownership *n* possessiō *f*, mancipium *nt*
ox *n* bōs *m*
ox herd *n* bubulcus *m*
oyster *n* ostrea *f*

Pp

pace n passus m; (speed) gradus m; **keep ~** gradum cōnferre ◆ vi incēdere; **~ up and down** spatiārī, inambulāre
pacific adj pācificus; (quiet) placidus
pacification n pācificātiō f
pacifist n imbellis m
pacify vt (anger) plācāre; (rising) sēdāre
pack n (MIL) sarcina f; (animals) grex m; (people) turba f ◆ vt (kit) colligere; (crowd) stīpāre; **~ together** coartāre; **~ up** colligere, compōnere ◆ vi vāsa colligere; **send packing** missum facere ◆ adj (animal) clītellārius
package n fasciculus m, sarcina f
packet n fasciculus m; (ship) nāvis āctuāria f
packhorse n iūmentum nt
packsaddle n clītellae fpl
pact n foedus nt, pactum nt
pad n pulvillus m
padding n tōmentum nt
paddle n rēmus m ◆ vi rēmigāre
paddock n saeptum nt
paean n paeān m
pagan adj pāgānus
page n (book) pāgina f; (boy) puer m
pageant n pompa f, spectāculum nt
pageantry n adparātus m
pail n situla f
pain n dolor m; **be in ~** dolēre ◆ vt dolōre adficere
painful adj acerbus; (work) labōriōsus
painfully adv acerbē, labōriōsē
painless adj dolōris expers
painlessly adv sine dolōre
painlessness n indolentia f
pains npl opera f; **take ~** operam dare; **take ~ with** (art) ēlabōrāre
painstaking adj dīligēns, operōsus
painstakingly adv dīligenter, summā cūrā
paint n pigmentum nt; (cosmetic) fūcus m ◆ vt pingere; (red) fūcāre; (in words) dēpingere; (portrait) dēpingere
paintbrush n pēnicillus m
painter n pictor m
painting n pictūra f
pair n pār nt ◆ vt coniungere, compōnere
palace n rēgia f
palatable adj suāvis, iūcundus
palate n palātum nt
palatial adj rēgius
palaver n colloquium nt, sermunculī mpl
pale n pālus m, vallus m, **beyond the ~** extrāneus ◆ adj pallidus; **look ~** pallēre; **grow ~** pallēscere;

~ brown subfuscus; **~ green** subviridis ◆ vi pallēscere
paleness n pallor m
palimpsest n palimpsēstus m
paling n saepēs f
palisade n (MIL) vallum nt
palish adj pallidulus
pall n (funeral) pallium nt ◆ vi taedēre
pallet n grabātus m
palliasse n strāmentum nt
palliate vt extenuāre, excūsāre
palliation n excūsātiō f
palliative n lēnīmentum nt
pallid adj pallidus
pallor n pallor m
palm n (hand) palma f; (tree) palma f ◆ vt: **~ off** impōnere
palmy adj flōrēns
palpable adj tractābilis; (fig) manifestus
palpably adv manifestō, propalam
palpitate vi palpitāre, micāre
palpitation n palpitātiō f
palsied adj membrīs captus
palsy n paralysis f
paltry adj vīlis, frīvolus
pamper vt indulgēre (dat)
pampered adj dēlicātus
pamphlet n libellus m
pan n patina f, patella f; (frying) sartāgō f; (of balance) lanx f
pancake n laganum nt
pander n lēnō m ◆ vi: **~ to** lēnōcinārī (dat)
panegyric n laudātiō f
panegyrist n laudātor m
panel n (wall) abacus m; (ceiling) lacūnār nt; (judges) decuria f
panelled adj laqueātus
pang n dolor m
panic n pavor m ◆ vi trepidāre
panic-stricken adj pavidus
panniers n clītellae fpl
panoply n arma ntpl
panorama n prōspectus m
panpipe n fistula f
pant vi anhēlāre
panther n panthēra f
panting n anhēlitus m
pantomime n mīmus m
pantry n cella penāria f
pap n mamma f
paper n charta f
papyrus n papyrus f

par *n*: **on a par with** pār (*dat*)
parable *n* parabolē *f*
parade *n* pompa *f*; (*show*) adparātus *m* ♦ *vt*
trādūcere, iactāre ♦ *vi* pompam dūcere,
incēdere
paradox *n* verba sēcum repugnantia;
paradoxes *pl* paradoxa *ntpl*
paragon *n* exemplar *nt*, specimen *nt*
paragraph *n* caput *nt*
parallel *adj* parallēlus; (*fig*) cōnsimilis
paralyse *vt* dēbilitāre; (*with fear*) percellere; **be**
paralysed torpēre
paralysis *n* dēbilitās *f*; (*fig*) torpēdō *f*
paramount *adj* prīnceps, summus
paramour *n* adulter *m*
parapet *n* lōrīca *f*
paraphernalia *n* adparātus *m*
paraphrase *vt* vertere
parasite *n* parasītus *m*
parasol *n* umbella *f*
parboiled *adj* subcrūdus
parcel *n* fasciculus *m* ♦ *vt*: **~ out** distribuere,
dispertīre
parch *vt* torrēre
parched *adj* torridus, āridus; **be ~** ārēre
parchment *n* membrāna *f*
pardon *n* venia *f* ♦ *vt* ignōscere (*dat*); (*offence*)
condōnāre
pardonable *adj* ignōscendus
pare *vt* dēglūbere; (*nails*) resecāre
parent *n* parēns *m/f*, genitor *m*, genetrīx *f*
parentage *n* stirps *f*, genus *nt*
parental *adj* patrius
parenthesis *n* interclūsiō *f*
parings *n* praesegmina *ntpl*
parish *n* (ECCL) paroecia *f*
parity *n* aequālitās *f*
park *n* hortī *mpl*
parlance *n* sermō *m*
parley *n* colloquium *nt* ♦ *vi* colloquī, agere
parliament *n* senātus *m*; **house of ~** cūria *f*
parliamentary *adj* senātōrius
parlour *n* exedrium *nt*
parlous *adj* difficilis, perīculōsus
parochial *adj* mūnicipālis
parody *n* carmen ioculāre *nt* ♦ *vt* calumniārī
parole *n* fidēs *f*
paronomasia *n* agnōminātiō *f*
paroxysm *n* accessus *m*
parricide *n* (*doer*) parricīda *m*; (*deed*) parricīdium
nt
parrot *n* psittacus *m*
parry *vt* ēlūdere, prōpulsāre
parsimonious *adj* parcus
parsimoniously *adv* parcē
parsimony *n* parsimōnia *f*, frūgālitās *f*
part *n* pars *f*; (*play*) partēs *fpl*, persōna *f*; (*duty*)
officium *nt*; **parts** loca *ntpl*; (*ability*) ingenium *nt*;
for my ~ equidem; **for the most ~** māximam
partem; **on the ~ of** ab; **act the ~ of** persōnam
sustinēre, partēs agere; **have no ~ in** expers
esse (*gen*); **in ~** partim; **it is the ~ of a wise man**
sapientis est; **play one's ~** officiō satisfacere;
take ~ in interesse (*dat*), particeps esse (*gen*);
take in good ~ in bonam partem accipere; **take**
someone's ~ adesse alicuī, dēfendere aliquem;

from all parts undique; **in foreign parts**
peregrē; **in two parts** bifāriam; (MIL) bipartītō;
in three parts trifāriam; (MIL) tripartītō;
of parts ingeniōsus ♦ *vt* dīvidere, sēparāre,
dirimere; **~ company** dīversōs discēdere ♦ *vi*
dīgredī, discēdere; (*things*) dissilīre; **~ with**
renūntiāre
partake *vi* interesse, particeps esse; **~ of** gustāre
partial *adj* (*biased*) inīquus, studiōsus; (*incomplete*)
mancus; **be ~ to** favēre (*dat*), studēre (*dat*); **win a**
~ victory aliquā ex parte vincere
partiality *n* favor *m*, studium *nt*
partially *adv* partim, aliquā ex parte
participant *n* particeps *m/f*
participate *vi* interesse, particeps esse
participation *n* societās *f*
particle *n* particula *f*
parti-coloured *adj* versicolor, varius
particular *adj* (*own*) proprius; (*special*)
praecipuus; (*exact*) dīligēns, accūrātus;
(*fastidious*) fastīdiōsus; **a ~ person** quīdam
♦ *n* rēs *f*; **with full particulars** subtīliter;
give all the particulars omnia exsequī; **in**
~ praesertim
particularity *n* subtīlitās *f*
particularize *vt* singula exsequī
particularly *adv* praecipuē, praesertim, in
prīmīs, māximē
parting *n* dīgressus *m*, discessus *m* ♦ *adj* ultimus
partisan *n* fautor *m*, studiōsus *m*
partisanship *n* studium *nt*
partition *n* (*act*) partītiō *f*; (*wall*) pariēs *m*;
(*compartment*) loculāmentum *nt* ♦ *vt* dīvidere
partly *adv* partim, ex parte
partner *n* socius *m*; (*in office*) collēga *m*
partnership *n* societās *f*; **form a ~** societātem
inīre
partridge *n* perdīx *m/f*
parturition *n* partus *m*
party *n* (POL) factiō *f*, partēs *fpl*; (*entertainment*)
convīvium *nt*; (MIL) manus *f*; (*individual*) homō
m/f; (*associate*) socius *m*, cōnscius *m*
party spirit *n* studium *nt*
parvenu *n* novus homō *m*
pass *n* (*hill*) saltus *m*; (*narrow*) angustiae *fpl*,
faucēs *fpl*; (*crisis*) discrīmen *nt*; (*document*)
diplōma *nt*; (*fighting*) petītiō *f*; **things have**
come to such a ~ in eum locum ventum
est, adeō rēs rediit ♦ *vi* īre, praeterīre; (*time*)
trānsīre; (*property*) pervenīre; **~ away** abīre;
(*die*) morī, perīre; (*fig*) dēfluere; **~ by** praeterīre;
~ for habērī prō (*abl*); **~ off** abīre; **~ on** pergere;
~ over trānsīre; **come to ~** fierī, ēvenīre; **let**
~ intermittere, praetermittere ♦ *vt* praeterīre;
(*riding*) praetervehī; (*by hand*) trādere; (LAW)
iubēre; (*limit*) excēdere; (*sentence*) interpōnere,
dīcere; (*test*) satisfacere (*dat*); (*time*) dēgere,
agere; **~ accounts** ratiōnēs ratās habēre; **~ the**
day diem cōnsūmere; **~ a law** lēgem ferre; **~ a**
decree dēcernere; **~ off** ferre; **~ over** praeterīre,
mittere; (*fault*) ignōscere (*dat*); **~ round** trādere;
~ through trānsīre
passable *adj* (*place*) pervius; (*standard*) mediocris
passably *adv* mediocriter

passage *n* iter *nt*, cursus *m*; (*land*) trānsitus *m*; (*sea*) trānsmissiō *f*; (*book*) locus *m*; **of ~** (*bird*) advena

passenger *n* vector *m*

passer-by *n* praeteriēns *m*

passing *n* obitus *m* ◆ *adj* admodum

passion *n* animī mōtus *m*, permōtiō *f*, ārdor *m*; (*anger*) īra *f*; (*lust*) libīdō *f*

passionate *adj* ārdēns, impotēns, ācer; īrācundus

passionately *adv* vehementer, ārdenter; īrācundē; **be ~ in love** amōre ārdēre

passive *adj* iners

passiveness *n* inertia *f*, patientia *f*

passport *n* diplōma *nt*

password *n* tessera *f*

past *adj* praeteritus; (*recent*) proximus ◆ *n* praeterita *ntpl* ◆ *prep* praeter (*acc*); (*beyond*) ultrā (*acc*)

paste *n* glūten *nt* ◆ *vt* glūtināre

pastime *n* lūdus *m*, oblectāmentum *nt*

pastoral *adj* pastōrālis; (*poem*) būcolicus

pastry *n* crustum *nt*

pasture *n* pāstus *m*, pāscuum *nt* ◆ *vt* pāscere

pat *vt* dēmulcēre ◆ *adj* opportūnus

patch *n* pannus *m* ◆ *vt* resarcīre

patchwork *n* centō *m*

pate *n* caput *nt*

patent *adj* apertus, manifestus ◆ *n* prīvilēgium *nt*

patently *adv* manifestō

paternal *adj* paternus

path *n* sēmita *f*, trāmes *m*

pathetic *adj* miserābilis

pathetically *adv* miserābiliter

pathfinder *n* explōrātor *m*

pathless *adj* āvius

pathos *n* misericordia *f*; (RHET) dolor *m*

pathway *n* sēmita *f*

patience *n* patientia *f*

patient *adj* patiēns ◆ *n* aeger *m*

patiently *adv* patienter, aequō animō

patois *n* sermō *m*

patrician *adj* patricius ◆ *n* patricius *m*

patrimony *n* patrimōnium *nt*

patriot *n* amāns patriae *m*

patriotic *adj* pius, amāns patriae

patriotically *adv* prō patriā

patriotism *n* amor patriae *m*

patrol *n* excubiae *fpl* ◆ *vi* circumīre

patron *n* patrōnus *m*, fautor *m*

patronage *n* patrōcinium *nt*

patroness *n* patrōna *f*, fautrīx *f*

patronize *vt* favēre (*dat*), fovēre

patronymic *n* nōmen *nt*

patter *vi* crepitāre ◆ *n* crepitus *m*

pattern *n* exemplar *nt*, exemplum *nt*, nōrma *f*; (*ideal*) specimen *nt*; (*design*) figūra *f*

paucity *n* paucitās *f*

paunch *n* abdōmen *nt*, venter *m*

pauper *n* pauper *m*

pause *n* mora *f*, intervallum *nt* ◆ *vi* īnsistere, intermittere

pave *vt* sternere; **~ the way** (*fig*) viam mūnīre

pavement *n* pavīmentum *nt*

pavilion *n* tentōrium *nt*

paw *n* pēs *m* ◆ *vt* pede pulsāre

pawn *n* (*chess*) latrunculus *m*; (COMM) pignus *nt*, fīdūcia *f* ◆ *vt* oppignerāre

pawnbroker *n* pignerātor *m*

pay *n* mercēs *f*; (MIL) stīpendium *nt*; (*workman*) manupretium *nt* ◆ *vt* solvere, pendere; (*debt*) exsolvere; (*in full*) persolvere; (*honour*) persolvere; (MIL) stīpendium numerāre (*dat*); (*penalty*) dare, luere; **pay down** numerāre; **pay for** condūcere; **pay off** dissolvere, exsolvere; **pay out** expendere; (*publicly*) ērogāre; **pay up** dēpendere; **pay a compliment to** laudāre; **pay respects to** salūtāre ◆ *vi* respondēre; **it pays** expedit

payable *adj* solvendus

paymaster *n* (MIL) tribūnus aerārius *m*

payment *n* solūtiō *f*; (*money*) pēnsiō *f*

pea *n* pīsum *n*; **like as two peas** tam similis quam lac lactī est

peace *n* pāx *f*; **~ and quiet** ōtium *nt*; **breach of the ~** vīs *f*; **establish ~** pācem conciliāre; **hold one's ~** reticēre; **sue for ~** pācem petere

peaceable *adj* imbellis, placidus

peaceably *adv* placidē

peaceful *adj* tranquillus, placidus, pācātus

peacefully *adv* tranquillē

peacemaker *n* pācificus *m*

peace-offering *n* piāculum *nt*

peach *n* Persicum *nt*

peacock *n* pāvō *m*

peak *n* apex *m*, vertex *m*

peal *n* (*bell*) sonitus *m*; (*thunder*) fragor *m* ◆ *vi* sonāre

pear *n* pirum *nt*; (*tree*) pirus *f*

pearl *n* margarīta *f*

pearly *adj* gemmeus; (*colour*) candidus

peasant *n* agricola *m*, colōnus *m*

peasantry *n* agricolae *mpl*

pebble *n* calculus *m*

pebbly *adj* lapidōsus

peccadillo *n* culpa *f*

peck *n* (*measure*) modius *m* ◆ *vt* vellicāre

peculate *vi* pecūlārī

peculation *n* pecūlātus *m*

peculiar *adj* (*to one*) proprius; (*strange*) singulāris

peculiarity *n* proprietās *f*, nota *f*

peculiarly *adv* praecipuē, praesertim

pecuniary *adj* pecūniārius

pedagogue *n* magister *m*

pedant *n* scholasticus *m*

pedantic *adj* nimis dīligens

pedantically *adv* dīligentius

pedantry *n* nimia dīligentia *f*

peddle *vt* circumferre

pedestal *n* basis *f*

pedestrian *adj* pedester ◆ *n* pedes *m*

pedigree *n* stirps *f*, stemma *nt* ◆ *adj* generōsus

pediment *n* fastīgium *nt*

pedlar *n* īnstitor *m*, circumforāneus *m*

peel *n* cortex *m* ◆ *vt* glūbere

peep *vi* dīspicere ◆ *n* aspectus *m*; **at ~ of day** prīmā lūce

peer *vi*: **~ at** intuērī ◆ *n* pār *m*; (*rank*) patricius *m*

peerless *adj* ūnicus, ēgregius

peevish *adj* stomachōsus, mōrōsus

peevishly *adv* stomachōsē, mōrōsē

peevishness *n* stomachus *m*, mōrōsitās *f*

121

peg n clāvus m; **put a round peg in a square hole** bovī clītellās impōnere ◆ vt clāvīs dēfīgere
pelf n lucrum nt
pellet n globulus m
pell-mell adv prōmiscuē, turbātē
pellucid adj perlūcidus
pelt n pellis f ◆ vt petere ◆ vi violenter cadere
pen n calamus m, stilus m; (cattle) saeptum nt ◆ vt scrībere
penal adj poenālis
penalize vt poenā adficere, multāre
penalty n poena f, damnum nt; (fine) multa f; **pay the ~** poenās dare
penance n supplicium nt
pencil n graphis f
pending adj sub iūdice ◆ prep inter (acc)
penetrable adj pervius
penetrate vt penetrāre
penetrating adj ācer, acūtus; (mind) perspicāx
penetration n (mind) acūmen nt
peninsula n paenīnsula f
penitence n paenitentia f
penitent adj: **I am ~** mē paenitet
penknife n scalpellum nt
penmanship n scrīptiō f, manus f
pennant n vexillum nt
penny n dēnārius m
pension n annua ntpl
pensioner n ēmeritus m
pensive adj attentus
pensiveness n cōgitātiō f
pent adj inclūsus
penthouse n (MIL) vīnea f
penurious adj parcus, avārus, tenāx
penuriousness n parsimōnia f, tenācitās f
penury n egestās f, inopia f
people n hominēs mpl; (nation) populus m, gēns f; **common ~** plēbs f ◆ vt frequentāre
peopled adj frequēns
pepper n piper nt
peradventure adv fortasse
perambulate vi spatiārī, inambulāre
perceive vt sentīre, percipere, intellegere
perceptible adj: **be ~** sentīrī posse, audīrī posse
perception n sēnsus m
perch n (bird's) pertica f; (fish) perca f ◆ vi īnsidēre
perchance adv fortasse, forsitan (subj)
percolate vi permānāre
percussion n ictus m
perdition n exitium nt
peregrinate vi peregrīnārī
peregrination n peregrīnātiō f
peremptorily adv praecīsē, prō imperiō
peremptory adj imperiōsus
perennial adj perennis
perfect adj perfectus, absolūtus; (entire) integer; (faultless) ēmendātus ◆ vt perficere, absolvere
perfection n perfectiō f, absolūtiō f
perfectly adv perfectē, ēmendātē; (quite) plānē
perfidious adj perfidus, perfidiōsus
perfidiously adv perfidiōsē
perfidy n perfidia f
perforate vt perforāre, terebrāre
perforation n forāmen nt
perforce adv per vim, necessāriō

perform vt perficere, peragere; (duty) exsequī, fungī (abl); (play) agere
performance n (process) exsecūtiō f, fūnctiō f; (deed) factum nt; (stage) fābula f
performer n āctor m; (music) tībīcen m, fidicen m; (stage) histriō m
perfume n odor m, unguentum m ◆ vt odōrāre
perfumer n unguentārius m
perfumery n unguenta ntpl
perfunctorily adv neglegenter
perfunctory adj neglegēns
perhaps adv fortasse, forsitan (subj), nesciō an (subj); (tentative) vel; (interrog) an
peril n perīculum m, discrīmen nt
perilous adj perīculōsus
perilously adv perīculōsē
perimeter n ambitus m
period n tempus nt, spatium nt; (history) aetās f; (end) terminus m; (sentence) complexiō f, ambitus m
periodic adj (style) circumscrīptus
periodical adj status
periodically adv certīs temporibus, identidem
peripatetic adj vagus; (sect) peripatēticus
periphery n ambitus m
periphrasis n circuitus m
perish vi perīre, interīre
perishable adj cadūcus, fragilis, mortālis
peristyle n peristȳlium nt
perjure vi: **~ oneself** pēierāre
perjured adj periūrus
perjurer n periūrus m
perjury n periūrium nt; **commit ~** pēierāre
permanence n cōnstantia f, stabilitās f
permanent adj stabilis, diūturnus, perpetuus
permanently adv perpetuō
permeable adj penetrābilis
permeate vt penetrāre ◆ vi permānāre
permissible adj licitus, concessus; **it is ~** licet
permission n potestās f; **ask ~** veniam petere; **give ~** veniam dare, potestātem facere; **by ~ of** permissū (gen); **with your kind ~** bonā tuā veniā; **without your ~** tē invītō
permit vt sinere, permittere (dat); **I am permitted** licet mihī
pernicious adj perniciōsus, exitiōsus
perorate vi perōrāre
peroration n perōrātiō f, epilogus m
perpendicular adj dīrēctus
perpendicularly adv ad perpendiculum, ad līneam
perpetrate vt facere, admittere
perpetual adj perpetuus, perennis, sempiternus
perpetually adv perpetuō
perpetuate vt continuāre, perpetuāre
perpetuity n perpetuitās f
perplex vt sollicitāre, cōnfundere
perplexing adj ambiguus, perplexus
perplexity n haesitātiō f
perquisite n pecūlium nt
persecute vt īnsectārī, exagitāre; persequī
persecution n īnsectātiō f
persecutor n īnsectātor m
perseverance n persevērantia f, cōnstantia f
persevere vi persevērāre, perstāre; **~ in** tenēre

Persian *n* Persa *m*
persist *vt* īnstāre, perstāre, persevērāre
persistence, persistency *n* pertinācia *f*, persevērantia *f*
persistent *adj* pertināx
persistently *adv* pertināciter, persevēranter
person *n* homō *m/f*; (*counted*) caput *nt*; (*character*) persōna *f*; (*body*) corpus *nt*; **in ~** ipse praesēns
personage *n* vir *m*
personal *adj* prīvātus, suus
personality *n* nātūra *f*; (*person*) vir ēgregius *m*
personally *adv* ipse, ipsō
personal property *n* pecūlium *nt*
personate *vt* persōnam gerere (*gen*)
personification *n* prosōpopoeia *f*
personify *vt* hūmānam nātūram tribuere (*dat*)
personnel *n* membra *ntpl*, sociī *mpl*
perspective *n* scaenographia *f*
perspicacious *adj* perspicāx, acūtus
perspicacity *n* perspicācitās *f*, acūmen *nt*
perspicuity *n* perspicuitās *f*
perspicuous *adj* perspicuus
perspiration *n* sūdor *m*
perspire *vi* sūdāre
persuade *vt* persuādēre (*dat*); (*by entreaty*) exōrāre
persuasion *n* persuāsiō *f*
persuasive *adj* blandus
persuasively *adv* blandē
pert *adj* procāx, protervus
pertain *vi* pertinēre, attinēre
pertinacious *adj* pertināx
pertinaciously *adv* pertināciter
pertinacity *n* pertinācia *f*
pertinent *adj* appositus; **be ~** ad rem pertinēre
pertinently *adv* appositē
pertly *adv* procāciter, protervē
perturb *vt* perturbāre
perturbation *n* animī perturbātiō *f*, trepidātiō *f*
peruke *n* capillāmentum *nt*
perusal *n* perlēctiō *f*
peruse *vt* perlegere; (*book*) ēvolvere
pervade *vt* permānāre per, complēre; (*emotion*) perfundere
pervasive *adj* crēber
perverse *adj* perversus, prāvus
perversely *adv* perversē
perversion *n* dēprāvātiō *f*
perversity *n* perversitās *f*
pervert *vt* dēprāvāre; (*words*) dētorquēre; (*person*) corrumpere
perverter *n* corruptor *m*
pessimism *n* dēspērātiō *f*
pest *n* pestis *f*
pester *vt* sollicitāre
pestilence *n* pestilentia *f*, pestis *f*
pestilential *adj* pestilēns, nocēns
pestle *n* pistillum *nt*
pet *n* dēliciae *fpl* ♦ *vt* in dēliciīs habēre, dēlēnīre
petard *n*: **be hoist with his own ~** suō sibī gladiō iugulārī
petition *n* precēs *fpl*; (*POL*) libellus *m* ♦ *vt* ōrāre
petrify *vt* (*fig*) dēfīgere; **be petrified** stupēre, obstupēscere
pettifogger *n* lēgulēius *m*
pettiness *n* levitās *f*

pettish *adj* stomachōsus
petty *adj* levis, minūtus
petulance *n* protervitās *f*
petulant *adj* protervus, petulāns
petulantly *adv* petulanter
pew *n* subsellium *nt*
phalanx *n* phalanx *f*
phantasy *n* commentīcia *ntpl*
phantom *n* simulacrum *nt*, īdōlon *nt*
phases *npl* vicēs *fpl*
pheasant *n* phāsiānus *m*
phenomenal *adj* eximius, singulāris
phenomenon *n* rēs *f*, novum *nt*, spectāculum *nt*
philander *vi* lascīvīre
philanthropic *adj* hūmānus, beneficus
philanthropically *adv* hūmānē
philanthropy *n* hūmānitās *f*, beneficia *ntpl*
Philippic *n* Philippica *f*
philologist *n* grammaticus *m*
philology *n* grammatica *ntpl*
philosopher *n* philosophus *m*, sapiēns *m*
philosophical *adj* philosophus; (*temperament*) aequābilis
philosophize *vi* philosophārī
philosophy *n* philosophia *f*, sapientia *f*
philtre *n* philtrum *nt*
phlegm *n* pituīta *f*; (*temper*) lentitūdō *f*
phlegmatic *adj* lentus
phoenix *n* phoenīx *m*
phrase *n* locūtiō *f*; (*GRAM*) incīsum *nt*
phraseology *n* verba *ntpl*, ōrātiō *f*
physic *n* medicāmentum *nt*; **physics** *pl* physica *ntpl*
physical *adj* physicus; (*of body*) corporis
physician *n* medicus *m*
physicist *n* physicus *m*
physique *n* corpus *nt*, vīrēs *fpl*
piazza *n* forum *nt*
pick *n* (*tool*) dolabra *f*; (*best part*) lēctī *mpl*, flōs *m* ♦ *vt* (*choose*) legere, dēligere; (*pluck*) carpere; **~ out** ēligere, excerpere; **~ up** colligere
pickaxe *n* dolabra *f*
picked *adj* ēlēctus, dēlēctus
picket *n* (*MIL*) statiō *f*
pickle *n* muria *f* ♦ *vt* condīre
picture *n* pictūra *f*, tabula *f* ♦ *vt* dēpingere; (*to oneself*) ante oculōs pōnere
picturesque *adj* (*scenery*) amoenus
pie *n* crustum *nt*
piebald *adj* bicolor, varius
piece *n* pars *f*; (*broken off*) fragmentum *nt*; (*food*) frustum *nt*; (*coin*) nummus *m*; (*play*) fābula *f*; **break in pieces** comminuere; **fall to pieces** dīlābī; **take to pieces** dissolvere; **tear in pieces** dīlaniāre
piecemeal *adv* membrātim, minūtātim
pied *adj* maculōsus
pier *n* mōlēs *f*
pierce *vt* perfodere, trānsfīgere; (*bore*) perforāre; (*fig*) pungere
piercing *adj* acūtus
piety *n* pietās *f*, religiō *f*
pig *n* porcus *m*, sūs *m/f*; **buy a pig in a poke** spem pretiō emere; **pig's** suillus
pigeon *n* columba *f*; **wood ~** palumbēs *f*
pig-headed *adj* pervicāx

pigment n pigmentum nt
pigsty n hara f
pike n dolō m, hasta f
pikeman n hastātus m
pile n acervus m, cumulus m; (funeral) rogus m; (building) mōlēs f; (post) sublica f ♦ vt cumulāre, congerere; ~ **up** exstruere, adcumulāre, coacervāre
pile-driver n fistūca f
pilfer vt fūrārī, surripere
pilferer n fūr m, fūrunculus m
pilgrim n peregrīnātor m
pilgrimage n peregrīnātio f
pill n pilula f
pillage n rapīna f, dēpopulātiō f, expīlātiō f ♦ vt dīripere, dēpopulārī, expīlāre
pillager n expīlātor m, praedātor m
pillar n columen nt, columna f
pillory n furca f
pillow n pulvīnus nt, culcita f
pilot n gubernātor m, ductor m ♦ vt regere, gubernāre
pimp n lēnō m
pimple n pustula f
pin n acus f ♦ vt adfīgere
pincers n forceps m/f
pinch vt pervellere, vellicāre; (shoe) ūrere; (for room) coartāre
pine n pīnus f ♦ vi tābēscere; ~ **away** intābēscere; ~ **for** dēsīderāre
pinion n penna f
pink adj rubicundus
pinnace n lembus m
pinnacle n fastīgium nt
pint n sextārius m
pioneer n antecursor m
pious adj pius, religiōsus
piously adv piē, religiōsē
pip n grānum nt
pipe n (music) fistula f, tībia f; (water) canālis m ♦ vi fistulā canere
piper n tībīcen m
pipkin n olla f
piquancy n sāl m, vīs f
piquant adj salsus, argūtus
pique n offēnsiō f, dolor m ♦ vt offendere
piracy n latrōcinium nt
pirate n pīrāta m, praedō m
piratical adj pīrāticus
piscatorial adj piscātōrius
piston n embolus m
pit n fovea f, fossa f; (THEAT) cavea f
pitch n pix f; (sound) sonus m ♦ vt (camp) pōnere; (tent) tendere; (missile) conicere
pitch-black adj piceus
pitched battle n proelium iustum nt
pitcher n hydria f
pitchfork n furca f
pitch pine n picea f
piteous adj miserābilis, flēbilis
piteously adv miserābiliter
pitfall n fovea f
pith n medulla f
pithy adj (style) dēnsus; ~ **saying** sententia f
pitiable adj miserandus
pitiful adj miser, miserābilis; misericors

pitifully adv miserē, miserābiliter
pitiless adj immisericors, immītis
pitilessly adv crūdēliter
pittance n (food) dēmēnsum nt; (money) stips f
pity n misericordia f; **take** ~ **on** miserērī (+acc of person, gen of things); **it is a** ~ **that** male accidit quod ♦ vt miserērī (gen); **I** ~ **me** miseret (gen)
pivot n cardō m
placability n plācābilitās f
placable adj plācābilis
placard n libellus m
placate vt plācāre
place n locus m; **in another** ~ alibī; **in the first** ~ prīmum; **in** ~ **of** locō (gen), pro (abl); **to this** ~ hūc; **out of** ~ intempestīvus; **give** ~ **to** cēdere (dat); **take** ~ fierī, accidere; **take the** ~ **of** in locum (gen) succēdere ♦ vt pōnere, locāre, collocāre; ~ **beside** adpōnere; ~ **over** (in charge) praepōnere; ~ **round** circumdare; ~ **upon** impōnere
placid adj placidus, tranquillus, quiētus
placidity n tranquillitās f, sedātus animus m
placidly adv placidē, quiētē
plagiarism n fūrtum nt
plagiarize vt fūrārī
plague n pestilentia f, pestis f
plain adj (lucid) clārus, perspicuus; (unadorned) subtīlis, simplex; (frank) sincērus; (ugly) invenustus ♦ n campus m, plānitiēs f; **of the** ~ campester
plainly adv perspicuē, simpliciter, sincērē
plainness n perspicuitās f; simplicitās f
plaint n querella f
plaintiff n petītor m
plaintive adj flēbilis, queribundus
plaintively adv flēbiliter
plait vt implicāre, nectere
plan n cōnsilium nt; (of a work) fōrma f, dēsignātiō f; (of living) ratiō f; (intent) prōpositum nt; (drawing) dēscrīptiō f ♦ vt (a work) dēsignāre, dēscrībere; (intent) cōgitāre, meditārī; cōnsilium capere or inīre; (with verb) in animō habēre (inf)
plane n (surface) plānitiēs f; (tree) platanus f; (tool) runcīna f ♦ adj aequus, plānus ♦ vt runcīnāre
planet n stēlla errāns f
plank n tabula f
plant n herba f, planta f ♦ vt (tree) serere; (field) cōnserere; (colony) dēdūcere; (feet) pōnere; ~ **firmly** īnfīgere
plantation n arbustum nt
planter n sator m, colōnus m
plaque n tabula f
plaster n albārium nt, tectōrium nt; (MED) emplastrum nt; ~ **of Paris** gypsum nt ♦ vt dealbāre
plasterer n albārius m
plastic adj ductilis, fūsilis
plate n (dish) catillus m; (silver) argentum nt; (layer) lāmina f ♦ vt indūcere
platform n suggestus m; rōstrum nt, tribūnal nt
platitude n trīta sententia f
platter n patella f, lanx f
plaudit n plausus m
plausibility n vērīsimilitūdō f
plausible adj speciōsus, vērī similis

play n lūdus m; (THEAT) fābula f; (voice) inclīnātiō f; (scope) campus m; (hands) gestus m; ~ **on words** agnōminātiō f; **fair** ~ aequum et bonum ♦ vi lūdere; (fountain) scatēre ♦ vt (music) canere; (instrument) canere (abl); (game) lūdere (abl); (part) agere; ~ **the part of** agere; ~ **a trick on** lūdificārī, impōnere (dat)
playbill n ēdictum nt
player n lūsor m; (at dice) āleātor m; (on flute) tībīcen m; (on lyre) fidicen m; (on stage) histriō m
playful adj lascīvus; (words) facētus
playfully adv per lūdum, per iocum
playfulness n lascīvia f; facētiae fpl
playground n ārea f
playmate n collūsor m
playwright n fābulārum scrīptor m
plea n causa f; (in defence) dēfēnsiō f, excūsātiō f
plead vi causam agere, causam ōrāre, causam dīcere; (in excuse) dēprecārī, excūsāre; ~ **with** obsecrāre
pleader n āctor m, causidicus m
pleasant adj iūcundus, dulcis, grātus; (place) amoenus
pleasantly adv iūcundē, suāviter
pleasantry n facētiae fpl, iocus m
please vt placēre (dat), dēlectāre; **try to** ~ īnservīre (dat); **just as you** ~ quod commodum est; **if you** ~ sīs; **pleased with** contentus (abl); **be pleased with oneself** sibī placēre ♦ adv amābō
pleasing adj grātus, iūcundus, amoenus; **be** ~ **to** cordī esse (dat)
pleasurable adj iūcundus
pleasure n voluptās f; (decision) arbitrium nt; **it is my** ~ libet; **derive** ~ voluptātem capere ♦ vt grātificārī (dat)
pleasure grounds n hortī mpl
pleasure-loving adj dēlicātus
plebeian adj plēbēius ♦ n: **the plebeians** plēbs f
plebiscite n suffrāgium nt
plectrum n plēctrum nt
pledge n pignus nt ♦ vt obligāre; ~ **oneself** prōmittere, spondēre; ~ **one's word** fidem obligāre, fidem interpōnere
Pleiads n Plēiadēs fpl
plenary adj īnfīnītus
plenipotentiary n lēgātus m
plenitude n cōpia f, mātūritās f
plentiful adj cōpiōsus, largus
plentifully adv cōpiōsē, largē
plenty n cōpia f, abundantia f; (enough) satis
pleonasm n redundantia f
pleurisy n lateris dolor m
pliable adj flexibilis, mollis, lentus
pliant adj flexibilis, mollis, lentus
pliers n forceps m/f
plight n habitus m, discrīmen nt ♦ vt spondēre
plod vi labōrāre, operam īnsūmere
plot n coniūrātiō f, īnsidiae fpl; (land) agellus m; (play) argūmentum nt ♦ vi coniūrāre, mōlīrī
plotter n coniūrātus m
plough n arātrum nt ♦ vt arāre; (sea) sulcāre; ~ **up** exarāre
ploughing n arātiō f
ploughman n arātor m
ploughshare n vōmer m

pluck n fortitūdō f ♦ vt carpere, legere; ~ **out** ēvellere; ~ **up courage** animum recipere, animō adesse
plucky adj fortis
plug n obtūrāmentum nt ♦ vt obtūrāre
plum n prūnum nt; (tree) prūnus f
plumage n plūmae fpl
plumb n perpendiculum nt ♦ adj dīrēctus ♦ adv ad perpendiculum ♦ vt (building) ad perpendiculum exigere; (depth) scrūtārī
plumber n artifex plumbārius m
plumb line n līnea f, perpendiculum nt
plume n crista f ♦ vt: ~ **oneself on** iactāre, prae sē ferre
plummet n perpendiculum nt
plump adj pinguis
plumpness n nitor m
plunder n (act) rapīna f; (booty) praeda f ♦ vi praedārī ♦ vt dīripere, expīlāre
plunderer n praedātor m, spoliātor m
plundering n rapīna f ♦ adj praedābundus
plunge vt mergere, dēmergere; (weapon) dēmittere ♦ vi mergī, sē dēmergere
plural adj plūrālis
plurality n multitūdō f, plūrēs pl
ply vt exercēre
poach vt surripere
pocket n sinus m
pocket money n pecūlium nt
pod n siliqua f
poem n poēma nt, carmen nt
poesy n poēsis f
poet n poēta m
poetess n poētria f
poetic adj poēticus
poetical adj = poetic
poetically adv poēticē
poetry n (art) poētica f; (poems) poēmata ntpl, carmina ntpl
poignancy n acerbitās f
poignant adj acerbus, acūtus
poignantly adv acerbē, acūtē
point n (dot) pūnctum nt; (place) locus m; (item) caput nt; (sharp end) aciēs f; (of sword) mucrō m; (of epigram) aculeī mpl; ~ **of honour** officium nt; **beside the** ~ ab rē; **to the** ~ ad rem; **from this** ~ hinc; **to that** ~ eō; **up to this** ~ hāctenus, adhūc; **without** ~ īnsulsus; **in** ~ **of fact** nempe; **make a** ~ **of doing** consultō facere; **on the** ~ **of death** moritūrus; **on the** ~ **of happening** inibī; **I was on the** ~ **of saying** in eō erat ut dīcerem; **matters have reached such a** ~ eō rēs recidit; **come to the** ~ ad rem redīre; **the** ~ **at issue** is illud quaeritur; **the main** ~ cardō m, caput nt; **turning** ~ articulus temporis m ♦ vt acuere, exacuere; (aim) intendere; (punctuate) distinguere; ~ **out** indicāre, dēmōnstrāre; ostendere
point-blank adj simplex ♦ adv praecīsē
pointed adj acūtus; (criticism) acūleātus; (wit) salsus
pointedly adv apertē, dīlūcidē
pointer n index m
pointless adj īnsulsus, frīgidus
pointlessly adv īnsulsē
point of view n iudicium nt, sententia f

poise n lībrāmen nt; (fig) urbānitās f ◆ vt lībrāre
poison n venēnum nt ◆ vt venēnō necāre; (fig) īnficere
poisoned adj venēnātus
poisoner n venēficus m
poisoning n venēficium nt
poisonous adj noxius
poke vt trūdere, fodicāre
polar adj septentriōnālis
pole n asser m, contus m; (ASTR) polus m
poleaxe n bipennis f
polemic n contrōversia f
police n lictōrēs mpl; (night) vigilēs mpl
policy n ratiō f, cōnsilium nt; **honesty is the best ~ ea māximē condūcunt quae sunt rēctissima**
polish n (appearance) nitor m; (character) urbānitās f; (LIT) līma f ◆ vt polīre; (fig) expolīre
polished adj polītus, mundus; (person) excultus, urbānus; (style) līmātus
polite adj urbānus, hūmānus, cōmis
politely adv urbānē, cōmiter
politeness n urbānitās f, hūmānitās f, cōmitās f
politic adj prūdēns, circumspectus
political adj cīvīlis, pūblicus; **~ life rēs pūblica f**
politician n magistrātus m
politics n rēs pūblica f; **take up ~ ad rem pūblicam accēdere**
polity n reī pūblicae fōrma f
poll n caput nt; (voting) comitia ntpl ◆ vi suffrāgia inīre
poll tax n tribūtum nt in singula capita impositum
pollute vt inquināre, contāmināre
pollution n corruptēla f
poltroon n ignāvus m
pomegranate n mālum Pūnicum nt
pomp n adparātus m
pomposity n māgnificentia f, glōria f
pompous adj māgnificus, glōriōsus
pompously adv māgnificē, glōriōsē
pompousness n māgnificentia f
pond n stagnum nt, lacūna f
ponder vi sēcum reputāre ◆ vt animō volūtāre, in mente agitāre
ponderous adj gravis, ponderōsus
ponderously adv graviter
poniard n pugiō m
pontiff n pontifex m
pontifical adj pontificālis, pontificius
pontoon n pontō m
pony n mannus m
pooh-pooh vt dērīdēre
pool n lacūna f, stagnum nt ◆ vt cōnferre
poop n puppis f
poor adj pauper, inops; (meagre) exīlis; (inferior) improbus; (pitiable) miser; **~ little misellus**
poorly adj aeger, aegrōtus ◆ adv parum, tenuiter
pop n crepitus m ◆ vi ēmicāre
pope n pāpa m
poplar n pōpulus f
poppy n papāver nt
populace n vulgus nt, plēbs f
popular adj grātus, grātiōsus; (party) populāris
popularity n populī favor m, studium nt
popularly adv vulgō

populate vt frequentāre
population n populus m, cīvēs mpl
populous adj frequēns
porcelain n fictilia ntpl
porch n vestibulum nt
porcupine n hystrīx f
pore n forāmen nt ◆ vi: **~ over** scrūtārī, incumbere in (acc)
pork n porcīna f
porous adj rārus
porridge n puls f
port n portus m ◆ adj (side) laevus, sinister
portage n vectūra f
portal n porta f
portcullis n cataracta f
portend vt portendere
portent n mōnstrum nt, portentum nt
portentous adj mōnstruōsus
porter n iānitor m; (carrier) bāiulus m
portico n porticus f
portion n pars f; (marriage) dōs f; (lot) sors f
portliness n amplitūdō f
portly adj amplus, opīmus
portrait n imāgō f, effigiēs f
portray vt dēpingere, exprimere, effingere
pose n status m, habitus m ◆ vt pōnere ◆ vi habitum sūmere
poser n nōdus m
posit vt pōnere
position n (GEOG) situs m; (body) status m, gestus m; (rank) dignitās f; (office) honōs m; (MIL) locus m; **be in a ~ to** habēre (inf); **take up a ~** (MIL) locum capere
positive adj certus; **be ~ about** adfirmāre
positively adv certō, adfirmātē, rē vērā
posse n manus f
possess vt possidēre, habēre; (take) occupāre, potīrī (abl)
possession n possessiō f; **possessions** pl bona ntpl, fortūnae fpl; **take ~ of** potīrī (abl), occupāre, manum inicere (dat); (inheritance) obīre; (emotion) invādere, incēdere (dat); **gain ~ of** potior (abl)
possessor n possessor m, dominus m
possibility n facultās f; **there is a ~** fierī potest
possible adj: **it is ~** fierī potest; **as big as ~** quam māximus
possibly adv fortasse
post n pālus m; (MIL) statiō f; (office) mūnus nt; (courier) tabellārius m; **leave one's ~** locō cēdere, signa relinquere ◆ vt (troops) locāre, collocāre; (at intervals) dispōnere; (letter) dare, tabellāriō dare; (entry) in cōdicem referre; **be posted** (MIL) in statiōne esse
postage n vectūra f
poster n libellus m
posterior adj posterior
posterity n posterī mpl; (time) posteritās f
postern n postīcum nt
posthaste adv summā celeritāte
posthumous adj postumus
posthumously adv (born) patre mortuō; (published) auctōre mortuō
postpone vt differre, prōferre
postponement n dīlātiō f
postscript n: **add a ~** adscrībere, subicere

postulate *vt* sūmere ✦ *n* sūmptiō *f*
posture *n* gestus *m*, status *m*
pot *n* olla *f*, matella *f*
pot-bellied *adj* ventriōsus
potency *n* vīs *f*
potent *adj* efficāx, valēns
potentate *n* dynastēs *m*, tyrannus *m*
potential *adj* futūrus
potentiality *n* facultās *f*
potentially *adv* ut fierī posse vidētur; ~ an emperor capāx imperiī
potently *adv* efficienter
potion *n* pōtiō *f*
pot-pourri *n* farrāgō *f*
potsherd *n* testa *f*
pottage *n* iūs *nt*
potter *n* figulus *m*; **potter's** figulāris
pottery *n* fictilia *ntpl*
pouch *n* pēra *f*, sacculus *m*
poultice *n* fōmentum *nt*, emplastrum *nt*
poultry *n* gallīnae *fpl*
pounce *vi* involāre, īnsilīre
pound *n* lībra *f*; **five pounds** (*weight*) **of gold** aurī quīnque pondo ✦ *vt* conterere; pulsāre
pour *vt* fundere; ~ **forth** effundere; ~ **in** īnfundere; ~ **on** superfundere; ~ **out** effundere ✦ *vi* fundī, fluere; ~ **down** ruere, sē praecipitāre
pouring *adj* (*rain*) effūsus
poverty *n* paupertās *f*, egestās *f*, inopia *f*; (*style*) iēiūnitās *f*
powder *n* pulvis *m*
powdery *adj* pulvereus
power *n* potestās *f*; (*strength*) vīrēs *fpl*; (*excessive*) potentia *f*; (*supreme*) imperium *nt*; (*divine*) nūmen *nt*; (*legal*) auctōritās *f*; (*of father*) manus *f*; **as far as is in my** ~ quantum in mē est; **have great** ~ multum valēre, posse; **have** ~ **of attorney** cognitōrem esse; **it is still in my** ~ **to** integrum est mihī (*inf*)
powerful *adj* validus, potēns
powerfully *adv* valdē
powerless *adj* impotēns, imbēcillus; **be** ~ nihil valēre
powerlessness *n* imbēcillitas *f*
practicable *adj* in apertō; **be** ~ fierī posse
practical *adj* (*person*) habilis
practical joke *n* lūdus *m*
practical knowledge *n* ūsus *m*
practically *adv* ferē, paene
practice *n* ūsus *m*, exercitātiō *f*; (*RHET*) meditātiō *f*; (*habit*) consuētūdō *f*, mōs *m*; **corrupt practices** malae artēs
practise *vt* (*occupation*) exercēre, facere; (*custom*) factitāre; (*RHET*) meditārī ✦ *vi* (*MED*) medicīnam exercēre; (*LAW*) causās agere
practised *adj* exercitātus, perītus
practitioner *n* (*MED*) medicus *m*
praetor *n* praetor *nt*; **praetor's** praetōrius
praetorian *adj* praetōrius
praetorian guards *npl* praetōriānī *mpl*
praetorship *n* praetūra *f*
praise *n* laus *f* ✦ *vt* laudāre
praiser *n* laudātor *m*
praiseworthy *adj* laudābilis, laude dignus
prance *vi* exsultāre
prank *n* lūdus *m*

prate *vi* garrīre
prating *adj* garrulus
pray *vi* deōs precārī, deōs venerārī ✦ *vt* precārī, ōrāre; ~ **for** petere, precārī; ~ **to** adōrāre
prayer, prayers *n* precēs *fpl*
prayerful *adj* supplex
preach *vt, vi* docēre, praedicāre
preacher *n* ōrātor *m*
preamble *n* exōrdium *nt*
prearranged *adj* cōnstitūtus
precarious *adj* dubius, perīculōsus
precariousness *n* discrīmen *nt*
precaution *n* cautiō *f*, prōvidentia *f*; **take precautions** cavēre, praecavēre
precede *vt* praeīre (*dat*), anteīre (*dat*), antecēdere
precedence *n* prīmārius locus *m*; **give ~ to** cēdere (*dat*); **take ~** (*thing*) antīquius esse; (*person*) prīmās agere
precedent *n* exemplum *nt*; (*LAW*) praeiūdicium *nt*; **breach of ~** īnsolentia *f*; **in defiance of ~** īnsolenter
preceding *adj* prior, superior
precept *n* praeceptum *nt*
preceptor *n* doctor *m*, magister *m*
precinct *n* terminus *m*, templum *nt*
precious *adj* cārus; pretiōsus; (*style*) pūtidus
precious stone *n* gemma *f*
precipice *n* locus praeceps *m*, rūpēs *f*
precipitancy *n* festīnātiō *f*
precipitate *vt* praecipitāre ✦ *adj* praeceps; praeproperus
precipitation *n* festīnātiō *f*
precipitous *adj* dēruptus, praeceps, praeruptus
precise *adj* certus, subtīlis; (*person*) accūrātus
precisely *adv* dēmum
precision *n* cūra *f*
preclude *vt* exclūdere, prohibēre
precocious *adj* praecox
precocity *n* festīnāta mātūritās *f*
preconceive *vt* praecipere; **preconceived idea** praeiūdicāta opīniō *f*
preconception *n* praeceptiō *f*
preconcerted *adj* ex compositō factus
precursor *n* praenūntius *m*
predatory *adj* praedātōrius
predecessor *n* dēcessor *m*; **my ~** cuī succēdō
predestination *n* fātum *nt*, necessitās *f*
predestine *vt* dēvovēre
predetermine *vt* praefīnīre
predicament *n* angustiae *fpl*, discrīmen *nt*
predicate *n* attribūtum *nt*
predict *vt* praedīcere, augurārī
prediction *n* praedictiō *f*
predilection *n* amor *m*, studium *nt*
predispose *vt* inclināre, praeparāre
predisposition *n* inclīnātiō *f*
predominance *n* potentia *f*, praestantia *f*
predominant *adj* praepotēns, praecipuus
predominantly *adv* plērumque
predominate *vi* pollēre, dominārī
pre-eminence *n* praestantia *f*
pre-eminent *adj* ēgregius, praecipuus, excellēns
pre-eminently *adv* ēgregiē, praecipuē, excellenter
preface *n* prooemium *nt*, praefātiō *f* ✦ *vi* praefārī

prefect n praefectus m
prefecture n praefectūra f
prefer vt (charge) dēferre; (to office) anteferre; (choice) antepōnere (acc and dat), posthabēre (dat and acc); (with verb) mālle
preferable adj potior
preferably adv potius
preference n favor m; **give ~ to** antepōnere, praeoptāre; **in ~ to** potius quam
preferment n honōs m, dignitās f
prefix vt praetendere ♦ n praepositiō f
pregnancy n graviditās f
pregnant adj gravida
prejudge vt praeiūdicāre
prejudice n praeiūdicāta opīniō f; (harmful) invidia f, incommodum nt; **without ~** cum bonā veniā ♦ vt obesse (dat); **be prejudiced against** invidēre (dat); male opīnārī dē (abl)
prejudicial adj damnōsus; **be ~ to** obesse (dat), nocēre (dat), officere (dat), dētrīmentō esse (dat)
preliminaries npl praecurrentia ntpl
preliminary adj prīmus ♦ n prōlūsiō f
prelude n prooemium nt
premature adj immātūrus; (birth) abortīvus
prematurely adv ante tempus
premeditate vt praecōgitāre, praemeditārī
premeditated adj praemeditātus
premier adj prīnceps, praecipuus
premise n (major) prōpositiō f; (minor) adsūmptiō f; **premises** pl aedēs fpl, domus f
premium n praemium nt; **be at a ~** male emī
premonition n monitus m
preoccupation n sollicitūdō f
preoccupied adj sollicitus, districtus
preordain vt praefīnīre
preparation n (process) adparātiō f, comparātiō f; (product) adparātus m; (of speech) meditātiō f; **make preparations for** instruere, exōrnāre, comparāre
prepare vt parāre, adparāre, comparāre; (speech) meditārī; (with verb) parāre; **prepared for** parātus ad (acc)
preponderance n praestantia f
preponderate vi praepollēre, vincere
preposition n praepositiō f
prepossess vt commendāre (dat and acc), praeoccupāre
prepossessing adj suāvis, iūcundus
prepossession n favor m
preposterous adj absurdus
prerogative n iūs nt
presage n ōmen nt ♦ vt ōminārī, portendere
prescience n prōvidentia f
prescient adj prōvidus
prescribe vt imperāre; (MED) praescrībere; (limit) fīnīre
prescription n (MED) compositiō f; (right) ūsus m
presence n praesentia f; (appearance) aspectus m; **~ of mind** praesēns animus m; **in the ~ of** cōram (abl); apud (abl); **in my ~** mē praesente
present adj praesēns, īnstāns; **be ~** adesse; **be ~ at** interesse (dat) ♦ n praesēns tempus nt; (gift) dōnum nt; **at ~** in praesentī, nunc; **for the ~** in praesēns ♦ vt dōnāre, offerre; (on stage) indūcere; (in court) sistere; **~ itself** occurrere
presentable adj spectābilis

presentation n dōnātiō f
presentiment n augurium nt
presently adv mox
preservation n cōnservātiō f
preserve vt cōnservāre, tuērī; (food) condīre
preside vi praesidēre (dat)
presidency n praefectūra f
president n praefectus m
press n prēlum nt ♦ vt premere; (crowd) stīpāre; (urge) īnstāre (dat); **~ for** flāgitāre; **~ hard** (pursuit) īnsequī, īnstāre (dat), īnsistere (dat); **~ out** exprimere; **~ together** comprimere
pressing adj īnstāns, gravis
pressure n pressiō f, nīsus m
prestige n auctōritās f, opīniō f
presumably adv sānē
presume vt sūmere, conicere ♦ vi audēre, confīdere; **I ~** opīnor, crēdō
presuming adj adrogāns
presumption n coniectūra f; (arrogance) adrogantia f, licentia f
presumptuous adj adrogāns, audāx
presumptuously adv adroganter, audācter
presuppose vt praesūmere
pretence n simulātiō f, speciēs f; **under ~ of** per speciem (gen); **under false pretences** dolō malō
pretend vt simulāre, fingere; **~ that ... not** dissimulāre
pretender n captātor m
pretension n postulātum nt; **make pretensions to** adfectāre, sibī adrogāre
pretentious adj adrogāns, glōriōsus
pretext n speciēs f; **under ~ of** per speciem (gen); **on the ~ that** quod (subj)
prettily adv pulchrē, bellē
prettiness n pulchritūdō f, lepōs m
pretty adj formōsus, pulcher, bellus ♦ adv admodum, satis
prevail vi vincere; (custom) tenēre, obtinēre; **~ upon** persuādēre (dat); (by entreaty) exōrāre
prevailing adj vulgātus
prevalent adj vulgātus; **be ~** obtinēre; **become ~** incrēbrēscere
prevaricate vi tergiversārī
prevarication n tergiversātiō f
prevaricator n veterātor m
prevent vt impedīre (+quōminus/quīn +subj), prohibēre (+acc and infin)
prevention n impedītiō f
previous adj prior, superior
previously adv anteā, antehāc
prevision n prōvidentia f
prey n praeda f ♦ vi: **~ upon** īnsectārī; (fig) vexāre, carpere
price n pretium nt; (of corn) annōna f; **at a high ~** māgnī; **at a low ~** parvī ♦ vt pretium cōnstituere (gen)
priceless adj inaestimābilis
prick vt pungere; (goad) stimulāre; **~ up the ears** aurēs adrigere
prickle n aculeus m
prickly adj aculeātus, horridus
pride n superbia f, fastus m; (boasting) glōria f; (object) decus nt; (best part) flōs m ♦ vt: **~ oneself on** iactāre, prae sē ferre

priest n sacerdōs m; (especial) flāmen m; **high ~** pontifex m, antistēs m
priestess n sacerdōs f; **high ~** antistita f
priesthood n sacerdōtium nt, flāminium nt
prig n homō fastīdiōsus m
priggish adj fastīdiōsus
prim adj modestior
primarily adv prīncipiō, praecipuē
primary adj prīmus, praecipuus
prime adj prīmus, ēgregius; **~ mover** auctor m ◆ n flōs m; **in one's ~** flōrēns ◆ vt īnstruere, ērudīre
primeval adj prīscus
primitive adj prīstinus, incultus
primordial adj prīscus
prince n rēgulus m; rēgis fīlius m; prīnceps m
princely adj rēgālis
princess n rēgis fīlia f
principal adj praecipuus, prīnceps, māximus ◆ n (person) prīnceps m/f; (money) sors f
principally adv in prīmīs, māximē, māximam partem
principle n prīncipium nt; (rule) fōrmula f, ratiō f; (character) fidēs f; **principles** pl īnstitūta ntpl, disciplīna f; **first principles** elementa ntpl, initia ntpl
print n nota f, signum nt; (foot) vestīgium nt ◆ vt imprimere
prior adj prior, potior
priority n: **give ~ to** praevertere (dat)
prise vt sublevāre; **~ open** vectī refringere
prison n carcer m, vincula ntpl; **put in ~** in vincula conicere
prisoner n reus m; (for debt) nexus m; (of war) captīvus m; **~ at the bar** reus m, rea f; **take ~** capere
pristine adj prīscus, prīstinus, vetus
privacy n sēcrētum nt
private adj (individual) prīvātus; (home) domesticus; (secluded) sēcrētus ◆ n (MIL) gregārius mīles m
privately adv clam, sēcrētō
private property n res familiāris f
privation n inopia f, egestās f
privet n ligustrum nt
privilege n iūs nt, immūnitās f
privileged adj immūnis
privy adj sēcrētus; **~ to** cōnscius (gen)
prize n praemium nt; (captured) praeda f; **~ money** manubiae fpl ◆ vt māgnī aestimāre
pro-Athenian adj rērum Athēniēnsium studiōsus
probability n vērī similitūdō f
probable adj vērī similis; **more ~** vērō propior
probably adv fortasse
probation n probātiō f
probationer n tīrō m
probe vt īnspicere, scrūtārī
probity n honestās f, integritās f
problem n quaestiō f; **the ~ is** illud quaeritur
problematical adj dubius, anceps
procedure n ratiō f, modus m; (LAW) fōrmula f
proceed vi pergere, prōcēdere, prōgredī; (narrative) īnsequī; **~ against** persequī, lītem intendere (dat); **~ from** orīrī, proficīscī ex
proceedings npl ācta ntpl

proceeds n fructus m, reditus m
process n ratiō f; (LAW) āctiō f; **in the ~ of time** post aliquod tempus
procession n pompa f; (fig) agmen nt
proclaim vt ēdīcere, prōnūntiāre, praedicāre, dēclārāre; **~ war upon** bellum indīcere (dat)
proclamation n ēdictum nt
proclivity n prōpēnsiō f
proconsul n prōcōnsul m
proconsular adj prōcōnsulāris
proconsulship n prōcōnsulātus m
procrastinate vt differre, prōferre ◆ vi cunctārī
procrastination n prōcrāstinātiō f, mora f
procreate vt generāre, prōcreāre
procreation n prōcreātiō f
procreator n generātor m
procumbent adj prōnus
procurator n prōcūrātor m
procure vt parāre, adipīscī, adquīrere; (by request) impetrāre
procurer n lēnō m
prod vt stimulāre
prodigal adj prōdigus ◆ n nepōs m
prodigality n effūsiō f
prodigally adv effūsē
prodigious adj ingēns, immānis
prodigy n prōdigium nt, portentum nt; (fig) mīrāculum nt
produce vt ēdere; (young) parere; (crops) ferre; (play) dare, docēre; (line) prōdūcere; (in court) sistere; (into view) prōferre; (from store) prōmere, dēprōmere ◆ n fructus m; (of earth) frūgēs fpl; (in money) reditus m
product n opus nt; **~ of** fructus (gen)
production n opus nt
productive adj fēcundus, ferāx, fructuōsus
productivity n fēcunditās f, ūbertās f
profanation n violātiō f
profane adj profānus, impius ◆ vt violāre, polluere
profanely adv impiē
profanity n impietās f
profess vt profitērī, prae sē ferre; **~ to be** profitērī sē
profession n professiō f; (occupation) ars f, haeresis f
professor n doctor m
proffer vt offerre, pollicērī
proficiency n prōgressus m, perītia f; **attain ~** prōficere
proficient adj perītus
profile n ōris līneāmenta ntpl; (portrait) oblīqua imāgō f
profit n lucrum nt, ēmolumentum nt, fructus m; **make a ~ out of** quaestuī habēre ◆ vt prōdesse (dat) ◆ vi: **~ by** fruī (abl), ūtī (abl); (opportunity) arripere
profitable adj fructuōsus, ūtilis
profitably adv ūtiliter
profligacy n flāgitium nt, perditī mōrēs mpl
profligate adj perditus, dissolūtus ◆ n nepōs m
profound adj altus; (discussion) abstrūsus
profoundly adv penitus
profundity n altitūdō f
profuse adj prōdigus, effūsus
profusely adv effūsē

profusion n abundantia f, adfluentia f; **in**
~ abundē
progenitor n auctor m
progeny n prōgeniēs f, prōlēs f
prognostic n signum nt
prognosticate vt ōminārī, augurārī, praedīcere
prognostication n ōmen nt, praedictiō f
programme n libellus m
progress n prōgressus m; **make** ~ prōficere ◆ vi
prōgredī
progression n prōgressus m
progressively adv gradātim
prohibit vt vetāre, interdīcere (dat)
prohibition n interdictum nt
project n prōpositum nt ◆ vi ēminēre, exstāre;
(land) excurrere ◆ vt prōicere
projectile n tēlum nt
projecting adj ēminēns
projection n ēminentia f
proletarian adj plēbēius
proletariat n plēbs f
prolific adj fēcundus
prolix adj verbōsus, longus
prolixity n redundantia f
prologue n prologus m
prolong vt dūcere, prōdūcere; (office) prōrogāre
prolongation n (time) propāgātiō f; (office)
prōrogātiō f
promenade n ambulātiō f ◆ vi inambulāre,
spatiārī
prominence n ēminentia f
prominent adj ēminēns, īnsignis; **be** ~ ēminēre
promiscuous adj prōmiscuus
promiscuously adv prōmiscuē
promise n prōmissum nt; **break a** ~ fidem
fallere; **keep a** ~ fidem praestāre; **make a**
~ fidem dare; **a youth of great** ~ summae
speī adulēscēns ◆ vt prōmittere, pollicērī; (in
marriage) dēspondēre; ~ **in return** reprōmittere
◆ vi: ~ **well** bonam spem ostendere
promising adj bonae speī
promissory note n syngrapha f
promontory n prōmunturium nt
promote vt favēre (dat); (growth) alere; (in rank)
prōdūcere
promoter n auctor m, fautor m
promotion n dignitās f
prompt adj alacer, prōmptus ◆ vt incitāre,
commovēre; (speaker) subicere
prompter n monitor m
promptitude n alacritās f, celeritās f
promptly adv extemplō, citō
promulgate vt prōmulgāre, palam facere
promulgation n prōmulgātiō f
prone adj prōnus; (mind) inclīnātus
prong n dēns m
pronounce vt ēloquī, appellāre; (oath)
interpōnere; (sentence) dīcere, prōnūntiāre
pronounced adj manifestus, īnsignis
pronouncement n ōrātiō f, adfirmātiō f
pronunciation n appellātiō f
proof n documentum nt, argūmentum nt; (test)
probātiō f ◆ adj immōtus, impenetrābilis
prop n adminiculum nt, firmāmentum nt ◆ vt
fulcīre
propaganda n documenta ntpl

propagate vt propāgāre
propagation n propāgātiō f
propel vt incitāre, prōpellere
propensity n inclīnātiō f
proper adj idōneus, decēns, decōrus; rēctus; **it**
is ~ decet
properly adv decōrē; rēctē
property n rēs f, rēs mancipī, bona ntpl; (estate)
praedium nt; (attribute) proprium nt; (slave's)
pecūlium nt
prophecy n vāticinium nt, praedictiō f
prophesy vt vāticinārī, praedīcere
prophet n vātēs m, fātidicus m
prophetess n vātēs f
prophetic adj dīvīnus, fātidicus
prophetically adv dīvīnitus
propinquity n (place) vīcīnitās f; (kin)
propinquitās f
propitiate vt plācāre
propitiation n plācātiō f, litātiō f
propitious adj fēlīx, faustus; (god) praesēns
proportion n mēnsūra f; **in** ~ prō portiōne, prō
ratā parte; **in** ~ **to** prō (abl)
proportionately adv prō portiōne, prō ratā
parte
proposal n condiciō f
propose vt prōpōnere; (motion) ferre,
rogāre; (penalty) inrogāre; (candidate) rogāre
magistrātum
proposer n auctor m, lātor m
proposition n (offer) condiciō f; (plan) cōnsilium
nt, prōpositum nt; (LOGIC) prōnūntiātum nt
propound vt expōnere, in medium prōferre
propraetor n prōpraetor m
proprietor n dominus m
propriety n decōrum nt; (conduct) modestia f;
with ~ decenter
propulsion n impulsus m
prorogation n prōrogātiō f
prorogue vt prōrogāre
prosaic adj pedester
proscribe vt prōscrībere
proscription n prōscrīptiō f
prose n ōrātiō f, ōrātiō solūta f
prosecute vt (task) exsequī, gerere; (at law)
accūsāre, lītem intendere (dat)
prosecution n exsecūtiō f; (at law) accūsātiō f;
(party) accūsātor m
prosecutor n accūsātor m
prosody n numerī mpl
prospect n prōspectus m; (fig) spēs f ◆ vi
explōrāre
prospective adj futūrus, spērātus
prosper vi flōrēre, bonā fortūnā ūtī ◆ vt
fortūnāre
prosperity n fortūna f, rēs secundae fpl, fēlīcitās
f
prosperous adj fēlīx, fortūnātus, secundus
prosperously adv prosperē
prostrate adj prōstrātus, adflīctus; **lie** ~ iacēre
◆ vt prōsternere, dēicere; ~ **oneself** prōcumbere,
sē prōicere
prostration n frāctus animus m
prosy adj longus
protagonist n prīmārum partium āctor m

protect *vt* tuērī, dēfendere, custōdīre, prōtegere
protection *n* tūtēla *f*, praesidium *nt*; (LAW)
patrōcinium *nt*; (POL) fidēs *f*; **put oneself under
the ~ of** in fidem venīre (*gen*); **take under one's
~ in** fidem recipere
protector *n* patrōnus *m*, dēfēnsor *m*, custōs *m*
protectress *n* patrōna *f*
protégé *n* cliēns *m*
protest *n* obtestātiō *f*; (POL) intercessiō *f* ♦ *vi*
obtestārī, reclāmāre; (POL) intercēdere
protestation *n* adsevērātiō *f*
prototype *n* archetypum *nt*
protract *vt* dūcere, prōdūcere
protrude *vi* prōminēre
protruding *adj* exsertus
protuberance *n* ēminentia *f*, tūber *nt*
protuberant *adj* ēminēns, turgidus
proud *adj* superbus, adrogāns, īnsolēns; **be
~** superbīre; **be ~ of** iactāre
proudly *adv* superbē
prove *vt* dēmōnstrāre, arguere, probāre; (*test*)
experīrī ♦ *vi* (*person*) sē praebēre; (*event*) ēvādere;
~ oneself sē praebēre, sē praestāre; **not proven**
nōn liquet
proved *adj* expertus
provenance *n* orīgō *f*
provender *n* pābulum *nt*
proverb *n* prōverbium *nt*
proverbial *adj* trītus; **become ~** in prōverbium
venīre
provide *vt* parāre, praebēre; **~ for** prōvidēre
(*dat*); **the law provides** lēx iubet; **~ against**
praecavēre
provided that *conj* dum, dummodo (*subj*)
providence *n* prōvidentia *f*; Deus *m*
provident *adj* prōvidus, cautus
providential *adj* dīvīnus; secundus
providentially *adv* dīvīnitus
providently *adv* cautē
providing *conj* dum, dummodo
province *n* prōvincia *f*
provincial *adj* prōvinciālis; (*contemptuous*)
oppidānus, mūnicipālis
provision *n* parātus *m*; **make ~ for** prōvidēre
(*dat*); **make ~** cavēre
provisionally *adv* ad tempus
provisions *n* cibus *m*, commeātus *m*, rēs
frūmentāria *f*
proviso *n* condiciō *f*; **with this ~** hāc lēge
provocation *n* inrītāmentum *nt*, offēnsiō *f*
provocative *adj* (*language*) molestus, invidiōsus
provoke *vt* inrītāre, lacessere; (*to action*) excitāre
provoking *adj* odiōsus, molestus
provost *n* praefectus *m*
prow *n* prōra *f*
prowess *n* virtūs *f*
prowl *vi* grassārī, vagārī
proximate *adj* proximus
proximity *n* propinquitās *f*, vīcīnia *f*
proxy *n* vicārius *m*
prude *n* fastīdiōsa *f*
prudence *n* prūdentia *f*
prudent *adj* prūdēns, cautus, sagāx
prudently *adv* prūdenter, cautē
prudery *n* fastīdiōsa quaedam pudīcitia *f*

prudish *adj* fastīdiōsus
prune *vt* amputāre
pruner *n* putātor *m*
pruning hook *n* falx *f*
pry *vi* inquīrere; **pry into** scrūtārī
pseudonym *n* falsum nōmen *nt*
psychology *n* animī ratiō *f*
Ptolemy *n* Ptolemaeus *m*
puberty *n* pūbertās *f*
public *adj* pūblicus; (*speech*) forēnsis; **~ life** rēs
pūblica *f*, forum *nt*; **in ~** forīs; **appear in ~** in
medium prōdīre; **make ~** in mediō pōnere,
forās perferre; **make a ~ case of** in medium
vocāre; **act for the ~ good** in medium
cōnsulere; **be a ~ figure** in lūce versārī, digitō
mōnstrārī ♦ *n* vulgus *nt*, hominēs *mpl*
publican *n* (*taxes*) pūblicānus *m*; (*inn*) caupō *m*
publication *n* ēditiō *f*, prōmulgātiō *f*; (*book*)
liber *m*
publicity *n* lūx *f*, celebritās *f*
publicly *adv* palam; (*by the state*) pūblicē
public opinion *n* fāma *f*
publish *vt* vulgāre, dīvulgāre; (*book*) ēdere
pucker *vt* corrūgāre
puerile *adj* puerīlis
puerility *n* ineptiae *fpl*
puff *n* aura *f* ♦ *vt* īnflāre ♦ *vi* anhēlāre
puffed up *adj* īnflātus, tumidus
pugilism *n* pugilātus *m*
pugilist *n* pugil *m*
pugnacious *adj* pugnāx
pugnacity *n* ferōcitās *f*
puissance *n* potentia *f*, vīrēs *fpl*
puissant *adj* potēns
pull *n* tractus *m*; (*of gravity*) contentiō *f* ♦ *vt*
trahere, tractāre; **~ apart** distrahere; **~ at**
vellicāre; **~ away** āvellere; **~ back** retrahere;
~ down dēripere, dētrahere; (*building*) dēmōlīrī;
~ off āvellere; **~ out** ēvellere, extrahere;
~ through *vi* pervincere; (*illness*) convalēscere;
~ up (*plant*) ēruere; (*movement*) coercēre; **~ to
pieces** dīlaniāre
pullet *n* pullus gallīnāceus *m*
pulley *n* trochlea *f*
pulmonary *adj* pulmōneus
pulp *n* carō *f*
pulpit *n* suggestus *m*
pulsate *vi* palpitāre, micāre
pulse *n* (*plant*) legūmen *nt*; (*of blood*) vēnae *fpl*; **feel
the ~** vēnās temptāre
pulverize *vt* contundere
pumice stone *n* pūmex *m*
pummel *vt* verberāre
pump *n* antlia *f* ♦ *vt* haurīre; **~ out** exhaurīre
pumpkin *n* cucurbita *f*
pun *n* agnōminātiō *f*
punch *n* ictus *m* ♦ *vt* pertundere, percutere
punctilious *adj* religiōsus
punctiliousness *n* religiō *f*
punctual *adj* accūrātus, dīligēns
punctuality *n* dīligentia *f*
punctually *adv* ad hōram, ad tempus
punctuate *vt* distinguere
punctuation *n* interpūnctiō *f*
puncture *n* pūnctiō *f* ♦ *vt* pungere

pundit n scholasticus m
pungency n ācrimōnia f; (in debate) acūleī mpl
pungent adj ācer, mordāx
punish vt pūnīre, animadvertere in (acc);
poenam sūmere dē (abl); **be punished** poenās
dare
punishable adj poenā dignus
punisher n vindex m, ultor m
punishment n poena f, supplicium nt; (censors')
animadversiō f; **capital** ~ capitis supplicium
nt; **corporal** ~ verbera ntpl; **inflict** ~ **on** poenā
adficere, poenam capere dē (abl), supplicium
sūmere dē (abl); **submit to** ~ poenam subīre;
undergo ~ poenās dare, pendere, solvere
punitive adj ulcīscendī causā
punt n pontō m
puny adj pusillus
pup n catulus m ♦ vi parere
pupil n discipulus m, discipula f; (eye) aciēs f,
pūpula f
pupillage n tūtēla f
puppet n pūpa f
puppy n catulus m
purblind adj luscus
purchase n emptiō f; (formal) mancipium nt ♦ vt
emere
purchaser n emptor m; (at auction) manceps m
pure adj pūrus, integer; (morally) castus; (mere)
merus
purely adv pūrē, integrē; (solely) sōlum, nīl nisi;
(quite) omnīnō, plānē
purgation n pūrgātiō f
purge vt pūrgāre, expūrgāre
purification n lūstrātiō f, pūrgātiō f
purify vt pūrgāre, expūrgāre
purist n fastīdiōsus m
purity n integritās f, castitās f
purloin vt surripere, fūrārī
purple n purpura f ♦ adj purpureus
purport n sententia f; (of words) vīs f; **what is the**
~ **of?** quō spectat?, quid vult? ♦ vt velle spectāre
ad
purpose n prōpositum nt, cōnsilium nt, mēns
f; **for that** ~ eō; **for the** ~ **of** ad (acc), ut (subj), eā
mente ut, eō cōnsiliō ut (subj); **on** ~ cōnsultō, dē
industriā; **to the** ~ ad rem; **to what purpose?**
quō?, quōrsum?; **to no** ~ frustrā, nēquīquam;
without achieving one's ~ rē īnfectā ♦ vt in
animō habēre, velle
purposeful adj intentus
purposeless adj inānis
purposely adv cōnsultō, dē industriā
purr n murmur nt ♦ vi murmurāre
purse n marsupium nt, crumēna f; **privy** ~ fiscus
m ♦ vt adstringere
pursuance n exsecūtiō f; **in** ~ **of** secundum (acc)

pursue vt īnsequī, īnsectārī, persequī; (closely)
īnstāre (dat), īnsistere (dat); (aim) petere; (course)
īnsistere
pursuer n īnsequēns m; (LAW) accūsātor m
pursuit n īnsectātiō f; (hunt) vēnātiō f; (ambition)
studium nt
purvey vt parāre; (food) obsōnāre
purveyance n prōcūrātiō f
purveyor n obsōnātor m
purview n prōvincia f
pus n pūs nt
push n pulsus m, impetus m ♦ vt impellere,
trūdere, urgēre; ~ **away** āmovēre; ~ **back**
repellere; ~ **down** dēprimere, dētrūdere;
~ **forward** prōpellere; ~ **in** intrūdere; ~ **on**
incitāre; ~ **through** perrumpere
pushing adj cōnfīdēns
pusillanimity n ignāvia f, timor m
pusillanimous adj ignāvus, timidus
pustule n pustula f
put vt (in a state) dare; (in a position) pōnere;
(in words) reddere; (argument) pōnere; (spur)
subdere; (to some use) adhibēre; **put an end**
to fīnem facere (dat); **put a question to**
interrogāre; **put against** appōnere; **put**
among intericere; **put aside** sēpōnere; **put**
away pōnere, dēmovēre; (store) repōnere; **put**
back repōnere; repellere; **put beside** adpōnere;
put between interpōnere; **put by** condere;
put down dēpōnere; (revolt) opprimere; **put**
forth extendere; (growth) mittere; **put forward**
ostentāre; (plea) adferre; **put in** immittere,
īnserere; (ship) adpellere; **put off** differre; **put**
on impōnere; (clothes) induere; (play) dare; **put**
out ēicere; (eye) effodere; (fire) exstinguere;
(money) pōnere; (tongue) exserere; **put out of**
the way dēmovēre; **put out to sea** in altum
ēvehī, solvere; **put over** superimpōnere;
put to adpōnere; (flight) dare in (acc), fugāre,
prōfligāre; in fugam conicere; (sea) solvere;
put together cōnferre; **put under** subicere;
put up (for sale) prōpōnere; (lodge) dēvertere,
dēversārī apud; **put up with** ferre, patī; **put**
upon impōnere
putrefaction n pūtor m
putrefy vi putrēscere
putrid adj putridus
puzzle n nōdus m ♦ vt impedīre, sollicitāre; **be**
puzzled haerēre
puzzling adj ambiguus, perplexus
pygmy n pygmaeus m
pyramid n pȳramis f
pyramidal adj pȳramidātus
pyre n rogus m
Pyrenees npl Pyrenaeī (montēs) mpl
python n pȳthōn m

Qq

quack *n* (*doctor*) circulātor *m* ◆ *vi* tetrinnīre
quadrangle *n* ārea *f*
quadruped *n* quadrupēs *m/f*
quadruple *adj* quadruplex
quaestor *n* quaestor *m*; **quaestor's** quaestōrius
quaestorship *n* quaestūra *f*
quaff *vt* ēpōtāre, haurīre
quagmire *n* palūs *f*
quail *n* (*bird*) coturnīx *f* ◆ *vi* pāvēscere, trepidāre
quaint *adj* novus, īnsolitus
quaintness *n* īnsolentia *f*
quake *vi* horrēre, horrēscere ◆ *n* (*earth*) mōtus *m*
quaking *n* horror *m*, tremor *m* ◆ *adj* tremulus
qualification *n* condiciō *f*; (*limitation*) exceptiō *f*
qualified *adj* (*for*) aptus, idōneus, dignus; (*in*) perītus, doctus
qualify *vi* prōficere ◆ *vt* temperāre, mītigāre
qualities *npl* ingenium *nt*
quality *n* nātūra *f*, vīs *f*; indolēs *f*; (*rank*) locus *m*, genus *nt*; **I know the ~ of** sciō quālis sit
qualm *n* religiō *f*, scrūpulus *m*
quandary *n* angustiae *fpl*; **be in a ~** haerēre
quantity *n* cōpia *f*, numerus *m*; (*metre*) vōcum mēnsiō *f*; **a large ~** multum *nt*, plūrimum *nt*; **a small ~** aliquantulum *nt*
quarrel *n* dissēnsiō *f*, contrōversia *f*; (*violent*) rixa *f*, iūrgium *nt* ◆ *vi* rixārī, altercārī
quarrelsome *adj* pugnāx, lītigiōsus
quarry *n* lapicīdinae *fpl*, metallum *nt*; (*prey*) praeda *f* ◆ *vt* excīdere
quart *n* duō sextāriī *mpl*
quartan *n* (*fever*) quartāna *f*
quarter *n* quarta pars *f*, quadrāns *m*; (*sector*) regiō *f*; (*direction*) pars *f*, regiō *f*; (*respite*) missiō *f*; **quarters** castra *ntpl*; (*billet*) hospitium *nt*; **come to close quarters** manum cōnserere; (*armies*) signa cōnferre; **winter quarters** hīberna *ntpl* ◆ *vt* quadrifidam dīvidere; (*troops*) in hospitia dīvidere
quarterdeck *n* puppis *f*
quarterly *adj* trimestris ◆ *adv* quartō quōque mēnse
quartermaster *n* (*navy*) gubernātor *m*; (*army*) castrōrum praefectus *m*
quarterstaff *n* rudis *f*
quash *vt* comprimere; (*decision*) rescindere
quatrain *n* tetrastichon *nt*
quaver *n* tremor *m* ◆ *vi* tremere
quavering *adj* tremebundus
quay *n* crepīdō *f*
queasy *adj* fastīdiōsus
queen *n* rēgīna *f*; (*bee*) rēx *m*

queer *adj* īnsolēns, rīdiculus
quell *vt* opprimere, domāre, dēbellāre
quench *vt* exstinguere, restinguere; (*thirst*) sēdāre, explēre
querulous *adj* querulus, queribundus
query *n* interrogātiō *f* ◆ *vt* in dubium vocāre ◆ *vi* rogāre
quest *n* investīgātiō *f*; **go in ~ of** investīgāre, anquīrere
question *n* interrogātiō *f*; (*at issue*) quaestiō *f*, rēs *f*; (*in doubt*) dubium *nt*; **ask a ~** rogāre, quaerere, scīscitārī, percontārī; **call in ~** in dubium vocāre, addubitāre; **out of the ~** indignus; **be out of the ~** improbārī, fierī nōn posse; **the ~ is** illud quaeritur; **there is no ~ that** nōn dubium est quīn (*subj*); **without ~** sine dubiō ◆ *vt* interrogāre; (*closely*) percontārī; (*doubt*) in dubium vocāre ◆ *vi* dubitāre
questionable *adj* incertus, dubius
questioner *n* percontātor *m*
questioning *n* interrogātiō *f*
queue *n* agmen *nt*
quibble *n* captiō *f* ◆ *vi* cavillārī
quibbler *n* cavillātor *m*
quibbling *adj* captiōsus
quick *adj* (*speed*) celer, vēlōx, citus; (*to act*) alacer, impiger; (*to perceive*) sagāx; (*with hands*) facilis; (*living*) vīvus; **be ~** properāre, festīnāre; **cut to the ~** ad vīvum resecāre; (*fig*) mordēre
quicken *vt* adcelerāre; (*with life*) animāre
quickening *adj* vītālis
quickly *adv* celeriter, citō; (*haste*) properē; (*mind*) acūtē; **as ~ as possible** quam celerrimē
quickness *n* celeritās *f*, vēlōcitās *f*; (*to act*) alacritās *f*; (*to perceive*) sagācitās *f*, sollertia *f*
quicksand *n* syrtis *f*
quick-tempered *adj* īrācundus
quick-witted *adj* acūtus, sagāx, perspicāx
quiescence *n* inertia *f*, ōtium *nt*
quiescent *adj* iners, ōtiōsus
quiet *adj* tranquillus, quiētus, placidus; (*silent*) tacitus; **be ~** quiēscere; silēre ◆ *n* quiēs *f*, tranquillitās *f*; silentium *nt*; (*peace*) pāx *f* ◆ *vt* pācāre, compōnere
quietly *adv* tranquillē, quiētē; tacitē, per silentium; aequō animō
quietness *n* tranquillitās *f*; silentium *nt*
quill *n* penna *f*
quince *n* cydōnium *nt*
quinquennial *adj* quinquennālis
quinquereme *n* quinquerēmis *f*
quintessence *n* flōs *m*, vīs *f*

quip *n* sāl *m*, facētiae *fpl*
quirk *n* captiuncula *f*; **quirks** *pl* trīcae *fpl*
quit *vt* relinquere ♦ *adj* līber, solūtus
quite *adv* admodum, plānē, prōrsus; **not ~** minus, parum; (*time*) nōndum
quits *n* parēs *mpl*
quiver *n* pharetra *f* ♦ *vi* tremere, contremere

quivering *adj* tremebundus, tremulus
quoit *n* discus *m*
quota *n* pars *f*, rata pars *f*
quotation *n* (*act*) commemorātiō *f*; (*passage*) locus *m*
quote *vt* prōferre, commemorāre
quoth *vt* inquit

Rr

rabbit n cunīculus m
rabble n turba f; (class) vulgus nt, plēbēcula f
rabid adj rabidus
rabidly adv rabidē
race n (descent) genus nt, stirps f; (people) gēns f, nōmen nt; (contest) certāmen nt; (fig) cursus m, curriculum nt; (water) flūmen nt; **run a ~** cursū certāre; **run the ~** (fig) spatium dēcurrere ♦ vi certāre, contendere
racecourse n (foot) stadium nt; (horse) spatium nt
racer n cursor m
racial adj gentīlis
rack n (torture) tormentum nt; (shelf) pluteus m; **be on the ~** (fig) cruciārī ♦ vt torquēre, cruciāre; **~ off** (wine) diffundere
racket n (noise) strepitus m
racy adj (style) salsus
radiance n splendor m, fulgor m
radiant adj splendidus, nitidus
radiantly adv splendidē
radiate vi fulgēre; (direction) dīversōs tendere ♦ vt ēmittere
radical adj īnsitus, innātus; (thorough) tōtus ♦ n novārum rērum cupidus m
radically adv omnīnō, penitus, funditus
radish n rādīx f
radius n radius m
raffish adj dissolūtus
raffle n ālea f ♦ vt āleā vēndere
raft n ratis f
rafter n trabs f, tignum nt
rag n pannus m
rage n īra f, furor m; **be all the ~** in ōre omnium esse; **spend one's ~** exsaevīre ♦ vi furere, saevīre; (furiously) dēbacchārī
ragged adj pannōsus
raid n excursiō f, incursiō f, impressiō f; **make a ~** excurrere ♦ vt incursiōnem facere in (acc)
rail n longurius m ♦ vt saepīre ♦ vi: **~ at** maledīcere (dat), convīcia facere (dat)
railing n saepēs f, cancellī mpl
raillery n cavillātiō f
raiment n vestis f
rain n pluvia f, imber m ♦ vi pluere; **it is raining** pluit
rainbow n arcus m
rainstorm n imber m
rainy adj pluvius
raise vt tollere, ēlevāre; (army) cōgere, cōnscrībere; (children) ēducāre; (cry) tollere; (from dead) excitāre; (laugh) movēre; (money) cōnflāre; (price) augēre; (siege) exsolvere; (structure)

extruere; (to higher rank) ēvehere; **~ up** ērigere, sublevāre
raisin n astaphis f
rajah n dynastēs m
rake n rastrum nt; (person) nepōs m ♦ vt rādere; **~ in** conrādere; **~ up** (fig) ēruere
rakish adj dissolūtus
rally n conventus m ♦ vt (troops) in ōrdinem revocāre; (with words) hortārī; (banter) cavillārī ♦ vi sē colligere
ram n ariēs m; (battering) ariēs m ♦ vt: **ram down** fistūcāre; **ram home** (fact) inculcāre
ramble n errātiō f ♦ vi vagārī, errāre
rambling adj vagus; (plant) errāticus; (speech) fluēns
ramification n rāmus m
rammer n fistūca f
rampage vi saevīre
rampant adj ferōx
rampart n agger m, vallum nt
ranch n lātifundium nt
rancid adj pūtidus
rancour n odium nt, acerbitās f, invidia f
random adj fortuītus; **at ~** temerē
range n ōrdō m, seriēs f; (mountain) iugum nt; (of weapon) iactus m; **within ~** intrā tēlī iactum; **come within ~** sub ictum venīre ♦ vt ōrdināre ♦ vi ēvagārī, pervagārī; (in speech) excurrere
rank n (line) ōrdō m; (class) ōrdō m; (position) locus m, dignitās f; **~ and file** gregāriī mīlitēs mpl; **keep the ranks** ōrdinēs observāre; **the ranks** (MIL) aciēs, aciēī f; **leave the ranks** ōrdine ēgredī, ab signīs discēdere; **reduce to the ranks** in ōrdinem redigere ♦ adj luxuriōsus; (smell) gravis, foetidus ♦ vt numerāre ♦ vi in numerō habērī
rankle vi exulcerāre
rankness n luxuriēs f
ransack vt dīripere, spoliāre
ransom n redemptiō f, pretium nt ♦ vt redimere
rant vi latrāre
ranter n rabula m, latrātor m
rap n ictus m ♦ vt ferīre
rapacious adj rapāx, avidus
rapaciously adv avidē
rapacity n rapācitās f, avid"tās f
rape n raptus m
rapid adj rapidus, vēlōx, citus, incitātus
rapidity n celeritās f, vēlōcitās f, incitātiō f
rapidly adv rapidē, vēlōciter, citō
rapine n rapīna f
rapt adj intentus

135

rapture n laetitia f, alacritās f
rare adj rārus; (occurrence) īnfrequēns; (quality) singulāris
rarefy vt extenuāre
rarely adv rārō
rarity n rāritās f; (thing) rēs īnsolita f
rascal n furcifer m, scelestus m
rascally adj improbus
rash adj temerārius, audāx, incōnsultus; praeceps
rashly adv temerē, incōnsultē
rashness n temeritās f, audācia f
rat n mūs m/f
rate n (cost) pretium nt; (standard) nōrma f; (tax) vectīgal nt; (speed) celeritās f; **at any ~** (concessive) utique, saltem; (adversative) quamquam, tamen ♦ vt (value) aestimāre; (scold) incrēpāre, obiūrgāre
rather adv potius, satius; (somewhat) aliquantum; (with comp) aliquantō; (with verbs) mālō; (correcting) immo; **~ sad** tristior; **I would ~** mālō; **I ~ think** haud sciō an; **~ than** magis quam, potius quam
ratification n (formal) sanctiō f
ratify vt ratum facere, sancīre; (LAW) iubēre
rating n taxātiō f, aestimātiō f; (navy) nauta m; (scolding) obiūrgātiō f
ratiocinate vi ratiōcinārī
ratiocination n ratiōcinātiō f
ration n dēmēnsum nt
rational adj animō praeditus; **be ~** sapere
rationality n ratiō f
rationally adv ratiōne
rations npl cibāria ntpl, diāria ntpl
rattle n crepitus m; (toy) crotalum nt ♦ vi crepitāre, increpāre
raucous adj raucus
ravage vt dēpopulārī, vāstāre, dīripere
rave vi furere, īnsānīre; (fig) bacchārī, saevīre
raven n cornīx f
ravenous adj rapāx, vorāx
ravenously adv avidē
ravine n faucēs fpl, hiātus m
raving adj furiōsus, īnsānus ♦ n furor m
ravish vt rapere; (joy) efferre
raw adj crūdus; (person) rudis, agrestis
ray n radius m; **the first ray of hope appeared** prīma spēs adfulsit
raze vt excīdere, solō aequāre
razor n novācula f
reach n (space) spatium nt; (mind) captus m; (weapon) ictus m; **out of ~ of** extrā (acc); **within ~** ad manum ♦ vt advenīre ad (acc); (space) pertinēre ad; (journey) pervenīre ad
react vi adficī; **~ to** ferre
reaction n: **what was his ~ to?** quō animō tulit?
read vt legere; (a book) ēvolvere; (aloud) recitāre; **~ over** perlegere
reader n lēctor m
readily adv facile, libenter, ultrō
readiness n facilitās f; **in ~** ad manum, in prōmptū, in expedītō
reading n lēctiō f
readjust vt dēnuō accommodāre

ready adj parātus, prōmptus; (manner) facilis; (money) praesēns; **get ~, make ~** parāre, expedīre, adōrnāre
reaffirm vt iterum adfirmāre
real adj vērus, germānus
real estate n fundus m, solum nt
realism n vēritās f
realistic adj vērī similis
reality n rēs f, rēs ipsa f, vērum nt; **in ~** rēvērā
realize vt intellegere, animadvertere; (aim) efficere, peragere; (money) redigere
really adv vērē, rēvērā, profectō; **really?** itane vērō?
realm n rēgnum nt
reap vt metere; **~ the reward of** frūctum percipere ex
reaper n messor m
reappear vi revenīre
rear vt alere, ēducāre; (structure) exstruere ♦ vi sē ērigere ♦ n tergum nt; (MIL) novissima aciēs f, novissimum agmen nt; **in the ~** ā tergō; **bring up the ~** agmen claudere, agmen cōgere ♦ adj postrēmus, novissimus
rearguard n novissimum agmen nt, novissimī mpl
rearrange vt ōrdinem mūtāre (gen)
reason n (faculty) mēns f, animus m, ratiō f; (sanity) sānitās f; (argument) ratiō f; (cause) causa f; (moderation) modus m; **by ~ of** propter (acc); **for this ~** idcircō, ideō, proptereā; **in ~** aequus, modicus; **with good ~** iūre; **without ~** temerē, sine causā; **without good ~** frūstrā, iniūriā; **give a ~ for** ratiōnem adferre (gen); **I know the ~ for** sciō cūr, quamobrem (subj); **there is no ~ for** nōn est cūr, nihil est quod (subj); **lose one's ~** īnsānīre ♦ vi ratiōcinārī, disserere
reasonable adj aequus, iūstus; (person) modestus; (amount) modicus
reasonably adv ratiōne, iūstē; modicē
reasoning n ratiō f, ratiōcinātiō f
reassemble vt colligere, cōgere
reassert vt iterāre
reassume vt recipere
reassure vt firmāre, cōnfirmāre
rebate vt dēdūcere
rebel n rebellis m ♦ adj sēditiōsus ♦ vi rebelliōnem facere, rebellāre, dēscīscere
rebellion n sēditiō f, mōtus m
rebellious adj sēditiōsus
rebound vi resilīre
rebuff n repulsa f ♦ vt repellere, āversārī
rebuild vt renovāre, restaurāre
rebuke n reprehēnsiō f, obiūrgātiō f ♦ vt reprehendere, obiūrgāre, increpāre
rebut vt refūtāre, redarguere
recalcitrant adj invītus
recall n revocātiō f, reditus m ♦ vt revocāre; (from exile) redūcere; (to mind) reminīscī (gen), recordārī (gen)
recant vt retractāre
recantation n receptus m
recapitulate vt repetere, summātim dīcere
recapitulation n ēnumerātiō f
recapture vt recipere
recast vt reficere, retractāre
recede vi recēdere

receipt *n* (*act*) acceptiō *f*; (*money*) acceptum *nt*; (*written*) apocha *f*
receive *vt* accipere, capere; (*in turn*) excipere
receiver *n* receptor *m*
recent *adj* recēns
recently *adv* nūper, recēns
receptacle *n* receptāculum *nt*
reception *n* aditus *m*, hospitium *nt*
receptive *adj* docilis
recess *n* recessus *m*, angulus *m*; (*holiday*) fēriae *fpl*
recharge *vt* replēre
recipe *n* compositiō *f*
recipient *n* quī accipit
reciprocal *adj* mūtuus
reciprocally *adv* mūtuō, inter sē
reciprocate *vt* referre, reddere
reciprocity *n* mūtuum *nt*
recital *n* nārrātiō *f*, ēnumerātiō *f*; (*LIT*) recitātiō *f*
recitation *n* recitātiō *f*
recite *vt* recitāre; (*details*) ēnumerāre
reciter *n* recitātor *m*
reck *vt* ratiōnem habēre (*gen*)
reckless *adj* temerārius, incautus, praeceps
recklessly *adv* incautē, temerē
recklessness *n* temeritās *f*, neglegentia *f*
reckon *vt* (*count*) computāre, numerāre; (*think*) cēnsēre, dūcere; (*estimate*) aestimāre; ~ **on** cōnfīdere (*dat*); ~ **up** dīnumerāre; (*cost*) aestimāre; ~ **with** contendere cum
reckoning *n* ratiō *f*
reclaim *vt* repetere; (*from error*) revocāre
recline *vi* recumbere; (*at table*) accumbere; (*pl*) discumbere
recluse *n* homō sōlitārius *m*
recognition *n* cognitiō *f*
recognizance *n* vadimōnium *nt*
recognize *vt* agnōscere; (*approve*) accipere; (*admit*) fatērī
recoil *vi* resilīre; ~ **from** refugere; ~ **upon** recidere in (*acc*)
recollect *vt* reminīscī (*gen*)
recollection *n* memoria *f*, recordātiō *f*
recommence *vt* renovāre, redintegrāre
recommend *vt* commendāre; (*advise*) suādēre (*dat*)
recommendation *n* commendātiō *f*; (*advice*) cōnsilium *nt*; **letter of** ~ litterae commendātīciae
recompense *vt* remūnerārī, grātiam referre (*dat*) ◆ *n* praemium *nt*, remūnerātiō *f*
reconcile *vt* compōnere, reconciliāre; **be reconciled** in grātiam redīre
reconciliation *n* reconciliātiō *f*, grātia *f*
recondite *adj* reconditus, abstrūsus
recondition *vt* reficere
reconnaissance *n* explōrātiō *f*
reconnoitre *vt, vi* explōrāre; **without reconnoitring** inexplōrātō
reconquer *vt* recipere
reconsider *vt* reputāre, retractāre
reconstruct *vt* restituere, renovāre
reconstruction *n* renovātiō *f*
record *n* monumentum *nt*; (*LIT*) commentārius *m*; **records** *pl* tabulae *fpl*, fāstī *mpl*, ācta *ntpl*; **break the** ~ priōrēs omnes superāre ◆ *vt* in

commentārium referre; (*history*) perscrībere, nārrāre
recount *vt* nārrāre, commemorāre
recourse *n*: **have** ~ **to** (*for safety*) cōnfugere ad; (*as expedient*) dēcurrere ad
recover *vt* recipere, recuperāre; (*loss*) reparāre; ~ **oneself** sē colligere; ~ **one's senses** ad sānitātem revertī ◆ *vi* convalēscere
recovery *n* recuperātiō *f*; (*from illness*) salūs *f*
recreate *vt* recreāre
recreation *n* requiēs *f*, remissiō *f*, lūdus *m*
recriminate *vi* in vicem accūsāre
recrimination *n* mūtua accūsātiō *f*
recruit *n* tīrō *m* ◆ *vt* (*MIL*) cōnscrībere; (*strength*) reficere
recruiting officer *n* conquīsītor *m*
rectify *vt* corrigere, ēmendāre
rectitude *n* probitās *f*
recumbent *adj* supīnus
recuperate *vi* convalēscere
recur *vi* recurrere, redīre
recurrence *n* reditus *m*, reversiō *f*
recurrent *adj* adsiduus
red *adj* ruber
redden *vi* ērubēscere ◆ *vt* rutilāre
reddish *adj* subrūfus
redeem *vt* redimere, līberāre
redeemer *n* līberātor *m*
redemption *n* redemptiō *f*
red-haired *adj* rūfus
red-handed *adj*: **catch** ~ in manifestō scelere dēprehendere
red-hot *adj* fervēns
red lead *n* minium *nt*
redness *n* rubor *m*
redolent *adj*: **be** ~ **of** redolēre
redouble *vt* ingemināre
redoubt *n* prōpugnāculum *nt*
redoubtable *adj* īnfestus, formīdolōsus
redound *vi* redundāre; **it redounds to my credit** mihī honōrī est
redress *n* remedium *nt*; **demand** ~ rēs repetere ◆ *vt* restituere
reduce *vt* minuere, attenuāre; (*to a condition*) redigere, dēdūcere; (*MIL*) expugnāre; ~ **to the ranks** in ōrdinem cōgere
reduction *n* imminūtiō *f*; (*MIL*) expugnātiō *f*
redundancy *n* redundantia *f*
redundant *adj* redundāns; **be** ~ redundāre
reduplication *n* gemīnātiō *f*
re-echo *vt* reddere, referre ◆ *vi* resonāre
reed *n* harundō *f*
reedy *adj* harundineus
reef *n* saxa *ntpl* ◆ *vt* (*sail*) subnectere
reek *n* fūmus *m* ◆ *vi* fūmāre
reel *vi* vacillāre, titubāre
re-enlist *vt* rescrībere
re-establish *vt* restituere
refashion *vt* reficere
refer *vt* (*person*) dēlēgāre; (*matter*) rēicere, remittere ◆ *vi*: ~ **to** spectāre ad; (*in speech*) attingere, perstringere
referee *n* arbiter *m*
reference *n* ratiō *f*; (*in book*) locus *m*
refine *vt* excolere, expolīre; (*metal*) excoquere
refined *adj* hūmānus, urbānus, polītus

refinement *n* hūmānitās *f*, cultus *m*, ēlegantia *f*
refit *vt* reficere
reflect *vt* reddere, repercutere ♦ *vi* meditārī;
~ **upon** cōnsīderāre, sēcum reputāre; (*blame*)
reprehendere
reflection *n* (*of light*) repercussus *m*; (*image*)
imāgō *f*; (*thought*) meditātiō *f*, cōgitātiō *f*;
(*blame*) reprehēnsiō *f*; **cast reflections on**
maculīs aspergere, vitiō vertere; **with due**
~ cōnsīderātē; **without** ~ incōnsultē
reflux *n* recessus *m*
reform *n* ēmendātiō *f* ♦ *vt* (*lines*) restituere; (*error*)
corrigere, ēmendāre, meliōrem facere ♦ *vi* sē
corrigere
reformation *n* corrēctiō *f*
reformer *n* corrēctor *m*, ēmendātor *m*
refract *vt* īnfringere
refractory *adj* contumāx
refrain *vi* temperāre, abstinēre (*dat*),
supersedēre (*inf*)
refresh *vt* recreāre, renovāre, reficere; (*mind*)
integrāre
refreshed *adj* requiētus
refreshing *adj* dulcis, iūcundus
refreshment *n* cibus *m*
refuge *n* perfugium *nt*; (*secret*) latebra *f*; **take**
~ **with** perfugere ad (*acc*); **take** ~ **in** confugere
refugee *n* profugus *m*
refulgence *n* splendor *m*
refulgent *adj* splendidus
refund *vt* reddere
refusal *n* recūsātiō *f*, dētrectātiō *f*
refuse *n* pūrgāmenta *ntpl*; (*fig*) faex *f* ♦ *vt* (*request*)
dēnegāre; (*offer*) dētrectāre, recūsāre; (*with verb*)
nōlle
refutation *n* refūtātiō *f*, reprehēnsiō *f*
refute *vt* refellere, redarguere, revincere
regain *vt* recipere
regal *adj* rēgius, rēgālis
regale *vt* excipere, dēlectāre; ~ **oneself** epulārī
regalia *n* īnsignia *ntpl*
regally *adv* rēgāliter
regard *n* respectus *m*, ratiō *f*; (*esteem*) grātia *f*;
with ~ **to** ad (*acc*), quod attinet ad ♦ *vt* (*look*)
intuērī, spectāre; (*deem*) habēre, dūcere; **send**
regards to salūtem dīcere (*dat*)
regarding *prep* dē (*abl*)
regardless *adj* neglegēns, immemor
regency *n* interrēgnum *nt*
regent *n* interrēx *m*
regicide *n* (*person*) rēgis interfector *m*; (*act*) rēgis
caedēs *f*
regime *n* administrātiō *f*
regimen *n* vīctus *m*
regiment *n* legiō *f*
region *n* regiō *f*, tractus *m*
register *n* tabulae *fpl*, album *nt* ♦ *vt* in tabulās
referre, perscrībere; (*emotion*) ostendere,
sūmere
registrar *n* tabulārius *m*
registry *n* tabulārium *nt*
regret *n* dolor *m*; (*for past*) dēsīderium *nt*; (*for fault*)
paenitentia *f* ♦ *vt* dolēre; **I** ~ **mē** paenitet, mē
piget (*gen*)
regretful *adj* maestus
regretfully *adv* dolenter

regrettable *adj* īnfēlīx, īnfortūnātus
regular *adj* (*consistent*) cōnstāns; (*orderly*)
ōrdinātus; (*habitual*) solitus, adsiduus; (*proper*)
iūstus, rēctus
regularity *n* moderātiō *f*, ōrdō *m*; (*consistency*)
cōnstantia *f*
regularly *adv* ōrdine; cōnstanter; iūstē, rēctē
regulate *vt* ōrdināre, dīrigere; (*control*) moderārī
regulation *n* lēx *f*, dēcrētum *nt*
rehabilitate *vt* restituere
rehearsal *n* meditātiō *f*
rehearse *vt* meditārī
reign *n* rēgnum *nt*; (*emperor's*) prīncipātus *m*; **in**
the ~ **of Numa** rēgnante Numā ♦ *vi* rēgnāre;
(*fig*) dominārī
reimburse *vt* rependere
rein *n* habēna *f*; **give full** ~ **to** habēnās
immittere ♦ *vt* īnfrēnāre
reindeer *n* rēnō *m*
reinforce *vt* firmāre, cōnfirmāre
reinforcement *n* subsidium *nt*; **reinforcements**
pl novae cōpiae *fpl*
reinstate *vt* restituere, redūcere
reinstatement *n* restitūtiō *f*, reductiō *f*; (*to legal*
privileges) postlīminium *nt*
reinvigorate *vt* recreāre
reiterate *vt* dictitāre, iterāre
reiteration *n* iterātiō *f*
reject *vt* rēicere; (*with scorn*) respuere, aspernārī,
repudiāre
rejection *n* rēiectiō *f*, repulsa *f*
rejoice *vi* gaudēre, laetārī ♦ *vt* dēlectāre
rejoicing *n* gaudium *nt*
rejoin *vt* redīre ad ♦ *vi* respondēre
rejoinder *n* respōnsum *nt*
rejuvenate *vt*: **be rejuvenated** repuerāscere
rekindle *vt* suscitāre
relapse *vi* recidere
relate *vt* (*tell*) nārrāre, commemorāre, expōnere;
(*compare*) cōnferre ♦ *vi* pertinēre
related *adj* propinquus; (*by birth*) cognātus; (*by*
marriage) adfīnis; (*fig*) fīnitimus
relation *n* (*tale*) nārrātiō *f*; (*connection*) ratiō *f*; (*kin*)
necessārius *m*, cognātus *m*, adfīnis *m*
relationship *n* necessitūdō *f*; (*by birth*) cognātiō *f*;
(*by marriage*) adfīnitās *f*; (*connection*) vīcīnitās *f*
relative *adj* cum cēterīs comparātus ♦ *n*
propinquus *m*, cognātus *m*, adfīnis *m*,
necessārius *m*
relatively *adv* ex comparātiōne
relax *vt* laxāre, remittere ♦ *vi* languēscere
relaxation *n* remissiō *f*, requiēs *f*, lūdus *m*
relay *n*: **relays of horses** dispositī equī *mpl*
release *vt* solvere, exsolvere, līberāre, expedīre;
(*LAW*) absolvere ♦ *n* missiō *f*, līberātiō *f*
relegate *vt* relēgāre
relent *vi* concēdere, plācārī, flectī
relentless *adj* immisericors, inexōrābilis;
(*things*) improbus
relevant *adj* ad rem
reliability *n* fīdūcia *f*
reliable *adj* fīdus
reliance *n* fīdūcia *f*, fidēs *f*
reliant *adj* frētus
relic *n* rēliquiae *fpl*

relief n levātiō f, levāmen nt, adlevāmentum nt; (aid) subsidium nt; (turn of duty) vicēs fpl; (art) ēminentia f; (sculpture) toreuma nt; **bas** ~ anaglypta ntpl; **in** ~ ēminēns, expressus; **throw into** ~ exprimere, distinguere

relieve vt levāre, sublevāre; (aid) subvenīre (dat); (duty) succēdere (dat), excipere; (art) distinguere

religion n religiō f, deōrum cultus m

religious adj religiōsus, pius; ~ **feeling** religiō f

religiously adv religiōsē

relinquish vt relinquere; (office) sē abdicāre (abl)

relish n sapor m; (sauce) condīmentum nt; (zest) studium nt ♦ vt dēlectārī (abl)

reluctance n: **with** ~ invītus

reluctant adj invītus

reluctantly adv invītus, gravātē

rely vi fīdere (dat), cōnfīdere (dat)

relying adj frētus (abl)

remain vi manēre, morārī; (left over) restāre, superesse

remainder n reliquum nt

remaining adj reliquus; **the** ~ cēterī pl

remains n rēliquiae fpl

remand vt (LAW) ampliāre

remark n dictum nt ♦ vt dīcere; (note) observāre

remarkable adj īnsignis, ēgregius, memorābilis

remarkably adv īnsignītē, ēgregiē

remediable adj sānābilis

remedy n remedium nt ♦ vt medērī (dat), sānāre

remember vt meminisse (gen); (recall) recordārī (gen), reminīscī (gen)

remembrance n memoria f, recordātiō f

remind vt admonēre, commonefacere

reminder n admonitiō f, admonitum nt

reminiscence n recordātiō f

remiss adj dissolūtus, neglegēns

remission n venia f

remissness n neglegentia f

remit vt remittere; (fault) ignōscere (dat); (debt) dōnāre; (punishment) condōnāre; (question) referre

remittance n pecūnia f

remnant n fragmentum nt; **remnants** pl rēliquiae fpl

remonstrance n obtestātiō f, obiūrgātiō f

remonstrate vi reclāmāre; ~ **with** obiūrgāre; ~ **about** expostulāre

remorse n paenitentia f, cōnscientia f

remorseless adj immisericors

remote adj remōtus, reconditus

remotely adv procul

remoteness n longinquitās f

removal n āmōtiō f; (going) migrātiō f

remove vt āmovēre, dēmere, eximere, removēre; (out of the way) dēmovēre ♦ vi migrāre, dēmigrāre

remunerate vt remūnerārī

remuneration n mercēs f, praemium nt

rend vt scindere, dīvellere

render vt reddere; (music) interpretārī; (translation) vertere; (thanks) referre

rendering n interpretātiō f

rendez-vous n cōnstitūtum nt

renegade n dēsertor m

renew vt renovāre, integrāre, īnstaurāre, redintegrāre

renewal n renovātiō f; (ceremony) īnstaurātiō f

renounce vt renūntiāre, mittere, repudiāre

renovate vt renovāre, reficere

renown n fāma f, glōria f

renowned adj praeclārus, īnsignis, nōtus

rent n (tear) fissum nt; (pay) mercēs f ♦ vt (hire) condūcere; (lease) locāre

renunciation n cessiō f, repudiātiō f

repair vt reficere, sarcīre ♦ vi sē recipere ♦ n: **keep in good** ~ tuērī; **in bad** ~ ruīnōsus

reparable adj ēmendābilis

reparation n satisfactiō f

repartee n facētiae fpl, salēs mpl

repast n cēna f, cibus m

repay vt remūnerārī, grātiam referre (dat); (money) repōnere

repayment n solūtiō f

repeal vt abrogāre ♦ n abrogātiō f

repeat vt iterāre; (lesson) reddere; (ceremony) īnstaurāre; (performance) referre

repeatedly adv identidem, etiam atque etiam

repel vt repellere, dēfendere

repellent adj iniūcundus

repent vi: **I** ~ mē paenitet (+ gen of thing)

repentance n paenitentia f

repentant adj paenitēns

repercussion n ēventus m

repertory n thēsaurus m

repetition n iterātiō f

repine vi conquerī

replace vt repōnere, restituere; ~ **by** substituere

replacement n supplēmentum nt

replenish vt replēre, supplēre

replete adj plēnus

repletion n satietās f

replica n apographon nt

reply vi respondēre ♦ n respōnsum nt

report n (talk) fāma f, rūmor m; (repute) opīniō f; (account) renūntiātiō f, litterae fpl; (noise) fragor m; **make a** ~ renūntiāre ♦ vt referre, dēferre, renūntiāre

repose n quiēs f, requiēs f ♦ vt repōnere, pōnere ♦ vi quiēscere

repository n horreum nt

reprehend vt reprehendere, culpāre

reprehensible adj accūsābilis, improbus

reprehension n reprehēnsiō f, culpa f

represent vt dēscrībere, effingere, exprimere, imitārī; (character) partēs agere (gen), persōnam gerere (gen); (case) prōpōnere; (substitute for) vicārium esse (gen)

representation n imāgō f, imitātiō f; **make representations to** admonēre

representative n lēgātus m

repress vt reprimere, cohibēre

repression n coercitiō f

reprieve n mora f, venia f ♦ vt veniam dare (dat)

reprimand vt reprehendere, increpāre ♦ n reprehēnsiō f

reprisals npl ultiō f

reproach vt exprobāre, obicere (dat) ♦ n exprobrātiō f, probrum nt; (cause) opprobrium nt

reproachful adj contumēliōsus

reprobate adj perditus

reproduce vt propāgāre; (likeness) referre

reproduction n prōcreātiō f; (*likeness*) imāgō f
reproductive adj genitālis
reproof n reprehēnsiō f, obiūrgātiō f
reprove vt reprehendere, increpāre, obiūrgāre
reptile n serpēns f
republic n lībera rēspūblica f, cīvitās populāris f
republican adj populāris
repudiate vt repudiāre
repudiation n repudiātiō f
repugnance n fastīdium nt, odium nt
repugnant adj invīsus, adversus
repulse n dēpulsiō f; (*at election*) repulsa f ♦ vt
repellere, āversārī, prōpulsāre
repulsion n repugnantia f
repulsive adj odiōsus, foedus
reputable adj honestus
reputation n fāma f, existimātiō f; (*for something*)
opīniō f (*gen*); **have a ~** nōmen habēre
repute n fāma f, existimātiō f; **bad ~** īnfāmia f
reputed adj: **I am ~ to be** dīcor esse
request n rogātiō f, postulātum nt; **obtain
a ~** impetrāre ♦ vt rogāre, petere; (*urgently*)
dēposcere
require vt (*demand*) imperāre, postulāre; (*need*)
egēre (*abl*); (*call for*) requīrere
requirement n postulātum nt, necessārium nt
requisite adj necessārius
requisition n postulātiō f ♦ vt imperāre
requital n grātia f, vicēs fpl
requite vt grātiam referre (*dat*), remūnerārī
rescind vt rescindere, abrogāre
rescript n rescrīptum nt
rescue vt ēripere, expedīre, servāre ♦ n salūs f;
come to the ~ of subvenīre (*dat*)
research n investīgātiō f
resemblance n similitūdō f, imāgō f, īnstar nt
resemble vt similem esse (*dat*), referre
resent vt aegrē ferre, indignārī
resentful adj īrācundus
resentment n dolor m, indignātiō f
reservation n (*proviso*) exceptiō f
reserve vt servāre; (*store*) recondere; (*in a deal*)
excipere ♦ n (MIL) subsidium nt; (*disposition*)
pudor m, reticentia f; (*caution*) cautiō f; **in ~** in
succenturiātus; **without ~** palam
reserved adj (*place*) assignātus; (*disposition*)
taciturnus, tēctus
reservedly adv circumspectē
reserves npl subsidia ntpl
reservoir n lacus m
reside vi habitāre; **~ in** incolere
residence n domicilium nt, domus f
resident n incola m/f
residual adj reliquus
residue, residuum n reliqua pars f
resign vt cēdere; (*office*) abdicāre mē, tē etc dē
(*abl*); **~ oneself** acquiēscere ♦ vi sē abdicāre
resignation n abdicātiō f; (*state of mind*) patientia
f, aequus animus m
resigned adj patiēns; **be ~ to** aequō animō ferre
resilience n mollitia f
resilient adj mollis
resist vt resistere (*dat*), adversārī (*dat*),
repugnāre (*dat*)
resistance n repugnantia f; **offer ~** obsistere
(*dat*)

resistless adj invictus
resolute adj fortis, cōnstāns
resolutely adv fortiter, cōnstanter
resolution n (*conduct*) fortitūdō f, cōnstantia
f; (*decision*) dēcrētum nt, sententia f; (*into parts*)
sēcrētiō f
resolve n fortitūdō f, cōnstantia f ♦ vt dēcernere,
cōnstituere; (*into parts*) dissolvere; **the senate
resolves** placet senātuī
resonance n sonus m
resonant adj canōrus
resort n locus celeber m; **last ~** ultimum
auxilium nt ♦ vi frequentāre, ventitāre; (*have
recourse*) dēcurrere, dēscendere, cōnfugere
resound vi resonāre, personāre
resource n subsidium nt; (*means*) modus m;
resources pl opēs fpl, cōpiae fpl
resourceful adj versūtus, callidus
resourcefulness n calliditās f, versūtus animus
m
respect n (*esteem*) honōs m, observantia f;
(*reference*) ratiō f; **out of ~** honōris causā;
pay one's respects to salūtāre; **show ~ for**
observāre; **in every ~** ex omnī parte, in omnī
genere; **in ~ of** ad (*acc*), ab (*abl*) ♦ vt honōrāre,
observāre, verērī
respectability n honestās f
respectable adj honestus, līberālis, frūgī
respectably adv honestē
respectful adj observāns
respectfully adv reverenter
respectfulness n observantia f
respective adj suus (*with quisque*)
respectively adv alius ... alius
respiration n respīrātiō f, spīritus m
respire vi respīrāre
respite n requiēs f, intercapēdō f, intermissiō f
resplendence n splendor m
resplendent adj splendidus, illūstris
resplendently adv splendidē
respond vi respondēre
response n respōnsum nt
responsibility n auctōritās f, cūra f
responsible adj reus; (*witness*) locuplēs; **be ~ for**
praestāre
responsive adj (*pupil*) docilis; (*character*) facilis
rest n quiēs f, ōtium nt; (*after toil*) requiēs f;
(*remainder*) reliqua pars f; **be at ~** requiēscere; **set
at ~** tranquillāre; **the ~** (*others*) cēteri mpl; **the
~ of** reliquī ♦ vi requiēscere, acquiēscere; **~ on**
nītī (*abl*), innītī in (*abl*) ♦ vt (*hope*) pōnere in (*abl*)
resting place n cubīle nt, sēdēs f
restitution n satisfactiō f; **make ~** restituere;
demand ~ rēs repetere
restive adj contumāx
restless adj inquiētus, sollicitus; **be ~** fluctuārī
restlessness n sollicitūdō f
restoration n renovātiō f; (*of king*) reductiō f
restore vt reddere, restituere; (*to health*)
recreāre; (*to power*) redūcere; (*damage*) reficere,
redintegrāre
restorer n restitūtor m
restrain vt coercēre, comprimere, cohibēre
restraint n moderātiō f, temperantia f, frēnī mpl;
with ~ abstinenter
restrict vt continēre, circumscrībere

restricted *adj* artus; ~ **to** proprius *(gen)*
restriction *n* modus *m*, finis *m*; *(limitation)*
  exceptiō *f*
result *n* ēventus *m*, ēventum *nt*, exitus *m*; **the ~ is**
  that quō fit ut ◆ *vi* ēvenīre, ēvādere
resultant *adj* cōnsequēns
resume *vt* repetere
resuscitate *vt* excitāre, suscitāre
retail *vt* dīvēndere, vēndere
retailer *n* caupō *m*
retain *vt* retinēre, tenēre, cōnservāre
retainer *n* satelles *m*
retake *vt* recipere
retaliate *vi* ulcīscī
retaliation *n* ultiō *f*
retard *vt* retardāre, remorārī
retention *n* cōnservātiō *f*
retentive *adj* tenāx
reticence *n* taciturnitās *f*
reticent *adj* taciturnus
reticulated *adj* rēticulātus
retinue *n* satellitēs *mpl*, comitātus *m*
retire *vi* recēdere, abscēdere; *(from office)* abīre;
  (from province) dēcēdere; *(MIL)* pedem referre, sē
  recipere
retired *adj* ēmeritus; *(place)* remōtus
retirement *n* *(act)* recessus *m*, dēcessus *m*; *(state)*
  sōlitūdō *f*, ōtium *nt*; **life of ~** vīta prīvāta
retiring *adj* modestus, verēcundus
retort *vt* respondēre, referre ◆ *n* respōnsum *nt*
retouch *vt* retractāre
retrace *vt* repetere, iterāre
retract *vt* revocāre, renūntiāre
retreat *n* *(MIL)* receptus *m*; *(place)* recessus *m*,
  sēcessus *m*; **sound the ~** receptuī canere ◆ *vi* sē
  recipere, pedem referre; regredī
retrench *vt* minuere, recīdere
retrenchment *n* parsimōnia *f*
retribution *n* poena *f*
retributive *adj* ultor, ultrīx
retrieve *vt* reparāre, recipere
retrograde *adj* *(fig)* dēterior
retrogression *n* regressus *m*
retrospect *n*: **in ~** respicientī
retrospective *adj*: **be ~** retrōrsum sē referre
retrospectively *adv* retrō
return *n* reditus *m*; *(pay)* remūnerātiō *f*; *(profit)*
  fructus *m*, pretium *nt*; *(statement)* professiō *f*;
  make a ~ of profitērī; **in ~ for** prō *(abl)*; **in ~** in
  vicem, vicissim ◆ *vt* reddere, restituere, referre
  ◆ *vi* redīre, revenīre, revertī; *(from province)*
  dēcēdere
reunion *n* convīvium *nt*
reunite *vt* reconciliāre
reveal *vt* aperīre, patefacere
revel *n* cōmissātiō *f*, bacchātiō *f*; **revels** *pl* orgia
  ntpl ◆ *vi* cōmissārī, bacchārī; ~ **in** luxuriārī
revelation *n* patefactiō *f*
reveller *n* cōmissātor *m*
revelry *n* cōmissātiō *f*
revenge *n* ultiō *f*; **take ~ on** vindicāre in *(acc)*
  ◆ *vt* ulcīscī
revengeful *adj* ulcīscendī cupidus
revenue *n* fructus *m*, reditus *m*, vectīgālia *ntpl*
reverberate *vi* resonāre
reverberation *n* repercussus *m*

revere *vt* venerārī, colere
reverence *n* venerātiō *f*; *(feeling)* religiō *f*;
  reverentia *f*
reverent *adj* religiōsus, pius
reverently *adv* religiōsē
reverie *n* meditātiō *f*, somnium *nt*
reversal *n* abrogātiō *f*
reverse *adj* contrārius ◆ *n* contrārium *nt*; *(MIL)*
  clādēs *f* ◆ *vt* invertere; *(decision)* rescindere
reversion *n* reditus *m*
revert *vi* redīre, revertī
review *n* recognitiō *f*, recēnsiō *f* ◆ *vt* *(MIL)*
  recēnsēre
revile *vt* maledīcere *(dat)*
revise *vt* recognōscere, corrigere; *(LIT)* līmāre
revision *n* ēmendātiō *f*; *(LIT)* līma *f*
revisit *vt* revīsere
revival *n* renovātiō *f*
revive *vt* recreāre, excitāre ◆ *vi* revīvīscere,
  renāscī
revocation *n* revocātiō *f*
revoke *vt* renūntiāre, īnfectum reddere
revolt *n* sēditiō *f*, dēfectiō *f* ◆ *vi* dēficere, rebellāre
revolting *adj* taeter, obscēnus
revolution *n* *(movement)* conversiō *f*; *(change)* rēs
  novae *fpl*; *(revolt)* mōtus *m*; **effect a ~** rēs novāre
revolutionary *adj* sēditiōsus, novārum rērum
  cupidus
revolve *vi* volvī, versārī, convertī ◆ *vt* *(in mind)*
  volūtāre
revulsion *n* mūtātiō *f*
reward *n* praemium *nt*, mercēs *f* ◆ *vt*
  remūnerārī, compēnsāre
rhapsody *n* carmen *nt*; *(epic)* rhapsōdia *f*
rhetoric *n* rhētorica *f*; **of ~** rhētoricus; **exercise**
  in ~ dēclāmātiō *f*; **practise ~** dēclāmāre;
  teacher of ~ rhētor *m*
rhetorical *adj* rhētoricus, dēclāmātōrius
rhetorically *adv* rhētoricē
rhetorician *n* rhētor *m*, dēclāmātor *m*
rhinoceros *n* rhīnocerōs *m*
rhyme *n* homoeoteleuton *nt*; **without ~ or**
  reason temerē
rhythm *n* numerus *m*, modus *m*
rhythmical *adj* numerōsus
rib *n* costa *f*
ribald *adj* obscēnus
ribaldry *n* obscēnitās *f*
ribbon *n* īnfula *f*
rice *n* oryza *f*
rich *adj* dīves, locuplēs; opulentus; *(fertile)* ūber,
  opīmus; *(food)* pinguis
riches *npl* dīvitiae *fpl*, opēs *fpl*
richly *adv* opulentē, largē, lautē
richness *n* ūbertās *f*, cōpia *f*
rid *vt* līberāre; **get rid of** dēpōnere, dēmovēre,
  exuere
riddle *n* aenigma *nt*; *(sieve)* cribrum *nt* ◆ *vt* *(with*
  wounds) cōnfodere
ride *vi* equitāre, vehī; ~ **a horse** in equō vehī; ~ **at**
  anchor stāre; ~ **away** abequitāre, āvehī; ~ **back**
  revehī; ~ **between** interequitāre; ~ **down**
  dēvehī; ~ **into** invehī; ~ **off** āvehī; ~ **out** ēvehī;
  ~ **past** praetervehī; ~ **round** circumvehī *(dat)*,
  circumequitāre; ~ **up and down** percquitāre;
  ~ **up to** adequitāre ad, advehī ad

rider *n* eques *m*
ridge *n* iugum *nt*
ridicule *n* lūdibrium *nt*, irrīsus *m* ◆ *vt* irrīdēre, illūdere, lūdibriō habēre
ridiculous *adj* rīdiculus, dērīdiculus
ridiculously *adv* rīdiculē
riding *n* equitātiō *f*
rife *adj* frequēns
riff-raff *n* faex populī *f*
rifle *vt* expīlāre, spoliāre
rift *n* rīma *f*
rig *vt* (*ship*) armāre, ōrnāre ◆ *n* habitus *m*
rigging *n* rudentēs *mpl*
right *adj* rēctus; (*just*) aequus, iūstus; (*true*) rēctus, vērus; (*proper*) lēgitimus, fās; (*hand*) dexter; **it is ~** decet (*+acc and infin*); **it is not ~** dēdecet (*+acc and infin*); **you are ~** vēra dīcis; **if I am ~** nisi fallor; **in the ~ place** in locō; **at the ~ time** ad tempus; **at ~ angles** ad parēs angulōs; **on the ~** ā dextrā ◆ *adv* rēctē, bene, probē; (*justifiably*) iūre; **~ up to** usque ad (*acc*); **~ on** rēctā ◆ *n* (*legal*) iūs *nt*; (*moral*) fās *nt* ◆ *vt* (*replace*) restituere; (*correct*) corrigere; (*avenge*) ulcīscī
righteous *adj* iūstus, sanctus, pius
righteously *adv* iūstē, sanctē, piē
righteousness *n* sanctitās *f*, pietās *f*
rightful *adj* iūstus, lēgitimus
rightfully *adv* iūstē, lēgitimē
right hand *n* dextra *f*
right-hand *adj* dexter; **~ man** comes *m*
rightly *adv* rēctē, bene; iūre
right-minded *adj* sānus
rigid *adj* rigidus
rigidity *n* rigor *m*; (*strictness*) sevēritās *f*
rigidly *adv* rigidē, sevērē
rigmarole *n* ambāgēs *fpl*
rigorous *adj* dūrus; (*strict*) sevērus
rigorously *adv* dūriter, sevērē
rigour *n* dūritia *f*; sevēritās *f*
rile *vt* inrītāre, stomachum movēre (*dat*)
rill *n* rīvulus *m*
rim *n* labrum *nt*
rime *n* pruīna *f*
rind *n* cortex *m*
ring *n* ānulus *m*; (*circle*) orbis *m*; (*of people*) corōna *f*; (*motion*) gȳrus *m* ◆ *vt* circumdare; (*bell*) movēre ◆ *vi* tinnīre, sonāre
ringing *n* tinnītus *m* ◆ *adj* canōrus
ringleader *n* caput *nt*, dux *m*
ringlet *n* cincinnus *m*
rinse *vt* colluere
riot *n* tumultus *m*, rixa *f*; **run ~** exsultāre, luxuriārī, tumultuārī, turbās efficere; (*revel*) bacchārī
rioter *n* cōmissātor *m*
riotous *adj* tumultuōsus, sēditiōsus; (*debauched*) dissolūtus; **~ living** cōmissātiō *f*, luxuria *f*
riotously *adv* tumultuōsē; luxuriōsē
rip *vt* scindere
ripe *adj* mātūrus; **of ~ judgment** animī mātūrus
ripen *vt* mātūrāre ◆ *vi* mātūrēscere
ripeness *n* mātūritās *f*
ripple *n* unda *f* ◆ *vi* trepidāre ·
rise *vi* orīrī, surgere; (*hill*) ascendere; (*wind*) cōnsurgere; (*passion*) tumēscere; (*voice*) tollī; (*in size*) crēscere; (*in rank*) ascendere;

(*in revolt*) coorīrī, arma capere; **~ and fall** (*tide*) reciprocāre; **~ above** superāre; **~ again** resurgere; **~ in** (*river*) orīrī ex (*abl*); **~ out** ēmergere; **~ up** exsurgere ◆ *n* ascēnsus *m*; (*slope*) clīvus *m*; (*increase*) incrēmentum *nt*; (*start*) ortus *m*; **give ~ to** parere
rising *n* (*sun*) ortus *m*; (*revolt*) mōtus *m* ◆ *adj* (*ground*) ēditus
risk *n* perīculum *nt*; **run a ~** perīculum subīre, ingredī ◆ *vt* perīclitārī, in āleam dare
risky *adj* perīculōsus
rite *n* rītus *m*
ritual *n* caerimōnia *f*
rival *adj* aemulus ◆ *n* aemulus *m*, rīvālis *m* ◆ *vt* aemulārī
rivalry *n* aemulātiō *f*
river *n* flūmen *nt*, fluvius *m* ◆ *adj* fluviātilis
riverbed *n* alveus *m*
riverside *n* rīpa *f*
rivet *n* clāvus *m* ◆ *vt* (*attention*) dēfīgere
rivulet *n* rīvulus *m*, rīvus *m*
road *n* via *f*, iter *nt*; **on the ~** in itinere, ex itinere; **off the ~** dēvius; **make a ~** viam mūnīre
roadstead *n* statiō *f*
roam *vi* errāre, vagārī; **~ at large** ēvagārī
roar *n* fremitus *m* ◆ *vi* fremere
roast *vt* torrēre ◆ *adj* āssus ◆ *n* āssum *nt*
rob *vt* spoliāre, exspoliāre, expīlāre; (*of hope*) dēicere dē
robber *n* latrō *m*, fūr *m*; (*highway*) grassātor *m*
robbery *n* latrōcinium *nt*
robe *n* vestis *f*; (*woman's*) stola *f*; (*of state*) trabea *f* ◆ *vt* vestīre
robust *adj* rōbustus, fortis
robustness *n* rōbur *nt*, firmitās *f*
rock *n* saxum *nt*; (*steep*) rūpēs *f*, scopulus *m* ◆ *vt* agitāre ◆ *vi* agitārī, vacillāre
rocky *adj* saxōsus, scopulōsus
rod *n* virga *f*; (*fishing*) harundō *f*
roe *n* (*deer*) capreolus *m*, caprea *f*; (*fish*) ōva *ntpl*
rogue *n* veterātor *m*
roguery *n* nēquitia *f*, scelus *nt*
roguish *adj* improbus, malus
role *n* partēs *fpl*
roll *n* (*book*) volūmen *nt*; (*movement*) gȳrus *m*; (*register*) album *nt*; **call the ~ of** legere; **answer the ~ call** ad nōmen respondēre ◆ *vt* volvere ◆ *vi* volvī, volūtārī; **~ down** *vt* dēvolvere ◆ *vi* dēfluere; **~ over** *vt* prōvolvere ◆ *vi* prōlābī; **~ up** *vt* convolvere
roller *n* (AGR) cylindrus *m*; (*for moving*) phalangae *fpl*; (*in book*) umbilīcus *m*
rollicking *adj* hilaris
rolling *adj* volūbilis
Roman *adj* Rōmānus ◆ *n*: **the Romans** Rōmānī *mpl*
romance *n* fābula *f*; amor *m*
romantic *adj* fābulōsus; amātōrius
Rome *n* Rōma *f*; **at ~** Rōmae; **from ~** Rōmā; **to ~** Rōmam
romp *vi* lūdere
roof *n* tēctum *nt*; (*of mouth*) palātum *nt* ◆ *vt* tegere, integere
rook *n* corvus *m*
room *n* conclāve *nt*, camera *f*; (*small*) cella *f*; (*bed*) cubiculum *nt*; (*dining*) cēnāculum *nt*; (*dressing*)

apodytērium *nt*; (*space*) locus *m*; **make ~ for** locum dare (*dat*), cēdere (*dat*)
roominess *n* laxitās *f*
roomy *adj* capāx
roost *vi* stabulārī
rooster *n* gallus gallīnāceus *m*
root *n* rādīx *f*; **take ~** coalēscere ♦ *vt*: **~ out** ērādīcāre
rooted *adj* (*fig*) dēfixus; **deeply ~** (*custom*) inveterātus; **be ~ in** īnsidēre (*dat*); **become deeply ~** inveterāscere
rope *n* fūnis *m*; (*thin*) restis *f*; (*ship's*) rudēns *m*; **know the ropes** perītum esse
rose *n* rosa *f*
rosemary *n* rōs marīnus *m*
rostrum *n* rōstra *ntpl*, suggestus *m*
rosy *adj* roseus, purpureus
rot *n* tābēs *f* ♦ *vi* putrēscere, pūtēscere ♦ *vt* putrefacere
rotate *vi* volvī, sē convertere
rotation *n* conversiō *f*; (*succession*) ōrdō *m*, vicissitūdō *f*; **in ~** ōrdine; **move in ~** in orbem īre
rote *n*: **by ~** memoriter
rotten *adj* putridus
rotund *adj* rotundus
rotundity *n* rotunditās *f*
rouge *n* fūcus *m* ♦ *vt* fūcāre
rough *adj* asper; (*art*) incultus, rudis; (*manners*) agrestis, inurbānus; (*stone*) impolītus; (*treatment*) dūrus, sevērus; (*weather*) atrōx, procellōsus ♦ *vi*: **~ it** dūram vītam vīvere
rough-and-ready *adj* fortuītus
rough draft *n* (LIT) silva *f*
roughen *vt* asperāre, exasperāre
rough-hew *vt* dolāre
roughly *adv* asperē, dūriter; (*with numbers*) circiter
roughness *n* asperitās *f*
round *adj* rotundus; (*spherical*) globōsus; (*cylindrical*) teres ♦ *n* (*circle*) orbis *m*; (*motion*) gȳrus *m*; (*series*) ambitus *m*; **go the rounds** (MIL) vigiliās circumīre ♦ *vt* (*cape*) superāre; **~ off** rotundāre; (*sentence*) concludere; **~ up** compellere ♦ *adv* circum, circā; **go ~** ambīre ♦ *prep* circum (*acc*), circā (*acc*)
roundabout *adj*: **~ story** ambāgēs *fpl*; **~ route** circuitus *m*, ānfrāctus *m*
roundly *adv* (*speak*) apertē, līberē
rouse *vt* excīre, excitāre; (*courage*) adrigere
rousing *adj* vehemēns
rout *n* fuga *f*; (*crowd*) turba *f* ♦ *vt* fugāre, fundere; in fugam conicere, prōflīgāre
route *n* cursus *m*, iter *nt*
routine *n* ūsus *m*, ōrdō *m*
rove *vi* errāre, vagārī
rover *n* vagus *m*; (*sea*) pīrāta *m*
row *n* (*line*) ōrdō *m*; (*noise*) turba *f*, rixa *f* ♦ *vi* (*boat*) rēmigāre ♦ *vt* rēmīs incitāre
rowdy *adj* turbulentus
rower *n* rēmex *m*
rowing *n* rēmigium *nt*
royal *adj* rēgius, rēgālis
royally *adv* rēgiē, rēgāliter

royalty *n* (*power*) rēgnum *nt*; (*persons*) rēgēs *mpl*, domus rēgia *f*
rub *vt* fricāre, terere; **rub away** conterere; **rub hard** dēfricāre; **rub off** dētergēre; **rub out** dēlēre; **rub up** expolīre
rubbing *n* trītus *m*
rubbish *n* quisquiliae *fpl*; (*talk*) nūgae *fpl*
rubble *n* rūdus *nt*
rubicund *adj* rubicundus
rudder *n* gubernāculum *nt*, clāvus *m*
ruddy *adj* rubicundus, rutilus
rude *adj* (*uncivilized*) barbarus, dūrus, inurbānus; (*insolent*) asper, importūnus
rudely *adv* horridē, rusticē; petulanter
rudeness *n* barbariēs *f*; petulantia *f*, importūnitās *f*
rudiment *n* elementum *nt*, initium *nt*
rudimentary *adj* prīmus, incohātus
rue *n* (*herb*) rūta *f* ♦ *vt*: **I rue** mē paenitet (*gen*)
rueful *adj* maestus
ruffian *n* grassātor *m*
ruffle *vt* agitāre; (*temper*) sollicitāre, commovēre
rug *n* strāgulum *nt*
rugged *adj* horridus, asper
ruggedness *n* asperitās *f*
ruin *n* ruīna *f*; (*fig*) exitium *nt*, perniciēs *f*; **go to ~** pessum īre, dīlābī ♦ *vt* perdere, dēperdere, pessum dare; (*moral*) corrumpere, dēprāvāre; **be ruined** perīre
ruined *adj* ruīnōsus
ruinous *adj* exitiōsus, damnōsus
rule *n* (*instrument*) rēgula *f*, amussis *f*; (*principle*) nōrma *f*, lēx *f*, praeceptum *nt*; (*government*) dominātiō *f*, imperium *nt*; **ten-foot ~** decempeda *f*; **as a ~** ferē; **lay down rules** praecipere; **make it a ~ to** īnstituere (*inf*); **~ of thumb** ūsus *m* ♦ *vt* regere, moderārī ♦ *vi* rēgnāre, dominārī; (*judge*) ēdīcere; (*custom*) obtinēre; **~ over** imperāre (*dat*)
ruler *n* (*instrument*) rēgula *f*; (*person*) dominus *m*, rēctor *m*
ruling *n* ēdictum *nt*
rumble *vi* mūgīre
rumbling *n* mūgītus *m*
ruminate *vi* rūminārī
rummage *vi*: **~ through** rīmārī
rumour *n* fāma *f*, rūmor *m*
rump *n* clūnis *f*
run *vi* currere; (*fluid*) fluere, mānāre; (*road*) ferre; (*time*) lābī ♦ *n* cursus *m*; **run about** discurrere, cursāre; **run across** incidere in (*acc*); **run after** sectārī; **run aground** offendere; **run away** aufugere, terga vertere; (*from*) fugere, dēfugere; **run down** dēcurrere, dēfluere ♦ *vt* (*in words*) obtrectāre; **run high** (*fig*) glīscere; **run into** incurrere in (*acc*), īnfluere in (*acc*); **run off with** abripere, abdūcere; **run on** pergere; **run out** (*land*) excurrere; (*time*) exīre; (*supplies*) dēficere; **run over** *vt* (*with car*) obterere; (*details*) percurrere; **run riot** luxuriārī; **run through** (*course*) dēcurrere; (*money*) disperdere; **run short** dēficere; **run up to** adcurrere ad; **run up against** incurrere in (*acc*); **run wild** lascīvīre ♦ *vt* gerere, administrāre

runaway *adj* fugitīvus
rung *n* gradus *m*
runner *n* cursor *m*
running *n* cursus *m* ◆ *adj* (water) vīvus
rupture *n* (fig) dissidium *nt* ◆ *vt* dīrumpere
rural *adj* rūsticus, agrestis
ruse *n* fraus *f*, dolus *m*
rush *n* (plant) cārex *f*, iuncus *m*; (movement)
impetus *m* ◆ *vi* currere, sē incitāre, ruere;
~ **forward** sē prōripere; prōruere; ~ **in** inruere,
incurrere; ~ **out** ēvolāre, sē effundere ◆ *adj*
iunceus

russet *adj* flāvus
rust *n* (iron) ferrūgō *f*; (copper) aerūgō *f* ◆ *vi*
rōbīginem trahere
rustic *adj* rūsticus, agrestis
rusticate *vi* rūsticārī ◆ *vt* relēgāre
rusticity *n* mōrēs rūsticī *mpl*
rustle *vi* increpāre, crepitāre ◆ *n* crepitus *m*
rusty *adj* rōbīginōsus
rut *n* orbita *f*
ruthless *adj* inexōrābilis, crūdēlis
ruthlessly *adv* crūdēliter
rye *n* secāle *nt*

Ss

sabbath *n* sabbata *ntpl*
sable *adj* āter, niger
sabre *n* acīnacēs *m*
sacerdotal *adj* sacerdōtālis
sack *n* saccus *m*; (MIL) dīreptiō *f* ◆ *vt* dīripere, expīlāre; spoliāre
sackcloth *n* cilicium *nt*
sacred *adj* sacer, sanctus
sacredly *adv* sanctē
sacredness *n* sanctitās *f*
sacrifice *n* sacrificium *nt*, sacrum *nt*; (act) immolātiō *f*; (victim) hostia *f*; (fig) iactūra *f* ◆ *vt* immolāre, sacrificāre, mactāre; (fig) dēvovēre, addīcere ◆ *vi* sacra facere; (give up) prōicere
sacrificer *n* immolātor *m*
sacrilege *n* sacrilegium *nt*
sacrilegious *adj* sacrilegus
sacristan *n* aedituus *m*
sacrosanct *adj* sacrōsanctus
sad *adj* maestus, tristis; (thing) tristis
sadden *vt* dolōre adficere
saddle *n* strātum *nt* ◆ *vt* sternere; (fig) impōnere
saddlebags *n* clītellae *fpl*
sadly *adv* maestē
sadness *n* tristitia *f*, maestitia *f*
safe *adj* tūtus, (out of danger) incolumis, salvus; (to trust) fīdus; ~ **and sound** salvus ◆ *n* armārium *nt*
safe-conduct *n* fidēs pūblica *f*
safeguard *n* cautiō *f*, prōpugnāculum *nt* ◆ *vt* dēfendere
safely *adv* tūtō, impūne
safety *n* salūs *f*, incolumitās *f*; **seek ~ in flight** salutem fugā petere
saffron *n* crocus *m* ◆ *adj* croceus
sag *vi* dēmittī
sagacious *adj* prūdēns, sagāx, acūtus
sagaciously *adv* prūdenter, sagāciter
sagacity *n* prūdentia *f*, sagācitās *f*
sage *n* sapiēns *m*; (herb) salvia *f* ◆ *adj* sapiēns
sagely *adv* sapienter
sail *n* vēlum *nt*; **set ~** vēla dare, nāvem solvere; **shorten ~** vēla contrahere ◆ *vi* nāvigāre; ~ **past** legere, praetervehī
sailing *n* nāvigātiō *f*
sailor *n* nauta *m*
sail yard *n* antenna *f*
saint *n* vir sanctus *m*
sainted *adj* beātus
saintly *adj* sanctus
sake *n*: **for the ~ of** grātiā (gen), causā (gen), propter (acc); (behalf) prō (abl)

salacious *adj* salāx
salad *n* morētum *nt*
salamander *n* salamandra *f*
salary *n* mercēs *f*
sale *n* vēnditiō *f*; (formal) mancipium *nt*; (auction) hasta *f*; **for** ~ vēnālis; **be for** ~ prōstāre; **offer for** ~ vēnum dare
saleable *adj* vēndibilis
salient *adj* ēminēns; ~ **points** capita *ntpl*
saline *adj* salsus
saliva *n* salīva *f*
sallow *adj* pallidus
sally *n* ēruptiō *f*; (wit) facētiae *fpl* ◆ *vi* ērumpere, excurrere
salmon *n* salmō *m*
salon *n* ātrium *nt*
salt *n* sal *m* ◆ *adj* salsus
saltcellar *n* salīnum *nt*
saltpetre *n* nitrum *nt*
salt-pits *n* salīnae *fpl*
salty *adj* salsus
salubrious *adj* salūbris
salubriously *adv* salūbriter
salubriousness *n* salūbritās *f*
salutary *adj* salūtāris, ūtilis
salutation *n* salūs *f*
salute *vt* salūtāre
salvage *vt* servāre, ēripere
salvation *n* salūs *f*
salve *n* unguentum *nt*
salver *n* scutella *f*
same *adj* īdem; ~ **as** īdem ac; **all the** ~ nihilōminus; **one and the** ~ ūnus et īdem; **from the** ~ **place** indidem; **in the** ~ **place** ibīdem; **to the** ~ **place** eōdem; **at the** ~ **time** simul, eōdem tempore; (adversative) tamen; **it is all the** ~ **to me** meā nōn interest
Samnites *n* Samnītēs, Samnītium *mpl*
sample *n* exemplum *nt*, specimen *nt* ◆ *vt* gustāre
sanctify *vt* cōnsecrāre
sanctimony *n* falsa rēligiō *f*
sanction *n* comprobātiō *f*, auctōritās *f* ◆ *vt* ratum facere
sanctity *n* sanctitās *f*
sanctuary *n* fānum *nt*, dēlubrum *nt*; (for men) asȳlum *nt*
sand *n* harēna *f*
sandal *n* (outdoors) crepida *f*; (indoors) solea *f*
sandalled *adj* crepidātus, soleātus
sandpit *n* harēnāria *f*
sandstone *n* tōfus *m*
sandy *adj* harēnōsus; (colour) flāvus

sane *adj* sānus
sangfroid *n* aequus animus *m*
sanguinary *adj* cruentus
sanguine *adj* laetus
sanitary *adj* salūbris
sanity *n* mēns sāna *f*
sap *n* sūcus *m* ♦ *vt* subruere
sapience *n* sapientia *f*
sapient *adj* sapiēns
sapling *n* surculus *m*
sapper *n* cunīculārius *m*
sapphire *n* sapphīrus *f*
sarcasm *n* aculeī *mpl*, dicācitās *f*
sarcastic *adj* dicāx, acūleātus
sardonic *adj* amārus
sash *n* cingulum *nt*
satchel *n* loculus *m*
sate *vt* explēre, satiāre
satellite *n* satelles *m*
satiate *vt* explēre, satiāre, saturāre
satiety *n* satietās *f*
satire *n* satura *f*; (*pl, of Horace*) sermōnēs *mpl*
satirical *adj* acerbus
satirist *n* saturārum scrīptor *m*
satirize *vt* perstringere, notāre
satisfaction *n* (*act*) explētiō *f*; (*feeling*) voluptās *f*; (*penalty*) poena *f*; **demand ~** rēs repetere
satisfactorily *adv* ex sententiā
satisfactory *adj* idōneus, grātus
satisfied *adj*: **be ~** satis habēre, contentum esse
satisfy *vt* satisfacere (*dat*); (*desire*) explēre
satrap *n* satrapēs *m*
saturate *vt* imbuere
satyr *n* satyrus *m*
sauce *n* condīmentum *nt*; (*fish*) garum *nt*
saucer *n* patella *f*
saucily *adv* petulanter
saucy *adj* petulāns
saunter *vi* ambulāre
sausage *n* tomāculum *nt*, hīllae *fpl*
savage *adj* ferus, efferātus; (*cruel*) atrōx, inhūmānus; saevus
savagely *adv* ferōciter, inhūmānē
savagery *n* ferōcitās *f*, inhūmānitās *f*
savant *n* vir doctus *m*
save *vt* servāre; **~ up** reservāre ♦ *prep* praeter (*acc*)
saving *adj* parcus; **~ clause** exceptiō *f* ♦ *n* compendium *nt*; **savings** *pl* peculium *nt*
saviour *n* līberātor *m*
savory *n* thymbra *f*
savour *n* sapor *m*; (*of cooking*) nīdor *m* ♦ *vi* sapere; **~ of** olēre, redolēre
savoury *adj* condītus
saw *n* (*tool*) serra *f*; (*saying*) prōverbium *nt* ♦ *vt* serrā secāre
sawdust *n* scobis *f*
say *vt* dīcere; **say that … not** negāre; **say no** negāre; **he says** (*quoting*) inquit; **he says yes** āit; **they say** ferunt (*+acc and infin*)
saying *n* dictum *nt*
scab *n* (*disease*) scabiēs *f*; (*over wound*) crusta *f*
scabbard *n* vāgīna *f*
scabby *adj* scaber
scaffold, scaffolding *n* fala *f*
scald *vt* ūrere

scale *n* (*balance*) lanx *f*; (*fish, etc*) squāma *f*; (*gradation*) gradūs *mpl*; (*music*) diagramma *nt* ♦ *vt* scālīs ascendere
scallop *n* pecten *m*
scalp *n* capitis cutis *f*
scalpel *n* scalpellum *nt*
scamp *n* verberō *m*
scamper *vi* currere
scan *vt* contemplārī; (*verse*) mētīrī
scandal *n* īnfāmia *f*, opprobrium *nt*; (*talk*) calumnia *f*
scandalize *vt* offendere
scandalous *adj* flāgitiōsus, turpis
scansion *n* syllabārum ēnārrātiō *f*
scant *adj* exiguus, parvus
scantily *adv* exiguē, tenuiter
scantiness *n* exiguitās *f*
scanty *adj* exiguus, tenuis, exīlis; (*number*) paucus
scapegoat *n* piāculum *nt*
scar *n* cicātrīx *f*
scarce *adj* rārus; **make oneself ~** sē āmovēre, dē mediō recēdere ♦ *adv* vix, aegrē
scarcely *adv* vix, aegrē; **~ anyone** nēmō ferē
scarcity *n* inopia *f*, angustiae *fpl*
scare *n* formīdō *f* ♦ *vt* terrēre; **~ away** absterrēre
scarecrow *n* formīdō *f*
scarf *n* fōcāle *nt*
scarlet *n* coccum *nt* ♦ *adj* coccinus
scarp *n* rūpēs *f*
scathe *n* damnum *nt*
scatter *vt* spargere; dispergere, dissipāre; (*violently*) disicere ♦ *vi* diffugere
scatterbrained *adj* dēsipiēns
scattered *adj* rārus
scene *n* spectāculum *nt*; (*place*) theātrum *nt*
scenery *n* locī faciēs *f*, speciēs *f*; (*beautiful*) amoenitās *f*
scent *n* odor *m*; (*sense*) odōrātus *m*; **keen ~** sagācitās *f* ♦ *vt* odōrārī; (*perfume*) odōribus perfundere
scented *adj* odōrātus
sceptic *n* Pyrrhōnēus *m*
sceptical *adj* incrēdulus
sceptre *n* scēptrum *nt*
schedule *n* tabulae *fpl*, ratiō *f*
scheme *n* cōnsilium *nt*, ratiō *f* ♦ *vt* māchinārī, mōlīrī
schemer *n* māchinātor *m*
schism *n* discidium *nt*, sēcessiō *f*
scholar *n* vir doctus *m*, litterātus *m*; (*pupil*) discipulus *m*
scholarly *adj* doctus, litterātus
scholarship *n* litterae *fpl*, doctrīna *f*
scholastic *adj* umbrātilis
school *n* (*elementary*) lūdus *m*; (*advanced*) schola *f*; (*high*) gymnasium *nt*; (*sect*) secta *f*, domus *f* ♦ *vt* īnstituere
schoolboy *n* discipulus *m*
schoolmaster *n* magister *m*
schoolmistress *n* magistra *f*
science *n* doctrīna *f*, disciplīna *f*, ars *f*
scimitar *n* acīnacēs *m*
scintillate *vi* scintillāre
scion *n* prōgeniēs *f*
Scipio *n* Scīpiō, Scīpiōnis *m*

scissors n forfex f
scoff vi irrīdēre; ~ **at** dērīdēre
scoffer n irrīsor m
scold vt increpāre, obiūrgāre
scolding n obiūrgātiō f
scoop n trulla f ◆ vt: ~ **out** excavāre
scope n (aim) fīnis m; (room) locus m, campus m; ample ~ laxus locus
scorch vt exūrere, torrēre
scorched adj torridus
score n (mark) nota f; (total) summa f; (reckoning) ratiō f; (number) vīgintī ◆ vt notāre ◆ vi vincere
scorn n contemptiō f ◆ vt contemnere, spernere
scorner n contemptor m
scornful adj fastīdiōsus
scornfully adv contemptim
scorpion n scorpiō m, nepa f
scot-free adj immūnis, impūnītus
scoundrel n furcifer m
scour vt (clean) tergēre; (range) percurrere
scourge n flagellum nt; (fig) pestis f ◆ vt verberāre, virgīs caedere
scout n explōrātor m, speculātor m ◆ vi explōrāre, speculārī ◆ vt spernere, repudiāre
scowl n frontis contractiō f ◆ vi frontem contrahere
scraggy adj strigōsus
scramble vi: ~ **for** certātim captāre; ~ **up** scandere
scrap n frūstum nt
scrape vt rādere, scabere; ~ **off** abrādere
scraper n strigilis f
scratch vt rādere; (head) perfricāre; ~ **out** exsculpere, ērādere
scream n clāmor m, ululātus m ◆ vi clāmāre, ululāre
screech n ululātus m ◆ vi ululāre
screen n obex m/f; (from sun) umbra f; (fig) vēlāmentum nt ◆ vt tegere
screw n clāvus m; (of winepress) cochlea f
scribble vt properē scrībere
scribe n scrība m
script n scrīptum nt; (handwriting) manus f
scroll n volūmen nt
scrub vt dētergēre, dēfricāre
scruple n rēligiō f, scrūpulus m
scrupulous adj rēligiōsus; (careful) dīligēns
scrupulously adv rēligiōsē, dīligenter
scrupulousness n rēligiō f; dīligentia f
scrutinize vt scrūtārī, intrōspicere in (acc), excutere
scrutiny n scrūtātiō f
scud vi volāre
scuffle n rixa f
scull n calvāria f; (oar) rēmus m
scullery n culīna f
sculptor n fictor m, sculptor m
sculpture n ars fingendī f; (product) statuae fpl ◆ vt sculpere
scum n spūma f
scurf n porrīgō f
scurrility n maledicta ntpl
scurrilous adj maledicus
scurvy adj (fig) turpis, improbus
scythe n falx f

sea n mare nt; aequor nt; **open sea** altum nt; **put to sea** solvere; **be at sea** nāvigāre; (fig) in errōre versārī ◆ adj marīnus; (coast) maritimus
seaboard n lītus nt
seafaring adj maritimus, nauticus
seafight n nāvāle proelium nt
seagull n larus m
seal n (animal) phōca f; (stamp) signum nt ◆ vt signāre; ~ **up** obsignāre
seam n sūtūra f
seaman n nauta m
seamanship n scientia et ūsus nauticārum rērum
seaport n portus m
sear vt adūrere, torrēre
search n investigātiō f ◆ vi investīgāre, explōrāre ◆ vt excutere, scrūtārī; **in ~ of** causa (gen); ~ **for** quaerere, exquīrere, investīgāre; ~ **into** inquīrere, anquīrere; ~ **out** explōrāre, indāgāre
searcher n inquīsītor m
searching adj acūtus, dīligēns
seashore n lītus nt
seasick adj: **be** ~ nauseāre
seasickness n nausea f
seaside n mare nt
season n annī tempus nt, tempestās f; (right time) tempus nt, opportūnitās f; **in ~** tempestīvē ◆ vt condīre
seasonable adj tempestīvus
seasonably adv tempestīvē
seasoned adj (food) condītus; (wood) dūrātus
seasoning n condīmentum nt
seat n sēdēs f; (chair) sedīle nt; (home) domus f, domicilium nt; **keep one's** ~ (riding) in equō haerēre ◆ vt collocāre; ~ **oneself** īnsidēre
seated adj: **be** ~ sedēre
seaweed n alga f
seaworthy adj ad nāvigandum ūtilis
secede vi sēcēdere
secession n sēcessiō f
seclude vt sēclūdere, abstrūdere
secluded adj sēcrētus, remōtus
seclusion n sōlitūdō f, sēcrētum nt
second adj secundus, alter; **a ~ time** iterum ◆ n temporis pūnctum nt; (person) fautor m; ~ **sight** hariolātiō f ◆ vt favēre (dat), adesse (dat)
secondary adj īnferior, dēterior
seconder n fautor m
second-hand adj aliēnus, trītus
secondly adv deinde
secrecy n sēcrētum nt, silentium nt
secret adj sēcrētus; occultus, arcānus; (stealth) fūrtīvus ◆ n arcānum nt; **keep** ~ dissimulāre, cēlāre; **in** ~ clam; **be** ~ latēre
secretary n scrība m, ab epistolīs, ā manū
secrete vt cēlāre, abdere
secretive adj tēctus
secretly adv clam, occultē, sēcrētō
sect n secta f, schola f, domus f
section n pars f
sector n regiō f
secular adj profānus
secure adj tūtus ◆ vt (MIL) firmāre, ēmūnīre; (fasten) religāre; (obtain) parāre, nancīscī
securely adv tūtō

security n salūs f, impūnitās f; (money) cautiō f, pignus nt, spōnsiō f; **sense of** ~ sēcūritās f; **give good** ~ satis dare; **on good** ~ (loan) nōminibus rēctis cautus; **stand** ~ **for** praedem esse prō (abl)
sedan n lectīca f
sedate adj placidus, temperātus, gravis
sedately adv placidē
sedateness n gravitās f
sedge n ulva f
sediment n faex f
sedition n sēditiō f, mōtus m
seditious adj sēditiōsus
seditiously adv sēditiōsē
seduce vt illicere, pellicere
seducer n corruptor m
seduction n corruptēla f
seductive adj blandus
seductively adv blandē
sedulity n dīligentia f
sedulous adj dīligēns, sēdulus
sedulously adv dīligenter, sēdulō
see vt vidēre, cernere; (suddenly) cōnspicārī; (performance) spectāre; (with mind) intellegere; **go and see** vīsere, invīsere; **see to** vidēre, cōnsulere (dat); curare (+acc and gerundive); **see through** dīspicere; **see that you are** vidē ut sīs, fac sīs; **see that you are not** vidē nē sīs, cavē sīs
seed n sēmen nt; (in a plant) grānum nt; (in fruit) acinum nt; (fig) stirps f, prōgeniēs f
seedling n surculus m
seed-time n sēmentis f
seeing that conj quōniam, siquidem
seek vt petere, quaerere
seeker n indāgātor m
seem vi vidērī
seeming adj speciōsus ♦ n speciēs f
seemingly adv ut vidētur
seemly adj decēns, decōrus; **it is** ~ decet
seep vi mānāre, percōlārī
seer n vātēs m/f
seethe vi fervēre
segregate vt sēcernere, sēgregāre
segregation n sēparātiō f
seize vt rapere, corripere, adripere, prehendere; (MIL) occupāre; (illness) adficere; (emotion) invādere, occupāre
seizure n ēreptiō f, occupātiō f
seldom adv rārō
select vt ēligere, excerpere, dēligere ♦ adj lēctus, ēlēctus
selection n ēlēctiō f, dēlēctus m; (lit) ecloga f
self n ipse; (reflexive) sē; **a second** ~ alter īdem
self-centred adj glōriōsus
self-confidence n cōnfīdentia f, fidūcia f
self-confident adj cōnfīdēns
self-conscious adj pudibundus
self-control n temperantia f
self-denial n abstinentia f
self-evident adj manifestus; **it is** ~ ante pedēs positum est
self-governing adj līber
self-government n lībertās f
self-important adj adrogāns
self-interest n ambitiō f
selfish adj inhūmānus, avārus; **be** ~ suā causā facere

selfishly adv inhūmānē, avārē
selfishness n inhūmānitās f, incontinentia f, avāritia f
self-made adj (man) novus
self-possessed adj aequō animō
self-possession n aequus animus m
self-reliant adj cōnfīdēns
self-respect n pudor m
self-restraint n modestia f
self-sacrifice n dēvōtiō f
selfsame adj ūnus et īdem
sell vt vēndere; (in lots) dīvēndere; **be sold** vēnīre
seller n vēnditor m
selvage n limbus m
semblance n speciēs f, imāgō f
semicircle n hēmicyclium nt
senate n senātus m; **hold a meeting of the** ~ senātum habēre; **decree of the** ~ senātus cōnsultum nt
senate house n cūria f
senator n senātor m; (provincial) decuriō m; **senators** pl patrēs mpl
senatorial adj senātōrius
send vt mittere; ~ **across** trānsmittere; ~ **ahead** praemittere; ~ **away** dīmittere; ~ **back** remittere; ~ **for** accersere; (doctor) adhibēre; ~ **forth** ēmittere; ~ **forward** praemittere; ~ **in** immittere, intrōmittere; ~ **out** ēmittere; (in different directions) dīmittere; ~ **out of the way** ablēgāre; ~ **up** submittere
senile adj senīlis
senility n senium nt
senior adj nātū māior; (thing) prior
sensation n sēnsus m; (event) rēs nova f; **lose** ~ obtorpēscere; **create a** ~ hominēs obstupefacere
sensational adj novus, prōdigiōsus
sense n (faculty) sēnsus m; (wisdom) prūdentia f; (meaning) vis f, sententia f; **common** ~ prūdentia f; **be in one's senses** apud sē esse, mentis suae esse; **out of one's senses** dēmēns; **recover one's senses** resipīscere; **what is the** ~ **of** quid sibī vult? ♦ vt sentīre
senseless adj absurdus, ineptus, īnsipiēns
senselessly adv īnsipienter
senselessness n īnsipientia f
sensibility n sēnsus m
sensible adj prūdēns, sapiēns
sensibly adv prūdenter, sapienter
sensitive adj mollis, inrītābilis, patibilis
sensitiveness n mollitia f
sensual adj libīdinōsus
sensuality n libīdō f, voluptās f
sensually adv libīdinōsē
sentence n (judge) iūdicium nt, sententia f; (GRAM) sententia f; **pass** ~ iūdicāre; **execute** ~ lēge agere ♦ vt damnāre; ~ **to death** capitis damnāre
sententious adj sententiōsus
sententiously adv sententiōsē
sentient adj patibilis
sentiment n (feeling) sēnsus m; (opinion) sententia f; (emotion) mollitia f
sentimental adj mollis, flēbilis
sentimentality n mollitia f
sentimentally adv molliter

sentries *npl* statiōnēs *fpl*, excubiae *fpl*
sentry *n* custōs *m*, vigil *m*; **be on ~ duty** in statiōne esse
separable *adj* dīviduus, sēparābilis
separate *vt* sēparāre, dīvidere, disiungere; *(forcibly)* dīrimere, dīvellere ♦ *vi* dīgredī ♦ *adj* sēparātus, sēcrētus
separately *adv* sēparātim, seōrsum
separation *n* sēparātiō *f*; *(violent)* discidium *nt*
September *n* mēnsis September *m*; **of ~** September
sepulchral *adj* fūnebris
sepulchre *n* sepulcrum *nt*
sepulture *n* sepultūra *f*
sequel *n* exitus *m*, quae sequuntur
sequence *n* seriēs *f*, ōrdō *m*
sequestered *adj* sēcrētus
serenade *vt* occentāre
serene *adj* tranquillus, sēcūrus
serenely *adv* tranquillē
serenity *n* sēcūritās *f*
serf *n* servus *m*
serfdom *n* servitūs *f*
sergeant *n* signifer *m*
series *n* seriēs *f*, ōrdō *m*
serious *adj* gravis, sērius, sevērus
seriously *adv* graviter, sēriō, sevērē
seriousness *n* gravitās *f*
sermon *n* ōrātiō *f*
serpent *n* serpēns *f*
serpentine *adj* tortuōsus
serrated *adj* serrātus
serried *adj* cōnfertus
servant *n* *(domestic)* famulus *m*, famula *f*; *(public)* minister *m*, ministra *f*; **family servants** familia *f*
servant maid *n* ancilla *f*
serve *vt* servīre *(dat)*; *(food)* ministrāre, adpōnere; *(interest)* condūcere *(dat)* ♦ *vi* *(MIL)* stīpendia merēre, mīlitāre; *(suffice)* sufficere; **~ as** esse prō *(abl)*; **~ in the cavalry** equō merēre; **~ in the infantry** pedibus merēre; **having served one's time** ēmeritus; **~ a sentence** poenam subīre; **~ well** bene merērī dē *(abl)*
service *n* *(status)* servitium *nt*, famulātus *m*; *(work)* ministerium *nt*; *(help)* opera *f*; *(by an equal)* meritum *nt*, beneficium *nt*; *(MIL)* mīlitia *f*, stīpendia *ntpl*; **be of ~ to** prōdesse *(dat)*, bene merērī dē; **I am at your ~** adsum tibī; **complete one's ~** stīpendia ēmerērī
serviceable *adj* ūtilis
servile *adj* servīlis; *(fig)* abiectus, humilis
servility *n* adūlātiō *f*
servitude *n* servitūs *f*
session *n* conventus *m*; **be in ~** sedēre
sesterce *n* sēstertius *m*; **10 sesterces** decem sēstertiī; **10,000 sesterces** dēna sēstertia *ntpl*; **1,000,000 sesterces** deciēs sēstertium
set *vt* pōnere, locāre, statuere, sistere; *(bone)* condere; *(course)* dīrigere; *(example)* dare; *(limit)* impōnere; *(mind)* intendere; *(music)* modulārī; *(sail)* dare; *(sentries)* dispōnere; *(table)* īnstruere; *(trap)* parāre ♦ *vi* *(ASTR)* occidere; **set about** incipere; **set against** oppōnere; **set apart** sēpōnere; **set aside** sēpōnere; **set down** *(writing)* perscrībere; **set eyes on** cōnspicere;

set foot on ingredī; **set forth** expōnere, ēdere; **set free** līberāre; **set in motion** movēre; **set in order** compōnere, dispōnere; **set off** *(decoration)* distinguere; *(art)* illūmināre; **set on** *(to attack)* immittere; **set on foot** īnstituere; **set on fire** incendere; **set one's heart on** exoptāre; **set out** *vi* proficīscī; **set over** praeficere, impōnere; **set up** statuere ♦ *adj* *(arrangement)* status; *(purpose)* certus; *(rule)* praescrīptus; *(speech)* compositus; **of set purpose** cōnsultō ♦ *n* *(persons)* numerus *m*; *(things)* congeriēs *f*; *(current)* cursus *m*
setback *n* repulsa *f*
settee *n* lectulus *m*
setting *n* *(ASTR)* occāsus *m*; *(event)* locus *m*
settle *n* sella *f* ♦ *vt* statuere; *(annuity)* praestāre; *(business)* trānsigere; *(colony)* dēdūcere; *(debt)* exsolvere; *(decision)* cōnstituere; *(dispute)* dēcīdere, compōnere ♦ *vi* *(abode)* cōnsīdere; *(agreement)* cōnstituere, convenīre; *(sediment)* dēsīdere; **~ in** īnsidēre *(dat)*
settled *adj* certus, explōrātus
settlement *n* *(of a colony)* dēductiō *f*; *(colony)* colōnia *f*; *(of dispute)* dēcīsiō *f*, compositiō *f*; *(to wife)* dōs *f*
settler *n* colōnus *m*
set to *n* pugna *f*
seven *num* septem; **~ each** septēnī; **~ times** septiēns
seven hundred *num* septingentī
seven hundredth *adj* septingentēsimus
seventeen *num* septendecim
seventeenth *adj* septimus decimus
seventh *adj* septimus; **for the ~ time** septimum
seventieth *adj* septuāgēsimus
seventy *num* septuāgintā; **~ each** septuāgēnī; **~ times** septuāgiēns
sever *vt* incīdere, sēparāre, dīvidere
several *adj* complūrēs, aliquot
severally *adv* singulī
severe *adj* gravis, sevērus, dūrus; *(style)* austērus; *(weather)* asper; *(pain)* ācer, gravis
severely *adv* graviter, sevērē
severity *n* gravitās *f*; asperitās *f*; sevēritās *f*
sew *vt* suere; **sew up** cōnsuere; **sew up in** īnsuere in *(acc)*
sewer *n* cloāca *f*
sex *n* sexus *m*
shabbily *adv* sordidē
shabbiness *n* sordēs *fpl*
shabby *adj* sordidus
shackle *n* compēs *f*, vinculum *nt* ♦ *vt* impedīre, vincīre
shade *n* umbra *f*; *(colour)* color *m*; **shades** *pl* mānēs *mpl*; **put in the ~** officere *(dat)* ♦ *vt* opācāre, umbram adferre *(dat)*
shadow *n* umbra *f*
shadowy *adj* obscūrus; *(fig)* inānis
shady *adj* umbrōsus, opācus
shaft *n* *(missile)* tēlum *nt*, sagitta *f*; *(of spear)* hastīle *nt*; *(of cart)* tēmō *m*; *(of light)* radius *m*; *(excavation)* puteus *m*
shaggy *adj* hirsūtus
shake *vt* quatere, agitāre; *(structure)* labefacere, labefactāre; *(belief)* īnfirmāre; *(resolution)* labefactāre, commovēre; **~ hands with**

dextram dare (*dat*) ◆ *vi* quatī, agitārī, tremere, horrēscere; ~ **off** dēcutere, excutere; ~ **out** excutere
shaking *n* tremor *m*
shaky *adj* īnstābilis, tremebundus
shall *aux vb use fut indic*
shallot *n* caepa Ascalōnia *f*
shallow *adj* brevis, vadōsus; (*fig*) levis
shallowness *n* vada *ntpl*; (*fig*) levitās *f*
shallows *n* brevia *ntpl*, vada *ntpl*
sham *adj* fictus, falsus, fūcōsus ◆ *n* simulātiō *f*, speciēs *f* ◆ *vt* simulāre
shambles *n* laniēna *f*
shame *n* (*feeling*) pudor *m*; (*cause*) dēdecus *nt*, ignōminia *f*; **it shames** pudet (+*acc of person*, *gen of thing*); **it is a ~** flāgitium est ◆ *vt* rubōrem incutere (*dat*) ◆ *interj* prō pudor!
shamefaced *adj* verēcundus
shameful *adj* ignōminiōsus, turpis
shamefully *adv* turpiter
shameless *adj* impudēns
shamelessly *adv* impudenter
shamelessness *n* impudentia *f*
shank *n* crūs *nt*
shape *n* fōrma *f*, figūra *f* ◆ *vt* fōrmāre, fingere; (*fig*) īnfōrmāre ◆ *vi*: ~ **well** prōficere
shapeless *adj* īnfōrmis, dēfōrmis
shapelessness *n* dēfōrmitās *f*
shapeliness *n* fōrma *f*
shapely *adj* fōrmōsus
shard *n* testa *f*
share *n* pars *f*; (*plough*) vōmer *m*; **go shares with** inter sē partīrī ◆ *vt* (*give*) partīrī, impertīre; (*have*) commūnicāre, participem esse (*gen*)
sharer *n* particeps *m/f*, socius *m*
shark *n* volpēs marīna *f*
sharp *adj* acūtus; (*fig*) ācer, acūtus; (*bitter*) amarus
sharpen *vt* acuere; (*fig*) exacuere
sharply *adv* ācriter, acūtē
sharpness *n* aciēs *f*; (*mind*) acūmen *nt*, argūtiae *fpl*; (*temper*) acerbitās *f*
shatter *vt* quassāre, perfringere, adflīgere; (*fig*) frangere
shave *vt* rādere; ~ **off** abrādere
shavings *n* rāmenta *ntpl*
she *pron* haec, ea, illa
sheaf *n* manipulus *m*
shear *vt* tondēre, dētondēre
shears *n* forficēs *fpl*
sheath *n* vāgīna *f*
sheathe *vt* recondere
shed *vt* fundere; (*blood*) effundere; (*one's own*) profundere; (*tears*) effundere; (*covering*) exuere; ~ **light on** (*fig*) lūmen adhibēre (*dat*)
sheen *n* nitor *m*
sheep *n* ovis *f*; (*flock*) pecus *nt*
sheepfold *n* ovīle *nt*
sheepish *adj* pudibundus
sheepishly *adv* pudenter
sheer *adj* (*absolute*) merus; (*steep*) praeruptus
sheet *n* (*cloth*) linteum *nt*; (*metal*) lāmina *f*; (*paper*) carta *f*, scheda *f*; (*sail*) pēs *m*; (*water*) aequor *nt*
shelf *n* pluteus *m*, pēgma *nt*
shell *n* concha *f*; (*egg*) putāmen *nt*; (*tortoise*) testa *f*
shellfish *n* conchŷlium *nt*

shelter *n* suffugium *nt*, tegmen *nt*; (*refuge*) perfugium *nt*, asŷlum *nt*; (*lodging*) hospitium *nt*; (*fig*) umbra *f* ◆ *vt* tegere, dēfendere; (*refugee*) excipere ◆ *vi* latēre; ~ **behind** (*fig*) dēlitēscere in (*abl*)
sheltered *adj* (*life*) umbrātilis
shelve *vt* differre ◆ *vi* sē dēmittere
shelving *adj* dēclīvis
shepherd *n* pastor *m*
shield *n* scūtum *nt*; clipeus *m*; (*small*) parma *f*; (*fig*) praesidium *nt* ◆ *vt* prōtegere, dēfendere
shift *n* (*change*) mūtātiō *f*; (*expedient*) ars *f*, dolus *m*; **make ~ to** efficere ut; **in shifts** per vicēs ◆ *vt* mūtāre; (*move*) movēre ◆ *vi* mūtārī; discēdere
shiftless *adj* iners, inops
shifty *adj* vafer, versūtus
shilling *n* solidus *m*
shimmer *vi* micāre ◆ *n* tremulum lūmen *nt*
shin *n* tībia *f*
shine *vi* lūcēre, fulgēre; (*reflecting*) nitēre; (*fig*) ēminēre; ~ **forth** ēlūcēre, ēnitēre; effulgēre; ~ **upon** adfulgēre (*dat*) ◆ *n* nitor *m*
shingle *n* lapillī *mpl*, glārea *f*
shining *adj* lūcidus, splendidus; (*fig*) illūstris
shiny *adj* nitidus
ship *n* nāvis *f*; **admiral's ~** nāvis praetōria; **decked ~** nāvis tēcta, nāvis cōnstrāta ◆ *vt* (*cargo*) impōnere; (*to a place*) nāvī invehere
shipowner *n* nāviculārius *m*
shipping *n* nāvēs *fpl*
shipwreck *n* naufragium *nt*; **suffer ~** naufragium facere
shipwrecked *adj* naufragus
shirk *vt* dēfugere, dētrectāre
shirt *n* subūcula *f*
shiver *n* horror *m* ◆ *vi* horrēre, tremere ◆ *vt* perfringere, comminuere
shivering *n* horror *m*
shoal *n* (*fish*) exāmen *nt*; (*water*) vadum *nt*; **shoals** *pl* brevia *ntpl*
shock *n* impulsus *m*; (*battle*) concursus *m*, cōnflīctus *m*; (*hair*) caesariēs *f*; (*mind*) offēnsiō *f* ◆ *vt* percutere, offendere
shocking *adj* atrōx, dētestābilis, flāgitiōsus
shoddy *adj* vīlis
shoe *n* calceus *m*
shoemaker *n* sūtor *m*
shoot *n* surculus *m*; (*vine*) pampinus *m* ◆ *vi* frondēscere; (*movement*) volāre; ~ **up** ēmicāre ◆ *vt* (*missile*) conicere, iaculārī; (*person*) iaculārī, trānsfigere
shop *n* taberna *f*
shore *n* lītus *nt*, ōra *f* ◆ *vt* fulcīre
short *adj* brevis; (*broken*) curtus; (*amount*) exiguus; **for a ~ time** parumper, paulisper; ~ **of** (*number*) intrā (*acc*); **be ~ of** indigēre (*abl*); **cut ~** interpellāre; **in ~** ad summam, dēnique; **very ~** perbrevis; **fall ~ of** nōn pervenīre ad, abesse ab; **run ~** dēficere; **to cut a long story ~** nē multīs morer, nē multa
shortage *n* inopia *f*
shortcoming *n* dēlictum *nt*, culpa *f*
short cut *n* via compendiāria *f*
shorten *vt* curtāre, imminuere, contrahere; (*sail*) legere
shorthand *n* notae *fpl*

shorthand writer n āctuārius m
short-lived adj brevis
shortly adv (time) brevī; (speak) breviter; ~ **after** paulō post, nec multō post
shortness n brevitās f, exiguitās f; (difficulty) angustiae fpl
short-sighted adj (fig) imprōvidus, imprūdēns
short-sightedness n imprūdentia f
short-tempered adj īrācundus
shot n ictus m; (range) iactus m
should vi (duty) dēbēre
shoulder n umerus m; (animal) armus m ✦ vt (burden) suscipere
shout n clāmor m, adclāmātiō f ✦ vt, vi clāmāre, vōciferārī; ~ **down** obstrepere (dat); ~ **out** exclāmāre
shove vt trūdere, impellere
shovel n rutrum nt
show n speciēs f; (entertainment) lūdī mpl, spectāculum nt; (stage) lūdicrum nt; **for** ~ **in** speciem; **put on a** ~ spectācula dare ✦ vt mōnstrāre, indicāre, ostendere, ostentāre; (point out) dēmōnstrāre; (qualities) praestāre; ~ **off** vi sē iactāre ✦ vt ostentāre
shower n imber m ✦ vt fundere, conicere
showery adj pluvius
showiness n ostentātiō f
showing off n iactātiō f
showy adj speciōsus
shred n fragmentum nt; **in shreds** minūtātim; **tear to shreds** dīlaniāre ✦ vt concīdere
shrew n virāgō f
shrewd adj acūtus, ācer, sagāx
shrewdly adv acūtē, sagāciter
shrewdness n acūmen nt, sagācitās f
shriek n ululātus m ✦ vi ululāre
shrill adj acūtus, argūtus
shrine n fānum nt, dēlubrum nt
shrink vt contrahere ✦ vi contrahī; ~ **from** abhorrēre ab, refugere ab, dētrectāre
shrivel vt corrūgāre ✦ vi exārēscere
shroud n integumentum nt; **shrouds** pl rudentēs mpl ✦ vt involvere
shrub n frutex m
shrubbery n fruticētum nt
shudder n horror m ✦ vi exhorrēscere; ~ **at** horrēre
shuffle vt miscēre ✦ vi claudicāre; (fig) tergiversārī
shun vt vītāre, ēvītāre, dēfugere
shut vt claudere; (with cover) operīre; (hand) comprimere; ~ **in** inclūdere; ~ **off** interclūdere; ~ **out** exclūdere; ~ **up** inclūdere
shutter n foricula f, lūmināre nt
shuttle n radius m
shy adj timidus, pudibundus, verēcundus
shyly adv timidē, verēcundē
shyness n verēcundia f
sibyl n sibylla f
sick adj aeger, aegrōtus; **be** ~ aegrōtāre; **feel** ~ nauseāre; **I am** ~ **of** mē taedet (gen)
sicken vt fastīdium movēre (dat) ✦ vi nauseāre, aegrōtāre
sickle n falx f
sickly adj invalidus

sickness n nausea f; (illness) morbus m, aegritūdō f
side n latus nt; (direction) pars f; (faction) partēs fpl; (kin) genus nt; **on all sides** undique; **on both sides** utrimque; **on one** ~ unā ex parte; **on our** ~ ā nōbis; **be on the** ~ **of** stāre ab, sentīre cum; **on the far** ~ **of** ultrā (acc); **on this** ~ hīnc; **on this** ~ **of** cis (acc), citrā (acc) ✦ vi: ~ **with** stāre ab, facere cum
sideboard n abacus m
sidelong adj oblīquus
sideways adv oblīquē, in oblīquum
sidle vi oblīquō corpore incēdere
siege n obsidiō f, oppugnātiō f; **lay** ~ **to** obsidēre
siege works npl opera ntpl
siesta n merīdiātiō f; **take a** ~ merīdiāre
sieve n crībrum nt
sigh n suspīrium nt; (loud) gemitus m ✦ vi suspīrāre, gemere
sight n (sense) vīsus m; (process) aspectus m; (range) cōnspectus m; (thing seen) spectāculum nt, speciēs f; **at** ~ ex tempore; **at first** ~ prīmō aspectū; **in** ~ in cōnspectū; **come into** ~ in cōnspectum sē dare; **in the** ~ **of** in oculīs (gen); **catch** ~ **of** cōnspicere; **lose** ~ **of** ē cōnspectū āmittere; (fig) oblīvīscī (gen) ✦ vt cōnspicārī
sightless adj caecus
sightly adj decōrus
sign n signum nt, indicium nt; (distinction) īnsigne nt; (mark) nota f; (trace) vestīgium nt; (proof) documentum nt; (portent) ōmen nt; (Zodiac) signum nt; **give a** ~ innuere ✦ vi signum dare, innuere ✦ vt subscrībere (dat); (as witness) obsignāre
signal n signum nt; **give the** ~ **for retreat** receptuī canere ✦ vi signum dare ✦ adj īnsignis, ēgregius
signalize vt nōbilitāre
signally adv ēgregiē
signature n nōmen nt, manus f, chīrographum nt
signet n signum nt
signet ring n anulus m
significance n interpretātiō f, significātiō f, vīs f; (importance) pondus nt
significant adj gravis, clārus
signification n significātiō f
signify vt significāre, velle; (omen) portendere; **it does not** ~ nōn interest
silence n silentium nt; **in** ~ per silentium ✦ vt comprimere; (argument) refūtāre
silent adj tacitus; (habit) taciturnus; **be** ~ silēre, tacēre; **be** ~ **about** silēre, tacēre; **become** ~ conticēscere
silently adv tacitē
silhouette n adumbrātiō f
silk n bombȳx m; (clothes) sērica ntpl ✦ adj bombȳcinus, sēricus
silken adj bombȳcinus
sill n līmen nt
silliness n stultitia f, ineptiae fpl
silly adj fatuus, ineptus; stultus; **be** ~ dēsipere
silt n līmus m
silver n argentum nt ✦ adj argenteus
silver mine n argentāria f
silver plate n argentum nt

silver-plated adj argentātus
silvery adj argenteus
similar adj similis
similarity n similitūdō f
similarly adv similiter
simile n similitūdō f
simmer vi lēniter fervēre
simper vi molliter subrīdēre
simple adj simplex; (mind) fatuus; (task) facilis
simpleton n homō ineptus m
simplicity n simplicitās f; (mind) stultitia f
simplify vt faciliōrem reddere
simply adv simpliciter; (merely) sōlum, tantum
simulate vt simulāre
simulation n simulātiō f
simultaneously adv simul, ūnā, eōdem
  tempore
sin n peccātum nt, nefās nt, dēlictum nt ♦ vi
  peccāre
since adv abhinc; **long ~** iamdūdum ♦ conj (time)
  ex quō tempore, postquam; (reason) cum (subj),
  quōniam; **~ he** quippe quī ♦ prep ab (abl), ex (abl),
  post (acc); **ever ~** usque ab
sincere adj sincērus, simplex, apertus
sincerely adv sincērē, ex animō
sincerity n fidēs f, simplicitās f
sinew n nervus m
sinewy adj nervōsus
sinful adj improbus, impius, incestus
sinfully adv improbē, impiē
sing vt canere, cantāre; **~ of** canere
singe vt adūrere
singer n cantor m
singing n cantus m ♦ adj canōrus
single adj ūnus, sōlus, ūnicus; (unmarried) caelebs
  ♦ vt: **~ out** ēligere, excerpere
single-handed adj ūnus
singly adv singillātim, singulī
singular adj singulāris; (strange) novus
singularly adv singulāriter, praecipuē
sinister adj īnfaustus, malevolus
sink vi dēsīdere; (in water) dēmergī; **~ in** inlābī,
  īnsīdere ♦ vt dēprimere, mergere; (well) fodere;
  (fig) dēmergere
sinless adj integer, innocēns, castus
sinner n peccātor m
sinuous adj sinuōsus
sip vt gustāre, lībāre
siphon n siphō m
sir n (to master) ere; (to equal) vir optime; (title)
  eques m
sire n pater m
siren n sīrēn f
sirocco n Auster m
sister n soror f; **sister's** sorōrius
sisterhood n germānitās f; (society) sorōrum
  societās f
sister-in-law n glōs f
sisterly adj sorōrius
sit vi sedēre; **sit beside** adsidēre (dat); **sit down**
  cōnsīdere; **sit on** īnsidēre (dat); (eggs) incubāre;
  sit at table accumbere; **sit up** (at night) vigilāre
site n situs m, locus m; (for building) ārea f
sitting n sessiō f
situated adj situs

situation n situs m; (circumstances) status m,
  condiciō f
six num sex; **six each** sēnī; **six or seven** sex
  septem; **six times** sexiēns
six hundred num sēscentī; **six hundred each**
  sēscēnī; **six hundred times** sēscentiēns
six hundredth adj sēscentēsimus
sixteen num sēdecim; **~ each** sēnī dēnī; **~ times**
  sēdeciēns
sixteenth adj sextus decimus
sixth adj sextus; **for the ~ time** sextum
sixtieth adj sexāgēsimus
sixty num sexāgintā; **~ each** sexāgēnī; **~ times**
  sexāgiēns
size n māgnitūdō f, amplitūdō f; (measure)
  mēnsūra f, fōrma f
skate vi per glaciem lābī; **~ on thin ice** (fig)
  incēdere per ignēs suppositōs cinerī dolōsō
skein n glomus nt
skeleton n ossa ntpl
sketch n adumbrātiō f, dēscrīptiō f ♦ vt
  adumbrāre, īnfōrmāre
skewer n verū nt
skiff n scapha f, lēnunculus m
skilful adj perītus, doctus, scītus; (with hands)
  habilis
skilfully adv perītē, doctē; habiliter
skill n ars f, perītia f, sollertia f
skilled adj perītus, doctus; **~ in** perītus (gen)
skim vt dēspūmāre; **~ over** (fig) legere,
  perstringere
skin n cutis f; (animal) pellis f ♦ vt pellem
  dētrahere (dat)
skinflint n avārus m
skinny adj macer
skip vi exsultāre ♦ vt praeterīre
skipper n magister m
skirmish n leve proelium nt ♦ vi vēlitārī
skirmisher n vēles m, excursor m
skirt n īnstita f; (border) limbus m ♦ vt contingere
  (dat); (motion) legere
skittish adj lascīvus
skulk vi latēre, dēlitēscere
skull n caput nt
sky n caelum nt; **of the sky** caelestis
skylark n alauda f
slab n tabula f
slack adj remissus, laxus; (work) piger, neglegēns
slacken vt remittere, dētendere ♦ vi laxārī
slackness n remissiō f; pigritia f
slag n scōria f
slake vt restinguere, sēdāre
slam vt adflīgere
slander n maledicta ntpl, obtrectātiō f; (LAW)
  calumnia f ♦ vt maledīcere (dat), īnfāmāre,
  obtrectāre (dat)
slanderer n obtrectātor m
slanderous adj maledicus
slang n vulgāria verba ntpl
slant vi in trānsversum īre
slanting adj oblīquus, trānsversus
slantingly adv oblīquē, ex trānsversō
slap n alapa f ♦ vt palmā ferīre
slapdash adj praeceps, temerārius
slash vt caedere ♦ n ictus m

slate n (roof) tēgula f; (writing) tabula f ◆ vt
  increpāre
slatternly adj sordidus, incōmptus
slaughter n caedēs f, strāgēs f ◆ vt trucīdāre
slaughterhouse n laniēna f
slave n servus m; (domestic) famulus m;
  (home-born) verna m; **be a ~ to** īnservīre (dat);
  household slaves familia f
slave girl n ancilla f
slavery n servitūs f
slavish adj servīlis
slavishly adv servīliter
slay vt interficere, occīdere
slayer n interfector m
sleek adj nitidus, pinguis
sleep n somnus m; **go to ~** obdormīscere ◆ vi
  dormīre; **~ off** vt ēdormīre
sleeper n dormītor m
sleepiness n sopor m
sleepless adj īnsomnis, vigil
sleeplessness n īnsomnia f
sleepy adj somniculōsus; **be ~** dormītāre
sleeve n manica f
sleight of hand n praestīgiae fpl
slender adj gracilis, exīlis
slenderness n gracilitās f
slice n frūstum nt ◆ vt secāre
slide n lāpsus m ◆ vi lābī
slight adj levis, exiguus, parvus ◆ n neglegentia f
  ◆ vt neglegere, offendere
slightingly adv contemptim
slightly adv leviter, paululum
slightness n levitās f
slim adj gracilis
slime n līmus m
slimness n gracilitās f
slimy adj līmōsus, mūcōsus
sling n funda f ◆ vt mittere, iaculārī
slinger n funditor m
slink vi sē subdūcere
slip n lāpsus m; (mistake) offēnsiuncula f; (plant)
  surculus m ◆ vi lābī; **~ away** ēlābī, dīlābī; **~ out**
  ēlābī; (word) excidere; **give the ~ to** ēlūdere;
  let ~ āmittere, ēmittere; (opportunity) ōmittere;
  there's many a ~ twixt the cup and the lip
  inter ōs et offam multa interveniunt
slipper n solea f
slippery adj lūbricus
slipshod adj neglegēns
slit n rīma f ◆ vt findere, incīdere
sloe n spīnus m
slope n dēclīve nt, clīvus m; (steep) dēiectus m ◆ vi
  sē dēmittere, vergere
sloping adj dēclīvis, dēvexus; (up) adclīvis
slot n rīma f
sloth n inertia f, segnitia f, dēsidia f, ignāvia f
slothful adj ignāvus, iners, segnis
slothfully adv ignāvē, segniter
slouch vi languidē incēdere
slough n (skin) exuviae fpl; (bog) palūs f
slovenliness n ignāvia f, sordēs fpl
slovenly adj ignāvus, sordidus
slow adj tardus, lentus; (mind) hebes
slowly adv tardē, lentē
slowness n tarditās f
sludge n līmus m

slug n līmāx f
sluggard n homō ignāvus m
sluggish adj piger, segnis; (mind) hebes
sluggishly adv pigrē, segniter
sluggishness n pigritia f, inertia f
sluice n cataracta f
slumber n somnus m, sopor m ◆ vi dormīre
slump n vīlis annōna f
slur n nota f; **cast ~ on** dētrectāre ◆ vt: **~ words**
  balbūtīre
sly adj astūtus, vafer, callidus; **on the sly** ex
  opīnātō
slyly adv astūtē, callidē
slyness n astūtia f
smack n (blow) ictus m; (with hand) alapa f; (boat)
  lēnunculus m; (taste) sapor m ◆ vt ferīre ◆ vi: **~ of**
  olēre, redolēre
small adj parvus, exiguus; **how ~** quantulus,
  quantillus; **so ~** tantulus; **very ~** perexiguus,
  minimus; **a ~ meeting of** īnfrequēns
smaller adj minor
smallest adj minimus
smallness n exiguitās f, brevitās f
small talk n sermunculus m
smart adj (action) ācer, alacer; (dress) concinnus,
  nitidus; (pace) vēlōx; (wit) facētus, salsus ◆ n
  dolor m ◆ vi dolēre; (fig) ūrī, mordērī
smartly adv ācriter; nitidē; vēlōciter; facētē
smartness n alacritās f; (dress) nitor m; (wit)
  facētiae fpl, sollertia f
smash n ruīna f ◆ vt frangere, comminuere
smattering n: **get a ~ of** odōrārī, prīmīs labrīs
  attingere; **with a ~ of** imbūtus (abl)
smear vt oblinere, ungere
smell n (sense) odōrātus m; (odour) odor m; (of
  cooking) nīdor m ◆ vt olfacere, odōrārī ◆ vi olēre
smelly adj olidus
smelt vt fundere
smile n rīsus m ◆ vi subrīdēre; **~ at** adrīdēre (dat);
  ~ upon rīdēre ad; (fig) secundum esse (dat)
smiling adj laetus
smirk vi subrīdēre
smith n faber m
smithy n fabrica f
smock n tunica f
smoke n fūmus m ◆ vi fūmāre
smoky adj fūmōsus
smooth adj lēvis; (skin) glaber; (talk) blandus;
  (sea) placidus; (temper) aequus; (voice) lēvis, teres
  ◆ vt sternere, līmāre
smoothly adv lēviter, lēniter
smoothness n lēvitās f, lēnitās f
smother vt opprimere, suffocāre
smoulder vi fūmāre
smudge n macula f
smug adj suī contentus
smuggle vt fūrtim importāre
smugness n amor suī m
smut n fūlīgō f
snack n cēnula f; **take a ~** gustāre
snag n impedīmentum nt, scrūpulus m
snail n cochlea f
snake n anguis m, serpēns f
snaky adj vīpereus

snap *vt* rumpere, praerumpere; ~ **the fingers**
digitīs concrepāre ♦ *vi* rumpī, dissilīre; ~ **at**
mordēre; ~ **up** corripere
snare *n* laqueus *m*, plaga *f*, pedica *f* ♦ *vt* inrētīre
snarl *n* gannītus *m* ♦ *vi* gannīre
snatch *vt* rapere, ēripere, adripere, corripere;
~ **at** captāre
sneak *n* perfidus *m* ♦ *vi* conrēpere; ~ **in** sē
īnsinuāre; ~ **out** ēlābī
sneaking *adj* humilis, fūrtīvus
sneer *n* irrīsiō *f* ♦ *vi* irrīdēre, dērīdēre
sneeze *n* sternūtāmentum *nt* ♦ *vi* sternuere
sniff *vt* odōrārī
snip *vt* praecīdere, secāre
snob *n* homō ambitiōsus *m*
snood *n* mitra *f*
snooze *vi* dormītāre
snore *vi* stertere
snoring *n* rhoncus *m*
snort *n* fremitus *m* ♦ *vi* fremere
snout *n* rōstrum *nt*
snow *n* nix *f* ♦ *vi* ningere; **snowed under** nive
obrutus; **it is snowing** ningit
snowy *adj* nivālis; (*colour*) niveus
snub *vt* neglegere, praeterīre
snub-nosed *adj* sīmus
snuff *n* (*candle*) fungus *m*
snug *adj* commodus
snugly *adv* commodē
so *adv* (*referring back*) sīc; (*referring forward*) ita; (*with
adj and adv*) tam; (*with verb*) adeō; (*consequence*)
ergō, itaque, igitur; **and so** itaque; **so great**
tantus; **so-so** sīc; **so as to** ut; **so be it** estō; **so
big** tantus; **so far** usque adeō, adhūc; **so far as**
quod; **so far from** adeō nōn; **so little** tantillus;
so long as dum; **so many** tot; **so much** *adj*
tantus ♦ *adv* tantum; (*with compar*) tantō; **so
often** totiēns; **so that** ut (*subj*); **so that … not**
(*purpose*) nē; (*result*) ut nōn; **and so on** deinceps;
not so very haud ita; **say so** id dīcere
soak *vt* imbuere, madefacere
soaking *adj* madidus
soap *n* sapō *m*
soar *vi* in sublīme ferrī, subvolāre; ~ **above**
superāre
sob *n* singultus *m* ♦ *vi* singultāre
sober *adj* sobrius; (*conduct*) modestus; (*mind*)
sānus
soberly *adv* sobriē, modestē
sobriety *n* modestia *f*, continentia *f*
so-called *adj* quī dīcitur
sociability *n* facilitās *f*
sociable *adj* facilis, cōmis
sociably *adv* faciliter, cōmiter
social *adj* sociālis, commūnis
socialism *n* populāris ratiō *f*
socialist *n* homō populāris *m/f*
society *n* societās *f*; (*class*) optimātēs *mpl*; (*being
with*) convīctus *m*; **cultivate the ~ of** adsectārī;
secret ~ sodālitās *f*
sod *n* caespes *m*, glaeba *f*
soda *n* nitrum *nt*
sodden *adj* madidus
soever *adv* -cumque
sofa *n* lectus *m*

soft *adj* mollis; (*fruit*) mītis; (*voice*) submissus;
(*character*) dēlicātus; (*words*) blandus
soften *vt* mollīre; (*body*) ēnervāre; (*emotion*)
lēnīre, mītigāre ♦ *vi* mollēscere, mītēscere
soft-hearted *adj* misericors
softly *adv* molliter, lēniter; blandē
softness *n* mollitia *f*, mollitiēs *f*
soil *n* sōlum *nt*, humus *f* ♦ *vt* inquināre, foedāre
sojourn *n* commorātiō *f*, mānsiō *f* ♦ *vi*
commorārī
sojourner *n* hospes *m*, hospita *f*
solace *n* sōlātium *nt*, levātiō *f* ♦ *vt* sōlārī,
cōnsōlārī
solar *adj* sōlis
solder *n* ferrūmen *nt* ♦ *vt* ferrūmināre
soldier *n* mīles *m*; **be a ~** mīlitāre; **common
~** manipulāris *m*, gregārius mīles *m*; **fellow
~** commīlitō *m*; **foot ~** pedes *m*; **old ~** veterānus
m ♦ *vi* mīlitāre
soldierly *adj* mīlitāris
soldiery *n* mīles *m*
sole *adj* sōlus, ūnus, ūnicus ♦ *n* (*foot*) planta *f*;
(*fish*) solea *f*
solecism *n* soloecismus *m*
solely *adv* sōlum, tantum, modō
solemn *adj* gravis; (*religion*) sanctus
solemnity *n* gravitās *f*; sanctitās *f*
solemnize *vt* agere
solemnly *adv* graviter; rītē
solicit *vt* flāgitāre, obsecrāre
solicitation *n* flāgitātiō *f*
solicitor *n* advocātus *m*
solicitous *adj* anxius, trepidus
solicitously *adv* anxiē, trepidē
solicitude *n* cūra *f*, anxietās *f*
solid *adj* solidus; (*metal*) pūrus; (*food*) firmus;
(*argument*) firmus; (*character*) cōnstāns,
spectātus; **become ~** concrēscere; **make
~** cōgere
solidarity *n* societās *f*
solidify *vt* cōgere ♦ *vi* concrēscere
solidity *n* soliditās *f*
solidly *adv* firmē, cōnstanter
soliloquize *vi* sēcum loquī
soliloquy *n* ūnīus ōrātiō *f*
solitary *adj* sōlus, sōlitārius; (*instance*) ūnicus;
(*place*) dēsertus
solitude *n* sōlitūdō *f*
solo *n* canticum *nt*
solstice *n* (*summer*) sōlstitium *nt*; (*winter*) brūma *f*
solstitial *adj* sōlstitiālis, brūmālis
soluble *adj* dissolūbilis
solution *n* (*of puzzle*) ēnōdātiō *f*
solve *vt* ēnōdāre, explicāre
solvency *n* solvendī facultās *f*
solvent *adj*: **be ~** solvendō esse
sombre *adj* obscūrus; (*fig*) tristis
some *adj* aliquī; (*pl*) nonnūllī, aliquot; ~ **people**
sunt quī (*subj*); ~ **… other** alius … alius; **for
~ time** aliquamdiū; **with ~ reason** nōn sine
causā ♦ *pron* aliquis; (*pl*) nonnūllī, sunt quī
(*subj*), erant quī (*subj*)
somebody *pron* aliquis; ~ **or other** nescioquis
somehow *adv* quōdammodō, nescio quōmodō
someone *pron* aliquis; (*negative*) quisquam; ~ **or
other** nescioquis; ~ **else** alius

something *pron* aliquid; ~ **or other** nescioquid; ~ **else** aliud
sometime *adv* aliquandō; *(past)* quondam
sometimes *adv* interdum, nonnumquam; ~ ... ~ modo ... modo
somewhat *adv* aliquantum, nōnnihil, paulum; *(with compar)* paulō, aliquantō
somewhere *adv* alicubi; *(to)* aliquō; ~ **else** alibī; *(to)* aliō; **from** ~ alicunde; **from** ~ **else** aliunde
somnolence *n* somnus *m*
somnolent *adj* sēmisomnus
son *n* filius *m*; **small son** fīliolus *m*
song *n* carmen *nt*, cantus *m*
son-in-law *n* gener *m*
sonorous *adj* sonōrus, canōrus
soon *adv* mox, brevi, citō; **as** ~ **as** ut prīmum, cum prīmum *(+fut perf)*, simul āc/atque *(+perf indic)*; ~ **as possible** quam prīmum; **too** ~ praemātūrē, ante tempus
sooner *adv* prius, mātūrius; *(preference)* libentius, potius; ~ **or later** sērius ōcius; **no** ~ **said than done** dictum factum
soonest *adv* mātūrissimē
soot *n* fūlīgō *f*
soothe *vt* dēlēnīre, permulcēre
soothing *adj* lēnis, blandus
soothingly *adv* blandē
soothsayer *n* hariolus *m*, vātēs *m/f*, haruspex *m*
sooty *adj* fūmōsus
sop *n* offa *f*; *(fig)* dēlēnīmentum *nt*
sophism *n* captiō *f*
sophist *n* sophistēs *m*
sophistical *adj* acūleātus, captiōsus
sophisticated *adj* lepidus, urbānus
sophistry *n* captiō *f*
soporific *adj* sopōrifer, somnifer
soprano *adj* acūtus
sorcerer *n* veneficus *m*
sorceress *n* venefica *f*, saga *f*
sorcery *n* venēficium *nt*; *(means)* venēna *ntpl*, carmina *ntpl*
sordid *adj* sordidus; *(conduct)* illīberālis
sordidly *adv* sordidē
sordidness *n* sordēs *fpl*; illīberālitās *f*
sore *adj* molestus, gravis, acerbus; **feel** ~ dolēre ◆ *n* ulcus *nt*
sorely *adv* graviter, vehementer
sorrel *n* lapathus *f*, lapathum *nt*
sorrow *n* dolor *m*, aegritūdō *f*; *(outward)* maeror *m*; *(for death)* lūctus *m* ◆ *vi* dolēre, maerere, lūgēre
sorrowful *adj* maestus, tristis
sorrowfully *adv* maestē
sorry *adj* paenitēns; *(poor)* miser; **I am ~ for** *(remorse)* mē paenitet, mē piget *(gen)*; *(pity)* mē miseret *(gen)*
sort *n* genus *nt*; **a ~ of** quīdam; **all sorts of** omnēs; **the ~ of** tālis; **this ~ of** huiusmodī; **the common ~** plēbs *f*; **I am not the ~ of man to** nōn is sum quī *(subj)*; **I am out of sorts** mihī displiceō ◆ *vt* dīgerere, compōnere; *(votes)* diribēre
sortie *n* excursiō *f*, excursus *m*, ēruptiō *f*; **make a ~** ērumpere, excurrere
sot *n* ēbriōsus *m*
sottish *adj* ēbriōsus, tēmulentus

sottishness *n* vīnolentia *f*
soul *n* anima *f*, animus *m*; *(essence)* vīs *f*; *(person)* caput *nt*; **not a ~** nēmō ūnus; **the ~ of** *(fig)* medulla *f*
soulless *adj* caecus, dūrus
sound *n* sonitus *m*, sonus *m*; *(articulate)* vōx *f*; *(confused)* strepitus *m*; *(loud)* fragor *m*; *(strait)* fretum *nt* ◆ *vt* *(signal)* canere; *(instrument)* īnflāre; *(depth)* scrūtārī, temptāre; *(person)* animum temptāre *(gen)* ◆ *vi* canere, sonāre; *(seem)* vidērī; ~ **a retreat** receptuī canere ◆ *adj* sānus, salūbris; *(health)* firmus; *(sleep)* artus; *(judgment)* exquīsītus; *(argument)* vērus; **safe and ~** salvus, incolumis
soundly *adv* *(beat)* vehementer; *(sleep)* artē; *(study)* penitus, dīligenter
soundness *n* sānitās *f*, integritās *f*
soup *n* iūs *nt*
sour *adj* acerbus, amārus, acidus; **turn ~** acēscere; *(fig)* coacēscere ◆ *vt* *(fig)* exacerbāre
source *n* fōns *m*; *(river)* caput *nt*; *(fig)* fōns *m*, orīgō *f*; **have its ~ in** orīrī ex; *(fig)* proficīscī ex
sourness *n* acerbitās *f*; *(temper)* mōrōsitās *f*
souse *vt* immergere
south *n* merīdiēs *f* ◆ *adj* austrālis ◆ *adv* ad merīdiem
south-east *adv* inter sōlis ortum et merīdiem
southerly *adj* ad merīdiem versus
southern *adj* austrālis
south-west *adv* inter occāsum sōlis et merīdiem
south wind *n* auster *m*
souvenir *n* monumentum *nt*
sovereign *n* rēx *m*, rēgīna *f* ◆ *adj* prīnceps, summus
sovereignty *n* rēgnum *nt*, imperium *nt*, prīncipātus *m*; *(of the people)* māiestās *f*
sow¹ *n* scrōfa *f*, sūs *f*
sow² *vt* serere; *(field)* cōnserere ◆ *vi* sementem facere
sower *n* sator *m*
sowing *n* sēmentis *f*
spa *n* aquae *fpl*
space *n* *(extension)* spatium *nt*; *(not matter)* ināne *nt*; *(room)* locus *m*; *(distance)* intervallum *nt*; *(time)* spatium *nt*; **open ~** ārea *f*; **leave a ~ of** intermittere ◆ *vt*: ~ **out** dispōnere
spacious *adj* amplus, capāx
spaciousness *n* amplitūdō *f*
spade *n* pāla *f*, rūtrum *nt*
span *n* *(measure)* palmus *m*; *(extent)* spatium *nt* ◆ *vt* iungere
spangle *n* bractea *f*
spangled *adj* distinctus
spar *n* tignum *nt*
spare *vt* parcere *(dat)*; *(to give)* suppeditāre; ~ **time for** vacāre *(dat)* ◆ *adj* exīlis; *(extra)* subsecīvus
sparing *adj* parcus
sparingly *adv* parcē
spark *n* scintilla *f*; *(fig)* igniculus *m*
sparkle *vi* scintillāre, nitēre, micāre
sparrow *n* passer *m*
sparse *adj* rārus
spasm *n* convulsiō *f*
spasmodically *adv* interdum

spatter vt aspergere

spawn n ōva ntpl

speak vt, vi loquī; (make speech) dīcere, contiōnārī, ōrātiōnem habēre; ~ **out** ēloquī; ~ **to** adloquī; (converse) colloquī cum; ~ **well of** bene dīcere (dat); **it speaks for itself** rēs ipsa loquitur

speaker n ōrātor m

speaking n: **art of** ~ dīcendī ars f; **practise public** ~ dēclāmāre ♦ adj: **likeness** ~ vīvida imāgō

spear n hasta f

spearman n hastātus m

special adj praecipuus, proprius

speciality n proprium nt

specially adv praecipuē, praesertim

species n genus nt

specific adj certus

specification n dēsignātiō f

specify vt dēnotāre, dēsignāre

specimen n exemplar nt, exemplum nt

specious adj speciōsus

speciously adv speciōsē

speciousness n speciēs f

speck n macula f

speckled adj maculīs distinctus

spectacle n spectāculum nt

spectacular adj spectābilis

spectator n spectātor m

spectral adj larvālis

spectre n larva f

speculate vi cōgitāre, coniectūrās facere; (COMM) forō ūtī

speculation n cōgitātiō f, coniectūra f; (COMM) ālea f

speculator n contemplātor m; (COMM) āleātor m

speech n ōrātiō f; (language) sermō m, lingua f; (to people or troops) cōntiō f; **make a** ~ ōrātiōnem/cōntiōnem habēre

speechless adj ēlinguis, mūtus

speed n celeritās f, cursus m, vēlōcitās f; **with all** ~ summā celeritāte; **at full** ~ māgnō cursū, incitātus; (riding) citātō equō ♦ vt adcelerāre, mātūrāre ♦ vi properāre, festīnāre

speedily adv celeriter, citō

speedy adj celer, vēlōx, citus

spell n carmen nt

spellbound adj: **be** ~ obstipēscere

spelt n far nt

spend vt impendere, īnsūmere; (public money) ērogāre; (time) agere, cōnsūmere, terere; (strength) effundere; ~ **itself** (storm) dēsaevīre; ~ **on** īnsūmere (acc & dat)

spendthrift n nepōs m, prōdigus m

sphere n globus m; (of action) prōvincia f

spherical adj globōsus

sphinx n sphinx f

spice n condīmentum nt; **spices** pl odōrēs mpl ♦ vt condīre

spicy adj odōrātus; (wit) salsus

spider n arānea f; **spider's web** arāneum nt

spike n dēns m, clāvus m

spikenard n nardus m

spill vt fundere, profundere ♦ vi redundāre

spin vt (thread) nēre, dēdūcere; (top) versāre; ~ **out** (story) prōdūcere ♦ vi circumagī, versārī

spindle n fūsus m

spine n spīna f

spineless adj ēnervātus

spinster n virgō f

spiral adj intortus ♦ n spīra f

spire n cōnus m

spirit n (life) anima f; (intelligence) mēns f; (soul) animus m; (vivacity) spīritus m, vigor m, vīs f; (character) ingenium nt; (intention) voluntās f; (of an age) mōrēs mpl; (ghost) anima f; **spirits** pl mānēs mpl; **full of** ~ alacer, animōsus

spirited adj animōsus, ācer

spiritless adj iners, frāctus, timidus

spiritual adj animī

spit n verū nt ♦ vi spuere, spūtāre; ~ **on** cōnspūtāre; ~ **out** exspuere

spite n invidia f, malevolentia f, līvor m; **in** ~ **of me** mē invītō; **in** ~ **of the difficulties** in his angustiīs ♦ vt incommodāre, offendere

spiteful adj malevolus, malignus, invidus

spitefully adv malevolē, malignē

spitefulness n malevolentia f

spittle n spūtum nt

splash n fragor m ♦ vt aspergere

spleen n splēn m; (fig) stomachus m

splendid adj splendidus, lūculentus; īnsignis; (person) amplus

splendidly adv splendidē, optimē

splendour n splendor m, fulgor m; (fig) lautitia f, adparātus m

splenetic adj stomachōsus

splice vt iungere

splint n ferula f

splinter n fragmentum nt, assula f ♦ vt findere

split vt findere ♦ vi dissilīre ♦ adj fissus ♦ n fissum nt; (fig) dissidium nt

splutter vi balbūtīre

spoil n praeda f ♦ vt (rob) spoliāre; (mar) corrumpere ♦ vi corrumpī

spoiler n spoliātor m; corruptor m

spoils npl spolia ntpl, exuviae fpl

spoke n radius m; **put a** ~ **in one's wheel** inicere scrūpulum (dat)

spokesman n interpres m, ōrātor m

spoliation n spoliātiō f, dīreptiō f

spondee n spondēus m

sponge n spongia f

sponsor n spōnsor m; (fig) auctor m

spontaneity n impulsus m, voluntās f

spontaneous adj voluntārius

spontaneously adv suā sponte, ultrō

spoon n cochlear nt

sporadic adj rārus

sporadically adv passim

sport n lūdus m; (in Rome) campus m; (fun) iocus m; (ridicule) lūdibrium nt; **make a** ~ **of** illūdere (dat) ♦ vi lūdere

sportive adj lascīvus

sportiveness n lascīvia f

sportsman n vēnātor m

sportsmanlike adj honestus, generōsus

spot n macula f; (place) locus m; (dice) pūnctum nt; **on the** ~ īlicō ♦ vt maculāre; (see) animadvertere

spotless adj integer, pūrus; (character) castus

spotted adj maculōsus

spouse n coniunx m/f

spout n (of jug) ōs nt; (pipe) canālis m ♦ vi ēmicāre
sprain vt intorquēre
sprawl vi sē fundere
sprawling adj fūsus
spray n aspergō f ♦ vt aspergere
spread vt pandere, extendere; (news) dīvulgāre; (infection) vulgāre ♦ vi patēre; (rumour) mānāre, incrēbrēscere; (feeling) glīscere
spreadeagle vt dispandere
spreading adj (tree) patulus
spree n cōmissātiō f
sprig n virga f
sprightliness n alacritās f
sprightly adj alacer, hilaris
spring n (season) vēr nt; (water) fōns m; (leap) saltus m ♦ vi (grow) crēscere, ēnāscī; (leap) salīre; ~ from orirī ex, proficīscī ex; ~ on to īnsilīre in (acc); ~ up exorīrī, exsilīre ♦ vt: ~ a leak rīmās agere; ~ a surprise on admīrātiōnēm movēre (dat) ♦ adj vērnus
springe n laqueus m
sprinkle vt aspergere; ~ on īnspergere (dat)
sprint vi currere
sprout n surculus m ♦ vi fruticārī
spruce adj nitidus, concinnus
sprung adj ortus, oriundus
spume n spūma f
spur n calcar nt; ~ of a hill prōminēns collis; on the ~ of the moment ex tempore ♦ vt incitāre; ~ the willing horse currentem incitāre; ~ on concitāre
spurious adj falsus, fūcōsus, fictus
spurn vt spernere, aspernārī, respuere
spurt vi ēmicāre; (run) sē incitāre ♦ n impetus m
spy n speculātor m, explōrātor m ♦ vi speculārī ♦ vt cōnspicere; **spy out** explōrāre
squabble n iūrgium nt ♦ vi rixārī
squad n (MIL) decuria f
squadron n (cavalry) āla f, turma f; (ships) classis f
squalid adj sordidus, dēfōrmis
squall n procella f
squally adj procellōsus
squalor n sordēs fpl, squālor m
squander vt dissipāre, disperdere, effundere
squanderer n prōdigus m
square n quadrātum nt; (town) ārea f ♦ vt quadrāre; (account) subdūcere ♦ vi cōnstāre, congruere ♦ adj quadrātus
squash vt conterere, contundere
squat vi subsīdere ♦ adj brevis atque obēsus
squatter n (on land) agripeta m
squawk vi crōcīre
squeak n strīdor m ♦ vi strīdēre
squeal n vāgītus m ♦ vi vāgīre
squeamish adj fastīdiōsus; **feel ~** nauseāre, fastīdīre
squeamishness n fastīdium nt, nausea f
squeeze vt premere, comprimere; ~ out exprimere
squint adj perversus ♦ n: **person with a ~** strabō m ♦ vi strabō esse
squinter n strabō m
squinting adj paetus
squire n armiger m; (landed) dominus m
squirm vi volūtārī
squirrel n sciūrus m

squirt vt ēicere, effundere ♦ vi ēmicāre
stab n ictus m, vulnus nt ♦ vt fodere, ferīre, percutere
stability n stabilitās f, firmitās f, cōnstantia f
stabilize vt stabilīre, firmāre
stable adj firmus, stabilis ♦ n stabulum nt, equīle nt; **shut the ~ door after the horse is stolen** clipeum post vulnera sūmere
stack n acervus m ♦ vt congerere, cumulāre
stadium n spatium nt
staff n scīpiō m, virga f; (augur's) lituus m; (officers) contubernālēs mpl
stag n cervus m
stage n pulpitum nt, proscēnium nt; (theatre) scēna f, theātrum nt; (scene of action) campus m; (of journey) iter nt; (of progress) gradus m ♦ adj scēnicus ♦ vt (play) dare, docēre
stage fright n horror m
stagger vi titubāre ♦ vt obstupefacere
stagnant adj iners
stagnate vi (fig) cessāre, refrīgēscere
stagnation n cessātiō f, torpor m
stagy adj scēnicus
staid adj sevērus, gravis
stain n macula f, lābēs f; (fig) dēdecus nt, ignōminia f ♦ vt maculāre, foedāre, contāmināre; ~ with īnficere (abl)
stainless adj pūrus, integer
stair n scālae fpl, gradus mpl
staircase n scālae fpl
stake n pālus m, stīpes m; (pledge) pignus nt; **be at ~** agī, in discrīmine esse ♦ vt (wager) dēpōnere
stale adj obsolētus, effētus; (wine) vapidus
stalemate n: **reach a ~** ad incitās redigī
stalk n (corn) calamus m; (plant) stīpes m ♦ vi incēdere ♦ vt vēnārī, īnsidiārī (dat)
stall n (animal) stabulum nt; (seat) subsellium nt; (shop) taberna f ♦ vt stabulāre
stallion n equus m
stalwart adj ingēns, rōbustus, fortis
stamina n patientia f
stammer n haesitātiō f ♦ vi balbūtīre
stammering adj balbus
stamp n fōrma f; (mark) nota f, signum nt; (of feet) supplōsiō f ♦ vt imprimere; (coin) signāre; (fig) inūrere; ~ one's feet pedem supplōdere; ~ out extinguere
stampede n discursus m; (fig) pavor m ♦ vi discurrere; (fig) expavēscere
stance n status m
stanchion n columna f
stand n (position) statiō f; (platform) suggestus m; **make a ~** resistere, restāre ♦ vi stāre; (remain) manēre; (matters) sē habēre ♦ vt statuere; (tolerate) ferre, tolerāre; ~ **against** resistere (dat); ~ **aloof** abstāre; ~ **by** adsistere (dat); (friend) adesse (dat); (promise) praestāre; ~ **convicted** manifestum tenērī; ~ **down** concēdere; ~ **fast** cōnsistere; ~ **one's ground** in locō perstāre; ~ **for** (office) petere; (meaning) significāre; (policy) postulāre; ~ **in awe of** in metū habēre; ~ **in need of** indigēre (abl); ~ **on** īnsistere in (abl); ~ **on end** horrēre; ~ **on one's dignity** gravitātem suam tuērī; ~ **out** ēminēre, exstāre; (against) resistere (dat); (to sea) in altum prōvehī; ~ **out of the way of** dēcēdere (dat); ~ **over** (case)

ampliāre; ~ **still** cōnsistere, īnsistere; ~ **to reason** sequī; ~ **trial** reum fierī; ~ **up** surgere, cōnsurgere; ~ **up for** dēfendere, adesse (*dat*); ~ **up to** respōnsāre (*dat*)

standard *n* (MIL) signum *nt*; (*measure*) nōrma *f*; ~ **author** scrīptor classicus *m*; **up to** ~ iūstus; **judge by the ~ of** referre ad

standard-bearer *n* signifer *m*

standing *adj* perpetuus ♦ *n* status *m*; (*social*) locus *m*, ōrdō *m*; **of long** ~ inveterātus; **be of long** ~ inveterāscere

stand-offish *adj* tēctus

standstill *n*: **be at a** ~ haerēre, frīgēre; **bring to a** ~ ad incitās redigere; **come to a** ~ īnsistere

stanza *n* tetrastichon *nt*

staple *n* uncus *m* ♦ *adj* praecipuus

star *n* stēlla *f*, astrum *nt*; sīdus *nt*; **shooting stars** acontiae *fpl*

starboard *adj* dexter

starch *n* amylum *nt*

stare *n* obtūtus *m* ♦ *vi* intentīs oculīs intuērī, stupēre; ~ **at** contemplārī

stark *adj* rigidus; simplex ♦ *adv* plānē, omnīnō

starling *n* sturnus *m*

starry *adj* stēllātus

start *n* initium *nt*; (*movement*) saltus *m*; (*journey*) profectiō *f*; **by fits and starts** carptim; **have a day's** ~ **on** diē antecēdere ♦ *vt* incipere, īnstituere; (*game*) excitāre; (*process*) movēre ♦ *vi* (*with fright*) resilīre; (*journey*) proficīscī; ~ **up** exsilīre

starting place *n* carcerēs *mpl*

startle *vt* excitāre, terrēre

starvation *n* famēs *f*

starve *vi* fāme cōnficī; (*cold*) frīgēre ♦ *vt* fāme ēnecāre

starveling *n* famēlicus *m*

state *n* (*condition*) status *m*, condiciō *f*; (*pomp*) adparātus *m*; (POL) cīvitās *f*, rēs pūblica *f*; **the** ~ **of affairs is** ita sē rēs habet; **I know the** ~ **of affairs** quō in locō rēs sit sciō; **of the** ~ pūblicus ♦ *adj* pūblicus ♦ *vt* adfirmāre, expōnere, profitērī; ~ **one's case** causam dīcere

stateliness *n* māiestās *f*, gravitās *f*

stately *adj* gravis, grandis, nōbilis

statement *n* adfirmātiō *f*, dictum *nt*; (*witness*) testimōnium *nt*

state of health *n* valētūdō *f*

state of mind *n* adfectiō *f*

statesman *n* vir reī pūblicae gerendae perītus *m*, cōnsilī pūblicī auctor *m*

statesmanlike *adj* prūdēns

statesmanship *n* cīvīlis prūdentia *f*

static *adj* stabilis

station *n* locus *m*; (MIL) statiō *f*; (*social*) locus *m*, ōrdō *m* ♦ *vt* collocāre, pōnere; (*in different places*) dispōnere

stationary *adj* immōtus, statārius, stabilis

statistics *n* cēnsus *m*

statuary *n* fictor *m*

statue *n* statua *f*, signum *nt*, imāgō *f*

statuette *n* sigillum *nt*

stature *n* fōrma *f*, statūra *f*

status *n* locus *m*

status quo *n*: **restore the** ~ ad integrum restituere

statutable *adj* lēgitimus

statute *n* lēx *f*

staunch *vt* (*blood*) sistere ♦ *adj* fīdus, cōnstāns

stave *vt* perrumpere, perfringere; ~ **off** arcēre

stay *n* firmāmentum *nt*; (*fig*) columen *nt*; (*sojourn*) mānsiō *f*, commorātiō *f* ♦ *vt* (*prop*) fulcīre; (*stop*) dētinēre, dēmorārī ♦ *vi* manēre, commorārī

stead *n* locus *m*; **stand one in good** ~ prōdesse (*dat*)

steadfast *adj* firmus, stabilis, cōnstāns; ~ **at home** tenēre sē domī

steadfastly *adv* cōnstanter

steadfastness *n* firmitās *f*, cōnstantia *f*

steadily *adv* firmē, cōnstanter

steadiness *n* stabilitās *f*; (*fig*) cōnstantia *f*

steady *adj* stabilis, firmus; (*fig*) gravis, cōnstāns

steak *n* offa *f*

steal *vt* surripere, fūrārī ♦ *vi*: ~ **away** sē subdūcere; ~ **over** subrēpere (*dat*); ~ **into** sē īnsinuāre in (*acc*); ~ **a march on** occupāre

stealing *n* fūrtum *nt*

stealth *n* fūrtum *nt*; **by** ~ fūrtim, clam

stealthily *adv* fūrtim, clam

stealthy *adj* fūrtīvus, clandestīnus

steam *n* aquae vapor *m*, fūmus *m* ♦ *vi* fūmāre

steed *n* equus *m*

steel *n* ferrum *nt*, chalybs *m* ♦ *adj* ferreus ♦ *vt* dūrāre; ~ **oneself** obdūrēscere

steely *adj* ferreus

steelyard *n* statēra *f*

steep *adj* arduus, praeceps, praeruptus; (*slope*) dēclīvis ♦ *vt* imbuere

steeple *n* turris *f*

steepness *n* arduum *nt*

steer *vi*, *vt* gubernāre, regere, dīrigere ♦ *n* iuvencus *m*

steering *n* gubernātiō *f*

steersman *n* gubernātor *m*; rector *m*

stellar *adj* stēllārum

stem *n* stīpes *m*, truncus *m*; (*ship*) prōra *f* ♦ *vt* adversārī (*dat*); ~ **the tide of** (*fig*) obsistere (*dat*)

stench *n* foetor *m*

stenographer *n* exceptor *m*, āctuārius *m*

stenography *n* notae *fpl*

stentorian *adj* (*voice*) ingēns

step *n* gradus *m*; (*track*) vestīgium *nt*; (*of stair*) gradus *m*; ~ **by** ~ gradātim; **flight of steps** gradus *mpl*; **take a** ~ gradum facere; **take steps to** ratiōnem inīre ut, vidēre ut; **march in** ~ in numerum īre; **out of** ~ extrā numerum ♦ *vi* gradī, incēdere; ~ **aside** dēcēdere; ~ **back** regredī; ~ **forward** prōdīre; ~ **on** insistere (*dat*)

stepdaughter *n* prīvigna *f*

stepfather *n* vītricus *m*

stepmother *n* noverca *f*

stepson *n* prīvīgnus *m*

stereotyped *adj* trītus

sterile *adj* sterilis

sterility *n* sterilitās *f*

sterling *adj* integer, probus, gravis

stern *adj* dūrus, sevērus; (*look*) torvus ♦ *n* puppis *f*

sternly *adv* sevērē, dūriter

sternness *n* sevēritās *f*

stew *vt* coquere

steward *n* prōcūrātor *m*; (*of estate*) vīlicus *m*

stewardship n prōcūrātiō f
stick n (for beating) fūstis m; (for walking)
  baculum nt ♦ vi haerēre; ~ **at nothing** ad
  omnia dēscendere; ~ **fast in** inhaerēre
  (dat), inhaerēscere in (abl); ~ **out** ēminēre;
  ~ **to** adhaerēre (dat); ~ **up** ēminēre; ~ **up for**
  dēfendere ♦ vt (with glue) conglūtināre; (with
  point) fīgere; ~ **into** īnfīgere; ~ **top on** praefīgere
stickler n dīligēns (gen)
sticky adj lentus, tenāx
stiff adj rigidus; (difficult) difficilis; **be** ~ rigēre
stiffen vt rigidum facere ♦ vi rigēre
stiffly adv rigidē
stiff-necked adj obstinātus
stiffness n rigor m
stifle vt suffocāre; (fig) opprimere, restinguere
stigma n nota f
stigmatize vt notāre
stile n saepēs f
still adj immōtus, tranquillus, quiētus;
  tacitus ♦ vt lēnīre, sēdāre ♦ adv etiam, adhūc,
  etiamnum; (past) etiam tum; (with compar)
  etiam; (adversative) tamen, nihilōminus
stillness n quiēs f; silentium nt
stilly adj tacitus
stilted adj (language) īnflātus
stilts n grallae fpl
stimulant n stimulus m
stimulate vt stimulāre, acuere, exacuere,
  excitāre
stimulus n stimulus m
sting n aculeus m; (wound) ictus m; (fig) aculeus m,
  morsus m ♦ vt pungere, mordēre
stingily adv sordidē
stinginess n avāritia f, sordēs fpl, tenācitās f
stinging adj (words) aculeātus, mordāx
stingy adj sordidus, tenāx
stink n foetor m ♦ vi foetere; ~ **of** olēre
stinking adj foetidus
stint n modus m; **without** ~ abundē ♦ vt
  circumscrībere
stipend n mercēs f
stipulate vt pacīscī, stipulārī
stipulation n condiciō f, pactum nt
stir n tumultus m ♦ vt movēre, agitāre; (fig)
  commovēre; ~ **up** excitāre, incitāre ♦ vi movērī
stirring adj impiger, tumultuōsus; (speech)
  ārdēns
stitch vt suere ♦ n sūtūra f; (in side) dolor m
stock n stirps f, genus nt, gēns f; (equipment)
  īnstrūmenta ntpl; (supply) cōpia f; (investment)
  pecūniae fpl; **livestock** rēs pecuāria f ♦ vt
  īnstruere ♦ adj commūnis, trītus
stockade n vallum nt
stock dove n palumbēs m/f
stock in trade n instrūmenta ntpl
stocks n (ship) nāvālia ntpl; (torture) compedēs fpl
stock-still adj plānē immōtus
stocky adj brevis atque obēsus
stodgy adj crūdus, īnsulsus
stoic n Stōicus m ♦ adj Stōicus
stoical adj dūrus, patiēns
stoically adv patienter
stoicism n Stōicōrum ratiō f, Stōicōrum
  disciplīna f
stoke vt agitāre

stole n stola f
stolid adj stolidus
stolidity n īnsulsitās f
stolidly adv stolidē
stomach n stomachus m; venter m ♦ vt patī,
  tolerāre
stone n lapis m, saxum nt; (precious) gemma
  f, lapillus m; (of fruit) acinum nt; **leave no**
  ~ **unturned** omnia experīrī; **kill two birds**
  with one ~ ūnō saltū duōs aprōs capere; **hewn**
  ~ saxum quadrātum; **unhewn** ~ caementum nt
  ♦ vt lapidibus percutere ♦ adj lapideus; ~ **blind**
  plānē caecus; ~ **deaf** plānē surdus
stonecutter n lapicīda m
stony adj (soil) lapidōsus; (path) scrūpōsus;
  (feeling) dūrus, ferreus
stool n sēdēcula f
stoop vi sē dēmittere; ~ **to** dēscendere in (acc)
stop n mora f; (punctuation) pūnctum nt; **come to**
  a ~ īnsistere; **put a** ~ **to** comprimere, dirimere
  ♦ vt sistere, inhibēre, fīnīre; (restrain) cohibēre;
  (hole) obtūrāre; ~ **up** occlūdere, interclūdere ♦ vi
  dēsinere, dēsistere; (motion) īnsistere
stopgap n tībīcen m
stoppage n interclūsiō f, impedīmentum nt
stopper n obtūrāmentum nt
store n cōpia f; (place) horreum nt; (for wine)
  apothēca f; **be in** ~ **for** manēre; **set great** ~ **by**
  māgnī aestimāre ♦ vt condere, repōnere;
  ~ **away** recondere; ~ **up** repōnere, congerere
storehouse n (fig) thēsaurus m
storekeeper n cellārius m
storeship n nāvis frūmentāria f
storey n tabulātum nt
stork n cicōnia f
storm n tempestās f, procella f; **take by**
  ~ expugnāre ♦ vt (MIL) expugnāre ♦ vi saevīre;
  ~ **at** īnsectārī, invehī in (acc)
stormbound adj tempestāte dētentus
stormer n expugnātor m
storming n expugnātiō f
stormy adj turbidus, procellōsus; (fig)
  turbulentus
story n fābula f, nārrātiō f; (short) fābella f;
  (untrue) mendācium nt
storyteller n nārrātor m; (liar) mendāx m
stout adj pinguis; (brave) fortis; (strong) validus,
  rōbustus; (material) firmus
stouthearted adj māgnanimus
stoutly adv fortiter
stove n camīnus m, fornāx f
stow vt repōnere, condere; ~ **away** vi in nāvī
  dēlitēscere
straddle vi vāricāre
straggle vi deerrāre, pālārī
straggler n pālāns m
straggling adj dispersus, rārus
straight adj rēctus, dīrēctus; (fig) apertus, vērāx;
  in a ~ **line** rēctā, ē regiōne; **set** ~ dīrigere ♦ adv
  dīrēctō, rēctā
straighten vt corrigere, extendere
straightforward adj simplex, dīrēctus; (easy)
  facilis
straightforwardness n simplicitās f
straightness n (fig) integritās f
straightway adv statim, extemplō

strain n contentiō f; (effort) labor m; (music) modī
mpl; (breed) genus nt ♦ vt intendere, contendere;
(injure) nimiā contentiōne dēbilitāre; (liquid)
dēliquāre, percōlāre ♦ vi ēnītī, vīrēs contendere
strained adj (language) arcessītus
strainer n cōlum nt
strait adj angustus ♦ n fretum nt; **straits** pl
angustiae fpl
straiten vt coartāre, contrahere; **straitened
circumstances** angustiae fpl
strait-laced adj tristis, sevērus
strand n lītus nt; (of rope) fīlum nt ♦ vt (ship) ēicere
strange adj novus, īnsolitus; (foreign) peregrīnus;
(another's) aliēnus; (ignorant) rudis, expers
strangely adv mīrē, mīrum in modum
strangeness n novitās f, īnsolentia f
stranger n (from abroad) advena f; peregrīnus
m; (visiting) hospes m, hospita f; (not of the family)
externus m; (unknown) ignōtus m
strangle vt strangulāre, laqueō gulam frangere
strap n lōrum nt, habēna f
strapping adj grandis
stratagem n cōnsilium nt, fallācia f
strategic adj (action) prūdēns; (position) idōneus
strategist n artis bellicae perītus m
strategy n ars imperātōria f; cōnsilia ntpl
straw n (stalk) culmus m; (collective) strāmentum
nt; **not care a ~ for** floccī nōn facere ♦ adj
strāmenticius
strawberry n frāgum nt
strawberry tree n arbutus m
stray vt aberrāre, deerrāre; vagārī ♦ adj
errābundus
streak n līnea f, macula f; (light) radius m;
(character) vēna f ♦ vt maculāre
stream n flūmen nt, fluvius m; **down ~** secundō
flūmine; **up ~** adversō flūmine ♦ vi fluere, sē
effundere; **~ into** īnfluere in (acc)
streamlet n rīvus m, rīvulus m
street n via f, platea f
strength n vīrēs fpl; (of material) firmitās f; (fig)
rōbur nt, nervī mpl; (MIL) numerus m; **know the
enemy's ~** quot sint hostēs scīre; **on the ~ of**
frētus (abl)
strengthen vt firmāre, corrōborāre; (position)
mūnīre
strenuous adj impiger, strēnuus, sēdulus
strenuously adv impigrē, strēnuē
strenuousness n industria f
stress n (words) ictus m; (meaning) vīs f; (importance)
mōmentum nt; (difficulty) labor m; **lay great ~ on**
in māgnō discrīmine pōnere ♦ vt exprimere
stretch n spatium nt, tractus m; **at a ~** sine ullā
intermissiōne ♦ vt tendere, intendere; (length)
prōdūcere, extendere; (facts) in māius crēdere;
~ a point indulgēre; **~ before** obtendere;
~ forth porrigere; **~ oneself** (on ground) sternī;
~ out porrigere, extendere ♦ vi extendī,
patēscere
strew vt (things) sternere; (place) cōnsternere
stricken adj saucius
strict adj (defined) ipse, certus; (severe) sevērus,
rigidus; (accurate) dīligēns
strictly adv sevērē; dīligenter; **~ speaking**
scīlicet, immo
strictness n sevēritās f; dīligentia f

stricture n vītuperātiō f
stride n passus m; **make great strides** (fig)
multum prōficere ♦ vi incēdere, ingentēs
gradūs ferre
strident adj asper
strife n discordia f, pugna f
strike vt ferīre, percutere; (instrument) pellere,
pulsāre; (sail) subdūcere; (tent) dētendere; (mind)
venīre in (acc); (camp) movēre; (fear into) incutere
in (acc); **~ against** offendere; **~ out** dēlēre; **~ up**
(music) incipere; **~ a bargain** pacīscī; **be struck**
vāpulāre ♦ vi (work) cessāre
striking adj īnsignis, īnsignītus, ēgregius
strikingly adv īnsignītē
string n (cord) resticula f; (succession) seriēs f;
(instrument) nervus m; (bow) nervus m; **have two
strings to one's bow** duplicī spē ūtī ♦ vt (bow)
intendere; (together) coniungere
stringency n sevēritās f
stringent adj sevērus
strip vt nūdāre, spoliāre, dēnūdāre; **~ off** exuere;
(leaves) stringere, dēstringere ♦ n lacinia f
stripe n virga f; (on tunic) clāvus m; **stripes** pl
verbera ntpl
striped adj virgātus
stripling n adulescentulus m
strive vi nītī, ēnītī, contendere; (contend) certāre
stroke n ictus m; (lightning) fulmen nt; (oar)
pulsus m; (pen) līnea f; **~ of luck** fortūna
secunda f ♦ vt mulcēre, dēmulcēre
stroll vi deambulāre, spatiārī
strong adj fortis, validus; (health) rōbustus,
firmus; (material) firmus; (smell) gravis;
(resources) pollēns, potēns; (feeling) ācer, māgnus;
(language) vehemēns, probrōsus; **be ~** valēre; **be
twenty ~** vīgintī esse numerō
strongbox n arca f
stronghold n arx f
strongly adv validē, vehementer, fortiter,
ācriter, graviter
strong-minded adj pertināx, cōnstāns
strophe n stropha f
structure n aedificium nt; (form) structūra f;
(arrangement) compositiō f
struggle n (effort) cōnātus m; (fight) pugna f,
certāmen nt ♦ vi nītī; certāre, contendere; (fight)
luctārī; **~ upwards** ēnītī
strut vi māgnificē incēdere
stubble n stipula f
stubborn adj pertināx, pervicāx
stubbornly adv pertināciter, pervicāciter
stubbornness n pertinācia f, pervicācia f
stucco n gypsum nt
stud n clāvus m; (horses) equī mpl
studded adj distinctus
student n discipulus m; **be a ~ of** studēre (dat)
studied adj meditātus, accūrātus; (language)
exquīsītus
studio n officīna f
studious adj litterīs dēditus, litterārum
studiōsus; (careful) attentus
studiously adv dē industriā
study vt studēre (dat); (prepare) meditārī; **~ under**
audīre ♦ n studium nt; (room) bibliothēca f
stuff n māteria f; (cloth) textile nt ♦ vt farcīre,
refercīre; (with food) sagīnāre

stuffing *n* sagina *f*; (*of cushion*) tōmentum *nt*
stultify *vt* ad inritum redigere
stumble *vi* offendere; ~ **upon** incidere in (*acc*), offendere
stumbling block *n* offēnsiō *f*
stump *n* stīpes *m*
stun *vt* stupefacere; (*fig*) obstupefacere, cōnfundere
stunned *adj* attonitus
stunt *vt* corporis auctum inhibēre
stunted *adj* curtus
stupefaction *n* stupor *m*
stupefied *adj*: **be ~** stupēre, obstupefierī
stupefy *vt* obstupefacere
stupendous *adj* mīrus, mīrificus
stupid *adj* stultus, hebes, ineptus
stupidity *n* stultitia *f*
stupidly *adv* stultē, ineptē
stupor *n* stupor *m*
sturdily *adv* fortiter
sturdiness *n* rōbur *nt*, firmitās *f*
sturdy *adj* fortis, rōbustus
sturgeon *n* acipēnser *m*
stutter *vi* balbūtire
stuttering *adj* balbus
sty *n* hara *f*
style *n* (*kind*) genus *nt*, ratiō *f*; (*of dress*) habitus *m*; (*of prose*) ēlocūtiō *f*, ōrātiō *f*; (*pen*) stilus *m* ♦ *vt* appellāre
stylish *adj* ēlegāns, lautus, expolītus
stylishly *adv* ēleganter
suasion *n* suāsiō *f*
suave *adj* blandus, urbānus
suavity *n* urbānitās *f*
subaltern *n* succenturiō *m*
subdivide *vt* dīvidere
subdivision *n* pars *f*, mōmentum *nt*
subdue *vt* subigere, dēvincere, redigere, domāre; (*fig*) cohibēre
subdued *adj* dēmissus, summissus
subject *n* (*person*) cīvis *m/f*; (*matter*) rēs *f*; (*theme*) locus *m*, argūmentum *nt* ♦ *adj* subiectus; ~ **to** obnoxius (*dat*) ♦ *vt* subicere; obnoxium reddere
subjection *n* servitūs *f*
subjective *adj* proprius
subject matter *n* māteria *f*
subjoin *vt* subicere, subiungere
subjugate *vt* subigere, dēbellāre, domāre
sublime *adj* sublīmis, ēlātus, excelsus
sublimely *adv* excelsē
sublimity *n* altitūdō *f*, ēlātiō *f*
submarine *adj* submersus
submerge *vt* dēmergere; (*flood*) inundāre ♦ *vi* sē dēmergere
submersed *adj* submersus
submission *n* obsequium *nt*, servitium *nt*; (*fig*) patientia *f*
submissive *adj* submissus, docilis, obtemperāns
submissively *adv* submissē, oboedienter, patienter
submit *vi* sē dēdere; ~ **to** pārēre (*dat*), obtemperāre (*dat*), patī, subīre ♦ *vt* (*proposal*) referre
subordinate *adj* subiectus, secundus ♦ *vt* subiungere, subicere

suborn *vt* subicere, subōrnāre
subpoena *vt* testimōnium dēnūntiāre (*dat*)
subscribe *vt* (*name*) subscrībere; (*money*) cōnferre
subscription *n* collātiō *f*
subsequent *adj* sequēns, posterior
subsequently *adv* posteā, mox
subserve *vt* subvenīre (*dat*), commodāre
subservience *n* obsequium *nt*
subservient *adj* obsequēns; (*thing*) ūtilis, commodus
subside *vi* dēsīdere, resīdere; (*fever*) dēcēdere; (*wind*) cadere; (*passion*) dēfervēscere
subsidence *n* lābēs *f*
subsidiary *adj* subiectus, secundus
subsidize *vt* pecūniās suppeditāre (*dat*)
subsidy *n* pecūniae *fpl*, vectīgal *nt*
subsist *vi* cōnstāre, sustentārī
subsistence *n* vīctus *m*
substance *n* (*matter*) rēs *f*, corpus *nt*; (*essence*) nātūra *f*; (*gist*) summa *f*; (*reality*) rēs *f*; (*wealth*) opēs *fpl*
substantial *adj* solidus; (*real*) vērus; (*important*) gravis; (*rich*) opulentus, dīves
substantially *adv* rē; māgnā ex parte
substantiate *vt* cōnfirmāre
substitute *vt* subicere, repōnere, substituere ♦ *n* vicārius *m*
substratum *n* fundāmentum *nt*
subterfuge *n* latebra *f*, perfugium *nt*
subterranean *adj* subterrāneus
subtle *adj* (*fine*) subtīlis; (*shrewd*) acūtus, astūtus
subtlety *n* subtīlitās *f*; acūmen *nt*, astūtia *f*
subtly *adv* subtīliter; acūtē, astūtē
subtract *vt* dētrahere, dēmere; (*money*) dēdūcere
subtraction *n* dētractiō *f*, dēductiō *f*
suburb *n* suburbium *nt*
suburban *adj* suburbānus
subvention *n* pecūniae *fpl*
subversion *n* ēversiō *f*, ruīna *f*
subversive *adj* sēditiōsus
subvert *vt* ēvertere, subruere
subverter *n* ēversor *m*
succeed *vi* (*person*) rem bene gerere; (*activity*) prosperē ēvenīre; ~ **in obtaining** impetrāre ♦ *vt* īnsequī, excipere, succēdere (*dat*)
success *n* bonus ēventus *m*, rēs bene gesta *f*
successful *adj* fēlīx; (*thing*) secundus; **be ~** rem bene gerere; (*play*) stāre
successfully *adv* fēlīciter, prosperē, bene
succession *n* (*coming next*) successiō *f*; (*line*) seriēs *f*, ōrdō *m*; **alternate ~** vicissitūdō *f*; **in ~ deinceps**, ex ōrdine
successive *adj* continuus, perpetuus
successively *adv* deinceps, ex ōrdine; (*alternately*) vicissim
successor *n* successor *m*
succinct *adj* brevis, pressus
succinctly *adv* breviter, pressē
succour *n* auxilium *nt*, subsidium *nt* ♦ *vt* subvenīre (*dat*), succurrere (*dat*), opem ferre (*dat*)
succulence *n* sūcus *m*
succulent *adj* sūcidus
succumb *vi* succumbere, dēficere
such *adj* tālis, ēiusmodī, hūiusmodī; (*size*) tantus; **at ~ a time** id temporis; ~ **great** tantus

suchlike *adj* hūiusmodī, ēiusdem generis
suck *vt* sūgere; ~ **in** sorbēre; ~ **up** exsorbēre, ēbibere
sucker *n* surculus *m*
sucking *adj* (*child*) lactēns
suckle *vt* nūtrīcārī, mammam dare (*dat*)
suckling *n* lactēns *m/f*
sudden *adj* subitus, repentīnus
suddenly *adv* subitō, repente
sue *vt* in iūs vocāre, lītem intendere (*dat*); **sue for** rogāre, petere, ōrāre
suffer *vt* patī, ferre, tolerāre; (*injury*) accipere; (*loss*) facere; (*permit*) patī, sinere ♦ *vi* dolōre adficī; ~ **defeat** cladem accipere; ~ **from** labōrāre ex, adficī (*abl*); ~ **for** poenās dare (*gen*)
sufferable *adj* tolerābilis
sufferance *n* patientia *f*, tolerantia *f*
suffering *n* dolor *m*
suffice *vi* sufficere, suppetere
sufficiency *n* satis
sufficient *adj* idōneus, satis (*gen*)
sufficiently *adv* satis
suffocate *vt* suffocāre
suffrage *n* suffrāgium *nt*
suffuse *vt* suffundere
sugar *n* saccharon *nt*
suggest *vt* admonēre, inicere, subicere; ~ **itself** occurrere
suggestion *n* admonitiō *f*; **at the ~ of** admonitū (*gen*); **at my ~** mē auctōre
suicidal *adj* fūnestus
suicide *n* mors voluntāria *f*; **commit ~** mortem sibī cōnscīscere
suit *n* (LAW) līs *f*, āctiō *f*; (*clothes*) vestītus *m* ♦ *vt* convenīre (*dat*), congruere (*dat*); (*dress*) sedēre (*dat*), decēre; **it suits** decet; **to ~ me** dē meā sententiā
suitability *n* convenientia *f*
suitable *adj* aptus (+ *dat or* 'ad' + *acc*), idōneus (+ *dat or* 'ad' + *acc*)
suitably *adv* aptē, decenter
suite *n* comitēs *mpl*, comitātus *m*
suitor *n* procus *m*, amāns *m*
sulk *vi* aegrē ferre, mōrōsum esse
sulky *adj* mōrōsus, tristis
sullen *adj* tristis, mōrōsus
sullenness *n* mōrōsitās *f*
sully *vt* īnfuscāre, contāmināre
sulphur *n* sulfur *nt*
sultriness *n* aestus *m*
sultry *adj* aestuōsus
sum *n* summa *f*; **sum of money** pecūnia *f* ♦ *vt* subdūcere, computāre; **sum up** summātim dēscrībere; **to sum up** ūnō verbō, quid plūra?
summarily *adv* strictim, summātim; sine morā
summarize *vt* summātim dēscrībere
summary *n* summārium *nt*, epitomē *f* ♦ *adj* subitus, praesēns
summer *n* aestās *f* ♦ *adj* aestīvus; **of ~** aestīvus
summit *n* vertex *m*, culmen *nt*; (*fig*) fastīgium *nt*; **the ~ of** summus
summon *vt* arcessere; (*meeting*) convocāre; (*witness*) citāre; ~ **up courage** animum sūmere
summons *n* (LAW) vocātiō *f* ♦ *vt* in iūs vocāre, diem dīcere (*dat*)
sumptuary *adj* sūmptuārius

sumptuous *adj* sūmptuōsus, adparātus, māgnificus, lautus
sumptuously *adv* sūmptuōsē, māgnificē
sun *n* sōl *m* ♦ *vt*: **sun oneself** aprīcārī
sunbeam *n* radius *m*
sunburnt *adj* adūstus
sunder *vt* sēparāre, dīvidere
sundial *n* sōlārium *nt*
sundry *adj* dīversī, complūrēs
sunlight *n* sōl *m*
sunlit *adj* aprīcus
sunny *adj* aprīcus, serēnus
sunrise *n* sōlis ortus *m*
sunset *n* sōlis occāsus *m*
sunshade *n* umbella *f*
sunshine *n* sōl *m*
sup *vi* cēnāre
superabundance *n* abundantia *f*
superabundant *adj* nimius
superabundantly *adv* satis superque
superannuated *adj* ēmeritus
superb *adj* māgnificus
superbly *adv* māgnificē
supercilious *adj* adrogāns, superbus
superciliously *adv* adroganter, superbē
superciliousness *n* adrogantia *f*, fastus *m*
supererogation *n*: **of** ~ ultrō factus
superficial *adj* levis; **acquire a ~ knowledge of** prīmīs labrīs gustāre
superficiality *n* levitās *f*
superficially *adv* leviter, strictim
superfluity *n* abundantia *f*
superfluous *adj* supervacāneus, nimius; **be ~** redundāre
superhuman *adj* dīvīnus, hūmānō māior
superimpose *vt* superimpōnere
superintend *vt* prōcūrāre, praeesse (*dat*)
superintendence *n* cūra *f*
superintendent *n* cūrātor *m*, praefectus *m*
superior *adj* melior, amplior; **be ~** praestāre, superāre ♦ *n* prīnceps *m*, praefectus *m*
superiority *n* praestantia *f*; **have the ~** superāre; (*in numbers*) plūrēs esse
superlative *adj* ēgregius, optimus
supernatural *adj* dīvīnus
supernaturally *adv* dīvīnitus
supernumerary *adj* adscrīptīcius; ~ **soldiers** accēnsī *mpl*
superscription *n* titulus *m*
supersede *vt* succēdere (*dat*), in locum succēdere (*gen*); ~ **gold with silver** prō aurō argentum suppōnere
superstition *n* rēligiō *f*, superstitiō *f*
superstitious *adj* rēligiōsus, superstitiōsus
supervene *vi* īnsequī, succēdere
supervise *vt* prōcūrāre
supervision *n* cūra *f*
supervisor *n* cūrātor *m*
supine *adj* supīnus; (*fig*) neglegēns, segnis
supinely *adv* segniter
supper *n* cēna *f*; **after** ~ cēnātus
supperless *adj* iēiūnus
supplant *vt* praevertere
supple *adj* flexibilis, mollis
supplement *n* appendix *f* ♦ *vt* amplificāre
supplementary *adj* additus

suppleness *n* mollitia *f*
suppliant *n* supplex *m/f*
supplicate *vt* supplicāre, obsecrāre
supplication *n* precēs *fpl*
supplies *npl* commeātus *m*
supply *n* cōpia *f* ♦ *vt* suppeditāre, praebēre; (*loss*) supplēre
support *n* firmāmentum *nt*; (*help*) subsidium *nt*, adiūmentum *nt*; (*food*) alimenta *ntpl*; (*of party*) favor *m*; (*of needy*) patrōcinium *nt*; **I ~** subsidio sum (*dat*); **lend ~ to rumours** alimenta rūmōribus addere ♦ *vt* fulcīre; (*living*) sustinēre, sustentāre; (*with help*) adiuvāre, opem ferre (*dat*); (*at law*) adesse (*dat*)
supportable *adj* tolerābilis
supporter *n* fautor *m*; (*at trial*) advocātus *m*; (*of proposal*) auctor *m*
supporting cast *n* adiūtōrēs *mpl*
suppose *vi* (*assume*) pōnere; (*think*) existimāre, opīnārī, crēdere; **~ it is true** fac vērum esse
supposedly *adv* ut fāma est
supposing *conj* sī; (*for the sake of argument*) sī iam
supposition *n* opīniō *f*; **on this ~** hōc positō
supposititious *adj* subditus, subditīvus
suppress *vt* opprimere, comprimere; (*knowledge*) cēlāre, reticēre; (*feelings*) coercēre, reprimere
suppression *n* (*of fact*) reticentia *f*
supremacy *n* imperium *nt*, dominātus *m*, prīncipātus *m*
supreme *adj* summus; **be ~** dominārī; **~ command** imperium *nt*
supremely *adv* ūnicē, plānē
sure *adj* certus; (*fact*) explōrātus; (*friend*) fīdus; **be ~ of** compertum habēre; **feel ~** persuāsum habēre, haud scīre an; pro certō habēre; **make ~ of** (*fact*) comperīre; (*action*) efficere ut; **to be ~ quidem; **~ enough** rē vērā
surely *adv* certō, certē, nonne; (*tentative*) scīlicet, sānē; **~ you do not think?** num putās?; **~ not** num
surety *n* (*person*) vās *m*, praes *m*, spōnsor *m*; (*deposit*) fīdūcia *f*; **be ~ for** spondēre prō
surf *n* fluctus *m*
surface *n* superficiēs *f*; **~ of the water** summa aqua
surfeit *n* satietās *f* ♦ *vt* satiāre, explēre
surge *n* aestus *m*, fluctus *m* ♦ *vi* tumēscere
surgeon *n* chīrūrgus *m*
surgery *n* chīrūrgia *f*
surlily *adv* mōrōsē
surliness *n* mōrōsitās *f*
surly *adj* mōrōsus, difficilis
surmise *n* coniectūra *f* ♦ *vi* suspicārī, conicere, augurārī
surmount *vt* superāre
surmountable *adj* superābilis
surname *n* cognōmen *nt*
surpass *vt* excellere, exsuperāre, antecēdere
surpassing *adj* excellēns
surplus *n* reliquum *nt*; (*money*) pecūniae residuae *fpl*
surprise *n* admīrātiō *f*; (*cause*) rēs inopīnāta *f*; **take by ~** dēprehendere ♦ *adj* subitus ♦ *vt* dēprehendere; (MIL) opprimere; **be surprised** dēmīrārī; **be surprised at** admīrārī
surprising *adj* mīrus, mīrābilis

surprisingly *adv* mīrē, mīrābiliter
surrender *vt* dēdere, trādere, concēdere ♦ *vi* sē dēdere; **~ unconditionally to** sē suaque omnia potestāti permittere (*gen*) ♦ *n* dēditiō *f*; (*legal*) cessiō *f*; **unconditional ~** permissiō *f*
surreptitious *adj* fūrtīvus
surreptitiously *adv* fūrtim, clam; **get in ~** inrēpere in (*acc*)
surround *vt* circumdare, cingere, circumvenīre, circumfundere
surrounding *adj* circumiectus; **surroundings** *n* vīcīnia *f*
survey *vt* contemplārī, cōnsīderāre; (*land*) mētārī ♦ *n* contemplātiō *f*; (*land*) mēnsūra *f*
surveyor *n* fīnītor *m*, agrimēnsor *m*, mētātor *m*
survival *n* salūs *f*
survive *vt* superāre; superesse (*dat*)
survivor *n* superstes *m/f*
susceptibility *n* mollitia *f*
susceptible *adj* mollis
suspect *vt* suspicārī; **be suspected in** suspiciōnem venīre
suspend *vt* suspendere; (*activity*) differre; (*person*) locō movēre; **be suspended** pendēre
suspense *n* dubitātiō *f*; **be in ~** animī pendēre, haerēre
suspicion *n* suspiciō *f*; **direct ~ to** suspiciōnem adiungere ad
suspicious *adj* (*suspecting*) suspiciōsus; (*suspected*) dubius, anceps
sustain *vt* (*weight*) sustinēre; (*life*) alere, sustentāre; (*hardship*) ferre, sustinēre; (*the part of*) agere
sustenance *n* alimentum *nt*, vīctus *m*
sutler *n* lixa *m*
suzerain *n* dominus *m*
swaddling clothes *n* incūnābula *ntpl*
swagger *vi* sē iactāre
swaggerer *n* homō glōriōsus *m*
swallow *n* hirundō *f* ♦ *vt* dēvorāre; **~ up** absorbēre
swamp *n* palūs *f* ♦ *vt* opprimere
swampy *adj* ūlīginōsus
swan *n* cycnus *m*; **swan's** cycnēus
swank *vi* sē iactāre
sward *n* caespes *m*
swarm *n* exāmen *nt*; (*fig*) nūbēs *f* ♦ *vi*: **~ round** circumfundī
swarthy *adj* fuscus, aquilus
swathe *vt* conligāre
sway *n* diciō *f*, imperium *nt*; **bring under one's ~** suae diciōnis facere ♦ *vt* regere ♦ *vi* vacillāre
swear *vi* iūrāre; **~ allegiance to** iūrāre in verba (*gen*)
sweat *n* sūdor *m* ♦ *vi* sūdāre
sweep *vt* verrere; **~ away** rapere; **~ out** ēverrere
sweet *adj* dulcis, suāvis
sweeten *vt* dulcem reddere
sweetheart *n* dēliciae *fpl*
sweetly *adv* dulciter, suāviter
sweetness *n* dulcitūdō *f*, suāvitās *f*
sweet-tempered *adj* suāvis, cōmis
swell *n* tumor *m* ♦ *vi* tumēre, tumēscere; (*fig*) glīscere ♦ *vt* inflāre
swelling *adj* tumidus ♦ *n* tumor *m*
swelter *vi* aestū labōrāre

swerve vi dēclīnāre, dēvertere ♦ n dēclīnātiō f
swift adj celer, vēlōx, incitātus
swiftly adv celeriter, vēlōciter
swiftness n celeritās f, vēlōcitās f
swill vt (rinse) colluere; (drink) ēpōtāre
swim vi nāre, innāre; (place) natāre; ~ **across**
  trānāre; ~ **ashore** ēnāre; ~ **to** adnāre
swimming n natātiō f
swindle vt circumvenīre, verba dare (dat) ♦ n
  fraus f
swine n sūs m/f
swineherd n subulcus m
swing n (motion) oscillātiō f ♦ vi oscillāre ♦ vt
  lībrāre
swinish adj obscēnus
swirl n vertex m ♦ vi volūtārī
switch n virga f ♦ vt flectere, torquēre
swivel n cardō f
swollen adj tumidus, turgidus, īnflātus
swoon n dēfectiō f ♦ vi intermorī
swoop n impetus m ♦ vi lābī; ~ **down on** involāre
  in (acc)
sword n gladius m; **put to the ~** occīdere; **with**
  fire and ~ ferrō ignīque
swordsman n gladiātor m
sworn adj iūrātus

sybarite n dēlicātus m
sycophancy n adsentātiō f, adūlātiō f
sycophant n adsentātor m, adūlātor m
syllable n syllaba f
syllogism n ratiōcinātiō f
sylvan adj silvestris
symbol n signum nt, īnsigne nt
symmetrical adj concinnus, aequus
symmetry n concinnitās f, aequitās f
sympathetic adj concors, misericors
sympathetically adv misericorditer
sympathize vi cōnsentīre; ~ **with** miserērī
  (gen)
sympathy n concordia f, consēnsus m;
  misericordia f
symphony n concentus m
symptom n signum nt, indicium nt
syndicate n societās f
synonym n verbum idem dēclārāns nt
synonymous adj idem dēclārāns
synopsis n summārium nt
syringe n clystēr m
system n ratiō f, fōrmula f; (PHILOS) disciplīna f
systematic adj ōrdinātus, cōnstāns
systematically adv ratiōne, ōrdine
systematize vt in ōrdinem redigere

Tt

tabernacle *n* tabernāculum *nt*
table *n* mēnsa *f*; (*inscribed*) tabula *f*; (*list*) index *m*;
  at ~ inter cēnam; **turn the tables on** pār parī
  referre
tablet *n* tabula *f*, tabella *f*
taboo *n* rēligiō *f*
tabulate *vt* in ōrdinem redigere
tacit *adj* tacitus
tacitly *adv* tacitē
taciturn *adj* taciturnus
taciturnity *n* taciturnitās *f*
tack *n* clāvulus *m*; (*of sail*) pēs *m* ♦ *vt*: ~ **on** adsuere
  ♦ *vi* (*ship*) reciprocārī, nāvem flectere
tackle *n* armāmenta *ntpl* ♦ *vt* adgredī
tact *n* iūdicium *nt*, commūnis sēnsus *m*,
  hūmānitās *f*
tactful *adj* prūdēns, hūmānus
tactfully *adv* prūdenter, hūmāniter
tactician *n* reī mīlitāris perītus *m*
tactics *n* rēs mīlitāris *f*, bellī ratiō *f*
tactless *adj* ineptus
tactlessly *adv* ineptē
tadpole *n* rānunculus *m*
tag *n* appendicula *f*
tail *n* cauda *f*; **turn** ~ terga vertere
tailor *n* vestītor *m*
taint *n* lābēs *f*, vitium *nt* ♦ *vt* inquināre,
  contāmināre, īnficere
take *vt* capere, sūmere; (*auspices*) habēre;
  (*disease*) contrahere; (*experience*) ferre; (*fire*)
  concipere; (*meaning*) accipere, interpretārī; (*in
  the act*) dēprehendere; (*person*) dūcere; ~ **after**
  similem esse (*dat, gen*); ~ **across** trānsportāre;
  ~ **arms** arma sūmere; ~ **away** dēmere, auferre,
  adimere, abdūcere; ~ **back** recipere; ~ **by
  storm** expugnāre; ~ **care that** curāre ut/ne
  (*subj*); ~ **down** dētrahere; (*in writing*) exscrībere;
  ~ **for** habēre prō; ~ **hold of** prehendere; ~ **in**
  (*as guest*) recipere; (*information*) percipere,
  comprehendere; (*with deceit*) dēcipere; ~ **in
  hand** incipere, suscipere; ~ **off** dēmere;
  (*clothes*) exuere; ~ **on** suscipere; ~ **out** eximere,
  extrahere; (*from store*) prōmere; ~ **over** excipere;
  ~ **place** fierī, accidere; ~ **prisoner** capere;
  ~ **refuge in** cōnfugere ad (*acc*); ~ **the field in**
  aciem dēscendere; ~ **to** sē dēdere (*dat*), amāre;
  ~ **to oneself** suscipere; ~ **up** sūmere, tollere;
  (*task*) incipere, adgredī ad; (*in turn*) excipere;
  (*room*) occupāre; ~ **upon oneself** recipere, sibī
  sūmere
taking *adj* grātus ♦ *n* (MIL) expugnātiō *f*
tale *n* fābula *f*, fābella *f*

talent *n* (*money*) talentum *nt*; (*ability*) ingenium
  nt, indolēs *f*
talented *adj* ingeniōsus
talk *n* sermō *m*; (*with another*) colloquium *nt*;
  common ~ fāma *f*; **be the ~ of the town** in
  ōre omnium esse ♦ *vi* loquī; (*to one*) colloquī
  cum; ~ **down to** ad intellectum audientis
  dēscendere; ~ **over** cōnferre, disserere dē
talkative *adj* loquāx
talkativeness *n* loquācitās *f*
tall *adj* prōcērus, grandis
tallness *n* prōcēritās *f*
tallow *n* sēbum *nt*
tally *n* tessera *f* ♦ *vi* congruere
talon *n* unguis *m*
tamarisk *n* myrīca *f*
tambourine *n* tympanum *nt*
tame *vt* domāre, mānsuēfacere ♦ *adj*
  mānsuētus; (*character*) ignāvus; (*language*)
  īnsulsus, frīgidus
tamely *adv* ignāvē, lentē
tameness *n* mānsuētūdō *f*; (*fig*) lentitūdō *f*
tamer *n* domitor *m*
tamper *vi*: ~ **with** (*person*) sollicitāre; (*writing*)
  interpolāre
tan *vt* imbuere
tang *n* sapor *m*
tangible *adj* tāctilis
tangle *n* nōdus *m* ♦ *vt* implicāre
tank *n* lacus *m*
tanned *adj* (*by sun*) adūstus
tanner *n* coriārius *m*
tantalize *vt* lūdere
tantamount *adj* pār, īdem
tantrum *n* īra *f*
tap *n* epitonium *nt*; (*touch*) plāga *f* ♦ *vt* (*cask*)
  relinere; (*hit*) ferīre
tape *n* taenia *f*
taper *n* cēreus *m* ♦ *vi* fastīgārī
tapestry *n* aulaea *ntpl*
tar *n* pix *f*
tardily *adv* tardē, lentē
tardiness *n* tarditās *f*, segnitia *f*
tardy *adj* tardus, lentus
tare *n* lolium *nt*
targe *n* parma *f*
target *n* scopus *m*
tariff *n* portōrium *nt*
tarn *n* lacus *m*
tarnish *vt* īnfuscāre, inquināre ♦ *vi* īnfuscārī
tarry *vi* morārī, commorārī, cunctārī
tart *adj* acidus, asper ♦ *n* scrīblīta *f*

tartly *adv* acerbē
tartness *n* asperitās *f*
task *n* pēnsum *nt*, opus *nt*, negōtium *nt*; **take to ~** obiūrgāre
taskmaster *n* dominus *m*
tassel *n* fimbriae *fpl*
taste *n* (*sense*) gustātus *m*; (*flavour*) sapor *m*; (*artistic*) iūdicium *nt*, ēlegantia *f*; (*for rhetoric*) aurēs *fpl*; **of ~** doctus; **in good ~** ēlegāns ♦ *vt* gustāre, dēgustāre ♦ *vi* sapere; **~ of** resipere
tasteful *adj* ēlegāns
tastefully *adv* ēleganter
tastefulness *n* ēlegantia *f*
tasteless *adj* īnsulsus, inēlegāns
tastelessly *adv* īnsulsē, inēleganter
tastelessness *n* īnsulsitās *f*
taster *n* praegustātor *m*
tasty *adj* dulcis
tattered *adj* pannōsus
tatters *n* pannī *mpl*
tattoo *vt* compungere
taunt *n* convīcium *nt*, probrum *nt* ♦ *vt* exprobrāre, obicere (*dat of pers, acc of charge*)
taunting *adj* contumēliōsus
tauntingly *adv* contumēliōsē
taut *adj* intentus; **draw ~** addūcere
tavern *n* taberna *f*, hospitium *nt*
tawdry *adj* vīlis
tawny *adj* fulvus
tax *n* vectīgal *nt*, tribūtum *nt*; **a 5 per cent tax** vīcēsima *f*; **free from tax** immūnis ♦ *vt* vectīgal impōnere (*dat*); (*strength*) contendere; **tax with** (*charge*) obicere (*acc & dat*), īnsimulāre
taxable *adj* vectīgālis
taxation *n* vectīgālia *ntpl*
tax collector *n* exāctor *m*
tax farmer *n* pūblicānus *m*
taxpayer *n* assiduus *m*
teach *vt* docēre, ērudīre, īnstituere; (*thoroughly*) ēdocēre; (*passive*) discere; **~ your grandmother** sūs Minervam
teachable *adj* docilis
teacher *n* magister *m*, magistra *f*, doctor *m*; (PHILOS) praeceptor *m*; (*of literature*) grammaticus *m*; (*of rhetoric*) rhētor *m*
teaching *n* doctrīna *f*, disciplīna *f*
team *n* (*animals*) iugum *nt*
tear *n* lacrima *f*; **shed tears** lacrimās effundere ♦ *vt* scindere; **~ down** revellere; **~ in pieces** dīlaniāre, discerpere, lacerāre; **~ off** abscindere, dēripere; **~ open** rescindere; **~ out** ēvellere; **~ up** convellere
tearful *adj* flēbilis
tease *vt* lūdere, inrītāre
teat *n* mamma *f*
technical *adj* (*term*) proprius
technique *n* ars *f*
tedious *adj* longus, lentus, odiōsus
tediously *adv* molestē
tedium *n* taedium *nt*, molestia *f*
teem *vi* abundāre
teeming *adj* fēcundus, refertus
teens *n*: **in one's ~** adulescentulus
teethe *vi* dentīre
tell *vt* (*story*) nārrāre; (*person*) dīcere (*dat*); (*number*) ēnumerāre; (*inform*) certiōrem facere;

(*difference*) intellegere; (*order*) iubēre (*+ acc and infin*), imperāre (*+ 'ut' +subj or + 'ne' +subj*); **~ the truth** vera dīcere; **~ lies** mentior ♦ *vi* valēre; **~ the difference between** discernere; **I cannot ~** nesciō
telling *adj* validus
temerity *n* temeritās *f*
temper *n* animus *m*, ingenium *nt*; (*bad*) īra *f*, īrācundia *f*; (*of metal*) temperātiō *f* ♦ *vt* temperāre; (*fig*) moderārī (*dat*)
temperament *n* animī habitus *m*, animus *m*
temperamental *adj* incōnstāns
temperance *n* temperantia *f*, continentia *f*
temperate *adj* temperātus, moderātus, sobrius
temperately *adv* moderātē
temperature *n* calor *m*, frīgus *nt*; **mild ~** temperiēs *f*
tempest *n* tempestās *f*, procella *f*
tempestuous *adj* procellōsus
temple *n* templum *nt*, aedēs *f*; (*head*) tempus *nt*
temporal *adj* hūmānus, profānus
temporarily *adv* ad tempus
temporary *adj* brevis
temporize *vi* temporis causā facere, tergiversārī
tempt *vt* sollicitāre, pellicere, invītāre
temptation *n* illecebra *f*
tempter *n* impulsor *m*
ten *num* decem; **ten each** dēnī; **ten times** deciēns
tenable *adj* inexpugnābilis, stabilis, certus
tenacious *adj* tenāx, firmus
tenaciously *adv* tenāciter
tenacity *n* tenācitās *f*
tenant *n* inquilīnus *m*, habitātor *m*; (*on land*) colōnus *m*
tenantry *n* colōnī *mpl*
tend *vi* spectāre, pertinēre ♦ *vt* cūrāre, colere
tendency *n* inclīnātiō *f*, voluntās *f*
tender *adj* tener, mollis ♦ *vt* dēferre, offerre
tenderhearted *adj* misericors
tenderly *adv* indulgenter
tenderness *n* indulgentia *f*, mollitia *f*
tendon *n* nervus *m*
tendril *n* clāviculus *m*
tenement *n* habitātiō *f*; **block of tenements** īnsula *f*
tenet *n* dogma *nt*, dēcrētum *nt*
tennis court *n* sphaeristērium *nt*
tenor *n* (*course*) tenor *m*; (*purport*) sententia *f*
tense *adj* intentus ♦ *n* tempus *nt*
tension *n* intentiō *f*
tent *n* tabernāculum *nt*; (*general's*) praetōrium *nt*
tentacle *n* bracchium *nt*
tentatively *adv* experiendō
tenterhooks *n*: **on ~** animī suspēnsus
tenth *adj* decimus; **for the ~ time** decimum; **men of the ~ legion** decumānī *mpl*
tenuous *adj* rārus
tenure *n* possessiō *f*
tepid *adj* tepidus; **be ~** tepēre
tergiversation *n* tergiversātiō *f*
term *n* (*limit*) terminus *m*; (*period*) spatium *nt*; (*word*) verbum *nt* ♦ *vt* appellāre, nuncupāre
terminate *vt* termināre, fīnīre ♦ *vi* dēsinere; (*words*) cadere
termination *n* fīnis *m*, terminus *m*

terminology n vocābulum ntpl
terms npl condiciō f, lēx f; **propose**
~ condiciōnem ferre; **be on good** ~ in grātiā
esse; **we come to** ~ inter nōs convenit
terrain n ager m
terrestrial adj terrestris
terrible adj terribilis, horribilis, horrendus
terribly adv horrendum in modum
terrific adj formīdolōsus; vehemēns
terrify vt terrēre, perterrēre, exterrēre
terrifying adj formīdolōsus
territory n ager m, fīnēs mpl
terror n terror m, formīdō f, pavor m; **object of**
~ terror m; **be a ~ to** terrōrī esse (dat)
terrorize vt metum inicere (dat)
terse adj pressus, brevis
tersely adv pressē
terseness n brevitās f
tessellated adj tessellātus
test n experīmentum nt, probātiō f; (standard)
obrussa f; **put to the** ~ experīrī, perīclitārī;
stand the ~ spectārī ◆ vt experīrī, probāre,
spectāre
testament n testāmentum nt
testamentary adj testāmentārius
testator n testātor m
testify vt testificārī
testifying n testificātiō f
testily adv stomachōsē
testimonial n laudātiō f
testimony n testimōnium nt
testy adj difficilis, stomachōsus
tether n retināculum nt, vinculum nt ◆ vt
religāre
tetrarch n tetrarchēs m
tetrarchy n tetrarchia f
text n verba ntpl
textbook n ars f
textile adj textilis
textual adj verbōrum
texture n textus m
than conj quam (abl); **other** ~ alius ac
thank vt grātiās agere (dat); ~ **you** bene facis; **no,**
~ **you** benīgnē
thankful adj grātus
thankfully adv grātē
thankfulness n grātia f
thankless adj ingrātus
thanklessly adv ingrātē
thanks n grātiae fpl, grātēs fpl; **return** ~ grātiās
agere, grātēs persolvere; ~ **to you** operā tuā,
beneficiō tuō; **it is** ~ **to sb that … not** per
aliquem stat quōminus (subj)
thanksgiving n grātulātiō f; (public) supplicātiō f
that pron (demonstrative) ille; (relat) quī ◆ conj
(statement) acc & infin; (command, purpose, result) ut;
(fearing) nē; (emotion) quod; **oh** ~ utinam
thatch n culmus m, strāmenta ntpl ◆ vt tegere,
integere
thaw vt dissolvere ◆ vi liquēscere, tabēscere
the art not expressed; (emphatic) ille; (with compar)
quō … eō
theatre n theātrum nt
theatrical adj scēnicus
theft n fūrtum nt
their adj eōrum; (ref to subject) suus

theme n māteria f, argūmentum nt
themselves pron ipsī; (reflexive) sē
then adv (time) tum, tunc; (succession) deinde,
tum, posteā; (consequence) igitur, ergō; **now and**
~ interdum; **only** ~ tum dēmum
thence adv inde
thenceforth adv inde, posteā, ex eō tempore
theologian n theologus m
theology n theologia f
theorem n prōpositum nt
theoretical adj contemplātīvus
theory n ratiō f; ~ **and practice** ratiō atque ūsus
there adv ibī, illīc; (thither) eō, illūc; **from** ~ inde,
illinc; **here and** ~ passim; ~ **is** est; (interj) ecce
thereabout, thereabouts adv circā, circiter,
prope
thereafter adv deinde, posteā
thereby adv eā rē, hōc factō
therefore adv itaque, igitur, ergō, idcircō
therein adv inibī, in eō
thereof adv ēius, ēius reī
thereon adv īnsuper, in eō
thereupon adv deinde, statim, inde, quō factō
therewith adv cum eō
thesis n prōpositum nt
thews n nervī mpl
they pron iī, hī, illī
thick adj dēnsus; (air) crassus
thicken vt dēnsāre ◆ vi concrēscere
thickening n concrētiō f
thicket n dūmētum nt
thickheaded adj stupidus, hebes
thickly adv dēnsē; ~ **populated** frequēns
thickness n crassitūdō f
thickset adj brevis atque obēsus
thick-skinned adj: **be** ~ callēre; **become**
~ occallēscere
thief n fūr m
thieve vt fūrārī, surripere
thievery n fūrtum nt
thievish adj fūrāx
thigh n femur nt
thin adj exīlis, gracilis, tenuis; (attendance)
īnfrequēns ◆ vt attenuāre, extenuāre; ~ **out**
rārefacere; ~ **down** dīluere
thine adj tuus
thing n rēs f; **as things are** nunc, cum haec ita
sint
think vi cōgitāre; (opinion) putāre, existimāre,
arbitrārī, rērī, crēdere; **as I** ~ meā sententiā;
~ **about** cōgitāre dē; ~ **highly of** māgnī
aestimāre; ~ **nothing of** nihilī facere; ~ **out**
excōgitāre; ~ **over** reputāre, in mente agitāre
thinker n philosophus m
thinking adj sapiēns ◆ n cōgitātiō f; ~ **that** ratus,
arbitrātus
thinly adv exīliter, tenuiter; rārē
thinness n exīlitās f, gracilitās f; (person) maciēs
f; (number) exiguitās f, īnfrequentia f; (air)
tenuitās f
thin-skinned adj inrītābilis
third adj tertius; **for the** ~ **time** tertium ◆ n tertia
pars f, triēns m; **two thirds** duae partēs, bēs m
thirdly adv tertiō
thirst n sitis f ◆ vi sitīre; ~ **for** sitīre
thirstily adv sitienter

thirsty *adj* sitiēns
thirteen *num* tredecim; **~ each** ternī dēnī; **~ times** terdeciēns
thirteenth *adj* tertius decimus
thirtieth *adj* trīcēsimus
thirty *num* trīgintā; **~ each** trīcēnī; **~ times** trīciēns
this *pron* hīc
thistle *n* carduus *m*
thither *adv* eō, illūc
thole *n* scalmus *nt*
thong *n* lōrum *nt*, habēna *f*
thorn *n* spīna *f*, sentis *m*
thorny *adj* spīnōsus
thorough *adj* absolūtus, germānus; (*work*) accūrātus
thoroughbred *adj* generōsus
thoroughfare *n* via *f*
thoroughly *adv* penitus, omnīnō, funditus
thoroughness *n* cūra *f*, diligentia *f*
thou *pron* tū
though *conj* etsī, etiamsī, quamvīs (*subj*), quamquam (+*indic*)
thought *n* (*faculty*) cōgitātiō *f*, mēns *f*, animus *m*; (*an idea*) cōgitātum *nt*, nōtiō *f*; (*design*) cōnsilium *nt*, prōpositum *nt*; (*expressed*) sententia *f*; (*heed*) cautiō *f*, prōvidentia *f*; (RHET) inventiō *f*; **second thoughts** posteriōrēs cōgitātiōnēs
thoughtful *adj* cōgitābundus; prōvidus
thoughtfully *adv* prōvidē
thoughtless *adj* incōnsīderātus, incōnsultus, imprōvidus, immemor
thoughtlessly *adv* temerē, incōnsultē
thoughtlessness *n* incōnsīderantia *f*, imprūdentia *f*
thousand *num* mīlle; **thousands** (*pl*) mīlia (*ntpl* +*gen*); **~ each** mīllēnī; **~ times** mīlliēns; **three ~** tria mīlia
thousandth *adj* mīllēsimus
thraldom *n* servitūs *f*
thrall *n* servus *m*
thrash *vt* verberāre
thrashing *n* verbera *ntpl*
thread *n* fīlum *nt*; **hang by a ~** (*fig*) fīlō pendēre ♦ *vt*: **~ one's way** sē īnsinuāre
threadbare *adj* trītus, obsolētus
threat *n* minae *fpl*, minātiō *f*
threaten *vt* minārī (*dat of pers*), dēnūntiāre ♦ *vi* imminēre, impendēre
threatening *adj* mināx, imminēns
threateningly *adv* mināciter
three *num* trēs; **~ each** ternī; **~ times** ter; **~ days** triduum *nt*; **~ years** triennium *nt*; **~ quarters** trēs partēs *fpl*, dōdrāns *m*
three-cornered *adj* triangulus, triquetrus
threefold *adj* triplex
three hundred *num* trecentī; **three hundred each** trecēnī; **three hundred times** trecentiēn
three hundredth *adj* trecentēsimus
three-legged *adj* tripēs
three-quarters *n* dōdrāns *m*, trēs partēs *fpl*
thresh *vt* terere, exterere
threshing floor *n* ārea *f*
threshold *n* līmen *nt*
thrice *adv* ter
thrift *n* frūgālitās *f*, parsimōnia *f*

thriftily *adv* frūgāliter
thrifty *adj* parcus, frūgī
thrill *n* horror *m* ♦ *vt* percellere, percutere ♦ *vi* trepidāre
thrilling *adj* mīrābilis
thrive *vi* vigēre, valēre, crēscere
thriving *adj* valēns, vegetus; (*crops*) laetus
throat *n* faucēs *fpl*, guttur *nt*; **cut the ~ of** iugulāre
throaty *adj* gravis, raucus
throb *vi* palpitāre, micāre ♦ *n* pulsus *m*
throe *n* dolor *m*; **be in the throes of** labōrāre ex
throne *n* solium *nt*; (*power*) rēgnum *nt*
throng *n* multitūdō *f*, frequentia *f* ♦ *vt* celebrāre; **~ round** stīpāre, circumfundī (*dat*)
throttle *vt* strangulāre
through *prep* per (*acc*); (*cause*) propter (*acc*), *abl* ♦ *adv*: **~ and ~** penitus; **go ~** trānsīre; **carry ~** exsequī, peragere; **go ~** trānsīre; **run ~** percurrere; **be ~ with** perfūnctum esse (*abl*)
throughout *adv* penitus, omnīnō ♦ *prep* per (*acc*)
throw *n* iactus *m*, coniectus *m* ♦ *vt* iacere, conicere; **~ about** iactāre; **~ across** trāicere; **~ away** abicere; (*something precious*) prōicere; **~ back** rēicere; **~ down** dēturbāre, dēicere; **~ into** inicere; **~ into confusion** perturbāre; **~ off** excutere, exsolvere; **~ open** patefacere; **~ out** ēicere, prōicere; **~ over** inicere; (*fig*) dēstituere; **~ overboard** iactūram facere (*gen*); **~ to** (*danger*) obicere; **~ up** ēicere; (*building*) exstruere; **~ a bridge over** pontem inicere (*dat*), pontem faciendum cūrāre in (*abl*); **~ light on** (*fig*) lūmen adhibēre (*dat*); **~ a rider** equitem excutere
throwing *n* coniectiō *f*, iactus *m*
thrum *n* līcium *nt*
thrush *n* turdus *m*
thrust *vt* trūdere, pellere, impingere; **~ at** petere; **~ away** dētrūdere; **~ forward** prōtrūdere; **~ home** dēfīgere; **~ into** īnfīgere, impingere; **~ out** extrūdere
thud *n* gravis sonitus *m*
thug *n* percussor *m*, sīcārius *m*
thumb *n* pollex *m*; **have under one's ~** in potestāte suā habēre
thump *n* plāga *f* ♦ *vt* tundere, pulsāre
thunder *n* tonitrus *m* ♦ *vi* tonāre, intonāre; **it thunders** tonāt
thunderbolt *n* fulmen *nt*
thunderer *n* tonāns *m*
thunderstruck *adj* attonitus
thus *adv* (*referring back*) sīc; (*referring forward*) ita; **~ far** hāctenus
thwack *vt* verberāre
thwart *vt* obstāre (*dat*), officere (*dat*), remorārī, frustrārī ♦ *n* (*boat's*) trānstrum *nt*
thy *adj* tuus
thyme *n* thymum *nt*; (*wild*) serpyllum *nt*
tiara *n* diadēma *nt*
ticket *n* tessera *f*
tickle *vt* titillāre
tickling *n* titillātiō *f*
ticklish *adj* lūbricus
tidal *adj*: **~ waters** aestuārium *nt*
tide *n* aestus *m*; (*time*) tempus *nt*; **ebb ~** aestūs recessus *m*; **flood ~** aestūs accessus *m*; **turn of**

the ~ commūtātiō aestūs; **the ~ will turn** (*fig*) circumagētur hīc orbis
tidily *adv* concinnē, mundē
tidiness *n* concinnitās *f*, munditia *f*
tidings *n* nūntius *m*
tidy *adj* concinnus, mundus
tie *n* (*bond*) vinculum *nt*, cōpula *f*; (*kin*) necessitūdō *f* ◆ *vt* ligāre; (*knot*) nectere; **tie fast** dēvincīre, cōnstringere; **tie on** illigāre; **tie to** adligāre; **tie together** colligāre; **tie up** adligāre; (*wound*) obligāre
tier *n* ōrdō *m*
tiff *n* dissēnsiō *f*
tiger *n* tigris *usu f*
tight *adj* strictus, astrictus, intentus; (*close*) artus; **draw ~** intendere, addūcere
tighten *vt* adstringere, contendere
tightly *adv* artē, angustē
tightrope *n* extentus fūnis; **~ walker** *n* fūnambulus *m*
tigress *n* tigris *f*
tile *n* tegula *f*, imbrex *f*, later *nt*
till *conj* dum, dōnec ◆ *prep* usque ad (*acc*), in (*acc*); **not ~** dēmum ◆ *n* arca *f* ◆ *vt* colere
tillage *n* cultus *m*
tiller *n* (*AGR*) cultor *m*; (*ship*) clāvus *m*, gubernāculum *nt*
tilt *vt* inclīnāre
tilth *n* cultus *m*, arvum *nt*
timber *n* (*for building*) māteria *f*; (*firewood*) lignum *nt*
timbrel *n* tympanum *nt*
time *n* tempus *nt*; (*lifetime*) aetās *f*; (*interval*) intervallum *nt*, spatium *nt*; (*of day*) hōra *f*; (*leisure*) ōtium *nt*; (*rhythm*) numerus *m*; **another ~** aliās; **at times** aliquandō, interdum; **at all times** semper; **at any ~** umquam; **at one ~ … at another** aliās … aliās; **at that ~** tunc, id temporis; **at the right ~** ad tempus, mātūrē, tempestīvē; **at the same ~** simul; tamen; **at the wrong ~** intempestīvē; **beating ~** percussiō *f*; **convenient ~** opportūnitās *f*; **for a ~** aliquantisper, parumper; **for a long ~** diū; **for some ~** aliquamdiū; **for the ~ being** ad tempus; **from ~ to ~** interdum, identidem; **have a good ~** geniō indulgēre; **have ~ for** vacāre (*dat*); **in ~** ad tempus, tempore; **in a short ~** brevī; **in good ~** tempestīvus; **in the ~ of** apud (*acc*); **keep ~** (*marching*) gradum cōnferre; (*music*) modulārī; **many times** saepe, saepenumerō; **pass ~**, **spend ~** tempus sūmere, dēgere; **several times** aliquotiēns; **some ~** aliquandō; **waste ~** tempus terere; **what is the time?** quota hōra est?; **~ expired** ēmeritus
time-honoured *adj* antīquus
timeliness *n* opportūnitās *f*
timely *adj* opportūnus, tempestīvus, mātūrus
timid *adj* timidus
timidity *n* timiditās *f*
timidly *adv* timidē
timorous *adj* timidus
timorously *adv* timidē
tin *n* stannum *nt*, plumbum album *nt* ◆ *adj* stanneus
tincture *n* color *m*, sapor *m* ◆ *vt* īnficere
tinder *n* fōmes *m*

tinge *vt* imbuere, īnficere, tingere
tingle *vi* horrēre
tingling *n* horror *m*
tinkle *vi* tinnīre ◆ *n* tinnītus *m*
tinsel *n* bractea *f*; (*fig*) speciēs *f*, fūcus *m*
tint *n* color *m* ◆ *vt* colōrāre
tiny *adj* minūtus, pusillus, perexiguus
tip *n* apex *m*, cacūmen *nt*, extrēmum *nt*; **the tip of** prīmus, extrēmus ◆ *vt* praefīgere; **tip over** invertere
tipple *vi* pōtāre
tippler *n* pōtor *m*, ēbrius *m*
tipsy *adj* tēmulentus
tiptoes *n*: **on ~** suspēnsō gradū
tirade *n* obiūrgātiō *f*, dēclāmātiō *f*
tire *vt* fatīgāre; **~ out** dēfatīgāre ◆ *vi* dēfetīscī, fatīgārī; **I ~ of** mē taedet (*gen*); **it tires** taedet (+ *acc of person, gen of thing*)
tired *adj* (dē)fessus, lassus; **~ out** dēfessus; **I am ~ of** mē taedet
tiresome *adj* molestus, difficilis
tiring *adj* labōriōsus, operōsus
tiro *n* tīrō *m*, rudis *m*
tissue *n* textus *m*
tit *n*: **give tit for tat** pār parī respondēre
Titan *n* Tītān *m*
titanic *adj* immānis
titbit *n* cuppēdium *nt*
tithe *n* decuma *f*
tithe gatherer *n* decumānus *m*
titillate *vt* titillāre
titillation *n* titillātiō *f*
title *n* (*book*) īnscrīptiō *f*, index *m*; (*inscription*) titulus *m*; (*person*) nōmen *nt*, appellātiō *f*; (*claim*) iūs *nt*, vindiciae *fpl*; **assert one's ~ to** vindicāre; **give a ~ to** īnscrībere
titled *adj* nōbilis
title deed *n* auctōritās *f*
titter *n* rīsus *m* ◆ *vi* rīdēre
tittle-tattle *n* sermunculus *m*
titular *adj* nōmine
to *prep* ad (*acc*), in (*acc*); (*attitude*) ergā (*acc*); (*giving*) *dat*; (*towns, small islands*, domus, rūs) *acc* ◆ *conj* (*purpose*) ut ◆ *adv*: **come to** animum recipere; **to and fro** hūc illūc
toad *n* būfō *m*
toady *n* adsentātor *m*, parasītus *m* ◆ *vt* adsentārī (*dat*)
toadyism *n* adsentātiō *f*
toast *n*: **drink a ~** prōpīnāre ◆ *vt* torrēre; (*drink*) prōpīnāre (*dat*)
today *adv* hodiē; **today's** hodiernus
toe *n* digitus *m*; **big toe** pollex *m*
toga *n* toga *f*
together *adv* ūnā, simul; **bring ~** cōgere, congerere; **come ~** convenīre, congregārī; **put ~** cōnferre, compōnere
toil *n* labor *m*; (*snare*) rēte *nt* ◆ *vi* labōrāre; **~ at** ēlabōrāre in (*abl*)
toilet *n* (*lady's*) cultus *m*
toilsome *adj* labōriōsus, operōsus
toil-worn *adj* labōre cōnfectus
token *n* īnsigne *nt*, signum *nt*, indicium *nt*
tolerable *adj* tolerābilis, patibilis; (*quality*) mediocris; (*size*) modicus
tolerably *adv* satis, mediocriter

tolerance n patientia f, tolerantia f
tolerant adj indulgēns, tolerāns
tolerantly adv indulgenter
tolerate vt tolerāre, ferre, indulgēre (dat)
toleration n patientia f; (freedom) lībertās f
toll n vectīgal nt; (harbour) portōrium nt
toll collector n exāctor m; portitor m
tomb n sepulcrum nt
tombstone n lapis m
tome n liber m
tomorrow adv crās; **tomorrow's** crāstinus; **the day after ~** perendiē; **put off till ~** in crāstinum differre
tone n sonus m, vōx f; (painting) color m
tongs n forceps m/f
tongue n lingua f; (shoe) ligula f; **on the tip of one's ~** in prīmōribus labrīs
tongue-tied adj ēlinguis, īnfāns
tonnage n amphorae fpl
tonsils n tōnsillae fpl
tonsure n rāsūra f
too adv (also) etiam, īnsuper, quoque; (excess) nimis ◆ compar adj: **too far** extrā modum; **too much** nimium; **too long** nimium diū; **too great to** māior quam quī (subj); **too late** sērius; **too little** parum (gen)
tool n īnstrūmentum nt; (AGR) ferrāmentum nt; (person) minister m
tooth n dēns m; **~ and nail** tōtō corpore atque omnibus ungulīs; **cast in one's teeth** exprobrāre, obicere; **cut teeth** dentīre; **in the teeth of** obviam (dat), adversus (acc); **with the teeth** mordicus
toothache n dentium dolor m
toothed adj dentātus
toothless adj ēdentulus
toothpick n dentiscalpium nt
toothsome adj suāvis, dulcis
top n vertex m, fastīgium nt; (tree) cacūmen nt; (toy) turbō m; **from top to toe** ab īmīs unguibus usque ad verticem summum; **the top of** summus ◆ vt exsuperāre; **top up** supplēre ◆ adj superior, summus
tope vi pōtāre
toper n pōtor m
topiary adj topiārius ◆ n topiārium opus nt
topic n rēs f; (RHET) locus m; **~ of conversation** sermō m
topical adj hodiernus
topmost adj summus
topography n dēscrīptiō f
topple vi titubāre; **~ over** prōlābī
topsail n dolō m
topsyturvy adv praeposterē; **turn ~** sūrsum deōrsum versāre, permiscēre
tor n mōns m
torch n fax f, lampas f
torment n cruciātus m; (mind) angor m ◆ vt cruciāre; (mind) discruciāre, excruciāre, angere
tormentor n tortor m
tornado n turbō m
torpid adj torpēns; **be ~** torpēre; **grow ~** obtorpēscere
torpor n torpor m, inertia f
torrent n torrēns m
torrid adj torridus

torsion n tortus m
torso n truncus m
tortoise n testūdō f
tortoiseshell n testūdō f
tortuous adj flexuōsus
torture n cruciātus m, supplicium nt; **instrument of ~** tormentum nt ◆ vt torquēre, cruciāre, excruciāre
torturer n tortor m, carnifex m
toss n iactus m ◆ vt iactāre, excutere; **~ about** agitāre; **be tossed** (at sea) fluitāre
total adj tōtus, ūniversus ◆ n summa f
totality n ūniversitās f
totally adv omnīnō, plānē
totter vi lābāre, titubāre; **make ~** labefactāre
tottering n titubātiō f
touch n tāctus m; **a ~ of** aliquantulum (gen); **finishing ~** manus extrēma f ◆ vt tangere, attingere; (feelings) movēre, tangere ◆ vi inter sē contingere; **~ at** nāvem appellere ad; **~ on** (topic) attingere, perstringere; **~ up** expolīre
touch-and-go adj anceps ◆ n discrīmen nt
touching adj (place) contiguus; (emotion) flexanimus ◆ prep quod attinet ad (acc)
touchstone n (fig) obrussa f
touchy adj inrītābilis, stomachōsus
tough adj dūrus
toughen vt dūrāre
toughness n dūritia f
tour n iter nt; (abroad) peregrīnātiō f
tourist n viātor m, peregrīnātor m
tournament n certāmen nt
tow n stuppa f; **of tow** stuppeus ◆ vt adnexum trahere, remulcō trahere
toward, towards prep ad (acc), versus (after noun, acc); (feelings) in (acc), ergā (acc); (time) sub (acc)
towel n mantēle nt
tower n turris f ◆ vi ēminēre
towered adj turrītus
town n urbs f, oppidum nt; **country ~** mūnicipium nt ◆ adj urbānus
town councillor n decuriō m
townsman n oppidānus m
townspeople npl oppidānī mpl
towrope n remulcum nt
toy n crepundia ntpl ◆ vi lūdere
trace n vestīgium nt, indicium nt ◆ vt investīgāre; (draw) dēscrībere; **~ out** dēsignāre
track n (mark) vestīgium nt; (path) callis m, sēmita f; (of wheel) orbita f; (of ship) cursus m ◆ vt investīgāre, indāgāre
trackless adj invius
tract n (country) tractus m, regiō f; (book) libellus m
tractable adj tractābilis, facilis, docilis
trade n mercātūra f, mercātus m; (a business) ars f, quaestus m; **freedom of ~** commercium nt ◆ vi mercātūrās facere, negōtiārī; **~ in** vēndere, vēnditāre
trader n mercātor m, negōtiātor m
tradesman n opifex m
tradition n fāma f, mōs māiōrum m, memoria f
traditional adj ā māiōribus trāditus, patrius
traditionally adv mōre māiōrum
traduce vt calumniārī, obtrectāre (dat)
traducer n calumniātor m, obtrectātor m

traffic n commercium nt; (on road) vehicula ntpl
♦ vi mercātūrās facere; ~ **in** vēndere, vēnditāre
tragedian n (author) tragoedus m; (actor) āctor
tragicus m
tragedy n tragoedia f; (fig) calamitās f, malum nt
tragic adj tragicus; (fig) tristis
tragically adv tragicē; male
tragicomedy n tragicocōmoedia f
trail n vestīgia ntpl ♦ vt trahere ♦ vi trahī
train n (line) agmen nt, ōrdō m; (of dress) īnstita f;
(army) impedīmenta ntpl; (followers) comitēs mpl,
satellitēs mpl, cohors f ♦ vt īnstituere, īnstruere,
docēre, adsuēfacere; exercēre; (weapon) dīrigere
trainer n (sport) lanista m, aliptēs m
training n disciplīna f, īnstitūtiō f; (practice)
exercitātiō f
trait n līneāmentum nt
traitor n prōditor m
traitorous adj perfidus, perfidiōsus
traitorously adv perfidiōsē
trammel vt impedīre
tramp n (man) planus m; (of feet) pulsus m ♦ vi
gradī
trample vi: ~ **on** obterere, prōterere, prōculcāre
trance n stupor m; (prophetic) furor m
tranquil adj tranquillus, placidus, quiētus,
sēdātus
tranquility n tranquillitās f, quiēs f, pāx f
tranquillize vt pācāre, sēdāre
tranquilly adv tranquillē, placidē, tranquillō
animō
transact vt agere, gerere, trānsigere
transaction n rēs f, negōtium nt
transactor n āctor m
transalpine adj trānsalpīnus
transcend vt superāre, excēdere
transcendence n praestantia f
transcendent adj eximius, ēgregius, excellēns
transcendental adj dīvīnus
transcendentally adv eximiē, ēgregiē, ūnicē
transcribe vt dēscrībere, trānscrībere
transcriber n librārius m
transcript n exemplar nt, exemplum nt
transfer n trānslātiō f; (of property) aliēnātiō
f ♦ vt trānsferre; (troops) trādūcere; (property)
abaliēnāre; (duty) dēlēgāre
transference n trānslātiō f
transfigure vt trānsfōrmāre
transfix vt trānsfīgere, trāicere, trānsfodere;
(mind) obstupefacere; **be transfixed** stupēre,
stupēscere
transform vt commūtāre, vertere
transformation n commūtātiō f
transgress vt violāre, perfringere ♦ vi
dēlinquere
transgression n dēlictum nt
transgressor n violātor m
transience n brevitās f
transient adj fluxus, cadūcus, brevis
transit n trānsitus m
transition n mūtātiō f; (speech) trānsitus m
transitory adj brevis, fluxus
translate vt vertere, reddere; ~ **into Latin** Latīnē
reddere
translation n: **a Latin** ~ **of Homer** Latīnē
redditus Homērus

translator n interpres m
translucent adj perlūcidus
transmarine adj trānsmarīnus
transmission n missiō f
transmit vt mittere; (legacy) trādere, prōdere
transmutable adj mūtābilis
transmutation n mūtātiō f
transmute vt mūtāre, commūtāre
transom n trabs f
transparency n perlūcida nātūra f
transparent adj perlūcidus; (fig) perspicuus
transparently adv perspicuē
transpire vi (get known) ēmānāre, dīvulgārī;
(happen) ēvenīre
transplant vt trānsferre
transport n vectūra f; (ship) nāvis onerāria
f; (emotion) ēlātiō f, summa laetitia f ♦ vt
trānsportāre, trānsvehere, trānsmittere; **be
transported** (fig) efferrī, gestīre
transportation n vectūra f
transpose vt invertere; (words) trāicere
transposition n (words) trāiectiō f
transverse adj trānsversus, oblīquus
transversely adv in trānsversum, oblīquē
trap n laqueus m; (fig) īnsidiae fpl ♦ vt dēcipere,
excipere; (fig) inlaqueāre
trappings npl ōrnāmenta ntpl, īnsignia ntpl;
(horse's) phalerae fpl
trash n nūgae fpl
trashy adj vīlis
Trasimene n Trasimēnus m
travail n labor m, sūdor m; (woman's) puerperium
nt ♦ vi labōrāre, sūdāre; parturīre
travel n itinera ntpl; (foreign) peregrīnātiō f ♦ vi
iter facere; (abroad) peregrīnārī; ~ **through**
peragrāre; ~ **to** contendere ad, in (acc),
proficīscī in (acc)
traveller n viātor m; (abroad) peregrīnātor m
traverse vt peragrāre, lūstrāre; ~ **a great
distance** multa mīlia passuum iter facere
travesty n perversa imitātiō f ♦ vt perversē
imitārī
tray n ferculum nt
treacherous adj perfidus, perfidiōsus; (ground)
lūbricus
treacherously adv perfidiōsē
treachery n perfidia f
tread vi incēdere, ingredī; ~ **on** īnsistere (dat) ♦ n
gradus m, incessus m
treadle n (loom) īnsilia ntpl
treadmill n pistrīnum nt
treason n māiestās f, perduelliō f; **be charged
with** ~ māiestātis accūsārī; **be guilty of high**
~ **against** māiestātem minuere, laedere (gen)
treasonable adj perfidus, perfidiōsus
treasure n gāza f, thēsaurus m; (person) dēliciae
fpl ♦ vt māximī aestimāre, dīligere, fovēre; ~ **up**
condere, congerere
treasure house n thēsaurus m
treasurer n aerārī praefectus m; (royal) dioecētēs
m
treasury n aerārium nt; (emperor's) fiscus m
treat n convīvium nt; dēlectātiō f ♦ vt (in any way)
ūtī (abl), habēre, tractāre, accipere; (patient)
cūrāre; (topic) tractāre; (with hospitality) invītāre;

~ with agere cum; **~ as a friend** amīcī locō habēre
treatise n liber m
treatment n tractātiō f; (MED) cūrātiō f
treaty n foedus nt; **make a ~** foedus ferīre
treble adj triplus; (voice) acūtus ◆ n acūtus sonus m ◆ vt triplicāre
tree n arbor f
trek vi migrāre ◆ n migrātiō f
trellis n cancellī mpl
tremble vi tremere, horrēre
trembling n tremor m, horror m ◆ adj tremulus
tremendous adj immānis, ingēns, vastus
tremendously adv immāne quantum
tremor n tremor m
tremulous adj tremulus
trench n fossa f
trenchant adj ācer
trenchantly adv ācriter
trend n inclīnātiō f ◆ vi vergere
trepidation n trepidātiō f
trespass n dēlictum nt ◆ vi dēlinquere; **~ on** (property) invādere in (acc); (patience, time, etc) abūtī (abl)
trespasser n quī iniussū dominī ingreditur
tress n crīnis m
trial n (essay) experientia f; (test) probātiō f; (LAW) iūdicium nt, quaestiō f; (trouble) labor m, aerumna f; **make ~ of** experīrī, perīculum facere (gen); **be brought to ~** in iūdicium venīre; **put on ~** in iūdicium vocāre; **hold a ~ on** quaestiōnem habēre dē (abl)
triangle n triangulum nt
triangular adj triangulus, triquetrus
tribe n tribus m; gēns f; (barbarian) nātiō f
tribulation n aerumna f
tribunal n iūdicium nt
tribune n tribūnus m; (platform) rōstra ntpl
tribuneship, tribunate n tribūnātus m
tribunician adj tribūnicius
tributary adj vectīgālis ◆ n: **be a ~ of** (river) īnfluere in (acc)
tribute n tribūtum nt, vectīgal nt; (verbal) laudātiō f; **pay a ~ to** laudāre
trice n: **in a ~** mōmentō temporis
trick n dolus m, fallācia f, fraus f, īnsidiae fpl, ars f; (conjurer's) praestīgiae fpl; (habit) mōs m ◆ vt fallere, dēcipere, ēlūdere; (with words) verba dare (dat); **~ out** ōrnāre, distinguere
trickery n dolus m, fraus f, fallāciae fpl
trickle n guttae fpl ◆ vi mānāre, dēstillāre
trickster n fraudātor m, veterātor m
tricky adj lūbricus, difficilis
trident n tridēns m, fuscina f
tried adj probātus, spectātus
triennial adj trietēricus
triennially adv quartō quōque annō
trifle n nūgae fpl, paululum nt ◆ vi lūdere, nūgārī; **~ with** lūdere
trifling adj levis, exiguus
triflingly adv leviter
trig adj lepidus, concinnus
trigger n manulea f
trim adj nitidus, concinnus ◆ vt putāre, tondēre; (lamp) oleum īnstillāre (dat) ◆ vi temporibus servīre

trimly adv concinnē
trimness n nitor, munditia f
trinket n crepundia ntpl
trip n iter nt ◆ vt supplantāre ◆ vi lābī, titubāre; **~ along** currere; **~ over** incurrere in (acc)
tripartite adj tripartītus
tripe n omāsum nt
triple adj triplex, triplus ◆ vt triplicāre
triply adv trifāriam
tripod n tripus m
trireme n trirēmis f
trite adj trītus
triumph n triumphus m; (victory) victōria f ◆ vi triumphāre; vincere; **~ over** dēvincere
triumphal adj triumphālis
triumphant adj victor; laetus
triumvir n triumvir m
triumvirate n triumvirātus m
trivial adj levis, tenuis
triviality n nūgae fpl
trochaic adj trochaicus
trochee n trochaeus m
Trojan n Trōiānus m
troop n grex f, caterva f; (cavalry) turma f ◆ vi cōnfluere, congregārī
trooper n eques m
troops npl cōpiae fpl
trope n figūra f, trānslātiō f
trophy n tropaeum nt; **set up a ~** tropaeum pōnere
tropic n sōlstitiālis orbis m; **tropics** pl loca fervida ntpl
tropical adj tropicus
trot vi tolūtim īre
troth n fidēs f
trouble n incommodum nt, malum nt, molestia f, labor m; (effort) opera f, negōtium nt; (disturbance) turba f, tumultus m; **take the ~ to** operam dare ut; **be worth the ~** operae pretium esse ◆ vt (disturb) turbāre; (make uneasy) sollicitāre, exagitāre; (annoy) incommodāre, molestiam exhibēre (dat); **~ oneself about** cūrāre, respicere; **be troubled with** labōrāre ex
troubler n turbātor m
troublesome adj molestus, incommodus, difficilis
troublesomeness n molestia f
troublous adj turbidus, turbulentus
trough n alveus m
trounce vt castīgāre
troupe n grex f, caterva f
trousered adj brācātus
trousers n brācae fpl
trow vi opīnārī
truant adj tardus ◆ n cessātor m; **play ~** cessāre, nōn compārēre
truce n indutiae fpl
truck n carrus m; **have no ~ with** nihil commercī habēre cum
truckle vi adsentārī
truculence n ferōcia f, asperitās f
truculent adj truculentus, ferōx
truculently adv ferōciter
trudge vi rēpere, pedibus incēdere
true adj vērus; (genuine) germānus, vērus; (loyal) fīdus, fidēlis; (exact) rēctus, iūstus

truism n verbum trītum nt
truly adv rēvērā, profectō, vērē
trumpery n nūgae fpl ♦ adj vīlis
trumpet n tuba f, būcina f
trumpeter n būcinātor m, tubicen m
trump up vt ēmentīrī, cōnfingere
truncate vt praecīdere
truncheon n fustis m, scīpiō m
trundle vt volvere
trunk n truncus m; (elephant's) manus f; (box)
cista f
truss n fascia f ♦ vt colligāre
trust n fidēs f, fīdūcia f; **breach of** ~ mala fidēs;
held in ~ fīdūciārius; **put** ~ **in** fidem habēre
(dat) ♦ vt cōnfīdere (dat), crēdere (dat); (entrust)
committere, concrēdere
trustee n tūtor m
trusteeship n tūtēla f
trustful adj crēdulus, fīdēns
trustfully adv fīdenter
trustily adv fīdēliter
trustiness n fidēs f, fidēlitās f
trusting adj fīdēns
trustingly adv fīdenter
trustworthily adv fidēliter
trustworthiness n fidēs f, integritās f
trustworthy adj fīdus, certus; (witness) locuplēs;
(authority) certus, bonus
trusty adj fīdus, fidēlis
truth n vēritās f, vērum nt; **in** ~ rē vērā
truthful adj vērāx
truthfully adv vērē
truthfulness n fidēs f
try vt (attempt) cōnārī; (test) experīrī, temptāre;
(harass) exercēre; (judge) iūdicāre, cognōscere;
try for petere, quaerere
trying adj molestus
tub n alveus m, cūpa f
tubby adj obēsus
tube n fistula f
tufa n tōfus m
tuft n crista f
tug vt trahere, tractāre
tuition n īnstitūtiō f
tumble vi concidere, corruere, prōlābī ♦ n cāsus
m
tumbledown adj ruīnōsus
tumbler n pōculum nt
tumid adj tumidus, īnflātus
tumour n tūber nt
tumult n tumultus m, turba f; (fig) perturbātiō f
tumultuous adj tumultuōsus, turbidus
tumultuously adv tumultuōsē
tumulus n tumulus m
tun n dolium nt
tuna n thunnus m
tune n modī mpl, carmen nt; **keep in**
~ concentum servāre; **out of** ~ absonus,
dissonus; (strings) incontentus ♦ vt (strings)
intendere
tuneful adj canōrus
tunefully adv numerōsē
tunic n tunica f; **wearing a** ~ tunicātus
tunnel n cunīculus m
turban n mitra f, mitella f
turbid adj turbidus

turbot n rhombus m
turbulence n tumultus m
turbulent adj turbulentus, turbidus
turbulently adv turbulentē, turbidē
turf n caespes m
turgid adj turgidus, īnflātus
turgidity n (RHET) ampullae fpl
turgidly adv īnflātē
turmoil n turba f, tumultus m; (mind)
perturbātiō f
turn n (motion) conversiō f; (bend) flexus m,
ānfrāctus m; (change) commūtātiō f, vicissitūdō
f; (walk) spatium nt; (of mind) adfectus m; (of
language) sententia f, cōnfōrmātiō f; ~ **of**
events mutātiō rērum f; **bad** ~ iniūria f; **good**
~ beneficium nt; ~ **of the scale** mōmentum nt;
take a ~ **for the worse** in pēiōrem partem vertī;
in turns invicem, vicissim, alternī; **in one's**
~ locō ōrdine ♦ vt vertere, convertere, flectere;
(change) vertere, mūtāre; (direct) intendere,
dīrigere; (translate) vertere, reddere; (on a lathe)
tornāre; ~ **the edge of** retundere; ~ **the head**
mentem exturbāre; ~ **the laugh against** rīsum
convertere in (acc); ~ **the scale** (fig) mōmentum
habēre; ~ **the stomach** nauseam facere; ~ **to**
account ūtī (abl), in rem suam convertere ♦ vi
versārī, circumagī; (change) vertere, mūtārī;
(crisis) pendēre; (direction) convertī; (scale)
prōpendēre; ~ **king's/queen's evidence**
indicium profitērī; ~ **against** vt aliēnāre ab
♦ vi dēscīscere ab; ~ **around** (se) circumvertere;
~ **aside** vt dēflectere, dēclīnāre ♦ vi dēvertere,
sē dēclīnāre; ~ **away** vt āvertere, dēpellere ♦ vi
āversārī, discēdere; ~ **back** vi revertī; ~ **down** vt
invertere; (proposal) rēicere; ~ **into** vi vertere in
(acc), mūtārī in (acc); ~ **out** vt ēicere, expellere
♦ vi cadere, ēvenīre, ēvādere; ~ **outside in**
excutere; ~ **over** vt ēvertere; (book) ēvolvere; (in
mind) volūtāre, agitāre; ~ **round** vt circumagere
♦ vi convertī; ~ **up** vt retorquēre; (earth) versāre;
(nose) corrūgāre ♦ vi adesse, intervenīre;
~ **upside down** invertere
turncoat n trānsfuga m
turning n flexus m, ānfrāctus m
turning point n discrīmen nt, mēta f
turnip n rāpum nt
turpitude n turpitūdō f
turquoise n callais f ♦ adj callainus
turret n turris f
turreted adj turrītus
turtle n testūdō f; **turn** ~ invertī
turtle dove n turtur m
tusk n dēns m
tussle n luctātiō f ♦ vi luctārī
tutelage n tūtēla f
tutelary adj praeses
tutor n praeceptor m, magister m ♦ vt docēre,
praecipere (dat)
tutorship n tūtēla f
twaddle n nūgae fpl
twang n sonus m ♦ vi increpāre
tweak vi vellicāre
tweezers n forceps m/f, volsella f
twelfth adj duodecimus ♦ n duodecima pars
f, ūncia f; **eleven twelfths** deūnx m; **five**

twelfths quīncūnx *m*; **seven twelfths** septūnx *m*

twelve *num* duodecim; ~ **each** duodēnī; ~ **times** duodeciēns

twelvemonth *n* annus *m*

twentieth *adj* vīcēsimus ♦ *n* vīcēsima pars *f*; (*tax*) vīcēsima *f*

twenty *num* vīgintī; ~ **each** vīcēnī; ~ **times** vīciēns

twice *adv* bis; ~ **as much** duplus, bis tantō; ~ **a day** bis diē, bis in diē

twig *n* virga *f*, rāmulus *m*

twilight *n* (*morning*) dīlūculum *nt*; (*evening*) crepusculum *nt*

twin *adj* geminus ♦ *n* geminus *m*, gemina *f*

twine *n* resticula *f* ♦ *vt* nectere, implicāre, contexere ♦ *vi* sē implicāre; ~ **round** complectī

twinge *n* dolor *m*

twinkle *vi* micāre

twirl *vt* intorquēre, contorquēre ♦ *vi* circumagī

twist *vt* torquēre, intorquēre ♦ *vi* torquērī

twit *vt* obicere (*dat*)

twitch *vt* vellicāre ♦ *vi* micāre

twitter *vi* pīpilāre

two *num* duo; **two each** bīnī; **two days** biduum *nt*; **two years** biennium *nt*; **two years old** bīmus; **two by two** bīnī; **two feet long** bipedālis; **in two parts** bifāriam, bipartītō

two-coloured *adj* bicolor

two-edged *adj* anceps

twofold *adj* duplex, anceps

two-footed *adj* bipēs

two-headed *adj* biceps

two-horned *adj* bicornis

two hundred *num* ducentī; **two hundred each** ducēnī; **two hundred times** ducentiēns

two hundredth *adj* ducentēsimus

two-oared *adj* birēmis

two-pronged *adj* bidēns, bifurcus

two-way *adj* bivius

type *n* (*pattern*) exemplar *nt*; (*kind*) genus *nt*

typhoon *n* turbō *m*

typical *adj* proprius, solitus

typically *adv* dē mōre, ut mōs est

typify *vt* exprimere

tyrannical *adj* superbus, crūdēlis

tyrannically *adv* superbē, crūdēliter

tyrannize *vi* dominārī, rēgnāre

tyrannous *adj see* **tyrannical**

tyrannously *adv see* **tyrannically**

tyranny *n* dominātiō *f*, rēgnum *nt*

tyrant *n* rēx *m*, crūdēlis dominus *m*; (*Greek*) tyrannus *m*

tyro *n* tīrō *m*, rudis *m*

Uu

ubiquitous *adj* omnibus locīs praesēns
ubiquity *n* ūniversa praesentia *f*
udder *n* ūber *nt*
ugliness *n* foedītās *f*, dēfōrmitās *f*, turpitūdō *f*
ugly *adj* foedus, dēfōrmis, turpis
ulcer *n* ulcus *nt*, vomica *f*
ulcerate *vi* ulcerārī
ulcerous *adj* ulcerōsus
ulterior *adj* ulterior
ultimate *adj* ultimus, extrēmus
ultimately *adv* tandem, ad ultimum
umbrage *n* offēnsiō *f*; **take ~ at** indignē ferre, patī
umbrageous *adj* umbrōsus
umbrella *n* umbella *f*
umpire *n* arbiter *m*, disceptātor *m*
unabashed *adj* intrepidus, impudēns
unabated *adj* integer
unable *adj* impotēns; **be ~** nōn posse, nequīre
unacceptable *adj* ingrātus
unaccompanied *adj* sōlus
unaccomplished *adj* īnfectus, imperfectus; *(person)* indoctus
unaccountable *adj* inexplicābilis
unaccountably *adv* sine causā, repentē
unaccustomed *adj* īnsuētus, īnsolitus
unacquainted *adj* ignārus *(gen)*, imperītus *(gen)*
unadorned *adj* inōrnātus, incōmptus; *(speech)* nūdus, ēnucleātus
unadulterated *adj* sincērus, integer
unadvisedly *adv* imprūdenter, incōnsultē
unaffected *adj* simplex, candidus
unaffectedly *adv* simpliciter
unaided *adj* sine auxiliō, nūdus
unalienable *adj* proprius
unalloyed *adj* pūrus
unalterable *adj* immūtābilis
unaltered *adj* immūtātus
unambiguous *adj* apertus, certus
unambitious *adj* humilis, modestus
unanimity *n* cōnsēnsiō *f*, ūnanimitās *f*
unanimous *adj* concors, ūnanimus; **be ~** idem omnēs sentīre
unanimously *adv* ūnā vōce, omnium cōnsēnsū
unanswerable *adj* necessārius
unanswerably *adv* sine contrōversiā
unappreciative *adj* ingrātus
unapproachable *adj* inaccessus; *(person)* difficilis
unarmed *adj* inermis
unasked *adj* ultrō, suā sponte
unassailable *adj* inexpugnābilis
unassailed *adj* intāctus, incolumis

unassuming *adj* modestus, dēmissus; **~ manners** modestia *f*
unassumingly *adv* modestē
unattached *adj* līber
unattempted *adj* intentātus; **leave ~** praetermittere
unattended *adj* sōlus, sine comitibus
unattractive *adj* invenustus
unauthentic *adj* incertō auctōre
unavailing *adj* inūtilis, inānis
unavenged *adj* inultus
unavoidable *adj* necessārius
unavoidably *adv* necessāriō
unaware *adj* īnscius, ignārus
unawares *adv* inopīnātō, dē imprōvīsō; incautus
unbalanced *adj* turbātus
unbar *vt* reserāre
unbearable *adj* intolerābilis, intolerandus
unbearably *adv* intoleranter
unbeaten *adj* invictus
unbecoming *adj* indecōrus, inhonestus; **it is ~** dēdecet
unbeknown *adj* ignōtus
unbelief *n* diffīdentia *f*
unbelievable *adj* incrēdibilis
unbelievably *adv* incrēdibiliter
unbelieving *adj* incrēdulus
unbend *vt* remittere, laxāre ♦ *vi* animum remittere, aliquid dē sevēritāte remittere
unbending *adj* inexōrābilis, sevērus
unbiassed *adj* integer, incorruptus, aequus
unbidden *adj* ultrō, sponte
unbind *vt* solvere, resolvere
unblemished *adj* pūrus, integer
unblushing *adj* impudēns
unblushingly *adv* impudenter
unbolt *vt* reserāre
unborn *adj* nōndum nātus
unbosom *vt* patefacere, effundere
unbound *adj* solūtus
unbounded *adj* īnfīnītus, immēnsus
unbridled *adj* īnfrēnātus; *(fig)* effrēnātus, indomitus, impotēns
unbroken *adj* integer; *(animal)* intractātus; *(friendship)* inviolātus; *(series)* perpetuus, continuus
unburden *vt* exonerāre; **~ oneself of** aperīre, patefacere
unburied *adj* inhumātus, īnsepultus
unbusinesslike *adj* iners
uncalled-for *adj* supervacāneus
uncanny *adj* mīrus, mōnstruōsus

uncared-for *adj* neglectus
unceasing *adj* perpetuus, adsiduus
unceasingly *adv* perpetuō, adsiduē
unceremonious *adj* agrestis, inurbānus
unceremoniously *adv* inurbānē
uncertain *adj* incertus, dubius, anceps; **be** ~ dubitāre, pendēre
uncertainly *adv* incertē, dubitanter
uncertainty *n* incertum *nt*; (*state*) dubitātiō *f*
unchangeable *adj* immūtābilis; (*person*) cōnstāns
unchanged *adj* immūtātus, īdem; **remain** ~ permanēre
uncharitable *adj* inhūmānus, malignus
uncharitableness *n* inhūmānitās *f*
uncharitably *adv* inhūmānē, malignē
unchaste *adj* impudīcus, libīdinōsus
unchastely *adv* impudīcē
unchastity *n* incestus *m*, libīdō *f*
unchecked *adj* līber, indomitus
uncivil *adj* inurbānus, importūnus, inhūmānus
uncivilized *adj* barbarus, incultus, ferus
uncivilly *adv* inurbānē
uncle *n* (*paternal*) patruus *m*; (*maternal*) avunculus *m*
unclean *adj* immundus; (*fig*) impūrus, obscēnus
uncleanly *adv* impūrē
uncleanness *n* sordēs *fpl*; (*fig*) impūritās *f*, obscēnitās *f*
unclose *vt* aperīre
unclothe *vt* nūdāre, vestem dētrahere (*dat*)
unclothed *adj* nūdus
unclouded *adj* serēnus
uncoil *vt* explicāre, ēvolvere
uncomely *adj* dēfōrmis, turpis
uncomfortable *adj* incommodus, molestus
uncomfortably *adv* incommodē
uncommitted *adj* vacuus
uncommon *adj* rārus, īnsolitus, inūsitātus; (*eminent*) ēgregius, singulāris, eximius
uncommonly *adv* rārō; ēgregiē, ūnicē
uncommonness *n* īnsolentia *f*
uncommunicative *adj* tēctus, taciturnus
uncomplaining *adj* patiēns
uncompleted *adj* imperfectus
uncompromising *adj* dūrus, rigidus
unconcern *n* sēcūritās *f*
unconcerned *adj* sēcūrus, ōtiōsus
unconcernedly *adv* lentē
uncondemned *adj* indemnātus
unconditional *adj* absolūtus
unconditionally *adv* nullā condiciōne
uncongenial *adj* ingrātus
unconnected *adj* sēparātus, disiūnctus; (*style*) dissolūtus
unconquerable *adj* invictus
unconquered *adj* invictus
unconscionable *adj* improbus
unconscionably *adv* improbē
unconscious *adj*: ~ **of** īnscius (*gen*), ignārus (*gen*); **become** ~ sōpīrī, animō linquī
unconsciousness *n* sopor *m*
unconsecrated *adj* profānus
unconsidered *adj* neglectus
unconstitutional *adj* illicitus
unconstitutionally *adv* contrā lēgēs, contrā rem pūblicam

uncontaminated *adj* pūrus, incorruptus, integer
uncontrollable *adj* impotēns, effrēnātus
uncontrollably *adv* effrēnātē
uncontrolled *adj* līber, solūtus
unconventional *adj* īnsolitus, solūtus
unconvicted *adj* indemnātus
unconvincing *adj* incrēdibilis, nōn vērī similis
uncooked *adj* crūdus
uncorrupted *adj* incorruptus, integer
uncouple *vt* disiungere
uncouth *adj* horridus, agrestis, inurbānus
uncouthly *adv* inurbānē
uncouthness *n* inhūmānitās *f*, rūsticitās *f*
uncover *vt* dētegere, aperīre, nūdāre
uncritical *adj* indoctus, crēdulus
uncultivated *adj* incultus; (*fig*) agrestis, rūsticus, impolītus
uncultured *adj* agrestis, rudis
uncut *adj* intōnsus
undamaged *adj* integer, inviolātus
undaunted *adj* intrepidus, fortis
undecayed *adj* incorruptus
undeceive *vt* errōrem tollere (*dat*), errōrem ēripere (*dat*)
undecided *adj* dubius, anceps; (*case*) integer
undecked *adj* (*ship*) apertus
undefended *adj* indēfēnsus, nūdus
undefiled *adj* integer, incontāminātus
undemonstrative *adj* taciturnus
undeniable *adj* certus
undeniably *adv* sine dubiō
undependable *adj* inconstāns, mōbilis
under *adv* īnfrā, subter ♦ *prep* sub (*abl*), īnfrā (*acc*); (*number*) intrā (*acc*); (*motion*) sub (*acc*); ~ **arms** in armīs; ~ **colour** (*pretext of*) speciē (*gen*), per speciem (*gen*); ~ **my leadership** mē duce; ~ **the circumstances** cum haec ita sint; **labour** ~ labōrāre ex; ~ **the eyes of** in cōnspectū (*gen*); ~ **the leadership of** *abl* + duce
underage *adj* impūbēs
undercurrent *n*: **an** ~ **of** lātēns
underestimate *vt* minōris aestimāre
undergarment *n* subūcula *f*
undergo *vt* subīre, patī, ferre
underground *adj* subterrāneus ♦ *adv* sub terrā
undergrowth *n* virgulta *ntpl*
underhand *adj* clandestīnus, fūrtīvus ♦ *adv* clam, fūrtim
underline *vt* subscrībere
underling *n* minister *m*, satelles *m/f*
undermine *vt* subruere; (*fig*) labefacere, labefactāre
undermost *adj* īnfimus
underneath *adv* īnfrā ♦ *prep* sub (*abl*), īnfrā (*acc*); (*motion*) sub (*acc*)
underprop *vt* fulcīre
underrate *vt* obtrectāre, extenuāre, minōris aestimāre
understand *vt* intellegere, comprehendere; (*be told*) accipere, comperīre; (*in a sense*) interpretārī; ~ **Latin** Latīnē scīre
understandable *adj* crēdibilis
understanding *adj* sapiēns, perītus ♦ *n* intellegentia *f*; (*faculty*) mēns *f*, intellectus *m*; (*agreement*) cōnsēnsus *m*; (*condition*) condiciō *f*

undertake *vt* suscipere, sūmere, adīre ad; (*business*) condūcere; (*case*) agere, dēfendere; (*promise*) recipere, spondēre
undertaker *n* dissignātor *m*
undertaking *n* inceptum *nt*, inceptiō *f*
undervalue *vt* minōris aestimāre
underwood *n* virgulta *ntpl*
underworld *n* īnferī *mpl*
undeserved *adj* immeritus, iniūstus
undeservedly *adv* immeritō, indignē
undeserving *adj* indignus
undesigned *adj* fortuītus
undesignedly *adv* fortuītō, temerē
undesirable *adj* odiōsus, ingrātus
undeterred *adj* immōtus
undeveloped *adj* immātūrus
undeviating *adj* dīrēctus
undigested *adj* crūdus
undignified *adj* levis, inhonestus
undiminished *adj* integer
undiscernible *adj* invīsus, obscūrus
undisciplined *adj* lascīvus, immoderātus; (*MIL*) inexercitātus
undiscovered *adj* ignōtus
undisguised *adj* apertus
undisguisedly *adv* palam, apertē
undismayed *adj* impavidus, intrepidus
undisputed *adj* certus
undistinguished *adj* ignōbilis, inglōrius
undisturbed *adj* tranquillus, placidus
undo *vt* (*knot*) expedīre, resolvere; (*sewing*) dissuere; (*fig*) īnfectum reddere
undoing *n* ruīna *f*
undone *adj* infectus; (*ruined*) perditus; **be ~** perīre, disperīre; **hopelessly ~** dēperditus
undoubted *adj* certus
undoubtedly *adv* sine dubiō, plānē
undress *vt* exuere, vestem dētrahere (*dat*)
undressed *adj* nūdus
undue *adj* nimius, immoderātus, inīquus
undulate *vi* fluctuāre
undulation *n* spīra *f*
unduly *adv* nimis, plūs aequō
undutiful *adj* impius
undutifully *adv* impiē
undutifulness *n* impietās *f*
undying *adj* immortālis, aeternus
unearth *vt* ēruere, dētegere
unearthly *adj* mōnstruōsus, dīvīnus, hūmānō māior
uneasily *adv* aegrē
uneasiness *n* sollicitūdō *f*, perturbātiō *f*
uneasy *adj* sollicitus, anxius, inquiētus
uneducated *adj* illitterātus, indoctus, rudis; **be ~** litterās nescīre
unemployed *adj* ōtiōsus
unemployment *n* cessātiō *f*
unencumbered *adj* expedītus, līber
unending *adj* perpetuus, sempiternus
unendowed *adj* indōtātus
unendurable *adj* intolerandus, intolerābilis
unenjoyable *adj* iniūcundus, molestus
unenlightened *adj* rudis, inērudītus
unenterprising *adj* iners
unenviable *adj* nōn invidendus
unequal *adj* impār, dispār

unequalled *adj* ūnicus, singulāris
unequally *adv* inaequāliter, inīquē
unequivocal *adj* apertus, plānus
unerring *adj* certus
unerringly *adv* certē
unessential *adj* adventīcius, supervacāneus
uneven *adj* impār; (*surface*) asper, inīquus, inaequābilis
unevenly *adv* inīquē, inaequāliter
unevenness *n* inīquitās *f*, asperitās *f*
unexamined *adj* (*case*) incognitus
unexampled *adj* inaudītus, ūnicus, singulāris
unexceptionable *adj* ēmendātus; (*authority*) certissimus
unexpected *adj* imprōvīsus, inopīnātus, īnspērātus
unexpectedly *adv* dē imprōvīsō, ex īnspērātō, inopīnātō, necopīnātō
unexplored *adj* inexplōrātus
unfading *adj* perennis, vīvus
unfailing *adj* perennis, certus, perpetuus
unfailingly *adv* semper
unfair *adj* inīquus, iniūstus
unfairly *adv* inīquē, iniūstē
unfairness *n* inīquitās *f*, iniūstitia *f*
unfaithful *adj* īnfidēlis, īnfīdus, perfidus
unfaithfully *adv* īnfidēliter
unfaithfulness *n* īnfidēlitās *f*
unfamiliar *adj* novus, ignōtus, īnsolēns; (*sight*) invīsitātus
unfamiliarity *n* īnsolentia *f*
unfashionable *adj* obsolētus
unfasten *vt* solvere, refīgere
unfathomable *adj* īnfīnītus, profundus
unfavourable *adj* inīquus, adversus, importūnus
unfavourably *adv* inīquē, male; **be ~ disposed** āversō animō esse
unfed *adj* iēiūnus
unfeeling *adj* dūrus, crūdēlis, ferreus
unfeelingly *adv* crūdēliter
unfeigned *adj* sincērus, vērus, simplex
unfeignedly *adv* sincērē, vērē
unfilial *adj* impius
unfinished *adj* īnfectus, imperfectus
unfit *adj* inūtilis, incommodus, aliēnus
unfix *vt* refīgere
unflinching *adj* impavidus, firmus
unfold *vt* explicāre, ēvolvere; (*story*) expōnere, ēnārrāre
unfolding *n* explicātiō *f*
unforeseen *adj* imprōvīsus
unforgettable *adj* memorābilis
unforgiving *adj* implācābilis
unformed *adj* īnfōrmis
unfortified *adj* immūnītus, nūdus
unfortunate *adj* īnfēlīx, īnfortūnātus
unfortunately *adv* īnfēlīciter, male; **~ you did not come** male accidit quod nōn vēnistī
unfounded *adj* inānis, vānus
unfrequented *adj* dēsertus
unfriendliness *n* inimīcitia *f*
unfriendly *adj* inimīcus, malevolus; **in an ~ manner** inimīcē
unfruitful *adj* sterilis; (*fig*) inānis, vānus
unfruitfulness *n* sterilitās *f*
unfulfilled *adj* īnfectus, inritus

unfurl vt explicāre, pandere
unfurnished adj nūdus
ungainly adj agrestis, rūsticus
ungallant adj inurbānus, parum cōmis
ungenerous adj illīberālis; ~ **conduct** illīberālitās f
ungentlemanly adj illīberālis
ungirt adj discinctus
ungodliness n impietās f
ungodly adj impius
ungovernable adj impotēns, indomitus
ungovernableness n impotentia f
ungraceful adj inconcinnus, inēlegāns
ungracefully adv inēleganter
ungracious adj inhūmānus, petulāns, importūnus
ungraciously adv acerbē
ungrammatical adj barbarus; **be ~** soloecismum facere
ungrateful adj ingrātus
ungrudging adj largus, nōn invītus
ungrudgingly adv sine invidiā
unguarded adj intūtus; (word) incautus, incōnsultus
unguardedly adv temerē, incōnsultē
unguent n unguentum nt
unhallowed adj profānus, impius
unhand vt mittere
unhandy adj inhabilis
unhappily adv infēlīciter, miserē
unhappiness n miseria f, tristitia f, maestitia f
unhappy adj infēlīx, miser, tristis
unharmed adj incolumis, integer, salvus
unharness vt disiungere
unhealthiness n valētūdō f; (climate) gravitās f
unhealthy adj invalidus, aeger; (climate) gravis, pestilens
unheard adj inaudītus; (LAW) indictā causā
unheard-of adj inaudītus
unheeded adj neglectus
unheeding adj immemor, sēcūrus
unhelpful adj difficilis, invītus
unhesitating adj audāx, prōmptus
unhesitatingly adv sine dubitātiōne
unhewn adj rudis
unhindered adj expedītus
unhinged adj mente captus
unhistorical adj fictus, commentīcius
unholiness n impietās f
unholy adj impius
unhonoured adj inhonōrātus
unhoped-for adj īnspērātus
unhorse vt excutere, equō dēicere
unhurt adj integer, incolumis
unicorn n monocerōs m
uniform adj aequābilis, aequālis ♦ n īnsignia ntpl; (MIL) sagum nt; **in ~** sagātus; **put on ~** saga sūmere
uniformity n aequābilitās f, cōnstantia f
uniformly adv aequābiliter, ūnō tenōre
unify vt coniungere
unimaginative adj hebes, stolidus
unimpaired adj integer, incolumis, illībātus
unimpeachable adj (character) integer; (style) ēmendātus
unimportant adj levis, nullīus mōmentī

uninformed adj indoctus, ignārus
uninhabitable adj inhabitābilis
uninhabited adj dēsertus
uninitiated adj profānus; (fig) rudis
uninjured adj integer, incolumis
unintelligent adj īnsipiēns, tardus, excors
unintelligible adj obscūrus
unintelligibly adv obscūrē
unintentionally adv imprūdēns, temerē
uninteresting adj frīgidus, āridus
uninterrupted adj continuus, perpetuus
uninterruptedly adv continenter, sine ullā intermissiōne
uninvited adj invocātus; ~ **guest** umbra f
uninviting adj iniūcundus, invenustus
union n coniūnctiō f; (social) cōnsociātiō f, societās f; (POL) foederātae cīvitātēs fpl; (agreement) concordia f, cōnsēnsus m; (marriage) coniugium nt
unique adj ūnicus, ēgregius, singulāris
unison n concentus m; (fig) concordia f, cōnsēnsus m
unit n ūniō f
unite vt coniungere, cōnsociāre, cōpulāre ♦ vi coīre; cōnsentīre, cōnspīrāre; (rivers) cōnfluere
unity n (concord) concordia f, cōnsēnsus m
universal adj ūniversus, commūnis
universally adv ūniversus, omnis; (place) ubīque
universe n mundus m, rērum nātūra f
university n acadēmia f
unjust adj iniūstus, inīquus
unjustifiable adj indignus, inexcūsābilis
unjustly adv iniūstē, iniūriā
unkempt adj horridus
unkind adj inhūmānus, inīquus
unkindly adv inhūmānē, asperē
unkindness n inhūmānitās f
unknowingly adv imprūdēns, īnscius
unknown adj ignōtus, incognitus; (fame) obscūrus
unlawful adj vetitus, iniūriōsus
unlawfully adv iniūriōsē, iniūriā
unlearn vt dēdiscere
unlearned adj indoctus, inērudītus
unless conj nisī
unlettered adj illitterātus
unlike adj dissimilis (+gen or dat), dispār
unlikely adj nōn vērīsimilis
unlimited adj īnfīnītus, immēnsus
unload vt exonerāre, deonerāre; (from ship) expōnere
unlock vt reserāre, reclūdere
unlooked-for adj īnspērātus, inexpectātus
unloose vt solvere, exsolvere
unlovely adj invenustus
unluckily adv infēlīciter
unlucky adj infēlīx, īnfortūnātus; (day) āter
unmake vt īnfectum reddere
unman vt mollīre, frangere, dēbilitāre
unmanageable adj inhabilis
unmanly adj mollis, ēnervātus, muliebris
unmannerliness n importūnitās f, inhūmānitās f
unmannerly adj importūnus, inhūmānus
unmarried adj (man) caelebs; (woman) vidua
unmask vt nūdāre, dētegere
unmatched adj ūnicus, singulāris

unmeaning adj inānis
unmeasured adj īnfīnītus, immoderātus
unmeet adj parum idōneus
unmelodious adj absonus, absurdus
unmentionable adj īnfandus
unmentioned adj indictus; **leave ~** ōmittere
unmerciful adj immisericors, inclēmēns
unmercifully adv inclēmenter
unmerited adj immeritus, indignus
unmindful adj immemor
unmistakable adj certus, manifestus
unmistakably adv sine dubiō, certē
unmitigated adj merus
unmixed adj pūrus
unmolested adj intāctus
unmoor vt solvere
unmoved adj immōtus
unmusical adj absonus, absurdus
unmutilated adj integer
unnatural adj (event) mōnstruōsus; (feelings) impius, inhūmānus; (style) arcessītus, pūtidus
unnaturally adv contrā nātūram; impiē, inhūmānē; pūtidē
unnavigable adj innāvigābilis
unnecessarily adv nimis
unnecessary adj inūtilis, supervacāneus
unnerve vt dēbilitāre, frangere
unnoticed adj: **be ~** latēre, fallere
unnumbered adj innumerus
unobjectionable adj honestus, culpae expers
unobservant adj tardus
unobserved adj: **be ~** latēre, fallere
unobstructed adj apertus, pūrus
unobtrusive adj verēcundus; **be ~** fallere
unobtrusiveness n verēcundia f
unoccupied adj vacuus, ōtiōsus
unoffending adj innocēns
unofficial adj prīvātus
unorthodox adj abnōrmis
unostentatious adj modestus, verēcundus
unostentatiously adv nullā iactātiōne
unpaid adj (services) grātuītus; (money) dēbitus
unpalatable adj amārus; (fig) iniūcundus, īnsuāvis
unparalleled adj ūnicus, inaudītus
unpardonable adj inexcūsābilis
unpatriotic adj impius
unpitying adj immisericors, ferreus
unpleasant adj iniūcundus, ingrātus, īnsuāvis, gravis, molestus
unpleasantly adv iniūcundē, ingrātē, graviter
unpleasantness n iniūcunditās f, molestia f
unpleasing adj ingrātus, invenustus
unploughed adj inarātus
unpoetical adj pedester
unpolished adj impolītus; (person) incultus, agrestis, inurbānus; (style) inconditus, rudis
unpopular adj invidiōsus, invīsus
unpopularity n invidia f, odium nt
unpractised adj inexercitātus, imperītus
unprecedented adj īnsolēns, novus, inaudītus
unprejudiced adj integer, aequus
unpremeditated adj repentīnus, subitus
unprepared adj imparātus
unprepossessing adj invenustus, illepidus
unpretentious adj modestus, verēcundus

unprincipled adj improbus, levis, prāvus
unproductive adj īnfēcundus, sterilis
unprofitable adj inūtilis, vānus
unprofitably adv frustrā, ab rē
unpropitious adj īnfēlīx, adversus
unpropitiously adv malīs ōminibus
unprotected adj indēfēnsus, intūtus, nūdus
unprovoked adj ultrō (adv)
unpunished adj impūnītus ◆ adv impūne
unqualified adj nōn idōneus; (unrestricted) absolūtus
unquestionable adj certus
unquestionably adv facile, certē
unquestioning adj crēdulus
unravel vt retexere; (fig) ēnōdāre, explicāre
unready adj imparātus
unreal adj falsus, vānus
unreality n vānitās f
unreasonable adj inīquus, importūnus
unreasonableness n inīquitās f
unreasonably adv inīquē
unreasoning adj stolidus, temerārius
unreclaimed adj (land) incultus
unrefined adj impolītus, inurbānus, rudis
unregistered adj incēnsus
unrelated adj aliēnus
unrelenting adj implācābilis, inexōrābilis
unreliable adj incertus, levis
unreliably adv leviter
unrelieved adj perpetuus, adsiduus
unremitting adj adsiduus
unrequited adj inultus, inānis
unreservedly adv apertē, sine ullā exceptiōne
unresponsive adj hebes
unrest n inquiēs f, sollicitūdō f
unrestrained adj līber, impotēns, effrēnātus, immoderātus
unrestricted adj līber, absolūtus
unrevenged adj inultus
unrewarded adj inhonōrātus
unrewarding adj ingrātus, vānus
unrighteous adj iniūstus, impius
unrighteously adv iniūstē, impiē
unrighteousness n impietās f
unripe adj immātūrus, crūdus
unrivalled adj ēgregius, singulāris, ūnicus
unroll vt ēvolvere, explicāre
unromantic adj pedester
unruffled adj immōtus, tranquillus
unruliness n licentia f, impotentia f
unruly adj effrēnātus, impotēns, immoderātus
unsafe adj perīculōsus, dubius; (structure) īnstābilis
unsaid adj indictus
unsatisfactorily adv nōn ex sententiā, male
unsatisfactory adj parum idōneus, malus
unsatisfied adj parum contentus
unsavoury adj īnsuāvis, taeter
unscathed adj incolumis, integer
unschooled adj indoctus, inērudītus
unscrupulous adj improbus, impudēns
unscrupulously adv improbē, impudenter
unscrupulousness n improbitās f, impudentia f
unseal vt resignāre, solvere
unseasonable adj intempestīvus, importūnus
unseasonableness n incommod}tās f

unseasonably *adv* intempestīvē, importūnē
unseasoned *adj* (food) nōn condītus; (wood) viridis
unseat *vt* (rider) excutere
unseaworthy *adj* īnfirmus
unseeing *adj* caecus
unseemly *adj* indecōrus
unseen *adj* invīsus; (ever before) invīsitātus
unselfish *adj* innocēns, probus, līberālis
unselfishly *adv* līberāliter
unselfishness *n* innocentia *f*, līberālitās *f*
unserviceable *adj* inūtilis
unsettle *vt* ad incertum revocāre, turbāre,
  sollicitāre
unsettled *adj* incertus, dubius; (mind) sollicitus,
  suspēnsus; (times) turbidus
unsew *vt* dissuere
unshackle *vt* expedīre, solvere
unshaken *adj* immōtus, firmus, stabilis
unshapely *adj* dēfōrmis
unshaven *adj* intōnsus
unsheathe *vt* dēstringere, stringere
unshod *adj* nūdis pedibus
unshorn *adj* intōnsus
unsightliness *n* dēfōrmitās *f*, turpitūdō *f*
unsightly *adj* foedus, dēfōrmis
unskilful *adj* indoctus, īnscītus, incallidus
unskilfully *adv* indoctē, īnscītē, incallide
unskilfulness *n* īnscītia *f*, imperītia *f*
unskilled *adj* imperītus, indoctus; ~ **in** imperītus
  (gen)
unslaked *adj* (lime) vīvus; (thirst) inexplētus
unsociable *adj* īnsociābilis, difficilis
unsoiled *adj* integer, pūrus
unsolicited *adj* voluntārius ♦ *adv* ultrō
unsophisticated *adj* simplex, ingenuus
unsound *adj* īnfirmus; (mind) īnsānus; (opinion)
  falsus, perversus
unsoundness *n* īnfirmitās *f*; īnsānitās *f*; prāvitās
  f
unsparing *adj* inclēmēns, immisericors; (lavish)
  prōdigus
unsparingly *adv* inclēmenter; prōdigē
unspeakable *adj* īnfandus, incrēdibilis
unspeakably *adv* incrēdibiliter
unspoilt *adj* integer
unspoken *adj* indictus, tacitus
unspotted *adj* integer, pūrus
unstable *adj* īnstabilis; (fig) incōnstāns, levis
unstained *adj* pūrus, incorruptus, integer
unstatesmanlike *adj* illīberālis
unsteadily *adv* incōnstanter; **walk** ~ titubāre
unsteadiness *n* (fig) incōnstantia *f*
unsteady *adj* īnstabilis; (fig) incōnstāns
unstitch *vt* dissuere
unstring *vt* retendere
unstudied *adj* simplex
unsubdued *adj* invictus
unsubstantial *adj* levis, inānis
unsuccessful *adj* īnfēlīx; (effort) inritus; **be**
  ~ **offendere; I am** ~ mihī nōn succēdit
unsuccessfully *adv* īnfēlīciter, rē īnfectā
unsuitable *adj* incommodus, aliēnus,
  importūnus; **it is** ~ dēdecet
unsuitableness *n* incommoditās *f*
unsuitably *adv* incommodē, ineptē
unsuited *adj* parum idōneus

unsullied *adj* pūrus, incorruptus
unsure *adj* incertus, dubius
unsurpassable *adj* inexsuperābilis
unsurpassed *adj* ūnicus, singulāris
unsuspected *adj* latēns, nōn suspectus; **be**
  ~ latēre, in suspiciōnem nōn venīre
unsuspecting *adj* imprōvidus, imprūdēns
unsuspicious *adj* nōn suspicāx, crēdulus
unswerving *adj* cōnstāns
unsworn *adj* iniūrātus
unsymmetrical *adj* inaequālis
untainted *adj* incorruptus, integer
untamable *adj* indomitus
untamed *adj* indomitus, ferus
untaught *adj* indoctus, rudis
unteach *vt* dēdocēre
unteachable *adj* indocilis
untenable *adj* inānis, īnfirmus
unthankful *adj* ingrātus
unthankfully *adv* ingrātē
unthankfulness *n* ingrātus animus *m*
unthinkable *adj* incrēdibilis
unthinking *adj* incōnsīderātus, imprōvidus
unthriftily *adv* prōdigē
unthrifty *adj* prōdigus, profūsus
untidily *adv* neglegenter
untidiness *n* neglegentia *f*
untidy *adj* neglegēns, inconcinnus, squālidus
untie *vt* solvere
until *conj* dum, dōnec ♦ *prep* usque ad (acc), in (acc);
  ~ **now** adhūc
untilled *adj* incultus
untimely *adj* intempestīvus, immātūrus,
  importūnus
untiring *adj* impiger; (effort) adsiduus
unto *prep* ad (acc), in (acc)
untold *adj* innumerus
untouched *adj* intāctus, integer
untoward *adj* adversus, malus
untrained *adj* inexercitātus, imperītus, rudis
untried *adj* intemptātus, inexpertus; (trial)
  incognitus
untrodden *adj* āvius
untroubled *adj* tranquillus, placidus, quiētus;
  (mind) sēcūrus
untrue *adj* falsus, fictus; (disloyal) īnfīdus, īnfidēlis
untrustworthy *adj* īnfīdus, mōbilis
untruth *n* mendācium *nt*, falsum *nt*
untruthful *adj* mendāx, falsus
untruthfully *adv* falsō, falsē
untuneful *adj* absonus
unturned *adj*: **leave no stone** ~ nihil
  intemptātum relinquere, omnia experīrī
untutored *adj* indoctus, incultus
unused *adj* (person) īnsuētus, īnsolitus; (thing)
  integer
unusual *adj* īnsolitus, inūsitātus, īnsolēns, novus
unusually *adv* īnsolenter, praeter
  cōnsuētūdinem
unusualness *n* īnsolentia *f*, novitās *f*
unutterable *adj* īnfandus, inēnārrābilis
unvarnished *adj* (fig) simplex, nūdus
unveil *vt* (fig) aperīre, patefacere
unversed *adj* ignārus (gen), imperītus (gen)
unwanted *adj* supervacāneus
unwarily *adv* imprudenter, incautē, incōnsultē

unwariness n imprūdentia f
unwarlike adj imbellis
unwarrantable adj inīquus, iniūstus
unwarrantably adv iniūriā
unwary adj imprūdēns, incautus, incōnsultus
unwavering adj stabilis, immōtus
unwearied, unwearying adj indēfessus, adsiduus
unweave vt retexere
unwedded adj (man) caelebs; (woman) vidua
unwelcome adj ingrātus
unwell adj aeger, aegrōtus
unwept adj indēflētus
unwholesome adj pestilēns, gravis
unwieldy adj inhabilis
unwilling adj invītus; be ~ nolle
unwillingly adv invītus
unwind vt ēvolvere, retexere
unwise adj stultus, īnsipiēns, imprūdēns
unwisely adv īnsipienter, imprūdenter
unwittingly adv imprūdēns, īnsciēns
unwonted adj īnsolitus, inūsitātus
unworthily adv indignē
unworthiness n indignitās f
unworthy adj indignus (abl)
unwounded adj intāctus, integer
unwrap vt ēvolvere, explicāre
unwritten adj nōn scrīptus; ~ law mōs m
unwrought adj īnfectus, rudis
unyielding adj dūrus, firmus, inexōrābilis
unyoke vt disiungere
up adv sūrsum; **up and down** sūrsum deōrsum; **up to** usque ad (acc), tenus (abl, after noun); **bring up** subvehere; (child) ēducāre; **climb up** ēscendere; **come up to** aequāre; **lift up** ērigere, sublevāre; **from childhood up** ā puerō; **it is all up with** āctum est dē; **well up in** gnārus (gen), perītus (gen); **what is he up to?** quid struit? ♦ prep (motion) in (acc) ♦ n: **ups and downs** (fig) vicissitūdinēs fpl
upbraid vt exprobrāre (dat of pers, acc of charge); obicere (dat and acc), increpāre, castīgāre
upbringing n ēducātiō f
upheaval n ēversiō f
upheave vt ēvertere
uphill adj acclīvis ♦ adv adversō colle, in adversum collem
uphold vt sustinēre, tuērī, servāre
upholstery n supellex f
upkeep n impēnsa f
upland adj montānus
uplift vt extollere, sublevāre
upon prep in (abl), super (abl); (motion) in (acc), super (acc); (dependence) ex (abl); ~ **this** quō factō
upper adj superior; **gain the ~ hand** superāre, vincere
uppermost adj suprēmus, summus
uppish adj superbus
upright adj rēctus, ērēctus; (character) integer, probus, honestus
uprightly adv rēctē; integrē
uprightness n integritās f
upriver adj, adv adversō flūmine
uproar n tumultus m; clāmor m

uproarious adj tumultuōsus
uproariously adv tumultuōsē
uproot vt ērādīcāre, exstirpāre, ēruere
upset vt ēvertere, invertere, subvertere; ~ **the apple cart** plaustrum percellere ♦ adj (fig) perturbātus
upshot n ēventus m
upside-down adv: **turn** ~ ēvertere, invertere; (fig) miscēre
upstart n novus homō m ♦ adj repentīnus
upstream adj, adv adversō flūmine
upward, upwards adv sūrsum; **upward(s) of** (number) amplius
urban adj urbānus, oppidānus
urbane adj urbānus, cōmis
urbanely adv urbānē, cōmiter
urbanity n urbānitās f
urchin n (boy) puerulus m; (animal) echīnus m
urge vt urgēre, impellere; (speech) hortārī, incitāre; (advice) suādēre; (request) sollicitāre; ~ **on** incitāre ♦ n impulsus m; dēsīderium nt
urgency n necessitās f
urgent adj praesēns, gravis; **be** ~ instāre
urgently adv graviter
urn n urna f
usage n mōs m, īnstitūtum nt, ūsus m
use n ūsus m; (custom) mōs m, cōnsuētūdō f; **be of use** ūsuī esse, prōdesse, condūcere; **out of use** desuētus; **go out of use** exolēscere; **in common use** ūsitātus; **it's no use** nīl agis, nīl agimus ♦ vt ūtī (abl); (improperly) abūtī; (for a purpose) adhibēre; (word) cōnsūmere, exhaurīre; **use up** cōnsūmere, exhaurīre; **used to** adsuētus (dat); solēre (inf); **I used to do** faciebam
useful adj ūtilis; **be** ~ ūsuī esse
usefully adv ūtiliter
usefulness n ūtilitās f
useless adj inūtilis; (thing) inānis, inritus; **be** ~ nihil valēre
uselessly adv inūtiliter, frustrā
uselessness n inānitās f
usher n (court) apparitor m; (theatre) dēsignātor m ♦ vt: ~ **in** indūcere, intrōdūcere
usual adj ūsitātus, solitus; **as** ~ ut adsolet, ut fert cōnsuētūdō, ex cōnsuētūdine; **out of the** ~ īnsolitus, extrā ōrdinem
usually adv ferē, plērumque; **he** ~ **comes** venīre solet
usufruct n ūsus et fructus m
usurer n faenerātor m
usurp vt occupāre, invādere in (acc), ūsurpāre
usurpation n occupātiō f
usury n faenerātiō f, ūsūra f; **practise** ~ faenerārī
utensil n īnstrūmentum nt, vās nt
utility n ūtilitās f, commodum nt
utilize vt ūtī (abl); (for a purpose) adhibēre
utmost adj extrēmus, summus; **at the** ~ summum; **do one's** ~ omnibus vīribus contendere
utter adj tōtus, extrēmus, summus ♦ vt ēmittere, ēdere, ēloquī, prōnūntiāre
utterance n dictum nt; (process) prōnūntiātiō f
utterly adv funditus, omnīnō, penitus
uttermost adj extrēmus, ultimus

Vv

vacancy n inānitās f; (*office*) vacuitās f; **there is a ~** locus vacat; **elect to fill a ~** sufficere
vacant adj inānis, vacuus; **be ~** vacāre
vacate vt vacuum facere
vacation n fēriae fpl
vacillate vi vacillāre, dubitāre
vacillation n dubitātiō f
vacuity n inānitās f
vacuous adj vacuus
vacuum n ināne nt
vagabond n grassātor m ♦ adj vagus
vagary n libīdō f
vagrancy n errātiō f
vagrant n grassātor m, vagus m
vague adj incertus, dubius
vaguely adv incertē
vain n vānus, inānis, inritus; (*person*) glōriōsus; **in ~** frustrā
vainglorious adj glōriōsus
vainglory n glōria f, iactantia f
vainly adv frustrā, nēquīquam
vale n vallis f
valet n cubiculārius m
valiant adj fortis, ācer
valiantly adv fortiter, ācriter
valid adj ratus; (*argument*) gravis, firmus
validity n vīs f, auctōritās f
valley n vallis f
valorous adj fortis
valour n virtūs f
valuable adj pretiōsus
valuation n aestimātiō f
value n pretium nt; (*fig*) vīs f, honor m ♦ vt aestimāre; (*esteem*) dīligere; **~ highly** magnī aestimāre; **~ little** parvī aestimāre, parvī facere
valueless adj vīlis, minimī pretī
valuer n aestimātor m
van n (*in battle*) prīma aciēs f; (*on march*) prīmum agmen nt
vanguard n prīmum agmen nt
vanish vi diffugere, ēvānēscere, dīlābī
vanity n (*unreality*) vānitās f; (*conceit*) glōria f
vanquish vt vincere, superāre, dēvincere
vanquisher n victor m
vantage n (*ground*) locus superior m
vapid adj vapidus, īnsulsus
vapidly adv īnsulsē
vaporous adj nebulōsus
vapour n vapor m, nebula f; (*from earth*) exhālātiō f
variable adj varius, mūtābilis
variableness n mūtābilitās f, incōnstantia f
variance n discordia f, dissēnsiō f, discrepantia f; **at ~** discors; **be at ~** dissidēre, inter sē discrepāre; **set at ~** aliēnāre

variant adj varius
variation n varietās f, vicissitūdō f
variegate vt variāre
variegated adj varius
variety n varietās f; (*number*) multitūdō f; (*kind*) genus nt; **a ~ of** dīversī
various adj varius, dīversus
variously adv variē
varlet n verberō m
varnish n pigmentum nt; (*fig*) fūcus m
varnished adj (*fig*) fūcātus
vary vt variāre, mūtāre; (*decorate*) distinguere ♦ vi mūtārī
vase n vās nt
vassal n ambāctus m; (*fig*) cliēns m
vast adj vastus, immānis, ingēns, immēnsus
vastly adv valdē
vastness n māgnitūdō f, immēnsitās f
vat n cūpa f
vault n (ARCH) fornix f; (*jump*) saltus m ♦ vi salīre
vaulted adj fornicātus
vaunt vt iactāre, ostentāre ♦ vi sē iactāre, glōriārī
vaunting n ostentātiō f, glōria f ♦ adj glōriōsus
veal n vitulīna f
vedette n excursor m
veer vi sē vertere, flectī
vegetable n holus nt
vehemence n vīs f, violentia f; (*passion*) ārdor m, impetus m
vehement adj vehemēns, violentus, ācer
vehemently adv vehementer, ācriter
vehicle n vehiculum nt
Veii n Veiī, Vēiōrum mpl
veil n rīca f; (*bridal*) flammeum nt; (*fig*) integumentum nt ♦ vt vēlāre, tegere
vein n vēna f
vellum n membrāna f
velocity n celeritās f, vēlōcitās f
venal adj vēnālis
vend vt vēndere
vendetta n simultās f
vendor n caupō m
veneer n (*fig*) speciēs f, fūcus m
venerable adj gravis, augustus
venerate vt colere, venerārī
veneration n venerātiō f, cultus m
venerator n cultor m
vengeance n ultiō f, poena f; **take ~ on** ulcīscī, vindicāre in (*acc*); **take ~ for** ulcīscī, vindicāre
vengeful adj ultor
venial adj ignōscendus
venison n dāma f, ferīna f
venom n venēnum nt; (*fig*) vīrus nt
venomous adj venēnātus

vent *n* spīrāculum *nt*; (*outlet*) exitus *m*; **give ~ to** profundere, ēmittere ◆ *vt* ēmittere; (*feelings on*) profundere in (*acc*), ērumpere in (*acc*)
ventilate *vt* perflāre; (*opinion*) in medium prōferre, vulgāre
ventilation *n* perflāre
venture *n* perīculum *nt*; (*gamble*) ālea *f*; **at a ~** temerē ◆ *vi* audēre ◆ *vt* perīclitārī, in āleam dare
venturesome *adj* audāx, temerārius
venturesomeness *n* audācia *f*, temeritās *f*
veracious *adj* vērāx, vēridicus
veracity *n* vēritās *f*, fidēs *f*
verb *n* verbum *nt*
verbally *adv* per colloquia; (*translate*) ad verbum, verbum prō verbo
verbatim *adv* ad verbum, totidem verbīs
verbiage *n* verba *ntpl*
verbose *adj* verbōsus
verbosity *n* loquendī prōfluentia *f*
verdant *adj* viridis
verdict *n* sententia *f*, iūdicium *nt*; **deliver a ~** sententiam prōnūntiāre; **give a ~ in favour of** causam adiūdicāre (*dat*)
verdigris *n* aerūgō *f*
verdure *n* viriditās *f*
verge *n* ōra *f*; **the ~ of** extrēmus; **on the ~ of** (*fig*) prope (*acc*) ◆ *vi* vergere
verification *n* cōnfirmātiō *f*
verify *vt* cōnfirmāre, comprobāre
verily *adv* profectō, certē
verisimilitude *n* vērī similitūdō *f*
veritable *adj* vērus
veritably *adv* vērē
verity *n* vēritās *f*
vermilion *n* sandīx *f*
vermin *n* bestiolae *fpl*
vernacular *adj* patrius ◆ *n* patrius sermō *m*
vernal *adj* vērnus
versatile *adj* versūtus, varius
versatility *n* versātile ingenium *nt*
verse *n* (*line*) versus *m*; (*poetry*) versus *mpl*, carmina *ntpl*
versed *adj* īnstructus, perītus, exercitātus
versification *n* ars versūs faciendī
versify *vt* versū inclūdere ◆ *vi* versūs facere
version *n* (*of story*) fōrma *f*; **give a Latin ~ of** Latīnē reddere
vertex *n* vertex *m*, fastīgium *nt*
vertical *adj* rēctus, dīrēctus
vertically *adv* ad līneam, rēctā līneā, ad perpendiculum
vertigo *n* vertīgō *f*
vervain *n* verbēna *f*
verve *n* ācrimōnia *f*
very *adj* ipse ◆ *adv* admodum, valdē, vehementer ◆ *superl*: **at that ~ moment** tum māximē; **not ~** nōn ita
vessel *n* (*receptacle*) vās *nt*; (*ship*) nāvigium *nt*
vest *n* subūcula *f* ◆ *vt*: **~ power in** imperium dēferre (*dat*); **vested interests** nummī locātī *mpl*
vestal *adj* vestālis ◆ *n* virgō vestālis *f*
vestibule *n* vestibulum *nt*
vestige *n* vestīgium *nt*, indicium *nt*
vestment *n* vestīmentum *nt*
vesture *n* vestis *f*
vetch *n* vicia *f*

veteran *adj* veterānus ◆ *n* (MIL) veterānus *m*; (*fig*) veterātor *m*
veto *n* interdictum *nt*; (*tribune's*) intercessiō *f* ◆ *vt* interdīcere (*dat*); (*tribune*) intercēdere (*dat*)
vex *vt* vexāre, sollicitāre, stomachum movēre (*dat*); **be vexed** aegrē ferre, stomachārī
vexation *n* (*caused*) molestia *f*; (*felt*) dolor *m*, stomachus *m*
vexatious *adj* odiōsus, molestus
vexatiously *adv* molestē
vexed *adj* īrātus; (*question*) anceps
via *prep* per (*acc*)
viaduct *n* pōns *m*
viands *n* cibus *m*
vibrate *vi* vībrāre, tremere
vibration *n* tremor *m*
vicarious *adj* vicārius
vice *n* (*general*) prāvitās *f*, perditī mōrēs *mpl*; (*particular*) vitium *nt*, flāgitium *nt*; (*clamp*) fībula *f*
viceroy *n* prōcūrātor *m*
vicinity *n* vīcīnia *f*, vīcīnitās *f*
vicious *adj* prāvus, vitiōsus, flāgitiōsus; (*temper*) contumāx
viciously *adv* flāgitiōsē; contumāciter
vicissitude *n* vicissitūdō *f*; **vicissitudes** *pl* vicēs *fpl*
victim *n* victima *f*, hostia *f*; (*fig*) piāculum *nt*; (*exploited*) praeda *f*; **be the ~ of** labōrāre ex; **fall a ~ to** morī (*abl*); (*trickery*) circumvenīrī (*abl*)
victimize *vt* nocēre (*dat*), circumvenīre
victor *n* victor *m*
victorious *adj* victor *m*, victrīx *f*; **be ~** vincere
victory *n* victōria *f*; **win a ~** victōriam reportāre; **win a ~ over** vincere, superāre
victory message *n* laureātae litterae *fpl*
victory parade *n* triumphus *m*
victual *vt* rem frūmentāriam suppeditāre (*dat*)
victualler *n* caupō *m*; (MIL) frūmentārius *m*
victuals *n* cibus *m*; (MIL) frūmentum *nt*, commeātus *m*
vie *vi* certāre, contendere; **vie with** aemulārī
view *n* cōnspectus *m*; (*from far*) prōspectus *m*; (*from high*) dēspectus *m*; (*opinion*) sententia *f*; **exposed to ~** in mediō; **entertain a ~** sentīre; **in ~ of** propter (*acc*); **in my ~** meā sententiā, meō iūdiciō; **end in ~** prōpositum *nt*; **have in ~ spectāre**; **point of ~** iūdicium *nt*; **with a ~ to** eō cōnsiliō ut ◆ *vt* īnspicere, spectāre, intuērī
vigil *n* pervigilium *nt*; **keep a ~** vigilāre
vigilance *n* vigilantia *f*, dīligentia *f*
vigilant *adj* vigilāns, dīligēns
vigilantly *adv* vigilanter, dīligenter
vigorous *adj* ācer, vegetus, integer; (*style*) nervōsus
vigorously *adv* ācriter, strēnuē
vigour *n* vīs *f*, nervī *mpl*, integritās *f*
vile *adj* turpis, impūrus, abiectus
vilely *adv* turpiter, impūrē
vileness *n* turpitūdō *f*, impūritās *f*
vilification *n* obtrectātiō *f*, calumnia *f*
vilify *vt* obtrectāre, calumniārī, maledīcere (*dat*)
villa *n* vīlla *f*
village *n* pāgus *m*, vīcus *m*; **in every ~** pāgātim
villager *n* pāgānus *m*, vīcānus *m*
villain *n* furcifer *m*, scelerātus *m*
villainous *adj* scelestus, scelerātus, nēquam
villainously *adv* scelestē
villainy *n* scelus *nt*, nēquitia *f*

vindicate *vt* (*right*) vindicāre; (*action*) pūrgāre; (*belief*) arguere; (*person*) dēfendere, prōpugnāre prō (*abl*)
vindication *n* dēfēnsiō *f*, pūrgātiō *f*
vindicator *n* dēfēnsor *m*, prōpugnātor *m*
vindictive *adj* ultor, ulcīscendī cupidus
vine *n* vītis *f*; **wild** ~ labrusca *f*
vinedresser *n* vīnitor *m*
vinegar *n* acētum *nt*
vineyard *n* vīnea *f*, vīnētum *nt*
vintage *n* vindēmia *f*
vintner *n* vīnārius *m*
violate *vt* violāre
violation *n* violātiō *f*
violator *n* violātor *m*
violence *n* violentia *f*, vīs *f*, iniūria *f*; **do** ~ **to** violāre; **offer** ~ **to** vim īnferre (*dat*)
violent *adj* violentus, vehemēns; (*passion*) ācer, impotēns; ~ **death** nex *f*
violently *adv* vehementer, per vim
violet *n* viola *f*
viper *n* vīpera *f*
viperous *adj* (*fig*) malignus
virgin *n* virgō *f* ♦ *adj* virginālis
virginity *n* virginitās *f*
virile *adj* virīlis
virility *n* virtūs *f*
virtually *adv* rē vērā, ferē
virtue *n* virtūs *f*, honestum *nt*; (*woman's*) pudīcitia *f*; (*power*) vis *f*, potestās *f*; **by** ~ **of** ex (*abl*)
virtuous *adj* honestus, probus, integer
virtuously *adv* honestē
virulence *n* vīs *f*, vīrus *nt*
virulent *adj* acerbus
virus *n* vīrus *nt*
visage *n* ōs *n*, faciēs *f*
vis-à-vis *prep* exadversus (*acc*)
viscosity *n* lentor *m*
viscous *adj* lentus, tenāx
visible *adj* ēvidēns, cōnspicuus, manifestus; **be** ~ appārēre
visibly *adv* manifestō
vision *n* (*sense*) vīsus *m*; (*power*) aspectus *m*; (*apparition*) vīsum *nt*, vīsiō *f*; (*whim*) somnium *nt*
visionary *adj* vānus ♦ *n* somniāns *m*
visit *n* adventus *m*; (*formal*) salūtātiō *f*; (*long*) commorātiō *f*; **pay a** ~ **to** invīsere ♦ *vt* vīsere; ~ **occasionally** intervīsere; **go to** ~ invīsere
visitation *n* (*to inspect*) recēnsiō *f*; (*to punish*) animadversiō *f*
visitor *n* hospes *m*, hospita *f*; (*formal*) salūtātor *m*
visor *n* buccula *f*
vista *n* prōspectus *m*
visual *adj* oculōrum
visualize *vt* animō cernere, ante oculōs pōnere
visually *adv* oculīs
vital *adj* (*of life*) vītālis; (*essential*) necessārius, māximī mōmentī
vitality *n* vīs *f*; (*style*) sanguis *m*
vitally *adv* praecipuē, imprīmīs
vitals *n* viscera *ntpl*
vitiate *vt* corrumpere, vitiāre
vitreous *adj* vitreus
vitrify *vt* in vitrum excoquere
vituperate *vt* vituperāre, obiūrgāre
vituperation *n* vituperātiō *f*, maledicta *ntpl*

vituperative *adj* maledicus
vivacious *adj* alacer, vegetus, hilaris
vivaciously *adv* hilare
vivacity *n* alacritās *f*, hilaritās *f*
vivid *adj* vīvidus, ācer
vividly *adv* ācriter
vivify *vt* animāre
vixen *n* vulpēs *f*
vocabulary *n* verbōrum cōpia *f*
vocal *adj*: ~ **music** vōcis cantus *m*
vocation *n* officium *nt*, mūnus *nt*
vociferate *vt, vi* vōciferārī, clāmāre
vociferation *n* vōciferātiō *f*, clāmor *m*
vociferous *adj* vōciferāns
vociferously *adv* māgnīs clāmōribus
vogue *n* mōs *m*; **be in** ~ flōrēre, in honōre esse
voice *n* vōx *f* ♦ *vt* exprimere, ēloquī
void *adj* inānis, vacuus; ~ **of** expers (*gen*); **null and** ~ inritus ♦ *n* ināne *nt* ♦ *vt* ēvomere, ēmittere
volatile *adj* levis, mōbilis
volatility *n* levitās *f*
volition *n* voluntās *f*
volley *n* imber *m*
volubility *n* volūbilitās *f*
voluble *adj* volūbilis
volume *n* (*book*) liber *m*; (*mass*) mōlēs *f*; (*of sound*) māgnitūdō *f*
voluminous *adj* cōpiōsus
voluntarily *adv* ultrō, suā sponte
voluntary *adj* voluntārius; (*unpaid*) grātuītus
volunteer *n* (MIL) ēvocātus *m* ♦ *vt* ultrō offerre ♦ *vi* (MIL) nōmen dare
voluptuary *n* dēlicātus *m*, homō voluptārius *m*
voluptuous *adj* voluptārius, mollis, dēlicātus, luxuriōsus
voluptuously *adv* molliter, dēlicātē, luxuriōsē
voluptuousness *n* luxuria *f*, libīdō *f*
vomit *vt* vomere, ēvomere; ~ **up** ēvomere
voracious *adj* vorāx, edāx
voraciously *adv* avidē
voracity *n* edācitās *f*, gula *f*
vortex *n* vertex *m*, turbō *m*
votary *n* cultor *m*
vote *n* suffrāgium *nt*; (*opinion*) sententia *f*; **take a** ~ (*senate*) discessiōnem facere ♦ *vi* (*election*) suffrāgium ferre; (*judge*) sententiam ferre; (*senator*) cēnsēre; ~ **against** (*bill*) antīquāre; ~ **for** (*candidate*) suffrāgārī (*dat*); (*senator's motion*) discēdere in sententiam (*gen*) ♦ *vt* (*senate*) dēcernere
voter *n* suffrāgātor *m*
votive *adj* vōtīvus
vouch *vi* spondēre; ~ **for** praestāre, testificārī
voucher *n* (*person*) auctor *m*; (*document*) auctōritās *f*
vouchsafe *vt* concēdere
vow *n* vōtum *nt*; (*promise*) fidēs *f* ♦ *vt* vovēre; (*promise*) spondēre
vowel *n* vōcālis *f*
voyage *n* nāvigātiō *f*, cursus *m* ♦ *vi* nāvigāre
vulgar *adj* (*common*) vulgāris; (*low*) plēbēius, sordidus, īnsulsus
vulgarity *n* sordēs *fpl*, īnsulsitās *f*
vulgarly *adv* vulgō; īnsulsē
vulnerable *adj* nūdus; (*fig*) obnoxius; **be** ~ vulnerārī posse
vulture *n* vultur *m*; (*fig*) vulturius *m*

wad *n* massa *f*
wade *vi* per vada īre; **~ across** vadō trānsīre
waft *vt* ferre, vehere
wag *n* facētus homō *m*, ioculātor *m* ♦ *vt* movēre, mōtāre, agitāre ♦ *vi* movērī, agitārī
wage *n* mercēs *f*; (*pl*) mercēs *f*, manupretium *nt*; (*fig*) pretium *nt*, praemium *nt* ♦ *vt* gerere; **~ war on** bellum īnferre (*dat*)/gerere
wager *n* spōnsiō *f* ♦ *vi* spōnsiōnem facere ♦ *vt* dēpōnere, oppōnere
waggery *n* facētiae *fpl*
waggish *adj* facētus, rīdiculus
waggle *vt* agitāre, mōtāre
wagon *n* plaustrum *nt*, carrus *m*
waif *n* inops *m/f*
wail *n* ēiulātus *m* ♦ *vi* ēiulāre, dēplōrāre, lāmentārī
wailing *n* plōrātus *m*, lāmentātiō *f*
waist *n* medium corpus *nt*; **hold by the ~** medium tenēre
wait *n*: **have a long ~** diū exspectāre; **lie in ~** īnsidiārī ♦ *vi* manēre, opperīrī, exspectāre; **~ for** exspectāre; **~ upon** (*accompany*) adsectārī, dēdūcere; (*serve*) famulārī (*dat*); (*visit*) salūtāre
waiter *n* famulus *m*, minister *m*
waive *vt* dēpōnere, remittere
wake *vt* excitāre, suscitāre ♦ *vi* expergīscī ♦ *n* vestīgia *ntpl*; **in the ~** pōne, ā tergō; **follow in the ~ of** vestīgiīs īnstāre (*gen*)
wakeful *adj* vigil
wakefulness *n* vigilantia *f*
waken *vt* excitāre ♦ *vi* expergīscī
walk *n* (*act*) ambulātiō *f*, deambulātiō *f*; (*gait*) incessus *m*; (*place*) ambulātiō *f*, xystus *m*; **~ of life** status *m*; **go for a ~** spatiārī, deambulāre ♦ *vi* ambulāre, īre, gradī; (*with dignity*) incēdere; **~ about** inambulāre; **~ out** ēgredī
wall *n* mūrus *m*; (*indoors*) pariēs *m*; (*afield*) māceria *f*; **walls** *pl* (*of town*) moenia *ntpl* ♦ *vt* mūnīre, saepīre; **~ up** inaedificāre
wallet *n* pēra *f*
wallow *vi* volūtārī
walnut *n* iūglāns *f*
wan *adj* pallidus
wand *n* virga *f*
wander *vi* errāre, vagārī; (*in mind*) ālūcinārī; **~ over** pervagārī
wanderer *n* errō *m*, vagus *m*
wandering *adj* errābundus, vagus ♦ *n* errātiō *f*, error *m*
wane *vi* dēcrēscere, senēscere

want *n* inopia *f*, indigentia *f*, egestās *f*, pēnūria *f*; (*craving*) dēsīderium *nt*; **in ~** inops; **be in ~** egēre ♦ *vt* (*lack*) carēre (*abl*), egēre (*abl*), indigēre (*abl*); (*miss*) dēsīderāre; (*wish*) velle
wanting *adj* (*missing*) absēns; (*defective*) vitiōsus, parum idōneus; **be ~** deesse, dēficere ♦ *prep* sine (*abl*)
wanton *adj* lascīvus, libīdinōsus ♦ *vi* lascīvīre
wantonly *adv* lascīvē, libīdinōsē
war *n* bellum *nt*; **regular war** iūstum bellum; **fortunes of war** fortūna bellī; **outbreak of war** exortum bellum; **be at war with** bellum gerere cum; **declare war** bellum indīcere; **discontinue war** bellum dēpōnere; **end war** (*by agreement*) compōnere; (*by victory*) cōnficere; **enter war** bellum suscipere; **give the command of a war** bellum mandāre; **make war** bellum īnferre; **prolong a war** bellum trahere; **provoke war** bellum movēre; **wage war** bellum īnferre; **wage war on** bellum īnferre (*dat*) ♦ *vi* bellāre
warble *vi* canere, cantāre
warbling *adj* garrulus, canōrus ♦ *n* cantus *m*
war cry *n* clāmor *m*
ward *n* custōdia *f*; (*person*) pupillus *m*, pupilla *f*; (*of town*) regiō *f* ♦ *vt*: **~ off** arcēre, dēfendere, prōpulsāre
warden *n* praefectus *m*
warder *n* custōs *m*
wardrobe *n* vestiārium *nt*
wardship *n* tūtēla *f*
warehouse *n* apothēca *f*
wares *n* merx *f*, mercēs *fpl*
warfare *n* bellum *nt*
warily *adv* prōvidenter, cautē
wariness *n* circumspectiō *f*, cautiō *f*
warlike *adj* ferōx, bellicōsus
warm *adj* calidus; (*fig*) ācer, studiōsus; **be ~** calēre; **become ~** calefierī, incalēscere; **keep ~** fovēre; **~ baths** thermae *fpl* ♦ *vt* calefacere, tepefacere, fovēre ♦ *vi* calefierī
warmly *adv* (*fig*) ferventer, studiōsē
warmth *n* calor *m*
warn *vt* monēre, admonēre
warning *n* (*act*) monitiō *f*; (*particular*) monitum *nt*; (*lesson*) documentum *nt*, exemplum *nt*
warp *n* stāmina *ntpl* ♦ *vt* dēprāvāre, īnflectere
warped *adj* (*fig*) prāvus
warrant *n* auctōritās *f* ♦ *vt* praestāre
warranty *n* cautiō *f*
warrior *n* bellātor *m*, bellatrīx *f*, mīles *m*
warship *n* nāvis longa *f*

wart n verrūca f
wary adj prōvidus, cautus, prūdēns
wash vt lavāre; (of rivers, sea) adluere; ~ **away**
dīluere; ~ **clean** abluere; ~ **out** (fig) ēluere ♦ vi
lavārī
washbasin n aquālis m
washing n lavātiō f
wasp n vespa f
waspish adj acerbus, stomachōsus
waste n dētrīmentum nt, intertrīmentum nt;
(extravagance) effūsiō f; (of time) iactūra f; (land)
sōlitūdō f, vastitās f ♦ adj dēsertus, vastus; **lay**
~ vastāre, populārī ♦ vt cōnsūmere, perdere,
dissipāre; (time) terere, absūmere; (with disease)
absūmere ♦ vi: ~ **away** tābēscere, intābēscere
wasteful adj prōdigus, profūsus; (destructive)
damnōsus, perniciōsus
wastefully adv prōdigē
wasting n tābēs f
wastrel n nebulō m
watch n (being awake) vigilia f; (sentry) statiō
f, excubiae fpl; **keep** ~ excubāre; **keep** ~ **on**,
keep ~ **over** custōdīre, invigilāre (dat); **set**
~ vigiliās dispōnere; **at the third** ~ ad tertiam
būcinam ♦ vt (guard) custōdīre; (observe) intuērī,
observāre, spectāre ad (acc); ~ **for** observāre,
exspectāre; (enemy) īnsidiārī (dat); ~ **closely**
adservāre
watcher n custōs m
watchful adj vigilāns
watchfully adv vigilanter
watchfulness n vigilantia f
watchman n custōs m, vigil m
watchtower n specula f
watchword n tessera f, signum nt
water n aqua f; **deep** ~ gurges m; **fresh** ~ aqua
dulcis; **high** ~ māximus aestus; **running**
~ aqua prōfluēns; **still** ~ stagnum nt; **fetch**
~ aquārī; **fetching** ~ aquātiō f; **cold** ~ frīgida f;
hot ~ calida f; **troubled waters** (fig) turbidae
rēs ♦ vt (land) inrigāre; (animal) adaquāre
water carrier n aquātor m; (Zodiac) Aquārius m
water clock n clepsydra f
waterfall n cataracta f
watering n aquātiō f; ~ **place** n (spa) aquae fpl
water pipe n fistula f
watershed n aquārum dīvortium nt
water snake n hydrus m
water spout n prēstēr m
watery adj aquōsus, ūmidus
wattle n crātēs f
wave n unda f, fluctus m ♦ vt agitāre, iactāre ♦ vi
fluctuāre
waver vi dubitāre, fluctuārī, nūtāre, vacillāre,
labāre, inclīnāre
wavering adj dubius, incōnstāns ♦ n dubitātiō
f, fluctuātiō f
wavy adj undātus; (hair) crispus
wax n cēra f ♦ vt cērāre ♦ vi crēscere
waxen adj cēreus
waxy adj cērōsus
way n via f; (route) iter nt; (method) modus m,
ratiō f; (habit) mōs m; (ship's) impetus m; **all
the way to, all the way from** usque ad, ab; **by
the way** (parenthesis) etenim; **get in the way
of** intervenīre (dat), impedīre; **get under way**
nāvem solvere; **give way** (structure) labāre; (MIL)
cēdere; **give way to** indulgēre (dat); **go out of
one's way to do** ultrō facere; **have one's way**
imperāre; **in a way** quōdam modō; **in this
way** ad hunc modum; **it is not my way to** nōn
meum est (inf); **lose one's way** deerrāre; **make
way** dē viā dēcēdere; **make way for** cēdere (dat);
make one's way into sē īnsinuāre in (acc); **on
the way** inter viam, in itinere; **out of the way**
āvius, dēvius; (fig) reconditus; **pave the way for**
praeparāre; **put out of the way** tollere; **right of
way** iter; **stand in the way of** obstāre (dat); **that
way** illāc; **this way** hāc; **ways and means** opēs
fpl, reditūs mpl
wayfarer n viātor m
waylay vt īnsidiārī (dat)
wayward adj protervus, incōnstāns, levis
waywardness n libīdō f, levitās f
we pron nōs
weak adj dēbilis, īnfirmus, imbēcillus; (health)
invalidus; (argument) levis, tenuis; (senses) hebes
weaken vt dēbilitāre, īnfirmāre; (resistance)
frangere, labefactāre ♦ vi imminuī, labāre
weakling n imbēcillus m
weakly adj invalidus, aeger ♦ adv īnfirmē
weak-minded adj mollis
weakness n dēbilitās f, īnfirmitās f; (of argument)
levitās f; (of mind) mollitia f, imbēcillitās f; (flaw)
vitium nt; **have a** ~ **for** delectārī (abl)
weal n salūs f, rēs f; (mark of blow) vībex f; **the
common** ~ rēs pūblica f
wealth n dīvitiae fpl, opēs fpl; **a** ~ **of** cōpia f,
abundantia f
wealthy adj dīves, opulentus, locuplēs, beātus;
make ~ locuplētāre, dītāre; (a husband) ♦ praedīves
wean vt lacte dēpellere; (fig) dēdocēre
weapon n tēlum nt
wear n (dress) habitus m; ~ **and tear**
intertrīmentum nt ♦ vt gerere, gestāre; (rub)
terere, conterere; ~ **out** cōnficere ♦ vi dūrāre;
~ **off** minuī
wearily adv cum lassitūdine, languidē
weariness n fatīgātiō f, lassitūdō f; (of) taedium
nt
wearisome adj molestus, operōsus, labōriōsus
weary adj lassus, fessus, dēfessus, fatīgātus ♦ vt
fatīgāre; **I am** ~ **of** me taedet (gen)
weasel n mustēla f
weather n tempestās f, caelum nt; **fine**
~ serēnitās f ♦ vt superāre
weather-beaten adj tempestāte dūrātus
weave vt texere
weaver n textor m, textrix f
web n (on loom) tēla f; (spider's) arāneum nt
wed vt (a wife) dūcere; (a husband) nūbere (dat)
wedding n nūptiae fpl
wedge n cuneus m ♦ vt cuneāre
wedlock n mātrimōnium nt
weed n inūtilis herba f ♦ vt runcāre
weedy adj exīlis
week n hebdomas f
ween vt arbitrārī, putāre
weep vi flēre, lacrimārī; ~ **for** dēflēre, dēplōrāre
weeping n flētus m, lacrimae fpl
weevil n curculiō m
weft n subtēmen nt; (web) tēla f

weigh *vt* pendere, exāmināre; (*anchor*) tollere; (*thought*) ponderāre; ~ **down** dēgravāre, opprimere; ~ **out** expendere ♦ *vi* pendere
weight *n* pondus *nt*; (*influence*) auctōritās *f*, mōmentum *nt*; (*burden*) onus *nt*; **have great** ~ (*fig*) multum valēre; **he is worth his** ~ **in gold** aurō contrā cōnstat
weightily *adv* graviter
weightiness *n* gravitās *f*
weighty *adj* gravis
weir *n* mōlēs *f*
weird *adj* mōnstruōsus ♦ *n* fātum *nt*
welcome *adj* grātus, exspectātus, acceptus ♦ *n* salūtātiō *f* ♦ *vt* excipere, salvēre iubēre ♦ *interj* salvē, salvēte
welfare *n* salūs *f*
well *n* puteus *m*; (*spring*) fōns *m* ♦ *vi* scatēre ♦ *adj* salvus, sānus, valēns; **be** ~ valēre ♦ *adv* bene, probē; (*transition*) age ♦ *interj* (*concession*) estō; (*surprise*) heia; ~ **and good** estō; ~ **begun is half done** dīmidium factī quī coepit habet; ~ **done!** probē!; ~ **met** opportūnē venis; ~ **on in years** aetāte prōvectus; **all is** ~ bene habet; **as** ~ etiam; **as** ~ **as** cum ... tum, et ... et; **let** ~ **alone** quiēta nōn movēre; **take** ~ in bonam partem accipere; **wish** ~ favēre (*dat*); **you may** ~ **say** iūre dīcis; **you might as** ~ **say** illud potius dīcās
well-advised *adj* prudēns
well-behaved *adj* modestus
wellbeing *n* salūs *f*
well-bred *adj* generōsus, līberālis
well-disposed *adj* benevolus, amīcus
well-informed *adj* ērudītus
well-judged *adj* ēlegāns
well-knit *adj* dēnsus
well-known *adj* nōtus, nōbilis; (*saying*) trītus
well-nigh *adv* paene
well-off *adj* beātus, fortūnātus; **you are** ~ bene est tibī
well-read *adj* litterātus
well-timed *adj* opportūnus
well-to-do *adj* beātus, dīves
well-tried *adj* probātus
well-turned *adj* rotundus
well-versed *adj* perītus, expertus
well-wisher *n* amīcus *m*, benevolēns *m*
well-worn *adj* trītus
welter *n* turba *f* ♦ *vi* miscērī, turbārī; (*wallow*) volūtārī
wench *n* muliercula *f*
wend *vt*: ~ **one's way** īre, sē ferre
west *n* occidēns *m*, sōlis occāsus *m* ♦ *adj* occidentālis
westerly, western *adj* occidentālis
westwards *adv* ad occidentem
west wind *n* Favōnius *m*
wet *adj* ūmidus, madidus; **be wet** madēre; **wet weather** pluvia *f* ♦ *vt* madefacere
wether *n* vervēx *m*
wet nurse *n* nūtrīx *f*
whack *n* ictus *m*, plāga *f* ♦ *vt* pulsāre, verberāre
whale *n* bālaena *f*
wharf *n* crepīdō *f*
what *pron* (*interrog*) quid; (*adj*) quī; (*relat*) id quod, ea quae; ~ **kind of?** quālis

whatever, whatsoever *pron* quidquid, quodcumque; (*adj*) quīcumque
wheat *n* trīticum *nt*
wheaten *adj* trīticeus
wheedle *vt* blandīrī, pellicere
wheedling *adj* blandus ♦ *n* blanditiae *fpl*
wheel *n* rota *f* ♦ *vt* flectere, circumagere ♦ *vi* sē flectere, circumagī
wheelbarrow *n* pabō *m*
wheeze *vi* anhēlāre
whelm *vt* obruere
whelp *n* catulus *m*
when *adv* (*interrog*) quandō, quō tempore ♦ *conj* (*time*) cum (*subj*), ubī (+*indic*)
whence *adv* unde
whenever *conj* quotiēns, utcumque, quandocumque, cum (+*perf indic/pluperf indic*); (*as soon as*) simul āc
where *adv* ubī; (*to*) quō; ~ ... **from** unde; ~ **to** quo (*interrog and relat*)
whereabouts *n* locus *m*; **your** ~ quō in locō sīs
whereas *conj* quōniam; (*contrast*) *not expressed*
whereby *adv* quō pāctō, quō
wherefore *adv* (*interrog*) quārē, cūr; (*relat*) quamobrem, quāpropter
wherein *adv* in quō, in quā
whereof *adv* cūius, cūius reī
whereon *adv* in quō, in quā
whereupon *adv* quō factō
wherever *conj* ubiubī, quācumque
wherewith *adv* quī, cum quō
wherry *n* linter *f*
whet *vt* acuere; (*fig*) exacuere
whether *conj* (*interrog*) utrum; (*single question*) num; (*condition*) sīve, seu; ~ ... **or** utrum ... an (*in indir question*); (*in cond clauses*) seu (sīve) ... seu (sīve); ~ ... **not** utrum ... necne (*in indir question*)
whetstone *n* cōs *f*
whey *n* serum *nt*
which *pron* (*interrog*) quis; (*of two*) uter; (*relat*) quī ♦ *adj* quī; (*of two*) uter
whichever *pron* quisquis, quīcumque; (*of two*) utercumque
whiff *n* odor *m*
while *n* spatium *nt*, tempus *nt*; **for a** ~ parumper; **a little** ~ paulisper; **a long** ~ diū; **it is worth** ~ expedit, operae pretium est; **once in a** ~ interdum ♦ *conj* (*during the time that*) dum (+ *pres indic*); (*all the time that*) dum (+*imperf indic*) ♦ *vt*: ~ **away** dēgere, fallere
whilst *conj* dum
whim *n* libīdō *f*, arbitrium *nt*
whimper *n* vāgītus *m* ♦ *vi* vāgīre
whimsical *adj* facētus, īnsolēns
whimsically *adv* facētē
whimsy *n* dēliciae *fpl*, facētiae *fpl*
whine *n* quiritātiō *f* ♦ *vi* quiritāre
whinny *n* hinnītus *m* ♦ *vi* hinnīre
whip *n* flagellum *nt*, flagrum *nt* ♦ *vt* flagellāre, verberāre
whirl *n* turbō *m* ♦ *vt* intorquēre, contorquēre ♦ *vi* contorquērī
whirlpool *n* vertex *m*, vōragō *f*
whirlwind *n* turbō *m*

whisper n susurrus m ◆ vt, vi susurrāre, īnsusurrāre; ~ **to** ad aurem admonēre, in aurem dīcere

whistle n (instrument) fistula f; (sound) sībilus m ◆ vi sībilāre

white adj albus; (shining) candidus; (complexion) pallidus; (hair) cānus; **turn ~** exalbēscere ◆ n album nt; (egg) albūmen nt

white-hot adj: **to be ~** excandēscere

whiten vt dealbāre ◆ vi albēscere

whiteness n candor m

whitewash n albārium nt ◆ vt dealbāre

whither adv quō; **whithersoever** quōcumque

whitish adj albulus

whizz n strīdor m ◆ vi strīdere, increpāre

who pron quis; (relat) quī

whoever pron quisquis, quīcumque

whole adj tōtus, cūnctus; (unhurt) integer, incolumis; (healthy) sānus ◆ n tōtum nt, summa f, ūniversitās f; **on the ~** plērumque

wholehearted adj studiōsissimus

wholeheartedly adv ex animō

wholesale adj māgnus, cōpiōsus; ~ **business** negōtiātiō f; ~ **dealer** mercātor m, negōtiātor m

wholesome adj salūtāris, salūbris

wholesomeness n salūbritās f

wholly adv omnīnō, tōtus

whoop n ululātus m ◆ vi ululāre

whose pron cūius

why adv cūr, quārē, quamobrem, qua de causa

wick n mergulus m

wicked adj improbus, scelestus; (to gods, kin, country) impius

wickedly adv improbē, scelestē, impiē

wickedness n improbitās f, scelus nt, impietās f

wicker adj vīmineus ◆ n vīmen nt

wide adj lātus, amplus; **be ~ of** aberrāre ab ◆ adv lātē; **far and ~** longē lātēque

widely adv lātē; (among people) vulgō

widen vt laxāre, dīlātāre

widespread adj effūsus, vulgātus

widow n vidua f

widowed adj viduus, orbus

widower n viduus m

widowhood n viduitās f

width n lātitūdō f, amplitūdō f

wield vt tractāre, gestāre, ūtī (abl)

wife n uxor f

wifely adj uxōrius

wig n capillāmentum nt

wild adj ferus, indomitus, saevus; (plant) agrestis; (land) incultus; (temper) furibundus, impotens, āmēns; (shot) temerārius; ~ **state** feritās f

wild beast n fera f

wilderness n sōlitūdō f, loca dēserta ntpl

wildly adv saevē

wildness n feritās f

wile n dolus m, ars f, fraus f

wilful adj pervicāx, contumāx; (action) cōnsultus

wilfully adv contumāciter; cōnsultō

wilfulness n pervicācia f, libīdō f

wilily adv astūtē, vafrē

wiliness n astūtia f

will n (faculty) voluntās f, animus m; (intent) cōnsilium nt; (decision) arbitrium nt; (of gods) nūtus m; (document) testāmentum nt; ~ **and pleasure** libīdō f; **against one's ~** invītus; **at ~** ad libīdinem suam; **good ~** studium nt; **ill ~** invidia f; **with a ~** summō studiō; **without making a ~** intestātus, intestātō ◆ vt (future) velle; (legacy) lēgāre; **as you ~** ut libet

willing adj libēns, parātus; **be ~** velle; **not be ~** nōlle

willingly adv libenter

willingness n voluntās f

willow n salix f ◆ adj salignus

willowy adj gracilis

wilt vi flaccēscere

wily adj astūtus, vafer, callidus

wimple n mitra f

win vt ferre, obtinēre, adipisci; (after effort) auferre; (victory) reportāre; (fame) cōnsequī, adsequī; (friends) sibī conciliāre; **win the day** vincere; **win over** dēlēnire, conciliāre ◆ vi vincere

wince vi resilīre

winch n māchina f, sucula f

wind¹ n ventus m; (north) aquilō m; (south) auster m; (east) eurus m; (west) favōnius m; **I get ~ of** subolet mihī; **run before the ~** vento sē dare; **take the ~ out of (someone's) sails** ad inritum redigere; **there is something in the ~** nescioquid olet; **which way the ~ blows** quōmodo sē rēs habeat

wind² vt torquēre; ~ **round** intorquēre ◆ vi flectī, sinuāre; ~ **up** (speech) perōrāre

windbag n verbōsus m

winded adj anhēlāns

windfall n repentīnum bonum nt

winding adj flexuōsus, tortuōsus ◆ n flexiō f, flexus m; **windings** pl (speech) ambāgēs fpl

windlass n māchina f, sucula f

window n fenestra f

windpipe n aspera artēria f

windward adj ad ventum conversus ◆ adv: **to ~** ventum versus

windy adj ventōsus

wine n vīnum nt; (new) mustum nt; (undiluted) merum nt

winebibber n vīnōsus m

wine cellar n apothēca f

wine merchant n vīnārius m

wine press n prēlum nt

wing n āla f; (MIL) cornū nt, āla f; (of bird) penna f; **take ~** ēvolāre; **take under one's ~** patrōnus fierī (gen), clientem habēre, in custōdiam recipere

winged adj ālātus, pennātus, volucer

wink n nictus m ◆ vi nictāre; ~ **at** cōnīvēre (dat)

winner n victor m

winning adj blandus, iūcundus

winningly adv blandē, iūcundē

winning post n mēta f

winnings n lucra ntpl

winnow vt ventilāre; (fig) excutere

winnowing-fan n vannus f

winsome adj blandus, suāvis

winter n hiems f; (mid) brūma f ◆ adj hiemālis, hībernus ◆ vi hībernāre

winter quarters n hīberna ntpl

wintry adj hiemālis, hībernus

wipe vt dētergēre; ~ **away** abstergēre; ~ **dry** siccāre; ~ **off** dētergēre; ~ **out** dēlēre; ~ **the nose** ēmungere

wire n fīlum aēneum nt

wiry adj nervōsus

wisdom n sapientia f; (in action) prūdentia f; (in judgment) cōnsilium nt

wise adj sapiēns, prūdēns

wisely adv sapienter, prūdenter

wish n optātum nt, vōtum nt; (for something missing) dēsīderium nt; **wishes** pl (greeting) salūs f ♦ vt optāre, cupere, velle; ~ **for** exoptāre, expetere, dēsīderāre; ~ **good-day** salvēre iubēre; **as you** ~ ut libet; **I** ~ **I could** utinam possim

wishful adj cupidus

wishing n optātiō f

wisp n manipulus m

wistful adj dēsīderī plenus

wistfully adv cum dēsīderiō

wistfulness n dēsīderium nt

wit n (humour) facētiae fpl, salēs mpl; (intellect) argūtiae fpl, ingenium nt; **caustic wit** dicācitās f; **be at one's wits' end** valdē haerēre; **be out of one's wits** dēlīrāre; **have one's wits about one** prūdens esse; **to wit** nempe, dīcō

witch n sāga f, strīga f

witchcraft n veneficium nt, magicae artēs fpl

with prep (person) cum (abl); (thing) abl; (in company) apud (acc); (fight) cum (abl), contrā (acc); **be angry** ~ īrāscī (dat); **begin** ~ incipere ab; **rest** ~ esse penes (acc); **end** ~ dēsinere in (acc); **what do you want** ~ **me?** quid mē vis?

withdraw vt dēdūcere, dētrahere; (fig) āvocāre; (words) retractāre ♦ vi discēdere, abscēdere, sē recipere, sē subdūcere

withdrawal n (MIL) receptus m

wither vt torrēre ♦ vi dēflōrēscere

withered adj marcidus

withhold vt abstinēre, retinēre, supprimere

within adv intus, intrā; (motion) intrō ♦ prep intrā (acc), in (abl)

without adv extrā, forīs; **from** ~ extrīnsecus; **be** ~ vacāre (abl), carēre (abl), expers (gen); **I admire** ~ **fearing** ita laudō ut nōn timeam; ~ **breaking the law** salvīs lēgibus; **you cannot see** ~ **admiring** vidēre nōn potes quīn laudēs; **you cannot appreciate** ~ **seeing for yourself** aestimāre nōn potes nisī ipse vīderis; ~ **doubt** sine dubiō; ~ **the order of** iniūssū (gen); ~ **striking a blow** rē integrā

withstand vt resistere (dat), obsistere (dat); (attack) ferre, sustinēre

withy n vīmen nt

witless adj excors, ineptus, stultus

witness n (person) testis m/f; (to a document) obsignātor m; (spectator) arbiter m; (evidence) testimōnium nt; **call as** ~ antestārī; **bear** ~ testificārī; **call to** ~ testārī ♦ vt testificārī; (see) vidēre, intuērī

witnessing n testificātiō f

witticism n dictum nt; **witticisms** pl facētiae fpl

wittily adv facētē, salsē

wittingly adv sciēns

witty adj facētus, argūtus, salsus; (caustic) dicāx

wizard n magus m, veneficus m

wizardry n magicae artēs fpl

wizened adj marcidus

woad n vitrum nt

wobble vi titubāre; (structure) labāre

woe n luctus m, dolor m, aerumna f; **woes** pl mala ntpl, calamitātēs fpl; **woe to** vae (dat)

woeful adj tristis, maestus, aerumnōsus

woefully adv triste, miserē

wolf n lupus m, lupa f; **wolf's** lupīnus

woman n fēmina f, mulier f; **old** ~ anus f; **married** ~ mātrōna f; **woman's** muliebris

womanish adj muliebris, effēminātus

womanly adj muliebris

womb n uterus m

wonder n admīrātiō f; (of a thing) admīrābilitās f; (thing) mīrāculum nt, mīrum nt, portentum nt ♦ vi mīrārī; ~ **at** admīrārī, dēmīrārī

wonderful adj mīrus, mīrābilis, admīrābilis; ~ **to relate** mīrābile dictu

wonderfully adv mīrē, mīrābiliter, mīrum quantum

wonderfulness n admīrābilitās f

wondering adj mīrābundus

wonderment n admīrātiō f

wondrous adj mīrus, mīrābilis

wont n mōs m, cōnsuētūdō f

wonted adj solitus

woo vt petere

wood n silva f, nemus nt; (material) lignum nt; **gather** ~ lignārī; **touch wood!** absit verbō invidia ♦ adj ligneus

woodcutter n lignātor m

wooded adj silvestris, saltuōsus

wooden adj ligneus

woodland n silvae fpl ♦ adj silvestris

woodman n lignātor m

wood nymph n dryas f

woodpecker n pīcus m

wood pigeon n palumbēs m/f

woodwork n tigna ntpl

woodworker n faber tignārius m

woody adj silvestris, silvōsus

wooer n procus m

woof n subtēmen nt

wool n lāna f

woollen adj lāneus

woolly adj lānātus

word n verbum nt; (spoken) vōx f; (message) nūntius m; (promise) fidēs f; (term) vocābulum nt; ~ **for** ~ ad verbum, verbum ē verbō; **a** ~ **with you!** paucīs tē volō!; **break one's** ~ fidem fallere; **bring back** ~ renūntiāre; **by** ~ **of mouth** ōre, verbō; **fair words** blanditiae fpl; **give one's** ~ fidem dare; **have a** ~ **with** colloquī cum; **have words with** iūrgāre cum; **have a good** ~ **for** laudāre; **in a** ~ ūnō verbō, dēnique; **keep one's** ~ fidem praestāre; **of few words** taciturnus; **take at one's** ~ crēdere (dat)

wording n verba ntpl

wordy adj verbōsus

work n (energy) labor m, opera f; (task) opus nt; (thing done) opus nt; (book) liber m; (trouble) negōtium nt; **works** (MIL) opera ntpl; (mechanism) māchinātiō f; (place) officīna f ♦ vi labōrāre ♦ vt (men) exercēre; (metal) fabricārī; (soil) subigere; (results) efficere; ~ **at** ēlabōrāre; ~ **in** admiscēre;

~ **off** exhaurire; ~ **out** ēlabōrāre; ~ **up** (*emotion*) efferre; ~ **one's way up** prōficere ♦ *vi* gerī

workaday *adj* cottīdiānus

workhouse *n* ergastulum *nt*

working *n* (*mechanism*) māchinātiō *f*; (*soil*) cultus *m*

workman *n* (*unskilled*) operārius *m*; (*skilled*) opifex *m*, faber *m*; **workmen** operae *fpl*

workmanship *n* ars *f*, artificium *nt*

workshop *n* fabrica *f*, officīna *f*

world *n* (*universe*) mundus *m*; (*earth*) orbis terrārum *m*; (*nature*) rērum nātūra *f*; (*mankind*) hominēs *mpl*; (*masses*) vulgus *nt*; **of the** ~ mundānus; **man of the** ~ homō urbānus *m*; **best in the** ~ rērum optimus, omnium optimus; **where in the** ~ ubī gentium

worldliness *n* quaestūs studium *nt*

worldly *adj* quaestuī dēditus

worm *n* vermis *m* ♦ *vi*: ~ **one's way** sē īnsinuāre

worm-eaten *adj* vermiculōsus

wormwood *n* absinthium *nt*

worn *adj* trītus

worried *adj* sollicitus, anxius

worry *n* cūra *f*, sollicitūdō *f* ♦ *vi* sollicitārī ♦ *vt* vexāre, sollicitāre; (*of dogs*) lacerāre

worse *adj* pēior, dēterior; **grow** ~ ingravēscere; **make matters** ~ rem exasperāre ♦ *adv* pēius, dēterius

worsen *vi* ingravēscere, dēteriōr fierī

worship *n* venerātiō *f*, deōrum cultus *m*; (*rite*) sacra *ntpl*, rēs dīvīnae *fpl* ♦ *vt* adōrāre, venerārī, colere

worst *adj* pessimus, dēterrimus; ~ **enemy** inimīcissimus *m*; **endure the** ~ ultima patī ♦ *vt* vincere

worsted *n* lāna *f*

worth *n* (*value*) pretium *nt*; (*moral*) dignitās *f*, frūgālitās *f*, virtūs *f*; (*prestige*) auctōritās *f* ♦ *adj* dignus; **for all one's** ~ prō virīlī parte; **how much is it worth?** quanti vēnit?; **it is** ~ **a lot** multum valet; **it is** ~ **doing** operae pretium est

worthily *adv* dignē, meritō

worthiness *n* dignitās *f*

worthless *adj* (*person*) nēquam; (*thing*) vīlis, inānis

worthlessness *n* levitās *f*, nēquitia *f*; vīlitās *f*

worthy *adj* dignus; (*person*) frūgī, honestus; ~ **of** dignus (*abl*)

wound *n* vulnus *nt* ♦ *vt* vulnerāre; (*feelings*) offendere

wounded *adj* saucius

wrangle *n* iūrgium *nt*, rixa *f* ♦ *vi* iūrgāre, rixārī, altercārī

wrap *vt* involvere, obvolvere; ~ **round** intorquēre; ~ **up** involvere

wrapper *n* involucrum *nt*

wrapping *n* integumentum *nt*

wrath *n* īra *f*, īrācundia *f*

wrathful *adj* īrātus

wrathfully *adv* īrācundē

wreak *vt*: ~ **vengeance on** saevīre in (*acc*), ulcīscī

wreath *n* corōna *f*, sertum *nt*

wreathe *vt* (*garland*) torquēre; (*object*) corōnāre

wreck *n* naufragium *nt* ♦ *vt* frangere; (*fig*) perdere; **be wrecked** naufragium facere

wreckage *n* fragmenta *ntpl*

wrecked *adj* (*person*) naufragus; (*ship*) frāctus

wrecker *n* perditor *m*

wren *n* rēgulus *m*

wrench *vt* intorquēre, extorquēre; ~ **away** ēripere; ~ **open** effringere

wrest *vt* extorquēre

wrestle *vi* luctārī

wrestler *n* luctātor *m*, athlēta *m*

wrestling *n* luctātiō *f*

wretch *n* scelerātus *m*, nēquam homō *m*; **poor** ~ miser homō *m*

wretched *adj* īnfēlīx, miser; (*pitiful*) flēbilis

wretchedly *adv* miserē

wretchedness *n* miseria *f*; maestitia *f*

wriggle *vi* sē torquēre

wriggling *adj* sinuōsus

wright *n* faber *m*

wring *vt* torquēre; ~ **from** extorquēre

wrinkle *n* rūga *f* ♦ *vt* corrūgāre

wrinkled *adj* rūgōsus

wrist *n* prīma palmae pars *f*

writ *n* (*legal*) auctōritās *f*

write *vt* scrībere; (*book*) cōnscrībere; ~ **off** indūcere; ~ **on** īnscrībere (*dat*); ~ **out** exscrībere, dēscrībere; ~ **out in full** perscrībere

writer *n* (*lit*) scrīptor *m*, auctor *m*; (*clerk*) scrība *m*

writhe *vi* torquērī

writing *n* (*act*) scrīptiō *f*; (*result*) scrīptum *nt*

wrong *adj* falsus, perversus, prāvus; (*unjust*) iniūstus, inīquus; **be** ~, **go** ~ errāre ♦ *n* iniūria *f*, culpa *f*, noxa *f*, malum *nt*; **do** ~ peccāre, dēlinquere; **right and** ~ (*moral*) honesta ac turpia *ntpl* ♦ *vt* laedere, nocēre (*dat*); (*by deceit*) fraudāre

wrongdoer *n* maleficus *m*, scelerātus *m*

wrongdoing *n* scelus *nt*

wrongful *adj* iniūstus, iniūriosus, inīquus

wrongfully *adv* iniūriā, iniūstē, inīquē

wrong-headed *adj* perversus

wrong-headedness *n* perversitās *f*

wrongly *adv* falsō, dēprāvātē, male, perperam

wroth *adj* īrātus

wrought *adj* factus

wry *adj* dētortus; **make a wry face** ōs dūcere

wryness *n* prāvitās *f*

Yy

yacht *n* phasēlus *m*
yard *n* (*court*) ārea *f*; (*measure*) trēs pedēs
yardarm *n* antenna *f*
yarn *n* fīlum *nt*; (*story*) fābula *f*
yawn *n* hiātus *m* ♦ *vi* hiāre, ōscitāre; (*chasm*) dehiscere
ye *pron* vōs
yean *vt* parere
year *n* annus *m*; **every ~** quotannīs; **for a ~** in annum; **half ~** sēmēstre spatium *nt*; **this year's** hōrnus; **twice a ~** bis annō; **two years** biennium *nt*; **three years** triennium *nt*; **four years** quadriennium *nt*; **five years** quinquennium *nt*
yearly *adj* annuus, anniversārius ♦ *adv* quotannīs
yearn *vi*: **~ for** dēsīderāre, exoptāre
yearning *n* dēsīderium *nt*
yeast *n* fermentum *nt*
yell *n* clāmor *m*; (*of pain*) ēiulātiō *f* ♦ *vi* clāmāre, eiulāre
yellow *adj* flāvus; (*pale*) gilvus; (*deep*) fulvus; (*gold*) luteus; (*saffron*) croceus
yelp *n* gannītus *m* ♦ *vi* gannīre
yeoman *n* colōnus *m*
yes *adv* ita verō (est), māximē; (*correcting*) immo
yesterday *adv* herī ♦ *n* hesternus diēs *m*; **yesterday's** hesternus; **the day before ~** nudius tertius

yet *adv* (*contrast*) tamen, nihilōminus, attamen; (*time*) adhūc, etiam; (*with compar*) etiam; **and yet** atquī, quamquam; **as yet** adhūc; **not yet** nōndum
yew *n* taxus *f*
yield *n* fructus *m* ♦ *vt* (*crops*) ferre, efferre; (*pleasure*) adferre; (*concession*) dare, concēdere; (*surrender*) dēdere ♦ *vi* cēdere; (*surrender*) sē dēdere, sē trādere; **~ to the wishes of** mōrem gerere (*dat*), obsequī (*dat*)
yielding *adj* (*person*) facilis, obsequēns; (*thing*) mollis ♦ *n* cessiō *f*; dēditiō *f*
yoke *n* iugum *nt* ♦ *vt* iungere, coniungere
yokel *n* agrestis *m*
yolk *n* vitellus *m*
yonder *adv* illīc ♦ *adj* ille, iste
yore *n*: **of ~** quondam, ōlim
you *pron* tū, vōs
young *adj* iuvenis, adulēscēns; (*child*) parvus; **younger** iūnior, nātū minor; **youngest** nātū minimus ♦ *n* fētus *m*, pullus *m*, catulus *m*
young man *n* iuvenis *m*; adulēscēns *m*
youngster *n* puer *m*
your *adj* tuus, vester
yourself *pron* ipse
youth *n* (*age*) iuventūs *f*, adulescentia *f*; (*person*) iuvenis *m*, adulēscēns *m*; (*collective*) iuventūs *f*
youthful *adj* iuvenīlis, puerīlis
youthfully *adv* iuvenīliter

Zz

zeal *n* studium *nt*, ārdor *m*
zealot *n* studiōsus *m*, fautor *m*
zealous *adj* studiōsus, ārdēns
zealously *adv* studiōsē, ārdenter
zenith *n* vertex *m*
zephyr *n* Favōnius *m*
zero *n* nihil *nt*

zest *n* (*taste*) sapor *m*; (*fig*) gustātus *m*,
  impetus *m*
zigzag *n* ānfrāctus *m* ✦ *adj* tortuōsus
zither *n* cithara *f*
zodiac *n* signifer orbis *m*
zone *n* cingulus *m*

GRAMMAR AND VERB TABLES

INTRODUCTION

This book is designed to help pupils and students of Latin to understand the grammar of the language. For beginners, the book provides an introduction to and explanation of the basic forms. More advanced students will find it an invaluable guide for reference and revision.

All parts of speech (nouns, pronouns, adjectives etc) are treated separately and clearly explained for the benefit of learners. Differences in usages are illustrated by extensive examples from many Latin authors. American students and teachers, please note: this book is designed for use by students around the world, many of whom use British case ordering (Nom, Voc, Acc, Gen, Dat, Abl).

A special section on word order in Latin, one of the greatest problems for students and pupils, has been included to guide the learner through both simple and compound sentences.

For ease of reference, all necessary structures, such as Indirect Statement, Conditional Sentences etc, have been listed under Contents. Each is then explained, for both English and Latin usage, to show the learner how to recognize the structure and translate it into English. Further examples of all structures are provided, for practice.

Handy, practical hints are given in the section on Translation Guidelines, to highlight the more common problems that confront students, and to assist in translation.

The final part of the grammar section lists the many "false friends" or confusable words that often lead students and pupils astray when translating from Latin. This section is of particular importance for examination candidates.

Tables of regular verbs provide information on verb formation and usage, while unique verbs are given in full with their meanings. A special feature of the grammar is a list of the 400 most common verbs, both regular and irregular. Irregular parts of verbs are highlighted and the conjugation number of each listed, so that by referring to the table indicated by this number, any part of the verb may be deduced.

Contents

Abbreviations used

abl	ablative	**nt, neut**	neuter
acc	accusative	**nom**	nominative
adv	adverb	**pl**	plural
conj	conjunction	**plup**	pluperfect
dat	dative	**prep**	preposition
dep	deponent	**pron**	pronoun
f, fem	feminine	**sing**	singular
gen	genitive	**voc**	vocative
indic	indicative		
intrans	intransitive		
m, masc	masculine		

Nouns

A noun is the name of a person, thing or quality.

Gender

- In Latin, as in English, the gender of nouns, representing persons or living creatures, is decided by meaning. Nouns denoting male people and animals are masculine

vir	a man
Gaius	Gaius
cervus	stag

- Nouns denoting female people and animals are feminine

femina	a woman
Cornelia	Cornelia
cerva	doe/hind

- However, the gender of things or qualities in Latin is decided by the ending of the noun.

  anulus (ring) *masc*
  sapientia (wisdom) *fem*
  barba (beard) *fem*
  gaudium (joy) *nt*

Number

- Nouns may be singular, denoting one, or plural, denoting two or more. This is shown by change of ending

SINGULAR	*PLURAL*
terr**a** (land)	terr**ae**
mod**us** (way)	mod**i**
op**us** (work)	op**era**

Cases

- There are six cases in Latin, expressing the relationship of the noun to the other words in the sentence.

  Nominative
  the subject of the verb: **Caesar** died

  Vocative
  addressing someone/thing: Welcome, **Alexander**

  Accusative
  the object of the verb: The cat ate **the mouse**

  Genitive
  belonging to someone/thing: The home **of my friend**

  Dative
  the indirect object of the verb: I gave the book **to my son**

  Ablative
  says by, with or from whom/what: This was agreed **by the Senate**

Declensions

- Latin nouns are divided into five groups or declensions by the ending of their stems. Each declension has six cases, both singular and plural, denoted by different endings. The endings of the genitive singular case help to distinguish the different declensions.

	STEMS	GENITIVE SINGULAR
1st Declension	-a	-ae
2nd Declension	-ŏ or u	-ī
3rd Declension	-i, u, consonant	-is
4th Declension	-ŭ	-ŭs
5th Declension	-ē	-ēi

First Declension

- All nouns end in **-a** in the nominative case and all are feminine except when the noun indicates a male, *eg* **poēta** (a poet), **agricola** (a farmer), etc.

	SINGULAR		PLURAL	
Nom	femina	the woman	feminae	women
Voc	femina	o woman	feminae	o women
Acc	feminam	the woman	feminās	women
Gen	feminae	of the woman	feminārum	of the women
Dat	feminae	to/for the woman	feminīs	to/for the women
Abl	feminā	by/with/from the woman	feminīs	by/with/from the women

- Note that **dea** (goddess) and **filia** (daughter), have their dative and ablative plurals **deābus** and **filiābus**

Second Declension

- Nouns of the second declension end in **-us**, or a few in **-er** or **-r**. All are masculine. Those few which end in **-um** are neuter.

	SINGULAR		PLURAL	
Nom	servus	slave	servī	slaves
Voc	serve		servī	
Acc	servum		servōs	
Gen	servī		servōrum	
Dat	servō		servīs	
Abl	servo		servīs	

	SINGULAR		PLURAL	
Nom	puer	boy	puerī	boys
Voc	puer		puerī	
Acc	puerum		puerōs	
Gen	puerī		puerōrum	
Dat	puerō		puetīs	
Abl	puerō		puerīs	

Second Declension (continued)

	SINGULAR		PLURAL	
Nom	bell**um**	war	bell**a**	wars
Voc	bell**um**		bell**a**	
Acc	bell**um**		bell**a**	
Gen	bell**ī**		bell**ōrum**	
Dat	bell**ō**		bell**īs**	
Abl	bell**ō**		bell**īs**	

- Note that proper names ending in -**ius** have vocative in -**ī**, **o Vergīlī** – o Virgil!

- **deus** (god), has an alternative vocative **deus**, and plural forms **di** in nominative and **dis** in dative and ablative.

Third Declension

- This is the largest group of nouns and may be divided into two broad categories, stems ending in a consonant and those ending in -**i**. All genders in this declension must be learnt.

Consonant Stems

- ending in -**l**

  consul, -is *m* (consul)

	SINGULAR	PLURAL
Nom	cōnsul	cōnsul**ēs**
Voc	cōnsul	cōnsul**ēs**
Acc	cōnsul**em**	cōnsul**ēs**
Gen	cōnsul**is**	cōnsul**um**
Dat	cōnsul**ī**	cōnsul**ibus**
Abl	cōnsul**e**	cōnsul**ibus**

- ending in -**n**

  legio, -onis *f* (legion)

	SINGULAR	PLURAL
Nom	legi**ō**	legi**ōnēs**
Voc	legi**ō**	legi**ōnēs**
Acc	legi**ōnem**	legi**ōnēs**
Gen	legi**ōnis**	legi**ōnum**
Dat	legi**ōnī**	legi**ōnibus**
Abl	legi**ōne**	legi**ōnibus**

  flumen, -inis *nt* (river)

	SINGULAR	PLURAL
Nom	flumen	flumin**a**
Voc	flumen	flumin**a**
Acc	flumen	flumin**a**
Gen	flumin**is**	flumin**um**
Dat	flumin**ī**	flumin**ibus**
Abl	flumin**e**	flumin**ibus**

- Note that the genitive plural of these nouns ends in -**um**.

- Stems ending in **–i**

    civis, -is *m/f* (citizen)

	SINGULAR	PLURAL
Nom	civis	civēs
Voc	civis	civēs
Acc	civem	civēs
Gen	civis	civium
Dat	civī	civibus
Abl	cive	civibus

- Note that these nouns have genitive plural in **-ium**.

Neuter Nouns

mare, -is *nt* (sea)

SINGULAR		PLURAL
Nom	mare	maria
Voc	mare	maria
Acc	mare	maria
Gen	maris	marium
Dat	mari	maribus
Abl	marī	maribus

animal, -is *nt* (animal)

SINGULAR		PLURAL
Nom	animal	animālia
Voc	animal	animālia
Acc	animal	animālia
Gen	animālis	animālium
Dat	animālī	animālibus
Abl	animālī	animālibus

- Note that the ablative singular of these neuter nouns ends in **-ī**.

- Nominative, vocative and accusative singular endings of neuter nouns are identical.

- Nominative, vocative and accusative plural endings of neuter nouns in **all** declensions end in **-ă**.

Monosyllabic Consonant Stems

- The following have their genitive plural in **-ium**:

arx, arcis f (citadel)	- arcium (of citadels)
gēns, gentis f (race)	- gentium (of races)
mōns, montis m (mountain)	- montium (of mountains)
nox, noctis f (night)	- noctium (of nights)
pōns, pontis m (bridge)	- pontium (of bndges)
urbs, urbis f (city)	- urbium (of cities)

NOUNS

Fourth Declension

- Nouns in this declension end in **-us** in the nominative singular and are mainly masculine. A few end in **-u** and are neuter.

  exercitus, -ūs *m* (army)

	SINGULAR	PLURAL
Nom	exercit**us**	exercit**ūs**
Voc	exercit**us**	exercit**ūs**
Acc	exercit**um**	exercit**ūs**
Gen	exercit**ūs**	exercit**uum**
Dat	exercit**uī**	exercit**ibus**
Abl	exercit**ū**	exercit**ibus**

  genū, -ūs *nt* (knee)

	SINGULAR	PLURAL
Nom	gen**ū**	gen**ua**
Voc	gen**ū**	gen**ua**
Acc	gen**ū**	gen**ua**
Gen	gen**ūs**	gen**uum**
Dat	gen**ū**	gen**ibus**
Abl	gen**ū**	gen**ibus**

- Note that a few common nouns are feminine, *eg* **domus** (house), **manus** (hand), **Idus** (Ides or 15th of the month).

- The form **domī** (at home) is an old form called locative, **domō** (from home) *abl sing*, **domōs** *acc pl* and **domōrum** *gen pl* are also used besides the fourth declension forms of **domus** (house).

Fifth Declension

- There are only a few nouns in this declension. All end in **-ēs** in the nominative case. Most are feminine, but **diēs** (day) and **meridiēs** (midday) are masculine.

  diēs, diēī *m* (day)

	SINGULAR	PLURAL
Nom	di**ēs**	di**ēs**
Voc	di**ēs**	di**ēs**
Acc	di**em**	di**ēs**
Gen	di**ēī**	di**ērum**
Dat	di**ēī**	di**ēbus**
Abl	di**ē**	di**ēbus**

Cases

Use Of Cases

Nominative Case

The nominative case is used where:

- the noun is the **subject** of the verb (→**1**)

- the noun is a **complement** (→**2**)

- the noun is **in apposition** to the subject (→**3**)

Accusative Case

The accusative case is used:

- for the **direct object** of the verb (→**4**)

- with verbs of teaching and asking which take accusative of person and thing (→**5**)

- Verbs of naming, making *etc* take two accusatives for the same person or thing (→**6**)

- in exclamations (→**7**)

- to show extent of space (→**8**)

- to show extent of time (→**9**)

- to show motion to a place or country usually with a preposition (→**10**)

- to show motion towards, without a preposition, before names of towns and small islands (→**11**)

    Note also: **domum** (home), **rus** (to the country), **foras** (outside)

- for an object with similar meaning to the verb (*cognate*) (→**12**)

Examples

1 **Sextus** ridet
Sextus laughs

2 Romulus **rex** factus est
Romulus was made king

3 Marcus Annius, **eques Romanus**, hoc dicit Marcus Annius, a Roman businessman, says this

4 canis **baculum** petit
the dog fetches the stick

5 **puerum litteras** docebo
I shall teach the boy literature

6 **Ancum Martium regem** populus creavit
The people made Ancus Martius king

7 o **tempora**, o **mores**
what times, what conduct!

8 murus decem **pedes** altus est
the wall is 10 foot high

9 Troia decem **annos** obsessa est
Troy was under siege for 10 years

10 **ad Hispaniam** effugerunt
they escaped to Spain

11 **Athenas** legati missi sunt
Ambassadors were sent to Athens

12 **vitam** bonam **vixit**
he lived a good life

NOUNS

Dative Case

- Indirect object (*ie* to or for whom an action is performed) (→**1**)

- used with verbs of obeying (**parēre**), resisting (**resistere**), pleasing (**placēre**), ordering (**imperāre**) etc (→**2**)

- verb compounds (beginning **ad-**, **ob-**, **prae-**, **sub-**) denoting helping or hindering take dative (→**3**)

    adesse – come to help
    subvenire – help

- indicates possession (→**4**)

- is used with adjectives meaning "like" (**similis**), "fit" (**aptus**), "near" (**proximus**) (→**5**)

- indicates a purpose (known as *predicative dative*) (→**6**)

- shows the agent of gerund/gerundive (→**7**)

Examples

1 pecuniam **domino** dedit
he gave the money to his master

2 maria terraque **Deo** parent
land and sea obey God

3 Pompeius **hostibus** obstitit
Pompey opposed the enemy

4 Poppaea amica est **Marciae**
Poppaea is Marcia's friend

5 feles **tigri similis** est
the cat is like a tiger

6 nemo mihi **auxilio** est
there is no-one to help me

7 omnia erant agenda **nobis**
everything had to be done by us

Genitive Case

- Indicates possession (→**1**)

- Denotes part of a whole (→**2**)

- Indicates a quality, always with an adjective (→**3**)

- Is used as a predicate, where a person represents a quality (→**4**)

- Is used with superlatives (→**5**)

- Precedes **causa** and **gratia** (for the sake of) (→**6**)

- Is used after certain adjectives (→**7**)

    sciens (knowing)
    inscius (ignorant of)
    cupidus (desiring)
    particeps (sharing) *etc*

- Is used with verbs of remembering (**memini**) and forgetting (**obliviscor**) (→**8**)

- Follows verbs of accusing, convicting *etc* (→**9**)

- Represents value or worth (→**10**)

Examples

1 domus **regis**
the king's house

uxor **Augusti**
the wife of Augustus

2 quid **novi**
what news?

plus **cibi**
more food

3 magnae **auctoritatis** es
your reputation is great

4 **stulti est** hoc facere
it is the mark of a fool to do this

5 Indus est **omnium fluminum** maximum
the Indus is the greatest of all rivers

6 tu me **amoris causa** servavisti
you saved me for love's sake

7 Verres, **cupidus pecuniae**, ex hereditate praedatus est
Verres, greedy for money, robbed the estate

8 **mortis** memento
remember death

9 ante **actarum rerum** Antonius accusatus est
Antony was accused of previous offences

10 frumentum **minimo** vendidit
he sold com of the lowest value

flocci non facio
I don't care at all

Ablative Case

- Indicates place, usually with the preposition "in" (→**1**)

  Note, however: **totā Asiā** – throughout Asia
  terrā marīque – by land and sea

- Indicates motion from, or down from a place, usually with prepositions **ex**, **de**, **a**(**b**) (→**2**)

- Note prepositions are omitted before names of towns, small islands and **domo** (from home), **rure** (from the country), **foris** (from outside) (→**3**)

- Represents time when or within which something happens (→**4**)

- Indicates origin, sometimes with prepositions **in**, **ex**, **a**(**b**) (→**5**)

- Is used to show material from which something is made (→**6**)

- Indicates manner (how something is done), usually with **cum** when there is no adjective, and without **cum** when there is an adjective (→**7**)

- Is used with verbs of depriving, filling, needing and with **opus est** (→**8**)

- Is used with deponent verbs **utor** (use), **abutor** (abuse), **fungor** (accomplish), **potior** (gain possession of) (→**9**)

- States cause (→**10**)

- To form **ablative absolute**, where a noun in the ablative is combined with a participle or another noun or adjective in the same case, to form an idea independent of the rest of the sentence. This is equivalent to an adverbial clause (→**11**)

Examples

1 Milo in **urbe** mansit
Milo remained in the city

2 **de equo** cecidit
He fell down from his horse

praedam **ex urbe ornatissima** sustulit
He stole booty from the rich city

3 **domo** cucurrerunt servi
The slaves ran from the house

4 **hac nocte** Agricola obiit
Agricola died on this night

decem annis Lacedaimonii non haec confecerunt
The Spartans did not complete this task within 10 years

5 Romulus et Remus, **Marte nati**
Romulus and Remus, sons of Mars

flumina **in Caucaso monte** orta
Rivers rising in the Caucasus mountains

6 statua **ex auro** facta est
The statue was made of gold

7 mulieres **cum virtute** vixerunt
The women lived virtuously

summa celeritate Poeni regressi sunt
The Carthaginians retreated at top speed

8 aliquem **vita** privare
to deprive someone of life

opus est mihi **divitiis**
I need wealth

9 **vi** et **armis** usus est
He used force of arms

10 leo **fame** decessit
The lion died of hunger

11 **exigua parte aestatis reliqua**, Caesar in Britanniam proficisci contendit
Although only a little of the summer remained, Caesar hurried to set out for Britain

Adjectives

An adjective adds a quality to the noun. It usually follows the noun but sometimes comes before it for emphasis. The adjective agrees with its noun in number, case and gender.

Gender

vir bonus (*masc*)	a good man
fēmina pulchra (*fem*)	a beautiful woman
bellum longum (*neut*)	a long war

Number

virī bonī (*pl*)	good men
fēminae pulchrae (*pl*)	beautiful women
bella longa (*pl*)	long wars

Case

virō bonō (*dat sing*	for a good man
fēminās pulchrās (*acc pl*)	beautiful women
bellī longī (*gen sing*)	of a long war

- Adjectives are declined like nouns and usually arranged in two groups:

  1. those with endings of the first and second declensions
  2. those with endings of the third declension

First and Second Declensions

bonus, bona, bonum (good)

SINGULAR

	Masc	Fem	Neut
Nom	bonus	bona	bonum
Voc	bone	bona	bonum
Acc	bonum	bonam	bonum
Gen	bonī	bonae	bonī
Dat	bonō	bonae	bonō
Abl	bonō	bonā	bonō

PLURAL

	Masc	Fem	Neut
Nom	bonī	bonae	bona
Voc	bonī	bonae	bona
Acc	bonōs	bonas	bona
Gen	bonōrum	bonārum	bonōrum
Dat	bonīs	bonīs	bonīs
Abl	bonīs	bonīs	bonīs

First and Second Declensions (continued)
miser, misera, miserum (unhappy)

SINGULAR

	Masc	*Fem*	*Neut*
Nom	mis**er**	mis**era**	mis**erum**
Voc	mis**er**	mis**era**	mis**erum**
Acc	mis**erum**	mis**eram**	mis**erum**
Gen	mis**erī**	mis**erae**	mis**erī**
Dat	mis**erō**	mis**erae**	mis**erō**
Abl	mis**erō**	mis**erā**	mis**erō**

PLURAL

	Masc	*Fem*	*Neut*
Nom	mis**erī**	mis**erae**	mis**era**
Voc	mis**erī**	mis**erae**	mis**era**
Acc	mis**erōs**	mis**erās**	mis**era**
Gen	mis**erōrum**	mis**erārum**	mis**erōrum**
Dat	mis**erīs**	mis**erīs**	mis**erīs**
Abl	mis**erīs**	mis**erīs**	mis**erīs**

- **liber** (free) and **tener** (tender) are declined like **miser**

pulcher, pulchra, pulchrum (beautiful)

SINGULAR

	Masc	*Fem*	*Neut*
Nom	pulch**er**	pulch**ra**	pulch**rum**
Voc	pulch**er**	pulch**ra**	pulch**rum**
Acc	pulch**rum**	pulch**ram**	pulch**rum**
Gen	pulch**rī**	pulch**rae**	pulch**rī**
Dat	pulch**rō**	pulch**rae**	pulch**rō**
Abl	pulch**rō**	pulch**rā**	pulch**rō**

PLURAL

	Masc	*Fem*	*Neut*
Nom	pulch**rī**	pulch**rae**	pulch**ra**
Voc	pulch**rī**	pulch**rae**	pulch**ra**
Acc	pulch**rōs**	pulch**rās**	pulch**ra**
Gen	pulch**rōrum**	pulch**rārum**	pulch**rōrum**
Dat	pulch**rīs**	pulch**rīs**	pulch**rīs**
Abl	pulch**rīs**	pulch**rīs**	pulch**rīs**

- **aeger** (sick), **crēber** (frequent), **integer** (whole), **niger** (black), **piger** (slow) and **sacer** (sacred) are declined like **pulcher**

- The following group of adjectives form their genitive singular in -**ius** and dative singular in -**i**:

alius, -a, -ud	another
alter, altera, alterum	one of two
neuter, neutra, neutrum	neither
nūllus, -a, -um	none
sōlus, -a, -um	alone
tōtus, -a, -um	whole
ūllus, -a, -um	any
ūnus, -a, -um	one
uter, utra, utrum	which of two?

sōlus (alone)

SINGULAR

	Masc	*Fem*	*Neut*
Nom	sōl**us**	sōl**a**	sōl**um**
Acc	sōl**um**	sōl**am**	sōl**um**
Gen	sōl**ius**	sōl**ius**	sōl**ius**
Dat	sōl**ī**	sōl**ī**	sōl**ī**
Abl	sōl**ō**	sōl**ā**	sōl**ō**

PLURAL

	Masc	*Fem*	*Neut*
Nom	sōl**ī**	sōl**ae**	sōl**a**
Acc	sōl**ōs**	sōl**as**	sōl**a**
Gen	sōl**ōrum**	sōl**arum**	sōl**ōrum**
Dat	sōl**īs**	sōl**īs**	sōl**īs**
Abl	sōi**īs**	sōl**īs**	sōl**īs**

Third Declension

Adjectives of the third declension, like nouns, may be divided into two broad types, those with consonant stems and those with vowel stems in -**i**.

Consonant Stems

These have **one** ending in nominative singular.

prūdēns (wise)

SINGULAR

	Masc	Fem	Neut
Nom	prūdēns	prūdēns	prūdēns
Voc	prūdēns	prūdēns	prūdēns
Acc	prūdent**em**	prūdent**em**	prūdēns
Gen	prūdent**is**	prūdent**is**	prūdent**is**
Dat	prūdent**ī**	prūdent**ī**	prūdent**ī**
Abl	prūdent**ī**	prūdent**ī**	prūdent**ī**

PLURAL

	Masc	Fem	Neut
Nom	prūdent**ēs**	prūdent**ēs**	prūdent**ia**
Voc	prūdent**ēs**	prūdent**ēs**	prūdent**ia**
Acc	prūdent**ēs**	prūdent**ēs**	prūdent**ia**
Gen	prūdent**ium**	prūdent**ium**	prūdent**ium**
Dat	prūdent**ibus**	prūdent**ibus**	prūdent**ibus**
Abl	prūdent**ibus**	prūdent**ibus**	prūdent**ibus**

- **dīligēns** (careful), **innocēns** (innocent), **potēns** (powerful), **frequēns** (frequent), **ingēns** (huge) are declined like **prūdēns**

amāns (loving)

SINGULAR

	Masc	Fem	Neut
Nom	amāns	amāns	amāns
Voc	amāns	amāns	amāns
Acc	amant**em**	amant**em**	amāns
Gen	amant**is**	amant**is**	amant**is**
Dat	amant**ī**	amant**ī**	amant**ī**
Abl	amant**e**	amant**e**	amant**e**

PLURAL

	Masc	Fem	Neut
Nom	amant**ēs**	amant**ēs**	amant**ia**
Voc	amant**ēs**	amant**ēs**	amant**ia**
Acc	amant**ēs**	amant**ēs**	amant**ia**
Gen	amant**ium**	amant**ium**	amant**ium**
Dat	amant**ibus**	amant**ibus**	amant**ibus**
Abl	amant**ibus**	amant**ibus**	amant**ibus**

- All present participles are declined like **amans**, although present participles of the other conjugations end in -**ēns**

- When participles are used as adjectives -**ī** is used instead of -**e** in ablative singular case

felix (lucky)

SINGULAR

	Masc	Fem	Neut
Nom	fēl**ix**	fēl**ix**	fēl**ix**
Voc	fēl**ix**	fēl**ix**	fēl**ix**
Acc	felic**em**	felic**em**	fēl**ix**
Gen	felic**is**	felic**is**	felic**is**
Dat	felic**ī**	felic**ī**	felic**ī**
Abl	felic**ī**	felic**ī**	felic**ī**

PLURAL

	Masc	Fem	Neut
Nom	fēlic**ēs**	fēlic**ēs**	fēlic**ia**
Voc	fēlic**ēs**	fēlic**ēs**	fēlic**ia**
Acc	fēlic**ēs**	fēlic**ēs**	fēlic**ia**
Gen	fēlic**ium**	fēlic**ium**	fēlic**ium**
Dat	fēlic**ibus**	fēlic**ibus**	fēlic**ibus**
Abl	fēlic**ibus**	fēlic**ibus**	fēlic**ibus**

- **audāx** (bold) and **ferōx** (fierce) are declined like **fēlix**

- Note that all the above adjectives have the same case endings in all genders except for the neuter accusative singular and the neuter nominative, vocative and accusative plural.

Vowel Stems

The following adjectives have **two** endings in nominative singular, one for masculine and feminine, one for neuter.
fortis, **forte** (brave)

SINGULAR

	Masc	Fem	Neut
Nom	fort**is**	fort**is**	fort**e**
Voc	fort**is**	fort**is**	fort**e**
Acc	fort**em**	fort**em**	fort**e**
Gen	fort**is**	fort**is**	fort**is**
Dat	fort**ī**	fort**ī**	fort**ī**
Abl	fort**ī**	fort**ī**	fort**ī**

PLURAL

	Masc	Fem	Neut
Nom	fort**ēs**	fort**ēs**	fort**ia**
Voc	fort**ēs**	fort**ēs**	fort**ia**
Acc	fort**ēs**	fort**ēs**	fort**ia**
Gen	fort**ium**	fort**ium**	fort**ium**
Dat	fort**ibus**	fort**ibus**	fort**ibus**
Abl	fort**ibus**	fort**ibus**	fort**ibus**

- **brevis** (short), **facilis** (easy), **gravis** (heavy), **levis** (light), **omnis** (all), **tristis** (sad), **turpis** (disgraceful), **talis** (of such a kind), and **qualis** (of which kind), are declined like **fortis**.

Third Declension (continued)

The following adjectives have **three** endings in nominative singular.
ācer, ācris, ācre (sharp)

SINGULAR

	Masc	Fem	Neut
Nom	ā**cer**	ā**cris**	ā**cre**
Voc	ā**cer**	ā**cris**	ā**cre**
Acc	ā**crem**	ā**crem**	ā**cre**
Gen	ā**cris**	ā**cris**	ā**cris**
Dat	ā**crī**	ā**crī**	ā**crī**
Abl	ā**crī**	ā**crī**	ā**crī**

PLURAL

	Masc	Fem	Neut
Nom	ā**crēs**	ā**crēs**	ā**cria**
Voc	ā**crēs**	ā**crēs**	ā**cria**
Acc	ā**crēs**	ā**crēs**	ā**cria**
Gen	ā**crium**	ā**crium**	ā**crium**
Dat	ā**cribus**	ā**cribus**	ā**cribus**
Abl	ā**cribus**	ā**cribus**	ā**cribus**

- **alacer** (lively), **equester** (of cavalry), and **volucer** (winged), are declined like **acer**, and **celer** (swift), declines similarly, but keeps -**e**- throughout (*eg* **celer, celeris, celere**)

Use of Adjectives

There are two ways of using adjectives.

- They can be used **attributively**, where the adjective in English comes before the noun: the new car

- An attributive adjective in Latin usually follows its noun but may sometimes come before it with a change of meaning (→**1**)

- They can be used **predicatively**, where the adjective comes after the verb: the car is new (→**2**)

- If an adjective describes two nouns, it agrees in gender with the nearer (→**3**)

- When an adjective describes two subjects of different sex it is often masculine plural (→**4**)

- When an adjective describes two subjects representing things without life it is often neuter plural (→**5**)

Examples

1 res **parvae**
small things

in parvis rebus
in unimportant matters

civis **Romanus** sum
I am a Roman citizen

2 Servi erant **fideles**
The slaves were faithful

3 Antonius, vir consilii **magni** et prudentiae
Antony, a man of great wisdom and prudence

4 frater et soror sunt **timidi**
Brother and sister are frightened

5 Calor et ventus per artus **praesentia** erant
Warmth and wind were present in the limbs

Comparative and Superlative

Adjectives also have comparative forms *eg* I am **luckier** than you, and superlative forms *eg* the **noblest** Roman of them all.

Formation

- The comparative is formed by adding **-ior** (*masc* and *fem*) and **-ius** (*neut*) to the consonant stem of the adjective and the superlative by adding **-issimus, -a, -um** to the stem:

POSITIVE	altus	high
	audāx	bold
	brevis	short
	prūdēns	wise
COMPARATIVE	altior	higher
	audācior	bolder
	brevior	shorter
	prūdentior	wiser
SUPERLATIVE	altissimus	highest
	audācissimus	boldest
	brevissimus	shortest
	prūdentissimus	wisest

- If the adjective ends in **-er** (*in masc nom sing*) add **-rimus** to form the superlative.

POSITIVE	ācer	sharp
	celer	swift
	miser	unhappy
	pulcher	beautiful
COMPARATIVE	ācrior	sharper
	celerior	swifter
	miserior	more unhappy
	pulchrior	more beautiful
SUPERLATIVE	ācerrimus	sharpest
	celerrimus	swiftest
	miserrimus	most unhappy
	pulcherrimus	most beautiful

Comparative and Superlative (continued)

- Six adjectives ending in -**ilis** (*in masc nom sing*) add -**limus** to the stem to form the superlative.

POSITIVE	facilis	easy
	difficilis	difficult
	similis	like
	dissimilis	unlike
	gracilis	slight
	humilis	low

COMPARATIVE	facilior	easier
	difficilior	more difficult
	similior	more like
	dissimilior	more unlike
	gracilior	more slight
	humilior	lower

SUPERLATIVE	facillimus	easiest
	difficillimus	most difficult
	simillimus	most like
	dissimillimus	most unlike
	gracillimus	most slight
	humillimus	lowest

Irregular comparison

- Some adjectives have irregular comparative and superlative forms:

POSITIVE	bonus	good
	malus	bad
	parvus	small
	magnus	big
	multus	much
	multī	many

COMPARATIVE	melior	better
	pēior	worse
	minor	smaller
	māior	bigger
	plūs	more
	plūrēs	more

SUPERLATIVE	optimus	best
	pessimus	worst
	minimus	smallest, least
	māximus	biggest
	plūrimus	most
	plūrimī	most

- Note that all adjectives ending in **-us** preceded by a vowel (except those ending in **-quus**) form comparative and superlative thus:

idōneus	suitable
magis idōneus	more suitable
māxime idōneus	most suitable
but	
antīquus	old
antīquior	older
antīquissimus	oldest

- Note the following comparatives and superlatives where there is no positive form:

exterior	outer	**extrēmus**	furthest
inferior	lower	**infīmus** or **īmus**	lowest
superior	upper, higher	**suprēmus** or **summus**	highest
posterior	later	**postrēmus**	latest

Declension of Comparative and Superlative

- All comparatives decline like adjectives of the third declension.

	SINGULAR		PLURAL	
	Masc/Fem	*Neut*	*Masc/Fem*	*Neut*
Nom	**altior**	**altius**	**altiōrēs**	**altiōra**
Voc	**altior**	**altius**	**altiōrēs**	**altiōra**
Acc	**altiōrem**	**altius**	**altiōrēs**	**altiōra**
Gen	**altiōris**	**altiōris**	**altiōrum**	**altiōrum**
Dat	**altiōrī**	**altiōrī**	**altiōribus**	**altiōribus**
Abl	**altiōre**	**altiōre**	**altiōribus**	**altiōribus**

- Note ablative singular in **-e**.

- All superlatives decline like adjectives of first and second declensions (*eg* **bonus, bona, bonum**).

Comparative and Superlative (continued)

Use

- The comparative is often followed by **quam** (than), or the thing or person compared is given in the ablative case (→**1**)

- Sometimes the comparative can be translated by "rather" or "quite" (→**2**)

- The comparative is often strengthened by "**multo**" (→**3**)

- Sometimes the superlative can be translated by "very", or even as a positive adjective in English (→**4**)

- "**quam**" with the superlative means "as ... as possible" (→**5**)

Examples

1 Marcus est **altior quam soror**
Marcus est **altior sorore**
Marcus is taller than his sister

2 Gallus erat **fortior**
the Gaul was rather brave

3 **multo carior**
much dearer

4 **vir sapientissimus**
a very wise man

   integerrima vita
   of virtuous life

5 **quam paucissimi**
as few people as possible

Adverbs

An adverb modifies a verb, adjective, another adverb or a noun. It answers questions such as "how?", "when?", "why?", "where?", "to what extent?".

Formation

Some are formed from nouns *eg* **furtim** (stealthily) or pronouns **aliās** (at other times) but most are formed from adjectives.

- Accusative singular neuter of adjectives of extent:

multum	much	**nimium**	too much
paulum	a little	**aliquantum**	somewhat
prīmum	first	**cēterum**	for the rest

- Adjectives in -us and -er change to -e:

altē	highly	**miserē**	wretchedly

- Ablative forms of these adjectives in -o or -a:

certē *or* **certō**	certainly	**verē**	in truth
dextrā	on the right	**verō**	certainly

- Adjectives of the third declension add -**ter**/-**iter**:

audacter	boldly	**celeriter**	quickly	**prudenter**	wisely

Position

- An adverb comes before the verb, adjective, adverb or noun that it modifies (→**1**)

- However adverbs of time often come at the beginning of the sentence (→**2**)

Examples

1 **vehementer** errabas, Verres
you were making a big mistake, Verres

nimium libera respublica
too free a state

bis consul
twice consul

2 **cras mane** putat se venturum esse
He thinks he will come tomorrow morning

saepe hoc mecum cogitavi
I often thought this over by myself

Common Adverbs

- **Manner** – "how?"

ita	thus	**crudeliter**	cruelly
sīc	thus	**iustē**	justly
aliter	otherwise	**liberē**	freely
fortē	by chance	**repentē**	suddenly
magnoperē	greatly		

- **Time** – "when?"

iam, nunc	now	**(n)umquam**	(n)ever
simul	at the same time	**iterum**	again
anteā	before	**saepe**	often
posteā	afterwards	**hodiē**	today
cōtīdiē	every day	**herī**	yesterday
diū	for a long time	**crās**	tomorrow
mox	soon	**postrīdiē**	next day
interim or **-ea**	meanwhile	**statim**	immediately
tum	then		

- **Place** – "where?"

ubi?	where?	**unde?**	where from	**quō?**	where to?
ibi	there	**inde**	from there	**eō**	to there
hīc	here	**hinc**	from here	**hūc**	to here
usquam	anywhere	**nusquam**	nowhere		

- **Others**

etiam	also	**fortasse**	perhaps
quoque	also	**consultō**	on purpose
quidem	indeed	**scīlicet**	no doubt

Comparison of Adverbs

The comparative form of the adverb is the nominative singular neuter of the comparative adjective. The superlative of the adverb is formed by changing -**us** of the superlative adjective to -**e**.

POSITIVE	COMPARITIVE	SUPERLATIVE
altē	**altius**	**altissimē**
highly	more highly	most highly
audacter	**audacius**	**audacissimē**
boldly	more boldy	most boldy
bene	**melius**	**optimē**
well	better	best
breviter	**brevius**	**brevissimē**
briefly	more briefly	most briefly
diū	**diūtius**	**diūtissimē**
for a long time	longer	longest
facile	**facilius**	**facillimē**
easily	more easily	most easily
magnoperē	**magis**	**maximē**
greatly	more	most
male	**peius**	**pessimē**
badly	worse	worst
miserē	**miserius**	**miserrimē**
wretchedly	more wretchedly	most wretchedly
multum	**plūs**	**plūrimum**
much	more	most
paulum	**minus**	**minimē**
a little	less	least
prope	**propius**	**proxime**
near	nearer	nearest
saepe	**saepius**	**saepissimē**
often	more often	most often

Notes on use of the comparative adjective may be applied also to the comparative adverb (see comparative adjective section).

Examples

rem totam brevius cognoscite
Find out about the whole matter more briefly

magis consilio quam virtute vicit
He won more because of his strategy than his courage

legiones diutius sine consule fuerunt
The legions were too long without a consul

multo plus
much more

optime
very well

mihi placebat Pomponius maxime vel minime
I liked Pomponius the most or disliked him the least

optimus quisque id optime facit
All the best people do it best

quam celerrime
as quickly as possible

Pronouns

Personal Pronouns

The pronouns **ego** (I), **nos** (we), **tu** (you, *sing*), **vos** (you, *pl*) decline as follows:

		SINGULAR		
Nom	**ego**	I	**tū**	you
Acc	**mē**	me	**tē**	you
Gen	**meī**	of me	**tuī**	of you
Dat	**mihi**	to/for me	**tibi**	to/for you
Abl	**mē**	by/with/from me	**tē**	by/with/from you

		PLURAL		
Nom	**nōs**	we	**vōs**	you
Acc	**nōs**	us	**vōs**	you
Gen	**nostrum**	of us	**vestrum**	of you
Dat	**nōbis**	to/for us	**vobis**	to/for you
Abl	**nōbis**	by/with/from us	**vōbis**	by/with/from you

Possessive

meus, -a, -um	my	**tuus, -a, -um**	your
noster, -ra, -rum	our	**vester, -ra, -rum**	your

- **nostri** and **vestri** are alternative forms of genitive plural.

- Possessives are sometimes used instead of the genitive of personal pronouns:
  odium tuum
  hatred of you

- For the third person pronoun, he/she/it, Latin uses **is**, **ea**, **id**:

	Masc		*Fem*		*Neut*	
			SINGULAR			
Nom	**is**	he	**ea**	she	**id**	it
Acc	**eum**	him	**eam**	her	**id**	it
Gen	**ēius**	of him	**ēius**	of her	**ēius**	of it
Dat	**eī**	to him	**eī**	to her	**eī**	to it
Abl	**eō**	by him	**ea**	by her	**eo**	by it

	Masc		*Fem*		*Neut*	
			PLURAL			
Nom	**eī**	they	**eae**	they	**ea**	they
Acc	**eōs**	them	**eās**	them	**ea**	them
Gen	**eōrum**	of them	**eārum**	of them	**eōrum**	of them
Dat	**eīs**	to them	**eīs**	to them	**eīs**	to them
Abl	**eīs**	by them	**eīs**	by them	**eīs**	by them

Use

- Pronouns as subjects (I, you) are not usually used in Latin. The person of the verb is indicated by the ending (*eg* **misimus** – we sent), **ego**, **nos** *etc* are used only for emphasis:

  ego vulgus odi, **tū** amas
  I hate crowds, you love them

- The genitive forms **nostrum** and **vestrum** are used partitively:

  multi **nostrum**   many of us   pauci **vestrum**   a few of you

Reflexive Pronouns

Acc	**mē**	myself	**tē**	yourself
Gen	**meī**		**tuī**	
Dat	**mihi**		**tibi**	
Abl	**mē**		**tē**	

Acc	**nōs**	ourselves	**vōs**	yourselves
Gen	**nostrum**		**vestrum**	
Dat	**nōbis**		**vōbis**	
Abl	**nōbis**		**vōbis**	

• These are identical in form to personal pronouns.

Acc	**sē**	himself/herself/itself/themselves
Gen	**suī**	
Dat	**sibi**	
Abl	**sē**	

• Reflexive pronouns are used to refer to the subject of the sentence:

quisque **se** amat
everybody loves themselves
me lavo
I wash myself

Determinative Pronouns

- **is** – he/that, **ea** – she, **id** – it: as above

- **idem** (the same)

SINGULAR

	Masc	Fem	Neut
Nom	īdem	eadem	idem
Acc	eundem	eandem	idem
Gen	ēiusdem	eīusdem	eīusdem
Dat	eīdem	eīdem	eīdem
Abl	eōdem	eadem	eōdem

PLURAL

Nom	eīdem	eaedem	eadem
Acc	eōsdem	eāsdem	eadem
Gen	eōrundem	eārundem	eōrundem
Dat	eīsdem	eīsdem	eīsdem
Abl	eīsdem	eīsdem	eīsdem

- **ipse** (himself/herself/itself/themselves)

SINGULAR

	Masc	Fem	Neut
Nom	ipse	ipsa	ipsum
Acc	ipsum	ipsam	ipsum
Gen	ipsīus	ipsīus	ipsīus
Dat	ipsī	ipsī	ipsī
Abl	ipsō	ipsā	ipsō

PLURAL

Nom	ipsī	ipsae	ipsa
Acc	ipsos	ipsās	ipsa
Gen	ipsōrum	ipsārum	ipsōrum
Dat	ipsīs	ipsīs	ipsīs
Abl	ipsīs	ipsīs	ipsīs

Demonstrative Pronouns

- **hic** (this/these)

SINGULAR

	Masc	*Fem*	*Neut*
Nom	**hīc**	**haec**	**hoc**
Acc	**hunc**	**hanc**	**hoc**
Gen	**hūius**	**hūius**	**hūius**
Dat	**huīc**	**huīc**	**huīc**
Abl	**hōc**	**hāc**	**hōc**

PLURAL

	Masc	*Fem*	*Neut*
Nom	**hī**	**hae**	**haec**
Acc	**hōs**	**hās**	**haec**
Gen	**hōrum**	**hārum**	**hōrum**
Dat	**hīs**	**his**	**hīs**
Abl	**hīs**	**hīs**	**hīs**

- **ille** (that/those)

SINGULAR

	Masc	*Fem*	*Neut*
Nom	**ille**	**illa**	**illud**
Acc	**illum**	**illam**	**illud**
Gen	**illīus**	**illīus**	**illīus**
Dat	**illī**	**illī**	**illī**
Abl	**illō**	**illā**	**illō**

PLURAL

	Masc	*Fem*	*Neut*
Nom	**illī**	**iilae**	**illa**
Acc	**illōs**	**illās**	**illa**
Gen	**illōrum**	**illārum**	**illōrum**
Dat	**illīs**	**illīs**	**illīs**
Abl	**illīs**	**illīs**	**illīs**

- Note that **īdem**, **hīc**, **ille** and all their parts may be adjectives as well as pronouns

Examples

1 **eadem** femina
the same woman

hic puer
this boy

tu autem **eadem** ages?
Are you going to do the same things?

2 patria est carior quam **nos ipsi**
Our native land is dearer than ourselves

3 **hac** remota, quomodo **illum** aestimemus?
When she is removed, how are we to judge him?

4 **nos** oportet opus conficere
We must complete the task

5 accusatores dicunt **te ipsam** testem **eius** criminis esse

The prosecutors claim that you yourself are the witness of that crime

6 sed **haec** omitto; ad **illa** quae **me** magis moverunt respondeo

But I pass over these matters; I reply to those which have affected me more deeply

7 pax **vobis**cum
Peace be with you!

8 puella intravit; **ea mihi** litteras dedit
The girl came in; she gave me a letter

PRONOUNS
Relative Pronouns

SINGULAR

	Masc		Fem		Neut	
Nom	**quī**	who	**quae**	who	**quod**	which/that
Acc	**quem**	whom	**quam**	whom	**quod**	which/that
Gen	**cūius**	whose	**cūius**	whose	**cūius**	of which
Dat	**cuī**	to whom	**cuī**	to whom	**cuī**	to which
Abl	**quō**	by whom	**quā**	by whom	**quō**	by which

PLURAL

	Masc		Fem		Neut	
Nom	**quī**	who	**quae**	who	**quae**	which
Acc	**quōs**	whom	**quās**	whom	**quae**	which
Gen	**quōrum**	whose	**quārum**	whose	**quōrum**	of which
Dat	**quibus**	to whom	**quibus**	to whom	**quibus**	to which
Abl	**quibus**	by whom	**quibus**	by whom	**quibus**	by which

- A relative pronoun attaches a subordinate clause to a word preceding it (its antecedent). It agrees with this word in number and gender but takes its case from its own clause (→**1**)

- **quidam, quaedam, quoddam** (a certain, somebody)
  quīcumque, quaecumoue, quodcumque (whoever/ whatever), decline in the same way as the relative above (→**2**)

Examples

1 **iuvenis cuius librum Sextus legit laetus erat**
The young man, whose book Sextus read, was happy

Fortunata, quae erat uxor Trimalchionis, saltare coeperat
Fortunata, who was Trimalchio's wife, had begun to dance

tum duo crotaiia protulit quae Fortunatae consideranda dedit
Then she brought out a pair of earrings which she gave to Fortunata to look at

2 **quidam** ex legatis
a certain ambassador

tu, **quicumque** es
you, whoever you are

Interrogative Pronouns

SINGULAR

	Masc		Fem		Neut	
Nom	**quis**	who?	**quis/quae**	who?	**quid**	what?
Acc	**quem**	whom?	**quam**	whom?	**quid**	what?
Gen	**cūius**	whose?	**cūius**	whose?	**cūius**	of what?
Dat	**cuī**	to whom?	**cuī**	to whom?	**cuī**	to what?
Abl	**quō**	by whom?	**quā**	by whom?	**quō**	by what?

PLURAL

	Masc		Fem		Neut	
Nom	**quī**	who?	**quae**	who?	**quae**	what?
Acc	**quōs**	whom?	**quās**	whom?	**quae**	what?
Gen	**quōrum**	whose?	**quārum**	whose?	**quōrum**	of what?
Dat	**quibus**	to whom?	**quibus**	to whom?	**quibus**	to what?
Abl	**quibus**	by whom?	**quibus**	by whom?	**quibus**	by what?

- The interrogative pronoun is used to ask questions and usually is the first word in the sentence (→**1**)

- **quisquis, quisquis, quidquid** (whoever, whatever)
  quisque, quisque, quidque (each)
  quisquam, quisquam, quicquam (anyone, anything)
  aliquis, aliquis, aliquid (someone, something)
  These pronouns decline in the same way as **quis** above (→**2**)

Examples

1 **quae fuit enim causa quamobrem isti mulieri venenum dare vellet Caelius?**
What was the reason why Caelius wanted to give that woman poison?

quid agam, iudices?
What am I to do, men of the jury?

quos ad cenam invitavisti?
Whom did you invite for dinner?

quorum agros Galli incenderunt?
Whose fields did the Gauls burn?

2 **quisque** is est
whoever he is

si **quemquam** video
if I see anyone

liber **alicuius**
someone's book

Prepositions

A preposition expresses the relationship of one word to another. Each Latin preposition governs a noun or pronoun in the accusative or ablative case. Some prepositions govern both cases. Some may also be used as adverbs eg **prope** (near).

Position

- Prepositions generally come before the noun, or an adjective or equivalent qualifying the noun *eg*

  ad villam   to the house
  ad Ciceronis villam   to Cicero's house

- **cum** follows a personal pronoun *eg*

  mēcum   with me

Prepositions governing the Accusative

On the following pages you will find some of the most frequent uses of prepositions in Latin. In the list below, the broad meaning is given on the left, with examples of usage following. Prepositions are given in alphabetical order.

ad
to/towards (*a place or person*)

oculos ad caelum sustulit
he raised his eyes to heaven

at, in the direction of, with regard to

ad Capuam profectus sum
I set out in the direction of Capua
ad portas
at the gates
ad duo milia occisi
about 2000 were killed
nil ad me attinet
it means nothing to me

adversum (-us)
opposite

sedens adversus te
sitting opposite you

towards

adversus Italiam
towards (*ie* facing) Italy

against

adversum flumen
against the stream

ante
before (*of place and time*),
used with ordinal number
in dates

ante meridiem
before midday
ante limen
before the doorway
ante diem quintum Kalendas Ianuarias
28th December (*ie* 5th before Kalends of January)

apud

at/near (usually with persons) **Crassus apud eum sedet**
Crassus is sitting near him

in the writing of **apud Platonem**
in Plato's writings

before (*authorities*) **apud pontifices**
before the high priests

circum (circa)

around, about (of place, people) **circum forum**
around the forum
circum Hectorem
around Hector
circa montes
around the mountains
circa decem milia Gallorum
about ten thousand Gauls

contra

against **contra hostes**
against the enemy
contra ventos
against the wind

opposite **contra Britanniam**
facing Britain

extra

outside of **extra muros**
outside the walls

beyond (*of place and time*) **extra iocum**
beyond a joke

inter

between **inter oppositos exercitus**
between the opposing armies
amans inter se
loving each other

among **inter saucios**
among the wounded
inter manus
within reach

during **inter hos annos**
during these years

intra

within (*of place and time*) **intra parietes**
within the walls
intra quattuor annos
within four years

ob

on account of **quam ob rem**
therefore
ob stultitiam
on account of your foolishness

Prepositions governing the Accusative (continued)

per
through

per noctem
through the night

by means of

per vos
by means of you

per aetatem periit
he died of old age

per deos iuro
I swear by the gods

post
after (*of time and place*)

post urbem conditam
after the foundation of the city

post tergum
behind your back

praeter
beyond

praeter naturam
beyond nature

besides

praeter se tres alios adduxit
he brought three others besides himself

except for

praeter paucos
except for a few

prope
near

prope me habitavit
he lived near me

propter
on account of

propter metum mortis
on account of fear of death

secundum
along (*of place*)

secundum flumen
along the river

immediately after (*time*)

secundum quietem
on waking from sleep

according to

secundum naturam
according to nature

trans
across

vexillum trans vallum traicere
to take the standard across the rampart

trans Rhenum
across the Rhine

ultra
beyond (*of time, degree etc*)

ultra vires
beyond one's power

Prepositions governing the Ablative

Those which are spatial represent the idea of rest in a place or motion from a place.

a(b)
from (*of place, people, direction, time*) **ab area hostes deiecti sunt**
the enemy were driven from the citadel
a nobis abesse
to be distant from us
a dextrā
from the right
a tertiā horā
from the third hour
by (*agent*) **ab amicis desertus**
abandoned by friends

cum
with **vade mecum**
go with me!
cum curā loqui
to speak with care
cum Augusto coniurare
to conspire with Augustus
summa cum laude
with distinction

dē
down from **dē caelō demittere**
to send down from heaven
away from **de tricliniō exire**
to go away from the dining room
about **cogitare de hāc rē**
to think about this matter
dē industriā
on purpose
during *or* at (*of time*) **dē nocte**
at night, during the night

ē(x)
out of (*from*) **ē carcere effugerunt**
they escaped from prison
ex equis desilire
to jump from their horses
quidam ex Hispania
someone from Spain
statua ex argentō facta
a statue made of silver
immediately after **ex consulatu**
immediately after his consulship
from **ex hōc diē**
from that day
ex aequō
equally

Prepositions governing the Ablative (continued)

pro
for/on behalf of

pro se quisque
each one for himself/ herself
pro patriā morī
to die for one's country

according to

pro viribus agere
to act according to one's ability

in front of

pro rostris
in front of the rostrum

sine
without

sine spē
without hope
sine pecuniā
without money

Prepositions governing Accusative and Ablative

in
with accusative

into   **in hanc urbem venire**
to come into the city

till   **in primam lucem dormivit**
he slept till dawn

against   **in rem publicam aggredi**
to attack the state

with ablative

in   **puella in illā domō laetē vivebat**
the girl lived happily in that house

on   **in capite coronam gerebat**
he wore a crown on his head
in animo habere
to intend (to have in one's mind)

within (of time)   **in omni aetate**
within every age

in (of condition)   **in parte facilis, in parte difficilis**
easy in parts, difficult in others

sub
with accusative

beneath   **sub iugum mittere**
to send beneath the yoke (*ie* into slavery)

below (*with verb of motion*)   **sub ipsum murum**
`   just below the wall

before (*of time*)   **sub vesperum**
just before nightfall

with ablative

under (*of place and power*)   **sub montibus constituere**
to station under the mountains
sub Nerone
under the power of Nero

super
with accusative

over, above (*of place*), in addition   **super capita hostium**
over the heads of the enemy
alii, super alios, advenerunt
they arrived one after the other

with ablative

concerning/about   **super his rebus scribam**
I shall write about these matters

Numerals

Cardinal and Ordinal Numbers

		CARDINAL	ORDINAL
1	I	ūnus, -a, -um	prīmus, -a, -um
2	II	duo, -ae, -o	secundus, -a, -um
3	III	trēs, tria	tertius, -a, -um
4	IV	quattuor	quartus, -a, -um
5	V	quīnque	quīntus, -a, -um
6	VI	sex	sextus, -a, -um
7	VII	septem	septimus, -a, -um
8	VIII	octō	octāvus, -a, -um
9	IX	novem	nōnus, -a, -um
10	X	decem	decimus, -a, -um
11	XI	ūndecim	ūndecimus, -a, -um
12	XII	duodecim	duodecimus, -a, -um
13	XIII	tredecim	tertius decimus, -a, -um
14	XIV	quattuordecim	quartus decimus, -a, -um
15	XV	quīndecim	quintus decimus, -a, -um
16	XVI	sēdecim	sextus decimus, -a, -um
17	XVII	septendecim	septimus decimus, -a, -um
18	XVIII	duodēvigintī	duodēvicēsimus, -a, -um
19	XIX	ūndevigmtī	undēvicēsimus, -a, -um
20	XX	vigintī	vicēsimus, -a, -um
21	XXI	vigintī ūnus	vicēsimus prīmus
30	XXX	trīginta	trīcēsimus
40	XL	quadrāgintā	quadrāgēsimus
50	L	quīnquāgintā	quīnquāgēsimus
60	LX	sexāgintā	sexāgēsimus
70	LXX	septuāgintā	septuāgēsimus
80	LXXX	octōgintā	octōgēsimus
90	XC	nōnagintā	nōnāgēsimus
100	C	centum	centēsimus
200	CC	ducentī, -ae, -a	ducentēsimus
300	CCC	trecentī, -ae, -a	trecentēsimus
400	CCCC	quadringentī -ae, -a,	quadringentēsimus
500	D (IↃ)	quīngentī, -ae, -a	quīngentesimus
600	DC	sescentī, -ae,	sescentesimus
700	DCC	septingentī, -ae, -a	septingentēsimus
800	DCCC	octingentī, -ae, –a	octingentēsimus
900	DCCCC	nōngentī, -ae, -a	nōngentēsimus
1000	M (CIↃ)	mīlle	mīllēsimus
2000	MM	duo mīlia	bis mīllesimus
1,000,000		deciēs centēna (centum)	mīlia

- Fractions are expressed as follows:

  dimidia pars 1/2
  tertia pars 1/3
  quārta pars 1/4

- Ordinal numbers (→**1**) decline like 1st and 2nd declension adjectives

- Cardinal numbers (→**2**) do not decline except for **ūnus**, **duo**, **trēs** and hundreds (**ducenti** etc)

- **unus** declines as 1st and 2nd declension adjectives except that the genitive singular ends in -**ius** and the dative in –**i**

- **duo** (two) declines as follows:

	Masc	*Fem*	*Neut*
Nom	**duo**	**duae**	**duo**
Acc	**duōs**	**duas**	**duo**
Gen	**duōrum**	**duārum**	**duōrum**
Dat	**duōbus**	**duābus**	**duōbus**
Abl	**duōbus**	**duābus**	**duōbus**

ambō, -ae, -a (both) declines in the same way

- **trēs** (three) declines as follows:

	Masc	*Fem*	*Neut*
Nom	**trēs**	**trēs**	**tria**
Acc	**trēs**	**trēs**	**tria**
Gen	**trium**	**trium**	**trium**
Dat	**tribus**	**tribus**	**tribus**
Abl	**tribus**	**tribus**	**tribus**

- Genitive of hundreds, *eg* **trecentī** ends -**um** (→**3**)

- **mīlia** (thousands) declines as follows:

Nom	**mīlia**
Acc	**mīlia**
Gen	**mīlium**
Dat	**mīlibus**
Abl	**mīlibus**

- **mīlle** (thousand) does not decline.

Examples

1 coquus **secundam** mensam paraverat
The cook had prepared the second course

legionis **nonae** milites magnam partem hostium interfecerunt
Soldiers of the ninth legion killed a large number of the enemy

2 **decem milia** passuum exercitus progressus est
The army advanced 10 miles

Cerberus, qui **tria** capita habebat, in antro recubuit
Cerberus, who had three heads, crouched in the cave

stellae **novem** orbes confecerunt
The stars completed nine orbits

duodeviginti onerariae naves huc accedebant
Eighteen cargo ships were approaching

Caesar **trecentos** milites trans Padanum traiecit
Caesar transported three hundred soldiers across the River Po

da mi basia **mille**
Give me a thousand kisses

3 **trecentum militum**
of three hundred soldiers

4 **duo milia passuum** (*gen*)
2000 paces *or* 2 miles

Distributive Numerals

These are used when repetition is involved as when multiplying (→**1**)

1	**singulī, -ae, -a**	*one each*
2	**bīnī, -ae, -a**	*two each*
3	**ternī (trinī)**	
4	**quaternī**	
5	**quīnī**	
6	**sēnī**	
7	**septēnī**	
8	**octonī**	
9	**novēnī**	
10	**dēni**	

Numeral Adverbs

1	**semel**	*once*
2	**bis**	*twice*
3	**ter**	
4	**quater**	
5	**quīnquiēs**	
6	**sexiēs**	
7	**septiēs**	
8	**octiēs**	
9	**noviēs**	
10	**deciēs**	

(→**2**)

Examples

1 **bini** gladiatores
(*describing pairs of gladiators*)

bina castra
two camps

quaternos denarios in **singulas** vini amphoras
4 denarii each for a bottle of wine

2 non plus quam **semel**
not more than once

decies centena milia sestertium or **decies** sestertium
1,000,000 sesterces

ter quattuor
twelve (*three times four*)

Dates

- Events of the year were usually recorded by using the names of the consuls holding office that year (→**1**)

- From the late republic the date of the foundation of Rome was established – 753 BC – and time was calculated from this date (→**2**)

- The four seasons were: (→**3**)

ver, veris (*nt*)	spring
aestās, -atis (*f*)	summer
autumnus, -i (*m*)	autumn
hiems, -is (*f*)	winter

- The months were reformed by Julius Caesar (7 of 31 days, 4 of 30, 1 of 28, and an extra day each leap year). Each month (**mensis, -is**, *m*) was identified by the following adjectives:

Iānuārius	January
Februārius	February
Martius	March
Āprīlis	April
Māius	May
Iūnius	June
Iulīus (Quintīlis)	July
Augustus (Sextīlis)	August
September	September
Octōber	October
November	November
December	December

- Three important days each month were:

Kalendae, -arum (*fpl*)	Kalends or 1st
Nonae, -arum (*fpl*)	Nones or 5th/7th
Idus, -uum (*fpl*)	Ides or 13th/15th

Examples

1 **Nerone iterum L. Pisone consulibus** pauca memoria digna evenerunt
Few incidents worth recording took place during the year when Nero and Lucius Piso were consuls (AD 57)

Lentulo Gaetulico C. Calvisio consulibus decreta sunt triumphi insignia Poppaeo Sabino
A triumph was voted to Poppaeus Sabinus during the consulship of Lentulus Gaetulicus and Gaius Calvisius

2 **ab urbe condita**
since the foundation of Rome

ante urbem conditam
before the foundation of the city

post urbem conditam
after the foundation of the city

3 ineunte **aestate**
in the beginning of summer

media **aestate**
midsummer

iam **hieme confecta**
when winter was already over

vere ineunte Antonius Tarentum navigavit
At the beginning of spring, Antony sailed to Tarentum

Dates (continued)

- In March, July, October and May, Nones fall on the 7th and Ides on the 15th day (5th and 13th in all other months).

- To refer to these dates, the ablative is used (→**1**)

- To refer to the day before these dates, use **pridiē** (→**2**)

- All other days were reckoned by counting (inclusively) the days before the next main date, "ante diem" + accusative of ordinal numbers and the next main date were used:
  9th of February is 5 days before the 13th of February (counting inclusively). 28th April is 4 days before 1st May (→**3**)

- An easy way to work out such dates is to add one to Nones and Ides and subtract the Latin number. Add two to the number of days in the month before the Kalends, again subtracting the given Latin number. You will then have the date in English.

- The day was divided into twelve hours **horae, -arum** (*fpl*). The hours of darkness into four watches of three hours each, **vīgiliae, -arum** (*fpl*), from 6–9 pm, 9–12 pm, 12–3 am, 3–6 am

- Other ways of expressing time:

primā luce	at dawn
solo orto	at sunrise
solis occasu	at sunset
media nocte	at midnight
noctu, nocte	at night
mane	in the morning
meridie	at midday
sub vesperum	towards evening
vespere	in the evening (→**4**)

Examples

❶ Kalendīs Martiis
on the 1st of March

Idibus Decembribus
on the 13th of December

Idibus Martiis Caesar a Bruto interfectus est
Caesar was killed by Brutus on the 15th of March

❷ pridie Nonas Ianuarias (**Non. Ian.**)
4th January

❸ ante diem quintum Idus Februarias
9th February

ante diem quartum Kalendas Maias
28th April

❹ prima hora
at the first hour (6–7 am)

tertia vigilia
during the third watch (midnight–3 am)

tertia fere vigilia navem solvit
He set sail after midnight (during the third watch)

ipse **hora circiter quarta diei** cum primis navibus Britanniam attigit
He himself reached Britain with the first ships around 10 o'clock in the morning

vespere vinum optimum convivae bibunt
In the evening, the guests drink vintage wine

Sentence Structure

Simple Sentences

Word order in English is stricter than in Latin. The usual English order – subject+verb+object – differentiates the meaning of sentences such as, "The cat caught the mouse" and "The mouse caught the cat". Latin order is more flexible since the endings of words clearly show their function, whatever their position in the sentence.

Compare the following:

feles murem cepit	the cat caught the mouse
murem cepit feles	it was the cat that caught the mouse

The sentences are identical in meaning, although the emphasis is different. This difference in word order often makes it difficult for English translators to unravel long Latin sentences. However there are certain principles to help:

- The normal *grammatical* word order in Latin is:
  Subject first, Predicate after (by Predicate understand "verb")

- Expressions qualifying the subject (*ie* adjectives) must be near the subject

- Expression qualifying the predicate (*eg* objects, adverbs, prepositional phrases) must be near the verb

> Thus the usual word order of a simple sentence is:
> (Connecting Word)
> **Subject**
> (Adjective)
> Object
> Adverbs *or* prepositional phrases
> **Predicate** (verb) (→**1**)

Examples

❶ at **hostes** magnam virtutem in extrema spe salutis **praestiterunt**
But the enemy showed great courage, finally hoping to save themselves

Ariovistus ad postulata Caesaris pauca **respondit**
Ariovistus briefly replied to Caesar's demands

iste **Hannibal** sic hanc Tertiam **dilexit**
Thus that Hannibal loved this Tertia

Simple Sentences (continued)

- Another principle is *emphasis*, where the words are in an unusual order, *eg* subject last, predicate first (→**1**)

- Questions usually begin with interrogatives (→**2**)

- Adjectives may precede or follow nouns. Check agreement of endings (→**3**)

- Genitives usually follow the governing word (→**4**)

- Words in apposition usually follow one another, although "rex" often comes first (→**5**)

- Adverbs usually come before their verb, adjective or adverb (→**6**)

- Prepositions usually come before their nouns (→**7**) but note, magna **cum** cura (with great care).

- Finally, watch out for the omission of words, particularly parts of **esse** (to be) (→**8**)

Examples

1 horum adventu **redintegratur | seditio** (subject last)
On their arrival trouble broke out once more

    confecerunt me | infirmitates meorum (verb first)
I have been upset by the illnesses of my slaves

2 **quid** hoc loco potes dicere, homo amentissime?
What can you say at this point, you madman?

    quis clarior in Graecia Themistocle?
Who (is) more famous in Greece than Themistocles?

3 **bello magno** victus
conquered in a great war

    magna domus
a large house

4 multi **nostrum**
many of us

    filius **Augusti**
Augustus' son

5 Cicero, **consul**
Cicero, the consul

    rex Tarquinius
King Tarquinius

6 **vix** cuiquam persuadebatur
hardly anyone could be persuaded

    multo carius
much dearer

7 **in** villam
into the house

    sub monte
under the mountain

8 **pudor inde et miseratio et patris Agrippae, Augusti avi memoria (est)**
A feeling of pity and shame came over them and they remembered her father Agrippa and her grandfather Augustus

Compound Sentences

A compound sentence is one with a main clause and one or more subordinate clauses. In Latin this is called a **period**, where the most important idea is kept to the end.

- conservate parenti filium, parentem filio, (1) ne aut senectutem iam prope desperatam contempsisse aut adulescentiam plenam spei | maximae non modo non aluisse vos verum etiam perculisse atque adflixisse videamini (2). (Cic. – Pro Caelio 32.80)

    1. Main clause
       save a son for his father, a father for his son.
    2. Negative purpose clause
       lest you appear either to have cast aside an old man near despair or that you have failed to sustain a young man full of the highest hopes, but have even struck him down and ruined him.

    Note that this sentence builds towards a climax at the end. The most important verbs here are **perculisse** and **adflixisse** rather than **videamini** (you may seem). Notice also the rhythm of the last two words. Repetition of similar phrases is common – **parenti filium, parentem filio**. This sentence is a good illustration of an orator's style.

- Historical style is much simpler, often a subordinate clause followed by a main clause:

    cum equites nostri funditoribus sagittariisque flumen transgressi essent (1), cum equitatu proelium commiserunt (2)

    1. Subordinate adverbial clause of time
       when our cavalry had crossed the river with slingers and archers
    2. Main clause
       they joined battle with the cavalry

- Participle phrase followed by the **main clause** and **subordinate** clause:

    nec patrum cognitionibus satiatus iudiciis (1), adsidebat in cornu tribunalis (2), ne praetorem curuli depelleret (Tac Ann I 75)

    1. Participle phrase
       nor was he (the emperor) satisfied with taking part in Senate trials
    2. Main clause
       he used to sit in the ordinary lawcourts
    3. Subordinate clause of purpose
       in case he pushed the praetor from his curule chair

Many other combinations of clauses are possible. It is important to relate the sentence to its context and to the passage as a whole as Latin sentences are linked logically. It is often helpful when translating a long sentence to pick out subjects and verbs in order to recognize the structure of the clauses and grasp the overall meaning of the sentence.

Direct Statement

The basic patterns involved in direct statement have been illustrated under **Simple Sentences** (see p 43).

Direct Questions

In Latin a direct question can be expressed as follows by:

- an interrogative pronoun (→**1**)

    quis? (who?), **quid**? (what?), **cur**? (why?)

- adding **-ne** to the first word, where no definite answer is indicated (→**2**)

- **nonne**, when the expected answer is YES (→**3**)

- **num**, when the expected answer is NO (→**4**)

- **utrum ... an(non)**
  -ne ... an(non) } (whether) ... or (not)
  ... an(non)
  in double questions (→**5**)

Examples

1 **quis** est
Who is it?

quid dicit?
What is he saying?

cur lacrimas?
Why are you crying?

2 times**ne** Verrem?
Are you scared of Verres?

3 **nonne** cladem audivisti?
Surely you heard of the defeat?
or You heard of the defeat, didn't you?

4 **num** heri venisti?
Surely you didn't come yesterday?
or You didn't come yesterday, did you?

5 utrum has condiciones accepistis **annon**?
Have you accepted these conditions or not?

Direct Command

- A direct command in Latin is expressed in the second person by the imperative if positive, by **nolī(te)** with the present infinitive if negative (→**1**)
- A direct command in the first or third persons is expressed by the present subjunctive, with **nē** if negative (→**2**)

Wishes

- Wishes are expressed in Latin by **utinam** with the subjunctive, **utinam nē** when negative (→**3**)
- **vellem** may also be used with imperfect or pluperfect subjunctive to express wishes (→**4**)

Examples

1 **venite** mecum
come with me

nolī me tangere
don't touch me

2 **vivamus** atque **amemus**
let us live and let us love

ne **fiat** lux
let there not be light

3 **utinam** frater redeat
I wish my brother would return (*future*)

utinam ne vere scriberem
I wish I were not writing the truth (*present*)

utinam brevi moratus esses
I wish you had stayed a little (*past*)

4 **vellem** me ad cenam **invitavisses**
I wish you had invited me to dinner

Indirect Statement

"You are making a mistake" is a *direct statement*. "I think that you are making a mistake" is an *indirect statement*.

- The indirect statement is the object clause of "I think". In indirect statement in Latin, the subject of the clause (*eg* te) goes into the accusative case, the verb is an infinitive (*errare*):

  Puto **te errare**
  I think that you are making a mistake

- This pattern is used after verbs of saying, thinking, perceiving, knowing (→**1**)

Examples

1

audire	hear	**negare**	say ... not
cognoscere	discover	**nescire**	not to know
credere	believe	**putare**	think
dicere	say	**scire**	know
intellegere	understand	**sentire**	perceive
meminisse	remember	**videre**	see
narrare	tell		

Translation

- The *present infinitive* refers to actions happening at the same time and may be translated – is, are, was, were.

- The *perfect infinitive* refers to prior action and may be translated – has, have, had.

- The *future infinitive* refers to future action and may be translated – will, would.

putamus	**te errāre**	We think	that you are making a mistake
	te errāvisse		that you have made a mistake
	te errātūrum esse		that you will make a mistake

putabamus	**te errāre**	We thought	that you were making a mistake
	te errāvisse		that you had made a mistake
	te errātūrum esse		that you would make a mistake

- Notice that when the main verb is *past tense*, translate the present infinitive – "was, were", the past infinitive – "had", the future infinitive – "would".

- The reflexive pronoun **sē** is used to refer to the subject of the main verb (→**1**)

- Translate **negō** – I say that... not (→**2**)

- Verbs of promising, hoping, threatening or swearing (*eg* **promitto**, **pollicēor**, **spērō**, **minor**, **iuro**) are followed by an accusative and future infinitive (→**3**)

Examples

1 senex dixit **se** thesaurum invenisse
The old man said that he had found treasure

2 **negavit** servum domum venturum esse
He said that the slave would not come home

3 **promisi me festinaturum esse**
I promised that I would hurry

sperabat se hoc confecturum esse
He hoped that he could complete this
or He hoped to complete this

Further Examples

creditores existimabant **eum** totam pecuniam **perdidisse**
His creditors thought that he had lost all his money

memini **simulacra** deorum de caelo **percussa esse**
I remember that the gods' statues were struck down from the heavens

vidistine **Catonem** in bibliotheca **sedere**?
Did you see Cato sitting in the library?

iuro **me** pro patria fortiter **pugnaturum esse**
I swear that I shall fight bravely for my country

iam ego credo **vos** verum **dixisse**
I now believe that you spoke the truth

negavit **nihil** umquam pulchrius statua **fuisse**
He said that nothing had ever been more beautiful than that statue

Indirect Question

"Where did he come from?" is a *direct question*. "I asked where he had come from" is an *indirect question*. Latin uses the same interrogative words (**quis** – who, **quid** – what *etc*) and the verb in indirect questions is always subjunctive

> rogavi **unde venisset**
> I asked where he had come from

- Latin uses six different forms of the subjunctive in this construction in a precise sequence depending on the main verb (→**1**)

Examples

1 rogo   **unde veniat**   I ask   where he comes from   *(present)*
        unde venerit   where he has come from   *(perfect)*
        unde venturus sit   where he will come from   *(future)*

   rogavi   **unde veniret**   I asked   where he was coming from   *(imperfect)*
        unde venisset   where he had come from   *(pluperfect)*
        unde venturus esset   where he would come from   *(future perfect)*

Translation

Translation of tenses in indirect question is *easy*, because English uses the same tenses as Latin, as can be seen on page 50.

- The reflexive pronoun **se** is used to refer to the subject of the main verb (→**1**)

- **utrum ... an** (if ... or), **utrum ... necne** (whether ... or not) are also used in indirect questions (→**2**)

- **num** is used to mean "if" in indirect questions (→**3**)

Examples

1 **rogavit quando se visuri essemus**
He asked when we would see him

2 roga **utrum** iverit **an** manserit
Ask whether he went or stayed

roga **utrum** manserit **necne**
Ask whether he stayed or not

rogavit **utrum** Scylla infestior **esset** Chaiybdis **necne**
He asked whether Charybdis was more dangerous than Scylla or not

3 nescio **num** venturi sint
I don't know if they will come

Further Examples

nescimus **quid facturi simus**
We don't know what we shall do

mirum est **quanta sit Roma**
It is amazing how big Rome is

or The size of Rome is amazing

exploratores cognoverunt **quanti essent** Poeni
Scouts discovered what the numbers of the Carthaginians were

incredibile est **quomodo** talia facere **potuerit**
It is incredible how he was able to do such things

nemo audivit **quid** rex **constituisset**
No one heard what the king had decided
or No one heard the king's decision

Indirect Command

"Come here" is a *direct command*. "I ordered you to come here" is an *indirect command*. Indirect commands in Latin are expressed by **ut** (when positive) or **nē** (when negative) and have their verbs in the subjunctive (→**1**)

- Latin uses two tenses of the subjunctive, present or imperfect, in this construction. It uses the present subjunctive if the main verb is present or future tense and imperfect subjunctive if the main verb is in the past tense. (→**2**)

Translation

- The English translation of the indirect command is the same, whichever tense is used in Latin – the infinitive (eg to come)

- The reflexive **se** is used to refer to the subject of the main verb (→**3**)

- Common verbs introducing indirect command are:

hortor	encourage
moneo	warn
oro	beg
persuadeo	persuade
rogo	ask

- Only **iubeo** (to order), **veto** (to tell... not), are usually used with the infinitive in Latin (→**4**)

Examples

1 tibi imperavi **ut venīrēs**
I ordered you to come

tibi imperavi **ne venires**
I forbade you to come

milites oravit **ne** in castris diutius **manerent**
He begged his soldiers not to stay in camp any longer

hoc rogo, mi Tiro, **ne** temere **naviges**
I beg you, my dear Tiro, not to sail carelessly

2 tibi **impero ut venias** (*present*)
I order you to come

tibi **imperavi ut venires** (*imperfect*)
I ordered you to come

deos precor **ut nobis parcant**
I beg the gods to spare us

amicos roga **ut veniant**, operamque **dent**, et messim hanc nobis **adiuvent**
Ask your friends to come and lend a hand and help us with this harvest

3 nos oravit ut **sibi** cibum daremus
He begged us to give him food

4 iubeo eos **navigare**
I order them to sail

veto eos **navigare**
I tell them not to sail

mater me **vetuit** in murum **ascendere**
Mother forbade me to climb on the wall

Antonius eos **iussit** adventum **suum exspectare**
Antony told them to await his arrival

Purpose or Final Clauses

There are two ways of expressing purpose in English:

> I am hurrying to the city to see the games
> *or* I am hurrying to the city so that I may see the games

- In Latin **ut** is used with the present or imperfect subjunctive, to express purpose. The present subjunctive is used if the main verb is in the present or future tense and the imperfect subjunctive if the main verb is in the past tense (→**1**)

- Negative purpose clauses are introduced by **ne** which can be translated "so that... not", "in case", "to avoid", "lest" *etc* (→**2**)

- If there is a comparative adjective or adverb in the Latin sentence **quō** is used instead of **ut** (→**3**)

- The relative **qui**, **quae**, **quod** may be used instead of **ut**, if it refers to an object in the main clause (→**4**)

- After negative **ne**, **quis** is used instead of **aliquis** to mean "anyone"

- Note that **se** is used to refer to the subject of the main verb (→**5**)

- **ad** is used with the gerundive to express purpose (→**6**)

- The supine -**um** is used after verbs of motion to express purpose (→**7**)

Examples

1 ad urbem festino **ut** ludos **videam**
I am hurrying to the city to see the games

ad urbem festinavi **ut** ludos **viderem**
I hurried to the city to see the games

filium multo cum fletu complexus, pepulit **ut abiret**
Embracing his son tearfully, he drove him to leave

2 Tiberius hoc recusavit **ne** Germanicus imperium **haberet**
Tiberius refused this lest Germanicus had power

pontem resciderunt **ne** hostes flumen **transirent**
They broke down the bridge in case the enemy crossed the river

3 puellae cantabant **quo** laetiores essent **hospites**
The girls sang to make their guests happier

4 rex sex milites delegit **qui** ad Graeciam **proficiscerentur**
The king chose six soldiers to set off for Greece

5 in silvis se abdidit **ne quis se** videret
He hid in the woods lest anyone should see him

sed **ut** venenum manifesto comprehendi **posset**, constitui locum iussit, **ut** eo **mitteret** amicos, **qui laterent**, cum venisset Licinius, venenumque traderet, comprehenderent
But *so that the poison could be seized openly*, he ordered that a place be appointed, *to send friends there, to hide*. When Licinius came to hand over the poison they could arrest him.

6 Verres ad Siciliam venit **ad urbes diripiendas**
Verres came to Sicily to plunder its cities

7 veniunt **spectatum**
They come to see

Result or Consecutive Clauses

> The road is so long that I am tired
> It was so hot that we could not work

In both these sentences, a result or consequence is expressed in English by using words such as

> **so ... that** (positive)
> **so that ... not** (negative)

- In Latin the following words are frequently used in the main clause

adeo	to such an extent
ita	thus, so
talis	of such a kind
tam	so
tantus	so great
tot	so many

- In the result clause, **ut** (so that) and **ut ... non** (so that ... not) are used with the present or imperfect subjunctive. Present subjunctive is used where the main verb is in the present and the imperfect subjunctive is used where the main verb is past (→**1**)

Note that **eum** is used to refer to "him" instead of **se** when referring to the subject of the main clause as in the first example (→**1**)

Examples

1 Gallus **tam** ferox est **ut** omnes Romani eum **timeant**
The Gaul is so fierce that all the Romans are scared of him

tanta erat tempestas **ut** nautae navem **non solverent**
So great was the storm that the sailors could not set sail

nemo est **adeo** stultus **ut non** discere **possit**
No one is so stupid that he can't learn

tot sententiae erant **ut nemo consentiret**
There were so many opinions that no one could agree

tales nos esse putamus **ut** ab omnibus **laudemur**
We think that we are the sort of people to be praised by everyone

Verbs of Fearing

In Latin, verbs of fearing (**timeo, metuo, paveo, vereor**) are followed by **nē, nē non** or **ut** with the present and perfect, imperfect and pluperfect subjunctive according to sequence of tenses:

- The present subjunctive represents present and future tenses in English

    I am afraid he is coming
    I am afraid he will come

- The perfect subjunctive represents the past tense in English

    I am afraid that he has come

- When the verb of fearing is in the past tense, imperfect and pluperfect subjunctive are used in Latin instead (→**1**)

- **nē** is used if the fear is expressed in a positive sentence (ie I am afraid he will come), **nē non, ut** is used if the fear is expressed negatively (ie I am afraid that he won't come) (→**2**)

- As in English, the infinitive can follow a verb of fearing, provided that the subjects of both are the same (→**3**)

Examples

1 veritus sum **ne veniret**
I was afraid he was coming

veritus sum **ne venisset**
I was afraid that he had come

2 **vereor ne** amicus **veniat**
I am afraid lest my friend comes
or lest my friend will come

vereor ne amicus **non veniat**
I am afraid that my friend won't come

vereor ut amicus **venerit**
I am afraid that my friend has not come

verebar ne amicus **non venisset**
I was afraid that my friend had not come

metuo ne virtutis maiorum nostrum **obliviscamur**
I am afraid that we shall forget the courage of our ancestors

paves ne ducas tu illam
You are afraid to marry her

Verres, **veritus ne** servi bellum in Sicilia **facerent**, multos in vincula coniecit
Verres, fearing that slaves might revolt in Sicily, threw many into prison

Romani **verebantur ne** fortiter **non pugnavissent**
The Romans were afraid that they had not fought bravely

3 timeo **abire**
I am afraid to go away

mulier **timebat manere** sola
The woman was scared to remain alone

Conditional Sentences

Compare the following two sentences in English:

> (a) If I tell you a lie, you will be angry
> (b) If I were to tell you a lie, you would be angry

The first is a *logical statement of fact*, stating what *will* happen, the second is a *hypothesis*, stating what *would happen*.

For the first type of sentence, Latin uses the indicative mood in both main and conditional clauses. For the second type, Latin uses the subjunctive mood in both main and conditional clauses.

Translate type (a) as follows:

> si hoc **dicis**, sapiens **es**
> if you say this, you are wise

> si hoc **dicebas**, sapiens **eras**
> if you were saying this, you were wise

> si hoc **dixisti**, erravisti
> if you said this, then you made a mistake

> si hoc **dixeris**, errabis
> if you say this, you will make a mistake

Notice that the same tenses in English are used as in Latin except in the last sentence. Latin is more precise – *you will have said this*, before you make a mistake, therefore Latin uses the *future perfect* tense.

• Consider also the following sentence:

> si me **amabis**, mecum **manebis**
> If you love me, you will stay with me

Latin uses the *future* tense in both clauses, English uses the *present* tense in the "if" clause. Both actions, "loving" and "remaining" *logically* refer to the *future*.

Translate type (b) as follows:

> (*present*)
> si hoc **dicas**, **erres**
> if you were to say this, you would be making a mistake

> (*imperfect*)
> si hoc **diceres**, **errares**
> if you said (or were saying) that, you would be making a mistake

> (*pluperfect*)
> si hoc **dixisses**, **erravisses**
> if you had said that, you would have made a mistake

Notice that both tenses of the subjunctive are the same in the above examples. Sometimes an imperfect may be used in one clause and the pluperfect in the other:

> si pudorem **haberes**, Roma **abiisses**
> if you had any sense of shame, you would have left Rome

Negative Conditional Sentences

- **nisi** (unless) is the negative of **si** (if) (→**1**)

- **si non** (if not), is less common and negates one word, or is used when the same verb is repeated (→**2**)

Examples

1 **nisi** id statim **feceris,** ego te **tradam** magistratui
Unless you do this immediately, I shall hand you over to the magistrate

nisi utilem **crederem,** non pacem **peterem**
Unless I thought it useful, I would not be seeking peace

2 **si** me **adiuveris,** laeta **ero; si** me **non adiuveris,** tristis **ero**
If you help me, I shall be happy; if you don't help me, I shall be sad

si navigatio **non morabitur,** mox te **videbo**
If my sailing is not delayed, I shall see you soon

Further Examples

(**b**) quis illum sceleratum fuisse **putavisset, si tacuisset**?
Who would have thought he was a rascal, if he had kept quiet?

(**b**) multi **agerent** et **pugnarent** si rei publicae **videretur**
Many would act and fight, if the state decided

(**a**) **gaudemus si** liberi in horto **ludunt**
We are happy if the children play in the garden

(**b**) **si quis** in caelum **ascendisset,** pulchritudinem siderum **conspexisset**
If anyone had gone up to heaven, he would have seen the beauty of the stars

Concessive Clauses

In English, Concessive clauses usually begin with "although":

> Although he is rich, he is not happy
> I shall succeed although it is difficult

- **quamquam** (although) is followed by the indicative (→**1**)

  Note that **tamen** (however) is often used in the main clause in concessive sentences

- **quamvis** (although) is always followed by the subjunctive (→**2**)

- **cum** in the sense "although" is always followed by the subjunctive (→**3**)

- **etsi** (although) takes the indicative or subjunctive according to the same rules as **si** (*see* p 56). The indicative is more common (→**4**)

Examples

1 medici **quamquam intellegunt**, numquam **tamen** aegris de morbo dicunt
Although doctors know, they never tell their patients about their illness

quamquam Aeneas dicere **volebat**, Dido solo fixos oculos aversa tenebat
Although Aeneas wished to speak, Dido turned away and kept her eyes fixed on the ground

2 **quamvis** frater **esset** molestus, Marcus eum amavit
Although his brother was a nuisance, Marcus loved him

feminae, **quamvis** in periculo **essent**, tamen liberos servaverunt
Although the women were in danger, yet they saved their children

3 **cum non didicissem** geometrias, litteras sciebam
Although I had not learnt geometry, I knew my letters

non poterant, **cum vellent**, Lucium liberare
They were not able, although they wished, to free Lucius

4 **etsi** servus **est**, certe persona est
Although he is a slave, he is a person

etsi victoriam non reportavissetis, tamen vos contentos esse oportebat
Although you had not won a victory, yet you should have been content

etsi domi **esset filius iuvenis**, agros ipse colebat
Although he had a young son at home, he cultivated the fields by himself

Causal Clauses

Clauses which begin with the words "because" or "since" and give a reason for something are often called causal clauses in English.

- Causal clauses have their verbs in the indicative when the *actual* cause is stated. They are introduced by **quod**, **quia** (because), and **quoniam** (since) (→**1**)

- **quod** is used with the subjunctive when the cause is only *suggested* (→**2**)

- **non quod** (+ *subj*) ... **sed quia** (+ *indic*) not because ... but because ..., is used when the first reason is discarded. The true reason is expressed in the indicative (→**3**)

- **cum** (since, as) is always followed by the subjunctive (→**4**)

- **qui** with the subjunctive can be used to mean "since" (→**5**)

Examples

1 non iratus sum **quod** in me **fuisti** asperior
I am not angry because you were too harsh towards me

in crypta Neapolitana vecti, timebamus **quia** longior et obscurior carcere **erat**
Travelling in the Naples tunnel, we were afraid because it was longer and darker than a prison

quoniam ita tu **vis**, ego Puteolos tecum proficiscar
Since you wish this, I shall set off with you to Pozzuoli

2 templa spoliare non poterant **quod** religione **impedirentur**
They could not plunder the temples because (they said) they were prevented by religious feelings

3 mater semper maxime laboravit **non quod** necessarium **esset sed quia** honestum esse **videbatur**
Mother always worked very hard, not because it was necessary but because it seemed proper

4 quae **cum** ita **sint**, Catilina, egredere ex urbe!
Since this is so, Catilina, leave the city!

Caesar, **cum** in continente hiemare **constituisset**, ad Galliam rediit
Since Caesar had decided to spend the winter on the mainland, he returned to Gaul

5 sapiens erat **qui** studiis totos annos **dedisset**
He was wise since he had devoted all his years to study

Temporal Clauses

Clauses denoting time are introduced by conjunctions, *eg* **ubi** (when) followed by verbs in the indicative. Some conjunctions, *eg* **cum** (when) may also take the subjunctive. (→**1**)

Conjunctions followed by the indicative:

ut	when, as
ubi	when

cum primum	
ubi primum	as soon as
ut primum	

simul ac	
simul atque	as soon as

quotiens	as often as, whenever
quamdiu	as long as, while
ex quo (**tempore**)	ever since

postquam	
posteaquam	after (**post** or **postea** may be separated from **quam**)

Examples

1 **ut** valetudo Germanici Romae **nuntiata est**, magna ira erat
When Germanicus' state of health was announced in Rome, there was great anger

ubi primum classis visa est, **complentur** non modo portus sed moenia ac tecta
As soon as the fleet was seen, not only the harbour but the walls and rooftops were filled (with people)

quod **ubi cognitum est** hostibus, universi nonam legionem nocte aggressi sunt
When this was discovered by the enemy, all of them attacked the ninth legion at night

quotiens proficiscor, pluit
Every time I set out, it rains

manebat **quamdiu poterat**
He stayed as long as he could

Septimus annus est, milites, **ex quo** Britanniam **vicistis**
It is seven years, soldiers, since you conquered Britain

postquam vallum **intravit**, portas stationibus **confirmavit**
After entering the fortification, he strengthened the gates with guards

post tertium diem **quam redierat**, mortuus est
He died three days after his return

Conjunctions which take the indicative or subjunctive:

cum

- **when** with indicative and often **tum** in the main clause (→**1**)

- **whenever** with the following pattern of tenses in the indicative: (→**2**)

    + **perfect** followed by **present** tense
    + **future perfect** followed by **future** tense
    + **pluperfect** followed by **imperfect** tense

- **when, as** with the imperfect or pluperfect subjunctive narrative (→**3**)

dum

- **while** with indicative

    the present tense is used when **dum** means "during the time that" (→**4**)

- Note that where the same tense (here, the future) is used in both clauses, **dum** means "all the time that". Latin uses future **vivam** more accurately than English "live" (→**5**)

Examples

1 **cum** tu Romae **eras, tum** ego domi eram
When you were in Rome, I was then at home

2 **cum surrexerat, cadebat**
Whenever he got up, he fell down

cum domum **veni**, amicum **visito**
Whenever I come home, I visit my friend

3 Socrates, **cum** triginta tyranni **essent**, non exibat
Socrates didn't go out when there were 30 tyrants

cum id Caesari **nuntiatum esset** ab urbe profectus est
When that message had been given to Caesar, he set out from the city

4 **dum** haec **geruntur** sex milia hominum ad Rhenum contenderunt
While this was going on, 6000 men marched to the Rhine

5 **dum vivam**, laeta **ero**
While I live, I shall be happy

Temporal Clauses (continued)

Conjunctions which take the indicative or subjunctive (continued)

dum, donec

- **until**   with subjunctive, often with the sense of purpose or suspense (→**1**)

antequam, priusquam

- **before**   with indicative (→**2**)

- **ante** and **prius** may be separated from **quam** especially in negative sentences (→**3**)

- **before**   with subjunctive, usually with a sense of purpose or limit (→**4**)

Examples

1   multa Antonio concessit **dum** interfectores patris **ulcisceretur**
He made many concessions to Antony until he could avenge his father's killers

Haterius in periculo erat **donec** Augustam auxilium **oraret**
Haterius was in danger until he begged for Augusta's help

2   **antequam finiam**, hoc dicam
Before I finish, I shall say this

priusquam gallus **cantabit**, ter me negabis
Before the cock crows, you will deny me three times

3   neque **prius** fugere destiterunt **quam** ad castra **pervenerunt**
They didn't stop running away before reaching their camp

4   consul Romam festinavit **antequam** Hannibal eo **perveniret**
The consul hurried to Rome before Hannibal could reach it

ita cassita nidum migravit **priusquam** agricola frumentum **meteret**
And so the lark abandoned her nest before the farmer could reap the corn

Comparative Clauses

- These are adverbial clauses which express likeness, agreement (or the opposite) with what is stated in the main clause (→**1**)

- When the comparative clause states a fact (as above) the verb is in the **indicative**. The commonest words of comparison are (→**2**)

    ut (as), **sicut** (just as), **aliter ac**, **aliter ut** (different from), **idem ac**, **idem atque**, **qui etc** (the same as)

- When the comparative clause is purely **imaginary**, the verb is **subjunctive**. The commonest words used with this type of clause are (→**3**)

    velut(**si**), **quasi**, **tamquam** (**si**) (as if)

Examples

1 eadem dixi ac prius dixeram
I said the same as I had said before

2 **ego ita ero, ut me esse oportet**
I shall be as I should be

sicut lupus agnos rapit, ita mater liberos servat
just as the wolf snatches the lamb, so the mother saves her children

haud aliter se gerebat ac solebat
He behaved as he usually did
or He behaved no differently from usual

idem abierunt qui venerant
The same men vanished as came

3 **velutsi haec res nihil ad se pertinuisset, tacebat**
He remained silent, as if this thing had nothing to do with him

hic flammae Aetnae minantur quasi ad caelum sublatae sint
Here Aetna's flames threaten, as if raised to the heavens

Cleopatram salutaverunt **tamquam si esset** regina
They greeted Cleopatra as if she were queen

Relative Clauses

- Relative clauses are more common in Latin than in English. They are introduced by the following:

qui, quae, quod	which, who, that
ubi	where, in which
unde	from where, from which

- These relatives come at the beginning of the clause but after prepositions.

- The relative agrees with a word which precedes it – its *antecedent* – in gender and number, but takes its case from its own clause (→**1**)

  > **qui** is masculine plural agreeing with antecedent **Romani**, nominative because it is the subject of **incenderunt**

- **quā** is feminine singular agreeing with **regio**, ablative after preposition in (→**2**)

- **quos** is masculine plural agreeing with **servos**, accusative because it is the object of **iudicavit** (→**3**)

- The relative **quod** refers to a sentence, and **id** is omitted (**id quod** – that which). This is often used in parenthesis, and not attached grammatically to the rest of the sentence.

  > After **cuius** (of, concerning which) the noun **laudationis** is repeated (→**4**)

- The relative sometimes agrees with the following word, especially with the verb **esse** (→**5**)

Examples

1 hi sunt Romani **qui** libros incenderunt
These are the Romans who burnt the books

2 haec est regio **in qua** ego sum natus
This is the region in which I was bom

3 servos **quos** ipse iudicavit, eos sua sponte liberavit
He willingly freed those slaves whom he himself had judged

4 deinde, **quod** alio loco antea dixi, quae est ista tandem laudatio, **cuius iaudationis** legati et principes et publice tibi navem aedificatam, et privatim se ipsos abs te spoliatos esse dixerunt? (**Cicero**, Verres V 58)
Well then, as I said earlier elsewhere, what does that praise consist of, namely that publicly the ambassadors and chief citizens said a ship had been built for you, but privately that they themselves had been robbed by you?

5 iusta gloria **qui** fructus virtutis est, bello quaeritur
True glory, which is the reward of courage, is looked for in war

Use of Subjunctive in Relative Clauses

- The subjunctive is used in relative clauses dependent on infinitives or subjunctives (→**1**)

- When **qui** is used with the subjunctive, it may express cause (→**2**)

    quippe is sometimes used with **qui** in this sense

- When **qui** *etc* is used with the present or imperfect subjunctive, it may express purpose (→**3**)

- **qui** with the subjunctive is used with the following (→**4**)

dignus est **qui**	he is worthy of
idoneus est **qui**	he is fit to
sunt **qui**	there are people who
nemo est **qui**	there is no one who

- At the beginning of a sentence, any part of **qui**, **quae**, **quod** may be used as a connective (instead of the demonstrative) with the previous sentence. Translate it in English by "this" or "that" (→**5**)

Examples

1 quis sit **cui** vita talis **placeat**?
Who is there that likes such a life?

2 multa de mea sententia questus est Caesar (**quippe**) **qui** Ravennae Crassum ante **vidisset**
Caesar complained a lot about my decision since he had seen Crassus at Ravenna previously

3 legatos misit **qui** pacem **peterent**
He sent ambassadors to ask for peace

4 **sunt qui** dicere **timeant**
There are some who are afraid to speak

nemo **idoneus** aderat **qui responderet**
There was nobody there capable of replying

5 **quod** cum **audivisset**, soror lacrimas fudit
When she heard this, my sister shed tears

quae cum ita **sint**, Vatinium defendam
Since this is so, I shall defend Vatinius

Negatives

There are several ways of forming a negative in Latin.

non

- This is the common negative in the indicative and usually stands before the verb, although it may be put in front of any word for emphasis (→**1**)
- Two negatives in the same sentence make an affirmative (→**2**)

haud

- This makes a single word negative, usually an adjective or an adverb (→**3**)
- It is also used in expressions such as **haud scio an** (I don't know whether), and **haud dubito** (I don't doubt) (→**4**)
- **haudquaquam** means not at all (→**5**)

Examples

1 ante horam tertiam noctis de foro **non discedit**
He didn't leave the forum before nine o'clock at night

Ambarri Caesarem certiorem faciunt se, vastatis agris, **non facile** vim hostium ab oppidis prohibere
The Ambarri informed Caesar that it was **not easy** for them, since their territory was destroyed, to keep the enemy force away from their towns

Caesar **non exspectandum** sibi statuit dum Helvetii pervenirent
Caesar decided **not to wait** till the Swiss arrived

2 **non** possum **non facere**
I must do

non sumus **ignari**
We are well aware

3 **haud** magnus
not great

haud procul
not far away

4 **haud scio an** ire mihi liceat
I don't know whether I am allowed to go

5 homo bonus, **haudquaquam** eloquens
A good man but not at all a good speaker

ne

- This is the negative of the imperative and subjunctive. It is also used in many subordinate clauses where the verb is in the subjunctive (→**1**)

- **Wishes** (→**2**)

- **Purpose** (→**3**)

- **Indirect command** (→**4**)

- **Fearing** (→**5**)

Examples

1 **ne** diutius **vivamus**
Let us **not live** any longer

2 utinam **ne** id **accidisset**
I wish that it **had not happened**

3 agnus celeriter fugit **ne** lupi se **caperent**
The lamb ran away quickly **in case** the wolves caught it

4 pater mihi imperavit **ne abirem**
Father told me **not to go away**

5 cives metuebant **ne** Tiberius libertatem sibi **non redderet**
The citizens were afraid that Tiberius **would not give** them **back** their freedom

veritus sum **ne** id quod accidit **adveniret**
I was afraid that what did in fact happen **might take place**

Negatives (continued)

Other Negatives

- **neque ... neque**   neither ... nor (→**1**)

- **neque ... quisquam**   neither anyone *or* and no one
  neque ... quidquam   neither anything *or* and nothing
  neque ... umquam   neither ever *or* and never
  nemo ... umquam   no one ever *or* never anyone
  nihil ... umquam   nothing ever *or* never anything (→**2**)

- Notice the following combinations:

nonnulli	some	*but*	**nulli ... non** all
nonnihil	somewhat	*but*	**nihil ... non** everything (→**3**)

- **non solum ... sed etiam**   not only ... but also
  non solum ... sed quoque   not only ... but also (→**4**)
- Roman authors repeat negatives for effect (→**5**)

Examples

1 **neque** illo adit **quisquam neque** eis ipsis **quidquam** praeter oram maritimam notum est
Neither did anyone approach that place, nor did they themselves know anything except the coast

2 **neque** post id tempus **umquam** summis nobiscum copiis hostes contenderunt
And after that the enemy never engaged in battle with us at full strength

ego **nihil umquam** feci solus
I never did anything alone

3 **nonnulli** amici
some friends

nulli amici **non** venerunt
all my friends came

4 Herennius Pontius, iam gravis annis, **non solum** militaribus **sed quoque** civilibus muneribus abscesserat
Herennius Pontius, now old, had withdrawn not only from military but also from civic duties

5 **nihil** audio quod audisse, **nihil** dico quod dixisse paeniteat; **nemo** apud me quemquam sinistris sermonibus carpit, **neminem** ipse reprehendo, **nisi** tamen me cum parum commode scribo; **nulla** spe, **nullo** timore sollicitor, **nullis** rumoribus inquietor; mecum tantum et cum libellis loquor (**Pliny** Ep 1, 9)
I hear nothing that I would regret having heard, I say nothing that I would regret having said; at home nobody nags me with vicious remarks, I don't blame anyone except myself when I write badly; no hope or fear worries me, no idle talk disturbs me; I speak only to myself and to my books

Translation Guidelines

Translating from Latin into English can be both a challenge and a pleasure. The word order of both languages is different: word order shows the relationship of words in English, in Latin it is shown by word endings. Sentences are generally shorter in English, structures simpler. Latin sentences often contain more subordinate clauses, sometimes embedded in other clauses, and often build up to form a long periodic sentence. Subject matter is two thousand years distant in time, although many ideas are still familiar to us today. The following guidelines are suggested to help in translation.

Guidelines

- *Establish the context* of the passage to be translated. Read the introduction in English carefully, find out *who* or *what* is being discussed, *when* and *where* the action took place.

- *Read through the whole passage* fairly quickly to gain some general understanding of the passage, however incomplete.

- *Focus on each sentence*, either taking each word as it comes, or establishing subject/verb/object according to your normal approach. Many find it helpful to pick out the verbs and work out the structure of the clauses. Watch for agreement of adjectives with nouns and how prepositional phrases fit in.

- *Watch conjunctions* **et**, **sed** *etc* and connectives such as **tamen** (however), and **igitur** (therefore). These help explain the logic of the passage as a whole.

- *Note punctuation*. It can be helpful in isolating clauses within the sentences, or marking off an ablative absolute.

- *Be open-minded*. Does **cum**, for example, mean "when", "since", or "although"? Don't decide till the whole sentence is worked out.

- *Use dictionaries carefully*. Check words of similar spelling, check endings. Once you have found the right Latin word, check all of its meanings before deciding on the correct translation.

- *Watch out for features of style eg* use of two adjectives with same meaning *etc*.

- Finally, *check your translation*. Does the narrative or logic of the passage seem consistent? Does your English sound natural? Does it represent the tone or style of the Latin passage? At this stage, fill in any blanks or make corrections.

Translation Problems

Finding the subject

- Look for a noun with a nominative ending. Check with verb ending for agreement. If there is no nominative, the subject will be indicated by the verb ending. Remember that, in Latin, the subject is continued from the previous sentence unless there is clear indication otherwise (→**1**)

Adjective agreement

- Check which adjective agrees with which noun in number, case and gender. Remember that it may be separated from its noun.

  > a   b   b   a
  > te **flagrantis atrox hora Caniculae** nescit tangere
  > The blazing Dog Star's fierce daytime heat can't touch you

Passive

- Often it is better to turn a Latin passive verb into an active verb in English (→**2**)

Tense

- English is not so precise as Latin in its use of tenses. Use the tense that seems most natural in English, for example, English past tense for historic present in Latin, or English present tense for Latin future perfect in a conditional clause (→**3**)

Examples

1 **consules** et armare plebem et inermem pati **timebant**. **sedabant** tumultum, sedando interdum **movebant**.
The consuls were afraid both to arm the people and to leave them unarmed. **They quelled** the riot, but sometimes, in quelling it, **they stirred it up again**.

2 hoc a te **demonstrari** et **probari** volo
I wish you to demonstrate and prove this
or I wish this to be demonstrated and proved by you

3 hoc faciam si **potuero** (*future perfect*)
I shall do this if I can (*present*)

Ablative absolute

hostibus victis can be translated:

when the enemy had been beaten
after beating the enemy
they beat the enemy and ...
although the enemy were beaten

Choose the version that makes most sense within the context of the passage.

Omission of esse

- Parts of **esse** (to be) are often omitted and have to be supplied in English (→**1**)

Omission of small words (ut, id, eo, hic *etc*)

- Check that you do not omit to translate these words – they are often very important (→**2**)

Neuter plurals

- **omnia** (everything) and **multa** (many things) are often mistranslated.

Impersonal passives

- It is worthwhile learning these (→**3**)

Examples

1 sed Germanicus quanto (**erat**) summae spei propior, tanto impensius pro Tiberio niti
But the nearer Germanicus **was** to succeeding, the more strenuously he exerted himself on behalf of Tiberius

2

eo	to there (*adv*), by, with or from him (*abl of pronoun*)
id ... quod	that which
hic	this (*pron*), here (*adv*)
fit ... ut	it happens ... that

3

allatum est	it was announced
cognitum est	it was discovered
pugnatum est	a battle was fought
traditum est	it was recorded
visum est	it seemed

Translation Problems (continued)

Similarity of English/Latin Words

A higher percentage of English words are derived from Latin than from any other source. This can be helpful when trying to deduce the meaning of a Latin word, *eg* **portus** (port). But **porta** (gate) may cause confusion. The following examples taken from actual examination scripts provide a cautionary note. The correct translation follows in brackets:

Examples

prima luce nuntius hic **Ameriam** venit
At dawn the messenger came to America
(*At dawn the messenger came to Ameria*)

sex et quinquaginta **milia passuum** in cisio pervolavit
56 thousand flew past in a chariot
(*He quickly travelled fifty-six miles in a chariot*)

ut mori **mallet**
He would rather be killed by a mallet
(*To prefer to die*)

legati **crediderunt**
The embassy got credit
(*The ambassadors believed*)

False Friends/Confusables

ad (+ *acc*)	to, towards	**constituō**	I decide
ab (+ *abl*)	from, by, with	**consist**	I stop
adeo	to such an extent	**crīmen**	charge
adeō	I approach	**scelus**	crime
aestās	summer	**cum** (*prep*)	with
aestus	heat, tide	**cum** (*conj*)	when, since, although
aetas	age	**dominus**	master
aura	breeze	**domus**	house
aures (*pl*)	ears	**equitēs** (*pl*)	horsemen
aurum	gold	**equus**	horse
avis	bird	**fama**	fame, report
avus	grandfather	**fames**	hunger
cadō	I fall	**forte**	by chance
caedō	I cut, kill	**fortis**	brave (not strong)
cēdō	I go, yield		
campus	plain	**fugāre**	to put to flight
castra (*pl*)	camp	**fugere**	to flee, escape
cēterum	but	**hōra**	hour
cēterī (*pl*)	the rest	**hōrum** (*gen pl*)	of these
coepī	I began	**iaceō**	I lie
coēgi	I forced	**iaciō**	I throw

imperātor	general (*not* emperor)	**quīdam**	a certain (person)
imperātus	ordered (*past participle*)	**quĭdem**	indeed
inveniō	I find (*not* come in)	**reddō, -ere**	I give back
		redeō, -īre	I go back
invitō	I invite	**serviō, -īre**	I serve
invītus	unwilling	**servō, -āre**	I save
iter, -ineris	journey	**sōl, -is**	sun
iterum	again	**soleō, -ēre**	I am accustomed
lātus, -a, -um	broad	** solitus sum**	
lātus, -a, -um	brought	**solum, -i**	soil
lătus, -eris	side	**sōlus, -a, -um**	alone
līber, -ri	book	**tamen**	however
līber, -a, -um	free	**tandem**	at last
līberī, -orum (*pl*)	children	**ut(ī)**	in order that, as, when
libertus, -i	freedman	**utī** (*dep*)	to use
magister, -ri	master	**vallis, -is**	valley
magistratus	magistrate	**vallum, -i**	wall, rampart
malus, -a, -um	bad	**victor**	winner
malum, -i	apple	**victus** (*past part*)	beaten
mālo, mālle	I prefer	**vinctus** (*past part*)	bound
manus, - ūs	hand, band	**vīs**	force
mānēs, -ium	spirits of dead	**vīres, -ium**	strength
miser, -a, -um	unhappy	**vir, -ī**	man
mīseram	I had sent (*plup of* **mitto**)	**virga, -ae**	stick
morior, -ī	I die	**virgo, -inis**	girl
moror, ārī	I delay	**vīta, -ae**	life
nauta	sailor	**vītō, -āre**	I avoid
nāvis	ship		
nēmō	no one		
nimium	too much		
occāsio	opportunity		
occāsus (**solis**)	setting (of sun)		
occidere	to fall, set		
occīdere	to kill		
opem	help		
opera, -ae	work		
opus, -eris	task		
opus est	it is necessary		
ōra, -ae	coast		
ōrō, -āre	I pray, beg		
ōs, ōris	face		
ŏs, ŏssis	bone		
parcō, -ere	I spare		
pareō, -ere	I obey		
pario, -ere	I give birth to		
parō, -are	I prepare		
passus, -us	a pace		
passus, -a, -um	suffered (*past participle of* **patior**)		
porta, -ae	gate		
portus, -us	port		
portō, -are	I carry		
quaerō, -ere	I seek		
queror, -ī	I complain		

Conjugations

There are four patterns of regular Latin verbs called conjugations. Each can be identified by the ending of the **present infinitive**:

- First conjugation verbs end in -**āre** (*eg* am**āre** – to love)

- Second conjugation verbs end in -**ēre** (*eg* hab**ēre** – to have)

- Third conjugation verbs end in -**ere** (*eg* mitt**ere** – to send)

- Fourth conjugation verbs end in -**īre** (*eg* aud**īre** – to hear)

Each regular verb has three **stems**:

- A **present stem** which is found by cutting off -**re** from the present infinitive (*eg* am**ā**re, hab**ē**re, mitt**e**re, aud**ī**re).

- A **perfect stem** which is formed by adding -**v** to the present stem in the first and fourth conjugations (*eg* am**āvī**, aud**īvī**), and by adding -**u** to the present stem in the second conjugation (*eg* hab**uī**).

  In the third conjugation there are several possible endings (*eg* scrips**ī**, dīx**ī**).

  Some short verbs lengthen the stem vowel (*eg* lēgī), others double the first consonant and vowel (*eg* cucurrī).

- A **supine stem** which is formed by cutting off -**um** from the supine forms (*eg* am**āt**um, hab**it**um, miss**um**, aud**īt**um).

Tenses

These forms of the verb show when an action takes place, in the present, in the past or in the future.

In Latin there are six tenses:

1	Present	
2	Imperfect	} formed from the present stem
3	Future	
4	Perfect	
5	Pluperfect	} formed from the perfect stem
6	Future Perfect	

Tenses Formed from the Present Stem

The following endings are added to the stem:

	PRESENT	IMPERFECT	FUTURE	
			Conj 1 and 2	Conj 3 and 4
sing				
1st person	-ō	-bam	-bō	-am
2nd person	-s	-bas	-bis	-ēs
3rd person	-t	-bat	-bit	-et
pl				
1st person	-mus	-bāmus	-bimus	-ēmus
2nd person	-tis	-bātis	-bitis	-ētis
3rd person	-nt	-bant	-bunt	-ent

Note that the above endings show the number and person of the subject of the verb. Subject pronouns are therefore not normally necessary in Latin.

Conjugations

1	2	3	4
INFINITIVE			
amare	habēre	mittere	audīre
PRESENT STEM			
ama-	habē-	mitte-	audī-
PRESENT			
amō	habeo	mittō	audiō
amās	habēs	mittis	audīs
amat	habet	mittit	audit
amāmus	habēmus	mittimus	audīmus
amātis	habētis	mittitis	audītis
amant	habent	mittunt	audiunt
IMPERFECT			
amābam	habēbam	mittēbam	audiēbam
amābās	habēbās	mittēbās	audiēbās
amābat	habēbat	mittēbat	audiēbat
amābāmus	habēbāmus	mittēbāmus	audiēbāmus
amābātis	habēbātis	mittēbātis	audiēbātis
amābant	habēbant	mittēbant	audiēbant
FUTURE			
amābō	habēbō	mittam	audiam
amābis	habēbis	mittēs	audiēs
amābit	habēbit	mittet	audiet
amābimus	habēbimus	mittēmus	audiēmus
amābitis	habēbitis	mittētis	audiētis
amābunt	habēbunt	mittent	audient

Tenses (continued)

Use:

The Present

In Latin, the present tense expresses what is going on now and can be translated into English in two ways (*eg* **laborat** – he works, he is working)

- The present is often used in Latin instead of a past tense to make the action more exciting (→**1**)

- Sometimes the Latin present tense is used to describe an action begun in the past and still continuing (→**2**)

The Imperfect

- Describes what went on or continued for a time (→**3**)

- Denotes an action repeated in the past (→**4**)

- Is used when an action is intended or interrupted (→**5**)

- Is sometimes translated "had" when used with **iam** (→**6**)

The Future

- Is used in Latin as in English to denote what will or is going to be or to happen (→**7**)

- Is occasionally used as a command (→**8**)

- After "**si**" (if) in conditional sentences, it is sometimes translated as present tense in English (→**9**)

Examples

1 **prima luce Caesar Gallos oppugnat**
Caesar attacked the Gauls at dawn

2 **Alexander iam tres annos regit**
Alexander has been ruling for three years now

3 **pluebat** – it was raining

4 **fortiter pugnabant**
They used to fight bravely
or They kept fighting bravely

5 **Romam intrabam**
I was about to enter Rome

6 **multos iam dies villam habitabat**
He had already lived in the house for many days

7 **hoc faciemus**
We shall do this
or We are going to do this

erit gloria
There will be glory

8 **non me vocabis**
Don't call me

9 **si id credes, errabis**
If you believe this, you will be making a mistake

Tenses Formed from the Perfect Stem

To the appropriate perfect stem add the following endings:

	PERFECT	PLUPERFECT	FUTURE PERFECT
sing			
1st person	-ī	-eram	-erō
2nd person	-istī	-erās	-eris
3rd person	-it	-erat	-erit
pl			
1st person	-imus	-erāmus	-erimus
2nd person	-istis	-erātis	-eritis
3rd person	-ērunt	-erant	-erint

Conjugations

1	2	3	4
PERFECT STEM			
amāv-	habu-	mīs-	audīv-
PERFECT			
amāvī	habuī	mīsī	audīvi
amāvistī	habuistī	mīsistī	audīvistī
amāvit	habuit	mīsit	audīvit
amāvimus	habuimus	mīsimus	audīvimus
amāvistis	habuistis	mīsistis	audīvistis
amāvērunt	habuērunt	mīserunt	audīvērunt
PLUPERFECT			
amāveram	habueram	mīseram	audīveram
amāverās	habuerās	mīserās	audīverās
amāverat	habuerat	mīserat	audīverat
amāverāmus	habuerāmus	mīserāmus	audīverāmus
amāverātis	habuerātis	mīserātis	audīverātis
amāverant	habuerant	mīserant	audīverant
FUTURE PERFECT			
amāverō	habuerō	mīserō	audīverō
amāveris	habueris	mīseris	audīveris
amāverit	habuerit	mīserit	audīverit
amāverimus	habuerimus	mīserimus	audīverimus
amāveritis	habueritis	mīseritis	audīveritis
amāverint	habuerint	mīserint	audīverint

Tenses (continued)

Use:

The Perfect

- In Latin, the perfect tense is equivalent to the simple past tense (*eg* **vīdī** – I saw) and the perfect tense (*eg* **vīdī** – I have seen) in English.

- It states past action particularly in narrative (→**1**)

- Expresses an action completed in the past which still has effect in the present (→**2**)

The Pluperfect

- Denotes an action completed in the past before another past action (→**3**)

The Future Perfect

- Denotes completing something in the future (→**4**)

- Is often used with **volō**, **possum**, **nolō** *etc* (→**5**)

- Denotes an action which precedes another action in the future, often in a subordinate clause (→**6**)

Examples

1 **veni, vidi, vici**
I came, I saw, I conquered

2 **spem in fide alicuius habuerunt**
They place their hope in someone's good faith

3 **Mithridates urbem Asiae clarissimam obsederat quam L. Lucullus virtute liberavit**
Mithridates had besieged the most famous city in Asia that Lucius Lucullus freed by his courage

4 **id fecero**
I shall have done it

5 **si potuero, faciam**
If I can, I shall do it

6 **qui prior venerit, prior discedet**
First to come will be first to go

The Passive

Verbs may be active or passive. In **active** forms of the verb, the subject carries out the action (*eg* Brutus **killed** Caesar). In **passive** forms of the verb, the subject receives the action (*eg* Caesar **was killed** by Brutus).

Conjugations

To form the passive tenses of regular verbs, substitute the following endings for those of the present, imperfect and future active tenses (conjugated on page 75):

- In the present 1st person sing the ending is -**or**.

- In the imperfect, the endings are added to -**ba**.

- In the future (conjugations 1 and 2), the endings are added to -**bo** (1st person sing), -**be** (2nd person sing), and -**bi** for other persons. In conjugations 3 and 4, the 1st person sing ending is -**ar**.

sing		*pl*	
1st person	-**r**	1st person	-**mur**
2nd person	-**ris**	2nd person	-**minī**
3rd person	-**tur**	3rd person	-**ntur**

Conjugations

1	2	3	4
PRESENT PASSIVE			
am**or**	habē**or**	mitt**or**	audi**or**
amā**ris**	habē**ris**	mitte**ris**	audī**ris**
ama**tur**	habē**tur**	mitti**tur**	audī**tur**
amā**mur**	habē**mur**	mitti**mur**	audī**mur**
amā**minī**	habē**minī**	mitti**minī**	audī**minī**
amā**ntur**	habē**ntur**	mittu**ntur**	audiu**ntur**
IMPERFECT PASSIVE			
amāba**r**	habēba**r**	mittēba**r**	audiēba**r**
amāba**ris**	habēbā**ris**	mittēbā**ris**	audiēbā**ris**
amāba**tur**	habēbā**tur**	mittēbā**tur**	audiēbā**tur**
amāba**mur**	habēbā**mur**	mittēbā**mur**	audiēbā**mur**
amāba**minī**	habēbā**minī**	mittēbā**minī**	audiēbā**minī**
amāba**ntur**	habēba**ntur**	mittēba**ntur**	audiēba**ntur**
FUTURE PASSIVE			
amābo**r**	habēbo**r**	mitta**r**	audia**r**
amābe**ris**	habēbe**ris**	mittē**ris**	audiē**ris**
amābi**tur**	habēbi**tur**	mittē**tur**	audiē**tur**
amābi**mur**	habēbi**mur**	mittē**mur**	audiē**mur**
amābi**minī**	habēbi**minī**	mittē**minī**	audiē**mini**
amābu**ntur**	habēbu**ntur**	mitte**ntur**	audie**ntur**

The Passive (continued)

Translation

Present Passive

1 I am loved   we are loved
  you (*sing*) are loved   you (*pl*) are loved
  he/she/it is loved   they are loved
2 I am held *etc*
3 I am sent *etc*
4 I am heard *etc*

Imperfect Passive

1 I was loved   we were loved
  you (*sing*) were loved   you (*pl*) were loved
  he/she/it was loved   they were loved
2 I was held *etc*
3 I was sent *etc*
4 I was heard *etc*

Future Passive

1 I shall be loved   we shall be loved
  you (*sing*) will be loved   you (*pl*) will be loved
  he/she/it will be loved   they will be loved
2 I shall be held *etc*
3 I shall be sent *etc*
4 I shall be heard *etc*

• "going to be" may also be used to translate the future.

Perfect, Pluperfect and Future Perfect Passive

These tenses consist of the past participle (formed from the supine stem) and tenses of the verb **sum** (to be). The past participle endings agree in number and gender with the subject of the verb.

Conjugations

1	2	3	4	
PERFECT PASSIVE				
amātus	habitus	missus	audītus	**sum**
-a, -um	-a, -um	-a, -um	-a, -um	**es**
				est
amāti	habitī	missī	audītī	**sumus**
-ae, -a	-ae, -a	-ae, -a	-ae, -a	**estis**
				sunt
PLUPERFECT PASSIVE				
amātus	habitus	missus	audītus	**eram**
				erās
				erat
amātī	habitī	missī	auditī	**erāmus**
				erātis
				erant
FUTURE PERFECT PASSIVE				
amātus	habitus	missus	audītus	**erō**
				eris
				erit
amātī	habitī	missī	audītī	**erimus**
				eritis
				erunt

The Passive (continued)

Translation

Perfect Passive

1	I have been loved	we have been loved
	you (*sing*) have been loved	you (*pl*) have been loved
	he/she/it has been loved	they have been loved
2	I have been held *or* I was held *etc*	
3	I have been sent *or* I was sent *etc*	
4	I have been heard *or* I was heard *etc*	

Pluperfect Passive

1	I had been loved	we had been loved
	you (*sing*) had been loved	you (*pl*) had been loved
	he/she/it had been loved	they had been loved
2	I had been held *etc*	
3	I had been sent *etc*	
4	I had been heard *etc*	

Future Perfect Passive

1	I shall have been loved	we shall have been loved
	you (*sing*) will have been loved	you (*pl*) will have been loved
	he/she/it will have been loved	they will have been loved
2	I shall have been held *etc*	
3	I shall have been sent *etc*	
4	I shall have been heard *etc*	

Examples

1 **milites a populo occisi sunt**
The soldiers were killed by the people

2 **populus milites occidit**
The people killed the soldiers

- Note that the subject of the passive verb in (**1**) becomes the object of the active verb in (**2**).

- Often in English it is better to translate the meaning actively as in (**2**).

- The **agent** of the action is translated by **a**(**b**) with the ablative case as in **a populo** (**1**) – by the people.

- The **thing** causing the action is translated by the ablative case alone

  saxo percussus erat
  He had been struck by a rock

The Subjunctive

So far all verbs described have belonged to the indicative mood, which states facts. The subjunctive mood represents ideas, possibilities or necessities and is often translated by auxiliary verbs such as **may**, **might**, **could**, **would**, **should** or **must**. There are four tenses active and passive – present, imperfect, perfect and pluperfect.

Formation of Active

The present subjunctive active is formed from the present stem, the imperfect from the infinitive. To these add the endings

> -**m**, -**s**, -**t**, -**mus**, -**tis**, -**nt**.

- Note that in first conjugation present the preceding vowel is -**e**, and in all others -**a**.
- The present subjunctive active is sometimes translated by using "**may**" (→**1**)
- The imperfect subjunctive active is sometimes translated by using "**might**" (→**2**)

Conjugations

1	2	3	4
PRESENT SUBJUNCTIVE ACTIVE			
ame**m**	habea**m**	mitta**m**	audia**m**
amē**s**	habeā**s**	mittā**s**	audiā**s**
ame**t**	habea**t**	mitta**t**	audia**t**
amē**mus**	habeā**mus**	mittā**mus**	audiā**mus**
amē**tis**	habeā**tis**	mittā**tis**	audiā**tis**
ame**nt**	habea**nt**	mitta**nt**	audia**nt**
IMPERFECT SUBJUNCTIVE ACTIVE			
amāre**m**	habēre**m**	mittere**m**	audīre**m**
amāre**s**	habērē**s**	mitterē**s**	audīrē**s**
amāre**t**	habēre**t**	mittere**t**	audīre**t**
amārē**mus**	habērē**mus**	mitterē**mus**	audīrē**mus**
amārē**tis**	habērē**tis**	mitterē**tis**	audīrē**tis**
amāre**nt**	habēre**nt**	mittere**nt**	audīre**nt**

Examples

1 **amem** – I may love

mittas – you (*sing*) may send

habeat – he may have

audiant – they may hear

2 **mitteretis** – you (*pl*) might send

haberem – I might have

amaret – she might love

audirent – they might hear

The Subjunctive (continued)

Formation of Passive

The passive of the present and imperfect subjunctive is easily formed by substituting the normal passive endings (**-r**, **-ris**, **-tur**, **-mur**, **-mini**, **-ntur**) for the active ones.

Conjugations

1	2	3	4
PRESENT SUBJUNCTIVE PASSIVE			
ame**r**	habea**r**	mitta**r**	audia**r**
amē**ris**	habeā**ris**	mittā**ris**	audiā**ris**
amē**tur**	habeā**tur**	mittā**tur**	audiā**tur**
amē**mur**	habeā**mur**	mittā**mur**	audiā**mur**
amē**minī**	habeā**minī**	mittā**minī**	audiā**minī**
ame**ntur**	habea**ntur**	mitta**ntur**	audia**ntur**
IMPERFECT SUBJUNCTIVE PASSIVE			
amāre**r**	habēre**r**	mittere**r**	audīre**r**
amārē**ris**	habērē**ris**	mitterē**ris**	audīrē**ris**
amārē**tur**	habērē**tur**	mitterē**tur**	audīrē**tur**
amārē**mur**	habērē**mur**	mitterē**mur**	audīrē**mur**
amārē**minī**	habērē**minī**	mitterē**minī**	audīrē**minī**
amāre**ntur**	habēre**ntur**	mittere**ntur**	audīre**ntur**

- The present subjunctive passive is sometimes translated by using "**may be**" (→**1**)

- The imperfect subjunctive passive is sometimes translated by using "**might be**" (→**2**)

Examples

1 **habeamur** – we may be held

   amer – I may be loved

   mittamini – you (*pl*) may be sent

   audiantur – they may be heard

2 **audiremini** – you (*pl*) might be heard

   amaretur – he might be loved

   haberentur – they might be held

   mitterer – I might be sent

Perfect and Pluperfect Subjunctive Active

Both perfect and pluperfect subjunctive active are formed from the perfect stem as follows:

Conjugations

1	2	3	4
PERFECT SUBJUNCTIVE ACTIVE			
amāverim	habuerim	mīserim	audīverim
amāveris	habueris	mīseris	audīveris
amāverit	habuerit	mīserit	audīverit
amāverimus	habuerimus	mīserimus	audīverimus
amāveritis	habueritis	mīseritis	audīveritis
amāverint	habuerint	mīserint	audīverint
PLUPERFECT SUBJUNCTIVE ACTIVE			
amāvissem	habuissem	mīsissem	audīvissem
amāvissēs	habuissēs	mīsissēs	audīvissēs
amāvisset	habuisset	mīsisset	audīvisset
amāvissēmus	habuissēmus	mīsissēmus	audīvissēmus
amāvissētis	habuissētis	mīsissētis	audīvissētis
amāvissent	habuissent	mīsissent	audīvissent

- The Perfect subjunctive active is sometimes translated by using "**may have**" with the past participle in English (→**1**)

- The Pluperfect subjunctive active is sometimes translated by using "**might have**" with the past participle in English (→**2**)

Examples

1 **miserit** – he may have sent

habuerint – they may have had

audiveris – you (*sing*) may have heard

amaveritis – you (*pl*) may have loved

2 **amavissemus** – we might have loved

habuisset – he might have had

audivissent – they might have heard

misissem – I might have sent

The Subjunctive (continued)

Perfect and Pluperfect Subjunctive Passive

Both perfect and pluperfect subjunctive passive are formed from the supine stem and the present and imperfect subjunctive of **sum** respectively:

Conjugation

1		2		3		4	

PERFECT SUBJUNCTIVE PASSIVE

amatus	**sim**	habitus	**sim**	missus	**sim**	audītus	**sim**
	sīs		**sīs**		**sīs**		**sīs**
	sit		**sit**		**sit**		**sit**
pl							
amatī	**sīmus**	habitī	**sīmus**	missī	**sīmus**	audītī	**sīmus**
	sītis		**sītīs**		**sītis**		**sītis**
	sint		**sint**		**sint**		**sint**

PLUPERFECT SUBJUNCTIVE PASSIVE

amatus	**essem**	habitus	**essem**	missus	**essem**	audītus	**essem**
	essēs		**essēs**		**essēs**		**essēs**
	esset		**esset**		**esset**		**esset**
pl							
amatī	**essēmus**	habitī	**essēmus**	missī	**essēmus**	audītī	**essēmus**
	essētis		**essētis**		**essētis**		**essētis**
	essent		**essent**		**essent**		**essent**

- The perfect subjunctive passive is sometimes translated by using "**may have been**" with the past participle in English (→**1**)

- The pluperfect subjunctive passive is sometimes translated by using "**might have been**" with the past participle in English (→**2**)

Examples

1 **habitus sis** – you (*sing*) may have been held

missi simus – we may nave been sent

auditus sim – I may have been heard

amati sint – they may have been loved

2 **amati essemus** – we might have been loved

habiti essent – they might have been held

missus esses – you (*sing*) might have been sent

auditus essem – I might have been heard

The Imperative

This is the mood of command. It has two forms, 2nd person *sing* and *pl*, active (→**1**) and passive (→**2**)

Conjugations

	1	2	3	4
IMPERATIVE ACTIVE				
sing	am**ā**	hab**ē**	mitt**e**	aud**ī**
pl	am**āte**	hab**ēte**	mitt**ite**	aud**īte**
IMPERATIVE PASSIVE				
sing	am**āre**	hab**ēre**	mitt**ere**	aud**īre**
pl	am**āmini**	hab**ēmini**	mitt**īmini**	aud**īminī**

Examples

1 **pecuniam mittite, o cives**
Citizens, send money! (active)

spem habe
Have hope! (active)

2 **in curia audimini**
Be heard in the senate! (passive)

ab omnibus semper amare, Romule
Always be loved by everyone, Romulus (passive)

The Infinitive

The infinitive was originally a noun and can be used in this way in Latin (*eg* **amare** – to love or loving). There are three types, present, future and perfect, both active and passive, formed as follows:

Active

	1	**2**
PRESENT	amā**re**	habē**re**
FUTURE	amāt**ūrus esse**	habit**ūrus esse**
PERFECT	amā**visse**	habu**isse**

	3	**4**
PRESENT	mitte**re**	audī**re**
FUTURE	miss**ūrus esse**	audīt**ūrus esse**
PERFECT	mīs**isse**	audī**visse**

Translation

to love	to have
to be going to love	to be going to have
to have loved	to have had
to send	to hear
to be going to send	to be going to hear
to have sent	to have heard

Passive

	1	**2**
PRESENT	amā**rī**	habē**rī**
FUTURE	amāt**um īrī**	habit**um īrī**
PERFECT	amāt**us esse**	habit**us esse**

	3	**4**
PRESENT	mit**tī**	audī**rī**
FUTURE	miss**um īrī**	audīt**um īrī**
PERFECT	miss**us esse**	audīt**us esse**

Translation

to be loved	to be had
to be going to be loved	to be going to be had
to have been loved	to have been had
to be sent	to be heard
to be going to be sent	to be going to be heard
to have been sent	to have been heard

- In the future active -**urus**, -**a**, -**um** and in the perfect passive -**us**, -**a**, -**um** agree in number and gender with the noun or pronoun in indirect speech.

Uses of the Infinitive

- It can be used as a neuter noun
- As the subject of the sentence (→**1**)
- With certain nouns such as **fas** (right), **nefas** (wrong) (→**2**)
- As the object of the following verbs: (→**3**)

volō	I wish	**cupiō**	I desire
nolō	I do not wish	**sinō**	I allow
possum	I am able to, can	**cogō**	I force
sciō	I know (how)	**audeō**	I dare
nesciō	I do not know	**conor**	I try
debeō	I ought	**desinō**	I stop
soleō	I am accustomed	**dubitō**	I hesitate
incipiō	I begin	**coepi**	I begin

- It can be used to describe a rapid series of events instead of using the perfect tense (→**4**)

Examples

1 **errare est humanum**
To err is human

2 **nefas est templa destruere**
It is wrong to destroy temples

3 **volo domum redire**
I wish to return home

desine mortuos commemorare
Stop remembering the dead

Romam exstinctam esse cupit
He wishes Rome blotted out

4 **ille non tollere oculos, non remittere stilum, tum fragor adventare et intra limen audiri**
He did not raise his eyes nor put down his pen, then the noise came closer and could be heard inside the door.

Participles

There are three participles (or verbal adjectives) in Latin: the present active, the perfect passive and the future active.

The Present Participle

This is formed from the present stem by adding **-ns** and lengthening the previous vowel. The genitive ending is **-ntis**.

Conjugations

1	2	3	4
amāns	habēns	mittēns	audiēns
loving	having	sending	hearing

• Note that these decline like group 3 adjectives ending in -ns with ablative singular, in -i when used as an adjective and in -e when used as a verb. They agree in number, case and gender with nouns or pronouns in the sentence.

Use

• It denotes an action going on at the same time as the main verb (→**1**)

• It can be used as a noun (→**2**)

Examples

1 **pro patria pugnantes iuvenes mortui sunt**
The young men died *while fighting* for their country

Romulo regnante, Roma urbs parva erat
While Romulus was ruling, Rome was a small city

2 **lacrimae adstantium**
the tears of *people standing by*

The Perfect Participle

This is formed from the supine stem by adding the endings -**us**, -**a**, -**m**. It declines like first and second declension adjectives (see pages 13–15)

Conjugation

1	2	3	4
amāt**us**	habit**us**	miss**us**	audīt**us**
(having	(having	(having	having
been) loved	been) held	been) sent	been) heard

Use

- It denotes an action that is completed before that of the main verb (→**1**)

- English is less precise in the use of tenses and frequently uses a present to translate a Latin past participle.

The Future Participle

This is formed by adding -**urus**, -**a**, -**um** to the supine stem. It declines like first and second declension adjectives.

Conjugations

1	2	3	4
amāt**ūrus**	habit**ūrus**	miss**ūrus**	audīt**ūrus**
going to love	going to have	going to send	going to hear

Use

- It denotes an action that is going to take place (→**2**)

- The forms **futurus** (going to be) and **venturus** (going to come) are often used as adjectives.

Examples

❶ equites Romani auditi ad senatum adducti sunt
The Roman businessmen *were heard* and then were brought before the Senate

castra capta incendimus
We *captured* the camp and burnt it
or *Capturing* the camp, we burnt it

❷ nos morituri te salutamus
We who are about to die salute you

VERBS

Gerunds and Gerundives

The **gerund** is a **verbal noun** and is active.

The **gerundive** is a **verbal adjective** and is passive.

The gerund is formed by adding -**ndum** to the present stem. It declines like a neuter noun -**ndum**, -**ndi**, -**ndo**, -**ndo**.

The gerundive declines like first and second declension adjectives -**us**, -**a**, -**um**.

Conjugations

1	2	3	4
GERUND			
ama**ndum**	habe**ndum**	mitte**ndum**	audie**ndum**
loving	having	sending	hearing
GERUNDIVE			
ama**ndus**	habe**ndus**	mitte**ndus**	audie**ndus**
requiring	requiring	requiring	requiring
to be loved	to be held	to be sent	to be heard

Use of Gerund and Gerundive

- The gerund is often used with the accusative case to express **purpose** (→**1**)
- If the verb has a direct object, the gerundive is used instead (→**2**)
- The gerund is used in the genitive case with nouns and adjectives (→**3**) such as
  ars (art), **spes** (hope), **cupidus** (eager), **peritus** (skilled)
- Both the gerund and the gerundive can be used in the genitive with **causa** to express **purpose** (→**4**)
- The gerundive can be used to imply **obligation** and the person is expressed by the dative case (→**5**)
- If the verb cannot take a direct object, the impersonal form is used (→**6**)
- Both the gerund and the gerundive can be used in the ablative case (→**7**)

Examples

1 **venit ad regnandum**
He came to rule

2 **venit ad pacem petendam**
He came to make peace

3 **spes videndi**
Hope of seeing

peritus equitandi
Skilled in riding

4 **dicendi causa**
to speak

pacis petendae causa
For the sake of making peace

5 **poenae nobis timendae sunt**
Punishment must be feared by us
or We must fear punishment

6 **mihi parendum est**
You must obey me

7 **docendo discimus**
We learn by teaching

me puniendo effugit
By punishing me he escaped

Impersonal Verbs

Impersonal verbs are used in the third person singular only

- To describe the weather (→**1**)

- To express feeling. The person affected appears in the accusative case and the cause in the genitive case (→**2**)

- To express permission or pleasure. The person affected appears in the dative case. The verb is often followed by a present infinitive (→**3**)

- To express happening, following *etc*. These are followed by **ut** with the subjunctive mood (→**4**)

fit ut	it happens that
accidit ut	it happens that
sequitur ut	it follows that

- Certain intransitive verbs are used impersonally in the passive (→**5**)

- Verbs of saying, believing *etc* are used impersonally in the perfect passive tense (→**6**)

- The verbs **interest** (it is of importance) and **refert** (it is of concern) are followed usually by **meā, tuā, nostrā, vestrā** (→**7**)

- Sometimes **interest** is followed by genitive of the person (→**8**)

- The following verbs are followed by a present infinitive. The person involved appears in the accusative case (→**9**)

me decet	it is fitting for me
me oportet	I must/ought

Examples

1 **pluit**
it is raining

fulgurat
there is lightning

tonat
there is thunder

ningit
it is snowing

2 **me miseret**
I am sorry for

me miseret sociorum
I am sorry for my comrades

me paenitet
I repent of

3 **mihi licet**
I am allowed to

nobis placet
it is pleasing to us
or we like

tibi videtur
it seems good to you
or you decide

4 **fit ut**
it happens that

fit ut fallar
it happens that I am mistaken

accidit ut
it happens that

5 **pugnatum est in mari**
the battle was fought at sea

vivitur in oculis omnium
life is lived in the sight of everyone

6 **nuntiatum est**
it has been announced

mihi dictum est Germanos transiisse Rhenum
I was told that the Germans had crossed the Rhine

7 **nihil mea refert**
it is of no interest to me

8 **Caesaris interest**
it is important to Caesar

9 **nos morari oportuit**
we ought to have waited

Deponent Verbs

Deponent verbs are passive in form but active in meaning. They also have present and future participles and future infinitives which are active. The perfect participle is also active in meaning. Otherwise the conjugation is similar to that of regular verbs.

First Conjugation

conārī (to try)

INDICATIVE		SUBJUNCTIVE	
PRESENT			
conor	I try *etc*	coner	I may try *etc*
conāris		conēris	
conātur		conētur	
conāmur		conēmur	
conāminī		conēmini	
conāntur		conentur	

IMPERFECT			
conābar	I was trying *etc*	conārer	I might try *etc*
conābāris		conārēris	
conābātur		conārētur	
conābāmur		conārēmur	
conābāminī		conārēmini	
conabantur		conārentur	

FUTURE	
conābor	I shall try *etc*
conāberis	
conābitur	
conābimur	
conābimini	
conābuntur	

PERFECT

| conātus | **sum** | I tried | conātus | **sim** | I may have tried |
| -a, -um | **es** | you tried *etc* | -a, -um | **sis** | you may have tried *etc* |

PLUPERFECT

| conātus | **eram** | I had tried | conātus | **essem** | I might have tried |
| -a, -um | **eras** | you had tried *etc* | -a, -um | **esses** | you might have tried *etc* |

FUTURE PERFECT

| conātus | **ero** | I shall have tried |
| -a, -um | **eris** | you will have tried *etc* |

IMPERATIVE

| con**āre** | *sing* | try |
| con**āminī** | *pl* | try |

INFINITIVES

Present	conār**ī**	to try
Future	conāt**urus esse**	to be going to try
Perfect	conāt**us esse**	to have tried

PARTICIPLES

Present	conā**ns**	trying
Future	conāt**urus**	going to try
Perfect	conāt**us**	having tried

| GERUND | conā**ndum** | trying |

| GERUNDIVE | conā**ndus** | requiring to be tried |

Deponent Verbs (continued)

Second, Third, Fourth Conjugations

These are conjugated like the passive form of verbs of the corresponding conjugations. A summary is provided as follows:

Second Conjugation

verērī (to fear, be afraid)

INDICATIVE

Present	ver**eor**	I am afraid
Imperfect	verēba**r**	I was afraid
Future	verēbo**r**	I shall be afraid
Perfect	verit**us sum**	I was afraid
Pluperfect	verit**us eram**	I had been afraid
Future Perfect	verit**us erō**	I shall have been afraid

SUBJUNCTIVE

Present	verē**ar**	I may be afraid
Imperfect	verēre**r**	I might be afraid
Perfect	verit**us sim**	I may have been afraid
Pluperfect	verit**us essem**	I might have been afraid

IMPERATIVE

Singular	ver**ēre**	be afraid
Plural	ver**ēminī**	be afraid

INFINITIVES

Present	verēr**ī**	to be afraid
Future	verit**ūrus esse**	to be going to be afraid
Perfect	verit**us esse**	to have been afraid

PARTICIPLES

Present	verē**ns**	fearing, being afraid
Future	verit**ūrus**	going to fear or be afraid
Perfect	verit**us**	having feared or been afraid (active)

GERUND	vere**ndum**	fearing
GERUNDIVE	vere**ndus**	requiring to be feared

Third Conjugation

sequī (to follow)

INDICATIVE

Present	sequ**or**	I follow
Imperfect	sequeba**r**	I was following
Future	sequa**r**	I shall follow
Perfect	secūt**us sum**	I followed
Pluperfect	secūt**us eram**	I had followed
Future Perfect	secūt**us erō**	I shall have followed

SUBJUNCTIVE

Present	sequa**r**	I may follow
Imperfect	seque**rer**	I might follow
Perfect	secūt**us sim**	I may have followed
Pluperfect	secūt**us essem**	I might have followed

IMPERATIVE

Singular	sequ**ere**	follow
Plural	sequ**iminī**	follow

INFINITIVES

Present	sequ**ī**	to follow
Future	secūt**ūrus esse**	to be going to follow
Perfect	secūt**us esse**	to have followed

PARTICIPLES

Present	sequ**ēns**	following
Future	secūt**ūrus**	going to follow
Perfect	secūt**us**	having followed

GERUND	seque**ndum**	following
GERUNDIVE	seque**ndus**	requiring to be followed

Deponent Verbs (continued)

Fourth Conjugation

mentīrī (to lie)

INDICATIVE

Present	ment**ior**	I lie
Imperfect	mentiēba**r**	I was lying
Future	mentia**r**	I shall lie
Perfect	mentī**tus sum**	I lied
Pluperfect	mentī**tus eram**	I had lied
Future Perfect	mentī**tus erō**	I shall have lied

SUBJUNCTIVE

Present	mentia**r**	I may lie
Imperfect	mentīre**r**	I might lie
Perfect	mentī**tus sim**	I may have lied
Pluperfect	mentī**tus essem**	I might have lied

IMPERATIVE

Singular	ment**ire**	lie
Plural	ment**iminī**	lie

INFINITIVES

Present	ment**irī**	to lie
Future	mentit**ūrus esse**	to be going to lie
Perfect	ment**itus esse**	to have lied

PARTICIPLES

Present	mentiē**ns**	lying
Future	mentī**turus**	going to lie
Perfect	mentī**tus**	having lied

GERUND	mentie**ndum**	lying
GERUNDIVE	mentie**ndus**	requiring to be lied to

Semi-deponent Verbs

A few verbs are passive in form and active in meaning in only the perfect tenses. All other tenses are active in form and meaning. These are:

audēre	to dare
gaudēre	to be glad
solēre	to be accustomed
confidere	to trust

INDICATIVE

Present	aud**eō**	I dare
Imperfect	aud**ēbam**	I was daring
Future	aud**ēbo**	I shall dare

SUBJUNCTIVE

Present	aude**am**	I may dare
Imperfect	audēre**m**	I might dare

IMPERATIVE

Singular	aud**ē**	dare
Plural	aud**ētē**	dare

INFINITIVE

Present	aud**ēre**	to dare

PRES PARTICIPLE	aud**ēns**	daring
GERUND	aude**ndum**	daring
GERUNDIVE	aude**ndus**	requiring to be dared

All other parts are **passive** in form:

INDICATIVE

Perfect	aus**us sum**	I dared
Pluperfect	aus**us eram**	I had dared
Future Perfect	aus**us erō**	I shall have dared

SUBJUNCTIVE

Perfect	aus**us sim**	I may have dared
Pluperfect	aus**us essem**	I might have dared

PARTICIPLES

Perfect	aus**us**	having dared
Future	aus**ūrus**	going to dare

INFINITIVES

Perfect	aus**us esse**	to have dared
Future	aus**ūrus esse**	to be going to dare

Unique Verbs

The following verbs are different from the conjugations described so far:

esse (to be)

Indicative

PRESENT

sum	I am
es	you (*sing*) are
est	he/she/it is
sumus	we are
estis	you (*pl*) are
sunt	they are

IMPERFECT

eram	I was
eras	you (*sing*) were
erat	he/she/it was
erāmus	we were
erātis	you (*pl*) were
erant	they were

FUTURE

erō	I shall be
eris	you (*sing*) will be
erit	he/she/it will be
erimus	we shall be
eritis	you (*pl*) will be
erunt	they will be

Subjunctive

PRESENT

sim	I may be
sīs	you (*sing*) may be
sit	he/she/it may be
sīmus	we may be
sītīs	you (*pl*) may be
sint	they may be

IMPERFECT

essem	I might be
essēs	you (*sing*) might be
esset	he/she/it might be
essēmus	we might be
essētis	you (*pl*) might be
essent	they might be

Indicative

PERFECT

fuī	I have been, was
fuistī	you (*sing*) have been/were
fuit	he/she/it has been/was
fuimus	we have been/were
fuistis	you (*pl*) have been/were
fuērunt	they have been/were

PLUPERFECT

fueram	I had been
fuerās	you (*sing*) had been
fuerat	he/she/it had been
fuerāmus	we had been
fuerātis	you (*pl*) had been
fuerant	they had been

FUTURE PERFECT

fuerō	I shall have been
fuerīs	you (*sing*) will have been
fuerit	he/she/it will have been
fuerīmus	we shall have been
fuerītis	you (*pl*) will have been
fuerint	they will have been

Subjunctive

PERFECT

fuerim	I may have been
fuerīs	you (*sing*) may have been
fuerit	he/she/it may have been
fuerīmus	we may have been
fuerītis	you (*pl*) may have been
fuerint	they may have been

PLUPERFECT

fuissem	I might have been
fuissēs	you (*sing*) might have been
fuisset	he/she/it might have been
fuissēmus	we might have been
fuissētis	you (*pl*) might have been
fuissent	they might nave been

Imperative

Singular	**es**	be
Plural	**este**	be

Infinitives

Present	**esse**	to be
Future	**futurus esse** / **fore**	to be going to be
Perfect	**fuisse**	to have been

Participle

futūrus	**going to be**

- Compounds of **esse** are listed in the principal parts on pages 113-121.

Unique Verbs (continued)

posse (to be able)

- This verb is formed from **pot-** and **-esse**. Note that **t** becomes **s** before another **s**.

Indicative

	PRESENT	
	possum	I am able
	potes	you (*sing*) are able
	potest	he/she/it is able
	possumus	we are able
	potestis	you (*pl*) are able
	possunt	they are able

	IMPERFECT	
	poteram	I was able *etc*
	poterās	
	poterat	
	poterāmus	
	poterātis	
	poterant	

	FUTURE	
	poterō	I shall be able *etc*
	poteris	
	poterit	
	poterimus	
	poteritis	
	poterunt	

Subjunctive

	PRESENT	
	possim	I may be able *etc*
	possis	
	possit	
	possīmus	
	possītīs	
	possint	

	IMPERFECT	
	possem	I might be able *etc*
	possēs	
	posset	
	possēmus	
	possētis	
	possent	

Indicative

PERFECT

potuī   I have been able *etc*
potuistī
potuit
potuimus
potuistis
potuērunt

PLUPERFECT

potueram   I had been able *etc*
potuerās
potuerat
potuerāmus
potuerātis
potuerant

FUTURE PERFECT

potuerō   I shall have been able *etc*
potueris
potuerit
potuerimus
potueritis
potuerint

Subjunctive

PERFECT

potuerim   I may have been able *etc*
potueris
potuerit
potuerimus
potueritis
potuerint

PLUPERFECT

potuissem   I might have been able *etc*
potuissēs
potuisset
potuissēmus
potuissētis
potuissent

Infinitives

posse   to be able
potuisse   to have been able

Unique Verbs (continued)

ferre (to bear)

Active

Indicative

PRESENT
ferō   I bear *etc*
fers
fert
ferimus
fertis
ferunt

IMPERFECT
ferēbam   I was bearing

FUTURE
feram   I shall bear

PERFECT
tuli   I bore

PLUPERFECT
tuleram   I had borne

FUTURE PERFECT
tulerō   I shall have borne

Subjunctive

PRESENT
feram   I may bear *etc*
ferās
ferat
ferāmus
ferātis
ferant

IMPERFECT
ferrem   I might bear

PERFECT
tulerim   I may have borne

PLUPERFECT
tulissem   I might have borne

Infinitives

Present	**ferre**	to bear
Future	**lātūrus esse**	to be going to bear
Perfect	**tulisse**	to have borne

Imperatives

Singular	**fer**	bear
Plural	**ferte**	bear

Supine   **lātum**

Passive

Indicative

PRESENT
feror   I am borne *etc*
ferris
fertur
ferimur
feriminī
feruntur

IMPERFECT
ferēbar   I was being borne

FUTURE
ferar   I shall be borne

PERFECT
lātus sum   I was borne

PLUPERFECT
lātus eram   I had been borne

FUTURE PERFECT
lātus erō   I shall have been borne

Subjunctive

PRESENT
ferar   I may be borne *etc*
ferāris
ferātur
ferāmur
feraminī
ferantur

IMPERFECT
ferrer   I might be borne

PERFECT
lātus sim   I may have been borne

PLUPERFECT
lātus essem   I might have been borne

Infinitives

Present	**ferri**	to be borne
Future	**lātum īrī**	to be going to be borne
Perfect	**lātus esse**	to have been borne

Imperatives

Singular	**ferre**	be borne
Plural	**feriminī**	be borne

Participles

Present	**ferēns**	bearing
Future	**lātūrus**	going to bear
Perfect	**lātus**	having been borne/carried

Gerund	**ferendum**	bearing
Gerundive	**ferendus**	requiring to be borne

Unique Verbs (continued)

fieri (to become, be made)
- This verb is the passive form of **facere** – to make.

Indicative

PRESENT
fīō	I become
fīs	you (*sing*) become
fit	he/she/it becomes
(**fimus**)	
(**fitis**)	
fiunt	

IMPERFECT
fiēbam	I was becoming

FUTURE
fīam	I shall become

PERFECT
factus sum	I became

PLUPERFECT
factus eram	I had become

FUTURE PERFECT
factus erō	I shall have become

Subjunctive

PRESENT
fīam	I may become *etc*
fīās	
fīat	
fīāmus	
fīātis	
fīant	

IMPERFECT
fierem	I might become

PERFECT
factus sim	I may have become

PLUPERFECT
factus essem	I might have become

Infinitives
Present	**fierī**	to become
Future	**factum īrī**	to be going to become
Perfect	**factus esse**	to have become

Participle
Perfect	**factus**	having become

Gerundive
faciendus	becoming

ire (to go)
- The stem is **i**-. Before a, o, u, it changes to **e**-.

Indicative

PRESENT
eo   I go *etc*
īs
īt
īmus
ītis
eunt

IMPERFECT
ībam   I was going

FUTURE
ībō   I shall go

PERFECT
īvī or **iī**   I went/have gone

PLUPERFECT
īveram   I had gone

FUTURE PERFECT
īverō   I shall have gone

Subjunctive

PRESENT
eam   I may go *etc*
eās
eat
eāmus
eātis
eant

IMPERFECT
īrem   I might go

PERFECT
īverim   I may have gone

PLUPERFECT
īvissem   I might have gone

Infinitives

Present	**īre**	to go
Future	**ītūrus esse**	to be going to go
Perfect	**īvisse** or **īsse**	to have gone

Imperative

Singular	**ī**	go
Plural	**īte**	go

Participles

Present	**iēns** (*gen* **euntis**)	going
Future	**itūrus**	going to go

Gerund

eundum   going

Unique Verbs (continued)

velle (to wish)

Indicative

PRESENT
volō   I wish/am willing *etc*
vīs
vult
volumus
vultis
volunt

IMPERFECT
volēbam   I was wishing
volēbās
volēbat
volēbāmus
volēbātis
volēbant

FUTURE
volam   I shall wish

PERFECT
voluī   I wished/have wished

PLUPERFECT
volueram   I had wished

FUTURE PERFECT
voluerō   I shall have wished

Subjunctive

PRESENT
velim   I may wish
velīs
velit
velīmus
velītis
velint

IMPERFECT
vellem   I might wish
vellēs
vellet
vellēmus
vellētis
vellent

PERFECT
voluerim   I may have wished

PLUPERFECT
voluissem   I might have wished

Infinitives

Present	**velle**	to wish
Perfect	**voluisse**	to have wished

Participle

     volēns, -entis   wishing

nōlle (not to wish, to be unwilling)

• This verb was originally **nōn volo**.

Indicative

PRESENT
nolō   I do not wish *etc*
nōn vis
nōn vult
nōlumus
nōn vultis
nōlunt

IMPERFECT
nōlēbam   I was not wishing
nōlēbas
nōlēbat
nōlēbāmus
nōlēbātis
nōlēbant

FUTURE
nōlam   I shall not wish

PERFECT
nōlui   I have not wished

PLUPERFECT
nōlueram   I had not wished

FUTURE PERFECT
nōluerō   I shall not have wished

Subjunctive

PRESENT
nōlim   I may not wish
nōlīs
nōlit
nōlīmus
nōlītis
nōlint

IMPERFECT
nōllem   I might not wish
nōllēs
nōllet
nōllēmus
nōllētis
nōllent

PERFECT
nōluerim   I may not have wished

PLUPERFECT
nōluissem   I might not have wished

Infinitives

Present	**nōlle**	not to wish
Perfect	**nōluisse**	not to have wished

Participle   **nōlens, -entis**   not wishing

Unique Verbs (continued)

malle (to prefer)
- This verb is formed from **ma volō** *or* **magis volō** (I wish more).

Indicative

PRESENT

mālō	I prefer
māvīs	
māvult	
mālumus	
māvultis	
mālunt	

IMPERFECT

mālēbam	I was preferring
mālēbās	
mālēbat	
malebamus	
mālēbātis	
mālēbant	

FUTURE

mālam	I shall prefer

PERFECT

mālui	I preferred

PLUPERFECT

mālueram	I had preferred

FUTURE PERFECT

māluerō	I shall have preferred

Subjunctive

PRESENT

mālim	I may prefer
mālīs	
mālit	
mālīmus	
mālītis	
mālint	

IMPERFECT

māllem	I might prefer
māllēs	
māllet	
māllēmus	
māllētis	
māllent	

PERFECT

māluerim	I may have preferred

PLUPERFECT

māluissem	I might have preferred

Infinitives

Present	**mālle**	to prefer
Perfect	**māluisse**	to have preferred

Defective Verbs

The following verbs have only a few forms which are used. These are shown below.

inquam (I say)

PRESENT
inquam
inquis
inquit
īnquimus
inquitis
inquiunt

This verb is mainly used in the third person singular
inquiēbat	he said
inquiet	he will say
inquit	he said

avēre	to hail, say "hello"
salvēre	to hail
valēre	to say goodbye

- These verbs are found mainly in infinitives as above or imperatives:

avē, salve	hello (*sing*)
avēte, salvēte	hello (*pl*)
valē (*sing*), **valēte** (*pl*)	goodbye

- Four verbs, **ōdī, meminī, coepī, nōvī** are found only in the perfect stem but are translated as follows:

ōdī	I hate	**meminī**	I remember
ōderam	I hated	**memineram**	I remembered
ōderō	I shall hate	**meminerō**	I shall remember
odisse	to hate	**meminisse**	to remember

coepī	I begin	**nōvī**	I know
coeperam	I began	**nōveram**	I knew
coeperō	I shall begin	**nōverō**	I shall know
coepisse	to begin	**nōvisse**	to know

Likewise subjunctive:

ōderim	I may hate	**meminerim**	I may remember
ōdissem	I might hate	**meminissem**	I might remember

coeperim	I may begin	**nōverim**	I may know
coepissem	I might begin	**nōvissem**	I might know

Principal Parts of Common Verbs

Latin verbs are most usefully listed under four principal parts, from which all other tenses *etc* may be formed or recognized

	1ST PERSON PRESENT ACTIVE	PRESENT INFINITIVE	1ST PERSON PERFECT ACTIVE	SUPINE
1st Conjugation	amō	amāre	amāvī	amātum
2nd Conjugation	habeō	habēre	habuī	habitum
3rd Conjugation	mittō	mittere	mīsī	missum
4th Conjugation	audiō	audīre	audīvī	auditum

400 of the most common verbs in Latin are listed below.

Included are the following:

- 120 regular verbs. Their conjugations are indicated by numbers 1–4. All parts of these verbs can be deduced from the model conjugations on pp 74–92.

- Nearly 300 verbs which are irregular in parts (highlighted in bold), mainly in the perfect and supine. Again their conjugation is indicated by the number of the group to which they belong. Regular parts of these verbs and person endings *etc* may be deduced from the models of conjugations 1–4. Many compound verbs are included (*eg* afficio from ad-facio).

- Eight unique verbs and their compounds. These are marked bold throughout and a page reference is given *in italics* for these.

- Defective verbs which are shown in full in the main text. Again a page reference *in italics* is provided

		Conj Page
abdō, abdere, **abdidī, abditum**	hide	3
abeō, abīre, abiī, abitum	go away	
abicio, abicere, **abiēcī, abiectum**	throw away	3
absum, abesse, afuī	be away	
accēdō, accēdere, **accessī, accessum**	approach	3
accidō, accidere, **accidī**	happen	3
accipio, accipere, **accēpī, acceptum**	receive	3
accūsō, accūsāre, accūsāvī, accūsātum	accuse	1
addō, addere, **addidī, additum**	add	3
adeō, adīre, adiī, aditum	approach	
adimō, adimere, **adēmī, ademptum**	take away	3

		Conj Page
adiuvō, adiuvare, **adiūvī, adiūtum**	help	1
administrō, administrāre, administrāvī, administratum	administer	1
adsum, adesse, adfuī	be present	
adveniō, advenīre, **advēnī, adventum**	reach	4
aedificō, aedificāre, aedificāvī, aedificātum	build	1
afferō, afferre, attulī, allātum	bring to	
afficiō, afficere, **affēcī, affectum**	affect	3
aggredior, aggredī, **aggressus sum**	attack	3
agnōscō, agnōscere, **agnōvī, agnitum**	recognize	3
agō, agere, **ēgī, āctum**	do/drive	3

			Conj Page
alō, alere, **aluī, altum**	feed		3
ambulō, ambulāre, ambulāvī, ambulātum	walk		1
āmittō, āmittere, **āmīsī, āmissum**	lose		3
amō, āmare, amāvī, amātum	love		1
animadvertō, animadvertere, **animadvertī, animadversum**	notice		3
aperiō, aperīre, **aperuī, apertum**	open		4
appareō, apparēre, appāruī, apparitum	appear		2
appellō, appellāre, appellāvī, appellātum	call		1
appropinquō, appropinquāre, appropinquāvī, appropinquātum	approach		1
arbitror, arbitrarī, arbitrātus sum	think		1
arcessō, arcessere, **arcessīvī, arcessītum**	send for		3
ārdeō, ārdēre, **ārsī, ārsum**	bum		2
armō, armāre, armāvī, armātum	arm		1
ascendō, ascendere, **ascendī, ascēnsum**	climb up		3
aspiciō, aspicere, **aspexī, aspectum**	look at		3
attingō, attingere, **attigī, attactum**	touch		3
audeō, audēre, ausus sum	dare		2
audiō, audīre, audīvī, audītum	hear		4
auferō, auferre, abstutī, ablātum	take away		
augeō, augēre, **auxī, auctum**	increase		2
bibō, bibere, **bibī**	drink		3

			Conj Page
cadō, cadere, **cecidī, cāsum**	fall		3
caedō, caedere, **cecīdī, caesum**	cut/kill		3
canō, canere, **cecinī, cantum**	sing		3
capiō, capere, **cēpī, captum**	take		3
careō, carere	lack		2
carpō, carpere, **carpsī, carptum**	pick		3
caveō, cavēre, **cāvī, cautum**	beware		2
cedō, cedere, **cessī, cessum**	go/give way	3
cēlō, cēlāre, cēlāvi, cēlātum	hide		1
cernō, cernere, **crēvi, crētum**	perceive		3
cieō, ciēre, **cīvī, citum**	rouse		2
cingō, cingere, **cinxī, cinctum**	surround		3
circumdō, circumdāre, **circumdēdī, circumdātum**	place round	1
clāmo, clamāre, clamāvī, clamātum	shout		1
claudō, claudere, **clausī, clausum**	close		3
coepī, coeptus	begin		*111*
cōgitō, cōgitāre, cōgitāvī, cōgitātum	think		1
cognoscō, cōgnōscere, **cōgnōvī, cōgnītum**	find out		3
cogō, cōgere, **coēgī, coāctum**	collect/ compel	3
colō, colere, **coluī, cultum**	look after/ worship	3
collocō, collocāre, collocāvī, collocātum	place		1
commoveō, commovēre, **commōvī, commōtum**	upset		2

			Conj Page
comparō, comparāre, **comparāvī, comparātum**	get ready		1
comperiō, comperīre, **comperī, compertum**	discover		4
compleō, complēre, **complēvī, complētum**	fill		2
comprehendō, comprehendere, **comprehendī, comprehēnsum**	grasp		3
concurrō, concurrere, **concurrī, concursum**	run together		3
condō, condere, **condidī, conditum**	found		3
conficiō, conficere, **confēcī, confectum**	finish		3
confīdō, confīdere, **confīsus sum**	trust		3
confīrmō, confīrmare, confīrmāvī, confīrmatūm	strengthen		1
confiteor, confitērī, confēssus sum	confess		2
congredior, congredī, **congressus sum**	meet		3
coniciō, conicere, **coniēcī, coniectum**	throw		3
coniungō, coniungere, **coniūnxi, coniūnctum**	join		3
coniūro, coniūrāre, coniūrāvī, coniūrātum	conspire		1
conor, conārī, conātus sum	try		1
consentiō, consentire, **consēnsī, consēnsum**	agree		4
consistō, consistere, **constitī, constitum**	stop		3
conspiciō, conspicere, **conspexī, conspectum**	catch sight of		3
constō, constāre, **constitī**	agree		1
constituō, constituere, **constituī, constitūtum**	decide		3
construō, construere, **construxī, constructum**	construct		3
consulo, consulere, **consului, consultum**	consult		3
consūmō, consūmere, **consūmpsī, consūmptum**	use up		3
contemnō, contemnere, **contempsī, contemptum**	despise		3
contendō, contendere, contendī, contentum	strive/hurry		3
contingō, contingere, **contigī, contactum**	touch		3
convenīo, convenīre, **convēni, conventum**	meet		4
corripio, corripere, **corripuī, correptum**	seize		3
crēdō, crēdere, **crēdidī, crēditum**	believe		3
crescō, crescere, **crēvī, crētum**	grow		3
culpō, culpāre, culpāvī, culpātum	blame		1
cunctor, cunctāri, cunctātus sum	delay		1
cupiō, cupere, **cupīvī, cupītum**	desire		3
cūrō, cūrare, cūravī, curātum	look after		1
currō, currere, **cucurrī, cursum**	run		3
custōdio, custōdīre, custōdīvī, custōdītum	guard		4
damnō, damnāre, damnāvī, damnātum	condemn		1
debeō, dēbēre, dēbuī, dēbitum	have to/owe		2
dēdō, dēdere, **dēdidī, dēditum**	hand over/ yield		3
dēducō, dēdūcere, **dēdūxī, dēdūctum**	bring/escort		3
dēfendō, dēfendere, **dēfendi, dēfensum**	defend		3

		Conj Page			Conj Page
dēficiō, dēficere, **dēfēcī, dēfectum**	revolt/fail	3	doceō, docēre, docuī, **doctum**	teach	2
dēiciō, dēicere, **dēiēcī, dēiectum**	throw down	3	doleō, dolēre, doluī, dolitum	grieve	2
dēlēctō, dēlectāre, dēlectāvī, dēlectatum	delight	1	dormiō, dormīre, dormīvī, dormītum	sleep	4
dēleō, dēlere, **dēlēvī, dēlētum**	destroy	2	dubitō, dubitāre, dubitāvī, dubitātum	doubt	1
dēligō, dēligere, **dēlēgī, dēlēctum**	choose	3	dūcō, dūcere, **dūxī, ductum**	lead	3
dēmōnstrō, dēmōnstrāre, dēmōnstrāvī, dēmōnstrātum	show	1			
dēpōnō, dēpōnere, **dēposuī, dēpositum**	lay down	3	ēdō, ēdere, **ēdī, ēsum**	eat	3
dēscendō, dēscendere, **dēscendī, dēscensum**	go down	3	efficiō, efficere, **effēcī, effectum**	complete	3
dēsero, dēsere, **dēseruī, dēsertum**	desert	3	effugiō, effugere, **effūgī**	escape	3
dēsiderō, dēsiderāre, dēsideravī, dēsiderātum	long for	1	ēgredior, ēgredī, **egressus sum**	go out	3
dēsiliō, dēsilere, **dēsiluī, dēsultum**	jump down	3	ēmō, ēmere, **ēmī, ēmptum**	buy	3
dēsino, dēsinere, **dēsiī, dēsitum**	stop/leave off	3	**eō, īre, īvī, itum**	go	*107*
dēsistō, dēsistere, **dēstitī**	stop/leave off	3	errō, errāre, erravī, errātum	wander/ be wrong	1
dēspērō, dēspērare, dēspērāvī, dēsperātum	despair	1	ērumpō, ērumpere, **ērūpī, ēruptum**	burst out	3
dēstruō, dēstruere, **dēstruxī, dēstructum**	destroy	3	excitō, excitāre, excitāvī, excitātum	arouse	1
dīcō, dīcere, **dīxī, dictum**	tell/say	3	**exeō, exīre, exiī, exitum**	go out	
dīligō, dīligere, **dīlexī, dīlēctum**	love	3	exerceō, exercēre, exercuī, exercitum	exercise/ train	2
dīmittō, dīmittere, **dīmīsī, dīmissum**	send away	3	exīstimō, exīstimāre, exīstimāvī, exīstimātum	think	1
discēdō, discēdere, **discessī, discessum**	go away	3	expellō, expellere, **expulī, expulsum**	drive out	3
discō, discere, **didicī**	learn	3	experior, experīrī, **expertus sum**	try/test	4
dīvidō, dīvidere, **dīvīsī, dīvīsum**	divide	3	exspectō, exspectāre, exspectāvī, exspectātum	wait for	1
dō, dāre, **dedī, datum**	give	1	exuō, exuere, **exuī, exūtum**	take off	3
			faciō, facere, **fēcī, factum**	do/make	3

		Conj Page				Conj Page
fallō, fallere, **fefellī**, falsum	deceive	3		hauriō, haurīre, **hausī**, haustum	drain away	4
faveō, favēre, **fāvī**, fautum	favour	2		horreō, horrēre, horruī	stand on end	2
ferō, ferre, tulī, lātum	bring/bear	104		hortor, hortārī, hortātus sum	encourage	1
festīnō, festīnāre, festīnāvi, festīnātum	hurry	1		iaceō, iacēre, iacui	lie down	2
fīgo, fīgere, **fīxī, fīxum**	fix	3		iaciō, iacere, **iēcī**, iactum	throw	3
fingō, fingere, **finxī**, fictum	invent	3		ignōscō, īgnoscere, **īgnōvī, ignōtum**	forgive	3
fiō, fierī, factus sum	become/ happen	106		immineō, imminēre	threaten	2
flectō, flectere, **flexī**, flexum	bend	3		impediō, impedīre, impedīvī, impedītum	hinder	4
fleō, flēre, **flēvī, flētum**	weep	2		impellō, impellere, **impulī, impulsum**	drive on	3
fluō, fluere, **flūxī**, flūxum	flow	3		imperō, imperāre, imperāvī, imperātum	order	1
frangō, frangere, **frēgī**, frāctum	break	3		incendō, incendere, **incendī, incēnsum**	burn	3
fruor, fruī, **frūctus** or **fruitus sum**	enjoy	3		incipiō, incipere, **coepī, coeptum**	begin	3
fugiō, fugere, **fūgī**, fugitum	flee/escape	3		incitō, incitāre, incitāvī, incitātum	drive on	1
fugō, fugāre, fūgāvī, fugātum	put to flight	1		inclūdō, inclūdere, **inclūsī, inclūsum**	include	3
fundō, fundere, **fūdī**, fūsum	pour	3		incolō, incolere, **incoluī**	live (in)	3
fungor, fungī, fūnctus sum	perform	3		**īnferō, inferre, intulī, illātum**	bring against	
gaudeō, gaudēre, **gāvīsus sum**	be glad	2		ingredior, ingredī, **ingressus sum**	enter	3
gemō, gemere, **gemuī**, gemitum	groan	3		īnstituō, īnstituere, **īnstituī, īnstitūtum**	set up	3
gerō, gerere, **gessī**, gestum	carry on/ wear	3		īnstruō, īnstruere, **īnstrūxī, īnstrūctum**	set/draw up	3
gignō, gignere, **genuī**, genitum	produce	3		intellegō, intellegere, **intellēxī, intellēctum**	realize	3
habeō, habēre, habuī, habitum	have/keep	2		interficiō, interficere, **interfecī, interfectum**	kill	3
habitō, habitāre, habitāvī, habitātum	live (in)	1		**intersum, interesse**	be among/ be important (impers)	
haereō, haerēre, **haesī**, haesum	stick	2		intrō, intrāre, intrāvī, intrātum	enter	1

		Conj *Page*
invenio, invenīre, **invēnī, inventum**	come upon/ find	4
invitō, invītāre, invītāvī, invītātum	invite	1
irrumpō, irrumpere, **irrūpī, irruptum**	rush into	3
iubeo, iubēre, **iussī, iussum**	order	2
iūdicō, iūdicāre, iūdicāvī, iūdicātum	judge	1
iungō, iungere, **iūnxī, iūnctum**	join	3
iūrō, iūrāre, iūrāvī, iūrātum	swear	1
iuvō, iuvāre, **iūvī, iūtum**	help	1
lābor, lābī, **lāpsus sum**	slip	3
labōrō, labōrāre, labōravī, labōrātum	work	1
lacessō, lacessere, **lacessīvī, lacessītum**	harass	3
lacrimō, lacrimāre, lacrimāvī, lacrimātum	weep	1
laedō, laedere, **laesī, laesum**	hurt	3
lateō, latēre, latuī	lie hidden	2
laudō, laudāre, laudāvī, laudātum	praise	1
lavō, lavāre, **lāvī, lautum**/lavātum/ **lōtum**	wash	1
legō, legere, **lēgī, lēctum**	read/choose	3
levō, levāre, levāvī, levātum	lighten	1
līberō, līberāre, līberāvi, līberātum	free	1
licet, licēre, licuit	it is allowed	2
locō, locāre, locāvī, locātum	place	1
loquor, loquī, **locūtus sum**	speak	3
lūdō, lūdere, **lūsī, lūsum**	play	3

		Conj *Page*
lustrō, lustrāre, lustrāvī, lustrātum	purify/scan	1
mālo, mālle, māluī	prefer	*110*
mandō, mandāre, mandāvī, mandātum	command/ trust	1
maneō, manēre, **mānsī, mānsum**	remain/stay	2
meminī, meminisse	remember	*111*
mentior, mentīrī, mentītus sum	tell lies	4
metūō, metuere, **metuī**	fear	3
minor, minārī, minātus sum	threaten	1
minuō, minuere, **minuī, minūtum**	lessen	3
miror, mirārī, mirātus sum	wonder (at)	1
misceō, miscēre, **miscui, mixtum**	mix	2
⎧ misereor, miserērī, miseritus sum miseret, miserēre, miseruit ⎩ (*eg* me miseret tui – I am sorry for you)	pity	2
mittō, mittere, **mīsī, missum**	send	3
mōlior, mōlīrī, molītus sum	strive/toil	4
moneō, monēre, monuī, monitum	advise/warn	2
morior, morī, **mortuus sum**	die	3
moror, morārī, morātus sum	delay/loiter	1
moveō, movēre, **mōvī, mōtum**	move	2
mūnio, mūnīre, mūnīvī/mūniī, mūnītum	fortify	4
mūtō, mūtāre, mūtāvī, mūtātum	change	1
nancīscor, nancīscī, **na(n)ctus sum**	obtain	3

			Conj Page
nārrō, nārrāre, nārrāvī, nārrātum		tell	1
nāscor, nāscī, **nātus sum**		be born	**3**
nāvigō, nāvigare, nāvigāvī, nāvigātum		sail	1
necō, necāre, necāvī, necātum		kill	1
negō, negāre, negāvī, negātum		refuse/deny	1
neglegō, neglegere, **neglēxi, neglēctum**		neglect	**3**
nescio, nescīre, nescīvī *or* iī, nescītum		not to know	4
noceō, nocēre, nocuī, nocitum		harm	2
nōlō, nōlle, nōluī		not to wish/ be unwilling	*109*
nōsco, nōscere, **nōvī, nōtum** (in perfect tenses translate as "know")		get to know	**3**
nūntio, nūntiāre, nūntiāvī, nūntiātum		announce	1
obeō, obīre, obīvī *or* **iī, obitum**		die	
obicio, obicere, **obiēcī, obiectum**		throw to/ oppose	**3**
oblīvīscor, oblīvīscī, **oblītus sum**		forget	**3**
obsideō, obsidēre, **obsēdī, obsessum**		besiege	**2**
obtineō, obtinēre, obtinuī, **obtentum**		hold/obtain	2
occidō, occidere, **occidī, occāsum**		fall	**3**
occīdō, occīdere, **occīdī, occīsum**		kill	**3**
occupō, occupāre, occupāvī, occupātum		seize	1
occurrō, occurrere, **occurrī, occursum**		meet	**3**
ōdī, ōdisse		hate	*111*
offerō, offerre, obtulī, oblātum		present	

			Conj Page
oportet, oportēre, oportuit	be proper/ ought		2
opprimō, opprimere, **oppressī, oppressum**	crush		**3**
oppugnō, oppugnāre, oppugnāvī, oppugnātum	attack		1
optō, optāre, optāvī, optātum	wish		1
orior, orīrī, **ortus sum**	arise		**4**
orō, orāre, orāvī, orātum	beg/plead		1
ornō, ornāre, ornāvī, ornātum	decorate/ equip		1
ostendō, ostendere, **ostendī, ostentum**	show		**3**
pācō, pācāre, pācāvī, pācātum	pacify		1
paenitet, paenitēre, paenituit	repent of		2
pandō, pandere, **pandī, passum**	spread out		**3**
parcō, parcere, **pepercī, parsum**	spare		**3**
pareō, parēre, paruī	obey		2
pariō, parere, **peperī, partum**	give birth to		**3**
parō, parāre, parāvī, parātum	prepare		1
pāscō, pāscere, **pāvī, pāstum**	feed		**3**
patefaciō, patefacere, **patefēcī, patefactum**	open		**3**
pateō, patēre, patuī	be open		2
patior, patī, **passus sum**	suffer/allow		**3**
paveō, pavēre, **pavī**	fear		2
pellō, pellere, **pepulī, pulsum**	drive		**3**
pendeō, pendēre, **pependī** (*intrans*)	hang		2
pendō, pendēre, **pependī, pēnsum**	weigh/pay		**3**

		Conj Page
perdō, perdere, **perdidī, perditum**	lose/destroy	3
pereo, perīre, periī, peritum	perish	
perficiō, perficere, **perfecī, perfectum**	complete	3
pergō, pergere, **perrēxī, perrēctum**	proceed	3
permittō, permittere, **permīsī, permissum**	allow	3
persuadeō, persuadēre, **persuasī, persuasum**	persuade	2
pertineō, pertinēre, pertinuī, **pertentum**	concern	2
perturbō, perturbāre, perturbāvī, perturbātum	confuse	1
perveniō, pervenīre, **pervēnī, perventum**	arrive at	4
petō, petere, **petīvī, petītum**	seek/ask	3
placeō, placēre, placuī, placītum	please	2
placet, placēre, placuit	it seems good	2
polliceor, pollicērī, **pollicitus sum**	promise	2
pōnō, pōnere, **posuī, positum**	place/put	3
portō, portāre, portāvī, portātum	carry	1
poscō, poscere, **poposcī**	ask for/demand	3
possum, posse, potui	to be able	102
postulō, postulāre, postulāvī, postulātum	demand	1
potior, potīrī, potitus sum	gain possession of	4
praebeō, praebēre, praebuī, praebitum	show	2
praeficiō, praeficere, **praefēcī, praefēctum**	put in command of	3
praestō, praestāre, **praestitī, praestatum**	stand out	1
premō, premere, **pressī, pressum**	press	3

		Conj Page
prōcēdō, prōcēdere, **prōcessī, prōcessum**	advance	3
prōdō, prōdere, **prōdidī, prōditum**	betray	3
proficīscor, proficīscī, **profectus sum**	set out	3
prōgredior, prōgredī, **progressus sum**	advance	3
prohibeō, prohibēre, prohibuī, prohibitum	prevent	2
prōmittō, prōmittere, **prōmīsī, prōmissum**	promise	3
prōvideō, prōvidēre, **prōvīdī, prōvisum**	take precautions	2
pugnō, pugnāre, pugnāvī, pugnātum	fight	1
pūniō, pūnīre, pūnīvī or iī, punītum	punish	4
putō, putāre, putāvī, putātum	think	1
quaerō, quaerere, **quaesīvī, quaesītum**	ask/seek	3
queror, querī, **questus sum**	complain	3
quiescō, quiescere, **quiēvī, quiētum**	keep quiet	3
rapiō, rapere, **rapuī, raptum**	snatch/seize	3
recipiō, recipere, **recēpī, receptum**	receive/recover	3
recusō, recusāre, recusāvī, recusātum	refuse	1
reddō, reddere, **reddidī, redditum**	give back/return	3
redeō, redīre, rediī, reditum	come back/return	
redūcō, redūcere, **redūxī, reductum**	bring back	3
regō, regere, **rēxī, rēctum**	rule	3
regredior, regredī, **regressus sum**	retreat	3
relinquō, relinquere, **relīquī, relictum**	leave	3

		Conj Page			Conj Page
remittō, remittere, **remīsī, remissum**	send back	3	serviō, servīre, servīvī, servītum	serve/ be a slave	4
reor, rērī, **ratus sum**	think	2	servō, servāre, servāvī, servātum	save	1
repellō, repellere, **reppulī, repulsum**	drive back	3	simulō, simulāre, simulāvī, simulātum	pretend	1
reperiō, reperīre, **repperī, repertum**	find	4	sinō, sinere, **sīvī, situm**	allow	3
resistō, resistere, **restitī**	resist	3	sistō, sistere, **stitī, statum**	set up	3
respiciō, respicere, **respexī, respectum**	look back	3	soleō, solere, **solitus sum**	be used to	2
respondeō, respondēre, **respondī, respōnsum**	answer	2	sollicitō, sollicitāre, sollicitāvī, sollicitātum	worry	1
restō, restāre, **restitī**	remain	1	solvō, solvere, **solvī, solūtum**	loosen	3
restituō, restituere, **restituī, restitūtum**	restore	3	sonō, sonāre, **sonuī, sonitum**	sound	1
retineō, retinēre, retinuī, **retentum**	hold back	2	spargō, spargere, **sparsī, sparsum**	scatter/ sprinkle	3
rideō, ridēre, **rīsī, rīsum**	laugh	2	spectō, spectāre, spectāvī, spectātum	look at	1
rogō, rogāre, rogāvī, rogātum	ask	1	spērō, spērāre, spērāvī, spērātum	hope	1
rumpō, rumpere, **rūpī, ruptum**	burst	3	spoliō, spoliāre, spoliāvī, spoliātum	rob/plunder	1
ruō, ruere, **ruī, rutum** (**ruitūrus** – *fut part*)	rush/fall	3	statuō, statuere, **statuī, statūtum**	set up	3
sciō, scīre, **scīvī/īī, scītum**	know	4	sternō, sternere, **strāvī, strātum**	cover/ overthrow	3
scrībō, scrībere, **scrīpsī, scriptum**	write	3	stō, stāre, **stetī, stātum**	stand	1
sēcernō, sēcernere, **secrevī, sēcrētum**	set apart	3	struō, struere, **strūxī, strūctum**	build	3
secō, secāre, **secuī, sectum**	cut	1	studeō, studēre, studuī	study	2
sedeō, sedēre, **sēdī, sessum**	sit	2	suādeō, suādēre, **suāsī, suāsum**	advise	2
sentiō, sentīre, **sēnsi, sēnsum**	feel/perceive	4	**subeō, subīre, subiī, subitum**	undergo	
sepeliō, sepelīre, sepelīvī, **sepultum**	bury	4	succedō, succēdēre, **successī, successum**	go up/relieve	3
sequor, sequī, **secūtus sum**	follow	3	**succurro, succurrere, succurri, succursum**	help	3
serō, serere, **sēvī, satum**	sow	3	**sum, esse, fuī, futūrus**		100
			sūmō, sūmere, **sūmpsī, sūmptum**	take	3

		Conj Page			Conj Page
superō, superare, superāvī, superātum	overcome	1	ulcīscor, ulcīscī, **ultus sum**	punish/ avenge	3
supersum, superesse, superfuī	survive		urgeō, urgēre, **ursī**	press/urge	2
surgō, surgēre, **surrēxī, surrēctum**	rise/get up	3	urō, urere, **ussī, ustum**	burn	3
			ūtor, ūtī, **ūsus sum**	use	3
suscipiō, suscipere, **suscēpī, susceptum**	undertake	3			
suspicor, suspicārī, suspicātus sum	suspect	1	valeō, valēre, valuī, valitum	be strong	2
sustineō, sustinēre, sustinuī, **sustentum**	sustain	2	vastō, vastāre, vastāvī, vastātum	destroy	1
			vehō, vehere, **vēxī, vectum**	carry	3
taceō, tacēre, tacuī, tacitum	be silent	2	vendō, vendere, **vendidī, venditum**	sell	3
taedet, taedēre, taeduit, **taesum est**	be tired of	2	veniō, venīre, **vēnī, ventum**	come	4
tangō, tangere, **tetigī, tactum**	touch	3	vereor, verērī, veritus sum	fear	2
tegō, tegere, **tēxī, tectum**	cover	3	vertō, vertere, **vertī, versum**	turn	3
tendō, tendere, tetendī, tentum or **tēnsum**	stretch	3	vescor, vescī	feed on	3
			vetō, vetāre, **vetuī, vetitum**	forbid	1
teneō, tenēre, tenuī, **tentum**	hold	2	videō, vidēre, **vīdī, vīsum**	see	2
terreō, terrēre, terruī, territum	terrify	2	vigilō, vigilāre, vigilāvī, vigilātum	stay awake	1
timeō, timēre, timuī	fear	2	vinciō, vincīre, **vinxī, vinctum**	bind	4
tollō, tollere, **sustulī, sublātum**	raise/remove	3	vincō, vincere, **vīcī, victum**	defeat/ conquer	3
tonō, tonāre, **tonuī**	thunder	1	vitō, vitāre, vitāvī, vitātum	avoid	1
torqueō, torquēre, **torsī, tortum**	twist	2	vivō, vivere, **vīxī, victum**	live	3
trādō, trādere, **trādidī, trāditum**	hand over	3	vocō, vocāre, vocāvī, vocātum	call/invite	1
trahō, trahere, **trāxī, tractum**	drag	3	**volō, velle, voluī**	wish/want	108
traicio, traicere, **traieci, traiectum**	take across	3	volvō, volvere, **volvī, volūtum**	roll	3
trānseō, trānsīre, trānsiī, trānsitum	cross over		voveō, vovēre, **vōvī, vōtum**	vow	2
tueor, tuērī, tuitus sum	look at	2			

GRAMMAR AND VERB TABLES INDEX

The following index lists comprehensively both grammatical terms and key words in English and Latin.